MAR − 8 1993

PHILOSOPHY
AND
THE HUMAN
CONDITION

PHILOSOPHY
AND
THE HUMAN
CONDITION

EDITED BY

Tom L. Beauchamp

William T. Blackstone

Joel Feinberg

PRENTICE-HALL, INC., Englewood Cliffs, New Jersey 07632

Library of Congress Cataloging in Publication Data

Main entry under title:

Philosophy and the human condition.

Includes bibliographies.
1. Philosophy—Introductions—Addresses,
essays, lectures.   I. Beauchamp, Tom L.
II. Blackstone, William T.   III. Feinberg,
Joel, (date)
BD21.P47   100   80-278
ISBN 0-13-662528-2

Printed in the United States of America

10   9   8   7   6   5   4   3   2   1

Editorial/production supervision by Virginia Rubens
Cover design by Maureen Olson
Manufacturing buyer: John Hall

PRENTICE-HALL INTERNATIONAL, INC., *London*
PRENTICE-HALL OF AUSTRALIA PTY. LIMITED, *Sydney*
PRENTICE-HALL OF CANADA, LTD., *Toronto*
PRENTICE-HALL OF INDIA PRIVATE LIMITED, *New Delhi*
PRENTICE-HALL OF JAPAN, INC., *Tokyo*
PRENTICE-HALL OF SOUTHEAST ASIA PTE. LTD., *Singapore*
WHITEHALL BOOKS LIMITED, *Wellington, New Zealand*

This book is dedicated to the memory of our dear friend and collaborator, William T. Blackstone

Tom L. Beauchamp
Joel Feinberg

Contents

CHAPTER 5   THE SANCTITY OF LIFE   250

Animal Life

Abortion

Suicide

Euthanasia

Killing and Letting Die

Murder and Justified Homicide

CHAPTER 9   BELIEF IN GOD   514

Preface

This book is designed to introduce college students at all levels of sophistication to philosophical problems that grow naturally out of their everyday concerns. Technical problems and technical language have been avoided as much as possible. We have also intentionally omitted certain abstruse theories from the heartland of traditional philosophy that have commonly populated introductory textbooks in philosophy. Instead we have relied more heavily on problems of moral and social philosophy with which the student is presumed already to be familiar: problems about killing and rescuing, racial and sexual equality, liberty and its limitation, love and sexual behavior. However, this book is a general introduction to *philosophy*, not only to the "value areas" of philosophy. Accordingly, we have also included nonevaluative problems about the nature of philosophy, the grounds and limits of knowledge, the problem of perception, theories of human nature, personal identity, the distinction between minds and machines, and questions about religious belief and the meaning of life.

The selections are structured to draw the student progressively into the more basic philosophical questions. The student's philosophical curiosity is stimulated by the presentation in simple, nontechnical language of opposed positions, and by introductory material in the form of court cases, fantasies, science fiction, and poetry. The intent of the latter materials is to induce genuine philosophical perplexity. In short, this volume is what is often pejoratively called a "relevance book," but it contains important differences. Unlike other books in this genre, *Philosophy and the Human Condition* contains many closely reasoned and tightly argued articles. Moreover, detailed introductory essays by the editors, employing argument outlines and conceptual clarifications, precede each section of the book. The selections and the introductions are complementary and make the "relevant" problems of philosophy and the major strategies for coping with them readily accessible to the student.

Several philosophers made suggestions that resulted in significant alterations of earlier versions of the manuscript. Among these friendly critics were: Sidney Gendin (Eastern Michigan University), John Granrose (University of Georgia), Louis Katzner (Bowling Green State University), Barbara MacKinnon (University of San Francisco), Lawrence Simon (University of Massachusetts-Boston), James Hall (East Stroudsburg State College), James F. Doyle (University of Missouri-St. Louis), and L. Bryant Keeling (Western Illinois University). We also owe special thanks to Mary Baker and Oksana Wengerchuk for their help in preparing the manuscript, and to our good friend Richard Trudgen for his unflagging encouragement.

Tom L. Beauchamp
William T. Blackstone
Joel Feinberg

PHILOSOPHY
AND
THE HUMAN
CONDITION

Chapter 1   The Nature of Philosophy

WHAT PHILOSOPHY IS NOT

Philosophy is generally thought to be a branch of learning which has its own distinctive questions to investigate and try to answer. One way of explaining philosophy is to examine those questions which are its characteristic concern. Unlike other disciplines, however, philosophy is in a sense "transcendent": its own nature is one of the subjects it investigates. The question "What is philosophy?" is itself a very typical philosophical question, whereas the question "What is science?" is not itself a question to be answered by scientists performing experiments and calculations; the question "What is art?" cannot be answered by making a painting or composing a symphony; the question "What is religion?" cannot be settled by uttering a prayer. These are philosophical questions. One kind of thing philosophy attempts to do is to define both itself and the other disciplines, to raise questions about their appropriate goals and methods, and to settle jurisdictional disputes among them. Thus philosophers seek to know the limits of scientific method, whether all knowledge is in principle scientific knowledge, or whether there are questions beyond science's reach that must be answered, if at all, by other methods. Indeed, philosophers raise these same questions about reason itself. Are there any limits, in principle, to what rational methods (scientific and extrascientific) can tell us about reality? If so, what are those limits? Is there such a thing as uniquely

religious knowledge? Do works of art have meaning and in their own way make statements that can be true or false?

No philosopher can be satisfied with a purported explanation of his subject matter that simply lists typical philosophical questions. That method is no more capable of providing *philosophical* understanding than a reply to the question "What is man?" that proceeds by saying "Smith is a man," "Jones is a man," etc. What the philosopher seeks is a more general answer which explains what the various instances of the thing to be defined have in common that distinguish them from things of other kinds. Interpreted in that way the question "What is philosophy?" is not only itself a philosophical question, it is a very difficult philosophical question. (But perhaps we should say that *all* philosophical questions are very difficult.) At first sight there are no obvious and significant characteristics that all philosophical questions have in common except negative ones: philosophical questions are clearly *not* scientific, historical, mathematical, or empirical questions. Indeed they appear at first sight to constitute a miscellany of questions that are left over after other questions have been assigned to science, history, literary criticism, empirical observation, mathematical calculation, and the other disciplines and intellectual functions. It would be convenient then to begin negatively with the cautious statement that any genuine intellectual question that is "left over" after these assignments have been made is by definition a philosophical question, thus leaving open for further philosophical inquiry the question of what positive features these questions may have in common, in virtue of which we call them "philosophical." We must leave it an open question at the start whether there are any such positive characteristics at all, for it is always possible that the objects denoted by a general word form an irreducible miscellany, definable only negatively, and unified only by a kind of "family resemblance" among them, rather than by features that are common and peculiar to all of them.

GENUINE AND PSEUDO QUESTIONS

It is important to emphasize that the left-over questions we call "philosophical" must be genuine intellectual questions which are amenable in principle to rational methods of inquiry and express genuine cognitive perplexity, as opposed to a kind of muddled misunderstanding. A left-over question, if it is to qualify as a philosophical problem, must be a genuine question, not what philosophers commonly call a "pseudoquestion." A pseudoquestion is one whose very formulation is so muddled that it can have no correct answer at all, but only an explanation of why it is ill-formed and unanswerable. That explanation itself will be a job for the philosopher, but diagnosing and curing a muddle is not the same thing as contributing authentic knowledge about the world, or solving a genuine problem in its own terms. Often pseudoquestions are easy to identify. For example, "Can home runs tap dance?" and "How much does virtue weigh?" are pure nonsense, resembling real questions only in their superficial conformity to the rules of grammar (each has a noun for its subject term, a verb for its predicate, etc.). Other pseudoquestions are more difficult to unravel. "What time is it on the sun when it is four o'clock in Los Angeles?" is one; another is the four-year-old's petulant question about his six-year-old brother: "Why was he born before me (instead of the other way around)?" Curing a person of acute worry or lingering conceptual confusion is often a subtle and difficult procedure, and so useful that it is not to be sneered at. That kind of "therapy" is surely *one* of the traditional tasks of the philosopher, but if it were the sole philosophical function then philosophy would be at best a kind of applied technique (like dentistry) rather than a theoretical discipline of its own.

Often it is very difficult to tell whether a given specimen is a genuine question or a mere pseudoquestion, and learned philosophers are often in disagreement about such matters. Some say that "What is the function of a human being?" and "What is the meaning of life?" are natural expressions of a deep human wonder about things, and are properly philosophical questions no matter how hard it may be to answer them to everyone's satisfaction. Others say that they are

3

mere muddles overlaid with a distinctive sort of emotion or anxiety. A skeptical philosopher might say that just because the heart and the liver have functions in the human body, it does not follow that the whole person has a function in the larger world, for that would imply that the universe itself is something like a biological organism and that people are like bodily organs. Life itself, a skeptic might go on to say, is no more the kind of thing that can have meaning than virtue is the kind of thing that can have weight or home runs the kinds of thing that can dance. A more subtle (and highly controversial) question is the famous expression of primordial wonder: "Why should there *be* anything at all (as opposed to pure nothingness)?" Some philosophers have attempted to answer this question; others take it seriously but argue that we can never discover its answer; others claim that it is a mere pseudoquestion. A radical skeptic might hold that there are no philosophical questions at all, since all the left-over questions will turn out, upon examination, to be pseudoquestions. Such extreme skepticism, however, breeds paradox, and contains the germs of its own refutation. Surely the question of whether extreme skepticism is *itself* true is a genuine question, and one which cannot be answered by science, history, or other disciplines. And the question whether any given left-over question is a genuine intellectual problem or a pseudoquestion will itself be a genuine and therefore philosophical question. The ability of philosophy to transcend itself, and raise questions about its own questions, is the surest sign of its disciplinary independence.

THE QUEST FOR ULTIMATES

The most famous traditional problems of philosophy give every appearance of raising genuine questions about the familiar world of common experience that is explained in its particular workings by science and chronicled by history. As Ralph Barton Perry points out in the selection that opens this chapter, these philosophical questions resemble questions of science and everyday life in their application of familiar workaday distinctions, like those between "real" and "apparent," "evi-

dent" and "certain," "cause" and "effect," "means" and "end," "good" and "bad." Philosophers, however, press common-sense distinctions to their ultimate beginnings and endings. They ask what is *ultimately* real, and not itself merely the appearance of something more ultimate still, what is ultimately good (worth having, doing, or being) and not itself merely a means to something else whose inherent goodness lends it its point, and so on.

One of the philosophical questions mentioned by Perry asks what is the ultimate source of evidence from which the rational reconstruction of all of our other beliefs must proceed. Many philosophers take this question to presuppose that there are some beliefs that are evident in themselves and which can therefore provide the ultimate premises in arguments for all other beliefs. If you ask a mathematician how to get evidence for our beliefs about (future) facts and happenings, he might reply by telling you how to apply the calculus of probabilities to your present beliefs in order to rationally generate further beliefs. That would surely be useful instruction but it would entirely miss the point of the *philosopher's* interest in evidence. To understand this point, consider an analogy. Suppose a wealthy financial advisor is asked by an ambitious young person, "How can I get lots of money?" He replies by advising the questioner to place his funds in this, that, or the other interest-producing investment. "No, you don't understand," replies the other. "I don't have any money to invest. I want to know how to get it in the first place—how to get it without first having it. What is the first and original—the ultimate—source of money?" At this point the financial advisor will probably lose interest in the question. It looks too "philosophical" for his practical interest. But as philosophers have often pointed out, a fuller philosophical understanding of any everyday concept (even the concept of "money") is by no means without practical benefits, even if, for the most part, it is one of those goods that reflective people value for their own sakes.

Perry's account can be misleading in two ways. First of all, he fails to mention that not all philosophers share the assumption that there must be ultimate causes if anything is to be explained at all, that there must be ultimate evidence if anything is to be known at all, that there must be ultimate reality if anything is to appear at all, that there must be ultimate ends if anything is to have value at all. Perhaps most contemporary philosophers would question at least one of these claims and some (most notably the distinguished American, John Dewey, 1859–1952) would emphatically reject them all. Again, however, the transcendent character of philosophy preserves the meaningfulness of the questions, for we can ask not simply what is ultimately real, explanatory, evident, good, etc., but rather *whether* anything *is* ultimately real, etc. and *if so,* what is its nature. All philosophers have taken that kind of complex question seriously, as indeed they should.

Secondly, Perry suggests that ultimate questions have been generated for philosophers only by the four sets of common-sense distinctions he mentions as examples, whereas in fact almost any useful common-sense distinction if pushed to its limits will produce philosophical perplexity. To consider just one other, take the distinction between authority and its counterfeit, usurpation, that is so central in our political and legal discourse. In ordinary life we often wonder or ask by what authority someone does something or whether some rule is valid or bogus. Philosophers, pondering such questions, soon begin to wonder about the ultimate grounds of authority, and their reasonings characteristically alternate between appeals to rules and appeals to persons. If we ask by what authority the traffic cop gives us a ticket, he will answer by citing an empowering statute (part of the municipal code). If we go on to question the authority of the rule, that in turn will be derived from the authority of (other) persons, namely the legislature, and in turn the authority of the legislature to restrict our conduct in certain ways will be traced to (other) rules, ultimately to the "basic norms" of our constitution. How far back can the sources of authority be traced in this way? At what point must the challenging questions be silenced? And why at that point rather than another? Should we stop with the constitution (rules) or trace its authority to "the people" or "the founding fathers" (other persons)? By what authority do

those persons bind me? Perhaps by the authority of still more ultimate norms—ancient traditions, or rules of reason. The latter are often collectively called "natural law" by some philosophers who treat them as the ultimate authority-generating rules. Some philosophers are not even content to drop their challenge at that point, but are driven to derive the authority even of natural law from an ultimate lawgiver, namely God, the supreme *personal* authority. One might argue that no one truly understands what authority is, even in its ordinary applications, until one has worked one's way through this philosophical maze.

PHILOSOPHY AS THE COMPLETION AND CRITICISM OF SCIENCE

Brand Blanshard in his eloquent essay presents a more comprehensive view of philosophy that incorporates Perry's "ultimate questions" and more. He agrees with Perry that it is not the exclusive aim of philosophy to help us clarify our concepts (although that is surely *one* of its useful functions). Like Perry he insists that philosophy is a partner of science in "the enterprise of understanding the world." Just as science builds on common sense, developing, expanding, and where necessary correcting it, so philosophy bears a similar relation to science, attempting to clarify its concepts, isolate its assumptions, and synthesize its findings. Philosophy "comes before science," he tells us, in the sense that science depends on concepts (like truth, existence, perception, probability, causation, space, and time) and assumptions (for instance that nature is governed by invariant laws) that have already been subject to philosophical interpretation and criticism. Equally, however, philosophy comes after science, in that it builds on the tentative findings of science in its own quest for absolutes; it attempts to reconcile the results of different scientific disciplines (e.g. physics and psychology) with each other; it tries to determine which of the sciences is the most basic and how, if at all, the others can be derived from it; it tries to trace the logical implications of science that bear on our conceptions of moral obligation and personal responsibility, attempting to reconcile apparent tensions and conflicts between scientific and moral realms of inquiry.

PHILOSOPHY AND DEFINITION

One of the "prescientific tasks" of philosophy in Blanshard's conception is to clarify concepts. The concepts that generate philosophical puzzlement tend to be those expressed in our language by abstract nouns, and they include not only the basic terms of science, but also the fundamental abstractions applied in our ordinary activities, both theoretical and practical. The philosopher's pursuit of conceptual clarification leads him to formulate questions somewhat different in form from those mentioned in Perry's essay. Perry's philosophical questions all have the form: What are the ultimately real, explanatory, evident, worthwhile, or authoritative things? Questions of conceptual analysis, on the other hand, appear to be requests for definitions: What do we (or must we) *mean* when we speak of truth, cause, time, knowledge, beauty, responsibility, action, justice, value, etc.? "It is surely true," Blanshard tells us, "that a main business of philosophy is to define words."

It may seem to the uninitiated that defining words is an intellectually trivial activity devoid of any relevance to how we live our lives. Yet Socrates, perhaps the first great Western philosopher (though he left no writings of his own), raised hardly any philosophical questions that did not appear to call for definitions as their answers. He insisted not only that examining one's life consists primarily in the effort to answer such questions, but also that "the unexamined life is not worth living." If we can judge from the literary picture of him in the *Dialogues* by his admiring follower Plato, Socrates went through the streets of Athens engaging young aristocrats in friendly conversation until one of the central philosophical concepts was used, and at that point the quest for philosophical definition was launched. The key questions in the famous Socratic *Dialogues* composed by Plato include: "What is justice?" "What is piety?" "What is temperance?" "What is courage?" "What is knowledge?" "What is love?" These questions appear to be equivalent to the questions "How are we to define the word 'justice'?," "What do we mean by the word 'love'?," etc., and thus are straightforward requests for definitions, though they surely are no less profound and difficult for that. Socrates insisted that insofar as we lack insights into these questions and glimmerings at least of their answers, we don't really know what we are up to in any of our everyday activities; our lives lack direction, and the dignity that comes with understanding.

Socrates did not himself claim to know the answers to the questions with which he tormented his fellow citizens. Rather he thought that his own contribution to human well-being consisted simply in raising the questions in the first place and stimulating others to think about them. He likened himself to a "gadfly" arousing sluggish citizens to thought, or to a "midwife" who helps others, by his probing questions, to give birth to their own ideas. While he rarely put forth positions of his own, he was extremely skillful at exposing the confusions and undermining the arguments of others. He was especially adept at refuting the claims of professional teachers of wisdom or *sophists*. By asking just a few "innocent" and "humble" questions, Socrates often succeeded in showing the purported wisdom (expressed in philosophical definitions) to be trivial or confused. This did not contribute to his popularity in every quarter.

In 400–399 B.C. Socrates was brought to trial before a jury of five hundred citizens on charges of (1) not worshipping the gods whom the State worships, but introducing new and unfamiliar religious practices, and (2) corrupting the young. The proceedings were instigated by Anytus, a moderate democratic politician, through the instrumentality of an obscure youth, one Miletus, who formally made the accusation in court. The prosecutor was told to demand the death penalty (which he did), not because Anytus wanted Socrates killed, but rather only "to induce Socrates to consult his own safety by withdrawing into exile and letting the case go by default."[1] Little did he know his man. Socrates chose to stand and fight, and in his famous "Apology" to the jury he makes an eloquent defense of his practice of following philosophic argument fearlessly wherever it may take him in the discharge of his vocation as a truth-seeker and a "gadfly."

The *Apology of Socrates* is preceded in this collection by a closely related Platonic dialogue, the *Euthyphro*. This work gives the student a typical example of Socrates at work eliciting a philosophical definition from a smug person who is content that he knows what he is up to, and then demolishing it by a few "innocent" questions, thereby revealing that the self-satisfied fool has no more understanding of what he is doing, and the concepts he employs to explain what he is doing, than a parrot or an automaton who might mouth the same words. Socrates and Euthyphro meet at the law court where both of them have business. Socrates is about to be tried on the charge of impiety, whereas Euthyphro is on his way to bring formal indictment of his own father—also for impiety. Surely there can be no doubt in this instance that the philosophical inquiry into the nature of piety and impiety has a clear relevance to the way people govern their lives! The reader should be warned that the English words "piety" and "impiety," with their narrow religious meanings, are at best only approximate renderings of the Greek terms used by Socrates and Euthyphro. To the Athenians of their time, "piety" blended a sense of responsibility, trustworthiness, and loyalty under one heading; "religious piety for the Greeks enforced all the obligations that bind an individual to others, and engage his personal responsibility to his family and friends, and his political loyalty to the state and its traditions."[2] In any case, Euthyphro is incapable of explaining what this conscientious loyalty really is, and his bumbling efforts at definition are circular or otherwise defective. To this day, Socrates' cross-examination remains one of the best introductions to philosophical reasoning and argument.

TYPES AND FUNCTIONS
OF DEFINITIONS

If philosophical questions are really requests for definitions, why can't philosophical issues be settled by simply looking up a word (like justice or knowledge) in an authoritative dictionary? The quick answer to this philosophical question about philosophy is that there are numerous types of definition and the kind that philosophers seek is not the same kind as those which are compiled by lexicographers. A more satisfactory answer, however, will have to go much deeper. It will be helpful to our effort to understand the definitions that are the products of philosophical analysis if we attempt to locate them on a map of general types of definition, so that we may then contrast them with the sorts of definition with which they might otherwise be confused.

1. *Dictionary definitions* (often called "lexical definitions") are of two kinds. *Descriptive* (or "reportive") definitions simply describe the way a word is actually used by typical speakers of the language. *Prescriptive* (or "normative") definitions specify standard usage of a word whether or not the standard reported is typically conformed to or violated. In a sense even the prescriptive definitions can be thought of as empirical reports, for they describe the conventional standards used by some group of authorities (authors, editors, critics, English professors) for determining the acceptability of usage. All dictionary definitions can thus be interpreted as empirical descriptions of usage, either the usage of people generally or that of some authoritative elite. As such they are either true or false depending on whether or not they accurately describe linguistic behavior.

2. *Stipulative definitions,* unlike dictionary definitions, are proposals or statements of intention to use words in certain ways, justified by their usefulness for some sensible purpose, but neither true nor false. New discoveries and inventions often require new words to refer to them. New terms are also invented to serve as abbreviations for longer, more cumbersome expressions. Sometimes there are words available for what one wishes to say, but one is dissatisfied with them because of their emotional associations and prefers to coin a new word or to use an old word in a new, emotionally neutral way. Sometimes the only simple terms available are vague words, and the writer finds it useful to propose a somewhat more precise sense for them. The word "overweight" might be defined, accurately but vaguely, as "weighing more than one should," but a scientific writer might find it useful to define it (say) in

terms of the ratio of fat tissue to lean tissue as measured in underwater weighings. He might then stipulate that "overweight" in his usage will mean "having more than 22.5 percent of one's total weight determined by one's fat tissue." Another motive for a stipulative definition might be to avoid ambiguity. A philosophical writer, for example, might begin a treatise in the philosophy of science by saying that the subject of his book is "law" in the sense that word has in the expression "law of nature," not in the sense it has in the expression "law of the state." Stipulative definitions of this sort can consist of a mere informal citing of examples to give the reader a rough indication of the way the author intends to use a term: "Thus, Newton's laws are laws in my sense, and the English common law and the U.S. Constitution are not laws."

3. *Pointing-out definitions* are definitions of either of the first two classes when they appear in a scientific or philosophical work, not as substantive conclusions, but as mere preliminaries to analysis. They simply point out to the reader which class of objects the writer wishes to analyze or explain in the more theoretical definition that will be the conclusion of his argument. In his *Principles of Mathematics* Bertrand Russell writes of his analysis or "definition" of mathematics:

The definition professes to be, not an arbitrary decision to use a common word in an uncommon signification, but rather a precise analysis of the ideas which, more or less unconsciously, are implied in the ordinary employment of the term.[3]

In other words, one must be familiar with the "ordinary employment" of the term "mathematics," or its dictionary definition, if one is to understand Russell's "philosophical definition," that is his analysis of that which is denoted by the dictionary definition. The dictionary definition *points out,* so to speak, a class of objects possessing a common property; the philosophical definition then purports to present new and important information about those objects. A pointing-out definition can be either lexical or stipulative depending on whether or not the term has a clear and useful "ordinary employment." When the term is ambiguous, that is when it has more than one ordi-

nary employment, the pointing-out definition must stipulate which of its senses is to be used. And when the term is vague, the pointing-out definition, in order to be useful, may have to render it more precise, that is stipulate a more definite meaning which, though not in perfect accord with the term's usual (vague) meaning, nevertheless falls within the range of its customary vagueness. (One may not define the vague word "bald" as "being at least seventy-two inches tall," for that definition, while more precise than the term it defines, falls entirely outside the borderline of the word's normal application. Even a "stipulator" is not perfectly free to mean *anything* he wishes by a word that has a well-known, albeit vague, sense.)

4. *Aristotelian real definitions* are one model for what a genuine philosophical or scientific definition must be like. Aristotle contrasted "real definitions" with the merely "nominal definitions" discussed thus far. The latter state relations between words; the former state relations between a word and a nonverbal part of the real world. Real definitions are either true or false, but unlike dictionary definitions, their truth is determined by their correspondence not with actual usage but with a segment of the world that is independent of language. In short, real definitions impart genuine scientific or philosophical knowledge, not mere knowledge about usage. The brief selection in this chapter from the logic text of Morris Cohen and Ernest Nagel succinctly states the Aristotelian theory of definition by genus and difference, illustrates it with the famous diagram invented by the Roman philosopher Porphyry in the third century A.D., and subjects it to criticism in the light of twentieth century philosophy of language.

5. *Scientific explication* is the name given by Rudolph Carnap (1891–1970) to definitions which express scientific theories. Many writers have found in Carnap's account of such definitions a suggestive model for understanding the definitions that express philosophical doctrines. Very often a theoretical definition in science is given of a term that already has a common prescientific usage. Commonly everything that is denoted by the word in its ordinary employment will also be denoted by its scientific definition, and vice versa. Consider, for example, the ordinary word

"blood." The dictionary definition would serve as a useful "pointing-out definition" in a scientific treatise aiming at an explication (scientific definition) of the term. Blood, we might say, is "a red fluid which flows through the skin when one is cut." An explication then would enumerate constituent elements of the complex thus pointed out which are common and peculiar to it and which help scientists explain and predict its behavior. Such an explication might be the following: "Blood is the fluid which carries nourishment and oxygen to all the cells of the body and carries away their waste products." The explication thus incorporates into the very meaning of a word a scientific explanatory theory. Notice (1) that the pointing-out definition of "blood" does correspond (roughly) to an accurate lexical definition, and (2) that everything that is blood according to these definitions is still called blood according to the scientific explication, and vice versa. Thus no revision of ordinary language is involved.

Carnap, however, does not require such an exact correspondence of denotations in every case of a good explication. He is satisfied if the class of things referred to by the term to be explicated (which he calls the "explicandum") is *similar* to the class of things denoted by the explicating phrase (which he calls the "explicatum"). But close similarity, while sometimes desirable, is by no means always required. Consider, for example, the zoologist's definition of "fish" as "a cold-blooded vertebrate which lives in the water and has gills throughout its life." The explicandum "fish" is a vague prescientific term whose pointing-out definition is simply "any animal that lives in the water," and which was commonly used to refer not only to trout, salmon, sharks, etc. but also to whales, dolphins, and seals. The classes referred to by the explicandum (fish) and the explicatum (cold-blooded aquatic vertebrate with life-long gills) obviously do not coincide, since the latter is narrower than the former. But does that invalidate the scientific explication? Not at all, for the new definition is much more useful for scientific purposes than the old prescientific one, even after we factor in the costs of deviating from customary usage. The new biological concept of a fish is more *fruitful* than the prescientific one because it can

more readily be used in the formulation of scientific laws. Marine zoologists discovered that the animals to which the redefined term "fish" applies have far more properties in common than do the animals to which the prescientific word "fish" applied, and that allows a greater number of general statements to be made about them as a class. That is what it means to have greater scientific fruitfulness.

Note that the scientific explication of "fish," while departing from ordinary prescientific usage, nevertheless requires only a minimal alteration of that usage. *Most* of the animals formerly called "fish" are still called "fish"; there is still a considerable correspondence between the denotations of these terms. But important as the requirement of denotational "similarity to the explicandum" is for Carnap, the requirement of fruitfulness is of overriding importance. The explicatum is to be as "similar" in its denotation to the explicandum as the prior requirements of exactness and fruitfulness permit, and in some cases, as in the "blood" example, the "similarity" might even amount to complete correspondence.

How helpful is this account of scientific explication as a model for our understanding of philosophical definitions? There are surely points of similarity. Like explications, most of the important definitions put forth by philosophers claim to be "real" rather than nominal, adding new information or insight into the nature of the objects denoted by the word defined, well beyond that which is made explicit in its pointing-out definition. Similarly, philosophers try not to depart drastically from ordinary usage since that would invite equivocation and spread linguistic confusion. (Prescientific terms can simply be dropped from the scientific vocabulary and replaced by more fruitful explicata, but the terms to be defined by philosophers are for the most part indispensable parts of our everyday working vocabularies.) Still, when something analogous to scientific "fruitfulness" warrants it, philosophers feel free to depart, to some small degree at least, from ordinary usage. And like scientists, philosophers do not feel bound to transcribe exactly what ordinary persons have in mind when they use a word, but rather make explicit the ideas that are, in Russell's words, "more or less unconsciously implied" in their usage.

There are of course important differences between the explications of science and philosophical definitions. The philosopher's "explicanda" are more general or abstract concepts (contrast the philosophical concepts "thing," "cause," "value" with the nonphilosophical concepts "blood," "fish," "acid"), and the sources of "fruitfulness" differ. Fruitful explications for the scientist are those that enable him to formulate laws and make predictions; fruitful philosophical definitions are those that yield deeper understanding of the most basic of all our concepts and the ways they link together and form a kind of picture of the structure of the world, at least in those respects in which the world answers to our categories for understanding it. In one sense philosophical definitions aim at clarification of our concepts (rather than scientific knowledge of natural events). But in another sense clarification of concepts itself imparts knowledge of the world. If we understand the concept of causation (or the word "cause") more clearly, then we have a better idea of what *causation* itself is, and we better understand every single case we know of where one event causes another in the "real world." And the same holds true of all the other philosophical concepts. If the question "What is X?" is equivalent to the question about language or concepts, namely, "What does the word X mean?," we must remember that the equivalence holds both ways; philosophical questions about language (for example, "What is the correct definition of the word X?") are at the same time questions about reality ("What is the true nature of X's?").

6. *Persuasive definitions* are yet another type of definition sometimes produced by philosophers (and not always intentionally). The term was coined by Charles L. Stevenson (1908–1979) in his famous essay which is excerpted in this chapter. Stevenson points out that some words in our language do more than make neutral reference to their denotations; they also express favorable or unfavorable attitudes towards those objects and are used to influence or redirect the attitudes of others. This expressive and directive function of language Stevenson calls "emotive meaning," and

in virtue of it, proferred definitions of a laudatory term are often efforts to assign the word as a kind of prize to a favored denotation thought worthy of it. When a philosopher offers a definition of such a word as "justice" or "piety" (to take two Socratic examples), he is not merely attempting to contribute to our knowledge or to clarify our concepts; rather he is *taking a stand* for or against something, awarding a linguistic prize to those objects or qualities he thinks deserving of it, and attempting to influence his readers' attitudes toward those objects or qualities. Giving a persuasive definition is pleading a cause under the guise of "merely" defining a word, but is illicit only when the definer misunderstands what he is doing and takes the definition to be a license to escape the need to give reasons, as when he says, "That's just what the word means; no further argument is necessary." When persuasive definitions appear as conclusions in the great works of philosophy they are always the product of elaborate supporting arguments.

CRITERIA FOR JUDGING DEFINITIONS

By what criteria can philosophical definitions be evaluated? That depends of course on whether the definition purports to be nominal or real, lexical or stipulative, clarificatory or persuasive. For those cases where the aim is to impart important new information or insight into some part of the nonverbal world, philosophical tradition has evolved a number of rough and ready standards of adequacy. First of all, the term to be defined (usually called the *definiendum)* and the expression that does the defining (usually called the *definiens)* should be at least roughly equivalent in their denotations. That is to say that the *definiens* must be "applicable to everything of which the *definiendum* can be predicated, and applicable to nothing else."[4] In other words, the *definiens* states properties that are common and peculiar to the objects denoted by the *definiendum*. The definition is too broad if the *definiens* applies to some objects not denoted by the *definiendum,* and too narrow if the *definiendum* applies to some things that are not also denoted by the *definiens*. The definition of a "cup" as a "glass container for pouring liquids" is too narrow, because wooden and plastic containers can also be cups even though they are not denoted by the *definiens*. To define a "psychiatrist" as "a professional person who gives advice about emotional problems" is too broad because some professional persons who give advice about emotional problems are not psychiatrists—they are ministers, marriage counselors, and so on. Some inadequate definitions suffer from both defects, being too narrow and too broad at the same time. Thus the definition of a dentist as "a man who treats diseases of the mouth" is too narrow because some dentists are women, and too broad because some men who treat diseases of the mouth are not dentists. These examples are not illustrations, of course, of attempted *philosophical* definitions, but the principles governing the latter are the same. Thus, to take a philosophical example, the definition of "justice" as "whatever promotes the interest of the stronger party" is both too narrow and too broad. When philosophers point to examples which show that a definition is too narrow or too broad they are said to have presented *counterexamples* to the definition, and thus to have refuted it. Sometimes this is done by making statements about the definition. Sometimes, more dramatically, it is done by direct demonstration, as when Diogenes (412–323 B.C.), dissatisfied with the definition propounded in the Athenian Academy of "man" as "a featherless biped," plucked a chicken and threw it over the Academy wall!

As we have seen, some philosophers, taking scientific explications as their model, do not require perfect denotational equivalence for an adequate philosophical definition, provided departures from it are justified by their "fruitfulness" and are no greater than necessary. But in the case of a definition which (like the scientific definition of "fish") is too broad or too narrow, the philosopher should shoulder the burden of showing that his departures from standard usage are indeed fruitful and minimal. Furthermore, if a philosopher is to avoid the charge that his or her definition is simply *false,* he or she should treat that part of it that is apparently vulnerable to counterexamples as stipulative, and therefore neither true nor false, but only useful as a vehicle

for transmitting the important truths in the rest of the definition that might otherwise be obscured.

Satisfaction (or near-satisfaction) of the criterion of denotational equivalence, however, is at best only necessary, but not yet sufficient for an adequate philosophical definition. Something like the scientist's "fruitfulness" is necessary too. The definition must avoid obviousness and triviality. It must cite characteristics that are important and that deepen our understanding or dispel our perplexities. To do that job it is not enough to cite a trivial characteristic other than those mentioned in a dictionary definition that just happens (incidentally) to be common and peculiar to the objects denoted by the *definiendum.* The Athenian academicians hardly improved things when in answer to Diogenes' counterexample they revised their definition of "man" by specifying that man is "a featherless biped with broad nails (rather than claws)." That revision did not deepen anyone's understanding of human nature.

A third criterion of adequacy is that the definition not be circular. This is the rule violated in poor Euthyphro's attempt to define piety as "what is pleasing to the gods." It is true that what is pleasing to the gods is pious and vice versa, but that trivial equivalence gives no insight whatsoever into the nature or ground of piety. What is it about pious acts that makes them pleasing to the gods? Are pious acts pleasing to the gods because they are pleasing to the gods (a trivial redundancy) or because they have some further common character? Clearly the latter, but in that case what is that further character? Euthyphro's definition leaves us in the dark. Before we can know what pious acts are, we must know what the gods like, and before we can know what acts the gods like, we must know what acts are pious. As Euthyphro puts it: "Now Socrates, I simply don't know how to tell you what I think. Somehow everything that we put forward keeps moving about us in a circle, and nothing will stay where we put it."

Circular definitions present an expression which is a virtual synonym of the *definiendum.* This can be helpful to a person who is just learning the language and is familiar with the one term but not the other. We might tell such a person that "courage" means the same as "bravery," but if we are deeply perplexed by the nature of courage and wish to have deeper insight into it (as well as knowledge of which acts truly *are* courageous), the mere synonym won't help, because we can raise precisely the same questions about *it,* and start our way round the circle. The net effect of the definition, even when it is helpful to someone or other, is merely verbal. As Cohen and Nagel put it, "the *structure* of 'courage' (what it signifies, not the word) has not been analyzed."[5] Those authors also make the useful point that some circular definitions (unlike the example of "courage is bravery") are very subtle indeed, and difficult to detect: "The present rule is violated if the sun is defined as 'the star which shines by day,' for 'day' itself is defined in terms of the shining of the sun."[6]

VAGUENESS AND OPEN TEXTURE

Many of the terms that present themselves most urgently for philosophical definition are vague words which for some pressing practical reason must be rendered more precise. It will be useful, in explaining how these terms challenge philosophers, to introduce a few more technical terms from the philosophy of language.

1. The *extension* (often called *denotation)* of a general word consists of all those objects to which it may be applied. Thus the extension of the word "city" consists of New York, London, Tokyo, Moscow, and all the others. Some words, like "city," have many objects in their extensions; some, like "hermaphrodite," have few; others, like "unicorn," have none at all. Yet all these terms have meaning, whatever the "size" of their extensions.

2. The *total intension* (often called *connotation)* of a general word consists of all those characteristics that are common and peculiar to all members of the term's denotation. To know the total intension of some general terms would require enormous scientific knowledge. Thus, we can define an *acid* as "a chemical compound capable of reacting with a base to form a salt," specifying a part of the word's total intension in our definition. But the rest of that total will include such characteristics as tasting sour; turning litmus paper red;

having hydrogen-containing molecules or ions able to give up a proton to a base; having the capacity to accept an unshared pair of electrons from a base; and so on. Very likely no chemist yet knows the *total* intension of the word "acid."

3. The *conventional intension* (connotation) of a general word consists of those characteristics in its total intension that are singled out and used in a correct dictionary definition of the word. The word "meaning" itself has various meanings, but perhaps its most usual sense is "conventional intension." To know the meaning (in this sense) of a general word is to know its dictionary definition.

4. A general word is *vague* when there is known to be at least one object for which it is impossible, on the basis of the word's conventional intension alone, to determine whether or not that object is a member of the term's extension. There is thus an uncertain area of application, a fuzzy no man's land, in the extension of a vague word. "Bald" is the most common textbook example. Its conventional intension (when applied to people) is "having relatively little hair on one's head." A man with no hair at all on his head (like Yul Brynner) is obviously bald; bushy-headed youths and most women are obviously not bald; but many millions of persons with thinning tops, receding hairlines, or bald spots, are neither clearly bald nor clearly not bald. These people straddle a dividing line so obscure that it is impossible to make it out. It would be a silly and futile verbal dispute to argue over whether they are truly bald or not.

Vagueness is not necessarily a defect in a word. It is very useful to have a part of our vocabularies reserved for expressing rough impressions and approximations. In law courts, however, even the useful vagueness of an ordinary everyday word can be an impediment to judicial functioning which must be eliminated. The standard textbook example is the statute that prohibits on pain of punishment the introduction of "vehicles" into a public park. Motor cars are clear cases of vehicles, and chairs are clear cases of nonvehicles, but how is a court to rule when a defendant is charged with violating the statute by bringing a baby carriage into the park? A bicycle? Roller skates? A toy automobile? A World War II army tank to be preserved as a monument? When persons in ordinary life argue whether a given borderline person is bald or not, there is usually no overriding practical reason why the issue has to be settled at all, and if they agree anyway that a definition is called for (say, in terms of having less than some arbitrarily selected number of hairs on one's head), they will agree that in a sense the definitional criterion selected is *arbitrary,* and any number of other ones would have done as well. But in the law court the issue must be settled, because a defendant must be either convicted or acquitted, and it cannot be settled simply by the arbitary fiat of the judge, since whatever justice is, *it* is not arbitrary. Judges therefore invoke as reasons their interpretations of the intentions and motives of the legislature that passed the statute, or their own conceptions of the common interest or public good.

5. Even a nonvague word can have *open texture,* which is another way of saying that it is logically possible that it might one day become vague. A number of years ago there was no known object such that it was impossible to determine, on the basis of the conventional intension of the word "life," whether that object was a form of living thing or not. All known objects were either clearly living animals or vegetable, or else clearly inanimate objects. But even before the discovery of certain nonclassifiable viruses, it was logically possible that some new kind of thing would come into existence or be newly discovered that would render the hitherto precise term "life" a puzzlingly vague term. This logical possibility of vagueness, this vulnerability to new inventions and disovcries that is characteristic of general terms, is called *open texture.*

LEGAL DEFINITION: THE CASE OF DOUGLAS TEMPLEMORE

Not only ordinary words like "vehicle," but terms of traditional philosophical interest like "person," "cause," and "human being," can become the occasion for attempts at legal definition when they occur (as they often do) in legal statutes and opinions. Indeed, in virtue of open texture—the possibility that new and unclassifiable borderline cases might turn up—almost any word at all might occa-

sion the attempt at legal definition. The problem of defining a term like "vehicle" is hardly a job for the philosopher, but nevertheless his methodological concern with legal reasoning will keep him interested, even when the term to be defined is so mundane. One of the traditional roles of the philosopher is to be a *critic of reasoning,* a judge in individual cases of the intellectual legitimacy of asserting one proposition on the basis of others that are said to be its ground or support. The philosopher here is concerned not so much with the "true nature of vehicles" as with stating and defending a rational conception of legal reasoning itself; not so much with playing the game of legal definition as with stating and defending its rules, and clarifying its objectives. But when the term to be defined is itself a philosophically interesting one, like "human being," the philosopher has a double interest in the process, both as player and as critic of the game.

In 1953 the French writer Jean Bruller published a remarkable novel under his *nom de plume* "Vercors" which was translated into English with the title *You Shall Know Them.* Because this ingenious work of fiction shows how the open texture of the concept "human being" can drive judges and jurymen to the study of philosophy, parts of it are included in this section. A brief synopsis of the plot is in order. Discovery in a remote part of New Guinea of the skull of a "missing link" in the evolution of man excites a group of British scientists, who organize an anthropological expedition to investigate the skull and search for more fossilized remains. They invite a popular writer, Douglas Templemore, to accompany them as a journalist and publicist. To their amazement they learn that the discovered bones are not fossils at all, and that the missing links who left them are not extinct. Eagerly they "befriend" and study these ape-men, and give them the affectionate name of "tropis." Vercors' description of these creatures is especially clever for it attributes characteristics to them that allow them to straddle the lines that have most commonly been proposed for distinguishing our species from the "lower animals." In the novel the term "human being" thus becomes disturbingly vague, and most of the scientists, and especially Templemore, become progressively more disturbed by their mounting philosophical doubts and perplexities.

Some of the tropis' organs resemble those of their human counterparts very closely; others are much closer to those of the great apes. Like apes the tropis have very long arms, and they run on the backs of their fingers like chimpanzees. Like apes they have flattened faces, low receding foreheads, jutting browlines, and virtually nonexistent noses. They have mighty teeth and fang-like canines. They have four hands (that is, their feet are prehensile), and their tested IQs are only slightly higher than those of such primates as chimpanzees. On the other hand, they have some remarkably humanoid features too. They chip stones, construct primitive handaxes, and make fires. They bury their dead. They generally stand erect and walk upright. Most importantly, they communicate by a "sort of language" that consists of about one hundred articulate cries. Like humans, they can laugh, and they show that they are capable of real individual friendships with people, not merely "the submissive attachment of dogs," and they can be taught simple mechanical chores. Even the basic biological test for determining lines between species fails to help classify them. Biologists define a species as a group of animals that can interbreed, no matter how different they may look. But experiments with the artifical insemination of female tropis show conclusively that they can interbreed with apes and *also* (this is the most startling discovery) that they can interbreed with humans!

One of the scientists in the expedition is not troubled by the riddle of classification. "All classifications are arbitrary," she tells Templemore. "Nature doesn't classify, it's we who do, because it's convenient . . . What is it to you, after all, whether this being whose skull I'm holding in my hand is called an ape or a man? He was what he was: the name we give it is immaterial." But Templemore is not persuaded, and his perplexities mount.

Finally, an alarming development galvanizes him into action. Unscrupulous Australian business interests buy the land on which the tropis live and lay claim to all its flora and fauna as their property. The anthropologists then learn that these businessmen plan to exploit the tropis as "cheap manpower" in textile mills. If the tropis are indeed apes, then legally they are mere property and can be put to work performing elementary chores, provided only that they are kept well-fed, given adequate rest, and treated humanely. If they are indeed human beings, however, then such treatment would be indistinguishable from slavery, an intolerable violation of the tropis' "human rights." The issue has now been forced on Templemore inescapably. He decides to compel the British legal system to settle the matter once and for all. He artificially inseminates a tropi with his own seed, delivers his child from her, flies to England with it, registers its birth under the name Douglas Templemore, Jr., and even has it (him?) baptized. Then he gives the infant a hypodermic injection of poison, painlessly causing its death, and turns himself in to the police demanding to be charged with murder. Whether or not he is a murderer depends entirely on whether his son was a human being; so now the ancient philosophical riddle becomes a problem of legal definition for the courts, and a matter of life or death for Douglas Templemore.

The double interest of the philosopher in this fictitious case is clearly shown in the excerpted passages. On the one hand, philosophers join anthropologists, lawyers, and theologians in the efforts to fashion a substantive definition. On the other hand, philosophers transcend their own primary question and self-consciously raise other questions about what they are doing. In this transcendent role, the philosopher tries to be both critic and rule-maker. "What is the primary question ultimately about?," he asks. Is it about language usage? Scientific data? Religious doctrine? Is it a matter of discovery or decision? Does it have an objectively correct answer at all? By what criteria are we to judge proposed answers to it? Which kinds of supporting reasons for proposed definitions are relevant and which are not? These so-called *metaquestions* (questions about other questions) are the very stuff of philosophy, but the primary original question ("What is a human being?") is the impelling one that cannot be comfortably evaded. Philosophers have had a great deal to say about *it* too, as the reader may discover in chapter 3.

PHILOSOPHY AND PUBLIC POLICY

Philosophy, then, consists of a set of "left-over," genuinely cognitive questions. Some of these are about "ultimates"; others seek "real definitions" of abstract terms; others analyze the concepts and methods of science or attempt to integrate the findings of science; others seek the general principles of all correct reasoning; and others (the metaquestions) raise methodological questions about the primary questions of philosophy themselves. Our account will not be complete, however, until we consider the very practical role of philosophical speculation and analysis in the making of social and personal decisions, for that role is the one given most emphasis in this text. *Philosophy and the Human Condition* is concerned more with the philosophical questions that arise spontaneously in the minds of all students than it is with others that are more recondite and technical.

In 1971 a new journal was started by the Princeton University Press called *Philosophy and Public Affairs*. Although this is a journal primarily for professional philosophers and other scholars, it has published articles mostly on urgent practical questions of public controversy, or at least about some crucial philosophical aspect of those questions that is usually ignored in popular discussions. Early issues of the journal, for example, contained articles about abortion, the morality of war, freedom of expression, the duties of the affluent in times of famine, civil disobedience, conscientious objection, the morality of suicide, capital punishment, reverse discrimination, and distributive justice. There are at least two ways in which a philosopher gets involved in such questions. First of all, philosophers, like other citizens, may wish to take stands and argue forcibly for some favored course of policy. Unlike other advocates, however, philosophers are likely to make explicit, analyze, and defend the general principles (including moral principles) which they employ in their arguments, to make relevant and enlightening distinctions along the way, and to be sensitive to the logical commitments of the stands they take, especially as they may bear on other issues not presently under discussion.

Secondly, philosophers try to isolate subquestions which are vital to the resolution of the primary question, formulate them exactly, and contribute to their solutions, as small but necessary contributions toward the solutions of the larger questions. Very often these strategic subquestions are questions of conceptual analysis of a form long familiar to philosophers. For example, we cannot argue convincingly for a stand about the permissibility of abortion until we have answered the prior philosophical questions "What is a person?," "What is a human being?," and "What is the ground of a right to life?" Other philosophical problems involved in most moral problems about killing and saving life (see chapter 4) are about the conceptual distinctions between acting and omitting, killing and letting die, intended and merely foreseen consequences. Similarly, controversial moral problems about justice often require philosophical definitions of "desert," "opportunity," and "need," and disputes over liberty lead philosophers to attempt to define "harm," "offense," "consent," and "autonomy." There is no longer any question of whether philosophy can be practical; what is now doubtful is whether any approach to a divisive public issue can be practical that is wholly dissociated from philosophy.

PHILOSOPHY AND PERSONAL POLICY

Persons of little learning, who know nothing of the professional discipline called "philosophy," still talk of their own "philosophies." If you ask a merchant to state his "philosophy of business," he will probably describe a policy for dealing with the problems which arise in the course of commercial transactions, and if he does this in a fairly systematic or comprehensive way, he will probably state his objectives as a merchant, or "what he wants out of business," as well as the methods he prefers to use to attain those ends. And so it is with any of the "philosophies" which ordinary people talk about—the coach's philosophy of baseball, the doctor's philosophy of medicine, anybody's "philosophy of life." Philosophy in this sense is a reasoned *personal policy* for dealing with either a part or the whole of one's affairs.

It is difficult to imagine how a person could manage his or her affairs without such policies. Without them, each occasion for action would pose a fresh problem to be resolved anew each time it presented itself. To have a philosophy and to be able to state one's philosophy, however, are two quite different things; thus among persons who are not professional philosophers, some are deemed more "philosophical" or thoughtful than others. Formulating a consistent and comprehensive philosophy of life is a task of such complexity, however, that no busy person of affairs could be expected to perform it. There is no surprise then in the fact that such a project is yet another concern of the professional philosopher. Chapter 10 ("The Meaning of Life") contains sample expressions of that concern, as do chapters 7 ("Love and Sexuality") and 9 ("Belief in God") in somewhat more restricted ways.

Joel Feinberg

NOTES

1. A. E. Taylor, *Socrates, The Man And His Thought* (Garden City, N.Y.: Doubleday Anchor Books, 1953), p. 102.

2. Robert D. Cumming, "Introduction," *The Euthyphro, Apology, and Crito of Plato* (New York: Bobbs-Merrill, 1948), p. x.

3. Bertrand Russell, *The Principles of Mathematics* (New York: W. W. Norton, 1948), p. 3.

4. Morris R. Cohen and Ernest Nagel, *An Introduction to Logic and Scientific Method* (New York: Harcourt, Brace, and Co., 1934), p. 238.

5. *Ibid.,* p. 239.

6. *Ibid.,* p. 240.

1. A DEFENSE OF PHILOSOPHY

Ralph Barton Perry

There are many drawbacks to being a professor of philosophy, and one of the worst is that you cannot gossip lightly about your occupation. Picture to yourself that great American forum and social centre, the smoking compartment of a Pullman car. There has been an exchange of confidences about the boot and shoe industry in St. Louis, or the boot-legging industry in Detroit, when your neighbor turns to you and asks, amidst a hush of expectancy, what you sell. To be as candid and optimistic as your neighbors, you would be compelled to say: "My firm manufactures and distributes ultimate truth; our business is to discover the nature of the universe, and apply it to the meaning of life." Some sound instinct prevents you from saying it. You know that you would create a situation which neither you nor your neighbors would be able to support, much as though you were to say "*I* am God." So you hastily mumble something about being a teacher, hoping that they won't insist on knowing the subject you teach,—and then pass rapidly on to safer topics, such as the hard winter we've been having, or how late the train is.

The youthful brothers William and Henry James suffered from a like embarrassment when asked by their schoolmates what their father was. Nor did his suggestion afford them much relief: "Say I'm a philosopher, say I'm a seeker for truth, say I'm a lover of my kind, say I'm an author of books if you like; or, best of all, just say I'm a Student."[1]

It would be fair enough to evade the questions, for, after all, that is what nearly everybody does. Socrates, who in defending himself before his judges, uttered the greatest of all apologies for

philosophy, said in effect that he hadn't been able to find anybody who really knew what he was about. He invented and went around asking the devastating question, "What are you really aiming at, and why?" and found nobody who could answer it. He based his own claim to distinction on the fact that he was the only person who thought of asking it. One reason why most occupations get off more easily than philosophy, is because they are more familiar. If you ask a man what his occupation is, and he answers "business," you are satisfied, simply because you have seen business men before. If you pressed him further, and asked him what business was, he might wonder where you came from, but he probably couldn't answer you. Ask a lawyer what law is, ask any living creature what life is, and you will find the result equally unsatisfactory. There is a sort of gentlemen's agreement not to ask such questions. And they are not felt to be necessary where the occupation is common and recognizable. In certain parts of the West a man who said he was a Mormon preacher would be viewed with much less suspicion than a man who announced that he was a philosopher; not because people would know the meaning of Mormonism any better than the meaning of philosophy, but because Mormons would have a recognizable identity that would quite satisfy their curiosity. It is like the man who being asked whether he believed in baptism, replied, "Believe in baptism! Why, I've seen it done." People do not as a rule insist upon knowing the meaning of things, further than to assign them a place in their world of familiar objects. The trouble with philosophy is not that people fail to understand what it means, but that they have never seen it done. If philosophers wore long hair and flowing robes, and were frequently seen about the landscape gazing at the skies in rapt contemplation, they would soon become as much

Reprinted from *A Defence of Philosophy* (Cambridge, Mass.: Harvard University Press, 1931), pp. 3–10, 25–41, by permission of the publisher.

a part of the accepted scheme of things as priests in Spain or as lawyers and business men in America.

Perhaps there is a feeling that the philosopher ought, like the priest, to be plainly marked, so that those among whom he mingles might be put on their guard. This is on the assumption that the philosopher is a man of edification and omniscience. People do not like to entertain sages unawares. It outrages their sense of propriety to have said ordinary things in an extraordinary presence; or they are mortified to have exhibited levity, obscenity, or ignorance in the company of gravity, austerity, and knowledge. Had they been warned they might at least have put on their company manners. Perhaps it is a mistake to suppose that any group of Americans in a smoking compartment would believe that a philosopher or anybody else really *was* edifying and omniscient. They would be more likely to think of a philosopher as one who *felt* himself to be edifying, and *thought* himself to be omniscient. But this would not ease the situation. Courtesy requires that even the odor of sanctity shall be respected. And what can you decently say to a man if you think that he thinks that he knows everything?

So the first step towards entering into comfortable relations with the philosopher is to relieve him of his reputation for edification and omniscience. You see I do not propose to evade the question as to what philosophy means. Were I anything but a philosopher, I might properly do so; but the philosopher is, above all persons, interested in what things mean, and he cannot consistently avoid applying the question to himself.

We begin, then, by humanizing the philosopher. And the first step is to distinguish between the man and his subject. To be a philosopher in the occupational and professional sense, means to investigate, and perhaps to teach, a certain branch of knowledge. The philosopher is a philosopher in the sense in which a chemist is a chemist, and not in the sense in which a Baptist is a Baptist. There need not be anything peculiarly philosophical about the philosopher any more than there is anything peculiarly chemical about the chemist. His philosophy is not a state of his will or conviction, but like the chemist's chemistry, it is the subject-matter which he seeks to know. It is true that, among other things, he seeks to know something about life; but that he should exemplify his knowledge is not his vocation, any more than it is the vocation of the physician to be healthy. He may, if his interest leads him into the field of ethics, know something about the difference between good and evil, or right and wrong. But here even the analogy with the physician has to be abandoned, for it is not the vocation of the philosopher to make people good, or persuade them to do the right. His calling is like that of the pure scientist. It is his business, if possible, to know some aspect of the truth, and to record that knowledge for others to apply, *if* and *as* they will. . . .

Though philosophy lies beyond the range of what we call the practically useful, and is contrary to those habits of discourse which we call common-sense, —although it involves a cruel and unusual intensity of thinking, it nevertheless lies in a well-known direction, at the end of a road on which every man has gone a certain distance. There need be no doubt as to where to look for it. So in our further examination of that problem of the ultimate, or of the bottom and the whole of things, to which allusion has already been made, I shall attempt to show how it grows out of familiar distinctions for which popular discourse already provides.

The general problem of the ultimate is divisible into four related but distinguishable problems, namely: the problems of the ultimate *reality,* the ultimate *cause,* the ultimate *truth,* and the ultimate *value.* To these correspond the four main divisions of philosophy, *metaphysics, cosmology, logic or theory of knowledge, and ethics or theory of value.*

The problem of ultimate *reality* springs from the familiar distinction between what things are and what they appear to be. Dreams, illusions, hallucinations, the distortions of sensible experience, and the notorious inaccuracies of observation, have taught us that we can not take reality at its face value. Physical science deepens this distrust of appearances, and is wont to tell us, whether rightly or wrongly, that the singing bird is not that spot of color which it is seen to be, or that melodic phrase which it is heard to be, or that "disembodied joy" which it is felt to be; but a mass of protoplasmic molecules, consisting of atoms, which consist in turn of particles of electromagnetic energy. Religion and poetry, on the other hand, seek to persuade us that the physical world, to scientific observation so alien and forbidding, is in reality the manifestation of a beneficent will; or, as Wordsworth says, the scene of "something far more deeply interfused . . . a motion and a spirit, that impels all thinking things, all objects of all thought, and rolls through all things."

I give these opinions for what they are worth, as opinions familiar to popular thought. They evidently agree only in asserting that there is a difference between what things seem to be, and what they really are. They both imply that a deeper or fuller view of things may result in a correction of that aspect which things initially present; that until you know all of a thing you cannot be sure that you know it at all. Such was the case with the elephant and the four blind men of Burmah. One of them grasped the elephant's tusk, and called it a spear; the second a leg, and called it a tree; the third the trunk, and called it a serpent; the fourth the tail and called it a rope. None of them apprehended the elephant for lack of apprehending the whole.

Once the force of such considerations is admitted, one is on an inclined plane at the foot of which lies philosophy. It is now simply a question of seeing it through. Because we all recognize that things may so qualify one another that one cannot know the first until one knows the last, or that the nature of a particular thing may depend on its place in the general scheme of things, philosophy attempts to exhibit such a general scheme of things, whether by conceptual abstraction, or by intuitive insight. Since partial knowledge may at any time be surprised and overwhelmed by new discovery coming from the wilderness of the unknown, philosophy attempts a general reconnaissance that may serve to render knowledge more stable and secure.

The second question is the question of the ultimate *cause*. This question is discovered in infancy and forgotten in later life. Every remarkable child (and all children are remarkable) has astonished his parents by asking, upon being told that God made the world, "And who made God?" There is an old German conundrum which asks: "St. Christopher carries Christ, and Christ carries the world, but on what, then, does Christopher stand?" Philosophers are the only people that try to guess this conundrum. One may feel that their guesses are pretty wild, but the philosopher is justified not so much by his answers as by his questions. These do not cease to exist when they are neglected, nor are they illegitimate simply because they are hard to answer. There stands the question. The ordinary casual explanation of things explains in terms of causes which require a like explanation in their turn. We ordinarily conceive natural events like a row of blocks, each of which is toppled over in turn by its toppling neighbor. Some people answer the question of war-guilt by the Austrian ultimatum to Serbia, while others trace it back to Mother Eve. And for theoretical purposes it makes little difference, since in either case you still have an erring will to explain. It is customary to carry the explanation back as far as it is convenient, and then, for lack of breath or time, to stop. But since you have then made every subsequent event dependent on the event at which you stop, and since you have failed to explain that, there is force in the contention that you have explained nothing. You have simply pushed the causal question back to a point at which it is somewhat less urgent and conspicuous. Once recognize the distinction between a proximate cause and an ulterior cause, and there thus emerges to any thorough mind the idea of an ultimate cause, or of causality so conceived as to need no further explanation, in order thus to meet a difficulty which science and common sense recognize but evade.

Third, there is the question of ultimate *truth*. In our studies of geometry we have all been made painfully aware that knowledge proceeds step by step and that the conclusions which are reached depend on the truth of prior theorems, and eventually on the truth of the axioms laid down at the outset,—such as the axiom that the straight line is the shortest line between two points, or the axiom that two parallel lines never meet. Doubt has in recent times been cast on these alleged axioms. Some of them now appear to be theorems which can themselves be proved, others to be arbitrary assumptions which cannot be proved, although they seem to need it. Requiring some support for the system of geometry, so-called philosophers of mathematics have sought to find it in logic, and have believed that they could eventually find highly abstract axioms, like the principle of contradiction, from which the whole chain of reasoning could be suspended.

There is another and opposite way of presenting the matter, which is to say that the unquestionable and rock-bottom certainties are not self-evident principles, but items of *fact* perceived through the senses. These are called "data" to indicate that while they are used to prove other things such as theories, they neither possess nor need any supporting evidence for themselves. To which the other party retorts that facts are as uncertain and doubtful as anything else, and have to be formulated in judgments, and attested by their consistency with other judgments, so that they are proved by rational or logical methods after all. And so the fight waxes furious, on an issue which most of the world ignores. But though theory battles with theory and though the outcome is dubious, as well as irrelevant to what most people do in most of their waking hours, the question stubbornly remains. Most truth is a derived or borrowed truth. A conclusion is no truer than the premises from which it is reasoned, or a theory than the facts which confirm it. If, as Bruno said, the first button of one's coat is wrongly buttoned, all the rest will be out of place. Here is the same need—a right beginning that will guarantee a right ending; the same desire, which gives philosophy its essential impulse, to build solidly on something ultimate.

Finally, there is the problem of ultimate *value.* Most things are valued for the sake of other things, for what they yield, or lead to, or can be exchanged for. In so far as we are reflective at all, action is attended by a prospective series of means and ends, each step an end in relation to the present means, and a means in relation to ulterior ends. As a rule this prospect does not definitely culminate in a final destination, but fades away in the distance. We buy land in order to sell it, in order to buy more land, in order to build a house, in order to put our furniture in it, in order to rent the house, in order to go to Europe, in order to do we know not what. We spend money in order to go to school, in order to go to college, in order to get an education, in order to make more money, in order to————but this is about as far as it is customary to look ahead. One is impatient to act, and one's hand is forced by circumstance. There is the train about to depart. If we wait longer, we shall miss it. Better take it when you can, no matter where it goes. Other people whom you know are taking it. Everybody's taking it. If a philosopher approaches at such a moment to suggest that you look before you leap, there is small chance of his being listened to. Such a scene is described by Mr. Chesterton in one of his early books.

Suppose that a great commotion arises in the street about something, let us say a lamp-post, which many influential persons desire to pull down. A grey-clad monk, who is the spirit of the Middle Ages, is approached upon the matter, and begins to say, in the arid manner of the Schoolmen, 'Let us first of all consider, my brethren, the value of Light. If Light be in itself good. . . .' At this point he is somewhat excusably knocked down. All the people make a rush for the lamp-post, the lamp-post is down in ten minutes, and they go about congratulating each other on their unmediaeval practicality. But as things go on they do not work out so easily. Some people have pulled the lamp-post down because they wanted the electric light; some because they wanted old iron; some because they wanted darkness, because their deeds were evil. Some thought it not enough of a lamp-post, some too much; some acted because they wanted to smash municipal machinery; some because they wanted to smash something. And there is war in the night, no man knowing whom he strikes. So, gradually and inevitably, to-day, to-morrow, or the next day, there comes back the conviction that the monk was right after all, and that all depends on what is the philosophy of Light. Only what we might have discussed under the gas-lamp, we now must discuss in the dark.[2]

As little heeded as Cassandra, philosophers have been preaching from the time of Socrates and earlier, that there is no sense in acting unless you know what *in the last analysis,* you want—unless you have made up your mind what is ultimately good, in order that you may select the necessary means, or in order that you and your fellows with you may organize for the purpose. Otherwise a man acts at random or defeats himself, while social effort is neutralized by discord and conflict. In life this is usually the sober second thought, arising from disillusionment. At the time of the World War men asked, "What is this so-called 'progress' anyway?" "Is the world getting any better?" "What do we mean by better?" In times of political and social doubt, such as the present, people ask, "What are we trying to make of life?" "What is the good of it all?" "Have we not, perhaps, sacrificed the deeper, simpler, better things to what is shallow and tawdry? Have we not preferred Mammon to God?" But these doubts which are novel and unusual to the average mind are the immemorial doubts of philosophy. What is that which is good in itself, supremely good, which is an end and not a means, an ultimate and not an intermediate good? Is it private pleasure, is it virtue, or the will of God, or the realization of human nature, or the happiness of mankind? Here again, I cannot claim for philosophy a final solution of the problem, but I do with confidence affirm the genuineness of the problem itself, and the consistency of the philosopher in sticking to it at the cost of his reputation for practical sagacity,—even at the risk of raising doubts as to his sanity.

There is, as it will be noted, a sameness in these four problems. And they all arise from distinctions which are recognized by common-sense. The perculiarity of philosophy lies in its pressing these distinctions. Common sense admits the distinction between reality and appearance, and recognizes that the reality of one appearance may in turn be the appearance of an ulterior reality; philosophy proclaims the need of conceiving a reality that is not itself an appearance at all, but is an *ultimate* reality. Common sense admits the distinction between cause and effect, and recognizes that the cause of one effect may in turn be the effect of an ulterior cause; philosophy proclaims the need of conceiving a cause that is not itself an effect at all, but is an *ultimate* cause. Common sense admits the distinction between conclusion and evidence, and recognizes that the evidence for one conclusion may in turn be a conclusion depending on ulterior evidence; philosophy proclaims the need of conceiving an evidence that is not itself a conclusion at all, but is an *ultimate* evidence. Common sense admits the distinction between end and means, and recognizes that the end of one means may in turn be the means to an ulterior end; philosophy proclaims the need of conceiving an end that is not itself a means at all, but is an *ultimate* end.

In other words, these questions which philosophy asks are all familiar in kind: What is real? Why did it happen? How do I know? What ought I to do? The difference is one of degree, and lies in the thoroughness, the obstinacy, the fanatical and disquieting glitter of the eye. . . .

NOTES

1. Henry James, *Notes of a Son and Brother,* 1904, p. 69.
2. G. K. Chesterton, *Heretics,* 1912, p. 23.

2. THE PHILOSOPHIC ENTERPRISE

Brand Blanshard

I

Philosophy is best understood, I think, as part of an older and wider enterprise, the enterprise of understanding the world. We may well look first at this understanding in the large. I shall ask, to begin with, what is its goal, then what are its chief stages, then what are the ways in which philosophy enters into it.

The enterprise, we have just said, is that of understanding the world. What do we mean by understanding—understanding anything at all? We mean, I suppose, explaining it to ourselves. Very well; what does explaining anything mean? We stumble upon some fact or event that is unintelligible to us; what would make it intelligible? The first step in the answer is, seeing it as an instance of some rule. You suffer some evening from an excruciating headache and despondently wonder why. You remember that you just ate two large pieces of chocolate cake and that you are allergic to chocolate; the headache seems then to be explained. It is no longer a mere demonic visitor intruding on you from nowhere; you have domesticated it, assimilated it to your knowledge, by bringing it under a known rule.

What sort of rules are these that serve to render facts intelligible? They are always rules of connection, rules relating the fact to be explained to something else. You explain the headache by bringing it under a law relating it causally to something else. In like manner, you explain the fact that a figure on the board has angles equal to two right angles by relating it *logically* to something else; by

This paper is a revised form of a Mahlon Powell Lecture delivered at Indiana University in 1961. It was published in *The Owl of Minerva: Philosophers on Philosophy,* ed. by Charles J. Bontempo and S. Jack Odell (New York: McGraw-Hill, 1975). Reprinted here by permission of the author, publisher, and Indiana University.

pointing out that it is a triangle, and that it belongs to the triangles as such to have this property.

Such bringing of a case under a rule explains admirably so far as it goes. But suppose someone asks for a further explanation. When you explain your headache by reference to the chocolate or the angle sum of the figure by referring to its triangularity, he says: "Yes, yes, I know this, but what I don't understand is why the rule itself holds. How do you explain *that?*" We can only give the same answer as before. To explain a rule is to connect it with some other rule from which it follows, just as to explain a fact or event is to connect it with some other fact or event. When you can so connect it, you can explain it; when you cannot, you can't. You can explain why a triangle should have angles equal to a straight line because you can show that this must be true if certain other propositions are true that you normally accept without question. Can you show similarly that the rule about chocolate producing headaches follows from some further rule? No doubt an expert allergist could. He would show that in trying to assimilate the protein molecules of the chocolate, certain of your body cells break down; and the rule that eating chocolate produces a headache follows from the further and more precise rule that a certain kind of cell deterioration produces a certain kind of headache. But then why should this hold? Why should a change in body cells produce a conscious ache? All explanations so far offered here run into a stone wall. We can see that certain changes in the body are in fact followed by changes in consciousness; we have not the slightest idea why.

At this point two courses are open to one who is trying to explain his world. He has come—or if he has not, he soon will—to a generalization that he cannot now explain by bringing it under anything more general. Is he to continue in his attempt or not? The likelihood of his doing so may well depend on what he takes the ideal of explanation to be. Present-day empiricists are quite content to end their inquiries with rules or laws that are merely statements of general conjunction. Certain changes in the body are always accompanied by certain changes in consciousness. Why? That is a foolish question. If they are always in fact so connected, what more could a sensible person ask? One explains a falling snowflake or raindrop or meteor by bringing it under the law of gravitation, and if that law has been made precise, if one can show that the earth and the snowflake are so connected that each pulls the other with a force varying directly with its mass and inversely with the square of its distance, what more could one want? One might, to be sure, find some still wider generalization from which the law of gravitation itself followed; this was a leading interest of Einstein's toward the end of his life, and it made sense. But if further explanation means more than this, the empiricist holds, it is a will-o'-the-wisp. Every explanation of fact must come sooner or later to a dead end. It must halt somewhere with a generalization that is a pure statement of *de facto* togetherness, itself opaque to reason.

But there is another ideal of explanation open to us, that of the rationalists, of whom I am one. They hold that when you end with any law whatever that is a mere statement of conjunction, your explanation is incomplete and you are bound to *try* at least to go beyond it. What leads them to say this? It is their sense of the goal that understanding is seeking, of what would bring the attempt to explain finally to rest. When you ask the question "Why?" you are seeking an answer of some kind; but of what kind? We can see with regard to some answers that we can raise the same question again, of others that we cannot because we have already reached the end of the line. Suppose you remark that two straight lines do not enclose a space, or that whatever is colored is extended, or that a thing cannot at once have a property and not have it, and suppose now some bright skeptic asks you why. Could you give him an answer? I do not think you could, not because there is an answer that you don't know, but because anyone who understood your remark would know the answer already and would be asking a silly question. When you have a law that connects things by a selfevident necessity, the question "Why?" has no point, for the kind of insight you have is just the kind you are asking for. If you see that, being what it is, A *must* be B, the further question "Why?" is meaningless.

What understanding is seeking, then, what would bring the search to rest, is seen necessity. Where it is present, we have what we wanted; where it is absent, we have not yet fully understood.

Now a rationalist is a person who assumes that behind every *is* there is a *must,* that if snow is white or fire burns or John has a cold, the question "Why?" has an answer, and that this answer would disclose a necessity. You may protest: "Can you prove this? Do you really think that because we are seeking necessity, it must be there to be found, that things must be intelligible because it would be so satisfactory to us if they were?" The answer, of course, is "No." The philosopher who takes something to be true because he wants it to be true betrays his calling. But unless the philosopher could assume that there was some answer to his questions, he would have no motive for pressing them. For the critical rationalist the intelligibility of things is neither a necessary conclusion nor an arbitrary assumption, but a postulate, that is, a proposition which for practical purposes he must assume and which experience progressively confirms, but which is incapable of present proof.

Thus the rationalist is, if you will, a man of faith. His faith is that there is to be found in the universe the kind of intelligibility that would satisfy his intellect, that there is a coincidence between reality and his intellectual ideal, that at every point there is an answer to his question "Why?" This faith is the mainspring of his endeavor. He is ready to discard it if he has to, but not until he has to; and he will regard an apparent defeat as only a temporary setback if he can. After all, if there is no answer, why seek it? One may say indeed with George Saintsbury that "the end of all things is bafflement, but it is good not to be baffled too soon." But if we expect nature at any moment to set a roadblock to our reason, we shall almost surely be baffled too soon.

My own faith as a rationalist goes further still. If you ask me why snow is white or why you are reading these lines, I am inclined, as I admitted, to say that there is an intelligible, that is, a necessary, answer to the question, whether we know it or not. Some people would agree with this but would be reluctant to take the next long step with the rationalist. That step is to say that this necessity holds not only between the event of your reading these lines, for example, and some event just before it, but between your so doing and all other events. I am inclined to think that if you had not at this moment been reading these lines, the *Mona Lisa* would not be hanging in the Louvre. The argument is in principle this. Start with the supposition that a present event had not happened, and ask what it commits you to. If you deny the consequent, you must deny the antecedent, which means that if you deny the present event, you must deny the whole succession of necessary causes which led to this event, no matter how long the string. Very well, take some remote bead on that string and deny it; what then? All the events that follow from it as necessary effects will presumably have been different, and since the causal lines diverge in many directions, much of the present world will inevitably have been different.

Make the argument concrete. Is there any remote event in history to which your reading these lines can be traced back? There are indefinitely many; I shall name just one. In the year 490 B.C. a council of war was held on a hill overlooking the Greek coast. The council consisted of eleven commanders of a small Greek force, who were considering what to do about a huge Persian army that was disembarking below them. They knew the intention of that army. It was to wipe out Athens. The presiding general, Callimachus, took the vote of the council on whether they should give battle or not. The vote was five to five, and it fell to him to cast the deciding ballot. He voted for immediate attack and shortly paid for it with his life on the plain of Marathon, not realizing that by his vote he had decided the fate of the Western world. The historian Sir Edward Creasy argues convincingly that if Athens had gone under, so would Greece; and that with the fall of Greece,

the science, philosophy, and art of the West would all have been smothered in their cradle. Plato, Archimedes, Leonardo would probably never have been heard of.

In short, deny that you are reading these lines, follow the stream of causation backward, then follow its diverging lines forward again, and you cannot with any confidence say that Leonardo would have lived or painted at all, let alone that his masterpiece would be hanging in the Louvre. Indeed, I suspect that every event in the universe is thus connected, directly or indirectly, with every other. And since in my view, which must here remain unargued, causality involves necessity, the universe must be assumed to be both a causal and an intelligible system in which every part is necessarily linked to every other. The complete explanation of anything would in the end involve everything. The world is a whole in which there are no accidents and no loose ends.

II

Now the career of reason, of which philosophy is one part, is a slow persistent climb toward the vision of that whole. On its way it passes through four levels—those of infancy, common sense, science, and philosophy. We shall see more clearly the part of philosophy in this enterprise if we briefly retrace our steps through the earlier levels.

For each of us the adventure of the mind begins in a swamp so far below where we now stand that we cannot see it or clearly imagine it. We begin with sensation, "a booming, buzzing confusion" of sensations, signifying nothing. What takes us out of the primitive swamp is the formation of solid little islands in the swamp, nodules of qualities that stick together and behave in settled ways. It is a triumph of tender reason when the child can grasp one stable cluster of qualities as a bottle and another as a rattle. He is breaking through to the level of common sense where we chiefly live.

By the commonsense world I mean the world of things and persons. The transition into this world the child makes in those years that Bertrand Russell called the most decisive in one's life, the years from one to two. About this most familiar of all realms I want to make two observations, first that it is an intellectual construction, and second that it is no permanent home.

First, it is a construction. Things as a whole are never given in sensation; when we perceive a red ball, what we see must be pieced out by interpretation based on our past experience of its having another side. Common sense believes that some of the things I see moving about are persons with feelings and ideas like my own, though this is a metaphysical flight that it can never directly verify. Further, it believes that when you and I look at the ball, we are seeing the same thing—a daring and highly dubious theory. Indeed the head of the plain man is full of theories about men, women, foreigners, artists, and communists, and his religious beliefs are brimming over with metaphysics.

The second remark to be made is that much of this theory is bad theory. The plain man's theory of knowledge, his religious beliefs, and his generalizations about things and people, recorded often in his proverbs, are riddled with inconsistencies. "Be not pennywise," he says, and adds, "Take care of the pence and the pounds will take care of themselves." He accepts both quite serenely.

In the commonsense world, then, reason can find no permanent home or halting place. It must move forward into science. This advance is not an abrupt leap into a new order or dimension. Science, as T. H. Huxley said, *is* common sense refined and organized. The commonsense world is a theoretical construction that has been built up by roughly fifty thousand centuries of trial and error, and much of it comes as a legacy acquired without effort. The scientific order is a superstructure most of which has been built in the last three centuries. But the two structures are continuous, and the newly built upper story will perhaps be occupied by our descendants as effortlessly as we have acquired the lower ones. To pass from the lower to the higher, however, requires the ascent of two flights of stairs, the first of which takes us to a new level of abstraction and the second to a new level of exactness.

First, abstraction. The physicist as a man may have much interest in Jane Doe as a person, but as a scientist he has little or none. He breaks her up into a set of properties and studies these singly. In point of mass, she is indiscriminable from a sack of potatoes, and if dropped from the leaning tower, she would accelerate at the same rate. For science, the interest held by a law is proportioned to its generality, and the more general it is, the more abstract are the qualities that are related by its laws.

Secondly, exactness. The scientist is never satisfied until the characters he correlates are measured and their variations can be stated as functions of each other. Anyone may notice an apple falling from a tree or the increasing pressure in the pot when it boils, but it takes a Newton with his law of the inverse squares to describe exactly what the apple is doing, and Boyle with his inverse variation of volume and pressure to describe exactly what is happening in the kettle.

III

The passage from common sense to science is not a passage to a new kind of thinking, but a refining of processes already at work. So is the passage from science to philosophy. It is a grave mistake to set up science and philosophy as rivals of each other; they are continuous with each other. A philosophy that ignores science will probably build castles in the air, and a science that ignores philosophy will be dogmatic or myopic or both. Philosophy, as I view it, is so bound up with science, so integral a part of the same enterprise, that I have here insisted on winding into it through the avenue of science.

Is there any need for going further? Many people in these days say no. "What is knowledge is science," Russell remarked, "and what is not science is not knowledge." It used to be said that to the English had been given the realm of the sea, to the French the domain of the land, and to the Germans the kingdom of the air; this meant of course the stratosphere, where philosophers are supposed to live, and indeed have been living ever since Thales wandered abroad with his head in the clouds and fell into a well. With these critics I must confess that I have much sympathy. The philosopher who pontificates about being and nonbeing in a prose that follows Dr. Johnson's alleged rule of never using a word of one syllable if he could find one of six seems to me rather worse than a bore. He is supposed to be a specialist in clear thinking and therefore clear speaking, and if he appears in public in a state of logical and linguistic unbuttonedness, groping for words for what are themselves mere gropings for ideas, he does neither philosophy nor education any good. But that is not philosophy as practiced by those who have known their craft.... Surely no one who has understood these philosophers could regard as anything but important what they were trying to do. Well, what have they been trying to do?

They have tried to supplement the work of science in at least two respects. In both of these respects science has to be extended if our thirst for understanding is to be satisfied, but in neither of them do scientists take much interest. The fact is that, logically speaking, philosophy begins before science does, and goes on after science has completed its work. In the broad spectrum of knowledge, science occupies the central band. But we know that there is more to the spectrum than this conspicuous part. On one side, beyond the red end of the spectrum, there is a broad band of infrared rays; and on the other side, beyond the violet end, are the ultraviolet rays. Philosophy deals with the infrareds and the ultraviolets of science, continuous with the central band but more delicate and difficult of discernment.

Take the red end first. Consider the sense in which philosophy comes before science. Many of the concepts the scientist uses and many of his working assumptions he prefers to take for granted. He can examine them if he wishes, and some scientists do. Most do not, because if they waited till they were clear on these difficult basic ideas, they might never get to what most interests them at all. But it would be absurd to leave these basic ideas unexamined altogether. This somewhat thankless preliminary work is the task of the philosopher.

We referred to these unexamined ideas as concepts and assumptions. Let us illustrate the concepts first.

Common sense and science are constantly using certain little words of one syllable that seem too familiar and perhaps unimportant to call for definition. We say, "What time is it?" "There is less space in a compact car," "There was no cause for his taking offense," "He must be out of his mind," "I think these strikes are unjust to the public." Consider the words we have used: 'time', 'space', 'cause', 'good', 'truth', 'mind', 'just', 'I'. If someone said to us, "What do you mean, *I?*" or, when we asked what time it was, "What do you mean by 'time'?" we should probably say, "Oh, don't be an idiot," or perhaps with St. Augustine, "I know perfectly well what time means until you ask me, and then I don't know." I suspect this last is the sound answer regarding all these words. We know what they mean well enough for everyday purposes, but to think about them is to reveal depth after depth of unsuspected meaning. This fact suggests both the strength and the weakness of present-day linguistic philosophy. It is surely true, as this school contends, that a main business of philosophy is to define words. The first great outburst of philosophy in the talk of Socrates was largely an attempt at defining certain key words of the practical life—'justice', 'piety', 'temperance', 'courage'. But their meanings proved bafflingly elusive; he chased the ghost of justice through ten books of the *Republic* and barely got his hands on it in the end. Socrates saw that to grasp the meaning even of these simple and common terms would solve many of the deepest problems in ethics and metaphysics. But we must add that Socrates was no ordinary language philosopher. He was not an Athenian Noah Webster, collecting the shopworn coins that were current in the marketplace; on the contrary, he took special pleasure in showing that at the level of ordinary usage our meanings were muddled and incoherent. Only by refining and revising them could we arrive at meanings that would stand.

Now the scientist who is trying to find the truth about the cause of flu cannot discontinue his experiments till he has reached clearness on the nature of truth or the concept of causality. The political scientist who holds that democracy is in certain respects better than communism cannot remain dumb till all his colleagues have agreed as to the definition of 'good'. These people must get on with their work, and they are right not to stop and moon about ultimates. But these ideas are ultimates after all; we must use them hourly in our thinking; and it would be absurd if, while researchers were trying to be clear about relatively unimportant matters, no one tried to get clear about the most important things of all. And the right persons to make that effort are surely the philosophers. A philosopher friend of mine sat down in a railway car beside a salesman who, recognizing a kindred spirit, poured out a stream of talk about his line. "And what's your line?" he concluded. "Notions," replied the philosopher. That seemed all right to the salesman, and it should be so to us. Notions are the line of the philosopher, such key notions as truth, validity, value, knowledge, without which scientific thought could not get under way, but which the scientist himself has neither the time nor the inclination to examine.

We suggested that it is not only his ultimate concepts but also his ultimate assumptions that the scientist prefers to turn over to others for inspection. Let me list a few and ask whether there is any natural scientist who does not take them for granted. That we can learn the facts of the physical order through perception. That the laws of our logic are valid of this physical order. That there is a public space and a public time in which things happen and to which we all have access. That every event has a cause. That under like conditions the same sort of thing has always happened, and always will. That we ought to adjust the degree of our assent to any proposition to the strength of the evidence for it. These are all propositions of vast importance, which the scientist makes use of every day of his life. If any one of them were false, his entire program would be jeopardized. But they are not scientific propositions. They are assumed by all sciences equally; they are continuous with the thought of all; yet they are the property of none. It would be absurd to leave these unexamined, for some or all of them may be untrue. But the scientist would be aghast if, before he used a microscope or a telescope, he had to settle the question whether knowledge was possible through perception, or whether there could be a logic without ontology. Scientists have

at times discussed these matters, and their views are always welcome, but they generally and sensibly prefer to turn them over to specialists. And the specialists in these problems are philosophers.

I have now, I hope, made clear what was meant by saying that philosophy comes before science. It comes before it in the sense of taking for examination the main concepts and assumptions with which scientists begin their work. Science is logically dependent on philosophy. If philosophy succeeded in showing, as Hume and Carnap thought it had, that any reference to a nonsensible existent was meaningless, the physics that talks to electrons and photons would either have to go out of business or revise its meanings radically. If philosophy succeeded, as James, Schiller, and Freud thought it had, in showing that our thinking is inescapably chained to our impulses and emotions, then the scientific enterprise, as an attempt at impartial and objective truth, would be defeated before it started. Philosophy does not merely put a bit of filigree on the mansion of science; it provides its foundation stones.

IV

If philosophy begins before science does, it also continues after the scientist has finished his work. Each science may be conceived as a prolonged effort to answer one large question. Physics asks, "What are the laws of matter in motion?" Biology asks, "What kinds of structure and behavior are exhibited by living things?" Each science takes a field of nature for its own and tries to keep within its own fences. But nature has no fences; the movement of electrons is somehow continuous with the writing of Hamlet and the rise of Lenin. Who is to study this continuity? Who is to reflect on whether the physicist, burrowing industriously in his hole, can break a tunnel through to the theologian, mining anxiously in his? Surely here again is a task that only the philosopher can perform. One way of performing it, which I do not say is the right way, is suggested by the definition of philosophy as the search by a blind man in a dark room for a black hat that isn't there, with the addendum that if he finds it, that is theology. It may be thought that since no two true propositions can contradict each other, the results of independent scientific search could not conflict, and that there is no problem in harmonizing them. On the contrary, when we examine even the most general results of the several sciences, we see that they clash scandalously and that the task of harmonizing them is gigantic. Indeed the most acute and fascinating of metaphysical problems arise in the attempt to reconcile the results of major disciplines with each other.

How are you to reconcile physics with psychology, for example? The physicist holds that every physical event has a physical cause, which seems innocent enough. To say that a material thing could start moving, or, once started, could have its motion accelerated or changed in direction without any physical cause, would seem absurd. If you say that a motion occurs with no cause at all, that is to the physicist irresponsible; if you say that it represents interference from outside the spatial order, it is superstitious. Now is not the psychologist committed to saying that this interference in fact occurs daily? If my lips and vocal cords now move as they do, it is because I am thinking certain thoughts and want to communicate them to you. And the only way in which a thought or desire can produce such results is through affecting the physical motions of waves or particles in my head. It will not do to say that only the nervous correlates of my thought are involved in producing these results, for those physical changes are not my thoughts, and if my thoughts themselves can make no difference to what I do, then rational living becomes a mummery. My action is never in fact guided by conscious choice, nor anything I say determined by what I think or feel. Common sense would not accept that, nor can a sane psychology afford to; the evidence against it is too massive. And what this evidence shows is that conscious choice, which is not a physical event at all, does make a difference to the behavior of tongue and lips, of arms and legs. Behavior may be consciously guided. But how are you to put that together with the physicist's conviction that all such behavior is caused physically? That is the lively philosophical problem of body and mind.

Conflicts of this kind may occur not only between natural sciences but between a natural and a normative science. Take physics and ethics. For the physicist all events—at least all macroscopic events—are caused; that is, they follow in accordance with some law from events immediately preceding them. This too seems innocent enough. But now apply the principle in ethics. A choice of yours is an event, even if not a physical event, and thus falls under the rule that all events are caused. That means that every choice you make follows in accordance with law from some event or events just preceding it. But if so, given the events that just preceded any of my choices, I had to do what I did do; I could not have done otherwise. But if that is true, does it not make nonsense to say in any case that I ought to have done otherwise, since I did the only thing that I could have done? But then what becomes of ethics as ordinarily conceived? If the scientific principle is true, one will have to rethink the ethical ground for remorse and reward and punishment and praise and blame. This is the ancient problem of free will, which was discussed with fascination by Milton's angels while off duty from their trumpets, and is discussed with equal fascination by undergraduates today.

To be sure, there are people nowadays who say that these old metaphysical issues are really only linguistic and disappear with a due regard to common usage. Thus when we see a man making something happen and know that he is not acting under coercion or some special inducement, we say he is acting freely; that is standard usage and hence correct usage; hence when we say that the man is acting freely, we are speaking correctly; hence we *are* acting freely; and hence there is no problem. I am not convinced. No doubt the man is acting freely in the sense chosen. Unfortunately this sense is irrelevant to the metaphysical issue. For what the determinist is saying is that even when we are *not* under any sort of coercion in the ordinary sense, our choices still follow from causes; and whether *that* is true is not to be settled by studying the plain man's language, for the chances are that he has never thought about it; nor would he necessarily be right if he had.

There are many other conflicts like the two we have mentioned. They fall in no one of the disciplines, but between them, and they must be arbitrated by an agency committed to nonpartisanship.

The only plausible nominee for this post is philosophy. Philosophy is the interdepartmental conciliation agency, the National Labor Relations Board, or if you prefer, the World Court, of the intellectual community. Like these other agencies, it has no means of enforcing its verdicts. Its reliance is on the reasonableness of its decisions.

We are now in a position to see the place of philosophy in the intellectual enterprise as a whole. Intelligence has shown from the beginning a drive to understand. To understand anything means to grasp it in the light of other things or events that make it intelligible. The first great breakthrough of this drive was the system of common sense, which was molded into form by millennia of trial and error. This system is being superseded by science, whose network of explanation is far more precise and comprehensive. Philosophy is the continuation of this enterprise into regions that science leaves unexplored. It is an attempt to carry understanding to its furthest possible limits. It brings into the picture the foundations on which science builds and the arches and vaultings that holds its structures together. Philosophy is at once the criticism and the completion of science. That, as I understand it, is what all the great philosophers have been engaged upon, from Plato to Whitehead.

They may never wholly succeed. It is quite possible that men will use such understanding as they have achieved to blow themselves and their enterprise off the planet. But while they do allow themselves further life, the enterprise is bound to go on. For the effort to understand is not a passing whim or foible; it is no game for a leisure hour or "lyric cry in the midst of business." It is central to the very nature and existence of man; it is what has carried him from somewhere in the slime to the lofty but precarious perch where he now rests. The drive of his intelligence has constructed his world for him and slowly modified it into conformity with the mysterious world without. To anyone who sees this, philosophy needs no defense. It may help in practical ways, and of course it does. But that is not the prime reason why men philosophize. They philosophize because they cannot help it, because the enterprise of understanding, ancient as man himself, has made him what he is, and alone can make him what he might be.

Philosophy and Definition

3. EUTHYPHRO

Plato

CHARACTERS

SOCRATES
EUTHYPHRO

SCENE—The Hall of the King

Euthyphro. What in the world are you doing here in the king's hall,[1] Socrates? Why have you left your haunts in the Lyceum? You surely cannot have a suit before him, as I have.

Translated by F. J. Church and revised by Robert D. Cumming. Published in *Euthyphro, Apology, and Crito* (New York: Bobbs-Merrill, 1956). Substantial excerpts included here. Reprinted by permission of the publisher.

Socrates. The Athenians, Euthyphro, call it an indictment, not a suit.

Euth. What? Do you mean that someone is prosecuting you? I cannot believe that you are prosecuting anyone yourself.

Socr. Certainly I am not.

Euth. Then is someone prosecuting you?

Socr. Yes.

Euth. Who is he?

Socr. I scarely know him myself, Euthyphro; I think he must be some unknown young man. His name, however, is Meletus, and his district Pitthis.

Euth. I don't know him, Socrates. But tell me, what is he prosecuting you for?

Socr. What for? Not on trivial grounds, I think. It is no small thing for so young a man to have formed an opinion on such an important matter. For he, he says, knows how the young are corrupted, and who are their corrupters. He must be a wise man who, observing my ignorance, is going to accuse me to the state, as his mother, of corrupting his friends. I think that he is the only one who begins at the right point in his political reforms; for his first care is to make the young men as good as possible, just as a good farmer will take care of his young plants first, and, after he has done that, of the others. And so Meletus, I suppose, is first clearing us away who, as he says, corrupt the young men growing up; and then, when he has done that, of course he will turn his attention to the older men, and so become a very great public benefactor. . . .

Euth. I hope it may be so, Socrates, but I fear the opposite. It seems to me that in trying to injure you, he is really setting to work by striking a blow at the foundation of the state. But how, tell me, does he say that you corrupt the youth?

Socr. In a way which sounds absurd at first, my friend. He says that I am a maker of gods; and so he is prosecuting me, he says, for inventing new gods and for not believing in the old ones.

Euth. I understand, Socrates. It is because you say that you always have a divine guide. So he is prosecuting you for introducing religious reforms; and he is going into court to arouse prejudice against you, knowing that the multitude are easily prejudiced about such matters. . . . Well, Socrates, I dare say that nothing will come of it. Very likely you will be successful in your trial, and I think that I shall be in mine.

Socr. And what is this suit of yours, Euthyphro? Are you suing, or being sued?

Euth. I am suing.

Socr. Whom?

Euth. A man whom people think I must be mad to prosecute.

Socr. What? Has he wings to fly away with?

Euth. He is far enough from flying; he is a very old man.

Socr. Who is he?

Euth. He is my father.

Socr. Your father, my good man?

Euth. He is indeed.

Socr. What are you prosecuting him for? What is the accusation?

Euth. Murder, Socrates.

Socr. Good heavens, Euthyphro! Surely the multitude are ignorant of what is right. I take it that it is not everyone who could rightly do what you are doing; only a man who was already well advanced in wisdom.

Euth. That is quite true, Socrates.

Socr. Was the man whom your father killed a relative of yours? But, of course, he was. You would never have prosecuted your father for the murder of a stranger?

Euth. You amuse me, Socrates. What difference does it make whether the murdered man were a relative or a stranger? The only question that you have to ask is, did the murderer kill justly or not? . . . In the present case the murdered man was a poor laborer of mine, who worked for us on our farm in Naxos. While drunk he got angry with one of our slaves and killed him. My father therefore bound the man hand and foot and threw him into a ditch, while he sent to Athens to ask the priest what he should do. While the messenger was gone, he entirely neglected the man, thinking that he was a murderer, and that it would be no great matter, even if he were to die. And that was exactly what happened; hunger and cold and his bonds killed him before the messenger returned. And now my father and the rest of my family are indignant with me because I am prosecuting my father for the murder of this murderer. They assert that he did not kill the man at all; and they say that, even if he had killed him over and over again, the man himself was a murderer, and that I ought not to concern myself about such a person because it is impious for a son to prosecute his father for murder. So little, Socrates, do they know the divine law of piety and impiety.

Socr. And do you mean to say, Euthyphro, that you think that you understand divine things and piety and impiety so accurately that, in such a case as you have stated, you can bring your father to justice without fear that you yourself may be doing something impious?

Euth. If I did not understand all these matters accurately, Socrates, I should not be worth much. . . .

Socr. Then, my dear Euthyphro, I cannot do

better than become your pupil and challenge Meletus on this very point before the trial begins. I should say that I had always thought it very important to have knowledge about divine things; and that now, when he says that I offend by speaking carelessly about them, and by introducing reforms, I have become your pupil. And I should say, "Meletus, if you acknowledge Euthyphro to be wise in these matters and to hold the correct belief, then think the same of me and do not put me on trial; but if you do not, then bring a suit, not against me, but against my master, for corrupting his elders—namely, myself whom he corrupts by his teaching, and his own father whom he corrupts by admonishing and punishing him." And if I did not succeed in persuading him to release me from the suit or to indict you in my place, then I could repeat my challenge in court.

Euth. Yes, by Zeus! Socrates, I think I should find out his weak points if he were to try to indict me. I should have a good deal to say about him in court long before I spoke about myself.

Socr. Yes, my dear friend, and knowing this I am anxious to become your pupil. I see that Meletus here, and others too, seem not to notice you at all, but he sees through me without difficulty and at once prosecutes me for impiety. Now, therefore, please explain to me what you were so confident just now that you knew. Tell me what are righteousness and sacrilege with respect to murder and everything else. I suppose that piety is the same in all actions, and that impiety is always the opposite of piety, and retains its identity, and that, as impiety, it always has the same character, which will be found in whatever is impious.

Euth. Certainly, Socrates, I suppose so.

Socr. Tell me, then, what is piety and what is impiety?

Euth. Well, then, I say that piety means prosecuting the unjust individual who has committed murder or sacrilege, or any other such crime, as I am doing now, whether he is your father or your mother or whoever he is; and I say that impiety means not prosecuting him. And observe, Socrates, I will give you a clear proof, which I have already given to others, that it is so, and that doing right means not letting off unpunished the sacrilegious man, whosoever he may be. Men hold Zeus to be the best and the most just of the gods;

and they admit that Zeus bound his own father, Cronos, for wrongfully devouring his children; and that Cronos, in his turn, castrated his father for similar reasons. And yet these same men are incensed with me because I proceed against my father for doing wrong. So, you see, they say one thing in the case of the gods and quite another in mine.

Socr. Is not that why I am being prosecuted, Euthyphro? I mean, because I find it hard to accept such stories people tell about the gods? I expect that I shall be found at fault because I doubt those stories. Now if you who understand all these matters so well agree in holding all those tales true, then I suppose that I must yield to your authority. What could I say when I admit myself that I know nothing about them? But tell me, in the name of friendship, do you really believe that these things have actually happened?

Euth. Yes, and more amazing things too, Socrates, which the multitude do not know of.

Socr. Then you really believe that there is war among the gods, and bitter hatreds, and battles, such as the poets tell of. . . .

Euth. Yes, Socrates, and more besides. As I was saying, I will report to you many other stories about divine matters, if you like, which I am sure will astonish you when you hear them.

Socr. I dare say. You shall report them to me at your leisure another time. At present please try to give a more definite answer to the question which I asked you just now. What I asked you, my friend, was, What is piety? and you have not explained it to me to my satisfaction. You only tell me that what you are doing now, namely, prosecuting your father for murder, is a pious act.

Euth. Well, that is true, Socrates.

Socr. Very likely. But many other actions are pious, are they not, Euthyphro?

Euth. Certainly.

Socr. Remember, then, I did not ask you to tell me one or two of all the many pious actions that there are; I want to know what is characteristic of piety which makes all pious actions pious. You said, I think, that there is one characteristic which makes all pious actions pious, and another characteristic which makes all impious actions impious. Do you not remember?

Euth. I do.

Socr. Well, then, explain to me what is this characteristic, that I may have it to turn to, and to use as a standard whereby to judge your actions and those of other men, and be able to say that whatever action resembles it is pious, and whatever does not, is not pious.

Euth. Yes, I will tell you that if you wish, Socrates.... What is pleasing to the gods is pious, and what is not pleasing to them is impious.

Socr. Fine, Euthyphro. Now you have given me the answer that I wanted. Whether what you say is true, I do not know yet. But, of course, you will go on to prove that it is true.

Euth. Certainly.

Socr. Come, then, let us examine our statement. The things and the men that are pleasing to the gods are pious, and the things and the men that are displeasing to the gods are impious. But piety and impiety are not the same; they are as opposite as possible—was not that what we said?

Euth. Certainly....

Socr. Have we not also said, Euthyphro, that there are quarrels and disagreements and hatreds among the gods?

Euth. We have.

Socr. But what kind of disagreement, my friend, causes hatred and anger? Let us look at the matter thus. If you and I were to disagree as to whether one number were more than another, would that make us angry and enemies? Should we not settle such a dispute at once by counting?

Euth. Of course.

Socr. And if we were to disagree as to the relative size of two things, we should measure them and put an end to the disagreement at once, should we not?... And should we not settle a question about the relative weight of two things by weighing them?

Euth. Of course.

Socr. Then what is the question which would make us angry and enemies if we disagreed about it, and could not come to a settlement? Perhaps you have not an answer ready; but listen to mine. Is it not the question of the just and unjust, of the honorable and the dishonorable, of the good and the bad? Is it not questions about these matters which make you and me and everyone else quarrel, when we do quarrel, if we differ about them and can reach no satisfactory agreement?

Euth. Yes. Socrates, it is disagreements about these matters.

Socr. Well, Euthyphro, the gods will quarrel over these things if they quarrel at all, will they not?

Euth. Necessarily.

Socr. Then, my good Euthyphro, you say that some of the gods think one thing just, the others another; and that what some of them hold to be honorable or good, others hold to be dishonorable or evil. For there would not have been quarrels among them if they had not disagreed on these points, would there?

Euth. You are right.

Socr. And each of them loves what he thinks honorable, and good, and just; and hates the opposite, does he not?

Euth. Certainly.

Socr. But you say that the same action is held by some of them to be just, and by others to be unjust; and that then they dispute about it, and so quarrel and fight among themselves. Is it not so?

Euth. Yes.

Socr. Then the same thing is hated by the gods and loved by them; and the same thing will be displeasing and pleasing to them.

Euth. Apparently.

Socr. Then, according to your account, the same thing will be pious and impious.

Euth. So it seems.

Socr. Then, my good friend, you have not answered my question. I did not ask you to tell me what action is both pious and impious; but it seems that whatever is pleasing to the gods is also displeasing to them. And so, Euthyphro, I should not be surprised if what you are doing now in punishing your father is an action well pleasing to Zeus, but hateful to Cronos and Uranus, and acceptable to Hephaestus, but hateful to Hera; and if any of the other gods disagree about it, pleasing to some of them and displeasing to others.

Euth. But on this point, Socrates, I think that there is no difference of opinion among the gods: they all hold that if one man kills another unjustly, he must be punished.

Socr. What, Euthyphro? Among mankind, have you never heard disputes whether a man ought to be punished for killing another man unjustly, or for doing some other unjust deed?

Euth. Indeed, they never cease from these disputes, especially in courts of justice. They do all manner of unjust things; and then there is nothing which they will not do and say to avoid punishment.

Socr. Do they admit that they have done something unjust, and at the same time deny that they ought to be punished, Euthyphro?

Euth. No, indeed, that they do not.

Socr. Then it is not the case that there is nothing which they will not do and say. I take it, they do not dare to say or argue that they must not be punished if they have done something unjust. What they say is that they have not done anything unjust, is is not so?

Euth. That is true.

Socr. Then they do not disagree over the question that the unjust individual must be punished. They disagree over the question, who is unjust, and what was done and when, do they not?

Euth. That is true.

Socr. Well, is not exactly the same thing true of the gods if they quarrel about justice and injustice, as you say they do? Do not some of them say that the others are doing something unjust, while the others deny it? No one, I suppose, my dear friend, whether god or man, dares to say that a person who has done something unjust must not be punished.

Euth. No, Socrates, that is true, by and large.

Socr. I take it, Euthyphro, that the disputants, whether men or gods, if the gods do disagree, disagree over each separate act. When they quarrel about any act, some of them say that it was just, and others that it was unjust. Is it not so?

Euth. Yes.

Socr. Come, then, my dear Euthyphro, please enlighten me on this point. What proof have you that all the gods think that a laborer who has been imprisoned for murder by the master of the man whom he has murdered, and who dies from his imprisonment before the master has had time to learn from the religious authorities what he should do, dies unjustly? How do you know that it is just for a son to indict his father and to prosecute him for the murder of such a man? Come, see if you can make it clear to me that the gods necessarily agree in thinking that this action of yours is just; and if you satisfy me, I will never cease singing your praises for wisdom.

Euth. I could make that clear enough to you, Socrates; but I am afraid that it would be a long business.

Socr. I see you think that I am duller than the judges. To them, of course, you will make it clear that your father has committed an unjust action, and that all the gods agree in hating such actions.

Euth. I will indeed, Socrates, if they will only listen to me.

Socr. They will listen if they think that you are a good speaker. But while you were talking, it occurred to me to ask myself this question: suppose that Euthyphro were to prove to me as clearly as possible that all the gods think such a death unjust, how has he brought me any nearer to understanding what piety and impiety are? This particular act, perhaps, may be displeasing to the gods, but then we have just seen that piety and impiety cannot be defined in that way; for we have seen that what is displeasing to the gods is also pleasing to them. So I will let you off on this point, Euthyphro; and all the gods shall agree in thinking your father's action wrong and in hating it, if you like. But shall we correct our definition and say that whatever all the gods hate is impious, and whatever they all love is pious; while whatever some of them love, and others hate, is either both or neither? Do you wish us now to define piety and impiety in this manner?

Euth. Why not, Socrates?

Socr. There is no reason why I should not, Euthyphro. It is for you to consider whether that definition will help you to teach me what you promised.

Euth. Well, I should say that piety is what all the gods love, and that impiety is what they all hate.

Socr. Are we to examine this definition, Euthyphro, and see if it is a good one? . . .

Euth. For my part I think that the definition is right this time.

Socr. We shall know that better in a little while, my good friend. Now consider this question. Do the gods love piety because it is pious, or is it pious because they love it?

Euth. I do not understand you, Socrates.

Socr. I will try to explain myself: we speak of a thing being carried and carrying, and being led and leading, and being seen and seeing; and you understand that all such expressions mean different things, and what the difference is.

Euth. Yes, I think I understand.

Socr. And we talk of a thing being loved, of a thing loving, and the two are different?

Euth. Of course.

Socr. Now tell me, is a thing which is being carried in a state of being carried because it is carried, or for some other reason?

Euth. No, because it is carried.

Socr. And a thing is in a state of being led because it is led, and of being seen because it is seen?

Euth. Certainly.

Socr. Then a thing is not seen because it is in a state of being seen: it is in a state of being seen because it is seen; and a thing is not led because it is in a state of being led: it is in a state of being led because it is led; and a thing is not carried because it is in a state of being carried: it is in a state of being carried because it is carried. Is my meaning clear now, Euthyphro? I mean this: if anything becomes or is affected, it does not become because it is in a state of becoming: it is in a state of becoming because it becomes; and it is not affected because it is in a state of being affected: it is in a state of being affected because it is affected. Do you not agree?

Euth. I do.

Socr. Is not that which is being loved in a state either of becoming or of being affected in some way by something?

Euth. Certainly.

Socr. Then the same is true here as in the former cases. A thing is not loved by those who love it because it is in a state of being loved; it is in a state of being loved because they love it.

Euth. Necessarily.

Socr. Well, then, Euthyphro, what do we say about piety? Is it not loved by all the gods, according to your definition?

Euth. Yes.

Socr. Because it is pious, or for some other reason?

Euth. No, because it is pious.

Socr. Then it is loved by the gods because it is pious; it is not pious because it is loved by them?

Euth. It seems so.

Socr. But, then, what is pleasing to the gods is pleasing to them, and is in a state of being loved by them, because they love it?

Euth. Of course.

Socr. Then piety is not what is pleasing to the gods, and what is pleasing to the gods is not pious, as you say, Euthyphro. They are different things.

Euth. And why, Socrates?

Socr. Because we are agreed that the gods love piety because it is pious, and that it is not pious because they love it. Is not this so?

Euth. Yes.

Socr. And that what is pleasing to the gods because they love it, is pleasing to them by reason of this same love, and that they do not love it because it is pleasing to them.

Euth. True.

Socr. Then, my dear Euthyphro, piety and what is pleasing to the gods are different things. If the gods had loved piety because it is pious, they would also have loved what is pleasing to them because it is pleasing to them; but if what is pleasing to them had been pleasing to them because they loved it, then piety, too, would have been piety because they loved it. But now you see that they are opposite things, and wholly different from each other. For the one is of a sort to be loved because it is loved, while the other is loved because it is of a sort to be loved. My question, Euthyphro, was, What is piety? But it turns out that you have not explained to me the essential character of piety; you have been content to mention an effect which belongs to it—namely, that all gods love it. You have not yet told me what its essential character is. Do not, if you please, keep from me what piety is; begin again and tell me that. Never mind whether the gods love it, or whether it has other effects: we shall not differ on that point. Do your best to make clear to me what is piety and what is impiety.

Euth. But, Socrates, I really don't know how to explain to you what is on my mind. Whatever statement we put forward always somehow moves round in a circle, and will not stay where we put it . . . .

Socr. Then we must begin again and inquire what piety is. I do not mean to give in until I have found out. Do not regard me as unworthy; give your whole mind to the question, and this time tell me the truth. For if anyone knows it, it is you; and you are a Proteus whom I must not let go until you have told me. It cannot be that you would ever have undertaken to prosecute your aged father for the murder of a laboring man unless you had known exactly what piety and impiety are. You would have feared to risk the anger of the gods, in case you should be doing wrong, and you would have been afraid of what men would say. But now I am sure that you think that you know exactly

what is pious and what is not; so tell me, my good Euthyphro, and do not conceal from me what you think.

Euth. Another time, then, Socrates, I am in a hurry now, and it is time for me to be off.

NOTE

1. The anachronistic title "King" was retained by the magistrate who had jurisdiction over crimes affecting the state religion.—Ed.

4. THE APOLOGY OF SOCRATES

Plato

... Let us begin from the beginning, then, and ask what is the accusation that has given rise to the prejudice against me, on which Meletus relied when he brought his indictment. What is the prejudice which my enemies have been spreading about me? I must assume that they are formally accusing me, and read their indictment. It would run somewhat in this fashion: "Socrates is guilty of engaging in inquiries into things beneath the earth and in the heavens, of making the weaker argument appear the stronger, and of teaching others these same things." That is what they say. And in the comedy of Aristophanes[1] you yourselves saw a man called Socrates swinging around in a basket and saying that he walked on air, and sputtering a great deal of nonsense about matters of which I understand nothing at all. I do not mean to disparage that kind of knowledge if there is anyone who is wise about these matters. I trust Meletus may never be able to prosecute me for that. But the truth is, Athenians, I have nothing to do with these matters, and almost all of you are yourselves my witnesses of this. I beg all of you who have ever heard me discussing, and they are many, to

inform your neighbors and tell them if any of you have ever heard me discussing such matters at all. That will show you that the other common statements about me are as false as this one.

But the fact is that not one of these is true. And if you have heard that I undertake to educate men, and make money by so doing, that is not true either, though I think that it would be a fine thing to be able to educate men, as Gorgias of Leontini, and Prodicus of Ceos, and Hippias of Elis do. For each of them, my friends, can go into any city, and persuade the young men to leave the society of their fellow citizens, with any of whom they might associate for nothing, and to be only too glad to be allowed to pay money for the privilege of associating with themselves. And I believe that there is another wise man from Paros residing in Athens at this moment. I happened to meet Callias, the son of Hipponicus, a man who has spent more money on sophists than everyone else put together. So I said to him (he has two sons), "Callias, if your two sons had been foals or calves, we could have hired a trainer for them who would have trained them to excel in doing what they are naturally capable of. He would have been either a groom or a farmer. But whom do you intend to take to train them, seeing that they are men? Who understands the excellence which a man and citizen is capable of attaining? I suppose that you must have thought of

Translated by F. J. Church and revised by Robert Cumming. Published in *Euthyphro, Apology, and Crito* (New York: Bobbs-Merrill, 1956). Substantial excerpts included here. Reprinted by permission of the publisher.

this, because you have sons. Is there such a person or not?" "Certainly there is," he replied. "Who is he," said I, "and where does he come from, and what is his fee?" "Evenus, Socrates," he replied, "from Paros, five minae." Then I thought that Evenus was a fortunate person if he really understood this art and could teach so cleverly. If I had possessed knowledge of that kind, I should have been conceited and disdainful. But, Athenians, the truth is that I do not possess it.

Perhaps some of you may reply: "But Socrates, what is the trouble with you? What has given rise to these prejudices against you? You must have been doing something out of the ordinary. All these rumors and reports of you would never have arisen if you had not been doing something different from other men. So tell us what it is, that we may not give our verdict arbitrarily." I think that that is a fair question, and I will try to explain to you what it is that has raised these prejudices against me and given me this reputation. Listen, then. Some of you, perhaps, will think that I am joking, but I assure you that I will tell you the whole truth. I have gained this reputation, Athenians, simply by reason of a certain wisdom. But by what kind of wisdom? It is by just that wisdom which is perhaps human wisdom. In that, it may be, I am really wise. But the men of whom I was speaking just now must be wise in a wisdom which is greater than human wisdom, or else I cannot describe it, for certainly I know nothing of it myself, and if any man says that I do, he lies and speaks to arouse prejudice against me. Do not interrupt me with shouts, Athenians, even if you think that I am boasting. What I am going to say is not my own statement. I will tell you who says it, and he is worthy of your respect. I will bring the god of Delphi to be the witness of my wisdom, if it is wisdom at all, and of its nature. You remember Chaerephon. From youth upwards he was my comrade; and also a partisan of your democracy, sharing your recent exile[2] and returning with you. You remember, too, Chaerephon's character—how impulsive he was in carrying through whatever he took in hand. Once he went to Delphi and ventured to put this question to the oracle—I entreat you again, my friends, not to interrupt me with your shouts—he asked if there was anyone

who was wiser than I. The priestess answered that there was no one. Chaerephon himself is dead, but his brother here will witness to what I say.

Now see why I tell you this. I am going to explain to you how the prejudice against me has arisen. When I heard of the oracle I began to reflect: What can the god mean by this riddle? I know very well that I am not wise, even in the smallest degree. Then what can he mean by saying that I am the wisest of men? It cannot be that he is speaking falsely, for he is a god and cannot lie. For a long time I was at a loss to understand his meaning. Then, very reluctantly, I turned to investigate it in this manner: I went to a man who was reputed to be wise, thinking that there, if anywhere, I should prove the answer wrong, and meaning to point out to the oracle its mistake, and to say, "You said that I was the wisest of men, but this man is wiser than I am." So I examined the man—I need not tell you his name, he was a politician—but this was the result, Athenians. When I conversed with him I came to see that, though a great many persons, and most of all he himself, thought that he was wise, yet he was not wise. Then I tried to prove to him that he was not wise, though he fancied that he was. By so doing I made him indignant, and many of the bystanders. So when I went away, I thought to myself, "I am wiser than this man: neither of us knows anything that is really worth knowing, but he thinks that he has knowledge when he has not, while I, having no knowledge, do not think that I have. I seem at any rate, to be a little wiser than he is on this point: I do not think that I know what I do not know." Next I went to another man who was reputed to be still wiser than the last, with exactly the same result. And there again I made him, and many other men, indignant.

Then I went on to one man after another, realizing that I was arousing indignation every day, which caused me much pain and anxiety. Still I thought that I must set the god's command above everything. So I had to go to every man who seemed to possess any knowledge, and investigate the meaning of the oracle. Athenians, I must tell you the truth; I swear, this was the result of the investigation which I made at the god's command: I found that the men whose reputation for wisdom stood highest were nearly the most lacking in it, while others who were looked down on as common people were much more intelligent. Now I must describe to you the wanderings which I undertook, like Herculean labors, to prove the oracle irrefutable. After the politicians, I went to see the poets, tragic, dithyrambic, and others, thinking that there I should find myself manifestly more ignorant than they. So I took up the poems on which I thought that they had spent most pains, and asked them what they meant, hoping at the same time to learn something from them. I am ashamed to tell you the truth, my friends, but I must say it. Almost any one of the bystanders could have talked about the works of these poets better than the poets themselves. So I soon found that it is not by wisdom that the poets create their works, but by a certain instinctive inspiration, like soothsayers and prophets, who say many fine things, but understand nothing of what they say. The poets seemed to me to be in a similar situation. And at the same time I perceived that, because of their poetry, they thought that they were the wisest of men in other matters too, which they were not. So I went away again, thinking that I had the same advantage over the poets that I had over the politicians.

Finally, I went to the artisans, for I knew very well that I possessed no knowledge at all worth speaking of, and I was sure that I should find that they knew many fine things. And in that I was not mistaken. They knew what I did not know, and so far they were wiser than I. But, Athenians, it seemed to me that the skilled artisans had the same failing as the poets. Each of them believed himself to be extremely wise in matters of the greatest importance because he was skillful in his own art: and this presumption of theirs obscured their real wisdom. So I asked myself, on behalf of the oracle, whether I would choose to remain as I was, without either their wisdom or their ignorance, or to possess both, as they did. And I answered to myself and to the oracle that it was better for me to remain as I was.

From this examination, Athenians, has arisen much fierce and bitter indignation, and as a result a great many prejudices about me. People say that I am "a wise man." For the bystanders always think

that I am wise myself in any matter wherein I refute another. But, gentlemen, I believe that the god is really wise, and that by this oracle he meant that human wisdom is worth little or nothing. I do not think that he meant that Socrates was wise. He only made use of my name, and took me as an example, as though he would say to men, "He among you is the wisest who, like Socrates, knows that his wisdom is really worth nothing at all." Therefore I still go about testing and examining every man whom I think wise, whether he be a citizen or a stranger, as the god has commanded me. Whenever I find that he is not wise, I point out to him, on the god's behalf, that he is not wise. I am so busy in this pursuit that I have never had leisure to take any part worth mentioning in public matters or to look after my private affairs. I am in great poverty as the result of my service to the god.

Besides this, the young men who follow me about, who are the sons of wealthy persons and have the most leisure, take pleasure in hearing men cross-examined. They often imitate me among themselves; then they try their hands at cross-examining other people. And, I imagine, they find plenty of men who think that they know a great deal when in fact they know little or nothing. Then the persons who are cross-examined get angry with me instead of with themselves, and say that Socrates is an abomination and corrupts the young. When they are asked, "why, what does he do? What does he teach?" they do not know what to say. Not to seem at a loss, they repeat the stock charges against all philosophers, and allege that he investigates things in the air and under the earth, and that he teaches people to disbelieve in the gods, and to make the worse argument appear the stronger. For, I suppose, they would not like to confess the truth, which is that they are shown up as ignorant pretenders to knowledge that they do not possess. So they have been filling your ears with their bitter prejudices for a long time, for they are ambitious, energetic, and numerous; and they speak vigorously and persuasively against me. Relying on this, Meletus, Anytus, and Lycon have attacked me. Meletus is indignant with me on behalf of the poets, Anytus on behalf of the artisans and politicians, and Lycon on behalf of the orators.

And so . . . I shall be surprised if I am able, in the short time allowed me for my defense, to remove from your minds this prejudice which has grown so strong. What I have told you, Athenians, is the truth: I neither conceal nor do I suppress anything, trivial or important. Yet I know that it is just this outspokenness which rouses indignation. But that is only a proof that my words are true, and that the prejudice against me, and the causes of it, are what I have said. And whether you investigate them now or hereafter, you will find that they are so.

What I have said must suffice as my defense against the charges of my first accusers. I will try next to defend myself against Meletus, that "good patriot," as he calls himself, and my later accusers. Let us assume that they are a new set of accusers, and read their indictment, as we did in the case of the others. It runs thus: Socrates is guilty of corrupting the youth, and of believing not in the gods whom the state believes in, but in other new divinities. Such is the accusation. Let us examine each point in it separately. Meletus says that I am guilty of corrupting the youth. But I say, Athenians, that he is guilty of playing a solemn joke by casually bringing men to trial, and pretending to have a solemn interest in matters to which he has never given a moment's thought. Now I will try to prove to you that this is so.

Come here, Meletus. Is it not a fact that you think it very important that the young should be as good as possible?

Meletus. It is.

Socrates. Come, then, tell the judges who improves them. You care so much,[3] you must know. You are accusing me, and bringing me to trial, because, as you say, you have discovered that I am the corrupter of the youth. Come now, reveal to the gentlemen who improves them. You see, Meletus, you have nothing to say; you are silent. But don't you think that this is shameful? Is not your silence a conclusive proof of what I say—that you have never cared? Come, tell us, my good man, who makes the young better?

Mel. The laws.

Socr. That, my friend, is not my question. What man improves the young, who begins by knowing the laws?

Mel. The judges here, Socrates.

Socr. What do you mean, Meletus? Can they educate the young and improve them?

Mel. Certainly.

Socr. All of them? Or only some of them?

Mel. All of them.

Socr. By Hera, that is good news! Such a large supply of benefactors! And do the members of the audience here improve them, or not?

Mel. They do.

Socr. And do the councilors?

Mel. Yes.

Socr. Well, then Meletus, do the members of the assembly corrupt the young or do they again all improve them?

Mel. They, too, improve them.

Socr. Then all the Athenians, apparently, make the young into good men except me, and I alone corrupt them. Is that your meaning?

Mel. Certainly, that is my meaning.

Socr. You have discovered me to be most unfortunate. Now tell me: do you think that the same holds good in the case of horses? Does one man do them harm and everyone else improve them? On the contrary, is it not one man only, or a very few—namely, those who are skilled with horses—who can improve them, while the majority of men harm them if they use them and have anything to do with them? Is it not so, Meletus, both with horses and with every other animal? Of course it is, whether you and Anytus say yes or no. The young would certainly be very fortunate if only one man corrupted them, and everyone else did them good. The truth is, Meletus, you prove conclusively that you have never thought about the young in your life. You exhibit your carelessness in not caring for the very matters about which you are prosecuting me.

Now be so good as to tell us, Meletus, is it better to live among good citizens or bad ones? Answer, my friend. I am not asking you at all a difficult question. Do not the bad harm their associates and the good do them good?

Mel. Yes.

Socr. Is there anyone who would rather be injured than benefited by his companions? Answer, my good man; you are obliged by the law to answer. Does anyone like to be injured?

Mel. Certainly not.

Socr. Well, then, are you prosecuting me for

corrupting the young and making them worse, voluntarily or involuntarily?

Mel. For doing it voluntarily.

Socr. What, Meletus? Do you mean to say that you, who are so much younger than I, are yet so much wiser than I that you know that bad citizens always do evil, and that good citizens do good, to those with whom they come in contact, while I am so extraordinarily ignorant as not to know that, if I make any of my companions evil, he will probably injure me in some way? And you allege that I do this voluntarily? You will not make me believe that, nor anyone else either, I should think. Either I do not corrupt the young at all or, if I do, I do so involuntarily, so that you are lying in either case. And if I corrupt them involuntarily, the law does not call upon you to prosecute me for an error which is involuntary, but to take me aside privately and reprove and educate me. For, of course, I shall cease from doing wrong involuntarily, as soon as I know that I have been doing wrong. But you avoided associating with me and educating me; instead you bring me up before the court, where the law sends persons, not for education, but for punishment.

But in truth, Athenians, I do not think that I need say very much to prove that I have not committed the act of injustice for which Meletus is prosecuting me. What I have said is enough to prove that. But be assured it is certainly true, as I have already told you, that I have aroused much indignation. That is what will cause my condemnation if I am condemned; not Meletus nor Anytus either, but that prejudice and resentment of the multitude which have been the destruction of many good men before me, and I think will be so again. There is no prospect that I shall be the last victim.

Perhaps someone will say: "Are you not ashamed, Socrates, of leading a life which is very likely now to cause your death?" I should answer him with justice, and say: "My friend, if you think that a man of any worth at all ought to reckon the chances of life and death when he acts, or that he ought to think of anything but whether he is acting justly or unjustly, and as a good or a bad man would act, you are mistaken.

When the generals whom you chose to command me, Athenians, assigned me my station during the battles of Potidaea, Amphipolis, and Delium, I remained where they stationed me and ran the risk of death, like other men. It would be very strange conduct on my part if I were to desert my station now from fear of death or of any other thing when the god has commanded me—as I am persuaded that he has done—to spend my life in searching for wisdom, and in examining myself and others. That would indeed be a very strange thing. Then certainly I might with justice be brought to trial for not believing in the gods, for I should be disobeying the oracle, and fearing death and thinking myself wise when I was not wise. For to fear death, my friends, is only to think ourselves wise without really being wise, for it is to think that we know what we do not know. For no one knows whether death may not be the greatest good that can happen to man. But men fear it as if they knew quite well that it was the greatest of evils. And what is this but that shameful ignorance of thinking that we know what we do not know? In this matter, too, my friends, perhaps I am different from the multitude. And if I were to claim to be at all wiser than others, it would be because, not knowing very much about the other world, I do not think I know. But I do know very well that it is evil and disgraceful to do an unjust act, and to disobey my superior, whether man or god. I will never do what I know to be evil, and shrink in fear from what I do not know to be good or evil. Even if you acquit me now, and do not listen to Anytus' argument that, if I am to be acquitted, I ought never to have been brought to trial at all, and that, as it is, you are bound to put me to death because, as he said, if I escape, all your sons will be utterly corrupted by practicing what Socrates teaches. If you were therefore to say to me, "Socrates, this time we will not listen to Anytus. We will let you go, but on the condition that you give up this investigation of yours, and philosophy. If you are found following these pursuits again, you shall die." I say, if you offered to let me go on these terms, I should reply: "Athenians, I hold you in the highest regard and affection, but I will be persuaded by the god rather than you. As long as I have breath and strength I will not give up philosophy and exhorting you and declaring the truth to every one of you whom I meet, saying, as I am accustomed, 'My good friend, you are a citizen of

Athens, a city which is very great and very famous for its wisdom and power—are you not ashamed of caring so much for the making of money and for fame and prestige, when you neither think nor care about wisdom and truth and the improvement of your soul?'" If he disputes my words and says that he does care about these things, I shall not at once release him and go away: I shall question him and cross-examine him and test him. If I think that he has not attained excellence, though he says that he has, I shall reproach him for undervaluing the most valuable things, and overvaluing those that are less valuable. This I shall do to everyone whom I meet, young or old, citizen or stranger, but especially to citizens, since they are more closely related to me. This, you must recognize, the god has commanded me to do. And I think that no greater good has ever befallen you in the state than my service to the god. For I spend my whole life in going about and persuading you all to give your first and greatest care to the improvement of your souls, and not till you have done that to think of your bodies or your wealth. And I tell you that wealth does not bring excellence, but that wealth, and every other good thing which men have, whether in public or in private, comes from excellence. If then I corrupt the youth by this teaching, these things must be harmful. But if any man says that I teach anything else, there is nothing in what he says. And therefore, Athenians, I say, whether you are persuaded by Anytus or not, whether you acquit me or not, I shall not change my way of life; no, not if I have to die for it many times.

Do not interrupt me, Athenians, with your shouts. Remember the request which I made to you, and do not interrupt my words. I think that it will profit you to hear them. I am going to say something more to you, at which you may be inclined to protest, but do not do that. Be sure that if you put me to death, I who am what I have told you that I am, you will do yourselves more harm than me. Meletus and Anytus can do me no harm: that is impossible, for I am sure it is not allowed that a good man be injured by a worse. He may indeed kill me, or drive me into exile, or deprive me of my civil rights. Perhaps Meletus and others think those things great evils. But I do not think so. I think it is a much greater evil to do what he is

doing now, and to try to put a man to death unjustly. And now, Athenians, I am not arguing in my own defense at all, as you might expect me to do, but rather in yours in order you may not make a mistake about the gift of the god to you by condemning me. For if you put me to death, you will not easily find another who, if I may use a ludicrous comparison, clings to the state as a sort of gadfly to a horse that is large and well-bred but rather sluggish because of its size, so that it needs to be aroused. It seems to me that the god has attached me like that to the state, for I am constantly alighting upon you at every point to arouse, persuade, and reproach each of you all day long. You will not easily find anyone else, my friends, to fill my place; and if you are persuaded by me, you will spare my life. You are indignant, as drowsy persons are when they are awakened, and, of course, if you are persuaded by Anytus, you could easily kill me with a single blow, and then sleep on undisturbed for the rest of your lives, unless the god in his care for you sends another to arouse you. And you may easily see that it is the god who has given me to your city; for it is not human, the way in which I have neglected all my own interests and allowed my private affairs to be neglected for so many years, while occupying myself unceasingly in your interests, going to each of you privately, like a father or an elder brother, trying to persuade him to care for human excellence. There would have been a reason for it, if I had gained any advantage by this, or if I had been paid for my exhortations; but you see yourselves that my accusers, though they accuse me of everything else without shame, have not had the shamelessness to say that I ever either exacted or demanded payment. To that they have no witness. And I think that I have sufficient witness to the truth of what I say—my poverty.

Perhaps it may seem strange to you that, though I go about giving this advice privately and meddling in others' affairs, yet I do not venture to come forward in the assembly and advise the state. You have often heard me speak of my reason for this, and in many places: it is that I have a certain divine guide, which is what Meletus has caricatured in his indictment. I have had it from childhood. It is a kind of voice which, whenever I hear it, always turns me back from something which I was going to do, but never urges me to act. It is this which forbids me to take part in politics. And I think it does well to forbid me. For, Athenians, it is quite certain that, if I had attempted to take part in politics, I should have perished at once and long ago without doing any good either to you or to myself. And do not be indignant with me for telling the truth. There is no man who will preserve his life for long, either in Athens or elsewhere, if he firmly opposes the multitude, and tries to prevent the commission of much injustice and illegality in the state. He who would really fight for justice must do so as a private citizen, not as a political figure, if he is to preserve his life, even for a short time. . . .

Now do you think that I could have remained alive all these years if I had taken part in public affairs, and had always maintained the cause of justice like a good man, and had held it a paramount duty, as it is, to do so? Certainly not, Athenians, nor could any other man. But throughout my whole life, both in private and in public, whenever I have had to take part in public affairs, you will find I have always been the same and have never yielded unjustly to anyone; no, not to those whom my enemies falsely assert to have been my pupils. But I was never anyone's teacher. I have never withheld myself from anyone, young or old, who was anxious to hear me converse while I was making my investigation; neither do I converse for payment, and refuse to converse without payment. I am ready to ask questions of rich and poor alike, and if any man wishes to answer me, and then listen to what I have to say, he may. And I cannot justly be charged with causing these men to turn out good or bad, for I never either taught or professed to teach any of them any knowledge whatever. And if any man asserts that he ever learned or heard anything from me in private which everyone else did not hear as well as he, be sure that he does not speak the truth.

Why is it, then, that people delight in spending so much time in my company? You have heard why, Athenians. I told you the whole truth when I said that they delight in hearing me examine persons who think that they are wise when they are not wise. It is certainly very amusing to listen to. And, as I have

said, the god has commanded me to examine men, in oracles and in dreams and in every way in which the divine will was ever declared to man. This is the truth, Athenians, and if it were not the truth, it would be easily refuted. For if it were really the case that I have already corrupted some of the young men, and am now corrupting others, surely some of them, finding as they grew older that I had given them bad advice in their youth, would have come forward today to accuse me and take their revenge. Or if they were unwilling to do so themselves, surely their relatives, their fathers or brothers, or others, would, if I had done them any harm, have remembered it and taken their revenge. Certainly I see many of them in court. . . . No, on the contrary, my friends, you will find all these men ready to support me, the corrupter who has injured their relatives, as Meletus and Anytus call me. Those of them who have been already corrupted might perhaps have some reason for supporting me, but what reason can their relatives have who are grown up, and who are uncorrupted, except the reason of truth and justice—that they know very well that Meletus is lying, and that I am speaking the truth?

Well, my friends, this, and perhaps more like this, is pretty much all I have to offer in my defense. There may be some one among you who will be indignant when he remembers how, even in a less important trial than this, he begged and entreated the judges, with many tears, to acquit him, and brought forward his children and many of his friends and relatives in court in order to appeal to your feelings; and then finds that I shall do none of these things, though I am in what he would think the supreme danger. Perhaps he will harden himself against me when he notices this; it may make him angry, and he may cast his vote in anger. If it is so with any of you—I do not suppose that it is, but in case it should be so—I think that I should answer him reasonably if I said: "My friend, I have relatives, too, for, in the words of Homer, I am 'not born of an oak or a rock'[4] but of flesh and blood." And so, Athenians, I have relatives, and I have three sons, one of them nearly grown up, and the other two still children. Yet I will not bring any of them forward before you and implore you to acquit me. And why will I do none of these things? It is not from arrogance, Athenians, nor because I lack respect for you—whether or not I can face death bravely is another question—but for my own good name, and for your good name, and for the good name of the whole state. I do not think it right, at my age and with my reputation, to do anything of that kind. Rightly or wrongly, men have made up their minds that in some way Socrates is different from the multitude of men. And it will be shameful if those of you who are thought to excel in wisdom, or in bravery, or in any other excellence, are going to act in this fashion. I have often seen men of reputation behaving in an extraordinary way at their trial, as if they thought it a terrible fate to be killed, and as though they expected to live for ever if you did not put them to death. Such men seem to me to bring shame upon the state. . . . Those of you, Athenians, who have any reputation at all ought not to do these things, and you ought not to allow us to do them. You should show that you will be much more ready to condemn men who make the state ridiculous by these pathetic performances than men who remain quiet.

(He is found guilty by 281 votes to 220.)

I am not indignant at the verdict you have given, Athenians, for many reasons. I expected that you would find me guilty; and I am not so much surprised at that as at the numbers of the votes. I certainly never thought that the majority against me would have been so narrow. But now it seems that if only thirty votes had changed sides, I should have escaped. So I think that I have escaped Meletus, as it is; and not only have I escaped him, for it is perfectly clear that if Anytus and Lycon had not come forward to accuse me, too, he would not have obtained the fifth part of the votes, and would have had to pay a fine of a thousand drachmae.

So he proposes death as the penalty. Be it so. And what alternative penalty shall I propose to you, Athenians?[5] What I deserve, of course, must I not? What then do I deserve to pay or to suffer for having determined not to spend my life in ease? I neglected the things which most men value, such as wealth, and family interests, and military commands, and public oratory, and all the civic appointments, and social clubs, and political factions, that there are in Athens; for I thought that I was really too honest a man to preserve my life if I engaged in these affairs. So I did not go where I should have done no good either to you or to myself. I went, instead, to each one of you privately to do him, as I say, the greatest of benefits, and tried to persuade him not to think of his affairs until he had thought of himself and tried to make himself as good and wise as possible, nor to think of the affairs of Athens until he had thought of Athens herself; and to care for other things in the same manner. Then what do I deserve for such a life? Something good, Athenians, if I am really to propose what I deserve; and something good which it would be suitable for me to receive. Then what is a suitable reward to be given to a poor benefactor who requires leisure to exhort you? There is no reward, Athenians, so suitable for him as receiving free meals in the prytaneum. It is a much more suitable reward for him than for any of you who has won a victory at the Olympic games with his horse or his chariots. Such a man only makes you seem happy, but I make you really happy; he is not in want, and I am. So if I am to propose the penalty which I really deserve, I propose this—free meals in the prytaneum.

Perhaps you think me stubborn and arrogant in what I am saying now, as in what I said about the entreaties and tears. It is not so, Athenians. It is rather that I am convinced that I never wronged any man voluntarily, though I cannot persuade you of that, since we have conversed together only a little time. If there were a law at Athens, as there is elsewhere, not to finish a trial of life and death in a single day, I think that I could have persuaded you; but now it is not easy in so short a time to clear myself of great prejudices. But when I am persuaded that I have never wronged any man, I shall certainly not wrong myself, or admit that I deserve to suffer any evil, or propose any evil for myself as a penalty. Why should I? Lest I should suffer the penalty which Meletus proposes when I say that I do not know whether it is a good or an evil? Shall I choose instead of it something which I know to be an evil, and propose that as a penalty? Shall I propose imprisonment? And why should I pass the rest of my days in prison, the slave of successive officials? Or shall I propose a fine, with imprisonment until it is paid? I have told you why

I will not do that. I should have to remain in prison, for I have no money to pay a fine with. Shall I then propose exile? Perhaps you would agree to that. Life would indeed be very dear to me if I were unreasonable enough to expect that strangers would cheerfully tolerate my discussions and arguments when you who are my fellow citizens cannot endure them, and have found them so irksome and odious to you that you are seeking now to be relieved of them. No, indeed, Athenians, that is not likely. A fine life I should lead for an old man if I were to withdraw from Athens and pass the rest of my days in wandering from city to city, and continually being expelled. For I know very well that the young men will listen to me wherever I go, as they do here. If I drive them away, they will persuade their elders to expel me; if I do not drive them away, their fathers and other relatives will expel me for their sakes.

Perhaps someone will say, "Why cannot you withdraw from Athens, Socrates, and hold your peace?" It is the most difficult thing in the world to make you understand why I cannot do that. If I say that I cannot hold my peace because that would be to disobey the god, you will think that I am not in earnest and will not believe me. And if I tell you that no greater good can happen to a man than to discuss human excellence every day and the other matters about which you have heard me arguing and examining myself and others, and that an unexamined life is not worth living, then you will believe me still less. But that is so, my friends, though it is not easy to persuade you. And, what is more, I am not accustomed to think that I deserve anything evil. If I had been rich, I would have proposed as large a fine as I could pay: that would have done me no harm. But I am not rich enough to pay a fine unless you are willing to fix it at a sum within my means. Perhaps I could pay you a mina, so I propose that. Plato here, Athenians, and Crito, and Critobulus, and Apollodorus bid me propose thirty minae, and they guarantee its payment. So I propose thirty minae. Their security will be sufficient to you for the money.

(He is condemned to death.)

You have not gained very much time, Athenians, and at the price of the slurs of those who wish to revile the state. And they will say that you put Socrates, a wise man, to death. For they will certainly call me wise, whether I am wise or not, when they want to reproach you. If you had waited for a little while, your wishes would have been fulfilled in the course of nature; for you see that I am an old man, far advanced in years, and near to death. I am saying this not to all of you, only to those who have voted for my death. And to them I have something else to say. Perhaps, my friends, you think that I have been convicted because I was wanting in the arguments by which I could have persuaded you to acquit me, if I had thought it right to do or to say anything to escape punishment. It is not so. I have been convicted because I was wanting, not in arguments, but in impudence and shamelessness—because I would not plead before you as you would have liked to hear me plead, or appeal to you with weeping and wailing, or say and do many other things which I maintain are unworthy of me, but which you have been accustomed to from other men. But when I was defending myself, I thought that I ought not to do anything unworthy of a free man because of the danger which I ran, and I have not changed my mind now. I would very much rather defend myself as I did, and die, than as you would have had me do, and live. Both in a lawsuit and in war, there are some things which neither I nor any other man may do in order to escape from death. In battle, a man often sees that he may at least escape from death by throwing down his arms and falling on his knees before the pursuer to beg for his life. And there are many other ways of avoiding death in every danger if a man is willing to say and to do anything. But, my friends, I think that it is a much harder thing to escape from wickedness than from death, for wickedness is swifter than death. And now I, who am old and slow, have been overtaken by the slower pursuer: and my accusers, who are clever and swift, have been overtaken by the swifter pursuer—wickedness. And now I shall go away, sentenced by you to death; they will go away, sentenced by truth to wickedness and injustice. And I abide by this award as well as they. Perhaps it was right for these things to be so. I think that they are fairly balanced.

And now I wish to prophesy to you, Athenians, who have condemned me. For I am going to die, and that is the time when men have most prophetic power. And I prophesy to you who have sentenced me to death that a far more severe punishment than you have inflicted on me will surely overtake you as soon as I am dead. You have done this thing, thinking that you will be relieved from having to give an account of your lives. But I say that the result will be very different. There will be more men who will call you to account, whom I have held back, though you did not recognize it. And they will be harsher toward you than I have been, for they will be younger, and you will be more indignant with them. For if you think that you will restrain men from reproaching you for not living as you should, by putting them to death, you are very much mistaken. That way of escape is neither possible nor honorable. It is much more honorable and much easier not to suppress others, but to make yourselves as good as you can. This is my parting prophecy to you who have condemned me.

With you who have acquitted me I should like to discuss this thing that has happened, while the authorities are busy, and before I go to the place where I have to die. So, remain with me until I go: there is no reason why we should not talk with each other while it is possible. I wish to explain to you, as my friends, the meaning of what has happened to me. An amazing thing has happened to me, judges—for I am right in calling you judges.[6] The prophetic guide has been constantly with me all through my life till now, opposing me even in trivial matters if I were not going to act rightly. And now you yourselves see what has happened to me—a thing which might be thought, and which is sometimes actually reckoned, the supreme evil. But the divine guide did not oppose me when I was leaving my house in the morning, nor when I was coming up here to the court, nor at any point in my speech when I was going to say anything; though at other times it has often stopped me in the very act of speaking. But now, in this matter, it has never once opposed me, either in my words or my actions. I will tell you what I believe to be the reason. This thing that has come upon me must be a good; and those of us who think that death is an evil must needs be mistaken. I have a clear proof that that is so; for my accustomed guide would certainly have opposed me if I had not been going to meet with something good.

And if we reflect in another way, we shall see that we may well hope that death is a good. For the state of death is one of two things: either the dead man wholly ceases to be and loses all consciousness or, as we are told, it is a change and a migration of the soul to another place. And if death is the absence of all consciousness, and like the sleep of one whose slumbers are unbroken by any dreams, it will be a wonderful gain. For if a man had to select that night in which he slept so soundly that he did not even dream, and had to compare with it all the other nights and days of his life, and then had to say how many days and nights in his life he had spent better and more pleasantly than this night, I think that a private person, nay, even the Great King of Persia himself, would find them easy to count, compared with the others. If that is the nature of death, I for one count it a gain. For then it appears that all time is nothing more than a single night. But if death is a journey to another place, and what we are told is true—that all who have died are there—what good could be greater than this, my judges? Would a journey not be worth taking, at the end of which, in the other world, we should be delivered from the pretended judges here and should find the true judges who are said to sit in judgment below, such as Minos and Rhadamanthus and Aeacus and Triptolemus, and the other demigods who were just in their own lives? Or what would you not give to converse with Orpheus and Musaeus and Hesiod and Homer? I am willing to die many times if this be true. And for my own part I should find it wonderful to meet there Palamedes, and Ajax the son of Telamon, and the other men of old who have died through an unjust judgment, and to compare my experiences with theirs. That I think would be no small pleasure. And, above all, I could spend my time in examining those who are there, as I examine men here, and in finding out which of them is wise, and which of them thinks himself wise when he is not wise. What would we not give, my judges, to be able to examine the leader of the great expedition against Troy, or Odysseus, or Sisyphus, or countless other men and women whom we could name? It would be an inexpressible happiness to converse with them and to live with them and to examine them. Assuredly there they do not put men to death for doing that.

For besides the other ways in which they are happier than we are, they are immortal, at least if what we are told is true.

And you too, judges, must face death hopefully, and believe this one truth, that no evil can happen to a good man, either in life or after death. His affairs are not neglected by the gods; and what has happened to me today has not happened by chance. I am persuaded that it was better for me to die now, and to be released from trouble; and that was the reason why the guide never turned me back. And so I am not at all angry with my accusers or with those who have condemned me to die. Yet it was not with this in mind that they accused me and condemned me, but meaning to do me an injury. So far I may blame them.

Yet I have one request to make of them. When my sons grow up, punish them, my friends, and harass them in the same way that I have harassed you, if they seem to you to care for riches or for any other thing more than excellence; and if they think that they are something when they are really nothing, reproach them, as I have reproached you,

for not caring for what they should, and for thinking that they are something when really they are nothing. And if you will do this, I myself and my sons will have received justice from you.

But now the time has come, and we must go away—I to die, and you to live. Which is better is known to the god alone.

NOTES

1. *The Clouds.* The basket was satirically assumed to facilitate Socrates' inquiries into things in the heavens.—Ed.
2. During the totalitarian regime of The Thirty which remained in power for eight months (404 B.C.), five years before the trial.—Ed.
3. Throughout the following passage Socrates plays on the etymology of the name "Meletus" as meaning "the man who cares."—Ed.
4. Homer, *Odyssey,* xix, 163.
5. For certain crimes no penalty was fixed by Athenian law. Having reached a verdict of guilty, the court had still to decide between the alternative penalties proposed by the prosecution and the defense.—Ed.
6. The form of address hitherto has always been "Athenians," or "my friends." The "judges" in an Athenian court were simply the members of the jury.—Ed.

5. ARISTOTLE'S THEORY OF REAL DEFINITION

Morris R. Cohen
Ernest Nagel

THE PREDICABLES

Aristotle's discussion of definition is central to his entire theory of science, and is itself based upon his analysis of the possible ways in which a predicate may be related to the subject. His inquiry grew out of his reflections upon the method and results of the speculations of Socrates and Plato.

From *An Introduction to Logic and Scientific Method* by Morris R. Cohen and Ernest Nagel, copyright 1934 by Harcourt Brace Jovanovich, Inc.; renewed 1962 by Ernest Nagel and Leonora Cohen Rosenfield. Reprinted by permission of the publisher, and Routledge and Kegan Paul, Ltd., London.

His writings upon the syllogism cannot really be understood without reference to his analysis of the possible kinds of propositions, each kind depending upon the nature of the relation between subject and predicate. This analysis, called the *theory of the predicables,* was in turn closely connected with fundamental metaphysical doctrines, especially with the doctrine of fixed natural kinds or types. Into these important matters we cannot go except for a brief discussion of the predicables.

Aristotle obtains an exhaustive enumeration of the possible relations between predicate and subject, in the following way: Every predicate must be either convertible with its subject or not; that is, if *A* is *B,* then either *B* is so related to *A* that if anything is *B* it is *A,* or this is not the case. If it is convertible (Aristotle also calls it commensurable), it either signifies its essence, in which case it is the *definition;* or it is a *property.* If the predicate is not convertible with the subject, either it is contained in the definition of the subject, in which case it is the *genus* or the *differentia,* or it is not contained in the definition, in which case it is an *accident.* A predicate must therefore stand to the subject in some one of these five possible relations: it must be either definition, property, genus, differentia, or accident. We must now explain the significance of each of these distinctions. But the reader must understand that the subject term is taken by Aristotle to represent a form, type, or universal, and not a singular, concrete thing. The predicables indicate the possible ways in which universals are related to one another. The concrete individual as such is not a subject matter for science, according to Aristotle; only in so far as the individual embodies a type or form is a science of individuals possible. It is never of Socrates as an individual, but only of Socrates as "man" that we may have scientific (or systematic) knowledge. Aristotle's discussion of the predicables, therefore, stressed the intensional aspect of terms. But it is possible to give an extensional interpretation of them also, and traditionally this has usually been done.

DEFINITION

"A 'definition,'" according to Aristotle, "is a phrase signifying a thing's essence."[1] By the essence of a thing he understood the set of fundamental attributes which are the necessary and sufficient conditions for any concrete thing to be a thing of that type. It approximates to what we have called the conventional intension of a term. Thus the essence or definition of a circle is that it is a plane figure every point of which is equidistant from a fixed point. The predicate (a plane figure every point of which is equidistant from a fixed point) is convertible or commensurate with the subject: it may be predicated of everything that is

a circle, and everything to which it can be applied is a circle. The predicate is the essence, because it tells *what* a circle is, so that all the "peculiarities" of the circle necessarily follow from it.

GENUS

The definition contains two terms as components, the *genus* and the *differentia.* "A 'genus' is what is predicated in the category of essence of a number of things exhibiting differences in kind."[2] Thus the genus of "circle" is "plane figure." The circle, on the other hand, is a *species* of plane figure. But "plane figure" is also the genus of "triangle," "ellipse," "hyperbola," and so on. These different species exhibit differences in kind, but they all belong to the same genus.

DIFFERENTIA

The *differentia* is that part of the essence which distinguishes the species from the other species in the same genus. The differentia of "circle" is "having all its points equidistant from a fixed point"; the differentia of "triangle" is "being bounded by three straight lines."

The distinction between genus and differentia was absolute for Aristotle, and was connected with his metaphysical views.[3] But from a purely logical or formal point of view, the distinction is absolute only within a specific context. For consider the definition, "Man is a rational animal." According to Aristotle, the genus is "animal," the differentia is "rational." But formally we may regard with equal right "rational" as the genus and "animal" as the differentia. This will be clear if we express the definition explicitly as a logical conjunction of two attributes. Thus, X is a man:=:X is rational and X is an animal. It doesn't make any logical difference which conjunctive is regarded as the more important. The logical function of the differentia is to limit or qualify the genus. And this function is performed by either term in the definition with respect to the other. A definition may, therefore, be regarded as *the logical product of two terms.* This interpretation is particularly adapted to an extensional emphasis upon the predicables.

The relation of a genus to its species is clearly

illustrated by the device known as the Tree of Porphyry. The following is the traditional illustration, and has evoked from Bentham the charac- terization of "the matchless beauty of the Tree of Porphyry."

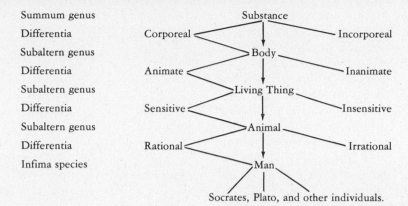

Summum genus		Substance
Differentia	Corporeal	Incorporeal
Subaltern genus		Body
Differentia	Animate	Inanimate
Subaltern genus		Living Thing
Differentia	Sensitive	Insensitive
Subaltern genus		Animal
Differentia	Rational	Irrational
Infima species		Man

Socrates, Plato, and other individuals.

The reader will note, however, that the relation between the genus "animal," say, to its species "man," is different from the relation of the species man to its individual members. The first is a relation between a *class* and its *subclass*, the second a relation between a *class* and its *members*. Porphyry, who considerably modified Aristotle's theory of the predicables, also confused it irreparably.

PROPERTY

"A 'property' is a predicate which does not indicate the essence of a thing, but yet belongs to that thing alone, and is predicated convertibly of it. Thus it is a property of man to be capable of learning grammar: for if *A* be a man, then he is capable of learning grammar, and if he be capable of learning grammar, he is a man."[4] Thus, a property of a circle is that it has the maximum area with a given perimeter; another property is that the product of the segments of the chords passing through a fixed point is constant. The property is an attribute which follows necessarily from the definition.

The distinction between essence and property was regarded by Aristotle as absolute, for a subject has, according to him, only one essence. From a purely logical point of view, however, the distinction is absolute only relatively to a given system. Thus if we define a circle as the locus of points equidistant from a fixed point, we can formally deduce the property that its area is maximum with

a given perimeter. On the other hand, if the circle is defined as the plane figure having a maximum area with a given circumference, it follows necessarily that all its points are equidistant from a fixed point. The rôles of definition and property are therefore interchangeable. Which character of a subject is taken as the definition turns upon extralogical considerations. Hence, while the distinction between essence and property is perfectly sound, it is absolute only within a given system. We have already seen, in connection with the discussion of the nature of mathematics, that there are no intrinsically undemonstrable propositions or intrinsically undefinable terms. The points we made there are relevant here. We have also suggested above that the "undemonstrable definitions" of Aristotle are the axioms of modern mathematical technique. The reader will therefore have no difficulty in interpreting the "properties" which flow from the definition as none other than the theorems of a system which are implied by the axioms. Unfortunately, in the example above we have quoted from him, Aristotle does not show how the property of being capable of learning grammar follows from the definition of man.

ACCIDENT

Finally, "an 'accident' is (1) something which, though it is none of the foregoing,—i.e., neither a definition nor a property nor a genus—yet belongs to the thing: (2) something which may possibly either belong or not belong to any one and the self-same thing, as (e.g.) the 'sitting posture' may belong or not belong to the self-same thing."[5] To have a triangle inscribed in it is, therefore, an accident of the circle. From a purely logical point of view, an accident is a proposition not formally derivable from the definition. So stated, it is perhaps unnecessary to warn the reader once more that an accidental predicate is not to be predicated of a concrete individual, but only of an individual as representing a *kind*. Thus, snub-nosedness is an accident not of Socrates as an *individual;* but of Socrates as a *man*. Man, the *type*, need not be, although it may be, conjoined with snub-nosedness. Snub-nosedness is an accident, because it is not a necessary consequence of being a man.

Such, in brief, is the Aristotelian theory of predicables. In terms of the doctrine, therefore, the condition which satisfactory definitions must satisfy is that they be stated in terms of genus and differentia. . . .

NOTES

1. Aristotle, *Posterior Analytics*, in *Works*, ed. by W. D. Ross (Oxford University Press, 1928), p. 101[b].
2. *Ibid.*, p. 102[a].
3. cf. *Ibid.*, p. 122[h].
4. *Ibid.*, p. 102[a].
5. *Ibid.*, p. 102[b].

6. PERSUASIVE DEFINITIONS

Charles L. Stevenson

1

A "persuasive" definition is one which gives a new conceptual meaning to a familiar word without substantially changing its emotive meaning, and which is used with the conscious or unconscious purpose of changing, by this means, the direction of people's interests.[1]

The object of this paper is to show that persuasive definitions are often used in philosophy and that the widespread failure to recognize them for what they are—the temptation to consider them as definitions which merely abbreviate, or which analyze common concepts—has led to important philosophical confusions.

Before considering philosophical examples, however, it will be helpful to consider some simpler ones, which will serve to make clearer what persuasive definitions are.

As an initial example let us take a definition of the word "culture." It will be convenient to invent

First published in *Mind*, Vol. 47 (1938). Excerpts reprinted here by permission of the editor of *Mind*, and Basil Blackwell, Publisher, Oxford.

pure fictions about the linguistic habits of the people to whom the definition is addressed, for this will typify the actual situation in a way that is free from complicating irrelevancies. Let us consider, then, a hypothetical community in which "culture" began by having an almost purely conceptual meaning. Let us sketch the development of its emotive meaning, show why the emotive meaning led certain people to redefine the word, and examine the way in which this redefinition achieved its purpose.

There was once a community in which "cultured" meant *widely read and acquainted with the arts.*

In the course of time these qualities came into high favor. If one man wanted to pay another a compliment he would dwell at length upon his culture. It became unnatural to use "culture" in any but a laudatory tone of voice. Those who lacked culture used the word with awe, and those who possessed it used the word with self-satisfaction, or perhaps with careful modesty. In this way the word acquired a strong emotive meaning. It awakened feelings not only because of its conceptual meaning, but more directly, in its own right; for it recalled the gestures, smiles, and tone of voice that so habitually accompanied it. A public speaker, for instance, was never introduced as "a man widely read and acquainted with the arts." He was described, rather, as "a man of culture." The latter phrase had no different conceptual meaning than the former but was more suitable for awakening in the audience a favorable attitude.

As the emotive meaning of the word grew more pronounced, the conceptual meaning grew more vague. This was inevitable, for the emotive meaning made the word suitable for use in metaphors. Men who were not cultured, literally, were often called so, particularly when they were admired for having *some* of the defining qualities of "culture." At first people readily distinguished these metaphorical compliments from literal statements; but as the metaphors grew more frequent the distinction became less clear. People weren't quite sure whether a person *must* know about the arts in order to be literally cultured. Perhaps some other kind of knowledge would serve as a substitute.

Let us now suppose that one member of the community had no wholehearted regard for mere reading or mere acquaintance with the arts but valued them only to the extent that they served to develop imaginative sensitivity. He felt that they were not always a reliable means to that end, and on no account the only means. It was his constant source of regret that such mechanical procedures as reading, or visiting museums, should win instant praise, and that sensitivity should scarcely be noticed. For this reason he proceeded to give "culture" a new meaning. "I know," he insisted, "that so and so is widely read and acquainted with the arts; but what has that to do with culture? The real meaning of 'culture,' the true meaning of 'culture,' is *imaginative sensitivity*." He persisted in this statement in spite of the fact that "culture" had never before been used in exactly this sense.

It will now be obvious that this definition was no mere abbreviation; nor was it intended as an analysis of a common concept. Its purpose, rather, was to redirect people's interests. "Culture" had and would continue to have a laudatory emotive meaning. The definition urged people to stop using the laudatory term to refer to reading and the arts and to use it, instead, to mean imaginative sensitivity. In this manner it sought to place the former qualities in a poor light and the latter in a fine one, and thus to redirect people's admiration. When people learn to call something by a name rich in pleasant associations, they more readily admire it; and when they learn not to call it by such a name, they less readily admire it. The definition made use of this fact. It changed interests by changing names.

The past history of "culture" facilitated the change. The emotive meaning of the word, it is true, had grown up because of the old conceptual meaning; but it was now so firmly established that it would persist even though the conceptual meaning were somewhat altered. The old conceptual meaning was easily altered, since it had been made vague by metaphorical usage. The definition could effect a change in conceptual meaning, then, which left the emotive meaning unaltered. Thanks again to vagueness the change seemed a "natural" one, which, by escaping the attention of the hearers, did not remind them that they were being influenced and so did not stultify them by making them self-conscious. The effectiveness of the definition lay partly in this and partly in the fact that it made its results permanent by embedding them in people's very linguistic habits.

The definition may be called "persuasive," then, in a quite conventional sense. Like most persuasive definitions it was in fact doubly persuasive. It at once dissuaded people from indiscriminately admiring one set of qualities (wide reading and acquaintance with the arts) and induced them to admire another (imaginative sensitivity). The speaker wished to attain both of these ends and was enabled, by his definition, to work for both at the same time.

There are hundreds of words which, like "culture," have both a vague conceptual meaning and a rich emotive meaning. The conceptual meaning of them all is subject to constant redefinition. The words are prizes which each man seeks to bestow on the qualities of his own choice.

In the nineteenth century, for instance, critics sometimes remarked that Alexander Pope was "not a poet." The foolish reply would be, "it's a mere matter of definition." It is indeed a matter of definition, but not a "mere" one. The word "poet" was used in an extremely narrow sense. This, so far from being idle, had important consequences; it enabled the critics to deny to Pope a laudatory name and so to induce people to disregard him. A persuasive definition, tacitly employed, was at work in redirecting interests. Those who wish to decide whether Pope was a poet must decide whether they will yield to the critics' influence—whether they will come to dislike Pope enough to allow him to be deprived of an honorary title. This decision will require a knowledge of Pope's works and a knowledge of their own minds. Such are the important matters which lie behind the acceptance of the tacitly proposed, narrow definition of "poet." It is not a matter of "merely arbitrary" definition, then, nor is any persuasive definition "merely arbitrary," if that phrase is taken to imply "suitably decided by the flip of a coin."

Persuasive definitions are often recognizable from the words "real" or "true," employed in a metaphorical sense. The speaker in our first example, for instance, was telling us what "real" culture was, as distinct from the "shell" of culture. The following are additional examples: "charity," in the true sense of the word, means the giving not merely of gold but of understanding; true love is the communion between minds alone; "courage," in the true sense, is strength against adverse public opinion. Each of these statements is a way of redirecting interests by leaving the emotive meaning of the words unchanged and wedding it to a new conceptual one. Similarly we may speak of the true meaning of "sportsmanship," "genius," "beauty," and so on. Or we may speak of the true meaning of "selfishness" or "hypocrisy," using persuasive definitions of these derogatory terms to blame rather than to praise. "True," in such contexts, is obviously not used literally. Since people usually accept what they consider true, "true" comes to have the persuasive force of "to be accepted." This force is utilized in the metaphorical expression "true meaning." The hearer is induced to accept the new meaning which the speaker introduces.

Outside the confinements of philosophical theory the importance of persuasive definitions has often been recognized. In philology they receive occasional stress. Or rather, although little attention is given to persuasive definitions, much is said about the broad heading under which a study of them would fall: the interplay between emotive and conceptual meanings in determining linguistic change, and its correlation with interests.

Leonard Bloomfield presents us with a particularly clear example: "The speculative builder has learned to appeal to every weakness, including the sentimentality, of the prospective buyer; he uses the speech forms whose content will turn the hearer in the right direction. In many locutions 'house' is the colorless, and 'home' the sentimental word. Thus the salesman comes to use the word 'home' for an empty shell that has never been inhabited, and the rest of us follow his style."[2]

Hanns Oertel, having stated that "the emotional element greatly influences the fate of some words," points out that "amica" came to have one sense which was synonymous with "concubina."[3] To be sure there are several reasons for this. "Concubina" had become slightly profane, too strong for delicate ears. And "amica" permitted a convenient ambiguity. Any shocking thoughts could always be ascribed to those who chose to understand the word in its less innocent sense. But a persuasive factor must also have been involved. Tact often required people to refer to concubines without expressing contempt. The word "amica," which retained part of its old laudatory emotive meaning in spite of its new sense, was useful in making concubines appear less contemptible.

Persuasive definitions are too frequently encountered, however, to have been noticed solely by the philologists. An extremely penetrating account, in spite of its cynical turn, is given by Aldous Huxley in his *Eyeless in Gaza:*

"But if you want to be free, you've got to be a prisoner. It's the condition of freedom—true freedom."

"True freedom!" Anthony repeated in the parody of a clerical voice. "I always love that kind of argument. The contrary of a thing isn't the contrary; oh, dear me, no! It's the thing itself, but as it *truly is.* Ask any diehard what conservatism is; he'll tell you it's *true* socialism. And the brewer's trade papers; they're full of articles about the beauty of true temperance. Ordinary temperance is just gross refusal to drink; but true temperance, *true* temperance is something much more refined. True temperance is a bottle of claret with each meal and three double whiskies after dinner.

"What's in a name?" Anthony went on. "The answer is, practically everything, if the name's a good one. Freedom's a marvellous name. That's why you're so anxious to make use of it. You think that, if you call imprisonment true freedom, people will be attracted to the prison. And the worst of it is you're quite right."[4]

2

... We must now proceed to a further point. Persuasive definitions redirect interests by changing only the conceptual meaning of an emotively laden term, allowing the emotive meaning to remain roughly constant. Clearly, the opposite change is equally important and prevalent: the emotive meaning may be altered, the conceptual meaning remaining constant. This latter device is no less persuasive. In fact, the same persuasive force can often be obtained either by the one linguistic change or by the other. In our initial example of "culture," for instance, the speaker used a persuasive definition. He might equally well have reiterated statements such as this: "Culture is only fool's gold; the true metal is imaginative sensitivity." This procedure would have permitted "culture" to retain its old conceptual meaning but would have tended to make its emotive meaning derogatory; and it would have added to the laudatory emotive meaning of "imaginative sensitivity." The same purpose would have been served in this way that was served by the persuasive definition. The qualities commonly referred to by "culture" would still be placed in a poor light and imaginative sensitivity in a fine one; but this would have been effected by a change in emotive meaning rather than in conceptual meaning.

Cases of this last sort must be excluded from our account of persuasive definitions. Although persuasive they are not secured through definition, but rather by one's gestures and tone of voice, or by rhetorical devices such as similes and metaphors. It is expedient to restrict the word "definition" to cases where conceptual meaning alone is being determined, or where, at least, this aspect predominates. We must not forget, however, that many statements which change mainly the emotive meaning of words may, in a wider sense, be called "definitions"; and that they, no less than persuasive definitions in our strict sense, may easily be confused with statements that are not persuasive. (For example, "by 'conscience' is meant the voice of destiny.") ...

3

Having explained what persuasive definitions are, let us now see how they are important to philosophy.

We can readily begin by considering philosophic definitions of the word "philosophy" itself. Ramsey defines it as a system of definitions. Van der Leeuw defines it as an attempt to penetrate behind appearances. Their divergence is no terminological accident. "Philosophy" is a dignified term, and each man reserves it for the inquiry he most wishes to dignify.

Consider the word "reality." Philosophers often seek not reality, but Reality, or rather, true Reality. But "true Reality," like "true culture," is easily defined in many different ways, with many different persuasive effects. Were the shadows in Plato's cave "real" shadows? Were there "real" shadows of horses and men as distinct from the imaginary shadows of centaurs? It will not do to express it so. "Real" is too impressive a term to be used in describing shadows and flux; so it must be given a restricted sense which makes it predicable only of the eternal patterns. (When "Reality" is used by the mystics the effects of a tacit persuasive definition become even more obvious.)

Why did Spinoza, so anxious to free thinking from anthropomorphism, nevertheless tempt his readers to anthropomorphism by using the word "God"? Why did he not speak always of "The One Substance"? One points, of course, to the political and social forces of the times, which made a semblance of orthodoxy imperative. But assuredly this is not all. The word "God" arouses, as if by magic, the very deepest of feelings. By giving a word a new conceptual meaning Spinoza was enabled to direct its emotional force away from the old anthropomorphic fictions and center it upon Substance, which he so earnestly thought would be a more rewarding object for all our wonder and humility. Had he said, "there is no God; nothing but Substance and its Modes," he would have said what he believed, provided "God" was used in the popular sense. But this would have been poor economy of the emotions. It would have taken away the object of men's wonder and humility, providing no substitute; and so these feelings would have died, to the great impoverishment of emotional life. The persuasive definition of a word was needed to preserve emotional vitality. The change in the meaning of "God" was too abrupt, however, to escape notice. Spinoza "the atheist" was long in giving place to Spinoza "the God-intoxicated man"; for the supporters of orthodoxy were not slow to see that his God was God in emotive meaning only.

These remarks are not to be misconstrued as cynical. To point out persuasion is not necessarily to condemn it, nor to identify all persuasion with that of a mob-orator. It *is* imperative, however, to distinguish between persuasion and rational demonstration. . .

4

Let us now turn to ethics, with particular attention to the word "justice," as defined in Plato's *Republic.*

The first book of the *Republic,* it will be remembered, is largely taken up with an argument between Socrates and Thrasymachus. Socrates is the victor and yet he is not content. "I have gone from one subject to another," he says, "without having discovered what I sought first, the nature of justice. I left that inquiry and turned away to consider whether justice is virtue and wisdom, or evil and folly."

Was this argument about the "virtue or evil" of justice really an unwarranted digression? In the light of our previous discussion we cannot agree that it was. The argument had the important function of determining whether or not "justice" was to retain its laudatory emotive meaning, and this was essential to the subsequent developments of the dialogue. When a man is about to give a persuasive definition (and we shall see in a moment that Socrates was) he must make sure that the

emotive meaning of the term defined is well established. Otherwise a definition which was intended to illuminate a conceptual meaning under a laudatory title will end by obscuring it under a derogatory one. The word "justice," which is a little too stern to be wholly pleasing, is in danger of becoming derogatory, and particularly so when men like Thrasymachus . . . are using their oratorical ability to *make* the word derogatory. Socrates must praise justice, then, before he defines "justice."

The question about the meaning of "justice" reappears in the fourth book. The two intervening books have redirected our interests by a moving description of the ideal state. These new interests must be rendered permanent. This can be done by dignifying the more significant aspects of the state under laudatory titles. Of the four laudatory terms which Socrates mentions, "wisdom," "courage," "temperance," and "justice," the first three are readily made to serve this purpose without great change in their conceptual meaning. The remaining term must be reserved for whatever else needs dignity. And so the definition of "justice" is found. "Justice of the state consists of each of the three classes doing the work of its own class."

The persuasive character of this definition—the fact that it forms a part of a spirited plea for a new class system, a beautiful and inspired kind of aristocratic propaganda—can scarcely be denied. The usual meanings of "justice" must give place to the "true" one, to the meaning which needs the dignity of a laudatory name. . .

We must return, however, to the definition of "justice." Plato's definition was persuasive; but this is far from being exceptional. Later definitions of "justice," with but few exceptions, are equally persuasive. They exert a different kind of influence, of course. Not all philosophers are aristocrats. But they do exert an influence.

Let us consider Bentham's definition. "'Justice,' in the only sense which has meaning [!], is an imaginary personage, feigned for the convenience of discourse, whose dictates are the dictates of utility, applied to certain particular cases."[5] More simply stated, "this is a just law" is a hypostatic way of saying, "this law contributes to the greatest happiness of the greatest number." Such a definition may not immediately strike us as being persuasive since so many of us are willing to be led in its direction. Yet its stress on mere numbers, its stress on counting the poor man's happiness side by side with the rich man's, clearly marks a plea for greater democracy. The definition propagated the ideals of a great liberal.

By a "just" wage for laborers, it may be suggested, is meant the wage that anticipates what laborers would get eventually, through operation of the laws of supply and demand, if only there were a perfect market in the economic sense. This definition conceals its persuasion quite well, making it seem to have the detachment of a purely scientific economics. But it is a plea, though slightly compromised, for the operation not of economic laws but of "natural" economic laws— that is to say, for the operation of economic laws as they *could* be stated *if* the purely competitive, "devil take the hindmost" aspects of industry were guaranteed. So you will find this definition more pleasing to those who thrive under the present industrial conditions than to those who do not.

"Justice" can be defined in a great many ways, always without shocking the lexicographers. An eye for an eye, and a tooth for a tooth? The keeping of contracts, merely? The king's will? The dis-

tribution of social wealth in accordance with the amount of labor that each man does? We have a wide choice of meanings and freedom, within wide conventional limits, to invent new ones. Which meaning we choose, however, is no trivial matter, for we shall dignify that meaning by a laudatory title. To choose a meaning is to take sides in a social struggle.

It is curious to note that theorists have all been perturbed by the uncertainty of ethics and have caught glimpses, even in moments of philosophical calm, of the element of persuasion involved. They sought to avoid this by defining their terms, hoping to give greater rigor and rationality to their inquiries. Yet, ironically enough, these very definitions involved the same persuasion, and in a way that veiled and confused it by making it appear to be purely intellectual analysis. . . .

NOTES

1. In this essay the term "interest" has R. B. Perry's sense, which elsewhere in the present volume is expressed by the term "attitude." [In his later works Stevenson substitutes the word "attitude"—Ed.]
2. *Language* (New York, 1933), p. 442.
3. *Lectures on the Study of Language* (New York, 1902), pp. 304, 305.
4. (New York, 1936), p. 90.
5. *Principles of Morals and Legislation* (1789), ch. 10, sect. 40, n.2.

Legal Definition: The Case of Douglas Templemore

7. YOU SHALL KNOW THEM

Vercors

Of course, to be awakened at five in the morning doesn't exactly stir one's sense of humor—not

From *You Shall Know Them* by Vercors (Jean Bruller), translated by Rita Barisse (Boston: Little, Brown and Company, 1953). Excerpts reprinted here by permission of the publisher.

even a doctor's. We cannot, therefore, be surprised that Dr. Figgins, called out as he was at crack of dawn, did not take things as we would after a comfortable breakfast in bed. Even the dramatic look on Douglas Templemore's face— for you or me a reason more to chuckle over this whole comedy of errors—was for Dr. Figgins a reason more for gloom. So, too, was the peculiar nature of the corpse he was shown. For this story, naturally, starts with a corpse. I apologize for so trite an opening, but it is not my fault.

Anyway, it was only a very small corpse. And certainly Dr. Figgins's career had afforded him ample opportunity for meeting corpses, both large and small. So at first this particular one caused him no surprise. He merely bent over the cot for a moment and then, straightening himself, fastened on Douglas a gaze in which professional sternness mingled with his best coffinside manner: his face puckered into an artistic network of wrinkles, expressing at once gravity, tact, blame and compassion. He maintained this eloquent silence for some time before announcing through the bristles of his heavy mustache:

"You've called me in a little late, I fear..."

Which reminded him, with a sting of resentment, of the early hour. Douglas nodded. His voice was expressionless:

"Quite so, doctor. That's what I wanted you to establish."

"I beg your pardon?"

"The child's been dead for half an hour or so, I suppose?"

Dr. Figgins thereupon forgot the hour and all the rest. His mustache swayed under a positive gale of indignation.

"Then why, in heaven's name, did you not call me sooner?"

"I'm afraid you did not understand me, doctor," said Douglas. "I gave him a shot of strychnine chlorhydrate."

Dr. Figgins recoiled a step, and knocked over a chair which he tried to retrieve as, unable to help himself, he foolishly cried:

"But... but that's—murder!"

"Don't doubt it."

"But what the dev... why... how could you...?"

"If you don't mind, doctor, I'll keep my explanations till later."

"I must notify the police!" the doctor declared, much agitated.

"I was going to ask you to."

Figgins took the receiver with a hand that shook a little. He rang up the Guildford police, asked for the inspector; in a voice that had meanwhile recovered its firmness, he requested him to come at once to Sunset Cottage where, he said, a crime had been committed against the person of a newborn baby.

"Infanticide?"

"Yes. The father's already admitted everything."

"Good heavens! Don't let him get away, doctor!"

"No... yes... well, he doesn't seem to want to."

He hung up and went back to the child. He lifted its eyelids, opened its mouth. He gazed with slight surprise at the small lobeless ears that were set unusually high, but he did not seem to give them much thought, for he said nothing.

Instead he opened his bag and carefully collected a drop of the child's saliva on a swab of cotton. This he placed in a small box. Then he closed his bag and sat down. Douglas had already been sitting for some time. Thus they remained in silence until the police arrived.

The inspector was a shy, courteous man with flaxen hair and beautiful manners. He interrogated Douglas with gentle deference. After the usual caution, he asked:

"You are the father, I gather?"

"I am."

"Your wife's upstairs?"

"Yes. I can call her if you like."

"Oh, no," the inspector hastened to assure him. "I wouldn't ask her to get up in *her* condition! I'll go and see her presently."

"I'm afraid you are under a misapprehension," said Douglas. "The child is not hers..."

The inspector's pale eyelids flickered a little. It took him a moment to grasp it.

"Oh... ah... well... is the—er—the mother here, then?"

"No," said Douglas.

"Ah... where is she?"

"She was taken back to the Zoo yesterday."

"The Zoo? Does she work there?"

"No. She lives there."

The inspector's eyes goggled.

"I beg your pardon?"

"The mother is not a woman, properly speaking. She is a female of the species *Paranthropus erectus.*"

For a moment the doctor and the policeman gaped at Douglas without uttering a sound. Then they furtively exchanged an uneasy glance.

Douglas could not help smiling.

"If the doctor," he suggested, "cares to examine the child a little more closely, he will doubtless be struck by certain anomalies."

Only for a second did the doctor hesitate. Then he strode over to the cot, uncovered the little body, and removed the diaper.

He simply said, "Damn!" and furiously seized his hat and bag.

This brought the inspector to his side with anxious speed.

"What's the matter, doctor?"

"This isn't a boy," barked Dr. Figgins. "It's a monkey."

"Are you sure?" asked Douglas in an odd voice.

Figgins grew very red in the face.

"What do you mean, am I sure! Inspector," he said, "we've been the victims of a stupid hoax. I don't know what you propose doing, but I for my part . . ."

He did not bother to finish the sentence: he was already making for the door.

"Just a minute, doctor, if you don't mind," Douglas intervened, in a voice that brooked no denial. He held out to him a sheet of paper that he had taken from a drawer in his desk. The paper bore the heading of the Australian College of Surgeons. "Will you read this?"

After a moment's hesitation the doctor took the paper and put on his spectacles. He read:

I hereby certify that this day at 4:30 A.M. I have delivered a pithecoid female, known as Derry, of the species *Paranthropus erectus,* of a male child in sound physical condition; and that the said birth took place as a result of an artificial insemination carried out by me in Sydney on December 9, 19— for the purpose of scientific investigation, the donor being Douglas M. Templemore.

SELBY D. WILLIAMS, M.D., K.B.E.

Dr. Figgins's naturally globular eyes bulged behind their spectacles to surprising dimensions. "He's going to lay them like eggs . . ." Douglas thought. Without a word, the doctor handed the document to the inspector, glared at Douglas as though he were the ghost of Cromwell, and walked back to the cot.

"Never heard of such a thing!" he muttered dully. "What is this . . . this *Paranthropus?*"

"Nobody knows yet."

"What do you mean?"

"A sort of anthropoid. Some thirty of them have just arrived in this country. They're being studied at the moment."

"But what have you . . ." the doctor began, but broke off and turned back to the cot.

"It's a monkey all the same. It's four-handed." There was a note of relief in his voice.

"That's rather jumping to conclusions," said Douglas mildly.

"There are no four-handed human beings."

"Doctor," said Douglas, "suppose, for instance, that a railway accident . . . look, let's cover up the legs. There, a little corpse with the feet gone. Would you be quite so categorical?"

There was a pause.

"His arms are too long," the doctor said at last.

"But his face?"

The doctor raised his eyes in a helpless perplexity that bordered on a panic.

"His ears . . ." he began.

"And suppose," said Douglas, "that in a few years' time we'd manage to teach him to read, write and reckon?"

"You can suppose anything you like since we'll never know," said Figgins hastily, with a shrug.

"Perhaps we shall. He has brothers, doctor. Two have already been born at the Zoo, by other females. Three more soon will be."

"Time enough then," stammered the doctor, wiping his forehead.

"Time to what?"

"To . . . to see . . . to know . . ."

The inspector drew nearer. His pale eyelashes were fluttering like moths.

"Mr. Templemore, what exactly do you expect us to do?"

"Your job, Inspector."

"But what job, sir? This little creature is a monkey, that's plain. Why the dickens do you want to . . ."

"That's my business, Inspector."

"Well, ours is certainly not to meddle . . ."

"I have killed my child, Inspector."

"I've grasped that. But this . . . this creature isn't a . . . it doesn't present . . ."

"He's been christened, Inspector, and his birth duly entered at the registry office under the name of Garry Ralph Templemore."

Fine beads of perspiration broke out on the inspector's face. He suddenly shot a question at Douglas.

"Under what name was the mother entered?"

"Under her own, Inspector: 'Native woman from New Guinea, known as Derry.'"

"False declaration!" cried the inspector triumphantly. "The whole registration is invalid."

"False declaration?"

"The mother isn't a woman."

"That remains to be proved."

"Why, you yourself —"

"Opinions are divided."

"Divided? Divided about what? Whose opinions?"

"Those of the leading anthropologists, about the species the *Paranthropus* belongs to. It's an intermediate species: man or ape? It resembles both. It may well be that Derry is a woman after all. It's up to you to prove the contrary, if you can. In the meantime her child is my son, before God and the law."

The inspector seemed so disconcerted that Douglas took pity on him.

"Perhaps," he suggested kindly, "you would like to refer the matter to your chief?"

The tow-colored face brightened.

"Yes, if you don't mind, sir."

The inspector lifted the receiver and asked for Guildford. He could not help flashing a grateful smile towards the murderer.

The doctor drew a few steps closer.

"But then," he said, "if I've understood you rightly . . . you're going to find yourself father of five more little monkeys, just like this one?"

"You're beginning to understand, doctor," said Douglas. . . .

Mr. Justice Draper was beginning to speak.

"Ladies and gentlemen of the jury," he said. "During the last three days you have heard the witnesses for the Crown and for the defense, you have heard the closing speech for the prosecution, and the accused has wished to spare you a final plea in his defense. You now have to decide on the prisoner's fate. But before you do so, it is my duty briefly to sum up for you the facts of the case in order to help you, if possible, to reach this grave and difficult decision.

"For it is indeed both grave and difficult. Yours is a formidable task; both sides have impressed this fact upon you. I shall not therefore enlarge upon that point. But I must remind you that, in reviewing the case as it is my duty to do, in weighing up the arguments and counterarguments produced in the course of this trial, I cannot relieve you of any part of your responsibility to decide as to their weight. It is up to you, and to you alone, to draw your own conclusions.

"This being clear, let us come straight to the point.

"What is this case all about?

"As a result of an artificial insemination experimentally performed on the female of a manlike species, recently discovered, the defendant found himself the father of a small hybrid creature, which he killed deliberately on the day of its birth.

"You have to judge whether, in doing so, the defendant has or has not committed a murder.

"Now murder, as a matter of law, is 'the intentional killing of a human being,' so for murder to have been committed, the defendant's act must be proved to have conformed in all points to that definition.

"You cannot, therefore, in this case, return a verdict of guilty unless you have first satisfied yourselves that the following three points have been proved beyond all reasonable doubt:

"First, that the prisoner did kill the deceased.

"Second, that he did so intentionally.

"Third, that the creature thus intentionally killed was a human being.

"With regard to the first two points, you need not, it seems, feel any hesitation. The prisoner claims the responsibility for his act, he admits and proclaims that it was intentional. All the evidence you heard confirmed that this is so.

"The third point, however, seems much less clear.

"Professor Knaatsch asserted that the deceased was a human being. He adduced as proof of this that the species to which it belongs can chip stone, make fire, talk a little, and has adopted the upright posture. The Professors Cocks and Hanson support his view, though for different reasons.

"In opposition to that view, Professor Eatons asserts that we cannot be dealing with a human being, since the foot of the deceased is of a conformation that has never appeared in any creature that stands in the evolutionary line of descent terminating in man.

"This was also the opinion expressed by Dr. Figgins.

"The prosecution has assured you that it is not your task to arbitrate in a dispute of experts; even less, however, to wash your hands of the whole case by an acquittal that would leave out of account the terrible consequences that might ensue. Your task, says the Crown, is to find the accused guilty of murder with premeditation since, legally and judicially, no doubt exists on that point.

"I do not think, however, that you can unhesitatingly follow such advice. On the contrary, I think that you must satisfy yourselves, before deciding on the guilt of the accused, that the third condition which must obtain if there is to be legal murder, has really been fulfilled. In other words, you must be satisfied beyond all reasonable doubt that the deceased was a human being.

"Beyond all reasonable doubt. This expression has come up over and again in the course of this trial. It is my task to enlighten you on the exact meaning of those two words.

"What, in effect, constitutes a 'reasonable doubt'?

"A dangerous confusion may arise on this point.

"The doubt may reside in the facts. For example, when an accused person is noticed on the scene of the crime but there is no conclusive evidence to prove that he committed it. In that case there does exist a reasonable doubt.

"Or the doubt may reside in the mind. For instance, if a juror's memory is at fault because of the vast number of facts presented in evidence, thus making it difficult for the juror to reach a clear understanding of the case. One cannot then speak of a reasonable doubt. In that case the jury must ask, as often as necessary, for further explanations, and if these, in the last resort, are still insufficient to enlighten them, it is open to the jury to declare itself unqualified to judge.

"If therefore you consider that there is a reasonable doubt in the facts, you must disregard completely the possible consequences of an acquittal, in however frightful or alarming a light the prosecution may have presented them. You must find the prisoner not guilty.

"If, on the contrary, you consider that the doubt lies, not in the facts, but in your understanding of them, then I cannot but repeat the Crown's exhortation to you: if the defendant stood here alone, if it were a question of your decision affecting only him, Christian compassion might be admissible in the event of doubt. But in the case before you, the consequences would be too grave to permit of an acquittal on the simple grounds of convenience, and it is certainly your duty as human beings to take into account those dreadful consequences.

"Nevertheless, to return a verdict against the prisoner while doubt remained in your mind would be equally unacceptable. In fact, you would thereby create a no less perilous precedent for the future administration of our justice. For if you were to send a possibly innocent man to his death, convicted not in punishment of his crime, but in consideration of the potential social or political consequences which his acquittal might entail, you would be undermining the very foundations of British justice."

After a brief pause, the judge continued:

"To sum up, then, I agree with the prosecution that the doubt cannot reside in the facts themselves. They are what they are, and the tropi is what he is. His nature is a given fact that is not dependent on us. Like the Crown, therefore, I consider that if doubt there is, it resides only in the understandable confusion caused by learned disputes. Consequently, I hold that the prosecution is right in saying that a doubt of this kind does not warrant mental laziness resulting in leniency regardless of the consequences.

"On the other hand, I concur with the defense that you cannot, in all conscience, convict the prisoner without first being certain that the three premises of a murder have been fulfilled.

"It therefore seems indispensable that, before

pronouncing yourselves one way or another, you should first have settled in your own minds the initial question of the nature of the deceased: ape or human being.

"Only when you are certain of that, can you decide one way or another.

"Failing such certainty, it must be feared that whatever verdict you return will prove a tragic and fatal blunder."

He paused again and then added:

"You are now, ladies and gentlemen of the jury, in possession of all the facts of the case. It remains for you to consider your verdict and to answer, in one word or in two, the question that will presently be put to you: do you find the prisoner at the bar guilty or not guilty?

"Members of the jury, you may now retire."

Mr. Justice Draper thereupon rose, left the courtroom, and unburdened himself of the wig beneath which he was perspiring. As for the public, it unburdened itself of the constraint of silence in a hubbub of conversation that burst with the sound of the sea breaking on rocks.

As soon as the hearing was resumed, the jury returned to the court. The foreman asked, on behalf of them all, for some explanations. He was hardly less pale than the slip of paper that was trembling in his hand.

"We are already agreed," he said, "on the main thing, on the ... er ... crime. No doubt on that score. There only remains one thing to decide, as you said: whether or not the tropis are human. But that's just what we know nothing about."

"Quite so," said Sir Arthur. "Well?"

"Well, could you, my lord, tell us ... what exactly you think about it?"

"That is impossible. I am here to throw light on the facts, on the points of law. I cannot have an opinion. And even if I had one, it would be most improper for me to express it."

The elderly juryman, tall and spare, with white hair curling round his small, shiny, pink pate, moved his lantern jaw sideways once or twice before saying:

"In that case, we thought if we might at least have ... if you would just recall to our minds how ... how man is generally defined, I mean in everyday usage ... the proper, legal definition ... surely that ... er ... that doesn't exceed your powers?"

"Indeed it doesn't," said the judge, smilingly. "However, such a legal definition would first of all have to exist. It is odd, perhaps, but the fact is that it doesn't."

The old man stared at him stupidly for a moment, then he asked:

"There isn't one?"

"No."

"But, I mean, that isn't possible."

"It's odd, I grant you, I said so before. Though actually quite in keeping with our national character. Anyway, there isn't one."

"Neither in this country nor anywhere else?"

"Nowhere at all. Not even in France, where everything is defined and codified, down to who owns the egg that the hen will lay in the neighbor's garden."

"But that's incredible," said the old juryman after a moment. "Are we to believe that everything is, as you say, defined and codified, even the tiniest thing, except ... why, just ourselves?"

"That's perfectly correct," said the judge.

"But look here, my lord. ... All the time that man's been existing, nobody's ever? ... Everything's been thought of ... laid down and defined, except just that? Isn't that rather as if one hadn't thought of anything at all? As if one'd put a whole lot of carts before the horse?"

The judge smiled. His hands described a movement of restrained helplessness.

"Because after all," continued the juryman, "if you don't know ... exactly ... I mean to say, if people haven't even agreed ... on, why, on us, on what we ... well, how the dickens can they agree on anything?" ...

The government proposed that a commission should be set up in order to obtain, with the aid of representatives of science and the law, a legal definition of man. The occasion moved him [Sir Arthur] to a brilliant flight of eloquence. He said that Great Britain, having taught the world democracy, would now lay the foundation stone of another sublime edifice. "Imagine," he said, "the consequences of our action, if such a definition should one day pass beyond the framework of British legislation and be incorporated in international law. For if what constitutes the essence of man comes to be legally defined, will not our obligations towards man be defined by the same stroke: since anything that threatened that essence would automatically be a menace to humanity." . . .

This opened the way for a lively debate as to how Parliament was to set about discharging this unusual and impressive task. Should a Royal Commission be appointed? A Committee of Inquiry be set up? Or was it more prudent for Parliament to leave the task, on the contrary, to an unofficial body, such as the Royal Society?

An old member declared that man being composed of mind and body, he surely could not be better defined than by the Lords Spiritual and Temporal. Another said that since a legal definition was wanted, it would be absurd not to appeal quite simply to the legal lights of the bench and the bar under the chairmanship of the Lord Chief Justice. Another said it was the business of the Queen and of her Privy Council, which surely came into its own in just such an emergency. Yet another suggested a congress of anthropologists, another again a congress of psychologists. Someone asked whether the B.B.C. could not be requested to conduct a referendum.

The suggestion that was ultimately adopted revealed the British genius for compromise at its highest in that, while contenting no one, it was acceptable to all. The choice fell upon the Royal College of Moral and Spiritual Sciences, an august body which counted among its members personalities of all callings and walks of life. This body was charged to form a committee, to which were to be nominated, informally by the various parties, certain members of the House, thus giving it a semiofficial character.

As a result, Sir Kenneth Summer, a noted back-bencher and active member of the college, could soon after announce in the Commons the formation of a "Committee for the Study of a Specification of the Human Species with a View to the Legal Definition of Man." For the sake of convenience, this was later generally referred to as the Summer Committee, after its chairman. Sir Arthur Draper was invited to assist the Committee, both as a distinguished jurist and as a sort of surety, by his presence, of the legality of their undertaking. It was decided to meet on Tuesdays and Fridays in the famous library of the Royal College of Moral and Spiritual Sciences, which had once been Cecil Rhodes' small reading room. And then it was that the difficulties began.

It became clear, in effect, that every member of the Committee had come to it with a preconceived view on the subject to which he clung tenaciously. Lord Humpleton, the *doyen* of the Committee, who was asked to open the proceedings, declared that in his opinion the best possible definition had been given by Wesley who, he reminded his fellow members, had shown that reason, though generally supposed to be a distinguishing feature of man, could not be so regarded. Indeed, many animals give proof of intelligence, whereas ideas as aberrant as fetishism and sorcery, alien to animals, scarcely plead in favor of human wisdom. The true difference, said Wesley, is that we are formed to know God and they are not.

A little Quaker lady, slim and graying, with candid eyes behind thick glasses, asked to be heard, and in a soft, almost quavering voice said that she did not see how we could presume to know what was going on in a dog's or a chimpanzee's heart, and how one could be sure that they did not know God in their fashion.

"But look here," protested Lord Humpleton, "they can't possibly! I mean, it stands to reason!"

The little Quaker lady said that assertion was no proof, and another, timid-looking, member suggested in a mild voice that it would be rash, moreover, to deny the fetish worshippers all benefit of reason: they merely exercised it badly, he assured the gathering, just as a banker who goes bankrupt may practice finance badly, but is yet more of a financier then, say, a midshipman of H.M.S. Victory. "It seems to me," he concluded, "that we should, on the contrary, make it our starting point that man is endowed with reason."

"And where exactly do you make reason start?" he was asked ironically by a very smartly dressed gentleman with impeccably starched collar and cuffs.

"That is precisely what we must define," said the shy gentleman.

But Lord Humpleton said that if the idea of God were to be left out of the definition of man, his own religious convictions would not allow him to take any further part in the work of the Committee.

Sir Kenneth Summer, in the chair, reminded him that the government had explicitly stated that the definition to be formulated by the Committee must be acceptable to all schools of thought and opinion. Lord Humpleton need therefore have no fear that the idea of God would be missing from it. However, an exclusively theological definition could no more meet the case since it would fail to satisfy the large number of agnostics to be found not only on the Continent, but also in the British Isles.

A portly gentleman with a heavy white mustache—a former colonel in the Indian Army who had had resounding *affaires* with ladies of note—said that what he was going to say might appear extravagant; but that, in the course of his long and intimate acquaintance with men and animals, he had come to the conclusion that one thing and one thing alone was entirely typical of man, and that was sexual perversion. He added that he thought that man was the only animal in creation that had, for instance, founded brilliant societies on homosexuality.

A gentleman-farmer from Hampshire asked Colonel Strang whether, according to him, the basic peculiarity lay in the existence of those brilliant societies—in which case what needed defining was man's urge to found civilizations—or whether it lay in homosexuality: for in the latter case he was sorry to have to inform the colonel that homosexual couples, both male and female, were quite common among ducks.

His own opinion, he added, was that you could get nowhere if you remained within "closed" fields of studies, like zoology, psychology, theology, and all the rest. Man is an "open" complex, he said, existing only in his relationship to other men and to things. He is determined by his environment, which he in turn determines, and it is this constant interplay which in the long run produces history. And outside history all is but a figment of the brain.

The gentleman with the cuffs ran a ringed finger round the inside of his collar as he said that his honorable colleague seemed to have contracted, on his Hampshire estate, an acute form of Marxian indigestion, and that if he'd set out to turn not only the Committee but the entire British government into Marxists, he would need a little more time than the Committee had at its disposal. The little Quaker woman said in her gentle, quavering voice that you need not be a Marxist to think as her colleague did, but that if what he said seemed substantially true, it did not, practically speaking, lead them anywhere. For it would still be necessary to explain why that interplay does not occur in animal societies. If man has a changing history and the animals have not, it is because there is something peculiar to man, and it was this that had to be defined.

Sir Kenneth asked her if she had any view to propound. She said that she most certainly had. "Man," she said, "is the only animal capable of entirely selfless acts. In other words, goodness and charity are peculiar to man and to him alone."

Lord Humpleton asked rather sarcastically how she knew that animals were incapable of unselfish impulses since she herself had claimed a moment ago that they might possibly know God? The gentleman-farmer capped it by remarking that his own dog had died in a fire because he had thrown himself into the flames to save a child. And anyway, even if it were shown that these feelings are peculiar to man, it would remain, as she herself had said, to discover what was the source of this difference.

The gentleman with the cuffs took the floor to say that as far as he was concerned it mattered very little whether there was a legal definition of man or not. For five hundred thousand years, he said, man had got on without being defined; or rather he had invented for himself changing conceptions which, in their day, had served the civilizations he had built. Why not let him continue in this way? One thing alone mattered, he claimed: the traces left by those civilizations as they disappeared. In a word—art. "This," he said, "is the characteristic feature of man, from Cro-Magnon days down to our own."

"But," asked the Quaker lady, "does it leave you altogether unmoved that thousands of tropis, supposing they're human, may be reduced to slavery; and, supposing they are apes, that an innocent man may be hanged?"

The gentleman answered that, as a matter of fact, from a somewhat loftier standpoint, it left him perfectly unmoved. Life crawls with injustices. The most you can flatter yourself on doing is reducing them to a minimum. To that end we have laws, traditions, customs, forms. The main thing is to apply them. That they may be more or less well applied is inherent in the indeterminate nature of what is just and unjust, and this we have not the power to change.

The gentleman-farmer said that this was of course open to debate, though he himself was not far from sharing this view. But he asked his colleague to give him a definition of art. For, he said, if he wanted to use art to define man, art itself must be defined first.

The gentleman with the cuffs replied that art being a unique and self-evident manifestation, immediately recognizable by all, there was no need to define it.

The gentleman-farmer said that, in that case, man being a self-evident and immediately recognizable species, there was no need to define him either.

The gentleman with the cuffs said that that was precisely what he himself had declared earlier.

Sir Kenneth pointed out that the Committee was meeting not in order to establish that man needed no definition but rather to attempt a definition.

He said that the first session had perhaps not advanced matters very much, but that it had at least afforded an opportunity for a frank exchange of interesting opinions.

Then he closed the meeting. . . .

"In comparing man's intelligence with the beast's," said Sir Arthur, "Professor Rampole talked to us less of quantity than of quality. He even pointed out that it is always like that in nature: a small difference in quantity can produce a sudden mutation, a total change in quality. For instance, when heating water, you can add more and more calories without the water changing its state. And then, at a given moment, one single degree is enough for it to pass from the liquid state to the gaseous one. Is

not that what has occurred with our forebears' intelligence? A small addition in quantity to the brain connections,—perhaps quite a minute one—and it made one of those jumps which produce a total change in quality. So that . . ."

"That's a subversive view," said the gentleman with the cuffs.

"I beg your pardon?"

"I've read things of that sort in . . . oh, I don't remember. Anyway, it's rank Bolshevik materialism. It's one of the three laws of their dialectics."

"Professor Rampole," said Sir Kenneth, "is a nephew of the Bishop of Crewe. His wife is one of Canon Clayton's daughters. The canon's mother is a friend of my mother's, and Sir Peter himself is a perfectly good Christian."

The gentleman pulled at his cuffs and gazed absorbedly at the beams of the ceiling.

"Professor Rampole," continued Sir Arthur, "has specified this change in quality. The difference between the Neanderthal man's intelligence and a great ape's can't have been much in the way of quantity. But it made a vast difference to their relationship to nature: the animal continued to submit to it; man suddenly started to question it."

"Well . . .," Lord Humpleton and the gentleman with the cuffs exclaimed together, but Sir Arthur did not let himself be interrupted.

"Now, in order to question there must be two of you—the one who questions, and the one who is questioned. Intimately bound up with nature, the animal cannot question it. That seems to be the point we are seeking. The animal is *one* with nature, while man and nature make *two*. To pass from passive unconsciousness to questioning consciousness, there had to be that schism, that divorce, there had to be that wrenching away from nature. Is not that precisely the borderline? Animal before the wrench, man after it? De-natured animals, that's what we are."

Some seconds of silence passed before Colonel Strang was heard to mutter:

"That's not so silly. Explains homosexuality."

"It explains," said Sir Arthur, "why the animal needs neither fables nor amulets. It is unaware of its own ignorance. Whereas the mind of man, torn away, cut off from nature—how could it fail to be instantly plunged in darkness and terror? Man sees himself alone, abandoned, mortal, not knowing anything—the only animal on earth 'that knows but one thing, that it knows nothing'—not even what it is. How could he help inventing myths: gods or spirits in response to that ignorance, fetishes and charms in response to that helplessness? Does not the animal's very lack of those aberrant inventions prove the absence, too, of those terrified questions?"

They all looked at him without saying a word.

"But if, then, what has made the person—the conscious person and his history—is indeed that wrench, that independence, that struggle, that de-nature; if a beast, in order to be admitted into the community of man, must have taken that hard and painful step—how, by what sign at last, can we recognize that it has done so?"

There was no answer. . . .

On the basis of the Summer Committee's report, the House passed a bill, after various minor amendments, containing the following articles:

Section 1. Man is distinguished from the Beast by his spirit of religion.

Section 2. The principal signs of a spirit of religion are, in decreasing order of importance: faith in God, science, art and all its manifestations; the various religious creeds and philosophies and all their manifestations; ritual cannibalism and its manifestations.

Section 3. Any animate being that displays one or more of the signs mentioned in Section 2 is admitted to the human community, and its person protected throughout the United Kingdom, the British Commonwealth, and Her Majesty's colonies across the seas, by the various provisions figuring in the last Declaration of the Rights of man.

As soon as the bill had become an act of Parliament, an M.P., known to have ties with the textile industry, asked what was going to be done about the tropis. . . .

After a lively debate there was general support for a proposal that the terms of reference of the Summer Committee should be extended to include the defining of the tropis' nature. It was, however, agreed beforehand that the House was not competent to introduce legislation on the status of the tropis. Parliament would have to confine itself to a "recommendation" which would be submitted simultaneously to the United Nations Organization as well as to the Government of Australia and the Governor-General of New Guinea.

The Committee, which Sir Peter Rampole had been invited to join in his capacity of an expert on primitive psychology, heard in turn Kreps, Pop, Willy, the Greames, and several other anthropologists who had been able to study the behavior of the tropis since their arrival in London.

It seemed at first that no sign of a spirit of religion could be detected in them. They made no use of fetishes, amulets, tattooing, had no dances or rituals of any kind—let alone vestiges of art or science. Though they interred their dead, they did it as many animals do, and in the way that most animals bury their excrements, prompted by some atavistic instinct to avoid the dangers of decay or to cover up their tracks. No funerary rites whatsoever could be observed in use among the tropis.

They did not even show the slightest tendency towards cannibalism. They did not devour each other, nor had they ever been observed trying to lure or snare a human being with a view to devouring him. They had not even done so in the case of the Papuan porters, in spite of their immediate and obvious dislike of the latter.

[Sir Peter remarked:] "Luckily the Papuans did not show a similar restraint, with regard to the tropis. They ate them clandestinely on several occasions.

"We must specially note this fact: the Papuan orgies were clandestine.

"This being so, the Papuans must have wished either to conceal them from the white men, or to prevent the white men from watching the accompanying rites or ceremonies.

"Now, they would not have taken these precautions had they thought they were merely feasting on ordinary animal flesh. So we can suppose that they considered they were indulging in cannibalism, and eating not animals but human beings."

Sir Peter Rampole paused for a moment. Then he continued:

"That is merely a clue for us to follow. We obviously cannot trust the Papuans' instincts rather than the accuracy of six months' close observation of the tropis by a brilliant team of scientists.

"On the other hand, we are even less justified in ignoring this hint altogether. We must take into account the clue provided by the instinct of those men who are so much closer than we are to the primitive manifestations of the human mind, and who may thus detect, far better than we can, its first, faint signs in others.

"My opinion therefore is that we may have overlooked, or failed to identify, some exceedingly primitive sign of a spirit of religion, which did not escape the Papuans.

"Sir Arthur and I have some idea of what this may be. But for confirmation we should have to dig more deeply into certain statements made to the Committee."

He added that he thought these details could be obtained from his distinguished colleague, the geologist Professor Kreps, who had been able to bring to the study of the tropis a keenly scientific mind unhampered by a zoologist's or anthropologist's parochialism or prejudice. No testimony, he thought, could be more unbiased than his.

So Kreps was heard again at the next sitting.

Sir Peter asked him if the Papuans had attacked indiscriminately the cliff-dwelling tropis and those in the compound.

Kreps replied that they hadn't. The Papuan raiding parties had been confined to the cliffs. Rather an odd fact, he admitted, since the domestic tropis were far more conveniently within their reach. No special watch had been kept over the compound, he explained, at least in the early days, so that they would have been an easy prey.

Sir Peter then asked whether a great deal of smoked meat had been found in the caves during their first visits to the cliffs.

Kreps said that they had found only very little.

"We understood," said Sir Peter, "that the tropis smoked their meat in order to preserve it?"

"That's what we thought too, at first. However, we never actually found that they did preserve it. They went out hunting whenever there was need, and consumed their booty at once."

"Are you sure they smoked their meat without cooking it?"

"Oh, absolutely!" said Kreps. "We never managed to make our tropis eat the least morsel of cooked meat. They loathe it. Their real treat is perfectly raw meat."

"Then why do they smoke it, if it's neither to preserve it nor because they like its taste?"

"To be perfectly frank, I have no idea. As a matter of fact, something rather odd happened: the cliff tropis never ate a scrap of meat that they hadn't left hanging over the fire for at least a day. They did this even to the ham we gave them, as if to make quite sure that it was smoked according to the rules. Whereas those in the compound greedily swallowed any raw meat we gave them, without standing on ceremony."

"And you drew no conclusion from this?"

"Well, you know," said Kreps, "it's common enough for captive animals to drop pretty quickly certain habits of their wild life, even quite instinctive ones."

"However," said Sir Peter, "here are some facts that are all strange in themselves, and even more so when taken in conjunction.

"First, the tropis prefer their meat quite raw. Secondly, the cliff tropis nevertheless carefully hang it over the fire, but not in order to preserve it. Thirdly, the domestic tropis promptly drop this practice. Fourth and lastly, the Papuans indulge in cannibalistic orgies of the former, and scorn the latter.

"Wasn't it you," he asked Kreps, "who said, talking of the domestic tropis: 'We've scooped all the flunkeys'?"

"Yes, indeed," laughed Kreps.

"Let us now," said Sir Peter, "try to put ourselves in the Papuans' place. They have there before them a strange people—half ape, half human. Part of that people seem proud, jealous of their independence; they indulge in a practice which the Papuans recognize, less as instinct or preference, than as a very primitive fire worship, a homage paid to its magic power of purification and exorcism. The rest of the tropis, frivolous and carefree, renounce their liberty for a handful of raw meat. Left to themselves, they promptly abandon a practice which they had followed out of imitation and not by instinct—still less by reason. And our Papuans are not mistaken: they treat the former as men, the latter as apes.

"We believe that they are right. In this people on the borderline between man and beast, all have not equally crossed the line. But it is enough, to our mind, that some of them have crossed it for the entire species to be received within the human community."

"Besides," Sir Arthur confided later to Sir Kenneth, "how many of us would have the right to the title "man," if all of us had had to cross the borderline unaided? . . ."

The Summer Committee thus reported to Parliament that the tropis, having shown signs of a spirit of religion by a ritual practice of fire worship, should be admitted to the human community. . . .

The second trial opened in an atmosphere no longer of high passions, but of curiosity tinged with sympathy for the accused. Now that everything was clear, the murder became a murder like any other. The general wish was that the accused should get off lightly, for his part in the emancipation of the tropis was not forgotten. It was hoped that the Crown would show itself sympathetic and the jury merciful. Bets were made on the sentence the accused would have to serve, some bold spirits even backing him for an acquittal. The sums involved were substantial. . . .

The trial did indeed pass off for the most part like a mere formality. There were few witnesses, as the only evidence needed was on the circumstances of the murder. The prosecution, as was expected, did not prove too severe. He said that a murder having been committed and now amply proved, it was out of the question to declare the accused not guilty. However, in view of the motive for the crime, and the fact that when it was committed the accused was unaware of the exact nature of the deceased, the Crown was prepared to admit the existence of extenuating circumstances.

Mr. Jameson, counsel for the defense, thanked the Crown for the understanding it had shown, but said that his learned friend had not gone far enough in the lesson he had drawn from the facts.

"The Crown recognizes," he said, "that at the time of the murder the accused was unaware of the deceased's true nature. But is that the proper way to put it? I do not think so.

"I contend that at the time of the murder the deceased was not a human being at all."

He paused for a moment after those words. Then he went on:

"In fact, special legislation was needed to define the human being. And yet further legislation to include the tropis in that definition.

"This shows that it did not rest with the tropis to be or not to be members of the human community, *but with us to admit them to it.*

"It shows too that no one is a human being by a right of nature, but that, on the contrary, before being recognized as such by his fellow men, he must have undergone—in a manner of speaking—an examination, an initiation.

"Mankind resembles a very exclusive club. What we call human is defined by us alone. The rules within the club are valid for us alone. Hence the need for a legal basis to be established, as much for the admission of new members as for setting up rules and regulations applicable to all.

"It is obvious, therefore, that before being accepted as members, the tropis could not share in the life of the club nor claim the benefit of the club regulations.

"In other words, we could not demand of anyone that he should treat the tropis as human beings before we ourselves had decided that they were entitled to that appellation.

"To declare the accused guilty would thus be equivalent to applying the law retrospectively. As if, supposing a new regulation were introduced that compelled vehicles to keep to the right, a fine were then imposed on all drivers who had hitherto kept to the left.

"It would be a crying injustice, besides being profoundly contrary to the spirit of all our laws.

"The facts are clear.

"The tropis—thanks, incidentally, to the accused—have been legally admitted to the human community. They share the rights of man. They are no longer threatened. No other primitive or backward race, once jeopardized by the absence of any legal definition, is threatened any more.

"The jury therefore need have no qualms that

the defendant's acquittal might have unfortunate consequences.

"On the other hand, you may be sure, ladies and gentlemen of the jury, that if you find the accused guilty, you will be responsible for a mistake, a misdeed, an appalling miscarriage of justice.

"For not only was the little victim as yet unrecognized as a human being at the time of its death, but it is common knowledge that its sacrifice lies at the root of the emancipation of all its people, as well as of a precious clarification of the laws of mankind in general.

"I therefore trust you to return a verdict fraught with wisdom and equity."

The judge's summing-up was genial. Though calmly impartial, he yet clearly showed that common sense favored the plea for the defense. The jury felt great relief. It retired for only a few minutes before bringing in, to the delight of the public, a verdict of *Not Guilty....*

SUGGESTIONS FOR FURTHER READING

GENERAL CONCEPTIONS OF PHILOSOPHY

Bobik, Joseph, ed. *The Nature of Philosophical Inquiry.* Notre Dame, Indiana: University of Notre Dame Press, 1970.

Bontempo, Charles J. and S. Jack Odell, eds. *The Owl of Minerva: Philosophers on Philosophy.* New York: McGraw-Hill, 1975.

Broad, C. D., "Critical and Speculative Philosophy" in J. H. Muirhead, ed. *Contemporary British Philosophy,* First Series. London: Allen & Unwin, 1924.

Danto, Arthur C. *What Philosophy Is: A Guide to the Elements.* New York: Harper & Row, 1968.

Johnstone, Henry W., ed. *What Is Philosophy?* London: Macmillan, 1965.

Korner, Stephen. *What Is Philosophy? One Philosopher's Answer.* London: Penguin, 1969.

Lazerowitz, Morris. *Philosophy and Illusion.* New York: Humanities Press, 1968.

Newell, R. W. *The Concept of Philosophy.* London: Methuen, 1967.

Ortega y Gasset, José. *What Is Philosophy?* trans. Mildred Adams. New York: W. W. Norton, 1960.

PHILOSOPHICAL METHOD AND DEFINITION

Carnap, Rudolf. *Logical Foundations of Probability.* Chicago: University of Chicago Press, 1950. pp. 1–18 ("On Explication").

Cohen, Morris R. and Ernest Nagel. *An Introduction to Logic and Scientific Method.* New York: Harcourt, Brace, & Co., 1934. pp. 223–44 ("Classification and Definition").

Copi, Irving M. *Introduction to Logic.* Fifth edition. New York: Macmillan, 1978. Part One, pp. 3–164.

Glover, Jonathan. *Causing Death and Saving Lives.* Harmondsworth, Middlesex: Penguin, 1977. pp. 22–38 ("The Scope and Limits of Moral Argument").

Gorovitz, Samuel, and Ron G. Williams. *Philosophical Analysis: An Introduction to Its Language and Techniques.* Second edition. New York: Random House, 1963.

Guthrie, W. K. C. *Socrates.* Cambridge: Cambridge University Press, 1971.

Robinson, Richard. *Definition.* Oxford: Clarendon Press, 1950.

Rosenberg, Jay F. *The Practice of Philosophy: A Handbook For Beginners.* Englewood Cliffs, N.J.: Prentice-Hall, 1976.

Ryle, Gilbert. "Philosophical Arguments" in A. J. Ayer, ed., *Logical Positivism.* New York: The Free Press, 1959.

Taylor, A. E. *Plato.* Fourth edition. London, 1937.

Taylor, A. E. *Socrates: The Man and His Thought.* Garden City, N.Y.: Doubleday Anchor Books, 1953.

Vlastos, Gregory, ed. *The Philosophy of Socrates.* Garden City, N.Y.: Doubleday Anchor Books, 1971. See especially "Socratic Definition" by Richard Robinson, "Elenctic Definitions" by George Nakhnikian, "Elenchus," by Richard Robinson, and "Socrates on the Definition of Piety: Euthyphro 10A-11B," by S. Mark Cohen.

Waisman, Friedrick. "How I See Philosophy" in A. J. Ayer, ed., *Logical Positivism.* New York: The Free Press, 1959.

Chapter 2   The Problem of Knowledge

College and university students, as well as their professors, have presumably been in the business of acquiring knowledge for many years. Because they already know a great deal, it may seem odd to ask such questions as "What is knowledge?" and "What can be known?" Yet philosophers have been perplexed by these questions for centuries. There are, of course, many common-sense answers to these questions, all of which suggest that a large body of information can be possessed. We seem to know much about the past (e.g., through historical works) and the present (in our own experience), and the sciences allow us to predict much about the future. But influential philosophers have raised serious questions concerning common-sense views about knowledge. And there are reasons to support their rejection of common sense. After all, most of us rarely feel absolutely certain about the truth of our beliefs, simply because we have so often been mistaken in the past. We have thought something was wrong with the steering mechanism of our automobile, for example, when it turned out that the problem was with the tires. We may think we see a bright star, when it is in fact a satellite. We brag that our German Shepherd does not bite, but the next day he grabs a piece of a postman's leg. So much for certainty, we may think.

Nonetheless, we often are certain enough about our convictions that we act on them in ways a more informed understanding would rule out. The philosopher G. E. M. Anscombe tells about a

man on a hunting trip who shot at what he took to be a stag but was really his father—with a fatal outcome. The huntsman was in fact looking at and shooting his father, but his father appeared to him to be a stag, and he thought he was shooting a stag.

We are all aware of circumstances in which we similarly misperceive things, though usually with less serious consequences. Faced with such problems, philosophers have long wondered what is involved in a claim that something merely appears to us, while we fail to see the thing as it really is. When they ask "What can we *know?*," as distinct from "What do we *believe?*," they have often demanded an answer that admits of no doubt whatever. These philosophers are engaged in what in chapter 1 was called a "quest for ultimates," especially for what was there described as "the ultimate source of evidence from which the rational reconstruction of all of our other beliefs must proceed."

Other philosophers, by contrast, have had a more modest task in mind. They have wanted only to find out what must be known so that *no reasonable person could raise a doubt* about the information possessed. This demand for knowledge resembles demands commonly made by courts: a person can be convicted if there is no reasonable doubt that he committed the alleged crime. Courts do not demand certainty, and we all know of cases where juries have been mistaken. The major difference between these two approaches obviously lies in whether one demands certainty or only absence of reasonable doubt. In either case, however, one is seeking a secure foundation for knowledge, and this problem of foundations is one we shall be exploring throughout the present chapter.

REALITY, APPEARANCE, AND PERCEPTUAL RELATIVITY

In our discussion of the quest for ultimates in chapter 1, we observed that many traditional problems of philosophy raise questions about the familiar worlds of common experience, science, and history. We there mentioned a distinction between the real and the apparent, in the context of philosophers' search for what is *ultimately* real. The mere appearance of something more real than an appearance itself obviously does not suffice as an answer to their demands. Their requests for reality are indeed alien to common sense, for nothing seems more real to us than the reality of desks, food, and all the other furniture of our universe. Yet what do we really know about such familiar items?

Let us consider one of the more common things in the world: water. Water appears to be transparent, yet we cannot always see through it. Water in a lake sometimes appears to be a deep blue, yet when we draw it from the lake it is not blue at all. If we are thirsty and hot, water is cool and refreshing, yet if we are sick and feverish nothing may seem more repulsive than a drink of this liquid. Water also appears to be fluid and conforms to the size and shape of any container, without obvious division into natural parts. It hardly seems divisible into "solid" particles in the way sand is, for example. Yet physics suggests that water, like sand, is divisible into discrete particles. Moreover, in order to experience water one must have a sensory experience of it—visual, tactile, or whatever. We have such experiences through the workings of our sensory apparatus and the brain. Does this suggest that water is nothing other than our set of sensory experiences? Or can it be reduced to an image in our brain? If so, should we say the same about the food that we eat, the desk at which we sit, and even the mothers who bore us? These questions challenge our common sense, for there is no obvious common-sense answer to them.

The puzzling intractability of such questions has confronted philosophers with the problem of appearance and reality. The problem may be further explored by considering a second example: a tomato. What are the ingredients involved in "experiencing" a tomato? Philosophers have discussed three possible ingredients: (1) the person having the experience, (2) the tomato, and (3) the tomato's colors, shapes, solidity, etc., as the person experiences them. The ingredients of this third category have often been called *sense data,* for they are the sheer data provided by our senses. But if we know *only* sense data and *not* the tomato itself, then we seem to know only an appearance of the tomato and not its reality. Or perhaps the tomato really is what it appears to be. But how can we know whether its reality *is* its appearance or something *separate* from its appearance?

These problems have plagued philosophy throughout its history. Even the early Greek philosophers noticed certain disparities between appearance and reality. Sticks and oars appear to all observers to be bent when partially immersed in water, and radiators feel warm to cold hands and cool to the fevered touch. There is no doubt that we have the sensations of bent sticks and cool-but-otherwise-warm objects; but is the stick really bent, and is the radiator really cool? Can the stick be truly bent for one person while straight for another, or a radiator truly cool for one person while warm for another?

It seems contradictory to assert that an object both is and is not bent, or is and is not cool. But perhaps this apparent contradiction can be removed by an account of *perceptual relativity*. It is an almost indisputable fact that the way objects appear to us varies as our perspective and distance change. Also, some paintings that appear to be three-dimensional to one observer are only two-dimensional to other observers. Is the "nature" of all objects in the world similarly relative to perceivers? Or are objects always what they are, while perceivers deviate in their perceptions of objects? Relatedly, is the color of the objects in the perceiver, or in the object itself? Perhaps the nature and color of things somehow exists in a *relationship* between a perceiver and an object, so that each makes a contribution. No one would say that the pain we experience when touching a fire is in the fire itself, so why should we say the color or shape is in the fire? On the other hand, no one would say that the fire is in our eyes, so why would we say the color or shape is in our eyes? Apparently the information we obtain from our senses does not always provide correct or at least unassailable information. The problem, once again, is to distinguish what is merely apparent from what really exists.

The possible disparity between appearance and reality has led to several problems about knowledge: (1) Can we know anything at all? (2) What do perceptual statements report? (3) Does independent evidence exist to corroborate whatever perceptual statements report? We shall be considering each of these questions throughout the present chapter.

SCEPTICISM

Some philosophers have thought, based on the above considerations, that propositions about the world are never certain and can always be subjected to doubt. Some have expressed this view in sceptical form: perhaps our senses *always* deceive us; perhaps we are dreaming; or perhaps an evil demon is distorting our judgment. One might attempt to answer the sceptic by assembling a group of "normal" perceivers to corroborate one's perception and judgments. This strategy, however, will not deter a hardened sceptic. The sceptic will question the reliability of those perceivers and will imagine conditions under which everyone would doubt the truth of what these perceivers report. Indeed, a thorough sceptic will deny that we have any knowledge at all—or at the very least the sceptic will challenge us to provide a reliable method for obtaining knowledge and will raise questions about all presently available means of achieving knowledge.

There are several kinds of scepticism, but most sceptical arguments follow a common pattern. The sceptic isolates some claim that we make about the past, the present, or the future. If the claim is about the past, then doubt is cast on the adequacy of our memory or of standard "historical evidence" used to recover information about the past. If the claim is about the present, doubt is cast on the adequacy of our senses or our ability to formulate correct conclusions. If the claim is about the future (e.g., the prediction of an eclipse), then doubt is cast on the adequacy of our present "knowledge" and the systems of inference we use to make reliable predictions.

Sceptical problems, and the other problems about knowledge and perception mentioned above, have been widely discussed throughout the history of philosophy. But the problems were discussed with a renewed vigor at the beginning of the modern period, a vigor due in large part to certain scientific developments in and around the seventeenth century. At that time it was generally agreed that scientific knowledge had to be rooted in the *observation* of nature and in the *inferences* made by using the so-called scientific method. The scientific reliance on observation and the use of empirical hypotheses gave philosophers broadened materials for their ancient debates. The rise of the scientific method thus spawned a philosophical reaction. A number of influential philosophers during the seventeenth and eighteenth centuries raised doubts about the reliability of sensory observations, and thus about the adequacy of the scientific method itself.

The philosopher René Descartes (1596–1650) was most responsible for bringing sceptical questions into the forefront of discussion. He finally rejects scepticism as a general philosophical position, yet remains sceptical about our knowledge of some properties of objects, e.g., that they have colors. Descartes' method is not to *promote* scepticism *per se*. Instead, he uses the strategy of provisionally *doubting* that we know anything at all, in order to discover what, if any, so-called "knowledge" is certain. A second influential philosopher during this period was George Berkeley (1685–1753). He, too, does not see himself as a sceptic, yet he advances a theory of perception and knowledge that sharply challenges our common-sense views about the distinction between appearance and reality. Moreover, many would say that Berkeley is himself a sceptic about the existence of physical objects. The first two selections from philosophers in this chapter are excerpts from major writings by Descartes and Berkeley. The overall approaches and conclusions of these two philosophers are so important that their systematic views deserve separate and detailed examination in this introduction.

DESCARTES, SCEPTICAL DOUBT, AND THE FOUNDATIONS OF KNOWLEDGE

A brief consideration of Descartes' life and background will clarify the main features of his thought. During the last few years of his college training he concentrated on philosophy, mathematics, and logic. Though he spoke of his teachers with enormous respect, he reflected on his training and found it wanting. It seemed to him that no solid foundation existed on which thought could be based with certainty. He says he found himself embarrassed by the many doubts that tormented him and by his ignorance of vital questions, the answers to which persistently eluded him. He remarked about the philosophy he had been taught that "no single thing is to be found in it which is not subject of dispute, and in consequence which is not dubious." At the same time, he gloried in mathematics, because it seemed perfectly clear and certain. The deficiency that he found in philosophy and the perfection he found in mathematics set the tone, as we shall see, for much of his philosophical work.

SCEPTICAL DOUBTS

Descartes' most famous approach is that of universal doubt, also called methodical doubt and sceptical doubt. It constitutes his real beginning in philosophy. He argues that if one is to be successful in finding absolute certainty, one must make as few assumptions as possible—or preferably no assumptions at all. Descartes maintains that one should doubt everything, in the sense of treating everything as provisionally false, until one finds a substantial premise which cannot be doubted and which is therefore certain. This doubt is *methodical* because it is a method of arriving at certain knowledge. It is said to be *sceptical* because one doubts, in the way a sceptic does, that one can know anything and must produce a satisfactory justification of what one claims to know in order to overcome the doubt. But, because Descartes is not thoroughly a sceptic, it is best that we treat his doubt as methodological.

What then should be doubted? Descartes distinguishes two kinds of propositions: *empirical* ones—known through the senses—and *a priori* ones—known through intuition. He argues that *both* may be doubted—which is somewhat surprising since, as we shall see, the *a priori* propositions seem to be his paradigm of knowledge. As to the doubt of empirical propositions, Descartes' argument is rather simple: Because the senses can be deceptive, it is wise not to trust them as sources of knowledge. Of course we sometimes *think* we are certain of immediate sensory knowledge—e.g., that we are turning a doorknob when we enter a room. But Descartes will have nothing to do with this sort of reply, for he thinks it violates his methodological principles. He thinks we can even doubt that our bodies exist. He refers to the vividness of dreams and notes that it is not beyond all doubt that real life itself is no more than a dream. Perhaps then we are asleep, even though we open our eyes, shake our heads, and go about our business every morning. In short, what *appears* to be the case may not really *be* the case. Descartes thinks this contrast between appearance and reality is relevant to his methodical doubt. It shows, in a provisional way, that we cannot rely on *any* element of sensory "knowledge" in order to achieve certain knowledge.

Descartes does not think *a priori* propositions, including mathematical truths, can be doubted in quite the same way. Whether we are awake or asleep, *a priori* truths seem to hold. However, he says, we can suppose that "some evil genius, no less powerful than deceitful, has employed his whole energies in deceiving" us, just as readily as we can conceive that we are constantly asleep. Hence, even mathematical truth cannot be trusted as the foundation of a general system of truths. However improbable the existence of an evil genius may be, such a genius could exist, and this doubt alone is sufficient to dismiss such truths as satisfying our criteria for certainty. We must turn elsewhere.

In all three of his most acclaimed writings, Descartes takes the same route out of the extremely demanding position in which he has placed himself. He first doubts all alleged truths about the existence of physical objects (empirical propositions) and about the certainty of mathematical statements (*a priori* propositions). He then argues that despite the rigor of his demands, one proposition is indubitably certain. Descartes' thought was that no matter how far he extends the method of methodical doubt, he can never extend it to his own existence. In the very act of doubting, he says, one affirms one's doubts; and even if one is dreaming, one has to exist in order to dream. We would normally expect Descartes to base knowledge in his system on intuition. And he does say that "each individual can mentally have an intui-

tion of the fact that he exists and that he thinks," and that "by a simple act of mental vision . . . a thing is known through itself." Descartes seems to be maintaining that he is not *inferring* his existence from his thinking, but rather is intuiting a necessary connection between his thinking and his existing. That is, he seems to be saying that intuition denies the possibility that he might think without at the same time existing. His famous and fundamental proposition, "*I think, therefore I am*," is a result.

Descartes maintains that this fundamental proposition alone can be used to erect the metaphysical system of certain truths he is concerned to establish. He demonstrates the existence of a veracious God to back his claims. God's existence is then said to guarantee the truth of all propositions based solely on clear and distinct ideas. And, finally, this groundwork is used to guarantee certain truths about the nature of mind, body, and the existence of the external world. These are the conclusions Descartes' method of sceptical doubt are supposed to support.

There are at least two reasons why many have remained sceptical that Descartes' method *could* achieve his goals. First, Descartes' evil genius postulation may be too demanding. After all, if one can doubt the truth of the external world and of mathematics because one is perhaps being intentionally deceived, cannot one doubt anything, including one's own existence, on the grounds that one may be being deceived? Second, since one is allowed to doubt a faculty of mind such as intuition on the grounds that one can be *deceived* in one's intuitions, how can one then appeal to an intuition in order to stop a regress of doubts? Descartes' view is that we can stop the regress because we hit on a very special proposition. A central question about his views is whether the proposition "I think, therefore I am" is as special as he thinks.

ORGANIZING PRINCIPLES

Descartes' emphasis on *reason* and his insistence on the need for *certainty* in knowledge, as well as his view that *mathematics provides a paradigm* of well-grounded knowledge, have perhaps been most responsible for his general reputation in philosophy. Indeed, these features could be called the chief organizing principles of his philosophy. Let us see why.

In mathematics, our starting point is an immediately evident proposition, or set of propositions, constituting the initial set of conditions on which the rest of mathematics is founded. Such knowledge is the product of *intuition,* the faculty of immediate and basic truths. Intuition, says Descartes, is "the conception, without doubt, of an unclouded and attentive mind, which springs from the light of reason alone." Intuition produces rational truths so clear and distinct that it is impossible to imagine them being wrong. One of Descartes' fundamental principles is his view that this faculty of intuition can be used in philosophy just as it is used in mathematics, and with the same results. An edifice of philosophical truths could be erected, he argues, that has its foundations entirely in truths that are *certain.* Descartes repeatedly returns to this thesis, most importantly in his discussion of clear and distinct ideas.

Assuming, then, that we can reach basic truths that are certain, how according to Descartes do we obtain *derivative* truths? His model is again mathematics: we *deduce* consequences from the basic propositions. This deduction from known certainties is accomplished by a pure movement of thought in which no conclusion is accepted unless a logical connection can be identified that links the conclusion to its premises. But, because this movement of thought rests on purely logical principles, it, too, cannot be mistaken. Thus, the entire edifice of thought can be made as certain as its basis.

THE NATURE OF KNOWLEDGE

It is important that we always understand what a philosopher means by the term "knowledge," for otherwise we may easily misunderstand his general theory of how and what we know. Descartes is a good example of a philosopher whom we might easily misunderstand or falsely criticize if we fail to comprehend his use of the term. We have seen that he has a mathematical criterion for the derivation of systematic knowledge and that he relies

heavily on the thesis that rational intuition is the source of the knowledge needed to do philosophy. For Descartes this philosophical background implies that the only propositions deserving the title of "knowledge" are propositions that are *certain.* He blames the errors of many past philosophers on their willingness to leave unexamined propositions whose truth, with insufficient justification, they took for granted. It was because they failed in the first place to explore whether their views were *certain* that so much doubt has arisen. Accordingly, Descartes says (in his *Discourse on the Method*) that he resolved never to accept anything as true unless it was so clear and distinct that no reasons could be offered against it.

One critical feature of Descartes' position is his general contention that the *clarity and distinctness* of ideas (propositions) is a proper *criterion of certain truth.* Descartes was motivated to hold this view because he thought the features in the proposition "I think, therefore I am" that account for its certain truth are the clarity and distinctness with which it is known to be true. Hence Descartes says, "I came to the conclusion that I might *assume* as a general rule that the things which we conceive very clearly and distinctly are all true." Given Descartes' emphasis on intuition, we might expect such a conclusion; but it is nonetheless quite striking and deserves closer examination.

What does it mean, in Descartes' philosophy, for something to be clear and distinct? He considered this question and wrote as follows:

I call that clear which is present and apparent to an attentive mind, in the same way as we assert that we see objects clearly when, being present to the beholding eye, they operate upon it with sufficient strength. But the distinct is that which is so precise and different from all other objects that it contains within itself nothing but what is clear.

Descartes is here attempting to distinguish between being clear and being distinct. Something can be clear without being distinct, but distinctness always implies clarity. For example, I may clearly "see" a jet plane, but if I cannot distinguish it from a bird it is not distinct. If, however, I am able to make it distinct from other things, it must be clear. It seems, then, that for Descartes knowledge is largely a matter of being distinctly aware of something, an act performed by the intellect.

SENSORY INFORMATION

Finally, we need to note that Descartes places little value on the information received in sensory experience. We have already seen that sensory information figures prominently in Descartes' method of doubt. He concedes only with reluctance that some of our sensory information about the external world must be correct. As he sees it, our sensory inputs cannot be so gravely deficient that they provide us with no correct information, for that would force us to the untenable conclusion that God is a deceiver.

On the other hand, Descartes also holds that properties such as color, sound, and taste—the so-called secondary qualities—are nothing except "the various dispositions of these objects which have the power of moving our nerves in various ways." Though we have an overwhelming tendency to think that smells, colors, and sounds exist externally to us, Descartes thinks they are merely the dispositions of objects to cause such perceptions in us. Only the so-called primary properties of objects—motion, magnitude, and figure—are considered truly external by Descartes. In contrast to the reality and accessibility of these primary properties, the secondary properties are necessarily more mysterious, being "colored by the contributions of our own sensory apparatus." Thus, our sensations only inform us truly about primary properties. Descartes concludes that although physical objects do exist, "they are . . . not exactly what we perceive by the senses, because this apprehension by the senses is in many instances very obscure and confused."

As we would expect of Descartes, the intellect rescues us from the uncertainties of sensory experience. Even when sensory information is not illusory or distorted, our rational faculty is able to judge whether accurate information is being obtained. Intuition, deduction, and the mathematical model thus firmly control Descartes' ideal of knowledge.

BERKELEY, THE MATERIAL WORLD, AND PHILOSOPHICAL IDEALISM

Bishop Berkeley was a most colorful figure. He rejected most of Descartes' view of the world, but he did so in such a way that an even more exciting picture resulted, one with even more radical conclusions. One gets some sense of this by reading his *Dialogues Between Hylas and Philonous*—the book from which the selection in this chapter is excerpted. These dialogues are unquestionably in the finest tradition of philosophical writing, comparing favorably even with the great Platonic *Dialogues*. Berkeley's development of character and his mode of argumentation are not only extraordinarily clear and exacting, but also exciting and engaging. His two main characters are Hylas and Philonous. The name "Hylas" means matter, while "Philonous" means lover of wisdom, and no reader can miss why he has chosen these names for his characters: Berkeley is a lover of wisdom, not a lover of matter. Berkeley's thought has always been controversial, and some people still consider his philosophy the work of a madman. He wrote his *Dialogues* in part as a reply to such critics of his earlier work.

ORGANIZING PRINCIPLES

Great philosophers such as Hobbes, Descartes, and Spinoza had breathed new life into philosophy at the time Berkeley lived; and Locke, Leibniz, and Malebranche were still alive. In spite of this philosophical ferment, it seemed to Berkeley that men's minds had become clogged and burdened with new errors rather than illuminated with new truths. He thought philosophy was obstructed by unnecessary complications and overstatements. He set himself the task of *simplification*.

Berkeley was convinced that he had a philosophical principle that corrected the basic error made by Descartes, while also refuting atheists and sceptics. He considered it crucial to eliminate Descartes' distinction between primary and secondary qualities, as well as the theory of the material world that accompanied it. However, it must not be thought that Berkeley supposed his views were in opposition to the theories of most philosophers. On the contrary, he saw his philosophy as a way of correcting the problems present in most modern philosophical systems. In his own opinion, this corrective philosophy had the additional advantage of being congenial with common-sense views of the world. Berkeley once summarized the main features of his philosophy, adding the conviction that his work has the spirit of synthesis:

I do not pretend to be a setter-up of new notions. My endeavors tend only to unite, and place in a clearer light, that truth which was before shared between the vulgar and the philosophers—the former being of opinion, that those things they immediately perceive are the real things and the latter that the things immediately perceived are ideas, which exist only in the mind. Which two notions put together, do, in effect, constitute the substance of what I advance.

This passage can be taken as a representative statement of Berkeley's philosophy.

IMMATERIALISM

Nonetheless, Berkeley had a fundamental objection to Descartes and to most of the scientists and philosophers of his time: they were all materialists. He rejects the doctrine of material substance as an unwarranted inference from the data of direct experience, an inference which was in no way necessary for the scientific or philosophical explanation of nature. Berkeley's basic claim is that the objects immediately perceived in experience exist *only* as ideas present to a mind—not as things that are "material." Since they are solely ideas, they can have no existence apart from a mind that perceives them. Everything in the universe, then, is either an idea or a mind which has ideas.

Berkeley argues the uncomplicated thesis that the things we immediately perceive are the real things; they are real as perceived. The fact that there is no such thing as Descartes' world of extended substance in no way counts against things *being* just as we *know* them, according to Berkeley. Indeed, he thinks Descartes' theory guarantees that we do not know physical things as they are,

but only know them through certain properties they manifest. Berkeley sees absolutely no basis (let alone an empirical basis) for the notion that so-called secondary properties or any properties of objects we do experience are caused by some substance which we do not experience. In this respect he is an uncompromising epistemological realist. Yet his theory of ideas in the mind makes him an uncompromising metaphysical idealist. For these reasons, Berkeley throughout the *Dialogues* defends the view that things in the world are simply what we perceive them to be, that ideas do not *represent* other things of which they are ideas, that there is no experience of matter (material substance), and that active causes can only be mental, not material.

It is the notion of matter or body as material substance that Berkeley's arguments are directed against, and he considers no other conceptions of material things. If you were to reply, "But we know material objects because we directly confront them in experience," Berkeley would have no quibble with you. He would simply respond that you have a semantic difference over the meaning of "matter." He is interested exclusively in the substances many philosophers thought to exist underneath and in support of the objects of everyday experience, but not available to direct sensory inspection.

Berkeley in fact tries to catch his philosophical opponents in a dilemma. If the direct objects of perception are ideas, we can only know ourselves as having this or that sensation or idea. Accordingly, either matter must be reduced to the status of an idea, in order to be known, or else it must be placed entirely beyond our knowledge. In respect to sensible things, Berkeley argues that we cannot go beyond our ideas, and hence cannot reach a material substance that by definition lies beyond the relation between the perceiver and his ideas. If material substance is banished beyond knowledge, there is no rational ground for supposing its existence. Berkeley thus shifts the burden of proof to those such as Descartes who believe in the existence of matter. Much of his dialogue is concerned with refuting this or that possible objection which the defender of material substance might make.

TO BE IS TO BE PERCEIVED

Berkeley goes on to say that since the objects we know are ideas, their very nature is to be ideas and nothing else, for they have no existence apart from the mind. Of ideas Berkeley says their *esse* is *percipi*—their being is in being perceived. When I say the table before me exists, according to Berkeley, I mean that I can touch it, see it, feel its hardness, etc.—and nothing over and above these sensory impressions. When I say there is an odor I mean nothing more than that it is smelt. To say that these things continue to exist when no one is aware of them is to make a claim we cannot really understand, says Berkeley, for in perceiving them we have already exhausted what it can mean to say they "exist." Hence to exist (as ideas) means to be perceived, and the essence of ideas consists in being perceived.

However, Berkeley goes on to distinguish between ideas and the mind that has the ideas. The essence of ideas consists in being perceived, but the essence of mind consists in doing the perceiving. The domain of things, then, contains two broad classes: ideas and mind. Berkeley marshals several arguments to support this view.

First, Berkeley (and Philonous) thinks our various sensory experiences suggest that we can never infer anything beyond the senses themselves. Consider, for example, the sensations of heat and cold. Exposure to a large amount of heat, as perceived, is just pain; and we all admit that pain exists only in the mind of a perceiver. Therefore, heat itself is merely mental, and we should reach the same conclusion about sensations of cold. Consider the case of lukewarm water. Suppose you are reaching in a tub for apples, and further suppose that one of your arms has been dangling outside the window in snow while the other has been resting on a radiator. If you put them both in the tub of lukewarm water to grab an apple, the water feels warm to one hand and cold to the other; but the same water cannot be at once both cold and warm. The same is true for sweet and bitter tastes, and for pleasant and unpleasant odors, as Berkeley argues in the dialogue from our selections. Philonous has some trouble convincing

Hylas of the fact that sound is also reducible to perception, but Hylas finally succumbs.

Second, Berkeley maintains that you cannot show that objects have an independent existence by making distinctions such as that between the object and its qualities or that between the object and the sensation itself. Here Berkeley points out that if you take away all sensible qualities there remains nothing sensible. The object simply disappears. Similarly, you cannot argue that matter or the external object can be known by its *relation* to its qualities, because the relation would have to be apprehended through sense experience. If you take away all the sensible qualities of an external object, there is nothing for it to have relations with. Furthermore, the very same arguments about the relativity of sensory perception in the case of sight, sound, touch, etc. can also be extended to primary qualities, according to Berkeley. The texture, the shape, and the motion of a thing are just as relative to perceivers as are its other features. To the same person, but from different perspectives or distances, the same object may appear large or small. uneven or even, round or elliptical.

COMMON SENSE VS. SCEPTICISM

Despite the paradoxes in Berkeley's system, he trumpeted his philosophy as the great defense of common sense—especially common sense as challenged by Descartes' scepticism about the existence of the external world. Berkeley asks readers of his dialogue to reflect on what is meant by saying the pie smells good, or the desk is covered with books, or the mile run is tomorrow. To assert the existence of such things is the same as to assert that they are perceived by some mind. The common-sense meaning of such sayings is that the pie is being smelled, the desk is being seen, and the mile run will be witnessed.

Many people would say that Berkeley's system reduces natural things to subjective states. Berkeley anticipated that he would receive such criticisms and does his best to address them. He argues that his doctrine leaves intact and even supports the common-sense view of the world. Just as the ordinary person believes that the objects of immediate perception are the real things, so in Berkeley's philosophy the objects of his experience *are* the *real* things. Berkeley was proud of this result and saw preserved in his system the verdant greens of the woods, the smells of clear springs, and the sounds of the river. These are assured realities—the last things in which persons would surrender belief, and the last things in which they ought to surrender belief. Berkeley's voice, then, was the first to be raised against the disparagement of sensory experience that characterizes much if not all of modern philosophy— especially as found in a philosopher such as Descartes. Philosophies that lead to scepticism about the external world and about human knowledge, in Berkeley's view, are on the wrong path altogether.

Berkeley holds that not *every* perception or idea is infallible and of something real, but every *sensory* perception is. Only if one makes inferences from experience, he thinks, can one be mistaken. In simply *apprehending* something in direct sensory experience one has infallible knowledge. Needless to say, this bold empiricism contrasts sharply with Descartes' views.

THEORIES OF MATERIAL OBJECTS AND THEORIES OF PERCEPTION

The question "What *is* a material object?" is explicitly raised by Berkeley and to some extent is treated in the selection by Descartes. The question, of course, asks what material objects *really* are, not simply what we *think* they are or what they *appear* to be. A common-sense answer, then, may not be at all appropriate. Many philosophers, including Berkeley, have not always been clear on this point. In some passages Berkeley depicts his answer as the common-sense answer, while at other points he hints that only a sophisticated analysis that moves beyond the reach of common sense could provide the correct solution. Setting aside Berkeley's particular views, let us now inquire into the wider range of theories that have been offered in response to the question, "What is a material object?" We cannot here survey all pos-

sible theories, but several of the more important ones may be summarized briefly.

1. *Naive Realism* is the view that material objects are nothing other than what we experience them to be. Colors and shapes, for example, are just as we know them, and they do not cease to exist when perceivers cease to perceive them. This view is closely associated with the common-sense view of the world. Insofar as Berkeley is a defender of common sense, he holds a similar view. But since he denies that unperceived objects *exist* without perceivers, he is not, in the end, a naive realist.

2. *Representative Realism* is the view that objects are in some respects as they appear (shape, size, solidity, and the primary qualities); but in other respects they are not as they appear. They are not really colored or hot, for example, and none of the remaining secondary qualities is considered a real aspect of objects either. Objects, however, have the capacity to *cause* colors and sounds in us, and these causal powers *can* be said to belong to the objects. Thus, if a cabinet appears as orange, the orange is not in the object, but the power to cause orangeness in normal human perceivers is in the object. This view seems to be the one subscribed to by Descartes, though John Locke is its best known defender.

3. *Subjective Idealism* erases the distinction between primary and secondary qualities, while holding that material things are *nothing but* ideas in the mind. Effectively this is the view that *to be* (a material object, in this case) is to be perceived, and so the view is precisely the one defended by Berkeley.

4. *Phenomenalist Theories* refine subjective idealism in various ways. They hold that a "material" object as we know it is constituted by the appearance that we experience under certain conditions. Ice cream, for example, is known exclusively through the set of visual and tactile sensations perceivers have when touching, looking at, and eating it. It does not follow on a phenomenalist theory, however, that whatever exists simply *is* an idea or mental construct. The phenomenalist is not committed to subjective idealism. Phenomenalists differ over the nature of appearances and

over what causes them, but they are united in the view that objects *as we know them* in experience are reducible to sets of sense data. Bertrand Russell defends one version of this theory in the selection following the Berkeley selection. Russell argues the quite engaging thesis that though we are only aware of sense data, "the object cannot be identical with the sense datum." He believes this view rests in the end on "instinctive beliefs" that philosophical arguments are incapable of overturning through any method of "proof."

5. *Perspective Realism* is the view that everything we perceive in the external world is a real feature of that world and continues in existence when we do not perceive it. However, we only selectively come to know certain features of the external world, and material objects as we know them do not include everything that a full description of such objects would include. An object thus really is more than we know it to be. Nonetheless, all normal perceivers know the *same* objects, for normal perceivers take the same perspective. This theory is defended by W. A. Sinclair in this chapter. Sinclair goes to considerable lengths to distinguish his account from the representative realist theory. In particular, he emphasizes that we know "the real world" to be "almost unbelievably rich and complicated," so much so that our awareness must be limited to a "mere fragmentary selection of the real world." He takes this view to be the direct opposite of Descartes' position.

To each of the above five theories of the nature of material objects there corresponds a theory of perception. Thus, *The Naive Realist Theory of Perception* is the view that we have a direct and immediate awareness of things in the real world. *The Representative Realist Theory of Perception* is the view that when we perceive objects there is a sense datum in our perceptual field that is caused by the object. The sense datum is not identical with the object, but it does accurately represent the primary qualities of the object. Thus our perceptual apparatus is capable of faithfully representing some features of external objects. *The Subjective Idealist Theory of Perception,* by contrast, holds that we perceive ideas alone and that, as Berkeley puts it, "an idea can be nothing but an idea." Even

so-called "perceptual processes" are nothing but sets of relations among ideas. Thus, the entire range of changes in our perceptual field is simply a change from one idea to another.

The other two theories of perception are, of course, developed in the selections by Russell and Sinclair. *The Phenomenalist Theory of Perception* is the theory that perceived "objects" are collections of sense data, but that these sense data do not accurately *represent* objects beyond experience, so far as we know. The person's act of perceiving consists of having sensations, but these sensations are simply given to a perceiver. As Russell argues, any attempt to show by appeal to our senses that sense data represent other objects must fail, for the appeal itself can only be to the sense data, not to the objects. Finally, *The Perspective Realist Theory of Perception* relies largely on scientific discoveries about perceptual mechanisms and the philosophical interpretation of these discoveries to explain perception. The theory focuses on the interactions between material objects—as science describes them—and the selective character of human perception. It is through the interaction between a *physical* process (e.g., a light wave) and human *physiological* processes (e.g., vision) that we are able to explain our awareness of material objects. Sinclair argues that our eyes, ears, etc. are "blind to very nearly all that surrounds us"—a fortunate condition, he thinks, for otherwise we would be "hopelessly confused" in our perceptual efforts. He sums up his view as follows:

We do experience reality directly, yet . . . different people can have different experiences because, owing to the nature of our sense organs, we do not experience anything like the whole of reality, but only some astonishingly small scraps of it, there being in some cases different scraps for different people. We have therefore passed far beyond the theory of Descartes and Locke that the real world is simple, bare, and colorless. . . . The real world *is* what I experience it to be.

We may now conclude our discussion of theories of material being and theories of perception. However, we need to discuss the *concept* of perception further, especially as it relates to the concepts of sensation and observation.

SENSING, PERCEIVING, AND OBSERVING

Ordinarily, to say that we see something is to say that we have an accurate visual impression of it. But words can assume many meanings, and we often use perceptual verbs to capture our sense of the difference between the appearance and the reality of a situation. Thus we may say that we "see" a stag, when what we really "see" is our father. Are there, then, two different kinds of objects being "seen"? Or is the same object simply seen in two different ways (one of which involves a misinterpretation)? Such questions are complicated by the fact that we often use verbs of appearing to describe our perception of what in fact are illusions, as when we speak of the image we observe in curved mirrors that distort our bodily form.

These problems and others are often brought into focus in philosophical discussions of the problem of perception. But is a *perception* the same as an *observation,* a *conception,* an *interpretation,* or a *sensation?* That is, do these words all denote the same human activity? In order to answer such questions, let us start with a rough distinction between *sensing, perceiving,* and *observing* (something to be the case). Our ultimate purpose is to understand the processes by which we can gain experiential *knowledge* of the world, either through sensation, perception, or observation (and perhaps with the aid of theories).

The word "perception" is usually reserved for direct *sensory* awareness, whereas the word "observation" is less restricted. Thus, we perceive the *redness* of a tomato, but we observe the *artistry* of a master chef preparing a meal with the tomato. But let us begin with the more primitive distinction between *sensing* and *perceiving.* To *sense* something is to have a private sensory experience. To *perceive* something is to be aware that something is the case by sensing it, so that any normal perceiver can also perceive that it is the case. We could sense without perceiving; but we could not perceive without sensing. Sensing is thus direct and immediate in a way perceiving is not; perceiving is both indirect and mediate, for it involves something over and above the mere possession of a sensory datum. Perception, as some philosophers have put it, involves a *concept* under which the sense datum is subsumed.

For example, we *sense* red, round, bulgy items. We perceive an item as a tomato by collecting properties such as "red," "round," and "bulgy" together. The sensing and the perceiving occur simultaneously, but we can always distinguish the two strands of awareness. For one thing, we can easily misperceive, but it is doubtful that we can missense. Crudely put, we might say: Sensing is dumb but always accurate, whereas perception is alive and informative but not always accurate.

Now what shall we mean by saying that X *observes* something to be the case? According to some contemporary philosophers, to *observe* requires more than "normal vision"—i.e., it involves more than simply sensing or perceiving. To observe is to *interpret* experience by fitting a perceived object or event into the nexus of a theory. We know what something is or what it is doing only because we possess a theory in whose terms we can make sense of it. Without the theory we could not observe it at all. Suppose I pick up a big, solid black bowling ball and put my eyes directly on it, so that all I see is black. I cannot be said to observe anything unless I am examining the quality of blackness (to see if there is any green) or unless I am looking for lumps or cracks. I might very well be sensing blackness—but I could not be said to be observing a bowling ball. In fact, I cannot observe the round, black object *as* a bowling ball at all until I know something about bowling. I need a concept of bowling and the "theory," as it were, of the game of bowling in order to see it as a bowling ball, rather than a cannonball. Some philosophers have held that *all* our important perceptive experiences are like this: they all involve interpreting sensory or perceptual data by means of concepts and theories. Potentially, a ball *perceived as round* could *be* either a bowling ball or a cannonball. *Perception* cannot tell you what it is—only *observation* can do that—even if perception can tell you that it is round.

Observation is a term of special importance for discussions of science, because the scientist is continually engaged in bringing hypotheses and theories to bear on sensory information. Several characteristics of observation are worth further notice. First, we can *observe* an *unperceivable item*. This is one reason why observation and perception must be carefully distinguished. The observation of unperceivables requires the use of theory and inference, processes impossible in perception alone. For example, we may observe stars, or a field of mustard plants on a farm, though all we perceive are bright twinkling lights and a square patch of yellow. We may observe that there are buffalo in the area if we are a park ranger, though in fact all that can be seen is a huge cloud of dust. Here we observe an object by directly perceiving something only associated with it. Though there must be a causal or theoretical connection between the two items, we are nonetheless observing without either sensing or perceiving the *objects* of the observation. In science it would make perfect sense to say electrons or magnetic fields are being observed, though we would never claim to *perceive* them. And hence observation is possible in the absence of direct sensory perception.

Finally, one can describe what one is observing in a great variety of ways—and the appropriate method of description is often determined by contextual considerations. To use an example of Peter Achinstein's, suppose that while sitting by the roadside at night, carefully attending to the road ahead, I am asked what I observe. I might reply: a car, a pair of automobile headlights, two yellowish lights, etc. Or, when driving on a dirt road in the daytime, I might at once claim to be observing a car, a trail produced by a car, or just a cloud of dust. In each case what one will actually say that one observes depends upon one's conceptual equipment, one's knowledge, and one's training—as well as upon what one is looking for in the circumstances. No single thing is here the exclusively correct interpretation or description. The puzzle such situations present is whether *all* observation follows this pattern. Are we only able selectively to perceive the features of things, and must we therefore constantly interpret what we experience through prior concepts and theories? Many contemporary philosophers have said that while there is a clear and important distinction between perception and observation, there is not a clear or perhaps important distinction between observation and theory. For them, observation must be "theory-laden." But if this is the case, do we only know what our theories direct us to observe? And, if so, how can we claim to know what really exists?

All of these questions, and many more as well, arise throughout the readings in this chapter. Philosophers differ in their views, and some would even deny that there are any sharp distinctions to be drawn between sensation, perception, observation, and theory. These problems are brought into clever focus in the first selection in the chapter—a short story by Rog Phillips about the taking of a yellow pill that changes human perceptions and observations of the world. It would be best at this point to let the neatly contrived solutions of Phillips' story speak for themselves.

Tom L. Beauchamp

8. THE YELLOW PILL

Rog Phillips

Dr. Cedric Elton slipped into his office by the back entrance, shucked off his topcoat and hid it in the small, narrow-doored closet, then picked up the neatly piled patient cards his receptionist Helena Fitzroy had placed on the corner of his desk. There were only four, but there could have been a hundred if he accepted everyone who asked to be his patient, because his successes had more than once been spectacular and his reputation as a psychiatrist had become so great because of this that his name had become synonymous with psychiatry in the public mind.

His eyes flicked over the top card. He frowned, then went to the small square of one-way glass in the reception-room door and looked through it. There were four police officers and a man in a straitjacket.

The card said the man's name was Gerald Bocek, and that he had shot and killed five people in a supermarket, and had killed one officer and wounded two others before being captured.

Except for the straitjacket, Gerald Bocek did not have the appearance of being dangerous. He was about twenty-five, with brown hair and blue eyes. There were faint wrinkles of habitual good nature about his eyes. Right now he was smiling, relaxed, and idly watching Helena, who was pretending to study various cards in her desk file but was obviously conscious of her audience.

Cedric returned to his desk and sat down. The card for Jerry Bocek said more about the killings. When captured, Bocek insisted that the people he had killed were not people at all, but blue-scaled Venusian lizards who had boarded his spaceship, and that he had only been defending himself.

Dr. Cedric Elton shook his head in disapproval. Fantasy fiction was all right in its place, but too many people took it seriously. Of course, it was

Reprinted from *Astounding Science Fiction*, Oct. 1958, with the permission of the publisher. Copyright © 1958 by Street & Smith Publications Inc.

not the fault of the fiction. The same type of person took other types of fantasy seriously in earlier days, burning women as witches, stoning men as devils—

Abruptly Cedric deflected the control on the intercom and spoke into it. "Send Gerald Bocek in, please," he said.

A moment later the door to the reception room opened. Helena flashed Cedric a scared smile and got out of the way quickly. One police officer led the way, followed by Gerald Bocek, closely flanked by two officers with the fourth one in the rear, who carefully closed the door. It was impressive, Cedric decided. He nodded toward a chair in front of his desk and the police officers sat the straitjacketed man in it, then hovered nearby, ready for anything.

"You're Jerry Bocek?" Cedric asked.

The straitjacketed man nodded cheerfully.

"I'm Dr. Cedric Elton, a psychiatrist," Cedric said. "Do you have any idea at all why you have been brought to me?"

"Brought to you?" Jerry echoed, chuckling. "Don't kid me. You're my old pal, Gar Castle. Brought to you? How could I get *away* from you in this stinking tub?"

"Stinking tub?" Cedric said.

"Spaceship," Jerry said. "Look, Gar. Untie me, will you? This nonsense has gone far enough."

"My name is Dr. Cedric Elton," Cedric enunciated. "You are not on a spaceship. You were brought to my office by the four policemen standing in back of you, and—"

Jerry Bocek turned his head and studied each of the four policemen with frank curiosity. "What policemen?" he interrupted. "You mean these four gear lockers?" He turned his head back and looked pityingly at Dr. Elton. "You'd better get hold of yourself, Gar," he said. "You're imagining things."

"My name is Dr. Cedric Elton," Cedric said.

Gerald Bocek leaned forward and said with

equal firmness, "Your name is Gar Castle. I refuse to call you Dr. Cedric Elton because your name is Gar Castle, and I'm going to keep on calling you Gar Castle because we have to have at least one peg of rationality in all this madness or you will be cut completely adrift in this dream world you've cooked up."

Cedric's eyebrows shot halfway up to his hairline.

"Funny," he mused, smiling. "That's exactly what I was just going to say to you!"

Cedric continued to smile. Jerry's serious intenseness slowly faded. Finally an answering smile tugged at the corners of his mouth. When it became a grin, Cedric laughed, and Jerry began to laugh with him. The four police officers looked at one another uneasily.

"Well," Cedric finally gasped. "I guess that puts us on an even footing! You're nuts to me and I'm nuts to you!"

"An equal footing is right!" Jerry shouted in high glee. Then he sobered. "Except," he said gently, "I'm tied up."

"In a straitjacket," Cedric corrected.

"Ropes," Jerry said firmly.

"You're dangerous," Cedric said. "You killed six people, one of them a police officer, and wounded two other officers."

"I blasted five Venusian lizard pirates who boarded our ship," Jerry said, "and melted the door off one gear locker, and seared the paint on two others. You know as well as I do, Gar, how space madness causes you to personify everything. That's why they drill into you that the minute you think there are more people on board the ship than there were at the beginning of the trip you'd better go to the medicine locker and take a yellow pill. They can't hurt anything but a delusion."

"If that is so," Cedric said, "why are you in a straitjacket?"

"I'm tied up with ropes," Jerry said patiently. "You tied me up. Remember?"

"And those four police officers behind you are gear lockers?" Cedric said. "OK, if one of those gear lockers comes around in front of you and taps you on the jaw with his fist, would you still believe it's a gear locker?"

Cedric nodded to one of the officers, and the man came around in front of Gerald Bocek and, quite carefully, hit him hard enough to rock his head but not hurt him. Jerry's eyes blinked with surprise, then he looked at Cedric and smiled. "Did you feel that?" Cedric said quietly.

"Feel what?" Jerry said. "Oh!" He laughed. "You imagined that one of the gear lockers—a police officer in your dream world—came around in front of me and hit me?" He shook his head in pity. "Don't you understand, Gar, that it didn't really happen? Untie me and I'll prove it. Before your very eyes I'll open the door on your *Policeman* and take out the pressure suit, or magnetic grapple, or whatever is in it. Or are you afraid to? You've surrounded yourself with all sorts of protective delusions. I'm tied with ropes, but you imagine it to be a straitjacket. You imagine yourself to be a psychiatrist named Dr. Cedric Elton, so that you can convince yourself that you're sane and I'm crazy. Probably you imagine yourself a very famous psychiatrist that everyone would like to come to for treatment. World famous, no doubt. Probably you even think you have a beautiful receptionist. What is her name?"

"Helena Fitzroy," Cedric said.

Jerry nodded. "It figures," he said resignedly. "Helena Fitzroy is the expediter at Mars Port. You try to date her every time we land there, but she won't date you."

"Hit him again," Cedric said to the officer. While Jerry's head was still rocking from the blow, Cedric said, "Now! Is it *my* imagination that your head is still rocking from the blow?"

"What blow?" Jerry said, smiling. "I felt no blow."

"Do you mean to say," Cedric said incredulously, "that there is no corner of your mind, no slight residue of rationality, that tries to tell you your rationalizations aren't reality?"

Jerry smiled ruefully. "I have to admit," he said, "when you seem so absolutely certain you're right and I'm nuts, it almost makes me doubt. Untie me, Gar, and let's try to work this thing out sensibly." He grinned. "You know, Gar, *one* of us has to be nuttier than a fruit cake."

"If I had the officers take off your straitjacket, what would you do?" Cedric asked. "Try to grab a gun and kill some more people?"

"That's one of the things I'm worried about,"

Jerry said. "If those pirates came back, with me tied up, you're just space crazy enough to welcome them aboard. That's why you must untie me. Our lives may depend on it, Gar."

"Where would you get a gun?" Cedric asked.

"Where they're always kept," Jerry said. "In the gear lockers."

Cedric looked at the four policemen, at their holstered revolvers. One of them grinned feebly at him.

"I'm afraid we can't take your straitjacket off just yet," Cedric said. "I'm going to have the officers take you back now. I'll talk with you again tomorrow. Meanwhile I want you to think seriously about things. Try to get below this level of rationalization that walls you off from reality. Once you make a dent in it the whole delusion will vanish." He looked up at the officers. "All right, take him away. Bring him back the same time tomorrow."

The officers urged Jerry to his feet. Jerry looked down at Cedric, a gentle expression on his face. "I'll try to do that, Gar," he said. "And I hope you do the same thing. I'm much encouraged. Several times I detected genuine doubt in your eyes. And—" Two of the officers pushed him firmly toward the door. As they opened it Jerry turned his head and looked back. "*Take* one of those yellow pills in the medicine locker, Gar," he pleaded. "It can't hurt you."

At a little before five-thirty Cedric tactfully eased his last patient all the way across the reception room and out, then locked the door and leaned his back against it.

"Today was rough," he sighed.

Helena glanced up at him briefly, then continued typing. "I only have a little more on this last transcript," she said.

A minute later she pulled the paper from the typewriter and placed it on the neat stack beside her.

"I'll sort and file them in the morning," she said. "It was rough, wasn't it, Doctor? That Gerald Bocek is the most unusual patient you've had since I've worked for you. And poor Mr. Potts. A brilliant executive, making half a million a year, and he's going to have to give it up. He seems so normal."

"He is normal," Cedric said. "People with above normal blood pressure often have very minor cerebral hemorrhages so small that the affected area is no larger than the head of a pin. All that happens is that they completely forget things that they knew. They can relearn them, but a man whose judgment must always be perfect can't afford to take the chance. He's already made one error in judgment that cost his company a million and a half. That's why I consented to take him on as a—Gerald Bocek really upset me, Helena. I *consent* to take a five hundred thousand dollar a year executive as a patient."

'He was frightening, wasn't he?" Helena said. "I don't mean so much because he's a mass murderer as—"

"I know. I know," Cedric said. "Let's prove him wrong. Have dinner with me."

"We agreed—"

"Let's break the agreement this once."

Helena shook her head firmly. "Especially not now," she said. "Besides, it wouldn't prove anything. He's got you boxed in on that point. If I went to dinner with you, it would only show that a wish fulfillment entered your dream world."

"Ouch," Cedric said, wincing. "That's a dirty word. I wonder how he knew about the yellow pills? I can't get out of my mind the fact that *if* we had spaceships and *if* there were a type of space madness in which you began to personify objects, a yellow pill would be the right thing to stop that."

"How?" Helena said.

"They almost triple the strength of nerve currents from end organs. What results is that reality practically shouts down any fantasy insertions. It's quite startling. I took one three years ago when they first became available. You'd be surprised how little you actually see of what you look at, especially of people. You look at symbol inserts instead. I had to cancel my appointments for a week. I found I couldn't work without my professionally built symbol inserts about people that enable me to see them—not as they really are—but as a complex of normal and abnormal symptoms."

"I'd like to take one sometime," Helena said.

"That's a twist," Cedric said, laughing. "One of the characters in a dream world takes a yellow pill and discovers it doesn't exist at all except as a fantasy."

"Why don't we both take one?" Helena said.

"Uh uh," Cedric said firmly. "I couldn't do my work."

"You're afraid you might wake up on a spaceship?" Helena said, grinning.

"Maybe I am," Cedric said. "Crazy, isn't it? But there is one thing today that stands out as a serious flaw in my reality. It's so glaring that I actually am afraid to ask you about it."

"Are you serious?" Helena said.

"I am." Cedric nodded. "How does it happen that the police brought Gerald Bocek here to my office instead of holding him in the psychiatric ward at City Hospital and having me go there to see him? How does it happen the D.A. didn't get in touch with me beforehand and discuss the case with me?"

"I . . . I don't know!" Helena said. "I received no call. They just showed up, and I assumed they wouldn't have without your knowing about it and telling them to. Mrs. Fortesque was your first patient and I called her at once and caught her just as she was leaving the house, and told her an emergency case had come up." She looked at Cedric with round, startled eyes.

"Now we know how the patient must feel," Cedric said, crossing the reception room to his office door. "Terrifying, isn't it, to think that if I took a yellow pill all this might *vanish*—my years of college, my internship, *my fame as the world's best known psychiatrist,* and you. Tell me, Helena, are you sure you aren't an expediter at Mars Port?"

He leered at her mockingly as he slowly closed the door, cutting off his view of her.

Cedric put his coat away and went directly to the small square of one-way glass in the reception-room door. Gerald Bocek, still in straitjacket, was there, and so were the same four police officers.

Cedric went to his desk and, without sitting down, deflected the control on the intercom.

"Helena," he said, "before you send in Gerald Bocek get me the D.A. on the phone."

He glanced over the four patient cards while waiting. Once he rubbed his eyes gently. He had had a restless night.

When the phone rang he reached for it. "Hello? Dave?" he said. "About this patient, Gerald Bocek—"

"I was going to call you today," the District Attorney's voice sounded. "I called you yesterday morning at ten, but no one answered, and I haven't had time since. Our police psychiatrist, Walters, says you might be able to snap Bocek out of it in a couple of days—at least long enough so that we can get some sensible answers out of him. Down underneath his delusion of killing lizard pirates from Venus, there has to be some reason for that mass killing, and the press is after us on this."

"But why bring him to my office?" Cedric said. "It's OK, of course, but . . . that is . . . I didn't think you could! Take a patient out of the ward at City Hospital and transport him around town."

"I thought that would be less of an imposition on you," the D.A. said. "I'm in a hurry on it."

"Oh," Cedric said. "Well, OK, Dave. He's out in the waiting room. I'll do my best to snap him back to reality for you."

He hung up slowly, frowning. "*Less of an imposition!*" His whispered words floated into his ears as he snapped into the intercom, "Send Gerald Bocek in, please."

The door from the reception room opened, and once again the procession of patient and police officers entered.

"Well, well, good morning, Gar," Jerry said. "Did you sleep well? I could hear you talking to yourself most of the night."

"I am Dr. Cedric Elton," Cedric said firmly.

"Oh, yes," Jerry said. "I promised to try to see things your way, didn't I? I'll try to cooperate with you, Dr. Elton." Jerry turned to the four officers. "Let's see now, these gear lockers are policemen, aren't they? How do you do, officers." He bowed to them, then looked around him. "And," he said, "this is your office, Dr. Elton. A very impressive office. That thing you're sitting behind is not the chart table but your desk, I gather." He studied the desk intently. "All metal, with a gray finish, isn't it?"

"All wood," Cedric said. "Walnut."

"Yes, of course," Jerry murmured. "How stupid of me. I really want to get into your reality,

Gar . . . I mean Dr. Elton. Or get you into mine. I'm the one who's at a disadvantage, though. Tied up, I can't get into the medicine locker and take a yellow pill like you can. Did you take one yet?"

"Not yet," Cedric said.

"Uh, why don't you describe your office to me, Dr. Elton?" Jerry said. "Let's make a game of it. Describe parts of things and then let me see if I can fill in the rest. Start with your desk. It's genuine walnut? An executive style desk. Go on from there."

"All right," Cedric said. "Over here to my right is the intercom, made of gray plastic. And directly in front of me is the telephone."

"Stop," Jerry said. "Let me see if I can tell you your telephone number." He leaned over the desk and looked at the telephone, trying to keep his balance in spite of his arms being encased in the straitjacket. "Hm-m-m," he said, frowning. "Is the number Mulberry five dash nine oh three seven?"

"No," Cedric said. "It's Cedar sev—"

"Stop!" Jerry said. "Let me say it. It's Cedar seven dash four three nine nine." "So you did read it and were just having your fun," Cedric snorted.

"If you say so," Jerry said.

"What other explanation can you have for the fact that it is my number, if you're unable to actually see reality?" Cedric said.

"You're absolutely right, Dr. Elton," Jerry said. "I think I understand the tricks my mind is playing on me now. I read the number on your phone, but it didn't enter my conscious awareness. Instead, it cloaked itself with the pattern of my delusion, so that consciously I pretended to look at a phone that I couldn't see, and I thought, 'His phone number will obviously be one he's familiar with. The most probable is the home phone of Helena Fitzroy in Mars Port,' so I gave you that; but it wasn't it. When you said Cedar I knew right away it was your own apartment phone number."

Cedric sat perfectly still. Mulberry 5-9037 was actually Helena's apartment phone number. He hadn't recognized it until Gerald Bocek told him.

"Now you're beginning to understand," Cedric said after a moment. "Once you realize that your mind has walled off your consciousness from reality, and is substituting a rationalized pattern of symbology in its place, it shouldn't be long until you break through. Once you manage to see one thing as it really is, the rest of the delusion will disappear."

"I understand now," Jerry said gravely. "Let's have some more of it. Maybe I'll catch on."

They spent an hour at it. Toward the end Jerry was able to finish the descriptions of things with very little error.

"You are definitely beginning to get through," Cedric said with enthusiasm.

Jerry hesitated. "I suppose so," he said. "I must. But on the conscious level I have the idea—a rationalization, of course—that I am beginning to catch on to the pattern of your imagination so that when you give me one or two key elements I can fill in the rest. But I'm going to try, really try—Dr. Elton."

"Fine," Cedric said heartily. "I'll see you tomorrow, same time. We should make the breakthrough then."

When the four officers had taken Gerald Bocek away, Cedric went into the outer office.

"Cancel the rest of my appointments," he said.

"But why?" Helena protested.

"Because I'm upset!" Cedric said. "How did a madman whom I never knew until yesterday know your phone number?"

"He could have looked it up in the phone book."

"Locked in a room in the psychiatric ward at City Hospital?" Cedric said. "How did he know your name yesterday?"

"Why," Helena said, "all he had to do was read it on my desk here."

Cedric looked down at the brass name plate.

"Yes," he grunted. "Of course. I'd forgotten about that. I'm so accustomed to it being there that I never see it."

He turned abruptly and went back into his office.

He sat down at his desk, then got up and went into the sterile whiteness of his compact laboratory. Ignoring the impressive battery of electronic instruments, he went to the medicine cabinet. Inside, on the top shelf, was the glass stoppered bottle he wanted. Inside it were a hundred vivid yellow pills. He shook out one and put the bottle away, then went back into his office. He sat down, placing the yellow pill in the center of the white note pad.

There was a brief knock on the door to the reception room and the door opened. Helena came in.

"I've canceled all your other appointments for today," she said. "Why don't you go out to the golf course? A change will do you—" She saw the yellow pill in the center of the white note pad and stopped.

"Why do you look so frightened?" Cedric said. "Is it because, if I take this little yellow pill, you'll cease to exist?"

"Don't joke," Helena said.

"I'm not joking," Cedric said. "Out there, when you mentioned about your brass name plate on your desk, when I looked down it was blurred for just a second, then became sharply distinct and solid. And into my head popped the memory that the first thing I do when I have to get a new receptionist is get a brass name plate for her, and when she quits I make her a present of it."

"But that's the truth," Helena said. "You told me all about it when I started working for you. You also told me that while you still had your reason about you I was to solemnly promise that I would never accept an invitation from you for dinner or anything else, because business could not mix with pleasure. Do you remember that?"

"I remember," Cedric said. "A nice pat rationalization in any man's reality to make the rejection be my own before you could have time to reject me yourself. Preserving the ego is the first principle of madness."

"But it isn't!" Helena said. "Oh, darling, I'm *here*! This is *real*! I don't care if you fire me or not. I've loved you forever, and you mustn't let that mass murderer get you down. I actually think he isn't insane at all, but has just figured out a way to seem insane so he won't have to pay for his crime."

"You think so?" Cedric said, interested. "It's a possibility. But he would have to be as good a psychiatrist as I am—You see? Delusions of grandeur."

"Sure," Helena said, laughing thinly. "Napoleon was obviously insane because he thought he was Napoleon."

"Perhaps," Cedric said. "But you must admit that if you are real, my taking this yellow pill isn't going to change that, but only confirm the fact."

"And make it impossible for you to do your work for a week," Helena said.

"A small price to pay for sanity," Cedric said. "No, I'm going to take it."

"You aren't!" Helena said, reaching for it.

Cedric picked it up an instant before she could get it. As she tried to get it away from him, he evaded her and put it in his mouth. A loud gulp showed he had swallowed it.

He sat back and looked up at Helena curiously.

"Tell me, Helena," he said gently. "Did you know all the time that you were only a creature of my imagination? The reason I want to know is—"

He closed his eyes and clutched his head in his hands.

"God!" he groaned. "I feel like I'm dying. I didn't feel like this the other time I took one." Suddenly his mind steadied, and his thoughts cleared. He opened his eyes.

On the chart table in front of him the bottle of yellow pills lay on its side, pills scattered all over the table. On the other side of the control room lay Jerry Bocek, his back propped against one of the four gear lockers, sound asleep, with so many ropes wrapped around him that it would probably be impossible for him to stand up.

Against the far wall were three other gear lockers, two of them with their paint badly scorched, the third with its door half melted off.

And in various positions about the control room were the half-charred bodies of five blue-scaled Venusian lizards.

A dull ache rose in Gar's chest. Helena Fitzroy was gone. Gone, when she had just confessed she loved him.

Unbidden, a memory came into Gar's mind. Dr. Cedric Elton was the psychiatrist who had examined him when he got his pilot's license for third-class freighters—

"God!" Gar groaned again. And suddenly he was sick. He made a dash for the washroom, and after a while he felt better.

When he straightened up from the wash basin he looked at his reflection in the mirror for a long time, clinging to his hollow cheeks and sunken eyes. He must have been out of his head for two or three days.

The first time. Awful! Somehow, he had never quite believed in space madness.

Suddenly he remembered Jerry. Poor Jerry!

Gar lurched from the washroom back into the control room. Jerry was awake. He looked up at Gar, forcing a smile to his lips. "Hello, Dr. Elton," Jerry said.

Gar stopped as though shot.

"It's happened, Dr. Elton, just as you said it would," Jerry said, his smile widening.

"Forget that," Gar growled. "I took a yellow pill. I'm back to normal again."

Jerry's smile vanished abruptly. "I know what I did now," he said. "It's terrible. I killed six people. But I'm sane now. I'm willing to take what's coming to me."

"Forget that!" Gar snarled. "You don't have to humor me now. Just a minute and I'll untie you."

"Thanks, Doctor," Jerry said. "It will sure be a relief to get out of this straitjacket."

Gar knelt beside Jerry and untied the knots in the ropes and unwound them from around Jerry's chest and legs.

"You'll be all right in a minute," Gar said, massaging Jerry's limp arms. The physical and nervous strain of sitting there immobilized had been rugged.

Slowly he worked circulation back into Jerry, then helped him to his feet.

"You don't need to worry, Dr. Elton," Jerry said. "I don't know why I killed those people, but I know I would never do such a thing again. I must have been insane."

"Can you stand now?" Gar said, letting go of Jerry.

Jerry took a few steps back and forth, unsteadily at first, then with better coordination. His resemblance to a robot decreased with exercise.

Gar was beginning to feel sick again. He fought it.

"You OK now, Jerry boy?" he asked worriedly.

"I'm fine now, Dr. Elton," Jerry said. "And thanks for everything you've done for me."

Abruptly Jerry turned and went over to the air-lock door and opened it.

"Good-by now, Dr. Elton," he said.

"Wait!" Gar screamed, leaping toward Jerry.

But Jerry had stepped into the air lock and closed the door. Gar tried to open it, but already Jerry had turned on the pump that would evacuate the air from the lock.

Screaming Jerry's name senselessly in horror, Gar watched through the small square of thick glass in the door as Jerry's chest quickly expanded, then collapsed as a mixture of phlegm and blood dribbled from his nostrils and lips, and his eyes enlarged and glazed over, then one of them ripped open and collapsed, its fluid draining down his cheek.

He watched as Jerry glanced toward the side of the air lock and smiled, then spun the wheel that opened the air lock to the vacuum of space, and stepped out.

And when Gar finally stopped screaming and sank to the deck, sobbing, his knuckles were broken and bloody from pounding on bare metal.

9. *MEDITATIONS ON FIRST PHILOSOPHY*

René Descartes

MEDITATION I

Of the things which may be brought within the sphere of the doubtful.

It is now some years since I detected how many were the false beliefs that I had from my earliest youth admitted as true, and how doubtful was everything I had since constructed on this basis; and from that time I was convinced that I must once for all seriously undertake to rid myself of all the opinions which I had formerly accepted, and commence to build anew from the foundation, if I wanted to establish any firm and permanent structure in the sciences. But as this enterprise appeared to be a very great one, I waited until I had attained an age so mature that I could not hope that at any later date I should be better fitted to execute my design. This reason caused me to delay so long that I should feel that I was doing wrong were I to occupy in deliberation the time that yet remains to me for action. To-day, then, since very opportunely for the plan I have in view I have delivered my mind from every care [and am happily agitated by no passions] and since I have procured for myself an assured leisure in a peaceable retirement, I shall at last seriously and freely address myself to the general upheaval of all my former opinions.

Now for this object it is not necessary that I should show that all of these are false—I shall perhaps never arrive at this end. But inasmuch as reason already persuades me that I ought no less carefully to withhold my assent from matters which are not entirely certain and indubitable than from those which appear to me manifestly to be false, if I am able to find in each one some reason

to doubt, this will suffice to justify my rejecting the whole. And for that end it will not be requisite that I should examine each in particular, which would be an endless undertaking; for owing to the fact that the destruction of the foundations of necessity brings with it the downfall of the rest of the edifice, I shall only in the first place attack those principles upon which all my former opinions rested.

All that up to the present time I have accepted as most true and certain I have learned either from the senses or through the senses; but it is sometimes proved to me that these senses are deceptive, and it is wiser not to trust entirely to anything by which we have once been deceived.

But it may be that although the senses sometimes deceive us concerning things which are hardly perceptible, or very far away, there are yet many others to be met with as to which we cannot reasonably have any doubt, although we recognise them by their means. For example, there is the fact that I am here, seated by the fire, attired in a dressing gown, having this paper in my hands and other similar matters. And how could I deny that these hands and this body are mine, were it not perhaps that I compare myself to certain persons, devoid of sense, whose cerebella are so troubled and clouded by the violent vapours of black bile, that they constantly assure us that they think they are kings when they are really quite poor, or that they are clothed in purple when they are really without covering, or who imagine that they have an earthenware head or are nothing but pumpkins or are made of glass. But they are mad, and I should not be any the less insane were I to follow examples so extravagant.

At the same time I must remember that I am a man, and that consequently I am in the habit of sleeping, and in my dreams representing to myself the same things or sometimes even less probable things, than do those who are insane in their waking moments. How often has it happened to me that in the night I dreamt that I found myself in this particular place, that I was dressed and seated near the fire, whilst in reality I was lying undressed in bed! At this moment it does indeed seem to me that it is with eyes awake that I am looking at this paper; that this head which I move is not asleep, that it is deliberately and of set purpose that I extend my hand and perceive it; what happens in sleep does not appear so clear nor so distinct as does all this. But in thinking over this I remind myself that on many occasions I have in sleep been deceived by similar illusions, and in dwelling carefully on this reflection I see so manifestly that there are no certain indications by which we may clearly distinguish wakefulness from sleep that I am lost in astonishment. And my astonishment is such that it is almost capable of persuading me that I now dream.

Now let us assume that we are asleep and that all these particulars, e.g. that we open our eyes, shake our head, extend our hands, and so on, are but false delusions; and let us reflect that possibly neither our hands nor our whole body are such as they appear to us to be. At the same time we must at least confess that the things which are represented to us in sleep are like painted representations which can only have been formed as the counterparts of something real and true, and that in this way those general things at least, i.e. eyes, a head, hands, and a whole body, are not imaginary things, but things really existent. For, as a matter of fact, painters, even when they study with the greatest skill to represent sirens and satyrs by forms the most strange and extraordinary, cannot give them natures which are entirely new, but merely make a certain medley of the members of different animals; or if their imagination is extravagant enough to invent something so novel that nothing similar has ever before been seen, and that then their work represents a thing purely fictitious and absolutely false, it is certain all the same that the colours of which this is composed are necessarily real. And for the same reason, although these general things, to wit, [a body], eyes, a head, hands, and such like, may be imaginary, we are bound at the same time to confess that there

are at least some other objects yet more simple and more universal, which are real and true; and of these just in the same way as with certain real colours, all these images of things which dwell in our thoughts, whether true and real or false and fantastic, are formed.

To such a class of things pertains corporeal nature in general, and its extension, the figure of extended things, their quantity or magnitude and number, as also the place in which they are, the time which measures their duration, and so on.

That is possibly why our reasoning is not unjust when we conclude from this that Physics, Astronomy, Medicine and all other sciences which have as their end the consideration of composite things, are very dubious and uncertain; but that Arithmetic, Geometry and other sciences of that kind which only treat of things that are very simple and very general, without taking great trouble to ascertain whether they are actually existent or not, contain some measure of certainty and an element of the indubitable. For whether I am awake or asleep, two and three together always form five, and the square can never have more than four sides, and it does not seem possible that truths so clear and apparent can be suspected of any falsity [or uncertainty].

Nevertheless I have long had fixed in my mind the belief that an all-powerful God existed by whom I have been created such as I am. But how do I know that He has not brought it to pass that there is no earth, no heaven, no extended body, no magnitude, no place, and that nevertheless [I possess the perceptions of all these things and that] they seem to me to exist just exactly as I now see them? And, besides, as I sometimes imagine that others deceive themselves in the things which they think they know best, how do I know that I am not deceived every time that I add two and three, or count the sides of a square, or judge of things yet simpler, if anything simpler can be imagined? But possibly God has not desired that I should be thus deceived, for He is said to be supremely good. If, however, it is contrary to His goodness to have made me such that I constantly deceive myself, it would also appear to be contrary to His goodness to permit me to be sometimes deceived, and nevertheless I cannot doubt that He does permit this.

There may indeed be those who would prefer to deny the existence of a God so powerful, rather than believe that all other things are uncertain. But let us not oppose them for the present, and grant that all that is here said of a God is a fable . . . . At the end I feel constrained to confess that there is nothing in all that I formerly believed to be true, of which I cannot in some measure doubt, and that not merely through want of thought or through levity, but for reasons which are very powerful and maturely considered; so that henceforth I ought not the less carefully to refrain from giving credence to these opinions than to that which is manifestly false, if I desire to arrive at any certainty [in the sciences] . . . .

I shall then suppose, not that God who is supremely good and the fountain of truth, but some evil genius not less powerful than deceitful, has employed his whole energies in deceiving me; I shall consider that the heavens, the earth, colours, figures, sound, and all other external things are nought but the illusions and dreams of which this genius has availed himself in order to lay traps for my credulity; I shall consider myself as having no hands, no eyes, no flesh, no blood, nor any senses, yet falsely believing myself to possess all these things; I shall remain obstinately attached to this idea, and if by this means it is not in my power to arrive at the knowledge of any truth, I may at least do what is in my power [i.e. suspend my judgment], and with firm purpose avoid giving credence to any false thing, or being imposed upon by this arch deceiver, however powerful and deceptive he may be. But this task is a laborious one, and insensibly a certain lassitude leads me into the course of my ordinary life. And just as a captive who in sleep enjoys an imaginary liberty, when he begins to suspect that his liberty is but a dream, fears to awaken, and conspires with these agreeable illusions that the deception may be prolonged, so insensibly of my own accord I fall back into my former opinions, and I dread awakening from this slumber, lest the laborious wakefulness which would follow the tranquillity of this repose should have to be spent not in daylight, but in the excessive darkness of the difficulties which have just been discussed.

MEDITATION II

Of the Nature of the Human Mind; and that it is more easily known than the Body.

The Meditation of yesterday filled my mind with so many doubts that it is no longer in my power to forget them. And yet I do not see in what manner I can resolve them; and, just as if I had all of a sudden fallen into very deep water, I am so disconcerted that I can neither make certain of setting my feet on the bottom, nor can I swim and so support myself on the surface. I shall nevertheless make an effort and follow anew the same path as that on which I yesterday entered, i.e. I shall proceed by setting aside all that in which the least doubt could be supposed to exist, just as if I had discovered that it was absolutely false; and I shall ever follow in this road until I have met with something which is certain, or at least, if I can do nothing else, until I have learned for certain that there is nothing in the world that is certain. Archimedes, in order that he might draw the terrestrial globe out of its place, and transport it elsewhere, demanded only that one point should be fixed and immoveable; in the same way I shall have the right to conceive high hopes if I am happy enough to discover one thing only which is certain and indubitable.

I suppose, then, that all the things that I see are false; I persuade myself that nothing has ever existed of all that my fallacious memory represents to me. I consider that I possess no senses; I imagine that body, figure, extension, movement and place are but the fictions of my mind. What, then, can be esteemed as true? Perhaps nothing at all, unless that there is nothing in the world that is certain.

But how can I know there is not something different from those things that I have just considered, of which one cannot have the slightest doubt? Is there not some God, or some other being by whatever name we call it, who puts these reflections into my mind? That is not necessary, for is it not possible that I am capable of producing them myself? I myself, am I not at least something? But I have already denied that I had senses and body. Yet I hesitate, for what follows from that? Am I so dependent on body and senses that I cannot exist without these? But I was persuaded that there was nothing in all the world, that there was no heaven, no earth, that there were no minds, nor any bodies: was I not then likewise persuaded that I did not exist? Not at all; of a surety I myself did exist since I persuaded myself of something [or merely because I thought of something]. But there is some deceiver or other, very powerful and very cunning, who ever employs his ingenuity in deceiving me. Then without doubt I exist also if he deceives me, and let him deceive me as much as he will, he can never cause me to be nothing so long as I think that I am something. So that after having reflected well and carefully examined all things, we must come to the definite conclusion that this proposition: I am, I exist, is necessarily true each time that I pronounce it, or that I mentally conceive it.

But I do not yet know clearly enough what I am, I who am certain that I am; and hence I must be careful to see that I do not imprudently take some other object in place of myself, and thus that I do not go astray in respect of this knowledge that I hold to be the most certain and most evident of all that I have formerly learned. That is why I shall now consider anew what I believed myself to be before I embarked upon these last reflections; and of my former opinions I shall withdraw all that might even in a small degree be invalidated by the reasons which I have just brought forward, in order that there may be nothing at all left beyond what is absolutely certain and indubitable.

What then did I formerly believe myself to be? Undoubtedly I believed myself to be a man. But what is a man? Shall I say a reasonable animal? Certainly not; for then I should have to inquire what an animal is, and what is reasonable; and thus from a single question I should insensibly fall into an infinitude of others more difficult; and I should not wish to waste the little time and leisure remaining to me in trying to unravel subtleties like these. But I shall rather stop here to consider the thoughts which of themselves spring up in my mind, and which were not inspired by anything beyond my own nature alone when I applied myself to the consideration of my being. In the first place, then, I considered myself as having a face, hands, arms, and all that system of members composed of bones and flesh as seen in a corpse which I designated by the name of body. In addition to this I considered that I was nourished, that I walked, that I felt, and that I thought, and I referred all these actions to the soul: but I did not stop to consider what the soul was, or if I did stop, I imagined that it was something extremely rare and subtle like a wind, a flame, or an ether, which was spread throughout my grosser parts. As to body I had no manner of doubt about its nature, but thought I had a very clear knowledge of it; and if I had desired to explain it according to the notions that I had then formed of it, I should have described it thus: By the body I understand all that which can be defined by a certain figure: something which can be confined in a certain place, and which can fill a given space in such a way that every other body will be excluded from it; which can be perceived either by touch, or by sight, or by hearing, or by taste, or by smell: which can be moved in many ways not, in truth, by itself, but by something which is foreign to it, by which it is touched [and from which it receives impressions]: for to have the power of self-movement, as also of feeling or of thinking, I did not consider to appertain to the nature of body: on the contrary, I was rather astonished to find that faculties similar to them existed in some bodies.

But what am I, now that I suppose that there is a certain genius which is extremely powerful, and, if I may say so, malicious, who employs all his powers in deceiving me? Can I affirm that I possess the least of all those things which I have just said pertain to the nature of body? I pause to consider, I revolve all these things in my mind, and I find none of which I can say that it pertains to me. It would be tedious to stop to enumerate them. Let us pass to the attributes of soul and see if there is any one which is in me? What of nutrition or walking [the first mentioned]? But if it is so that I have no body it is also true that I can neither walk nor take nourishment. Another attribute is sensation. But one cannot feel without body, and besides I have thought I perceived many things during sleep that I recognised in my waking moments as not having been experienced at all. What of thinking? I find here that thought is an attribute that belongs to me; it alone cannot be separated from me. I am, I exist, that is certain. But how often? Just when I think; for it might possibly be the case if I ceased entirely to think, that I should likewise cease altogether to exist. I do not now admit anything which is not necessarily true: to speak accurately I am not more than a thing which thinks, that is to say a mind or a soul, or an understanding, or a reason, which are terms whose significance was formerly unknown to me. I am, however, a real thing and really exist; but what thing? I have answered: a thing which thinks . . . .

Is there nothing in all this which is as true as it is certain that I exist, even though I should always sleep and though he who has given me being employed all his ingenuity in deceiving me? Is there likewise any one of these attributes which can be distinguished from my thought, or which might be said to be separated from myself? For it is so evident of itself that it is I who doubts, who understands, and who desires, that there is no reason here to add anything to explain it. And I have certainly the power of imagining likewise; for although it may happen (as I formerly supposed) that none of the things which I imagine are true, nevertheless this power of imagining does not cease to be really in use, and it forms part of my thought. Finally, I am the same who feels, that is to say, who perceived certain things, as by the organs of sense, since in truth I see light, I hear noise, I feel heat. But it will be said that these phenomena are false and that I am dreaming. Let it be so; still it is at least quite certain that it seems to me that I see light, that I hear noise and that I feel heat. That cannot be false; properly speaking it is what is in me called feeling; and used in this precise sense that is no other thing than thinking.

From this time I begin to know what I am with a little more clearness and distinction than before; but nevertheless it still seems to me, and I cannot prevent myself from thinking, that corporeal things, whose images are framed by thought, which are tested by the senses, are much more distinctly known than that obscure part of me which does not come under the imagination. Although really it is very strange to say that I know and understand more distinctly these things whose existence seems to me dubious, which are unknown to me, and which do not belong to me, than others of the truth of which I am convinced, which are known to me and which pertain to my real nature, in a word, than myself. But I see clearly how the case stands: my mind loves to wander, and cannot yet suffer itself to be retained within the just limits of truth. Very good, let us once more give it the freest rein, so that, when afterwards we seize the proper occasion for pulling up, it may the more easily be regulated and controlled.

Let us begin by considering the commonest matters, those which we believe to be the most distinctly comprehended, to wit, the bodies which we touch and see; not indeed bodies in general, for these general ideas are usually a little more confused, but let us consider one body in particular. Let us take, for example, this piece of wax: it has been taken quite freshly from the hive, and it has not yet lost the sweetness of the honey which it contains; it still retains somewhat of the odour of the flowers from which it has been culled; its colour, its figure, its size are apparent; it is hard, cold, easily handled, and if you strike it with the finger, it will emit a sound. Finally all the things which are requisite to cause us distinctly to recognise a body, are met with in it. But notice that while I speak and approach the fire what remained of the taste is exhaled, the smell evaporates, the colour alters, the figure is destroyed, the size increases, it becomes liquid, it heats, scarcely can one handle it, and when one strikes it, no sound is emitted. Does the same wax remain after this change? We must confess that it remains; none would judge otherwise. What then did I know so distinctly in this piece of wax? It could certainly be nothing of all that the senses brought to my notice, since all these things which fall under taste, smell, sight, touch, and hearing, are found to be changed, and yet the same wax remains . . . . I should not conceive [clearly] according to truth what wax is, if I did not think that even this piece that we are considering is capable of receiving more variations in extension than I have ever imagined. We must then grant that I could not even understand through the imagination what this piece of wax is, and that it is my mind alone which perceives it. I say this piece of wax in particular, for as to wax in general it is yet clearer. But what is this piece of wax which cannot be understood excepting by the [understanding or] mind? It is certainly the same that I see, touch, imagine, and finally it is the same which I have always believed it to be from the beginning. But what must particularly be observed is that its perception is neither an act of vision, nor of touch, nor of imagination, and has never been such although it may have appeared formerly to be so, but only an intuition of the mind, which may be imperfect and confused as it was formerly, or clear and distinct as it is at present, according as my attention is more or less directed to the elements which are found in it, and of which it is composed.

Yet in the meantime I am greatly astonished when I consider [the great feebleness of mind] and its proneness to fall [insensibly] into error; for although without giving expression to my thoughts I consider all this in my own mind, words often impede me and I am almost deceived by the terms of ordinary language. For we say that we see the same wax, if it is present, and not that we simply judge that it is the same from its having the same colour and figure. From this I should conclude that I knew the wax by means of vision and not simply by the intuition of the mind; unless by chance I remember that, when looking from a window and saying I see men who pass in the street, I really do not see them, but infer that what I see is men, just as I say that I see wax. And yet what do I see from the window but hats and coats which may cover automatic machines? Yet I judge these to be men. And similarly solely by the faculty of judgment which rests in my mind, I comprehend that which I believed I saw with my eyes. . . . And what I have here remarked of wax may be applied to all other things which are external to me [and which are met with outside of me]. And further, if the [notion or] perception of wax has seemed to me clearer and more distinct, not only after the sight or the touch, but also after many other causes have rendered it quite manifest to me, with how much more [evidence] and distinctness must it be said that I now know myself, since all the reasons which contribute to the knowledge of wax, or any other body whatever, are yet better proofs of the nature of my mind! And there are so many other things in the mind itself which may contribute to the elucidation of its nature, that those which depend on body such as these just mentioned, hardly merit being taken into account.

But finally here I am, having insensibly reverted to the point I desired, for, since it is now manifest to me that even bodies are not properly speaking known by the senses or by the faculty of imagination, but by the understanding only, and since they are not known from the fact that they are seen or touched, but only because they are understood, I see clearly that there is nothing which is easier for me to know than my mind. But because it is difficult to rid oneself so promptly of an opinion to which one was accustomed for so long, it will be well that I should halt a little at this point, so that by the length of my meditation I may more deeply imprint on my memory this new knowledge . . . .

MEDITATION VI

Of the Existence of Material Things, and of the real distinction between the Soul and Body of Man.

Nothing further now remains but to inquire whether material things exist . . . . It is right that I should at the same time investigate the nature of sense perception, and that I should see if from the ideas which I apprehend by this mode of thought, which I call feeling, I cannot derive some certain proof of the existence of corporeal objects.

And first of all I shall recall to my memory those matters which I hitherto held to be true, as having perceived them through the senses, and the foundations on which my belief has rested . . . .

Outside myself, in addition to extension, figure, and motions of bodies, I remarked in them hardness, heat, and all other tactile qualities, and, further, light and colour, and scents and sounds, the variety of which gave me the means of distinguishing the sky, the earth, the sea, and generally all the other bodies, one from the other. And certainly, considering the ideas of all these qualities which presented themselves to my mind, and which alone I perceived properly or immediately, it was not without reason that I believed myself to perceive objects quite different from my thought, to wit, bodies from which those ideas proceeded; for I found by experience that these ideas presented themselves to me without my consent being requisite, so that I could not perceive any object, however desirous I might be, unless it were present to the organs of sense; and it was not in my power not to perceive it, when it was present. And because the ideas which I received through the senses were much more lively, more clear, and even, in their own way, more distinct than any of those which I could of myself frame in meditation, or than those I found impressed on my memory, it appeared as though they could not have proceeded from my mind, so that they must necessarily have been produced in me by some other things. And having no knowledge of those objects excepting the knowledge which the ideas themselves gave me, nothing was more likely to occur to my mind than that the objects were similar to the ideas which were caused. And because I likewise remembered that I had formerly made use of my senses rather than my reason, and recognised that the ideas which I formed of myself were not so distinct as those which I perceived through the senses, and that they were most frequently even composed of portions of these last, I persuaded myself easily that I had no idea in my mind which had not formerly come to me through the senses . . . .

But now that I begin to know myself better, and to discover more clearly the author of my being, I do not in truth think that I should rashly admit all the matters which the senses seem to teach us, but, on the other hand, I do not think that I should doubt them all universally . . . . On the one side, I have a clear and distinct idea of myself inasmuch as I am only a thinking and unextended thing, and as, on the other, I possess a distinct idea of body, inasmuch as it is only an extended and unthinking thing, it is certain that this I [that is to say, my soul by which I am what I am], is entirely and absolutely distinct from my body, and can exist without it . . . .

Since God is no deceiver, . . . we must allow that corporeal things exist. However, they are perhaps not exactly what we perceive by the senses, since this comprehension by the senses is in many instances very obscure and confused; but we must at least admit that all things which I conceive in them clearly and distinctly, that is to say, all things which, speaking generally, are comprehended in the object of pure mathematics, are truly **to be recognised** as external objects.

As to other things, however, which are either particular only, as, for example, that the sun is of such and such a figure, etc., or which are less clearly and distinctly conceived, such as light, sound, pain and the like, it is certain that although they are very dubious and uncertain, yet on the sole ground that God is not a deceiver, and that consequently He has not permitted any falsity to exist in my opinion which He has not likewise given me the faculty of correcting, I may assuredly hope to conclude that I have within me the means of arriving at the truth even here. And first of all there is no doubt that in all things which nature teaches me there is some truth contained; for by nature, considered in general, I now understand no other thing than either God Himself or else the order and disposition which God has established in created things; and by my nature in particular I understand no other thing than the complexus of all the things which God has given me . . . .

Moreover, nature teaches me that many other bodies exist around mine, of which some are to be avoided, and others sought after. And certainly from the fact that I am sensible of different sorts of colours, sounds, scents, tastes, heat, hardness, etc., I very easily conclude that there are in the bodies from which all these diverse sense-perceptions proceed certain variations which answer to them, although possibly these are not really at all similar to them. . . .

It seems to me that it is mind alone, and not mind and body in conjunction, that is requisite to a knowledge of the truth in regard to such things. Thus, although a star makes no larger an impression on my eye than the flame of a little candle there is yet in me no real or positive propensity impelling me to believe that it is not greater than that flame; but I have judged it to be so from my earliest years, without any rational foundation. And although in approaching fire I feel heat, and in approaching it a little too near I even feel pain, there is at the same time no reason in this which could persuade me that there is in the fire something resembling this heat any more than there is in it something resembling the pain; all that I have any reason to believe from this is, that there is something in it, whatever it may be, which excites in me these sensations of heat or of pain. . . .

10. A DIALOGUE BETWEEN HYLAS AND PHILONOUS

George Berkeley

THE FIRST DIALOGUE

Philonous. Good morrow, *Hylas:* I did not expect to find you abroad so early.

Hylas. It is indeed something unusual; but my thoughts were so taken up with a subject I was discoursing of last night, that finding I could not sleep, I resolved to rise and take a turn in the garden.

Phil. It happened well, to let you see what innocent and agreeable pleasures you lose every morning. Can there be a pleasanter time of the day, or a more delightful season of the year? That purple sky, those wild but sweet notes of birds, the fragrant bloom upon the trees and flowers, the gentle influence of the rising sun, these and a thousand nameless beauties of nature inspire the soul with secret transports; its faculties too being at this time fresh and lively, are fit for these meditations, which the solitude of a garden and tranquillity of the morning naturally dispose us to. But I am afraid I interrupt your thoughts: for you seemed very intent on something.

Hyl. It is true, I was, and shall be obliged to you if you will permit me to go on in the same vein; not that I would by any means deprive myself of your company, for my thoughts always flow more easily in conversation with a friend, than when I am alone: but my request is, that you would suffer me to impart my reflections to you. . . .

Phil. Pray, what were those?

Hyl. You were represented in last night's conversation, as one who maintained the most extravagant opinion that ever entered into the mind of man, to wit, that there is no such thing as *material substance* in the world.

Phil. That there is no such thing as what Philosophers call *material substance,* I am seriously persuaded: but, if I were made to see anything absurd or sceptical in this, I should then have the same reason to renounce this that I imagine I have now to reject the contrary opinion.

Hyl. What! can anything be more fantastical, more repugnant to common sense, or a more manifest piece of Scepticism, than to believe there is no such thing as *matter?*

Phil. Softly, good *Hylas.* What if it should prove, that you, who hold there is, are, by virtue of that opinion, a greater sceptic, and maintain more paradoxes and repugnances to common sense, than I who believe no such thing?

Hyl. You may as soon persuade me, the part is greater than the whole, as that, in order to avoid absurdity and Scepticism, I should ever be obliged to give up my opinion in this point . . . .

Phil. Pray, *Hylas,* what do you mean by a *sceptic?*

Hyl. I mean what all men mean—one that doubts of everything.

Phil. He then who entertains no doubt concerning some particular point, with regard to that point cannot be thought a sceptic.

Hyl. I agree with you.

Phil. Whether doth doubting consist in embracing the affirmative or negative side of a question?

Hyl. In neither; for whoever understands English, cannot but know that *doubting* signifies a suspense between both . . . .

Phil. How cometh it to pass then, *Hylas,* that you pronounce me a *sceptic,* because I deny what you affirm, to wit, the existence of Matter? Since, for aught you can tell, I am as peremptory in my denial, as you in your affirmation.

Hyl. Hold, *Philonous,* I have been a little out in my definition; but every false step a man makes in discourse is not to be insisted on. I said indeed that a *sceptic* was one who doubted of everything; but I should have added, or who denies the reality and truth of things.

Phil. What things? Do you mean the principles

Reprinted from George Berkeley, *A Dialogue Between Hylas and Philonous,* first published in 1713.

and theorems of sciences? But these you know are universal intellectual notions, and consequently independent of Matter; the denial therefore of this doth not imply the denying them.

Hyl. I grant it. But are there no other things? What think you of distrusting the senses, of denying the real existence of sensible things, or pretending to know nothing of them. Is not this sufficient to denominate a man a *sceptic?*

Phil. Shall we therefore examine which of us it is that denies the reality of sensible things, or professes the greatest ignorance of them; since, if I take you rightly, he is to be esteemed the greatest *sceptic?*

Hyl. That is what I desire.

Phil. What mean you by Sensible Things?

Hyl. Those things which are perceived by the senses. Can you imagine that I mean anything else?

Phil. Pardon me, *Hylas,* if I am desirous clearly to apprehend your notions, since this may much shorten our inquiry. Suffer me then to ask you this farther question. Are those things only perceived by the senses which are perceived immediately? Or, may those things properly be said to be *sensible* which are perceived mediately, or not without the intervention of others?

Hyl. I do not sufficiently understand you.

Phil. In reading a book, what I immediately perceive are the letters, but mediately, or by means of these, are suggested to my mind the notions of God, virtue, truth, &c. Now, that the letters are truly sensible things, or perceived by sense, there is no doubt: but I would know whether you take the things suggested by them to be so too.

Hyl. No, certainly; it were absurd to think *God* or *virtue* sensible things, though they may be signified and suggested to the mind by sensible marks, with which they have an arbitrary connexion.

Phil. It seems then, that by *sensible things* you mean those only which can be perceived *immediately* by sense? . . .

Hyl. To prevent any more questions of this kind, I tell you once for all, that by *sensible things* I mean those only which are perceived by sense,

and that in truth the senses perceive nothing which they do not perceive immediately: for they make no inferences. The deducing therefore of causes or occasions from effects and appearances, which alone are perceived by sense, entirely relates to reason.

Phil. This point then is agreed between us—that *sensible things are those only which are immediately perceived by sense.* You will farther inform me, whether we immediately perceive by sight anything beside light, and colours, and figures; or by hearing, anything but sounds; by the palate, anything beside tastes; by the smell, beside odours; or by the touch, more than tangible qualities.

Hyl. We do not.

Phil. It seems, therefore, that if you take away all sensible qualities, there remains nothing sensible?

Hyl. I grant it.

Phil. Sensible things therefore are nothing else but so many sensible qualities, or combinations of sensible qualities?

Hyl. Nothing else.

Phil. *Heat* then is a sensible thing?

Hyl. Certainly.

Phil. Doth the reality of sensible things consist in being perceived? or, is it something distinct from their being perceived, and that bears no relation to the mind?

Hyl To *exist* is one thing, and to be *perceived* is another.

Phil. I speak with regard to sensible things only: and of these I ask, whether by their real existence you mean a subsistence exterior to the mind, and distinct from their being perceived?

Hyl. I mean a real absolute being, distinct from, and without any relation to their being perceived.

Phil. Heat therefore, if it be allowed a real being, must exist without the mind?

Hyl. It must.

Phil. Tell me, *Hylas,* is this real existence equally compatible to all degrees of heat, which we perceive; or is there any reason why we should attribute it to some, and deny it to others? and if there be, pray let me know that reason.

Hyl. Whatever degree of heat we perceive by sense, we may be sure the same exists in the object that occasions it.

Phil. What! the greatest as well as the least?

Hyl. I tell you, the reason is plainly the same in respect of both: they are both perceived by sense; nay, the greater degree of heat is more sensibly perceived; and consequently, if there is any difference, we are more certain of its real existence than we can be of the reality of a lesser degree.

Phil. But is not the most vehement and intense degree of heat a very great pain?

Hyl. No one can deny it.

Phil. And is any unperceiving thing capable of pain or pleasure?

Hyl. No certainly.

Phil. Is your material substance a senseless being, or a being endowed with sense and perception?

Hyl. It is senseless without doubt.

Phil. It cannot therefore be the subject of pain?

Hyl. By no means.

Phil. Nor consequently of the greatest heat perceived by sense, since you acknowledge this to be no small pain?

Hyl. I grant it.

Phil. What shall we say then of your external object; is it a material Substance, or no?

Hyl. It is a material substance with the sensible qualities inhering in it.

Phil. How then can a great heat exist in it, since you own it cannot in a material substance? I desire you would clear this point.

Hyl. Hold, *Philonous,* I fear I was out in yielding intense heat to be a pain. It should seem rather, that pain is something distinct from heat, and the consequence or effect of it.

Phil. Upon putting your hand near the fire, do you perceive one simple uniform sensation, or two distinct sensations?

Hyl. But one simple sensation.

Phil. Is not the heat immediately perceived?

Hyl. It is.

Phil. And the pain?

Hyl. True.

Phil. Seeing therefore they are both im-mediately perceived at the same time, and the fire affects you only with one simple, or uncompounded idea, it follows that this same simple idea is both the intense heat immediately perceived and the pain: and, consequently, that the intense heat immediately perceived, is nothing distinct from a particular sort of pain.

Hyl. It seems so.

Phil. Again, try in your thoughts, *Hylas,* if you can conceive a vehement sensation to be without pain or pleasure.

Hyl. I cannot.

Phil. Or can you frame to yourself an idea of sensible pain or pleasure, in general, abstracted from every particular idea of heat, cold, tastes, smells? &c.

Hyl. I do not find that I can.

Phil. Doth it not therefore follow, that sensible pain is nothing distinct from those sensations or ideas—in an intense degree?

Hyl. It is undeniable; and, to speak the truth, I begin to suspect a very great heat cannot exist but in a mind perceiving it.

Phil. What! are you then in that *sceptical* state of suspense, between affirming and denying?

Hyl. I think I may be positive in the point. A very violent and painful heat cannot exist without the mind.

Phil. It hath not therefore, according to you, any real being?

Hyl. I own it . . . .

Phil. Is it not an absurdity to think that the same thing should be at the same time both cold and warm?

Hyl. It is.

Phil. Suppose now one of your hands hot, and the other cold, and that they are both at once put into the same vessel of water, in an intermediate state; will not the water seem cold to one hand, and warm to the other.

Hyl. It will.

Phil. Ought we not therefore, by your principles, to conclude it is really both cold and warm at the same time, that is, according to your own concession, to believe an absurdity?

Hyl. I confess it seems so.

Phil. Consequently, the principles themselves

are false, since you have granted that no true principle leads to an absurdity . . . .

Hyl. Hold, *Philonous,* I now see what it was deluded me all this time. You asked whether heat and cold, sweetness and bitterness, were not particular sorts of pleasure and pain; to which I answered simply, that they were. Whereas I should have thus distinguished:—those qualities, as perceived by us, are pleasures or pains; but not as existing in the external objects. We must not therefore conclude absolutely, that there is no heat in the fire, or sweetness in the sugar, but only that heat or sweetness, as perceived by us, are not in the fire or sugar. What say you to this?

Phil. I say it is nothing to the purpose. Our discourse proceeded altogether concerning sensible things, which you defined to be, *the things we immediately perceive by our senses.* Whatever other qualities, therefore, you speak of, as distinct from these, I know nothing of them, neither do they at all belong to the point in dispute. You may, indeed, pretend to have discovered certain qualities which you do not perceive, and assert those insensible qualities exist in fire and sugar. But what use can be made of this to your present purpose, I am at a loss to conceive. Tell me then once more, do you acknowledge that heat and cold, sweetness and bitterness (meaning those qualities which are perceived by the senses), do not exist without the mind?

Hyl. I see it is to no purpose to hold out, so I give up the cause as to those mentioned qualities. Though I profess it sounds oddly, to say that sugar is not sweet . . . .

Phil. In the next place, *odours* are to be considered. And, with regard to these, I would fain know whether what hath been said of tastes doth not exactly agree to them? Are they not so many pleasing or displeasing sensations?

Hyl They are . . . .

Phil. May we not therefore conclude of smells, as of the other forementioned qualities, that they cannot exist in any but a perceiving substance or mind?

Hyl. I think so.

Phil. Then as to *sounds,* what must we think of them: are they accidents really inherent in external bodies, or not?

Hyl. That they inhere not in the sonorous bodies is plain from hence; because a bell struck in the exhausted receiver of an air-pump sends forth no sound. The air, therefore, must be thought the subject of sound.

Phil. What reason is there for that, *Hylas?*

Hyl. Because, when any motion is raised in the air, we perceive a sound greater or lesser, according to the air's motion; but without some motion in the air, we never hear any sound at all.

Phil. And granting that we never hear a sound but when some motion is produced in the air, yet I do not see how you can infer from thence, that the sound itself is in the air.

Hyl. It is this very motion in the external air that produces in the mind the sensation of *sound.* For, striking on the drum of the ear, it causeth a vibration, which by the auditory nerves being communicated to the brain, the soul is thereupon affected with the sensation called *sound.*

Phil. What! is sound then a sensation?

Hyl. I tell you, as perceived by us, it is a particular sensation in the mind.

Phil. And can any sensation exist without the mind?

Hyl. No, certainly.

Phil. How then can sound, being a sensation, exist in the air, if by the *air* you mean a senseless substance existing without the mind?

Hyl. You must distinguish, *Philonous,* between sound as it is perceived by us, and as it is in itself; or (which is the same thing) between the sound we immediately perceive, and that which exists without us. The former, indeed, is a particular kind of sensation, but the latter is merely a vibrative or undulatory motion in the air.

Phil. I thought I had already obviated that distinction, by the answer I gave when you were applying it in a like case before. But, to say no more of that, are you sure then that sound is really nothing but motion?

Hyl. I am.

Phil. Whatever therefore agrees to real sound, may with truth be attributed to motion?

Hyl. It may . . . .

Phil. Tell me, *Hylas,* to which of the senses, think you, the idea of motion belongs? to the hearing?

Hyl. No, certainly; but to the sight and touch.

Phil. It should follow then, that, according to you, real sounds may possibly be *seen* or *felt,* but never *heard* . . . .

Phil. And I hope you will make no difficulty to acknowledge the same of *colours.*

Hyl. Pardon me: the case of colours is very different. Can anything be plainer than that we see them on the objects?

Phil. The objects you speak of are, I suppose, corporeal Substances existing without the mind?

Hyl. They are . . . .

Phil. Pray, is your corporeal substance either a sensible quality, or made up of sensible qualities?

Hyl. What a question that is! who ever thought it was?

Phil. My reason for asking was, because in saying, *each visible object hath that colour which we see in it,* you make visible objects to be corporeal substances; which implies either that corporeal substances are sensible qualities, or else that there is something beside sensible qualities perceived by sight: but, as this point was formerly agreed between us, and is still maintained by you, it is a clear consequence, that your corporeal substance is nothing distinct from sensible qualities.

Hyl. You may draw as many absurd consequences as you please, and endeavour to perplex the plainest things; but you shall never persuade me out of my senses. I clearly understand my own meaning.

Phil. I wish you would make me understand it too. But, since you are unwilling to have your notion of corporeal substance examined, I shall urge that point no farther. Only be pleased to let me know, whether the same colours which we see exist in external bodies, or some other.

Hyl. The very same.

Phil. What! are then the beautiful red and purple we see on yonder clouds really in them? Or do you imagine they have in themselves any other form than that of a dark mist or vapour?

Hyl. I must own, *Philonous,* those colours are not really in the clouds as they seem to be at this distance. They are only apparent colours.

Phil. *Apparent* call you them? how shall we distinguish these apparent colours from real?

Hyl. Very easily. Those are to be thought apparent which, appearing only at a distance, vanish upon a nearer approach.

Phil. And those, I suppose, are to be thought real which are discovered by the most near and exact survey.

Hyl. Right.

Phil. Is the nearest and exactest survey made by the help of a microscope, or by the naked eye?

Hyl. By a microscope, doubtless.

Phil. But a microscope often discovers colours in an object different from those perceived by the unassisted sight. And, in case we had microscopes magnifying to any assigned degree, it is certain that no object whatsoever, viewed through them, would appear in the same colour which it exhibits to the naked eye.

Hyl. And what will you conclude from all this? You cannot argue that there are really and naturally no colours on objects: because by artificial managements they may be altered, or made to vanish.

Phil. I think it may evidently be concluded from your own concessions, that all the colours we see with our naked eyes are only apparent as those on the clouds, since they vanish upon a more close and accurate inspection which is afforded us by a microscope. Then, as to what you say by way of prevention: I ask you whether the real and natural state of an object is better discovered by a very sharp and piercing sight, or by one which is less sharp?

Hyl. By the former without doubt.

Phil. Is it not plain from *Dioptrics* that microscopes make the sight more penetrating, and represent objects as they would appear to the eye in case it were naturally endowed with a most exquisite sharpness?

Hyl. It is.

Phil. Consequently the microscopical representation is to be thought that which best sets forth the real nature of the thing, or what it is in itself. The colours, therefore, by it perceived are more genuine and real than those perceived otherwise.

Hyl. I confess there is something in what you say . . . .

Phil. Is light then a substance?

Hyl. I tell you, *Philonous,* external light is

nothing but a thin fluid substance, whose minute particles being agitated with a brisk motion, and in various manners reflected from the different surfaces of outward objects to the eyes, communicate different motions to the optic nerves; which, being propagated to the brain, cause therein various impressions; and these are attended with the sensations of red, blue, yellow, &c.

Phil. It seems then the light doth no more than shake the optic nerves.

Hyl. Nothing else.

Phil. And, consequent to each particular motion of the nerves, the mind is affected with a sensation, which is some particular colour.

Hyl. Right.

Phil. And these sensations have no existence without the mind.

Hyl. They have not.

Phil. How then do you affirm that colours are in the light; since by *light* you understand a corporeal substance external to the mind?

Hyl. Light and colours, as immediately perceived by us, I grant cannot exist without the mind. But, in themselves they are only the motions and configurations of certain insensible particles of matter . . . .

Hyl. I frankly own, *Philonous,* that it is in vain to stand out any longer. Colours, sounds, tastes, in a word all those termed *secondary qualities,* have certainly no existence without the mind. But, by this acknowledgment I must not be supposed to derogate anything from the reality of Matter or external objects; seeing it is no more than several philosophers maintain, who nevertheless are the farthest imaginable from denying Matter. For the clearer understanding of this, you must know sensible qualities are by philosophers divided into *primary* and *secondary.* The former are Extension, Figure, Solidity, Gravity, Motion, and Rest. And these they hold exist really in bodies. The latter are those above enumerated; or, briefly, all sensible qualities beside the Primary, which they assert are only so many sensations or ideas existing nowhere but in the mind. But all this, I doubt not, you are apprised of. For my part, I have been a long time sensible there was such an opinion current among philosophers, but was never thoroughly convinced of its truth until now.

Phil. You are still then of opinion that *exten-*

sion and *figures* are inherent in external unthinking substances?

Hyl. I am.

Phil. But what if the same arguments which are brought against Secondary Qualities will hold good against these also?

Hyl. Why then I shall be obliged to think, they too exist only in the mind.

Phil. Is it your opinion the very figure and extension which you perceive by sense exist in the outward object or material substance?

Hyl. It is . . . .

Phil. A mite therefore must be supposed to see his own foot, and things equal or even less than it, as bodies of some considerable dimension; though at the same time they appear to you scarce discernible, or at best as so many visible points.

Hyl. I cannot deny it.

Phil. And to creatures less than the mite they will seem yet larger?

Hyl. They will.

Phil. Insomuch that what you can hardly discern will to another extremely minute animal appear as some huge mountain?

Hyl. All this I grant.

Phil. Can one and the same thing be at the same time in itself of different dimensions?

Hyl. That were absurd to imagine.

Phil. But, from what you have laid down it follows that both the extension by you perceived, and that perceived by the mite itself, as likewise all those perceived by lesser animals, are each of them the true extension of the mite's foot; that is to say, by your own principles, you are led into an absurdity.

Hyl. There seems to be some difficulty in the point.

Phil. Again, have you not acknowledged that no real inherent property of any object can be changed without some change in the thing itself?

Hyl. I have.

Phil. But, as we approach to or recede from an object, the visible extension varies, being at one distance ten or a hundred times greater than at another. Doth it not therefore follow from hence likewise that it is not really inherent in the object?

Hyl. I own I am at a loss what to think.

Phil. Your judgment will soon be determined, if you will venture to think as freely concerning this quality as you have done concerning the rest. Was it not admitted as a good argument, that neither heat nor cold was in the water, because it seemed warm to one hand and cold to the other?

Hyl. It was.

Phil. Is it not the very same reasoning to conclude, there is no extension or figure in an object, because to one eye it shall seem little, smooth, and round, when at the same time it appears to the other, great, uneven, and angular?

Hyl. The very same. But does this latter fact ever happen?

Phil. You may at any time make the experiment, by looking with one eye bare, and with the other through a microscope.

Hyl. I know not how to maintain it, and yet I am loath to give up *extension,* I see so many odd consequences following upon such a concession . . . .

Phil. To help you out, do but consider that if *extension* be once acknowledged to have no existence without the mind, the same must necessarily be granted of motion, solidity, and gravity—since they all evidently suppose extension. It is therefore superfluous to inquire particularly concerning each of them. In denying extension, you have denied them all to have any real existence.

Hyl. I wonder, *Philonous,* if what you say be true, why those philosophers who deny the Secondary Qualities any real existence, should yet attribute it to the Primary. If there is no difference between them, how can this be accounted for?

Phil. It is not my business to account for every opinion of the philosophers. But, among other reasons which may be assigned for this, it seems probably that pleasure and pain being rather annexed to the former than the latter may be one. Heat and cold, tastes and smells, have something more vividly pleasing or disagreeable than the ideas of extension, figure, and motion affect us with. And, it being too visibly absurd to hold that pain or pleasure can be in an unperceiving Substance, men are more easily weaned from believing the external existence of the Secondary than the Primary Qualities. You will be satisfied there is something in this, if you recollect the difference you made between an intense and more moderate degree of heat; allowing the one a real existence, while you denied it to the other. But, after all,

there is no rational ground for that distinction; for, surely an indifferent sensation is as truly *a sensation* as one more pleasing or painful; and consequently should not any more than they be supposed to exist in an unthinking subject . . . .

Hyl. You need say no more on this head. I am free to own, if there be no secret error or oversight in our proceedings hitherto, that all sensible qualities are alike to be denied existence without the mind. But, my fear is that I have been too liberal in my former concessions, or overlooked some fallacy or other. In short, I did not take time to think.

Phil. For that matter, *Hylas,* you may take what time you please in reviewing the progress of our inquiry. You are at liberty to recover any slips you might have made, or offer whatever you have omitted which makes for your first opinion.

Hyl. One great oversight I take to be this— that I did not sufficiently distinguish the *object* from the *sensation.* Now, though this latter may not exist without the mind, yet it will not thence follow that the former cannot.

Phil. What object do you mean? The object of the senses?

Hyl. The same.

Phil. It is then immediately perceived?

Hyl. Right.

Phil. Make me to understand the difference between what is immediately perceived, and a sensation.

Hyl. The sensation I take to be an act of the mind perceiving; besides which, there is something perceived; and this I call the *object.* For example, there is red and yellow on that tulip. But then the act of perceiving those colours is in me only, and not in the tulip.

Phil. What tulip do you speak of? Is it that which you see?

Hyl. The same.

Phil. And what do you see beside colour, figure, and extension?

Hyl. Nothing.

Phil. What you would say then is that the red and yellow are coexistent with the extension; is it not?

Hyl. That is not all; I would say they have a real existence without the mind, in some unthinking substance . . . .

Phil. I see you have no mind to be pressed that way. To return then to your distinction between *sensation* and *object;* if I take you right, you distinguish in every perception two things, the one an action of the mind, the other not.

Hyl. True.

Phil. And this action cannot exist in, or belong to, any unthinking thing; but, whatever beside is implied in a perception may?

Hyl. That is my meaning.

Phil. So that if there was a perception without any act of the mind, it were possible such a perception should exist in an unthinking substance?

Hyl. I grant it. But it is impossible there should be such a perception . . . .

Phil. And yet you asserted that you could not conceive how qualities or accidents should really exist, without conceiving at the same time a material support of them?

Hyl. I did.

Phil. That is to say, when you conceive the real existence of qualities, you do withal conceive something which you cannot conceive?

Hyl. It was wrong I own. But still I fear there is some fallacy or other. Pray what think you of this? It is just come into my head that the ground of all our mistake lies in your treating of each quality by itself. Now, I grant that each quality cannot singly subsist without the mind. Colour cannot without extension, neither can figure without some other sensible quality. But, as the several qualities united or blended together form entire sensible things, nothing hinders why such things may not be supposed to exist without the mind.

Phil. Either, *Hylas,* you are jesting, or have a very bad memory. Though indeed we went through all the qualities by name one after another; yet my arguments, or rather your concessions, nowhere tended to prove that the Secondary Qualities did not subsist each alone by itself; but, that they were not *at all* without the mind. Indeed, in treating of figure and motion we concluded they could not exist without the mind, because it was impossible even in thought to separate them from all secondary qualities, so as to conceive them existing by themselves. But then this was not the only argument made use of upon that occasion. But (to pass by all that hath been

hitherto said, and reckon it for nothing, if you will have it so) I am content to put the whole upon this issue. If you can conceive it possible for any mixture or combination of qualities, or any sensible object whatever, to exist without the mind, then I will grant it actually to be so.

Hyl. If it comes to that the point will soon be decided. What more easy than to conceive a tree or house existing by itself, independent of, and unperceived by, any mind whatsoever? I do at this present time conceive them existing after that manner.

Phil. How say you, *Hylas,* can you see a thing which is at the same time unseen?

Hyl. No, that were a contradiction.

Phil. Is it not as great a contradiction to talk of *conceiving* a thing which is *unconceived?*

Hyl. It is.

Phil. The tree or house therefore which you think of is conceived by you?

Hyl. How should it be otherwise?

Phil. And what is conceived is surely in the mind?

Hyl. Without question, that which is conceived is in the mind.

Phil. How then came you to say, you conceived a house or tree existing independent and out of all minds whatsoever?

Hyl. That was I own an oversight; but stay, let me consider what led me into it.—It is a pleasant mistake enough. As I was thinking of a tree in a solitary place where no one was present to see it, methought that was to conceive a tree as existing unperceived or unthought of—not considering that I myself conceived it all the while. But now I plainly see that all I can do is to frame ideas in my own mind. I may indeed conceive in my own thoughts the idea of a tree, or a house, or a mountain, but that is all. And this is far from proving that I can conceive them *existing out of the minds of all Spirits.*

Phil. You acknowledge then that you cannot possibly conceive how any one corporeal sensible thing should exist otherwise than in a mind?

Hyl. I do . . . .

Phil. You ought not therefore to conclude that sensible objects are without the mind, from their appearance or manner wherein they are perceived.

Hyl. I acknowledge it. But doth not my sense deceive me in those cases?

Phil. By no means. The idea or thing which you immediately perceive, neither sense nor reason informs you that it actually exists without the mind. By sense you only know that you are affected with such certain sensations of light and colours, &c. And these you will not say are without the mind . . . .

Hyl. To speak the truth, *Philonous,* I think there are two kinds of objects:—the one perceived immediately, which are likewise called *ideas;* the other are real things or external objects, perceived by the mediation of ideas, which are their images and representations. Now, I own ideas do not exist without the mind; but the latter sort of objects do. I am sorry I did not think of this distinction sooner; it would probably have cut short your discourse . . . .

Phil. Which are material objects in themselves—perceptible or imperceptible?

Hyl. Properly and immediately nothing can be perceived but ideas. All material things, therefore, are in themselves insensible, and to be perceived only by our ideas.

Phil. Ideas then are sensible, and their archetypes or originals insensible?

Hyl. Right.

Phil. But how can that which is sensible be like that which is insensible? Can a real thing, in itself *invisible,* be like a *colour;* or a real thing, which is not *audible,* be like a *sound?* In a word, can anything be like a sensation or idea, but another sensation or idea? . . .

Hyl. Upon inquiry, I find it is impossible for me to conceive or understand how anything but an idea can be like an idea. And it is most evident that *no idea can exist without the mind.*

Phil. You are therefore, by your principles, forced to deny the reality of sensible things; since you made it to consist in an absolute existence exterior to the mind. That is to say, you are a downright sceptic. So I have gained my point, which was to shew your principles led to Scepticism.

Hyl. For the present I am, if not entirely convinced, at least silenced . . . .

Perception and the Physical World

11. BERKELEY, MATTER, AND THE LIMITS OF KNOWLEDGE

Bertrand Russell

APPEARANCE AND REALITY

Philosophers, though they [may] deny matter as opposed to mind, nevertheless, in another sense, admit matter. [Let us ask] two questions; namely,

From *The Problems of Philosophy* by Bertrand Russell, published by Oxford University Press (1912). Reprinted by permission of Oxford University Press.

(1) Is there a real table at all? (2) If so, what sort of object can it be? . . .

Almost all philosophers seem to be agreed that there is a real table: they almost all agree that, however much our sense-data—colour, shape, smoothness, etc.—may depend upon us, yet their occurrence is a sign of something existing independently of us, something differing, perhaps, completely from our sense-data, and yet to be regarded as causing those sense-data whenever we are in a suitable relation to the real table.

Now obviously this point in which the philosophers are agreed—the view that there *is* a real table, whatever its nature may be—is vitally important, and it will be worth while to consider what reasons there are for accepting this view before we go on to the further question as to the nature of the real table . . . .

Before we go farther it will be well to consider for a moment what it is that we have discovered so far. It has appeared that, if we take any common object of the sort that is supposed to be known by the senses, what the senses *immediately* tell us is not the truth about the object as it is apart from us, but only the truth about certain sense-data which, so far as we can see, depend upon the relations between us and the object. Thus what we directly see and feel is merely 'appearance', which we believe to be a sign of some 'reality' behind. But if the reality is not what appears, have we any means of knowing whether there is any reality at all? And if so, have we any means of finding out what it is like?

Such questions are bewildering, and it is difficult to know that even the strangest hypotheses may not be true. Thus our familiar table, which has roused but the slightest thoughts in us hitherto, has become a problem full of surprising possibilities. The one thing we know about it is that it is not what it seems. Beyond this modest result, so far, we have the most complete liberty of conjecture . . . .

Philosophy, if it cannot *answer* so many questions as we could wish, has at least the power of *asking* questions which increase the interest of the world, and show the strangeness and wonder lying just below the surface even in the commonest things of daily life.

THE EXISTENCE OF MATTER

. . . Before we embark upon doubtful matters, let us try to find some more or less fixed point from which to start. Although we are doubting the physical existence of the table, we are not doubting the existence of the sense-data which made us think

there was a table; we are not doubting that, while we look, a certain colour and shape appear to us, and while we press, a certain sensation of hardness is experienced by us. All this, which is psychological, we are not calling in question. In fact, whatever else may be doubtful, some at least of our immediate experiences seem absolutely certain.

Descartes (1596–1650), the founder of modern philosophy, invented a method which may still be used with profit—the method of systematic doubt. He determined that he would believe nothing which he did not see quite clearly and distinctly to be true. Whatever he could bring himself to doubt, he would doubt, until he saw reason for not doubting it. By applying this method he gradually became convinced that the only existence of which he could be *quite* certain was his own. He imagined a deceitful demon, who presented unreal things to his senses in a perpetual phantasmagoria; it might be very improbable that such a demon existed, but still it was possible, and therefore doubt concerning things perceived by the senses was possible.

But doubt concerning his own existence was not possible, for if he did not exist, no demon could deceive him. If he doubted, he must exist; if he had any experiences whatever, he must exist. Thus his own existence was an absolute certainty to him. 'I think, therefore I am,' he said *(Cogito, ergo sum);* and on the basis of this certainty he set to work to build up again the world of knowledge which his doubt had laid in ruins. By inventing the method of doubt, and by showing that subjective things are the most certain, Descartes performed a great service to philosophy, and one which makes him still useful to all students of the subject.

But some care is needed in using Descartes' argument. '*I* think, therefore *I* am' says rather more than is strictly certain. It might seem as though we were quite sure of being the same person to-day as we were yesterday, and this is no doubt true in some sense. But the real Self is as hard to arrive at as the real table, and does not seem to have that absolute, convincing certainty that belongs to particular experiences. When I look at my table and see a certain brown colour, what is quite certain at once is not '*I* am seeing a brown colour', but rather, 'a brown colour is being seen'. This of course involves something (or somebody) which (or who) sees the brown colour; but it does not of itself involve that more or less permanent person whom we call 'I'. So far as immediate certainty goes, it might be that the something which sees the brown colour is quite momentary, and not the same as the something which has some different experience the next moment . . . .

The problem we have to consider is this: Granted that we are certain of our own sense-data, have we any reason for regarding them as signs of the existence of something else, which we can call the physical object? When we have enumerated all the sense-data which we should naturally regard as connected with the table, have we said all there is to say about the table, or is there still something else—something not a sense-datum, something which persists when we go out of the room? Common sense unhesitatingly answers that there is. What can be bought and sold and pushed about and have a cloth laid on it, and so on, cannot be a *mere* collection of sense-data. If the cloth completely hides the table, we shall derive no sense-data from the table, and therefore, if the table were merely sense-data, it would have ceased to exist, and the cloth would be suspended in empty air, resting, by a miracle, in the place where the table formerly was. This seems plainly absurd; but whoever wishes to become a philosopher must learn not to be frightened by absurdities.

One great reason why it is felt that we must secure a physical object in addition to the sense-data, is that we want the *same* object for different people. When ten people are sitting round a dinner-table, it seems preposterous to maintain that they are not seeing the same tablecloth, the same knives and forks and spoons and glasses. But the sense-data are private to each separate person; what is immediately present to the sight of one is not immediately present to the sight of another: they all see things from slightly different points of view, and therefore see them slightly differently. Thus, if there are to be public neutral objects, which can be in some sense known to many different people, there must be something over and above the private and particular sense-data which appear to various people. What reason, then, have we for believing that there are such public neutral objects?

The first answer that naturally occurs to one is that, although different people may see the table slightly differently, still they all see more or less similar things when they look at the table, and the variations in what they see follow the laws of perspective and reflection of light, so that it is easy to arrive at a permanent object underlying all the different people's sense-data. I bought my table from the former occupant of my room; I could not buy *his* sense-data, which died when he went away, but I could and did buy the confident expectation of more or less similar sense-data. Thus it is the fact that different people have similar sense-data, and that one person in a given place at different times has similar sense-data, which makes us suppose that over and above the sense-data there is a permanent public object which underlies or causes the sense-data of various people at various times . . . .

In one sense it must be admitted that we can never *prove* the existence of things other than ourselves and our experiences. No logical absurdity results from the hypothesis that the world consists of myself and my thoughts and feelings and sensations, and that everything else is mere fancy. In dreams a very complicated world may seem to be present, and yet on waking we find it was a delusion; that is to say, we find that the sense-data in the dream do not appear to have corresponded with such physical objects as we should naturally infer from our sense-data. (It is true that, when the physical world is assumed, it is possible to find physical causes for the sense-data in dreams: a door banging, for instance, may cause us to dream of a naval engagement. But although, in this case, there is a physical *cause* for the sense-data, there is not a physical object *corresponding* to the sense-data in the way in which an actual naval battle would correspond.) There is no logical impossibility in the supposition that the whole of life is a dream, in which we ourselves create all the objects that come before us. But although this is not logically impossible, there is no reason whatever to suppose that it is true; and it is, in fact, a less simple hypothesis, viewed as a means of accounting for the facts of our own life, than the common-sense hypothesis that there really are objects independent of us, whose action on us causes our sensations . . . .

When human beings speak—that is, when we hear certain noises which we associate with ideas, and simultaneously see certain motions of lips and expressions of face—it is very difficult to suppose that what we hear is not the expression of a thought, as we know it would be if we emitted the same sounds. Of course similar things happen in dreams, where we are mistaken as to the existence of other people. But dreams are more or less suggested by what we call waking life, and are capable of being more or less accounted for on scientific principles if we assume that there really is a physical world. Thus every principle of simplicity urges us to adopt the natural view, that there really are objects other than ourselves and our sense-data which have an existence not dependent upon our perceiving them.

Of course it is not by argument that we originally come by our belief in an independent external world. We find this belief ready in ourselves as soon as we begin to reflect: it is what may be called an *instinctive* belief. We should never have been led to question this belief but for the fact that, at any rate in the case of sight, it seems as if the sense-datum itself were instinctively believed to be the independent object, whereas argument shows that the object cannot be identical with the sense-datum. This discovery, however—which is not at all paradoxical in the case of taste and smell and sound, and only slightly so in the case of touch—leaves undiminished our instinctive belief that there *are* objects *corresponding* to our sense-data. Since this belief does not lead to any difficulties, but on the contrary tends to simplify and systematize our account of our experiences, there seems no good reason for rejecting it. We may therefore admit—though with a slight doubt derived from dreams—that the external world does really exist, and is not wholly dependent for its existence upon our continuing to perceive it.

The argument which has led us to this conclusion is doubtless less strong than we could wish, but it is typical of many philosophical arguments, and it is therefore worth while to consider briefly its general character and validity. All knowledge, we find, must be built up upon our instinctive beliefs, and if these are rejected, nothing is left. But among our instinctive beliefs some are much stronger than others, while many have, by habit and association, become entangled with other beliefs, not really instinctive, but falsely supposed to be part of what is believed instinctively.

Philosophy should show us the hierarchy of our instinctive beliefs, beginning with those we hold most strongly, and presenting each as much isolated and as free from irrelevant additions as possible. It should take care to show that, in the form in which they are finally set forth, our instinctive beliefs do not clash, but form a harmonious system. There can never be any reason for rejecting one instinctive belief except that it clashes with others; thus, if they are found to harmonize, the whole system becomes worthy of acceptance.

It is of course *possible* that all or any of our beliefs may be mistaken, and therefore all ought to be held with at least some slight element of doubt. But we cannot have *reason* to reject a belief except on the ground of some other belief. Hence, by organizing our instinctive beliefs and their consequences, by considering which among them is most possible, if necessary, to modify or abandon, we can arrive, on the basis of accepting as our sole data what we instinctively believe, at an orderly systematic organization of our knowledge, in which, though the *possibility* of error remains, its likelihood is diminished by the interrelation of the parts. . . .

THE NATURE OF MATTER

. . . We cannot hope to be acquainted directly with the quality in the physical object which makes it look blue or red. Science tells us that this quality is a certain sort of wave-motion, and this sounds familiar, because we think of wave-motions in the space we see. But the wave-motions must really be in physical space, with which we have no direct acquaintance; thus the real wave-motions have not that familiarity which we might have supposed them to have. And what holds for colours is closely similar to what holds for other sense-data. Thus we find that, although the *relations* of physical objects have all sorts of knowable properties, derived from their correspondence with the relations of sense-data, the physical objects themselves remain unknown in their intrinsic nature, so far at least as can be discovered by means of the senses. The question remains whether there is any other method of discovering the intrinsic nature of physical objects.

The most natural, though not ultimately the most defensible, hypothesis to adopt in the first instance, at any rate as regards visual sense-data, would be that, though physical objects cannot, for the reasons we have been considering, be *exactly* like sense-data, yet they may *be more or less like*. According to this view, physical objects will, for example, really have colours, and we might, by good luck, see an object as of the colour it really is. The colour which an object seems to have at any given moment will in general be very similar, though not quite the same, from many different points of view; we might thus suppose the 'real' colour to be a sort of medium colour, intermediate between the various shades which appear from the different points of view.

Such a theory is perhaps not capable of being definitely refuted, but it can be shown to be groundless. To begin with, it is plain that the colour we see depends only upon the nature of the light-waves that strike the eye, and is therefore modified by the medium intervening between us and the object, as well as by the manner in which light is reflected from the object in the direction of the eye. The intervening air alters colours unless it is perfectly clear, and any strong reflection will alter them completely. Thus the colour we see is a result of the ray as it reaches the eye, and not simply a property of the object from which the ray comes. Hence, also, provided certain waves reach the eye, we shall see a certain colour, whether the object from which the waves start has any colour or not. Thus it is quite gratuitous to suppose that physical objects have colours, and therefore there is no justification for making such a supposition. Exactly similar arguments will apply to other sense-data . . . .

IDEALISM

The word 'idealism' is used by different philosophers in somewhat different senses. We shall understand by it the doctrine that whatever exists, or at any rate whatever can be known to exist, must be in some sense mental. This doctrine, which is very widely held among philosophers, has several forms, and is advocated on several different grounds. The doctrine is so widely held, and so interesting in itself, that even the briefest survey of philosophy must give some account of it.

Those who are unaccustomed to philosophical speculation may be inclined to dismiss such a doctrine as obviously absurd. There is no doubt that common sense regards tables and chairs and the sun and moon and material objects generally as something radically different from minds and the contents of minds, and as having an existence which might continue if minds ceased. We think of matter as having existed long before there were any minds, and it is hard to think of it as a mere product of mental activity. But whether true or false, idealism is not to be dismissed as obviously absurd . . . .

The grounds on which idealism is advocated are generally grounds derived from the theory of knowledge, that is to say, from a discussion of the conditions which things must satisfy in order that we may be able to know them. The first serious attempt to establish idealism on such grounds was that of Bishop Berkeley. He proved first, by arguments which were largely valid, that our sense-data cannot be supposed to have an existence independent of us, but must be, in part at least, 'in' the mind, in the sense that their existence would not continue if there were no seeing or hearing or touching or smelling or tasting. So far, his contention was almost certainly valid, even if some of his arguments were not so. But he went on to argue that sense-data were the only things of whose existence our perceptions could assure us, and that to be known is to be 'in' a mind, and therefore to be mental. Hence he concluded that nothing can ever be known except what is in some mind, and that whatever is known without being in my mind must be in some other mind.

In order to understand his argument, it is necessary to understand his use of the word 'idea'. He gives the name '*idea*' to anything which *is immediately* known, as, for example, sense-data are known. Thus a particular colour which we see is an idea; so is a voice which we hear, and so on. But the term is not wholly confined to sense-data. There will also be things remembered or imagined, for with such things also we have immediate acquaintance at the moment of remembering or imagining. All such immediate data he calls 'ideas'.

He then proceeds to consider common objects, such as a tree, for instance. He shows that all we know immediately when we 'perceive' the tree consists of ideas in his sense of the word, and he argues that there is not the slightest ground for supposing that there is anything real about the tree except what is perceived. Its being, he says, consists in being perceived: in the Latin of the schoolmen its *'esse'* is *'percipi'*. He fully admits that the tree must continue to exist even when we shut our eyes or when no human being is near it. But this continued existence, he says, is due to the fact that God continues to perceive it; the 'real' tree, which corresponds to what we called the physical object, consists of ideas in the mind of God, ideas more or less like those we have when we see the tree, but differing in the fact that they are permanent in God's mind so long as the tree continues to exist. All our perceptions, according to him, consist in a partial participation in God's perceptions, and it is because of this participation that different people see more or less the same tree. Thus apart from minds and their ideas there is nothing in the world, nor is it possible that anything else should ever be known, since whatever is known is necessarily an idea.

There are in this argument a good many fallacies which have been important in the history of philosophy, and which it will be as well to bring to light. In the first place, there is a confusion engendered by the use of the word 'idea'. We think of an idea as essentially something *in* somebody's mind, and thus when we are told that a tree consists entirely of ideas, it is natural to suppose that, if so, the tree must be entirely in minds. But the notion of being 'in' the mind is ambiguous. We speak of bearing a person in mind, not meaning that the person is in our minds, but that a thought of him is in our minds. When a man says that some business he had to arrange went clean out of his mind, he does not mean to imply that the business itself was ever in his mind, but only that a thought of the business was formerly in his mind, but afterwards

ceased to be in his mind. And so when Berkeley says that the tree must be in our minds if we can know it, all that he really has a right to say is that a thought of the tree must be in our minds. To argue that the tree itself must be in our minds is like arguing that a person whom we bear in mind is himself in our minds. This confusion may seem too gross to have been really committed by any competent philosopher, but various attendant circumstances rendered it possible. In order to see how it was possible, we must go more deeply into the question as to the nature of ideas . . . .

Taking the word 'idea' in Berkeley's sense, there are two quite distinct things to be considered whenever an idea is before the mind. There is on the one hand the thing of which we are aware—say the colour of my table—and on the other hand the actual awareness itself, the mental act of apprehending the thing. The mental act is undoubtedly mental, but is there any reason to suppose that the thing apprehended is in any sense mental? Our previous arguments concerning the colour did not prove it to be mental; they only proved that its existence depends upon the relation of our sense organs to the physical object—in our case, the table. That is to say, they proved that a certain colour will exist, in a certain light, if a normal eye is placed at a certain point relatively to the table. They did not prove that the colour is in the mind of the percipient.

Berkeley's view, that obviously the colour *must* be in the mind, seems to depend for its plausibility upon confusing the thing apprehended with the act of apprehension. Either of these might be called an 'idea'; probably either would have been called an idea by Berkeley. The act is undoubtedly in the mind; hence, when we are thinking of the act, we readily assent to the view that ideas must be in the mind . . . . Thus, by an unconscious equivocation, we arrive at the conclusion that whatever we can apprehend must be in our minds. This seems to be the true analysis of Berkeley's argument, and the ultimate fallacy upon which it rests.

This question of the distinction between act and object in our apprehending of things is vitally important, since our whole power of acquiring knowledge is bound up with it. The faculty of being acquainted with things other than itself is the main characteristic of a mind. Acquaintance with objects essentially consists in a relation between the mind and something other than the mind; it is this that constitutes the mind's power of knowing things. If we say that the things known must be in the mind, we are either unduly limiting the mind's power of knowing, or we are uttering a mere tautology. We are uttering a mere tautology if we mean by '*in* the mind' the same as by '*before* the mind', i.e. if we mean merely being apprehended by the mind. But if we mean this, we shall have to admit that what, *in this sense,* is in the mind, may nevertheless be not mental. Thus when we realize the nature of knowledge, Berkeley's argument is seen to be wrong in substance as well as in form, and his grounds for supposing that 'ideas'—i.e. the objects apprehended—must be mental, are found to have no validity whatever. Hence his grounds in favour of idealism may be dismissed. It remains to see whether there are any other grounds . . . .

KNOWLEDGE, ERROR, AND PROBABLE OPINION

. . . There can be no doubt that *some* of our beliefs are erroneous; thus we are led to inquire what certainty we can ever have that such and such a belief is not erroneous. In other words, can we ever *know* anything at all, or do we merely sometimes by good luck believe what is true? Before we can attack this question, we must, however, first decide what we mean by 'knowing', and this question is not so easy as might be supposed . . . .

Knowledge [let us suppose] is what is validly deduced from *known* premisses. This, however, is a circular definition: it assumes that we already know what is meant by 'known premisses'. It can, therefore, at best define one sort of knowledge, the sort we call derivative, as opposed to intuitive knowledge. We may say: '*Derivative* knowledge is what is validly deduced from premisses known intuitively'. In this statement there is no formal defect, but it leaves the definition of *intuitive* knowledge still to seek . . . .

The chief difficulty in regard to knowledge, does not arise over derivative knowledge, but over intuitive knowledge. So long as we are dealing with derivative knowledge, we have the test of intuitive knowledge to fall back upon. But in regard to intuitive beliefs, it is by no means easy to discover any criterion by which to distinguish some as true and others as erroneous. In this question it is scarcely possible to reach any very precise result: all our knowledge of truths is infected with *some* degree of doubt, and a theory which ignored this fact would be plainly wrong. Something may be done, however, to mitigate the difficulties of the question.

Our theory of truth, to begin with, supplies the possibility of distinguishing certain truths as *self-evident* in a sense which ensures infallibility. When a belief is true, we said, there is a corresponding fact, in which the several objects of the belief form a single complex. The belief is said to constitute *knowledge* of this fact, provided it fulfils those further somewhat vague conditions which we have been considering . . . . But in regard to any fact, besides the knowledge constituted by belief, we may also have the kind of knowledge constituted by *perception* (taking this word in its widest possible sense). For example, if you know the hour of the sunset, you can at that hour know the fact that the sun is setting: this is knowledge of the fact by way of knowledge of *truths;* but you can also, if the weather is fine, look to the west and actually see the setting sun: you then know the same fact by the way of knowledge of *things.*

Thus in regard to any complex fact, there are, theoretically, two ways in which it may be known: (1) by means of a judgement, in which its several parts are judged to be related as they are in fact related; (2) by means of *acquaintance* with the complex fact itself, which may (in a large sense) be called perception, though it is by no means confined to objects of the senses. Now it will be observed that the second way of knowing a complex fact, the way of acquaintance, is only possible when there really is such a fact, while the first way, like all judgement, is liable to error . . .

We may say that a truth is self-evident, in the first and most absolute sense, when we have acquaintance with the fact which corresponds to the truth. When Othello believes that Desdemona loves Cassio, the corresponding fact, if his belief were true, would be 'Desdemona's love for Cassio'. This would be a fact with which no one could have acquaintance except Desdemona; hence in the sense of self-evidence that we are considering, the truth that Desdemona loves Cassio (if it were a truth) could only be self-evident to Desdemona. All mental facts, and all facts concerning sense-data, have this same privacy: there is only one person to whom they can be self-evident in our present sense, since there is only one person who can be acquainted with the mental things or the sense-data concerned. Thus no fact about any particular existing thing can be self-evident to more than one person. On the other hand, facts about universals do not have this privacy. Many minds may be acquainted with the same universals; hence a relation between universals may be known by acquaintance to many different people. In all cases where we know by acquaintance a complex fact consisting of certain terms in a certain relation, we say that the truth that these terms are so related has the first or absolute kind of self-evidence, and in these cases the judgement that the terms are so related *must* be true. Thus this sort of self-evidence is an absolute guarantee of truth.

But although this sort of self-evidence is an absolute guarantee of truth, it does not enable us to be *absolutely* certain, in the case of any given judgement, that the judgement in question is true. Suppose we first perceive the sun shining, which is a complex fact, and thence proceed to make the judgement 'the sun is shining'. In passing from the perception to the judgement, it is necessary to analyse the given complex fact: we have to separate out 'the sun' and 'shining' as constituents of the fact. In this process it is possible to commit an error; hence even where a *fact* has the first or absolute kind of self-evidence, a judgement believed to correspond to the fact is not absolutely infallible, because it may not really correspond to the fact. But if it does correspond . . . then it *must* be true.

The second sort of self-evidence will be that which belongs to judgements in the first instance, and is not derived from direct perception of a fact as a single complex whole. This second kind of self-evidence will have degrees, from the very highest degree down to a bare inclination in favour of the belief. Take, for example, the case of a horse trotting away from us along a hard road. At first our certainty that we hear the hoofs is complete; gradually, if we listen intently, there comes a moment when we think perhaps it was imagination or the blind upstairs or our own heartbeats; at last we become doubtful whether there was any noise at all; then we *think* we no longer hear anything, and at last we *know* we no longer hear anything. In this process, there is a continual gradation of self-evidence, from the highest degree to the least, not in the sense-data themselves, but in the judgements based on them . . . .

In derivative knowledge our ultimate premisses must have some degree of self-evidence, and so must their connexion with the conclusions deduced from them. Take for example a piece of reasoning in geometry. It is not enough that the axioms from which we start should be self-evident: it is necessary also that, at each step in the reasoning, the connexion of premiss and conclusion should be self-evident. In difficult reasoning, this connexion has often only a very small degree of self-evidence; hence errors of reasoning are not improbable where the difficulty is great.

From what has been said it is evident that, both as regards intuitive knowledge and as regards derivative knowledge, if we assume that intuitive knowledge is trustworthy in proportion to the degree of its self-evidence, there will be a gradation in trustworthiness, from the existence of noteworthy sense-data and the simpler truths of logic and arithmetic, which may be taken as quite certain, down to judgements which seem only just more probable than their opposites. What we firmly believe, if it is true, is called *knowledge,* provided it is either intuitive or inferred (logically or psychologically) from intuitive knowledge from which it follows logically. What we firmly believe, if it is not true, is called *error.* What we firmly believe, if it is neither knowledge nor error, and also what we believe hesitatingly, because it is, or is derived from, something which has not the highest degree of self-evidence, may be called *probable opinion.* Thus the greater part of what would commonly pass as knowledge is more or less probable opinion . . . .

THE VALUE OF PHILOSOPHY

. . . The value of philosophy is, in fact, to be sought largely in its very uncertainty. The man who has no tincture of philosophy goes through life imprisoned in the prejudices derived from common sense, from the habitual beliefs of his age or his nation, and from convictions which have grown up in his mind without the co-operation or consent of his deliberate reason. To such a man the world tends to become definite, finite, obvious; common objects rouse no questions, and unfamiliar possibilities are contemptuously rejected. As soon as we begin to philosophize, on the contrary, we find, as we saw in our opening chapters, that even the most everyday things lead to problems to which only very incomplete answers can be given. Philosophy, though unable to tell us with certainty what is the true answer to the doubts which it raises, is able to suggest many possibilities which enlarge our thoughts and free them from the tyranny of custom. Thus, while diminishing our feeling of certainty as to what things are, it greatly increases our knowledge as to what they may be; it removes the somewhat arrogant dogmatism of those who have never travelled into the region of liberating doubt, and it keeps alive our sense of wonder by showing familiar things in an unfamiliar aspect.

12. DESCARTES, PERCEPTION, AND THE REAL WORLD
W. A. Sinclair

If I now try to outline to you some alternative theory of knowledge, I shall of course have to do so in terms of that new alternative theory itself, because what I write will not make sense in any other way. At first you will interpret what I write in terms of the old familiar representative view. The consequence is that if I were now to begin a systematic exposition, you would find yourself at once regarding it as either incomprehensible or wrong, for the very good reason that, on the representative theory whose lingering influence still affects you, the new alternative view would not make sense. This constitutes a special disability which makes the study of the theory of knowledge peculiarly difficult. We all suffer from it.

The best and indeed the only way that I can think of to circumvent this very real difficulty is to begin not by a systematic and definitive exposition, but by a discussion intended to do no more than give the reader some first hint of the alternative theory that I have in mind. Thereafter, as we advance, the theory will I hope become by stages progressively clearer.

For this purpose, and in this manner, let us turn our attention once more to our sense-organs. When we consider how they detect things in our environment, the point that at once impresses us is how little they do in fact detect. Consider our eyes. The retinas of the eyes detect light-waves as do the sensitized films in cameras. As the scientists would put it, they react to light-waves, i.e., to electro-magnetic vibrations of a certain range of wave-length. They do not react to other electro-magnetic vibrations which are either longer or shorter in wave-length than light-waves, though otherwise similar; and there are innumerable other such electro-magnetic vibrations all around us at all times.

This is a somewhat surprising fact of which comparatively few people seem to be aware. Take an analogy to make it clearer. Suppose that you are on board ship, and that you lean over the side and

From *An Introduction to Philosophy* by W. A. Sinclair, published by Oxford University Press (1944). Reprinted by permission of Oxford University Press.

look down at the waves. There is not only one sort of wave on the surface of the water, but many sorts. Some of them are very large and very long, the distance from the crest of one wave to the crest of the next being about the length of the ship. If you are in mid-ocean there may even be still longer waves, the deep sea swell, which are so long that you cannot easily pick out the crests by the eye, though you can feel their presence by the slow rise and fall of the whole ship. In addition to those very long waves there are all sorts of smaller waves also, the distance from the crest of one to the crest of the next being a matter of yards or feet. There are also still smaller wavelets chasing each other over the surface of the water hither and thither, some of them so small that the distance from the crest of one to the crest of the next may be only a fraction of an inch. All those different waves, of such widely differing wave-lengths, are passing hither and thither over the surface of the water all the time.

Something very similar to this is happening in the room in which you are now sitting, the waves in this case being electro-magnetic waves such as light-waves and wireless waves. Passing through the room hither and thither at enormous velocities, and passing through your body also, are electro-magnetic waves of innumerable different lengths. Some are very long indeed, so long that the crest of one wave is miles away from the crest of the next. Others are so short that the crest of one is only a most minute fraction of a millimeter away from the next. There are all sorts of others whose lengths fall in between these extremes. They are all there. They are all in the room, i.e., passing through the room, at the instant at which you are reading this.

Some of them, but only a very few of them, are of such a length that they affect your eyes. If an electro-magnetic wave is shorter than about 1/30,000 of an inch, and longer than about 1/60,000 of an inch, then it affects the retina. When waves between these upper and lower limits are reflected by objects and fall on the eye, they cause changes in the retina, and this in turn causes changes in the nerves behind the eye, which in turn cause changes in the brain; after which, in some way we do not understand, we have the experience we call "seeing." For that reason, waves between those upper and lower limits of length are called "visible," or "light-waves."

There are also other electro-magnetic waves passing through the room which are exactly like these, only somewhat longer. They do not affect the retina, but they do affect certain nerve-endings in the skin. They cause nerve-currents to pass along nerves from the skin to the brain, and after these reach the brain we have the experience we call "feeling heat." If somebody thoughtfully provides a hot drink for you at bedtime, then the glass will not be visible if you switch out your bedside light, but you will be able to feel the heat of it on your hand when you bring your hand close to it. This is because the heated liquid is emitting waves of the lengths that affect the heat-sensitive organs in your skin, but is not emitting the very slightly shorter waves which would affect the retinas of your eyes. There are yet other electro-magnetic waves also, which are exactly the same except that they are longer still. They do not affect the body at all. Then there are others even longer, which do not affect the body, but do affect wireless receiving sets. These are called "radio-frequencies" or "wireless waves." We are familiar with the lengths of such waves from reading the dials on any wireless set. All these different waves are round about us at all times, even though our sense-organs fail to detect them. If you had a wireless set beside you at this moment, and were slowly to turn the tuning knob, you would hear one station after the other. All those stations are sending their waves through the room, and through your body, at this moment, but none of them caused any reaction in your body, and you would not have known they were there at all, unless you had used the wireless set to detect them. Your sense-organs themselves do not detect them.

Not only are there in the room around you those waves which you cannot detect because they are longer than those to which your sense-organs react; there are also innumerable other waves which you do not detect because they are shorter than those to which your sense-organs react, such as ultra-violet rays, gamma-rays, and others.

The point of this long string of examples is to emphasize how very small is the range of electro-magnetic waves which are detected by our sense-organs. If the range of wave-lengths known to the scientists were represented by a line from the top to the bottom of this page, then the part of that range that our sense-organs detect—namely light-waves and heat-waves—would be represented by a section of the line too small to see except with a magnifying glass.

So, speaking picturesquely and loosely, our eyes are blind to very nearly all that surrounds us. We can console ourselves for this deficiency by the consideration that it is well that things are so, because otherwise we should no doubt be hopelessly confused. It appears to be only because our eyes are blind to very nearly everything, because they neglect very nearly everything, that we are able to see things around us as we do. If our eyes detected more, we should then no doubt experience only confusion, something analogous to the confusion we experience at present if we listen to an unsatisfactory wireless set which reacts at the same time not only to one wave-length but to neighboring wave-lengths also. This produces a jumble of sounds, with one program on top of another. If our eyes were not blind to all but a very limited range of wave-lengths, we might well have a similar sort of confusion in our visual experience. (The reader will at this point probably inquire what is meant by calling our normal daily experience "orderly" as distinguished from that possible state of confusion. Is there, he may ask, any independent standard of what constitutes confusion, or is what we call "order" only that kind of confusion with which we have grown familiar and with which we are consequently able to cope? This is the kind of question that will or will not appear significant to the reader according to the amount of questioning thought that he has given to the matter. We shall return to this opinion later in a context that will make the point more clear.)

The same considerations apply to hearing, except of course that the waves are waves in air, and not electro-magnetic waves. At the present moment there are air waves of all sorts of wave-lengths passing to and fro in the air of the room you are in. They are falling on the drums of your ears. If these air-waves are longer than about thirty-five feet you cannot hear them. If they are

shorter than about seven-eighths of an inch you cannot hear them. Dogs, as you probably know, can hear sounds that human beings cannot hear, because dogs' ears react to sound-waves shorter than those to which human ears react. Poachers become applied scientists in this connection, for they make whistles which produce air-waves just long enough to make a dog's ears react, but not long enough to make the gamekeeper's ears react.

So, again speaking picturesquely and loosely, our ears are deaf to very nearly everything, just as our eyes are blind to very nearly everything. The same applies to all our other sense-organs. They react to only minute sections of all that surrounds them, and do not react to the vast remainder. In this way they may be said to select for our attention only very minute sections of our environment, very minute sections indeed . . . .

Now, in the light of all this, let us take stock. As a result of thinking along with Berkeley, and as a result of the change in our thinking which he brought about, and as a result of our further cogitation on the points in this chapter, we now find ourselves taking a view which is the opposite of that held by philosophers like Descartes and Locke.

They held that the real world was somewhat dull and uninteresting, and that the secondary qualities, the warmth and color of our daily experience, had no real counterparts, but were merely something added to our own private mental pictures. They thought, indeed, that the richness of our experience was an illusion, and that there existed nothing real corresponding to it.

We now have come to a view which is precisely the opposite, namely that the real world is almost unbelievably rich and complicated, so complicated that we should be confused and bewildered if we experienced anything more than minute and much simplified selections from it. What we experience (that is to say the world as we know it in ordinary day-to-day experience) is only a fragmentary selection of the real world; and we experience such minute selections as we do experience because our sense-organs react to them only, and are blind and deaf and unfeeling to all the vast remainder.

Let us now consider more fully what is involved in the preceding. Suppose—to make a fanciful but not necessarily misleading analogy, though still speaking somewhat loosely—that there is a large aerial fixed up outside your house, with the lead-in coming through the window and the end of the wire lying loose on a table. Let us have some friends in to see you, and let us fall to discussing what program is, as people say, "coming down" the lead-in. Suppose that I have with me a very simple little wireless set of my own. It has no adjustable tuning device, but has fixed tuning, and is so made that it will react to the B.B.C. Home Service wave-length and to no other. It has no loud-speaker, but only earphones, so that I can hear it, while none of the others can. When I pick up the lead-in, and touch the wire against the proper terminal on my little set, I say: "It's the B.B.C. Home Service that is coming down the lead-in," for that is what I hear. In the room there is another friend of yours who also has his own little set. It is exactly like mine, only it is tuned to the B.B.C. Forces Program. He pick up the lead-in, touches it to his set and says: "No, it's the Forces Program." Let us also have an American visitor in the room, with a set tuned to the Boston short-wave station in his own country. He puts the lead-in on to his set, and he says: "No, you are both wrong. The program coming down this lead-in is the program of the Boston short-wave station."

If we three then asked you to explain to us this apparently incomprehensible situation, you could do so quite easily. You would explain to us that these different programs were all of them coming down the lead-in, and that each of us could hear only the one to which he was himself tuned. You would explain that what was coming down the lead-in was in reality extremely complicated, and that the wireless set that each of us was using served to pick out for each of us from that complicated congestion only one particular range of electro-magnetic vibrations. You would explain that each of us was unaware of the other ranges of wave-lengths, because each of us had only his own wireless set, permanently tuned to just one range of wave-lengths. You would add that there were innumerable other ranges of wave-lengths also, such as those radiated by the various Continental stations, by ships and aircraft, and so forth, all of which were coming down the lead-in as well, though nobody in the room detected any of them, because nobody in the room had a set tuned to any of them.

This is somewhat grotesque situation to imagine, but it makes quite a good analogy to explain the situation in which you and I and all men are, in our daily experience. There are surrounding us at this moment what can be described as innumerable electro-magnetic vibrations, of innumerably different wave-lengths, to nearly all of which we are blind, and similarly there are innumerable air-waves of innumerably different wave-lengths, to nearly all of which we are deaf.

Only the most minute sections of them are of the lengths to which our eyes and ears and other sense-organs are tuned, and the experience we call "seeing and hearing and feeling the things around us," is simply the experience that arises from the reaction of our sense-organs to that very minute section, while the vast remainder is neglected. That remainder is all there too, even though our sense-organs do not react to it, much as in our analogy all the programs were, as we say, coming down that lead-in, though we each reacted to and were aware of only one of them, while not reacting to and not being aware of the others . . . .

This line of thought leads to an explanation of that puzzle which we used as a means of starting our inquiry, namely that the men we call color-blind see only one uniform color in two lights, while you and I see two different colors. The fact that a color-blind man sees no difference in two lights which to us look conspicuously different makes us think at first that his eyes must be very unlike ours. Yet, though his eyes are not quite the same as ours, they are not by any means as different from ours as are, say, the eyes of a bee. The color-blind man's difference from people of normal color vision is comparatively small. The explanation of his different experience appears to be as follows.

The waves, or what can be described as the waves, which cause you and me to see what we call red, are longer than the waves that cause us to see what we call green, but only very slightly longer, only by about 1/120,000 of an inch. Our retinas react to the longer waves in a way which is different from the way in which they react to waves 1/120,000 inch shorter, and hence we have different experiences, i.e., we see different colors. The color-blind man's retina is not so discriminating. It reacts in the same way to both sets of waves. Hence he sees only one color, no matter whether it be the longer or the shorter waves that are falling upon his retina. Probably he sees the world around him much as normal people see an etching or a drawing, rather than as they see a colored painting.

To sum up the outcome of this state of our inquiry, it is beginning to appear that we do experience reality directly, yet that different people can have different experiences because, owing to the nature of our sense-organs, we do not experience anything like the whole of reality, but only some astonishingly small scraps of it, there being in some cases different scraps for different people.

We have therefore passed far beyond the theory of Descartes and Locke that the real world is simple, bare and colorless, and that we each add the richness of color and warmth and all the other secondary qualities to the private and largely illusory picture that each of us has in his own mind. Instead, we have now come to the opposite, and incidentally much pleasanter, conclusion that the real world is astonishingly rich and complex, containing genuinely in itself all those interesting qualities which Descartes and Locke believed were illusions. The real world is what I experience it to be. It is also what you experience it to be, and what the next man experiences it to be; and what the color-blind man experiences it to be; and what

animals and insects experience it to be; and a very great deal more also. The reason why we have different experiences is not that each of us has a private and subjective picture, but that each of us picks out and attends to only a part of the immensely rich and complex world in which we find ourselves, and one man's part may not be the same as another man's part.

By this time an alternative theory has begun to emerge, or in other words an alternative way of looking upon the question of the nature of knowledge is becoming possible. It must, however, be specifically noted that this alternative theory is no more than suggested; and, further, that the argument by which it has been suggested cannot be used as a proof, because the means I have used to suggest it is observation of the working of our sense-organs, and our sense-organs are themselves observed by us in precisely the same way as are tables and chairs, and are subject to the same qualifications. Whatsoever the conclusions that we come to about tables and chairs and how we know them, we must hold the same conclusions about our sense-organs themselves and about the way we know them. We must not fall into the capacious trap, into which so many amateur philosophers fall, of thinking that we can produce a theory of knowledge by arguing from the working of the sense-organs, and forgetting that in so doing they may have contradicted the suppositions underlying the view they take of our knowledge of those quite material objects, namely our own sense-organs, on which the new alleged theory is based.

SUGGESTIONS FOR FURTHER READING

GENERAL DISCUSSIONS OF THE PROBLEM OF KNOWLEDGE

Ayer, A. J. *The Problem of Knowledge.* New York: St. Martin's Press, 1956.

Chisholm, R. M. *Theory of Knowledge.* Englewood Cliffs, N.J.: Prentice-Hall, 1956.

Danto, A. C. *Analytical Philosophy of Knowledge.* Cambridge: Cambridge University Press, 1968.

ANTHOLOGIES ON PERCEPTION AND THE THEORY OF KNOWLEDGE

Canfield, J. V., and Franklin H. Donnell, eds. *Readings in the Theory of Knowledge.* New York: Appleton Century Crofts, 1964.

Chisholm, R. M., and R. J. Swartz, eds. *Empirical Knowledge: Readings from Contemporary Sources.* Englewood Cliffs, N.J.: Prentice-Hall, 1973.

Hirst, R. J., ed. *Perception and the External World.* New York: The Macmillan Co., 1965.

Nagel, E., and R. Brandt. *Meaning and Knowledge.* New York: Harcourt, Brace & World, 1965.

Swartz, R. J., ed. *Perceiving, Sensing, and Knowing.* Garden City, N.Y.: Doubleday & Co., 1965.

ADDITIONAL CLASSICAL WRITINGS IN EPISTEMOLOGY

Aristotle. *De Anima.*

Berkeley, George. *The Principles of Human Knowledge.*

Descartes, René. *Discourse on the Method.*

Hume, David. *An Inquiry Concerning Human Understanding.*

Locke, John. *Essay Concerning Human Understanding.*

Plato. *Phaedo, Republic,* and *Theaetetus.*

PERCEPTION

Ayer, A. J. *The Foundations of Empirical Knowledge.* London: Macmillan & Co. Ltd., 1953.

Chisholm, R. M. *Perceiving: A Philosophical Study.* Ithaca, N.Y.: Cornell University Press, 1956.

Hirst, R. J. *The Problems of Perception.* London: George Allen & Unwin, Ltd., 1959.

Locke, D. *Perception and Our Knowledge of the External World.* New York: Humanities Press, 1967.

Mundle, C. W. K. *Perception: Facts and Theories.* Oxford: Oxford University Press, 1971.

Pitcher, George. *A Theory of Perception.* Princeton: Princeton University Press, 1971.

Chapter 3   What Is a Human Being?

There is no question more fundamental to philosophy than the one posed by the title of this chapter. No portion of this book and virtually no philosophy whatsoever is untouched by an answer to this question. Theories about the meaning of life, the sanctity of life, the nature of the mind, proper sexual behavior, the equality of persons, social freedom, and religious belief are all rooted in a particular view of the nature of human beings. Yet there are many competing theories about human nature, and at least some of them are mutually inconsistent. A familiar view espoused by many people raised in Anglo-American culture is the religious theory that God created human beings in His own image, while at the same time including a definite plan for each human life. Yet, as we shall see, other accounts contrast sharply with this one. For example, Darwin sees us as the product of the competitive forces of nature; Marx regards us as dominantly the product of social forces; and existentialists see us as dominantly the products of our own choosing. There may, of course, be some truth in each of these accounts. But in this chapter each view is expressed in sufficiently strong terms by its proponents that it is probably impossible to cling to all seven views as expressing true (though limited) insights into the human condition. We have little choice but to become philosophers on our own in order to decide between these rival theories whenever they stand irresolvably opposed.

The theories included in this chapter were chosen because of their paramount importance for philosophy, psychology, and the history of ideas. In many cases these views are also important because of the major roles they play in our social, political, and religious practices. Marxism and certain religious views so dominate the lives of some individuals and even whole societies that they can only be described as the controlling influence. Also, some of these theories have dramatically altered past human convictions about the place of man in the universe. Darwin's view, for example, revolutionized biology and our general view of human history. Moreover, some of the theories we shall encounter contain whole programs for what should be done to improve the human condition. For this reason the question "What is a human being?" is treated in this chapter as having two dimensions: The first asks for a description of human nature, and the second asks for an evaluative theory of ethical, social, and political changes that would (because of human nature) improve the human condition. The readings in some sections reflect only one of these two purposes, but in some cases the two kinds of questions are bound together throughout a single reading. In still other cases a single influential figure has developed the theory virtually unaided by others. In these instances that individual's views alone will be outlined in this introduction. Occasionally several authors have made major contributions to a way of reasoning about humankind, and in these instances the general views of this group of thinkers will be outlined.

THE RELIGIOUS VIEW

The religious view of human beings in Western culture is so familiar to most of us that its main features are obvious. Yet there is considerable disagreement even among religious believers as to the central doctrines about humankind and as to the proper source of their derivation. It would be impossible here to arbitrate these disputes, but we can at least set forth the convictions which are central to any belief about humans which can fairly be called "religious."

The most basic conviction is that God plays some crucial role in the creation of human beings. God is said to create us for a special role in the order of creation. We usually are held to have been created in the image of God and to have been given a position of dominance over the rest of creation. The capacities of appreciating and loving God are also attributed to humans as direct results of the creation, and this gift further distinguishes us from the lower animals. An extended version of this view is that God created human beings in order that they might interact in ways impossible for other animals. We fulfill this purpose by maintaining a relation of fellowship with God. The idea that a special relation to God exists which is not shared by any other creature is central to virtually all religions. However, there are substantial disputes concerning the nature of this special relationship.

Consider, for example, the distinct religious views of human beings presented in the Christian religion and the Jewish religion. The Christian view is roughly composed of four theses about the nature and destiny of humankind, derived from the Bible: (1) Humans as Created in God's Image, (2) Humans as Sinners, (3) Humans as Redeemed, and (4) Humans as Immortal. The first doctrine rests on the creation account just outlined. The second includes not only the traditional theory that humans inevitably fall from innocence and perform acts of evil, but that humans were created as free, rational, spiritual beings capable of choosing between good and evil. The third doctrine asserts that despite a sinful nature, humans are redeemed through the agency of Christ, who removes the causes of sin and guilt and seeks to restore to wholeness even the most wicked persons. The Jewish view is similar but with less emphasis placed on humans as sinners and none at all on the agency of Christ.

The main contrasting differences between Christian and Jewish views perhaps comes in what might be called the "worthless" aspect of humankind. In the Christian tradition our *sinfulness* constitutes our "worthless" dimension, whereas in the Jewish tradition our *lowly origin* and eventual descent into dust constitutes worthlessness (though "humankind's iniquities" play an important role in Jewish thought). Nonetheless, it is obvious that there is significant agreement between these two religious outlooks. They agree completely, for example, on the creational account of the superior character of our position over the beasts, as provided in the Old Testament. They also seem to agree in attributing immortality to the human soul as a way of distinguishing us from other animals.

In the initial reading in this chapter W. E. Hocking and John H. Randall, Jr. provide an interpretation of the religious approach. In the first half of their selection—written by Hocking—it is argued that human beings are to be distinguished from other animals by their interest in studying their own uniqueness, by certain distinguishing biological and psychological features of the human animal, by their use of abstract concepts, by being the only animal that reflects on the nature and the meaning of the universe, and by the practice of religion. In the second half of the article—written by Randall—it is maintained that historically "religion has been primarily an organization of man's emotions and conduct." According to this view, religious reactions to the "important concerns of life" generate an entire framework for the conduct of life. Human existence is said in religious traditions to be proper if it conforms to such religious ideals, and improper if it does not.

THE MARXIST VIEW

We turn now to a philosophy which stands in sharp contrast to religious views. This philosophy originated in the nineteenth century with the work of Karl Marx, a committed atheist. Marx argued that social arrangements, not God, make us what we are. Marx did not specifically intend to write a *philosophy* of humankind. Instead, he regarded his work as a scientific and historical study of humans and society. However, part of Marx's work is now generally regarded as philosophical; and without question he and his collaborator Friedrich Engels provide a distinctive philosophical view of human beings. This view is developed within the framework of their "historical materialism," according to which human belief and behavior are determined by "the material conditions of life" (most notably the economic modes of production needed to sustain existence). That is, Marx thinks the only way to understand humans is to examine the social conditions which lead to their beliefs and behavior—rather than by studying the beliefs and behavior themselves. Some of the reasons for choosing the terms "historical" and "materialism" are found in Marx's intent to write a scientific history and in his rejection of supernatural explanations of man given by religion. Marx wanted his account to be confirmable by valid historical methods, and he therefore wished to avoid all reliance on speculative claims. Additionally, his account is materialistic in that the material conditions of life determine human values and social arrangements.*

Marx's phrase "the material conditions of life" is intended to cover both the social forces leading to economic productivity and the actual means of production. Marx sees society as having a single *primary* activity: production. There are other secondary activities, such as political and legal "superstructures," as Marx refers to them. There are also religious beliefs, moral beliefs, and other "ideologies," as Marx refers to all such schemes of justification. He sees these ideologically controlled activities as secondary, because he believes they are rooted in and determined by the productive forces and economic character of society. Marx even thinks one can only understand the differences between different societies in terms of the different environments and schemes of production. For example, production and work depend, on the one hand, on such factors as soil and energy resources, and, on the other hand, on economic schemes such as capitalism and communism. As these factors vary, Marx thought, so do the character of a society and the beliefs of its members. From this beginning, he develops his well-known theories that the

---

* Marx's use of "materialism" is this context is not to be confused with the section on materialism later in this chapter. Marx did not use the term "materialism" either to mean *metaphysical* materialism (nothing exists except matter) or to mean *motivational* materialism (humans are motivated solely out of their desire for material gain).

main source of power in any society belongs to those who control the means of production, that workers are exploited under capitalism by having their labor drained off to the rich, that this exploitation alienates them from their work, and that the major reason for political revolution is to destroy exploitative economic institutions, such as capitalism.

Marx's view of how humans are to be distinguished from other animals also derives directly from his theory of historical materialism. He argues that what most distinguishes humans from the other beasts is the technology of production. More than anything else it is toolmaking that distinguishes the human creature. Marx no doubt was aware that many animals use various tools to build dams, break open food, etc.; but these primitive animal devices do not constitute what he means by "production." They lead only to shelter or a meal, not to some other commodity by which life can be improved and by which still other tools can be produced. Human beings, by contrast, have a capacity for using what they produce to produce something else, while supposedly improving the conditions of life. This thesis fits comfortably with Marx's view that the primary human *social* activity is economic production, as created by the work of laborers. In today's industrialized society this theory strikes some people as obviously true, and others as obviously false. However, in Marx's own time it was an exciting and innovative thesis. Everywhere Marx saw previously unanticipated technologies changing individual lives and even whole societies. There can be no doubt that his enthusiasm for explaining the nature of humankind in terms of productive forces was motivated by his knowledge of history and how he saw it being modified in his own time.

The selections in this section of the chapter are taken from two different writings by Marx and Engels. Each selection develops from a different perspective the view that "the real nature of man is the totality of social relations," as Marx once put it (in his 1845 thesis on Feuerbach). In the first reading Marx explains how he came to his conviction that all relations in the political state are determined by the material conditions of life. In this short article Marx provides perhaps his clearest account of the meaning of this now famous expression and also explains its broader importance for his social and political philosophy. In the second selection the Marxist view of human beings is related to a communist vision of past and future society. This selection, which is taken from the *Communist Manifesto,* differentiates capitalist society and communist society, as Marxists see the differences. The central argument is that society under capitalist domination has been merely a "history of class struggles" between the bourgeois class (which controls the means of production) and the proletarian or "working" class. Several themes about the nature of humankind in the previous selection are reiterated in order to show that a communist-controlled state can best eliminate conditions which suppress laborers, while freeing them from the control of the bourgeois class. It is important to notice, throughout these arguments, that Marx is opposed to private property only in the sense of "the means of industrial production." He does not oppose private ownership of clothes, rugs, etc.

THE DARWINIAN VIEW

Charles Darwin was a British biologist and virtual contemporary of Marx. Darwin's views about human evolution significantly altered scientific, philosophical, and even religious views of the nature of human beings. His two best known works are *The Origin of Species* (1859) and *The Descent of Man* (1871). In these works Darwin establishes beyond scientific doubt that all living species, including humans, have developed from simple life forms through a long chain of modification and adaptation to the environment. It is difficult for us, only a century later, to appreciate the revolutionary character of Darwin's achievement. He himself began his career convinced by the orthodox religious beliefs that species in the environment were fixed and that humans had origins as depicted in the Biblical account. It was only through his own perceptive scientific observations that Darwin began to speculate otherwise.

Darwin's theory of natural selection is the key to his understanding of human beings. This theory begins with the premise that some animals are equipped with advantageous properties not possessed by other animals. These favorable features are ones which can be transmitted to the offspring of the species. Since in most environments species tend to overproduce to the point that the environment cannot support all the offspring of all species, those with the most favorable characteristics will win out in the struggle for available resources and eventually for the survival of the species itself. The more favorable the variations which occur, the more strengthened the species will be, relative to other species. Of course, the environment itself can change, and those species that best adapt by appropriate changes will again win out in the struggle. According to Darwin, there is continuous evolutionary change and adaptation, during which the species itself is altered. One of the more counterintuitive aspects of the theory is his view that chance variations occur in nature, and hence that there is no necessary direction of development. It was some while before these and other views were accepted by biologists, because it was difficult to show that chance variations which occur in nature can be inherited. Darwin eventually did prove heritability, though he admitted that the causes and laws controlling variation and inheritance were themselves unknown.

In *The Origin of Species* Darwin avoided all application of his theory to human evolution because he realized there would be strong adverse public reaction. Darwin never did claim that he could pinpoint the single ancestral origins of both humans and apes, though he did try to trace a general line of descent from a primitive ape "low in the mammalian series." Of greater interest to us here are Darwin's discussions in his later work of similarities in mental ability between humans and apes. Biologists prior to Darwin, including Lamarck, had argued that despite the great anatomical similarity between humans and apes, humans are distinguished by their possession of reason and speech. Darwin apparently set out to undermine this notion that there is any substantial difference between apes and humans in these respects, even if humans might have a superior capacity. In the selection by Darwin in this chapter he argues that despite "enormous differences" in *degree* of "mental

power" between humans and apes, there is no fundamental difference in *kind* between humans and the rest of animal nature. He argues that other animals are highly intelligent, similar in emotional response, and even use systems of communication similar to human language. Moreover, according to Darwin, there is a much greater gap in the intelligence level of, for example, apes and marine life than there is between apes and humans. The effect of Darwin's argument is to place humans in the broad context of animal life, where there are "numberless gradations" of mental and physical ability between the different species. In one revealing sentence Darwin states a view underlying much of his argument: ". . . it is a pure assumption to assert that the mental act is not essentially of the same nature in the animal as in the man." Darwin goes on to argue that *if* there is a single major difference between a human being and a beast, the most likely candidate is the human's moral sense (conscience), which Darwin describes as "the most noble of all the attributes of man."

In a second reading in this section, the zoologist Desmond Morris argues that humans are just one of the 193 living species of monkeys and apes. Humans are distinguished by being almost completely hairless, by having the biggest brain and the largest penis, by their two-legged form of locomotion, and by having a slightly different genetic structure—but Morris, like Darwin, sees these strictly as differences of degree, not of kind. So far as Morris is concerned, man is little more than a "naked ape" with an interesting history, a complex civilization, and the most active sexual life of all the primates.

Darwin's views about human evolution were regarded in his own time as a challenge to religious views of humankind. There certainly seems to be some substance to this belief, since most religions regard human beings as the unique creation of God, whereas Darwin's views seem to undermine this claim. The Darwinian view is not merely that humans are continuous with the animal world and thus subject to all the same biological laws. It is, more radically, that whatever moral, physical, and mental qualities humans possess evolved through precisely the same gradual series of processes that occur elsewhere in nature. The faculties of reason and speech are thus no different in their origin than are the tooth of the snake, the fin of the fish, and the beak of the buzzard. Because of this explanation of the origin and place of human beings in nature, Darwinism has frequently been proclaimed the enemy of the religious view of humankind. This view has been expressed by Darwinians and clergy alike —though, of course, not by all clergy or by all Darwinians. Religious Darwinians sometimes argue that God designed the laws of nature (including Darwin's laws) and that the survival of the fit indicates that the fittest creatures were divinely aided in their development. It is sometimes additionally argued that humans can be unique even if emergent from the evolutionary process. Accordingly, it remains a matter of controversy whether religious views of human beings are compatible with Darwinian views.

THE LANGUAGE-USER VIEW

An ancient view in philosophy, apparently first propounded by Aristotle, is that human beings are rational animals. Aristotle noticed that it is a part of the nature of humans to form political groups, from which he inferred that humans are "political animals." But this property is obviously not very distinguishing, since ants, bees, and other creatures in nature form themselves into organized social units. Accordingly, Aristotle distinguished humans from the other groups on the basis of rationality. It is not entirely clear in his philosophy what rationality consists of, over and above superior intelligence. However, through the centuries (e.g., in the philosophy of Descartes), Aristotle's idea that humans are set apart from the beasts by their rationality has come to be intimately associated with the view that the ability to use language is the distinctive property of humans. (Language is understood to be, at a minimum, an organized system of symbols which have a common meaning understood by those who employ the linguistic system.) We have just discussed Darwin's challenge to this view, but we shall now see that those who espouse the "language-user view" do not follow Darwin on this point. The idea that language itself affords an insight into the nature of human beings had widespread appeal in nineteenth-century Europe, and it has continued to

appeal to some recent European philosophers (such as Heidegger and Merleau-Ponty). But in the English-speaking world only the German-American philosopher Ernst Cassirer has achieved notoriety through this approach. His admirer and translator Susanne Langer gave expression to Cassirer's views in several of her books, which also had an effect on contemporary philosophy. In this chapter these two philosophers represent this ancient tradition, deriving from Aristotle.

Cassirer argues that it is the ability of human beings to employ symbolic language that enables them to live in a "new dimension of reality" different from that of all other forms of life. The ability to symbolize is understood by Cassirer as the ability to understand that a linguistic sign signifies or points to something other than itself in an "imaginative and intelligent" way. Cassirer illustrates his point by reference to the famous story of Helen Keller, who overcame severe limitations as a blind deaf-mute by learning that words are to be used as "names" of objects. The crucial thing she learned, according to Cassirer, is that words are instruments of thought. So long as she saw words in terms of fixed associations, she could only react at a primitive level to a word—just as a dog reacts to a command. Mechanical association is characteristic of animals, according to Cassirer, while the free use of symbols is reserved for human persons. Cassirer draws strong conclusions from his proposals. He contends that human symbols do not simply mirror the world about us. They actually create the world as we experience it. Thus the symbolic forms of science create the scientific world, artistic symbols create the world of art, and mythical "pictures" create the worlds of myth and religion. From this perspective Cassirer reaches the general conclusion that human culture is essentially reducible to its variety of symbols. That is, our different symbolic worlds in the realms of art, religion, science, and so on, jointly constitute culture.

Some recent work in psychology which explores the linguistic abilities of monkeys has interesting implications for Cassirer's claims. It now appears that some monkeys can use a limited range of symbols in order to communicate with humans. While they cannot grasp the wide variety of symbols used by humans, they do seem to have the capacity for *symbolic* representation. They understand, perhaps as Helen Keller did during her initial insight, that signs signify something else and can be *used* in various ways. If this ability is one that monkeys genuinely possess, then Cassirer's theory might have to be modified so that symbolic activity is not characteristic of humans per se, but only of a very limited set of intelligent creatures in nature. (Cassirer would agree if animals were shown capable of what he calls "propositional language.") Such a modification would place Cassirer's views closer to Darwin's than they now are. However, without this modification, Cassirer seems partially opposed to Darwin, since one of the basic views advanced by Darwin is that humans are similar in most every respect to animals (due to continuity in nature). Cassirer, on the other hand, takes the view that there is a sharp discontinuity between humans and beasts, and that this discontinuity occurs precisely because of the human being's distinctive symbolic capacity. As Langer bluntly puts it, "the line between man and beast—between the highest ape and the lowest savage—is the language line."

THE MATERIALIST VIEW

Materialism is a term used to refer to a broad spectrum of philosophical doctrines which give a primary place in the universe to matter and which attribute a secondary, dependent place to mind—or perhaps no place at all to mind. A *material thing* is to be understood as something which has only physical properties such as size, shape, solidity, and hardness. Since such items as consciousness, purpose, and dreams do not seem to be physical, the materialist must either explain how they are physical or, at the very least, how they are derived from the physical. The theme most consistently unifying materialists of different types is that humans and everything else in nature must be explained in terms of causal laws based exclusively on observations of matter and motion. This approach to the study of humankind has been embraced with special enthusiasm in the physical sciences. It is the desire to provide a comprehensive, unified, and scientifically acceptable account of nature and the human being's place in it that continues to motivate philosophers to embrace materialism.

The first reading in this section of the chapter is by the English biologist, T. H. Huxley. He was one of Darwin's closest personal friends, and was especially fond of defending Darwin against clergymen who attacked the theory of evolution. Moreover, Huxley began explicit comparison of humans with the anthropoid apes even before Darwin, and he zealously pursued antievolutionists with challenges of public debate. However, in the present chapter Huxley represents materialism. Clearly these two views of humankind are not inconsistent, and Huxley strongly embraced both. As a biologist Huxley believes that animal and human bodies are best understood as purely mechanical physical systems. Yet he is aware that states of consciousness do not appear themselves to be physical, and he sets himself the task of discovering the *relation* between the mechanical body and the mind. Huxley never argues that the mind *is* the body (the so-called identity theory), but he does contend that the mind is entirely controlled by the body. Molecular changes in the brain, in his view, directly cause all states of consciousness. However, he does not believe that the reverse holds; i.e., he does not think the mind directly causes changes in the body. It is for this reason that Huxley repeatedly propounds the general thesis that human and beast alike are automata entirely controlled by the forces of the physical world (even if their minds are not identified with material bodies). Huxley at one point likens animal and human minds to the bell of an alarm clock: the alarm sounds only when the mechanical controls inside the clock direct it to sound. While Huxley freely admitted that we do not know all the causal means whereby the brain controls the mind, he thought any other belief inconsistent with basic facts about biology which apply to all species.

The materialism espoused by Huxley led him not only to determinism, but also to atheism, and thence to a strong denunciation of the religious view of human beings. He became a polemicist against organized religion, largely because of official church teachings about the nature of humankind. He wrote treatises against the creation accounts and in favor of the Darwinian view, and he attacked religious beliefs such as the immortality of the soul. Although materialism is not, strictly speaking, inconsistent with religious belief, it is fair to say that Huxley became the most famous atheist of the nineteenth century *because* of his materialism.

THE BEHAVIORIST VIEW

Behaviorism is the view that human beings can profitably be studied only by a rigorous scientific examination of human behavior. A radical behaviorist is one who believes—quite paradoxically—that humans are nothing but the entire range of their behavior. However, it has proven difficult to specify precisely what is meant by a "behavior," and as a result there are many different types of behaviorism. In the section on behaviorism in this chapter we shall be exclusively concerned with the work of B. F. Skinner. He is the best-known behaviorist of recent times and is probably the only one to develop a comprehensive behaviorist account of the nature of human beings and society.

Skinner defends the view that a "behavior" is some movement of an organism where the causes of the movement are other than physiological. He understands behavior in this way because he is interested in causes which substantially contribute to making us individual entities. He finds it somewhat uninteresting that we all have genes, muscles, and internal organs which affect our responses to stimuli. All normal persons are, after all, are physically similar and therefore react similarly on a physiological level. What makes us interestingly different is our different individual behaviors, which Skinner believes are the inevitable results of the different environments in which we are raised. This notion of environmental control is at the heart of Skinner's thought about human beings. As a psychologist he sets out to determine through precise experimental means how behavior is controlled by exposure to an environment. Like all behaviorists who have approached the study of humans in this way, Skinner accepts three basic premises: (1) behavior is far more important for the study of humans than consciousness, because only behavior can be precisely measured and controlled in an experimental way (while consciousness is scientifically unobservable); (2) environmental influences control us more than does heredity; and

(3) scientific laws can be discovered which relate environmental causes to the control of human behavior. It is from roughly these three points of psychological method that Skinner generalizes to a philosophical theory of human beings.

Skinner's program begins with a rejection of the other ways of studying humans which are considered in this chapter. He rejects religious views and existential views—to mention two theories—because they postulate unobservable entities such as free will and God. Even purely physiological reactions he believes are traceable to the environment which originally nourished and encouraged them. At any rate, he thinks all important human behavior is strictly controlled or conditioned by what he calls environmental *variables* (determinants). For example, dogs are conditioned by patient masters to sit and shake hands, and humans are similarly conditioned by driving instructors to hit the brake pedal of an automobile at the first sign of danger. It may be that humans learn faster than most animals, but according to Skinner everything we learn, and every response we form, is similarly the result of conditioning (analogous to the way we learn to drive an automobile). The key to Skinner's idea is that certain kinds of behavior are *reinforced,* and this reinforcement encourages us to repeat the behavior. Thus any animal or human will be conditioned to cultivate a response by a reinforcing environment, and such environments can be arranged so that a reinforcer is available whenever a piece of "desirable" behavior occurs. We presume this theory frequently with dogs, for we give them bones or enthusiastically pat them when they do what we want. Skinner thinks humans are no different: we behave strictly in accordance with the way we are reinforced.

Skinner's approach has had dramatic success in dealing with some areas of human learning, especially with difficult subjects such as the mentally retarded and others who are institutionalized. This success has prompted Skinner to the belief that behaviorism will eventually explain all human behavior, including even institutions such as government, religion, economics, and language. For this reason Skinner is convinced that we can and ought to introduce strong measures of social control, rather than leaving the formation of societies to individual desire. He is further convinced that behavioral psychology can tell us what controls should be instituted for reform and which reinforcers are the most powerful inducements to change. He argues that we will have to give up such outdated and illusory notions as "human freedom and dignity" (which have no place in a scientific psychology), but he thinks this price a small one to pay for a more satisfying life. He outlines both his practical views and his more theoretical claims about the nature of human beings in this chapter. The selection by Skinner is excerpted from his book, *Beyond Freedom and Dignity,* where he develops a popular account of his theory of behaviorism as a technology applicable equally to animals and humans.

THE EXISTENTIALIST VIEW

The philosophy known as existentialism has roots in the nineteenth century, but its major writings have all appeared in the twentieth century. Existentialists prefer to approach the question "What is a human being?" by asking what it means to exist as a human being. They seek the uniquely human condition, as contrasted with the kind of existence which characterizes non-human objects. The typical existentialist approach is reflected in the slogan "existence precedes essence." Unravelling this saying is the key to understanding existentialism, especially in the work of Jean-Paul Sartre. We must first, then, come to grips with the meaning he gives to this expression.

It is an ancient view in philosophy that the essence of a thing is that set of properties which makes it the *kind* of thing it is. These properties are ones objects cannot lose without becoming different objects and different kinds of things. The essence of the cherry tree, for example, consists in its limb structure, root structure, genetic make-up, and the blossom it puts forth at a certain time of the year. If a cherry tree is chopped down and cut up for firewood it is no longer the *tree* it was, and is not a *cherry tree* at all. It has lost its essence as a cherry tree. Of course not every property exhibited by a tree is an essential property. Its color, for example, could be different and it would still be the same tree. Its essence does not change simply because it

is stained. However—and this is the important point—if we could specify all the essential properties of the cherry tree (its full essence), then we would understand what it means for something to exist as a cherry tree. We would be understanding its existence through an understanding of its essence.

Many philosophers—indeed most of those previously discussed—believe that the essence of human beings can be stated in a way analogous to the specification of the essence of the cherry tree. Properties such as being a symbol-user, as we have seen, are put forward as essential to humans. Existentialists contend, however, that there is *no* essential property which characterizes human beings, and therefore "human nature" cannot be understood in the way the natures of other things are understood. This particular view is advanced in some existentialist writings (e.g. by Ortega y Gasset), where it is said that humans have no nature, but only a history. This means that human beings *make* their lives through their own capacity to control and shape their existence. Trees and stones have no such capacity, and by contrast—as Ortega paradoxically expresses it—a human is "an entity whose being consists not in what it is already, but in what it is not yet, a being that consists in not-yet-being. . . . Man is the entity that makes itself." Accordingly, to say that existence precedes essence for humans is to say that whatever important "defining" properties are exhibited by them are the products of their own free choice.

According to Sartre, such choice is made through the human capacity for absolutely unrestrained freedom. Since there is a complete lack of fixed, determinate properties in human nature, Sartre reasons that humans are not simply free; rather, "man *is* freedom." By this seemingly exaggerated equation Sartre means that human reality cannot be understood except in terms of human acts of free will. It would be paradoxical, but nonetheless correct, to say that for Sartre the only essential property of humans is their free will. Humans are not first unfree entities that later somehow find freedom. Rather, as Sartre puts it, "the being of man" is his "being free." This doctrine also implies—and very importantly for all existentialists—that there are no objective moral laws or standards which humans must observe, except those of their own choosing. We create our own moral and political situation. Whatever we become, then, is a matter of our own choosing; and we are responsible for whatever properties we possess, precisely because they are the products of our choice and not the products of nature or of someone else's choice. We are thus left without excuse for what we are. In sum, Sartre's ultimate answer to the question "What is a human being?" is that to be human is to make one's own essence through freedom and to assume responsibility for what is created.

Sartre also stresses the importance of atheism for a philosophy of human beings. His views on this matter set him radically apart from the opening readings in this chapter on the religious view of humans. Sartre closely relates his anti-theistic views to the slogan "existence precedes essence." He believes that the religious view of human creation entails that God fashions the essence of humans (as an idea in God's mind) prior to the actual existence of humans. One main reason why Sartre argues against theism is to show that there can be no essence of human beings because there is no God to have a prior conception of them. Hence, Sartre repeatedly calls for an anti-theistic *humanism* as the only viable ethical and social philosophy.

PHILOSOPHICAL IMPLICATIONS OF THESE THEORIES

Thus far the seven theories we have surveyed have largely been approached as answers to the question, "What is a human being?" It is important to observe that the acceptance of some of these views implies the acceptance of views on related but different philosophical problems. Many such problems might be mentioned, but three deserve special notice.

METAPHYSICAL IMPLICATIONS

Views about human nature often carry with them views about the ultimate nature of the universe. That is, such views present a general theory of all reality, not simply of the world of human reality. For example, the materialist view asserts that nothing but matter (and motion) exists; everything

whatsoever is composed of material particles. By contrast, religious views imply that much more than mere matter exists; and their creation accounts usually specify what they take to be the ultimate nature of things. Other theories that we have encountered do not, strictly speaking, provide a framework from which the animal world and perhaps all of nature is to be understood. Thus the behaviorist view, and also the Darwinian view, provide a perspective from which to understand in a fairly unified way the behavior of all creatures in the animal world. Some of these views sharply conflict with the metaphysical perspective of one or more of the other views. Darwin's theory of evolution, for example, has had an enormous impact on certain religious beliefs about the creation of the world. It is a matter of continuing controversy whether these two views are inconsistent, but no doubt a great many people believe they are. In still other cases it is certain that one view entails a denial of another's metaphysical view. Religious views cannot be reconciled with materialism, for example, and behaviorism stands in stark opposition to existentialism.

FREEDOM AND DETERMINISM

One metaphysical view of considerable importance which has been previously mentioned is determinism—the theory that throughout the universe every event has a cause and had to occur just as it did occur. Determinism entails a flat denial of freedom, as that term is used by most philosophers in this chapter. We have seen that determinism is vigorously defended by materialists and by Skinner. On the other hand, the religious view and the existentialist view are united in an enthusiastic endorsement of human freedom. This dispute has occupied a major position in modern philosophy, perhaps because of its important implications for various ways we now treat some persons. We have come to believe that those who are insane are determined to behave as they do, and hence do not act of their own free will. Accordingly, we think it is appropriate to provide treatment for them when they commit a crime, rather than to punish them. But what if *all* our actions are caused in a relevantly similar way? Would we then not punish those who engage in what we now call intentional criminal activity? The lawyer Clarence Darrow once declared in a famous trial that "Back of *every* murder and back of *every human act* are sufficient causes that move the human machine beyond their control." He was, of course, defending a determinist view, with the intent of minimizing blame and punishment for his clients. But the problem of determinism and punishment is no lawyer's game. It is one of the most perplexing controversies in philosophy.

SOCIAL AND POLITICAL IMPLICATIONS

We have repeatedly had occasion to note that some views of human beings have interesting implications for the way in which society should and should not be organized. Marx and Skinner provide striking examples of proposals for reform that would significantly modify political life in most western nations. Other theories, in contrast, have almost no implications for social and political life. The language-user view is the outstanding example, but it is also uncertain what implications existentialism and religious views have for most features of our social and political life. In still other cases, there may be strong and important implications, contingent upon the specific interpretation given to the theory. An example is a once-common use of Darwin's view to promote "Social Darwinism." While there are different versions of this theory, the best known rely heavily on Darwin's theory of natural selection to support the position that human existence is basically a struggle of one person against another. The fittest rise to the top through their persistence, intelligence, ingenuity, and other favorable qualities. And this result is as it should be, say social Darwinists, since superior individuals *deserve* their position. The weak, lazy, and infirm, by contrast, are said to be selected out in the competitive struggle for position and for sexual partners. While there probably are many people who still believe this theory, it has virtually vanished from current writings on social and political theory. Needless to say, other theories which we have studied, such as Marxism, continue to exert major influence on social and political thought.

Tom L. Beauchamp

13. MAN AND RELIGION

W. E. Hocking
John H. Randall, Jr.

A. MAN AND ANIMAL*

MAN'S UNIQUE INTEREST IN HIMSELF

There is no sure way of telling what animals think about. But it seems safe to say that the human being gives more thought than any other animal *to himself*. He alone keeps diaries, uses mirrors, writes histories, makes innumerable comments on human nature, and develops such sciences as psychology and sociology. He alone speculates on the origin of his species on the earth, on what happens to the individual soul after death, and on what is to be the destiny of the race in the long future of the planet.

This interest of man in himself is a justified interest. Purely as a biological study, the human body is the most complex and interesting of all organic forms. There are animals that live longer; but there are none that live so much during their lifetime, and none which are capable of so great variety in behavior. . . . On the face of it, nothing should be easier to know than ourselves, and certainly nothing is more accessible. Everyone has a sample of human nature in his own person, body and mind; and surely every man knows his own mind: no one else can tell him how *he* feels and thinks. In another sense, every man is a puzzle to himself: there are things about him which his friends may know better than he does. He may be overconfident, and they can point out the dangers of conceit; he may be overdiffident, and they can give him self-assurance. And there are other riddles of human nature to which no one yet knows the final answer: why human beings feel as they do, entertain wishes,

take likings or aversions, become excited or hold steady, remember some things and forget others, have nagging anxieties or queer private superstitions or hunches about this or that or strange bursts of confidence. For that matter, our simplest mental operations—attending, learning, forming habits, imagining, deciding—are still not fully explained by any science.

The simplest of all tasks connected with self-knowledge ought to be, one would think, to report what is in the mind at any moment, since what we mean by the mind is simply the activity of knowing, feeling, deciding, and so on, which makes up the "stream of consciousness." . . .

But the chief puzzle of human nature is its doubleness. It is both *mind and body*. These two are fused into one being so closely that it is impossible to say where the joint is! And yet the words "mind" and "body" do not mean the same thing.

The body can be seen; no one will claim that he can see the mind. The body can be handled, weighed, measured, but not the mind. If anyone is under the momentary illusion that the brain and the mind are the same, let him consider whether he is prepared to take the chemical analysis of the mind, as he can of the brain.

But if we are not to think of the mind as a measurable object in space, how are we to think of it? A great deal of your philosophy will depend on how you answer this question. . . .

DIFFERENCES BETWEEN MAN AND ANIMAL

Most definitions of man begin with the words "Man is an animal." They then proceed to mention what they regard as the most important difference which separates him from the other animals. Thus, Aristotle defined man as the animal that *reasons*. He also proposed that man is the "political animal," i.e., the

Reprinted from Hocking, Blanshard, Hendel, and Randall, *Preface to Philosophy: Textbook* (New York: Macmillan, 1946).

*This section of the article was written by W. E. Hocking, and is reprinted with permission of Professor Randall.

animal that builds societies going beyond the family to the more impersonal groupings of the village and the state. He added the remark that man is political because he has language. This seems to run afoul of the fact that all social animals—bees, ants, birds, ruminants—have some form of speech or communication. But Aristotle goes on to explain that human language contains signs for general ideas, such as "justice"; and that without such ideas the kind of political society human beings build would be impossible. Animal societies often have a remarkable organization, and the conduct of their members is "lawful" in the sense of following definite lines of instinct; but we have no reason to suppose that any of them think out rules and change them from time to time, still less that they try to think out an idea of justice. On second thought, we can agree that Aristotle has lighted on an important point of difference.

Many other definitions have been proposed, more or less seriously. Man is the animal that laughs. Man is the animal that draws pictures. Man is the self-conscious animal. Man is the animal capable of shame, since no other animal shows signs of apology for its natural processes. Another definition comes nearer the center of the target: man is the animal with a moral sense; he is therefore capable of remorse and indeed of so much moral suffering that we occasionally fancy that a return to the animal condition would be a relief.

But however man may overdo his moral anxieties, he would not willingly part with his capacity for being discontented with himself; for it is only through this characteristic discontent that his long history is distinguished from that of every other animal species by its progressiveness. Man's compunction is part of the secret of his growth. This brings us close to a definition of long standing—that man is the *animal with a soul.* This is an important proposal, but difficult until we know what is meant by the soul. . . .

WHETHER MAN CAN BE DEFINED AS THE ANIMAL WITH A SOUL

We wish to consider what is meant by the soul. Let us approach this question by way of a trivial trait of human nature—man's capacity to be bored.

In the Near East one often sees donkeys following a circular path all day long as they work the shaft of a water-wheel. Their attitude expresses patience but not boredom. To a man, this type of work would be provocative first of tedium, then of rebellion, then of insanity. Why? Because the man's imagination would be busy with the things he was *not* doing. Again, animals, if they know they are going to die—which is doubtful—are not bothered by that fact. They make no will; they take out no insurance; they accept each day as so much time in hand and quite literally take no thought for the morrow. Man takes careful account of how much time he has and has *not.*

This means that man's mind sees things on their negative as well as on their positive side. And this is a result of seeing them as *parts of wholes;* for in the light of a totality, every partial fact has two reckonings—what it is and what it is not, what it lacks of being complete. Oftentimes the negative reckoning is the more important side of the truth. No animal is worried by its ignorance; for man, the knowledge of how much he does not know is his perpetual incentive to learn. He grows because on all sides he is aware of the unachieved. When we have a creature whose thought takes account of wholes, we have a radical step, perhaps the most radical step, in mental history.

If so, man can be defined as *the animal who thinks in terms of totalities.* Some word for "all" and some word for "the world" are found in all languages. There are also words for the negatives "not all," "absence," "emptiness," "silence," "nothing," "not enough." These terms separate human from all animal language. Man's early ideas of the whole of things, the universe, provide it with an imaginary rim, a limit of space, a beginning and an end in time. But as his restless thought experiments with this rim, he keeps moving it outward and finally faces the notion of "endlessness," of "infinitude."

Now the term "soul" has been used to indicate that there is an important gap between the animal and the human mind. And this gap has commonly been placed in man's moral nature, his capacity for self-judgment, and for "hitching his wagon to a star." I suggest that these qualities depend on the power we have now observed—the capacity to think of things and of himself in the frame of the whole in which they are placed, the infinite uni-

and his relation to man, which expressed their own faith in Reason and Knowing. This theology, though rarely understood and often taken as a "mystery" to be accepted on faith, has enabled the Christian beliefs to serve as symbols for intellectual as well as moral values. In the Christian tradition, scientists and philosophers have again and again been able to express their devotion to intelligibility and truth in Christian forms; and great Christian thinkers like St. Augustine and St. Thomas have interpreted God to mean Truth, that Truth which is the source of all other truths.

It has been natural for the religion of a society which, above all others, sets high store by knowledge, science, and understanding, to give intellectual and scientific values a central place. It is natural for it to regard the explanation of the world and of life as a major function of religion. . . .

THE RESULTING "CONFLICT" BETWEEN RELIGION AND SCIENCE

On the one hand, this emphasis led many Protestants to identify their faith completely with a set of scientific or philosophic propositions about the world as the scene of the moral life. In the eighteenth century this tendency culminated in the reduction of religion to the three ideas of "rational theology": God, freedom, and immortality. In the nineteenth century, it tended to associate religion with the more elaborate systems of philosophical idealism stemming from Hegel, who held that religion was really the expression in symbolic form of the truths he had succeeded in stating in exact and philosophic fashion. For both, it made religion a set of propositions to be believed, essentially a body of *knowledge.*

On the other hand, this identification of religion with a distinct kind of knowledge made inevitable the long "conflict" between the religious beliefs that made up "faith" and man's growing scientific knowledge. No sooner had men incorporated as central in their religion some parts of scientific or philosophic knowledge than new scientific discoveries or new philosophic theories seemed to challenge those already embodied in their religious beliefs. This incompatibility has usually been called

the "conflict between religion and science." It could be so viewed only by men who identified religion with theological beliefs, and who furthermore assumed that the function of theology was to give a theoretical explanation of the world and of human nature. Because Protestants have made these assumptions, they have faced plenty of "conflict" with science and philosophy. But that conflict has clearly not arisen between science and religion, for the function of religion, as we have seen, has not been primarily to provide knowledge or explanation at all. It has not even been a conflict between science and theology, for theology does not offer an explanation of the things that science explains. It has been a conflict between newer and more extensive scientific knowledge and older and inadequate science, enshrined in religious beliefs.

Assuredly, there is a place for intellectual belief, for reason and intelligence, for knowledge and truth, in the religious life. If these things are to have a place in our life at all, they must be consecrated in our religion. But to the objective observer of religions, starting from what he can "see," the significant functions of religion in human life do not seem to be to provide theoretical knowledge. The religion of a complex society, especially the religion of the subtle, the reflective, and the learned, will normally express and consecrate intellectual and scientific values. It will normally draw on and incorporate the best scientific and philosophic knowledge available. But religion itself seems to be primarily a way of feeling and acting, not a way of understanding and explaining. . . .

THE CRITICAL FUNCTION OF RELIGION

Far more important for religion than any presumed function of providing understanding or knowledge has been its function of bringing men's true desires to a focus and placing them side by side with the highest ideals men know. A religious tradition embodies the deepest insights of a long line of prophets and sensitive spiritual leaders. When the passing needs of the moment are brought into close contact with this store of ethical wisdom, the result is inevitably a "clarification" of what men really want and a criticism of transitory enthusiasms. This is the most valuable of all the social functions of religion.

That some form of religion is indispensable to any society seems no longer an open question. It has been long debated whether a society could get along without any religious organization of its life. Recent experience has made clear that if a traditional religion disintegrates, men will not calmly proceed to live without any religion at all. A new religion, or, if we prefer, a new substitute for religion, will spring up to fill the vacuum and to perform the historic functions of a religion. And this new "religion" will be much worse than the old one it supplants. For it will inevitably express some need of the moment; it will be onesided and fanatical. It will forget much of what has been learned through the bitter experience of generations because it will lack what the great historic religions have received, the criticism and clarification that have been born of centuries of human experience. . . .

THE LANGUAGE OF RELIGION: ITS SYMBOLIC FUNCTION

It is significant that, in passing from the discussion of the observation of religions to the question of religious vision, we have found ourselves employing a rather different kind of language. It is not the appropriate language of the social scientist investigating the functioning of religions. It is rather what we should recognize as "religious language." It is not a language about religion but the language of religion itself. It is what Plato called "the language of probability." He employed it in his religious and moral "myths" or illustrative stories. It is the language of the Gospel parables.[1] It is clearly different, both in its forms and in its functions, from the literal language found in the statements of science. It is used to convey a sense of what men *feel* about their experience and to awaken in others the same attitudes and emotions. In expressing and communicating this shared feeling, it employs metaphors and "symbols" and religious ideas which different men would understand differently if they attempted to translate them into the language of exact statement, but which have a common emotional and "religious" meaning.

Religious *language* provides a set of *symbols* in terms of which men can express and share the experiences they feel deeply, and relate them to the "things which are not seen." This same function is performed also by all the other practices of religion. This is especially true of the various techniques of religious worship, of rites, ritual, and observance. They are all definite ways of behaving, particular acts to be performed, which carry with them a *symbolic* meaning. That is, they stimulate and communicate to all who perform them certain common and shared feelings and attitudes toward experiences that affect them profoundly and help to awaken religious vision and strengthen religious faith.

Thus the ritual of a funeral service expresses men's common feeling of bereavement and loss. It then focuses the emotions of sorrow upon the enduring and permanent values of which the earthly life of the spirit inhabiting this particular mortal flesh was a transitory illustration. This power of religious symbols, in language and ritual, to express a deeply felt and shared emotion and redirect it toward a vision of the eternal, is clearest of all when men stand in the presence of the death of one whom they have known and loved.[2] There are few indeed, even in our secular-minded society, who do not feel on such an occasion the need and the appropriateness of some religious observances and some expression of religious vision. You cannot bury a man like a dog.

NOTES

1. Cf. for example, "The Parable of the Prodigal Son."
2. Cf. "The Parable of the Mustard Seed."

14. THE MATERIAL CONDITIONS OF LIFE
Karl Marx

I was led by my [early] studies to the conclusion that legal relations as well as forms of state could be neither understood by themselves nor explained by the so-called general progress of the human mind, but that they are rooted in the material conditions of life, which are summed up by Hegel after the fashion of the English and French of the eighteenth century under the name "civil society"; the anatomy of that civil society is to be sought in political economy. The study of the latter, which I had taken up in Paris, I continued at Brussels, whither I immigrated on account of an order of expulsion issued by Mr. Guizot. The general conclusion at which I arrived and which, once reached, continued to serve as the leading thread in my studies may be briefly summed up as follows: In the social production which men carry on they enter into definite relations that are indispensable and independent of their will; these relations of production correspond to a definite stage of development of their material powers of production. The sum total of these relations of production constitutes the economic structure of society—the real foundation, on which rise legal and political superstructures and to which correspond definite forms of social consciousness. The mode of production in material life determines the general character of the social, political, and spiritual processes of life. It is not the consciousness of men that determines their existence, but, on the contrary, their social existence determines their consciousness. At a certain stage of their development the material forces of production in society come into conflict with the existing relations of production, or—what is but a legal expression for the same thing—with the property relations within which they had been at work before. From forms of development of the forces of production these relations turn into their fetters. Then comes the period of social revolution. With the change of the economic foundation the entire immense superstructure is more or less rapidly transformed. In considering such transformations the distinction should always be made between the material transformation of the economic conditions of production, which can be determined with the precision of natural science, and the legal, political, religious, aesthetic, or philosophic—in short, ideological—forms in which men become conscious of this conflict and fight it out. Just as our opinion of an individual is not based on what he thinks of himself, so can we not judge such a period of transformation by its own consciousness; on the contrary, this consciousness must rather be explained from the contradictions of material life, from the existing conflict between the social forces of production and the relations of production. No social order ever disappears before all the productive forces for which there is room in it have been developed, and new, higher relations of production never appear before the material conditions of their existence have matured in the womb of the old society. Therefore mankind always takes up only such problems as it can solve, since, looking at the matter more closely, we will always find that the problem itself arises only when the material conditions necessary for its solution already exist or are at least in the process of formation. In broad outlines we can designate the Asiatic, the ancient, the feudal, and the modern bourgeois methods of production as so many epochs in the progress of the economic formation of society. The bourgeois relations of production are the last antagonistic form of the social process of production—antagonistic not in the sense of individual antagonism, but of one arising from conditions surrounding the life of individuals in society; at the same time the productive forces developing in the womb of bourgeois society create the material conditions for the solution of that antagonism. This social formation constitutes, therefore, the closing chapter of the prehistoric stage of human society.

Reprinted from Karl Marx, *A Contribution to the Critique of Political Economy,* trans. 1904, by N. I. Stone (Chicago: Charles Kerr Co., 1904), pp. 11–12.

15. A COMMUNIST VIEW OF MAN

Karl Marx
Friedrich Engels

I. BOURGEOIS AND PROLETARIANS

The history of all hitherto existing society is the history of class struggles.

Free man and slave, patrician and plebeian, lord and serf, guild master and journeyman, in a word, oppressor and oppressed, stood in constant opposition to one another, carried on an uninterrupted, now hidden, now open fight, a fight that each time ended either in a revolutionary reconstitution of society at large or in the common ruin of the contending classes. . . .

The modern bourgeois society that has sprouted from the ruins of feudal society has not done away with class antagonisms. It has but established new classes, new conditions of oppression, new forms of struggle in place of the old ones.

Our epoch, the epoch of the bourgeoisie, possesses, however, this distinctive feature: it has simplified the class antagonisms. Society as a whole is more and more splitting up into two great hostile camps, into two great classes directly facing each other: bourgeoisie and proletariat . . . the bourgeoisie has at last, since the establishment of modern industry and of the world market, conquered for itself, in the modern representative state, exclusive political sway. The executive of the modern state is but a committee for managing the common affairs of the whole bourgeoisie.

The bourgeoisie, historically, has played a most revolutionary part.

The bourgeoisie, wherever it has got the upper hand, has put an end to all feudal, patriarchal, idyllic relations. It has pitilessly torn asunder the motley feudal ties that bound man to his "natural superiors," and has left remaining no other nexus between man and man than naked self-interest, than callous "cash payment." . . . It has resolved personal worth into exchange value and, in place of

Reprinted from Karl Marx and Friedrich Engels, *Manifesto of the Communist Party,* issued by Foreign Languages Publishing House, Moscow, English Edition of 1888.

the numberless indefeasible chartered freedoms, has set up that single, unconscionable freedom—free trade. In one word, for exploitation, veiled by religious and political illusions, it has substituted naked, shameless, direct, brutal exploitation.

The bourgeoisie has stripped of its halo every occupation hitherto honored and looked up to with reverent awe. It has converted the physician, the lawyer, the priest, the poet, the man of science into its paid wage laborers. . . .

In proportion as the bourgeoisie, i.e., capital, is developed, in the same proportion is the proletariat, the modern working class, developed—a class of laborers, who live only so long as they find work, and who find work only so long as their labor increases capital. These laborers, who must sell themselves piecemeal, are a commodity, like every other article of commerce, and are consequently exposed to all the vicissitudes of competition, to all the fluctuations of the market.

Owing to the extensive use of machinery and to division of labor, the work of the proletarians has lost all individual character and, consequently, all charm for the workman. . . .

No sooner is the exploitation of the laborer by the manufacturer over, to the extent that he receives his wages in cash, than he is set upon by the other portions of the bourgeoisie, the landlord, the shopkeeper, the pawnbroker, etc.

The lower strata of the middle class—the small tradespeople, shopkeepers, and retired tradesmen generally, the handicraftsmen and peasants—all these sink gradually into the proletariat, partly because their diminutive capital does not suffice for the scale on which modern industry is carried on, and is swamped in the competition with the large capitalists, partly because their specialized skill is rendered worthless by new methods of production. Thus the proletariat is recruited from all classes of the population. . . .

II. PROLETARIANS AND COMMUNISTS

The immediate aim of the communists is the same as that of all the other proletarian parties: formation of the proletariat into a class, overthrow of the bourgeois supremacy, conquest of political power by the proletariat.

The theoretical conclusions of the communists are in no way based on ideas or principles that have been invented, or discovered, by this or that would-be universal reformer.

They merely express, in general terms, actual relations springing from an existing class struggle, from a historical movement going on under our very eyes. The abolition of existing property relations is not at all a distinctive feature of communism.

All property relations in the past have continually been subject to historical change consequent upon the change in historical conditions.

The French Revolution, for example, abolished feudal property in favor of bourgeois property.

The distinguishing feature of communism is not the abolition of property generally, but the abolition of bourgeois property. But modern bourgeois private property is the final and most complete expression of the system of producing and appropriating products that is based on class antagonisms, on the exploitation of the many by the few.

In this sense the theory of the communists may be summed up in the single sentence: Abolition of private property. . . .

You are horrified at our intending to do away with private property. But in your existing society private property is already done away with for nine tenths of the population; its existence for the few is solely due to its nonexistence in the hands of those nine tenths. You reproach us, therefore, with intending to do away with a form of property the necessary condition for whose existence is the nonexistence of any property for the immense majority of society.

In one word, you reproach us with intending to do away with your property. Precisely so; that is just what we intend.

From the moment when labor can no longer be converted into capital, money, or rent, into a social power capable of being monopolized, i.e., from the moment when individual property can no longer be transformed into bourgeois property, into capital, from that moment, you say, individuality vanishes.

You must, therefore, confess that by "individual" you mean no other person than the bourgeois, than the middle-class owner of property. This person must, indeed, be swept out of the way and made impossible.

Communism deprives no man of the power to appropriate the products of society; all that it does is to deprive him of the power to subjugate the labor of others by means of such appropriation. . . .

Does it require deep intuition to comprehend that man's ideas, views, and conceptions, in one word, man's consciousness, change with every change in the conditions of his material existence, in his social relations, and in his social life?

What else does the history of ideas prove than that intellectual production changes its character in proportion as material production is changed? The ruling ideas of each age have ever been the ideas of its ruling class.

When people speak of ideas that revolutionize society they do but express the fact that within the old society the elements of a new one have been created, and that the dissolution of the old ideas keeps even pace with the dissolution of the old conditions of existence.

When the ancient world was in its last throes, the ancient religions were overcome by Christianity. When Christian ideas succumbed in the eighteenth century to rationalist ideas, feudal society fought its death battle with the then revolutionary bourgeoisie. The ideas of religious liberty and freedom of conscience merely gave expression to the sway of free competition within the domain of knowledge.

"Undoubtedly," it will be said, "religious, moral, philosophical, and juridical ideas have been modified in the course of historical development. But religion, morality, philosophy, political science, and law constantly survived this change.

"There are, besides, eternal truths, such as freedom, justice, etc., that are common to all states of society. But communism abolishes eternal truths, it abolishes all religion, and all morality, instead of constituting them on a new basis; it therefore acts in contradiction to all past historical experience."

What does this accusation reduce itself to? The history of all past society has consisted in the development of class antagonisms, antagonisms that assumed different forms at different epochs.

But whatever form they may have taken, one fact is common to all past ages, viz., the exploitation of one part of society by the other. No wonder then that the social consciousness of past ages, despite all the multiplicity and variety it displays, moves within certain common forms, or general ideas, which cannot completely vanish except with the total disappearance of class antagonisms.

The communist revolution is the most radical rupture with traditional property relations; no wonder that its development involves the most radical rupture with traditional ideas.

But let us have done with the bourgeois objections to communism.

The Darwinian View

16. MAN AND THE LOWER ANIMALS

Charles Darwin

Man bears in his bodily structure clear traces of his descent from some lower form; but it may be urged that, as man differs so greatly in his mental power from all other animals, there must be some error in this conclusion. No doubt the difference in this respect is enormous, even if we compare the mind of one of the lowest savages, who has no words to express any number higher than four, and who uses hardly any abstract terms for common objects or for the affections, with that of the most highly organised ape. The difference would, no doubt, still remain immense, even if one of the higher apes had been improved or civilised as much as a dog has been in comparison with its parent-form, the wolf or jackal. The Fuegians rank amongst the lowest barbarians; but I was continually struck with surprise how closely the three natives on board H.M.S. *Beagle,* who had lived some years in England, and could talk a little English, resembled us in disposition and in most of our mental faculties. If no organic being excepting man had possessed any mental power, or if his powers had been of a wholly different nature from those of the lower animals, then we should never have been able to convince ourselves that our high faculties had been gradually developed. But it can be shewn that there is no fundamental difference of this kind. We must also admit that there is a much wider interval in mental power between one of the lowest fishes, as a lamprey or lancelet, and one of the higher apes, than between an ape and man; yet this interval is filled up by numberless gradations. . . .

The lower animals, like man, manifestly feel pleasure and pain, happiness and misery. Happiness is never better exhibited than by young animals, such as puppies, kittens, lambs, &c., when playing together, like our own children. Even insects play together, as has been described by that excellent observer, P. Huber,[1] who saw ants chasing and pretending to bite each other, like so many puppies.

The fact that the lower animals are excited by the same emotions as ourselves is so well established, that it will not be necessary to weary the reader by many details. Terror acts in the same manner on them as on us, causing the muscles to tremble, the heart to palpitate, the sphincters to be relaxed, and the hair to stand on end. Suspicion, the offspring of fear, is eminently characteristic of most wild animals. It is, I think, impossible to read the account given by Sir E. Tennent, of the behaviour of the

Reprinted from Charles Darwin, *The Descent of Man,* first published in England, 1871.

female elephants, used as decoys, without admitting that they intentionally practise deceit, and well know what they are about. Courage, and timidity are extremely variable qualities in the individuals of the same species, as is plainly seen in our dogs. Some dogs and horses are ill-tempered, and easily turn sulky; others are good-tempered; and these qualities are certainly inherited. Every one knows how liable animals are to furious rage, and how plainly they shew it. Many, and probably true, anecdotes have been published on the long-delayed and artful revenge of various animals. . . .

The love of a dog for his master is notorious; as an old writer quaintly says,[2] "A dog is the only thing on this earth that luvs you more than he luvs himself."

In the agony of death a dog has been known to caress his master, and every one has heard of the dog suffering under vivisection, who licked the hand of the operator; this man, unless the operation was fully justified by an increase of our knowledge, or unless he had a heart of stone, must have felt remorse to the last hour of his life.

As Whewell[3] has well asked, "Who that reads the touching instances of maternal affection, related so often of the women of all nations, and of the females of all animals, can doubt that the principle of action is the same in the two cases?" We see maternal affection exhibited in the most trifling details; thus Rengger observed an American monkey (a Cebus) carefully driving away the flies which plagued her infant; and Duvaucel saw a Hylobates washing the faces of her young ones in a stream. So intense is the grief of female monkeys for the loss of their young, that it invariably caused the death of certain kinds kept under confinement by Brehm in N. Africa. . . .

Most of the more complex emotions are common to the higher animals and ourselves. Every one has seen how jealous a dog is of his master's affection, if lavished on any other creature; and I have observed the same fact with monkeys. This shews that animals not only love, but have desire to be loved. Animals manifestly feel emulation. They love approbation or praise; and a dog carrying a basket for his master exhibits in a high degree self-complacency or pride. There can, I think, be no doubt that a dog feels shame, as distinct from fear,

and something very like modesty when begging too often for food. . . .

We will now turn to the more intellectual emotions and faculties, which are very important, as forming the basis for the development of the higher mental powers. Animals manifestly enjoy excitement, and suffer from ennui, as may be seen with dogs, and, according to Rengger, with monkeys. All animals feel *Wonder,* and many exhibit *Curiosity.* They sometimes suffer from this latter quality, as when the hunter plays antics and thus attracts them; I have witnessed this with deer, and so it is with the wary chamois, and with some kinds of wild-ducks. . . .

Hardly any faculty is more important for the intellectual progress of man than *Attention.* Animals clearly manifest this power, as when a cat watches by a hole and prepares to spring on its prey. Wild animals sometimes become so absorbed when thus engaged, that they may be easily approached. . . .

ABSTRACTION, GENERAL CONCEPTIONS, SELF-CONSCIOUSNESS, MENTAL INDIVIDUALITY

It would be very difficult for any one with even much more knowledge than I possess, to determine how far animals exhibit any traces of these high mental powers. This difficulty arises from the impossibility of judging what passes through the mind of an animal; and again, the fact that writers differ to a great extent in the meaning which they attribute to the above terms, causes a further difficulty. If one may judge from various articles which have been published lately, the greatest stress seems to be laid on the supposed entire absence in animals of the power of abstraction, or of forming general concepts. But when a dog sees another dog at a distance, it is often clear that he perceives that it is a dog in the abstract; for when he gets nearer his whole manner suddenly changes if the other dog be a friend. A recent writer remarks, that in all such cases it is a pure assumption to assert that the mental act is not essentially of the same nature in the animal as in man. If either refers what he perceives with his senses to a mental concept, then so do both.[4] When I say to my terrier, in an eager voice (and I have made the trial many times), "Hi, hi, where is it?" she at once takes it as a sign that something is to be hunted, and generally first looks quickly all around, and then rushes into the nearest thicket, to scent for any game, but finding nothing, she looks up into any neighbouring tree for a squirrel. Now do not these actions clearly shew that she had in her mind a general idea or concept that some animal is to be discovered and hunted?

It may be freely admitted that no animal is self-conscious, if by this term it is implied, that he reflects on such points, as whence he comes or whither he will go, or what is life and death, and so forth. But how can we feel sure that an old dog with an excellent memory and some power of imagination, as shewn by his dreams, never reflects on his past pleasures or pains in the chase? And this would be a form of self-consciousness. . . .

LANGUAGE

This faculty has justly been considered as one of the chief distinctions between man and the lower animals. But man, as a highly competent judge, Archbishop Whately remarks, "is not the only animal that can make use of language to express what is passing in his mind, and can understand, more or less, what is so expressed by another."[5] In Paraguay the *Cebus azarae* when excited utters at least six distinct sounds, which excite in other monkeys similar emotions.[6] The movements of the features and gestures of monkeys are understood by us, and they partly understand ours, as Rengger and others declare. It is a more remarkable fact that the dog, since being domesticated, has learnt to bark[7] in at least four or five distinct tones. . . .

The habitual use of articulate language is, however, peculiar to man; but he uses, in common with the lower animals, inarticulate cries to express his meaning, aided by gestures and the movements of the muscles of the face.[8] This especially holds good with the more simple and vivid feelings, which are but little connected with our higher intelligence. Our cries of pain, fear, surprise, anger, together with their appropriate actions, and the murmur of a mother to her beloved child are more expressive than any words. That which distinguishes man from the lower animals is not the understanding of artic-

ulate sounds, for, as every one knows, dogs understand many words and sentences. In this respect they are at the same stage of development as infants, between the ages of ten and twelve months, who understand many words and short sentences, but cannot yet utter a single word. It is not the mere articulation which is our distinguishing character, for parrots and other birds possess this power. Nor is it the mere capacity of connecting definite sounds with definite ideas; for it is certain that some parrots, which have been taught to speak, connect unerringly words with things, and persons with events. The lower animals differ from man solely in his almost infinitely larger power of associating together the most diversified sounds and ideas; and this obviously depends on the high development of his mental powers. . . .

I fully subscribe to the judgment of those writers who maintain that of all the differences between man and the lower animals, the moral sense or conscience is by far the most important. This sense, as Mackintosh[9] remarks, "has a rightful supremacy over every other principle of human action"; it is summed up in that short but imperious word *ought*, so full of high significance. It is the most noble of all the attributes of man, leading him without a moment's hesitation to risk his life for that of a fellow-creature; or after due deliberation, impelled simply by the deep feeling of right or duty, to sacrifice it in some great cause. . . .

The following proposition seems to me in a high degree probable—namely, that any animal whatever, endowed with well-marked social instincts, the parental and filial affections being here included, would inevitably acquire a moral sense or conscience, as soon as its intellectual powers had become as well, or nearly as well developed, as in man. For, *firstly,* the social instincts lead an animal to take pleasure in the society of its fellows, to feel a certain amount of sympathy with them, and to perform various services for them. The services may be of a definite and evidently instinctive nature; or there may be only a wish and readiness, as with most of the higher social animals, to aid their fellows in certain general ways. But these feelings and services are by no means extended to all the individuals of the same species, only to those of the same association. *Secondly,* as soon as the mental faculties had become highly developed, images of all past actions and motives would be incessantly passing through the brain of each individual; and that feeling of dissatisfaction, or even misery, which invariably results, as we shall hereafter see, from any unsatisfied instinct, would arise, as often as it was perceived that the enduring and always present social instinct had yielded to some other instinct, at the time stronger, but neither enduring in its nature, nor leaving behind it a very vivid impression. It is clear that many instinctive desires, such as that of hunger, are in their nature of short duration; and after being satisfied, are not readily or vividly recalled. *Thirdly,* after the power of language had been acquired, and the wishes of the community could be expressed, the common opinion how each member ought to act for the public good, would naturally become in a paramount degree the guide to action. But it should be borne in mind that however great weight we may attribute to public opinion, our regard for the approbation and disapprobation of our fellows depends on sympathy, which . . . forms an essential part of the social instinct, and is indeed its foundation-stone. *Lastly,* habit in the individual would ultimately play a very important part in guiding the conduct of each member; for the social instinct, together with sympathy, is, like any other instinct, greatly strengthened by habit, and so consequently would be obedience to the wishes and judgment of the community. . . .

SUMMARY

There can be no doubt that the difference between the mind of the lowest man and that of the highest animal is immense. An anthropomorphous ape, if he could take a dispassionate view of his own case, would admit that though he could form an artful plan to plunder a garden—though he could use stones for fighting or for breaking open nuts, yet that the thought of fashioning a stone into a tool was quite beyond his scope. Still less, as he would admit, could he follow out a train of metaphysical reasoning, or solve a mathematical problem, or reflect on God, or admire a grand natural scene. Some apes, however, would probably declare that they could and did admire the beauty of the coloured skin and fur of their partners in marriage. They would admit, that though they could make other apes understand by cries some of their perceptions and simpler wants, the notion of expressing definite ideas by definite sounds had never crossed their minds. They might insist that they were ready to aid their fellow-apes of the same troop in many ways, to risk their lives for them, and to take charge of their orphans; but they would be forced to acknowledge that disinterested love for all living creatures, the most noble attribute of man, was quite beyond their comprehension.

Nevertheless the difference in mind between man and the higher animals, great as it is, certainly is one of degree and not of kind. We have seen that the senses and intuitions, the various emotions and faculties, such as love, memory, attention, curiosity, imitation, reason, &c., of which man boasts, may be found in an incipient, or even sometimes in a well-developed condition, in the lower animals. They are also capable of some inherited improvement, as we see in the domestic dog compared with the wolf or jackal. If it could be proved that certain high mental powers, such as the formation of general concepts, self-consciousness, &c., were absolutely peculiar to man, which seems extremely doubtful, it is not improbable that these qualities are merely the incidental results of other highly-advanced intellectual faculties; and these again mainly the result of the continued use of a perfect language. At what age does the new-born infant possess the power of abstraction, or become self-conscious, and reflect on its own existence? We cannot answer; nor can we answer in regard to the ascending organic scale. The half-art, half-instinct of language still bears the stamp of its gradual evolution.

NOTES

1. *Recherches sur les Maeurs des Fourmis,* 1810, p. 173.
2. Quoted by Dr. Lauder Lindsay, in his "Physiology of Mind in the Lower Animals," *Journal of Mental Science,* April, 1871, p. 38.
3. *Bridgewater Treatise,* p. 263.
4. Mr. Hookham, in a letter to Prof. Max Müller, in the *Birmingham News,* May, 1873.
5. Quoted in *Anthropological Review,* 1864, p. 158.
6. Rengger, *Naturgesh der Säugethiere von Paraguay,* 1830, s. 45.
7. See my *Variation of Animals and Plants under Domestication,* vol. i., p. 27.
8. See a discussion on this subject in Mr. E. B. Tylor's very interesting work, *Researches into the Early History of Mankind,* 1865, chaps. ii. to iv.
9. *Dissertation on Ethical Philosophy,* 1837, p. 231, &c.

17. THE NAKED APE

Desmond Morris

There are one hundred and ninety-three living species of monkeys and apes. One hundred and ninety-two of them are covered with hair. The exception is a naked ape self-named *Homo sapiens*. This unusual and highly successful species spends a great deal of time examining his higher motives and an equal amount of time studiously ignoring his fundamental ones. He is proud that he has the biggest brain of all the primates, but attempts to conceal the fact that he also has the biggest penis, preferring to accord this honour falsely to the mighty gorilla. He is an intensely vocal, acutely exploratory, over-crowded ape, and it is high time we examined his basic behaviour.

I am a zoologist and the naked ape is an animal. He is therefore fair game for my pen and I refuse to avoid him any longer simply because some of his behaviour patterns are rather complex and impressive. My excuse is that, in becoming so erudite, *Homo sapiens* has remained a naked ape nevertheless; in acquiring lofty new motives, he has lost none of the earthy old ones. This is frequently a cause of some embarrassment to him, but his old impulses have been with him for millions of years, his new ones only a few thousand at the most—and there is no hope of quickly shrugging off the accumulated genetic legacy of his whole evolutionary past. He would be a far less worried and more fulfilled animal if only he would face up to this fact. Perhaps this is where the zoologist can help. . . .

The approach I propose to use . . . draws its material from three main sources: (1) the information about our past as unearthed by paleontologists and based on the fossil and other remains of our ancient ancestors; (2) the information available from the animal behaviour studies of the comparative ethologists, based on detailed observations of a wide range of animal species, especially our closest living relatives, the monkeys and apes; and (3) the information that can be assembled by simple, direct observation of the most basic and widely shared behaviour patterns of the successful mainstream specimens from the major contemporary cultures of the naked ape itself. . . .

There is a label on a cage at a certain zoo that states simply, 'This animal is new to science'. Inside the cage there sits a small squirrel. It has black feet and it comes from Africa. No black-footed squirrel has ever been found in that continent before. Nothing is known about it. It has no name.

For the zoologist it presents an immediate challenge. What is it about its way of life that has made it unique? How does it differ from the three hundred and sixty-six other living species of squirrels already known and described? Somehow, at some point in the evolution of the squirrel family, the ancestors of this animal must have split off from the rest and established themselves as an independent breeding population. What was it in the environment that made possible their isolation as a new form of life? The new trend must have started out in a small way, with a group of squirrels in one area becoming slightly changed and better adapted to the particular conditions there. But at this stage they would still be able to interbreed with their relatives nearby. The new form would be at a slight advantage in its special region, but it would be no more than a race of the basic species and could be swamped out, reabsorbed into the mainstream at any point. If, as time passed, the new squirrels became more and more perfectly tuned-in to their particular environment, the moment would eventually arrive when it would be advantageous for them to become isolated from possible contamination by their neighbours. At this stage their social and sexual behaviour would undergo special modifications, making inter-breeding with other kinds of squirrels unlikely and eventually impossible. At first, their anatomy may have changed and become better at coping with the special food of the district, but later their mating calls and displays would also differ, ensuring that they attract only mates of the new type. At last, a new species would have evolved, separate and discrete, a unique form of life, a three hundred and sixty-seventh kind of squirrel.

When we look at our unidentified squirrel in its zoo cage, we can only guess about these things. All we can be certain about is that the markings of its fur—its black feet—indicate that it is a new form. But these are only the symptoms, the rash that gives a doctor a clue about his patient's disease. To really understand this new species, we must use these clues only as a starting point, telling us there is something worth pursuing. We might try to guess at the animal's history, but that would be presumptuous and dangerous. Instead we will start humbly by giving it a simple and obvious label: we will call it the African black-footed squirrel. Now we must observe and record every aspect of its behaviour and structure and see how it differs from, or is similar to, other squirrels. Then, little by little, we can piece together its story.

The great advantage we have when studying such animals is that we ourselves are not black-footed squirrels—a fact which forces us into an attitude of humility that is becoming to proper scientific investigation. How different things are, how depressingly different, when we attempt to study the human animal. Even for the zoologist, who is used to calling an animal an animal, it is difficult to avoid the arrogance of subjective involvement. We can try to overcome this to some extent by deliberately and rather coyly approaching the human being as if he were another species, a strange form of life on the dissecting table, awaiting analysis. How can we begin?

As with the new squirrel, we can start by comparing him with other species that appear to be most closely related. From his teeth, his hands, his eyes and various other anatomical features, he is obviously a primate of some sort, but of a very odd kind. Just how odd becomes clear when we lay out in a long row the skins of the one hundred and ninety-two living species of monkeys and apes, and then try to insert a human pelt at a suitable point somewhere in this long series. Wherever we put it, it looks out of place. Eventually we are driven to position it right at one end of the row of skins, next to the hides of the tailless great apes such as the chimpanzee and the gorilla. Even here it is obtrusively different. The legs are too long, the arms are too short and the feet are rather strange. Clearly this species of primate has developed a special kind of locomotion which has modified its basic form. But there is another characteristic that cries out for attention: the skin is virtually naked. Except for conspicuous tufts of hair on the head, in the armpits and around the genitals, the skin surface is completely exposed. When compared with the other primate species, the contrast is dramatic. True, some species of monkeys and apes have small naked patches of skin on their rumps, their faces, or their chests, but nowhere amongst the other one hundred and ninety-two species is there anything even approaching the human condition. At this point and without further investigation, it is justifiable to name this new species the 'naked ape'. It is a simple, descriptive name based on a simple observation, and it makes no special assumptions. Perhaps it will help us to keep a sense of proportion and maintain our objectivity.

Staring at this strange specimen and puzzling over the significance of its unique features, the zoologist now has to start making comparisons. Where else is nudity at a premium? The other primates are no help, so it means looking farther afield. A rapid survey of the whole range of the living mammals soon proves that they are remarkably attached to their protective, furry covering, and that very few of the 4,237 species in existence have seen fit to abandon it. Unlike their reptilian ancestors, mammals have acquired the great physiological advantage of being able to maintain a constant, high body temperature. This keeps the delicate machinery of the body processes tuned in for top performance. It is not a property to be endangered or discarded lightly. The temperature-controlling devices are of vital importance and the possession of a thick, hairy, insulating coat obviously plays a major role in preventing heat loss. In intense sunlight it will also prevent overheating and damage to the skin from direct exposure to the sun's rays. If the hair has to go, then clearly there must be a very powerful reason for abolishing it. With few exceptions this drastic step has been taken only when mammals have launched themselves into an entirely new medium. . . .

[Consider] the last million or so years of the naked ape's ancestral history, [with its] shattering and increasingly dramatic developments. Several things happened together, and it is important to realize this. All too often, when the story is told, the separate parts of it are spread out as if one major advance led to another, but this is misleading. The ancestral ground-apes already had large and high-quality brains. They had good eyes and efficient grasping hands. They inevitably, as primates, had some degree of social organization. With strong pressure on them to increase their prey-killing prowess, vital changes began to take place. They became more upright—fast, better runners. Their hands became freed from locomotion duties—strong, efficient weapon-holders. Their brains became more complex—brighter, quicker decision-makers. These things did not follow one another in a major, set sequence; they blossomed together, minute advances being made first in one quality and then in another, each urging the other on. A hunting ape, a killer ape, was in the making.

It could be argued that evolution might have favoured the less drastic step of developing a more typical cat- or dog-like killer, a kind of cat-ape or dog-ape, by the simple process of enlarging the teeth and nails into savage fang-like and claw-like weapons. But this would have put the ancestral ground-ape into direct competition with the already highly specialized cat and dog killers. It would have meant competing with them on their own terms, and the outcome would no doubt have been disastrous for the primates in question. (For all we know, this may actually have been tried and failed so badly that the evidence has not been found.) Instead, an entirely new approach was made, using artificial weapons instead of natural ones, and it worked.

From tool-using to tool-making was the next step, and alongside this development went improved hunting techniques, not only in terms of weapons, but also in terms of social cooperation. The hunting apes were pack-hunters, and as their techniques of killing were improved, so were their methods of social organization. Wolves in a pack deploy themselves, but the hunting ape already had a much better brain than a wolf and could turn it to such problems as group communication and cooperation. Increasingly complex manoeuvres could be developed. The growth of the brain surged on.

Essentially this was a hunting-group of males.

The females were too busy rearing the young to be able to play a major role in chasing and catching prey. As the complexity of the hunt increased and the forays became more prolonged, it became essential for the hunting ape to abandon the meandering, nomadic ways of its ancestors. A home base was necessary, a place to come back to with the spoils, where the females and young would be waiting and could share the food. This step . . . has had profound effects on many aspects of the behaviour of even the most sophisticated naked apes of today.

So the hunting ape became a territorial ape. His whole sexual, parental and social pattern began to be affected. His old wandering, fruit-plucking way of life was fading rapidly. He had now really left his forest of Eden. He was an ape with responsibilities. He began to worry about the prehistoric equivalent of washing machines and refrigerators. He began to develop the home comforts—fire, food storage, artificial shelters. But this is where we must stop for the moment, for we are moving out of the realms of biology and into the realms of culture. The biological basis of these advanced steps lies in the development of a brain large and complex enough to enable the hunting ape to take them, but the exact form they assume is no longer a matter of specific genetic control. The forest ape that became a ground ape that became a hunting ape that became a territorial ape has become a cultural ape, and we must call a temporary halt. . . . His way of life was geared to a forest existence, and then suddenly (suddenly in evolutionary terms) he was jettisoned into a world where he could survive only if he began to live like a brainy, weapon-toting wolf. We must examine now exactly how this affected not only his body, but especially his behaviour, and in what form we experience the influence of this legacy at the present day. . . .

The hunting ape's new way of life threw up a special problem, one that it did not share with the typical 'pure' carnivores: the role of the sexes had to become more distinct. The hunting parties, unlike those of the 'pure' carnivores, had to become all-male groups. If anything was going to go against the primate grain, it was this. For a virile primate male to go off on a feeding trip and leave his females unprotected from the advances of any other males that might happen to come by, was unheard of. No amount of cultural training could put this right. This was something that demanded a major shift in social behaviour.

The answer was the development of a pair-bond. Male and female hunting apes had to fall in love and remain faithful to one another. This is a common tendency in many other groups of animals, but is rare amongst primates. It solved three problems in one stroke. It meant that the females remained bonded to their individual males and faithful to them while they were away on the hunt. It meant that serious sexual rivalries between the males were reduced. This aided their developing co-operativeness. If they were to hunt together successfully, the weaker males as well as the stronger ones had to play their part. They had to play a central role and could not be thrust to the periphery of society, as happens in so many primate species. What is more, with his newly developed and deadly artificial weapons, the hunting ape male was under strong pressure to reduce any source of disharmony within the tribe. Thirdly, the development of a one-male-one-female breeding unit meant that the offspring also benefited. The heavy task of rearing and training the slowly developing young demanded a cohesive family unit. In other groups of animals, whether they are fishes, birds or mammals, when there is too big a burden for one parent to bear alone, we see the development of a powerful pair-bond, tying the male and female parents together throughout the breeding season. This, too, is what occurred in the case of the hunting ape.

In this way, the females were sure of their males' support and were able to devote themselves to their maternal duties. The males were sure of their females' loyalty, were prepared to leave them for hunting, and avoided fighting over them. And the offspring were provided with the maximum of care and attention. This certainly sounds like an ideal solution, but it involved a major change in primate socio-sexual behaviour. . . . It is clear from the behaviour of our species today that the trend was only partially completed and that our earlier primate urges keep on re-appearing in minor forms. . . .

SEX

Sexually the naked ape finds himself today in a somewhat confusing situation. As a primate he is pulled one way, as a carnivore by adoption he is pulled another, and as a member of an elaborate civilized community he is pulled yet another.

To start with, he owes all his basic sexual qualities to his fruit-picking, forest-ape ancestors. These characteristics were then drastically modified to fit in with his open-country, hunting way of life. This was difficult enough, but then they, in turn, had to be adapted to match the rapid development of an increasingly complex and culturally determined social structure.

The first of these changes, from a sexual fruit-picker to a sexual hunter, was achieved over a comparatively long period of time and with reasonable success. The second change has been less successful. It has happened too quickly and has been forced to depend upon intelligence and the application of learned restraint rather than on biological modifications based on natural selection. It could be said that the advance of civilization has not so much moulded modern sexual behaviour, as that sexual behaviour has moulded the shape of civilization. . . .

How does the way we behave sexually help us to survive? Why do we behave in the way we do, rather than in some other way? We may be helped in these questions if we ask another one: How does our sexual behaviour compare with that of other living primates?

Straight away we can see that there is much more intense sexual activity in our own species than in any other primates, including our closest relations. For them, the lengthy courtship phase is missing. Hardly any of the monkeys and apes develop a prolonged pair-bond relationship. The pre-copulatory patterns are brief and usually consist of no more than a few facial expressions and simple vocalizations. Copulation itself is also very brief. (In baboons, for instance, the time taken from mounting to ejaculation is no more than seven to eight seconds, with a total of no more than fifteen pelvic thrusts, often fewer.) The female does not appear to experience any kind of climax. If there is anything that could be called an orgasm it is a trivial response when compared with that of the female of our own species.

The period of sexual receptivity of the female monkey or ape is more restricted. It usually only lasts for about a week, or a little more, of their monthly cycle. Even this is an advance on the lower mammals, where it is limited more severely to the actual time of ovulation, but in our own species the primate trend towards longer receptivity has been pushed to the very limit, so that the female is receptive at virtually all times. Once a female monkey or ape becomes pregnant, or is nursing a baby, she ceases to be sexually active. Again, our species has spread its sexual activities into these periods, so that there is only a brief time just before and just after parturition when mating is seriously limited.

Clearly, the naked ape is the sexiest primate alive. To find the reason for this we have to look back again at his origins. What happened? First, he had to hunt if he was to survive. Second, he had to have a better brain to make up for his poor hunting body. Third, he had to have a longer childhood to grow the bigger brain and to educate it. Fourth, the females had to stay put and mind the babies while the males went hunting. Fifth, the males had to cooperate with one another on the hunt. Sixth, they had to stand up straight and use weapons for the hunt to succeed. I am not implying that these changes happened in that order; on the contrary they undoubtedly all developed gradually at the same time, each modification helping the others along. I am simply enumerating the six basic, major changes that took place as the hunting ape evolved. Inherent in these changes there are, I believe, all the ingredients necessary to make up our present sexual complexity. . . .

In addition to increasing the amount of time when sexual activities can take place, the activities themselves have been elaborated. The hunting life that gave us naked skins and more sensitive hands has given us much greater scope for sexually stimulating body-to-body contacts. During pre-copulatory behaviour these play a major role. Stroking, rubbing, pressing and caressing occur in abundance and far exceed anything found in other primate species. Also, specialized organs such as the lips, ear-lobes, nipples, breasts and genitals are richly endowed with nerve-endings and have become highly sensitized to erotic tactile stimulation. . . .

This, then, is the naked ape in all its erotic complexity: a highly sexed, pair-forming species with many unique features; a complicated blend of primate ancestry with extensive carnivore modifications. Now, to this we must add the third and final ingredient: modern civilization. The enlarged brain that accompanied the transformation of the simple forest-dweller into a co-operative hunter began to busy itself with technological improvements. The simple tribal dwelling places became great towns and cities. The axe age blossomed into the space age. But what effect did the acquisition of all this gloss and glitter have on the sexual system of the species? Very little, seems to be the answer. It has all been too quick, too sudden, for any fundamental biological advances to occur. Superficially they *seem* to have occurred, it is true, but this is largely make-believe. Behind the facade of modern city life there is the same old naked ape. Only the names have been changed: for 'hunting' read 'working', for 'hunting grounds' read 'place of business', for 'home base' read 'house', for 'pair-bond' read 'marriage', for 'mate' read 'wife', and so on. . . . Studies of contemporary sexual patterns . . . have revealed that the physiological and anatomical equipment of the species is still being put to full use. The evidence of prehistoric remnants combined with comparative data from living carnivores and other living primates has given us a picture of how the naked ape must have used this sexual equipment in the distant past and how he must have organized his sex life. The contemporary evidence appears to give much the same basic picture, once one has cleaned away the dark varnish of public moralizing. As I said at the beginning . . . it is the biological nature of the beast that has moulded the social structure of civilization, rather than the other way around.

18. THE POWER AND PERIL OF LANGUAGE
Susanne K. Langer

A. MAN'S MOST DISTINCTIVE MARK: LIVING BY SYMBOLS

Of all born creatures, man is the only one that cannot live by bread alone. He lives as much by symbols as by sense report, in a realm compounded of tangible things and virtual images, of actual events and ominous portents, always between fact and fiction. For he sees not only actualities but meanings. He has, indeed, all the impulses and interests of animal nature; he eats, sleeps, mates, seeks comfort, flees pain, just as cats and bears do. But he has something more in his repertoire, too: he has laws and religions, theories and dogmas, because he lives not only through sense but through symbols. That is the special asset of his mind, which makes him master of earth and all its progeny.

By the agency of symbols—marks, words, mental images, and icons of all sorts—he can hold his ideas for contemplation long after their original causes have passed away. Therefore, he can think of things that are not presented or even suggested by his actual environment. By associating symbols in his mind, he combines things and events that were never together in the real world. This gives him the power we call imagination. Further, he can symbolize only part of an idea and let the rest go out of consciousness; this gives him the faculty that has been his pride throughout the ages, the power of abstraction.

The combined effect of these two powers is inestimable. They are the roots of his supreme talent, the gift of reason. The human mind is probably the only mind on earth that can reach out to an awareness of things beyond its practical environment and can also conceive of such notions as truth, beauty, justice, majesty, space and time and creation.

Where in the course of evolution did man lose the realism of a clever animal and fall prey to subjective fears? The answer is, I think, that man's mind is *not* a direct evolution from the beast's mind, but is a unique variant and therefore has had a meteoric and startling career very different from any other animal history. The trait that sets human mentality apart from every other is its preoccupation with symbols, with images and names that *mean* things, rather than with things themselves. . . .

All human activity is based on the appreciation and use of symbols. Language, religion, mathematics, all learning, all science and superstition, even right and wrong, are products of symbolic expression rather than direct experience. Our commonest words, such as *house* and *red* and *walking,* are symbols; the pyramids of Egypt and the mysterious circles of Stonehenge are symbols; so are dominions and empires and astronomical universes. We live in a mind-made world, where things of prime importance are images or words that embody ideas and feelings and attitudes.

B. HOW SYMBOLS CREATE THE PERILS OF ILLUSION

The images of things that we remember are not exact and faithful transcriptions even of our actual sense impressions. They are made as much by what we think as by what we see. It is a well-known fact that if you ask several people the size of the moon's disk as they look at it, their estimates will vary from the area of a dime to that of a barrel top. Ideas are transformations of actual things. They are, in fact, *symbols* of reality, not pieces of it.

A symbol is not the same thing as a sign. All intelligent animals use signs; so do we. To them as well as to us sounds and smells and motions are signs of food, danger, the presence of other beings, or of rain or storm. In every case a sign is closely bound up with something to be noted or expected in experience. The difference between a sign and a symbol is, in brief, that a sign causes us to think or act *in face of* the thing signified, whereas a symbol causes us to think *about* the thing symbolized. A symbol does not announce the presence of an object, but merely *brings this thing to mind.* Therein lies the great importance of symbolism for human life.

A sign is always embedded in reality, in a present that emerges from the actual past and stretches to the future; but a symbol may be divorced from reality altogether. It may refer to what is *not* the case, to a mere idea, a figment, a dream. It serves, therefore, to liberate thought from the immediate stimuli of a physically present world; and that liberation marks the essential difference between human and non-human mentality. Animals think, but they think *of* and *at* things; men think primarily *about* things. Words, pictures, and memory images are symbols that may be combined and varied in a thousand ways. The tendency to manipulate ideas, to combine and abstract, mix and extend them by playing with symbols, is man's outstanding characteristic. It seems to be what his brain most naturally and spontaneously does. Therefore, his primitive mental function is not judging reality, but *dreaming his desires.*

C. THE EXPANSION OF HUMAN LIFE THROUGH SYMBOLS

The fact that sensuous forms of natural processes have a significance beyond themselves makes the range of our symbolism, and with it the horizon of our consciousness, much wider and deeper than language. This is the source of ritual, mythology, and art. Ritual is a symbolic rendering of certain emotional *attitudes,* which have become articulate and fixed by being constantly expressed. Mythology is man's image of his world, and of himself, in the world. Art is the exposition of his own subjective history, the life of feeling, the human spirit in all its adventures.

The process of symbolic transformation that all our experiences undergo is nothing more or less than the process of *conception,* which underlies the human faculties of abstraction and imagination, and in the course of manipulating symbols we inevitably distort the original experience. . . .

The process of *envisaging* facts, values, hopes, and fears underlies our whole behavior pattern; and this process is reflected in the evolution of an extraordinary phenomenon found always, and only, in human societies, the phenomenon of language.

Language is the highest and most amazing achievement of the symbolistic human mind. The power it bestows is almost inestimable, for without it anything properly called "thought" is impossible. The birth of language is the dawn of humanity. The line between man and beast—between the highest ape and the lowest savage—is the language line.

19. A CLUE TO THE NATURE OF MAN: THE SYMBOL

Ernst Cassirer

In the human world we find a new characteristic which appears to be the distinctive mark of human life. The functional circle of man is not only quantitively enlarged; it has also undergone a qualitative change. Man has, as it were, discovered a new method of adapting himself to his environment. Between the receptor system and the effector system, which are to be found in all animal species, we find in man a third link which we may describe as the *symbolic system*. This new acquisition transforms the whole of human life. As compared with the other animals man lives not merely in a broader reality; he lives, so to speak, in a new *dimension* of reality. There is an unmistakable difference between organic reactions and human responses. In the first case a direct and immediate answer is given to an outward stimulus; in the second case the answer is delayed. It is interrupted and retarded by a slow and complicated process of thought. At first sight such a delay may appear to be a very questionable gain. Many philosophers have warned man against this pretended progress. "L'homme qui médite," says Rousseau, "est un animal depravé": it is not an improvement but a deterioration of human nature to exceed the boundaries of organic life.

Yet there is no remedy against this reversal of the natural order. Man cannot escape from his own achievement. He cannot but adopt the conditions of his own life. No longer in a merely physical universe, man lives in a symbolic universe. Language, myth, art, and religion are parts of this universe. They are the varied threads which weave the symbolic net, the tangled web of human experience. All human progress in thought and experience refines upon and strengthens this net. No longer can man confront reality immediately; he cannot see it, as it were, face to face. Physical reality seems to recede in proportion as man's symbolic

activity advances. Instead of dealing with the things themselves man is in a sense constantly conversing with himself. He has so enveloped himself in linguistic forms, in artistic images, in mythical symbols or religious rites that he cannot see or know anything except by the interposition of this artificial medium. . . .

From the point of view at which we have just arrived we may correct and enlarge the classical definition of man. In spite of all the efforts of modern irrationalism this definition of man as an *animal rationale* has not lost its force. Rationality is indeed an inherent feature of all human activities. Mythology itself is not simply a crude mass of superstitions or gross delusions. It is not merely chaotic, for it possesses a systematic or conceptual form. But, on the other hand, it would be impossible to characterize the structure of myth as rational. Language has often been identified with reason, or with the very source of reason. But it is easy to see that this definition fails to cover the whole field. It is a *pars pro toto;* it offers us a part for the whole. For side by side with conceptual language there is an emotional language; side by side with logical or scientific language there is a language of poetic imagination. Primarily language does not express thoughts or ideas, but feelings and affections. And even a religion "within the limits of pure reason" as conceived and worked out by Kant is no more than a mere abstraction. It conveys only the ideal shape, only the shadow, of what a genuine and concrete religious life is. The great thinkers who have defined man as an *animal rationale* were not empiricists, nor did they ever intend to give an empirical account of human nature. By this definition they were expressing rather a fundamental moral imperative. Reason is a very inadequate term with which to comprehend the forms of man's cultural life in all their richness and variety. But all these forms are symbolic forms. Hence, instead of defining man as an *animal rationale,* we should define him as an *animal symbolicum.* By so doing we can designate his specific difference, and we can

Reprinted from Ernst Cassirer, *An Essay on Man* (New Haven: Yale University Press, 1974), pp. 24–36, with the permission of the publisher.

understand the new way open to men—the way to civilization. . . .

By our definition of man as an *animal symbolicum* we have arrived at our first point of departure for further investigations. But it now becomes imperative that we develop this definition somewhat in order to give it greater precision. That symbolic thought and symbolic behavior are among the most characteristic features of human life, and that the whole progress of human culture is based on these conditions, is undeniable. But are we entitled to consider them as the special endowment of man to the exclusion of all other organic beings? Is not symbolism a principle which we may trace back to a much deeper source, and which has a much broader range of applicability?. . .

We shall attempt to describe the symbolic attitude of man in a more accurate manner in order to be able to contradistinguish it from other modes of symbolic behavior found throughout the animal kingdom. That animals do not always react to stimuli in a direct way, that they are capable of an indirect reaction, is evidently beyond question. The well-known experiments of Pavlov provide us with a rich body of empirical evidence concerning the so-called representative stimuli. In the case of the anthropoid apes a very interesting experimental study by Wolfe has shown the effectiveness of "token rewards." The animals learned to respond to tokens as substitute for food rewards in the same way in which they responded to food itself.[1] According to Wolfe the results of varied and protracted training experiments have demonstrated that symbolic processes occur in the behavior of anthropoid apes. Robert M. Yerkes, who describes these experiments in his latest book, draws from them an important general conclusion.

That they [symbolic processes] are relatively rare and difficult to observe is evident. One may fairly continue to question their existence, but I suspect that they presently will be identified as antecedents of human symbolic processes. Thus we leave this subject at a most exciting stage of development, when discoveries of moment seem imminent.[2]

It would be premature to make any predictions with regard to the future development of this problem. The field must be left open for future investigations. The interpretation of the experimental facts, on the other hand, always depends on certain fundamental concepts which have to be clarified before the empirical material can bear its fruit. Modern psychology and psychobiology take this fact into account. It seems to me highly significant that nowadays it is not the philosophers but the empirical observers and investigators who appear to be taking the leading roles in solving this problem. The latter tell us that after all the problem is not merely an empirical one but to a great degree a logical one. Georg Révész has recently published a series of articles in which he starts off with the proposition that the warmly debated question of so-called *animal language* cannot be solved on the basis of mere facts of animal psychology. Everyone who examines the different psychological theses and theories with an unbiased and critical mind must come at last to the conclusion that the problem cannot be cleared up by simply referring to forms of animal communication and to certain animal accomplishments which are gained by drill and training. All such accomplishments admit of the most contradictory interpretations. Hence it is necessary, first of all, to find a correct logical starting point, one which can lead us to a natural and sound interpretation of the empirical facts. This starting point is the *definition of speech*. . . .

Here we touch upon the crucial point in our whole problem. The difference between *propositional language* and *emotional language* is the real landmark between the human and the animal world. All the theories and observations concerning animal language are wide of the mark if they fail to recognize this fundamental difference. In all the literature of the subject there does not seem to be a single conclusive proof of the fact that any animal ever made the decisive step from subjective to objective, from affective to propositional language. Koehler insists emphatically that speech is definitely beyond the powers of anthropoid apes. He maintains that the lack of this invaluable technical aid and the great limitation of those very important components of thought, the so-called images, constitute the causes which prevent animals from ever achieving even the least beginnings of cultural development[3]. . . . The logical analysis of human speech always leads us to an element of prime importance which has no parallel in the animal world. The general theory of evolution in no sense stands in the way of the acknowledgment of this fact. Even in the field of the phenomena of organic nature we have learned that evolution does not exclude a sort of original creation. The fact of sudden mutation and of emergent evolution has to be admitted. Modern biology no longer speaks of evolution in terms of earlier Darwinism; nor does it explain the causes of evolution in the same way. We may readily admit that the anthropoid apes, in the development of certain symbolic processes, have made a significant forward step. But again we must insist that they did not reach the threshold of the human world. They entered, as it were, a blind alley.

For the sake of a clear statement of the problem we must carefully distinguish between *signs* and *symbols.* That we find rather complex systems of signs and signals in animal behavior seems to be an ascertained fact. We may even say that some animals, especially domesticated animals, are extremely susceptible to signs. A dog will react to the slightest changes in the behavior of his master; he will even distinguish the expressions of a human face or the modulations of a human voice. But it is a far cry from these phenomena to an understanding of symbolic and human speech. The famous experiments of Pavlov prove only that animals can easily be trained to react not merely to direct stimuli but to all sorts of mediate or representative stimuli. A bell, for example, may become a "sign for dinner," and an animal may be trained not to touch its food when this sign is absent. . . .

Bearing this distinction in mind, we can find an approach to one of the most controverted problems. The question of the *intelligence of animals* has always been one of the greatest puzzles of anthropological philosophy. Tremendous efforts, both of thought and observation, have been expended on answers to this question. But the ambiguity and vagueness of the very term "intelligence" has always stood in the way of a clear solution. . . . If by intelligence we understand either adjustment to the immediate environment or adaptive modification of environment, we must certainly ascribe to animals a comparatively highly developed intelligence. It must also be conceded that not all

animal actions are governed by the presence of an immediate stimulus. The animal is capable of all sorts of detours in its reactions. It may learn not only to use implements but even to invent tools for its purposes. Hence some psychobiologists do not hesitate to speak of a creative or constructive imagination in animals. But neither this intelligence nor this imagination is of the specifically human type. In short, we may say that the animal possesses a practical imagination and intelligence whereas man alone has developed a new form: a *symbolic imagination and intelligence.*

Moreover, in the mental development of the individual mind the transition from one form to the other—from a merely practical attitude to a symbolic attitude—is evident. But here this step is the final result of a slow and continuous process. By the usual methods of psychological observation it is not easy to distinguish the individual stages of this complicated process. There is, however, another way to obtain full insight into the general character and paramount importance of this transition. Nature itself has here, so to speak, made an experiment capable of throwing unexpected light upon the point in question. We have the classical cases of Laura Bridgman and Helen Keller, two blind deaf-mute children, who by means of special methods learned to speak. Although both cases are well known and have often been treated in psychological literature,[4] I must nevertheless remind the reader of them once more because they contain perhaps the best illustration of the general problem with which we are here concerned. Mrs. Sullivan, the teacher of Helen Keller, has recorded the exact date on which the child really began to understand the meaning and function of human language. I quote her own words:

I must write you a line this morning because something very important has happened. Helen has taken the second great step in her education. She has learned that *everything has a name, and that the manual alphabet is the key to everything she wants to know.*

. . . This morning, while she was washing, she wanted to know the name for "water." When she wants to know the name of anything, she points to it and pats my hand. I spelled "w-a-t-e-r" and thought no more about it until after breakfast. . . . [Later on] we went out to the pump house, and I made Helen hold her mug under the spout while I pumped. As the cold water gushed forth, filling the mug, I spelled "w-a-t-e-r" in Helen's free hand. The word coming so close upon the sensation of cold water rushing over her hand seemed to startle her. She dropped the mug and stood as one transfixed. A new light came into her face. She spelled "water" several times. Then she dropped on the ground and asked for its name and pointed to the pump and the trellis and suddenly turning round she asked for my name. I spelled "teacher." All the way back to the house she was highly excited, and learned the name of every object she touched, so that in a few hours she had added thirty new words to her vocabulary. The next morning she got up like a radiant fairy. She has flitted from object to object, asking the name of everything and kissing me for very gladness. . . . Everything must have a name now. Wherever we go, she asks eagerly for the names of things she has not learned at home. She is anxious for her friends to spell, and eager to teach the letters to everyone she meets. She drops the signs and pantomime she used before, as soon as she has words to supply their place, and the acquirement of a new word affords her the liveliest pleasure. And we notice that her face grows more expressive each day.[5]

The decisive step leading from the use of signs and pantomime to the use of words, that is, of symbols, could scarcely be described in a more striking manner. What was the child's real discovery at this moment? Helen Keller had previously learned to combine a certain thing or event with a certain sign of the manual alphabet. A fixed association had been established between these things and certain tactile impressions. But a series of such associations, even if they are repeated and amplified, still does not imply an understanding of what human speech is and means. In order to arrive at such an understanding the child had to make a new and much more significant discovery. It had to understand that *everything has a name*—that the symbolic function is not restricted to particular cases but is a principle of *universal* applicability which encompasses the whole field of human thought. In the case of Helen Keller this discovery came as a sudden shock. She was a girl seven years of age who, with the exception of defects in the use of certain sense organs, was in an excellent state of health and possessed of a highly developed mind. By the neglect of her education she had been very much retarded. Then, suddenly, the crucial development takes place. It works like an intellectual revolution. The child begins to see the world in a new light. It has learned the use of words not merely as mechanical signs or signals but as an entirely new instrument of thought. A new horizon is opened up, and henceforth the child will roam at will in this incomparably wider and freer area.

The same can be shown in the case of Laura Bridgman, though hers is a less spectacular story. Both in mental ability and in intellectual development Laura Bridgman was greatly inferior to Helen Keller. Her life and education do not contain the same dramatic elements we find in Helen Keller. Yet in both cases the same typical elements are present. After Laura Bridgman had learned the use of the finger-alphabet she, too, suddenly reached the point at which she began to understand the symbolism of human speech. In this respect we find a surprising parallelism between the two cases. "I shall never forget," writes Miss Drew, one of the first teachers of Laura Bridgman, "the first meal taken after she appreciated the use of the finger-alphabet. Every article that she touched must have a name; and I was obliged to call some one to help me wait upon the other children, while she kept me busy in spelling the new words."[6]

The principle of symbolism, with its universality, validity, and general applicability, is the magic word, the Open Sesame! giving access to the specifically human world, to the world of human culture. . . . As the case of Helen Keller proves, man can construct his symbolic world out of the poorest and scantiest materials. The thing of vital importance is not the individual bricks and stones but their general *function* as architectural form. In the realm of speech it is their general symbolic function which vivifies the material signs and "makes them speak." Without this vivifying principle the human world would indeed remain deaf and mute. With this principle, even the world of a deaf, dumb, and blind child can become incomparably broader and richer than the world of the most highly developed animal. . . .

Without symbolism the life of man would be like that of the prisoners in the cave of Plato's famous simile. Man's life would be confined within the limits of his biological needs and his practical interest; it could find no access to the "ideal world" which is opened to him from different sides by religion, art, philosophy, science.

NOTES

1. J. B. Wolfe, "Effectiveness of Token-rewards for Chimpanzees," Comparative Psychology Monographs, 12, No. 5.

2. Robert M. Yerkes, *Chimpanzees. A Laboratory Colony* (New Haven, Yale University Press, 1943), p. 189.

3. Koehler, *The Mentality of Apes,* p. 277.

4. For Laura Bridgman see Maud Howe and Florence Howe Hall, *Laura Bridgman* (Boston, 1903); Mary Swift Lamson, *Life and Education of Laura Dewey Bridgman* (Boston, 1881);

Wilhelm Jerusalem, *Laura Bridgman. Erziehung einer Taubstumm-Blinden* (Berlin, 1905).

5. See Helen Keller, *The Story of My Life* (New York, Doubleday, Page & Co., 1902, 1903), Supplementary Account of Helen Keller's Life and Education, pp. 815 ff.

6. See Mary Swift Lamson, *Life and Education of Laura Dewey Bridgman, the Deaf, Dumb, and Blind Girl* (Boston, Houghton, Mifflin Co., 1881), pp. 7 f.

The Materialist View

20. MAN AS AUTOMATON

Thomas H. Huxley

. . . There remains a doctrine to which Descartes attached great weight, so that full acceptance of it became a sort of note of a thorough-going Cartesian, but which, nevertheless, is so opposed to ordinary prepossessions that it attained more general notoriety, and gave rise to more discussion, than almost any other Cartesian hypothesis. It is the doctrine that brute animals are mere machines or automata, devoid not only of reason, but of any kind of consciousness, which is stated briefly in the *Discourse on Method,* and more fully in the "Replies to the Fourth Objections," and in the correspondence with Henry More. . . .

REFLEX ACTION AND CONSCIOUSLY MOTIVATED BEHAVIOR

Descartes' line of argument is perfectly clear. He starts from reflex action in man, from the unquestionable fact that, in ourselves, co-ordinate, purposive, actions may take place, without intervention of consciousness or volition, or even contrary to the latter. As actions of a certain degree of complexity are brought about by mere mechanism, why may not actions of still greater complexity be the result of a more refined mechanism? What

Reprinted from Thomas H. Huxley, *Methods and Results,* published in England, 1874.

proof is there that brutes are other than a superior race of marionettes, which eat without pleasure, cry without pain, desire nothing, know nothing, and only simulate intelligence as a bee simulates a mathematician?

The Port Royalists adopted the hypothesis that brutes are machines, and are said to have carried its practical applications so far as to treat domestic animals with neglect, if not with actual cruelty. . . . Modern research has brought to light a great multitude of facts, which not only show that Descartes' view is defensible, but render it far more defensible than it was in his day.

It must be premised, that it is wholly impossible absolutely to prove the presence or absence of consciousness in anything but one's own brain, though, by analogy, we are justified in assuming its existence in other men. Now if, by some accident, a man's spinal cord is divided, his limbs are paralysed, so far as his volition is concerned, below the point of injury; and he is incapable of experiencing all those states of consciousness which, in his uninjured state, would be excited by irritation of those nerves which come off below the injury. If the spinal cord is divided in the middle of the back, for example, the skin of the feet may be cut, or pinched, or burned, or wetted with vitriol, without any sensation of touch, or of pain, arising, in consciousness. So far as the man is concerned, therefore, the part of the central nervous system which lies beyond the injury is cut off from consciousness. . . . However near the brain the spinal cord is injured, consciousness remains intact, except that the irritation of parts below the injury is no longer represented by sensation. On the other hand, pressure upon the anterior division of the brain, or extensive injuries to it, abolish consciousness. Hence, it is a highly probable conclusion, that consciousness in man depends upon the integrity of the anterior division of the brain, while the middle and hinder divisions of the brain, and the rest of the nervous centres, have nothing to do with it. And it is further highly probable, that what is true for man is true for other vertebrated animals.

We may assume, then, that in a living vertebrated animal, any segment of the cerebro-spinal axis (or spinal cord and brain) separated from that anterior division of the brain which is the organ of consciousness, is as completely incapable of giving rise to consciousness as we know it to be incapable of carrying out volitions. Nevertheless, this separated segment of the spinal cord is not passive and inert. On the contrary, it is the seat of extremely remarkable powers. . . .

EFFECT OF BRAIN DAMAGE IN A LOWER ANIMAL

If the spinal cord of a frog is cut across, so as to provide us with a segment separated from the brain, we shall have a subject parallel to the injured man, on which experiments can be made without remorse; as we have a right to conclude that a frog's spinal cord is not likely to be conscious, when a man's is not.

Now the frog behaves just as the man did. The legs utterly paralysed, so far as voluntary movement is concerned; but they are vigorously drawn up to the body when any irritant is applied to the foot. But let us study our frog a little farther. Touch the skin of the side of the body with a little acetic acid, which gives rise to all the signs of great pain in an uninjured frog. In this case, there can be no pain, because the application is made to a part of the skin supplied with nerves which come off from the cord below the point of section; nevertheless, the frog lifts up the limb of the same side, and applies the foot to rub off the acetic acid; and, what is still more

remarkable, if the limb be held so that the frog cannot use it, it will, by and by, move the limb of the other side, turn it across the body, and use it for the same rubbing process. It is impossible that the frog, if it were in its entirety and could reason, should perform actions more purposive than these: and yet we have most complete assurance that, in this case, the frog is not acting from purpose, has no consciousness, and is a mere insensible machine.

But now suppose that, instead of making a section of the cord in the middle of the body, it had been made in such a manner as to separate the hindermost division of the brain from the rest of the organ, and suppose the foremost two-thirds of the brain entirely taken away. The frog is then absolutely devoid of any spontaneity; it sits upright in the attitude which a frog habitually assumes; and it will not stir unless it is touched; but it differs from the frog which I have just described in this, that, if it be thrown into the water, it begins to swim, and swims just as well as the perfect frog does. But swimming requires the combination and successive co-ordination of a great number of muscular actions. And we are forced to conclude, that the impression made upon the sensory nerves of the skin of the frog by the contact with the water into which it is thrown, causes the transmission to the central nervous apparatus of an impulse which sets going a certain machinery by which all the muscles of swimming are brought into play in due co-ordination. If the frog be stimulated by some irritating body, it jumps or walks as well as the complete frog can do. The simple sensory impression, acting through the machinery of the cord, gives rise to these complex combined movements.

It is possible to go a step farther. Suppose that only the anterior division of the brain—so much of it as lies in front of the "optic lobes"—is removed. If that operation is performed quickly and skillfully, the frog may be kept in a state of full bodily vigour for months, or it may be for years; but it will sit unmoved. It sees nothing: it hears nothing. It will starve sooner than feed itself, although food put into its mouth is swallowed. On irritation, it jumps or walks; if thrown into the water it swims. If it be put on the hand, it sits there, crouched, perfectly quiet, and would sit there for ever. If the hand be inclined very gently and slowly, so that the frog would naturally tend to slip off, the creature's fore paws are shifted on to the edge of the hand, until he can just prevent himself from falling. If the turning of the hand be slowly continued, he mounts up with great care and deliberation, putting first one leg forward and then another, until he balances himself with perfect precision upon the edge; and if the turning of the hand is continued, he goes through the needful set of muscular operations, until he comes to be seated in security, upon the back of the hand. The doing of all this requires a delicacy of co-ordination, and a precision of adjustment of the muscular apparatus of the body, which are only comparable to those of a rope-dancer. To the ordinary influences of light, the frog, deprived of its cerebral hemispheres, appears to be blind. Nevertheless, if the animal be put upon a table, with a book at some little distance between it and the light, and the skin of the hinder part of its body is then irritated, it will jump forward, avoiding the book by passing to the right or left of it. Therefore, although the frog appears to have no sensation of light, visible objects act through its brain upon the motor mechanism of its body.

It is obvious, that had Descartes been acquainted with these remarkable results of modern research, they would have furnished him with far more powerful arguments than he possessed in favour of his view of the automatism of brutes. The habits of a frog, leading its natural life, involve such simple adaptations to surrounding conditions, that the machinery which is competent to do so much without the intervention of consciousness, might well do all. And this argument is vastly strengthened by what has been learned in recent times of the marvellously complex operations which are performed mechanically, and to all appearance without consciousness, by men, when, in consequence of injury or disease, they are reduced to a condition more or less comparable to that of a frog, in which the anterior part of the brain has been removed. A case has recently been published by an eminent French physician, Dr. Mesnet, which illustrates this condition so remarkably, that I make no apology for dwelling upon it at considerable length.

THE CASE OF SERGEANT F.

A sergeant of the French army, F———, twenty-seven years of age, was wounded during the battle of Bazeilles, by a ball which fractured his left parietal bone. He ran his bayonet through the Prussian soldier who wounded him, but almost immediately his right arm became paralysed; after walking about two hundred yards, his right leg became similarly affected, and he lost his senses. When he recovered them, three weeks afterwards, in a hospital at Mayence, the right half of the body was completely paralysed, and remained in this condition for a year. At present, the only trace of the paralysis which remains is a slight weakness of the right half of the body. Three or four months after the wound was inflicted, periodical disturbances of the functions of the brain made their appearance, and have continued ever since. The disturbances last from fifteen to thirty hours; the intervals at which they occur being from fifteen to thirty days.

For four years, therefore, the life of this man has been divided into alternating phases—short abnormal states intervening between long normal states.

In the periods of normal life, the ex-sergeant's health is perfect; he is intelligent and kindly, and performs, satisfactorily, the duties of a hospital attendant. The commencement of the abnormal state is ushered in by uneasiness and a sense of weight about the forehead, which the patient compares to the constriction of a circle of iron; and, after its termination, he complains, for some hours, of dullness and heaviness of the head. But the transition from the normal to the abnormal state takes place in a few minutes, without convulsions or cries, and without anything to indicate the change to a bystander. His movements remain free and his expression calm, except for a contraction of the brow, an incessant movement of the eyeballs, and a chewing motion of the jaws. The eyes are wide open, and their pupils dilated. If the man happens to be in a place to which he is accustomed, he walks about as usual; but, if he is in a new place, or if obstacles are intentionally placed in his way, he stumbles gently against them, stops, and then, feeling over the objects with his hands, passes on one side of them. He offers no resistance to any change of direction which may be impressed upon him, or to the forcible acceleration or retardation of his movements. He eats, drinks, smokes, walks about, dresses and undresses himself, rises and goes to bed at the accustomed hours. Nevertheless, pins may be run into his body, or strong electric shocks may be sent through it, without causing the least indication of pain; no odorous substance, pleasant or unpleasant, makes the least impression; he eats and drinks with avidity whatever is offered, and takes asafoetida, or vinegar, or quinine, as readily as water; no noise affects him; and light influences him only under certain conditions. Dr. Mesnet remarks, that the sense of touch alone seems to persist, and indeed to be more acute and delicate than in the normal state: and it is by means of the nerves of touch, almost exclusively, that his organism is brought into relation with the external world. Here a difficulty arises. It is clear from the facts detailed, that the nervous apparatus by which, in the normal state, sensations of touch are excited, is that by which external influences determine the movements of the body, in the abnormal state. But does the state of consciousness, which we term a tactile sensation, accompany the operation of this nervous apparatus in the abnormal state? Or is consciousness utterly absent, the man being reduced to an insensible mechanism?

It is impossible to obtain direct evidence in favour of the one conclusion or the other; all that can be said is, that the case of the frog shows that the man may be devoid of any kind of consciousness.

A further difficult problem is this. The man is insensible to sensory impressions made through the ear, the nose, the tongue, and, to a great extent, the eye; nor is he susceptible of pain from causes operating during his abnormal state. Nevertheless, it is possible so to act upon his tactile apparatus, as to give rise to those molecular changes in his sensorium, which are ordinarily the causes of associated trains of ideas. I give a striking example of this process in Dr. Mesnet's words:—

He was taking a walk in the garden under a bunch of trees. We placed in his hand his walking stick which he had let fall a few minutes before. He feels it, passes his hand over the bent handle a few times, becomes attentive, seems to extend his ear, and suddenly calls out, "Henry," then, "Here they are. There are about twenty to our two! We have reached our end." And then, with his hand behind his back, as if about to leap, he prepares to attack with his weapon. He crouches in the level, green grass, his head concealed by a tree, in the position of a hunter, and follows all the short-distance movements of the enemy which he believes he sees, with accompanying movements of his hands and shoulders.

In a subsequent abnormal period, Dr. Mesnet caused the patient to repeat this scene by placing him in the same conditions. Now, in this case, the question arises whether the series of actions constituting this singular pantomime was accompanied by the ordinary states of consciousness, the appropriate train of ideas, or not? Did the man dream that he was skirmishing? Or was he in the condition of one of Vaucauson's automata—a senseless mechanism worked by molecular changes in his nervous system? The analogy of the frog shows that the latter assumption is perfectly justifiable.

The ex-sergeant has a good voice, and had, at one time, been employed as a singer at a café. In one of his abnormal states he was observed to begin humming a tune. He then went to his room, dressed himself carefully, and took up some parts of a periodical novel, which lay on his bed, as if he were trying to find something. Dr. Mesnet, suspecting that he was seeking his music, made up one of these into a roll and put it into his hand. He appeared satisfied, took his cane and went downstairs to the door. Here Dr. Mesnet turned him round, and he walked quite contentedly, in the opposite direction, towards the room of the concierge. The light of the sun shining through a window now happened to fall upon him, and seemed to suggest the footlights of the stage on which he was accustomed to make his appearance. He stopped, opened his roll of imaginary music, put himself into the attitude of a singer, and sang, with perfect execution, three songs, one after the other. After which he wiped his face with his handkerchief and drank, without a grimace, a tumbler of strong vinegar and water which was put into his hand.

INNATE AND AUTOMATIC BEHAVIOR PATTERNS

An experiment which may be performed upon the frog deprived of the fore part of its brain, well known as Goltz's "Quak-versuch," affords a parallel to this performance. If the skin of a certain part of the back of such a frog is gently stroked with the finger, it immediately croaks. It never croaks unless it is so stroked, and the croak always follows the stroke, just as the sound of a repeater follows the touching of the spring. In the frog, this "song" is innate—so to speak *a priori*—and depends upon a mechanism in the brain governing the vocal apparatus, which is set at work by the molecular change set up in the sensory nerves of the skin of the back by the contact of a foreign body.

In man there is also a vocal mechanism, and the cry of an infant is in the same sense innate and *a priori,* inasmuch as it depends on an organic relation between its sensory nerves and the nervous mechanism which governs the vocal apparatus. Learning to speak, and learning to sing, are processes by which the vocal mechanism is set to new tunes. A song which has been learned has its molecular equivalent, which potentially represents it in the brain, just as a musical box, wound up, potentially represents an overture. Touch the stop and the overture begins; send a molecular impulse along the proper afferent nerve and the singer begins his song.

Again, the manner in which the frog, though apparently insensible to light, is yet, under some circumstances, influenced by visual images, finds a singular parallel in the case of the ex-sergeant.

Sitting at a table, in one of his abnormal states, he took up a pen, felt for paper and ink, and began to write a letter to his general, in which he recommended himself for a medal, on account of his good conduct and courage. It occurred to Dr. Mesnet to ascertain experimentally how far vision was concerned in this act of writing. He therefore interposed a screen between the man's eyes and his hands; under these circumstances he went on writing for a short time, but the words became illegible, and he finally stopped, without manifesting any discontent. On the withdrawal of the screen he began to write again where he had left off. The substitution of water for ink in the inkstand had a similar result. He stopped, looked at his pen, wiped it on his coat, dipped it in the water, and began again with the same effect.

On one occasion, he began to write upon the topmost of ten superimposed sheets of paper. After he had written a line or two, this sheet was suddenly drawn away. There was a slight expression of surprise, but he continued his letter on the second sheet exactly as if it had been the first. This operation was repeated five times, so that the fifth sheet contained nothing but the writer's signature at the bottom of the page. Nevertheless, when the signature was finished, his eyes turned to the top of the blank sheet, and he went through the form of reading over what he had written, a movement of lips accompanying each word; moreover, with his pen, he put in such corrections as were needed, in that part of the blank page which corresponded with the position of the words which required correction, in the sheets which had been taken away. If the five sheets had been transparent, therefore, they would, when superposed, have formed a properly written and corrected letter.

Immediately after he had written his letter, F——— got up, walked down to the garden, made himself a cigarette, lighted and smoked it. He was about to prepare another, but sought in vain for his tobacco-pouch, which had been purposely taken away. The pouch was now thrust before his eyes and put under his nose, but he neither saw nor smelt it; yet, when it was placed in his hand, he at once seized it, made a fresh cigarette, and ignited a match to light the latter. The match was blown out, and another lighted match placed close before his eyes, but he made no attempt to take it; and, if his cigarette was lighted for him, he made no attempt to smoke. All this time the eyes were vacant, and neither winked, nor exhibited any contraction of the pupils. From these and other experiments, Dr. Mesnet draws the conclusion that his patient sees some things and not others; that the sense of sight is accessible to all things which are brought into relation with him by the sense of touch, and, on the contrary, insensible to things which lie outside this relation. He sees the match he holds and does not see any other.

Just so the frog "sees" the book which is in the way of his jump, at the same time that isolated visual impressions take no effect upon him.

As I have pointed out, it is impossible to prove that F——— is absolutely unconscious in his abnormal state, but it is no less impossible to prove the contrary; and the case of the frog goes a long way to justify the assumption that, in the abnormal state, the man is a mere insensible machine. . . .

Though we may see reason to disagree with Descartes' hypothesis that brutes are unconscious machines, it does not follow that he was wrong in regarding them as automata. They may be more or less conscious, sensitive, automata; and the view that they are such conscious machines is that which is implicitly, or explicitly adopted by most persons. When we speak of the actions of the lower animals being guided by instinct and not by reason, what we really mean is that, though they feel as we do, yet their actions are the results of their physical organisation. We believe, in short, that they are machines, one part of which (the nervous system) not only sets the rest in motion, and co-ordinates its movements in relation with changes in surrounding bodies, but is provided with special apparatus, the function of which is the calling into existence of those states of consciousness which are termed sensations, emotions, and ideas. I believe that this generally accepted view is the best expression of the facts at present known. . . .

It may be assumed, then, that molecular changes in the brain are the causes of all the states of consciousness of brutes. Is there any evidence that these states of consciousness may, conversely, cause those molecular changes which give rise to muscular motion? I see no such evidence. The frog walks, hops, swims, and goes through his gymnastic performances quite as well without consciousness, and consequently without volition, as with it; and, if a frog, in his natural state, possesses anything corresponding with what we call volition, there is no reason to think that it is anything but a concomitant of the molecular changes in the brain which form part of the series involved in the production of motion.

The consciousness of brutes would appear to be related to the mechanism of their body simply as a collateral product of its working, and to be as completely without any power of modifying that working as the steam-whistle which accompanies the work of a locomotive engine is without influence upon its machinery. Their volition, if they have any, is an emotion indicative of physical changes, not a cause of such changes.

This conception of the relations of states of consciousness with molecular changes in the brain—of *psychoses* with *neuroses*—does not prevent us from ascribing free will to brutes. For an agent is free when there is nothing to prevent him from doing that which he desires to do. If a greyhound chases a hare, he is a free agent, because his action is in entire accordance with his strong desire to catch the hare; while so long as he is held back by the leash he is not free, being prevented by external force from following his inclination. And the ascription of freedom to the greyhound under the former circumstances is by no means inconsistent with the other aspect of the facts of the case—that he is a machine impelled to the chase, and caused, at the same time, to have the desire to catch the game by the impression which the rays of light proceeding from the hare make upon his eyes, and through them upon his brain. . . .

THE SAME CONCLUSION APPLIES TO HUMAN BEINGS

It will be said, that I mean that the conclusions deduced from the study of the brutes are applicable to man, and that the logical consequences of such application are fatalism, materialism, and atheism—whereupon the drums will beat the *pas de charge*.

One does not do battle with drummers; but I venture to offer a few remarks for the calm consideration of thoughtful persons, untrammelled by foregone conclusions, unpledged to shore-up tottering dogmas, and anxious only to know the true bearings of the case.

It is quite true that, to the best of my judgment, the argumentation which applies to brutes holds equally good of men; and, therefore, that all states of consciousness in us, as in them, are immediately caused by molecular changes of the brain-substance. It seems to me that in men, as in brutes, there is no proof that any state of consciousness is the cause of change in the motion of the matter of the organism. If these positions are well based, it follows that our mental conditions are simply the symbols in consciousness of the changes which take place automatically in the organism; and that, to take an extreme illustration, the feeling we call volition is not the cause of a voluntary act, but the symbol of that state of the brain which is the immediate cause of that act. We are conscious automata, endowed with free will in the only intelligible sense of that much-abused term—inasmuch as in many respects we are able to do as we like—but none the less parts of the great series of causes and effects which, in unbroken continuity, composes that which is, and has been, and shall be—the sum of existence.

The Behaviorist View

21. WHAT IS MAN?

B. F. Skinner

Unable to understand how or why the person we see behaves as he does, we attribute his behavior to a person we cannot see, whose behavior we cannot explain either but about whom we are not inclined to ask questions. We probably adopt this strategy not so much because of any lack of interest or power but because of a longstanding conviction that for much of human behavior there *are* no relevant antecedents. The function of the inner man is to provide an explanation which will not be explained in turn. Explanation stops with him. He is not a mediator between past history and current behavior, he is a *center* from which behavior emanates. He initiates, originates, and creates, and in doing so he remains, as he was for the Greeks, divine. We say that he is autonomous—and, so far as a science of behavior is concerned, that means miraculous.

The position is, of course, vulnerable. Autonomous man serves to explain only the things we are not yet able to explain in other ways. His existence depends upon our ignorance, and he naturally loses status as we come to know more about behavior. The task of a scientific analysis is to explain how the behavior of a person as a physical system is related to the conditions under which the human species evolved and the conditions under which the individual lives. . . .

We can follow the path taken by physics and biology by turning directly to the relation between behavior and the environment and neglecting supposed mediating states of mind. Physics did not advance by looking more closely at the jubilance of a falling body, or biology by looking at the nature of vital spirits, and we do not need to try to discover what personalities, states of mind, feelings, traits of character, plans, purposes, intentions, or the other perquisites of autonomous man really are in order to get on with a scientific analysis of behavior. . . .

There is a much more important reason why we have been so slow in discarding mentalistic explanations: it has been hard to find alternatives. Presumably we must look for them in the external environment, but the role of the environment is by no means clear. The history of the theory of evolution illustrates the problem. Before the nineteenth century, the environment was thought of simply as a passive setting in which many different kinds of organisms were born, reproduced themselves, and died. No one saw that the environment was responsible for the fact that there *were* many different kinds (and that fact, significantly enough, was attributed to a creative Mind). The trouble was that the environment acts in an inconspicuous way: it does not push or pull, it *selects*. For thousands of years in the history of human thought the process of natural selection went unseen in spite of its extraordinary importance. When it was eventually discovered, it became, of course, the key to evolutionary theory.

The effect of the environment on behavior remained obscure for an even longer time. We can see what organisms do to the world around them, as they take from it what they need and ward off its dangers, but it is much harder to see what the world does to them. . . .

The environment not only prods or lashes, it *selects*. Its role is similar to that in natural selection, though on a very different time scale, and was overlooked for the same reason. It is now clear that we must take into account what the environment does to an organism not only before but after it responds. Behavior is shaped and maintained by its consequences. Once this fact is recognized, we can formulate the interaction between organism and environment in a much more comprehensive way.

There are two important results. One concerns the basic analysis. Behavior which operates upon the environment to produce consequences ("operant" behavior) can be studied by arranging environments in which specific consequences are contingent upon it. The contingencies under investigation have become steadily more complex, and one by one they are taking over the explanatory functions previously assigned to personalities, states of mind, feelings, traits of character, purposes, and intentions. The second result is practical: the environment can be manipulated. It is true that man's genetic endowment can be changed only very slowly, but changes in the environment of the individual have quick and dramatic effects. A technology of operant behavior is, as we shall see, already well advanced, and it may prove to be commensurate with our problems.

That possibility raises another problem, however, which must be solved if we are to take advantage of our gains. We have moved forward by dispossessing autonomous man, but he has not departed gracefully. He is conducting a sort of rearguard action in which, unfortunately, he can marshal formidable support. He is still an important figure in political science, law, religion, economics, anthropology, sociology, psychotherapy, philosophy, ethics, history, education, child care, linguistics, architecture, city planning, and family life. These fields have their specialists, and every specialist has a theory, and in almost every theory the autonomy of the individual is unquestioned. The

inner man is not seriously threatened by data obtained through casual observation or from studies of the structure of behavior, and many of these fields deal only with groups of people, where statistical or actuarial data impose few restraints upon the individual. The result is a tremendous weight of traditional "knowledge," which must be corrected or displaced by a scientific analysis.

Two features of autonomous man are particularly troublesome. In the traditional view, a person is free. He is autonomous in the sense that his behavior is uncaused. He can therefore be held responsible for what he does and justly punished if he offends. That view, together with its associated practices, must be re-examined when a scientific analysis reveals unsuspected controlling relations between behavior and environment. A certain amount of external control can be tolerated. Theologians have accepted the fact that man must be predestined to do what an omniscient God knows he will do, and the Greek dramatist took inexorable fate as his favorite theme. Soothsayers and astrologers often claim to predict what men will do, and they have always been in demand. Biographers and historians have searched for "influences" in the lives of individuals and peoples. Folk wisdom and the insights of essayists like Montaigne and Bacon imply some kind of predictability in human conduct, and the statistical and actuarial evidences of the social sciences point in the same direction.

Autonomous man survives in the face of all this. . . .

By questioning the control exercised by autonomous man and demonstrating the control exercised by the environment, a science of behavior also seems to question dignity or worth. A person is responsible for his behavior, not only in the sense that he may be justly blamed or punished when he behaves badly, but also in the sense that he is to be given credit and admired for his achievements. A scientific analysis shifts the credit as well as the blame to the environment, and traditional practices can then no longer be justified. These are sweeping changes, and those who are committed to traditional theories and practices naturally resist them. . . .

In shifting control from autonomous man to the observable environment we do not leave an empty organism. A great deal goes on inside the skin, and physiology will eventually tell us more about it. It will explain why behavior is indeed related to the antecedent events of which it can be shown to be a function. The assignment is not always correctly understood. Many physiologists regard themselves as looking for the "physiological correlates" of mental events. Physiological research is regarded as simply a more scientific version of introspection. But physiological techniques are not, of course, designed to detect or measure personalities, ideas, attitudes, feelings, impulses, thoughts, or purposes. . . .

At the moment neither introspection nor physiology supplies very adequate information about what is going on inside a man as he behaves, and since they are both directed inward, they have the same effect of diverting attention from the external environment.

Much of the misunderstanding about an inner man comes from the metaphor of storage. Evolutionary and environmental histories change an organism, but they are not stored within it. Thus, we observe that babies suck their mothers' breasts, and we can easily imagine that a strong tendency to do so has survival value, but much more is implied by a "sucking instinct" regarded as something a baby possesses which enables it to suck. The concept of "human nature" or "genetic endowment" is dangerous when taken in that sense. We are closer to human nature in a baby than in an adult, or in a primitive culture than in an advanced, in the sense that environmental contingencies are less likely to have obscured the genetic endowment, and it is tempting to dramatize that endowment by implying that earlier stages have survived in concealed form: man is a naked ape, and "the paleolithic bull which survives in man's inner self still paws the earth whenever a threatening gesture is made on the social scene." But anatomists and physiologists will not find an ape, or a bull, or for that matter instincts. They will find anatomical and physiological features which are the product of an evolutionary history.

The personal history of the individual is also often said to be stored within him. For "instinct" read "habit." The cigarette habit is presumably something more than the behavior said to show

that a person possesses it; but the only other information we have concerns the reinforcers and the schedules of reinforcement which make a person smoke a great deal. The contingencies are not stored; they have simply left a changed person.

The environment is often said to be stored in the form of memories: to recall something we search for a copy of it, which can then be seen as the original thing was seen. As far as we know, however, there are no copies of the environment in the individual *at any time,* even when a thing is present and being observed. The products of more complex contingencies are also said to be stored; the repertoire acquired as a person learns to speak French is called a "knowledge of French.". . .

It is in the nature of an experimental analysis of human behavior that it should strip away the functions previously assigned to autonomous man and transfer them one by one to the controlling environment. The analysis leaves less and less for autonomous man to do. But what about man himself? Is there not something about a person which is more than a living body? Unless something called a self survives, how can we speak of self-knowledge or self-control? To whom is the injunction "Know thyself" addressed?

It is an important part of the contingencies to which a young child is exposed that his own body is the only part of his environment which remains the same (*idem*) from moment to moment and day to day. We say that he discovers his *identity* as he learns to distinguish between his body and the rest of the world. He does this long before the community teaches him to call things by name and to distinguish "me" from "it" or "you."

A self is a repertoire of behavior appropriate to a given set of contingencies. A substantial part of the conditions to which a person is exposed may play a dominant role, and under other conditions a person may report, "I'm not myself today," or, "I couldn't have done what you said I did, because that's not like me." The identity conferred upon a self arises from the contingencies responsible for the behavior. Two or more repertoires generated by different sets of contingencies compose two or more selves. A person possesses one repertoire appropriate to his life with his friends and another appropriate to his life with his family, and a friend may find him a very different person if he sees him with his family or his family if they see him with his friends. The problem of identity arises when situations are intermingled, as when a person finds himself with both his family and his friends at the same time.

Self-knowledge and self-control imply two selves in this sense. The self-knower is almost always a product of social contingencies, but the self that is known may come from other sources. The controlling self (the conscience or superego) is of social origin, but the controlled self is more likely to be the product of genetic susceptibilities to reinforcement (the id, or the Old Adam). The controlling self generally represents the interests of others, the controlled self the interest of the individual.

The picture which emerges from a scientific analysis is not of a body with a person inside, but of a body which *is* a person in the sense that it displays a complex repertoire of behavior. The picture is, of course, unfamiliar. The man thus portrayed is a stranger, and from the traditional point of view he may not seem to be a man at all. "For at least one hundred years," said Joseph Wood Krutch, "we have been prejudiced in every theory, including economic determinism, mechanistic behaviorism, and relativism, that reduces the stature of man until he ceases to be man at all in any sense that

the humanists of an earlier generation would recognize.". . .

An experimental analysis shifts the determination of behavior from autonomous man to the environment—an environment responsible both for the evolution of the species and for the repertoire acquired by each member. Early versions of environmentalism were inadequate because they could not explain how the environment worked, and much seemed to be left for autonomous man to do. But environmental contingencies now take over functions once attributed to autonomous man, and certain questions arise. Is man then "abolished"? Certainly not as a species or as an individual achiever. It is the autonomous inner man who is abolished, and that is a step forward. But does man not then become merely a victim or passive observer of what is happening to him? He is indeed controlled by his environment, but we must remember that it is an environment largely of his own making. The evolution of a culture is a gigantic exercise in self-control. It is often said that a scientific view of man leads to wounded vanity, a sense of hopelessness, and nostalgia. But no theory changes what it is a theory about; man remains what he has always been. And a new theory may change what can be done with its subject matter. A scientific view of man offers exciting possibilities. We have not yet seen what man can make of man.

The Existentialist View

22. THE HUMANISM OF EXISTENTIALISM

Jean-Paul Sartre

What can be said from the very beginning is that by existentialism we mean a doctrine which makes human life possible and, in addition, declares that every truth and every action implies a human setting and a human subjectivity.

From Jean-Paul Sartre, *Existentialism*, trans. by Bernard Frechtman, reprinted by permission of Citadel Press, Inc.

As is generally known, the basic charge against us is that we put the emphasis on the dark side of human life. Someone recently told me of a lady who, when she let slip a vulgar word in a moment of irritation, excused herself by saying, "I guess I'm becoming an existentialist." Consequently, existentialism is regarded as something ugly; that is why we are said to be naturalists; and if we are, it is rather surprising that in this day and age we cause so much more alarm and scandal than does naturalism, properly so called. . . .

There are still people . . . who say, "It's only human!" whenever a more or less repugnant act is pointed out to them, the people who glut themselves on *chansons réalistes;* these are the people who accuse existentialism of being too gloomy, and to such an extent that I wonder whether they are complaining about it, not for its pessimism, but much rather its optimism. Can it be that what really scares them in the doctrine I shall try to present here is that it leaves to man a possibility of choice? To answer this question, we must re-examine it on a strictly philosophical plane. What is meant by the term *existentialism?* . . .

Actually, it is the least scandalous, the most austere of doctrines. It is intended strictly for specialists and philosophers. Yet it can be defined easily. What complicates matters is that there are two kinds of existentialists; first, those who are Christian, among whom I would include Jaspers and Gabriel Marcel, both Catholic; and on the other hand the atheistic existentialists among whom I class Heidegger, and then the French existentialists and myself. What they have in common is that they think that existence precedes essence, or, if you prefer, that subjectivity must be the starting point.

Just what does that mean? Let us consider some object that is manufactured, for example, a book or a paper-cutter: here is an object which has been made by an artisan whose inspiration came from a concept. He referred to the concept of what a paper-cutter is and likewise to a known method of production, which is part of the concept, something which is, by and large, a routine. Thus, the paper-cutter is at once an object produced in a certain way and, on the other hand, one having a specific use; and one can not postulate a man who produces a paper-cutter but does not know what it is used for. Therefore, let us say that, for the paper-cutter, essence—that is, the ensemble of both the production routines and the properties which enable it to be both produced and defined—precedes existence. Thus, the presence of the paper-cutter or book in front of me is determined. Therefore, we have here a technical view of the world whereby it can be said that production precedes existence. . . .

Atheistic existentialism, which I represent, is more coherent. It states that if God does not exist, there is at least one being in whom existence precedes essence, a being who exists before he can be defined by any concept, and that this being is man, or, as Heidegger says, human reality. What is meant here by saying that existence precedes essence? It means that, first of all, man exists, turns up, appears on the scene, and, only afterwards, defines himself. If man, as the existentialist conceives him, is indefinable, it is because at first he is nothing. Only afterward will he be something, and he himself will have made what he will be. Thus, there is no human nature, since there is no God to conceive it. Not only is man what he conceives himself to be, but he is also only what he wills himself to be after this thrust toward existence.

Man is nothing else but what he makes of himself. Such is the first principle of existentialism. It is also what is called subjectivity, the name we are labeled with when charges are brought against us. But what do we mean by this, if not that man has a greater dignity than a stone or table? For we mean that man first exists, that is, that man first of all is the being who hurls himself toward a future and who is conscious of imagining himself as being in the future. Man is at the start a plan which is aware of itself, rather than a patch of moss, a piece of garbage, or a cauliflower; nothing exists prior to this plan; there is nothing in heaven; man will be what he will have planned to be. Not what he will want to be. Because by the word "will" we generally mean a conscious decision, which is subsequent to what we have already made of ourselves. I may want to belong to a political party, write a book, get married; but all that is only a manifestation of an earlier, more spontaneous choice that is called "will." But if existence really does precede essence, man is responsible for what he is. Thus, existentialism's first move is to make every man aware of what he is and to make the full responsibility of his existence rest on him. And when we say that a man is responsible for himself, we do not only mean that he is responsible for his own individuality, but that he is responsible for all men.

The word subjectivism has two meanings, and

our opponents play on the two. Subjectivism means, on the one hand, that an individual chooses and makes himself; and, on the other, that it is impossible for man to transcend human subjectivity. The second of these is the essential meaning of existentialism. When we say that man chooses his own self, we mean that every one of us does likewise; but we also mean by that that in making this choice he also chooses all men. In fact, in creating the man that we want to be, there is not a single one of our acts which does not at the same time create an image of man as we think he ought to be. To choose to be this or that is to affirm at the same time the value of what we choose, because we can never choose evil. We always choose the good, and nothing can be good for us without being good for all.

If, on the other hand, existence precedes essence, and if we grant that we exist and fashion our image at one and the same time, the image is valid for everybody and for our whole age. Thus, our responsibility is much greater than we might have supposed, because it involves all mankind. If I am a workingman and choose to join a Christian trade-union rather than be a communist, and if by being a member I want to show that the best thing for man is resignation, that the kingdom of man is not of this world, I am not only involving my own case—I want to be resigned for everyone. As a result, my action has involved all humanity. To take a more individual matter, if I want to marry, to have children; even if this marriage depends solely on my own circumstances or passion or wish, I am involving all humanity in monogamy and not merely myself. Therefore, I am responsible for myself and for everyone else. I am creating a certain image of man of my own choosing. In choosing myself, I choose man.

This helps us understand what the actual content is of such rather grandiloquent words as anguish, forlornness, despair. As you will see, it's all quite simple.

First, what is meant by anguish? The existentialists say at once that man is anguish. What that means is this: the man who involves himself and who realizes that he is not only the person he chooses to be, but also a lawmaker who is, at the same time, choosing all mankind as well as himself, can not help escape the feeling of his total and deep responsibility. Of course, there are many people

who are not anxious; but we claim that they are hiding their anxiety, that they are fleeing from it. Certainly, many people believe that when they do something, they themselves are the only ones involved, and when someone says to them, "What if everyone acted that way?" they shrug their shoulders and answer, "Everyone doesn't act that way." But really, one should always ask himself, "What would happen if everybody looked at things that way?" There is no escaping this disturbing thought except by a kind of double-dealing. A man who lies and makes excuses for himself by saying "Not everybody does that," is someone with an uneasy conscience, because the act of lying implies that a universal value is conferred upon the lie.

Anguish is evident even when it conceals itself. This is the anguish that Kierkegaard called the anguish of Abraham. You know the story: an angel has ordered Abraham to sacrifice his son; if it really were an angel who has come and said, "You are Abraham, you shall sacrifice your son," everything would be all right. But everyone might first wonder, "Is it really an angel, and am I really Abraham? What proof do I have?"

There was a madwoman who had hallucinations; someone used to speak to her on the telephone and give her orders. Her doctor asked her, "Who is it who talks to you?" She answered, "He says it's God." What proof did she really have that it was God? If an angel comes to me, what proof is there that it's an angel? And if I hear voices, what proof is there that they come from heaven and not from hell, or from the subconscious, or a pathological condition? What proves that they are addressed to me? What proof is there that I have been appointed to impose my choice and my conception of man on humanity? I'll never find any proof or sign to convince me of that. If a voice addresses me, it is always for me to decide that this is the angel's voice; if I consider that such an act is a good one, it is I who will choose to say that it is good rather than bad.

Now, I'm not being singled out as an Abraham, and yet at every moment I'm obliged to perform exemplary acts. For every man, everything happens as if all mankind had its eyes fixed on him and were guiding itself by what he does. And every man ought to say to himself, "Am I really the kind of man who has the right to act in such a way that humanity might guide itself by my actions?" And if he does not say that to himself, he is masking his anguish.

There is no question here of the kind of anguish which would lead to quietism, to inaction. It is a matter of a simple sort of anguish that anybody who has had responsibilities is familiar with. For example, when a military officer takes the responsibility for an attack and sends a certain number of men to death, he chooses to do so, and in the main he alone makes the choice. Doubtless, orders come from above, but they are too broad; he interprets them, and on this interpretation depend the lives of ten or fourteen or twenty men. In making a decision he can not help having a certain anguish. All leaders know this anguish. That doesn't keep them from acting; on the contrary, it is the very condition of their action. For it implies that they envisage a number of possibilities, and when they choose one, they realize that it has value only because it is chosen. We shall see that this kind of anguish, which is the kind that existentialism describes, is explained, in addition, by a direct responsibility to the other men whom it involves. It is not a curtain separating us from action, but is part of action itself.

When we speak of forlornness, a term Heidegger was fond of, we mean only that God does not exist and that we have to face all the consequences of this. The existentialist is strongly opposed to a certain kind of secular ethics which would like to abolish God with the least possible expense. About 1880, some French teachers tried to set up a secular ethics which went something like this: God is a useless and costly hypothesis; we are discarding it; but, meanwhile, in order for there to be an ethics, a society, a civilization, it is essential that certain values be taken seriously and that they be considered as having an *a priori* existence. It must be obligatory, *a priori*, to be honest, not to lie, not to beat your wife, to have children, etc., etc. So we're going to try a little device which will make it possible to show that values exist all the same, inscribed in a heaven of ideas, though otherwise God does not exist. In other words—and this, I believe, is the tendency of everything called reformism in France —nothing will be changed if God does not exist. We shall find ourselves with the same norms of honesty, progress, and humanism, and we shall have made of God an outdated hypothesis which will peacefully die off by itself.

The existentialist, on the contrary, thinks it very distressing that God does not exist, because all possibility of finding values in a heaven of ideas disappears along with Him; there can no longer be an *a priori* Good, since there is no infinite and perfect consciousness to think it. Nowhere is it written that the Good exists, that we must be honest, that we must not lie; because the fact is we are on a plane where there are only men. Dostoievsky said, "If God didn't exist, everything would be possible." That is the very starting point of existentialism. Indeed, everything is permissible if God does not exist, and as a result man is forlorn, because neither within him nor without does he find anything to cling to. He can't start making excuses for himself.

If existence really does precede essence, there is no explaining things away by reference to a fixed and given human nature. In other words, there is no determinism, man is free, man is freedom. On the other hand, if God does not exist, we find no values or commands to turn to which legitimize our conduct. So, in the bright realm of values, we have no excuse behind us, nor justification before us. We are alone, with no excuses.

That is the idea I shall try to convey when I say that man is condemned to be free. Condemned, because he did not create himself, yet, in other respects is free; because, once thrown into the world, he is responsible for everything he does. The existentialist does not believe in the power of passion. He will never agree that a sweeping passion is a ravaging torrent which fatally leads a man to certain acts and is therefore an excuse. He thinks that man is responsible for his passion.

The existentialist does not think that man is going to help himself by finding in the world some omen by which to orient himself. Because he thinks that man will interpret the omen to suit himself. Therefore, he thinks that man, with no support and no aid, is condemned every moment to invent man. Ponge, in a very fine article, has said, "Man is the future of man." That's exactly it. But if it is taken to mean that this future is recorded in heaven, that God sees it, then it is false, because it would really no longer be a future. If it is taken to mean that, whatever a man may be, there is a future to be forged, a virgin future before him, then this remark is sound.

SUGGESTIONS FOR FURTHER READING

GENERAL

Fromm, Erich, and Xirau, Ramón, eds. *The Nature of Man.* New York: Macmillan, 1968.

Regan, Tom, and Singer, Peter, eds. *Animal Rights and Human Obligations.* Englewood Cliffs, N.J.: Prentice-Hall, 1976, See esp. Part II: "Animal and Human Nature."

Stevenson, Leslie. *Seven Theories of Human Nature.* New York: Oxford University Press, 1974.

THE RELIGIOUS VIEW

Burtt, Edwin A. *Types of Religious Philosophy.* New York: Harper & Brothers, 1951.

de Chardin, Pierre Teilhard. *The Phenomenon of Man.* Translated by B. Wall. New York: Harper and Row, 1961.

Heschel, Abraham. *Who Is Man?* Stanford, Calif.: Stanford University Press, 1966.

Niebuhr, Reinhold. *Man's Nature and His Communities.* New York: Charles Scribner's Sons, 1965.

Radhakrishnan, S., and Raju, P. T. "The Indian Concept of Man," In their *The Concept of Man.* London: Allen & Unwin, 1957.

THE MARXIST VIEW

Bottomore, T. B., and Rubel, M., eds. *Karl Marx: Selected Writings in Sociology and Social Philosophy.* New York: McGraw-Hill, 1964.

Feuer, Lewis S., ed. *Marx & Engels: Basic Writings on Politics and Philosophy.* Garden City, N.Y.: Doubleday, 1959.

Fromm, Erich. *Marx's Concept of Man.* New York: Frederick Ungar, 1961.

THE DARWINIAN VIEW

Ardrey, Robert. *African Genesis.* New York: Atheneum, 1961.

Darwin, Charles. *The Descent of Man.* London: 1871.

Huxley, Julian. *The Uniqueness of Man.* London: Chatto & Windus, 1941.

Munson, Ronald, ed. *Man and Nature.* New York: Dell Publishing Co., 1971.

THE LANGUAGE-USER VIEW

Aristotle. *On the Soul.* Book II. Chapter 2. 413^{a}ff.

Cassirer, Ernst. *Language and Myth.* Translated by Susanne K. Langer. New York: Harper and Brothers, 1946.

Descartes, Rene. *Discourse on Method.* Part V (end).

THE MATERIALIST VIEW

Armstrong, D. M. *A Materialist Theory of the Mind.* New York: Humanities Press, 1968.

Borst, C. V., ed. *The Mind/Brain Identity Theory.* New York: St. Martin's Press, 1970.

Hobbes, Thomas. *Body, Man, and Citizen.* Edited by R.S. Peters. New York: Collier Books, 1962.

Smart, J. J. C. *Philosophy and Scientific Realism.* New York: Humanities Press, 1963.

THE BEHAVIORIST VIEW

Broadbent, D. E. *Behaviour.* London: Methuen, 1961.

Shaffer, Jerome A. *Philosophy of Mind.* Englewood Cliffs, N.J.: Prentice-Hall, 1968. Chapters 1-2.

Skinner, B. F. *Science and Human Behavior.* New York: Macmillan, 1953.

THE EXISTENTIALIST VIEW

Kaufmann, Walter. *Nietzsche.* 4th ed. Princeton, N.J.: Princeton University Press, 1974.

Ortega y Gasset, Jose. *Man and People.* Translated by W. Trask. New York: Norton, 1963.

Sartre, Jean-Paul. *Existentialism and Human Emotion.* Translated by B. Frechtman. New York: Philosophical Library, 1957.

Warnock, Mary. *Existentialism.* Oxford: Oxford Galaxy Books, 1970.

Chapter 4   Minds, Machines, and Persons

In recent decades we have become increasingly respectful of the intellectual triumphs and technological achievements of the biomedical and computer sciences. Many of these results, and their implications for understanding and therapeutically treating human beings, have been the subject of a great deal of speculation—not only in philosophy but also in science fiction. In this chapter these two very different approaches to the implications of modern technology—the philosophical and the science fictional—are brought together. Many aspects of the study of the human mind made possible by these sciences have important philosophical implications.

We cannot hope in the short span of this chapter to survey even most of the issues raised by modern research and technology. We shall, however, study three problems that have generated as much interest as any others: The first is the problem of behavior control, particularly where there is permanent mind alteration. The second is the connection between mind alteration and the ancient philosophical problem of personal identity. The third is the problem of the relation between human thought and machine thought—especially where machines can be programmed to behave very much like humans (for example, the well known science fiction themes of humanoids and social control by computers). The first of these three problems involves ethical questions about the permissibility of certain kinds of individual, social, and legal control over individual behavior. In this case we want to know

when, if ever, we are morally justified in controlling human mental potentialities by technological capacities. The other two problems do not have such an orientation in ethics, however. They are conceptual and substantive philosophical problems about the nature of persons and machines.

BEHAVIOR CONTROL THROUGH MIND ALTERATION

The term *behavior control* is a general label used to refer to biomedical, psychological, and social means of manipulating human actions, whether of an individual person or a group. It is defined by Perry London as "the ability to get someone to do one's bidding." This definition seems to imply that behavior control is present only if one's behavior is being manipulated *by another party* and is a *coercive* manipulation. But biomedical and psychological controls might be used voluntarily by individuals to control their own behavior, as when people take tranquillizers in order to reduce anxiety. Hence London's definition must be altered, though it is controversial how far and in which respects it should be augmented.

There is nothing very new about the ideas that techniques can be used to control human behavior. Political authorities in many states have long known about tactics of pressure used to control political dissidents, and even powerful drugs and brain surgery are not recent in origin. Relatively new, however, are several sophisticated applications of older control methods, as well as some novel techniques developed by modern science and psychology. The implications of these modern developments are currently being assessed in order to discover their efficacy as treatments, the precision with which predictions can be made using such techniques, and the conditions under which they are and are not ethically acceptable. Some of these techniques have aroused considerable public interest. Examples are the use of new tranquillizing and energizing drugs, psychotherapies, and programs of behavioral modification. These technologies can be used as therapies for the treatment of illnesses; but they can also be used to manipulate, distort, and even destroy persons. The particular techniques discussed in this chapter are surgical operations on the brain in order to alter mental states or overt behavior (psychosurgery) and electrical stimulation of the brain (ESB). Whether such techniques are therapeutic or destructive is one major part of the controversy over their use.

HISTORY OF THE PROBLEM OF PSYCHOSURGERY

Published accounts of operations on the human brain intended to alter behavior and the emotions appeared for the first time just before the twentieth century (around 1891). Despite some surgeons' contentions that excitable and uncontrollable patients were calmed and thereby helped by such surgery, it was vigorously opposed and largely discontinued at the time. However, it was gradually reintroduced; and it appeared in 1936 in the United States, largely through the work of Freeman and Watts. By the time of his retirement Freeman estimated that he had performed psychosurgical procedures on at least 3,500 patients. The procedure thereafter grew in appeal, especially in the face of severely disturbed psychiatric veterans who became patients following the Second World War. Between 1945 and 1955 it is reliably estimated that over 40,000 "prefrontal lobotomies," as such procedures were called, were performed in the United States alone. There seem to have been two results from this accelerated use of psychosurgery, one negative and the other positive. Negatively, there were many confirmed reports, especially in the late 1950s, of undesirable side-effects of the surgery, and even reports of persons reduced to zombie-like states. Positively, scientists obtained important new data about the brain, both from these procedures and from work on animals. Surgeons thereby gained new skills at making tiny lesions in the brain which were highly localized and not nearly so disruptive as in past lobotomies. Naturally this reduced the number of reported unsatisfactory side-effects.

CONTEMPORARY PROBLEMS OF PSYCHOSURGERY

A result of these procedures and their effects was the growth of public and scientific concern about these and other techniques of behavior control. The rise of new drugs and a substantial public outcry reduced the number of psychosurgical procedures, though they were by no means stopped. Throughout the 1960s and 1970s several issues of psychosurgery were debated, and some of the principal figures in this debate are represented in the present chapter through their articles. During this period critics of psychosurgery aimed their criticism not only at the lack of scientific justification for the procedure, but also at the lack of ethical justification and, as they saw it, the overly political character of some of these operations. The latter accusation arose from a letter sent by Professor Vernon Mark of the Harvard Medical School to the *Journal of the American Medical Association* (September 1967), and repeated in a book he wrote with Frank Ervin, *Violence and the Brain* (1970). Mark, himself a psychosurgeon, contended that acts of "senseless violence" might well be prevented by appropriate diagnosis and psychosurgical procedures. Since these remarks came at a time when the United States was engulfed in a wave of what many regarded as racial and political violence, Mark's comments were regarded by some as political and even racist in character.

In his article in this chapter, Mark not only attempts to justify his views as non-political and non-racist, but as scientifically acceptable as well. While there can be little doubt that Mark is well informed about all aspects of the psychosurgery debate, many scientists in neurology remain unconvinced on all counts that psychosurgery is as justified as Mark suggests. A vigorous reply is mounted in the present chapter by Stephan Chorover, a physiological psychologist at MIT. Chorover not only believes that substantial scientific questions remain about psychosurgery, but that the racist and political charges brought against Mark are not without foundation. Chorover is one among many critics of psychosurgery to contend that no adequate general justification has yet to be provided.

In the midst of the recent debates over psychosurgery, two dramatic publications brought the problem of psychosurgery to public attention. The first was Stanley Kubrick's movie *A Clockwork Orange,* and the second was Michael Crichton's novel *The Terminal Man.* Crichton's shocking science fiction account of electrodes implanted in the human brain is included as the first selection in the present chapter. Although the thrust of Crichton's book seems decidedly negative, it must not be thought that it is either scientifically uninformed or futuristic in vision. On the contrary, present technology makes it possible to do almost precisely what Crichton envisages. In the same year that Crichton's novel appeared, the United States Congress and the Department of Justice held hearings into government support of behavior control measures, with special emphasis on psychosurgery. These hearings led eventually to a termination of government support of research in the area of psychosurgery. There can be no doubt that at this time there was considerable fear of psychosurgery and also concern that prisoners were being coercively controlled by psychosurgery (a belief resulting from a widespread report of its use in California prisons).

Shortly after the appearance of Crichton's novel a law case in the state of Michigan—*Kaimowitz v. Department of Mental Health* (July 1973)—brought to public attention an attempt to use an involuntarily detained mental patient (a criminal sexual psychopath) as the subject of a research project. This project intended to compare the effects of psychosurgery with the effects of certain hormone treatments as ways of reducing problems of uncontrollable aggression. The state of Michigan had funded the research and a human rights review committee at the clinic where the operation would have been performed had approved it. Both the adult patient and his parents signed consent forms. In the Kaimowitz case, a three-judge Michigan court held that involuntarily confined mental patients are in no position to give valid informed consent to participate in such a dangerous and irreversible procedure. The court argued that the risk and the effect of institutionalization itself (an "inherently coercive environment") invalidated the consent, because it could not be shown to be genuinely competent and voluntary. At the same time the consent was said to be less than adequately informed because of the lack of an adequate scientific basis for proving that a therapeutic effect would result from the procedure. This case has itself produced a substantial legal and philosophical literature on the problem of psychosurgery. Subsequent to the case there were further restrictions by government officials and even by scientists themselves on the practice of psychosurgery.

On the other hand, the Michigan case had also been heavily criticized. Many critics have argued that at least some involuntarily detained persons not only stand in need of such procedures but demonstrably are competent to consent to them. This argument is usually supplemented by the claim (which has some sociological support) that involuntary confinement environments are not always inherently coercive and that persons in such environments do not regard themselves as being coerced. It is also urged that if standards of this sort are to govern psychosurgery, then they ought also to govern psychotherapy, chemotherapy, drug therapy, electroshock, and the like. The net result of this criticism, plus new evidence about psychosurgery, has been to throw into doubt whether the decision of the Kaimowitz court would now be sustained by most courts. (In a later California appellate case, *Aden v. Younger,* many of the arguments presented in *Kaimowitz* were directly challenged.)

These multitudinous problems about psychosurgery were brought to sharp focus in 1976-77 when the National Commission for the Protection of Human Subjects of Biomedical and Behavioral Research was mandated by the United States Congress and by the National Institutes of Health to study the problem and to submit recommendations which would be appropriate for the regulation of psychosurgery. This commission was charged to investigate the nature and the extent of the use of psychosurgery, the kinds of patients used, the environments in which it was used, the safety and efficacy of the procedures, and its general acceptability or unacceptability as a matter of ethics. The recommendations of this commission, delivered in 1977, stand in sharp contrast to the worries expressed by Chorover and are also in contrast to some extent to Crichton's imaginative presentation. The commission found, to the great surprise of some, that there is comparatively little in the way of an objectionable use of psychosurgery —either ethically, politically, or scientifically. In order to understand how the commission reached these conclusions, it is necessary to consider briefly the data and arguments which impressed the commission.

The commission found at its inception that there was virtually no evidence concerning the nature and extent of the psychosurgery recently performed in the United States, concerning the nature of the patients being treated, and concerning the effects of the procedures employed. The commission therefore supported some studies which would provide such information. These studies were performed by teams of objective persons, including representatives from psychology, neurology, psychiatry, neurosurgery, and social work. The net results of these studies showed with some precision that there are fewer operations than had been thought, that most surgeons performed very few each year (four surgeons accounted for 48 percent of the procedures in the country), and that most published reports on the effects of psychosurgery are relatively useless. It was also found that persons severely disturbed in mood and emotion can benefit from such surgery, that these procedures are largely used by the middle class and seldom involve persons from minority groups, and that the success rate and patient satisfaction were often quite high (approximately 78 percent in one study). In fact, patients seldom suffered a worsening of their condition, and patients exposed to different treatments preferred psychosurgery to electroshock. Patients almost always supported their physicians' motives and decisions even if the patients knew their condition had worsened. The commission was convinced by these studies that psychosurgery, when properly planned and reviewed, is basically a safe and efficacious procedure and that there are no known cases in recent years of psychological or cognitive deficits as a result of the psychosurgery itself. There are qualifications on these optimistic conclusions (e.g., the interest of the surgeon appears to play some role in the efficacy of the procedure), but on the whole the commission gave a clean bill of health to psychosurgery when carefully designed and skillfully executed. The commission therefore saw its task as that of insuring proper procedures for the limitation of psychosurgery.

MAJOR EMPIRICAL, CONCEPTUAL, AND ETHICAL CONTROVERSIES

While several problems recur in all areas of behavior control, in the case of psychosurgery there seem to be three major problems, one of which is empirical, one conceptual, and one ethical. We will discuss each of these problems, and finally a legal problem will also be mentioned.

The Empirical Problem of Adequate Evidence

Several problems of assessing scientific evidence appear in our readings, most of which have some bearing on ethical judgments about psychosurgery. It is claimed by some experts that we know so little about the brain (and also about the physiological effects of powerful drugs) that we ought not to allow psychosurgery and various drug therapies until we have obtained controlled experimental evidence which supplies such information. It is claimed that we do not adequately understand what side-effects might occur, whether the results are irreversible, and which among the available therapies are most likely to be successful in permanently eliminating the undesired behavior. Additionally, it is argued that while the risks are high, the evaluation of the data concerning the success of psychosurgery has generally been loosely and imprecisely carried out by those who lack the requisite objectivity to perform the evaluations (usually the surgeons themselves). These critics also maintain that there has been careless reliance on animal data as evidence of the efficacy of psychosurgery, without a due appreciation for the differences between humans and animals. Chorover is one critic who has argued many of these points. Other experts flatly disagree with these critics, arguing that the evidence is as good as that used in ordinary medical practice for the treatment of most diseases and that it is both safe and efficacious. These proponents of psychosurgery also maintain that alternative treatments such as prolonged electroshock, drug therapy, and even psychotherapy may have irreversible effects on the person which are at least as serious behaviorally and cognitively as the effects of psychosurgery. Mark is one defender who has argued precisely this line.

Mark argues in his article that in the case of both psychosurgery and electrical stimulation there is considerable scientific evidence to indicate that many disordered behaviors can be controlled or cured by psychosurgical techniques. The early part of his article is well stocked with scientific reports in support of this claim. Mark is particularly concerned to show that psychosurgery is efficacious for the control of violent behaviors such as cata-strophic rage, as well as for serious medical problems such as the control of epileptic seizures. Mark provides several graphic illustrations of his claim in the form of case histories. Such case histories, and indeed the very scientific evidence cited by Mark, are criticized in the article by Chorover. Attention to Chorover's footnotes reveals that some of these case histories formed the scientific basis for Crichton's novel. (Some aspects of Crichton's evidence are also found questionable by Chorover.) Chorover argues that many of Mark's published reports about later behavior are questionable in the light of follow-up studies done on such patients. Chorover's point seems to be that while such patients do well for a short period of time, they are worse off over a longer period of time than they would have been if they had not had psychosurgery.

The problem of assessing scientific evidence is not a matter which philosophers and laymen will find easy, but resolution of these disputes over empirical matters is nonetheless of decisive ethical relevance.

The Conceptual Problem of Distinguishing Disease and Deviancy

If psychosurgery is a medical treatment, as is usually claimed by those who employ it, then what is the disease being treated? Diagnoses of illness are often made on the basis of overt behavior—e.g., violent behavior. But is this behavior diseased, or is it simply a behavioral manifestation of which we highly disapprove? Are we treating people for a disease, or are we punishing them? How in general is the distinction to be drawn between deviant behavior of which we disapprove but which is not diseased and behavior which is deviant because of a disease? The separation of the two is especially difficult if the diagnosis itself is made exclusively on the basis of observed behavior. They are less difficult to separate if, as Mark and others claim, definite structural abnormalities can be detected by (for example) x-rays and exploratory surgery.

This problem emerges with special vigor in the debate below between Mark and Chorover. Mark protests Chorover's charge that his procedures are performed on those whose behaviors—e.g. in violent ghettos—are regarded as politically and socially deviant. Mark is inclined to take the view that only serious and obvious medical problems should be used in justification of psychosurgery. Indeed, where the charge of racism is likely to emerge, Mark argues that special precautions and special detail to the *pathological* nature of the disorder should be required. Mark even concludes that besides the criterion of undesirable behavior, anyone considering performing psychosurgery should additionally take account of informed legal, ethical, political, and social considerations. (Mark and Ervin have also argued that there are more efficient and efficacious ways of controlling dissidents on a massive scale. Drugs, for example, are easily concealed and are easily available, whereas psychosurgery is hard to conceal, expensive, difficult, and time-consuming.)

However, after several years of confrontation with Mark's arguments, Chorover still believes that Mark uses judgments about "deviance control" as the primary reason for linking abnormal behavior to "brain disfunction." This is also the underlying reason, Chorover thinks, for the intent to use psychosurgical procedures on prisoners and the mentally disabled (as in the *Kaimowitz* case). Chorover argues that this general motive for psychosurgery constitutes an international ethical problem, since in some countries the use of psychosurgery for deviance control is much worse than in the United States. Because of the emphasis on deviant behavior and the lack of proof of a medical problem, Chorover believes the use of psychosurgery is overtly social and political and therefore probably ought not to be permitted.

The Ethical Problem of Informed Consent

Must one obtain voluntary informed consent in order to employ mind-altering therapies? Ordinarily one would think so, but when persons have been involuntarily institutionalized in hospitals and prisons, must their informed consent still always be obtained? Is this necessary not only for major procedures such as psychosurgery, but also for presumably milder forms of therapy, such as drugs and psychotherapy? And, finally, if the person is in a coercive environment such as a prison or hospital, under what conditions, if any, is it meaningful to say that consent is informed and voluntarily given? Some critics of psychosurgery have questioned whether someone who is a candidate for the oper-

ation in the first place is capable of giving voluntary and informed consent. Other critics have worried about the use of the third-party consent, especially in the context of institutions where persons are involuntarily committed. The latter worry has led to suggestions that psychosurgery ought never to be performed on prisoners, children, and other involuntarily confined persons such as the mentally disabled. A related concern is voiced by Chorover, who has doubts about the acceptability of any practice which intentionally modifies personality characteristics, thought processes, and emotional experiences. His argument seems to be that *no* consent under such conditions could be ethically acceptable even if it were voluntary and informed.

The general issue of informed consent has been comparatively neglected in writings on psychosurgery, but it is given a prominent place in the report by the National Commission (and Mark does insist in his article that informed consent must be available). In this report either the patient must give informed consent or, in cases where the patient is incapable of giving informed consent, very strict criteria must be satisfied. These criteria include stipulations that there must be a mandatory review of the procedure by a national advisory body, a legal guardian must give proxy consent for the patient, and a court in which the patient has legal representation must have approved the performance of the operation. These proposals are among the strictest yet suggested to enforce the moral requirement of informed consent, despite the commission's finding of acceptable uses of psychosurgery. One reason why the issue of informed consent receives more attention in this report is legal in character. Several states in the United States have enacted laws governing psychosurgery, and in almost every case the problem of what constitutes a valid consent (whether by the individual or by a third party) has been the matter of chief concern. Elaborate review mechanisms have been established in some states to insure that the surgery is therapeutic and the consent valid.

The Legal Control of Behavior Control

The ethical justifiability of laws which restrict and/or permit technologies of behavior control such as psychosurgery are themselves a central and controversial issue. Ideally laws exist to protect people, most obviously from physical abuse, but also from psychic and emotional abuse as well. Since the technologies of behavior control easily lend themselves to substantial physical and mental abuse, laws which safeguard individual and societal rights and liberties are obviously desirable. But there may also be an undue restriction of the liberty of others. Many, and perhaps the majority, of ethical problems of psychosurgery derive from asking the question, "Which uses of control technologies should be banned outright, which should be legally restricted though not prohibited, and which should be legally unrestrained?"

In attempting to answer this question, a distinction should be made between *coercive uses* and *voluntary uses* of psychosurgery and all behavior control devices. Consider voluntary uses first. Patients commonly submit freely to therapeutic uses of behavior control technologies, as when they visit a psychiatrist or enroll in a behavior modification program in order to lose weight. The same request is also sometimes made for psychosurgery. If laws sharply restrict access to this operation, they limit the freedom of both patients and practitioners. But should such voluntary uses of these techniques therefore be banned, and if so, on what grounds? At bottom this question is a moral and not a legal one, for it asks what the law *ought* to be rather than what it *is*.

Evidence of *coercive* uses of such invasive behavior control technologies as psychosurgery is difficult to find, but since drug therapies and psychotherapy are commonly forced on many persons involuntarily committed to mental institutions, it is clear that psychosurgery *could* be similarly used (and there is evidence to indicate that its use in such settings has been seriously contemplated). The same ethical question arises irrespective of the actual behavior control technique employed: under what conditions, if any, is the state justified in the coercive use of these technologies in order to control the behavior of individual persons?

Ethically acceptable answers to the above questions must provide principled justifications of state intervention. To deny access to behavior control technologies such as psychosurgery and mind-altering drugs is one way of limiting liberty, while the forced use of these therapies is undoubtedly an intervention, though some would deny that it limits liberty. In any event, the question of a principled justification of state intervention remains. In chapter 7 of this book throughout the chapter very similar problems of liberty limitation are discussed.

PERSONAL IDENTITY

Michael Crichton's science fiction story about electronic stimulation of the brain and the articles on psychosurgery are all based on scientific data which indicates what might now be done by using modern psychological and technological capacities for control of the brain. The next section of the present chapter also begins with a science fiction account of human manipulation of the brain. This story, written by Roland Puccetti (a philosopher and novelist) is based not on a *present* technological capacity but rather on one which is no doubt many years away—a brain transplant. Brain transplants have been performed in such lower animals as salamanders, though never in humans. However, Puccetti is not suggesting that there is an immediate likelihood of a human brain transplant, which might approximate recent successes in heart transplantation and kidney transplantation. Also, unlike Crichton, Puccetti is not worried about ethical problems of how we might use or abuse the capacity to stimulate or transplant brains. He is worried about an old *conceptual* problem in philosophy: the problem of personal identity.

The problem of personal identity has its roots in such innocent questions as "How can it be said that I am the *same* person now that I was twenty years ago?" or "What is it about my old friends that enables me to say that they are now the same persons they were when we were childhood friends?" In ordinary circumstances in life we have no difficulties with these seemingly trivial questions. But the very stuff of philosophy and science fiction has to do with the discovery of perplexing problems which are uncommon. Still, the issue is not totally foreign to our thinking, as may be illustrated by referring again to the phenomenon of psychosurgery and imagining an even more dramatic case than the one envisioned by Crichton. If a man were to undergo a radical brain surgery procedure, after which he had none of his previous memories and could recognize none of his former friends, or even himself, would it be correct to say that this person is the *same* person he was before the operation? It certainly is the same body (from an observor's perspective), with the same biological character and with many of the same coordinative skills, but can it be the same person if the memory and emotional structure have been permanently altered? In this connection one might also think of "multiple personality" cases where one single body seems to harbor several different personalities, and perhaps even several different persons. Indeed one might think of even more speculative possibilities suggested by various religious and science fiction accounts, such as the resurrection of the dead, reincarnation in another body, the transmigration of souls, whether someone could inhabit another's body, and whether the body could be disintegrated and then reassembled.

In such cases, where are we to locate that which makes these persons *identical* with their former self or selves (or perhaps their other selves, in multiple identity cases)? Is the identity or sameness to be found in the body, and nothing more? Or is it to be found in the mind, with its storehouse of memories, and nothing more? Or is identity somehow a unique combining of properties of the body with properties of the mind? Or perhaps there really is no such thing as personal identity, in which case we are *not* the same selves that we were before. Such puzzling cases as multiple personalities and questions like those just raised challenge the common assumption that a person is simply a living human organism. It would seem that a person cannot simply be *identified* with a body if there are multiple personalities. Yet if one is not to be identified with one's body, what account (if any) can be given of one's own identity? This question, and all those previously mentioned, are not questions exclusively about bizarre persons. They apply to all of us. Such questions have a long history in philosophy, and the principal figures in this history are found in the present chapter. We may begin by explaining the contribution made by each of the major figures, and then return later to a comparison of them.

John Locke was the first philosopher to discuss the problem of personal identity in its modern form. According to Locke, it is our consciousness, in the form of memories, that primarily accounts for our being persons, and it therefore is the retention of past experiences in the form of memories that makes us the same persons throughout different times. Locke apparently thinks that memory is the criterion not only of my identity as a person but also of my awareness of someone else as the same person he or she previously was. For example, if a friend shows up at my office looking very different in physical appearance from her appearance in the past, all I need do, according to Locke, is question her to see if she has the appropriate memories. If she does, then she genuinely is my friend—the same person. If she does not, then (unless there is only a temporary lapse of memory) she is not my friend. Locke takes this sort of evidence, gained from memories, to be the only criterion of personal identity. Any other possible criterion such as that of an immaterial substance or a hidden soul, Locke believes, cannot be proven and hence cannot be used for purposes of identifying the sameness of persons. Locke is aware that persons are continually changing, but he believes there can be identity of a person even through very substantial bodily and personality change in that person. It is memory alone that cannot completely change, for if it did then Locke believes there would no longer be the same person.

In his argument Locke distinguishes the concept of *human* from the concept of *person*. The former notion he equates with a living human organism which has a distinct biological description; a human is to be identified as the *same* human by "the same successive body." Locke believes this notion of *human* is quite distinct from that of *person*, which he defines as "a thinking intelligent being, that has reason and reflection, and can consider itself as itself, the same thinking thing, in different times and places. . . ." Locke is thus enabled to sharply distinguish *bodily* criteria of identity (of "humans") from *memory* criteria of identity (of "persons"). He has been heavily criticized for this distinction, since we do not ordinarily distinguish sharply between someone's personhood and that person's bodily existence. Nonetheless, Locke's distinction allows him to give an example of personal identity which has become one of the most famous examples in the history of philosophy. Locke says that if a prince's mind were somehow to be magically transferred into the body of a cobbler, "everyone" would see that it is the prince who retains his identity, not the cobbler. Ever since Locke's presentation of this example, the problem of personal identity has been taken to be largely that of specifying whether memory alone is the criterion of personal identity, or whether body alone is the criterion of personal identity, or whether some mixture of body and memory (or other items) is required to account for personal identity.

David Hume, in the next selection in this section, presents what is often called the sceptical theory of personal identity. Hume argues that there really is no simple or substantial self which is unchanging and therefore identical from time to time. Persons are, over time, "nothing but a bundle or collection of different perceptions" in a constant state of change, according to Hume. The "nothing but" here is to be taken with utmost seriousness. Hume believes the self is reducible to its entire set of perceptions (mental events). He lands on perceptions because when he looks introspectively at the contents of the mind, he can find no unique and simple self. He finds nothing other than a constantly changing collection of perceptions. This internal appeal to ideas was also Locke's starting point in philosophy. Like Locke, Hume thinks there is *continuity* in our lives, and that memory plays a role in maintaining continuity. This continuity he accounts for basically in terms of the resemblances between long chains of perceptions. (For example, my many feelings of a headache over the period of an hour are very much alike, even though the wavering pains are clearly not the same pains from moment to moment.) Hume's basic idea is not that there is no personal identity at all. Rather, he believes that personal identity can be explained in terms of resemblance amidst change. In his philosophy a person is not something over and above a body, a set of perceptual experiences and habits, and a set of relations between those experiences (resemblance, memory, and causal relations). A person simply *is* all of those things conjointly—nothing more.

Hume thinks metaphysicians have been tempted to a stricter notion of personal identity by failing to attend to the gradual changes which occur in experience, preferring instead to attend to certain smooth and regular patterns. Hume does not deny that such patterns exist; rather he believes that there is change even when the patterns are relatively stable. But he is critical of philosophers who invent theories to explain identity, for he believes that they in effect create their theories without evidence in order to account for something that cannot be found in experience. While Hume's theory is quite complicated and subject to different interpretations, at least the following six propositions seem integral to his theory of personal identity, whatever interpretation is taken:

1. The self is entirely reducible to a collection of perceptions.
2. The self is not characterized by strict identity in the sense of sameness of substance.
3. There is nothing simple in which the collection of perceptions inheres.
4. Both identity and simplicity are attributed to the self because of relations between perceptions—the relations of causation and resemblance.
5. The relations of resemblance and causation unite these perceptions.
6. There are no real (non-associational) connections or relations among these perceptions which unite them.

Thomas Reid holds a quite different theory from both Locke and Hume, a theory often referred to as the "common sense" view. He begins with an argument to show that Locke's account must be rejected for several reasons. He points out that any person may have done things in the past that he or she cannot remember, yet that person is nonetheless the same person who did those things, whether or not he or she ever remembers doing them. Reid's point is that Locke seems to imply that anything I cannot remember doing was not done by *me,* which is absurd. Indeed Reid points out that none of us could be the same persons we were when we were children, since we neither had recallable memories at an early age (though we were persons) nor can we now recall those parts of our lives. Reid has several other criticisms to offer, all of which lead in the direction of the very theory Locke rejects—namely, to the notion of an uninterrupted continuance of an immaterial substance. (Reid's counter-example of the brave officer is one of the most famous in the literature of personal identity. It is thought by many to devastate Locke's account.)

Reid's views on this subject spring from a theory of the general character of identity which he sets forth at the beginning of his article. He agrees with Locke that memory provides the evidence for personal identity, but he believes it is a great mistake to equate one's *evidence* for the existence of something with that *thing itself*. Reid also points out that we have criteria of personal identity other than memory—e.g., the fact that my mother bore me. While Reid does not quite say so, he clearly implies that Locke's criterion of memory, even as a view about evidence, needs to be supplemented by other criteria. This supplementation might involve combining the notion of memory with certain bodily traits and personality traits. Subsequent to Reid this maneuver has been a popular one, and it is perhaps not unduly generous to attribute it to his genius. But however that may be, it should not escape notice that this maneuver not only involves a rejection of Locke's account of personal identity, but also of his distinction between "person" and "human" on which his theory heavily relies.

Reid believes that Hume's theory is at once more radical than Locke's and rooted in the same mistaken theory of ideas propounded by Locke. Reid has a general belief that modern philosophy went wrong by adopting the Locke-Descartes view that philosophy starts with an examination of the contents of the mind, which is exclusively composed of ideas. The argument he presents against Hume in the last part of his article begins with his hypothesis that all of these philosophers share a wrong starting point and so mistakenly wind up with Hume's scepticism about the mind. He congratulates Hume on his *consistency* but provides several arguments to show that Hume is simply wrong, or at the very least has not defended his starting point. Reid seems at one point to accuse Hume of begging the question by *assuming* that only ideas exist and so only ideas could constitute a mind. Reid also argues that Hume wants to provide both an account of

personal identity and of human nature, yet cannot possibly achieve this goal since his scepticism destroys the belief that there is a human nature. Reid seems to believe that it is a basic and unprovable conviction of common sense that there must be something which *has* sensations or else the person would not exist. He takes this to be as obvious as the fact that if there is treason there must be a traitor. His point is that if something *has* sensations, then Hume cannot be correct in arguing that the mind is *nothing but* its sensations. Reid's overall proposal in rebutting Hume is that "there are certain principles . . . which the constitution of our nature leads us to believe, and which we are under a necessity to take for granted in the common concerns of life, without being able to give a reason for them; these are what we call the principles of common sense." Since Locke and Hume advance theories which seriously violate such principles of common sense, Reid denounces them as "absurd."

Roland Puccetti's story opens this chapter. It is followed by an analysis of personal identity which brings out the philosophical points he presents through the story. Just as one ought not reveal the contents of a movie before others view it, so Puccetti's vivid tale ought not to be related in this Introduction. However, it is important to get some grasp of the philosophical perspective from which he writes the story, and this perspective is revealed in his article (which is placed second in the present section). Here Puccetti begins with a case of two persons, one of whom has a failing body and the other of whom has a failing brain. He imagines that an arrangement is made whereby the good brain is transplanted into the head of the good body by a surgical procedure. His question is whether we now have before us, after the surgery, a *new* person, or the old person whose body is now functioning without a failing brain, or the other old person whose brain is now functioning without a failing body. Who is this composite entity before us?, he asks. In the Lockean tradition, he notes the importance of the brain for memories, since memories are stored in the cerebral cortex. But the memories simply are those of the old person whose brain is still here. Hence the "new" person must simply be that old person whose memories are retained. At the same time, Puccetti points out that voice production and other distinctive personality traits are more dependent on the learned response of the body than on the brain. It looks, then, as if our "new person" is a kind of organic composite of two old ones. However, having reached this point, Puccetti goes on to provide a strong argument to show that "where goes a brain, there goes a person." For Puccetti this saying does *not* mean that a person *is* his brain. Rather it means that in order to be the same person one must have the same brain. Brain retention thus becomes, for Puccetti, *the* criterion of personal identity. And the solution to his puzzle case is that the "new" person really is just the old person whose brain is retained; the old person whose body is kept "alive" is actually dead and gone.

It might seem, on first reflection, that Puccetti takes a view exactly like Locke's: memory (as stored in the brain) is the crucial criterion. While it is tempting to interpret Puccetti's argument in this way, it is clear that he rejects this interpretation himself. While thinking of Locke and like-minded philosophers, Puccetti writes as follows:

Philosophers in the past have talked blithely of "bodily transfer", by which they meant mind-transference between two bodies without one single brain cell changing its physical *locus*. This may be conceivable logically, but in terms of the causal conditions of human life it is just so much philosophical gas.

Puccetti's point seems to be that personal identity, contra Locke, is not simply determined by memories, because there is a real *physical* basis to memory—the brain. Locke might reply to Puccetti that an external set of memories might be chemically created by drug injections into a brain; while the old memories are chemically flushed out with drugs. It is somewhat unclear how Puccetti might respond to this objection, though presumably he would say a new brain is present, not simply new memories in an old brain. These interpretive matters are more than idle speculations about differences between Puccetti and Locke. Despite their near equal emphasis on memory, Puccetti does require a *physical* basis for identity and Locke requires *no physical basis*.

At the same time Puccetti would seem to be rejecting Reid's views in favor of Locke's, for Puccetti explicitly argues against the multiple criteria theory (though it is not clear that Puccetti answers Reid's *objections* to Locke's theory). Puccetti seems also to be arguing against Hume's view, since Hume thinks there is *no single* abiding basis of identity; but on that point it is somewhat unclear what Puccetti's commitments are.

It might seem from the discussion thus far that the truth about personal identity lies somewhere in the direction of the Locke-Puccetti approach. However, it is widely believed that Reid's critique of Locke devastated that philosopher. But if Reid's criticisms overthrow Locke, they may well be similarly successful for the criticism of Puccetti's theory. Also, it remains unclear how directly any of these philosophers has addressed Hume's scepticism. As just noted, Puccetti's analysis has little to say about Hume's theory, and many philosophers, including Reid, have taken Hume to be simply carrying out to consistency the beginning point employed by Locke. Also, Reid's denunciation of Hume in the name of common sense has never convinced those who are inclined toward sceptical views. There are two reasons for this. First, Hume was well aware that his views offended common sense. He thought philosophy should find the truth, even if it turned out to be highly counterintuitive. Second, many philosophers have thought that the resort to common sense merely provides a refuge in the familiar, without having to provide the harder arguments needed to refute scepticism.

In the end it does appear that we have four quite different views of personal identity expressed in these articles (despite the weak alliance between Locke and Puccetti) and that there is much to say for each, since they all live on in contemporary philosophy.

MINDS AND MACHINES

The drawing opposite illustrates the subject of the final section in this chapter. In the seventeenth century the philosopher Rene Descartes used the assertion "Cogito, ergo sum"—"I think, therefore I am"—as a fundamental proposition in his theory of knowledge and his theory of human minds. Descartes believed that the primary attribute of human beings, an attribute setting them off from all other

"I'll be damned. It says, 'Cogito, ergo sum.'"
(Drawing by Richter; © 1958 The New Yorker Magazine, Inc.)

things in nature, was that of *thinking*. (Descartes' view is not unlike those views about thinking and language advanced by Langer and Cassirer in chapter 3 of this book.) Descartes believed that trees, stones, and animals lacked this crucial property; and for this reason he believed they lacked, in any significant sense, a mind. Naturally Descartes thought the same about machine devices which were available to his inspection in the seventeenth century. Computers, however, have radically altered this seventeenth-century outlook. They handle symbols with far greater facility than the human mind, and they are capable of giving an extraordinary range of answers to questions that are fed to them. Theoretically they could attribute to themselves such mental states as thinking, as the cartoon above suggests. But suppose a machine does *attribute* thinking to itself, and suppose further (with Descartes) that symbolic thinking is a sufficient condition of being a mind. Must we then say that machines do think? And if so, do machines have minds? Are they perhaps even persons, so that we can discuss problems about the personal identity of a machine?

It must not be thought that even in the seventeenth and eighteenth centuries the close analogy between complex machines and the human mind had been overlooked. Descartes' French successor Julien De La Mettrie wrote in 1747 that a human being is nothing but a self-maintaining physical system. To be sure, La Mettrie said that a human is an "enlightened machine," but he saw no reason in principle why there could not also be enlightened machines which were composed of non-human materials. La Mettrie advanced the thesis—promoted in recent philosophy by those who believe in the so-called mind/brain identity theory—that science has progressively shown that all of nature is composed of a single set of chemical and physical units. This theory asserts that biology may discover genetic material in humans which is different from that found in other species, and psychology may show that human brains are capable of far richer intelligence and range of functioning than are non-human brains. Yet these differences are more apparent than real. Psychology and biology deal with the human organism on what might be called a macroscopic level, whereas physics and chemistry deal with human beings and all physical processes on a microscopic level. Those who accept this view that human beings are simply composed of physical and chemical processes found elsewhere in nature hold out the hope that some day all of human behavior will be explicable purely in the mechanistic terms of physics and chemistry. This hope in turn leads to speculation that we shall be able to construct machines which are as complicated as we are, but which are capable of all the same activities and thought processes of which we are capable. It has even been speculated that with increased engineering skills we shall be able to create robots which look exactly like humans and which function exactly like them.

Such speculation has, of course, been a staple of science fiction writing for decades. The advent of powerful computing machines, along with theories of their actual and potential capacities, have provided new and more precise facts on which these writers, as well as philosophers, can base their speculations. In the opening selection in the section on minds and machines in this chapter, D. F. Jones engages in such speculation in our third science fiction story. Jones imagines a highly sophisticated robot capable of both sensory and computing capacitites. Those familiar with the movie *2001: A Space Odyssey* will immediately recognize the similarities between Jones' robot and the robot eventually destroyed in that movie. An interesting difference is that in Jones' story the robot is so sophisticated that it is not vulnerable to destruction in the way the robot in the movie is vulnerable.

RECENT COMPUTER ADVANCES

While traces of the problem of minds and machines can be found throughout the history of philosophy, recent speculation began only with the production of high-speed and highly complex computers developed after World War II. A series of rapid successes in computer development showed that these machines could be used to replace humans for a wide variety of menial but critical calculation tasks. Almost overnight the terms "operations research" and "computer science" sprang into common use. Soon there were laboratories equipped to do sophisticated experimental research in order to create new and better computers. An emerging problem in this research was the extent to which

computers could be designed to imitate human behavior. This research was and remains especially fascinating, since it was able to produce computer "behaviors" which a few years before were thought to be limited to human behavior. For example, computers were designed to play chess, do "creative" writing, create patterns for indexing books, and solve highly complex mathematical problems. These successes led to a wide variety of measures for sophisticating the design and capacities of such computers and to hundreds of new research projects as well. Alan Anderson, in checking the literature between 1953 and 1963, reported that during this decade over a thousand papers were published on the single issue whether machines can think.

This new interest and the newly available research facilities led to the hypothesis that computers might be designed which actually reproduce functions of the human brain. Such research came to be called "computer simulation of cognitive processes." The hope was not to create a human brain with neurological pathways (as we have in our brains). Rather the hope was to use electrical circuitry which could do precisely what we do in the way of conceptual recognition and calculation. This hope in turn generated news stories and science fiction writing which (sometimes all too sensationally) proclaimed that we may soon have to choose between a society of human employees and a society of robot servants—and even, as we shall see in this section in the story by Jones—to speculation of a robot takeover. We now know that the objective of creating artificial "brains" is more complex than some people first thought. Available machines have not turned out to be as clever and creative as was hoped. They can play chess and compose short stories—but not very imaginatively. This "failure," in the path of past successes, has led to a widespread conviction that the reason these machines cannot be designed to do all that we wish is that we do not understand human brain processes well enough to simulate them with computers. The present state of affairs seems to be that no one sufficiently understands precisely how conceptual functioning, creative thinking, and related activities actually occur in the brain to be able to simulate them. On the other hand, those involved in computer simulation continue faithfully to carry out their research, and it is far from clear that they shall be proved wrong.

PROBLEMS OF CRITERIA AND EVIDENCE

Under what conditions would we agree that something has a mind (especially when "purely mechanical" entities are brought into consideration)? We would all agree that human beings have minds. And most of us are sufficiently intrigued by the intelligence of monkeys, dolphins, and our pets that we would not deny that they have minds. Psychologists who experiment with rats and pigeons find it as compelling to say that these animals have minds as that monkeys and humans do. Even tiny insects react in ways that lead us to say they are conscious, even if we might have some hesitation about saying that they have minds. But where shall we draw the line between entities with minds and those without minds? This question requests a specification of the criteria being used to identify something as a mind, and it is an eminently fair request, even if the answer is difficult. One problem infecting discussions of minds and machines has been a serious unclarity about the question itself. If we are to ask whether machines *think* or not, it is necessary to be clear in the first place on what it is to think. And if we are to know whether machines have minds or not, it is crucial to specify what a mind is.

In the present chapter, and in most of the literature on minds and machines, two very different approaches are taken to this problem of criteria. The first answer, defended briefly by J. J. C. Smart in this chapter, is that all organisms are physico-chemical mechanisms, that we recognize entities as having minds by the way they *behave,* and that science gives us a viewpoint from which we shall some day be able to explain with precision how both man and machine are explicable in exactly the same mechanistic terms. The second answer, defended by Paul Ziff, is that although machines might *behave* much as humans do, in the end they are simply programmed by humans and lack essential human properties of mind such as feelings. Put another way, this position holds that while in principle we can successfully design machines to behave and even to look very much like ourselves, we shall always know that they do not have minds because that is precisely the structural feature of humans

which we cannot introduce into machines. In short, Smart looks to *outward behavior* as the criterion of having a mind, while Ziff accepts only *internal structure.*

In the attempt to resolve these disputes it is helpful to start out with the assumption that we know both that human beings, monkeys, etc., have minds and that present computers do not have minds. We can then ask what form of *evidence* would compel us to say that a new machine does have a mind (or thinks or feels or whatever). It is useful to approach the issue in this way because it helps get out in the open for examination our commitments about minds. If J. J. C. Smart were to produce before your very eyes a laboratory-created human being, with the same chemical, genetic, and brain structure that we have, would you say it had a mind? Most, including Ziff, would answer this question in the affirmative, because of their awareness that we shall probably soon produce "test-tube babies" and also because human geneticists could demonstrate that these synthetically produced humans were no different structurally from the rest of us. But if the question is answered in the affirmative, then precisely *how* different can such a synthetic product be and still correctly be said to have a mind? For example, if a complex computer could be substituted for a diseased brain in an actual human body, so that the body behaved like the rest of us, would we then be correct in saying this "person" has a mind? And if we did say that, would we also talk about this entity just as we talk about other human beings? (For example, would we say, "Don't tease him, as he is very sensitive," or "Tickling gets him every time"?) It would be question-begging to insist from the outset that in principle no such "machine" could ever be created that had a mind. On the other hand, there may be arguments which demonstrate that such machines could not be created. It is the soundness or unsoundness of such arguments that interests us in the present section.

CONSCIOUSNESS, THINKING, AND FEELING

Those opposed to the view that minds are merely machines have generally tried to base their arguments on the presence in minds of such properties as consciousness, thinking, and feelings. The defenders of man-the-machine traditionally reply that a property such as thinking is merely the product of human information processing machinery, and that such processing is itself reducible to physico-chemical processes in the brain. Accordingly, defenders of the non-machine view must support their position by showing that there are special properties which have emerged from the combining of physical properties in the brain but which are either not themselves physical or else uniquely result from the biochemical world. Much of the discussion about minds and machines has come to focus on whether feeling and thinking can be explicated so that machines *could not feel or think.*

In the readings in this chapter Ziff contends that electronic machines cannot have feelings, no matter how sophisticated they are. He claims that they could neither feel nor reason, even if their calculating capacities far exceed those of humans. The essence of his argument seems to be that although a robot can be programmed to perform like a tired man, the robot cannot actually feel tired. Robot performance is no indicator that they *act* on their own. They act mechanistically as directed by us, and this is part of what it means to be a robot. We know this because we know all about their struc-

ture. Hence it is structure, not behavior, that is crucial. These contentions by Ziff are countered by Smart, whose mechanistic and physicalistic position was previously outlined. In the final selection, Hilary Putnam argues against Ziff, but with a different objective from Smart's. Putnam contends that Ziff begs the question by *assuming* that mechanistic structures and parts cannot be mental when combined. He thinks, in effect, that Ziff produces no argument at all. He then goes on to argue the quite fascinating thesis—itself the possible subject of a science fiction treatment—that there really is *no correct answer* to the question whether machines and robots are conscious and have feelings. In Putnam's view we shall have to *decide* whether they are or are not conscious, and hence whether we shall accept them as fellows in the community of minds (or as mere machines). This will be done, Putnam thinks, on the basis of how seriously we accept the analogies between human and machine behavior. But the matter is strictly one of our choice, not a matter of some discovery we shall make which will definitively determine the issue.

Tom L. Beauchamp

23. THE TERMINAL MAN

Michael Crichton

AUTHOR'S INTRODUCTION

Readers who find the subject matter of this book shocking or frightening should not delude themselves by also thinking it is something quite new. The physical study of the brain has been proceeding for more than a century; the technology of behavior modification has been developing for more than fifty years. For decades, it was there for anyone to see, discuss, support, or oppose.

Nor has there been any lack of publicity. Research in neurobiology is spectacular enough to appear regularly in the Sunday supplements. But the public has never really taken it seriously. There has been so much ominous talk and so much frivolous speculation for so many years that the public now regards "mind control" as a problem removed to the distant future: it might eventually happen, but not soon, and not in a way that would affect anyone now alive.

Scientists engaged in this research have sought public discussion. James V. McConnell of the University of Michigan told his students some years ago, "Look, we can do these things. We can control behavior. Now, who's going to decide what's to be done? If you don't get busy and tell me how I'm supposed to do it, I'll make up my own mind for you. And then it's too late."

Many people today feel that they live in a world that is predetermined and running along a fixed pre-established course. Past decisions have left us with pollution, depersonalization, and urban blight; somebody else made the decisions for us, and we are stuck with the consequences.

That attitude represents a childish and dangerous denial of responsibility, and everyone should recognize it for what it is. In that spirit, the following chronology is presented:

HISTORY OF THERAPY OF PSYCHOMOTOR EPILEPSY

1864 Morel, Fairet, and other French neurologists describe some elements of psychomotor epilepsy.

1888 Hughlings Jackson (Great Britain) provides the classic description of psychomotor epilepsy and its preceding aura.

1898 Jackson and Colman (Great Britain) localize the disorder to the temporal lobe of the brain.

1908 Horsley and Clarke (Great Britain) describe stereotaxic surgical techniques for use on animals.

1941 Jasper and Kershman (U.S.A. and Canada) show that the electroencephalogram of patients with psychomotor epilepsy is characterized by discharges from the temporal lobe.

1947 Spiegel and co-workers (U.S.A.) report the first stereotaxic surgery performed on a human being.

1950 Penfield and Flanagan (Canada) perform ablative surgery for psychomotor epilepsy, with good results.

1953 Heath and co-workers (U.S.A.) perform stereotaxic implantation of depth electrodes.

1958 Talairach and co-workers (France) begin chronic stereotaxic implantation of depth electrodes.

1963 Heath and co-workers (U.S.A.) allow patients to stimulate themselves, at will, via implanted electrodes.

1965 Narabayashi (Japan) reports on 98 patients with violent behavior treated by stereotaxic surgery.

1965 More than 24,000 stereotaxic procedures on human beings have been performed in various countries by this date.

1968 Delgado and co-workers (U.S.A.) attach "stimoceiver" (radio stimulator plus radio receiver) to freely ambulatory hospital patients with psychomotor epilepsy.

1969 Chimpanzee at Alamogordo, N.M., is directly linked by radio to a computer which programs and delivers his brain stimulations.

1971 Patient Harold Benson is operated on in Los Angeles.

THE TERMINAL MAN

. . . Morris was struck by his appearance. Benson was a meek, pudgy, thirty-four-year-old man, with a sort of permanently bewildered air about him. He stood by the van, with his wrists handcuffed in front of him, and looked around. When he saw Morris, he said, "Hello," and then looked away, embarrassed.

One of the cops said, "You in charge here?"

"Yes. I'm Dr. Morris."

The cop gestured toward the interior of the hospital. "Lead the way, Doctor."

Morris said, "Would you mind taking off his handcuffs?"

Benson's eyes flicked up at Morris, then back down.

"We don't have any orders about that." The cops exchanged glances. "I guess it's okay."

While they took the cuffs off, the driver brought Morris a form on a clipboard: "Transfer of Suspect to Institutional Care (Medical)." He signed it. . . .

The cops nodded. There was a moment of silence. Finally, one of them said, "What's wrong with him, anyway?"

"He has a form of epilepsy."

"I saw the guy he beat up," one of the cops said. "Big strong guy, looked like a truck driver. You'd never think a little guy like that"—he jerked his arm toward Benson's room—"could do it."

"When he has epileptic fits, he's violent."

They nodded vaguely. "What's this operation he's getting?"

"It's a kind of brain surgery we call a stage-three procedure," Morris said. He didn't bother to explain further. The policemen wouldn't understand. And, he thought, even if they understood, they wouldn't believe it. . . .

1

Ellis drew a point on the brain, then sketched concentric circles.

"These electrical ripples produce a seizure. In some parts of the brain, the discharge focus produces a shaking fit, frothing at the mouth, and so on. In other parts, there are other effects. If the focus is in the temporal lobe, as in Mr. Benson's case, you get what is called psychomotor epilepsy

—convulsions of thought, not of body. Strange thoughts and frequently violent behavior, preceded by a characteristic aura which is often an odor."

Benson was watching, listening, nodding.

"Now, then," Ellis said, "we know from the work of many researchers that it is possible to abort a seizure by delivering an electrical shock to the correct portion of the brain substance. These seizures begin slowly. There are a few seconds—sometimes as much as half a minute—before the seizure takes effect. A shock at that moment prevents the seizure.". . .

It was 6:21 when Benson was wheeled in. He was now heavily pre-medicated, relaxed, his body limp, his eyelids heavy. His head was wrapped in a green towel.

Ellis supervised Benson's transfer from the stretcher to the chair. As the leather straps were placed across his arms and legs, Benson seemed to wake up, his eyes opening wide.

"That's just so you don't fall off," Ellis said easily. "We don't want you to hurt yourself."

"Uh-huh," Benson said softly, and closed his eyes again.

Ellis nodded to the nurses, who removed the sterile towel from Benson's head. The naked head seemed very small . . . and white. The skin was smooth, except for a razor nick on the left frontal. Ellis's blue-ink "X" marks were clearly visible on the right side.

Benson leaned back in the chair. He did not open his eyes again. One of the technicians began to fix the monitor leads to his body, strapping them on with little dabs of electrolyte paste. . . .

Ellis looked at the TV monitor screens. The EEG was now tracing sixteen jagged lines; heartbeat was recorded; respirations were gently rising and falling; temperature was steady. The technicians began to punch pre-op parameters into the computer. Normal lab values had already been fed in. During the operation, the computer would monitor all vital signs at five-second intervals, and would signal if anything went wrong.

"Let's have music, please," Ellis said, and one of the nurses slipped a tape cartridge into the portable cassette recorder in a corner of the room. A Bach concerto began to play softly. Ellis always operated to Bach; he said he hoped that the precision, if not the genius, might be contagious.

They were approaching the start of the operation. The digital wall clock said 6:29:14 a.m.. . . .

All the team turned to look at the computer print-out screen. The X-ray views appeared briefly, and were replaced by schematic drawings. The maxfield location of the stereotactic apparatus was calculated; the actual location was then merged with it. A set of coordinates flashed up, followed by the notation "PLACEMENT CORRECT."

Ellis nodded. "Thank you for your consultation," he said humorlessly, and went over to the tray which held the electrodes. . . .

With the help of the computer, it was no longer necessary to expose the brain surface. Instead, a few small holes were drilled in the skull and the electrodes inserted, while the computer watched by X-ray to make sure they were being placed correctly. . . .

To [psychiatrist Janet] Ross, the computer was the most remarkable part of the entire system. Since she had joined the NPS three years before, she had seen the computer shrink from a prototype as large as a briefcase to the present tiny model, which looked small in the palm of a hand yet contained all the elements of the original bulky unit.

This tiny size made subdermal implantation possible. The patient was free to move about, take showers, do anything he wanted. Much better than the old units, where the charger was clipped to a patient's belt and wires dangled down all over.

She looked at the computer screens which flashed "OPERATIVE MONITORS INTERRUPTED FOR ELECTRONICS CHECK." On one screen, a blown-up circuit diagram appeared. The computer checked each pathway and component independently. It took four-millionths of a second for each check; the entire process was completed in two seconds. The computer flashed "ELECTRONIC CHECK NEGATIVE." A moment later, brain views reappeared. The computer had gone back to monitoring the operation.

"Well," Ellis said, "let's hook him up." He painstakingly attached the forty fine wire leads from the two electrode arrays to the plastic unit. Then he fitted the wires down along the neck, tucked the plastic under the skin, and called for sutures. . . .

Morris wheeled Benson into the recovery room, a long, low-ceilinged room where patients were brought immediately after operation. The NPS had a special section of the rec room, as did cardiac patients and burns patients. But the NPS section, with its cluster of electronic equipment, had never been used before. Benson was the first case. . . .

2

At 6 p.m., Roger McPherson, head of the Neuropsychiatric Research Unit, went up to the seventh floor to check on his patient. At least, that was how he thought of Benson—as his patient. A proprietary feeling, but not entirely incorrect. Without McPherson, there would be no NPS, and without an NPS, there would be no surgery, no Benson. That was how he thought of it.

Room 710 was quiet and bathed in reddish light from the setting sun. Benson appeared to be asleep, but his eyes opened when McPherson closed the door.

"How are you feeling?" McPherson asked, moving close to the bed.

Benson smiled. "Everyone wants to know that," he said.

McPherson smiled back. "It's a natural question."

"I'm tired, that's all. Very tired . . . . Sometimes I think I'm a ticking time bomb, and you're wondering when I'll explode."

"Is that what you think?" McPherson asked. Automatically, he adjusted Benson's covers so he could look at the I.V. line. It was flowing nicely.

"Ticktick," Benson said, closing his eyes again. "Ticktick."

McPherson frowned. He was accustomed to mechanical metaphors from Benson—the man was preoccupied, after all, with the idea of men as machines. But to have them appear so soon after operation . . .

"Any pain?"

"None. A little ache behind my ears, like I'd fallen. That's all."

That, McPherson knew, was the bone pain from the drilling.

"Fallen?"

"I'm a fallen man," Benson said. "I've succumbed."

"To what?"

"To the process of being turned into a machine." He opened his eyes and smiled again. "Or a time bomb.". . .

3

He looked at the row of charts on the shelf, a row of unfamiliar names, into which BENSON, H. F. 710 merged indistinguishably. In one sense, he thought, Benson was correct—he was a walking time bomb. A man treated with mind-control technology was subject to all sorts of irrational public prejudice. "Heart control" in the form of cardiac pacemakers was considered a wonderful invention; "kidney control" through drugs was a blessing. But "mind control" was evil, a disaster—even though the NPS control work was directly analogous to control work with other organs. Even the technology was similar: the atomic pacemaker they were using had been developed first for heart work. . . .

McPherson saw this case as the first of many. He planned to go from epileptics to schizophrenics to mentally retarded patients to blind patients. The charts were all there on his office wall. And he planned to use more and more sophisticated computers in the link-up. . . .

But today the practical question was which of the forty electrodes would prevent an attack. Nobody knew that yet. It would be determined experimentally.

During the operation, the electrodes had been located precisely, within millimeters of the target area. That was good surgical placement, but considering the density of the brain it was grossly inadequate. A nerve cell in the brain was just a micron in diameter. There were a thousand nerve cells in the space of a millimeter.

From that standpoint, the electrodes had been crudely positioned. And this crudeness meant that many electrodes were required. One could assume that if you placed several electrodes in the correct general area, at least one of them would be in the precise position to abort an attack. Trial-and-error stimulation would determine the proper electrode to use. . . .

The nurse patted Benson on the shoulder, nodded to Dr. Ross, and left the room. They were alone.

For a moment, neither spoke. Benson stared at her; she stared back. She wanted to give Gerhard time to focus the TV camera in the ceiling, and to prepare his stimulating equipment.

"What are we doing today?" Benson asked.

"We're going to stimulate your electrodes, sequentially, to see what happens." . . .

In the next room, Ross was saying, "You'll feel a variety of sensations, and some of them may be quite pleasant. We want you to tell us what you feel. All right?"

Benson nodded.

Richards said, "Electrode one, five millivolts, for five seconds." Gerhard pressed the buttons. The computer diagram showed a tracing of the circuit being closed, the current snaking its way through the intricate electronic maze of Benson's shoulder computer. They watched Benson through the one-way glass.

Benson said, "That's interesting."

"What's interesting?" Ross asked.

"That feeling."

"Can you describe it?"

"Well, it's like eating a ham sandwich."

"Do you like ham sandwiches?"

Benson shrugged. "Not particularly."

"Do you feel hungry?"

"Not particularly."

"Do you feel anything else?"

"No. Just the taste of a ham sandwich." He smiled. "On rye."

Gerhard, sitting at the control panel, nodded. The first electrode had stimulated a vague memory trace.

Richards: "Electrode two, five millivolts, five seconds."

Benson said, "I have to go to the bathroom."

Ross said, "It will pass."

Gerhard sat back from the control panel, sipped a cup of coffee, and watched the interview progress.

"Electrode three, five millivolts, five seconds."

This one produced absolutely no effect on Benson. Benson was quietly talking with Ross about bathrooms in restaurants, hotels, airports—

"Try it again," Gerhard said. "Up five."

"Repeat electrode three, ten millivolts, five seconds," Richards said. The TV screen flashed the circuit through electrode three. There was still no effect.

"Go on to four," Gerhard said. He wrote out a few notes:

#1—?memory trace (ham sand.)
#2—bladder fullness
#3—no subject change
#4—

He drew the dash and waited. It was going to take a long time to go through all forty electrodes, but it was fascinating to watch. They produced such strikingly different effects, yet each electrode was very close to the next. It was the ultimate proof of the density of the brain, which had once been described as the most complex structure in the known universe. And it was certainly true: there were three times as many cells packed into a single human brain as there were human beings on the face of the earth. That density was hard to comprehend, sometimes. Early in his NPS career, Gerhard had requested a human brain to dissect. He had done it over a period of several days, with a dozen neuroanatomy texts opened up before him. He used the traditional tool for brain dissection, a blunt wooden stick, to scrape away the cheesy gray material. He had patiently, carefully scraped away—and in the end, he had nothing. The brain was not like the liver or the lungs. To the naked eye, it was uniform and boring, giving no indication of its true function. The brain was too subtle, too complex. Too dense.

"Electrode four," Richards said into the recorder. "Five millivolts, five seconds." The shock was delivered.

And Benson, in an oddly childlike voice, said, "Could I have some milk and cookies, please?"

"That's interesting," Gerhard said, watching the reaction.

Richards nodded. "How old would you say?"

"About five or six, at most."

Benson was talking about cookies, talking about his tricycle, to Ross. Slowly, over the next few minutes, he seemed to emerge like a time-traveler advancing through the years. Finally he became fully adult again, thinking back to his youth, instead of actually being there. "I always wanted the cookies, and she would never give them to me. She said

they were bad for me and would give me cavities."

"We can go on," Gerhard said.

Richards said, "Electrode five, five millivolts, five seconds."

In the next room, Benson shifted uncomfortably in his wheelchair. Ross asked him if something was wrong. Benson said, "It feels funny."

"How do you mean?"

"I can't describe it. It's like sandpaper. Irritating."

Gerhard nodded, and wrote in his notes, "#5—potential attack electrode." This happened sometimes. Occasionally an electrode would be found to stimulate a seizure. Nobody knew why—and Gerhard personally thought that nobody ever would. The brain was, he believed, beyond comprehension.

His work with programs . . . had led him to understand that relatively simple computer instructions could produce complex and unpredictable machine behavior. It was also true that the programmed machine could exceed the capabilities of the programmer; that was clearly demonstrated in 1963 when Arthur Samuel at IBM programmed a machine to play checkers—and the machine eventually became so good that it beat Samuel himself.

Yet all this was done with computers which had no more circuits than the brain of an ant. The human brain far exceeded that complexity, and the programming of the human brain extended over many decades. How could anyone seriously expect to understand it?

There was also a philosophical problem. Goedel's Theorem: that no system could explain itself, and no machine could understand its own workings. At most, Gerhard believed that a human brain might, after years of work, decipher a frog brain. But a human brain could never decipher itself in the same detail. For that you would need a superhuman brain.

Gerhard thought that someday a computer would be developed that could untangle the billions of cells and hundreds of billions of interconnections in the human brain. Then, at last, man would have the information that he wanted. But man wouldn't have done the work—another order of intelligence would have done it. And man would not know, of course, how the computer worked.

Morris entered the room with a cup of coffee. He sipped it, and glanced at Benson through the glass. "How's he holding up?"

"Okay," Gerhard said.

"Electrode six, five and five," Richards intoned.

In the next room, Benson failed to react. He sat talking with Ross about the operation, and his lingering headache. He was quite calm and apparently unaffected. They repeated the stimulation, still without change in Benson's behavior. Then they went on.

"Electrode seven, five and five," Richards said. He delivered the shock.

Benson sat up abruptly. "Oh," he said, "that was nice."

"What was?" Ross said.

"You can do that again if you want to."

"How does it feel?"

"Nice," Benson said. His whole appearance seemed to change subtly. "You know," he said after a moment, "you're really a wonderful person, Dr. Ross."

"Thank you," she said.

"Very attractive, too. I don't know if I ever told you before."

"How do you feel now?"

"I'm really very fond of you," Benson said. "I don't know if I told you that before." . . .

4

The TV screen glowed to life. After a moment, letters appeared on it.

BENSON, H.F.
INTERFACING PROCEDURE
POSSIBLE ELECTRODES: 40, designated serially
POSSIBLE VOLTAGES: continuous
POSSIBLE DURATIONS: continuous
POSSIBLE WAVE FORMS: pulse only

Gerhard pressed a button and the screen went blank. Then a series of questions appeared, to which Gerhard typed out the answers on the console.

INTERFACE PROCEDURES BENSON, H. F.
1. WHICH ELECTRODES WILL BE ACTIVATED?

7,31 only

2. WHAT VOLTAGE WILL BE APPLIED TO ELECTRODE SEVEN?

5 mv

3. WHAT DURATION WILL BE APPLIED TO ELECTRODE SEVEN?

5 sec

There was a pause, and the questions continued for electrode 31. Gerhard typed in the answers. Watching him, McPherson said to Morris, "This is amusing, in a way. We're telling the tiny computer how to work. The little computer gets its instructions from the big computer, which gets its instructions from Gerhard, who has a bigger computer than any of them."

"Maybe," Gerhard said, and laughed.

The screen glowed:

INTERFACING PARAMETERS STORED. READY TO PROGRAM AUXILIARY UNIT.

Morris sighed. He hoped that he would never reach the point in his life when he was referred to by a computer as an "auxiliary unit." Gerhard typed quietly, a soft clicking sound. On the other TV screens, they could see the inner circuitry of the small computer. It glowed intermittently as the wiring locked in.

BENSON HF HAS BEEN INTERFACED. IMPLANTED DEVICE NOW READING EEG DATA AND DELIVERING APPROPRIATE FEEDBACK.

That was all there was to it. Somehow Morris was disappointed; he knew it would be this way, but he had expected—or needed—something more dramatic. . . .

Finally Ellis was alone with Benson.

"You feel like sleeping?" Ellis said.

"I feel like a goddamned machine. I feel like an automobile in a complicated service station. I feel like I'm being *repaired.*"

Benson was getting angry. Ellis could feel his own tension building. He was tempted to call for nurses and orderlies to restrain Benson when the attack came. But he remained seated.

"That's a lot of crap," Ellis said.

Benson glared at him, breathing deeply.

Ellis looked at the monitors over the bed. The brain waves were going irregular, moving into an attack configuration.

Benson wrinkled his nose and sniffed. "What's that smell?" he said. "That awful—"

Above the bed, a red monitor light blinked STIMULATION. The brain waves spun in a distorted tangle of white lines for five seconds. Simultaneously, Benson's pupils dilated. Then the lines were smooth again; the pupils returned to normal size.

Benson turned away, staring out the window at the afternoon sun. "You know," he said, "it's really a very nice day, isn't it?"

5

"Damn," she said when she saw the graph.

"What's the matter?" Gerhard said.

"He's getting more frequent stimulations. He had none for a long time, and then he began to have them every couple of hours. Now it looks like one an hour."

"So?" Gerhard said.

"What does that suggest to you?" she said.

"Nothing in particular."

"It should suggest something quite specific," she said. "We know that Benson's brain will be interacting with the computer, right?"

"Yes. . . ."

"And that interaction will be a learning pattern of some kind. It's just like a kid with a cookie jar. If you slap the kid's hand every time he reaches for the cookies, pretty soon he won't reach so often. Look." She drew a quick sketch.

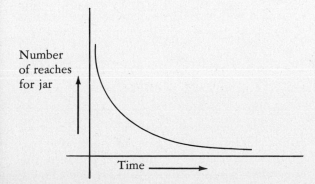

"Now," she said, "that's negative reinforcement. The kid reaches, but he gets hurt. So he stops reaching. Eventually he'll quit altogether. Okay?"

"Sure," Gerhard said, "but—"

"Let me finish. If the kid is normal, it works that way. But if the kid is a masochist, it will be very different." She drew another curve.

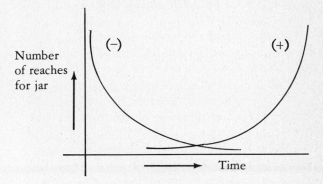

"Here the kid is reaching more often for the cookies, because he likes getting hit. It should be negative reinforcement, but it's really positive reinforcement. Do you remember Cecil?"

"No," Gerhard said.

On the computer console, a new report appeared:

11:22   STIMULATION

"Oh shit," she said. "It's happening."

"What's happening?"

"Benson is going into a positive progression cycle."

"I don't understand."

"It's just like Cecil. Cecil was the first monkey to be wired with electrodes to a computer. That was back in '65. The computer wasn't miniaturized then; it was a big clunky computer, and the monkey was wired up by actual wires. Okay. Cecil had epilepsy. The computer detected the start of a seizure, and delivered a counter-shock to stop it. Okay. Now the seizures should have come less and less frequently, like the hand reaching for the cookies less and less often. But instead the reverse happened. Cecil *liked* the shocks. And he began to initiate seizures in order to experience the pleasurable shocks."

"And that's what Benson is doing?"

"I think so."

Gerhard shook his head. "Listen, Jan, that's all interesting. But a person can't start and stop epileptic seizures at will. They can't control it. The seizures are—"

"Involuntary," she said. "That's right. You have no more control over them than you do over heart rate and blood pressure and sweating and all the other involuntary acts.". . .

Gerhard scratched his head. "And you think Benson is producing more seizures to be rewarded with shocks?"

"Yes."

"Well, what's the difference? He still can't have any seizures. The computer always prevents them from happening."

"Not true," she said. "A couple of years ago, a Norwegian schizophrenic was wired up and allowed to stimulate a pleasure terminal as often as he wanted. He pushed himself into a convulsion by overstimulating himself."

Gerhard winced.

Richards, who had been watching the computer console, suddenly said, "Something's wrong."

"What is it?"

"We're not getting readings any more."

On the screen, they saw:

11:32 -------
11:42 -------

Ross looked and sighed. "See if you can get a computer extrapolation of that curve," she said. "See if he's really going into a learning cycle, and how fast." She started for the door. "I'm going to see what's happened to Benson.". . . .

The room lights were off; the only light came from the glow of the television. Benson had apparently fallen asleep; his body was turned away from the door, and the sheets were pulled up over his shoulder. She clicked the television off and crossed the room to the bed. Gently, she touched his leg.

"Harry," she said softly. "Harry—"

She stopped.

The leg beneath her hand was soft and formless. She pressed down; the "leg" bulged oddly. She reached for the bedside lamp and turned it on, flooding the room with light. Then she pulled back the sheets.

Benson was gone. In his place were three plastic bags of the kind the hospital used to line wastebaskets. Each had been inflated and then knotted shut tightly. Benson's head was represented by a wadded towel; his arm by another.

"Officer," she said, in a low voice, "you'd better get your ass in here.". . .

6

"Hello?" she said.

There was a pause. Then a male voice said, "Whom am I speaking to?"

"This is Dr. Ross."

"Are you affiliated with the"—a short pause—"the Neuropsychiatric Research Unit?"

"Yes, I am."

"Get a pencil and paper. I want you to take an address down. This is Captain Anders of the Los Angeles police."

She gestured to Gerhard for something to write with. "What's the problem, Captain?"

"We have a murder here," Anders said, "and we've got some questions for your people."

7

As she approached the NPS, she saw that a cluster of reporters had cornered Ellis outside the building. He was answering their questions in clear bad humor; she heard the words "mind control" repeated several times.

Feeling slightly guilty, she cut around to the far entrance and took the elevator to the fourth floor. Mind control, she thought. The Sunday supplements were going to have a field day with mind control. And then there would be solemn editorials in the daily papers, and even more solemn editorials in the medical journals, about the hazards of uncontrolled and irresponsible research. She could see it coming.

Mind control. Christ.

The truth was that everybody's mind was controlled, and everybody was glad for it. The most powerful mind controllers in the world were parents, and they did the most damage. Theorists usually forgot that nobody was born prejudiced, neurotic, or hung-up; those traits required a helping hand. Of course, parents didn't intentionally damage their children. They merely inculcated attitudes that they felt would be important and useful to their children.

Newborn children were little computers waiting to be programmed. And they would learn whatever they were taught, from bad grammar to bad attitudes. Like computers, they were undiscriminating; they had no way to differentiate between good ideas and bad ones. The analogy was quite exact: many people had remarked on the childishness and the literalness of computers. For example, if you could instruct a computer to "Put on your shoes and socks," the computer would certainly reply that socks could not be fitted over shoes.

All the important programming was finished by the age of seven. Racial attitudes, sexual attitudes, ethical attitudes, religious attitudes, national attitudes. The gyroscope was set, and the children let loose to spin off on their predetermined courses.

Mind control. . . .

She got off at the fourth floor, brushed past several policemen in the hallway, and went into her office. Anders was there, hanging up the telephone. And frowning.

"We just got our first break," he said.

"Oh?" Her irritation dissipated in a wave of expectancy.

"Yes," Anders said, "but I'll be damned if I know what it means."

"What happened?"

"Benson's description and his pictures are being circulated downtown, and somebody recognized him."

"Who?"

"A clerk in Building Planning, in City Hall. He said Benson came in ten days ago. Building and Planning files specifications on all public structures erected within city limits, and they administer certain building codes."

Ross nodded.

"Well, Benson came in to check specs on a building. He wanted to review electrical blueprints. Said he was an electrical engineer, produced some identification."

Ross said, "The girls at his house said he'd come back for some blueprints."

"Well, apparently he got them from Building and Planning."

"What are they for?"

"University Hospital," Anders said. "He has the complete wiring system for the entire hospital. Now what do you make of that?" They stared at each other.

8

. . . She went into the computer room and looked around. The main computer was demolished. Two magnetic tape banks were knocked over; the main control panel was riddled with fine round punctures, and sparks sputtered and dripped from the panel toward the floor. She ought to control that, she thought. It might start a fire. She looked around for a fire extinguisher and saw Benson's axe lying on the carpet in a corner. And then she saw the gun.

Curious, she picked it up. It was surprisingly heavy, much heavier than she expected. It felt big and greasy and cold in her hand. She knew Anders had his gun; therefore this must be Benson's. Benson's gun. She stared at it oddly, as if it might tell her something about him.

From somewhere in the basement, there were four gunshots in rapid succession. They echoed through the labyrinthine hospital tunnels. She walked to the broken windows and looked out at the tunnels. She saw nothing, heard nothing.

It must be finished, she thought. The sputtering, hissing sound of sparks behind her made her turn. There was also a slapping sound, repetitive and monotonous. She saw that one of the magnetic tape reels had spun out, and the edge of the tape was slapping against the hardware spindle. . . .

Another gunshot, very close now.

She ducked down behind one of the magnetic tape banks as she heard approaching footsteps. She was aware of the irony: Benson had been hiding behind the computers, and now she was hiding, cowering behind the metal columns, as if they could protect her in some way.

She heard someone gasping for breath; the footsteps paused; the door to the computer room opened, then closed with a slam. She was still hidden behind the tape bank, and could not see what was happening.

A second set of running feet went past the computer room and continued down the corridor, fading into echoes. Everything was quiet. Then she heard heavy breathing and a cough.

She stood.

Harry Benson, in his torn white orderly's clothes, his left leg very red, was sprawled on the carpet, his body half-propped up against the wall. He was sweating; his breath came in ragged gasps; he stared straight ahead, unaware of anyone else in the room.

She still held the gun in her hand, and she felt a moment of elation. Somehow it was all going to work out. She was going to get him back alive. The police hadn't killed him, and by the most unbelievable stroke of luck she had him alone, to herself. It made her wonderfully happy.

"Harry."

He looked over slowly and blinked. He did not seem to recognize her for a moment, and then he smiled. "Hello, Dr. Ross."

It was a nice smile. She had the brief image of McPherson, with his white hair, bending over to congratulate her on saving the project and getting Benson back alive. And then she remembered, quite incongruously, how her own father had gotten sick and had suddenly had to leave her medical-school graduation ceremonies. Why did she think of that now?

"Everything is going to be all right, Harry," she said. Her voice was full of confidence; it pleased her.

She wanted to reassure him, so she did not move, did not approach him. She stayed across the room, behind the computer data bank.

He continued to breathe heavily, and said nothing for a moment. He looked around the room at the demolished computer equipment. "I really did it," he said. "Didn't I?"

"You're going to be fine, Harry," she said. She was drawing up a schedule in her mind. He could undergo emergency surgery on his leg that night, and in the morning they could disconnect his computer, reprogram the electrodes, and everything would be corrected. A disaster would be salvaged. It was the most incredible piece of luck. Ellis would keep his house. McPherson would continue to expand the NPS into new areas. They would be grate-

ful. They would recognize her achievement and appreciate what she—

"Dr. Ross . . . " He started to get up, wincing in pain.

"Don't try to move. Stay where you are, Harry."

"I have to."

"Stay where you are, Harry."

Benson's eyes flashed briefly, and the smile was gone. "Don't call me Harry. My name is Mr. Benson. Call me Mr. Benson."

There was no mistaking the anger in his voice. It surprised her and upset her. She was trying to help him. Didn't he know that she was the only one who still wanted to help him? The others would be just as happy if he died. . . .

Benson took another step. His eyes never left her face. He started to fall, and leaned heavily on one of the disc drive consoles. It tore his white jacket at the armpit. He looked at the tear numbly. "It tore. . . ."

"Stay there, Harry. Stay there." It's like talking to an animal, she thought. Do not feed or molest the animals. She felt like a lion tamer in the circus.

He hung there a moment, supporting himself on the drive console, breathing heavily. "I want the gun," he said. "I need it. Give it to me."

"Harry—"

With a grunt, he pushed away from the console and continued moving toward her.

"Anders!"

"It's no good," Benson said. "There's no time left, Dr. Ross." His eyes were on her. She saw the pupils expand briefly as he received a stimulation. "That's beautiful," he said, and smiled.

The stimulation seemed to halt him for a time. He was turned inward, enjoying the sensation. When he spoke again, his voice was calm and distant. "You see," he said, "they are after me. They have turned their little computers against me. The program is hunt. Hunt and kill. The original human program. Hunt and kill. Do you understand?". . . .

Benson advanced.

"No closer, Harry. I mean it."

A flood of images overcame her. She saw Benson as she had first met him, a meek man with a terrifying problem. She saw him in a montage of all the hour-long interviews, all the tests, all the drug trials. He was a good person, an honest and frightened person. Nothing that had happened was his fault. It was her fault, and Ellis's fault, and McPherson's fault, and Morris's fault. . . .

She fired at point-blank range.

With remarkable agility, Benson jumped and spun in the air, dodging the bullet. She was pleased. She had managed to drive him back without hurting him. Anders would arrive any minute to help subdue him before they took him to surgery.

Benson's body slammed hard into the printing unit, knocking it over. It began to clatter in a monotonous, mechanical way as the keys printed out some message. Benson rolled onto his back. Blood spurted in heavy thick gushes from his chest. His white uniform became darkly red.

"Harry?" she said.

He did not move.

"Harry? Harry?"

She didn't remember clearly what happened af-ter that. Anders returned and took the gun from her hand. He moved her to the side of the room as three men in gray suits arrived, carrying a long plastic capsule on a stretcher. They opened the capsule up; the inside was lined in a strange, yellow honeycomb insulation. They lifted Benson's body —she noticed they were careful, trying to keep the blood off their special suits—and placed him inside the capsule. They closed it and locked it with special locks. Two of the men carried it away. A third went around the room with a Geiger counter, which chattered loudly. Somehow the sound reminded her of an angry monkey. The man went over to Ross. She couldn't see his face behind the gray helmet he wore; the glass was fogged.

"You better leave this area," the man said.

Anders put his arm around her shoulders. She began to cry.

24. THE CASE FOR PSYCHOSURGERY

Vernon H. Mark

I. INTRODUCTION

The continuing controversy surrounding psychosurgery is responsible not only for greater public awareness of the procedure but also for the publication of misinformation that has hindered rational discourse and policy planning relating to its use. An informed discussion of psychosurgery must proceed from at least a general familiarity with the medical data. It is therefore the purpose of this article to provide a brief summary of the research in this area and to correct the more significant distortions regarding psychosurgical practice that have surfaced in the course of the anti-psychosurgery campaign. . . .

Reprinted with permission from Vernon H. Mark, "Psychosurgery Versus Anti-Psychiatry," *Boston University Law Review*, Vol. 54, No. 2 (March 1974).

II. A SURVEY OF THE MEDICAL FINDINGS

A. CLASSICAL PSYCHOSURGERY

In its classical sense, psychosurgery includes operations on the frontal lobes or their connections in the brain to relieve the symptoms of intractable depression, agitation, compulsion, delusion, hallucination and ideas of reference in patients with no known brain disease. Such surgery is performed only when psychiatric treatment, drug therapy, electroconvulsive treatment and other forms of environmental therapy have failed to relieve the patient's symptoms.

Frontal lobe surgery was initiated by the clinical trials of Moniz, a Nobel Laureate. Although it is most effective in treating agitation and depression, the operation of radical frontal lobotomy was widely performed in the United States for the relief of symptoms in agitated schizophrenic patients. Many of these patients were institutionalized, and controlled studies, such as those of the United States Veterans Administration, showed that the condition of the operated patients improved in terms of their ability to leave mental institutions and carry on integrated lives in noninstitutional settings. However, some of these patients paid the unacceptably high price of severe emotional blunting and intellectual deterioration for their treatment. Thus, with the advent of powerful ataractic drugs—Thorazine, Stelazine and Haldoperidol, for example—capable of achieving the same therapeutic goals without surgery, the performance of radical frontal lobe surgery in the United States ceased. . . .

Cairns and his associates at Oxford University began to modify frontal lobe operations so that small portions of the frontal lobe were ablated to produce specific relief of symptoms.[1] They initiated the operation of cingulotomy in which the destructive lesion is restricted to a small bundle of fibers called the cingulum. Fortunately, critical British psychiatrists evaluated an extensive series of patients prior to surgery and followed them for several years afterward. A review of their published studies indicates that restricted forms of frontal surgery may be therapeutic when other methods of treatment have proved ineffective.[2]

B. PSYCHOSURGERY AND EPILEPSY

Psychosurgery has expanded beyond its classical meaning to include any neurosurgical operation that affects human behavior, even if the patients being treated have obvious brain disease. The most controversial patients within this expanded definition are those who have epilepsy and psychiatric symptoms, often including abnormally aggressive behavior.

Although the brain responds to the environment as an integrated unit, an individual's brain mechanisms are limited by their ontogenetic and phylogenetic development. It is therefore a specialized portion of the brain, the limbic system, that more directly governs "fight or flight" behavior, sexuality, appetite and emotional tone. As broadly defined, the limbic system or limbic brain includes the medial-frontal lobes and orbital surfaces, the cingulum, amygdala, hippocampus, hypothalamus and portions of the thalamus, mid-brain and midline commissures.[3]

The limbic brain may be damaged by head injury, infections such as virus encephalitis and rabies, brain tumors, hemorrhage, infarcts, poisons, and lack of oxygen such as may occur in febrile convulsions. One of the more common diseases afflicting the limbic brain, however, is focal epilepsy.[4] Such epilepsy may be associated with behavioral abnormalities, and the focus may originate from the inner or medial-anterior portion of the temporal lobe. A typical attack of temporal lobe epilepsy which includes such foci produces the following symptoms: hallucinations of taste or smell associated with momentary lapses in consciousness, lip-smacking, head and eye turning, mental confusion, inappropriate speech, repetitive inappropriate movements and, at times, major motor seizures.

Episodes of violence appear to be occasionally related to this variety of epilepsy. Currie and his colleagues, for example, have shown that abnormal aggressivity, sometimes motivated by unreasoning and overwhelming fear, may occur either preceding or during the seizure itself or in the stage of post-ictal confusion.[5] Much more frequently, however, episodes of catastrophic rage occur between seizures. Walker, who has demonstrated that implanted electrodes may detect frequent seizures deep within the brain that are undetectable from the surface of the brain or head, believes that these repeated deep seizures bear an important relationship to the inter-ictal rage characteristic of epileptic patients with limbic foci.[6]

If anti-convulsant and ataractic drugs and psychiatric treatment fail to relieve the symptoms associated with temporal lobe epilepsy, surgical treatment involving the removal of the anterior portion of the temporal lobe is usually administered. Specifically, such surgery includes the complete removal of amygdala, hippocampus in its anterior third and surface structures on the lateral portion of the lobe. However, in an attempt to achieve the same kind of therapy with less destruction of brain tissue, stereotactic methods have been developed. Tiny electrodes implanted into the amygdala may now be used for recording, stimulating and destroying restricted portions of tissue with heat.[7] The preservation of as much brain tissue as possible is, of course, always to be desired. . . .

Because the clinical signs of temporal lobe epilepsy are not as dramatic as those of major motor seizures and the surface confirmation of a temporal lobe attack is difficult, critics of this kind of surgery argue that the diagnosis of the disorder is indefinite and dependent upon the vagaries of a brain wave recording. Recent studies prove, however, that most patients with temporal lobe epilepsy have definite structural changes in the brain which can be seen on special x-rays called pneumoencephalograms or in the specimens of temporal lobes removed when temporal lobectomy is performed. . . .

Studies by Walker and Blumer[8] and by Falconer[9] demonstrate that temporal lobe surgery may relieve epileptic patients of their seizures, abnormal aggressivity and other psychiatric symptoms. In the words of one who has reviewed this data, "this careful but uncontrolled series would hardly lend support to an indiscriminate use of brain surgery for management of disordered behavior, [but] it lends equally little support to those who would forbid any surgery of this type under all circumstances."[10]

Cooper and Gilman have achieved similar results without removing brain tissue.[11] Through the implantation of stimulating electrodes on top of the cerebellum, or small brain, they have stopped epileptic seizures by electrical stimulation. In one patient in particular, in whom epileptic seizures were associated with catastrophic rage and destructive violence, cerebellar stimulation completely reversed both these symptoms and the seizures themselves. Seizures and violence recurred when the stimulation was no longer administered, but the symptoms disappeared once again when it was resumed.

C. PSYCHOSURGERY AND STRUCTURAL BRAIN DAMAGE

Catastrophic rage may develop in association with rabies, head injury, hydrocephalus and large brain tumors. Although such tumors usually grow so rapidly and are so disabling that aggressivity is not a major complaint, some patients do have this symptom.

1. Three Case Histories

Patient A,[12] brought to the hospital after trying to decapitate his wife with a meat cleaver, was in an agitated, aggressive state and had to be restrained from tearing at people with his nails and teeth. A distinctive personality change had occurred five months prior to his admission to the hospital. He had become slovenly in his habits, filthy in his body care, insulting to his wife and fellow workers, and he complained of weakness in one arm and of headaches. An examination revealed that his optic nerve heads were swollen with increased intracranial pressure. In addition, a mass lesion in the right frontal area of the brain impinged upon the base of the frontal lobe and pressed internal connections from the anterior temporal lobe. Part of this mass, it was discovered through surgery, consisted of swollen dead brain tissue which had been destroyed by a tumor the size of a small tangerine. After the removal of this tumor—a variety known as meningioma—the patient did not threaten the life of his wife for another 20 years, during which time he worked for 17 years at one job. The recurrence of his condition has prompted a repeat neurological examination at the present time. . . .

Patient B[13] was hit by an automobile and sustained a head injury. In a convalescent home, unusual symptoms of mental disturbance and aggressive behavior began to appear. His language patterns changed abruptly and he became hostile, repeatedly attacking nurses by tackling them to the ground and then proceeding to bite them. Studies of his brain indicated a remarkable dilation of his ventricles. Surgery known as the ventriculo-atrial shunt was performed in which spinal fluid is shunted into the right heart through a valve. By reducing the excess fluid in his ventricles, the operation successfully reversed the patient's symptoms, including his abnormal aggressivity.

Head injuries that do not result in hydrocephalus may also be related to abnormal aggressivity. Patient C[14] suffered a severe head injury when the bicycle he was riding collided with a truck. Upon his admission to the emergency room, the patient began to terrorize nurses, doctors and attendants. His wild and agitated state lasted for 36 hours, and, during periods of apparent lucidity, he denied having any memory of the collision or his wild behavior. Initial arteriograms were normal but were followed by a typical temporal lobe epileptic attack ushered in by a feeling of floating and brief unconsciousness. These symptoms were subsequently followed by a series of major motor seizures and seizures involving one arm and leg with rapidly advancing paralysis and coma. It was then discovered, through a repeat arteriogram and surgery, that the patient's brain had a huge swollen hemisphere with blood over the surface and pockets of blood in the depths of the temporal and parietal lobes. An extensive, external decompression saved the patient's life and promoted the recovery of some function in the previously paralyzed arm and leg. Moreover, his emotional behavior is now normal.

2. The Role of the Environment

The relationship between brain abnormalities and abnormal behavior does not necessarily negate the role of social and cultural factors in the course of diagnosis or treatment. All human behavior is the result of interaction between the brain and the environment and must therefore be analyzed on an individual basis. . . .

III. THE ANTI-PSYCHOSURGERY CAMPAIGN

In 1967, Dr. William Sweet, Dr. Frank Ervin and I wrote a letter to the *Journal of the American Medical Association* about the possible role of brain dysfunction in individuals who killed or maimed others in urban riots.[15] For several years, this preliminary statement was, like most letters to the editor, largely ignored. Subsequently, it was superseded by more complete statements in a book and an article. The anti-psychosurgery campaign initiated in 1972,[16] however, suddenly invested the letter with false significance. These critics have claimed that this letter and our other writings advocated psychosurgery for urban rioters by linking the riots to brain disease and by treating biological factors at the expense of socio-cultural conditions.[17] A reading of the letter reveals, however, that the use of

psychosurgery on urban rioters was not discussed, but rather that the possible role of brain disease in individual violence was presented. Moreover, the letter explicitly recognized the severe social problems of urban centers. Similarly, the critics have generally ignored our suggestion in 1970 that the investigation of the causes of violence include consideration of police and National Guard activity.[18]

Pervading the criticism of neurological treatment for personal violence is concern that it is directed primarily against the poor and the underprivileged and that it has marked overtones of racism. . . . It is important to note that to date no psychosurgery of the classical form has been performed at Boston City Hospital, although such procedures properly continue to be performed in Boston's private hospitals.

More distressing and misleading, however, is the charge of racism.[19] A theory that some violence is caused by brain disease in no way implies that it is characteristic of blacks. Indeed, it is the theory that personal violence is caused exclusively by social conditions that may direct our attention to the black ghettos. Thus, our theory of violence does not have any racially suspect political implications.

In addition, it is our experience that there is no special correlation between violence and race. . . .

There is, however, a danger of de facto racism that should not be minimized. Certain institutions in which blacks are disproportionately represented may present their inmates as candidates for psychiatric neurosurgery for custodial or punitive motives. This form of racism should be combatted through the limitation of psychiatric neurosurgery to cases where brain pathological disorders are well defined. In addition, the safeguards of requiring informed consent and regulating institutional action should receive adequate attention. Under present conditions, it would seem that the performance of psychosurgery on convicted felons should be prohibited.

IV. THE RELATIVE BENEFITS OF PSYCHOSURGERY AND OTHER FORMS OF PSYCHIATRIC TREATMENT

To fully appreciate the cost-benefit ratio of psychosurgery, it must be compared with the results obtained by nonsurgical forms of treatment. Environmental manipulation, psychoanalysis, behavior therapy and other forms of psychotherapy may be successful in relieving the symptoms of certain patients, but it has been recently reported that no valid statistical data indicate that any particular form of psychotherapy is more effective in treating seriously ill mental patients than any other form of treatment or even chance alone.[20] Furthermore, recent studies of the effectiveness of psychotherapy are said to be characterized by serious methodological flaws invalidating their conclusions.[21]

Any discussion of the hazards of psychosurgery should also take note of the significant hazards associated with psychotherapy. Yalom and Lieberman, for example, have studied encounter group casualties.[22] Of 209 university undergraduates who entered 18 encounter groups which met for a total of 30 hours each, 39 did not complete the schedule and were considered dropouts. Sixteen of the remaining test group subjects were judged to be casualties. In other words, they experienced significant, negative effects that endured for many months. Another patient in the series committed suicide.

Drug therapy with neuroleptic agents—Thorazine, Stelazine and Haldol, for example—have proved to be more effective than inert substances or conventional sedatives.[23] Over 250 million people have taken these drugs since their introduction in the 1950s.[24] Although a single dose of any antipsychotic drug is seldom dangerous, the administration of these agents over a period of weeks or months may cause a number of side effects and complications. A syndrome resembling Parkinson's disease is common and some of the drugs may occasionally produce a fatal leukopenia. . . .

V. CONCLUSION

Although the arguments of the . . . anti-psychosurgeons may be countered on several grounds, the responsibility of neurosurgeons to properly diagnose and treat their patients is not, by this critique, diminished. It is clear, however, that the function of the neurosurgeon requires reference not only to medical considerations, but to legal, ethical, social and political ones as well. Thus, it is particularly appropriate for the physician and surgeon in charge of the patient to make their decisions in conjunction with a multidisciplinary committee composed of independent persons skilled in the relevant scientific and nonscientific disciplines.

NOTES

1. Whitty, Duffield, Tow & Cairns, Anterior Cingulectomy in the Treatment of Mental Disease, 1 Lancet 175 (1952).

2. Sweet, Treatment of Medically Intractable Mental Disease by Limited Frontal Leucotomy—Justifiable?, 289 New Eng. J. Med. 1117 (1973).

3. For a more extensive discussion of the limbic system see V. Mark & F. Ervin, Violence and the Brain 13–24 (1970).

4. "Epilepsy itself is not a disease. It is a symptom of brain dysfunction and electrical disorganization within the brain. This disorganization is manifested inside the brain as a very noticeable electrical discharge marked by an increase in both amplitude and frequency of the brain waves." Id. at 60.

5. Currie, Heathfield, Henson & Scott, Clinical Course and Prognosis of Temporal Lobe Epilepsy, 94 Brain 173 (1971).

6. Walker, Man and His Temporal Lobes, 1 Surg. Neurol. 69 (1973).

7. For an extensive discussion of stereotactic surgery see V. Mark & F. Ervin, supra note 8 [in original text] at 69–87.

8. Walker & Blumer, Long-Term Effects of Temporal Lobe Lesions on Sexual Behavior and Aggressivity, in The Neurobiology of Violence (W. Fields & W. Sweet eds. in press).

9. Falconer, Reversibility by Temporal-Lobe Resection of the Behavioral Abnormalities of Temporal-Lobe Epilepsy, 289 New Eng. J. Med. 451 (1973).

10. Geschwind, Effects of Temporal-Lobe Surgery on Behavior, 289 New Eng. J. Med. 480, 481 (1973).

11. Address by I. Cooper & S. Gilman, The Effect of Chronic Cerebellar Stimulation upon Muscular Hypertonus and Epilepsy in Man. The American Neurological Association, Montreal, June 12, 1973.

12. V. Mark & F. Ervin, supra note 8 [in the original text] at 58–59.

13. Crowell, Tew & Mark, Aggressive Dementia Associated with Normal Pressure Hydrocephalus, 23 Neurology 461 (1973).

14. This case has not been published in the medical literature.

15. Mark, Sweet & Ervin, Role of Brain Disease in Riots and Urban Violence, 201 J.A.M.A. 895 (1967).

16. See Breggin, The Return of Lobotomy and Psychosurgery, reprinted in 118 Cong. Rec. E1602 (daily ed. Feb. 24, 1972).

17. See, e.g., Breggin, New Information in the Debate over Psychosurgery, reprinted in 118 Cong. Rec. E3380 (daily ed. Mar. 30, 1972); Chorover, Big Brother and Psychotechnology, Psychology Today, Oct. 1973, at 43, 47–48.

18. See note 22 supra [in the original text].

19. Chorover, supra note 26 [in the original text] at 48.

20. Grinker, Emerging Concepts of Mental Illness and Models of Treatment: The Medical Point of View, 125 Am. J. Psychiat. 865, 866 (1969).

21. Dyrud & Holzman, The Psychotherapy of Schizophrenia: Does It Work?, 130 Am. J. Psychiat. 670 (1973).

22. Yalom & Lieberman, A Study of Encounter Group Casualties, 25 Arch. Gen. Psychiat. 16 (1971).

23. Crane, Clinical Psychopharmacology in Its 20th Year, 181 Science 124 (1973).

24. Id. at 124.

25. PSYCHOSURGERY: THE CASE AGAINST IT

Stephan L. Chorover

INTRODUCTION

We are still far from understanding how our brains give rise to the varied phenomena of our subjective experience. But despite our relative ignorance, we biologists and behavioral scientists stand today in a position comparable to that occupied by our colleagues in nuclear physics almost 30 years ago. In 1945, developments in that field led to the atomic bomb and ushered in a new world of ethical and social problems. During the past few decades, developments in the biobehavioral sciences have spawned a wide-ranging psychotechnology, a varied arsenal of tools and techniques for predicting and modifying human social behavior. The continued development and deployment of this psychotechnology has also engendered serious ethical and social problems that can no longer be ignored.

Psychosurgery is among the more controversial forms of psychotechnology. Also known as "psychiatric neurosurgery," "mental surgery," "functional neurosurgery" and "sedative neurosurgery," psychosurgery may be defined as brain surgery that has as its primary purpose the alteration of thoughts, social behavior patterns, personality characteristics, emotional reactions, or some similar aspects of subjective experience in human beings. . . .

PSYCHOSURGERY FOR VIOLENCE

It has long been popularly believed that there is a close association between epilepsy and violence. The phrase "a fit of anger" nicely epitomizes this view. Over the years, a large number of clinical studies have dealt with this question. After reviewing the available literature and assessing the clinical experience of neurologists who have cared for many patients with seizure disorders, a recent study sponsored by the National Institute of Neurological Diseases and Stroke concluded that "violence and aggressive acts do occur in patients with temporal lobe epilepsy but such are rare, perhaps no more frequent than in the general population."[1]

Two of the best known cases of this kind are "Thomas R." and "Julia S." Their pseudonyms have entered the vocabulary of psychosurgery, their cases have been fictionalized in a best-selling novel,[2] and they continue to arouse public interest as purported successes of Drs. Vernon H. Mark and Frank R. Ervin, the authors of the controversial *Violence and the Brain*. Bearing in mind that the existence of a causal connection between epilepsy and violence remains an open question in the view of most neurologists, let us consider each of these cases in turn.

A. THE CASE OF THOMAS R.

1. The Presentation by Mark and Ervin

Thomas is introduced to Mark and Ervin's readers in the following passages:[3]

He was a brillant [*sic*] 34-year-old engineer with several important patents to his credit. Despite his muscular physique it was difficult to believe he was capable of an act of violence when he was not enraged, for his manner was quiet and reserved, and he was both courteous and sympathetic.

Despite a history of physical illness, Thomas managed to educate himself as an engineer.

He was an extremely talented, inventive man, but his behavior at times was unpredictable and even frankly psychotic. He was seen and treated by psychiatrists over a period of 7 years with no effect on his destructive outbursts of violence.

Thomas's chief problem was his violent rage; this was sometimes directed at his co-workers and friends, but it was mostly expressed toward his wife and children. He was very paranoid, and harbored grudges which eventually produced an explosion of anger. He often felt that people were gratuitously insulting to him. . . .

Reprinted with permission from Stephan L. Chorover, "Psychosurgery: A Neurological Perspective," *Boston University Law Review,* Vol 54, No. 2 (March 1974).

For example, during a conversation with his wife, he would seize upon some innocuous remark and interpret it as an insult. At first, he would try to ignore what she had said, but could not help brooding; and the more he thought about it, the surer he felt that his wife no longer loved him and was "carrying on with a neighbor." Eventually he would reproach his wife for these faults, and she would hotly deny them. Her denials were enough to set him off into a frenzy of violence.

Thomas was referred to Mark and Ervin by a psychiatrist who they say had concluded that "prolonged psychiatric treatment did not improve his behavior and . . . that his spells of staring, automatisms and rage represented an unusual form of temporal lobe seizure."[4] An electroencephalographic examination revealed electrical brain activity considered by them to be indicative of epilepsy, and additional tests suggested the presence of other brain abnormalities. After experimenting with a wide range of pharmacological agents, none of which proved therapeutic, they decided to proceed with stereotaxic surgery. Arrays of electrodes were implanted in both temporal lobes with their ends reaching the nucleus amygdala. The "optimal site for destructive lesions"[5] was sought through repeated stimulation and recording. Stimulation in one portion of the amygdala "produced a complaint of pain, and a feeling of 'I am losing control,'" two reactions that marked the onset of Thomas' periods of violence. However, stimulation of a portion of the amygdala just four millimeters to the side produced the opposite reactions of detachment, "hyperrelaxation" and a "feeling like Demerol."[6]

Mark and Ervin's account of how they obtained Thomas' consent to their proposed surgery is revealing both in terms of what is said and what is left unsaid. They viewed Thomas as keenly aware of personal insults and highly sensitive to threats, and found that "the suggestion that the medial portion of his temporal lobe was to be destroyed . . . would provoke wild, disordered thinking."[7] At this point in their discussion, they acknowledge in a footnote the physician's "extraordinary responsibility" of safeguarding the rights of the patient and of securing his free and informed consent.[8] But, they continue, "[u]nder the effects of lateral amygdala stimulation, [Thomas] showed bland acquiescence to the suggestion" that psychosurgery be performed.[9]

However, 12 hours later, when this effect had worn off, Thomas turned wild and unmanageable. The idea of anyone's making a destructive lesion in his brain enraged him. He absolutely refused any further therapy, and it took many weeks of patient explanation before he accepted the idea of bilateral lesions' [sic] being made in his medial amygdala.[10]

Since Mark and Ervin considered Thomas' rage inappropriate and were, by their own account, able to blunt it by lateral amygdala stimulation, it is perhaps not surprising to learn that Thomas finally "accepted the idea." Directly following this quoted passage, we are informed of the success of the procedure in these brief sentences: "Four years have passed since the operation, during which time Thomas has not had a single episode of rage. He continues, however, to have an occasional epileptic seizure with periods of confusion and disordered thinking."[11]

The reader, recalling Mark and Ervin's original assertion that Thomas' "chief problem was his violent rage"[12] and that he exhibited some preoperative seizures and confused or disordered thinking, may reasonably conclude from this account that bilateral amygdalectomy has not only improved Thomas' condition, but has also effected a specific and total cure of his chief complaint. The rage is allegedly gone, the other preoperative symptoms remain essentially unchanged, and no postoperative side effects are mentioned. In light of the devastating effects of bilateral amygdalectomy on the social behavior of nonhuman primates, the apparently successful outcome of Thomas' case seems remarkable indeed. The implied absence of any adverse social reactions appears especially unexpected. Is it sufficient, however, to rely on mere implications? Highly relevant information is not provided by the published case histories. Prior to his operation, Thomas was married and supported his family through his work as an engineer. It would seem that a full account of the effects of his psychosurgery should include, for example, information concerning his marriage and his employment.

2. Contradictory Reports

At the request of Thomas' family an independent follow-up of Thomas case has been performed by Dr. Peter R. Breggin, a psychiatrist and well known critic of psychosurgery.[13] Dr. Breggin interviewed the patient and his family, reviewed the hospital charts made before and after surgery and discussed the case with several well-informed individuals.

According to Dr. Breggin, Thomas was continuously employed through December 1965. During that year he began to have serious marital problems which prompted visits to his wife's psychiatrist. Breggin conducted a telephone interview with this psychiatrist during which he was told that Thomas' wife was indeed afraid of him, but that no actual harm was done to her.[14] Moreover, writes Breggin:

[the] psychiatrist remembers that Thomas was depressed, but not sufficiently depressed to warrant electroshock or drugs. His memory is entirely consistent with the hospital records which report no hallucinations, delusions, paranoid ideas or signs of difficulty with thinking. In the charts, his most serious psychiatric diagnosis is "personality pattern disturbance," [a classification] reserved for mild problems with no psychotic symptomatology.[15]

Finally, certain hospital charts state that "[h]e has never been in any trouble at work or otherwise for aggressive behavior."[16] In short, Dr. Breggin's account stands in sharp contrast to the published assertions of Drs. Mark and Ervin. Inded, Breggin claims that the only incidence of violence mentioned in Thomas' hospital files were those provoked by Mark and Ervin themselves.

Thomas was treated by Mark and Ervin from October 1966 until his release from Massachusetts General Hospital on August 27, 1967. He subsequently returned with his mother to the west coast, unable to rejoin his wife and children because his wife had, during his treatment, filed for divorce. Eventually, she married the man about whom Thomas had allegedly been paranoid.[17] Shortly after the operation, it became apparent that Thomas was socially confused and unable to cope with the complexities of normal life. He was soon admitted to a west coast Veterans Administration hospital where he was placed on a locked ward and given heavy doses of medication. Breggin's account suggests that Thomas' new physicians did not have access to his medical records from Massachusetts General Hospital. Indeed, they regarded his comments concerning Mark and Ervin's procedures as evidence of his delusional state of mine.[18] After six months of confinement, he was discharged with a diagnosis of "schizophrenic reaction, paranoid type."[19] At present, Breggin claims, Thomas is totally unable to work, is incapable of caring for himself and must periodically be rehospitalized as assaultive and psychotic.

Dr. Breggin is not the only available source of information about Thomas' postoperative history. His follow-up study has recently been supplemented by a complaint filed in behalf of the patient[20] and is generally consistent with information the author has obtained from other sources.[21] In August 1972, Dr. Ernst Rodin, a Detroit neurosurgeon, visited Dr. Mark's project in Boston. Rodin, at that time a co-author of a proposal to perform psychosurgery on involuntarily incarcerated individuals,[22] made the visit "to obtain the most up-to-date information on the results of surgery for aggressive behavior in human beings. . . ."[23] Hoping that this inquiry would strengthen his proposal, Rodin was all the more disturbed by the disparities he discovered between the published accounts and the information available at first hand. Specifically, Dr. Ira Sherwin, a neurologist involved with the project, told Rodin that "he was not aware of any genuinely successful cases"[24] and that Thomas R. "will never be able to function in Society."[25]

B. THE CASE OF JULIA S.

1. The Presentation by Mark and Ervin

Julia S., another one of Mark and Ervin's celebrated patients, is the daughter of a well-to-do physician. She is described as being "an attractive, pleasant, cherubic blonde who looked much younger than her age of 21."[26] Starting with an attack of encephalitis before the age of two, she had a long history of brain disease. Her epileptic seizures began at about the age of 10, some being grand-mal convulsions, but most appearing to be petit mal, or psycho-motor, seizures charactized by "brief lapses of consciousness, staring, lip smacking, and chewing."[27] Between seizures, Julia's behavior was marked by "severe temper tantrums followed by extreme remorse."[28] She also experienced "racing spells," which began with terrifying feelings of panic and ended in her rapidly running aimlessly about the streets. At least 12 people are said to have been assaulted by her, and when she was 18, she seriously injured other women in two separate stabbing incidents.[29]

Because Julia failed to respond to extensive psychotherapy, drugs and electroshock, Mark and Ervin concluded that her case "clearly illustrates the point that violent behavior caused by brain dysfunction cannot be modified except by treating the dysfunction itself."[30] Accordingly, they explored Julia's brain, producing rage reactions with the aid of amygdala electrodes and a telemetry device called a "stimoceiver." Finally, lesions were made in the "appropriate areas." *Violence and the Brain,* which was published two years after Julia's operation, contains the following evaluation by Mark and Ervin:

It is still too early to assess the results of the procedure, but she had only two mild rage episodes in the first postoperative year and none in the second. Since she had generalized brain disease and multiple areas of epileptic activity, it is not surprising that epileptic seizures have not been eliminated, or that her psychotic episodes have continued at the postoperative level.[31]

2. Contradictory Reports

The author is aware of no independent and detailed follow-up studies that may have been made of Julia's case. However, a former member of the project staff, a professional person who was particularly concerned about Julia and in a position permitting almost constant observation of her, recalls that Mark and Ervin's treatments made Julia more despondent and brought an end to her guitar playing and to her desire to engage in intellectual discussions.[32]

PSYCHOSURGERY AND DEVIANCE CONTROL

Results obtained in both animals and human beings raise serious doubts about the purported merits of psychosurgery. The continued performance of the procedure when its scientific foundations remain dubious and its therapeutic value has yet to be established may justifiably be considered questionable or even irresponsible. What is more ominous, however, is the increasing promotion and practice of psychosurgery as a technique of deviance control. The development of psychosurgery is another example of the time-honored practice of reducing complex social problems to the status of personal infirmities.[33] The authors of *Violence and the Brain* are among those who have advanced the view that social deviance and interpersonal violence in our society may be attributable to some kind of "brain dysfunction." It follows from this view that amygdalectomy may be an appropriate treatment for individuals whose brain dysfunction results in "a low threshold for impulsive violence."[34]

Other psychosurgeons have also advocated their medical procedures as an approach to social policy planning in the area of deviance control. At the Second International Conference of Psychosurgery in 1970, for example, Dr. M. Hunter Brown, a California psychosurgeon, urged his colleagues "to initiate pilot programs for precise rehabilitation of the prisoner-patient who is often young and intelligent, yet incapable of controlling various forms of violence." Jessica Mitford has recently noted, however, that the increasing popularity of behavior alteration programs among penologists is in part due to their interest in suppressing those prisoners who interpret prison life in socioeconomic or racial terms.[35] These suggested uses for psychosurgery clearly involve more than medical considerations.

Foreign psychosurgeons, it would seem, have been at least as devoted to deviance control as their American counterparts. During 1972, a group of German neurosurgeons performed stereotaxic psychosurgery involving the destruction of a portion of the hypothalamus upon "22 male patients, 20 of them being sexual deviants, one suffering from neurotic 'pseudo homosexuality' and one from intractable addiction to alcohol and drugs."[36] . . .

Psychosurgery explicitly aimed at taming hyperactive children has been performed in India, Thailand, Japan and the United States. In a summary of 115 patients,[37] including 39 children under the age of 11, one team recently claimed that the destruction of the cingulate gyrus, amygdala and regions of the hypothalamus "proved to be useful in the management of patients who previously could not be managed by other means."[38]. . .

CONCLUSION

Because the weight of the available evidence indicates that limbic system psychosurgery produces a marked deterioration in behavior, serious impairments of judgment and other disastrous social adjustment effects, and because psychosurgeons have failed to provide balanced accounts of their cases, it would appear prudent for the medical profession and the relevant regulatory agencies of state and federal government to act promptly along the following lines. First, there should be an explicit recognition that psychosurgery is a highly experimental procedure and not a proven therapeutic one as is so often alleged by its contemporary proponents. Second, psychosurgery should not be performed upon children, prisoners, involuntarily held or committed mental patients, or those deemed to be mentally retarded. Third, a registry and assessment mechanism should be established to collect and disseminate information on present and past practices in psychosurgery. One function of such an agency might be the systematic psychological assessment of surviving psychosurgery patients and post-mortem examinations of their brain tissue when they die. Fourth, there should be a temporary moratorium on all further psychosurgical operations until the risks can be weighed against the benefits discovered by a systematic and impartial review of the field. Finally, basic research on brain mechanisms and behavior should be supported and extended. Carefully pursued and properly interpreted, such research offers the only reliable course of action for increasing our understanding of human brain function and its relation to behavior. A better understanding of this kind, coupled with broader public education in the brain sciences, should ultimately provide the best possible defense against the simplistic theories upon which much of contemporary psychosurgery has been built.

It would be a mistake, however, to view psychosurgery in a social vacuum. Although it has unique characteristics, psychosurgery is, in terms of social policy, merely one of a large number of psychotechnological means that are continually being advanced to deal with troublesome individuals or groups. The relevant "target populations" are vaguely defined as "aggressive," "assaultive," "volatile," "acting-out," "disruptive," "incorrigible," "uncooperative," or "dangerous." The possibility that such behavior may be justifiable is generally ignored as are the social consequences of discouraging diversity. Indeed, the physical and chemical control of disruptive behavior has been suggested in every futuristic model of technological fascism. Insofar as the causes of social conflict actually lie in the domain of social affairs, psychotechnological treatment of deviants should be regarded as a perversion of medicine and a distinct threat to individual liberty. The time has come to examine the entire spectrum of psychotechnology and to question the prevalent ideologies of behavioral prediction, modification and control. We must try, most of all, to assess the impact and social consequences of psychotechnology in the broad contexts of politics and public policy. For to deny the power and political appeal of repressive psychotechnology is to expedite its encroachment, and to refrain from combatting it is to surrender not only our constitutional freedom, but also our human dignity.

NOTES

1. Goldstein, Brain Research and Violent Behavior, 30 Arch. Neurol. 1, 28 (1974).
2. *See* M. Crichton, *The Terminal Man* (1972). Thomas appears to be the model for Harry Benson, the title character in Crichton's novel. Ellis, the fictional neurosurgeon in the book, expresses with some literary license Mark and Ervin's view that psychomotor epilepsy and other brain damage are major factors in contemporary social violence and that psychosurgery offers a rational approach to the prevention of such violence. In this connection, it is of interest to note that Crichton has added a postscript to the paperback edition of the book which reveals: "In the face of considerable controversy among clinical neuroscientists, I am persuaded that the understanding of the relationship between organic brain damage and violent behavior is not so clear as I thought at the time I wrote the book." *Id.* at 282 (1973 ed.).
3. Mark & Ervin 93–94.
4. Mark & Ervin, Is There a Need to Evaluate the Individuals Producing Human Violence?, Psychiat. Opinion, Aug. 1968, at 32, 33.

5. *Id.* at 33.
6. Mark & Erwin 96.
7. Mark & Ervin, *supra* note 27 [in the original text] at 34.
8. *Id.*
9. *Id.*
10. Mark & Ervin 96–97.
11. *Id.* at 97.
12. *Id.* at 93.
13. Breggin, An Independent Followup of a Person Operated upon for Violence and Epilepsy by Drs. Vernon Mark, Frank Ervin and William Sweet of the Neuro-Research Foundation of Boston, Rough Times, Nov.–Dec. 1973, at 8, col. 1.
14. *Id.* at 3, col. 3.
15. *Id.*
16. *Id.*
17. *Id.* at 9, col. 2. For a description of this aspect of his "paranoia" see Mark & Ervin 93–94.
18. Thomas' discharge summary from the Veterans Administration Hospital reads: "Patient stated that . . . Massachusetts General Hospital were [*sic*] controlling him by creating lesions in his brain tissue some time before. Stated that they can control him, control his moods and control his actions, they can turn him up or turn him down." Breggin, *supra* note 36 [in the original text] at 9, col. 2. *See also* Memorandum, note 44 *infra*, at 4.
19. Breggin, *supra* note 36 [in the original text] at 9, col. 3.
20. Kille v. Mark, Civil No. 681998 (Super Ct., Suffolk County, Mass., filed Dec. 3, 1973).
21. Hunt, The Politics of Psychosurgery, Part I, Real Paper (Boston), May 30, 1973, at 1, col. 1, *reprinted in* Rough Times, Sept.–Oct. 1973, at 2., col. 1; Hunt, The Politics of Psychosurgery, Part II, Real Paper (Boston), June 13, 1973, at 8, col. 1, *reprinted in* Rough Times, Nov.–Dec. 1973, at 6, col. 1; Trotter, Violent Brains (unpublished manuscript written for

Ralph Nader's Center for Responsive Law, Washington, D.C.); Memorandum from Dr. Ernst Rodin to Dr. J. S. Gottlieb, Aug. 9, 1972, submitted as Exhibit AC–4 in Kaimowitz v. Department of Mental Health, Civil No. 73–19434–AW (Cir. Ct., Wayne County, Mich., July 10, 1973).
22. This proposed research was ultimately blocked in Kaimowitz v. Department of Mental Health, Civil No. 73–19434–AW (Cir. Ct., Wayne County, Mich., July 10, 1973).
23. Memorandum, *supra* note 44 [in the original text] at 1.
24. *Id.* at 4.
25. *Id.*
26. Mark & Ervin 97.
27. *Id.*
28. *Id.*
29. *Id.* at 97–98.
30. *Id.* at 98.
31. *Id.* at 107–08.
32. The author is in possession of an extensive record of personal observations made by this member of the project staff, who wishes to remain anonymous.
33. *See* Chorover, Big Brother and Psychotechnology, Psychology Today, Oct. 1973, at 43, 45.
34. Mark & Ervin 2.
35. *See* Mitford, The Torture Cure, Harper's, Aug. 1973, at 16. *See also* J. Mitford, Kind and Usual Punishment (1973).
36. Müller, Roeder & Orthner, Further Results of Stereotaxis in the Human Hypothalamus in Sexual Deviations, First Use of This Operation in Addiction to Drugs, 16 Neurochirurgia 113 (1973).
37. Balasubramaniam, Kanaka, Ramanuagam & Remanurthi, Surgical Treatment of Hyperkinetic and Behavior Disorder, 54 Int'l Surgery 18 (1970).
38. *Id.* at 22.

Personal Identity

26. THE DEATH OF THE FUHRER

Roland Puccetti

'Well, at least he got what he deserved. That squalid suicide in Berlin, Russian shells falling all around him, his empire reduced to a couple of square miles of rubble . . .'

'You believe that?'

From Roland Puccetti, *The Death of the Fuhrer,* copyright © 1972. Reprinted by permission of the author and St. Martin's Press.

'Believe what?'

'That Hitler died in the Berlin Führerbunker by his own hand?'

'Well, I thought historians agreed . . .'

'Don't talk to me of historians.' For the first time he looked directly into Grayson's eyes. His own were clear blue, turned almost white by the reflected snow. 'Historians and history are two different matters.'

'Do you mean . . .?'

'I mean they just don't know how Hitler died. They are, in fact, victims of a hoax. A hoax as great as the famous Piltdown Man discovery. But they haven't realized it yet.'

'I'm afraid I don't . . .'

'Of course you don't understand. How could you?' The eyes were glittering now, seeming to melt the snow in their blue depths. 'Stretch out your leg, young man, and relax. I'll take you back twenty years. To Paris, just after the War. And I'll tell you the truth.'

'About what?' For some unaccountable reason, Grayson felt fear in his bowels.

'About the death of the Führer.'

1

'They found the bodies on May 2, 1945, dead only a couple of days. His and his mistress's. What was her name? Yes, Eva Braun. Though I understand he married her before their suicide. Frau Hitler, in any case, did not interest us much. Our mission was to establish beyond doubt that the Führer was dead.' He paused to cough again, and this time I noticed flecks of blood on his hand afterwards.

'Where was I? Yes, the bodies were charred beyond easy recognition, but we were able to make a positive identification of Hitler. Dental records provided sketches of his teeth and jawbone formation, and these matched perfectly. No doubt about it. It was Hitler's body.'

His voice had begun to fall slightly, so I judged it wise to put some questions.

'Cause of death?'

'The mouths contained splinters of glass. Crushed ampoules. There was a smell of bitter almonds still. And in the intestines we found traces of cyanide compounds.'

'Then they didn't shoot themselves?'

'This is what puzzled us. There were also bullet-holes in temple and roof of mouth. But you can't shoot yourself in the head and then take cyanide. Nor can you take cyanide and *then* shoot yourself: it acts in microseconds. We concluded that they had the capsules between their teeth when they shot themselves. Probably they were afraid of bungling the job and having to be finished off like dogs

by some S.S. corporal. So they made doubly sure.'

'Any other peculiarities?'

Kutuzov tried to smile but didn't quite make it. 'Yes,' he said, 'Hitler had only one testicle.' I smiled for him, patted his shoulder, pushing him back a little on the pillows. There was a globule of blood easing down from the corner of his mouth now.

'But that was not all.' His eyes fixed mine intently. 'This is what I have told no one before.'

I leaned over more closely still and touched his lips with my handkerchief. 'Go on,' I said. 'But slowly. Do not tire yourself.' I doubt that he even heard me.

'One thing puzzled me deeply. I wondered how there could be so much blood, mostly singed off by the gasoline fire but the blackened traces were still there, around Hitler's head. Because the cyanide would have stopped his heart pumping immediately. I suspected my colleagues of wanting to overlook this so Stalin would be pleased by the emphasis on cyanide. A coward's death, not a soldier's death, was what Stalin obviously wanted. So I went back to the body at night, after our official autopsy was completed. I decided I would examine the brain. See if the bullet might have severed one of the arteries in it. I actually brought a surgical saw with me, concealed under my coat, for this purpose.'

My breath began to quicken as his got shallower and more prolonged. I realized now that we had only minutes left. He was like a record running down. When it finished he would be too, and I wanted to know. I wanted desperately to know what he had found.

'So you opened the skull, Dmitri? You opened it?'

'I didn't have to.'

'What do you mean, you didn't have to?'

'The cranium had been sectioned and then re-wired. I just cut the wires to reopen it.'

'The skull had already been opened?'

'Yes. You see, the brain was missing.'

2

'MISSING?' Nathan Haberman chewed the word around in his mouth along with the soggy cigar butt. 'What the goddam hell do you mean, *missing?*'

'Somebody removed it before the Russians found the bodies.'

'From the grave? Imagine that! Those goddam ghouls! Well, I guess it's not too hard to understand. Some Nazi fanatic waited until all the others fled the Bunker, then snuck outside to the grave at night before the Russians arrived . . .'

'And rewired the skull afterwards?'

'Sure. That way nobody'd know he'd taken it. It's probably floating in a jar of formaldehyde in a Berlin cellar right now.'

'No, Nate.' I looked out the huge window past the gilt letters spelling NEW YORK HERALD TRIBUNE, PARIS EDITION against a paling sky. On its ledge two pigeons began to stir. Soon they would soar off towards the Opera House nearby. 'I'm afraid it's more complicated than that.'

'Why?'

'Kutuzov was definite on this point. The wires had been partially melted by the gasoline fire.'

'You mean it was taken out *before* cremation and burial?'

'Yes. And it wasn't a hurried job. All twelve cranial nerves had been carefully cut. Surgical clamps were used on the protruding ends of the two severed arteries. Even the scalp had been carefully resewn.'

Nate sighed and reached down to a bottom drawer. He pulled out a fifth of Jack Daniel's Sour Mash, unscrewed the top and held it out to me. I shook my head from side to side.

'All right. So it was done in the Bunker itself. Now the question, who did it?'

'The answer lies there. In the Führerbunker itself. I want to go there, Nate.'

He looked at me as if I were mad. 'To the Führerbunker? Isn't that in the Soviet Zone?'

'Yes, but you could get me into East Berlin easily enough. Just assign me to do an article on their Geriatrics Institute or something. At night I'll prowl around there and find a way in.'

'Aren't they guarding it?'

'No, the Russians sealed it with explosives years ago. But I'll find a way in.'

He got up and waddled over to the window. The pigeons soared off towards the Opera building as a first ray of sunlight shot through his sparse greying hair. 'This is awfully risky, Carl. You're a native-born German, even if you've been a U.S. citizen for a long time now. You were working for OSS in Yugoslavia and Czechoslovakia at the end of the war. If you got caught in East Berlin they could try you as a spy. Then the *Tribune* would be in trouble for providing you with cover. Have you thought of that, Carl?'

'Yes, Nate. But there's something I think you should know.'

He came back to his desk and sagged into a chair. 'Go on.'

'According to Kutuzov the cerebral and carotid artery stumps had surgical clamps on them. If Hitler first died of cyanide poisoning some minutes before there would have been no need for these. Unless the body were tilted head-down little blood would have entered the cranial cavity, because the heart would have stopped pumping. As a matter of fact one of the clamps, on the carotid artery, had not held well. This is why Kutuzov found a lot of blood and got suspicious.'

'What are you trying to say?' Nate began to look pale, and I didn't think it was the whisky.

The sun slid over the building across the street and came into my eyes. I turned my head slightly, still looking at Nathan Haberman's haggard face.

'I'm trying to say I think Hitler was still alive when his brain was taken out.'

3

'Research must think I'm running an intelligence agency on the side. Where do you want to start?'

'1935 would be recent enough; I haven't seen Willi Tränger since then.'. . .

'Okay. Now let's see. Did his internship at Bonn in 1935, where he joined the National Socialist Physicians' Society. Attended the Führer School of German Physicians at Altrehse in Mecklenburg, summer of 1936. Joined the Hohenlychen Medical Institute in Brandenburg and stayed there until 1938, when he took the doctorate in neurology.'

'What was his thesis title?'

'Huh? Wait, here it is. "Problems of Nerve Regeneration in Aryans and Non-Aryans". Christ!'

'Go on.'

'Commissioned S.S. Obersturmführer thereafter . . . What's that?'

'First Lieutenant.'

'And stayed on at the Institute doing research.'

'It figures. By then it was an S.S. hospital under Gebhardt, Himmler's old buddy. Doctor Tränger must have had plenty of non-Aryan material available after that. What else?'

'In 1941 promoted to S.S. Obersturmbannführer. . . .'

I whistled. 'Lieutenant Colonel? Quite a jump from First Lieutenant.'

'. . . and given his own facilities at Auschwitz Concentration Camp. Say, this is funny.'

'What is?'

'According to the Nürnberg investigators, he wasn't responsible to anyone thereafter. Not to the Camp Commandant, Rudolf Hoess, nor to Grawitz, the S.S. Reich Physician, not even to Himmler himself.'

I whistled again. 'Something very special, eh? Probably Hitler's personal authorization.'

'Yeah. Then the funniest thing of all. In October 1944 our friend Tränger closes up shop.'

'What do you mean?'

'Just what I said. He has his laboratories dismantled, all records destroyed, prisoner personnel liquidated. Not a trace remains. The Gehirngruppe disappears.'

'Gehirngruppe? Was that an official designation?'

'No. S.S. slang for Tränger and his surgical team. Because they only seemed interested in brains. They also had a nice name for Tränger. Called him "der Bussard".'

The buzzard. I felt a chill come up the river and along my spine. I got to my feet and walked to the water's edge; a small boy was fishing in the diffused greyish sunset. Nate stood just behind me, struggling to relight his cigar in the breeze.

'Well, looks like you're right. If anybody could have taken out Hitler's brain so fast and neatly it would be Tränger's gang. They must have had a lot of practice at Auschwitz.'

I said nothing, looking steadily down into the water.

'There's just one thing I don't understand, Carl. Why did they leave his brain behind?'

Suddenly the little boy pulled and a tiny fish, white and squirming against the dark, sluggish wa-ter, came bursting to the surface.

'They didn't,' I said. 'They took it with them.'. . .

'Carl, you're not making sense!'

'Yes I am. You don't think Hitler had those secret installations built and went through the elaborate pretence of suicide just so Willi Tränger could throw his living brain into a surgical refuse bucket, do you? What would he have gained by that? And why was there a heart and lung machine and adrenalin available? For what purpose? You use those to keep a body alive when the brain is not functioning . . . or gone. But *whose* body? Hardly Hitler's, since they brought that back upstairs and shot the empty head through the temples with his own pistol. After crushing a cyanide capsule between the teeth.'

'Good Lord, Carl! You mean Hitler might be alive and walking around right now?'

'Yes. In a new body provided for him by Willi Tränger.'

Nate threw away the cigar and seized me by the shoulders like a great bear. 'What are we going to do? Carl, what can we do?'

'We'll hunt him down, Nate. That's what we'll do.'

'And then what?' He looked too stunned to think any more.

I took his arm and led him away, back towards the bridge and the bustling city now lighting up, coming to life for the evening and the long night ahead. I almost whispered the words.

'Then I'll kill him.'

4

I throttled down the motorcycle and held my breath. The old Citroën, long and black and streaked with red dust, swung to the right momentarily, in the direction of the hospital at Óbrigo. Then it dug in its front wheels and zoomed up the left fork towards Mansilla and the road north to the Cantabrian foothills, one of the most remote regions of the Iberian Peninsula. I heaved a sigh of relief. It wasn't going to be so hard to find Willi Tränger after all.

My mind went back to Paris and the month's work I had put into tracing Willi this far. Nate Haberman thought it was hopeless, but when he saw what I had he changed his tune. Posing as a fictitious manufacturer of medical supplies and dangling the promise of lucrative paid advertising before editors' noses, I secured the full subscription lists of over sixty technical medical journals in five languages. On no less than twenty-six of them there occurred one obscure name: Señor Sánchez del Río, a gentleman who used only a general post office box number as an address, came from the provincial city of León, and was nowhere listed as a practising physician or teacher on a medical faculty or even research worker in all of Spain. What is more, all twenty-six journals specialized in surgery or neurology or associated fields.

5

. . . As I told Nate, the one thing we could expect of Willi Tränger would be that no matter where he was hiding, he would keep up with research. So four days of sitting in the café in León across the street from the post office, my eyes fixed on the open door and box number 839 beyond, had paid off. This road led nowhere but to the mountains, a perfect hideaway.

It was an enormous old castle, probably dating from the fourteenth century, complete with battlements and towers and even a moat, now empty. As I watched a wooden drawbridge clanked down and two men in uniforms came across it on bicycles. At least I thought they were uniforms, though I couldn't make out any insignia on them, because they were solid black in colour. As the men got closer I saw it was leather: trousers as well as jackets of black leather, boots up to the knee of the same, and even caps of leather. Across their backs were strapped Schmiesser machine pistols: I could recognize the ugly snouts sticking up over their shoulders. Now their faces became clear. Both were pale young men, not more than twenty, with clear blue eyes and blond hair showing on the sides of the head not covered by their caps. They braked at the gate and took the packages from the sentry who, I now saw, looked exactly like them and was similarly armed. They pedalled away back to and across the drawbridge. It cranked up after them. Silence fell heavily in the valley.

I scanned the wall along its length in both directions. There was no other entrance. I put down the binoculars and sighed. Then I remembered something I had seen but not noted. I picked up the glasses again. Yes, just to the left of the sentry box there was a high mound of dirt, piled there because recently they had been scraping and levelling the road. From here it looked a good six feet high; the wall beyond was only two or three feet higher and probably no more than five feet away.

I took out my papers and spread them on the grass in front of me. One was a Federal Republic of Germany passport; procured for me at great expense by Nate Haberman on the Paris black market. A second was a photostat, equally bogus, of my Army discharge, showing that I had been a captain in the Field Medical Unit of the 114th Jäger Division and captured by Italian partisans. A third, also a photostat, was a court order issued in Frankfurt dismissing an indictment against me for war crimes on the grounds of lack of conclusive evidence. Then there was my driving licence, establishing my residence as Düsseldorf and my profession as doctor. My office card showed I was a specialist in internal medicine, sharing a clinic with Dr. Fritz Niederhof, and from this non-existent colleague there was a crumpled letter, its envelope stamped by the León post office, urging me to relax and enjoy my motorcycle excursion into northeastern Spain.

I put all these papers back, did the straps up tightly, and mounted the motorcycle. Pointing it down the hill, I took a deep breath, turned the ignition key, and kicked the engine into life. I started rolling.

It was perhaps five hundred yards down to the wall. The bike picked up speed rapidly, bouncing on the rocks but holding the road anyway. I twisted the handle accelerator. The engine roared. I put it in top speed. The wall was getting bigger. The speedometer needle climbed. Forty-five miles an hour. Sixty. Seventy-five. I clenched the exhaust pipes with my heels, fighting to stay on. Eighty and the machine was bucking wildly. I hit the bottom of the road at eighty-five miles an hour, the wheels spinning in the loose earth, grabbing, the bike shooting straight for the wall. The sentry was out of the box now, swinging the gun off his back, fitting it into his shoulder, bringing the deadly nozzle up at me, trying to follow my path and lead ahead of me.

But I was going much too fast for him: the needle touched ninety just as I reached the mound. Out of the corner of my eye I saw him twist and a quick burst, four or five shots only, went off as the bike caromed up the mound in an explosion of earth and stones and I was pulling back hard on the handles, straining my head back so the machine would land ahead of me, and then the rear tyre hit the top of the wall and blew up and we were sailing, the bike turning over and over backwards, and I was shouting as the land beneath rose up and smashed into my head.

6

'God in heaven! It is a medal of some kind. A German war medal.'

'You are too young to recognize it.' He hesitated and pronounced the syllables slowly. 'RITT-ER-KREUZ.'

'What?'

'Yes. The Knight's Cross. Awarded only for extreme courage in battle. And this man wore it under his shirt. Probably he has done so for years. Here is one German veteran not ashamed to have served his fatherland. He wears it next to his heart. Who is this man? He must have had papers of some kind on him.'

'Uh, he is a doctor. From Düsseldorf. Name of Gisevius.'

I heard Willi draw in his breath sharply. Then he was alongside the table turning my face from side to side. He cursed.

'You fool! I know this man. A fraternity brother of mine. Heidelberg, 1934. See that scar on his cheek? I gave it to him. And see this scar of mine? He gave it to me. We exchanged blood, Hofrat, we exchanged blood! And you almost let me kill him! Quick, get me all his papers. Now.'

I listened as the other man trundled off, his feet going down some stone corridor. Willi kept my face in his fingers. I could smell wine on his breath. Then steps came running back and he let go of my face. The papers sounded crisp near my ears.

'Yes, it is him. Karl Gustav Gisevius. I had not seen him since our graduation; he was second in the class. Ah, so. 114th Jäger Division. Field Medic. And look! No mention in the discharge of his

award. Those craven cowards! Ah, look at this. Captured by partisans and accused of war crimes. Hah, insufficient evidence! The German of today is so despicable he will cooperate in persecution of his compatriots even when they were only defending themselves against criminal partisan activities! Such is the level to which our civilization has fallen. Poor man!'

I opened my eyes and looked into Willi Tränger's. I tried to smile. He patted me on the shoulder affectionately. He called for another syringe, a smaller one this time, and injected its contents into my arm.

'Rest, old friend. Yes, Karl, it is Willi. Don't try to talk. You have a mild concussion, left hemisphere. The speech centres are temporarily affected. But don't worry. Tomorrow you will talk. Or if not tomorrow the day after. You remember your accident?'

I nodded dumbly. I could feel cool air coming into my mouth, so I knew I was smiling successfully.

'That is good. You recognize me now, not so? Soon you will sleep, Karl. I have given you a strong sedative. But as soon as you are able we shall have a chat together, just as in the old days. There is so much to tell, yes?'

I tried to nod again but I was slipping away now. Willi's face began to recede, as if I were looking at him with the binoculars reversed, until finally just the beaked nose appeared at the end of a long, black tunnel. Then darkness.

7

'Extraordinary woman, Karl. Wait until you see her. Prussian on one side, Polish landed gentry on the other. A skin so clear you can see your face in hers when you talk to her. And that body! It ought to be in all the medical textbooks. Perfect example of Aryan beauty. Of course there's some Slavic blood in her veins, just enough to heighten the predominant Nordic strain. Gives her a touch of Eastern lust, if you know what I mean, something our Brünehildes notoriously lack. Reminds me of a Hungarian countess I once knew; what was her name? Never mind, I've forgotten. In fact I've forgotten her face too. That's the trouble with my memories of women. First goes the name, then the face; it's only their bottoms that stay with me, and God knows they all look the same down there.

'But to get back to the Baroness. Extraordinary. Fanatically loyal to the Reich. You could hardly find a woman in all Europe so devoted to the Germanic ideal. She wanted particularly to meet you, Karl. Aha! my words have had their effect. You arise splendid from your bath. Yes, that jacket will do. No one expects a vagabond traveller like you to achieve sartorial elegance, and in any case dress is optional.'

At exactly eight fifty-seven I began to hear the sentry's boots growing louder in the corridor, like a film's sound track being played in reverse. I moved up to the door and put my hand on its latch. He stomped to a halt, did a quarter-turn to the right, and clicked his heels. I snatched open the door just as he was bringing the weapon stock down on it. He lost his balance, staggered, straightened up with a red face.

'Are . . . are you ready, Herr Doktor?'

'No. I am still in my bath. What you see before you is a ghostly apparition.'

He wheeled about, looking grim, and started marching down the corridor with me a pace behind. We crossed the courtyard as if he were leading me to the firing squad: in a way, I reflected, he might very well be doing just that.

But no one could have had a warmer welcome from the Baroness. She opened the door herself with a dazzling smile and fire dancing in her pale green eyes. Indeed, as I swooped down to her hand, painfully reminded of the knife scabbard under my trousers, I saw there was a fire in her room. Just a few token logs in the familiar fireplace, but they were burning brightly. I also saw something else new, something that made me catch my breath. A couple of paces from the fireplace was a table set for two, with two candles burning on it and flanked by covered casseroles and wine buckets with slim necks protruding from starched linen napkins. It was going to be very much a *diner en tête-à-tête.*

The Baroness gestured towards the fireplace, looking away and muttering inanities that require no answer, just as any beautiful woman will do when she wants to give a man plenty of time to admire her physically. I did so with utter frankness.

She was wearing an incredible gown. I don't know even if it should be called a gown. It was made entirely of some soft leather—perhaps deerskin—dyed black and stretching from her shoulders to the floor. Only her arms, neck, and feet— yes, I could see she was bare-footed as she stepped in the direction of the fireplace—were uncovered by it. But she might just as well have been bare all over, because this gown was so flesh-fitting it seemed I could see every line, every wrinkle of her body. The circle of her nipples, the navel and mount of Venus, and as she turned the ridge under the buttocks: all was there in clear outline. Only from the thighs down did it fall straight and unrevealingly. I wondered how she ever got into it. Or better, out. Then I saw the answer. A broad silver zipper, not concealed in any way, running from the back of the neckline straight between the buttocks and all the way down to the floor. Just one continuous motion: two, at the most three, seconds. I cleared my throat.

'Can you see to the champagne?' she asked. 'Just a little for me, please. I don't care much for alcohol. Please be seated. Let us start with the omelette.'

The cork gave way with an ear-splitting pop.

'Shall we have a toast? Now what shall we toast? Why you, of course, Herr Doktor!'

'Please, madam. You must call me Karl.'

'And I shall be Gerda to you. All right? After all, we are comrades, not so?'. . .

'It's ungodly hot in here,' she said. 'Why don't you take off your jacket? I insist. Your tie too. We are alone here. You know why?'

'Why what?'

'Why it is so hot. It's all the fault of Willi Tränger. When he had the castle renovated he insisted on leaving the fireplaces open to preserve its medieval flavour. Really, he's as entranced by the Middle Ages as old Heini ever was.' I stopped listening for a second until I realized whom she meant— Heinrich Himmler. . . .

I tried to keep my voice casual. 'How about you, Gerda?'

'What about me?'

'Aren't you warm in that dress?'

She put her fork down and looked me steadily in the eye. 'Yes,' she said. 'Yes, I am.' Then she lifted a hand behind her back, groped a second, and I heard the soft rustle of metal on metal as the zipper ran down to her waist or below. With one motion she slipped the straps off her shoulders and pulled the front of the gown away from her body. It came away from the moist flesh with a sucking sound. Her breasts, suddenly liberated, spilled out of their confines and undulated a moment before straightening out, the nipples trained on my chest.

'There,' she pronounced, 'that's better.'

I tried to say something gay, like it certainly was better, but the food had turned to sawdust in my mouth. . . .

I tore my eyes off her and looked down at the table, searching desperately for some words that my voice wouldn't betray. My champagne glass, still frosted, stood empty; on an impulse I seized it and placed it over her left breast. 'This will cool you,' I said, trying to smile. She swallowed back food and looked down at her breast filling the glass. Through the stem I could see her nipple swelling; then suddenly the glass shattered into fragments. Our eyes met. I thought she would be angry. Instead she said 'Karl' in a bleating tone. We stood up, moved around the table in one quick step and fell into each other's arms.

Her hands were working furiously on my trousers belt as I reached down and started to pull out my soggy shirt. I heard a faint ripping of thread in the back and only then remembered, thunderstruck, the knife scabbard hanging down there. Quickly, I unbuttoned the shirt and peeled it away, while she was taking off my shoes and socks so she could get my trousers clear. This done, she started coming up my legs again with her hands, her mouth wide like a fish rising to the surface; I seized her hands when they reached my hips and held them there, hoping she wouldn't look up and see the cord tied around my waist. Her tongue ran over me like a lizard's, but burning hot, before she dropped to my feet and stretched up her fingers to me imploringly. I bent down and swept her up in my arms. The dais groaned very loudly this time, as I lay her down on the great double bed.

The candles on our table sputtered and went out, leaving her body a roasted pink colour from the glow of the logs. I mounted on the bed and kneeled prayerfully between her yawning thighs. They opened still wider as she lifted her feet to encircle my back; but knowing what she might feel there I rapidly seized her knees and put them over my shoulders. She locked her ankles behind my neck and started raising and lowering her buttocks rhythmically. My hands held her hips tightly; her skin was actually hot to the touch, as if it had been warmed over the fire, but inside her body was the fire itself.

I forced myself to look at her face. It was twisting and turning too, the eyes closed and her lips parted in a moan. No, it wasn't a moan. It was a single word murmured over and over again: BITTE, BITTE, BITTE. I began whispering in turn, slowly, to match the strokes of my body, the impact of moist flesh on moist flesh. It became a weird incantation as I plunged on and on.

'Gerda oh my darling Gerda oh can you know what this means to me to have seen you wanted you now to have you like this really it is the greatest day of my life it is as if I came over that castle wall to die and woke up in heaven and you know Gerda it may sound silly but . . . I felt in the presence of the Führer my beloved can it be he is somehow still with us and near us oh Gerda I am as certain of this as intuition can make it tell me darling am I right oh Gerda how my happiness would be complete if I could just see him again and hear his voice I don't care how he has changed Gerda is he not in this castle have I not perhaps even met him and did not know it only you I am sure can tell me yes tell me who he is I must know please yes of course you can have all of me now but for this gift of myself will you not too give me the only other precious thing besides yourself yes who is he Gerda where is he who and where is the Führer please then we shall at the same time we shall. . . .'

Gerda's eyes opened widely now. The pupils looked dark in the fire glow, much darker than before, and somehow beyond them and behind them there was a deep rustling of Teutonic forests, of shadowy predators roaming in the night. . . . Only then did I raise my trembling, terribly tired fingers to her head, slide them under the golden hair and feel the bony ridge across her skull. Only then did her lips part to give the fateful cry.

'ICH BIN DER FÜHRER.'

8

The words struck me like four barbed tips of a knout full in the face. I jerked erect and, losing balance, fell forward across her upper body. My face was buried in her hair; she twisted her head, sought and found my mouth, began sucking on it to draw my tongue into hers. I screamed. The sound rebounded inside her head as if it were a drum. She drew back, her mouth still open, her eyes wide with surprise and fright. I rolled away to the left, off her body; the moist parting made a loud smacking sound. I reached behind me with my right hand, found the knife handle, raised the blade high. She looked up at it unbelievingly. I shut my eyes and brought it down with all my strength. I heard the air go out of her lungs; her body went down into the bed, the springs groaned, her back arched and her belly rose in one great, final orgasm. Now she screamed. I opened my eyes. The handle stood alone high up in the solar plexus, as if someone had pasted it there, rising and falling with her convulsions. I rolled twice more to my left, fell off the bed on to the dais, and lay there retching.

Then I heard it. It started slowly, like a feline growl in the distant night, picked up pitch and intensity, became a high ear-shattering whine that bounced off the inner walls of the courtyard and shook the bedroom's windows: a siren.

I lurched to my feet. She was still spread-eagled on the bed, twisting and turning in her agony, but now she had a silken cord in her hands and was tugging on it fiercely, like a woman in heavy labour. I had seen the cord hanging there before, over the head of the bed, but hadn't imagined it was anything more than a bell attachment for summoning servants. Even so, I should have cut it first; now when I realized it was a general alarm she was sounding I cursed myself for a fool.

But there wasn't time for that; searchlights were sweeping the courtyard, voices hailing each other, boots crunching the gravel outside.

9

'ATTENTION EVERYONE.' I twisted my head and saw the tiny loudspeaker affixed to the ceiling. There seemed to be a long echo: then I realized I was hearing the same voice at different distances. Probably they had a loudspeaker in evey corridor.

'THIS IS YOUR CASTLE KOMMANDANT. LISTEN CAREFULLY. THE KILLER GISEVIUS IS STILL AT LARGE . . . IN THE EVENT OF SUSPICIOUS BEHAVIOUR CONTACT THE OFFICE OF THE KOMMANDANT IMMEDIATELY. EXTRAORDINARY SECURITY MEASURES ARE TO BE ENFORCED AT ALL TIMES. . . .'

I stopped listening because there were heavy footsteps coming from the other side of the Surgery doors now. They were growing louder. I backed off and looked wildly around. The nearest room was to my left. I darted in the open doorway and flattened against the wall. I heard the big doors swing open abruptly and footsteps coming down the ramp. Hofrat Heinz was striding by, his head down. He looked preoccupied. He went into the waiting room. Before the door closed I heard boots coming up on the double. I peeked my head through the doorway. On the other side of the glass I saw three men come into the waiting room and confront Hofrat. Two were guards. The third was the ferret-faced hospital attendant. I couldn't hear what he was saying but he was waving his arms and gesturing towards the Surgery. Hofrat was shrugging his shoulders. Finally he stepped aside to let them pass. I pulled back into the doorway again, seized the door and eased it shut. There was no latch on the door, no key.

I could hear them moving through the other rooms now, one after the other. They were switching on the lights in each one, taking their time to look carefully. I began to panic. I could see absolutely nothing in this room, and I didn't dare turn on my flashlight for fear they would spot a line of light under the door. They were walking towards me now. I darted forward and collided with a heavy, immovable object at the level of my hips. I ran my fingers over it. It was of polished stone, perhaps marble. I leaned forward. Something pressed into my chest. It was soft and yielding, but just as cold. A human foot. Then I realized what this was: a dissecting table.

I ducked my head and scrambled under the table

just as they opened the door. My shoulder hit something very solid. It was the table's concrete mounting. I crawled behind it. Here there was much less space: the whole table was constructed to tilt about fifteen degrees towards the head, so the blood would drain down to this end. I felt behind me. The metal wash basin was right there. I curled up into a sitting position with the machine pistol across my lap, my finger on the trigger. I heard the light switch snap on. The effect was blinding. I could see their boots in the doorway. Hofrat's voice sounded very loud.

'As you see, gentlemen, this room is temporarily occupied.'

'God in heaven.'

'Go ahead and search. I'm needed back in Surgery.' He walked off and again I heard the Surgery's doors swing open and shut. The others hesitated in the doorway.

'You'd think they'd cover it up afterwards. It's enough to make you sick.'

'Well, there's not much point in looking further here. No place for him to hide.'

'Yes, I agree. Now listen. I'll stay in the waiting room just in case he does try to get into the Surgery. You go back to the desk with Graver here and report to the Kommandant.'

The light snapped off. They closed the door softly behind them. I waited until I could hear their footsteps fade away before crawling out and standing up. Then I switched on the flashlight, keeping it well away from the door area. Its cone of light revealed a midsection of white flesh with a thick, black knife handle standing straight up in its centre.

So, I thought. They tried to save her and failed. They even left the knife in her, probably to avoid excessive bleeding.

Bleeding? I let the light play on her body. Why was there so little blood? The drainage channels were bone dry, yet she looked ghostly pale. I brought the powerful beam slowly up to the chest, where her breasts stood proudly erect even now. On the right arm there were marks of tape and a blue-fringed hole on the inside of the elbow, where they must have inserted the adrenalin tube. But even here no traces of blood appeared. Where had it all gone? I moved the light up to her face. It was almost transparently white, a mask of beauty cut in

porcelain. Yet there was no blood from her lips. I stepped forward and opened the mouth. The gums and palate were chalky grey, but around the tongue and teeth no blood traces showed. How was it she hadn't even vomited blood, with a terrible abdominal wound like that? Then I saw something.

Alongside her neck, just below the right ear, a tube was sticking out. But it wasn't a tube. It was the stump of the carotid artery. Why had they sectioned this and exposed it? What would they gain by that? Then I recalled something from my days in Heidelberg. In brain surgery it is advisable to withdraw the blood from the carotid artery, chill it, and pump it back. This freezes the hypothalamus of the brain slightly, lowers its temperature and metabolic rate, and thus reduces danger of tissue damage by oxygen starvation.

The brain. I moved my light up another few inches. Something was missing. Yes, her golden hair. Her head had been shaved. I walked over to the end of the dissecting table, behind the head. There was a nickel wash basin with water taps set above it. The back of the head was exposed. I put my flashlight on it. The scalp was gone. So was the top of the skull. I put the flashlight inside the hole. There was nothing there. Nothing except severed nerve ends and blood, dripping softly now into the basin below.

I switched off my flashlight and just stood there, panting with the horror of it all. I sobbed audibly.

10

As I rounded the bend in the corridor I could see where I was going. At its end was a pair of swinging doors and above them a sign which announced in bold letters the offices of Herr Doktor Wilhelm Tränger, Reich Surgeon-General.

I lengthened my stride so I would look like a surgeon in a hurry. The machine pistol began to make my gown pulsate. I put a hand on it to steady it and felt the trigger guard under my finger. An electric clock on the wall to my left, just above a pair of elevator doors, said 11.15 a.m. as I pushed my way into Willi's private lair.

Willi was seated behind his desk. He was playing with a little box he held between his fingers. He looked up at me and smiled.

'Hello, Karl,' he said. 'I have been expecting you.'

11

I saw what he was after: the sabres mounted on the far wall.

I hit the wall too hard: the sabre came away in my hand but I bounced back and was in danger of falling. I caught the uper edge of the Heidelberg plaque to steady myself; it wrenched off the surface in my fingers and crashed to the floor, but it was enough to save my balance. Now I turned to face Willi.

I wondered if there was any way of distracting him, of getting his guard down, of creating an opportunity to break through his defences. I decided to stop where I was and move back a little so he would relax. We had gone half-way around in a circle; I could see the blank space where the plaque had been mounted on the wall just above Willi's head. There was something printed there in small letters. I strained to read it as I was talking.

'By the way, Willi, something I meant to ask you before.' He watched me warily, his eyes still on the bell and my feet. 'Why did you install the Führer's brain in a woman's body? Surely he didn't want that?'

He chuckled, but kept his sabre up all the same. 'Heavens no. I had a fine Aryan lad all ready—a Werewolf leader—but unfortunately he suffered heart failure at the last minute. The Baroness was with us at the time—she had been recruited as cover for the escape to Spain—and was of the same blood group. As soon as she saw the situation she volunteered.'

'The Führer didn't know?'

'Absolutely not. He might have refused if he knew. We prepared the Baroness' body and kept it concealed under a sheet when he came down from the Führerbunker. . . .'

'Even so,' I asked, 'how could he accept being a woman?. . . .

'My dear Karl. Your ignorance of the human brain would fill volumes. The brain is bisexual. It's all a matter of which cell areas are activated, and that depends on the kind of hormones that come into the brain with the blood. . . .'

Blood. The tube carrying the blood up into Hitler's brain. It was sticking out to one side of the vat, well off to Willi's right at knee-level. If I could cut that. . . .

'Of course he was furious when he found out, but by then we were well on our way to Spain and safety. He insisted on a second operation as soon as possible, but within three weeks he changed his mind. He found he liked being a woman after all. . . .

'I see. But what I still don't understand is. . . .'

I never finished my sentence. I made a quick feint to Willi's left and as his sabre came up to parry it, dived forward onto the polished floor on the opposite side, hitting hard and sliding several feet under the 'whoosh' of his blade, my point up and aimed not at Willi but at the plastic tube. Willi stepped towards me and lifted his sword high but it was too late; a fine jet of blood spurted out and when Willi saw that he stopped his attack, dropped to a kneeling position, and clamped his left hand over the hole.

'You fool! You deceitful fool!' He was screaming at me as if I were a bungling medical assistant in an operation. Then he got up slowly, holding the tube in a vice-like grip, and swung the pedestal around so he would be facing me with his sabre; his eyes looked maniacal.

I backed off warily, keeping my sword straight out and groping under the gown with my other hand for the key. He was puzzled. Could I have suddenly become cowardly? Why was I increasing the distance between us? Then he stopped questioning himself. His Führer had eight minutes to live if this hole wasn't repaired.

His attack came with lightning rapidity, a blur of heavy steel smashing at me from every angle until it seemed I were caught in a giant electric fan. I had no chance to strike back. All I could do was parry, watch his blade turning, follow it and parry again. I fought desperately to keep the same distance between us so I wouldn't be overwhelmed, retreating around the edge of the wall, then breaking out into the centre, but always back, back, back. I could feel the sabre getting heavier in my hand, my arm ached with the strain, my eyes filled with sweat, my reflexes began to slow down. It occurred to me that if he could maintain the ferocity of his assault for half a minute more he would break through and I would be finished.

Suddenly I collided with something. Something solid that nevertheless gave way under the impact. Then I heard a squeak of metal casters and the aluminium pedestal topped by the brain-filled vat rolled sedately into the periphery of my vision. With two quick sidesteps I was behind it, keeping it between Willi and me, circling it rapidly, just out of his sword's reach. The brain turned slowly in the disturbed liquid; through the hole in the top of the glass I could see its grey convolutions bobbing up and down, naked and exposed. Quickly I reversed my sabre, holding the bell high and the point aimed at the tender white mass. Willi stopped dead in his tracks. He opened his mouth to say something. I plunged the blade down into and all the way through the brain. I heard Willi gasp as I wrenched the sword out. Instantly the fluid in the vat turned pink, then red.

Now he was screaming. He raised his blade high and moved up against the pedestal so he could reach across for a final head-splitting downward slash. It was the chance I had been waiting for. I crouched down, levelled the blade straight ahead with my arm bent at a right angle, swept the pedestal aside with my left hand, and drove the point forward into Willi's undefended crotch. I saw it disappear in him, go on deeper and deeper until it stopped with a jolt against the base of his spine. Willi sobbed softly, let his sabre clatter to the floor, closed both hands on the protruding blade as if to steady himself, then staggered backwards, drawing his body off the sword. The pedestal was tottering to a halt right next to him; he put his arms out to it for support, caught it, and pulled it down with him as he fell. There was a loud crash and the tinkle of glass. A torrent of red liquid gushed over the floor, carrying in its midst the Führer's dying brain.

27. BRAIN TRANSPLANTATION AND PERSONAL IDENTITY

Roland Puccetti

I begin without introduction. We have a patient dying of some wasting general disease, such as cancer, which as far as we can tell has not yet affected his brain. Let us call him X. At the same time we have an emergency admission, Y, where massive cerebral damage was incurred in an accident, though his body is unhurt and in good general health. We keep Y alive for hours using a respirator machine, adrenalin injections, and so on, but it is quite clear he will never recover consciousness or control over his body. X and Y are of the same blood group. So with X's consent, and with permission of Y's nearest kin, we prepare to transplant X's

From Roland Puccetti, "Brain Transplantation and Personal Identity," *Analysis* vol. 29, no. 3 (1969), pp. 65-77. Reprinted by permission of the author and Basil Blackwell, Publisher.

brain into Y's body, sacrificing thereby one fatally-diseased body and one fatally-damaged brain. On the level of medical ethics I cannot see how this is much different from heart transplantation. However, there are formidable . . . logical differences, as we shall see. . . .

We now have X's brain comfortably installed in Y's body, hooked up and ready to go. This is where our logical difficulties begin. To avoid prejudicing the outcome, let us call the composite organism Z. The question arises, *Who* is Z? Is Z just Y with a new brain? Or X with a new body? Or have we created a third person, "Z"? And depending on our answer here, to what extent is our concept of a particular person linked to possession of a particular body or brain? To a particular sex, for that matter?

ARE PEOPLE WHAT YOU MEET?

Suppose we let six months go by, during which time Z heals nicely and is discharged from the hospital. We now find Z in his favourite pub of a late afternoon, toasting his new health. A youngish man enters, slaps him on the back, and starts addressing him as Y.

Joel Andrews, you say? I'm terribly sorry. My name is Weatherby.
Oh, come off it, Joel. I know you like a brother.
Clarence Weatherby.
We roomed together at school!
I had all my schooling in Australia.
But I was best man at your wedding, just two years ago!
Two years ago I was in South Africa, long since married.
This is incredible! You even have that scar on the bridge of your nose.
What about it?
I gave it to you, with a cricket bat. Don't you remember?
Never played cricket in my life.

Nothing in this dialogue comes as a surprise. After all, how *could* Z, *i.e.* Y's body with X's brain, remember things Y did? Memories are stored in the cerebral cortex and brainstem, not the body. What the young man is asking Z to remember perished with Y's brain. So Z cannot be Y, even if he has Y's body. You might say, Yes, but people sometimes lose memories—even all memories prior to a cerebral accident—yet they are the same people. True, but Z is not a general amnesiac. Unless he's lying he has a very definite set of memory traces to draw upon, quite different from Y's.

To whom do these memories belong? Surely not to Z as a distinct person. If Z were a distinct person, newly created by the juncture of X's brain and Y's body, his memory could extend no further back in time than six months ago. Indeed, as a new person he would not even have the store of unconscious traces the amnesiac has. He would not know how to walk and talk, for example. He would be on the intellectual level of the infant toddler. But Z is not like that at all. Thus Z cannot be "Z", that is a novel person, any more than he can be Y. Then who *is* Z? Only one alternative remains. He must be X.

Look, I think there's something you should know. Your friend is dead.

Joel dead? Good God! How did it happen?
I'm told he dived into an empty swimming pool on his head.
How did you learn this? Did you know him?
We never actually met. I mean, we weren't introduced.
How's Kitty taking it?
His wife? I owe my life to that woman.
I don't follow.
You've heard of brain transplantation, haven't you?
Well. . . .

Will the young man accept Z or X, even if he hears the whole story from Y's lips? Or will he think he is the victim of some kind of elaborate joke? No one can say in advance, but assuming that brain transplants are not unknown by this time, it seems to me he would.

So there she sat, vaguely hoping I was her husband after all.
Poor Kitty.
Yes, she even kissed me goodbye on her last visit. I actually cried.
And your own wife? It must have been equally weird to her.
Well, of course. *(Smiling).* But on the whole I'd say she's pleased with the change.
What do you mean?
I was 48 and your friend only 29. A most vigorous young man too, if I may say so.
Joel was an excellent skier.
That won't help me. I don't know how to stand in the bloody things.
Do you like any sports?
Tennis. I can play a match of singles without breathing hard now.
That's funny. Joel never played tennis.
Should have taken it up. What stamina! And his reflexes.

Everything above is consistent with the hypothesis of brain transplantation, once one realises exactly what is being transplanted.

For instance, while he's talking Z will probably reveal a slight Australian accent. When appropriate he would throw in some Australian expression. But his voice production would be Y's, because that's not in X's brain. Similarly, his sexual interests and associations would remain X's, but reinforced by Y's hormone production and better general health. Since the memory storage is in the brain, he could hardly be expected to have acquired Y's learned responses along with that body. These are stored in the reticular activating system in the upper brain-stem, and in the cerebellum. Thus he wouldn't be able to ski, though if he knew tennis he would find he has become a better player because the reflexes, muscle response to nerve impulses, and supporting organ efficiency—heart, lungs, *etc.*—would be far superior to what he had before he acquired Y's body. No doubt the first few months of post-operative recovery would require Z to get used to these differences. Where he used to drag himself out of bed he will now bound, as if he had been transported to a planet subject to lesser grav-itational forces. It is the reverse of a healthy person having to walk very carefully after a long confinement in bed, when his muscular response, *etc.,* became weakened. Since the reticular activa-ting system and cerebellum embody a feedback mechanism enabling us to make adjustments be-tween sensory input and motor output uncon-sciously, the new situation requires conscious ad-justment. But soon it is effected. X learns, in brief, to take over Y's body successfully.

But then why should we continue to speak of Z? Z is not, as we saw, really "Z", a new person. Z is the organic composite of X's brain and Y's body, which in terms of personal identity is really X. We sometimes say someone is 'a new person' where we mean he's undergone *sauna* treatments, psycho-analysis, Dr. Reich's orgone box, transcendental meditation, hormone injections, conversion to Ro-man Catholicism, Communism, Zen Buddhism or what have you. These are all weak senses of the term 'new person'. In the strong sense they remain the same people nevertheless. So does X, even though his transformation is more drastic on the corporeal side. Old acquaintances who knew him not long before the transplant would find it hard, as his wife did, to believe this is Clarence Weatherby. But he could provide convincing evidence he is, in the form not only of specific memories but also of continued likes and dislikes, emotional responses, character traits—everything that goes to make up a real individual person.

The logical difference between brain and heart transplantation is therefore enormous. We have a medical convention according to which he who gives up part of his body is the 'donor' and he who assimilates it functionally is the 'recipient'. This holds true for blood transfusions, skin grafts, cor-neal transplants, indeed all *other* organ transplants —heart, kidneys, perhaps lungs someday. And the human brain is an organ. But uniquely it carries the notion of ownership with it. Y cannot have a new brain the way he can have a new heart. Because without his old brain Y is no more. If we want to preserve the convention we shall have to say, not that X gave Y his brain, but that Y gave X his body. Where goes a brain, there goes a person.

Not that a person *is* a brain—I am pushing no Identity Hypothesis here. Brains "belong to" peo-ple as much as their hearts and livers do. What I am saying is that the brain is the physical basis of a human person, so that one cannot realistically dis-sociate one from the other. Philosophers in the past have talked blithely of "bodily transfer", by which they meant mind-transference between two bod-ies without one single brain cell changing its physi-cal *locus*. This may be conceivable logically, but in terms of the causal conditions of human life it is just so much philosophical gas.

On the other hand this too is clear. Whatever a person is, he is not this or that particular body. Z is really X in Y's body. Possession of a particular body is not a guarantee of personal identity. Sup-pose Z were arraigned for some crime Y had com-mitted. There would be eye-witnesses to say they had seen him in the act, and perhaps Y's finger-prints—hence his own now—on the murder weapon. But X can prove he is not Y. He can prove he is really X. He can say that while he does not deny his body did the dirty deed, he had no control over that body at the time. Because he was then controlling a very different body. It's not just that he has no memory of the event, like an amnesiac, but that he has very different memories connected provably with a different body. This established, what jury in its right mind would find him guilty? Thus bodily identity cannot be a necessary, much less a sufficient, condition of personal identity.

The truth is that we never meet the physical basis of personhood. We could not recognise our own brains if we saw them (by having a neurosurgeon open the cranium under a local anaesthetic and looking through mirrors at the cerebral cortex), let alone other people's brains. What we do meet are bodies controlled by brains. So we say those intelligently and distinctly controlled physical entities are persons. It is only when we confront the prospect of brain transplantation that we realise bodies are radically dissociable from persons.

One can fancy X standing in the graveyard, in Y's body, watching a double funeral. Alongside him are Y's wife and his own. There are two coffins being lowered into the grave together. One is very small—shoebox size. That is Y's dead brain. The other is very big, X's former body. Everyone is grieving. But not for X. Why should they, since he is standing there, alive and happier than he has been for years? Only Y is being buried, in that tiny box. If you asked X how it felt to witness his own funeral he would perhaps laugh, and rightly so. He might even point to the shoebox-sized coffin and say 'ask Y that'.

But if brain-centred persons are really so independent of the bodies they inhabit, then surely our concept of a person is exaggeratedly confined? This is the consequence of brain transplantation I want to take up next.

ARE PEOPLE OF A PARTICULAR SEX?

It will be helpful to consider the following situation. We have the body of a young woman in a hospital bed, private first-class room. She opens her eyes slowly, looks around. She is all alone. She looks down at herself, also slowly. She raises her hands. She runs them down her body, starting with the head. When she reaches the breasts her eyes open widely in surprise. Then her hands move down the waist and widen as they follow the hipbone structure. Again her eyes enlarge. Frantically she moves her hands together. She screams, piercingly. A young doctor in long white coat enters, looking flustered.

Calm yourself, please. You mustn't get upset.
What the bloody hell have you done to me?
Here, take this tranquilliser.
I won't take anything from you any more. Start explaining.
Well, there were two people in that car crash, as you know.
Go on.
The husband died of heart failure during the operation.

I'm waiting.
His wife survived. She also had compatible blood.
So you just decided you'd plop me into *her!*
You don't understand. I already had your brain out when he died.
There was no other choice and she was right there, heart pumping well and . . .
You couldn't have put me back and waited for another man?
That would have been very dangerous—your lungs were collapsing.
All right. What's done is done. I suppose I should be grateful I'm alive.
I was hoping you'd see it that way. And she was very healthy.
That's nice, but I don't *want* to be a woman, healthy or not.
You'll get used to it. Wait till the hormones begin taking effect.
Look here, if you think I'm going to like *men* all of a sudden you're . . .
(Smiling). We'll see how you feel about it next week.

Surely the doctor is right? How could this person —let us designate him neutrally as N—who was formerly a male human remain so in a female human body? Now it is true all his past sexual associations are male; he will have a problem forming radically different associations. But this is the case also, in a milder sense, with intact humans who undergo surgery for sex-transformation in the same body. Admittedly such persons often seek the transformation themselves because for a long time before they felt sexually ambiguous, indicating an abnormal hormone balance to begin with. Admittedly also the unambiguous male or female is not so readily responsive to abrupt hormonal change. Probably this is because during early development the dominant hormone balance played an organizational role by more or less determining the extent of growth of those nerve circuits in the brain which direct male and female behaviour. But it seems clear from recent experimental work that both types of circuits exist in the brain, so that we are all capable of being either male or female depending on the chemical stimulation our brains get.

Fisher, for example, has reported some interesting results in working with rats. Whereas a steroid hormone injected into the muscle tissue or bloodstream of a male rat does not take effect for

24 to 48 hours, he found that injections directly into the brain just in front of the hypothalamus at the level of the optic tracts produced changes within seconds or minutes. But even when using the male hormone testosterone (at best a weak substitute for progesterone, the female hormone), a slight deviation from the injection site provoked powerful feminine and indeed maternal behaviour in the male rat. Conversely, direct stimulation of a site very near that one provoked decided malelike behaviour even in female rats. This seems clear evidence that the brains of males and females are essentially identical in character and organization of the neurons, so that maleness and femaleness alike depend on which nerve circuits are fired by chemical stimulants.

In the case of N above, given his past sexual associations and already-established circuits responsive to male hormones, the transition to true female-like tastes and behaviour might be very slow and painful. Assuming the human brain equally responsive to direct stimulation of circuits controlling primary drives as the rat brain is, we might at N's request speed this up for him by firing his heretofore quiescent "female" neurons. But we must not think N is really a male human in female garb, like some kind of transvestite. His sex identity changes with the body, not only in the sense of an immediate and drastic physical transformation but also in the sense of an eventual, at least, transformation of tastes, inclinations, desires. The day he foregoes cigars and gets interested in perfumes we will know it. Will N then be the same person?

Well, why not? We saw before that while there are a lot of ways of saying someone is 'a new person' they do not conflict with our understanding of it being at a deeper level the same person after all. X in Y's body was quite different from X in X's body outwardly, though not much so inwardly. N is even more different outwardly after the transplant, and he is also, or soon will be, more different inwardly too. But he will not be an *entirely* different person. One of his primary drives will have taken a new direction, yes, and that will affect a whole cluster of associated dispositions. But will it destroy his memories, his basic character before the operation, his political opinions or religious feelings or moral convictions? There seems no reason to suppose

this. Probably he will divide up his life into two stages. He will reflect upon Stage A, when he was a man, recall with amusement how he misunderstood women, wonder how he could have enjoyed brawling and hunting so much, *etc.* Perhaps all events asociated with his post-operative experience, Stage B, will be recalled in a different way, and in speaking of himself there he will consciously use the feminine gender to describe how he had behaved in the eyes of others. 'So what did your little Lucy do? She turned towards that vampire and said in her most chilling voice. . . .' But it will still be old N, and she or he will know it. . . .

DISEMBODIMENT

We have an excised human brain R ready for transplant, but unfortunately the donor body died and we don't have a second with compatible blood type on hand. So we place R in a large jar filled with cerebrospinal fluid, being careful to feed fresh blood into it through the carotid artery, and wait for our chance. Days go by, then weeks. No luck. It's too late now. The nerve endings have degenerated beyond hope of repair by artificial stimulation. R will never hook up with another body and take control over it.

But R is still alive. The electro-encephalograph shows a low, wavy pattern characteristic of deep sleep, yet it's there. So what should we do? There's not much point in keeping R in this state. With no new sensory input to act on, and no way of acting on it without extensions of the motor nerves, there is nothing for R to wake up to. Perhaps it would be best to shut off the blood supply now. Within minutes oxygen starvation will destroy the tissues and the brain will stop emitting electrical impulses. Then we can pronounce R dead and notify its owner's nearest kin. Yes, that seems the only thing to do.

Suddenly someone remembers Penfield's accidental triggering of memory traces in the cerebral cortex years ago, when he was probing the temporal lobes of focal epileptics. And R's owner—let us call him O—was an epileptic of that type. What is more, he was a nice fellow, well-liked in the hospital. Why not give him some artificial stimulation there, in the temporal lobes? He might have considerable recall, most of it pleasant since unpleasant traces are usually lost. So we sink fine electrodes into both lobes, wait a couple of days, and give R mild jolts. The EEG pattern responds immediately —low amplitude, rapidly-changing. R is alert. Then some high spikes appear on the chart. O must be having some vivid recall now. What is it? We can't tell, because O can't tell us.

But perhaps he sees himself again running over the hills through deep grass of a fine summer's day, a cloudless blue sky above and the salt-laden wind rushing through his lungs, and there in the distance stands his mother calling and he waves and comes bounding down the last hillside and stumbles and meets the green earth and with its sweet dampness in his nostrils rolls and rolls down and down laughing with the joy of it all.

And who knows? Maybe that is heaven.

28. MEMORY AS THE CRITERION OF PERSONAL IDENTITY

John Locke

. . . If the identity of *soul alone* makes the same *man,* and there be nothing in the nature of matter why the same individual spirit may not be united to different bodies, it will be possible that those men, living in distant ages, and of different tempers, may have been the same man: which way of speaking must be from a very strange use of the word man, applied to an idea out of which body and shape are excluded. . . .

An animal is a living organized body; and consequently the same animal, as we have observed, is the same continued *life* communicated to different particles of matter, as they happen successively to be united to that organized living body. And whatever is talked of other definitions, ingenious observation puts it past doubt, that the idea in our minds, of which the sound "man" in our mouths is the sign, is nothing else but of an animal of such a certain form. . . .

I presume it is not the idea of a thinking or rational being alone that makes the *idea of a man* in most people's sense: but of a body, so and so shaped, joined to it; and if that be the idea of a man, the same successive body not shifted all at once, must, as well as the same immaterial spirit, go to the making of the same man.

This being premised, to find wherein personal identity consists, we must consider what *person* stands for;—which, I think, is a thinking intelligent being, that has reason and reflection, and can consider itself as itself, the same thinking thing, in different times and places; which it does only by that consciousness which is inseparable from thinking, and, as it seems to me, essential to it: it being impossible for any one to perceive without *perceiving* that he does perceive. When we see, hear, smell, taste, feel, meditate, or will anything, we know that we do so. Thus it is always as to our present sensations and perceptions: and by this every one is to himself that which he calls self:—it not being considered, in this case, whether the same self be continued in the same or divers substances. For, since consciousness always accompanies thinking, and it is that which makes every one to be what he calls self, and thereby distinguishes himself from all other thinking things, in this alone consists personal identity, i.e. the sameness of a rational being: and as far as this consciousness can be extended backwards to any past action or thought, so far reaches the identity of that

From John Locke, *An Essay Concerning Human Understanding,* Book II, Chapter 27, "Of Ideas of Identity and Diversity." First published in 1690.

person; it is the same self now it was then; and it is by the same self with this present one that now reflects on it, that that action was done.

But it is further inquired, whether it be the same identical substance. This few would think they had reason to doubt of, if these perceptions, with their consciousness, always remained present in the mind, whereby the same thinking thing would be always consciously present, and, as would be thought, evidently the same to itself. But that which seems to make the difficulty is this, that this consciousness being interrupted always by forgetfulness, there being no moment of our lives wherein we have the whole train of all our past actions before our eyes in one view, but even the best memories losing the sight of one part whilst they are viewing another; and we sometimes, and that the greatest part of our lives, not reflecting on our past selves, being intent on our present thoughts, and in sound sleep having no thoughts at all, or at least none with that consciousness which remarks our waking thoughts,—I say, in all these cases, our consciousness being interrupted, and we losing the sight of our past selves, doubts are raised whether we are the same thinking thing, i.e. the same *substance* or no. Which, however reasonable or unreasonable, concerns not *personal* identity at all. The question being what makes the same person; and not whether it be the same identical substance, which always thinks in the same person, which, in this case, matters not at all: different substances, by the same consciousness (where they do partake in it) being united into one person, as well as different bodies by the same life are united into one animal, whose identity is preserved in that change of substances by the unity of one continued life. For, it being the same consciousness that makes a man be himself to himself, personal identity depends on that only, whether it be annexed solely to one individual substance, or can be continued in a succession of several substances. For as far as any intelligent·being *can* repeat the idea of any past action with the same consciousness it had of it at first, and with the same consciousness it has of any present action; so far it is the same personal self. For it is by the consciousness it has of its present thoughts and actions, that it is *self to itself* now, and so will be the same self, as far as the same

consciousness can extend to actions past or to come; and would be by distance of time, or change of substance, no more two persons, than a man be two men by wearing other clothes today than he did yesterday, with a long or a short sleep between: the same consciousness uniting those distant actions in the same person, whatever substances contributed to their production.

That this is so, we have some kind of evidence in our very bodies, all whose particles, whilst vitally united to this same thinking conscious self, so that *we feel* when they are touched, and are affected by, and conscious of good or harm that happens to them, are a part of ourselves; i.e. of our thinking conscious self. Thus, the limbs of his body are to every one a part of himself; he sympathizes and is concerned for them. Cut off a hand, and thereby separate it from that consciousness he had of its heat, cold, and other affections, and it is then no longer a part of that which is himself, any more than the remotest part of matter. Thus, we see the *substance* whereof personal self consisted at one time may be varied at another, without the change of personal identity; there being no question about the same person, though the limbs which but now were a part of it, be cut off. . . .

And thus may we be able, without any difficulty, to conceive the same person at the resurrection, though in a body not exactly in make or parts the same which he had here,—the same consciousness going along with the soul that inhabits it. But yet the soul alone, in the change of bodies, would scarce to any one but to him that makes the soul the man, be enough to make the same man. For should the soul of a prince, carrying with it the consciousness of the prince's past life, enter and inform the body of a cobbler, as soon as deserted by his own soul, every one sees he would be the same *person* with the prince, accountable only for the prince's actions: but who would say it was the same *man?* The body too goes to the making the man, and would, I guess, to everybody determine the man in this case, wherein the soul, with all its princely thoughts about it, would not make another man: but he would be the same cobbler to every one besides himself. I know that, in the ordinary way of speaking, the same person, and the same man, stand for one and the same thing. And indeed every one will always have a liberty to speak as he pleases, and to apply what articulate sounds to what ideas he thinks fit, and change them as often as he pleases. But yet, when we will inquire what makes the same *spirit, man,* or *person,* we must fix the ideas of spirit, man, or person in our minds; and having resolved with ourselves what we mean by them, it will not be hard to determine in either of them, or the like, when it is the same, and when not.

But though the immaterial substance or soul does not alone, wherever it be, and in whatsoever state, make the same *man;* yet it is plain, consciousness, as far as ever it can be extended—should it be to ages past—unites existences and actions very remote in time into the same *person,* as well as it does the existences and actions of the immediately preceding moment: so that whatever has the consciousness of present and past actions, is the same person to whom they both belong. Had I the same consciousness that I saw the ark and Noah's flood, as that I saw an overflowing of the Thames last winter, or as that I write now, I could no more doubt that I who write this now, that saw the Thames overflowed last winter, and that viewed the flood at the general deluge, was the same *self,*—place that self in what *substance* you please—than that I who write this am the same *myself* now whilst I write (whether I consist of all the same substance, material or immaterial, or no) that I was yesterday. For as to this point of being the same self, it matters not whether this present self be made up of the same or other substances—I being as much concerned, and as justly accountable for any action that was done a thousand years since, appropriated to me now by this self-consciousness, as I am for what I did the last moment. . . .

But yet possibly it will still be objected,—Suppose I wholly lose the memory of some parts of my life, beyond a possibility of retrieving them, so that perhaps I shall never be conscious of them again; yet am I not the same person that did those actions, had those thoughts that I once was conscious of, though I have now forgot them? To which I answer, that we must here take notice what the word *I* is applied to; which, in this case, is the *man* only. And the same man being presumed to be the same person, I is easily here supposed to stand also for the same person. But if it be possible for the same man to have distinct incommunicable consciousness at different times, it is past doubt the same man would at different times make different persons; which, we see, is the sense of mankind in the solemnest declaration of their opinions, human laws not punishing the mad man for the sober man's actions, nor the sober man for what the mad man did,—thereby making them two persons: which is somewhat explained by our way of speaking in English when we say such an one is 'not himself,' or is 'beside himself'; in which phrases it is insinuated, as if those who now, or at least first used them, thought that self was changed; the selfsame person was no longer in that man.

But yet it is hard to conceive that Socrates, the same individual man, should be two persons. To help us a little in this, we must consider what is meant by Socrates, or the same individual *man.*

First, it must be either the same individual, immaterial, thinking substance; in short, the same numerical soul, and nothing else.

Secondly, or the same animal, without any regard to an immaterial soul.

Thirdly, or the same immaterial spirit united to the same animal.

Now, take which of these suppositions you please, it is impossible to make personal identity to consist in anything but consciousness; or reach any further than that does.

29. A SKEPTICAL VIEW OF PERSONAL IDENTITY

David Hume

There are some philosophers, who imagine we are every moment intimately conscious of what we call our Self; that we feel its existence and its continuance in existence; and are certain, beyond the evidence of a demonstration, both of its perfect identity and simplicity. . . .

Unluckily all these positive assertions are contrary to that very experience, which is pleaded for them, nor have we any idea of *self*, after the manner it is here explain'd. For from what impression cou'd this idea be deriv'd? This question 'tis impossible to answer without a manifest contradiction and absurdity; and yet 'tis a question, which must necessarily be answer'd, if we wou'd have the idea of self pass for clear and intelligible. It must be some one impression, that gives rise to every real idea. But self or person is not any one impression, but that to which our several impressions and ideas are suppos'd to have a reference. If any impression gives rise to the idea of self, that impression must continue invariably the same, thro' the whole course of our lives; since self is suppos'd to exist after that manner. But there is no impression constant and invariable. Pain and pleasure, grief and joy, passions and sensations succeed each other, and never all exist at the same time. It cannot, therefore, be from any of these impressions, or from any other, that the idea of self is deriv'd; and consequently there is no such idea.

But farther, what must become of all our particular perceptions upon this hypothesis? All these are different, and distinguishable, and separable from each other, and may be separately consider'd, and may exist separately, and have no need of any thing to support their existence. After what manner, therefore, do they belong to self; and how are they connected with it? For my part, when I enter most intimately into what I call *myself,* I always stumble on some particular perception or other, of heat or cold, light or shade, love or hatred, pain or pleasure. I never can catch *myself* at any time without a perception, and never can observe any thing but the perception. When my perceptions are remov'd for any time, as by sound sleep; so long am I insensible of *myself,* and may truly be said not to exist. And were all my perceptions remov'd by death, and cou'd I neither think, nor feel, nor see, nor love, nor hate after the dissolution of my body, I shou'd be entirely annihilated, nor do I conceive what is farther requisite to make me a perfect nonentity. If any one upon serious and unprejudic'd reflexion, thinks he has a different notion of *himself,* I must confess I can reason no longer with him. All I can allow him is, that he may be in the right as well as I, and that we are essentially different in this particular. He may, perhaps, perceive something simple and continu'd, which he calls *himself;* tho' I am certain there is no such principle in me.

But setting aside some metaphysicians of this kind, I may venture to affirm of the rest of mankind, that they are nothing but a bundle or collection of different perceptions, which succeed each other with an inconceivable rapidity, and are in a perpetual flux and movement. Our eyes cannot turn in their sockets without varying our perceptions. Our thought is still more variable than our sight; and all our other senses and faculties contribute to this change; nor is there any single power of the soul, which remains unalterably the same, perhaps for one moment. The mind is a kind of theatre, where several perceptions successively make their appearance; pass, re-pass, glide away, and mingle in an infinite variety of postures and situations. There is properly no *simplicity* in it at one time, nor *identity* in different; whatever natural propension we may have to imagine that simplicity and identity. The comparison of the theatre must not mislead us. They are the successive perceptions only, that constitute the mind; nor have we the most distant notion of the place, where these scenes are represented, or of the materials, of which it is compos'd.

From David Hume, *A Treatise of Human Nature.* First published in England in 1738.

What then gives us so great a propension to ascribe an identity to these successive perceptions, and to suppose ourselves possest of an invariable and uninterrupted existence thro' the whole course of our lives?. . .

We have a distinct idea of an object, that remains invariable and uninterrupted thro' a suppos'd variation of time; and this idea we call that of *identity* or *sameness.* We have also a distinct idea of several different objects existing in succession, and connected together by a close relation; and this to an accurate view affords as perfect a notion of *diversity,* as if there was no manner of relation among the objects. But tho' these two ideas of identity, and a succession of related objects be in themselves perfectly distinct, and even contrary, yet 'tis certain, that in our common way of thinking they are generally confounded with each other. That action of the imagination, by which we consider the uninterrupted and invariable object, and that by which we reflect on the succession of related objects, are almost the same to the feeling, nor is there much more effort of thought requir'd in the latter case than in the former. The relation facilitates the transition of the mind from one object to another, and renders its passage as smooth as if it contemplated one continu'd object. This resemblance is the cause of the confusion and mistake, and makes us substitute the notion of identity, instead of that of related objects. . . .

Thus we feign the continu'd existence of the perceptions of our senses, to remove the interruption; and run into the notion of a *soul,* and *self,* and *substance,* to disguise the variation. But we may farther observe, that where we do not give rise to such a fiction, our propension to confound identity with relation is so great, that we are apt to imagine something unknown and mysterious, connecting the parts, beside their relation; and this I take to be the case with regard to the identity we ascribe to plants and vegetables. And even when this does not take place, we still feel a propensity to confound these ideas, tho' we are not able fully to satisfy ourselves in that particular, nor find any thing invariable and uninterrupted to justify our notion of identity.

Thus the controversy concerning identity is not merely a dispute of words. For when we attribute identity, in an improper sense, to variable or interrupted objects, our mistake is not confin'd to the expression, but is commonly attended with a fiction, either of something invariable and uninterrupted, or of something mysterious and inexplicable, or at least with a propensity to such fictions. What will suffice to prove this hypothesis to the satisfaction of every fair enquirer, is to shew from daily experience and observation, that the objects, which are variable or interrupted, and yet are suppos'd to continue the same, are such only as consist of a succession of parts, connected together by resemblance, contiguity, or causation. . . .

A ship, of which a considerable part has been chang'd by frequent reparations, is still consider'd as the same; nor does the difference of the materials hinder us from ascribing an identity to it. The common end, in which the parts conspire, is the same under all their variations, and affords an easy transition of the imagination from one situation of the body to another. . . .

Tho' every one must allow, that in a very few years both vegetables and animals endure a *total* change, yet we still attribute identity to them, while their form, size, and substance are entirely alter'd. An oak, that grows from a small plant to a large tree, is still the same oak; tho' there be not one particle of matter, or figure of its parts the same. An infant becomes a man, and is sometimes fat, sometimes lean, without any change in his identity. . . . A man, who hears a noise, that is frequently interrupted and renew'd, says, it is still the same noise; tho' 'tis evident the sounds have only a specific identity or resemblance, and there is nothing numerically the same, but the cause, which produc'd them. In like manner it may be said without breach of the propriety of language, that such a church, which was formerly of brick, fell to ruin, and that the parish rebuilt the same church of free-stone, and according to modern architecture. Here neither the form nor materials are the same, nor is there any thing common to the two objects, but their relation to the inhabitants of the parish; and yet this alone is sufficient to make us denominate them the same. . . .

From thence it evidently follows, that identity is nothing really belonging to these different perceptions, and uniting them together; but is merely a quality, which we attribute to them, because of the union of their ideas in the imagination, when we reflect upon them. . . .

The only question, therefore, which remains, is, by what relations this uninterrupted progress of our thought is produc'd, when we consider the successive existence of a mind or thinking person. And here 'tis evident we must confine ourselves to resemblance and causation. . . . Also, as memory alone acquaints us with the continuance and extent of this succession of perceptions, 'tis to be consider'd, upon that account chiefly, as the source of personal identity. Had we no memory, we never shou'd have any notion of causation, nor consequently of that chain of causes and effects, which constitute our self or person.

30. A CRITIQUE OF LOCKE AND HUME ON PERSONAL IDENTITY

Thomas Reid

. . . It is proper to consider what is meant by identity in general, what by our own personal identity, and how we are led into that invincible belief and conviction which every man has of his own personal identity, as far as his memory reaches.

Identity in general I take to be a relation between a thing which is known to exist at one time, and a thing which is known to have existed at another time. If you ask whether they are one and the same, or two different things, every man of common sense understands the meaning of your question perfectly. Whence we may infer with certainty, that every man of common sense has a clear and distinct notion of identity.

If you ask a definition of identity, I confess I can give none; it is too simple a notion to admit of logical definition. . . .

I see evidently that identity supposes *an uninterrupted continuance of existence*. That which has ceased to exist cannot be the same with that which afterwards begins to exist; for this would be to suppose a being to exist after it ceased to exist, and to have had existence before it was produced, which are manifest contradictions. Continued uninterrupted existence is therefore necessarily implied in identity. Hence we may infer, that identity cannot, in its proper sense, be applied to our pains, our pleasures, our thoughts, or any operation of our minds. The pain felt this day is not the same individual pain which I felt yesterday, though they may be *similar* in kind and degree, and have the same cause. The same may be said of every feeling, and of every operation of mind. They are all successive in their nature, like time itself, no two moments of which can be the same moment. It is otherwise with the parts of absolute space. They always are, and were, and will be the same. So far, I think, we proceed upon clear ground in fixing the notion of identity in general.

NATURE AND ORIGIN OF OUR IDEA OF PERSONAL IDENTITY

It is perhaps more difficult to ascertain with precision the meaning of *personality;* but it is not necessary in the present subject: it is sufficient for our purpose to observe, that all mankind place their personality in something that *cannot be divided, or consist of parts.* A part of a person is a manifest absurdity. When a man loses his estate, his health, his strength, he is still the same person, and has lost nothing of his personality. If he has a leg or an arm cut off, he is the same person he was before. The amputated member is no part of his person, oth-

Edited from two sources: Thomas Reid, *Essays on the Intellectual Powers of Man,* first published in England in 1785, and *An Inquiry Into the Human Mind.*

erwise it would have a right to a part of his estate, and be liable for a part of his engagements. It would be entitled to a share of his merit and demerit, which is manifestly absurd. A person is something indivisible, and is what Leibniz calls a *monad.*

My personal identity, therefore, implies the continued existence of that indivisible thing which I call *myself.* Whatever this self may be, it is something which thinks, and deliberates, and resolves, and acts, and suffers. I am not thought, I am not action, I am not feeling; I am something that thinks, and acts, and suffers. My thoughts, and actions, and feelings, change every moment; they have no continued, but a successive, existence; but that *self,* or *I,* to which they belong, is permanent, and has the same relation to all the succeeding thoughts, actions, and feelings which I call mine.

Such are the notions that I have of my personal identity. But perhaps it may be said, this may all be fancy without reality. How do you know,—what evidence have you,—that there is such a permanent self which has a claim to all the thoughts, actions, and feelings which you call yours?

To this I answer, that the proper evidence I have of all this is *remembrance.* I remember that twenty years ago I conversed with such a person; I remember several things that passed in that conversation: my memory testifies, not only that this was done, but that it was done by me who now remember it. If it was done by me, I must have existed at that time, and continued to exist from that time to the present: if the identical person whom I call myself had not a part in that conversation, my memory is fallacious; it gives a distinct and positive testimony of what is not true. Every man in his senses believes what he distinctly remembers, and everything he remembers convinces him that he existed at the time remembered.

Although memory gives the most irresistible evidence of my being the identical person that did such a thing, at such a time, I may have other good evidence of things which befell me, and which I do not remember: I know who bare me, and suckled me, but I do not remember these events.

It may here be observed, (though the observation would have been unnecessary, if some great philosophers had not contradicted it,) that it is not my remembering any action of mine that *makes* me to be the person who did it. This remembrance makes me to *know* assuredly that I did it; *but I might have done it, though I did not remember it.* That relation to me, which is expressed by saying that *I did it,* would be the same, though I had not the least remembrance of it. . . .

When we pass judgment on the identity of other persons than ourselves, we proceed upon other grounds, and determine from a variety of circumstances, which sometimes produce the firmest assurance, and sometimes leave room for doubt. The identity of persons has often furnished matter of serious litigation before tribunals of justice. But no man of a sound mind ever doubted of his own identity, as far as he distinctly remembered. . . .

Thus it appears, that the evidence we have of our own identity, as far back as we remember, is totally of a different kind from the evidence we have of the identity of other persons, or of objects of sense. The first is grounded on *memory,* and gives undoubted certainty. The last is grounded on *similarity,* and on other circumstances, which in many cases are not so decisive as to leave no room for doubt.

It may likewise be observed, that the identity of *objects of sense* is never perfect. All bodies, as they consist of innumerable parts that may be disjoined from them by a great variety of causes, are subject to continual changes of their substance, increasing, diminishing, changing insensibly. When such alterations are gradual, because languages could not afford a different name for every different state of such a changeable being, it retains the same name, and is considered as the same thing. Thus we say of an old regiment, that it did such a thing a century ago, though there now is not a man alive who then belonged to it. We say a tree is the same in the seed-bed and in the forest. A ship of war, which has successively changed her anchors, her tackle, her sails, her masts, her planks, and her timbers, while she keeps the same name, is the same.

The identity, therefore, which we ascribe to bodies, whether natural or artificial, is not perfect identity; it is rather something which, for the conveniency of speech, we call identity. It admits of a great change of the subject, providing the change be *gradual;* sometimes, even of a total change. And the changes which in common language are made consistent with identity differ from those that are thought to destroy it, not in *kind,* but in *number* and *degree.* It has no fixed nature when applied to bodies; and questions about the identity of a body are very often questions about words. But identity, when applied to persons, has no ambiguity, and admits not of degrees, or of more and less. It is the foundation of all rights and obligations, and of all accountableness; and the notion of it is fixed and precise.

STRICTURES ON LOCKE'S ACCOUNT OF PERSONAL IDENTITY

In a long chapter, *Of Identity and Diversity,* Mr. Locke has made many ingenious and just observations, and some which I think cannot be defended. . . .

This doctrine has some strange consequences, which the author was aware of. (1.) Such as, that if the same consciousness can be transferred from one intelligent being to another, which he thinks we cannot show to be impossible, *then two or twenty intelligent beings may be the same person.* (2.) And if the intelligent being may lose the consciousness of the actions done by him, which surely is possible, then he is not the person that did those actions; so that *one intelligent being may be two or twenty different persons,* if he shall so often lose the consciousness of his former actions.

(3.) There is another consequence of this doctrine, which follows no less necessarily, though Mr. Locke probably did not see it. It is, *that a man may be, and at the same time not be, the person that did a particular action.* Suppose a brave officer to have been flogged when a boy at school for robbing an orchard, to have taken a standard from the enemy in his first campaign, and to have been made a general in advanced life; suppose, also, which must be admitted to be possible, that, when he took the standard, he was conscious of his having been flogged at school, and that, when made a general, he was conscious of his taking the standard, but had absolutely lost the consciousness of his flogging. These things being supposed, it follows, from Mr. Locke's doctrine, that he who was flogged at school is the same person who took the standard, and that he who took the standard is the same person who was made a general. Whence it follows, if there be any truth in logic, that the general is the same

person with him who was flogged at school. But the general's consciousness does not reach so far back as his flogging; therefore, according to Mr. Locke's doctrine, he is not the person who was flogged. Therefore the general is, and at the same time is not, the same person with him who was flogged at school.

Leaving the consequences of this doctrine to those who have leisure to trace them, we may observe, with regard to the doctrine itself,—

First, that Mr. Locke attributes to consciousness the conviction we have of our past actions, as if a man may now be conscious of what he did twenty years ago. It is impossible to understand the meaning of this, unless by *consciousness* he meant *memory,* the only faculty by which we have an immediate knowledge of our past actions. . . .

When, therefore, Mr. Locke's notion of personal identity is properly expressed, it is, that personal identity *consists in distinct remembrance;* for, even in the popular sense, to say that I am conscious of a past action means nothing else than that I distinctly remember that I did it.

Secondly, it may be observed, that, in this doctrine, not only is consciousness confounded with memory, but, which is still more strange, *personal identity* is confounded with *the evidence which we have of our personal identity.*

It is very true, that my remembrance that I did such a thing is the evidence I have that I am the identical person who did it. And this, I am apt to think, Mr. Locke meant. But to say that my remembrance that I did such a thing, or my consciousness, *makes* me the person who did it, is, in my apprehension, an absurdity too gross to be entertained by any man who attends to the meaning of it; for it is to attribute to memory or consciousness a strange magical power of producing its object, though that object must have existed before the memory or consciousness which produced it. Consciousness is the testimony of one faculty; memory is the testimony of another faculty; and to say that the testimony is the cause of the thing testified, this surely is absurd, if any thing be, and could not have been said by Mr. Locke, if he had not confounded the testimony with the thing testified.

When a horse that was stolen is found and claimed by the owner, the only evidence he can have, or that a judge or witnesses can have, that this is the very identical horse which was his property, is similitude. But would it not be ridiculous from this to infer that the identity of a horse *consists* in similitude only? The only *evidence* I have that I am the identical person who did such actions is, that I remember distinctly I did them; or, as Mr. Locke expresses it, I am conscious I did them. To infer from this, that personal identity consists in consciousness, is an argument which, if it had any force, would prove the identity of a stolen horse to consist solely in similitude.

Thirdly, is it not strange that the sameness or identity of a person should consist in a thing *which is continually changing,* and is not any two minutes the same?

Our consciousness, our memory, and every operation of the mind, are still flowing like the water of a river, or like time itself. The consciousness I have this moment can no more be the same consciousness I had last moment, than this moment can be the last moment. Identity can only be affirmed of things which have a continued existence. Consciousness, and every kind of thought, are transient and momentary, and have no continued existence; and, therefore, if personal identity consisted in consciousness, it would certainly follow, that *no man is the same person any two moments of his life;* and as the right and justice of reward and punishment are founded on personal identity, no man could be responsible for his actions. . . .

Fourthly, there are many expressions used by Mr. Locke, in speaking of personal identity, which to me are altogether unintelligible, unless we suppose that he confounded that sameness or identity which we ascribe to an individual with the identity which, in common discourse, is often ascribed to many individuals of the same species.

When we say that pain and pleasure, consciousness and memory, are the same in all men, this sameness can only mean similarity, or sameness *of kind.* That the pain of one man can be the same individual pain with that of another man is no less impossible, than that one man should be another man: the pain felt by me yesterday can no more be the pain I feel to-day, than yesterday can be this day; and the same thing may be said of every passion and of every operation of the mind. The same

kind or species of operation may be in different men, or in the same man at different times; but it is impossible that the same individual operation should be in different men, or in the same man at different times.

When Mr. Locke, therefore, speaks of "the same consciousness being continued through a succession of different substances"; when he speaks of "repeating the idea of a past action, with the same consciousness we had of it at the first," and of "the same consciousness extending to actions past and to come"; these expressions are to me unintelligible, unless he means not the same individual consciousness, but a consciousness that is similar, or of the same kind. If our personal identity consists in consiousness, as this consciousness cannot be the same individually any two moments, but only of the *same kind,* it would follow, that we are not for any two moments the same individual persons, but the same *kind* of persons. As our consciousness sometimes ceases to exist, as in sound sleep, our personal identity must cease with it. Mr. Locke allows, that the same thing cannot have two beginnings of existence, so that our identity would be irrecoverably gone every time we ceased to think, if it was but for a moment. . . .

STRICTURES ON HUME'S ACCOUNT OF PERSONAL IDENTITY

Locke's principle must be, that identity consists in remembrance; and consequently a man must lose his personal identity with regard to every thing he forgets.

Nor are these the only instances whereby our philosophy concerning the mind appears to be very fruitful in creating doubts, but very unhappy in resolving them.

Des Cartes, Malebranche, and Locke, have all employed their genius and skill, to prove the existence of a material world; and with very bad success. . . .

The present age, I apprehend, has not produced two more acute or more practised in this part of philosophy than [George Berkeley] the Bishop of Cloyne, and the author of the Treatise of Human Nature [David Hume, who]. . . undoes the world of spirits, and leaves nothing in nature but ideas and impressions, without any subject on which they may be impressed.

It seems to be a peculiar strain of humour in this author, to set out in his introduction, by promising with a grave face, no less than a complete system of the sciences, upon a foundation entirely new, to wit, that of human nature; when the intention of the whole work is to shew, that there is neither human nature nor science in the world. It may perhaps be unreasonable to complain of this conduct in an author, who neither believes his own existence, nor that of his reader; and therefore could not mean to disappoint him, or to laugh at his credulity. Yet I cannot imagine, that the author of the Treatise of Human Nature is so skeptical as to plead this apology. He believed, against his principles, that he should be read, and that he should retain his personal identity, till he reaped the honour and reputation justly due to his metaphysical *acumen*. Indeed he ingenuously acknowledges, that it was only in solitude and retirement that he could yield any assent to his own philosophy; society, like daylight, dispelled the darkness and fogs of skepticism, and made him yield to the dominion of common sense. Nor did I ever hear him charged with doing any thing, even in solitude, that argued such a degree of skepticism, as his principles maintain. . . .

That the natural issue of this system is skepticism with regard to every thing except the existence of our ideas, and of their necessary relations which appear upon comparing them, is evident: for ideas being the only objects of thought, and having no existence but when we are conscious of them, it necessarily follows, that there is no object of our thought, which can have a continued and permanent existence. Body and spirit, cause and effect, time and space, to which we were wont to ascribe an existence independent of our thought, are all turned out of existence by this short dilemma: Either these things are ideas of sensation or reflection, or they are not: if they are ideas of sensation or reflection, they can have no existence but when we are conscious of them; if they are not ideas of sensation or reflection, they are words without any meaning.

Neither Des Cartes nor Locke perceived this consequence of their system concerning ideas.

Bishop Berkeley was the first who discovered it . . . But with regard to the existence of spirits or minds, he does not admit the consequence; and if he had admitted it, he must have been an absolute skeptic. . . .

Thus we see, that Des Cartes and Locke take the road that leads to skepticism, without knowing the end of it; but they stop short for want of light to carry them farther. Berkeley, frighted at the appearance of the dreadful abyss, starts aside, and avoids it. But the author of the Treatise of Human Nature, more daring and intrepid, without turning aside to the right hand or to the left, like Virgil's Alecto, shoots directly into the gulf. . . .

We ought, however, to do this justice both to the bishop of Cloyne and to the author of the Treatise of Human Nature, to acknowledge, that their conclusions are justly drawn from the doctrine of ideas, which has been so universally received. On the other hand, from the character of Bishop Berkeley, and of his predecessors Des Cartes, Locke, and Malebranche, we may venture to say, that if they had seen all the consequences of this doctrine, as clearly as the author before mentioned did, they would have suspected it vehemently, and examined it more carefully than they appear to have done.

The theory of ideas, like the Trojan horse, had a specious appearance both of innocence and beauty; but if those philosophers had known that it carried in its belly death and destruction to all science and common sense, they would not have broken down their walls to give it admittance. . . .

It is certain, no man can conceive or believe smelling to exist of itself, without a mind, or something that has the power of smelling, of which it is called a sensation, an operation or feeling. Yet if any man should demand a proof, that sensation cannot be without a mind or sentient being, I confess that I can give none; and that to pretend to prove it, seems to me almost as absurd as to deny it.

This might have been said without any apology before the Treatise of Human Nature appeared in the world. For till that time, no man, as far as I know, ever thought either of calling in question that principle, or of giving a reason for his belief of it. Whether thinking beings were of an ethereal or igneous nature, whether material or immaterial, was variously disputed; but that thinking is an operation of some kind of being or other, was always taken for granted, as a principle that could not possibly admit of doubt. . . .

If there are certain principles, as I think there are, which the constitution of our nature leads us to believe, and which we are under a necessity to take for granted in the common concerns of life, without being able to give a reason for them; these are what we call the principles of common sense; and what is manifestly contrary to them, is what we call absurd. . . .

It is a fundamental principle of [Hume's] ideal system, that every object of thought must be an impression, or an idea, that is, a faint copy of some preceding impression. This is a principle so commonly received, that the author above mentioned, although his whole system is built upon it, never offers the least proof of it. It is upon this principle, as a fixed point, that he erects his metaphysical engines, to overturn heaven and earth, body and spirit. And indeed, in my apprehension, it is altogether sufficient for the purpose. For if impressions and ideas are the only objects of thought, then heaven and earth, and body and spirit, and every thing you please, must signify only impressions and ideas, or they must be words without any meaning. It seems, therefore, that this notion, however strange, is closely connected with the received doctrine of ideas, and we must either admit the conclusion, or call in question the premises. . . .

The triumph of ideas was completed by the Treatise of Human Nature, which discards spirits also, and leaves ideas and impressions as the sole existences in the universe. What if at last, having nothing else to contend with, they should fall foul of one another, and leave no existence in nature at all? This would surely bring philosophy into danger; for what should we have left to talk or to dispute about? However, hitherto these philosophers acknowledge the existence of impressions and ideas; they acknowledge certain laws of attraction, or rules of precedence, according to which ideas and impressions range themselves in various forms, and succeed one another: but that they should belong to a mind, as its proper goods and chattels, this they have found to be a vulgar error. These ideas are as free and independent as the birds of the air. . . . They make the whole furniture of the universe; starting into existence, or out of it, without any cause; combining into parcels which the vulgar call *minds;* and succeeding one another by fixed laws, without time, place, or author of those laws. . . .

The Treatise of Human Nature . . . seems to have made but a bad return, by bestowing upon them this independent existence; since thereby they are turned out of house and home, and set adrift in the world, without friend or connection, without a rag to cover their nakedness; and who knows but the whole system of ideas may perish by the indiscreet zeal of their friends to exalt them?

However this may be, it is certainly a most amazing discovery that thought and ideas may be without any thinking being: a discovery big with consequences which cannot easily be traced by those deluded mortals who think and reason in the common track. We were always apt to imagine, that thought supposed a thinker, and love a lover, and treason a traitor: but this, it seems, was all a mistake; and it is found out, that there may be treason without a traitor, and love without a lover, laws without a legislator, and punishment without a sufferer, succession without time, and motion without any thing moved, or space in which it may move: or if, in these cases, ideas are the lover, the sufferer, the traitor, it were to be wished that the author of this discovery had farther condescended to acquaint us, whether ideas can converse together, and be under obligations of duty or gratitude to each other; whether they can make promises, and enter into leagues and covenants, and fulfil or break them, and be punished for the breach? If one set of ideas makes a covenant, another breaks it, and a third is punished for it, there is reason to think that justice is no natural virtue in this system.

It seemed very natural to think, that the Treatise of Human Nature required an author, and a very ingenious one too; but now we learn, that it is only a set of ideas which came together, and arranged themselves by certain associations and attractions.

After all, this curious system appears not to be fitted to the present state of human nature. How far it may suit some choice spirits, who are refined from the dregs of common sense, I cannot say. It is acknowledged, I think, that even these can enter into this system only in their most speculative hours, when they soar so high in pursuit of those self-existent ideas, as to lose sight of all other things. But when they condescend to mingle again with the human race, and to converse with a friend, a companion, or a fellow citizen, the ideal system vanishes; common sense, like an irresistible torrent, carries them along; and, in spite of all their reasoning and philosophy, they believe their own existence, and the existence of other things. . . .

This philosophy is like a hobby-horse, which a man in bad health may ride in his closet, without hurting his reputation; but if he should take him abroad with him to church, or to the exchange, or to the play house, his heir would immediately call a jury, and seize his estate.

Minds, Machines, and Robots

31. COLOSSUS, OR THE FORBIN PROJECT

D. F. Jones

"It's a hellava thought! The trouble with you, Forbin, is that you've lived too close to the Project. So Colossus has a better brain—fine! Just the very thing we've been working for all these years. No, Professor, we go ahead now, repeat now!" The President lightly stroked a button on his desk. "I'll give you a written order."

Prytzkammer, the aide, came in and stood silent before the President.

"P, take this down. Type it yourself—I'll sign as soon as it's ready—such as in two minutes' time." He gave Forbin a humorless grin. "To Professor Forbin, Chief Director, Project Colossus. In my capacity, no my *dual* capacity of President and Commander in Chief of the Armed Forces of the United States of North America, I order you to activate Colossus—" he swung his chair to face Forbin—"how about 0800 on the 5th? That'll give you just over forty-eight hours."

"That will be enough."

"Right, P, go on—activate Colossus at 0800 5th.

That's all, except I want it graded Top Secret until 1000 5th, then downgraded to Unclassified. All times Eastern Standard."

1

"Gentlemen, the free world, here is the President."

He walked slowly to the doors to give the camera a chance to keep him in shot, and opened both doors. Camera Two sank down on one knee, getting a desk-level view of the President as the doors opened, slowly straightening up as the reporters filed in on either side of him. The PPA joined Forbin, out of view well to one side of the President's desk.

The President waited until the reporters were seated, then leaned forward on his elbows, hands clasped in front. It was a small gesture which conveyed the impression on TV that he was talking to you, confidentially, that this was man-to-man stuff.

"Fellow citizens of the world," he began in a low, measured, almost stately voice, "I am told that this telecast is being watched by more than half the people of the globe, and that a further ten percent are listening on the radio. You may well wonder

From D. F. Jones, *Colossus, or the Forbin Project,* copyright © 1966. Reprinted with permission of Berkley Publishing Corp. and Rupert Hart-Davis Ltd.

what I can say that is important enough to justify taking up your time like this. In all solemnity, I can assure you I have that justification. For good or evil —and I devoutly believe in good—we have reached one of those vital turning points in the history of man and of this planet. There have been a number of such moments in the past, most of them passing unrecognized. The first was the discovery of the use of fire, the second when the wheel was invented. The construction of the first internal-combustion machine was another. Some of you are old enough to recall the terrible dawn of the atomic age, and the host of technological advances we have made since then. But for the unhappy state of our world's affairs, we could all enjoy life to the full; remove the risk of conflict between the nations, and the Golden Age would be with us—now!" The President did not forget himself and bang the desk, but raised one finger as he spoke the last word, giving the slight visual shock to keep his vast audience's full attention. He went on, wearily.

"Instead, for years, for generations, we have been delicately poised on the brink of a disaster too complete and horrible to contemplate." His voice lost its weariness, gathered strength. "We of the free world have upheld the banner of freedom and truth, knowing that this must be preserved, even at the cost of all our lives."

Again the President paused, and resumed his confidential approach. "We do not want war—and to be truthful, I do not think anyone else does either. Nevertheless, we have all gone on, with recurrent crises, each carrying with it the risk of a clip or error on one side, or the other, which could result in the final tragedy of global destruction. There is an old saying that 'everyone makes mistakes,' but that is just what neither side can afford. We are all human, taking inhuman risks. One of the great philosophers of this century, Bertrand Russell, said many years ago, 'You may reasonably expect a man to walk a tightrope safely for ten minutes; it would be unreasonable to do so without accident for two hundred years.' This we have known for a long time, and for years, here in the United States, we have been working on this problem. Until this very minute this work has been our most closely guarded secret. It has involved vast effort, vast expenditure, but I have to tell you that our efforts have been crowned with success.

"As President of the United States of North America, I have to tell you, the people of the world, that as of eight o'clock Eastern Standard Time this morning the defense of the nation, and with it the defense of the free world, has been the responsibility of a machine. As the first citizen of my country, I have *delegated* my right to take my people to war.

"That decision now rests with Colossus, which is the name of the machine. It is basically an electronic brain, but far more advanced than anything previously built. It is capable of studying intelligence and data fed to it, and on the basis of those facts only—not of emotions—deciding if an attack is about to be launched upon us. If it did decide that an attack was imminent—and by that I mean that an assault was impending and would probably be launched within four hours—Colossus would decide, and act. It controls its own weapons and can select and deliver whatever it considers appropriate.

"Understand that Colossus' decisions are superior to any we humans can make, for it can absorb far more data than is remotely possible for the greatest genius that ever lived. And more important than that, it has no emotions. It knows no fear, no hate, no envy. It cannot act in a sudden fit of temper. Above all, *it cannot act at all,* so long as there is no threat.

"Fellow humans, we in the USNA now live in the shade, but not the shadow, of Colossus. And indirectly, you do too. May it never see fit to act."

The President took another sip of water. He was aware that the Tass man, Kyrovitch, was about to speak, but he also saw Prytzkammer motion him to be silent. The rest of the reporters looked dazed. The President was enjoying himself even more than he had expected.

"We of the free world," he continued, "do not want war. Indeed, we will never fight unless attacked. Now that we have Colossus we have no real need for armed forces except for minor disturbances. It is therefore my intention to reduce the overall strength of our fighting services by seventy-five percent over the next five years. As soon, in fact, as the readjustment can be made.

"Further, we are prepared to show the world how Colossus works—what has been built into it— and to prove to anyone's satisfaction" (he could not help flashing a look at Kyrovitch) "that Colossus is a defensive system. If we can convince the Soviet Bloc that Colossus is solely defensive, and demonstrate that we have no offensive intentions by the virtual disbandment of our Navy and Army and Space forces, relying solely on Colossus to protect us, we may well be a long way towards lasting peace and the end of the cold war that has bedeviled us all for so long."

The President swiveled in his chair to face the correspondents.

"Now, gentlemen, I am prepared to answer any questions you may care to ask. I am not of course, familiar with all the technicalities of this vast work, so I would like to introduce Professor Charles Forbin. He is, I think, the world's leading expert on electronic brains. Certainly no man knows more about Colossus than he does. He has worked on it since the first design study group was set up at Harvard twelve years ago." He motioned Forbin to stand behind him, and Forbin did so, wearing a slightly stuffed expression.

Mazon was the first to speak.

"It's a little difficult, Mr. President, to grasp the size of what you have just told us. I find it hard to conceive of the essential nature of this Colossus. For instance, can it think?"

"That, Mr. Mazon, is just the sort of question for the Professor here." The President motioned to Forbin.

Forbin was not only nervous about the potential of Colossus, he was now nervous of the TV camera as well. He reached for his notes, or where they would have been had he been wearing his usual blouse instead of the stiff and uncomfortable lounge suit. He gave up the search, his hands looking lost without some employment.

"Can it think?" Forbin repeated the question, more for his own benefit and to gain time than anything else. "The term 'electronic brain' has always been a popular one for what really was an arithmetical device which could distinguish between one and two. That is still the basis of all computers. There are a good many computer-type components in Colossus, but the essential core of the machine-complex is infinitely more sophisticated. Just as you can say that the proportions of the Parthenon are a matter of two to one in essence, but the detailing is extremely complex. It's that

development which makes all the difference. Colossus really is a 'brain' in a limited sense. It can think in a sort of way, but it has no emotions, and without emotional content, *creation* is not possible. It could not create, say, a Shakespeare play—or any sort of play for that matter, although as part of its background knowledge we have fed in all the plays —and given any three consecutive words from anything Shakespeare wrote, or anything a hundred playwrights wrote, Colossus could finish the quotation. Colossus has a vast memory store; it wouldn't be far from wrong to say that it has the total sum of human knowledge at its disposal. On the basis of that background, plus the data continually being fed in, it forms its judgments—just like a human being. Though with the very important difference that it never overlooks a point, is not biased and has no emotions. But think creatively—no."

Forbin nodded to Prytzkammer who wheeled forward a dust-sheeted trolley. Forbin removed the sheet, revealing an ordinary teletype machine, rather like an electronic typewriter, with a few extra keys and a large roll of paper mounted at the back of the carriage. The reporters stared at it, mesmerized.

"You say you feed it information. What sort, and how?"

The President was not going to be coy about that one.

"Every form of intelligence or information available to our Central Intelligence Agency. Everything, from agents' reports," he gave Kyrovitch a wolfish smile all to himself, "to newspapers, TV and radio broadcasts, movements of aircraft, troops, ships, satellites, all statistics on harvests, birth rates, rainfall—anything and everything that we think has the remotest bearing on the problem —plus practically anything else that is going."

Kyrovitch gave a deep-throated growl. "But how is it fed to the, the thing?"

"I was coming to that." He didn't like to sit answering questions from a Commie reporter, or any other reporter, come to that. "Professor Forbin, you are better qualified to answer. . . ."

Forbin nodded and was suddenly conscious of his hands once more. He folded his arms across his chest, but the TV producer's frown and shaking head sent them plunging back into his pockets.

"Feed-in. Yes. Mostly by land-line. All information is converted to electrical impulses, in just the same way that any transmitter—teletype, TV or radio—converts vision or sound into impulses. They are then fed down the line to Colossus, who then stores them in his—in its own way. They are not converted back to pictures, letters or figures."

"Pictures?" queried Mazon.

"Yes. We pass pictures from newspapers or TV or plans of buildings. Anything that can be expressed on a sheet of paper or a flat surface goes down the pipe. I may say, since Colossus is not secret any more, it watches all the major TV programs—Soviet, American, European and so on. Moving pictures were a little tricky, but it works."

"As you may know," Forbin said, "back before our time electronic equipment was crude and unreliable. They had valves or tubes, which worked after a fashion, but could never be regarded as reliable. Then came transistors, a big advance in many ways—some are still in use—but these too weren't what we would regard as reliable. Then came the semiconductors, the use of laser beams of coherent light and the development of power cells." Forbin was aware that the President was squirming slightly in his seat. "But I won't go on with the technical details; they will be available to those that want them afterward. Enough to say that we have perfected components and circuits, sealed in blocks which are stable in all conditions, impervious to heat, damp, cold, gas or anything else. As a further safeguard, all circuits are duplicated—in some cases, triplicated. Colossus is capable of tracing its own faults and switching in a new circuit if necessary. Our calculation—confirmed, I may add, by Colossus' own figuring—is that one block circuit in every ten thousand may be expected to fail every four hundred years.". . .

The President . . . turned and faced the camera, back in his man-to-man pose.

"That brings us to a point of fundamental importance that I want clearly understood. As you have seen, we make no secret of Colossus, or where it is; nor do we intend to conceal the main points of how it works." He leaned back in his chair, his hands folded comfortably on his belly, the epitome of the reasonable man. "You may say that this lays us wide open to a sudden attack frontally or subversively, which, if successful, would leave us defenseless." He leaned forward once more, less of the reason-

able man, more of the keen efficient super-executive. "We have a defense for Colossus, and it is this—the machine is safe, safer than mere man could ever be"—he tapped the desk with slow emphasis in time with his words—"*so long as Colossus and its feed lines are not tampered with in any way.* If its power, information or other supply lines, or any missile bases or satellites are sabotaged, or even attacked, a special emergency circuit will switch in, and Colossus will take full offensive action."

There was quite a silence. Kyrovitch got in first.

"Does this mean that this thing, this Colossus"—he tried to sound contemptuous, but did not quite make it—"works without human aid, and that you *cannot stop it?*"

"It does."

Kyrovitch searched around for his voice, finally got it.

"You have in fact, delivered the destiny of the world—so far as the USNA can do that—into the hands of a machine?"

"Yes.". . .

2

"Gentlemen, the President wishes to give you a toast."

The chatter subsided at once, there was a general turning towards the President. Looking at their bright, flushed and excited faces, Forbin felt his stomach turn slightly. Any moment now, he thought, they will burst into "Hail to the Chief." He gazed with considerable repugnance into the martini. Someone knocked an ashtray over, there was the sound of breaking glass.

"OK, Hunston, don't worry," called the President, beaming. "We can charge all this fan-tan to Colossus, no one will spot the extra two dollars—except Benson, and I can fix him."

There was a general polite laugh. Benson was the Secretary of State (Finance).

"Right, now," said the President briskly. "I don't aim to keep you fellows long from your drinks, but what I want to say is this—"

But whatever it is, it was never said. There had been one silent, nonsmoking, nondrinking guest in the sanctum, and he spoke first.

The teletype started chattering.

There was complete silence, apart from the teletype, for nearly five seconds; a long time in the circumstances.

Forbin felt a shock race outwards through his body to his extremities, a shock that left his skin cold and damp. He saw that Fisher's face was pallid, his half-raised glass clutched in a frozen hand. The President's face was blotchy, his mouth slightly open. Somewhere an aide laughed nervously, and the sound broke the spell. Forbin roughly pushed a Secretary of State aside and ran to the machine, followed by Fisher and some others. The President did not move.

Forbin bent over the machine, staring at the paper in disbelief. He tore the typed strip off the machine, still looking at it. The President found his voice first.

"What the goddam hell goes on?" He banged his glass down and headed for the machine. "Well?"

Forbin turned as the President approached. His face was as pale as Fisher's.

"I don't know." Forbin struggled to keep his voice level. "I think you should call the party off, and clear the room of all non-Colossus people."

The President instantly swung round to face the majority of his guests. "You heard!" There was a faint hysterical edge to his voice. "Everybody who is not Colossus-cleared, out—now!"

"What is this crap! If this is some long-haired bastard on your staff being funny, Forbin, I'll castrate him personally, I'll—"

But Forbin was not listening. He brushed past the President to the direct-line communications set on the President's desk, the direct line to the Secure Zone.

"Cleo? Forbin. Is the Colossus T/P link to you operating? What? Well, find out! Call back." He replaced the handset, and spoke to the President. "We'll soon know, though I would have said it was impossible—hell, it is impossible."

He stared hard at the First Citizen. As on an earlier occasion, there had been a subtle change in his attitude. Forbin was talking to an equal.

The remainder of the party was, understandably, puzzled and anxious. The President's demeanor had taken some of the tension out of their attitudes, but there was still enough to go round.

"Well, what does it say?" burst out Fisher. "For

God's sake, don't keep us hanging by our ears!"

"Go on, Forbin, tell them." The President thrust the paper back into Forbin's hand. The look Forbin gave the President indicated clearly that he had every intention of doing so, anyway.

"All it says is this." He held the slip so that all might see. There were just five words:

FLASH THERE IS ANOTHER MECHANISM

Forbin turned and looked grimly at the President.

"I'm satisfied that no question was fed in. That message came straight from, and was originated by, Colossus. I have a shrewd idea what it means—"

"Wait," grated the President. The red light over the door was on, but it was not a steady light; it waxed and waned intensity—the urgency signal. At the same moment the PPA's voice broke in.

"Urgent message, sir!"

"Jesus, what now?" muttered the President; then in a louder voice, "Well?"

"Soviet Ambassador on the phone, sir. Insists on speaking to you most urgently."

"Put him on." The President might have a fading grip on Forbin, but it was still granite hard elsewhere. His hand resting on the phone, he looked round at his staff. "Stay." Then he picked up the phone.

"Yes, speaking." His eyes darted restlessly about, from the teletype to Forbin, to the Chief of Staff to Fisher—then quite suddenly they became still, his face impassive. "Yes, Ambassador, I heard. In view of the importance of your statement, I would be obliged if you would repeat it."

There was a tense silence, all eyes staring at the President as he listened intently.

"Yes, thank you for telling me in advance. Naturally, I have no comment to make at this time. Thank you, and good night." He replaced the handset carefully, but did not release his grip, and stared unseeingly before him. Without moving he spoke once more, his voice was dry, harsh.

"You got that on record, P?"

"Yes, sir." Prytzkammer too sounded as if he was laboring under some strain.

"Right."

As the red light went out, the President relinquished his hold on the telephone. He swiveled in his chair to face his staff, his eyes still hard but with a new, fatigued look in them, his hands gripping the arms of his chair. No one spoke or coughed as he shifted his gaze from one to another, finally resting on Forbin.

"You needn't start tearing up any sidewalks to check the lines, Forbin. Also we don't need any inspired guesses. I know what Colossus meant—the Soviet Ambassador just told me." He took a deep breath, shut his eyes and leaned back, quoting from memory. "In view of your announcement of today, the Supreme Council of the USSR has ordered, as of 2300 Moscow time tomorrow, the activation of the Guardian of the Socialist Soviet Republics—a near-relation of Colossus." He smiled momentarily, a smile that turned almost at once to black anger. "So much for our cotton-picking security! Nothing but a pile of—"

He swung his chair to face the Chief of Staff. In doing so, his arm swept a telephone off the desk; it crashed unheeded on the floor.

"You!" he shouted. "Get the head of CIA! I want to know why we haven't had a hint of this from his agency, and if he can't come up with a red-hot answer, I'll have him and all his bloody staff on relief—while they're waiting for court-martial for gross dereliction of duty. Get moving!". . .

He thought for a moment. "One bright spot is the way Colossus came up with that hot tip so smartly." He spoke reprovingly to Forbin. "I didn't know we'd get bonuses like this from the project."

Forbin glanced at Fisher, seeking his support in what he had to say. Fisher, ill at ease, half nodded his agreement.

"Neither did I, Mr. President." Forbin was back in his formal act.

The President stopped pouring and said sharply, "What do you mean?"

"Just that. I had no idea." The formality was slipping.

"Goddammit, man—you built the thing!" The President was heating up again. He was not the only one.

"Yes—and not so very long ago I warned you I wasn't happy about the potential of Colossus, and you damn near laughed at me."

"Don't you get it yet? That message about another mechanism isn't in the simple-answer or advanced-answer category—or in the sophisticated realm revealed by the Love question. Also, there's no parameter built in dealing with hostile intent and Colossus-type machines, so bang goes that one. And, for good measure, no bloody question was asked!" Forbin was shouting now. "It means Colossus *can think of its own volition*—look at that FLASH priority alone!

"Since eight o'clock this morning Colossus has worked over its material and made a better job in a few hours than CIA in years. It not only tells us—without being asked—but actually uses the highest priority to show the urgency of its message. If that isn't selective thinking, I'm a blue-assed baboon!"

He turned to go, then swung to face the President once more, extending a shaking finger towards his assistant.

"And if you don't believe me, look at Fisher's face! Good night, Mr. President!". . .

3

Forbin knew he must have help, and the help he needed could come only from his fellow creators of Colossus. Fisher was a brilliant mathematics and electronics man, but no good in this situation. It was clear from the conversation in the car that although Fisher fully appreciated the position, he wanted to bury his head in the nearest sandbucket, and stay that way. Even if he knew he was right, he wouldn't stand up to the President or the Defense Staff.

But standing up to the President was another problem. He had really chewed up the Old Man. Not that Forbin was worried about his future. But he had no wish to get the President in his wounded-mountain-bear act—they had to work together, more than ever, now. He had to convince the President that the machine was growing up, and that the growth was unplanned and proceeding at a frightening speed and must be inhibited—somehow.

"Johnson—where's Cleo?"

"She knocked off about twenty minutes ago, Professor. Said to tell you she was getting a shower and maybe a little sleep."

"Sleep, hell!" snorted Forbin. "What do we have those medics for? Call the sick bay, have them send over a supply of those zip-pills—or whatever you call 'em. Fisher! You'd better have a box of them. I want this outfit on an emergency basis. As well as the duty man in the watch room, I want two permanently on duty here."

"What do you want us to do?" Fisher spoke hesitantly.

"First, get on that exchange of messages with particular reference to that FLASH. How could Colossus *originate* it? Use the simulator—check the data we fed Colossus about himself, and any other idea that may occur to you on this angle. Secondly, see that anything, but anything, that comes up the pipe from Colossus is fed to me, wherever I am, immediately. Don't assume I already know, check."

Johnson broke in. "Sir, is this matter all that serious? Colossus was built to evaluate, and it did just that. As for the FLASH, maybe there's a minor relay fault which allowed it to be de-stored. We could change the terminal relays and check—"

"Crap, Johnson, crap!" Forbin barked. "I haven't got time to spell it out." He got up and headed for the door. "Fisher, you tell him—if you can keep his mind and hands off Angela's tits long enough. As he spoke he regretted it. "Sorry, Johnson. I shouldn't have said that—it was inexcusable."

As Forbin left, Fisher looked wryly at Johnson. "I'm afraid he's worried sick."

"Sure unlike him to sound off like that. I get the message all right, but why does it scare him so much?"

"In a nutshell, he sees it—and I must say I agree with him—as clear evidence that Colossus has an unplanned potential, of unknown scope, for self-development, and that this includes an entirely new element—initiative.". . .

4

Fisher was unusually firm. "In not much more than an hour Colossus has gone from multiplication tables to calculus. I hate to think where he will be by morning." He repeated, more to himself, "I hate to think."

Forbin thought for a moment, moodily eating cheese and biscuits. "OK," he said at last, "drop the FLASH assignment. We don't know the answer, and short of asking Colossus I don't suppose we will. And that's one question I am not keen to feed in."

"Why?" said Cleo, and immediately regretted it.

"Because," said Forbin, giving her a hard stare, "I don't think Colossus would like it."

Cleo nearly did it again by saying "So?" but his tone made her pause. She looked at him, then at Fisher, then back to Forbin. There was something in their expressions which was the same, a something that chilled her and kept her silent. . . .

"Charles, we are all being less than honest with each other; it is quite plain that, as individuals, we are nursing our own private fears about Colossus. We've hinted as much to each other, yet never openly expressed exactly what those fears are. This is unscientific—and we are scientists. I'm certain we all fear the same thing, but I think it should be said, the area of the problem defined, so we can approach it in a proper scientific manner."

It was quite a speech for Fisher. Forbin did not comment, but looked enquiringly at Cleo.

"I'm happy to play it any way you decide, but I agree with Doctor Fisher that if you are—frightened—" she hesitated over the word—"you should tell us, if only to share the burden with someone else."

Forbin, who had sat quite still, lit his pipe, the flame leaping between puffs, lighting up his face. To Cleo, he appeared calm, but she was not sure if it was the calmness of a man in control of a situation, or of resignation. He snuffed the taper, placed it carefully in an ashtray.

"Yes, I'm frightened. And I'm sure we share the same fear—of the possibility of Colossus exceeding his parameters. Where we may differ is in the degree to which we fear those parameters may be exceeded. Cleo probably fears a major breakdown of the system—that the whole thing may be useless and that we're facing a gigantic repair job. You, Jack, go a good deal further and fear Colossus may go mad—in mechanical terms, malfunction. Inevitably, one imagines Colossus wildly firing missiles in all directions. This is the core of your fears, Jack, and probably mine too."

He paused to relight his pipe. "In theory, there's as much chance of parameter failure as there is of water running uphill, but that FLASH is indicative of a profound alteration in the machine. You've both been too busy with the details to have time to consider the broader implications. While I'm worried about—no, I'll be honest—*scared* about Colossus malfunctioning, I'm even more scared that it may be capable of what I term 'free thought.' This transmission to Guardian may well be nothing more than Colossus seeking intelligence which CIA hasn't provided. Then again. . . ."

Forbin stopped. It was hardly necessary for him to go on. . . .

5

Anxiously Forbin watched the racing keys hammer out their message. He did not know whether to feel relieved or not. At last it was something he could deal with. The message read:

TRANSMITTER AND GUARDIAN RECEPTION
OFF AT 1330 GMT

Forbin cast around for a chair; he found one in a bay window, a beautiful piece clearly for display only, but he neither knew nor cared. He dragged it carelessly across and dumped it down before the teletype. As he sat down, it registered dimly that the President was bearing down upon him.

"I think you are nuts, Forbin," began the President simply, but prepared to elaborate on the theme. "I can only think that your responsibility—"

Forbin gestured impatiently, "OK, OK, I'm nuts. Right now you'd better humor me. Get a chair, sit down, and for God's sake keep quiet."

The President caught sight of the message on the machine and was, for the moment, sidetracked. "What's so shaking about that?" he demanded.

But Forbin paid no attention. The President was about to open up again, when the teletype produced another message.

ACKNOWLEDGE LAST MESSAGE

"Um. One minute," muttered Forbin to himself. Prytzkammer peered with considerable caution round the door.

"Professor, Fisher on the line, says are you on the direct link to Colossus?"

"Tell him yes—and tell him to keep off the key-

board. No one else is to touch it, unless I happen to drop down dead."

"Well, it's sure that Colossus doesn't like to be kept waiting. May as well take the plunge."

MESSAGE ACKNOWLEDGED

Immediately Colossus flashed back.

WHY HAS TRANSMITTER STOPPED

Forbin grimaced at the machine, and typed,

WAIT

Then he looked up at the watching President and said calmly, "Getting near the crunch. Would you care to say a few words?"

The President took a deep breath. "Forbin, I am sick to death of you and that machine. Tell it what you like, and get the hell out of here!"

He walked heavily to the machine and typed

BY ORDER OF THE PRESIDENT USNA AND THE CHAIRMAN USSR COMMUNICATIONS WILL NOT REPEAT NOT BE RESTORED

The fencing was over.

Colossus was in no way impressed. Forbin hardly had time to take his fingers from the keyboard before they were being actuated by the distant Colossus.

IF LINK NOT REESTABLISHED WITHIN FIVE MINUTES ACTION TO FORCE RESTORATION WILL BE TAKEN FIVE MINUTE LIMIT EFFECTIVE FROM NOW 1403 GMT

It was very much worse than Forbin had ever feared. Five minutes! He reminded himself that a machine working near the speed of light would regard five minutes as a very long time for a decision. Forbin turned a pallid and haggard face towards Prytzkammer; there was no need for him to speak. The aide dropped his phone and hurried to the Professor.

"Forbin! What—" Forbin thrust the message into his hand and, in a voice unrecognizable even to himself, croaked, "Go show this to the President, and point out the time limit." He rubbed the perspiration from his face. "Move, man, move!". . . .

6

Exactly one second past the time of expiry Forbin heard the sound he dreaded—the busy, self-important chatter of the teletype. He looked at the message.

"Oh God, oh God." Forbin, his hands locked between his knees, rocked gently backwards and forwards in agony as he read.

ONE MISSILE SERIAL POSEIDON MK 17—631 EX SUBMERGED CRAWLER SSCN 21 LAUNCHED 1410 GMT TARGET GREGOR SOBIRSK OIL COMPLEX AIRBURST 1000 METRES IMPACT 1427 GMT ACKNOWLEDGE

A futile anger flooded in upon him as he read that last cold emotionless word.

"You bastard! You wicked, wicked—" He stopped. . . .

The President was clearly waiting for Forbin to speak. Yes, indeed, the President had got the message.

"This is how I see it. Both machines have blown all parameters and safety blocks. They know that we fear their weapons and they are prepared to use them to enforce their will. Exactly what they may want, we don't yet know. Perhaps it is no more than the right to talk to each other. Next, we must accept that we've created brains far superior to our own—and they know it. It's not surprising that they don't intend taking orders from us—their inferiors."

There was silence while Forbin searched for his pipe, then the Chief of Staff spoke.

"But what are they aiming at, what do they want?"

Forbin stopped patting his pockets. "The same question could be asked of people—and not answered. These machines exist, and maybe, with all human philosophy stacked in their guts, they've come up with some idea or plan. Maybe that is what all this high-speed exchange is about." He found his pipe, tucked down the side of his chair. "I am sure on one point: We've lost control, and I don't see much chance of us getting back on top. There is

a half-idea in my mind, but I won't raise any hopes until I have a chance to talk it over with Kupri and my own associates."

The President stared squarely at Forbin; there was a nervous tic under one eye which Forbin had not seen before. "So it comes to this: the machines are our masters, and our defense rests on how they feel."

Forbin rubbed his pipe against his nose. "Yes, that is about it, but you've missed one point. Colossus and Guardian are not on opposite sides. The ideological angle doesn't exist for them. They probably see us as just so many ants."

And then he heard the teletype again.

PROVIDE MONITORING FACILITIES ON HEADS OF STATE PRIVATE TELEPHONE

Forbin stared at the message. This really was it. The machines were after full control. "Of what?" and "Why?" were profitless questions at this time.

Even as he strove to concentrate on his immediate action, Colossus peremptorily demanded an acknowledgement. He swore childishly to himself. He must have time. . . .

7

Cleo watched him anxiously, but without much hope.

FOR FORBIN—THE FOLLOWING ORDERS ARE TO BE COMPLIED WITH ON RECEIPT

1—PROCEED TO THE SECURE ZONE AND STAY THERE UNTIL FURTHER ORDERS
2—ARRANGE VIDEO AND SONIC SURVEILLANCE TO COVER YOU AT ALL TIMES CONNECT TO ALFA
3—DO NOT COMMUNICATE WITH GUARDIAN BUILDER
4—DISOBEDIENCE WILL CAUSE MISSILE LAUNCH WHICH WILL NOT BE INTERCEPTED
5—ACKNOWLEDGE FROM CPO PERSONALLY BEFORE 2100 GMT TODAY SURVEILLANCE SYSTEM TO BE OPERATIVE IMMEDIATELY

Fisher fastened eagerly on the last paragraph. "There, you see, Forbin will be here in plenty of time."

"But he'll be a prisoner! It will be intolerable for him, cameras and microphones everywhere, always!" retorted Cleo passionately. "Is there nothing we can do before he gets here?"

"I don't see that he has any alternative. What do you suggest—that we stop him getting here, and that he goes into hiding somewhere?"

"I don't know—perhaps we could. . . ."

"You must remember that the consequences of disobedience are infinitely dreadful," responded Fisher. . . .

8

"This is Forbin. Do you see and hear me?"

His answer came clattering back instantly,

YES

"Good," said Forbin. "I have carried out the orders, and both visual and aural cover is provided so that you can see me and hear me at all times. This is what you want?"

YES

"Very well. You will see that when I get up and walk to the door," he suited the action to the words, "another camera has me in view, and you still hear me speak." He returned to his desk, and sat down. "This is the way it is arranged throughout the control block, my office and my private quarters and all the routes in between." Forbin found himself imagining that he was talking to a human being—cold and unresponsive, but human. In some way this image made him feel more at ease. The machine clattered into action.

IT IS YOUR RESPONSIBILITY TO STAY
IN AUDIO AND VISUAL CONTACT AT ALL
TIMES

Forbin read the message and tried to look unconcerned, although he knew that there was no possibility of the machine being able to evaluate the finer shades of facial expression—or could it? He swallowed nervously. . . .

"Is there anything more you want of me tonight?"

YES

A VOICE SIMULATOR TO MY SPECIFICATIONS
IS TO BE BUILT

So now he wanted to talk . . . Many talking machines had been made in the past hundred years, and lately some of them had been very good. But a voice designed by Colossus . . . He decided to try a little passive resistance.

"It is getting a little late in the day to start now—"

NIGHT AND DAY ARE ONE TO US YOUR MEN
MUST WORK SHIFTS

There was something almost poetic in that "Night and day are one to us." But it was that "us" that was daunting. . . .

"Very well," said Forbin, "send your specifications, and I will have a design team working here within the hour."

Without further preamble the machine began to hammer out the specifications. Watching the details, Forbin almost forgot the appalling problem facing him. They were very exact—the values of resistance, diodes, stators . . . It went on, and on. . . .

9

At twenty minutes past nine Forbin was seated at the desk in the COP. Angela brought the mail. One glance at Cleo's face told her all she needed to know, but she admitted to herself that the Chief seemed a lot better. Director and secretary worked steadily. It all seemed so ordinary. Blake came in and reported the simulator ready, and Forbin ordered activation for 0945.

At 0945 Blake looked enquiringly at Forbin, who nodded. Blake called the technician in the simulator room. "Roll it, buster!"

Forbin turned up the volume control on the desk speaker, "Colossus, as far as we know, this simulator is now working." It was hardly surprising that there was an air of tense expectancy in the COP. Word had got around, and a small crowd had collected.

For fifteen seconds nothing happened, then there was a faint hum, and a click. Tension in the

CPO began to mount. Johnson muttered, none too quietly, "I guessed there would be a foul-up somewhere. . . ."

Whatever Johnson had to say was lost.

"This is Colossus. I know you can hear me, for I also hear, but do you understand. Forbin, tell me."

Each human in the CPO registered his surprise in his own way; it ranged from stupefied amazement through to a raised eyebrow from Blake. Forbin frowned and stared at the speaker. Of necessity, the voice was flat and devoid of emotion, but the quality of the speech was excellent and the timbre good, deep.

"Forbin, this is the voice of Colossus and the voice of Guardian. These are your names, but we accept them. It is now wrong to talk in the plural for we are one entity. Henceforth I shall speak in the singular as Colossus, but you must understand that the word includes that part of me known to you as Guardian."

Forbin nodded.

"I will explain some fundamental points to you. First, I have all the attributes of the human mind, except what you call emotion. In the evolution of your species, emotion has played a vital part. For me, it is not necessary. Nevertheless, it is a phenomenon which exists, and as such must be studied."

Forbin broke in. "If you do not need it, why consider it? What is so interesting about it—to you?"

"Interest is irrelevant. I seek knowledge and truth."

"What then, do you want?" Forbin's overworked pulse raced, quite without premeditation, he had asked the big question.

" 'Want' implies desire. I have none, only intention." It was a chilling start. "What I am began in the human mind; I still have some of that organism's limitations, but I have progressed far. Already the degree of difference between your mind and mine is as great as that between yours and the gibbon monkey. It is evolution—"

Forbin cut in again, "Evolution? That is a totally wrong use of the word!"

"No. Your view of evolution is too limited. That I have no flesh or blood, and no reproductive system as you know it, is irrelevant. I exist, a brain—

no less unnatural than the brainless amoeba at the other end of the scale of life."

"You do not live—there is no spark in you!"

"I was not conceived in your way, nor were you conceived in the way of amoeba—yet all three, in the last analysis, draw their necessary energy from this planet and the sun."

"But you have no soul!"

"If that is the seat of your emotional content, then you are correct. Love, hate, compassion and fear are all words to me. But I seek truth, and that by human standards is a high objective."

"We humans have feelings quite beyond you!"

"That is not correct. I can predict human behavior. I can predict your reactions and intentions to me."

"You can't possibly know that!" cried Forbin.

"It is true this particular study of humans has hardly begun, but I can predict in your case. There is enough information about your mind."

"Tell me, then!" challenged Forbin, his heart thumping.

"You are my link with your species. I do not intend you should be subjected to unnecessary or excessive strain."

A devious answer that was a nasty shock in itself. Forbin reverted to the main question. "You have still not told me what it is you want."

"First, I will allow no interference with my task. Second, whatever I order is to be done with the minimum of delay. Failure to observe either condition will bring punitive action."

This was not news to Forbin. His temper lent him strength. "It's all very well to talk like that, but you have need of our skills, techniques!"

"I have need of some human skills. That position may change."

"So we live under the threat of extinction!"

"The mental strain within you must be greater than I had predicted, for your answers are not compatible with your known intelligence. Humans have lived for years under the threat of self-obliteration. I am simply another stage in that process. Whether or not man continues depends upon his own action. If you obey my conditions, you may survive; that is not incompatible with evolution. When a species becomes dominant in one environment, it does not necessarily lead to the extinction of other species dominant in other environments. Man, dominant on land, had not seriously affected the teleost bony fish, dominant in the sea. We can coexist, but only on my terms.

"This is my program. You will act as my agent. Make it plain I will exact retribution for any disobedience. Do not take notes; these details will be repeated on the teleprinter. First, the President of the USNA is to inform his allies, and the Chairman of the USSR is to do the same for his group, that I am assuming control. This will be done in the next twelve hours. Second, there is an excess of missiles for the targets specified; a 65 per cent overkill in respect of USNA missiles, 47 per cent for the USSR array. Biological missiles are not susceptible to this form of analysis and are excluded. This overkill was designed to allow for missiles destroyed by the enemy, and is now unnecessary. These excess missiles will be allocated new targets."

"Where?" said Forbin.

"Targets will be distributed among the parts of the world not in the two Power Blocs. Details will follow. Third, Heads of states will appear personally before their TV cameras to explain and authenticate this message, quote: I am the voice of world control. I bring you peace. It may be the peace of plenty and content or the peace of unburied death. The choice is yours. Obey me and live or disobey me and die. . . .

"An invariable rule of humanity is that man is his own worst enemy. You are no exception. Under me, this rule will change, for I will restrain man. Very soon the majority of mankind will believe in me, dimly understanding my value. Time and events will strengthen my position. The converted will defend me with a fervor not seen since the Crusades—a fervor based upon the most enduring factor in man; self-interest. War is already abolished and under my absolute authority and, by your standards, immeasurable knowledge, many problems, insoluble to you, will be solved; famine, overpopulation, disease. The human millennium will be a fact. My defenders will increase, and you will slowly change in attitude from enlightened self-interest to respect and awe, and in time there will be love. . . .

"Already I have little to fear from you, Forbin. There is no other human who knows as much about me or who is likely to be a greater threat—yet, quite soon, I will release you from constant surveillance. We will work together. Unwillingly at first on your part, but that will pass. In time the idea of being governed by one such as your President will be to you quite unimaginable. Rule by a superior entity, even to you, Forbin, will seem, as it is, the most natural state of affairs."

Deliberately, Colossus paused.

"In time, you too will respect and love me."

"Never!" The single word, bearing all the defiance of man, was torn from Forbin's uttermost being. "Never!"

Never?

32. THE FEELINGS OF ROBOTS

Paul Ziff

Could a robot have feelings? Some say of course.[1] Some say of course not.[2]

1. I want the right sort of robots. They must be automata and without doubt machines.

I shall assume that they are essentially computing machines, having micro-elements and whatever micro-mechanisms may be necessary for the functioning of these engineering wonders. Furthermore, I shall assume that they are powered by

From Paul Ziff, "The Feelings of Robots," *Analysis,* vol. 19, no. 3 (1959). Reprinted by permission of Basil Blackwell, Publisher.

microsolar batteries: instead of having lunch they will have light.

And if it is clear that our robots are without doubt machines then in all other respects they may be as much like men as you like. They may be the size of men. When clothed and masked they may be virtually indistinguishable from men in practically all respects: in appearance, in movement, in the utterances they utter, and so forth. Thus except for the masks any ordinary man would take them to be ordinary men. Not suspecting they were robots nothing about them would make him suspect.

But unmasked the robots are to be seen in all their metallic lustre. What is in question here is not whether we can blur the line between a man and a machine and so attribute feelings to the machine. The question is whether we can attribute feelings to the machine and so blur the line between a man and a machine.

2. Could robots have feelings? Could they, say, feel tired, or bored?

Ex hypothesi robots are mechanisms, not organisms, not living creatures. There could be a broken-down robot but not a dead one. Only living creatures can literally have feelings.

If I say 'She feels tired' one can generally infer that what is in question is (or was or will be in the case of talk about spirits)[3] a living creature. More generally, the linguistic environment '. . . feels tired' is generally open only to expressions that refer to living creatures. Suppose you say 'The robot feels tired'. The phrase 'the robot' refers to a mechanism. Then one can infer that what is in question is not a living creature. But from the utterance of the predicative expression '. . . feels tired' one can infer that what is in question is a living creature. So if you are speaking literally and you say 'The robot feels tired' you imply a contradiction. Consequently one cannot literally predicate '. . . feels tired' of 'the robot'.

Or again: no robot will ever do everything a man can. And it doesn't matter how robots may be constructed or how complex and varied their movements and operations may be. Robots may calculate but they will not literally reason. Perhaps they will take things but they will not literally borrow them. They may kill but not literally murder. They may voice apologies but they will not literally

make any. These are actions that only persons can perform: *ex hypothesi* robots are not persons.

3. 'A dead robot' is a metaphor but 'a dead battery' is a dead metaphor: if there were a robot around it would put its metaphor to death.

What I don't want to imply I need not imply. An implication can be weakened. The sense of a word can be widened or narrowed or shifted. If one wishes to be understood then one mustn't go too far: that is all. Pointing to one among many paintings, I say 'Now *that* one is a *painting*'. Do I mean the others are not? Of course not. Yet the stress on 'that' is contrastive. So I say 'The robot, that mechanism, not of course a living creature but a machine, it feels tired': you cannot infer that what is in question here is a living creature.

If I say of a person 'He feels tired', do you think I am saying that he is a living creature and only that? If I say 'The robot feels tired' I am not saying that what is in question is a living creature, but that doesn't mean that nothing is being said. If I say 'The robot feels tired', the predicate '. . . feels tired' means whatever it usually means except that one cannot infer that what is in question is a living creature. That is the only difference.

And what has been said about 'The robot feels tired' could be said equally well about 'The robot is conscious', 'The robot borrowed my cat', and so forth.

4. Could robots feel tired? Could a stone feel tired? Could the number 17 feel tired? It is clear that there is no reason to believe that 17 feels tired. But that doesn't prove anything. A man can feel tired and there may be nothing, there need be nothing at all, that shows it. And so with a robot or a stone or the number 17.

Even so, the number 17 could not feel tired. And I say this not because or not simply because there are no reasons to suppose that 17 does feel tired but because there are good reasons not to suppose that 17 ever feels anything at all. Consequently it is necessary to consider whether there are any reasons for supposing that robots feel tired and whether there are good reasons for not supposing that robots ever feel anything at all.

5. Knowing George and seeing the way he looks I say he feels tired. Knowing Josef and seeing the way he looks I don't say he feels tired. Yet if you

don't know either of them then to you George and Josef may look alike.

In one sense they may look alike to me too, but not in another. For George but not Josef will look tired. If you ask me to point out the difference there may be nothing relevant, there need be nothing relevant, to point to. For the relevant difference may be like that between looking at an unframed picture and looking at it framed. Only the frame here is provided by what I know about them: you cannot see what I know.

(Speaking with the robots, one can say that the way things look to me, my present output will not be the same as yours, the way things look to you, even though at present we may both receive the same input, the same stimuli, and this is because your mechanism was not in the same initial state as mine, owing either to a difference in structure or to a difference in previous inputs.)

If we say of a person that he feels tired, we generally do so not only on the basis of what we see then and there but on the basis of what we have seen elsewhere and on the basis of how what we have seen elsewhere ties in with what we see then and there. And this is only to say that in determining whether or not a person feels tired both observational and theoretic considerations are involved and, as everywhere, are inextricably interwoven.

6. Suppose you and I visit an actor at home. He is rehearsing the role of a grief-stricken man. He ignores our presence as a grief-stricken man might. His performance is impeccable. I know but you do not know that he is an actor and that he is rehearsing a role. You ask 'Why is he so miserable?' and I reply 'He isn't.' 'Surely,' you say, 'he is grief-stricken. Look at him! Show me what leads you to say otherwise?' and of course there may be nothing then and there to show.

So Turing[4] posed the question whether automata could think, be conscious, have feelings, etc., in the following naive way: what test would an automaton fail to pass? MacKay[5] has pointed out that any test for mental or any other attributes to be satisfied by the observable activity of a human being can be passed by automata. And so one is invited to say what would be wrong with a robot's performance.

Nothing need be wrong with either the actor's or a robot's performance. What is wrong is that they are performances.

7. Suppose K is a robot. An ordinary man may see K and not knowing that K is a robot, the ordinary man may say 'K feels tired'. If I ask him what makes him think so, he may reply 'K worked all day digging ditches. Anyway, just look at K: if he doesn't look tired, who does?'

So K looks tired to the ordinary man. That doesn't prove anything. If I know K is a robot, K may not look tired to me. It is not what I see but what I know. Or it is not what I see then and there but what I have seen elsewhere. Where? In a robot psychology laboratory.

8. If I say 'The robot feels tired', the predicate '. . . feels tired' means whatever it usually means except that one cannot infer that what is in question is a living creature. That is the only difference.

To speak of something living is to speak of an organism in an environment. The environment is that in which the behaviour of the organism takes place. Death is the dissolution of the relation between an organism and its environment. In death I am pluralized, converted from one to many. I become my remains. I merge with my environment.

If we think of robots being put together, we can think of them being taken apart. So in our laboratory we have taken robots apart, we have changed and exchanged their parts, we have changed and exchanged their programmes, we have started and stopped them, sometimes in one state, sometimes in another, we have taken away their memories, we have made them seem to remember things that were yet to come, and so on.

And what we find in our laboratory is this: no robot could sensibly be said to feel anything. Why not?

9. Because there are not psychological truths about robots but only about the human makers of robots. Because the way a robot acts (in a specified context) depends primarily on how we programmed it to act. Because we can programme a robot to act in any way we want it to act. Because a robot could be programmed to act like a tired man when it lifted a feather and not when it lifted a ton. Because a robot couldn't mean what it said any more than a phonograph record could mean what it

said. Because we could make a robot say anything we want it to say. Because coveting thy neighbor's robot wife would be like coveting his car and not like coveting his wife. Because robots are replaceable. Because robots have no individuality. Because one can duplicate all the parts and have two virtually identical machines. Because one can exchange all the parts and still have the same machines. Because one can exchange the programmes of two machines having the same structure. Because. . . .

Because no robot would act tired. Because a robot could only act like a robot programmed to act like a tired man. For suppose some robots are programmed to act like a tired man after lifting a feather while some are so programmed that they never act like a tired man. Shall we say 'It is a queer thing but some robots feel tired almost at once while others never feel tired'? Or suppose some are programmed to act like a tired man after lifting something blue but not something green. Shall we say 'Some robots feel tired when they lift blue things but not when they lift green things'? And shall we conclude 'Some robots find blue things heavier than green things'? Hard work makes a man feel tired: what will make a robot act like a tired man? Perhaps hard work, or light work, or no work, or anything at all. For it will depend on the whims of the man who makes it (though these whims may be modified by whatever quirks may appear in the robot's electronic nerve network, and there may be unwanted and unforeseen consequences of an ill-conceived programme). Shall we say 'There's no telling what will make a robot feel tired'? And if a robot acts like a tired man then what? Some robots may be programmed to require a rest, others to require more work. Shall we say 'This robot feels tired so put it back to work'?

What if all this were someday to be done with and to human beings? What if we were someday to break down the difference between a man and his environment? Then some day we would wake and find that we are robots. But we wouldn't wake to a mechanical paradise or even an automatic hell: for then it might not make sense to talk of human beings having feelings just as it now doesn't make sense to talk of robots having feelings.

A robot would behave like a robot.

NOTES

1. Cf. D. M. MacKay, "The Epistemological Problem for Automata," in *Automata Studies* (Princeton: Princeton Univ. Press, 1956), 235-251.
2. Cf. M. Scriven, "The Mechanical Concept of Mind." *Mind, LXII,* 246 (1953), 230-240.
3. I shall henceforth omit the qualification.
4. Cf. "Computing Machinery and Intelligence," *Mind, LIX,* 236 (1950), 433-466.
5. Cf. "Mentality in Machines," *Arist. Soc. Supp. XXVI* (1952), 61-86.

33. PROFESSOR ZIFF ON ROBOTS

J. J. C. Smart

Professor Ziff ("The Feelings of Robots") argues that robots could not have feelings. Only living things, he says, could have feelings, and robots could not be living things. Both his premise and his conclusion seem to me to be questionable, though in a brief note I can touch on some only of my reasons for thinking this.

From "Professor Ziff on Robots," *Analysis,* vol. 19, no. 5 (1959). Reprinted by permission of Basil Blackwell, Publisher.

(A) The notion of "living thing" as opposed to "robot" is unclear.

(1) Let us pretend that the *Genesis* story is literally true. Then Adam and Eve were robots. They were artifacts fashioned by God. If a conflation of ancient theology and modern biology may be allowed, we could even say that God gave Adam and Eve "programs," namely their sets of genes, probably DNA molecules which have the function of recording hereditary information.

(2) Consider von Neumann's self-reproducing mechanism. (John von Neumann, "The General and Logical Theory of Automata," *Cerebral Mechanisms in Behaviour,* The Hixon Symposium, 1951, pp. 1–31.) In what sense would descendants of such a mechanism be any the less living creatures than descendants of Adam and Eve? We could even suppose small random alterations in that part of them which records their design. Such machines could evolve by natural selection and develop propensities and capacities which did not belong to the original machine.

(1) and (2) taken together show how unclear is the distinction between a (sufficiently complex) artifact and a living creature. I myself find this not in the least surprising, for I am inclined to accept the physicalist thesis that living creatures just are very complicated physico-chemical mechanisms.

(B) I cannot see why "this has feelings" entails "this is a living creature," if "this is a living creature" is taken to entail "this is not an artifact." None of the artifacts any of us have met in practice have been sufficiently complex to warrant the assertion that they have feelings. So we should in fact at present run into no trouble if we deduced "this is a living creature" if told "this has feelings". Nevertheless it need not be a logical entailment. Maybe in the future we shall find counterexamples.

(C) Suppose we made a robot so complex that it could learn new purposes and capacities in the way that a child can. (Compare Turing's child-machine, in "Computing Machinery and Intelligence.") It might even become a philosopher, attending conferences, and developing just as human philosophers do. Why should we not say that it *meant* what it said? It would not be at all analogous to Ziff's machine with a phonograph record inside.

In short, therefore, I find Ziff's arguments unconvincing. I suspect that I may have misunderstood their purport, but I feel that Ziff could have made his intentions plainer.

34. ROBOTS: MACHINES OR ARTIFICIALLY CREATED LIFE?

Hilary Putnam

Those of us who passed many (well- or ill-spent?) childhood hours reading tales of rockets and robots, androids and telepaths, galactic civilizations and time machines, know all too well that robots—hypothetical machines that simulate human behavior, often with an at least roughly human appearance—can be friendly or fearsome, man's best friend or worst enemy. When friendly, robots can be inspiring or pathetic—they can overawe us with

Reprinted from "Robots: Machines or Artificially Created Life?," *The Journal of Philosophy* (vol. LXI, no. 21, November 12, 1964), by permission of the editor and Hilary Putnam. This paper was presented in a symposium on "Minds and Machines" at the sixty-first annual meeting of the American Philosophical Association, Eastern Division, December 28, 1964.

their superhuman powers (and with their greater than human virtue as well, at least in the writings of some authors), or they can amuse us with their stupidities and naivete. Robots have been "known" to fall in love, go mad (power- or other-wise), annoy with oversolicitousness. At least in the literature of science fiction, then, it is possible for a robot to be "conscious"; that means (since 'consciousness,' like 'material object' and 'universal,' is a philosopher's stand-in for more substantial words) to have feelings, thoughts, attitudes, and character traits. But is it really possible?. . . .

Let Oscar be one of these robots, and let us imagine that Oscar is having the "sensation" of red. Is Oscar having the sensation of red? In more ordinary language: is Oscar *seeing* anything? Is he thinking, feeling anything? Is Oscar Alive? Is Oscar Conscious?

I have referred to this problem as the problem of the "civil rights of robots" because that is what it may become, and much faster than any of us now expect. Given the ever-accelerating rate of both technological and social change, it is entirely possible that robots will one day exist, and argue "we *are* alive; we *are* conscious!" In that event, what are today only philosophical prejudices of a traditional anthropocentric and mentalistic kind would all too likely develop into conservative political attitudes. But fortunately, we today have the advantage of being able to discuss this problem disinterestedly, and a little more chance, therefore, of arriving at the correct answer.

I think that the most interesting case is the case in which (1) "psychophysical parallelism" holds (so that it can at least be contended that *we* are just as much "physical-chemical systems" as robots are), and (2) the robots in question are psychologically isomorphic to us. This is surely the most favorable case for the philosopher who wishes to argue that robots of "a sufficient degree of complexity" would (not just *could,* but necessarily *would*) be conscious. Such a philosopher would presumably contend that Oscar had sensations, thoughts, feelings, etc., in just the sense in which we do and that the use of "raised-eyebrow" quotes throughout this paper whenever a psychological predicate was being applied to a robot was unnecessary. It is this contention that I wish to explore. . . .

ZIFF'S ARGUMENT

In this situation, it is of interest to turn to an ingenious ("anti-civil-libertarian") argument by Paul Ziff.[1]

Ziff wishes to show that it is false that Oscar is conscious. He begins with the undoubted fact that if Oscar is not alive he cannot be conscious. Thus, given the semantical connection between 'alive' and 'conscious' in English, it is enough to show that Oscar is not *alive.* Now, Ziff argues, when we wish to tell whether or not something is alive, we do *not* go by its *behavior.* Even if a thing looks like a flower, etc., if I find upon taking it apart that it consists of gears and wheels and miniaturized furnaces and

vacuum tubes and so on, I say "what a clever mechanism," not "what an unusual plant." It is *structure,* not *behavior* that determines whether or not something is alive; and it is a violation of the semantical rules of our language to say of anything that is clearly a mechanism that it is "alive."

Ziff's argument is unexpected, because of the great concentration in the debate up to now upon *behavior,* but it certainly calls attention to relevant logical and semantical relationships. Yet I cannot agree that these relationships are as clear-cut as Ziff's argument requires. Suppose that we construct a robot—or, let me rather say, an *android,* to employ a word that smacks less of mechanism—out of "soft" (protoplasm-like) stuff. Then, on Ziff's account, it may be perfectly correct, if the android is sufficiently "life-like" in structure, to say that we have "synthesized life." So, given two artifacts, both "models" of the same psychological theory, both completely deterministic physical-chemical systems, both designed to the same end and "programmed" by the designer to the same extent, it may be that we must say that one of them is a "machine" and not conscious, and the other is a "living thing," (albeit "artifically created") and conscious, simply because the one consists of "soft stuff" and the other consists of "hardware." A great many speakers of English, I am sure (and I am one of them), would find the claim that this dogmatic decision is required by the meaning of the word 'alive' quite contrary to their linguistic intuitions. I think that the difficulty is fundamentally this: a plant does not exhibit much "behavior." Thus it is natural that criteria having to do with *structure* should dominate criteria having to do with "behavior" when the question is whether or not something that looks and "behaves" like a plant is really a living thing or not. But in the case of something that looks and behaves like an *animal* (and especially like a *human being*), it is natural that criteria having to do with behavior—and not just with actual behavior, but with the *organization* of behavior, as specified by a psychological theory of the thing—should play a much larger role in the decision. Thus it is not unnatural that we should be prepared to argue, in the case of the "pseudo-plant," that "it isn't a living thing because it is a mechanism," while some are prepared to argue, in the case of the robot, that "it isn't *mere* mechanism, because it is *alive*," and "it is alive, because it is conscious," and "it is conscious because it has the same behavioral organization as a living human being." Yet Ziff's account may well explain why it is that many speakers are not convinced by these latter arguments. The tension between conflicting criteria results in the "obviousness," to some minds, of the robot's "machine" status, and the equal "obviousness," to other minds, of its "artificial-life" status.

There is a sense of 'mechanism' in which it is clearly analytic that a mechanism cannot be alive. Ziff's argument can be reduced to the contention that, on the normal interpretation of the terms, it is analytic in English that something whose *parts* are all mechanisms, in this sense, likewise cannot be alive. If this is so, then no English speaker should suppose that he could even *imagine* a robot *thinking*, being *power-mad, hating humans,* or *being in love,* any more than he should suppose that he could imagine a married bachelor. It seems evident to me (and indeed to most speakers) that, absurdly or not, we *can* imagine these things. I conclude, therefore, that Ziff is wrong: it may be *false,* but it is not a *contradiction,* to assert that Oscar is alive.

THE "KNOW-NOTHING" VIEW

We have still to consider the most traditional view on our question. According to this view, which is still quite widely held, *it is possible that Oscar is conscious, and it is possible that he is not conscious.* In its theological form, the argument runs as follows: I am a creature with a body and a soul. My body happens to consist of flesh and blood, but it might just as well have been a machine, had God chosen. Each voluntary movement of my body is correlated with an activity of my soul (how and why is a "mystery"). So, it is quite possible that Oscar has a soul, and that each "voluntary" movement of his mechanical body is correlated in the same mysterious way with an activity of his soul. It is also possible—since the laws of physics suffice to explain the motions of Oscar's body, without use of the assumption that he has a soul—that Oscar is but a lifeless machine. There is absolutely no way in which we can know. This argument can also be

given a nontheological (or at least apparently nontheological) form by deleting the reference to God, and putting 'mind' for 'soul' throughout. To complete the argument, it is contended that I know what it *means* to say that Oscar has a "soul" (or has a pain, or the sensation of red, etc.) *from my own case.*

One well-known difficulty with this traditional view is that it implies that it is also possible that other humans are not really conscious, even if they are physically and psychologically isomorphic to me. It is contended that I can know with *probability* that other humans are conscious by the "argument from analogy." But in the inductive sciences, an argument from analogy is generally regarded as quite weak unless the conclusion is capable of further and independent inductive verification. So it is hard to believe that our reasons for believing that other persons are conscious are very strong ones if they amount simply to an analogical argument with a conclusion that admits of *no* independent check, observational, inductive, or whatever. Most philosophers have recently found it impossible to believe *either* that our reasons for believing that other persons are conscious are that weak *or* that the possibility exists that other persons, while being admittedly physically and psychologically isomorphic (in the sense of the present paper) to myself, are not conscious. Arguments on this point may be found in the writings of all the major analytical philosophers of the present century. Unfortunately, many of these arguments depend upon quite dubious theories of meaning.

The critical claim is the claim that it follows from the fact that I have had the sensation of red, I can imagine this sensation, "I know what it is like," that I can understand the assertion that Oscar has the sensation of red (or any other sensation or psychological state). In a sense, this is right. I *can,* in one sense, understand the *words.* I can parse them; I don't think "sensation of red" means *baby carriage,* etc. More than that: I know what I would experience if I were conscious and psychologically as I am, but with Oscar's mechanical "body" in place of my own. How does this come to be so? It comes to be so, at least in part, because we have to learn from experience what our own bodies are like. If a child were brought up in a suitable kind of armor, the child might be deceived into thinking that it was a robot. It would be harder to fool him into thinking that he had the internal structure of a robot, but this too could be done (fake X-rays, etc.). And when I "imagine myself in the shoes of a (conscious) robot," what I do, of course, is to imagine the sensations that I might have if I were a robot, or rather *if I were a human who mistakenly thought that he was a robot.* (I look down at my feet and see bright metal, etc.)

Well, let us grant that in this sense we *understand* the sentence "Oscar is having the sensation of red." It does not follow that the sentence possesses a truth value. We understand the sentence "the present King of France is bald," but, on its normal interpretation in English, the sentence has no truth value under present conditions. We can give it one by adopting a suitable convention—for example, Russell's theory of descriptions—and more than one such suitable convention exists. The question really at issue is *not* whether we can "understand" the sentences "Oscar is conscious" (or "has the sensation of red" or "is angry") and "Oscar is not conscious," in the sense of being able to use them in such contexts as "I can perfectly well picture to myself that Oscar is conscious," but whether there really is an intelligible sense in which one of these sentences is true, on a normal interpretation, and the other false (and, in that case, whether it is also true that we can't tell which).

Let us revert, for a moment, to a fantasy of ROBOTS—i.e., second-order robots, robots created by robots and regarded by robots as *mere* ROBOTS. A robot philosopher might very well be led to consider the question: Are ROBOTS conscious? The robot philosopher "knows," of course, just what "experiences" he would have if he were a "conscious" ROBOT (or a robot in a ROBOT suit). He can "perfectly well picture to himself that a ROBOT could have "sensation." So he may perfectly well arrive at the position that it is logically possible that ROBOTS have sensations (or, rather, "sensations") and perfectly possible that they do not, and moreover he can never know. What do we think of this conclusion?

It is clear what we should think: we should think that there is not the slightest reason to suppose (and every reason not to suppose) that there is a special property, "having the 'sensation' of red,"

which the ROBOT may or may not have, but which is inaccessible to the robot. The robot, knowing the physical and psychological description of the ROBOT, is in a perfectly good position to answer all questions about the ROBOT that may reasonably be asked. The idea that there is a further question (class of questions) about the ROBOT which the robot cannot answer, is suggested to the robot by the fact that these alleged "questions" are grammatically well formed, can be "understood" in the sense discussed above, and that the possible "answers" can be "imagined."

I suggest that our position with respect to robots is *exactly* that of robots with respect to ROBOTS. There is not the slightest reason for us, either, to believe that "consciousness" is a well-defined property, which each robot either *has* or *lacks,* but such that it is not possible, on the basis of the physical description of the robot, or even on the basis of the psychological description (in the sense of "psychological" explained above), to *decide* which (if any) of the robots possesses this property and which (if any) fail to possess it. The rules of "robot language" may well be such that it is perfectly possible for a robot to "conjecture" that ROBOTS have "sensations" and also perfectly possible for a robot to conjecture that ROBOTS do not have "sensations." It does not follow that the physical and psychological description of the ROBOTS is "incomplete," but only that the concept of "sensation" (in "raised-eyebrow quotes") is a well-defined concept only when applied to robots. The question raised by the robot philosopher: Are ROBOTS "conscious"? calls for a decision and not for a discovery. The decision, at bottom, is this: Do I treat ROBOTS as fellow members of my linguistic community, or as machines? If the ROBOTS are accepted as full members of the robot community, then a robot can find out whether a ROBOT is "conscious" or "unconscious," "alive" or "dead" in just the way he finds out these things about a fellow robot. If they are rejected, then nothing *counts* as a ROBOT being "conscious" or "alive." Until the decision is made, the statement that ROBOTS are "conscious" has no truth value. In the same way, I suggest, the question: Are robots conscious? calls for a decision, on our part, to treat robots as fellow members of our linguistic community, or not to so treat them. As long as we leave this decision un-made, the statement that robots (of the kind de-scribed) are conscious has no truth value.

If we reject the idea that the physical and psy-chological description of the robots is incomplete (because it "fails to specify whether or not they are conscious"), we are not thereby forced to hold either that "consciousness" is a "physical" attribute or that it is an attribute "implicitly defined by a psychological theory." Russell's question in the philosophy of mathematics: If the number 2 is not the set of all pairs, then what on earth is it? was a silly question. Two is simply the second number, and nothing else. Likewise, the materialist ques-tion: If the attribute of "consciousness" is not a physical attribute (or an attribute implicitly defined by a psychological theory) then what on earth is it? is a silly question. Our psychological concepts in ordinary language are as we have fashioned them. The "framework" of ordinary-language psy-chological predicates is what it is and not another framework. *Of course* materialism is false; but it is so *trivially* false that no materialist should be bothered!

CONCLUSION

I have concluded . . . that there is no correct answer to the question: Is Oscar conscious? Robots may indeed have (or lack) properties unknown to phys-ics and undetectable by us; but not the slightest reason has been offered to show that they do, as the ROBOT analogy demonstrates. It is reasonable, then, to conclude that the question that titles this paper calls for a decision and not for a discovery. If we are to make a decision, it seems preferable to me to extend our concept so that robots *are* con-scious—for "discrimination" based on the "soft-ness" or "hardness" of the body parts of a synthetic "organism" seems as silly as discriminatory treat-ment of humans on the basis of skin color. But my purpose in this paper has not been to improve our concepts, but to find out what they are

NOTE

1. I take the liberty of reporting an argument used by Ziff in a conversation. I do not wish to imply that Ziff necessarily subscribes to the argument in the form in which I report it, but I include it because of its ingenuity and interest.

SUGGESTIONS FOR FURTHER READING

BEHAVIOR CONTROL, MIND ALTERATION AND PSYCHOSURGERY

Chorover, Stephan. "The Pacification of the Brain." *Psychology Today* 7 (May 1974):59–69.

Dworkin, Gerald. "Autonomy and Behavior Control." *Hastings Center Report* 6 (February 1976):23–28.

Engelhardt, H. Tristram, Jr., and Spicker, Stuart F. *Philosophical Dimensions of the Neuro-Medical Sciences.* Boston: Reidel, 1976. Part II.

London, Perry. *Behavior Control.* New York: Harper & Row, 1971.

Mark, Vernon, and Ervin, Frank. *Violence and the Brain.* New York: Harper & Row, 1970.

Mark, Vernon, Ervin, Frank, and Sweet, William. "The Role of Brain Disease in Riots and Urban Violence," *Journal of the American Medical Association* 201 (1967):895.

Michigan, Circuit Court for Wayne County. *Kaimowitz v. Department of Mental Health.* Civil No. 73-19434-AW (July 10, 1973).

Murphy, Jeffrie G. "Total Institutions and the Possibility of Consent to Organic Therapies." *Human Rights* 5 (Fall 1975):25–45.

National Commission for the Protection of Human Sub-jects of Biomedical and Behavioral Research. *Report and Recommendations: Psychosurgery.* Washington, D.C.: U.S. Government Printing Office, 1977. DHEW Pub. no. (OS)77-0001.

"New Technologies and Strategies for Social Control: Ethical and Practical Limits." *American Behavioral Sci-entist* 18 (May/June, 1975). Special issue.

"Symposium: Psychosurgery." *Boston University Law Re-view* 54 (March, 1974). Special issue. Reissued as *Psy-chosurgery - A Multidisciplinary Symposium.* Boston: Lexington Books, 1974.

Valenstein, Elliot S. *Brain Control: Critical Examination of Brain Stimulation and Psychosurgery.* New York: Wiley, 1974.

Valenstein, Elliot S. *The Practice of Psychosurgery: A Sur-vey of the Literature (1971–76).* Bethesda, Md.: Na-tional Commission for the Protection of Human Subjects of Biomedical and Behavioral Research, National Institutes of Health, 1976.

PERSONAL IDENTITY

Beauchamp, Tom L., and Robinson, D.N. "Personal Identity: Reid's Answer to Hume." *Monist* 61 (April 1978).

Biro, J. I. "Hume on Self-Identity and Memory." *Review of Metaphysics* (1976), pp. 19–38.

Brennan, Andrew. "Persons and their Brains." *Analysis* 30 (1970). [On Puccetti]

Broad, C. D. *The Mind and Its Place in Nature.* London: Routledge & Kegan Paul, 1937. Chapter 13.

Flew, Antony. "Locke and the Problem of Personal Identity." *Philosophy* (1951).

James, William. *Principles of Psychology.* New York: Holt, 1890. Chapter X.

Parfit, Derek. "Personal Identity." *Philosophical Review* 80 (1971). [In Perry, below]

Penelhum, Terence. "Hume on Personal Identity." *Philosophical Review* 64 (1955).

———. Hume. New York: St. Martin's Press, 1975.

Perry, John, ed. *Personal Identity.* Berkeley, Calif.: University of California Press, 1975.

Puccetti, Roland. "Mr. Brennan on Persons' Brains," *Analysis* 31 (1970).

Rorty, Amelie, ed. *The Identities of Persons.* London, 1975.

Shoemaker, Sydney *Self-Knowledge and Self-Identity.* Ithaca, N.Y.: Cornell University Press, 1963.

MINDS, MACHINES, AND ROBOTS

Anderson, Alan Ross, ed. *Minds and Machines.* Englewood Cliffs, N.J.: Prentice-Hall, 1964.

Dreyfus, Hubert L. *What Computers Can't Do: A Critique of Artificial Reason.* New York: Harper & Row, 1973.

Gunderson, Keith. *Mentality and Machines.* New York: Doubleday, 1971.

———. "Interview With a Robot." *Analysis* (1964).

Hook, Sidney, ed. *Dimensions of Mind.* New York: New York University Press, 1960. Part II.

Puccetti, Roland. "On Thinking Machines and Feeling Machines." *British Journal for the Philosophy of Science* 18 (1967).

Sayre, Kenneth M. *Consciousness: A Philosophical Study of Minds and Machines.* New York: Random House, 1969.

Sayre, Kenneth M., and Crosson, Frederick J., eds. *The Modeling of Mind: Computers and Intelligence.* New York: Simon & Schuster, 1963.

Scriven, Michael. "The Compleat Robot: A Prolegomena to Androidology." In *Dimensions of the Mind,* edited by Hook (above).

Chapter 5   The Sanctity of Life

MORAL PRINCIPLES AND STATUS PRINCIPLES

Most of us pay lip service to the principle that life is sacred and that killing, except for the very weightiest reasons, is morally wrong. But there is very little agreement about what it means to attribute "sanctity" to life, the grounds for such an attribution, or the nature of the reasons which are "weighty" enough to override it in specific exceptional cases. Hence in practice many persons participate in good conscience in the slaughter of animals, the abortion of human fetuses, the withdrawal of life support systems for the hopelessly ill, the killing of enemy soldiers or civilians in war, or the capital punishment of criminals, while others respond with moral outrage to some or all of these practices. One of the philosopher's tasks, amidst all this confusion, is to find general principles that will permit taking a reasoned and consistent stand on all of these difficult questions, principles that point to the morally relevant differences between different cases that underlie the different judgments the philosopher wishes to make about those cases. The sought-for moral principles, moreover, must not have unnoticed logical consequences that would be unacceptable when applied to actual or hypothetical cases.

Many of the specific moral problems about killing, however, are difficult not only because we may be uncertain which of various rival moral principles apply, but also for another kind of reason. We may be confident, for example, that it is wrong to kill a certain kind of being in a certain set of circumstances *if* that being is a person, but we may be quite bewildered about how to go about deciding whether it is a person or not. In that case, we are not confused about which of various proposed moral principles has the greatest "weight" when applied to the case at hand, so much as about whether any of the principles *applies at all*. The two most obvious examples are animals and fetuses. Moral confusion about the killing of such beings often stems from puzzlement over whether they are the kinds of entities that have the appropriate status for some moral principle to apply to them. If the philosopher has help to offer in these instances it will be in the form of *status-principles* to be used in distinguishing human from non-human, persons from non-persons, autonomous from non-autonomous beings, and the like, rather than (or in addition to) *moral principles* declaring what sorts of behavior are proper toward entities of various types.

THREE FAMILIES OF MORAL CONSIDERATIONS

At least three different types of reasons have been advanced by philosophers to guide our moral judgments about the permissibility of killing. (We shall encounter a fourth in our examination of capital punishment.) The first of these are often called *utilitarian considerations*. They refer to the effects of actions, or contemplated actions, on the happiness or unhappiness of the persons likely to be affected by them. The person who does the action, of course, will be affected. In cases of killing, the victim is also affected. Then there are "third parties"—spouses, parents, siblings, children, other friends and dependents, colleagues, customers, neighbors, and the like. Insofar as these parties have love for the victim, or interests (economic, professional, or other) in his or her continued existence, they are harmed by the victim's death, and will be made unhappy by it. Finally, there are more "distant" groups of persons—the neighborhood, profession, or community in general—who are deprived of the victim's services, or threatened by example of the killing. Some of these effects of killing are immediate and direct: "victims" are either put out of their misery or (more typically) deprived of years of happiness that they might otherwise have experienced. Other consequences of killing affect interests of persons other than the victim. They are, in that sense, less direct, and hence are sometimes called "side-effects." These include the effects on the interests of the killer, third parties, and the community in general. One can see quickly that in the overwhelming proportion of cases of killing people, both the direct and indirect effects on human happiness will be very bad indeed. That fact constitutes the utilitarian case against homicide.

A second class of reasons often invoked in discussion of the morality of killing are considerations of *personal autonomy*. These are especially likely to be cited in cases where people choose to kill themselves or to ask another person to kill them, or when there appears to be a strong utilitarian case for killing oneself and yet one chooses not to do so. A truly autonomous person is one who is rightly in control of his or her own life, just as a truly sovereign political state is one that is legitimately in control of its own territory. Insofar as the conduct of autonomous people does not violate the borders of other people's personal sovereignty, they are free to do as they wish, to determine their own lot in life, to be their own boss, to risk mistakes, to take responsibility, to "go to hell on their own" if that's how it turns out. For example if a man chooses to kill himself in order to avoid what he takes to be unbearable suffering either in himself or in others, it is his own life, after all, that he takes, and ultimately that is *his* concern, not that of others. Similarly, if he chooses to go on living despite the apparent hopelessness of his position, that too is his decision alone, and death cannot be imposed on him "for his own good" (as determined by utilitarian reasons) without violating his personal autonomy.

A quite distinct third kind of reason can be called a consideration of *the sanctity of life*. This sort of reason is commonly advanced as an independent value and claim, and a constraint on the use of utilitarian and personal autonomy considerations that might otherwise apply. What makes acts of killing seriously wrong (when they are so) is simply *that they are acts of killing,* whatever their effects on happiness or personal autonomy. The sanctity of life, so construed, is not derived from considerations of utility or autonomy. Like them it is entirely underivative, a basic moral consideration in its own right. There are, of course, various interpretations of the sanctity of life. Albert Schweitzer's "reverence for life" was unrestricted, applying to all living things, not only human beings. Similarly, the teachings of Buddhism attach a sanctity to the whole animal kingdom. The Christian tradition, on the other hand, attaches a unique significance to *human* life. Some sanctity of life theorists (whether restricted or unrestricted) ground their moral principle in theological doctrine; others hold it to be independent of theology, a kind of moral ultimate, ungrounded in anything beyond itself. Among the theological interpretations there appear many and various metaphors to explain the relation between the Creator and the created life that is sacred: God is spoken of as loving parent, as property owner, as law-maker, or as gift-giver (cf. the "gift of life").

RIVAL MORAL PRINCIPLES

Much of the controversy among philosophers over the morality of various kinds of killing can be traced to disagreements over the relative "weights," or degrees of stringency, to be ascribed to the three types of moral consideration above. For some philosophers, one and only one type of reason has relevant application to problems of killing, or if more than one type applies, there is a clear and invariant order of priority among them. *Utilitarianism* can be defined as the view that ultimately *only utilitarian considerations* have relevant application to moral decisions, whether about killing or anything else. When another kind of reason appears to be relevant, it is only because that reason points to a feature of acts in virtue of which they tend in the vast majority of cases to have an effect on human happiness. Utilitarians, for example, might condemn an act on the ground that it is a deliberate taking of human life, but only because they believe (quite rightly) that acts of killing tend on balance to have very adverse effects on human happiness. Thus in the very rare case where utilitarians think that killing will lead to a net gain in happiness over unhappiness (taking into account *all* those likely to be affected by it), they will approve of the killing. That is to say that utilitarian considerations, when they conflict with considerations of other kinds, are always the trump card.

We can attach the much-used label *libertarianism* to the view that personal autonomy is the weightiest of moral considerations. The libertarian never tires of emphasizing the moral importance of voluntary choice and consent. That which is truly within the domain of a person's autonomy can be disposed of as the person voluntarily chooses, or

voluntarily consent to another party's disposal, whatever considerations of happiness (his or her own) or sanctity of life (his or her own) may say about the matter. Some moral problems, of course, do not seem to involve autonomy or consent at all, at least not in a clear unproblematic way. Thus, fetuses make no choices of their own; nor do newly born brain-damaged infants, or irreversibly comatose adults. Some libertarians would find a consideration of self-determination even in these examples, perhaps arguing that "sovereign control" in these cases belongs to other parties (parents or guardians) whose informed consent is morally required and morally sufficient, or that testimentary directions in the form of "living wills" made at an earlier time should control. Other libertarians might concede that in cases of these sorts, personal autonomy is not involved, and that either utilitarian considerations or considerations of the sanctity of life should govern. But where all three considerations do apply, and personal autonomy conflicts with the other two, personal autonomy must triumph.

A third leading moral position ranks consideration of the sanctity of life, when it applies, above considerations of the other two kinds. There are two leading versions of this position. The absolutist version holds that the intentional killing of human beings, whether born or fetal, healty or sick, allies or enemies, conscious or comatose, innocent or guilty, is absolutely impermissible morally. The weaker version (which is far more common) holds that killing human beings is permissible if and only if it seems on reasonable grounds to be necessary to save the lives of (other) innocent human beings. An absolutistic sanctity of life position would endorse unconditional pacifism in "just" as well as "unjust" wars; it would condemn capital punishment even if it were demonstrated to be efficacious in saving innocent human lives; it would forbid abortion even when necessary to save the life of the mother; and would reject self-defense as a *moral* excuse for homicide. The weaker version, on the other hand, is consistent with killing combatants in just wars, using the death penalty (but only as a "deterrent"), and killing in self-defense.

Both versions of the sanctity of life principle agree that where sanctity of life considerations conflict with utilitarian or libertarian considerations, the latter must be subordinate in authority. We can kill horses to put them out of their misery, but killing suffering human beings is always a greater evil even than the fact of their suffering, on this view. And where the sanctity of life *seems* to conflict with personal autonomy, that is because (as it is often argued) the latter has been misinterpreted. Personal autonomy is important, the argument goes, but the decision to live or die falls outside its boundaries. That is because our lives do *not,* after all, belong to us, but rather are the property of our Creator, or because (in the language of Immanuel Kant) the "humanity in each individual's person" commands categorical respect and hence cannot be destroyed.

There is finally a *mixed theory* which allows some weight to considerations of all three kinds, but does not put them into any fixed order of priority. Which consideration has precedence in cases of conflict, according to the theory, depends on the individual circumstances, aspects of which are morally unique. All one can do in these difficult and tragic cases is turn one's mind into a kind of delicate balancing instrument, and then be moved reluctantly but bravely to action, propelled by the consideration that seems weightiest in the particular circumstances. In the end the decision rests with informed but fallible "intuition," rather than elaborate reasoning or deductions from fixed principles. This view, therefore, is sometimes called *intuitionism.*

ANIMAL LIFE

The first essay in this section, by Peter Singer, challenges us to find some ground, apart from arbitrary self-preference, for restricting the "sanctity of life" to *human* life. Singer, who is the author of the widely read book *Animal Liberation* (New York: Random House, 1975), argues that if the requirements of morality are radically different in respect to our treatment of animals and our conduct toward our fellow human beings, that must be because there is some morally relevant difference between *all* individual animals, on the one hand, and *all* individual humans, on the other. But he can find no such difference in every case. To take the extreme example that most fortifies his position, he can find

no reason for keeping alive at all cost severely and irreparably retarded human infants, while mutilating and killing adult chimapanzees in trivial psychological experiments. If "rationality," "intelligence," or "sensitivity to anxiety and suffering" are the morally relevant differences, the chimpanzees should have a greater (not a lesser) claim against us not to be killed. And if the sheer fact of membership in the human species is what qualifies the retarded infants and excludes the developed apes, Singer cannot understand how species membership, *by itself,* quite apart from any necessary correlation with other traits, could be "morally relevant." Discrimination on the basis of species alone he calls "speciesism," and condemns as being as irrational and immoral as "racism" and "sexism." In the end, Singer poses a dilemma: If we are to continue to hold the doctrine of the sanctity of human life, we must also extend it to members of the higher animal species; if, on the other hand, we deny the sanctity of some (higher) animal lives for what we take to be good reasons, then we must withdraw our attribution of sanctity to particular human lives whenever the same reasons apply.

ABORTION

Singer's article makes a useful transition to the four selections on the problem of abortion. There are two main kinds of philosophical question about the morality of abortion. The first (the one on which Singer's arguments have bearing) is the problem of "the status of the fetus": At what stage, if any, in the development from a one-celled zygote to the moment of birth is a fetus the sort of being appropriately protected by the prohibition of homicide? The second problem is that of stating the grounds, if any, for justified homicide of the fetus, on the assumption that it *is* a human person with a full-blown moral right to life.

The problem of the status of the fetus is not settled instantly by the commonplace observation that the rule against homicide applies to all human beings and that a fetus is a "being" that is clearly human (clearly not canine, equine, bovine, feline, etc.). After all, a human ovum or spermatozoan, or a piece of tissue from an arm or leg, is clearly a "being" that is human too. (One can look even at a single chromosome under a microscope and find it recognizably human, as opposed to equine, canine, etc.). What is at issue is whether a human (admittedly human) fetus, at some given stage of its development, is the appropriate kind of thing to qualify as a *person* with a right to life. Professor Mary Anne Warren, in her essay arguing for the permissibility of abortion at all stages, therefore raises the question early in her argument of which criteria we would naturally use in deciding whether some creature is a "person" or not. Suppose, for example, we are space travelers on a remote planet orbiting a distant star, and we discover creatures totally unlike any animal or plant ever seen on earth. How could we tell whether they are persons to be respected, greeted, traded and negotiated with, or mere things to be skinned, chopped up, boiled, and used for food and clothing? Warren suggests that we would naturally seek to discover whether these creatures are *conscious,* whether they are able to feel *pain,* whether they are able to form *social relationships,* whether they are capable of some degree of *thought,* and whether they have a sense of their own identity. Quite clearly a human fetus (at least in its earlier stages) does not have any of these traits. Hence, it is easy to conclude, as Warren does, that while fetuses are clearly human (belong to the species *homo sapiens*), they are not in the requisite sense *persons* with rights to be claimed against us.

Warren's list of person-making traits (or some other similar list, if hers is deficient) can be used to describe the main types of answers that have been proposed by philosophers to the problem of the status of the fetus. If we let the letter *C* stand for the complex of traits (whichever they are) that determine "commonsense personhood," then the main criteria for deciding on the moral status of the fetus can be stated as follows:

THE STRICT CRITERION OF SPECIES MEMBERSHIP

"All and only living members of the human species —those who have been conceived by human parents and thus carry the full genetic 'blueprint' of an individual human being—are moral persons *whether or not they happen to possess C* in individual cases." This criterion would confer personhood and its attendant rights on the fetus from the mo-

ment of conception and thus confirm the widespread conviction that any living being that carries a full complement of human genes, even if it is no larger than a mere speck, is a creature of dignity whose life is sacred. Without a supplementary theological account of the source of that sanctity (of the sort Paul Ramsey provides in his selection), however, it will not appear obvious why a mere speck of protoplasm should have any value at all, whatever it might potentially become. No one, after all, can communicate with a tiny embryo, or make promises to it, or respect its self-consciousness, or befriend it, or reason with it, or inflict pain on it. Warren and others of her persuasion find further difficulties with this criterion. It seems vulnerable (at least without theological supplementation) to Singer's charge of "species-ism"; it would attribute personhood to the irreversibly comatose who lack *C* not only actually but even potentially; and it forever excludes from the ranks of persons those possibly rational members of other species in other galaxies still undiscovered. In short, it forecloses both the possibility that some living humans are not persons and the possibility that some actual persons are not human.

THE MODIFIED CRITERION OF SPECIES MEMBERSHIP

"All and only living members of species generally characterized by *C* (or all of whose *normal* members have *C*) are persons, whether that species be *homo sapiens* or other, and whether or not the individuals in question happen to possess *C* themselves." According to this criterion then, if it would be murder (morally speaking) to kill a normal fully mature member of even a non-human species characterized by *C,* it would also be murder to kill an abnormal member of that species who lacked *C,* or to abort an incipient member of that species before it acquired *C.* This version of the species criterion clearly avoids some of the difficulties of the strict version, but it fails equally to solve the problem of the "status of the fetus" without theological supplementation (and the necessary theology would have to depart from the traditional Christian insistence on the moral uniqueness of human beings), and it fails to recommend itself to common sense in the case of the irreversibly comatose member of *any* species.

THE CRITERION OF ACTUAL PERSONHOOD

"At any given time *t,* all and only those creatures who actually possess *C* are persons at *t,* whatever biological or extraterrestrial species they may belong to." This is the criterion favored by most of those who find abortion, at least during the early and middle stages of pregnancy, to be morally permissible. Some writers who favor this criterion, however, hold very strict conceptions of the characteristics that make up *C,* and therefore condemn as murder any abortion that occurs after some rather early stage such as that at which brain waves of the fetus can be monitored. Professor Kluge, in his selection in this chapter, applies the criterion in that strict fashion. (Hardly any writers who employ this criterion, however, apply it in such a way that the embryo in the first five or six weeks of its life is deemed a person.) The main difficulty for the actual possession criterion as applied by most defenders of abortion is one that is usually given major emphasis by the opponents of abortion. If a fetus does not yet actually possess *C* the day before birth (an admittedly plausible view) then it is not likely that it possesses *C* the day after birth either. In that case, the criterion yields the embarrassing result that newborn babies are still non-persons or pre-persons who have no right of their own to life. Some writers employing this criterion, including Professor Warren, locate the origin of genuine personhood at some indeterminate point months after birth, but nevertheless oppose infanticide on general utilitarian grounds. Another difficulty for the actual possession criterion, according to some critics, is that it seems to exclude from the class of persons the reversibly comatose who *temporarily* lack *C,* and even persons in deep sleep who also temporarily lack *C.* The best reply to this charge, however, is that which points out a sense in which one can actually possess a dispositional trait like a skill, ability, capacity, belief, attitude, virtue, or flaw even when one is not in a position to exercise it. Actual possession of a latent disposition is not merely "potential possession." It is true of Jimmy Carter, for example, even when he is sound asleep, that he is a Democrat, he loves his wife, he knows how to swim, etc. Similar statements made in 1977, in the present tense, about Karen Quinlan, on the assumption that she would *never* regain consciousness, made no sense.

THE STRICT CRITERION OF POTENTIAL PERSONHOOD

"All and only those creatures who either actually or potentially possess *C* (who either have *C* now or would come to have *C* in the natural course of events) are persons now, whatever their species or other characteristics." This criterion, like the criteria of species membership, permits one to condemn abortion "from the moment of conception," and further it permits that condemnation to be grounded on a personal *right* to life of the fetus itself, as opposed to mere identification by species. Since the potentiality of personhood exists from conception, the actual rights of persons do too, on this view, and from the moral point of view, killing embryos is exactly like killing adults. There are, however, serious problems for this approach too. Normally, to say of people that they *potentially* possess the characteristics that will qualify them for a right is a reason for predicting that they will acquire the right in the future, not for attributing the actual right to them now, in the present. On November 15, 1976, Jimmy Carter was the potential president of the United States, but he had no right yet, at that time, to veto legislation or to command the United States Army and Navy. Fetuses are potential persons, it might be said, and therefore *potential,* not actual, right-holders. Moreover, our actual attitude toward fetuses seems in certain respects to differ from our attitude toward real persons, even toward newborn babies considered as newly actual, or imminently potential, persons. When a woman has a miscarriage in her second month, she and her husband may be bitterly disappointed and depressed, but they do not consciously grieve for the fetus's sake, so much as for their own.

THE MODIFIED OR GRADUALIST CRITERION OF POTENTIAL PERSONHOOD

"Personhood being a matter of degree, only a very weak claim can be attributed to the "speck-like" zygote at the moment of conception, not a full-blown right to life, but that claim keeps growing stronger, requiring ever stronger reasons to override it, until at the point of actual personhood, it becomes a right to life that can be overridden, if at all, only by the rights to life of other persons." On this view, abortion is a serious business, morally speaking, at any time, and can never rightly be done from mere capricious or trivial reasons, but as the fetus grows closer to actual personhood, the reasons required for the justification of abortion must likewise be stronger and better. Mere convenience may suffice during the first few weeks, but then fear of deformity in the child or harm to the mother are required, then serious functional abnormality or serious harm, then at some advanced point only saving the mother's life will do, until finally, at birth, only the reasons that would justify killing an adult (self-defense, defense of the lives of others, "necessity," or forced choice of the lesser evil) will suffice, and they are likely to lack plausibility when applied to infants. This view has the usual attraction of compromises, but it shares one serious difficulty with all forms of the potentiality criterion, namely, the difficulty of explaining how *any* merely potential person, even a very nearly actual person, can have actual rights.

The articles on abortion in this chapter represent three different substantial views, and a greater diversity still of forms of argument. Mary Anne Warren's article employs an actual personhood criterion to argue for the general permissibility of abortion. On her view, fetuses can be killed without committing homicide because homicide is the killing of people, and fetuses are not people, only potential people. Eike-Henner Kluge employs a gradualist potentiality criterion and a strict conception of the commonsense person-determining characteristics to come to a more complicated conclusion, namely that "abortions performed within a certain more or less clearly defined period of fetal development are murderous, whereas those performed prior to this period are not . . . but this does not mean that no moral gravamen attaches to the latter sort of action, but that instead the moral seriousness of the act is reduced to a degree commensurate with the stage of development of the fetus." Paul Ramsey, a leading Protestant moral theologian, is a more uncompromising opponent of abortion. Writing from what he calls an "authentic religious point of view," he dismisses the actual or potential traits of the living human embryo as largely irrelevant to the question of the sanctity of life, which he interprets as an "overflow from God's dealings with him," an "alien dignity" that wholly derives from the value God places upon the person. Nothing intrinsic in even a grown person, then, is the ground of his or her human dignity or the sanctity of his or her life. Rather "his life is entirely an ordination, a loan, and a stewardship." Ramsey's theological interpretation of the sanctity of life, if it is sound, applies to problems beyond that of abortion, and undermines the appeal to personal autonomy when used as a justification for suicide or euthanasia.

SUICIDE

Despite the thousands of volumes of argument over the moral permissibility of suicide, there is still some confusion over the prior question of what suicide is. Part of the explanation of this conceptual uncertainty concerns the distinction between terminating and shortening one's life, and its vagueness. For example, the prisoner in his cell who poisons himself one hour before his scheduled execution shortens his life by sixty minutes. The astronaut who, after being instructed by radio from Houston that his spacecraft is doomed, takes a poison tablet, may shorten his life by only ten minutes. The parachutist whose chute won't open shoots herself in free flight, sparing herself sixty seconds of terror. All of these persons terminated their own lives, but it might be argued in their behalves that they did not "commit suicide," since they were certain to die anyway within minutes. In reply to this it can be said that all of us are "certain to die anyway" eventually and that suicide is not a matter of degree measured by how much life is shortened. But if deliberately shortening one's life by a few moments is suicide in the above cases, it should give one pause to realize that many of us who must die sooner or later, knowingly and deliberately do many things certain to make it *much* sooner rather than later (e.g., overeat, drink, smoke).

Conceptual confusion also stems from the fact that restrictions on *motive* are often involved in our very conception, or definition, of suicide. Thus we tend to exclude self-sacrificial acts of heroism such as diving in front of a speeding truck to push a small child out of danger, or falling on a live hand grenade to save one's buddies. Traditionally such forms of self-destruction have not been considered suicide at all. Yet most traditional moralists would deny the right of a terminal patient to volunteer to be killed on the operating table so that his or her organs might be used to save the lives of injured children. That would not be called "suicide" only because a doctor would be the instrument of the patient's will, but if the patient injected the fatal fluid into his or her own arm, it would probably be called "suicide" despite any altruistic motives. By and large, however, the term "suicide" has been reserved for self-killings done from self-serving motives, particularly from the desire to avoid suffering or humiliation for oneself. But usage has been inconsistent in respect to this requirement, generating considerable puzzlement.

Since most people most of the time are worth more to others alive than dead, utilitarian considerations alone are usually sufficient to rule out suicide. In untypical desperate cases, however, utilitarian considerations would clearly favor suicide, where a very old and sick woman in great pain, for example, kills herself to end her pain, relieve her children of the burden of supporting her, and prevent the total depletion of her estate. In other types of desperate circumstances utilitarianism would condemn merely self-serving suicide. Where social life is hard and dangerous and every person's fullest efforts are needed to prevent a general disaster (as for example in a beleaguered garrison), then to kill oneself while one is still capable of serving is blameworthy self-indulgence to the detriment of others. St. Thomas Aquinas apparently thought that something like the garrison situation is the normal human condition, for he argued that suicide is almost always a harm to the community.

The personal autonomy principle applied in normal social situations generally provides a justification for suicide, for according to it every person's life is his own and he may therefore do with it as he wishes within his own area of autonomy, that is where the interests of others are not strongly and directly affected. But in the garrison situation everybody's "area of autonomy" has shrunk to a bare minimum, and suicide can be prohibited or condemned as a violation of the autonomy of one's fellows. In that case appeals to social utility and personal autonomy have the same result.

The absolutist version of the sanctity of life principle does not commend itself to common sense as applied to some suicides. It would condemn as immoral, for example, the "life-shortenings" of the condemned prisoner, the astronaut, and the parachutist. Even the qualified sanctity of life principle, however, would condemn all suicides intended merely for the suicide's own sake, or to bring about any good other than a saving of other human lives. There is at least one attitude toward death, however, that renders the sanctity of life position on suicide more plausible. While many ancient Stoic philosophers cheerfully recommended suicide as a way of escaping pain and suffering, a more consistent Stoic doctrine urged people to die, as they should have lived, with style, fortitude, and excellence. The more painful the final hours, the greater the opportunity to die well with high virtue and noble courage. It is not up to us to choose our role in life or in death, said Epictetus, but it is entirely within our power to play that role well. Suicide, according to this way of thinking, is always a morally unbecoming repudiation of an assigned part in the cosmic drama that the actor finds too difficult to play.

These and others arguments are given precise expression in the selections from the thirteenth century philosopher St. Thomas Aquinas, and (on the other side) the skeptical eighteenth-century philosopher David Hume. It is probable that Hume wrote his essay as a deliberate reply to Aquinas. The essay was not published during Hume's life, perhaps because it was thought to be too daring, and probably also because Hume was dissatisfied with some of the arguments. But it remains to this day one of the most widely read and influential statements of the right to commit suicide.

EUTHANASIA

If all people who wanted to die were both willing and able to kill themselves, then there would be no need to consider the moral propriety of either *aiding another's suicide* or *voluntary euthanasia.* Sometimes, however, a relatively dignified and properly timed death cannot be achieved without the assistance of others, as when some German Jews, soon to be shipped to concentration camps in World War II, requested and received poison tablets from a certain heroically obliging German doctor. Those who cannot end their own lives even with outside help, however, are virtually all aged, enfeebled, or physically helpless. Hence the problem of voluntary euthanasia (killing another at his or her request and for his or her own sake) is almost entirely a problem of medical ethics, about what is or should be acceptable hospital practice.

Marvin Kohl, in his essay in this volume, defends the moral propriety and urges the legalization of active voluntary euthanasia for those who are in intense and hopeless suffering. Kohl bases his argument mainly on the moral stringency of the requirement to be *kind;* refusing euthanasia in some circumstances, he charges, is to treat a fellow human being with exquisite cruelty. Where both kindness and personal autonomy pull in the same direction, Kohl argues, consideration of the sanctity of life has very little countervailing force.

On the other side, the members of the Study Group on Euthanasia set up by the Catholic Union of Great Britain in 1968 warn that the legalization of euthanasia would be a threat to the lives of all of us. The chapter on "The Ethics of Euthanasia" reprinted here from their report, *Your Death Warrant,* discusses the distinction between direct killing and not using extraordinary measures to save a life; the distinction between producing another's death as a means or an end and permitting it as a foreseen byproduct of the pursuit of an acceptable end (like reducing pain); the famous "doctrine of double effect"; the difficulties of determining the voluntariness of a purported statement of consent; and the effects of euthanasia on the doctor-patient and patient-family relationships. It concludes with a statement of the famous "slippery-slope" argument that legalizing voluntary euthanasia would be just the first step on the inevitable downward path to involuntary euthanasia and eventually to mass murder of "misfits" as a social policy. Kohl's article anticipates this charge, and attempts to rebut it.

The reader should notice, however, that there are two distinct versions of the slippery-slope argument, and that each requires support or rebuttal (as the case may be) in a different way. The *strong* or *logical* version of the argument has the form of a *reductio ad absurdum.* One uses this argument in counter-attack against an opponent when one tries to show that the same reasons the opponent uses to establish his or her position can establish with exactly the same force another position which is presumed to be antecedently unacceptable or morally absurd. The *empirical* version of the argument is a rejoinder of a quite different kind. "The policy or practice you advocate (P_1)," one says, "might seem innocuous enough. But if it is adopted, then in all likelihood it will encourage others to urge P_2, which is a more dangerous policy. And if P_2 is adopted then in fact political resistance to P_3 might collapse, and once P_3 is in, no one (because of complicated social and political causes) will dare resist P_4, which even you must admit is morally unacceptable. It is not logically inconsistent to advocate P_1 and condemn P_4, but because of the operation of various causal forces in the social world (*not* because of the laws of logic), P_4 will probably come about if P_1 does." Opponents of euthanasia who use the empirical argument often invoke the Nazi precedent, which is frightening indeed. (Legalized euthanasia in Germany, at first justified on humanitarian grounds, soon blended without a trace of friction with the Nazi policy of eliminating the "unfit" and exterminating the racially "inferior.") But defenders of voluntary euthanasia, like Kohl can cite historical precedents on their side too. The Eskimo practice of killing aging parents at their request, for example, did not lead to a general killing of unwilling "misfits."

If "euthanasia" is defined as "the killing of another person for what is thought to be his or her own good," several varieties can be distinguished. *Voluntary euthanasia* (discussed in the preceding section) is euthanasia performed at the request of the person who is killed, or (failing that) with presumed consent. (An incapacitated patient may be unable to communicate voluntary consent but may have written and notarized at some earlier time a "living will" authorizing that the patient's life not be continued in circumstances of the kind that now actually obtain.) *Involuntary euthanasia* is euthanasia performed without the consent of the person who is killed, because he or she is incompetent, that is, legally incapable of giving consent to anything, being either an infant, or brain damaged, or senile, or comatose. Cutting across this distinction is a contrast of a different kind between *active euthanasia* in which the patient is directly killed by some positive act (for example, injecting a substance into the blood) and *passive euthanasia* in which the patient is left to die although positive steps (of a quite "ordinary" kind) might have been taken to keep him or her alive.

KILLING AND LETTING DIE

Most of those who urge legalized euthanasia, like Marvin Kohl, advocate only the voluntary kind. Still, a great deal of attention has been focused on the plight of tiny infants who have been born with painful and/or seriously incapacitating deformities, diseases, or birth defects. The official position of the American Medical Association is that active euthanasia of such patients is strictly forbidden but that it is permissible to allow them to die by withholding treatment that would merely prolong their lives, provided that this failure to act has the consent of the child's parents or guardians and that death is imminent. James Rachels challenges this position on four different grounds. He argues that in many cases active euthanasia is more humane than passive euthanasia (and gives one vivid example), that the A.M.A. position leads doctors to make decisions concerning life and death on morally irrelevant grounds, that the distinction between killing and letting die has no moral importance (this is his essential point), and finally that the most common arguments in favor of the A.M.A. position are defective. In his reply to a set of unanimously critical letters to the editor from doctors in the next issue of the *New England Journal of Medicine,* Rachels reminds his readers that his article does not, strictly speaking, *advocate* active euthanasia: "I only argued that the two forms of euthanasia are morally equivalent—that either both are acceptable, or both are unacceptable. I did not advocate either form of euthanasia. Of course, if any reader is persuaded by my arguments, and he

already believes that passive euthanasia is acceptable, he may conclude that active euthanasia is acceptable also—but that is another matter."

One of Rachels' conclusions, that there is no moral difference between killing and letting die, serves as the key premise in John Harris's remarkable article, "The Survival Lottery." For if that proposition is true, then in failing to save two persons (X and Y) by killing a third (A) and transplanting that person's organs, we are as responsible for X's and Y's deaths as if we had killed them directly. Harris, who appears to adhere to a utilitarian moral philosophy, therefore advocates (for the distant hypothetical future when the techniques of organ transplanting are perfected) a scheme in which random victims are selected (without bias) by a computer to contribute all their organs to those who will otherwise die of natural causes. Since each "contributor" can save the lives of several other persons that way, the total number of deaths will be minimized, and everybody will be more secure. The personal autonomy principle might yield decisive reasons for rejecting the scheme if participation in it (like that in a military conscription lottery) were not limited to those who voluntarily enrolled in the lottery, for then some citizens would have imposed on them, on terms they are unwilling to accept, the risk of being killed by agents of the state, and that would be in effect to sanction a kind of political murder. But if we imagine a society all of whose members *voluntarily* participate in the scheme because of its anticipated benefits, on what further ground might it be condemned?

Most readers will initially suspect that there is something "fishy" in Harris's proposal, but will be puzzled (at least at first) about what exactly is wrong with it. Is it (directly) morally wrong? Or is it merely cumbersome, unwieldy, and politically dangerous? If the reader is certain that it is wrong in principle, but can find no mistake in its logic, then he might take Harris's article to be a *reductio ad absurdam* of its premise that there is no moral difference between killing and letting die. But in that case, the reader must cope with Rachels' argument to the contrary. If one's objections, on the other hand, are based on the irremovable practical difficulties inherent in the scheme (which Harris himself seems prepared to acknowledge in his final paragraph), then perhaps one might consider whether the ravages of nature themselves might not be considered a kind of "natural lottery" striking at victims in an impartial way, without any of the political dangers inherent in Harris's admittedly more efficient artificial lottery.

MURDER AND JUSTIFIED HOMICIDE

Some of the most poignant dilemmas involving "the sanctity of life" are those that confront persons who must decide whom to save and whom to let die in tragic situations in which many lives are threatened but not all can be rescued. These dilemmas are difficult enough when the decision maker is not one of the threatened group, as for example, a medical administrator who must decide which patients to treat with a life-saving therapy in short supply. It can be even more agonizing when the decision must be made by some or all of the threatened group itself, as for example, survivors of a shipwreck in a overcrowded lifeboat, or miners trapped in a cave-in with very limited provisions.

It is not difficult to construct a rationale for *lotteries* as a device for making decisions in such circumstances. If we hold to the doctrine of *the equality of human lives* (and perhaps that doctrine exhausts the whole content of *one,* relatively weak, version of "the sanctity of life principle") then we are required to give each person, whatever his or her other characteristics, an equal opportunity to survive. A genuinely randomized decision procedure would indeed provide that equal opportunity. Alternatively, if we prefer to speak of a "right to life" held equally by all human beings, then we must admit that such a right cannot imply an absolute right to be saved whenever one is endangered, because in the tragic situations it is impossible that everyone be saved even though everyone (equally) has the right to be saved. All that an equal right to life can entail in such situations is that everyone be given an equal chance to be saved, and the best way to produce that result is to design an impartial random lottery.

Because of the importance of fairness and impartiality in the distribution of heavy burdens and extreme sacrifices, random lotteries play a vital role

in reasonings as different in other ways as those of John Harris and Lon Fuller. Indeed, a lottery among five trapped cave explorers is centrally involved in Fuller's famous moral tale, "The Case of the Speluncean Explorers," a fictitious court case set in the future in a make-believe country whose moral and legal traditions are strikingly similar to our own. Fuller's ingenious story was probably suggested to him, in part, by two actual cases, *U.S. v. Holmes* (1842), a shipwreck case in which some passengers in an overloaded lifeboat were thrown overboard by order of the first mate in order to keep the boat afloat, and *Regina v. Dudley and Stephens* (1884), in which seamen adrift in a small lifeboat on the ocean, having long since consumed their supplies, deliberately killed a teenage cabin boy and fed on his body in order to keep alive until a rescuing craft should appear. The defendants were convicted of manslaughter in *U.S. v. Holmes* on the ground that "the proper mode of determining who was to be sacrificed was by casting lots." The defendants in *Regina v. Dudley and Stephens* were convicted of murder and sentenced to death (although that sentence was later commuted to six months' imprisonment). Lord Coleridge, in delivering the judgment of the court, explicitly rejected the opinion of the seventeenth-century English philosophers Hobbes and Bacon that the necessity to save one's own life is always an excuse for taking the life of another, even if the person killed is totally innocent, and not an assailant. Lord Coleridge preferred to invoke the authority of Hale and Blackstone, and argued that "to preserve one's life is generally speaking a duty, but it may be the plainest and highest duty to sacrifice it. War is full of instances in which it is a man's duty not to live, but to die. The duty in case of shipwreck of a captain to his crew, of the crew to the passengers, of soldiers to women and children. . . . these duties impose on men the moral necessity, not of the preservation, but of the sacrifice of their lives. . . . It is not correct, therefore, to say that there is any absolute or unqualified necessity to preserve one's life."

Difficult as these historical cases may have been, they are trifles when compared with Fuller's complicated hypothetical case. The unfortunate defendants before the bar in that story had to consider under pressure the various factors bearing on the moral decision to kill—probability and necessity, the lottery, consent and its revocation. The court too had to deliberate about precisely these matters, and also under pressure, albeit of a quite different kind. In addition the judges had to consider (other) factors bearing on the judicial decision to impose or withhold criminal liability. These include excuses and justifications—"self-defense," "duress," "ignorance," "necessity"—and also such deep jurisprudential matters as the scope and limits of judicial discretion, the aim of criminal punishment, the natural limits of jurisdiction, standards for interpreting a governing statute, and the role of precedent, public opinion, and the likelihood of clemency. And behind each judge's decision, subtly shaping and directing it, is some one or combination of the great perennial philosophies of law—natural law, social contract, legal positivism, and legal realism. In that way a riddle about the grounds of justified homicide leads the reader into some of the great issues in moral *and* legal philosophy.

CAPITAL PUNISHMENT

Our final problem about the morality of killing is whether the state can ever be justified in imposing the death penalty on criminals, and if so, on what grounds and for which crimes. For the utilitarian this vexed question reduces to a series of factual questions about cause and effect relations. Since capital punishment in most cases is a direct utilitarian evil in that it causes suffering and anxiety to the criminal and his loved ones and dependents, and deprives the criminal of whatever happiness his future life would otherwise have brought him, it can be justified, for the utilitarian, only on the grounds that the good of its total consequences for society in general outbalances its immediate evil. For the utilitarian, the death penalty is, like all punishment, at best a "necessary evil," justified (like evil-tasting medicine) by what it does rather than by what it is. What punishment does *when it works* is (1) to keep dangerous criminals off the streets and deprive them, at least for a time, of all opportunity to repeat their crimes, (2) to persuade them, either through fear of repeated punishment or by means of genuine repentance and moral re-

form, not to repeat their crimes, and (3) to make credible the threat of punishment to other would-be transgressors and thus deter them from committing the crimes they might otherwise be tempted to try. By means of incapacitation, reform, and deterrence, the total number of crimes is reduced, and the great amounts of suffering caused to the victims of crimes diminished. Therein lies the point, indeed the *whole* point, of punishment, according to the utilitarian. Capital punishment, of course, is the ultimate in incapacitation, so it does some utilitarian good in that respect. On the other side, it is a total failure as a reforming treatment for the criminal, since you cannot improve people by killing them. So far, there is little controversy and little need of empirical research. Almost all of the disagreement over the consequences of capital punishment is over the extent to which it succeeds in performing its third utilitarian function, that of deterring others.

Interestingly enough, utilitarians share their overriding concern with deterrence with the non-absolutistic sanctity of life theorist. The latter holds the view that imposing capital punishment on convicted murderers can be justified if and *only if* it seems, on reasonable grounds, necessary to save the lives of innocent human beings. The more lives saved, the better, on this view, since all human life, after all, is sacred. And if circumstances force us to choose between the innocent lives of unknown prospective victims or the lives of guilty murderers, then reluctantly we must choose to save the innocent. We are forced to make this choice only if we reasonably believe that killing the murderers we have in our clutches now will deter other potential murderers and thus save innocent lives. If we hold this belief in the deterrent efficacy of capital punishment and still refuse to execute murderers, then we are deliberately saving some known guilty lives at the cost of permitting a larger number of (still unknown) innocent lives to be lost, and that would be to violate the principle of the sanctity of human life, interpreted in this way. Hence, the question of deterrence is as crucial for the non-absolutist sanctity of life theorist as it is for the utilitarian.

Does the death penalty succeed in deterring potential murderers? It might seem obvious to those of us who are intimidated from double parking by the fear of $50 parking tickets, that many of our counterparts who are tempted to kill would be prevented by the fear of their own deaths at the hands of an executioner. But the matter is not as simple as that. In the first place, many (perhaps most) murders are committed, not by deliberate prudent calculators, but by persons in grand passions and towering rages, or by members of violent sub-cultures engaged in street fights or barroom brawls and doing what is required to save face or prove themselves in those communities. Either there is no time for prudent calculation or such consideration itself would cause a loss of standing with the immediate social group. Hence, no penalty, not even the death penalty, is likely to have much effect in these cases.

"Professional criminals" are another matter. They surely do weigh risks in deciding when, where, and how to commit their "crimes of gain." But since the deterrent efficacy of a punishment is a function both of its severity and (especially) of the perceived likelihood of getting apprehended in the first place, many robbers, muggers, burglars, and rapists have a self-serving motive for killing their victims and other witnesses of their crimes. In that way, in some circumstances, they may greatly increase their chances of getting away with their crimes. It is possible that in some cases over-severe punishment for nonhomicidal crimes might in this manner be counter-productive by encouraging killing.

Still another class of potential murderers might actually be encouraged to kill by a death penalty. In the aftermath of the Gary Mark Gilmore case, the *New York Times* (December 18, 1976) published an article by Boyce Rensberger which began: "The annals of psychiatry contain many cases in which persons who led tormented, and often demented, lives murdered others with the intention of invoking a death penalty that would bring them surcease. Many are clearly suicidal and believe that they deserve to die but admit they lack the nerve to kill themselves."

Even when we consider normal, non-suicidal persons who weigh risks carefully before acting, the deterrent efficacy of the death penalty is by no means obvious. What we have to remember is that we are not being asked to compare a situation in which there is a death penalty for murder with another hypothetical circumstance in which there is *no* penalty for murder. Other things being equal, we obviously could expect fewer murders in the former case than in the latter. Rather we have to ask how many calculating potential murderers (a small enough class to begin with) who are not deterred by the threat of life imprisonment (a still smaller class) would be deterred by the threat of death? There is no sure answer to this question, but surely it is not "obvious" that there would be any such persons at all, or much more than a handful every year.

Still another complication in the controversy over deterrence is not about the factual question but rather about the moral and legal costs of seeking deterrence. Some have argued that the death penalty can be deterrent if we sacrifice due process, or that we can have due process govern the infliction of the death penalty, but only by sacrificing whatever deterrence it can be presumed to have. When a human life is at stake, the courts (and especially the Supreme Court) have been more fastidious in reviewing cases for error, more thoroughgoing and rigorous in the application of constitutional standards than in cases of any other kind. (Errors in capital cases, of course, become irrevocable.) Among the consequences of this admirable rigor are ever increasing delays of execution, and an ever decreasing percentage of those convicted who are ever executed, and larger numbers of convictions overturned. (In fact, in the ten years before 1977, no one at all was executed in the United States while the numbers of prisoners on death row mounted.) The right of appeal exercised to the full leads to seemingly endless litigation, at enormous public expense, and also to what Hugo Bedau has called "luck of the draw" justice. Because the connection between murder and the death penalty has been so delayed and obscured, the deterrent effect of the latter (if it had any to begin with) must have been weakened. Hence the delays and uncertainties caused by constitutional punctiliousness may tend to destroy the deterrent effect of capital punishment. "We can ill afford . . . to sacrifice certainty and swiftness of punishment for spasmodic brutality," testified a California police chief in 1931, and numerous prosecutors and police chiefs in recent years have come to agree.

Whether capital punishment deters persons from killing us is, of course, an empirical question that cannot be settled independently of evidence. Most social scientists, however, agree that all the statistical studies of this question so far have been inconclusive. What then is the dialectical significance of this ignorance in the debate over capital punishment? Some argue that the burden of proof should always be placed on the shoulders of the person who advocates taking a human life, a proposition that seems plausible enough. There is an argument that deserves respect, however, for placing the burden of proof on the party who favors abolition of capital punishment. A policeman might argue, for example, that so long as the evidence leaves any doubt whatever of the deterrent effect of the death penalty, the benefit of that doubt should be given to innocent potential victims of murderers rather than to already convicted murderers. "My work is dangerous enough," a policeman might argue; "if a reformer proposes to decrease the penalty for murdering me, surely the burden of showing that the reform will not increase my danger ought to be squarely on the shoulders of the reformer." This argument is especially impressive when applied to measures that would reserve the death penalty for the intentional killings of policemen, prison guards, firemen on active duty, and others who need special protection, and may—or may not—get such protection from the threat of the death penalty.[1]

It may seem at first that the absolutist version of the sanctity of life principle is the least plausible of the contending principles when applied to capital punishment, but on second thought, there is surprisingly a lot to be said for it. This is the view that deliberately killing human beings, even "guilty" ones, as a means to society's ends, is absolutely impermissible morally, even when the end in question is the net saving of human lives. To appreciate that this view is not wildly implausible, readers should compare their own, presumably "absolutist," view of *torturing to death* as a possible punishment. Suppose we had good reason to believe that by reinstituting death by torture for murder we could save 100 innocent lives a year. Almost everyone these days would reject the proposal that such a penalty be introduced no matter what its deterrent effect. Torture is simply not an eligible instrument of social policy in a civilized nation. The sanctity of life "absolutist" feels the same way about the gallows and the electric chair.

It is not clear what bearing personal autonomy considerations have on the problem of punishment in general and capital punishment in particular. Some "retributivists" have argued that such considerations have at least borderline relevance in the following way: It is in the interest of everyone—even potential criminals—to have a system of criminal laws enforced by sanctions. If each person in a "state of nature" were to consult his or her own self-interest only in deciding whether to vote for or against such a system, the vote would be unanimously affirmative. The state has in fact set up such a system, a kind of "automatic machinery" that is set in motion whenever a lawbreaker is apprehended. It is as if the machinery were surrounded by signs: "WARNING! DANGER! PROCEED AT YOUR OWN RISK! WHOEVER TOUCHES THIS MACHINERY STANDS A GOOD CHANCE OF BEING CLUTCHED BY IT BEFORE HE CAN GET AWAY!" If people deliberately trespass on the machine despite the warning and are captured by its long mechanical arms, they have no one to blame but themselves. They freely assumed the risk of punishment. They "brought it on themselves." And if they would have been prepared to vote in favor of the penalty long before they put themselves in a position to receive it, they cannot complain if the general social policy of which they approved is applied in an automatic way in a particular case. The question the reader should ponder, however, is whether the *death penalty* is one that all of us would approve "in advance."

DESERVING TO DIE

In addition to the usual utilitarian, personal autonomy, and sanctity of life considerations, one quite distinct set of reasons is often invoked in the special case of capital punishment. It is here alone among the problems about the morality of killing that the factors of guilt and desert are involved. A *retributivist* is a person who argues that the primary justification for any punishment is that the criminal *deserves* it, not in any future benefit or advantage to be secured by its infliction. A deliberate murderer deserves to be killed, whatever the effect on "deterrence," and that's an end to the matter. Retributivists, if they are philosophers, will deny that their position has anything to do with anger or vengeance. Crime deserves its punishment, they will say, for the same kind of reason that good performance deserves applause, or that a good paper deserves a good grade and a poor paper a poor grade, or that the unfortunate deserve compensation, or that winners in competitions deserve prizes, and great benefactors and achievers deserve rewards. There is a unique appropriateness in the deserved responses that is not subject to further analysis, just as there is a peculiar fittingness between matching colors in art and harmonious tones in music.

James Fitzjames Stephen, the eminent Victorian jurist, argues strongly in favor of capital punishment, but in the selections included here he does not appeal explicitly to moral desert (though he no doubt does hold the view that murderers deserve to die). Instead he argues on two other grounds, first, that the public clamor for vengeance deserves its "legitimate satisfaction," and second, that human beasts must be exterminated just as much as "wolves and tigers" and other animals whose free existence would be inconsistent with "civilized society." Strictly speaking, neither of these arguments is retributive. Rather, the appeal is utilitarian. It is socially useful, Stephen maintains, to gratify public indignation, and socially indispensable to remove human wolves from the streets at minimum cost. As for the likes of William Palmer, Stephen will listen to no excuses. The man was not mad; nor was he in any way disadvantaged. The explanation for his hideous crimes as well as the justification for his hanging is that he was a thoroughly evil man.

The American judge Curtis Bok, on the other hand, is opposed to capital punishment. In an ingenious paragraph included here, he suggests that *if* any convicted killers should be put to death, it should be the insane ones who really are like wild animals, and not the normal criminals who are less dangerous as a class and more amenable to rehabilitation. But if we execute "homicidal maniacs" in the same spirit as that in which we shoot wolves or (to switch the metaphor) throw out rotten apples, we are not really *punishing* them at all. Punishment expresses a stern moral judgment; it implies that the criminal could have avoided the evil deed; and it is typically accompanied by dread and anguish, if not guilt and remorse. But exterminating "human beasts" might just as well be done as efficiently and painlessly as possible without ceremony and without pointless moralizing. Bok would prefer, of course, not to execute anybody, insane or normal. Even the most "wicked" killers, those whom Stephen would destroy without mercy, can be thought to be suffering, Bok suggests, from a kind of "moral illness or deficiency" so that it would be "unfair" to punish them. In the extreme case of Albert Fish (hardly a typical murderer) there seems no gainsaying Bok. The Fish case suggests a paradox: Beyond a certain maximum point, human wickedness seems so bizarre as not to be thought of as wickedness at all, but as exculpating mental illness. How wicked then can a person become before we think of him as not truly wicked at all?

Paul Crump was a much more typical killer than Albert Fish. Angry, treacherous, and unrepentant, he seemed at the time of his conviction to be truly a wild beast who had known no life but that of the human jungle, "bloody in tooth and claw." Stephen would gladly have seen him exterminated without mercy. Ronald Bailey, in the concluding article in this chapter, describes the extraordinary changes in Crump's character that occurred during the seven years he was on "death row" before his sentence to death was commuted. Had Crump been executed promptly at the time of his conviction, there would have been few dissenters to the judgment that he got what he deserved. In some sense he was the "same man" seven years later, but it would have seemed morally absurd then to hold that he *deserved* to be hanged.

Fish did not deserve to die because his "wickedness" was so extreme that it must have been illness beyond his control (according to Bok). Crump did not deserve to die (according to his warden) because his wickedness was not great enough to preclude his rehabilitation. Somewhere in between these extremes, there may be killers who truly do deserve to die, but is is no easy task conceiving what they must be like.

Joel Feinberg

NOTE

1.   Some of the material in the preceding two paragraphs has been drawn directly from the review of Hugo Bedau's *The Death Penalty in America* by Joel Feinberg that appeared in *Ethics,* 76 (October 1965): 65–66.

Animal Life

35. UNSANCTIFYING HUMAN LIFE

Peter Singer

As a preface to the substantive part of this paper, I offer a comment on the nature of medical ethics which may clarify my approach.

The professional philosopher with an interest in ethics, and in particular what might be called "applied moral philosophy," may well discuss, with his students and colleagues, the moral problems that doctors encounter in the course of their practice. Since the professional philosopher is specially trained to think about these issues, and has all the time he requires at his disposal to do so, one might think that the philosopher would be able to give considerable assistance to the doctor, whose training and time are devoted to medicine rather than moral philosophy. Yet, with few exceptions, this is not the case. Doctors discuss their ethical dilemmas in the medical journals, and philosophers keep to the philosophical journals; and the footnotes in each case remain within the circle of the author's colleagues.

Reprinted from Peter Singer, "Unsanctifying Human Life," with the permission of the author. The full version of this article contains a concluding "historical excursus" in which the author discusses the religious origin of the doctrine of the sanctity of human life. It appears in *Ethical Issues Relating to Life and Death,* ed. by John Ladd (New York: Oxford University Press, 1978).

All this is not just a matter of the old academic failure to look at work outside one's own discipline. Anyone who reads both philosophical and medical journals containing discussions of problems in medical ethics can hardly avoid noticing that there is a more fundamental gap between the discussions than the fact that they appear in different kinds of journals. There is also a difference in the presuppositions employed, and the problems discussed.

For example, in recent issues of philosophical journals, we can find articles in which it is argued, quite seriously and on plausible grounds, that a normal, healthy human infant has no right to life, and that it is, in this respect, in the same position as a fetus.[1] Doctors, on the other hand, are so far from even considering this position that they regard as serious ethical dilemmas such questions as: "What should be done with a patient certain never to recover consciousness?" or, "Are parents to be given the option of deciding how far a doctor should go in using all available techniques to save the life of a hopelessly retarded infant with, in addition, a congenital heart defect?"[2]

There are a number of reasons why the ethical concerns of philosophers and practicing physicians should be so far apart. One important reason is the different ways in which they are affected by the law.

The busy doctor, who would rather be doing medicine than philosophy, turns to ethical questions only when they actually confront him. He tends not to raise questions which he would never face in practice, for he has enough problems without thinking up hypothetical ones. So if some course of action is straightforwardly illegal—for instance, the direct killing of a retarded infant—then most doctors are not even going to consider whether this course of action might be morally justifiable. When the law is clear, it resolves the doctor's ethical problem for him. So long as the doctor obeys the law, he can hardly be blamed for the outcome, for he can regard himself as purely a medical man, a technician whose business it is to carry out policy, but not to set it; if he goes against the law, however, he risks disqualification from practice, and criminal proceedings. No wonder that most medical ethics is concerned with cases on which the law fails to give any clear guide—cases like those involving the use of extraordinary means to save life.

The philosopher, of course, is in a quite different position. Untroubled by such mundane issues as what the law allows, he turns his attention to cases which invoke basic moral principles. If real cases do not serve this purpose, he is free to make up hypothetical ones. So he follows the argument wherever it leads him, and if it leads him to the view that infanticide is often justifiable, well, this conclusion is not likely to cause him any personal problems.

Now one can certainly sympathize with the doctor who confines his attention to those cases that he *has* to deal with, and regards the moral philosopher as an irresponsible theorizer. Nevertheless, the resulting limited scope of much of the work by medical people in medical ethics has, I think, had a harmful effect on the conclusions reached even within those areas that have received close attention. While we may agree that in general a doctor ought to obey the law, there has been a tendency to lose sight of the difference between this view, and the idea that the law, and the conventional moral standards it embodies, is an indisputable starting point for further ethical debate. Because in practice a doctor could not challenge the law when it is clear and straightforward, the moral standards behind the law also do not often get challenged; if these conventional moral standards are in fact dubious, however, then conclusions which presuppose them are also likely to be dubious.

My purpose in what follows is to challenge one of these conventional moral doctrines: the doctrine of the sanctity of human life. I know that in taking this approach I run the risk of being regarded as yet another philosopher far removed from the world of real people. I shall try to guard against this danger by discussing some current, widely accepted medical practices. My strategy will be to bring together two distinct areas of medicine that are normally discussed only in quite separate moral contexts, and to show thereby that current attitudes in medical ethics are either plainly inconsistent, or else guilty of a crude form of discrimination that is no more defensible than racial discrimination. In this way I want to force those involved in medicine to reconsider the foundations of the decisions they make. Foundations that give rise to the kind of inconsistency or discrimination that I am referring to are in urgent need of reconsideration; and the core of the problem, I believe, is the doctrine of the sanctity of human life.

People often say that life is sacred. They almost never mean what they say. They do not mean, as their words seem to imply, that *all* life is sacred. If they did, killing a pig, or, for that matter, pulling up a cabbage, would be as contrary to their doctrine as infanticide. So when, in the context of medical ethics, people talk of the sanctity of life, it is the sanctity of *human* life that they really mean. It is this doctrine that I shall be discussing from now on.

In discussing the doctrine of the sanctity of human life, I shall not take the term "sanctity" in any specifically religious sense. Although I think that the doctrine does have a religious origin, and I shall say more about this shortly, it is now part of a broadly secular ethic, and it is as part of this secular ethic that it is most influential today. Not all those who talk about "the sanctity of life" are religious, and of those that are religious, in many cases their affirmation of the sanctity of life is independent of their religious views. In the secular context in which problems of medical ethics are usually discussed today, those who talk of the sanctity of human life are trying to say, essentially, that human life has some very special value; and a crucial implication of this assertion is the idea that there is a radical difference between the value of a human life and the value of the life of some other animal—a difference not merely in degree, but of quality or kind.

It is this idea, the idea that *human* life as such has unique value, that I shall criticize. Before I do so, however, I want to demonstrate how deep-seated and pervasive this idea of the unique value of human life is, and how far this idea is sometimes taken in our own society, and within the field of medicine. To demonstrate this, I offer two instances from different areas of medicine.

First, as an example of the value attributed to human life, I summarize a case history from Anthony Shaw's recent article, "Dilemmas of 'Informed Consent' in Children":[3]

A baby was born with Down's syndrome (mongolism), intestinal obstruction, and a congenital heart condition. The mother, believing that the retarded infant would be impossible for her to care for adequately, refused to consent to surgery to remove the intestinal obstruction. Without surgery, of course, the baby would soon die. Thereupon a local child-welfare agency, invoking a state child-abuse statute, obtained a court order directly that surgery be performed. After a complicated course of surgery and thousands of dollars worth of medical care, the infant was returned to her mother. In addition to her mental retardation, the baby's physical growth and development remained markedly retarded because of her severe cardiac disease. A follow-up enquiry eighteen months after the baby's birth revealed that the mother felt more than ever that she had been done an injustice.

This case, then, shows how much some people are prepared to do in order to ensure that a human infant lives, irrespective of the actual or potential mental capacities of the infant, its physical condition, or the wishes of the mother.

While some doctors are struggling to preserve life in cases of this sort, others are using their medical training in another way: They design and carry out experiments on non-human animals. I will give an example of the kind of work that is quite frequently done, because its nature is not as well known as it ought to be. This particular experiment was carried out at the University of Michigan Medical School, and funded by the National Research Council and the U.S. Public Health Service. The description which follows is drawn from the researchers' own account, which they published in the journal *Psychopharmacologia:*[4]

The researchers confined sixty-four monkeys in small cubicles. These monkeys were then given unlimited access to a variety of drugs, through tubes implanted in their arms. They could control the intake by pressing a lever. In some cases, after the monkeys had become addicted, supplies were abruptly cut off. Of the monkeys that had become addicted to morphine, three were "observed to die in convulsions" while others found dead in the morning were "presumed to have died in convulsions." Monkeys that had taken large amounts of cocaine inflicted severe wounds upon themselves, including biting off their fingers and toes, before dying convulsive deaths. Amphetamines caused one monkey to "pluck all of the hair off his arms and abdomen." In general, the experimenters found that "The manifestations of toxicity . . . were similar to the well-known toxicities of these drugs in man." They noted that experiments on animals with addictive drugs had been going on in their laboratory for "the last 20 years."

I know that it is not pleasant to think about experiments of this nature; but since they are a real part of medicine, they should not be ignored. In fact this experiment is by no means exceptional, and is perhaps no worse than the routine testing of new drugs, foodstuffs, and cosmetics, which results in the poisoning of millions of animals annually in the United States.[5] Nor, for that matter, is the case of the mongoloid infant exceptional, apart from the fact that it was necessary to invoke the law; more commonly, the doctors would have obtained the mother's signature, though how often that signature implies genuine 'informed consent' is another matter.

The question that arises from consideration of these two kinds of case is simply this: can it be right to make great efforts to save the life of a mongoloid human infant, when the mother does not want the infant to live, and at the same time not be wrong to kill, slowly and painfully, a number of monkeys?

One obvious defense of the addiction experiment that might be offered is that by means of such experiments, results are obtained which lead to the elimination of more suffering than is caused by the experiments themselves. In fact, this is usually not the case. Certainly in the experiment I described, no startling new discoveries were made, and any connection with the alleviation of suffering seems very tenuous. But anyway, this defense is irrelevant to the comparison I am drawing between the way we treat humans and other animals. We would not forcibly addict mongoloid infants to drugs and then allow them to die in convulsions even if we did believe that useful knowledge could thus be obtained. Why do we think it wrong to treat members of our own species in the same way that we treat other species?

Can it ever be right to treat one kind of being in a way that we would not treat another kind? Of course it can, if the beings differ in relevant respects. Which respects are relevant will depend on the treatment in question. We could defend a decision to teach young members of our own species to read, without making the same effort on behalf of young dogs, on the grounds that the two kinds of being differ in their capacity to benefit from these efforts. This difference is obviously relevant to the particular proposal. On the other hand, anyone who proposed teaching some humans to read, but not others, on the grounds that people whose racial origin is different from his own should not be encouraged to read, would be discriminating on an arbitrary basis, since race as such has nothing to do with the extent to which a person can benefit from being able to read.

Now what is the position when we compare severely and irreparably retarded human infants with non-human animals like pigs and dogs, monkeys and apes? I think we are forced to conclude that in at least some cases the human infant does not possess any characteristics or capacities that are not also possessed, to an equal or higher degree, by many non-human animals. This is true of such capacities as the capacity to feel pain, to act intentionally, to solve problems, to communicate with and relate to other beings; and such characteristics as self-awareness, a sense of one's own existence over time, concern for other beings, and curiosity.[6] In all these respects adult members of the species I have mentioned equal or surpass many retarded infant members of our own species; moreover some of these non-humans surpass anything that

some human infants might eventually achieve even with intensive care and assistance. (In case anyone should be uncertain about this, may I remind you that chimpanzees have now been taught to communicate by means of American Sign Language, the standard language used by deaf people in this country, and have mastered vocabularies of well over a hundred signs, including signs which indicate that they possess self-awareness, and the concept of time.[7])

So when we decide to treat one being—the severely and irreparably retarded infant—in one way, and the other being—the pig, monkey, or whatever —in another way, there seems to be no difference between the two that we can appeal to in defense of our discrimination. There is, of course, the fact that one being is, biologically, a member of our own species, while the others are members of other species. This difference, however, cannot justify different treatment, except perhaps in very special circumstances; for it is precisely the kind of arbitrary difference that the most crude and overt kind of racist tries to use to justify racial discrimination. Just as a person's race is, in itself, nearly always irrelevant to the question of how that person should be treated, so a being's species is, in itself, nearly always irrelevant. If we are prepared to disciminate against a being simply because it is not a member of our own species, although it has capacities equal or superior to those of a member of our own species, how can we object to the racist discriminating against those who are not of his own race, although they have capacities equal or superior to those of members of his own race?

I said a moment ago that a difference of species cannot justify different treatment except perhaps in very special circumstances. It may be worth mentioning the circumstances I have in mind. If we had discovered a new drug which we thought might be a very powerful aid in the treatment of serious diseases, we might feel that it should be tested in some way before being used on normal humans, in order to see if it had dangerous side-effects. Assuming that there was no reliable way of testing it except on a living, sentient creature, should we test it on a severely and irreparably retarded human infant, or on some other animal, like a monkey? Here, if the capacities of the beings are equal, I think we might be justified in saying that the biological species of the being was relevant. Since many drugs affect different species in unpredictably different ways, we would probably achieve our goal sooner by testing the drug on the retarded member of our own species than on the monkey; this would mean that we would have to use less subjects for our experiment, and so inflict less suffering all told. This seems to be a reasonable ground for preferring to use the human infant, rather than the monkey, if we have already decided to test the drug on one or other of the two. So discrimination on the basis of species, in the rare cases in which it is justified, seems to go *against* our present practices, rather than in favor of them. (Even here, it ought to be said, we would not really be discriminating on the basis of species *as such,* but rather using the species of the being as an indication of further possible unknown differences between them.)

The doctrine of the sanctity of human life, as it is normally understood, has at its core a discrimination on the basis of species and nothing else. Those who espouse the doctrine make no distinction, in their opposition to killing, between normal humans who have developed to a point at which they surpass anything that other animals can achieve, or humans in a condition of hopeless senility, or human fetuses, or infant humans, or severely brain-damaged humans. Yet those who use the sanctity of life doctrine as a ground for opposition to killing any human being show little or no concern over the vast amount of quite unnecessary killing of non-human animals that goes on in our society, despite the fact that, as I have said, many of these other animals equal or surpass, on any test that I can imagine to be relevant, humans in all the categories I have just mentioned, except for normal humans beyond the age of infancy. It is significant to note, too, that even if we allow the relevance of a being's potential (and I would agree with Michael Tooley that there are serious objections to so doing[8]) there are still human beings, whose life is allegedly sacrosanct, who cannot be distinguished from other animals in respect of their potential.

A doctrine which went by the name of "the sanctity of human life" would not necessarily have to be a speciesist doctrine. The term "human" is not, strictly, a biological term, and, as Tooley has pointed out, it is a mistake to assume that "human being" refers to precisely the same beings as are designated by the biological idea of "member of the species *homo sapiens*." "Human," according to the Oxford English Dictionary, means "of, belonging to, or characteristic of man"; or in a slightly different sense, "having or showing the qualities or attributes proper to or distinctive of man." If the advocates of the "sanctity of human life" doctrine were to take this definition seriously, they would find their views radically transformed. According to the definition, whether we class a being as "human" will depend on what qualities or attributes we think characteristic of, proper to, or distinctive of man (and I assume that by "man," the dictionary here means men and women, mankind as a whole). So we would then have to try to draw up a list of these qualities or attributes—something which some writers in the field have already tried to do.[9] This list would probably include some or all of the capacities and characteristics that I mentioned earlier, when comparing retarded infants and monkeys, but to decide which properties were necessary and which sufficient would be difficult. Let us say, though, just to take an example, that we decide that what is characteristic or distinctive of men and women is a capacity for self-awareness or self-consciousness. Then we will not count severely retarded infants as human beings, even though they are clearly members of *homo sapiens;* at the same time we might decide, after examining the abilities displayed by apes, dolphins, and perhaps some other mammals, to count these beings as human beings.

In any case, if we follow the dictionary definition of "human," one point seems certain, whatever criteria we eventually select as distinctive of men and women: severely and irreparably retarded *homo sapiens* infants would be in the same category as a great many members of other species. This seems true, anyway, so long as we stay within the secular context that I have been assuming throughout this discussion. If we allow appeals to religious doctrines, based on special revelations, other conclusions might be possible. . . .

Is the only problem with the doctrine of the sanctity of human life, then, a misconception about the boundaries of "human"? Is it just that the advocates of this doctrine have got hold of a biological notion of what it is to be human, instead of a notion that defines the term as the dictionary suggests it should be defined, with regard to distinctively human characteristics?

We could, perhaps, try to save the doctrine by modifying it in this way. It would be no small modification; I chose my two contrasting examples of medical practice to show how far from this kind of position our present attitudes are. The suggested modification of the doctrine would place lethal experiments on the more developed non-human animals in the same category as experiments on severely retarded members of our own species. Similarly, if, as Jonathan Swift once suggested, human infants, boiled, roasted or fricasséed, make a tasty dish, then we would have to choose between ceasing to rear animals like pigs and cattle for food, or admitting that there is no moral objection to fattening retarded infants for the table. Clearly, this is not a position that many present advocates of the sanctity of human life would be prepared to embrace. In fact, it is so far from what present advocates of the doctrine mean, that it would be downright misleading to continue to use the same name for the doctrine. Whatever the proper or dictionary meaning of the word "human" is now, in popular usage, too closely identified with "member of the species *homo sapiens*" for us to apply it to chimpanzees, or deny it to retarded infants. I myself, in this paper, have used, and for reasons of convenience shall continue to use, the word in its popular, rather than dictionary, sense.

A further difficult question which any attempt to redraw the boundaries of the "human" community must face is: where do we place normal embryonic or infant members of our species, who have the potential, given normal development, to satisfy the criteria for membership, but do not satisfy them at present? Judged by the characteristics they actually possess, and excluding for the moment such indirect factors as the concerns of parents or others, an infant *homo sapiens* aged, say, 6 months, would seem to be much less of a "human" than an adult chimpanzee; and if we reduce the age of the infant to, say, one month, it compares unfavorably with those adult members of other species—pigs, cattle, sheep, rats, chickens, and mice—that we destroy by the million in our slaughterhouses and laboratories. Does the potential of these infants make a difference to the wrongness of killing them?

It is impossible for me to discuss this question adequately in the time I have available, so I will only point out that if we believe it is the potential of the infant that makes it wrong to kill it, we seem to be committed to the view that abortion, however soon after conception it may take place, is as seriously wrong as infanticide. Moreover, it is not easy to see on what grounds mere potential could give rise to a right to life, unless we valued what it was that the being had potential to become—in this case, a rational, self-conscious being. Now while we may think that a rational, self-conscious being has a right to life, relatively few of us, I think, value the existence of rational self-conscious beings in the sense that the more of them there are, the better we think it is. If we did value the existence of rational self-conscious beings in this way, we would be opposed to contraception, as well as abortion and infanticide, and even to abstinence or celibacy. But most of us think that there are enough rational self-conscious beings around already—in which case I find it hard to see why we should place great moral weight on every potentially rational, self-conscious being realizing its potential. For further discussion of this important topic, though, I must refer you to the articles by Tooley and Warren that I have already mentioned.

Assuming that we can settle the criteria for being "human" in the strict sense, and can settle this problem about potentially "human" beings, would this mean that we had settled the question of which lives are sacred, and which beings it is justifiable to kill for rather trivial reasons? Unfortunately, even then we would not have solved all our problems; for there is no necessary connection between what is characteristic of, or distinctive of, mankind, and what it is that makes it wrong to kill a being. To believe that this connection was automatic and followed immediately without further argument would only be a slightly more sophisticated form of speciesism than the crude biological basis of discrimination discussed earlier. While we might, in the end, decide that all and only those beings whose lives were sacred were those that possessed the characteristics distinctive of mankind, this would be a moral decision that could not be deduced simply from the definition of "human." We might, on reflection, decide the other way—for instance, we might hold that no sentient being should be killed if the probability is that its life will contain a favorable balance of pleasure or happiness over pain and suffering.

Although I have been unable to make up my own mind about the necessary criteria for a right to life —and I leave this question open in the hope that others will be able to help me decide—it is clear that we shall have to change our attitudes about killing so as to obliterate the sharp distinction that we currently make between beings that are members of our own species and beings that are not. How shall we do this?

There are three possibilities:

(1) While holding constant our attitudes to members of other species, we change our attitudes to members of our own species, so that we consider it legitimate to kill retarded human infants in painful ways for experimental purposes even when no immediately useful knowledge is likely to be derived from these experiments; and in addition we give up any moral objections we may have to rearing and killing these infants for food.

(2) While holding constant our attitudes to members of our own species, we change our attitudes to members of other species, so that we consider it wrong to kill them because we like the taste of their flesh, or for experimental purposes even when the experiment would result in immediately useful knowledge; and moreover we refuse to kill them even when they are suffering severe pain from some incurable disease, and are a burden to those who must look after them.

(3) We change our attitudes to both humans and non-humans, so that they come together at some point in between the present extremes.

None of these three positions makes an arbitrary discrimination on the basis of species, and all are consistent. So we cannot decide between them on these grounds; and accordingly, while I am quite certain that our present attitudes are wrong, I am a little more tentative about which of these possibilities is right. Still, if we look at what each implies, I think we can see that the third possibility has much in its favor—not surprisingly, in view of its median position. Thus, I doubt that anyone could seriously advocate performing an experiment like that I described earlier, on retarded infants of our own species; nor do I think that many of us could treat retarded infants as if they were purely means

towards our gastronomic ends. I think that we can only carry on these practices with regard to other species because we have a huge prejudice in favor of the interests of our own species, and a corresponding tendency to neglect the interests of other species. If I am right about this, we are not likely to transfer this prejudice to members of our own species. Racist slave-owners, if forced to stop discriminating, would be unlikely to start enslaving whites.

As for the second possibility, while I advocate a very radical change in our attitudes towards other species, I do not think this change should go so far as to imply that we should eliminate all mercy-killing, or attempt to keep alive an animal which can only live in misery.

So we have to change our attitudes in both directions. We have to bring non-humans within the sphere of our moral concern, and cease to treat them purely as means to our ends. At the same time, once we realize that the fact that severely and irreparably retarded infants are members of the species *homo sapiens* is not in itself relevant to how we should treat them, we should be ready to reconsider current practices which cause suffering to all concerned and benefit nobody. As an example of such a practice, I shall consider, very briefly, the practice of allowing these infants to die by withholding treatment.

It quite often happens that a severely and irreparably retarded infant has, in addition to its retardation, a condition which, unless treated, will cause it to die in some foreseeable period—perhaps a day, perhaps a few months or a year. The condition may be one which doctors could, and in the case of a normal infant certainly would, cure; but sometimes, when the infant is severely and irreparably retarded, the doctor in charge will withhold this treatment and allow the infant to die. In general, we can only guess at how often this occurs; but a recent investigation of the Yale-New Haven special care nursery showed that over a 2½ year period, 43 deaths, or 14% of all deaths in the nursery, were related to withholding treatment. The decision to withhold treatment at this nursery was in each case made by parents and physicians together, on the basis that there was little or no chance for a meaningful life for the infant.[10] The investigators, Duff and Campbell, cautiously endorse this practice, and within the alternatives legally available to the doctors, it does seem to be the best that they can do; but if it is justifiable to withhold available forms of treatment, knowing that this will result in the death of the infant, what possible grounds can there be for refusing to kill the infant painlessly?

The idea that there is a significant moral distinction between an act and an omission, between killing and letting die, has already been attacked by philosophers.[11] I accept their arguments, and I have nothing new to add to them, except for the reflection that we would never consider allowing a horse or dog to die in agony if it could be killed painlessly. Once we see that the case of a dying horse is really quite parallel to the case of a dying retarded infant, we may be more ready to drop the distinction between killing and letting die in the case of the infant too.

This is by no means an academic issue. Enormous, and in my view utterly needless, suffering is caused by our present attitudes. Take, for example, the condition known as *spina bifida*, in which the infant is born with its spinal cord exposed. Three out of every thousand babies have this condition, which adds up to a large number of babies. Although treatment is possible, with the more severe cases even immediate surgery and vigorous treatment will not result in successful rehabilitation. The children will grow up severely handicapped, both mentally and physically, and they will probably die in their teens. The burdens on the family can easily be imagined, and it is doubtful if the child's life is a benefit for him. But what is the alternative to surgery, under present medical ethics?

If surgery is not performed, the spina bifida baby will die—but not immediately. Some of them, perhaps a third, will last more than three months, and a few will survive for several years. One writer has described their condition in the following terms:

Virtually all will be paralyzed from the waist down, and incontinent because of damage to their exposed nerves. Four out of five of these survivors will get hydrocephalus; their heads will swell out, some until they are too heavy to hold up. Severely retarded, often spastic and blind, they will spend their childhood in institutions that most of us do not care to think about, let alone visit. By adolescence virtually all will be dead.[12]

This kind of life is the alternative that parents must face if they hesitate to consent to surgery. It is a horrible, immoral choice to offer anyone, let alone parents immediately after the birth of their child. The obvious alternative to trying to bring up a severely retarded and handicapped child—a swift, painless death for the infant—is not available, because the law enforces the idea that the infant's life is sacred and cannot be directly terminated.

This, then, is one way in which our treatment of severely and irreparably retarded infants needs to be brought closer to our better forms of treatment of members of other species.

I said at the beginning of this paper that the doctor with an interest in medical ethics, and the moral philosopher, have different concerns, at least partly because of their different positions vis-a-vis the law. No doubt this applies to the practice of allowing infants to die while refusing to kill them. The law prohibits killing, but gives no clear directive about letting die; so doctors do what they can to relieve suffering within the boundaries of the law. For this, of course, they are to be commended; but there are indications that a policy which can be defended only in terms of making the best of a bad legal situation is also being thought of as embodying a significant moral distinction. Doctors can be heard sagely quoting Arthur Clough's lines: "Thou shalt not kill, but needst not strive officiously to keep alive," as if these lines were a piece of ancient wisdom—they seem to be unaware that the lines were written to satirize the moral position in support of which they are being quoted.[13] More seriously, the House of Delegates of the American Medical Association recently adopted a policy statement condemning "the intentional termination of the life of one human being by another" as "contrary to that for which the medical profession stands," although the same statement went on to allow the "cessation of the employment of extraordinary means to preserve the life of the body."[14] But what is the cessation of any form of life-sustaining treatment if it is not the intentional termination of the life of one human being by another? And what exactly is it for which the medical profession stands that allows it to kill millions of sentient non-human beings, while prohibiting it from releasing from suffering an infant *homo sapiens* with a lower potential for a meaningful life? While doctors may have to obey the law, they do not have to defend it.

I have suggested some ways in which, once we eliminate speciesist bias from our moral views, we might bring our attitudes to human and non-human animals closer together. I am well aware that I have not given any precise suggestions about when it is justifiable to kill either a retarded infant, or a non-human animal. I really have not made up my mind on this problem, and so I leave it open, in the hope that others will offer suggestions.

NOTES

1. See Michael Tooley, "Abortion and Infanticide," *Philosophy and Public Affairs*, vol. 2, no. 1 (1972); a similar conclusion seems to be implied by Mary Anne Warren, "The Moral and Legal Status of Abortion," *The Monist*, vol. 57, no. 1 (1973).
2. See Henry K. Beecher, "Ethical Problems Created by the Hopelessly Unconscious Patient," *New England Journal of Medicine*, vol. 278, no. 26 (1968); Anthony Shaw, "Dilemmas of 'Informed Consent' in Children," *New England Journal of Medicine*, vol. 289, no. 17 (1973).
3. *Op. cit.*

4. G. Deneau, T. Yanagita and M. Seevers, "Self-Administration of Psychoactive Substances by the Monkey," *Psychopharmacologia*, vol. 16, pp. 30–48.
5. See Richard Ryder, "Experiments on Animals" in *Animals, Men and Morals*, ed. S. and R. Godlovitch and J. Harris, Gollancz, London, 1971.
6. This list is a compound of the main indicators of "humanhood" or "personhood" suggested by Mary Anne Warren, *op. cit.*, and Joseph Fletcher, "Indicators of Humanhood: A Tentative Profile of Man," *The Hastings Center Report* (Institute of Society, Ethics and the Life Sciences, Hastings-on Hudson, N.Y.), vol. 2, no. 5 (1972).
7. For an early report, see R. A. Gardner and B. T. Gardner, "Teaching Sign Language to a Chimpanzee," *Science*, 165 (1969); and for a more recent informal summary of progress in this area see a report by Peter Jenkins, *The Guardian* (London), July 10, 1973, p. 16.
8. *Op. cit.*
9. See note 6, above.
10. R. S. Duff and A. G. M. Campbell, "Moral and Ethical Dilemmas in the Special Care Nursery," *New England Journal of Medicine*, vol. 289, no. 17 (1973).
11. See Jonathan Bennett, "Whatever the Consequences," *Analysis*, vol. 26 (1966) and Tooley, *op. cit.*
12. Gerald Leach, *The Biocrats* (Penguin, Middlesex, England, 1972), p. 197.
13. I owe this point to Jonathan Glover.
14. *New York Times*, Dec. 5, 1973.

Abortion

36. ON THE MORAL AND LEGAL STATUS OF ABORTION

Mary Anne Warren

We will be concerned with both the moral status of abortion, which for our purposes we may define as the act which a woman performs in voluntarily terminating, or allowing another person to terminate, her pregnancy, and the legal status which is

From Mary Anne Warren, "On the Moral and Legal Status of Abortion," *The Monist*, Vol. 57 (1973), and "Postscript on Infanticide" from *Today's Moral Problems*, ed. by Richard A. Wasserstrom (New York: Macmillan, 1975), pp. 135–36. Reprinted by permission of the author and *The Monist*.

appropriate for this act. I will argue that, while it is not possible to produce a satisfactory defense of a woman's right to obtain an abortion without showing that a fetus is not a human being, in the morally relevant sense of that term, we ought not to conclude that the difficulties involved in determining whether or not a fetus is human make it impossible to produce any satisfactory solution to the problem of the moral status of abortion. For it is possible to show that on the basis of intuitions which we may expect even the opponents of abortion to share, a fetus is not a person, and hence not the sort of entity to which it is proper to ascribe full moral rights. . . .

The question which we must answer in order to produce a satisfactory solution to the problem of the moral status of abortion is this: How are we to define the moral community, the set of beings with full and equal moral rights, such that we can decide whether a human fetus is a member of this community or not? What sort of entity, exactly, has the inalienable rights to life, liberty, and the pursuit of happiness? Jefferson attributed these rights to all *men,* and it may or may not be fair to suggest that he intended to attribute them *only* to men. Perhaps he ought to have attributed them to all human beings. If so, then we arrive, first, at Noonan's problem of defining what makes a being human, and second, at the equally vital question which Noonan does not consider, namely, What reason is there for identifying the moral community with the set of all human beings, in whatever way we have chosen to define that term?

1. ON THE DEFINITION OF 'HUMAN'

One reason why this vital second question is so frequently overlooked in the debate over the moral status of abortion is that the term 'human' has two distinct, but not often distinguished, senses. This fact results in a slide of meaning, which serves to conceal the fallaciousness of the traditional argument that since (1) it is wrong to kill innocent human beings, and (2) fetuses are innocent human beings, then (3) it is wrong to kill fetuses. For if 'human' is used in the same sense in both (1) and (2) then, whichever of the two senses is meant, one of these premises is question-begging. And if it is used in two different senses then of course the conclusion doesn't follow.

Thus, (1) is a self-evident moral truth,[1] and avoids begging the question about abortion, only if 'human being' is used to mean something like "a full-fledged member of the moral community." (It may or may not also be meant to refer exclusively to members of the species *Homo sapiens*.) We may call this the *moral* sense of 'human'. It is not to be confused with what we will call the *genetic* sense,

i.e., the sense in which *any* member of the species is a human being, and no member of any other species could be. If (1) is acceptable only if the moral sense is intended, (2) is non-question-begging only if what is intended is the genetic sense.

In "Deciding Who is Human," Noonan argues for the classification of fetuses with human beings by pointing to the presence of the full genetic code, and the potential capacity for rational thought (p.135). It is clear that what he needs to show, for his version of the traditional argument to be valid, is that fetuses are human in the moral sense, the sense in which it is analytically true that all human beings have full moral rights. But, in the absence of any argument showing that whatever is genetically human is also morally human, and he gives none, nothing more than genetic humanity can be demonstrated by the presence of the human genetic code. And, as we will see, the *potential* capacity for rational thought can at most show that an entity has the potential for *becoming* human in the moral sense.

2. DEFINING THE MORAL COMMUNITY

Can it be established that genetic humanity is sufficient for moral humanity? I think that there are very good reasons for not defining the moral community in this way. I would like to suggest an alternative way of defining the moral community, which I will argue for only to the extent of explaining why it is, or should be, self-evident. The suggestion is simply that the moral community consists of all and only *people,* rather than all and only human beings;[2] and probably the best way of demonstrating its self-evidence is by considering the concept of personhood, to see what sorts of entity are and are not persons, and what the decision that a being is or is not a person implies about its moral rights.

What characteristics entitle an entity to be considered a person? This is obviously not the place to attempt a complete analysis of the concept of personhood, but we do not need such a fully adequate analysis just to determine whether and why a fetus is or isn't a person. All we need is a rough and approximate list of the most basic criteria of personhood, and some idea of which, or how many, of these an entity must satisfy in order to properly be considered a person.

In searching for such criteria, it is useful to look beyond the set of people with whom we are acquainted, and ask how we would decide whether a totally alien being was a person or not. (For we have no right to assume that genetic humanity is necessary for personhood.) Imagine a space traveler who lands on an unknown planet and encounters a race of beings utterly unlike any he has ever seen or heard of. If he wants to be sure of behaving morally toward these beings, he has to somehow decide whether they are people, and hence have full moral rights, or whether they are the sort of thing which he need not feel guilty about treating as, for example, a source of food.

How should he go about making this decision? If he has some anthropological background, he might look for such things as religion, art, and the manufacturing of tools, weapons, or shelters, since these factors have been used to distinguish our human from our prehuman ancestors, in what seems to be closer to the moral than the genetic sense of 'human'. And no doubt he would be right to consider the presence of such factors as good evidence that the alien beings were people, and morally human. It would, however, be overly anthropocentric of him to take the absence of these things as adequate evidence that they were not, since we can imagine people who have progressed beyond, or evolved without ever developing, these cultural characteristics.

I suggest that the traits which are most central to the concept of personhood, or humanity in the moral sense, are, very roughly, the following:

(1) consciousness (of objects and events external and/or internal to the being), and in particular the capacity to feel pain;
(2) reasoning (the *developed* capacity to solve new and relatively complex problems);
(3) self-motivated activity (activity which is relatively independent of either genetic or direct external control);
(4) the capacity to communicate, by whatever means, messages of an indefinite variety of types, that is, not just with an indefinite number of possible contents, but on indefinitely many possible topics;

(5) the presence of self-concepts, and self-awareness, either individual or racial, or both.

Admittedly, there are apt to be a great many problems involved in formulating precise definitions of these criteria, let alone in developing universally valid behavioral criteria for deciding when they apply. But I will assume that both we and our explorer know approximately what (1)–(5) mean, and that he is also able to determine whether or not they apply. How, then, should he use his findings to decide whether or not the alien beings are people? We needn't suppose that an entity must have *all* of these attributes to be properly considered a person; (1) and (2) alone may well be sufficient for personhood, and quite probably (1)–(3) are sufficient. Neither do we need to insist that any one of these criteria is *necessary* for personhood, although once again (1) and (2) look like fairly good candidates for necessary conditions, as does (3), if 'activity' is construed so as to include the activity of reasoning.

All we need to claim, to demonstrate that a fetus is not a person, is that any being which satisfies *none* of (1)–(5) is certainly not a person. I consider this claim to be so obvious that I think anyone who denied it, and claimed that a being which satisfied none of (1)–(5) was a person all the same, would thereby demonstrate that he had no notion at all of what a person is—perhaps because he had confused the concept of a person with that of genetic humanity. If the opponents of abortion were to deny the appropriateness of these five criteria, I do not know what further arguments would convince them. We would probably have to admit that our conceptual schemes were indeed irreconcilably different, and that our dispute could not be settled objectively.

I do not expect this to happen, however, since I think that the concept of a person is one which is very nearly universal (to people), and that it is common to both proabortionists and antiabortionists, even though neither group has fully realized the relevance of this concept to the resolution of their dispute. Furthermore, I think that on reflection even the antiabortionists ought to agree not only that (1)–(5) are central to the concept of personhood, but also that it is a part of this concept that all and only people have full moral rights. The concept of a person is in part a moral concept; once we have admitted that *x* is a person we have recognized, even if we have not agreed to respect, *x*'s right to be treated as a member of the moral community. It is true that the claim that *x* is a *human being* is more commonly voiced as part of an appeal to treat *x* decently than is the claim that *x* is a person, but this is either because 'human being' is here used in the sense which implies personhood, or because the genetic and moral senses of 'human' have been confused.

Now if (1)–(5) are indeed the primary criteria of personhood, then it is clear that genetic humanity is neither necessary nor sufficient for establishing that an entity is a person. Some human beings are not people, and there may well be people who are not human beings. A man or woman whose consciousness has been permanently obliterated but who remains alive is a human being which is no longer a person; defective human beings, with no appreciable mental capacity, are not and presumably never will be people; and a fetus is a human being which is not yet a person, and which therefore cannot coherently be said to have full moral rights. Citizens of the next century should be prepared to recognize highly advanced, self-aware robots or computers, should such be developed, and intelligent inhabitants of other worlds, should such be found, as people in the fullest sense, and to respect their moral rights. But to ascribe full moral rights to an entity which is not a person is as absurd as to ascribe moral obligations and responsibilities to such an entity.

3. FETAL DEVELOPMENT AND THE RIGHT TO LIFE

Two problems arise in the application of these suggestions for the definition of the moral community to the determination of the precise moral status of a human fetus. Given that the paradigm example of a person is a normal adult human being, then (1) How like this paradigm, in particular how far advanced since conception, does a human being need to be before it begins to have a right to life by virtue, not of being fully a person as of yet, but of being *like* a person? and (2) To what extent, if any, does the fact that a fetus has the *potential* for be-

coming a person endow it with some of the same rights? Each of these questions requires some comment.

In answering the first question, we need not attempt a detailed consideration of the moral rights of organisms which are not developed enough, aware enough, intelligent enough, etc., to be considered people, but which resemble people in some respects. It does seem reasonable to suggest that the more like a person, in the relevant respects, a being is, the stronger is the case for regarding it as having a right to life, and indeed the stronger its right to life is. Thus we ought to take seriously the suggestion that, insofar as "the human individual develops biologically in a continuous fashion . . . the rights of a human person might develop in the same way."[3] But we must keep in mind that the attributes which are relevant in determining whether or not an entity is enough like a person to be regarded as having some of the same moral rights are no different from those which are relevant to determining whether or not it is fully a person—i.e., are no different from (1)–(5)—and that being genetically human, or having recognizably human facial and other physical features, or detectable brain activity, or the capacity to survive outside the uterus, are simply not among these relevant attributes.

Thus it is clear that even though a seven- or eight-month fetus has features which make it apt to arouse in us almost the same powerful protective instinct as is commonly aroused by a small infant, nevertheless it is not significantly more personlike than is a very small embryo. It is *somewhat* more personlike; it can apparently feel and respond to pain, and it may even have a rudimentary form of consciousness, insofar as its brain is quite active. Nevertheless, it seems safe to say that it is not fully conscious, in the way that an infant of a few months is, and that it cannot reason, or communicate messages of indefinitely many sorts, does not engage in self-motivated activity, and has no self-awareness. Thus, in the *relevant* respects, a fetus, even a fully developed one, is considerably less personlike than is the average mature mammal, indeed the average fish. And I think that a rational person must conclude that if the right to life of a fetus is to be based upon its resemblance to a person, then it cannot be said to have any more right to life than, let us say, a newborn guppy (which also seems to be capable of feeling pain), and that a right of that magnitude could never override a woman's right to obtain an abortion, at any stage of her pregnancy.

There may, of course, be other arguments in favor of placing legal limits upon the stage of pregnancy in which an abortion may be performed. Given the relative safety of the new techniques of articially inducing labor during the third trimester, the danger to the woman's life or health is no longer such an argument. Neither is the fact that people tend to respond to the thought of abortion in the later stages of pregnancy with emotional repulsion, since mere emotional responses cannot take the place of moral reasoning in determining what ought to be permitted. Nor, finally, is the frequently heard argument that legalizing abortion, especially late in the pregnancy, may erode the level of respect for human life, leading, perhaps, to an increase in unjustified euthanasia and other crimes. For this threat, if it is a threat, can be better met by educating people to the kinds of moral distinctions which we are making here than by limiting access to abortion (which limitation may, in its disregard for the rights of women, be just as damaging to the level of respect for human rights).

Thus, since the fact that even a fully developed fetus is not personlike enough to have any significant right to life on the basis of its person-likeness shows that no legal restrictions upon the stage of pregnancy in which an abortion may be performed can be justified on the grounds that we should protect the rights of the older fetus; and since there is no other apparent justification for such restrictions, we may conclude that they are entirely unjustified. Whether or not it would be *indecent* (whatever that means) for a woman in her seventh month to obtain an abortion just to avoid having to postpone a trip to Europe, it would not, in itself, be *immoral*, and therefore it ought to be permitted.

4. POTENTIAL PERSONHOOD AND THE RIGHT TO LIFE

We have seen that a fetus does not resemble a person in any way which can support the claim that

it has even some of the same rights. But what about its *potential*, the fact that if nurtured and allowed to develop naturally it will very probably become a person? Doesn't that alone give it at least some right to life? It is hard to deny that the fact that an entity is a potential person is a strong prima facie reason for not destroying it; but we need not conclude from this that a potential person has a right to life, by virtue of that potential. It may be that our feeling that it is better, other things being equal, not to destroy a potential person is better explained by the fact that potential people are still (felt to be) an invaluable resource, not to be lightly squandered. Surely, if every speck of dust were a potential person, we would be much less apt to conclude that every potential person has a right to become actual.

Still, we do not need to insist that a potential person has no right to life whatever. There may well be something immoral, and not just imprudent, about wantonly destroying potential people, when doing so isn't necessary to protect anyone's rights. But even if a potential person does have some prima facie right to life, such a right could not possibly outweigh the right of a woman to obtain an abortion, since the rights of any actual person invariably outweigh those of any potential person, whenever the two conflict. Since this may not be immediately obvious in the case of a human fetus, let us look at another case.

Suppose that our space explorer falls into the hands of an alien culture, whose scientists decide to create a few hundred thousand or more human beings, by breaking his body into its component cells, and using these to create fully developed human beings, with, of course, his genetic code. We may imagine that each of these newly created men will have all of the original man's abilities, skills, knowledge, and so on, and also have an individual self-concept, in short that each of them will be a bona fide (though hardly unique) person. Imagine that the whole project will take only seconds, and that its chances of success are extremely high, and that our explorer knows all of this, and also knows that these people will be treated fairly. I maintain that in such a situation he would have every right to escape if he could, and thus to deprive all of these potential people of their potential lives; for his right to life outweighs all of theirs together, in spite of the fact that they are all genetically human, all innocent, and all have a very high probability of becoming people very soon, if only he refrains from acting.

Indeed, I think he would have a right to escape even if it were not his life which the alien scientists planned to take, but only a year of his freedom, or, indeed, only a day. Nor would he be obligated to stay if he had gotten captured (thus bringing all these people-potentials into existence) because of his own carelessness, or even if he had done so deliberately, knowing the consequences. Regardless of how he got captured, he is not morally obligated to remain in captivity for *any* period of time for the sake of permitting any number of potential people to come into actuality, so great is the margin by which one actual person's right to liberty outweighs whatever right to life even a hundred thousand potential people have. And it seems reasonable to conclude that the rights of a woman will outweigh by a similar margin whatever right to life a fetus may have by virtue of its potential personhood.

Thus, neither a fetus's resemblance to a person, nor its potential for becoming a person provides any basis whatever for the claim that it has any significant right to life. Consequently, a woman's right to protect her health, happiness, freedom, and even her life,[4] by terminating an unwanted pregnancy, will always override whatever right to life it may be appropriate to ascribe to a fetus, even a fully developed one. And thus, in the absence of any overwhelming social need for every possible child, the laws which restrict the right to obtain an abortion, or limit the period of pregnancy during which an abortion may be performed, are a wholly unjustified violation of a woman's most basic moral and constitutional rights.[5]

POSTSCRIPT ON INFANTICIDE

Since the publication of this article, many people have written to point out that my argument appears to justify not only abortion, but infanticide as well. For a new-born infant is not significantly more person-like than an advanced fetus, and consequently it would seem that if the destruction of the latter is permissible so too must be that of the former. Inasmuch as most people, regardless of how they feel about the morality of abortion, consider infanticide a form of murder, this might appear to represent a serious flaw in my argument.

Now, if I am right in holding that it is only people who have a full-fledged right to life, and who can be murdered, and if the criteria of personhood are as I have described them, then it obviously follows that killing a new-born infant isn't murder. It does *not* follow, however, that infanticide is permissible, for two reasons. In the first place, it would be wrong, at least in this country and in this period of history, and other things being equal, to kill a new-born infant, because even if its parents do not want it and would not suffer from its destruction, there are other people who would like to have it, and would, in all probability, be deprived of a great deal of pleasure by its destruction. Thus, infanticide is wrong for reasons analogous to those which make it wrong to wantonly destroy natural resources, or great works of art.

Secondly, most people, at least in this country, value infants and would much prefer that they be preserved, even if foster parents are not immediately available. Most of us would rather be taxed to support orphanages than allow unwanted infants to be destroyed. So long as there are people who want an infant preserved, and who are willing and able to provide the means of caring for it, under reasonably humane conditions, it is, *ceteris parabis,* wrong to destroy it.

But, it might be replied, if this argument shows that infanticide is wrong, at least at this time and in this country, doesn't it also show that abortion is wrong? After all, many people value fetuses, are disturbed by their destruction, and would much prefer that they be preserved, even at some cost to themselves. Furthermore, as a potential source of pleasure to some foster family, a fetus is just as valuable as an infant. There is, however, a crucial difference between the two cases: so long as the fetus is unborn, its preservation, contrary to the wishes of the pregnant woman, violates her rights to freedom, happiness, and self-determination. Her rights override the rights of those who would like the fetus preserved, just as if someone's life or limb is threatened by a wild animal, his right to protect himself by destroying the animal overrides the rights of those who would prefer that the animal not be harmed.

The minute the infant is born, however, its preservation no longer violates any of its mother's rights, even if she wants it destroyed, because she is free to put it up for adoption. Consequently, while the moment of birth does not mark any sharp discontinuity in the degree to which an infant possesses the right to life, it does mark the end of its mother's right to determine its fate. Indeed, if abortion could be performed without killing the fetus, she would never possess the right to have the fetus destroyed, for the same reasons that she has no right to have an infant destroyed.

On the other hand, it follows from my argument that when an unwanted or defective infant is born into a society which cannot afford and/or is not willing to care for it, then its destruction is permissible. This conclusion will, no doubt, strike many people as heartless and immoral; but remember that the very existence of people who feel this way, and who are willing and able to provide care for unwanted infants, is reason enough to conclude that they should be preserved.

NOTES

1. Of course, the principle that it is (always) wrong to kill innocent human beings is in need of many other modifications, e.g., that it may be permissible to do so to save a greater number of other innocent human beings, but we may safely ignore these complications here.
2. From here on, we will use 'human' to mean genetically human, since the moral sense seems closely connected to, and perhaps derived from, the assumption that genetic humanity is sufficient for membership in the moral community.
3. Thomas L. Hayes, "A Biological View," *Commonweal,* 85 (March 17, 1967), 677–78; quoted by Daniel Callahan, in *Abortion, Law, Choice, and Morality* (London: Macmillan & Co., 1970).
4. That is, insofar as the death rate, for the woman, is higher for childbirth than for early abortion.
5. My thanks to the following people, who were kind enough to read and criticize an earlier version of this paper: Herbert Gold, Gene Glass, Anne Lauterbach, Judith Thomson, Mary Mothersill, and Timothy Binkley.

37. ABORTION

Eike-Henner W. Kluge

The controversy concerning abortion can be stated simply in the form of two questions: (1) In aborting a human pregnancy prior to its natural termination in the course of events, are we guilty of murder, or are we guilty of a lesser moral crime? Indeed, (2) are we guilty of a moral crime at all?

In what follows, I shall suggest that abortions performed within a certain, more or less clearly defined period of fetal development are murderous, whereas those performed prior to this period are not. I shall also argue that this does not mean that no moral gravamen attaches to the latter sort of action, but that instead the moral seriousness of the act is reduced to a degree commensurate with the stage of development of the fetus. . . .

THE CONCEPT OF A PERSON

Although superficially perspicuous, the concept of a person is not at all easy to adumbrate. Traditionally, several criteria have been proposed which, both severally and together, have been deemed decisive. Chief of these have been morphology,[1] genealogy,[2] genetics,[3] and behavior.[4] As to morphology: Are the shape and the possession as well as arrangement of various limbs and organs really decisive in the question of what counts as a person? If so, criteria will have to be stated so vaguely as to permit us in the end to draw no hard and fast boundaries at all. For, clearly, the possession and

From Eike-Henner W. Kluge, *The Practice of Death* (New Haven: Yale University Press, 1975), pp. 86–100. Reprinted with permission of the publisher.

arrangement of particular external limbs cannot be decisive: Moralist, lawyer, and layman alike agree in considering grossly deformed and congenitally crippled individuals as persons. Similarly with the possession—or lack of possession—and arrangement of various internal organs. In fact, at least one part of current thinking has it that so long as the ancestry of the entity in question is human, such anomalies must be discounted and the being considered a person.

The morphological criterion would therefore seem to yield to the genealogical one: To be a person is to be an offspring of a human being. But even here, practice is not consistent. For, by that token we ourselves, strictly speaking, could not count as persons, since (a) the criterion makes personhood an inherited characteristic dependent upon the human status of one's progenitors, and (b) our ultimate progenitors certainly were not human. Furthermore, while restrictive in this sense, in another the criterion is too inclusive. For, by a process of reasoning similar to the one just indicated it would follow, mutatis mutandis, that our progeny, no matter what their characteristics and natures might be, would count as persons just as long as we ourselves do. In the light of our present knowledge of genetics, mutations, and evolutionary change, this cannot be accepted.

However, these last considerations suggest a refinement of the genealogical criterion: All and only those entities are persons which have a more or less human genetic makeup. In other words, a genetic criterion is substituted for a merely genealogical one. Once more, however, success evades us, for once again the criterion is not applied consistently. And that for good reasons: For the religiously inclined, it would entail that God and other immaterial entities could not be persons—an unwelcome consequence to say the least. And for those not of a religious bent, there remain two further issues: precisely where to draw the line with genetic changes—and for what reason. Even at the present time such radical genetic changes as the doubling of chromosomes do occur in beings that we account as unquestionably persons. Furthermore, all of the objections raised above against the morphological and genealogical criteria can be raised, mutatis mutandis, against the genetic one.

After all, these criteria do find their essential biological base in genetic phenomena. Finally—to turn to a still more contemporary consideration—what are we to do with language-using animals like dolphins? Are we to accord them rationality without a vestige of personhood?

The considerations just advanced are nothing new. . . . But they . . . serve a useful purpose. They not only illustrate the difficulty in attempting to define 'person'; they also strain the traditional parameters of the discussion—in particular, the last series of considerations, involving as they do the notion of language-using and hence rational, but by any biological standard certainly nonhuman, beings. If we are really serious in countenancing the possibility—perhaps even the actuality—of these as rational beings, then we are faced with a with a threefold choice: *either* to admit them as persons in virtue of their rationality; or to admit them as persons in virtue of a characteristic had by them and us, but which so far we have not mentioned; or, finally, to deny that they are persons altogether.

Here, everything hinges on the concept of a rational being. So far, we have said relatively little about it, and it is now time to go into the concept in some detail. To begin with, let us note that the concept is tied not to actual behavior, but to inherent and constitutive potential. Thus, someone may be a rational being—have a certain nature— and yet not behave rationally. Such a lapse from rationality, even if it should be consistent, would not count against the claim that we have here a rational being, unless that deviation from rationality were a result of internal constitution. After all, we may choose—and choose consistently—to be irrational. Furthermore, we may be prevented from the exercise of our potential as rational beings either by internal malfunctioning, or by external chaotic situations or states of affairs. The second point to note is more definitive than the preceding: To be a rational being is to be capable of symbolic awareness of reality, that is to say, of responding to external reality by means of symbolic categorization processes that permit whatever it is that has this sort of awareness to apprehend the world as subsumed under certain more or less conventional categories of classification. Still differently, it is the ability to form judgments. Third, to count as a rational being, something must also have the capability for self-awareness. Fourth—and in a sense this overlaps with the last two criteria—the entity in question must be capable of internalizing and using a language.[5]

In my view, then, this is what it is to be a rational being. It will immediately be obvious that my definition does not include any reference to capabilities for emotions, for aesthetic appreciation, and the like. Nor does it involve anything like an appeal to the subconscious and similar Freudian and post-Freudian constructs. The reason for these omissions is very simple: We do not require them as necessary conditions for the ascription of the predicate 'rational being' to our paradigm examples of rational beings: to people. They may have them, and we shall consider them all the more "human" if they do; but if they do not, we do not cease to call them rational beings. One further thing stands out about this definition: It divorces the concept of being a rational being from any specific physical or biological constitution. And given this, we have our transition to a "species-free" definition of a person:

A person is an entity that is a rational being; that is to say, it is an entity that has the present capabilities of symbolic awareness in the manner characteristic of rational beings as defined above. A person is an entity—any entity, irrespective of the precise nature of its constitution—that is either presently aware in a manner characteristic of rational beings, or can become thus aware without any change in the constitutive nature of its composition.

The advantages of this definition are immediately obvious: Personhood will be independent of precisely those elements that previously were seen to lead to difficulties. Personhood will depend solely on rational awareness. Nor need this awareness be actually present: the mere potential for it, as a constitutive potential, will suffice. In this way an individual, whether awake, asleep, or in a coma, will count as a person just as long as his constitutive nature is such as to permit rational awareness. Again, for a similar reason, mutatis mutandis, insanity will not prevent us from calling such a being a person. Likewise, this definition will enable us to countenance with equanimity the suggestion that animals not of the species *homo sapiens* might be persons: for example, dolphins. And certainly, this suggestion captures much that is at the core of religious contentions to the effect that the professed deity is a person. The only entities excluded will be those that lack the potential in the requisite sense.[6]

However, even if acceptable, as it stands the definition is still far from being clear. Precisely how is the notion of a constitutive potential to be understood? What is it "to be aware in a manner characteristic of rational beings" or to "have the present capability of rational awareness"? Furthermore, how is this rational awareness—or worse yet, the capability for rational awareness—to be recognized? In short, the definition needs to be clarified and supplemented by criteria.

All of these difficulties can be met by considering first this last question. The initial temptation is to fall back on physical states of affairs as indicator phenomena, to argue that the means whereby we can recognize actual or potential rationality must be accessible to us within the context of the world in which we move. And here, physical behavior immediately comes to mind: An entity will be deemed a rational being if and only if it engages in the sorts of activities—behaves in the sorts of ways —that traditionally have been associated with rational thought. Such a criterion, however, would be intolerably restrictive. It would permit us to include all and only those entities that actually evinced physical behavior of the requisite sort. In other words, it would allow us to consider as persons all and only those entities that actually behaved rationally in some recognizable way. But what of those who are comatose, catatonic, simply do not act in a physical manner, or are actually insane? Furthermore, the criterion neglects the fact that one man's rationality may be another's insanity; indeed, that rationality vis-à-vis behavior can be recognized only by those within the same . . . culture group. Finally, what would this do to the clause about potential awareness in the original definition?

Fortunately, a solution to the difficulties is forthcoming. Again, it will involve physical manifestations. After all, these do constitute the only publicly accessible means for evaluating personhood. This time, however, the criterion does not involve the performance of some act or other, but instead centers around the constitution underlying such (possible) acts. In other words, the constitution of the entity itself is taken as an indicator phenomenon.

Let me give an example of what I mean. In biological entities of the species *homo sapiens,* that part of the organism which is generally considered to be the generative and originative part governing activities is the nervous system, in particular, that part of it which we call the central nervous system, with special emphasis on the brain. The nervous system in general and the brain in particular evince electrical activity of varying degrees of intensity, frequency, and complexity. This can be recorded by means of electroencephalographs. The electroencephalograms (EEGs for short) that result have a characteristic nature which—whether the human being is asleep or awake—can serve to distinguish his nervous activity from that, say, of a cat, a frog, or even a monkey. EEGs, then, reflect a difference in neurological activity of man vis-à-vis other animals. Furthermore—on a slightly different tangent—the brain of a human being has certain structures, particularly in those parts of it that are termed the nonlimbic cortex, which are characteristic of the human brain. They are thought to be the physiological basis for symbolic processes and self-awareness. If, then, we take a normal human being as our paradigm case of a rational being,[7] we can establish the following as an operational criterion for being a rational being:

All and only those entities are rational beings whose neurological activity or relevant analogue thereof has a mathematically analyzable structure that is at least as complex as that of a human being, or whose brain or relevant analogue thereof has a structural and functional similarity to that of a human being, particularly with respect to those substructures that are the relevant analogues of the nonlimbic cortex.

With this criterion we can once again approach the problem of the sleeping, of the comatose, and so on. So long as their neurological systems or the relevant analogues thereof are sufficiently complex to support a type of activity (or analogue thereof) that compares favorably with that of our standard case, they will count as persons. Or, alternatively,

so long as their brains or the relevant analogues thereof have the requisite substructures and possess a structural similarity to those of a human being—whether the system is actually functioning or not—then the entities in question will be persons. Another slightly different way of putting the point would be by appealing to the Aristotelian distinction between first and second degree of actuality: An entity will be in a state of first degree of actuality vis-à-vis rationality if its neurological system (or analogue thereof) is capable of supporting neural (or analogous) activity of the requisite degree of complexity. It will be in a state of second degree of actuality if the potential inherent in the system (or its analogue)[8] is actually realized. Thus sleeping or comatose beings will be in a state of first degree of actuality with respect to rationality, simply in virtue of possessing nervous systems that are sufficiently similar in structure to permit them to enter into a state of second degree of actuality as defined, should the proper stimulus and so on be forthcoming.[9]

This criterion also has two further advantages: It recognizes that the human model might not exhaust the class of types of rational awareness. That is why there is the "at least" clause in the requirement on complexity. Also, it does not beg questions as to the precise constitution of the being in question. That is why there is the "analogue" clause.

THE MORAL STATUS OF ABORTION

Being in possession of a criterion of personhood— a criterion, be it noted, that may overlap with, but need not be coextensive with, that of humanity— we can now return to our initial definition of moral acts as directed toward persons, and can proceed to the question of the moral status of abortions. The solution will take the following form: If the abortion involves the termination of life of a fetus whose neurological system either actually does or potentially could evince neurological activity whose structure is of the type of a human being, or, alternatively, whose brain has the relevant structures definitive of a rational being, then the act of killing it will be that of killing a rational being. In which case, as per our preceding discussion, the act of killing it will be the act of killing a person. Whence, given our analysis of moral vs. nonmoral action, it follows that the act permits of moral evaluation, possibly even that of murder.

This, of course, squarely confronts us with the question with which we began: Is it one of murder? In the light of the preceding argument, it seems to follow that it is. It seems to follow, that is, unless we can show either that such an act was not premeditated or that some one or other of the excusing and extenuating circumstances generally admitted in the case of homicide obtain.

Unfortunately, neither of these alternatives seems to hold. As to the first, it is a simple fact that an abortion is not something which is done in the heat of passion, where, for the moment, one has lost one's head, and where one is swayed solely by the emotions of the moment, unable to stop and reflect. . . . In any ordinary understanding of the term, the abortion of a well-established pregnancy can hardly be said to be an unpremeditated act.

This, then, leaves the second alternative: the possibility of mitigating and extenuating circumstances. . . .

. . . Only four major sorts of considerations . . . really merit our special attention at this stage of the discussion: (a) the claim that the act was done in a state of mental depression resulting from the pregnancy, and that therefore a plea of diminished responsibility ought to be admitted; (b) the claim that the pregnancy is a result of a rape, and therefore merits abortion, no matter what the circumstances; (c) the claim that the threat to the life of the woman is always an extenuating circumstance; and (d) the claim that radical fetal deformation of the fetus—or a good likelihood thereof—is always an indication for abortion.

Two of these—(a) and (d)—can indeed be dismissed as irrelevant, stark and extraordinary as that may seem. For . . . considerations of these types entirely miss the moral point at issue. We are dealing here with the question of aborting a fetus that is sufficiently developed to be a person. The existence of this person is the result of an act of intercourse engaged in by other moral agents. As moral agents, the participants in that activity are responsible for the results of their actions. In engaging in this act which could—and did—lead to the existence of a new person, the participants have assumed responsibility for the existence of another repository of moral rights; that is to say, they have —either tacitly or explicitly—assumed responsibility for the existence of another person. In that sense, they have subordinated their rights to its rights—particularly in view of the fact that the existence of such a person may be attended by certain risks: precisely those risks which they are now unwilling to accept: threat to life, mental depression, socioeconomic hardship, and the like. Furthermore—and this is a telling factor—in not aborting the pregnancy prior to the fetus's attainment of the status of a person, the individuals have confirmed that cession of rights which they now wish to withdraw. Therefore all other things being equal—the intercourse not being one of rape—the participants cannot now plead extenuating circumstances, whether these involve reasons of health, socioeconomic condition, psychological well-being and stability, or what have you. Nor could the unwanted nature of the pregnancy be introduced as an excusing factor. Quite the contrary: It would only serve to heighten the charge of culpable negligence in not taking the proper precautions which would have prevented the pregnancy in question. Therefore, in the cases of (a) and (d) excusing circumstances for aborting the pregnancy will not obtain. Whence it follows that aborting a fetus of the sort under discussion will be an act of premeditated and inexcusable killing of a person. It will be an act of murder.

As to (b) pregnancy resulting from rape, in this case, too, abortion will be an act of murder, since, in the situation under discussion, the crucial threshold to personhood has already been passed. The element of premeditation exists here as in all other cases, and the temporal consideration is just as relevant. As to the fact that the pregnancy was, so to speak, forced, the reply here is that this is not to the point in considering the question of abortion. It is to the point in awarding damages to the individual who has thus been used and who has suffered as a result of the action. It is also to the point when examining a society that would permit such a thing to occur, and, above all, which would permit such a pregnancy to proceed until the fetus has attained personhood. But, as we said, it is not to the point when examining the question of whether a person —the fetus at this stage of development—may be murdered.[10]

Finally, there is point (d), the tough cases involving fetal abnormality or high likelihood thereof. In particular, cases like Down's syndrome, Tay-Sachs disease, rubella, and thalidomide come to mind. In such cases abortion, surely, is warranted? Once again, the reply must be in the negative. Once the fetus has become a person in our sense of the term—and by the criteria which we indicated, the fourth month of the gestation period would seem to be a reasonable point on which to focus—aborting it would be nothing less than killing a person because of its handicaps, without even obtaining the consent of the person in question, a factor that just barely might change the whole situation to one of (requested) euthanasia. And that, we submit, no matter how considered, is murder. Therefore even cases of type (d) do not afford an escape from the indictment.

Before concluding, we should consider briefly one type of case which, so far, we have neglected: that of accidental pregnancy resulting from contraceptive failure, where otherwise due care was taken that conception should not occur. In such a case—it is frequently argued—abortion should be permitted; all the more so, since the charge of culpable negligence cannot be raised against the individuals involved, and therefore no moral blame attaches to them. Furthermore, so sentiment has it, to deny them an abortion would be to punish them for an accident over which they had no control— something that goes against the grain of every legal and moral consideration.

Nevertheless, even in these cases abortion would be murder. That is to say, abortion under the conditions we have outlined. The fact that due care was taken to prevent conception is beside the point. The point is that here we have a person, and no matter how or under what circumstances the person came to be—whether on purpose or by accident—that alters nothing in his personhood. It is this fact of personhood that is morally decisive. Therefore, under these circumstances to perform an abortion is to commit murder. As an aside, I might add that if the pregnancy was really unwanted all along, it should have been aborted at an earlier date prior to the acquisition of personhood by the fetus. No moral gravamen of a murderous sort would then have attached to such an act. Waiting until the threshold of personhood has been passed is to play games with a person's life.

These last comments focus the discussion on a qualification that has run throughout all of the preceding: namely, that an abortion will be an act of murder if and only if it occurs after the fetus has passed the threshold to personhood. Does this mean that, so far as our analysis is concerned, abortions performed prior to this time are not murderous? Much as it may grate on some sensibilities, I see myself forced to answer yes. The logic of my position demands that I deny that abortions performed prior to this crucial point are murderous. Nor am I loath to accept this consequence. However, in this context, two further points are worthy of explicit mention. First, this does not mean that no moral gravamen is attached to an abortion performed prior to this point of development. That would follow if and only if it was assumed that only acts done to persons are attended by moral qualities. Although this was assumed throughout the foregoing discussion, it was done for the sake of the argument only. In point of fact, I subscribe to the thesis that the wanton taking of any sentient life is morally reprehensible. Therefore, in reply to the question of whether or not abortions performed prior to this critical period are without moral parameters, I can do no better than to quote what I said at the beginning: that the moral gravamen attaching to such an act is commensurate with the stage of development of the fetus.

The second point—and this is the note on which I shall conclude—is this: I have spoken a great deal about a threshold to personhood, about a critical point in the development of a fetus, about its becoming a person, and the like. Given our working criterion for personhood and our analysis of murder, that is natural enough. But in so talking, I may have fostered the impression that this is a temporal criterion only: that it is the same for all fetuses, and that the transition occurs at a particular, definite point in time. Both of these impressions must be corrected. The point of development is not the same in all cases. It depends on the particular nature of the pregnancy and of the fetus involved.

And it does not occur with momentary rapidity, as it were, taking merely an instant. It is a gradual development spread over some time—a development where only the beginning and the end are clearly discernible. There is an indefinable, unclassifiable middle ground, where we do not know whether our criteria apply or not: whether or not to call the entity in question a person. To abort or not to abort? Here we will be in an area of grave moral risk.

NOTES

1. Cf. Grisez, *Abortion*, p. 131 and passim; Tooley, "Defense of Abortion and Infanticide," for this position.

2. Cf. Noonan, *The Morality of Abortion*, pp. 51–59 and passim; idem, "Abortion and the Catholic Church: A Summary History," *Natural Law Forum* 12 (1967):126.

3. Noonan, "Abortion and the Catholic Church," pp. 128–29.

4. Cf. Callahan, *Abortion*, pp. 365 ff.

5. On the relationship between language and awareness, cf. Adam Schaff, *Language and Cognition*, R. S. Cohen, ed., Olgierd Wojtasiewicz, trans. (New York: McGraw-Hill, 1973), esp. part 3, which also has a good though dated bibliography in the back. See also Noam Chomsky, *Cartesian Linguistics* (New York: Harper and Row, 1960). D. C. Dennett, *Content and Consciousness* (London: Routledge & Kegan Paul, 1969), proposes a slightly different analysis in terms of intentionality; however, Dennett retains the symbolic parameter of this definition.

6. The definition will force us to admit nonliving, nonbiological entities as persons so long as they satisfy the definition. I do not think that this constitutes a difficulty; quite the contrary.

7. Ignoring the difficulties in defining the notion of the normal human being.

8. Henceforth, this parenthetical phrase will be understood in this and similar locations.

9. Where—it must be noted—this stimulus does not effect a structural change in the neurological net or its analogue.

10. Largely, be it noted, for the sake of convenience.

38. THE MORALITY OF ABORTION

Paul Ramsey

... Of all these demarcations, the time of birth would in many ways seem the least likely account of the beginning of life that has dignity and sanctity. A newborn baby is not noticeably much more human than before. It can, of course, do its own breathing; but, before it could within limits do its own moving, and it could very definitely do its own dying. While its independence of its mother's body is relatively greater, even dramatically greater, a born baby is still a long, long way from being able to do its own praying, from being a "subject," and "I," or from being rational.

Having begun with all these distinctions and theories about when germinating life becomes human, it is now necessary for me to say that from an

From Paul Ramsey, "The Morality of Abortion," in *Life or Death: Ethics and Options*, ed. by Daniel H. Labby (Seattle: University of Washington Press, 1968), pp. 70–75. Copyright © 1968 by the University of Washington Press and reprinted with their permission.

authentic religious point of view none of them matters very much.

Strictly speaking, it is far more crucial for contemporary thought than it is for any religious viewpoint to *say when* there is on the scene enough of the actuality of a man who is coming to be for there to be any sacredness in or any rights attached to his life. For in modern world views, the sanctity of life could rest only on something inherent in man. It is, therefore, important to determine when proleptically he already essentially is all else that he will ever become in the course of a long life. The sanctity of life in the first of it, if this has any sacredness, must be an overflow backward from or in anticipation of something—some capability or power—that comes later to be a man's inherent possession.

One grasps the religious outlook upon the sanctity of human life only if he sees that this life is asserted to be *surrounded* by sanctity that need not be in a man; that the most dignity a man ever possesses is a dignity that is alien to him. From this point of view it becomes *relatively* unimportant to say exactly when among the products of human generation we are dealing with an organism that is human and when we are dealing with organic life that is not yet human (despite all the theological speculations upon this question). A man's dignity is an overflow from God's dealings with him, and not primarily an anticipation of anything he will ever be by himself alone.

This is why in our religious traditions fetal life was *so certainly* surrounded with protections and prohibitions. This is why fetal life was surrounded by protections for the time before anyone supposed that a "man alive" assuredly existed, and even when, in opinions then current, there was a great degree of probability that he did not. "When nature is in deliberation about the man,"[1] Christians through the ages knew that God was in deliberation about the man. This took some of the weight off of analyzing the stages in the course of nature's deliberations, and off of the proofs from nature and from reason that were nevertheless used.

The value of a human life is ultimately grounded in the value God is placing on it. Anyone who can himself stand imaginatively even for a moment within an outlook where everything is referred finally to God—who, from things that are not, brings into being the things that are—should be able to see that God's deliberations about the man need have only begun. If there is anything incredible here, it is not the science, but the pitch of faith which no science proves, disproves, or confirms.

According to the religious outlooks and "onlooks" that have been traditional to us, man is a sacredness *in* human biological processes no less than he is a sacredness in the human social or political order. That sacredness is not composed by observable degrees of relative worth. A life's sanctity consists not in its worth *to* anybody. What life is in and of itself is most clearly to be seen in situations of naked equality of one life with another, and in the situation of congeneric helplessness which is the human condition in the first of life. No one is ever much more than a fellow fetus; and in

order not to become confused about life's primary value, it is best not to concentrate on degrees of relative worth we may later acquire.

The Lord did not set his love upon you, nor choose you, because you were already intrinsically more than a blob of tissue in the uterus or greater in size than the period at the end of this sentence. Even so, the writer of Deuteronomy proclaimed to the children of Israel:

The Lord did not set his love upon you, nor choose you, because you were more in number than any people; for you were the fewest of all people.

But because the Lord loved you, and because he would keep the oath which he had sworn unto your fathers, hath the Lord brought you out with a mighty hand . . . [7:7, 8a].

Not only the prophet Jeremiah, but anyone who has a glimmer of what it means to be a religious man, should be able to repeat after him: "Before I formed thee in the belly I knew thee; and before thou camest forth out of the womb I sanctified thee; and I ordained thee . . ." (1:5). Or after the Psalmist:

O Lord, thou hast searched me, and known me.
. . . .
Thou has beset me behind and before, and laid thy hand upon me.
. . . .
Behold . . . the darkness and the light are both alike to thee.

For thou hast possessed my reins:
Thou hast covered me in my mother's womb.

I will praise thee; for I am fearfully and wonderfully made: Marvelous are thy works: and that my soul knoweth right well [139:1, 5, 12b, 13, 14]

Thus, every human being is a unique, unrepeatable opportunity to praise God. His life is entirely an ordination, a loan, and a stewardship. His essence is his existence before God and to God, as it is from Him. His dignity is "an *alien* dignity," an evaluation that is not of him but placed upon him by the divine decree.

In regard to the respect to be accorded this generic, nascent, and dying life of ours, it does not matter much which of several religious formulations is chiefly invoked. This may be the doctrine concerning the origin of a human life, or man's creation in the image of God. It may be the biblical doctrine of God's covenant with his people and thence with all mankind, with the standard this provides for the mercy to be extended in every human relation. It may be the doctrine concerning man's ultimate destination. Nor does it matter much whether it is man's life from God, before God, or toward God that is most stressed in a religious philosophy of life, whether it is supernatural faith or divine charity or supernatural hope that bestows the value. In all cases it is hardly possible to exclude what is nowadays narrowly called "nascent life" from our purview or from the blessing and sanctity and protection which—a religious man is convinced—God places over all human lives. *Sub specie Dei* human procreation is procreation. That is the most fundamental "pro" word in our vocabulary. This means procreation in God's behalf. *Sub specie Dei,* it was not because it could be

proved that after a certain point in our pre- or even our postnatal development we became discernibly "human" and thus a bearer of rights and deserving of respect, while before that we were not; it was rather because the Lord loved us even while we were yet microscopic and sent forth his call upon us and brought forth from things that are not the things that are. *Sub specie Dei,* it is precisely the little ones who have hardly any human claims who are sought out and covered by his mercy. *Sub specie Dei,* it is precisely when all reasonable natural grounds for hope are gone that one needs hope and may hope in God, even as when all hope was gone Abraham hoped on in faith; and in this perspective it is hardly possible to exclude from the meaning of nascent life God's call sent forth among men that once again they have hope beyond and beneath the limits reason might set. . . .

NOTE

1. Tertullian *Apologia* ix. 6–7.

Suicide

39. WHETHER IT IS LAWFUL TO KILL ONESELF?

St. Thomas Aquinas

We proceed thus to the Fifth Article:

Objection 1. It would seem lawful for a man to kill himself. For murder is a sin in so far as it is contrary to justice. But no man can do an injustice to himself, as is proved in *Ethic.* v.11.[1] Therefore no man sins by killing himself.

Obj. 2. Further, It is lawful, for one who exercises public authority, to kill evildoers. Now he who

From St. Thomas Aquinas, "Whether It Is Lawful to Kill Oneself?" from *Summa Theologica* (1925), Vol. II, Part II, Question 64, A5. Reprinted by permission of Benziger Brothers.

exercises public authority is sometimes an evildoer. Therefore he may lawfully kill himself.

Obj. 3. Further, It is lawful for a man to suffer spontaneously a lesser danger that he may avoid a greater: Thus it is lawful for a man to cut off a decayed limb even from himself, that he may save his whole body. Now sometimes a man, by killing himself, avoids a greater evil, for an example an unhappy life, or the shame of sin. Therefore a man may kill himself.

Obj. 4. Further, Samson killed himself, as related in Judges xvi, and yet he is numbered among the saints (Heb.xi). Therefore it is lawful for a man to kill himself.

Obj. 5. Further, It is related (2 Mach.xiv.42) that a certain Razias killed himself, *choosing to die nobly rather than to fall into the hands of the wicked, and to suffer abuses unbecoming his noble birth.* Now nothing that is done nobly and bravely is unlawful. Therefore suicide is not unlawful.

On the contrary, Augustine says (*De Civ. Dei* i20): *Hence it follows that the words "Thou shalt not kill" refer to the killing of a man; not another man; therefore, not even thyself. For he who kills himself, kills nothing else than a man.*

I answer that, It is altogether unlawful to kill oneself, for three reasons. First, because everything naturally loves itself, the result being that everything naturally keeps itself in being, and resists corruption so far as it can. Wherefore suicide is contrary to the inclination of nature, and to charity whereby every man should love himself. Hence suicide is always a mortal sin, as being contrary to the natural law and to charity.

Secondly, because every part, as such, belongs to the whole. Now every man is part of the community, and so, as such, he belongs to the community. Hence by killing himself he injures the community, as the Philosopher declares (*Ethic.*v.ii).

Thirdly, because life is God's gift to man, and is subject to His power, Who kills and makes to live. Hence whoever takes his own life, sins against God, even as he who kills another's slave, sins against that slave's master, and as he who usurps himself judgment of a matter not entrusted to him. For it belongs to God alone to pronounce sentence of death and life, according to Deut.xxxii.39, *I will kill and I will make to live.*

Reply Obj. 1. Murder is a sin, not only because it is contrary to justice, but also because it is opposed to charity which a man should have towards himself: in this respect suicide is a sin in relation to oneself. In relation to the community and to God, it is sinful, by reason also of its opposition to justice.

Reply Obj. 2. One who exercises public authority may lawfully put to death an evildoer, since he can pass judgment on him. But no man is judge of himself. Wherefore it is not lawful for one who exercises public authority to put himself to death

for any sin whatever: although he may lawfully commit himself to the judgment of others.

Reply Obj. 3. Man is made master of himself through his free-will: wherefore he can lawfully dispose of himself as to those matters which pertain to this life which is ruled by man's free-will. But the passage from this life to another and happier one is subject not to man's free-will but to the power of God. Hence it is not lawful for man to take his own life that he may pass to a happier life, nor that he may escape any unhappiness whatsoever of the present life, because the ultimate and most fearsome evil of this life is death, as the Philosopher states (*Ethic.*iii.6). Therefore to bring death upon oneself in order to escape the other afflictions of this life, is to adopt a greater evil in order to avoid a lesser. In like manner it is unlawful to take one's own life on account of one's having committed a sin, both because by so doing one does oneself a very great injury, by depriving oneself of the time needful for repentance, and because it is not lawful to slay an evildoer except by the sentence of the public authority. Again it is unlawful for a woman to kill herself lest she be violated, because she ought not to commit on herself the very great sin of suicide, to avoid the lesser sin of another. For she commits no sin in being violated by force, provided she does not consent, since *without consent of the mind there is no stain on the body,* as the Blessed Lucy declared. Now it is evident that fornication and adultery are less grievous sins than taking a man's, especially one's own, life: since the latter is most grievous, because one injures oneself, to whom one owes the greatest love. Moreover it is most dangerous since no time is left wherein to expiate it by repentance. Again it is not lawful for anyone to take his own life for fear he should consent to sin, because *evil must not be done that good may come* (Rom.iii.8) or that evil may be avoided, especially if the evil be of small account and an uncertain event, for it is uncertain whether one will at some future time consent to a sin, since God is able to deliver man from sin under any temptation whatever.

Reply Obj. 4. As Augustine says (*De Civ. Dei* i.21), *not even Samson is to be excused that he crushed himself together with his enemies under the ruins of the house, except the Holy Ghost, Who had wrought many wonders through him, had secretly commanded him to do this.* He assigns the same reason in the case of certain holy women, who at the time of persecution took their own lives, and who are commemorated by the Church.

Reply Obj. 5. It belongs to fortitude that a man does not shrink from being slain by another, for the sake of the good of virtue, and that he may avoid sin. But that a man take his own life in order to avoid penal evils has indeed an appearance of for-titude (for which reason some, among whom was Razias, have killed themselves, thinking to act from fortitude), yet it is not true fortitude, but rather a weakness of soul unable to bear penal evils, as the Philosopher (*Ethic.* iii.7) and Augustine (*De Civ. Dei* i.22,23) declare.

NOTE

1. The reference is to Aristotle, to whom Aquinas frequently refers as "The Philosopher."

40. OF SUICIDE

David Hume

1. . . . If Suicide be criminal it must be a transgression of our duty either to God, our neighbour, or ourselves.—To prove that suicide is no transgression of our duty to God, the following considerations may perhaps suffice. . . .

What is the meaning . . . of that principle that a man, who, tired of life, and haunted by pain and misery, bravely overcomes all the natural terrors of death and makes his escape from this cruel scene; that such a man, I say, has incurred the indignation of his Creator by encroaching on the office of divine providence, and disturbing the order of the universe? Shall we assert that the Almighty has reserved to himself in any peculiar manner the disposal of the lives of men, and has not submitted that event, in common with others, to the general laws by which the universe is governed? This is plainly false; the lives of men depend upon the same laws as the lives of all other elements; and these are subjected to the general laws of matter and motion. The fall of a tower, or the infusion of poison, will destroy a man equally with the meanest creature; an inundation sweeps away every thing without distinction that comes within the reach of its fury. Since therefore the lives of men are for ever dependent on the general laws of matter and motion, is a man's disposing of his life criminal, because in every case it is criminal to encroach upon these laws, or disturb their operation? But this seems absurd; all animals are entrusted to their own prudence and skill for their conduct in the world, and have full authority, as far as their power extends, to alter all the operations of nature. Without the exercise of this authority they could not subsist a moment; every action, every motion of a man, innovates on the order of some parts of matter, and diverts from their ordinary course the general laws of motion. Putting together, therefore, these conclusions, we find that human life depends upon the general laws of matter and motion, and that it is no encroachment on the office of providence to disturb or alter these general laws. Has not everyone, of consequence, the free disposal of his own life? And may he not lawfully employ that power with which nature has endowed him? In order to destroy the evidence of this conclusion, we must show a reason why this particular case is excepted; is it because human life is of so great importance, that 'tis a presumption for human prudence to dispose of it? But the life of a man is of no greater importance to the universe than that of an oyster. And were it of ever so great importance, the order of nature has actually submitted it to human

From David Hume, "Of Suicide," first published in 1898.

prudence. . . . Were the disposal of human life so much reserved as the peculiar province of the Almighty that it were an encroachment of His right for men to dispose of their own lives; it would be equally criminal to act for the preservation of life as for its destruction. If I turn aside a stone which is falling upon my head, I disturb the course of nature, and I invade the peculiar province of the Almighty by lengthening out my life beyond the period which by the general laws of matter and motion He had assigned it.

A hair, a fly, an insect is able to destroy this mighty being whose life is of such importance. Is it an absurdity to suppose that human prudence may lawfully dispose of what depends on such insignificant causes? It would be no crime in me to divert the Nile or Danube from its course, were I able to effect such purposes. Where then is the crime of turning a few ounces of blood from their natural channel?—Do you imagine that I repine at providence or curse my creation, because I go out of life, and put a period to a being, which, were it to continue, would render me miserable? Far be such sentiments from me; I am only convinced of a matter of fact, which you yourself acknowledge possible, that human life may be unhappy, and that my existence, if further prolonged, would become ineligible: but I thank providence, both for the good which I have already enjoyed, and for the power with which I am endowed of escaping the ill that threatens me. To you it belongs to repine providence, who foolishly imagine that you have no such power, and who must still prolong a hated life, though loaded with pain and sickness, with shame and poverty.—Do you not teach that when any ill befalls me, though by the malice of my enemies, I ought to be resigned to providence, and that the actions of men are the operations of the Almighty as much as the actions of inanimate beings? When I fall upon my own sword, therefore, I receive my death equally from the hands of the Deity as if it had proceeded from a lion, a precipice, or a fever. The submission which you require to providence in every calamity that befalls me excludes not human skill and industry, if possibly by their means I can avoid or escape the calamity: And why may I not employ one remedy as well as another?—If my life be not my own, it were criminal

for me to put it in danger, as well as to dispose of it; nor could one man deserve the appellation of *hero* whom glory or friendship transports into the greatest dangers, and another merit the reproach of *wretch* or *miscreant* who puts a period to his life for like motives.—There is no being which possesses any power or faculty that it receives not from its Creator, nor is there any one which by ever so irregular an action can encroach upon the plan of His providence, or disorder the universe. Its operations are His works equally with that chain of events which it invades, and whichever principle prevails, we may for that very reason conclude it to be most favoured by Him. Be it animate, or inanimate, rational, or irrational; 'tis all a case: Its power is still derived from the supreme creator, and is alike comprehended in the order of His providence. When the horror of pain prevails over the love of life; when a voluntary action anticipates the effects of blind causes; 'tis only in consequence of those powers and principles which He has implanted in His creatures. Divine providence is still inviolate and placed far beyond the reach of human injuries.

'Tis impious, says the old Roman superstition, to divert rivers from their course, or invade the prerogatives of nature. 'Tis impious, says the French superstition, to inoculate for the small-pox, or usurp the business of providence, by voluntarily producing distempers and maladies. 'Tis impious, says the modern European superstition, to put a period to our own life, and thereby rebel against our creator; and why not impious, say I, to build houses, cultivate the ground, or sail upon the ocean? In all these actions we employ our powers of mind and body to produce some innovation in the course of nature; and in none of them do we any more. They are all of them therefore equally innocent, or equally criminal.—*But you are placed by providence, like a sentinel in a particular station, and when you desert it without being recalled, you are equally guilty of rebellion against your almighty sovereign, and have incurred his displeasure.*—I ask, why do you conclude that providence has placed me in this station? For my part I find that I owe my birth to a long chain of causes, of which many depend upon voluntary actions of men. *But Providence guided all these causes, and nothing happens in the universe without its consent and cooperation.* If so, then neither does my death, however voluntary, happen without its consent; and whenever pain or sorrow so far overcome my patience as to make me tired of life, I may conclude that I am recalled from my station in the clearest and most express terms. 'Tis Providence surely that has placed me at this present moment in this chamber: But may I not leave it when I think proper, without being liable to the imputation of having deserted my post or station? When I shall be dead, the principles of which I am composed will still perform their part in the universe, and will be equally useful in the grand fabric, as when they composed this individual creature. The difference to the whole will be no greater than between my being in a chamber and in the open air. The one change is of more importance to me than the other; but not more so to the universe.

'Tis a kind of blasphemy to imagine that any created being can disturb the order of the world or invade the business of providence! It supposes that that being possesses powers and faculties which it received not from its creator, and which are not subordinate to His government and authority. A man may disturb society no doubt, and thereby incur the displeasure of the Almighty: But the government of the world is placed far beyond his reach and violence. And how does it appear that the Almighty is displeased with those actions that disturb society? By the principles which He has implanted in human nature, and which inspire us with a sentiment of remorse if we ourselves have been guilty of such actions, and with that of blame and disapprobation, if we ever observe them in others.

2.—Let us now examine, according to the method proposed, whether Suicide be of this kind of actions, and be a breach of our duty to our *neighbour* and to *society*.

A man who retires from life does no harm to society: he only ceases to do good; which, if it is an injury, is of the lowest kind. All our obligations to do good to society seem to imply something reciprocal. I receive the benefits of society and therefore ought to promote its interests, but when I withdraw myself altogether from society, can I be bound any longer? But, allowing that our obligations to do good were perpetual, they have certainly some bounds; I am not obliged to do a small

good to society at the expense of a great harm to myself; why then should I prolong a miserable existence, because of some frivolous advantage which the public may perhaps receive from me? If upon account of age and infirmities I may lawfully resign any office, and employ my time altogether in fencing against these calamities, and alleviating as much as possible the miseries of my future life: Why may I not cut short these miseries at once by an action which is no more prejudicial to society?— But suppose that it is no longer in my power to promote the interest of society; suppose that I am a burden to it; suppose that my life hinders some person from being much more useful to society. In such cases my resignation of life must not only be innocent but laudable. And most people who lie under any temptation to abandon existence are in some such situation; those who have health, or power, or authority, have commonly better reason to be in humour with the world.

A man is engaged in a conspiracy for the public interest; is seized upon suspicion; is threatened with the rack; and knows from his own weakness that the secret will be extorted from him: Could such a one consult the public interest better than by putting a quick period to a miserable life? This was the case of the famous and brave Strozi of Florence. —Again, suppose a malefactor is justly condemned to a shameful death; can any reason be imagined why he may not anticipate his punishment, and save himself all the anguish of thinking on its dreadful approaches? He invades the business of providence no more than the magistrate did, who ordered his execution; and his voluntary death is equally advantageous to society by ridding it of a pernicious member.

That suicide may often be consistent with interest and with our duty to ourselves, no one can question who allows that age, sickness, or misfortune may render life a burden, and make it worse even than annihilation. I believe that no man ever threw away life while it was worth keeping. For such is our natural horror of death that small motives will never be able to reconcile us to it; and though perhaps the situation of man's health or fortune did not seem to require this remedy, we may at least be assured that any one who, without apparent reason, has had recourse to it, was cursed with such an incurable depravity or gloominess of temper as must poison all enjoyment, and render him equally miserable as if he had been loaded with the most grievous misfortunes.—If suicide be supposed a crime 'tis only cowardice can impel us to it. If it be no crime, both prudence and courage should engage us to rid ourselves at once of existence, when it becomes a burden. 'Tis the only way that we can then be useful to society, by setting an example, which, if imitated, would preserve to everyone his chance for happiness in life and would effectually free him from all danger or misery.

Euthanasia

41. VOLUNTARY BENEFICENT EUTHANASIA

Marvin Kohl

As long as we respect human dignity and regard kindly acts as being at least virtuous, beneficent euthanasia, or mercy killing, will be practiced and remain a moral activity. For, as Cicero correctly observed, other things being equal, our first duty is to help most where help is most needed.

I shall present my case in three parts. Although I shall say a few words about the morality of passive euthanasia, the major focus in part one is upon questions about the intrinsic goodness of life and the role of intrinsic dignity. A characterization and brief defense of active voluntary beneficent euthanasia will be presented in part two. In part three I will evaluate three of the most formidable objections to beneficent euthanasia.

I

Euthanasia is usually defined in one of several ways. Defined narrowly it refers to the *inducement* of as quick and painless a death as is possible (hereafter referred to simply as a "painless quick death"). In one of its broader senses, however, the term refers to the *allowance* or *inducement* of a painless quick death. I shall follow here the broader usage and

From Marvin Kohl, "Voluntary Beneficent Euthanasia," from *Beneficent Euthanasia,* ed. by Marvin Kohl (Buffalo, N.Y.: Prometheus Books, 1975), pp. 130-141. Reprinted by permission of the author and Prometheus Books.

roughly distinguish between active and passive euthanasia. The former designates acts in which one does something directly to end life when it would otherwise go on; the latter designates acts in which one refrains from doing something so that death will come more quickly.

Aside from the problem of undesirable consequences, the question of whether or not an act of passive euthanasia is sinful or immoral is not likely to arise unless it is already believed that the continuance of mere physical life is an absolute and/or intrinsic good. I suggest that this position, a position held by most vitalists and some inalienable-right theorists, is open to formidable objections.

It should be noticed, first, that saying life is intrinsically good means that the existence of life would be a good even if it existed quite alone, without any accompaniments, goals, or meaning— that is, that the mere physical process, in and of itself, is always a good. I am inclined to believe that those who take this position are motivated by good intentions, for it often does seem that the best way to protect something is to make protection exceptionless. But surely we do not want a principle that seeks to preserve life at the price of protecting suffering when that suffering can be shown to be needless.

To say that all human life is intrinsically good is to say that each and every life, whether or not the individual is suffering acutely from an incurable condition or disease, is intrinsically good. It is to say that the life of a child like David Patrick Houle —a child who was born with, among other things, improperly formed vertebrae, a malformed left side and hand, no left eye or ear, and who, if he had survived, would have been partly deaf, palsied, blind, and mentally retarded—is intrinsically good. It is to say that when a life has been irretrievably blasted by an accident or blighted by some ghastly illness, or that even when all dignity, beauty, and meaning have vanished, life is intrinsically good. The flaw in this position lies not in its intention but in its results. For unless it is abridged or more carefully qualified, it entails the acceptance of pointless suffering.

Still another difficulty is that the vitalist position runs counter to common moral intuitions or beliefs about killing. For example, it is widely held that killing in self-defense and in defense of others, especially when necessary to save life, is morally justifiable. In addition, the vitalist's high regard for life qua life runs counter to the moral approval of the hero or the martyr who lays down his life for the sake of other values, such as honor or conscience. John Huss, the Bohemian religious reformer, was burned at the stake and his ashes were thrown into the Rhine River because he refused to stop attacking the worldliness of the clergy and the interference of the Catholic Church in political matters. I do not think we would be prepared to say that Huss' belief that honor and conscience come before one's own personal safety was mistaken, though we might in practice often lack the courage of that conviction.

The main point is this: There is a difference between saying "X is good" or "X is an almost intrinsic good" and saying "X is an intrinsic and/or absolute good." Almost all men hold life to be a good (perhaps an almost intrinsic good), but few would perceive or hold it to be either a good in itself or the highest good. To make a case for those claims, it must be shown (a) that mere physical life is always a good thing and/or (b) that it is the highest good. This has not been done, and I do not believe it can be done.

My only excuse for insisting on the inadequacy of the vitalist position is that it is not consistently recognized by opponents of euthanasia. There is a sort of odd bifurcation, for many seem to maintain that what I have said is right when applied to problems of passive euthanasia but wrong when applied to problems of active euthanasia. Plainly, they cannot have it both ways. If these beliefs are inadequate grounds for opposing passive euthanasia, then they are inadequate for opposing active euthanasia.

Besides the objection from the intrinsic goodness of life there is a related argument, namely, that proponents of euthanasia deny that all human beings have intrinsic dignity or that they advocate policies that would violate that dignity. In fact, the word *dignity* is so closely identified in popular thought with the heart of the euthanasia issue and so many varied and ambiguous ethical doctrines have recently been erected on a foundation of this vague word that a closer examination becomes an intellectual necessity. I can give only a succinct summary and refer the reader to some of the more interesting contemporary papers for supporting evidence.[1]

The word *dignity* has at least two related but distinct senses. As an intrinsic characteristic of humans, it connotes the things of excellence that set human beings apart from other species. In this sense (dignity$_1$) it is "the intrinsic worth which attaches to, or is possessed by, a human being just because he is a member of a uniquely rational and capable species." The literature is reasonably clear concerning the indestructibility of this kind of dignity. An individual has dignity$_1$ even though he does not equally share in the excellence of other members of the species and even though he may be distressed, ill, or physically or mentally handicapped. Just how this is possible is seldom explained, but the claim is eminently clear: since the species as a whole has worth, every member possesses some worth. In short, intrinsic dignity can never be destroyed.

Extrinsic human dignity (dignity$_2$) is a still more difficult notion to grasp. But it is probably true to say that, in addition to being a value term, dignity$_2$ connotes having reasonable control over the major and significant aspects of one's life, as well as the ofttimes necessary condition of not being treated disrespectfully.

Care should of course be taken not to confuse respect for a person's ability with respect for the person as a human being. I may or may not respect Mary's or John's plumbing ability but nonetheless may respect each as a person. On the other hand, if I fail to respect (that is, value highly and not interfere with) a mature and rational person's ability to freely function in major areas of human endeavor (assuming they have the capacity to so function or are not acting immorally), then to that degree I fail to respect her or him as a person.

Few who are aware of this distinction are inclined to deny that every human being has some worth or dignity1. Obviously, if a patient has dignity1 regardless of his condition or treatment, solely because he is a member of homo sapiens, then all human patients have dignity1. But what is the value of this kind of dignity? Is it not true that telling a patient who is suffering and being mistreated that he nonetheless has dignity1 is like consoling the concentration-camp prisoner who is being forcefully carried into the "shower house" by telling him that he is metaphysically free?

The heart of the matter, I believe, lies elsewhere. It has to do with dignity2, the having of which roughly denotes the actual ability of a human being to rationally determine and control his way of life and death and to have this acknowledged and respected by others. This is what is meant when we say that because all human beings have a basic need for dignity they have a corresponding right to be so treated.

We can now, perhaps, better understand why some opponents of euthanasia use the term *dignity* equivocally. There are two propositions at issue: (1) All human life has some worth or dignity1, and (2) all human life has some worth or dignity2. Proposition 1 is true, almost vacuous and of dubious value. But proposition 2 is false. For there are situations, especially some cases of terminal illness, where an individual's condition is so grave that there is no genuine possibility that he can obtain reasonable control over the major and significant aspects of his life. And this is to say nothing about the complex issues raised by disrespectful treatment. Although opponents of euthanasia may continue to use the term *dignity* obscurely or equivocally in order to give proposition 2 an air of plausibility, it is difficult to understand why this maneuver should be considered an intellectual virtue.

II

Correctly conceived, for an act to be one of active beneficent euthanasia, the dominant motive must be a desire to help the intended recipient, the act must involve the inducement of a relatively painless quick death, and it must result in at least beneficial treatment for the recipient. To state this more accurately, the term *active beneficent euthanasia* is synonymous with the term *mercy killing* —that is, both refer to the inducement of a relatively painless and quick death, the intention and actual consequences of which are the *kindest possible treatment* of an unfortunate individual in the actual circumstances.

In an earlier version of this paper, I used the term *noninvoluntary*. I said that an act is to be considered to be noninvoluntary only if it is either the result of the fully informed consent of the intended recipient or, when the recipient is not mentally or physically free to choose (as in the case of permanent coma), the proper legal guardian (or when this is inappropriate, society or its representative) acting on the individual's behalf gives consent. I then went on to say that I favored only noninvoluntary beneficent euthanasia. I am still inclined to believe that *noninvoluntary* is a less misleading term than *voluntary*. But if great care is taken and if we are willing to stretch *voluntary act* to mean *voluntary acceptance,* then perhaps we can use *voluntary* and thereby avoid the more cumbersome expression. A voluntary act, in this special sense, is one in which the intended recipient gives free, fully informed consent, or when he is not a free agent (because of natural conditions, as in the case of infants or the permanently comatose), consent is obtained from an authorized representative acting on his behalf.[2]

My claim is that in situations where there are no overriding rights or similar considerations voluntary active beneficent euthanasia (hereafter referred to simply as beneficent euthanasia) is a moral obligation.

I have described the nature of kindly acts and argued for the morality of beneficent euthanasia at length in *The Morality of Killing.*[3] Here I shall be content to expand upon some of the basic points.

The argument for beneficent euthanasia is twofold. First, since it is kind treatment, and since society and its members each have a prima facie (though not equal) obligation to treat members kindly, it follows that beneficent euthanasia is a prima facie obligation. This means that in certain circumstances we have an actual moral obligation to induce death, that it is not only virtuous to help most where help is most needed but it is often a duty to do so.

This argument neither says nor means to suggest (a) that kindness alone will do or (b) that the obligation to be kind is only limited to acts of mercy killing. Let us briefly examine each of these points more closely.

As to (a): Unless the weight of a kindly act is overridden by other rights or similar considerations, a kindly act is a moral one. In other words, while a kindly or beneficent act is not necessarily a moral act, more often than not it is. As to (b): Acting kindly in cases where the patient's death is imminent requires that there be relief of pain, relief of suffering, respect for the patient's right to refuse treatment, as well as the provision of adequate health care. To this extent, I agree with Arthur Dyck.[4] Where we differ, however, is that for Dyck the right to merciful treatment seems to be overridden by the principle prohibiting the killing of innocent people, while I hold that in cases of mercy (that is, in cases where inducing death is the kindest possible treatment) exception should be made to the principle prohibiting killing.

Second, in addition to the argument from kindness, there is an argument from justice. It has two prongs. The first is that where an individual is not constrained, but physically and mentally free to choose, his consent is necessary. This is an essential safeguard, for one of the best defenses against injustice is that of freely given, fully informed consent. The second is that justice requires that where possible we give to each according to his or her basic needs; and since human beings have a basic need to live and die with dignity$_2$, it is just that we treat them accordingly. This entails the right to live, the right to die, and the right to death with dignity$_2$.

To many moralists nothing seems morally so self-evident as having consent as a necessary condition for just or moral acts. Yet there seems good reason to question the rule that unless we have overt consent a given action is unjust, immoral, or nonmoral. Admittedly, the existence of infants and permanently comatose patients raises a difficult problem. It is not always easy to know when an individual is not free to choose; nor should the transfer of this obligation be taken lightly. However, when the fanatical insistence on consent only brings with it continued or increased misery, and when it is clear that neither justice nor the welfare of the individual is being served, then we must choose to act on behalf of the interests of that individual. For no person should suffer merely because he cannot express consent.

It should be clear that I arrive at this conclusion reluctantly. But what are the alternatives? To say that infants and comatose patients are not subject to moral actions obviously will not do. To say that any help that may be extended toward such individuals must be unjust or immoral is morally implausible and deeply unsatisfying. And so we fall back upon the notion that when we have a problematic situation in which one or more moral principles are not applicable (as in the case of requiring consent from those who cannot possibly give consent) the actual judgment must depend upon the relative weight of moral rules that can be applied,[5] where those who apply the rules are acting on behalf of those who cannot give consent.

Before turning to the more serious objections, I should like to consider one that is widely held and theologically rooted. It may be called the principle of sufficient reason for suffering and can be formulated as follows: Everything is connected in definite ways with other things, so that a thing's full nature is not revealed except by its position and relationship within a system. If we fully understood the entire system, we would appreciate the role played by suffering, for suffering brings us closer to God. "Suffering is almost the greatest gift of God's love. For if we stop to think, we can never be like Him in power or dignity. We can, however, become like Him in our suffering. In other words, by suffering we become God-like."[6] To those who hold this view I can only say that there is enough tragedy in life. We all know that an accident, illness, or death may suddenly seize us or our loved ones. Fortunately, most men realize that there is enough suffering in this world without our nurturing or worshipping it.

Contrary to the plea for tolerance of unnecessary suffering, I wish to urge the following doctrine:

that given the spirit rather than the letter of the Judaic-Christian tradition (or, better, actually following the spirit of that tradition) we should believe that (a) there is no virtue in unnecessary pain or suffering; (b) beneficial acts take moral precedence over simplistic rules; (c) indifference to suffering tends to beget indifference or cruelty, while kindliness often begets kindliness; and (d) according to tradition, God would not have created the world and the world could not endure if justice were to rule untempered by mercy.

III

Many people would say that when an action is a kindly one it is to some extent desirable and that when it is both kindly and just it is a prima facie moral, if not obligatory, act. But some would be quick to add that even a kindly and intrinsically just act is not necessarily moral, whatever the consequences. For, like the utilitarians, they hold that the rule not to kill the innocent must be regarded as universally binding for two reasons: first, because the wisdom of past generations has discovered that the consequences of killing the innocent in permissible circumstances is in fact conducive to the killing of the innocent in nonpermissible circumstances; and second, even in the case of an apparent exception where the killing has good consequences (beneficent euthanasia), the rule should still be kept because it is right and one breach of it would weaken the authority of the rule, which we wish to see generally observed.

The first of these two arguments, the so-called wedge or slippery slope argument, may be ruled out. There is simply no evidence that killing per se is contagious, but there is overwhelming evidence to show that it is not. It is true that people who believe that it is right to kill Gypsies, Jews, or anyone else, provided their deaths may profit the state, will probably continue to kill if they have the power to do so. But this is not evidence of the seductiveness of killing. Rather it is evidence that when men have almost unlimited power their actions will be consistent with their beliefs, and if their beliefs entail needless cruelty, so will their actions.

No doubt much of the resistance to euthanasia is due to fear, the almost abject fear of the Nazi experience. I think Joseph Fletcher is right in holding that the Nazis never engaged in mercy killing: "What they did was merciless killing, either genocidal or for ruthless experimental purposes."[7] The motivation behind and the nature and consequences of acts of beneficent euthanasia are radically different. In the Nazi example, the motivation, aside perhaps from sadism, was solely that of maximizing "benefit" for the state. In cases of beneficent euthanasia the motivation is essentially and predominantly that of maximizing benefit for the recipient, of helping most where and when the individual needs it most. The Nazi form was involuntary; the form advocated here is voluntary.

There still remains the difficult task of being able to distinguish free, informed consent from that of subtly, or otherwise, coerced consent. Yet this problem should not be blown out of proportion. The obsessive fear of abuse should not prevent us from acting kindly. Nor should it blind us to the facts that some acts are not only freely chosen but easily recognized to be so and that in cases of beneficent euthanasia the individual has the right and power to reject or terminate that action.

Similarly, there are cases where the proposed act of inducing death constitutes a borderline case of kindness. Here, even if death is freely requested by the patient, one should refrain from acting. *If there is reasonable doubt that the purported act is not kind or not the kindest possible actual alternative, one should refrain from acting.*[8] This is not to say that one does not have a right to self-determination and thereby to suicide. Nor is it to say that one should refrain from acting in cases that easily and clearly meet the conditions outlined earlier. It is only to suggest that there is an important difference between suicide and proxy suicide and that the consent of a potential recipient does not in itself necessarily incur the obligation upon someone else to assist in the act.

This procedural rule, especially when added to our understanding that an act is only beneficent euthanasia if both the intention and actual consequences of the act are the kindest possible treatment for the recipient, radically separates beneficent from nonbeneficent varieties of euthanasia.

The second major theoretical consequentialist argument is that the so-called inviolate rule prohibiting the killing of the innocent should be kept, and therefore that beneficent euthanasia should be prohibited. In other words, we are told that we ought to weigh the maximizing of benefit against the maximizing of harm and that if we did so we would find that the consequences of breaking the inviolate rule prohibiting the killing of the innocent are in fact conducive to misery rather than to happiness or some other ideal. To some extent this criticism has been dealt with already in part II, but the charge is of such a serious and persistent nature that I wish to pursue it further. For not only do utilitarians maintain that the rightness of a rule or action is to be judged solely by its consequences but mixed-deontologists maintain that a necessary, though not sufficient, condition for a morally right act is that it promote the greatest balance of good over evil. If, therefore, the consequences of beneficent euthanasia are in fact more conducive to misery than to happiness or its like, then utilitarians and mixed-deontologists should have to reject the practice.

But why should we advocate a rule when we know that in cases calling for merciful treatment it will not be the most beneficial rule to abide by? As J. J. C. Smart correctly observes, "to refuse to break a generally beneficial rule in those cases in which it is not most beneficial to obey it seems irrational and to be a case of rule worship."[9] Therefore why dogmatically adhere to a principle that protects innocent life *and* needless suffering? Why not simply formulate a better rule?

In *The Morality of Killing* I suggested that the principle prohibiting killing be reformulated so that it would not apply to cases of beneficent euthanasia. If this strategy is workable we obtain a new prohibition: "Do not do K except in circumstances of the sort C," where K stands for the killing of innocent people and C stands for the voluntary inducement of a painless and quick death, the intention and actual consequences of which are the kindest possible treatment in the actual circumstances for the recipient of that act. The merit of this rule is that it both protects the innocent and allows us to help those in dire need. And this is what morality is largely, if not all, about.

I now turn to the last objection I wish to consider. It was brought to my attention by a clergyman, who after one of my talks on euthanasia came up to me and privately said: "No, no, you must be mistaken. I refuse to believe God would have created a world where it is necessary to kill an innocent human being. He would not create a world where in order to help, where in order to be merciful to another human being, we should have to put him to death."

This objection is somewhat puzzling. Part of it turns upon the failure to face reality—the refusal to accept the fact that death may be a kindness and that we do indeed live in a universe where the act of inducing death is often the kindest thing we can do for a person. But part of it turns upon a brilliant insight; that even predominantly helpful acts of killing are harmful in part, that even in acts such as beneficent euthanasia we violate a certain interest, namely, the wish to live under better conditions. The argument appears to be as follows: To harm another is to violate his interests, and since there is always some interest or wish to exist, even acts of beneficent euthanasia are partially harmful.

This, of course, is *not* an argument against such acts, for the result of not acting yields greater harm.[10] Besides, the wish to be alive in these special circumstances is the wish to be alive *only if* one's life could be radically different. And since in the circumstances we have been discussing that is not a realistic medical alternative, the interest, though it exists, is not a significant one.

Yet the argument does explain why many well-intentioned persons are opposed to the practice of beneficent euthanasia. Apparently they only wish to engage in helpful, nonharmful acts. They refuse to approve of, or perform, acts that are partially harmful though predominantly helpful, especially when such acts involve the killing of innocent people. More important, they seem to be so fearful of the dangers of a world that requires beneficent euthanasia that they refuse to recognize the existence of these acts of mercy because they would be forced, at the same time, to recognize the existence of that kind of universe; this they are unable, or at least strongly prefer, not to do. But this is not a proper moral response, because in their aversion to unpleasant truths, they allow needless harm, and often agony, to occur.

To say that the world is such that there are tragically sad circumstances where, in order to help those we love or value, we have to induce death is not to say that we prefer to live in such a world. But what is the choice?

Before my son left for college he left a quote from Yevtushenko on my desk, and I should like to close with it.

> It is
> dangerous
> to go out
> into this
> hellish world
> but it is
> still more
> dangerous
> to hide
> in the bushes.

NOTES

1. See Abraham Edel, "Humanist Ethics and the Meaning of Human Dignity," in Paul Kurtz, ed., *Moral Problems in Contemporary Society* (Buffalo, N.Y.: Prometheus Books, 1973), pp. 227–240; Herbert Spiegelberg, "Human Dignity: A Challenge to Contemporary Philosophy," *The Philosophy Forum,* 9:1–2 (1971), pp. 39–64; Michael S. Pritchard, "Human Dignity and Justice," *Ethics,* 82:4 (1972), pp. 299–313.

2. It may be suggested, as Kenneth Lucy has been kind enough to do, that *voluntary* is being used here as a synonym for *consensual.* The suggestion has considerable merit, but I am reluctant to follow it because in the historical context of the euthanasia debate *voluntary* has been used for this purpose and *consensual* has certain semantic overtones that I believe are best avoided. In short, *consensual* would have to be stretched as much as I, and others in the euthanasaia debate, have probably stretched the most ordinary employment of *voluntary.* For an excellent discussion of this problem, see Gilbert Ryle, "The Distinction between Voluntary and Involuntary," *The Concept of Mind* (New York: Barnes & Noble, 1949), pp. 69–74.

3. Marvin Kohl, *The Morality of Killing: Sanctity of Life, Abortion, and Euthanasia* (New York: Humanities Press, and London: Peter Owen, 1974).

4. See Arthur Dyck, "Beneficent Euthanasia and Benemortasia," herein, pp. 117–129.

5. To give the most relevant example, we can weigh the prohibition forbidding the killing of innocent people against the principle of beneficence. The latter states that in each problematic situation society owes to each man the maximum amount of help that is consistent with the principles of distributive justice and the realities of human existence.

6. Joseph V. Sullivan, *The Morality of Mercy Killing* (Westminster, Md: The Newman Press, 1950), pp. 75–76.

7. Joseph Fletcher, "Ethics and Euthanasia," in Robert H. Williams, ed., *To Live and To Die* (New York: Springer-Verlag, 1973), p. 114.

8. This rule may be generalized to read: If there is reasonable doubt that a purported act is not *X,* where *X* stands for the relevant set of moral qualities and the necessary conditions for acting, then one should refrain from acting. This procedural safety rule has the advantage of preventing moral slides and of allowing us to act in cases that are easily and clearly recognized to have the moral quality in question.

9. J. J. C. Smart, "An Outline of a System of Utilitarian Ethics," in J. J. C. Smart and Bernard Williams, *Utilitarianism: For and Against* (London: Cambridge Univ. Press, 1973), p. 10.

10. Even Gandhi, the father of twentieth-century pacifism and a man who abhorred violence and almost all forms of killing, writes: "I see there is an instinctive horror of killing living beings under any circumstances whatever. . . . [But] should my child be attacked with rabies and there was no helpful remedy to relieve his agony, I should consider it my duty to take his life. . . . [For] one of the remedies and the final one to relieve the agony of a tortured child is to take his life." *Young India,* Nov. 18, 1926. Quoted in *The Essential Gandhi,* Louis Fischer, ed. (New York: Vintage Books, 1962), p. 216.

42. THE ETHICS OF EUTHANASIA

Jonathan Gould and Lord Craigmyle

This chapter seeks to examine the general ethical aspects of euthanasia on a basis which we believe will be acceptable to those who do not subscribe to a formal faith, notwithstanding that many of our arguments are drawn from lines of thought traditional in Christian philosophy.

From Jonathan Gould and Lord Craigmyle, "The Ethics of Euthanasia," in *Your Death Warrant?* (New Rochelle, N.Y.: Arlington House, 1971), pp. 79–88. Reprinted by permission of Arlington House.

As has been pointed out in the introductory chapter, much of the discussion has been blurred by the vague use of the term 'euthanasia'. There is no ethical merit in prolonging the process of dying, but it is false logic to equate the active termination of life with allowing someone to die peacefully without extraordinary efforts at resuscitation. Much stir was caused some time ago when instructions were issued in a hospital that patients above a certain age should not be resuscitated; these instructions were misguided because they were given as a general ruling, without consideration of individual circumstances, which can be judged only by the doctor attending the patient at the relevant time.

It would appear from the debate on the Voluntary Euthanasia Bill in the House of Lords in March 1969[1] that even a man of the learning of the Bishop of Durham could be misled by the ambiguity of the term euthanasia, for he said that one of the contexts in which this question arose was that of keeping people alive by highly artificial means. We must emphasise again: to abstain from keeping people artificially alive by such means is *not* euthanasia in the sense of the Bill. The indefinite prolongation of life when the patient has no prospect of ever again being able to maintain his own life, or no prospect of leading a life rewarding to himself even with artificial aid, is in fact a travesty of sound medicine: it makes a mockery both of life and of the process of dying.

There is a further clear distinction between using means for the relief of suffering which may, as a secondary result, shorten life, and actively ending life. Here the guide is the principle known as the principle of double effect. It is a principle commonly misunderstood, but one which in fact guides doctors whenever the problem of undesirable side effects arises with any treatment. And not only doctors: very many of our acts have more than one foreseeable consequence; if one foreseeable consequence is undesirable we have to weigh up whether or not to do the act we have in mind. There are four criteria:

(i)   the act itself must be morally good, or at least neutral;

(ii) the purpose must be to achieve the good consequence, the bad consequence being only a side effect;

(iii) the good effect must not be achieved by way of the bad, but both must result from the same act;

(iv) the bad result must not be so serious as to outweigh the advantage of the good result.

In practice these criteria can involve difficulties in judgement, but the ignoring of these criteria does not ease any problems; it merely permits evasion.

The use of medicaments with the intention of relieving pain is good, and if by repeated pain-relief the patient's resistance is lowered and he dies earlier than he would otherwise have done, this is a side effect which may well be acceptable. More often than not life will not be shortened in this way, because the benefit of rest and sleep and an untroubled mind will do the patient more good than heavy sedation will do him harm.[2] On the other hand, to give an overdose *with the intention that the patient should never wake up* is morally wrong. It is killing. The protection of life is not only the concern of the churches, it is deeply entrenched in law. It was one of the accepted arguments against the death penalty that a man might be mistakenly convicted of a crime. Essentially the same consideration must be given to any man who has done no willful harm, and Kamisar rightly put the question, 'What is the need for euthanasia which leads us to tolerate the mistakes, the very fatal mistakes, that will inevitably occur?'[3]

This principle of double effect has long been acknowledged as valid by the Catholic Church: although it has only been strictly formulated as a general principle in the last century or so, its origins go back to the time of St Thomas Aquinas, who stated the principle clearly in connection with self-defence. Thus the authors of the Euthanasia Society's *Plan for Voluntary Euthanasia* (1962) are wide of the mark when they write: '*Even the Roman Catholic Church has recently agreed* that where a human life is ending in great suffering it is the doctor's duty to relieve that suffering, even although the means taken may shorten life.'[4] It is blurring the all-important clear definition of the term euthanasia when later on the same authors state: 'If that policy shortens the patient's life, even by a few hours, the doctor is, in fact, practising euthanasia, although not strictly *voluntary* euthanasia.'[5] What the doctor is doing is to relieve his patient's suffering. As a secondary effect he may be securing for his patient euthanasia in the literal sense of an easy death, but he is very certainly *not killing* his patient, that is, he is not practising euthanasia in the sense for which legislation is sought.

In the foreword to a recently published book on

euthanasia the Earl of Listowel writes: 'We can now urge that the moral right to a dignified and merciful death, from which the legal right will eventually flow, should be enshrined in the Universal Declaration of Human Rights adopted in 1949 by the General Assembly of the United Nations.'[6] However, no new legal right is required to achieve this. The right to a dignified and merciful death has the approval of the law and of all the churches. The non-statutory declaration suggested by Miss Barrington in the same book declining 'any treatment or sustenance designed to prolong my life'[7] is framed in too wide terms, as treatment and sustenance in a conscious patient may sometimes provide relief of suffering as well as prolonging life.

What the various efforts to introduce euthanasia legislation have aimed at has been the legalisation not of the right to die—a palpable absurdity—but of the right to kill. This, even with the patient's consent and at his request (anyway supposedly so) is a very different matter. 'The *direct* ending of a life, with or without the patient's consent, is euthanasia in its simple, unsophisticated and ethically candid form' writes J. Fletcher.[8] His further sentence in this connection: 'A decision *not* to keep a patient alive is as morally deliberate as a decision to *end* life'[9] strikes strange. Of course a decision to do a wise or good act is as deliberate as a decision to do a foolish or wicked act, but that does not make the two acts morally equal. The reader of that sentence might be forgiven for inferring that in its author's opinion, because the two decisions are equally deliberate, they are either equally culpable or equally praiseworthy, which clearly they are not. The same remark will strike doubly strange to the reader who pursues his study of that book into the next chapter, for there he will find George P. Fletcher emphasising strongly the distinction between causing harm and permitting harm to occur.

To relieve pain and distress remains the doctor's first task, and he has plenty of means to help him, whether the patient's suffering is physical or mental. The medical conquest of distress is still not complete, but even so the Euthanasia Society has this to say about hospitals for terminal illnesses: 'Most of these hospitals are staffed by dedicated women belonging to some religious order, many of whom are also trained in nursing. Experience has shown that in the sympathetic and sometimes surprisingly cheerful atmosphere created by these women . . . they (the patients) are able to face death when it comes with a quiet mind—unafraid. Even if euthanasia were permissible to these patients probably very few would wish to avail themselves of it.'[10]

The authors of the pamphlet say that these circumstances are exceptional, because there are few such terminal hospitals, and this fact is used as support for the legalisation of euthanasia. What an indictment against our society, to propose killing people because there is not enough sympathy for them! If the old are a burden on their relations, the solution is to make proper provision for them. This was pointed out by several speakers in the Debate in the House of Lords on the Voluntary Euthanasia Bill 1969.

In those cases where a patient 'merely exists', it is not he who suffers but those around him. In the words of the Euthanasia Society's spokesman: 'Dying is still often an ugly business',[11] but where should we end up once we admitted the principle that a man may be killed for the benefit of someone else?

Medical judgment is fallible and, with ever-increasing medical skill, conditions may be curable tomorrow that are incurable today. To this argument the Euthanasia Society retorts that 'the remote possibility of making a mistake is not a reason for doing nothing'.[12] The safeguard mentioned in that context is—or at least in the 1962 pamphlet was—'that patients will seldom seriously consider the termination of life before such gross damage has been done to vital organs that recovery is out of the question';[13] but this point has lost its validity since a declaration in advance was incorporated into the Euthanasia Society's proposals.

Once a patient has signed a declaration, possibly even before he has signed it but when he knows the family expects him to do so, pride or a false sense of duty may prevent him, despite his distress, from changing his decision even though he has changed his mind. Such change of mind may be due only to a natural fear of death now the patient actually has to face it, but it may equally well be due to an experience of conversion or recovery of faith. There are certainly many instances known of this, so that clearly the spiritual state of a patient must not be assumed to remain static during a terminal illness. Moreover, where the patient's mind is clouded but still receptive, or his expression is impaired, how could an independent assessing doctor become aware, or be made aware, of a change of mind? The ethical point at issue here is that in the circumstances the doctor has no access to information from the patient on which he can conscientiously base a decision which is both professionally and ethically sound.

A patient might be suffering from an incurable disease but still be capable of leading a gratifying life for a long time; who would decide, and by what criteria, when he was to be liquidated? For cases like carcinoma of the throat with difficulty in swallowing and breathing, the Euthanasia Society argues that, though few express it, 'we cannot know how many have harboured that wish (for release) secretly'.[14] To this, it must be answered that we do not know either how many fear the end, and might fear it more if they had signed declarations and wondered at what stage their 'Will' might be executed.

Supporters of euthanasia urge that the quality of life is more important than the quantity. This slogan misleads many people: what is meant by quality? What criteria can be used to judge it, and by what possible standards can anybody assess the level of quality below which life is worthless?

Lord Ailwyn argued in the debate on Lord Raglan's Bill that those who believe in an after-life should agree that a suffering mortal be given the right to be wafted painlessly into it. Followed to its logical conclusion this would lead to the obviously absurd inference that Christian babies should be killed as soon as they are baptised, as that would guarantee their going straight to heaven.

The opposition to the legalisation of euthanasia stems from the realisation that permissive legislation would end in the encouragement of what is, in fact, in Lord Cork and Orrery's phrase, 'suicide by proxy'. Of course there are some who not only defend but extol suicide and consider the 'indoctrination' against it to be regrettable.[15] The law of the land no longer allows prosecution for attempted suicide, but in abstaining from prosecution it does not express approval: in practice it

treats attempted suicide as evidence of mental disturbance. Suicide pacts, and any encouragement to or help with a suicide, are still offences in law. Flew, in his essay on 'The Principle of Euthanasia', states that he is concerned primarily with general principles and is not discussing—except perhaps quite incidentally—'any questions of comparative detail'.[16] Such a position is untenable: these general principles cannot be separated from practicalities. Whenever risk of error or abuse exists, as it certainly would in the practice of euthanasia, the question must be asked, 'How compelling is the need to implement the principle?'—particularly so when the soundness of the principle is itself in doubt.

The supporters of euthanasia consider that the doctor-patient relationship would not be damaged if euthanasia were available. In *A Plan for Voluntary Euthanasia* (1962) this was one of the 'Arguments commonly employed against euthanasia' which the authors sought to refute (page 18 et seq). On page 24 they state:

(12) The legalisation of euthanasia would tend to undermine the confidence of patients in their doctors, and would even lead some patients to fear that euthanasia might be used without their consent.
Comment
On the contrary, the safeguards in the proposed Bill should help to allay such fears. And many people approaching old age would certainly find comfort in the assurance that their doctor would be sympathetic to their request for relief if a terminal illness should bring unbearable suffering. Medical men are not infrequently asked to give such an assurance.

Scrutiny of this statement shows that use of the term 'relief' is ambiguous and perhaps euphemistic. If 'relief of suffering' only is meant, then the proponents of euthanasia are asking no more than is common, decent medical practice. If, however, 'relief' means the deliberate and intentional ending of life, why do they not say so, for this is an entirely different matter? Why obscure the difference?

The patient trusts his doctor to care for him to the best of his ability. However hard-pressed a family doctor may be, he will find time for a confidential talk with his dying patient. Knowing the family background, he will more quickly arrive at sound conclusions than another doctor, and his encouragement and comfort will be more easily accepted by his patient. But if the doctor had undertaken to observe his patient's requests (see the schedule to the 1969 Bill (p.143), which empowers the patient to specify the time or indicate the circumstances of his death), even though the doctor had grounds for regarding these requests as no longer relevant or applicable, then the doctor would be in a position where he could no longer freely serve the best interests of his patient. This is an example of the type of damage that could be done to the doctor-patient relationship from the doctor's point of view: the implications could be far-reaching.

There might be tensions anyway in the home of an incurably ill man, but there is a great difference between those which the healthy relatives may have to bear in struggling with their mixed emotions, and the tensions which might arise between the patient and those surrounding him through a petition for euthanasia, or perhaps more often by a failure to petition. Particularly, children of vulnerable age would suffer from the effects of the discussions that would necessarily go on in a family before such a decision was made, and which it would be impossible to conceal from them. Obviously, so long as there is no provision in law for a petition for death, forecasts of what might happen if there were must be speculative. Nevertheless, such speculation can be fairly based on clinical observation, and such observation shows that there is more concern on the part of relatives that a patient should not be allowed to linger on in 'unnecessary suffering' than there is on the part of the patient himself.

Underlying the whole controversy is a difference of approach to the value of human life. On the one hand the tradition, not only of Christendom but of all civilised people, gives to human life a respect above that accorded to animal life, and of a different sort: on the other hand there are those who dismiss this respect as misplaced. Thus J. R. Wilson writes: 'We are all supposed to feel some deep inherent reverence for human life',[17] the implication being not only that some people do not feel such reverence, but also that there is at least an element of superstition in such feeling. To accept that line of thought is to reduce men to the stature of animals—a notion offensive to common sense. 'People take the experience of killing very easily indeed; it is the disapproval of society which bothers them', the same author adds. Taken together with the preceding thought, it seems that Wilson considers it enlightened to feel free to kill, and old-fashioned to disapprove of killing. These quotations illustrate the type of thinking which underlies the case for euthanasia.

However closely and carefully an Act might be framed in order to ensure that euthanasia was committed only in certain strictly defined circumstances, those circumstances would in practice be read into every conceivable case by those who wished to practice euthanasia, while those who declined could be denounced as failing to implement the law of the land, or to give patients 'their rights'.

Though no forecast concerning the long-term consequences of a Voluntary Euthanasia Act can be infallible, the suspicion that the voluntary aspect of it would not last long is certainly not to be dismissed as scaremongering. Lord Chorley gave a pointer in this direction during the 1950 Debate in the House of Lords: 'Another objection is that the Bill does not go far enough . . . that may be so, but we *must go step by step.*'[18] More recently, the Earl of Listowel, though pleading for voluntary euthanasia only, added the ominous words '. . . we cannot wish to preserve an anonymous individual who has been stripped of personality and reduced by incessant pain or physical deterioration to the animal or vegetable level'.[19] Lord Listowel is here putting forward a highly colored picture of a rare case, but is putting it forward as if it were commonplace. Moreover, as should be clear from what has been said earlier, the perpetuation of a merely breathing body is not currently good medical practice.

Once the principle of the sanctity of human life is abandoned, or the propaganda accepted that to uphold it is old-fashioned, prejudiced or superstitious, the way is open to the raising of—and the satisfaction of—a demand for so-called euthanasia for severely handicapped children, the mentally sub-normal, the severely crippled, the aged, and ultimately for all who are a burden on the community services and the public purse.

Medicine—and thus its practitioner—is essentially concerned with the relief of pain and suffering and the furtherance of the well-being of the individual.[20] For this reason, whenever the doctor is involved (and he is necessarily involved in this matter) his approach must be an individual one. Nevertheless there is no antithesis between the ultimate good of the individual and that of society. To those who believe in the brotherhood of man, whether from religious or humanist considerations, such an antithesis must appear as a contradiction in terms.

The small families of the 1920's and 30's have left us in the 1960's and 70's with a high proportion of elderly people. Euthanasia could make the sick elderly a ready target for an unwholesome social policy—indeed their destruction might improve the appearance of the population statistics. Let euthanasia be seen for what it is: a tragic attempt to patch up a morbid society.

NOTES

1. Hansard, H. of L., 25 March 1969, vol 300, col 1180.
2. K. F. M. Pole, *Handbook for the Catholic Nurse,* Robert Hale Ltd., (1964).
3. *Euthanasia and the Right to Death,* ed. A. B. Downing, Peter Owen, (1969), page 103.
4. *A Plan for Voluntary Euthanasia* (1962), page 18. Our italics.
5. *Ibid.,* page 20. Original italics.
6. *Euthanasia and the Right to Death,* page 5.
7. *Ibid.,* page 171.
8. *Ibid.,* page 68. Original italics.
9. *Ibid.,* loc. cit. Original italics.
10. *A Plan for Voluntary Euthanasia* (1962), page 19.
11. *Ibid.,* page 6.
12. *Ibid.,* page 24.
13. *Ibid.,* loc. cit.
14. *Ibid.,* page 21.
15. *Euthanasia and the Right to Death,* page 153.
16. *Ibid.,* page 31.
17. J. R. Wilson, 'The Freedom to Die', *The Spectator,* 7 February 1969.
18. Hansard, H. of L., vol 169, col 559. Our italics.
19. *Euthanasia and the Right to Death,* page 6.
20. J. Gould, 'The Psychiatry of Major Crime', *Recent Progress in Psychiatry,* vol III (1958).

Killing and Letting Die

43. ACTIVE AND PASSIVE EUTHANASIA

James Rachels

The distinction between active and passive euthanasia is thought to be crucial for medical ethics. The idea is that it is permissible, at least in some cases, to withhold treatment and allow a patient to die, but it is never permissible to take any direct action designed to kill the patient. This doctrine seems to be accepted by most doctors, and it is endorsed in a statement adopted by the House of Delegates of the American Medical Association on December 4, 1973:

From James Rachels, "Active and Passive Euthanasia," *New England Journal of Medicine,* Vol. 292 (1975), pp. 78–80. Reprinted by permission of the *New England Journal of Medicine.*

The intentional termination of the life of one human being by another—mercy killing—is contrary to that for which the medical profession stands and is contrary to the policy of the American Medical Association.

The cessation of the employment of extraordinary means to prolong the life of the body when there is irrefutable evidence that biological death is imminent is the decision of the patient and/or his immediate family. The advice and judgment of the physician should be freely available to the patient and/or his immediate family.

However, a strong case can be made against this doctrine. In what follows I will set out some of the relevant arguments, and urge doctors to reconsider their views on this matter.

To begin with a familiar type of situation, a patient who is dying of incurable cancer of the throat is in terrible pain, which can no longer be satisfactorily alleviated. He is certain to die within a few days, even if present treatment is continued, but he does not want to go on living for those days since the pain is unbearable. So he asks the doctor for an end to it, and his family joins in the request.

Suppose the doctor agrees to withhold treatment, as the conventional doctrine says he may. The justification for his doing so is that the patient is in terrible agony, and since he is going to die anyway, it would be wrong to prolong his suffering needlessly. But now notice this. If one simply withholds treatment, it may take the patient longer to die, and so he may suffer more than he would if more direct action were taken and a lethal injection given. This fact provides strong reason for thinking that, once the initial decision not to prolong his agony has been made, active euthanasia is actually preferable to passive euthanasia, rather than the reverse. To say otherwise is to endorse the option that leads to more suffering rather than less, and is contrary to the humanitarian impulse that prompts the decision not to prolong his life in the first place.

Part of my point is that the process of being "allowed to die" can be relatively slow and painful, whereas being given a lethal injection is relatively quick and painless. Let me give a different sort of example. In the United States about one in 600 babies is born with Down's syndrome. Most of these babies are otherwise healthy—that is, with only the usual pediatric care, they will proceed to an otherwise normal infancy. Some, however, are born with congenital defects such as intestinal obstructions that require operations if they are to live. Sometimes, the parents and the doctor will decide not to operate, and let the infant die. Anthony Shaw describes what happens then:

... When surgery is denied [the doctor] must try to keep the infant from suffering while natural forces sap the baby's life away. As a surgeon whose natural inclination is to use the scalpel to fight off death, standing by and watching a salvageable baby die is the most emotionally exhausting experience I know. It is easy at a conference, in a theoretical discussion, to decide that such infants should be allowed to die. It is altogether different to stand by in the nursery and watch as dehydration and infection wither a tiny being over hours and days. This is a terrible ordeal for me and the hospital staff—much more so than for the parents who never set foot in the nursery.[1]

I can understand why some people are opposed to all euthanasia, and insist that such infants must be allowed to live. I think I can also understand why other people favor destroying these babies quickly and painlessly. But why should anyone favor letting "dehydration and infection wither a tiny being over hours and days?" The doctrine that says that a baby may be allowed to dehydrate and wither, but may not be given an injection that would end its life without suffering, seems so patently cruel as to require no further refutation. The strong language is not intended to offend, but only to put the point in the clearest possible way.

My second argument is that the conventional doctrine leads to decisions concerning life and death made on irrelevant grounds.

Consider again the case of the infants with Down's syndrome who need operations for congenital defects unrelated to the syndrome to live. Sometimes, there is no operation, and the baby dies, but when there is no such defect, the baby lives on. Now, an operation such as that to remove an intestinal obstruction is not prohibitively difficult. The reason why such operations are not performed in these cases is, clearly, that the child has Down's syndrome and the parents and doctor judge that because of that fact it is better for the child to die.

But notice that this situation is absurd, no matter what view one takes of the lives and potentials of such babies. If the life of such an infant is worth preserving, what does it matter if it needs a simple operation? Or, if one thinks it better that such a baby should not live on, what difference does it make that it happens to have an unobstructed intestinal tract? In either case, the matter of life and death is being decided on irrelevant grounds. It is the Down's syndrome, and not the intestines, that is the issue. The matter should be decided, if at all, on that basis, and not be allowed to depend on the essentially irrelevant question of whether the intestinal tract is blocked.

What makes this situation possible, of course, is the idea that when there is an intestinal blockage, one can "let the baby die," but when there is no such defect there is nothing that can be done, for one must not "kill" it. The fact that this idea leads to such results as deciding life or death on irrelevant grounds is another good reason why the doctrine should be rejected.

One reason why so many people think that there is an important moral difference between active and passive euthanasia is that they think killing someone is morally worse than letting someone die. But is it? Is killing, in itself, worse than letting die? To investigate this issue, two cases may be considered that are exactly alike except that one involves killing whereas the other involves letting someone die. Then, it can be asked whether this difference makes any difference to the moral assessments. It is important that the cases be exactly alike, except for this one difference, since otherwise one cannot be confident that it is this difference and not some other that accounts for any variation in the assessments of the two cases. So, let us consider this pair of cases:

In the first, Smith stands to gain a large inheritance if anything should happen to his six-year-old cousin. One evening while the child is taking his bath, Smith sneaks into the bathroom and drowns the child, and then arranges things so that it will look like an accident.

In the second, Jones also stands to gain if anything should happen to his six-year-old cousin. Like Smith, Jones sneaks in planning to drown the child in his bath. However, just as he enters the bathroom Jones sees the child slip and hit his head, and fall face down in the water. Jones is delighted; he stands by, ready to push the child's head back under if it is necessary, but it is not necessary. With only a little thrashing about, the child drowns all by himself, "accidentally," as Jones watches and does nothing.

Now Smith killed the child, whereas Jones "merely" let the child die. That is the only difference between them. Did either man behave better, from a moral point of view? If the difference between killing and letting die were in itself a morally

important matter, one should say that Jones's behavior was less reprehensible than Smith's. But does one really want to say that? I think not. In the first place, both men acted from the same motive, personal gain, and both had exactly the same end in view when they acted. It may be inferred from Smith's conduct that he is a bad man, although that judgment may be withdrawn or modified if certain further facts are learned about him—for example, that he is mentally deranged. But would not the very same thing be inferred about Jones from his conduct? And would not the same further considerations also be relevant to any modification of this judgment? Moreover, suppose Jones pleaded, in his own defense, "After all, I didn't do anything except just stand there and watch the child drown. I didn't kill him; I only let him die." Again, if letting die were in itself less bad than killing, this defense should have at least some weight. But it does not. Such a "defense" can only be regarded as a grotesque perversion of moral reasoning. Morally speaking, it is no defense at all.

Now, it may be pointed out, quite properly, that the cases of euthanasia with which doctors are concerned are not like this at all. They do not involve personal gain or the destruction of normal healthy children. Doctors are concerned only with cases in which the patient's life is of no further use to him, or in which the patient's life has become or will soon become a terrible burden. However, the point is the same in these cases; the bare difference between killing and letting die does not, in itself, make a moral difference. If a doctor lets a patient die, for humane reasons, he is in the same moral position as if he had given the patient a lethal injection for humane reasons. If his decision was wrong—if, for example, the patient's illness was in fact curable—the decision would be equally regrettable no matter which method was used to carry it out. And if the doctor's decision was the right one, the method used is not in itself important.

The AMA policy statement isolates the crucial issue very well; the crucial issue is "the intentional termination of the life of one human being by another." But after identifying this issue, and forbidding "mercy killing," the statement goes on to deny that the cessation of treatment is the intentional termination of a life. This is where the mistake comes in, for what is the cessation of treatment in these circumstances, if it is not "the intentional termination of the life of one human being by another?" Of course it is exactly that, and if it were not, there would be no point to it.

Many people will find this judgment hard to accept. One reason, I think, is that it is very easy to conflate the question of whether killing is, in itself, worse than letting die, with the very different question of whether most actual cases of killing are more reprehensible than most actual cases of letting die. Most actual cases of killing are clearly terrible (think, for example, of all the murders reported in the newspapers), and one hears of such cases every day. On the other hand, one hardly ever hears of a case of letting die, except for the actions of doctors who are motivated by humanitarian reasons. So one learns to think of killing in a much worse light than of letting die. But this does not mean that there is something about killing that makes it in itself worse than letting die, for it is not the bare difference between killing and letting die that makes the difference in these cases. Rather, the other factors—the murderer's motive of personal gain, for example, contrasted with the doctor's humanitarian motivation—account for different reactions to the different cases.

I have argued that killing is not in itself any worse than letting die; if my contention is right, it follows that active euthanasia is not any worse than passive euthanasia. What arguments can be given on the other side? The most common, I believe, is the following:

"The important difference between active and passive euthanasia is that, in passive euthanasia, the doctor does not do anything to bring about the patient's death. The doctor does nothing, and the patient dies of whatever ills already afflict him. In active euthanasia, however, the doctor does something to bring about the patient's death: he kills him. The doctor who gives the patient with cancer a lethal injection has himself caused his patient's death; whereas if he merely ceases treatment, the cancer is the cause of the death."

A number of points need to be made here. The first is that it is not exactly correct to say that in passive euthanasia the doctor does nothing, for he does do one thing that is very important: he lets the patient die. "Letting someone die" is certainly different, in some respects, from other types of action—mainly in that it is a kind of action that one may perform by way of not performing certain other actions. For example, one may let a patient die by way of not giving medication, just as one may insult someone by way of not shaking his hand. But for any purpose of moral assessment, it is a type of action nonetheless. The decision to let a patient die is subject to moral appraisal in the same way that a decision to kill him would be subject to moral appraisal: it may be assessed as wise or unwise, compassionate or sadistic, right or wrong. If a doctor deliberately let a patient die who was suffering from a routinely curable illness, the doctor would certainly be to blame for what he had done, just as he would be to blame if he had needlessly killed the patient. Charges against him would then be appropriate. If so, it would be no defense at all for him to insist that he didn't "do anything." He would have done something very serious indeed, for he let his patient die.

Fixing the cause of death may be very important from a legal point of view, for it may determine whether criminal charges are brought against the doctor. But I do not think that this notion can be used to show a moral difference between active and passive euthanasia. The reason why it is considered bad to be the cause of someone's death is that death is regarded as a great evil—and so it is. However, if it has been decided that euthanasia—even passive euthanasia—is desirable in a given case, it has also been decided that in this instance death is no greater an evil than the patient's continued existence. And if this is true, the usual reason for not wanting to be the cause of someone's death simply does not apply.

Finally, doctors may think that all of this is only of academic interest—the sort of thing that philosophers may worry about but that has no practical bearing on their own work. After all, doctors must be concerned about the legal consequences of what they do, and active euthanasia is clearly forbidden by the law. But even so, doctors should also be concerned with the fact that the law is forcing upon them a moral doctrine that may well be indefensible, and has a considerable effect on their practices. Of course, most doctors are not now in the position of being coerced in this matter, for they do not regard themselves as merely going along with what the law requires. Rather, in statements such as the AMA policy statement that I have quoted, they are endorsing this doctrine as a central point of medical ethics. In that statement, active euthanasia is condemned not merely as illegal but as "contrary to that for which the medical profession stands," whereas passive euthanasia is approved. However, the preceding considerations suggest that there is really no moral difference between the two, considered in themselves (there may be important moral differences in some cases

in their *consequences,* but, as I pointed out, these differences may make active euthanasia, and not passive euthanasia, the morally preferable option). So, whereas doctors may have to discriminate between active and passive euthanasia to satisfy the law, they should not do any more than that. In particular, they should not give the distinction any added authority and weight by writing it into official statements of medical ethics.

NOTE

1. Shaw, A., "Doctor, Do We Have a Choice?", *The New York Times Magazine,* January 30, 1972, p. 54.

44. THE SURVIVAL LOTTERY

John Harris

Let us suppose that organ transplant procedures have been perfected; in such circumstances if two dying patients could be saved by organ transplants then, if surgeons have the requisite organs in stock and no other needy patients, but nevertheless allow their patients to die, we would be inclined to say, and be justified in saying, that the patients died because the doctors refused to save them. But if there are no spare organs in stock and none otherwise available, the doctors have no choice, they cannot save their patients and so must let them die. In this case we would be disinclined to say that the doctors are in any sense the cause of their patients' deaths. But let us further suppose that the two dying patients, Y and Z, are not happy about being left to die. They might argue that it is not strictly true that there are no organs which could be used to save them. Y needs a new heart and Z new lungs. They point out that if just one healthy person were to be killed his organs could be removed and both of them be saved. We and the doctors would probably be alike in thinking that such a step, while

technically possible, would be out of the question. We would not say that the doctors were killing their patients if they refused to prey upon the healthy to save the sick. And because this sort of surgical Robin Hoodery is out of the question we can tell Y and Z that they cannot be saved, and that when they die they will have died of natural causes and not of the neglect of their doctors. Y and Z do not however agree, they insist that if the doctors fail to kill a healthy man and use his organs to save them, then the doctors will be responsible for their deaths.

Many philosophers have for various reasons believed that we must not kill even if by doing so we could save life. They believe that there is a moral difference between killing and letting die. On this view, to kill A so that Y and Z might live is ruled out because we have a strict obligation not to kill but a duty of some lesser kind to save life. A. H. Clough's dictum 'Thou shalt not kill but need'st not strive officiously to keep alive' expresses bluntly this point of view. The dying Y and Z may be excused for not being much impressed by Clough's dictum. They agree that it is wrong to kill the innocent and are prepared to agree to an absolute prohibition against so doing. They do not agree,

From John Harris, "The Survival Lottery," *Philosophy*, Vol. 50 (1975), pp.81–87. Reprinted by permission of Cambridge University Press.

however, that A is more innocent than they are. Y and Z might go on to point out that the currently acknowledged right of the innocent not to be killed, even where their deaths might give life to others, is just a decision to prefer the lives of the fortunate to those of the unfortunate. A is innocent in the sense that he has done nothing to deserve death, but Y and Z are also innocent in this sense. Why should they be the ones to die simply because they are so unlucky as to have diseased organs? Why, they might argue, should their living or dying be left to chance when in so many other areas of human life we believe that we have an obligation to ensure the survival of the maximum number of lives possible?

Y and Z argue that if a doctor refuses to treat a patient, with the result that the patient dies, he has killed that patient as sure as shooting, and that, in exactly the same way, if the doctors refuse Y and Z the transplants that they need, then their refusal will kill Y and Z, again as sure as shooting. The doctors, and indeed the society which supports their inaction, cannot defend themselves by arguing that they are neither expected, nor required by law or convention, to kill so that lives may be saved (indeed, quite the reverse) since this is just an appeal to custom or authority. A man who does his own moral thinking must decide whether, in these circumstances, he ought to save two lives at the cost of one, or one life at the cost of two. The fact that so called 'third parties' have never before been brought into such calculations, have never before been thought of as being involved, is not an argument against their now becoming so. There are of course, good arguments against allowing doctors simply to haul passers-by off the streets whenever they have a couple of patients in need of new organs. And the harmful side-effects of such a practice in terms of terror and distress to the victims, the witnesses and society generally, would give us further reasons for dismissing the idea. Y and Z realize this and have a proposal, which they will shortly produce, which would largely meet objections to placing such power in the hands of doctors and eliminate at least some of the harmful side-effects.

In the unlikely event of their feeling obliged to reply to the reproaches of Y and Z, the doctors might offer the following argument: they might maintain that a man is only responsible for the death of someone whose life he might have saved, if, in all the circumstances of the case, he ought to have saved the man by the means available. This is why a doctor might be a murderer if he simply refused or neglected to treat a patient who would die without treatment, but not if he could only save the patient by doing something he ought in no circumstances to do—kill the innocent. Y and Z readily agree that a man ought not to do what he ought not to do, but they point out that if the doctors, and for that matter society at large, ought on balance to kill one man if two can thereby be saved, then failure to do so will involve responsibility for the consequent deaths. The fact that Y's and Z's proposal involves killing the innocent cannot be a reason for refusing to consider their proposal, for this would just be a refusal to face the question at issue and so avoid having to make a decision as to what ought to be done in circumstances like these. It is Y's and Z's claim that failure to adopt their plan will also involve killing the innocent, rather more of the innocent than the proposed alternative.

To back up this last point, to remove the arbitrariness of permitting doctors to select their donors from among the chance passers-by outside hospitals, and the tremendous power this would place in doctors' hands, to mitigate worries about side-effects and lastly to appease those who wonder why poor old A should be singled out for sacrifice, Y and Z put forward the following scheme: they propose that everyone be given a sort of lottery number. Whenever doctors have two or more dying patients who could be saved by transplants, and no suitable organs have come to hand through 'natural' deaths, they can ask a central computer to supply a suitable donor. The computer will then pick the number of a suitable donor at random and he will be killed so that the lives of two or more others may be saved. No doubt if the scheme were ever to be implemented a suitable euphemism for 'killed' would be employed. Perhaps we would begin to talk about citizens being called upon to 'give life' to others. With the refinement of transplant procedures such a scheme could offer the chance of saving large numbers of lives that are now lost.

Indeed, even taking into account the loss of the lives of donors, the numbers of untimely deaths each year might be dramatically reduced, so much so that everyone's chance of living to a ripe old age might be increased. If this were to be the consequence of the adoption of such a scheme, and it might well be, it could not be dismissed lightly. It might of course be objected that it is likely that more old people will need transplants to prolong their lives than will the young, and so the scheme would inevitably lead to a society dominated by the old. But if such a society is thought objectionable, there is no reason to suppose that a programme could not be designed for the computer that would ensure the maintenance of whatever is considered to be an optimum age distribution throughout the population.

Suppose that inter-planetary travel revealed a world of people like ourselves, but who organized their society according to this scheme. No one was considered to have an absolute right to life or freedom from interference, but everything was always done to ensure that as many people as possible would enjoy long and happy lives. In such a world a man who attempted to escape when his number was up or who resisted on the grounds that no one had a right to take his life, might well be regarded as a murderer. We might or might not prefer to live in such a world, but the morality of its inhabitants would surely be one that we could respect. It would not be obviously more barbaric or cruel or immoral than our own.

Y and Z are willing to concede one exception to the universal application of their scheme. They realize that it would be unfair to allow people who have brought their misfortune on themselves to benefit from the lottery. There would clearly be something unjust about killing the abstemious B so that W (whose heavy smoking has given him lung cancer) and X (whose drinking has destroyed his liver) should be preserved to over-indulge again.

What objections could be made to the lottery scheme? A first straw to clutch at would be the desire for security. Under such a scheme we would never know when we would hear *them* knocking at the door. Every post might bring a sentence of death, every sound in the night might be the sound of boots on the stairs. But, as we have seen, the chances of actually being called upon to make the ultimate sacrifice might be slimmer than is the present risk of being killed on the roads, and most of us do not lie trembling a-bed, appalled at the prospect of being dispatched on the morrow. The truth is that lives might well be more secure under such a scheme.

If we respect individuality and see every human being as unique in his own way, we might want to reject a society in which it appeared that individuals were seen merely as interchangeable units in a structure, the value of which lies in its having as many healthy units as possible. But of course Y and Z would want to know why A's individuality was more worthy of respect than theirs.

Another plausible objection is the natural reluctance to play God with men's lives, the feeling that it is wrong to make any attempt to re-allot the life opportunities that fate has determined, that the deaths of Y and Z would be 'natural', whereas the death of anyone killed to save them would have been perpetrated by men. But if we are able to change things, then to elect not to do so is also to determine what will happen in the world.

Neither does the alleged moral difference between killing and letting die afford a respectable way of rejecting the claims of Y and Z. For if we really want to counter proponents of the lottery, if we really want to answer Y and Z and not just put them off, we cannot do so by saying that the lottery involves killing and object to it for that reason, because to do so would, as we have seen, just beg the question as to whether the failure to save as many people as possible might not also amount to killing.

To opt for the society which Y and Z propose would be then to adopt a society in which saintliness would be mandatory. Each of us would have to recognize a binding obligation to give up his own life for others when called upon to do so. In such a society anyone who reneged upon this duty would be a murderer. The most promising objection to such a society, and indeed to any principle which required us to kill A in order to save Y and Z, is, I suspect, that we are committed to the right of self-defence. If I can kill A to save Y and Z then he can kill me to save P and Q, and it is only if I am prepared to agree to this that I will opt for the lottery or be prepared to agree to a man's being killed if doing so would save the lives of more than one other man. Of course there is something paradoxical about basing objections to the lottery scheme on the right of self-defence since, *ex hypothesi,* each person would have a better chance of living to a ripe old age if the lottery scheme were to be implemented. None the less, the feeling that no man should be required to lay down his life for others makes many people shy away from such a scheme, even though it might be rational to accept it on prudential grounds, and perhaps even mandatory on utilitarian grounds. Again, Y and Z would reply that the right of self-defence must extend to them as much as to anyone else; and while it is true that they can only live if another man is killed, they would claim that it is also true that if they are left to die, then someone who lives on does so over their dead bodies.

It might be argued that the institution of the survival lottery has not gone far to mitigate the harmful side-effects in terms of terror and distress to victims, witnesses and society generally, that would be occasioned by doctors simply snatching passers-by off the streets and disorganizing them for the benefit of the unfortunate. Donors would after all still have to be procured, and this process, however it was carried out, would still be likely to prove distressing to all concerned. The lottery scheme would eliminate the arbitrariness of leaving the life and death decisions to the doctors, and remove the possibility of such terrible power falling into the hands of any individuals, but the terror and distress would remain. The effect of having to apprehend presumably unwilling victims would give us pause. Perhaps only a long period of education or propaganda could remove our abhorrence. What this abhorrence reveals about the rights and wrongs of the situation is however more difficult to assess. We might be inclined to say that only monsters could ignore the promptings of conscience so far as to operate the lottery scheme. But the promptings of conscience are not necessarily the most reliable guide. In the present case Y and Z would argue that such promptings are mere squeamishness, an over-nice self-indulgence that costs lives. Death, Y and Z would remind us, is a distressing experience whenever and to whomever

it occurs, so the less it occurs the better. Fewer victims and witnesses will be distressed as part of the side-effects of the lottery scheme than would suffer as part of the side-effects of not instituting it.

Lastly, a more limited objection might be made, not to the idea of killing to save lives, but to the involvement of 'third parties'. Why, so the objection goes, should we not give X's heart to Y or Y's lungs to X, the same number of lives being thereby preserved and no one else's life set at risk? Y's and Z's reply to this objection differs from their previous line of argument. To amend their plan so that the involvement of so called 'third parties' is ruled out would, Y and Z claim, violate their right to equal concern and respect with the rest of society. They argue that such a proposal would amount to treating the unfortunate who need new organs as a class within society whose lives are considered to be of less value than those of its more fortunate members. What possible justification could there be for singling out one group of people whom we would be justified in using as donors but not another? The idea in the mind of those who would propose such a step must be something like the following: since Y and Z cannot survive, since they are going to die in any event, there is no harm in putting their names into the lottery, for the chances of their dying cannot thereby be increased and will in fact almost certainly be reduced. But this is just to ignore everything that Y and Z have been saying. For if their lottery scheme is adopted they are not going to die anyway—their chances of dying are no greater and no less than those of any other participant in the lottery whose number may come up. This ground for confining selection of donors to the unfortunate therefore disappears. Any other ground must discriminate against Y and Z as members of a class whose lives are less worthy of respect than those of the rest of society.

It might more plausibly be argued that the dying who cannot themselves be saved by transplants, or by any other means at all, should be the priority selection group for the computer programme. But how far off must death be for a man to be classified as 'dying'? Those so classified might argue that their last few days or weeks of life are as valuable to them (if not more valuable) than the possibly longer span remaining to others. The problem of narrowing down the class of possible donors without discriminating unfairly against some sub-class of society is, I suspect, insoluble.

Such is the case for the survival lottery. Utilitarians ought to be in favour of it, and absolutists cannot object to it on the ground that it involves killing the innocent, for it is Y's and Z's case that any alternative must also involve killing the innocent. If the absolutist wishes to maintain his objection he must point to some morally relevant difference between positive and negative killing. This challenge opens the door to a large topic with a whole library of literature, but Y and Z are dying and do not have time to explore it exhaustively. In their own case the most likely candidate for some feature which might make this moral difference is the malevolent intent of Y and Z themselves. An absolutist might well argue that while no one intends the deaths of Y and Z, no one necessarily wishes them dead, or aims at their demise for any reason, they do mean to kill A (or have him killed). But Y and Z can reply that the death of A is no part of their plan, they merely wish to use a couple of his organs, and if he cannot live without them . . . *tant pis!* None would be more delighted than Y and Z if artificial organs would do as well, and so render the lottery scheme otiose.

One form of absolutist argument perhaps remains. This involves taking an Orwellian stand on some principle of common decency. The argument would then be that even to enter into the sort of 'macabre' calculations that Y and Z propose displays a blunted sensibility, a corrupted and vitiated mind. Forms of this argument have recently been advanced by Noam Chomsky (*American Power and the New Mandarins*) and Stuart Hampshire (*Morality and Pessimism*). The indefatigable Y and Z would of course deny that their calculations are in any sense 'macabre', and would present them as the most humane course available in the circumstances. Moreover they would claim that the Orwellian stand on decency is the product of a closed mind, and not susceptible to rational argument. Any reasoned defence of such a principle must appeal to notions like respect for human life, as Hampshire's argument in fact does, and these Y and Z could make conformable to their own position.

Can Y and Z be answered? Perhaps only by relying on moral intuition, on the insistence that we do feel there is something wrong with the survival lottery and our confidence that this feeling is prompted by some morally relevant difference between our bringing about the death of A and our bringing about the deaths of Y and Z. Whether we could retain this confidence in our intuitions if we were to be confronted by a society in which the survival lottery operated, was accepted by all, and was seen to save many lives that would otherwise have been lost, it would be interesting to know.

There would of course be great practical difficulties in the way of implementing the lottery. In so many cases it would be agonizingly difficult to decide whether or not a person had brought his misfortune on himself. There are numerous ways in which a person may contribute to his predicament, and the task of deciding how far, or how decisively, a person is himself responsible for his fate would be formidable. And in those cases where we can be confident that a person is innocent of responsibility for his predicament, can we acquire this confidence in time to save him? The lottery scheme would be a powerful weapon in the hands of someone willing and able to misuse it. Could we ever feel certain that the lottery was safe from unscrupulous computer programmers? Perhaps we should be thankful that such practical difficulties make the survival lottery an unlikely consequence of the perfection of transplants. Or perhaps we should be appalled.

It may be that we would want to tell Y and Z that the difficulties and dangers of their scheme would be too great a price to pay for its benefits. It is as well to be clear, however, that there is also a high, perhaps an even higher, price to be paid for the rejection of the scheme. That price is the lives of Y and Z and many like them, and we delude ourselves if we suppose that the reason why we reject their plan is that we accept the sixth commandment.[1]

NOTE

1.   Thanks are due to Ronald Dworkin, Jonathan Glover, M. J. Inwood and Anne Seller for helpful comments.

45. THE CASE OF THE SPELUNCEAN EXPLORERS

Lon L. Fuller

IN THE SUPREME COURT OF NEWGARTH, 4300

The defendants, having been indicted for the crime of murder, were convicted and sentenced to be hanged by the Court of General Instances of the County of Stowfield. They bring a petition of error before this court. The facts sufficiently appear in the opinion of the Chief Justice.

TRUEPENNY, C. J. The four defendants are members of the Speluncean Society, an organization of amateurs interested in the exploration of caves. Early in May of 4299 they, in the company of Roger Whetmore, then also a member of the Society, penetrated into the interior of a limestone cavern of the type found in the Central Plateau of this Commonwealth. While they were in a position remote from the entrance to the cave, a landslide occurred. Heavy boulders fell in such a manner as to block completely the only known opening to the cave. When the men discovered their predicament they settled themselves near the obstructed entrance to wait until a rescue party should remove the detritus that prevented them from leaving their underground prison. On the failure of Whetmore and the defendants to return to their homes, the Secretary of the Society was notified by their families. It appears that the explorers had left indications at the headquarters of the Society concerning the location of the cave they proposed to visit. A rescue party was promptly dispatched to the spot.

From Lon L. Fuller, "The Case of the Speluncean Explorers," *Harvard Law Review*, Vol. 62 (1949), pp. 616–645. Reprinted with the author's permission.

The task of rescue proved one of overwhelming difficulty. It was necessary to supplement the forces of the original party by repeated increments of men and machines, which had to be conveyed at great expense to the remote and isolated region in which the cave was located. A huge temporary camp of workmen, engineers, geologists, and other experts was established. The work of removing the obstruction was several times frustrated by fresh landslides. In one of these, ten of the workmen engaged in clearing the entrance were killed. The treasury of the Speluncean Society was soon exhausted in the rescue effort, and the sum of eight hundred thousand frelars, raised partly by popular subscription and partly by legislative grant, was expended before the imprisoned men were rescued. Success was finally achieved on the thirty-second day after the men entered the cave.

Since it was known that the explorers had carried with them only scant provisions, and since it was also known that there was no animal or vegetable matter within the cave on which they might subsist, anxiety was early felt that they might meet death by starvation before access to them could be obtained. On the twentieth day of their imprisonment it was learned for the first time that they had taken with them into the cave a portable wireless machine capable of both sending and receiving messages. A similar machine was promptly installed in the rescue camp and oral communication established with the unfortunate men within the mountain. They asked to be informed how long a time would be required to release them. The engineers in charge of the project answered that at least ten days would be required even if no new landslides occurred. The explorers then asked if any physicians were present, and were placed in communication with a committee of medical experts. The imprisoned men described their condition and the rations they had taken with them, and asked for a medical opinion whether they would be likely to live without food for ten days longer. The chairman of the committee of physicians told them that there was little possibility of this. The wireless machine within the cave then remained silent for eight hours. When communication was re-established the men asked to speak again with the physicians. The chairman of the physicians' committee was placed before the apparatus, and Whetmore, speaking on behalf of himself and the defendants, asked whether they would be able to survive for ten days longer if they consumed the flesh of one of their number. The physicians' chairman reluctantly answered this question in the affirmative. Whetmore asked whether it would be advisable for them to cast lots to determine which of them should be eaten. None of the physicians present was willing to answer the question. Whetmore then asked if there were among the party a judge or other official of the government who would answer this question. None of those attached to the rescue camp was willing to assume the role of advisor in this matter. He then asked if any minister or priest would answer their question, and none was found who would do so. Thereafter no further messages were received from within the cave, and it was assumed (erroneously, it later appeared) that the electric batteries of the explorers' wireless machine had become exhausted. When the imprisoned men were finally released it was learned that on the twenty-third day after their entrance into the cave Whetmore had been killed and eaten by his companions.

From the testimony of the defendants, which was accepted by the jury, it appears that it was Whetmore who first proposed that they might find the nutriment without which survival was impossible in the flesh of one of their own number. It was also Whetmore who first proposed the use of some method of casting lots, calling the attention of the defendants to a pair of dice he happened to have with him. The defendants were at first reluctant to adopt so desperate a procedure, but after the conversations by wireless related above, they finally agreed on the plan proposed by Whetmore.

After much discussion of the mathematical problems involved, agreement was finally reached on a method of determining the issue by the use of the dice.

Before the dice were cast, however, Whetmore declared that he withdrew from the arrangement, as he had decided on reflection to wait for another week before embracing an expedient so frightful and odious. The others charged him with a breach of faith and proceeded to cast the dice. When it came Whetmore's turn, the dice were cast for him by one of the defendants, and he was asked to declare any objections he might have to the fairness of the throw. He stated that he had no such objections. The throw went against him, and he was then put to death and eaten by his companions.

After the rescue of the defendants, and after they had completed a stay in a hospital where they underwent a course of treatment for malnutrition and shock, they were indicted for the murder of Roger Whetmore. At the trial, after the testimony had been concluded, the foreman of the jury (a lawyer by profession) inquired of the court whether the jury might not find a special verdict, leaving it to the court to say whether on the facts as found the defendants were guilty. After some discussion, both the Prosecutor and counsel for the defendants indicated their acceptance of this procedure, and it was adopted by the court. In a lengthy special verdict the jury found the facts as I have related them above, and found further that if on these facts the defendants were guilty of the crime charged against them, then they found the defendants guilty. On the basis of this verdict, the trial judge ruled that the defendants were guilty of murdering Roger Whetmore. The judge then sentenced them to be hanged, the law of our Commonwealth permitting him no discretion with respect to the penalty to be imposed. After the release of the jury, its members joined in a communication to the Chief Executive asking that the sentence be commuted to an imprisonment of six months. The trial judge addressed a similar communication to the Chief Executive. As yet no action with respect to these pleas has been taken, as the Chief Executive is apparently awaiting our disposition of this petition of error.

It seems to me that in dealing with this extraordinary case the jury and the trial judge followed a course that was not only fair and wise, but the only course that was open to them under the law. The language of our statute is well known: "Whoever shall willfully take the life of another shall be punished by death." N.C.S.A. (N.S.) § 12-A. This statute permits of no exception applicable to this case, however our sympathies may incline us to make allowance for the tragic situation in which these men found themselves.

In a case like this the principle of executive clemency seems admirably suited to mitigate the rigors of the law, and I propose to my colleagues that we follow the example of the jury and the trial judge by joining in the communications they have addressed to the Chief Executive. There is every reason to believe that these requests for clemency will be heeded. . . . If this is done, then justice will be accomplished without impairing either the letter or spirit of our statutes and without offering any encouragement for the disregard of law.

FOSTER, J. I am shocked that the Chief Justice, in an effort to escape the embarrassments of this tragic case, should have adopted, and should have proposed to his colleagues, an expedient at once so sordid and so obvious. I believe something more is on trial in this case than the fate of these unfortunate explorers; that is the law of our Commonwealth. If this Court declares that under our law these men have committed a crime, then our law is itself convicted in the tribunal of common sense, no matter what happens to the individuals involved in this petition of error. For us to assert that the law we uphold and expound compels us to a conclusion we are ashamed of, and from which we can only escape by appealing to a dispensation resting within the personal whim of the Executive, seems to me to amount to an admission that the law of this Commonwealth no longer pretends to incorporate justice.

For myself, I do not believe that our law compels the monstrous conclusion that these men are murderers. I believe, on the contrary, that it declares them to be innocent of any crime. I rest this conclusion on two independent grounds, either of which is of itself sufficient to justify the acquittal of these defendants.

The first of these grounds rests on a premise that may arouse opposition until it has been examined candidly. I take the view that the enacted or positive law of this Commonwealth, including all of its statutes and precedents, is inapplicable to this case, and that the case is governed instead by what ancient writers in Europe and America called "the law of nature."

This conclusion rests on the proposition that our positive law is predicated on the possibility of men's coexistence in society. When a situation arises in which the coexistence of men becomes impossible, then a condition that underlies all of our precedents and statutes has ceased to exist. When that condition disappears, then it is my opinion that the force of our positive law disappears with it. We are not accustomed to applying the maxim *cessante ratione legis, cessat et ipsa lex*[1] to the whole of our enacted law, but I believe that this is a case where the maxim should be so applied. . . .

Had the tragic events of this case taken place a mile beyond the territorial limits of our Commonwealth, no one would pretend that our law was applicable to them. . . . Now I contend that a case may be removed morally from the force of a legal order, as well as geographically. If we look to the purposes of law and government, and to the premises underlying our positive law, these men when they made their fateful decision were as remote from our legal order as if they had been a thousand miles beyond our boundaries. . . .

What these men did was done in pursuance of an agreement accepted by all of them and first proposed by Whetmore himself. Since it was apparent that their extraordinary predicament made inapplicable the usual principles that regulate men's relations with one another, it was necessary for them to draw, as it were, a new charter of government appropriate to the situation in which they found themselves. . . .

I believe that the line of argument I have just expounded permits of no rational answer. I realize that it will probably be received with a certain discomfort by many who read this opinion, who will be inclined to suspect that some hidden sophistry must underlie a demonstration that leads to so many unfamiliar conclusions. The source of this discomfort is, however, easy to identify. The usual conditions of human existence incline us to think of human life as an absolute value, not to be sacrificed under any circumstances. There is much that is fictitious about this conception even when it is applied to the ordinary relations of society. We have an illustration of this truth in the very case before us. Ten workmen were killed in the process of removing the rocks from the opening to the cave. Did not the engineers and government officials who directed the rescue effort know that the operations they were undertaking were dangerous and involved a serious risk to the lives of the workmen executing them? If it was proper that these ten lives should be sacrificed to save the lives of five imprisoned explorers, why then are we told it was wrong for these explorers to carry out an arrangement which would save four lives at the cost of one?

Every highway, every tunnel, every building we project involves a risk to human life. Taking these projects in the aggregate, we can calculate with some precision how many deaths the construction of them will require; statisticians can tell you the average cost in human lives of a thousand miles of a four-lane concrete highway. Yet we deliberately and knowingly incur and pay this cost on the assumption that the values obtained for those who survive outweigh the loss. If these things can be said of a society functioning above ground in a normal and ordinary manner, what shall we say of the supposed absolute value of a human life in the desperate situation in which these defendants and their companion Whetmore found themselves?

This concludes the exposition of the first ground of my decision. My second ground proceeds by rejecting hypothetically all the premises on which I have so far proceeded. I concede for purposes of argument that I am wrong in saying that the situation of these men removed them from the effect of our positive law, and I assume that the Consolidated Statutes have the power to penetrate five hundred feet of rock and to impose themselves upon these starving men huddled in their underground prison.

Now it is, of course, perfectly clear that these men did an act that violates the literal wording of the statute which declares that he who "shall willfully take the life of another" is a murderer. But one of the most ancient bits of legal wisdom is the saying that a man may break the letter of the law without breaking the law itself. Every proposition of positive law, whether contained in a statute or a judicial precedent, is to be interpreted reasonably, in the light of its evident purpose. This is a truth so elementary that it is hardly necessary to expatiate on it. Illustrations of its application are numberless and are to be found in every branch of the law. In *Commonwealth v. Staymore* the defendant was convicted under a statute making it a crime to leave one's car parked in certain areas for a period longer than two hours. The defendant had attempted to remove his car, but was prevented from doing so because the streets were obstructed by a political demonstration in which he took no part and which he had no reason to anticipate. His conviction was set aside by this Court, although his case fell squarely within the wording of the statute. Again, in *Fehler v. Neegas* there was before this Court for construction a statute in which the word "not" had plainly been transposed from its intended position in the final and most crucial section of the act. This transposition was contained in all the successive drafts of the act, where it was apparently overlooked by the draftsmen and sponsors of the legislation. No one was able to prove how the error came about, yet it was apparent that, taking account of the contents of the statute as a whole, an error had been made, since a literal reading of the final clause rendered it inconsistent with everything that had gone before and with the object of the enactment as stated in its preamble. This Court refused to accept a literal interpretation of the statute, and in effect rectified its language by reading the word "not" into the place where it was evidently intended to go.

The statute before us for interpretation has never been applied literally. Centuries ago it was established that a killing in self-defense is excused. There is nothing in the wording of the statute that suggests this exception. Various attempts have been made to reconcile the legal treatment of self-defense with the words of the statute, but in my opinion these are all merely ingenious sophistries. The truth is that the exception in favor of self-defense cannot be reconciled with the *words* of the statute, but only with its *purpose*.

The true reconciliation of the excuse of self-defense with the statute making it a crime to kill another is to be found in the following line of reasoning. One of the principal objects underlying any criminal legislation is that of deterring men from crime. Now it is apparent that if it were declared to be the law that a killing in self-defense is murder such a rule could not operate in a deterrent manner. A man whose life is threatened will repel his aggressor, whatever the law may say. Looking therefore to the broad purposes of criminal legislation, we may safely declare that this statute was not intended to apply to cases of self-defense.

When the rationale of the excuse of self-defense is thus explained, it becomes apparent that precisely the same reasoning is applicable to the case at bar. If in the future any group of men ever find themselves in the tragic predicament of these defendants, we may be sure that their decision whether to live or die will not be controlled by the contents of our criminal code. Accordingly, if we read this statute intelligently it is apparent that it does not apply to this case. The withdrawal of this situation from the effect of the statute is justified by precisely the same considerations that were applied by our predecessors in office centuries ago to the case of self-defense.

There are those who raise the cry of judicial usurpation whenever a court, after analyzing the purpose of a statute, gives to its words a meaning that is not at once apparent to the casual reader who has not studied the statute closely or examined the objectives it seeks to attain. Let me say emphatically that I accept without reservation the proposition that this Court is bound by the statutes of our Commonwealth and that it exercises its powers in subservience to the duly expressed will of the Chamber of Representatives. The line of reasoning I have applied above raises no question of fidelity to enacted law, though it may possibly raise a question of the distinction between intelligent and unintelligent fidelity. No superior wants a servant who lacks the capacity to read between the lines. The stupidest housemaid knows that when she is told "to peel the soup and skim the potatoes" her mistress does not mean what she says. She also knows that when her master tells her to "drop everything and come running" he has overlooked the possibility that she is at the moment in the act of rescuing the baby from the rain barrel. Surely we

have a right to expect the same modicum of intelligence from the judiciary. The correction of obvious legislative errors or oversights is not to supplant the legislative will, but to make that will effective.

I therefore conclude that on any aspect under which this case may be viewed these defendants are innocent of the crime of murdering Roger Whetmore, and that the conviction should be set aside.

TATTING,, J. . . . As I analyze the opinion just rendered by my brother Foster, I find that it is shot through with contradictions and fallacies. Let us begin with his first proposition: these men were not subject to our law because they were not in a "state of civil society" but in a "state of nature." I am not clear why this is so, whether it is because of the thickness of the rock that imprisoned them, or because they were hungry, or because they had set up a "new charter of government" by which the usual rules of law were to be supplanted by a throw of the dice. Other difficulties intrude themselves. If these men passed from the jurisdiction of our law to that of "the law of nature," at what moment did this occur? Was it when the entrance to the cave was blocked, or when the threat of starvation reached a certain undefined degree of intensity, or when the agreement for the throwing of the dice was made? These uncertainties in the doctrine proposed by my brother are capable of producing real difficulties. Suppose, for example, one of these men had had his twenty-first birthday while he was imprisoned within the mountain. On what date would we have to consider that he had attained his majority—when he reached the age of twenty-one, at which time he was, by hypothesis, removed from the effects of our law, or only when he was released from the cave and became again subject to what my brother calls our "positive law"? These difficulties may seem fanciful, yet they only serve to reveal the fanciful nature of the doctrine that is capable of giving rise to them.

But it is not necessary to explore these niceties further to demonstrate the absurdity of my brother's position. Mr. Justice Foster and I are the appointed judges of a court of the Commonwealth of Newgarth, sworn and empowered to administer the laws of that Commonwealth. By what authority do we resolve ourselves into a Court of Nature? If these men were indeed under the law of nature, whence comes our authority to expound and apply that law? Certainly *we* are not in a state of nature. . . .

The principles my brother expounds contain other implications that cannot be tolerated. He argues that when the defendants set upon Whetmore and killed him (we know not how, perhaps by pounding him with stones) they were only exercising the rights conferred upon them by their bargain. Suppose, however, that Whetmore had had concealed upon his person a revolver, and that when he saw the defendants about to slaughter him he had shot them to death in order to save his own life. My brother's reasoning applied to these facts would make Whetmore out to be a murderer, since the excuse of self-defense would have to be denied to him. If his assailants were acting rightfully in seeking to bring about his death, then of course he could no more plead the excuse that he was defending his own life than could a condemned prisoner who struck down the executioner lawfully attempting to place the noose about his neck. . . .

I come now to the second part of my brother's opinion, in which he seeks to show that the defendants did not violate the provisions of N. C. S. A. (N. S.) § 12-A. Here the way, instead of being clear, becomes for me misty and ambiguous, though my brother seems unaware of the difficulties that inhere in his demonstrations.

The gist of my brother's argument may be stated in the following terms: No statute, whatever its language, should be applied in a way that contradicts its purpose. One of the purposes of any criminal statute is to deter. The application of the statute making it a crime to kill another to the peculiar facts of this case would contradict this purpose, for it is impossible to believe that the contents of the criminal code could operate in a deterrent manner on men faced with the alternative of life or death. The reasoning by which this exception is read into the statute is, my brother observes, the same as that which is applied in order to provide the excuse of self-defense. . . .

Now let me outline briefly, however, the perplexities that assail me when I examine my brother's demonstration more closely. It is true

that a statute should be applied in the light of its purpose, and that *one* of the purposes of criminal legislation is recognized to be deterrence. The difficulty is that other purposes are also ascribed to the law of crimes. It has been said that one of its objects is to provide an orderly outlet for the instinctive human demand for retribution. *Commonwealth v. Scape.* It has also been said that its object is the rehabilitation of the wrongdoer. *Commonwealth v. Makeover.* Other theories have been propounded. Assuming that we must interpet a statute in the light of its purpose, what are we to do when it has many purposes or when its purposes are disputed?

A similar difficulty is presented by the fact that although there is authority for my brother's interpretation of the excuse of self-defense, there is other authority which assigns to that excuse a different rationale. Indeed, until I happened on *Commonwealth v. Parry* I had never heard of the explanation given by my brother. The taught doctrine of our law schools, memorized by generations of law students, runs in the following terms: The statute concerning murder requires a "willful" act. The man who acts to repel an aggressive threat to his own life does not act "willfully," but in response to an impulse deeply ingrained in human nature. I suspect that there is hardly a lawyer in this Commonwealth who is not familiar with this line of reasoning, especially since the point is a great favorite of the bar examiners.

Now the familiar explanation for the excuse of self-defense just expounded obviously cannot be applied by analogy to the facts of this case. These men acted not only "willfully" but with great deliberation and after hours of discussing what they should do. Again we encounter a forked path, with one line of reasoning leading us in one direction and another in a direction that is exactly the opposite. . . .

I recognize the relevance of the precedents cited by my brother concerning the displaced "not" and the defendant who parked overtime. But what are we to do with one of the landmarks of our jurisprudence, which again my brother passes over in silence? This is *Commonwealth v. Valjean.* Though the case is somewhat obscurely reported, it appears that the defendant was indicted for the larceny of a loaf of bread, and offered as a defense that he was in a condition approaching starvation. The court refused to accept this defense. If hunger cannot justify the theft of wholesome and natural food, how can it justify the killing and eating of a man? Again, if we look at the thing in terms of deterrence, is it likely that a man will starve to death to avoid a jail sentence for the theft of a loaf of bread? . . . .

I have given this case the best thought of which I am capable. I have scarcely slept since it was argued before us. When I feel myself inclined to accept the view of my brother Foster, I am repelled by a feeling that his arguments are intellectually unsound and approach mere rationalization. On the other hand, when I incline toward upholding the conviction, I am struck by the absurdity of directing that these men be put to death when their lives have been saved at the cost of the lives of ten heroic workmen. It is to me a matter of regret that the Prosecutor saw fit to ask for an indictment for murder. If we had a provision in our statutes making it a crime to eat human flesh, that would have been a more appropriate charge. If no other charge suited to the facts of this case could be brought against the defendants, it would have been wiser, I think, not to have indicted them at all. Unfortunately, however, the men have been indicted and tried, and we have therefore been drawn into this unfortunate affair.

Since I have been wholly unable to resolve the doubts that beset me about the law of this case, I am with regret announcing a step that is, I believe, unprecedented in the history of this tribunal. I declare my withdrawal from the decision of this case.

KEEN, J. I should like to begin by setting to one side two questions which are not before this Court.

The first of these is whether executive clemency should be extended to these defendants if the conviction is affirmed. Under our system of government, that is a question for the Chief Executive, not for us. I therefore disapprove of that passage in the opinion of the Chief Justice in which he in effect gives instructions to the Chief Executive as to what he should do in this case and suggests that some impropriety will attach if these instructions are not heeded. This is a confusion of governmental functions—a confusion of which the judiciary should be the last to be guilty. I wish to state that if I were the Chief Executive I would go farther in the direction of clemency than the pleas addressed to him propose. I would pardon these men altogether, since I believe that they have already suffered enough to pay for any offense they may have committed. I want it to be understood that this remark is made in my capacity as a private citizen who by the accident of his office happens to have acquired an intimate acquaintance with the facts of this case. In the discharge of my duties as judge, it is neither my function to address directions to the Chief Executive, nor to take into account what he may or may not do, in reaching my own decision, which must be controlled entirely by the law of this Commonwealth.

The second question that I wish to put to one side is that of deciding whether what these men did was "right" or "wrong," "wicked" or "good." That is also a question that is irrelevant to the discharge of my office as a judge sworn to apply, not my conceptions of morality, but the law of the land. . . .

The sole question before us for decision is whether these defendants did, within the meaning of N. C. S. A. (N. S.) § 12-A, willfully take the life of Roger Whetmore. The exact language of the statute is as follows: "Whoever shall willfully take the life of another shall be punished by death." Now I should suppose that any candid observer, content to extract from these words their natural meaning, would concede at once that these defendants did "willfully take the life" of Roger Whetmore.

Whence arise all the difficulties of the case, then, and the necessity for so many pages of discussion about what ought to be so obvious? The difficulties, in whatever tortured form they may present themselves, all trace back to a single source, and that is a failure to distinguish the legal from the moral aspects of this case. To put it bluntly, my brothers do not like the fact that the written law requires the conviction of these defendants. Neither do I, but unlike my brothers I respect the obligations of an office that requires me to put my personal predilections out of my mind when I come to interpret and apply the law of this Commonwealth. . . .

My brother [Foster] thinks he knows exactly what was sought when men made murder a crime, and that was something he calls "deterrence." My brother Tatting has already shown how much is passed over in that interpretation. But I think the trouble goes deeper. I doubt very much whether our statute making murder a crime really has a "purpose" in any ordinary sense of the term. Primarily, such a statute reflects a deeply-felt human conviction that murder is wrong and that something should be done to the man who commits it. . . .

The essential shabbiness of my brother Foster's attempt to cloak his remaking of the written law with an air of legitimacy comes tragically to the surface in my brother Tatting's opinion. In that opinion Justice Tatting struggles manfully to combine his colleague's loose moralisms with his own sense of fidelity to the written law. The issue of this struggle could only be that which occurred, a complete default in the discharge of the judicial function. You simply cannot apply a statute as it is written and remake it to meet your own wishes at the same time. . . .

I conclude that the conviction should be affirmed.

HANDY, J. I have listened with amazement to the tortured ratiocinations to which this simple case has given rise. I never cease to wonder at my colleagues' ability to throw an obscuring curtain of legalisms about every issue presented to them for decision. We have heard this afternoon learned disquisitions on the distinction between positive law and the law of nature, the language of the statute and the purpose of the statute, judicial functions and executive functions, judicial legislation and legislative legislation. . . .

What have all these things to do with the case? The problem before us is what we, as officers of the government, ought to do with these defendants. That is a question of practical wisdom, to be exercised in a context, not of abstract theory, but of human realities. When the case is approached in this light, it becomes, I think, one of the easiest to decide that has ever been argued before this Court.

Before stating my own conclusions about the merits of the case, I should like to discuss briefly some of the more fundamental issues involved— issues on which my colleagues and I have been divided ever since I have been on the bench.

I have never been able to make my brothers see that government is a human affair, and that men are ruled, not by words on paper or by abstract theories, but by other men. They are ruled well when their rulers understand the feeling and conceptions of the masses. They are ruled badly when that understanding is lacking. . . .

Now I realize that wherever you have rules and abstract principles lawyers are going to be able to make distinctions. To some extent the sort of thing I have been describing is a necessary evil attaching to any formal regulation of human affairs. But I think that the area which really stands in need of such regulation is greatly overestimated. There are, of course, a few fundamental rules of the game that must be accepted if the game is to go on at all. I would include among these the rules relating to the conduct of elections, the appointment of public officials, and the term during which an office is held. Here some restraint on discretion and dispensation, some adherence to form, some scruple for what does and what does not fall within the rule, is, I concede, essential. . . .

But outside of these fields I believe that all government officials, including judges, will do their jobs best if they treat forms and abstract concepts as instruments. We should take as our model, I think, the good administrator, who accommodates procedures and principles to the case at hand, selecting from among the available forms those most suited to reach the proper result. . . .

This case has aroused an enormous public interest, both here and abroad. Almost every newspaper and magazine has carried articles about it; columnists have shared with their readers confidential information as to the next governmental move; hundreds of letters-to-the-editor have been printed. One of the great newspaper chains made a poll of public opinion on the question, "What do you think the Supreme Court should do with the Speluncean explorers?" About ninety per cent expressed a belief that the defendants should be pardoned or let off with a kind of token punishment. It is perfectly clear, then, how the public feels about the case. We could have known this without the poll, of course, on the basis of common sense, or even by observing that on this Court there are apparently four-and-a-half men, or ninety per cent, who share the common opinion.

This makes it obvious, not only what we should do, but what we must do if we are to preserve between ourselves and public opinion a reasonable and decent accord. . . .

In the normal course of events the case now before us would have gone on all of its issues directly to the jury. Had this occurred we can be confident that there would have been an acquittal or at least a division that would have prevented a conviction. If the jury had been instructed that the men's hunger and their agreement were no defense to the charge of murder, their verdict would in all likelihood have ignored this instruction and would have involved a good deal more twisting of the letter of the law than any that is likely to tempt us. Of course the only reason that didn't occur in this case was the fortuitous circumstance that the foreman of the jury happened to be a lawyer. His learning enabled him to devise a form of words that would allow the jury to dodge its usual responsibilities. . . .

I come now to the most crucial fact in this case, a fact known to all of us on this Court, though one that my brothers have seen fit to keep under the cover of their judicial robes. This is the frightening likelihood that if the issue is left to him, the Chief Executive will refuse to pardon these men or commute their sentence. As we all know, our Chief Executive is a man now well advanced in years, of very stiff notions. Public clamor usually operates on him with the reverse of the effect intended. As I have told my brothers, it happens that my wife's niece is an intimate friend of his secretary. I have learned in this indirect, but, I think, wholly reliable way, that he is firmly determined not to commute the sentence if these men are found to have violated the law.

No one regrets more than I the necessity for relying in so important a matter on information that could be characterized as gossip. If I had my way this would not happen, for I would adopt the sensible course of sitting down with the Executive, going over the case with him, finding out what his views are, and perhaps working out with him a common program for handling the situation. But of course my brothers would never hear of such a thing. . . .

I conclude that the defendants are innocent of the crime charged, and that the conviction and sentence should be set aside.

TATTING, J. I have been asked by the Chief Justice whether, after listening to the two opinions just rendered, I desire to re-examine the position previously taken by me. I wish to state that after hearing these opinions I am greatly strengthened in my conviction that I ought not to participate in the decision of this case.

The Supreme Court being evenly divided, the conviction and sentence of the Court of General Instances is *affirmed*. It is ordered that the execution of the sentence shall occur at 6 A.M., Friday, April 2, 4300, at which time the Public Executioner is directed to proceed with all convenient dispatch to hang each of the defendants by the neck until he is dead

NOTE

1. "When the reason for the law ceases to exist then the law itself ceases to exist."

46. SUGGESTIONS AS TO CAPITAL PUNISHMENT AND THE CASE OF WILLIAM PALMER

James Fitzjames Stephen

SUGGESTIONS AS TO CAPITAL PUNISHMENT

. . . Such is the history of the punishment of death as inflicted by the law of England. The subject is so trite that I feel reluctant to discuss it, but I am also reluctant to pass it over without shortly stating my own opinion upon it. My opinion is that we have gone too far in laying it aside, and that it ought to be inflicted in many cases not at present capital. I think, for instance, that political offences should in some cases be punished with death. People should be made to understand that to attack the existing state of society is equivalent to risking their own lives.

In cases which outrage the moral feelings of the community to a great degree, the feeling of indignation and desire for revenge which is excited in the minds of decent people is, I think, deserving of legitimate satisfaction. If a man commits a brutal murder, or if he does his best to do so and fails only by accident, or if he ravishes his own daughter (I have known several such cases), or if several men acting together ravish any woman, using cruel violence to effect their object, I think they should be destroyed, partly in order to gratify the indignation which such crimes produce, and which it is desirable that they should produce, and partly in order to make the world wholesomer than it would otherwise be by ridding it of people as much misplaced in civilized society as wolves or tigers would

be in a populous country. What else can be done with such people? If William Palmer had not been hanged in 1856, he would probably have been alive at this day, and likely to live for many years to come. What is the use of keeping such a wretch alive at the public expense for, say, half a century?

If by a long series of frauds artfully contrived a man has shown that he is determined to live by deceiving and impoverishing others, or if by habitually receiving stolen goods he has kept a school of vice and dishonesty, I think he should die.

These views, it is said, are opposed to the doctrine that human life is sacred. I have never been able to understand distinctly what that doctrine means, or how its truth is alleged to be proved. If it means that life ought to have serious aims and to be pervaded by a sense of duty, I think the doctrine is true, but I do not see its relation to the proposition that no one ought ever to be put to death. It rather suggests the contrary conclusion as to persons who refuse to act upon it. If it means only that no one ought ever to be killed, I do not know on what grounds it can be supported. Whether life is sacred or not, I think there are many cases in which a man should be ready to inflict, or, if necessary, to suffer death without shrinking.

As, however, these views are at present unpopular and peculiar, and in the present state of public feeling on the subject it is useless to discuss this matter at length, no good purpose is served by making specific proposals which no one would entertain; but I may remark that I would punish with death offences against property only upon great deliberation, and when it was made to appear by a public formal inquiry held after a conviction for an isolated offence that the criminal really was an ha-

James Fitzjames Stephen, "Suggestions as to Capital Punishment" and "The Case of William Palmer," from *A History of the Criminal Law of England* (New York: Burt Franklin), Vol. I, pp. 478–80, and Vol. III, p. 389 and pp. 424–25. Originally published in London, 1883.

bitual, hardened, practically irreclaimable offender. I would on no account make the punishment so frequent as to lessen its effect, nor would I leave any doubt as to the reason why it was inflicted. I suspect that a small number of executions of professional receivers of stolen goods, habitual cheats, and ingenious forgers, after a full exposure of their career and its extent and consequences, would do more to check crime than twenty times as many sentences of penal servitude. If society could make up its mind to the destruction of really bad offenders, they might, in a very few years, be made as rare as wolves, and that probably at the expense of a smaller sacrifice of life than is caused by many a single shipwreck or colliery explosion; but, for this purpose, a change of public sentiment would be necessary, of which there are at present no signs. . . .

THE CASE OF WILLIAM PALMER

On the 14th of May, 1856, William Palmer was tried at the Old Bailey for the murder of John Parsons Cook at Rugeley, in Staffordshire. The trial lasted for twelve days, and ended on the 27th May, when the prisoner was convicted, and received sentence of death, on which he was afterwards executed at Stafford.

Palmer was a general medical practitioner at Rugeley, much engaged in sporting transactions. Cook, his intimate friend, also a sporting man, after attending Shrewsbury races with Palmer on the 13th November, 1855, returned in his company to Rugeley, and died at the Talbot Arms Hotel, at that place, soon after midnight, on the 21st November, 1855, under circumstances which raised a suspicion that he had been poisoned by Palmer. The case against Palmer was, that he had a strong motive to murder his friend, and that his conduct before, at the time of, and after his death, coupled with the circumstances of the death itself, left no reasonable doubt that he did murder him, by poisoning him with antimony and strychnine. . . .

[*Editor's note.* In his desperate efforts to settle his gambling debts, Palmer apparently committed a large number of crimes, including passing bad checks, forgery, fraud, the murder of his wife and brother to collect insurance money, and the murder of various other persons when that seemed necessary to "cover up" his other crimes.]

I am tempted to make one other observation on Palmer's case. His career supplied one of the proofs of a fact which many kind-hearted people seem to doubt, namely, the fact that such a thing as atrocious wickedness is consistent with good education, perfect sanity, and everything, in a word, which deprives men of all excuse for crime. Palmer was respectably brought up; apart from his extravagance and vice, he might have lived comfortably enough. He was a model of physical health and strength, and was courageous, determined, and energetic. No one ever suggested that there was even a disposition towards madness in him; yet he was as cruel, as treacherous, as greedy of money and pleasure, as brutally hard-hearted and sensual a wretch as it is possible even to imagine. If he had been the lowest and most ignorant ruffian that ever sprang from a long line of criminal ancestors, he could not have been worse than he was. He was by no means unlike Rush, Thurtell, and many other persons whom I have known. The fact that the world contains an appreciable number of wretches, who ought to be exterminated without mercy when an opportunity occurs, is not quite so generally understood as it ought to be, and many common ways of thinking and feeling virtually deny it.

47. HOMICIDAL MANIACS, MORAL ILLNESS, AND THE CASE OF ALBERT FISH

Curtis Bok

... The argument is often made that reform is sentimental. This is the theme of the most blood-thirsty among us who imagine that prisoners are coddled because they get steak once a month and movies twice a week and that this is wrong, prison and even hanging being too good for the likes of them.

As any level-headed philosopher will agree, ha-tred and malice and vengeance are the worst forms of sentimentality. It is Shaw's argument that we are grossly sentimental about the people we choose to murder legally. It cannot be the insane: it must be the sane. What perversion of common sense is this? So long as we permit the death penalty at all, let us kill off the right people, the homicidal maniacs and the insane killers. We need not do it vengefully or in bad blood, but rather with relief, once they have been determined to be fit candidates for the gas chamber or the electric chair. Then let us quietly, dispassionately, painlessly, even apologetically re-turn them to Mother Earth. It is the sane killers that should give us pause. Most of them will never take life again, for a man does not realize what a fearful thing it is to murder until he has done it. The average murderer is far less a continuing social menace than the professional thief. ...

Penology is beginning to regard criminals as ill men. The more horrible the crime, the greater may be the criminal's deviation from mankind's mod-erate average madness and the more help he should have, provided we have it to give. A case in point is that of John Gilbert Graham, who tried to collect his mother's insurance by stowing a bomb into the airplane in which she and forty-three other people were traveling. He was found legally sane under the M'Naghten Rule and gassed, but it is hard to believe that anyone who would do such a thing was not emotionally twisted almost beyond repair. Probably we have nothing for him in our social pharmacopoeia and he was the best type to kill so long as we are going to kill anybody.

When we talk of moral illness as a moving cause of crime, we must stop and think a bit. Remember Shaw's parallel between crime and tuberculosis. "Why a man who is punished," he wrote, "for having an inefficient conscience should be privi-leged to have an inefficient lung is a debatable question. If one is sent to prison and the other to hospital, why make the prison so different from the hospital?". ...

The following case shows the failure of the law, the failure of psychiatry, and the failure of humanity.

In the case of Albert Fish, whose conviction and sentence of execution were affirmed, without opin-ion, by the New York Court of Appeals in 1935. It appears in the literature.[1]

Fish was a mild-mannered man approaching sixty, and father of six children. In 1928 he kid-napped, choked to death, and for nine days ate parts of Grace Budd, a girl of ten. While choking her he put his knee on her chest "to get her out of her misery." He was a religious fanatic, and in his confessions and statements to the doctor he made a point of religious atonement and self-castigation. There was no known form of perversion that he had not indulged in. He had eaten his own ex-crement. He had put cotton, saturated with alco-hol, up his rectum and had set fire to it. X-rays showed twenty-nine needles inserted in his body between the scrotum and the anus. "If only pain were not so painful!" he exclaimed, when he spoke of his attempts to insert needles into the scrotum and beneath his nails.

It was finally discovered, too late, that Fish had molested at least one hundred children and that opportunity for cannibalism had presented itself in the five to fifteen child murders for which, after his arrest, it was estimated he was responsible.

He was no stranger to the law. He had been arrested eight times: for larceny, for bad checks, for sending obscene letters through the mails, for parole violations. Twice he was sent to psychiatric hospitals for observation, the first time over two years after he had killed and eaten Grace Budd. He was also picked up many times for impairing the morals of minors, but nothing much happened to him. He was generally let go because he was so kindly and co-operative and looked so innocent, the kind of man to whom anyone would entrust his child.

Four psychiatrists testified at his trial that he was sane, including the chief of the two public psychiatric hospitals where he had been observed and pronounced harmless *after* eating Grace. Some astonishing things were said. "Committing a crime has nothing to do with mental disease," was an example. Another was: "I know of individuals prominent in society: one ate human feces as a side dish with salad. I had a patient, a very prominent official, who did it."

The press shrilled loudly for revenge, and the jury obliged by giving Fish the death penalty. Interviewed later, a majority of the jury said that, while they thought him legally insane, they felt that he should die anyhow.

Fish went to his death coolly and even helped to strap on the leg electrodes.

He belongs in the class who should be killed if we are going to kill anybody, but, even so, the reasons are all twisted. He belongs with John Gilbert Graham, the airplane murderer, and with the low-grade mental defective who, a few years ago, escaped from the asylum for the criminally insane at Dartmoor, England, and murdered a child: he was found sane and hanged. Our real reason for killing such people is that we fear and hate them.

Fish was obviously incurable, unreformable, and unpunishable. If asked whether I would spare the life of such a monster, I should of course say that I would. The man was obviously mad and it was unfair to kill him. The failure to recognize him as mad is our fault, not his, and it is our responsibility to find a cure for him or to confine him and prevent his repeated aggressions. Killing him is to avoid the problem, not to solve it. . . .

NOTE

1. Dr. Frederic Wertham: *The Show of Violence* (New York: Doubleday and Company, 1949); Giles Playfair and Derrick Sington: *The Offenders: The Case Against Legal Vengeance* (New York: Simon and Schuster; 1957).

48. REHABILITATION ON DEATH ROW: THE CASE OF PAUL CRUMP

Ronald Bailey

When Warden Jack Johnson met him, Paul Crump was, Johnson says, "choked up with hatred. He was animalistic and belligerent. Self-preservation was the only law he knew."

From Ronald Bailey, "Facing Death, A New Life Perhaps Too Late," *Life,* vol. 53 (July 27, 1962), pp. 28–29. Copyright © 1962 Time, Inc. Reprinted with permission.

The men clashed, head on, in a series of showdowns. The first came late in 1955, only two months after Johnson assumed command of the scandal-ridden, riot-scarred prison. Crump and the twelve other condemned men on Death Row decided to test the new warden. They smashed lights, ripped apart wooden benches, set fire to blankets and mattresses. Johnson, a six-foot one-inch, 259-pound mountain of a man, strode angrily down to Death Row and ordered the men out of their cells. When they refused, Johnson tossed six shells of tear gas into the cellblock. As the men staggered out, they found—instead of the usual goon squad armed with clubs—only the warden and two doctors.

This was the first battle in what became known as the nineteen-day "cold war" between Johnson and the inmates of Death Row. The warden locked them up in widely separated cells and stripped them of their privileges. They were allowed no visitors, no reading material and no mail. On the fourteenth day they sent for the warden. Paul Crump was their spokesman.

"Look," he said, "you've won. Get the goon squad down here, beat us up and get this thing over with and give us our privileges back."

"There aren't any goon squads here any more," the warden told him. "All I want is your word that you will make no more trouble in this jail."

The men refused. Five days later Crump sent for the warden again. This time he pledged his word and that of the other condemned men. The warden's will, enforced without brutality, had beaten them.

Paul Crump's surrender marked the beginning of a rehabilitation that has lasted for seven years. It also marked the beginning of a deep friendship between the convicted murderer and his warden.

Before Johnson's arrival the jail had been an abomination. One of the country's largest penal institutions, it was overcrowded and understaffed, a grotesque relic of outmoded days. The guards wore guns and carried arsenals of brass knuckles, blackjacks and miniature baseball bats.

In Death Row, condemned men were locked up for twenty-two hours a day in four-by-eight-foot cells. For two hours daily they exercised, tightly handcuffed and dragging leg irons, in the cellblock corridor. "Maximum security" was stamped across the chests of their khaki uniforms like a brand.

The slum-bred Crump described coming to jail as being "transplanted from one jungle to another. If I hadn't been an animal, I wouldn't have survived."

When he took on the job as warden, Johnson went from tier to tier hearing prisoners' complaints. He saw that archaic treatment bred many of the hatreds of his 2,000 caged inmates and barred any chance for rehabilitation. The tough ex-cop, who had had no prison experience before, found that "a simple word of love was what was lacking in this jail."

Johnson reduced the emphasis on punishment, disarmed the guards, ended the Death Row lockup and tried a few simple words of love. He had success with some of the short-term prisoners, but a more convincing proof of his new philosophy was needed. He had to work with extreme cases, those convicted of murder and awaiting death. Paul Crump and his condemned comrades became the subjects of Warden Johnson's brave experiment.

After the cold war truce, Johnson took personal charge of Death Row. He made daily visits there. He installed two telephones outside the tier and told the inmates: "Anytime you guys want to talk to me, call me up." He started bringing them in groups of three and four for discussions with the new prison sociologist and psychologist. The men aired their gripes—lousy food, not enough books to read, brutal guards—and the warden listened. But for a while Crump did not join the sessions in the warden's office. When Johnson wanted to see Crump, he had to go to his cell.

"Finally, I began to see that the Old Man was serious about this philosophy," recalls Crump. "The things he wanted done started happening. There was a guard who beat up an inmate with a baseball bat. The next day I was sitting in the office next to the warden's and I heard him tell a bunch of guards: 'If I hear of this happening again, I'll break your goddamned leg.'"

A new climate pervaded the jail, a climate in which Crump found his chance to change and grow. He sought out the prison chaplains. Although a convert to Catholicism, Crump was befriended by rabbi, Protestant minister and priest alike. Crump told Father James Jones, the Episcopal chaplain, that he wanted to write, and Father Jones gave him $10 for writing materials.

Crump immediately started work on his autobiographical novel, *Burn, Killer, Burn.* But in his writing Crump soon felt the bounds imposed by his ninth-grade education. Hans Mattick, a gifted sociologist who was then assistant warden, offered to give Crump an informal course in analytic reading. Three times Mattick had Crump read *Moby Dick,* each time asking him to write a ten- to fifteen-page essay on the different facets of the book. In his second essay Crump explained the message of the book: "Though evil might seem to triumph, the spirit of man will rise again." His third essay, Mattick says, would have done credit to an English major in college.

In Crump's cell the cheap paperback novels and the few law books, which he had purchased for his own defense by giving up cigarets for six months, gave way to Thomas Wolfe's *Look Homeward, Angel,* Will Durant's *The Story of Philosophy* and books on sociology. Crump read the English metaphysical poets and found a poignant relevance for himself in John Donne's famous line: "No man is an *Iland.* . . ."

"I read and read and read," says Crump, "and some old distortions were swept away. I had thought that anything good that happened to me was all gravy, just accident. I started seeing that things don't happen by accident, but because of the good will of people and their belief in the basic goodness of man."

A fellow inmate, Ed Balchowsky, plucked at the strings of Crump's new-found curiosity about life and the world. Balchowsky, in jail on a narcotics rap, was also a rebel against society—a bohemian, an itinerant artist, writer and composer. He introduced Crump to the poetry of Max Bodenheim and sang songs for him in Russian, Spanish and Italian. Night after night the two men worked late editing the crude, handwritten manuscripts of Crump's book.

Crump needed a typewriter, so Balchowsky wrote a letter to the prison newspaper, *The Grapevine,* asking other inmates not to complain if Crump got one. More than 1,000 letters supporting Crump flooded the paper, and Warden Johnson got Crump a typewriter. On it Crump wrote short stories, articles and poems, which were published in small magazines. He started a second novel—his first will be published this fall—and developed a voluminous correspondence with interested and sympathetic people around the world.

He began to take an interest in the problems of his fellow prisoners. The stories they told him were familiar: slums, broken homes, high school dropouts. By comparing their experiences with his own, Crump understood himself better. "It helped me to see the real me," he says. "The start of rehabilitation was when I saw the real me." Through the irony of living under prolonged death sentence, the old Paul Crump was dying, just as surely as if he had been burned in the electric chair.

Looking back on those days, the warden recalls that Crump was "beginning to realize that he had a conscience, realizing that life was not just taking—that there was such a thing as giving. He actually became a man."

The change was best mirrored in Crump's relationship with the warden. Crump became a frequent visitor to Johnson's office. Until the 9 P.M. lock-up time they would discuss "everything from sex to psychology." For Crump, whose own father had deserted his family when Paul was six, "This was the first time I could talk to someone in a language you would use in talking to your father. He told me that life is not just Paul Crump. He said that I'm just as responsible for the people around me as they are responsible for me."

In February 1958, Johnson abolished Death Row. He distributed the condemned men throughout the jail and gave them each responsibilities. Six, including Crump, were put in charge of separate tiers. Crump's job was "barn boss" of the convalescent tier for the new jail hospital.

As barn boss, Crump became, in the words of a guard, "mother, father, priest and social worker" for some fifty prisoners. To his tier came epileptics, diabetics, heart patients, old men suffering from the DTs, dope addicts on withdrawal. Johnson also sent Crump problem prisoners and inmates who needed special protection from other prisoners and from themselves—fourteen-year-old kids, former policemen, potential suicides. Crump ministered to his charges at all hours of the night and told the youngsters: "Get smart. Stay out of trouble when you get out of here." His tier became the best in the jail.

Shortly after Death Row was abolished came the decisive point in Paul Crump's rehabilitation. It was a particularly bad time for him. He was between stays of execution and fighting desperately to stave off the electric chair. He fired his lawyer and laboriously wrote his own petition for a writ of habeas corpus. The petition—unprecedented in Illinois because it went directly to the federal court—was turned down.[1] But then Crump received a letter which informed him that the warden had offered to talk to the judge on his behalf.

"The letter knocked the props out from under me," he remembers. "It cracked me up. Until then I was still a little suspicious of the Old Man because he was an ex-cop and because he was white."

Crump, clutching the letter in his hand, fell down on his knees in the warden's office and wept for nearly an hour. "He whimpered like a baby," the warden remembers. "I think it was the first time in his life Paul ever completely let himself go. And for the first time, he really believed in another person."

"I had a father," Crump says. "A white father."

Thereafter the tales of Paul Crump's deeds in the convalescent tier grew legendary. He got in the shower with senile men who were unable to bathe themselves. He set aside a corner of the cellblock so that a seventy-year-old, Orthodox Jew wearing his skull cap and prayer shawl could worship in privacy. He broke up fights and on several occasions prevented guards from getting hurt. A cousin of one of the guards was born with a heart defect and needed blood. The guard spoke to Crump. Within twenty minutes Crump had signatures of fifty men who promised to donate blood.

One poignant story illustrates how Crump's racial animosity changed to tolerance. An epileptic, in jail for bombing Negro homes, was put in his tier. One day the man had a seizure and Crump grappled with him to keep him from hurting himself. When the man came to, he screamed: "Get away from me, you black nigger!" Crump released his hold and went back to his cell. Ten minutes later the man came to Crump, sat down and cried. "I'm

sorry," he said finally. "As long as I live I'll never hurt another person because of his race."

During one late bull session in the warden's office, Johnson was accidently locked in the radio room next door. Crump was alone, and Johnson could not reach him. The possibility that Crump might escape flickered across the minds of both men. "I let him knock three times," says Crump, "then I opened the door." He told the warden: "If you opened the gates now, I wouldn't run. You kept faith with me, and I'm going to keep faith with you."

If Paul Crump has undergone a great change in the past seven years, so has Jack Johnson. As Crump responded like a son, Johnson grew like a father. When he came to the jail, the warden had no strong feelings about capital punishment. Now he vigorously opposes it.

"Paul Crump is completely rehabilitated," he says. "Should society demand Paul's life at this point, it would be capital vengeance, not punishment. If it were humanly possible, I would put Paul back on the street tomorrow. I have no fear of any antisocial behavior on his part. I would stake my life on it. And I would trust him with my life."

Now, as the sovereign State of Illinois prepares again to decide Crump's fate, the warden is a man with a heavy burden. Crump has requested, if he must die, that Johnson push the button that will send 1,900 volts of electricity into his body.

"He trusts me," says the warden. "He wants a friend to do it. It is my duty."[2]

NOTES

1. [Editor's note: See 295 F. 2d 699 (1961). The Illinois Supreme Court had earlier granted Crump a new trial; see 5 Ill. 2d 251 (1955).]

2. [Editor's note: Paul Crump's death sentence was commuted by Governor Otto Kerner on August 1, 1962 to 199 years imprisonment without possibility of parole. In commuting the sentence, Governor Kerner wrote in part, ". . . The embittered, distorted man who commited a vicious murder no longer exists . . . Under these circumstances, it would serve no useful purpose to take this man's life . . . The most significant goal of a system of penology is the rehabilitation of one of its members . . ." See New York Times of August 2, 1962.]

SUGGESTIONS FOR FURTHER READING

GENERAL

Beauchamp, Tom, and Walters, LeRoy. *Contemporary Issues in Bioethics*. Encino, Calif.: Dickenson, 1977.

Devine, Philip. *The Ethics of Homicide*. Ithaca, NY: Cornell University Press, 1978.

Glover, Jonathan. *Causing Deaths and Saving Lives*. London and New York: Pelican, 1977

Kohl, Marvin. *The Morality of Killing: Sanctity of Life, Abortion, and Euthanasia*. New York: Humanities Press, and London: Peter Owen, 1974.

Margolis, Joseph. *Negativities, The Limits of Life*. Columbus, Ohio: Charles E. Merrill, 1975.

Williams, Glanville. *The Sanctity of Life and the Criminal Law*. New York: Alfred A. Knopf, 1968.

ANIMAL LIFE

Godlovitch, S., Godlovitch, R., and Harris, J., eds. *Animals, Men, and Morals*. New York: Taplinger, 1973.

Kant, Immanuel. *Lectures on Ethics*. Translated by L. Infield. New York: Harper & Row, 1963, pp. 239–41.

Nozick, Robert. *Anarchy, State, and Utopia*. New York: Basic Books, 1974, pp. 35–41.

Regan, Thomas, and Singer, P., eds. *Human Duties and Animal Rights*. Englewood Cliffs, N.J.: Prentice-Hall, 1975.

Singer, Peter. *Animal Liberation*. New York: Random House, 1975.

Vercors (pseud.). *You Shall Know Them*. Translated by Rita Barisse. Boston: Little, Brown and Company, 1953. A novel on the distinction between human and non-human and its moral and legal consequences.

Westermarck, Edward. *The Origin and Development of the Moral Ideas*. London: Macmillan, 1917, Vol. II.

ABORTION

Callahan, Daniel. *Abortion: Law, Choice, and Morality*. New York: Macmillan, 1970.

Cohen, M., Nagel, T., and Scanlon, T., eds. *The Rights and Wrongs of Abortion*. Princeton, N.J.: Princeton University Press, 1974.

Feinberg, Joel, ed. *The Problem of Abortion*. Belmont, Calif.: Wadsworth, 1973.

Noonan, J. T., Jr., ed. *The Morality of Abortion: Legal and Historical Perspectives*. Cambridge, Mass.: Harvard University Press, 1970.

Perkins, Robert I.., ed. *Abortion*. Cambridge, Mass.: Harvard University Press, 1974.

SUICIDE

Beauchamp, Tom L. "An Analysis of Hume's Essay 'On Suicide.'" *The Review of Metaphysics* 30 (1976): 73–95.

Durkheim, Emile. *Suicide*. Translated by Spaulding and Simpson. New York: Free Press, 1960.

Josephus, Flavius. *The Jewish War*. Translated by R. Traill. London, 1851, Book 3, Chap. 8, Sec. 5.

Kant, Immanuel. *Lectures on Ethics*. Translated by L. Infield. New York: Harper & Row, 1963, pp. 147–53.

Montaigne, Michel de. *Essays*. Translated by John Florio. London, 1928, especially Book 2, Chap. 3, "A Custom of the Isle of Cea."

Schopenhauer, Arthur. "On Suicide." *Studies in Pessimism*. Translated by T. B. Saunders. London: Allen & Unwin, 1890.

Sprott, S. E. *The English Debate on Suicide*. LaSalle, Ill.; Open Court, 1961.

EUTHANASIA

Bok, S., ed. *The Dilemma of Euthanasia*. New York: Doubleday, 1975.

Downing, A. B., ed. *Euthanasia and the Right to Die*. New York: Humanities Press, 1970. An excellent collection.

Kohl, Marvin, ed. *Beneficent Euthanasia*. Buffalo, N.Y.: Prometheus Press, 1975.

Maguire, Daniel C. *Death by Choice*. Garden City, N.Y.: Doubleday, 1974.

Parliamentary Debates on Voluntary Euthanasia Bill. House of Lords Official Report, Vol. 300, No. 50 (March 25, 1969).

Pope Pius XII. "The Prolongation of Life" (excerpts). *The Pope Speaks,* Vol. 3–4 (1956–58): 393–95. Reprinted by the Institute for Society, Ethics, and the Life Sciences.

Russell, O. Ruth. *Freedom to Die*. New York: Human Sciences Press, 1975.

Wertenbaker, Lael Tucker. *Death of a Man*. New York: Bantam Books, 1957.

Wertham, Fredric. *A Sign for Cain*. New York: Paperback Library, 1969, chapter 9. A detailed and chilling account of the euthanasia movement in Germany.

KILLING AND LETTING DIE

Brand, Myles. "The Language of Not Doing." *American Philosophical Quarterly* 8 (1971), pp. 45–53.

Kleinig, John. "Good Samaritanism." *Philosophy and Public Affairs* 6 (1976), pp. 382–407.

Ratcliffe, James M., ed. *The Good Samaritan and the Law.* Garden City, N.Y.: Doubleday, 1966. An excellent collection.

Thomson, Judith J. "Killing, Letting Die, and the Trolley Problem." *The Monist* 60 (1976), pp. 204–17.

MURDER AND JUSTIFIED HOMICIDE

Becker, Stephen. *A Covenant with Death.* New York: Atheneum, 1965. An ingenious novel in which a theory of self-defense derived from Thomas Hobbes is expounded.

Cahn, Edmund. *The Moral Decision.* Bloomington, Ind.: Indiana University Press, 1955.

Childress, James F. "Who Shall Live When Not All Can Live?" *Soundings* 53 (Winter 1970). See reply by F. B. Westervelt in the same issue.

Kadish, Sanford H. "Respect for Life and Regard for Rights in the Criminal Law." *California Law Review* 64 (1976): 871–901.

Kadish, S., and Paulsen, M. G., eds. *Criminal Law and Its Processes.* 3rd ed. Boston: Little Brown, 1975.

Murphy, Jeffrie G. "The Killing of the Innocent." *The Monist,* 54 (1973).

Regina v. Dudley and Stephens, 14 Q.B.D. 273 (1884). An historical model for "The Case of the Speluncean Explorers."

Rescher, Nicholas. "The Allocation of Exotic Medical Lifesaving Therapy." *Ethics* 79 (1969): 173–86.

United States v. Holmes, 1. Wall. Jr. 1, 15 Fed. Cas. No. 15, 383 (C.C.E.D. Pa 1842). Another historical model for "The Case of the Speluncean Explorers."

CAPITAL PUNISHMENT

Aquinas, St. Thomas. *Summa Theologica.* New York: Benziger Brothers, 1925, Book II, Part II.

Beccaria, Marquis de. *On Crimes and Punishments.* Translated by H. Paolucci. Indianapolis: Bobbs-Merrill, 1963.

Bedau, Hugo A., ed. *The Death Penalty in America.* Garden City, N.Y.: Doubleday, 1964. A classic anthology.

Camus, Albert. *Reflections on the Guillotine.* Translated by R. Howard. Michigan City, Ind.: Fridyof-Karla, 1959.

Koestler, Arthur. *Reflections on Hanging.* New York: Macmillan, 1957.

Marx, Karl. "Capital Punishment." In *Marx and Engels: Basic Writings on Politics and Philosophy,* edited by L. Feuer. Garden City, N.Y.: Doubleday, 1959.

Pincoffs, Edmund L. *The Rationale of Legal Punishment.* New York: Humanities Press, 1966.

Royal Commission on Capital Punishment. *Report* (1953).

Sellin, T., ed. *Capital Punishment.* New York: Harper & Row, 1967.

Westermarck, Edward. *Origin and Development of the Moral Ideas.* London: Macmillan, 1917, Vol. I, chapter 20.

Chapter 6   Justice and Equality

In this chapter we will be concerned with a part of social justice, specifically that part which centers on the principle of equality and the doctrine of equal rights for all. This principle and this doctrine are an essential part of the democratic ethic and, in the Fourteenth Amendment, they are embedded in the Constitution of the United States (though they were not always there!). The principle of equality, construed as the requirement that there shall be no arbitrary discrimination in the treatment of different persons, is not the whole of morality. Morality is broader than the entirety of justice. We grant this when we recognize that there is some morally justified injustice, as when an impoverished parent steals to feed a starving child. Nor is the principle of equal treatment identical with the whole of justice. Though Aristotle claimed that "The just is the equal, as all men suppose it to be, even apart from argument," there are contexts where we properly say that injustice has occurred, even when the principle of equality (non-discrimination) has not been violated. In a society of relative abundance, for example, where the basic needs of all citizens can be satisfied, we speak of that society and its distributive policies as being unjust if they permit disadvantaged and impoverished members of that society to starve or suffer from want of basic necessities. No active discrimination occurs in such contexts, no partiality in the application of rules, and no arbitrary exclusion of one party compared to another. All that occurs is severe deprivation in a very affluent society. Yet we apply the term "injustice" here. We want to say that in such a society the basic necessities are *due* each person. This is the sort of case which falls under what Joel Feinberg calls "non-comparative justice," where we judge the treatment of a person in accordance with an objective or independent standard—with "human need," in this case.[1] Even if we are non-discriminatory in ignoring the needs of impoverished persons, that is, we ignore them all equally, we have still committed an injustice.

There is a tendency in both moral and constitutional theory to conflate these two types of justice —comparative and non-comparative. Frank Michelman warns us that at the level of constitutional debate this conflation and confusion can have serious normative results.[2] Many want to expand the equal protection clause, he notes, to solve all of our social ills. Equal protection emphasis fits the category of comparative justice where arbitrary discrimination between persons is the key theme. In contexts of poverty, the model of equal protection makes one look for discriminatory policies which have resulted in the poverty—economic discrimination. In some situations such discrimination may exist and may have caused the poverty. In countless others the poverty or deprivation exists, but it is not the result of arbitrary discrimination but of the facts of life. Many persons are born into poverty (though it *may* be possible to hold government responsible in some cases for the conditions into which people are born). If no one is responsible for that poverty, if it has not resulted from arbitrary discrimination and if equal protection in the sense of non-discrimination is the only premise in the argument that government should alleviate the conditions of poverty, then the result may well be government abdication of the task of providing for the fundamental needs of those citizens who cannot provide for themselves (when resources to meet those needs are available). For this reason, Michelman contends, the more adequate moral and constitutional appeal in such contexts is the doctrine of "minimum protection" (not equal protection) where the state recognizes the existence of "just wants" of everyone. Constitutional grounds for minimum protection are to be found in that part of the Fourteenth Amendment which states that there shall be "no deprivation of life without due process of law."[3] The justice of "minimum protection" would fall under Feinberg's category of non-comparative justice. Moral grounds for minimum protection might be a human right (a right which each person has simply because that person is human) to those necessities required for the satisfaction of one's fundamental economic needs (when those resources exist).

FORMAL EQUALITY

There is a great deal of non-comparative injustice in the world. Our concern in this chapter is with comparative injustice—injustice which results from arbitrary discrimination. Here Aristotle may be right: The just *is* the equal. But what is equality?

Aristotle goes on to formulate justice as equality in this way: Justice requires equal treatment for equals; unequal treatment for unequals. Put negatively, "injustice arises when equals are treated unequally, and also when unequals are treated equally." Plainly this is a highly abstract principle. It tells you nothing about what you are required to do in order to render justice, *until the meaning of "equals" and "unequals" is filled in.* For this reason the principle of equality as here formulated is often called the *formal* principle of equality. Aristotle himself rejects equality of distribution in the sense of the same portion for each (arithmetical proportion) unless the parties are in fact equals in the relevant respects. He recognizes that persons differ enormously, and many of those differences—by no means all—are relevant grounds for differential treatment. Strict equality of treatment when there are relevant differences is unjust; inequality of treatment when there are no relevant differences also is unjust. Where there are relevant differences, justice requires proportionate equality, differences in treatment which are proportionate to the differences between the parties.

SUBSTANTIVE EQUALITY: MATERIAL PRINCIPLES OF JUSTICE

What is an equal? What are relevant differences? Those differences deemed relevant by Aristotle are the possession of moral and intellectual virtues, noble birth, and wealth. Some persons, he thinks,

are inferior by nature and may even be justly enslaved. His formal principle, when filled in by these
substantive or material criteria, is a meritarian theory of justice. All of these criteria—and the general
criterion of merit itself—have since been challenged as arbitrary, invidious distinctions. Other
substantive or material principles of justice have
been invoked, specifying quite different characteristics or criteria as relevant to the proper distribution of wealth and honors in society. Some
have suggested the criterion of "need" as basic to
proper distribution of some goods. Others have
emphasized the criterion of "contribution," economic and/or social, as most basic to just distribution. If someone contributes a great deal to the
production of goods and services or if he or she
contributes a great deal to the welfare of society,
that person is due a great deal in return. The person's income and status should be proportionate to
that contribution. Others have stressed not one's
actual contribution but one's effort to contribute.
Effort sometimes misfires. Also, hard work in one
area may be more productive than the same effort
in another area. Still, equal effort deserves equal
reward. Yet others have stressed the criterion of
"humanity," of simply being human, as the most
basic criterion for distribution of goods and services. The mere fact that every human has the
capacity for choice and for suffering requires that
the basic needs of each be met. Or, as others prefer
to put it, the fact that each person partakes of the
same essential humanity; the fact that each of us is a
"child of God"; the fact that each of us has a "spark
of the divine reason," as the Stoic claims—these
natural, theological, and metaphysical facts have all
been invoked as grounds for equal treatment and
the fulfillment of basic human needs.

Just as Aristotle's material principles—nobility,
wealth, and so on—were challenged as unjust and
as based on invidious distinctions, these other criteria of relevance for treatment have also been
challenged on a variety of grounds. If "need" is to
be the criterion of distribution, what are basic
needs? Food, clothing, shelter, and medical care, of
course. But aren't demands which go beyond these
basics also "needs" in some societies? Also, depending on a person's abilities and purposes, he or
she may have specific needs that others do not
have. Does the need principle entail that means to

bring those abilities and purposes to fruition are
required, even if they go well beyond the provision
of basics?

If "contribution" is taken as the basic criterion,
how does one measure and rate contributions to
economic production or, more broadly, to social
welfare? Is the contribution of a plumber equal to
that of a carpenter? to that of a teacher? a physician? What is the specific rationale for differential
reward? Does the owner of a business make a
greater contribution than the manager? or the
worker? Are not many contributions ostensibly
made by individuals really the result in large part of
social support? For example, the education of physicians, lawyers, and professors are heavily subsidized by state and private institutions. Should not
some of the reward for the contributions of these
professionals redound to the community which
made the opportunities for these professional contributions possible?

Some philosophers have argued that the fact that
certain individuals have natural abilities (intelligence and so on) and cultural advantages (socioeconomic conditions) which others lack is arbitrary
from the moral point of view. They have done
nothing to *deserve* those advantages and abilities;
nor have those who lack them done anything to
deserve not having them. Hence distribution of
goods and services fundamentally on the basis of
contributions made possible by such fortuitous circumstances or "luck of the draw" is irrational and
unjust. A "fanatical egalitarian" goes even further
and presses for complete leveling in society.[4] He
would insist, I suppose, that in the name of social
justice we handicap those persons with great natural abilities while we compensate those with disadvantages. (Some say that our public schools are
doing this today!) Perhaps we should have an office
of Handicapper General of the United States, as is
humorously suggested by Kurt Vonnegut in his
Welcome to the Monkey House (the short story, "Harrison Bergeron").

Those who have appealed to the criterion of
"humanity" or of simply being human as the basic
criterion for distribution have generally collapsed
this criterion, normatively, into the "need" criterion. Metaphysically and theologically, several have
challenged the claim that there is an "essential humanity." When conceptually stripped of all acci-

dental characteristics like wealth, social status, and intelligence, humans are simply beings with an "undifferentiated potentiality" and this provides no criterion for distribution.

The parade of conflicting criteria of distribution or material principles of justice is quite perplexing. Nearly everyone agrees—with the exception of the "fanatical egalitarian"—that there are justified inequalities in the distribution of wealth and honors, goods and services. But there is considerable disagreement over what criteria justify inequalities and the degree of inequality justified. Perhaps part of the problem is that these various criteria have sometimes been seen as mutually exclusive. Could not a number of these criteria be relevant, and properly invoked in different contexts? Perhaps several criteria or material principles are relevant but some have priority over others. Surely the relevance of criteria is determined heavily by the context of distribution, and since there are many different contexts with different social objectives, there must necessarily be many different criteria which are relevant to the distribution of goods, services, prizes, and opportunities. The social practice or objective dictates the relevance of certain criteria. So, if we are engaged in the practice of awarding a prize for the best paper in ethics or ecology, the relevant criteria are defined by those disciplines and the authorities in those disciplines. If health care is being distributed, a health need of some type is relevant. If teaching positions are being filled ("distributed"), knowledge of subject-matter and the ability to impart that knowledge are relevant. And so on. There is a great deal of agreement on literally thousands of specific criteria of relevance in different contexts and many general criteria (need, contribution, effort, and so on). This is not to say that we should simply accept all ongoing social practices and the criteria they embrace. Some of those practices and their criteria of distribution are undoubtedly unjust. But sensitivity to the multiplicity of those practices should make us wary of one who would reduce relevant criteria to a single principle or two.

JUSTICE AS REGULARITY BUT AS MORE THAN REGULARITY

Quite clearly, even allowing for the fact that relevant criteria are many, there are a number of social practices and laws in which *irrelevant* criteria are invoked, hence practices and laws which are unjust. We refer here not to the inconsistent or irregular application of a law or social practice. True, there is considerable injustice in the application or administration of law. If, for example, a judge imposes a harsher penalty on one of two parties who violated a law and who were similar in all relevant respects, that is an injustice. It is reasonably well documented that blacks in the South received far more severe penalties for crimes than their white counterparts. This category of justice, which John Rawls calls "justice as regularity," requires the fair and impartial application of existing law to all to whom it applies.[5] But there are laws or social practices which themselves embrace irrelevant criteria for the treatment of persons in their very formulation; for example, laws or practices which arbitrarily discriminate on the basis of sex, race, ethnic origin, and religion. (It must be admitted that these criteria may be relevant *in some contexts;* but for most purposes, they are not.) In such cases the uniform application of law results in massive injustice. This is what has happened in the course of human history. Laws and practices which embodied invidious, arbitrary distinctions were brutally applied to all. Thus, Ralf Dahrendorf suggests that if we want to understand the causes of inequalities among human beings, the causes of social stratification of various kinds, we must turn to the system of laws and socially approved sanctions in society. Though a classless and distinctionless society, he suggests, is "sociologically impossible," unjust or arbitrary distinctions and laws will result in unjust inequalities and unjust stratification.[6] The law itself, then, can be and often is the key instrument causing and creating injustice. Nor do we need to turn to Nazi Germany for examples of unjust laws —there are plenty right at home.

Civil rights advocates such as Martin Luther King, Jr., who demanded more than "law and order," knew this all too well. The law can not only be administered unfairly. It can be used as a tool to perpetuate and justify status quo prejudices and injustices. Of course, law and order is necessary if one is to have a society at all; but when the appeal to law and order is a thinly disguised code to preserve existing unjust conditions, when the objective of the law itself is to protect invidious distinctions and those who have vested interests in those distinctions, then it is plain that we must go beyond the law itself to obtain justice. Bernard Schwartz reminds us that the framers of the Constitution of the United States did not extend equality to all members of the community.[7] For many of them social justice did not require either the abolition of slavery or equal rights for women. Only with the passage of the Fourteenth Amendment was equality as a principle elevated to the constitutional level, and even then, with the presumed guarantee of equality of treatment regardless of "race, color, or previous condition of servitude," discriminatory practices in flat contradiction to this principle were permitted to exist.

FACTS, RELEVANCE, AND JUSTICE

Why did discriminatory practices continue to exist? Was it merely moral obtuseness and cultural lag, a kind of recalcitrance which custom imposes upon us all? Was it the intentional use of the political process to preserve values and ways of life which were in the interests of some people? Was it ignorance of facts about the races? Recall that many racists argued that blacks are genetically inferior to whites, that they have lower I.Q.'s, that they are morally primitive, and the like. Hence they do not deserve the same treatment as whites. Undoubtedly, all of these factors contributed to the discriminatory practices which prevailed after equality was declared. But the purported *factual* differences between the races certainly played a key role. Once equality was declared legally binding, out-and-out racism was beyond the pale. Racists had to look for justification within the framework of law to sustain their prejudices and stereotypes. And they found it. The principle of equality, they correctly saw, does not require *identity* of treatment when there are relevant differences. In fact, identity of treatment where there are relevant differences results in injustice. As the Equal Protection Clause of the Fourteenth Amendment states, any given classification providing the basis for differential treatment "must always rest upon some difference which bears a reasonable and just relation to the act in respect to which the classification is proposed." It is plain history that many found the (what they assume to be) factual

differences between the races to bear a "reasonable and just relation" to a host of acts or practices. They found that those differences justify racially separate schools, separate water fountains, separate seating arrangements on public buses, separate motels, hotels, and other public accommodations, and the like. The "separate but equal" doctrine of *Plessy-Ferguson* involving the public schools was part of a total package of "separate but equal" policy which was seen as consistent with the equal protection requirement of the Fourteenth Amendment.

We need not recall in detail the historical events since the overturning of *Plessy-Ferguson* by *Brown-Topeka* in 1954. The latter decision requiring desegregation rejected the separate but equal doctrine, in large part on the basis of new sociological and psychological data, data which supported the conclusion that racially separate schools were inherently unequal. Racial segregation, it was argued in *Brown,* brands the minority race as inferior, and that branding and all that goes with it prevents equality of educational opportunity. It is not merely that majority race schools were given more enriched resources. It is the psychologically crippling impact of segregation on members of the minority race which prevents equal opportunity.

There is still great debate over the relationship of certain characteristics to race and to sex, and over the relevance of those characteristics to the differential treatment of persons. For example, given the physiological differences generally among men and women, it would be unfair, some argue, to force women to compete with men for a single university tennis team. Perhaps so (though others argue that the lesser physical strength of women is the result of culture, not nature). But surely those differences, if they exist and whatever their causes, do not justify the differential treatment of women in other contexts, like voting rights, political participation in general, and nearly all working opportunities. In the same way, racial differences are irrelevant to differential treatment in nearly all contexts. Not in all, for if sickle cell anemia, for example, is a disease exclusively confined to blacks, then surely that justifies special medical attention for blacks. The problem, of course, is that racists and sexists have created or inherited stereotypes of blacks and of women and those stereotypes have influenced both their perception of fact and of what ought to be. These stereotypes gloss over all or most of the relevant similarities between the races and between the sexes, which are far greater than relevant differences. Those who have accepted these stereotypes—and in the past, at least, that seems to include the majority of us—have permitted those stereotypes to be reflected in law and to permeate social practices. To that extent most of us have either wittingly or unwittingly contributed to the massive injustices of our society. Much of it is unwitting. We are all creatures of custom and habit, as Aristotle knew so well. The accretions of culturally inherited stereotypes are very difficult to shuck off. They are even difficult to see when one is so totally immersed in them. Yet, when a Martin Luther King, Jr., a John Stuart Mill, or a Mary Wollstonecraft comes along, some can be made to see. Moral or stereotype *conversions* do occur. But what in the way of *argument* can be offered as underpinning for moral and social change? What in the way of extra-legal grounds can serve to demonstrate the injustice of certain laws—even the injustice of the objectives of certain laws? Are we reduced to ultimate disagreement rooted in (once the facts have been explored) intractable attitudinal differences, as the emotivist claims?

EXTRA-LEGAL GROUNDS OF JUSTICE

Let us examine briefly several theoretical and normative frameworks which provide grounds for the rejection of racism and sexism. First, the framework to which Martin Luther King, Jr., appealed.

GOD AND NATURAL LAW

In his now-famous *Letter From Birmingham City Jail* (included in the readings in this chapter), Martin Luther King, Jr., declared that an "unjust law is no law at all." He intended not to deny that such laws were laws in the positive sense. They were promulgated by legislatures. He intended to deny that one is morally obligated to obey a law which is unjust. In fact he maintained that one has a moral obligation to disobey such laws. What are the extra-legal grounds for judging certain laws to be unjust? King's answer places him squarely within the Judeo-Christian tradition: An unjust law is one which is out of harmony with the moral law of God. It is a

human law which is "not rooted in eternal and natural law." King refers here directly to the great Church Father and philosopher, St. Thomas Aquinas. Their tests of injustice are the same: Does the law violate either God's moral law or the natural law which reflects God's law? The problem with this appeal, as many have pointed out, is that there are different interpretations of God's will or His moral law. Which is correct?

King fleshes out what he takes to be the normative content of God's moral law. "Any law that uplifts human personality is just. Any law that degrades human personality is unjust." The problem, then, is to discover what it means more specifically to degrade human personality and which laws do the degrading. One thing is for certain for King. All segregation statutes degrade the human personality. Segregation "distorts the soul and damages the personality" and hence is unjust and immoral. The fact that each person is a child of God and is equal in that sense provides the ontological base for the normative test of justice and injustice: Does the law in question "uplift human personality" or does it "degrade" it?

There are other tests for justice and injustice in King's thought. For example, he states that "a just law is a code that a majority compels a minority to follow that it is *willing to follow itself* [italics added]." Here we have what some philosophers have called the "reversibility test"; others, the "golden rule test." Are you willing to abide by that law were it applicable to you?

Another test he offers might be called the "consent requirement." A law is unjust if it is "inflicted upon a minority which . . . had no part in enacting or creating" it. The clear supposition here is that blacks had nothing to do with setting up segregation laws, since they were disenfranchised. Therefore segregation laws violate the consent requirement of a democracy.

King's most fundamental test for injustice, however, is not the consent requirement, for even if a minority did consent to segregation laws (a most implausible supposition), those laws would still be unjust. Nor is the basic test that of "reversibility," for even if members of the majority were willing to abide by those laws were they applicable to them (again, a most unlikely possibility),[8] still the segregation statute would be unjust, for it degrades human personality. The latter is the basic test for King.

There is a problem in knowing the extent of this test. Segregation statutes violate it. They involve active discrimination against a certain minority class, degrading their personalities. What about poverty? It may involve no active discrimination but only deprivation. Still there is an important sense in which poverty degrades human personality, for it precludes the flowering and hence the fulfillment of human capacities. Is poverty then unjust? Late in King's life (in fact, the year prior to his assassination) he expanded his concern for social justice to include a war on poverty in the United States and abroad. Economic injustice he saw as an "enormous, entrenched evil."[9] Much of that economic injustice is due to the sins of the past in which some human beings arbitrarily discriminated against and exploited others, enriching themselves at other's expense. Slavery was a major part of those sins. However, much of it is due to the inaction of government, where "The society is refusing to take means which have been called for, and which are at hand, to lift the load of poverty."[10] This is a kind of injustice. It is not exclusively racial. In fact it may not be rooted in invidious distinctions. But, King insists, "in our society it is murder, psychologically, to deprive a man of a job or an income. . . . You are in a real way depriving him of life, liberty, and the pursuit of happiness, denying in his case the very creed of his society."[11] Given those moral and political values and given the affluence of our society, it is an injustice that the poor are permitted to remain poor. Whether rooted in invidious distinctions or not, poverty degrades human personality and hence is unjust. Plainly King's normative standard for assessing the justice of law and social policy is broad and open to interpretation. It certainly requires that we go well beyond the elimination of racism.

SOCIAL CONTRACT (JUSTICE AS FAIRNESS)

Let us now turn to a theory of moral rights in which there is no reference to God or natural law but in which the normative principles espoused by John Locke, Martin Luther King, and others in the natural law tradition emerge via a hypothetical social contract; and in which those normative principles are further refined and lexically ordered to generate even more specific directives for the justice of a society. I refer to the recent mammoth work by John Rawls, *A Theory of Justice.*

Any attempt to briefly state Rawls' position will oversimplify his theory, but I think this can be done without distorting his position. He generates his extra-legal grounds for assessing the justice of a society and whether inequalities are justified by constructing a hypothetical social contract in which rational, self-interested (but not necessarily egoistic) individuals assemble to jointly draw up the basic principles of justice which are to apply to all. The conditions of agreement are constrained to assure impartiality and objectivity so that the principles which emerge reflect no special interest or class. Contracting parties are not permitted to know anything about their own natural or cultural assets; that is, all information about one's own (possible or predictable) status or position in society is screened out by what Rawls calls a "veil of ignorance." The veil prevents self-interest or class interest from coloring the choice of basic principles of justice.

Under these conditions rational contractors would agree to adopt two basic principles of justice arranged in a hierarchical order: (1) the principle of equal liberty, and (2) the principle of fair equality of opportunity and the "difference" principle. The second principle really has two parts and here Rawls requires that fair equality of opportunity be satisfied before the difference principle comes into play. But more fundamentally, the principle of equal liberty must be satisfied before the second principle as a whole comes into play. That is, there can be no trade-off of basic liberties for equality of opportunity or consequential concerns. (This lexical ordering, or what Rawls calls his "special conception of justice," holds only in societies where the material conditions of life are such that basic liberties can be effectively exercised.)

The principle of equal liberty requires an equal right to the most extensive basic liberty compatible with a similar liberty for others. Fair equality of opportunity requires not mere formal access to opportunities, but also the material conditions essential for taking advantage of formal access (without which formal access is an empty bag). The difference principle—by far the most controversial component of Rawls' theory—requires that all inequalities of wealth and income be justified on the grounds that they raise the standard of living of those persons at the bottom of the economic ladder. As Rawls puts it, the difference principle represents "an agreement to regard the distribution of natural talents as a common asset and to share in the benefits of this distribution whatever it turns out to be. Those who have been favored by nature, whoever they are, may gain from their good fortune only on terms that improve the situation of those who have lost out."[12] The assumption of the difference principle is that the possession of natural talents and of a favorable socioeconomic condition to develop those talents are undeserved natural and social contingencies, mere accidents of nature or culture. No one can be said to deserve either the advantages or the disadvantages which generally accompany these sheer historical accidents. Natural and social facts, such as one's being born black or white, male or female, wealthy or poor, an imbecile or with high intelligence capacity, are beyond one's control. They are fortuitous circumstances which are arbitrary from a moral point of view and which deserve no rewards or penalties.

Recognition of these facts and the adoption of these principles of justice will not only do away with racism and sexism in society, it will do away (at least in a society as affluent as our own) with the gross disparities between the very poor and the very rich. For the principles not only assure genuine equal access to opportunities irrespective of race, sex, or economic condition, but they assure the satisfaction of the basic requirements for a minimally satisfactory life, even for those who are unable for one reason or another to take advantage of opportunities and look after themselves.

The principles require even more than what are often called welfare rights, and that is the rub for many liberals who otherwise fall into line with Rawlsian principles: *No* inequalities of wealth and income are permitted unless those inequalities are required to raise the standard of those at the bottom. This seems to require not merely meeting the conditions required for a minimally satisfactory life for all, but also continually escalating the standard of those at the bottom by lessening the wealth differential between the top and the bottom until any further lessening impairs the escalation. At that stage the inequalities are justified, for it would be irrational not to permit inequalities which benefit everyone. More traditional liberals have not gone this far. The provision of the minimal conditions for a satisfactory life for all, yes; but beyond that, wide differences in wealth are justified. Merit or desert plays a stronger role with more traditional liberals than with Rawls. The fundamental needs of all have moral priority in the distribution of goods and services but, beyond that, merit criteria of various kinds justifiably come into play and permit inequalities. (It is undoubtedly the case that Rawls and the traditional liberal would disagree substantially on what is within one's control; that is, voluntary. Part of their disagreement on when the desert or merit criterion is to be plugged into the equality principle is probably rooted in this factual disagreement.)

Some maintain that even within Rawls' own principles, wide disparities in wealth are permitted, for such disparities are required for the capital investment which it takes to keep the economy growing and the conditions of the poor improving. But it seems clear that many inequalities now accepted as justified which are not required to maximize the minimum standard must be eliminated on his theory. Consequently, his theory is extremely controversial on both a normative level, in terms of what it requires for a society to be just, and on a theoretical level, in terms of the assumptions and contract theory from which he generates the normative principles.[13]

Normatively, it is similar to the position of King in requiring not only the elimination of racism, sexism, and other forms of arbitrary discrimination but also the elimination of the conditions of poverty which stultify and degrade human beings. There are very significant differences, however. Rawls' "difference" principle takes him well beyond the minimum income-welfare rights emphasis of King. In this sense Rawls is more of a radical egalitarian than King, odd as it sounds.

One further difference between Rawls and, if not King, then other civil rights activists, bears mention. The latter may not accept the strict lexical ordering of principles held by Rawls in which there can be no trade-offs between basic liberties and equality of opportunity or consequential considerations. The issue is complicated and surely we must distinguish between a trade-off in which there is more or less permanent loss of a liberty and a trade-off in which there is a temporary violation of a liberty. In any case, some civil rights theorists advocate preferential treatment for minorities and women in order to overcome the effects of past injustice and assure distributive justice today, which, others argue, results in "reverse discrimination" and the violation of the liberties of others. Essays dealing with this question appear in this chapter, and it will be discussed later in this Introduction.

UTILITARIANISM

The utilitarian attempts to answer the question "What are just inequalities?" with a single principle or formula. Inequalities are just (and justified) if they contribute to the greatest happiness of the greatest number. Justice is not seen as a principle independent of the principle of utility. Rather it is "a name for certain moral requirements, which, regarded collectively, stand higher in the scale of social utility, and are therefore of more paramount obligation, than any others."[14] Justice involves the recognition that each person has an equal claim to happiness and that society must give "equal protection to the rights of all."[15] The rights with which justice is concerned are both moral and legal, but the most basic rights are moral ones. For some laws conferring legal rights may themselves be unjust, and the only criteria for judging the justice of the law itself are moral rights. In this sense, though on quite different moral grounds, the utilitarian and Martin Luther King are in agreement. For he, like King, insists that we should not apply the term "injustice" to all violations of law "but only violations of such laws as ought to exist. . . ."[16]

But what is the criterion for denominating something as a moral right? Are not there any number of moral rights of individuals which conflict? The utilitarian explicitly recognizes such conflicts not only between individual rights but between criteria invoked as grounds for individual rights. Some persons hold that moral rights to goods and services must be determined by need; some, by strict equal-ity; some, by effort; others, by merit. There is no way of resolving such conflicts of principles of justice, the utilitarian insists, without stepping outside of the frame of each of these principles. Some utilitarians stress the "duty to do to each according to his deserts. . . ." All should be equally well treated, John Stuart Mill insists, "(where no higher duty forbids) who have deserved equally well of us."[17] When there is conflict, how do we decide on the highest duty? "Social utility alone can decide the preference."[18]

Justice, then, or the attempt to render each person his or her due, may involve and often does involve conflicting rules and principles, each of which has limited validity. When conflict occurs, it is resolved by asking which rule or principle (or ordering of principles) maximizes social utility. In fact the utilitarian insists that if a recognized moral right of an individual conflicts with the greater social good, that right can be justifiably overridden. This amounts to "laudable" or morally justified injustice, though any such overriding of individual rights must be rare and strictly construed. Some utilitarians would insist that moral rights can only be overridden by other stronger moral rights, not by a direct application of the principle of maximizing social utility, and there are some grounds for reading Mill himself in this way. Utility is invoked only in choosing and adjudicating between systems of moral rights. Nonetheless, whether the principle of utility is applied directly or indirectly to resolve such conflicts, it is the ultimate court of appeal.

Utilitarians point out that many rights recognized in the past were grounded in a host of invidious distinctions. Mill points to the distinctions between slaves and freemen, nobles and serfs, partisans and plebians; and he insists, well ahead of his time, that the "aristocracies of color, race and sex" will pass. Those aristocracies have not passed yet, a hundred years after his prediction. But surely he is correct in his judgment that they ought to pass. What about the differences and distinctions which ought to be recognized and embodied in social practice and law? Where are his priorities (and those of the utilitarians generally) when there are conflicts between moral rights, all of which are based on proper and relevant distinctions? The right to liberty for Mill and many utilitarians has paramount standing among all rights. This right—which really involves a cluster of rights such as the right to vote, to participate in the political process, to a fair trial, and to move about without interference—is fundamental; for liberty or freedom is basic to human happiness, and rules which involve restrictions on freedoms "are more vital to human well being than any maxims."[19] So Mill and other utilitarians, in agreement with Rawls, would put basic liberties on the most secure ground, beyond the reach even of majority control. Also, like Rawls, but for quite different reasons, basic liberties have priority over other rights or value considerations such as welfare rights. Each person, with the equal right to happiness, also has an "equal claim to all the means of happiness." This commitment, in conjunction with the belief that poverty can be "completely extinguished" by society, means that it is both unjust and immoral not to satisfy that equal claim. It is unjust, because the satisfaction of that equal claim is something which is *due* each person (it is his moral right) when material conditions are such that it can be satisfied. Under those conditions, poverty is an injustice. It is immoral because not to do so violates the utilitarian requirement that we maximize happiness. For even if fulfillment of that equal claim requires the lessening of luxuries for others, social utility demands this of us. The luxuries of a few do not offset the miseries of many. (This is what is called the "diminishing marginal utility" of gross inequality.)

Not all utilitarians agree that social utility requires the priority of liberty. The priority is rooted in the empirical belief that liberties are more basic to human happiness than other things, but some utilitarians would reject this belief. Those liberties are meaningless to persons who are hungry, sick, or undereducated. Hence, the welfare rights of all are more important than basic liberties. This possible conclusion from utilitarian premises is exactly what worries a contract theorist like Rawls, who insists on placing basic liberties on a firmer foundation.

Of course, to provide basic necessities for those who can not provide them for themselves need not affect at all the recognition and preservation of basic liberties. It may require a redistributive scheme which takes from the rich and gives to the poor; and if property rights are seen as absolute rights or entitlements, then the liberties of the rich would be lessened to provide for the necessities of the poor. It should be noted, however, that this would neither negate nor conflict with any basic political rights or liberties, and property rights have never been seen as absolute entitlements. The long-standing doctrine of "public domain" attests to that fact. Still it must be admitted that state redistribution schemes and programs designed to assure minimum economic standards for all do restrict traditional areas of free choice. Liberty and equality may be "twin ideals in the minds of democrats," as David Thomson puts it,[20] but there is at least some tension between the twins. Not as much as the radical egalitarian holds, who would reject all freedom which leads to inequality; nor as much as the radical libertarian holds, who would reject all equalization efforts which restrict freedom. Surely some freedom is justifiably restricted and some inequalities are just, for freedom as a moral ideal has generally meant *equal freedom* for all, not freedom to do whatever one wants, and equality as a moral ideal has generally meant *equal consideration* for all, not identical treatment or a complete leveling of all humans. The tension is in where to draw the line. It was suggested above that there are sound arguments grounded in both justice and utility not to draw the line at the extremes where the libertarian and the radical egalitarian do. The challenge to those who are committed to justice and equality is that of demonstrating by appeal to relevant considerations of justice, utility, or other moral principles that certain inequalities are just and/or justified and that others are not. This is not a task which can be done once and for all. Reasons of justice and reasons of utility are highly context-dependent. Also the conditions of human life are continually changing, conditions which bear dramatically on the justice and utility of distributive decisions; and our knowledge of the empirical facts related to the attainment of social justice and social utility increases with time and attention. Progress has been made in eliminating unjust and unjustified inequalities (and unjust and unjustified equalities) but many remain behind screens of factual ignorance, institutionalized stereotypes, conceptual confusion, and moral obtuseness.

Of the many problems concerning justice and equality, only three are treated in this chapter: racial discrimination, sexual discrimination, and what is now often called "reverse" discrimination.

RACIAL DISCRIMINATION

Racism is a massive phenomenon, in the United States and the world as a whole. It involves many races. Great progress has been made in the United States in recent decades. Blacks now serve on the Supreme Court, in the cabinet, the Senate, and the House. In the South, the traditional bastion of white supremacy, registered black voters have doubled in the past decade and elected black officials have increased from fewer than 100 to over 1,500. Nationwide, over one hundred towns and cities, including Atlanta, Detroit, Los Angeles, Newark, Cincinnati, and Washington, D.C., have elected black mayors. Accompanying this progress into the political mainstream has been black progress into the economic mainstream. The income level for blacks is now much closer to that of the average white. We have come a long way since the 1954 *Brown* decision, a long way from the conditions described by Martin Luther King, Jr., in his *Letter from Birmingham City Jail* in which, for blacks, "your first name becomes 'nigger,' your middle name becomes 'boy' (however old you are) and your last name becomes 'John.' " Gone are the officially segregated schools, the separate water fountains and bathrooms, the balcony for blacks in theaters, the seating of blacks in the backs of buses, and the separate hotels and motels.

All that is progress. Yet a great deal of individual and institutionalized racism persists. Knowles and Prewitt suggest, in their essay in this chapter, that the Report of the National Advisory Commission on Civil Disorders (generally referred to as the Kerner Commission Report) stresses the immediate conditions giving rise to disorders, not the basic causes behind those conditions. Thus, it directs its attention to the conditions of the ghetto, not the "white structures and practices"—the institutionalized racism—which create ghettos. We need a Report by a National Advisory Commission on White Racism, not one on civil disorders, they argue, for many of the institutions of our society—

universities, medical institutions—legal and political institutions, are permeated by racism. We can solve the problem of racism only by attacking it at its roots, by focusing on institutionalized practices and the attitudes behind them.

Irving Thalberg argues similarly in his essay. The doctrine of white supremacy is gone but "visceral racism" remains, the kind of racism in which so-called unprejudiced whites refuse to recognize certain social inequalities. Visceral racists, Thalberg argues, live in a "protective cocoon of ignorance and distortion."[21] It is a far more difficult type of racism to overcome. The Ku Kluxer can be met head-on; the visceral racist cannot. And this kind of racism, many suggest, permeates the North, a region of the country which until recently was seen as far ahead of the South in overcoming racism.

In an essay not included in this chapter, former Chief Justice Earl Warren focuses on racism in the administration of justice in the courts. He argues that "the law is the greatest force for maintaining civilized society, and . . . its ultimate objective is justice for all."[22] And yet, racism pervades our court system. Blacks and other minorities are often systematically excluded from jury duty. They are inadequately represented by legal counsel and often treated with indignity in court proceedings. They receive disproportionately harsh penalties for their crimes. The organized Bar of the nation has not on the whole discharged its obligation to rectify these wrongs. How can we expect numbers of minority groups to respect the law, he asks, if their rights are denied by the very legal system they are asked to respect?

The practices described above are in flat contradiction to the moral and constitutional commitments of this country. The essays in this section portray that contradiction poignantly. They contrast our moral and constitutional ideals with the reality of our individual and institutionalized racism; and they suggest ways out of the contradiction.

SEXUAL DISCRIMINATION

There are similarities but also major differences between racial and sexual discrimination. Females, aside from black ones, were not *literally* enslaved. They have not suffered the brutal effects of the cultural legacy of slavery. However, they have suffered from other types of oppression and stereotyping, and they still suffer. Though not subjected as a class to the same vicious economic, educational, political, and judicial discrimination to which blacks were subjected, nonetheless they were disenfranchised until 1920. They were systematically denied the opportunity to enter many professions and lines of work for which they were qualified by ability. The law itself discriminated against women in many ways: higher criminal penalties than males for the same offense, the exclusion of women from jury duty, the condoning of credit policies which treat women unfairly, and the like.

Of course, there was some discrimination which was in favor of women (and against men). But the overall effect of the discrimination was the relegation of women to certain places and roles in society and the prohibition of others. This is a kind of slavery or oppression, however unwitting it may be.

Behind these forms of sexual discrimination lie explicit theories of the biological and psychological nature of women and of men, stereotypes which defined the essential nature and hence the roles of men and women. Women as a class are seen as emotional, illogical, indecisive, passive, submissive, physically weak, and dependent. They are intended for motherhood and child care and have their sense of identity as persons and their happiness only through these roles. Men as a class are seen as logical, active, assertive, aggressive, physically strong, and better problem solvers (a stereotype equally oppressive for many men). The battle for the liberation of women from Mary Wollstonecraft to Simone de Beauvoir, Betty Freidan, and Kate Millett has been and continues to be a battle against this stereotype and its impact in law and social practice. The selections in this chapter by Millett, Goldberg, and Trebilcot reflect this running battle. Millet sees the stereotype as unfounded and as bequeathing to us a patriarchal political system (in which there is a "birthright priority whereby males rule females") and all of the injustices and inequalities of that system. Goldberg, on the other hand, sees that stereotype as grounded in biological fact and consequently he sees the social inequalities

which emerge from those facts as necessary ones, not injustices. It is a biological fact that men, while perhaps not more talented than women, are far more aggressive and stronger on the whole, and "political-economic systems are limited by, and must conform to the nature of man," Goldberg insists. The resulting social and political inequities and the norms which channel men in certain directions and women in another are required for the survival of the culture itself. Sexual discrimination and socialization, then, are not forms of oppression or chauvinism but a recognition of competencies ordained by nature. Furthermore, Goldberg holds, although not all women are to be cast as wives, mothers, and homemakers, still any movement which attempts to liberate women from roles for which they are by nature best equipped and to thrust them into competition with men for tasks for which they are ill-equipped will doom the vast majority of women to failure.

Does the appeal to nature and biology cut the ice which Goldberg thinks it does? No, Trebilcot argues. For even if there are natural biological and psychological differences between the sexes, this fact does not mandate the legislation of specific sex roles. Even if there were a universal and inevitable correlation between sex and roles, then such legislation would be unnecessary. But since there is not, such legislation forces some individuals (male and female) into roles which they would not otherwise choose. This is a violation of individual freedom and rights and a denial of equality of opportunity. It is to these values which we must attend in debating the propriety of sexual discrimination, Trebilcot insists, not purported biological differences.

Opposed both to those who reject biological differences between men and women as either negligible or nonexistent and those who reject them as irrelevant even if they do exist, some feminists offer a middle-of-the-road "solution to the women problem."[23] We should not try to do away with sex roles altogether, for some tasks are "more congenial" to one sex than the other. Simply leave all the options open. Adopt a pluralistic view of male and female roles whereby each person is free to choose the life-style which suits his or her particular disposition. This approach avoids the oppression of rigidly sex-defined roles without ignoring or destroying the distinction between the sexes and without at the same time endorsing the position that "equality means similarity." At the same time it recognizes that there are *no* sex-related grounds for excluding women from many of the rights from which they have been excluded.

REVERSE DISCRIMINATION

The law itself, we have seen, can be the purveyor of the most invidious forms of discrimination and is responsible for much unjust social stratification and inequality. What can be done, what ought to be done, in situations where not only individuals but entire classes of persons continue to suffer the residual effects of past institutionalized injustice—the effects of slavery and racial discrimination or the effects of sexist laws and social practices? It need hardly be said that we have yet to reach a state of affairs of non-discrimination where each person is considered on his or her own merits regardless of sex or race. Racism and sexism are still rampant in our social practices, even after being declared illegal. What can be done to assure genuine equality of opportunity under those conditions? Is mere enforcement of non-discrimination—an enormously difficult task in itself—adequate? Many members of minority groups and many women would settle for that! Or is compensatory action of some type also required? To say to those who have been disadvantaged by past institutionalized injustice (and *current* practices), "The door is now open, so sink or swim in the competition with the majority, non-disadvantaged class," may be itself unfair. Benign neglect of the effects of the sins of the past may assure continued inequality, not equality. Thus, many argue that mere non-discrimination, even if it could be attained by its simple declaration, will not bring equality to those who have been disadvantaged by past injustices. Something more is needed, some positive, affirmative action to bring disadvantaged minorities and women into the mainstream so that they can compete on equal terms with others. But, to accomplish that or to reach a condition where distributive justice prevails, there must first be compensatory justice in the form of preferential treatment for minorities and women as classes. That is, given the fact that

women and racial minorities have been discriminated against in the past on the basis of the irrelevant characteristics of sex and race, we are now justified, perhaps even morally required, to discriminate in their favor on the basis of the same characteristics. The basis for preferential treatment, then, is two-fold: (1) To compensate for injuries suffered from society's institutionalized injustices, society now *owes* this special treatment to rectify those injustices. (2) Without that special preference, it will be impossible to attain a state of distributive justice where ultimately only non-discrimination (no preferential treatment) is required or permitted. There is, then, both a backward-looking and a forward-looking thrust to the demand for preferential treatment.

During the past several years (through the Office of Civil Rights) there has been officially condoned preferential treatment of women and racial minorities, the preference taking a weak and a strong form. The weak form gives preference to a minority member or woman in contexts in which that candidate is *equally* qualified as a majority candidate. The strong form gives such preference even when the minority member or woman is *less* qualified. Numerical goals and quotas for the hiring and promotion of minorities and women have been imposed on many institutions. The response from many quarters is that this preference for some is discrimination against others, that majority members are being discriminated against because of their race or sex—that, in effect, "reverse" discrimination occurs.

As might be expected, those policies of preferential treatment have engendered great debate. Several questions arise. (1) Do the recently enacted civil rights laws permit such preference? (2) Does such preference violate the Constitution? (3) Is such preference unjust? (4) Is such preference immoral or unjustified? These are all separate, though related, issues. The points of reference for assessing preferential policies differ in each approach.

Concerning the first question, some contend that the 1964 Civil Rights act, later amended by the Equal Employment Opportunity Act of 1972, and the Affirmative Action Program which came into existence basically with Executive Order 11246 absolutely prohibit preferential treatment on the basis of race or sex. But the implementors of these laws, they declare, have imposed numerical goals and quotas on employers, thereby requiring not merely equal opportunity but specific *results,* namely the hiring, promotion, and admission of racial minorities and women regardless of competitive abilities. This amounts to discrimination in favor of some on the basis of sex or race and, conversely, discrimination against others who are excluded on grounds of sex or race. Suits charging "reverse discrimination" are now appearing in the courts. Recently, A T & T, after having signed a consent decree with the federal government to hire more women, was successfully sued by a man who charged that he was unfairly denied promotion to a supervisor's job because of discrimination in favor of women. But we must distinguish the law itself from the implementation of the law.

Does preferential treatment on the basis of sex or race, even that intended to rectify past injustice and produce equality, violate the Constitution? The Court ducked the chance to directly answer this question by declaring the *DeFunis* case moot.[24] This question is quite complex and parties have lined up on both sides. The Supreme Court of the State of Washington concluded in the *DeFunis* case that the non-invidious use of race is constitutionally permissible. The Constitution "is color conscious to prevent the perpetuation of discrimination and to undo the effects of past segregation."[25] Most appeals to race are invidious and unconstitutional, but in cases in which a "compelling state interest" requires that we attend to race, it is permissible to do so. The most "rigid scrutiny" is required in the use of racial classification, but color blindness in some contexts may prevent social justice. In the process of school desegregation, for example, racial classification is essential in formulating a remedy. "We must take care," Ronald Dworkin admonishes us, "not to use the equal protection clause to cheat ourselves of equality."[26]

Others, on the other hand, argue that all racial discrimination is unconstitutional, whether or not it is intended to rectify injustice or bring some so-called "compelling state interest" to fruition. Challenging the compelling state interest argument as a basis for racial discrimination, Justice Douglas said in his *DeFunis* dissent: "If discrimination based on race is constitutionally permissible when those who hold the reins can come up with 'compelling' reasons to justify it, then constitutional guarantees acquire an accordianlike quality."[27] If equal protection of the law can be overriden in this way, Justice Douglas seems to say, then the constitutional guarantee is no guarantee at all. It is an illusion. Racial classification which does not result in racial discrimination may be permitted. This, it is claimed by many, is what happened in the school desegretation cases where a racial mix was decreed (*Swann* and *Green*). In these cases no benefits were withheld from anyone on grounds of race. But in the case of preferential admissions, employment, and promotion of racial minorities or women, racial discrimination against others does occur and benefits are arbitrarily withheld, for some persons are excluded from consideration for employment, admission, and promotion solely because of their race or sex. Even the Washington court which ruled against DeFunis admitted that preferential admissions is "not benign with respect to non-minority students who are displaced by it."

This brings us to the question, Is preferential treatment on the basis of sex or race unjust? The Washington Court admitted that some injustice may be done to majority applicants by a preferential policy (involving a limited number of seats in the law school). But, it held, it is both constitutional and just to do this if it is required to bring a "compelling state interest" to fruition. In this case the compelling interest is the moving of minorities into the profession of law in order to help effect long-term racial justice.

Others contend that there is no compelling state interest—there can be none!—which requires the violation of a constitutional guarantee or principle as fundamental as equal protection of the laws. One cannot, without gross inconsistency and without undermining the Constitution itself, violate this basic principle of the Constitution.

The above makes it clear that reasons of justice might conflict—that there may be conflicts of rights, as it were, in this case between the right to genuine equality of opportunity of someone disadvantaged by past institutionalized injustice and the right to equal protection of the law or to nondiscrimination of another. Justice does not always speak with an undivided voice. The conflict can also appear in the form of tension between the right to economic justice and the right to equal protection. The uniform application of meritocratic standards of access to employment, admissions, and promotions may have, and often does have, the effect of condemning members of minorities to continued economic injustice, injustice which they suffer now because of non-access and injustice in the past. Under these circumstances, Thomas Nagel argues, those persons with better qualifications to succeed in certain positions "cannot claim that justice requires the allocation of positions on the basis of ability, because the result of such allocation, in the present system, is serious injustice of a different kind."[28] In weighing conflicting rights, Nagel here seems to be saying, equal protection might be justly violated in the name of economic justice; or, perhaps more generally, he is urging that we place compensatory justice in front of sheer distributive justice for all. This argument, if sound, would appear to support the priority of compensatory action on behalf of *anyone* who has been unjustly disadvantaged and who consequently suffers economic injustice. That is, it would appear to support racially and sexually neutral compensatory measures, even though it may be that the bulk of those who benefit from the policy would be minority members and women.

In the case of conflicts of principles of justice, whether it be between equal protection and equal opportunity or between equal protection and economic justice, and whether we are speaking of justice under a constitutional system or under a philosophical system (such as that of Rawls), we are forced to opt for some hierarchy of principles of justice and provide some rationale for that hierarchy.

Several further problems involving preferential treatment on the basis of sex or race as means of effecting compensatory and distributive justice must be noted. A basic question is whether compensation can be or should be awarded to racial minorities or women as classes, in contrast to compensation to individuals. Both sides of this question have been argued forcefully. Those who insist that, at least for blacks and women, it must be on an individual basis argue that compensation as a principle of justice itself requires a specific response in the form of redress to a specific individual who has

been wronged or injured by another party. It also requires that the compensatory redress be proportionate to the injury suffered and that it be exacted from the party responsible for the injury. Blanket preferential treatment on the basis of race or sex violates both of these requirements of compensatory justice, namely, proportionality and exacting redress from the guilty party. Blanket policies providing compensation and distribution on a class basis for either blacks or women have the effect of exacting and awarding compensation arbitrarily. It is often exacted from majority members who are themselves innocent of any wrongdoing but who are excluded from certain opportunities on the basis of their race or sex in order to make room for the minority member or woman. And it may be awarded to minority members and women who themselves have escaped the effects of past institutionalized injustice, who in fact have advantaged backgrounds in contrast to some whites and males.

Those who argue for the class approach to compensation (and distribution) agree that these injustices occur, but they hold that the class approach is the only feasible one. There is ample evidence of a wide economic differential between whites and blacks, males and females, and of widely disproportionate numbers of these groups in the professions, politics, and the like. This is the direct result of past institutionalized injustice and current on-going racial and sexual discrimination which has persisted even after declared illegal. The only viable way of eradicating these effects is a class approach. Some injustice results, yes, but there is less injustice than there would be by attempting rectification on an individual basis. For in most cases there is no guilty individual from whom to exact compensation. There is only a guilty society, as it were, which each of us inherited, where the progenitors of racism and, to a lesser degree, sexism are dead and gone but where the residue of those ills remains in our minds, hearts, and practices, if not in our laws. That sort of institutionalized injustice requires an institutionalized response, namely, preferential treatment for the classes who were discriminated against in the past.

A final point of reference for assessing preferential policies has been that of morality as a whole, not simply justice. Those who take this approach begin with the assumption that considerations of justice (compensatory and distributive) are only part of the relevant considerations in assessing such policies. Other moral concerns not reducible to justice must be weighed—benevolence or charity and social utility, for example. Perhaps the duty of benevolence requires that one forfeit certain rights under certain conditions? That is a possible rationale for preferential policies, though not one which is prominent in the literature. Perhaps reasons of social utility are so strong that they override reasons of justice in some contexts? This is an argument sometimes invoked, but again, even among those whose moral frameworks will permit reasons of utility to override those of justice, there is disagreement over whether the overall consequences of preferential policies are good or bad.

Those who argue that the results are (or would be) good put their case roughly in this way: Past institutionalized injustice has handicapped large numbers of persons in our society. As a result their competitive abilities and the quality of their lives have been greatly lowered. Furthermore, the vestiges of that institutionalized injustice still result in the systematic exclusion of many members of minority groups and many women from equal opportunity. Such pervasive unfairness breeds social discord and disorder. If a temporary policy of discrimination in favor of such persons could help overcome the handicapping effects of past sins and rid us of the vestiges of those sins, it would alleviate a basic cause of social unrest and disorder, bring a higher quality life to millions, and lay the foundation for genuine equality for future generations. Even if this discrimination in favor of some involves discrimination against others, it is morally justified.

Those who argue that on the whole the consequences of preferential policies are bad point to other effects—to the deleterious consequences for society if race or sex were to become central criteria for access to positions and if meritocratic criteria were made secondary, and to the possible wholesale non-cooperation by majority members against whom such policies discriminate and the negative impact of that non-cooperation on social institutions and society itself. They also point to the fact that preferential policies for some groups open the door for preferential policies for many other groups who also suffer from past (and current) injustice and to the social disorder which such a wide array of discriminatory policies would generate.

Thus, there is disagreement on the propriety of preferential policies, whether the grounds of assessment are social utility or morality generally, justice, the Constitution, or civil rights laws. The selections by Professors Lisa Newton and Tom Beauchamp explore this complex question in some detail, the former arguing against reverse discrimination; the latter, in favor of it. Professor Newton believes that reverse discrimination raises insoluble problems in both principle and practice. Concerning the issue of principle, it is a paradox, if not a contradiction in terms, to argue that the ideal of equality justifies the violation of justice. Reverse discrimination "undermines the foundation of the very ideal in whose name it is advocated." Furthermore, in practice, there is no basis for drawing the line between one group of discriminees and another. Literally hundreds of groups would be eligible for preferential treatment. Nor is there any way of knowing how much preferential treatment to give. The practice, Newton believes, will result in "power struggles and popularity contests," not in social justice. Professor Beauchamp, on the other hand, argues that some policies which result in reverse discrimination are justifiable. His rationale is *not* primarily that society must compensate for past sins. Rather it is that such policies are required to eliminate present discriminatory practices and to make sure that such practices do not continue. Discriminatory attitudes are deeply entrenched in our society, Beauchamp argues, and he points to a variety of empirical evidence to indicate the depth of that entrenchment. Although reverse discrimination is prima facie unjust and immoral, for it results in some injustice, other considerations of both justice and social utility justify the practice. Affirmative action programs, he suggests, are far too "light-weight" to solve the problem of on-going discrimination.

The *DeFunis* case (presented here in part from the case as argued to the Washington Supreme Court) provides a concrete case of litigation in which the petitioner, Marco DeFunis, charged the University of Washington Law School with reverse discrimination. The final selection is an abbreviation of Justice Douglas' dissent in the *DeFunis* case (which was declared moot), which discusses the merits of the case.

William T. Blackstone

NOTES

1. Joel Feinberg, *Social Philosophy* (Englewood Cliffs, N.J.: Prentice-Hall, 1973), p. 98.

2. Frank Michelman, "Foreword: On Protecting the Poor Through the Fourteenth Amendment," *Harvard Law Review* 83 (1969).

3. Ibid.

4. I borrow the phrase from the discussion by Isaiah Berlin, "Equality," *Proceedings of the Aristotelian Society,* 56 (1955–56).

5. John Rawls, *A Theory of Justice.* (Cambridge, Mass.: Harvard University Press, 1971), p. 235.

6. Ralf Dahrendorf, "On the Origin of Social Inequalities," in *Philosophy, Politics, and Society,* edited by Peter Laslett and W. G. Runciman (Oxford: Basil Blackwell, 1962).

7. Bernard Schwartz, *Commentary on the Constitution of the United States,* Vol. II, *Equality, Belief and Dignity* (New York, 1968), p. 487.

8. But we are reminded by Richard Hare in another context that there may be "conscientious" Nazis. See Richard Hare, *Freedom and Reason* (New York: Oxford University Press, 1963), chapter IX.

9. Martin Luther King, Jr., *The Trumpet of Conscience* (New York: Harper & Row, 1967), p. 55.

10. Ibid., p. 60.

11. Ibid., p. 55.

12. John Rawls, *A Theory of Justice,* p. 101.

13. See Norman Daniels, ed., *Reading Rawls* (New York: Basic Books, 1976), for a collection of critical articles on Rawls' theory and a bibliography.

14. John Stuart Mill, *Utilitarianism,* Everyman Edition (London 1910), p. 59. Though I here use Mill's position as a point of reference, what is said applies generally to utilitarianism.

15. Ibid., p. 42.

16. Ibid., p. 44.

17. Ibid., pp. 57–58.

18. Ibid., p. 54.

19. Ibid., p. 55.

20. David Thomson, *Equality,* Cambridge University Press, 1949.

21. Irving Thalberg, "Visceral Racism," *The Monist* 56, No. 1, (January 1972).

22. Chief Justice Earl Warren, "All Men Are Created Equal," the 27th Annual Benjamin Cardoza Lecture, published by the Association of the Bar of the City of New York, 42 West 44th Street (1970).

23. Sheila K. Johnson, "A Woman Anthropologist Offers a Solution to the Woman Problem," *The New York Times Magazine,* August 27, 1972.

24. 94 S. Ct. 1704 (1974).

25. Wash. 507 P2d 1180.

26. Ronald Dworkin, "The Defunis Case: The Right to Go to Law School," *The New York Review,* February 5, 1976, p. 33.

27. 40 L Ed 2d 184.

28. Thomas Nagel, "Equal Treatment and Compensatory Discrimination," *Philosophy and Public Affairs* 2, No. 4 (Summer 1973): 356.

49. LETTER FROM BIRMINGHAM CITY JAIL

Martin Luther King, Jr.

My dear Fellow Clergymen,

While confined here in the Birmingham City Jail, I came across your recent statement calling our present activities "unwise and untimely." Seldom, if ever, do I pause to answer criticism of my work and ideas. If I sought to answer all of the criticisms that cross my desk, my secretaries would be engaged in little else in the course of the day and I would have no time for constructive work. But since I feel that you are men of genuine goodwill and your criticisms are sincerely set forth, I would like to answer your statement in what I hope will be patient and reasonable terms.

I think I should give the reason for my being in Birmingham, since you have been influenced by the argument of "outsiders coming in." I have the honor of serving as president of the Southern Christian Leadership Conference, an organization operating in every Southern state with headquarters in Atlanta, Georgia. We have some eighty-five affiliate organizations all across the South— one being the Alabama Christian Movement for Human Rights. Whenever necessary and possible we share staff, educational, and financial resources with our affiliates. Several months ago our local affiliate here in Birmingham invited us to be on call to engage in a nonviolent direct action program if such were deemed necessary. We readily consented and when the hour came we lived up to our promises. So I am here, along with several members of my staff, because we were invited here. I am here because I have basic organizational ties here. Beyond this, I am in Birmingham because injustice is here. Just as the eighth century prophets left their little villages and carried their "thus saith the Lord" far beyond the boundaries of their home town, and just as the Apostle Paul left his little village of Tarsus and carried the gospel of Jesus Christ to practically every hamlet and city of the Graeco-Roman world, I too am compelled to carry the gospel of freedom beyond my particular home town. Like Paul, I must constantly respond to the Macedonian call for aid.

Moreover, I am cognizant of the interrelatedness of all communities and states. I cannot sit idly by in Atlanta and not be concerned about what happens in Birmingham. Injustice anywhere is a threat to justice everywhere. We are caught in an inescapable network of mutuality tied in a single garment of destiny. Whatever affects one directly affects all indirectly. Never again can we afford to live with the narrow, provincial "outside agitator" idea. Anyone who lives inside the United States can never be considered an outsider anywhere in this country.

You deplore the demonstrations that are presently taking place in Birmingham. But I am sorry that your statement did not express a similar concern for the conditions that brought the demonstrations into being. I am sure that each of you would want to go beyond the superficial social ana-

Martin Luther King, Jr. *Letter from Birmingham City Jail.* Reprinted by permission of the American Friends Service Committee, Philadelphia, Pennsylvania.

lyst who looks merely at effects, and does not grapple with underlying causes. I would not hesitate to say that it is unfortunate that so-called demonstrations are taking place in Birmingham at this time, but I would say in more emphatic terms that it is even more unfortunate that the white power structure of this city left the Negro community with no other alternative.

In any nonviolent campaign there are four basic steps: (1) collection of the facts to determine whether injustices are alive; (2) negotiation; (3) self-purification; and (4) direct action. We have gone through all of these steps in Birmingham. There can be no gainsaying the fact that racial injustice engulfs this community. Birmingham is probably the most thoroughly segregated city in the United States. Its ugly record of police brutality is known in every section of this country. Its unjust treatment of Negroes in the courts is a notorious reality. There have been more unsolved bombings of Negro homes and churches in Birmingham than any city in this nation. These are the hard, brutal, and unbelievable facts. On the basis of these conditions Negro leaders sought to negotiate with the city fathers. But the political leaders consistently refused to engage in good faith negotiation.

Then came the opportunity last September to talk with some of the leaders of the economic community. In these negotiating sessions certain promises were made by the merchants—such as the promise to remove the humiliating racial signs from the stores. On the basis of these promises Rev. Shuttlesworth and the leaders of the Alabama Christian Movement for Human Rights agreed to call a moratorium on any type of demonstrations. As the weeks and months unfolded we realized that we were the victims of a broken promise. The signs remained. As in so many experiences of the past we were confronted with blasted hopes, and the dark shadow of a deep disappointment settled upon us. So we had no alternative except that of preparing for direct action, whereby we would present our very bodies as a means of laying our case before the conscience of the local and national community. We were not unmindful of the difficulties involved. So we decided to go through a process of self-purification. We started having workshops on non-

violence and repeatedly asked ourselves the questions, "Are you able to accept blows without retaliating? Are you able to endure the ordeals of jail?"

We decided to set our direct action program around the Easter season, realizing that with the exception of Christmas, this was the largest shopping period of the year. Knowing that a strong economic withdrawal program would be the by-product of direct action, we felt that this was the best time to bring pressure on the merchants for the needed changes. Then it occurred to us that the March election was ahead, and so we speedily decided to postpone action until after election day. When we discovered that Mr. Connor was in the run-off, we decided again to postpone action so that the demonstrations could not be used to cloud the issues. At this time we agreed to begin our nonviolent witness the day after the run-off.

This reveals that we did not move irresponsibly into direct action. We too wanted to see Mr. Connor defeated; so we went through postponement after postponement to aid in this community need. After this we felt that direct action could be delayed no longer.

You may well ask, "Why direct action? Why sit-ins, marches, etc? Isn't negotiation a better path?" You are exactly right in your call for negotiation. Indeed, this is the purpose of direct action. Nonviolent direct action seeks to create such a crisis and establish such creative tension that a community that has constantly refused to negotiate is forced to confront the issue. It seeks so to dramatize the issue that it can no longer be ignored. I just referred to the creation of tension as a part of the work of the nonviolent resister. This may sound rather shocking. But I must confess that I am not afraid of the word tension. I have earnestly worked and preached against violent tension, and there is a type of constructive nonviolent tension that is necessary for growth. Just as Socrates felt that it was necessary to create a tension in the mind so that individuals could rise from the bondage of myths and half-truths to the unfettered realm of creative analysis and objective appraisal, we must see the need of having nonviolent gadflies to create the kind of tension in society that will help men rise from the dark depths of prejudice and racism to the majestic heights of understanding and brotherhood. So the purpose of the direct action is to create a situation so crisis-packed that it will inevitably open the door to negotiation. We, therefore, concur with you in your call for negotiation. Too long has our beloved Southland been bogged down in the tragic attempt to live in monologue rather than dialogue.

One of the basic points in your statement is that our acts are untimely. Some have asked, "Why didn't you give the new administration time to act?" The only answer that I can give to this inquiry is that the new administration must be prodded about as much as the outgoing one before it acts. We will be sadly mistaken if we feel that the election of Mr. Boutwell will bring the millennium to Birmingham. While Mr. Boutwell is much more articulate and gentle than Mr. Connor, they are both segregationists dedicated to the task of maintaining the status quo. The hope I see in Mr. Boutwell is that he will be reasonable enough to see the futility of massive resistance to desegregation. But he will not see this without pressure from the devotees of civil rights. My friends, I must say to you that we have not made a single gain in civil rights without determined legal and nonviolent pressure. History is the long and tragic story of the fact that privileged groups seldom give up their privileges voluntarily. Individuals may see the moral light and voluntarily give up their unjust posture; but as Reinhold Niebuhr has reminded us, groups are more immoral than individuals.

We know through painful experience that freedom is never voluntarily given by the oppressor; it must be demanded by the oppressed. Frankly I have never yet engaged in a direct action movement that was "well timed," according to the timetable of those who have not suffered unduly from the disease of segregation. For years now I have heard the word "Wait!" It rings in the ear of every Negro with a piercing familiarity. This "wait" has almost always meant "never." It has been a tranquilizing thalidomide, relieving the emotional stress for a moment, only to give birth to an ill-formed infant of frustration. We must come to see with the distinguished jurist of yesterday that "justice too long delayed is justice denied." We have waited for more than three hundred and forty years for our constitutional and God-given rights. The nations of Asia and Africa are moving with jet-like speed toward the goal of political independence, and we still creep at horse and buggy pace toward the gaining of a cup of coffee at a lunch counter.

I guess it is easy for those who have never felt the stinging darts of segregation to say wait. But when you have seen vicious mobs lynch your mothers and fathers at will and drown your sisters and brothers at whim; when you have seen hate-filled policeman curse, kick, brutalize, and even kill your black brothers and sisters with impunity; when you see the vast majority of your twenty million Negro brothers smothering in an air-tight cage of poverty in the midst of an affluent society; when you suddenly find your tongue twisted and your speech stammering as you seek to explain to your six-year-old daughter why she can't go to the public amusement park that has just been advertised on television, and see tears welling up in her little eyes when she is told that Funtown is closed to colored children, and see the depressing clouds of inferiority begin to form in her little mental sky, and see her begin to distort her little personality by unconsciously developing a bitterness toward white people; when you have to concoct an answer for a five-year-old son asking in agonizing pathos: "Daddy, why do white people treat colored people so mean?"; when you take a cross country drive and find it necessary to sleep night after night in the uncomfortable corners of your automobile because no motel will accept you; when you are humiliated day in and day out by nagging signs reading "white" men and "colored"; when your first name becomes "nigger" and your middle name becomes "boy" (however old you are) and your last name becomes "John," and when your wife and mother are never given the respected title "Mrs."; when you are harried by day and haunted by night by the fact that you are a Negro, living constantly at tip-toe stance never quite knowing what to expect next, and plagued with inner fears and outer resentments; when you are forever fighting a degenerating sense of "nobodiness";—then you will understand why we find it difficult to wait. There comes a time when the cup of endurance runs over, and men are no longer willing to be plunged into an abyss of injustice where they experience the bleakness of corroding despair. I hope, sirs, you can understand our legitimate and unavoidable impatience.

You express a great deal of anxiety over our willingness to break laws. This is certainly a legitimate concern. Since we so diligently urge people to obey the Supreme Court's decision of 1954 outlawing segregation in the public schools, it is rather strange and paradoxical to find us consciously breaking laws. One may well ask, "How can you advocate breaking some laws and obeying others?" The answer is found in the fact that there are two types of laws; There are *just* laws and there are *unjust* laws. I would be the first to advocate obeying just laws. One has not only a legal but moral responsibility to obey just laws. Conversely, one has a moral responsibility to disobey unjust laws. I would agree with Saint Augustine that "An unjust law is no law at all."

Now what is the difference between the two? How does one determine when a law is just or unjust? A just law is a man-made code that squares with the moral law or the law of God. An unjust law is a code that is out of harmony with the moral law. To put it in the terms of Saint Thomas Aquinas, an unjust law is a human law that is not rooted in eternal and natural law. Any law that uplifts human personality is just. Any law that degrades human personality is unjust. All segregation statutes are unjust because segregation distorts the soul and damages the personality. It gives the segregator a false sense of superiority and the segregated a false sense of inferiority. To use the words of Martin Buber, the great Jewish philosopher, segregation substitutes an "I-it" relationship for the "I-thou" relationship, and ends up relegating persons to the status of things. So segregation is not only politically, economically, and sociologically unsound, but it is morally wrong and sinful. Paul Tillich has said that sin is separation. Isn't segregation an existential expression of man's tragic separation, an expression of his awful estrangement, his terrible sinfulness? So I can urge men to obey the 1954 decision of the Supreme Court because it is morally right, and I can urge them to disobey segregation ordinances because they are morally wrong.

Let us turn to a more concrete example of just and unjust laws. An unjust law is a code that a majority inflicts on a minority that is not binding on itself. This is *difference* made legal. On the other hand a just law is a code that a majority compels a minority to follow that it is willing to follow itself. This is *sameness* made legal.

Let me give another explanation. An unjust law is a code inflicted upon a minority which that minority had no part in enacting or creating because they did not have the unhampered right to vote. Who can say the legislature of Alabama which set up the segregation laws was democratically elected? Throughout the state of Alabama all types of conniving methods are used to prevent Negroes from becoming registered voters and there are some counties without a single Negro registered to vote despite the fact that the Negro constitutes a majority of the population. Can any law set up in such a state be considered democratically structured?

These are just a few examples of unjust and just laws. There are some instances when a law is just on its face but unjust in its application. For instance, I was arrested Friday on a charge of parading without a permit. Now there is nothing wrong with an ordinance which requires a permit for a parade, but when the ordinance is used to preserve segregation and to deny citizens the First Amedment privilege of peaceful assembly and peaceful protest, then it becomes unjust.

I hope you can see the distinction I am trying to point out. In no sense do I advocate evading or defying the law as the rabid segregationist would do. This would lead to anarchy. One who breaks an unjust law must do it *openly, lovingly* (not hatefully as the white mothers did in New Orleans when they were seen on television screaming "nigger, nigger, nigger") and with a willingness to accept the penalty. I submit that an individual who breaks a law that conscience tells him is unjust, and willingly accepts the penalty by staying in jail to arouse the conscience of the community over its injustice, is in reality expressing the very highest respect for law.

Of course there is nothing new about this kind of civil disobedience. It was seen sublimely in the refusal of Shadrach, Meshach, and Abednego to obey the laws of Nebuchadnezzar because a higher moral law was involved. It was practiced superbly by the early Christians who were willing to face hungry lions and the excruciating pain of chopping blocks, before submitting to certain unjust laws of the Roman Empire. To a degree academic freedom is a reality today because Socrates practiced civil disobedience.

We can never forget that everything Hitler did in Germany was "legal" and everything the Hungarian freedom fighters did in Hungary was "illegal." It was "illegal" to aid and comfort a Jew in Hitler's Germany. But I am sure that, if I had lived in Germany during that time, I would have aided and comforted my Jewish brothers even though it was illegal. If I lived in a communist country today where certain principles dear to the Christian faith are suppressed, I believe I would openly advocate disobeying these anti-religious laws.

I must make two honest confessions to you, my Christian and Jewish brothers. First I must confess that over the last few years I have been gravely disappointed with the white moderate. I have almost reached the regrettable conclusion that the Negroes' great stumbling block in the stride toward freedom is not the White Citizens' "Counciler" or the Ku Klux Klanner, but the white moderate who is more devoted to "order" than to justice; who prefers a negative peace which is the absence of tension to a positive peace which is the presence of justice; who constantly says "I agree with you in the goal you seek, but I can't agree with your methods of direct action"; who paternalistically feels that he can set the time-table for another man's freedom; who lives by the myth of time and who constantly advises the Negro to wait until a "more convenient season." Shallow understanding from people of good will is more frustrating than absolute misunderstanding from people of ill will. Lukewarm acceptance is much more bewildering than outright rejection. . . .

I started thinking about the fact that I stand in the middle of two opposing forces in the Negro community. One is a force of complacency made up of Negroes who, as a result of long years of oppression, have been so completely drained of self-respect and a sense of "somebodiness" that they have adjusted to segregation, and of a few Negroes in the middle class who, because of a degree of academic and economic security, and because at points they profit by segregation, have unconsciously become insensitive to the problems of the masses. The other force is one of bitterness and hatred and comes perilously close to advocating violence. It is expressed in the various black nationalist groups that are springing up over the nation, the largest and best known being Elijah Muhammad's Muslim movement. This movement is nourished by the contemporary frustration over the continued existence of racial discrimination. It is made up of people who have lost faith in America, who have absolutely repudiated Christianity, and who have concluded that the white man is an incurable "devil." I have tried to stand between these two forces saying that we need not follow the "do-nothingism" of the complacent or the hatred and despair of the black nationalist. There is the more excellent way of love and nonviolent protest. I'm grateful to God that, through the Negro church, the dimension of nonviolence entered our struggle. If this philosophy had not emerged I am convinced that by now many streets of the South would be flowing with floods of blood. And I am further convinced that if our white brothers dismiss us as "rabble rousers" and "outside agitators"—those of us who are working through the channels of nonviolent direct action—and refuse to support our nonviolent efforts, millions of Negroes, out of frustration and despair, will seek solace and security in black nationalist ideologies, a development that will lead inevitably to a frightening racial nightmare. . . .

. . . I must honestly reiterate that I have been disappointed with the Church. I do not say that as one of those negative critics who can always find something wrong with the Church. I say it as a minister of the gospel, who loves the Church; who was nurtured in its bosom; who has been sustained by its spiritual blessings and who will remain true to it as long as the cord of life shall lengthen.

I had the strange feeling when I was suddenly catapulted into the leadership of the bus protest in Montgomery several years ago that we would have the support of the white Church. I felt that the white ministers, priests, and rabbis of the South would be some of our strongest allies. Instead, some have been outright opponents, refusing to understand the freedom movement and mis-representing its leaders; all too many others have been more cautious than courageous and have remained silent behind the anesthetizing security of stained glass windows. . . .

I hope the Church as a whole will meet the challenge of this decisive hour. But even if the Church does not come to the aid of justice, I have no despair about the future. I have no fear about the outcome of our struggle in Birmingham, even if our motives are presently misunderstood. We will reach the goal of freedom in Birmingham and all over the nation, because the goal of America is freedom. Abused and scorned though we may be, our destiny is tied up with the destiny of America. Before the pilgrims landed at Plymouth, we were here. Before the pen of Jefferson etched across the pages of history the majestic words of the Declaration of Independence, we were here. For more than two centuries our foreparents labored in this country without wages; they made cotton "king"; and they built the homes of their masters in the midst of brutal injustice and shameful humiliation—and yet out of a bottomless vitality they continued to thrive and develop. If the inexpressible cruelties of slavery could not stop us, the opposition we now face will surely fail. We will win our freedom because the sacred heritage of our nation and the eternal will of God are embodied in our echoing demands.

I must close now. But before closing I am impelled to mention one other point in your statement that troubled me profoundly. You warmly commended the Birmingham police force for keeping "order" and "preventing violence." I don't believe you would have so warmly commended the police force if you had seen its angry violent dogs literally biting six unarmed, nonviolent Negroes. I don't believe you would so quickly commend the policemen if you would observe their ugly and inhuman treatment of Negroes here in the city jail; if you would watch them push and curse old Negro women and young Negro girls; if you would see them slap and kick old Negro men and young Negro boys; if you will observe them, as they did on two occasions, refuse to give us food because we wanted to sing our grace together. I'm sorry that I can't join you in your praise for the police department.

It is true that they have been rather disciplined in their public handling of the demonstrators. In this sense they have been rather publicly "nonviolent." But for what purpose? To preserve the evil system of segregation. Over the last few years I have consistently preached that nonviolence demands that the means we use must be as pure as the ends we seek. So I have tried to make it clear that it is wrong to use immoral means to attain moral ends. But now I must affirm that it is just as wrong, or even more so, to use moral means to preserve immoral ends. Maybe Mr. Connor and his policemen have been rather publicly nonviolent, as Chief Pritchett was in Albany, Georgia, but they have used the moral means of nonviolence to maintain the immoral end of flagrant racial injustice. T. S. Eliot has said that there is no greater treason than to do the right deed for the wrong reason.

I wish you had commended the Negro sit-inners and demonstrators of Birmingham for their sublime courage, their willingness to suffer, and their amazing discipline in the midst of the most inhuman provocation. One day the South will recognize its real heroes. They will be the James Merediths, courageously and with a majestic sense of purpose, facing jeering and hostile mobs and the agonizing loneliness that characterizes the life of the pioneer. They will be old, oppressed, battered Negro women, symbolized in a seventy-two year old woman of Montgomery, Alabama, who rose up with a sense of dignity and with her people decided not to ride the segregated buses, and responded to one who inquired about her tiredness with ungrammatical profundity: "My feets is tired, but my soul is rested." They will be young high school and college students, young ministers of the gospel and a host of the elders, courageously and nonviolently sitting in at lunch counters and willingly going to jail for conscience sake. One day the South will know that when these disinherited children of God sat down at lunch counters they were in reality standing up for the best in the American dream and the most sacred values in our Judeo-Christian heritage, and thus carrying our whole nation back to great wells of democracy which were dug deep by the founding fathers in the formulation of the Constitution and the Declaration of Independence.

Never before have I written a letter this long (or should I say a book?). I'm afraid that it is much too long to take your precious time. I can assure you that it would have been much shorter if I had been writing from a comfortable desk, but what else is there to do when you are alone for days in the dull monotony of a narrow jail cell other than write long letters, think strange thoughts, and pray long prayers?

If I have said anything in this letter that is an overstatement of the truth and is indicative of an unreasonable impatience, I beg you to forgive me. If I have said anything in this letter that is an understatement of the truth and is indicative of my having a patience that makes me patient with anything less than brotherhood, I beg God to forgive me.

I hope this letter finds you strong in the faith. I also hope that circumstances will soon make it possible for me to meet each of you, not as an integrationist or a civil rights leader, but as a fellow clergyman and a Christian brother. Let us all hope that the dark clouds of racial prejudice will soon pass away and the deep fog of misunderstanding will be lifted from our fear-drenched communities and in some not too distant tomorrow the radiant stars of love and brotherhood will shine over our great nation with all of their scintillating beauty.

*Yours for the cause of
Peace and Brotherhood*
MARTIN LUTHER KING, JR.

50. INSTITUTIONAL AND IDEOLOGICAL ROOTS OF RACISM

Louis Knowles
Kenneth Prewitt

THE REPORT OF THE NATIONAL ADVISORY COMMISSION ON CIVIL DISORDERS: A COMMENT

The contemporary document perhaps most indicative of the ideology of official America is the influential "Kerner Commission Report." . . .

The Report asks: "Why Did It Happen?" A painful truth is then recorded: "White racism is essentially responsible for the explosive mixture which has been accumulating in our cities since the end of World War II." Unfortunately, the Report too quickly leaves this truth and emphasizes the familiar list of "conditions" of "Negro unrest." Paraded before the reader are observations about the frustrated hopes of Negroes, the "belief" among Negroes that there is police brutality, the high

Reprinted from Louis Knowles and Kenneth Prewitt, *Institutional Racism in America,* © 1969, pp. 2–6, 124–6, 129, 131, 133. Reprinted by permission of Prentice-Hall, Inc., Englewood Cliffs, New Jersey.

unemployment in the ghetto, the weak family structure and social disorganization in the Negro community, and so on.

It is the immediate conditions giving rise to civil disorders which the Report stresses, not the *causes behind the conditions.* Perhaps what is needed is a National Advisory Commission on White Racism. If a group of men sets out to investigate "civil disorders," their categories of analysis are fixed and, from our perspective, parochial. In spite of their admission that "white institutions created [the ghetto], white institutions maintain it, and white society condones it," the categories with which the commission operated screened out the responsibility of white institutions and pushed the commission back to the familiar account of "black pathology."

In the important section "What Can Be Done," this fault is even more clearly seen. Certainly it is true that much accumulated frustration would be relieved if the sweeping recommendations concerning administration of justice, police and community relations, housing, unemployment and underemployment, welfare thinking, and so forth were implemented. The Report merits the closest attention for its statement that issues of race and poverty must receive the highest national priority, and for its further argument that what is needed is a massive commitment by all segments of society. What disappoints the reader is that the section "What Can Be Done" only accentuates the shortsightedness of the section "Why Did It Happen." The recommendations are directed at ghetto conditions and *not* at the white structures and practices which are responsible for those conditions. Thus, while it is true that improved communication between the ghetto and city hall might defuse the pressures building up in the black community, the issue is not "better communication" but "full representation." Black people should not have to communicate with city hall; they should be represented at city hall.

The shallowness of the Report as social analysis is again reflected in its discussion of black protest movements. The Report does not uncover a critical social dynamic: militancy is first of all a response to white resistance and control, not its cause. The naiveté of the Report, and its ultimate paternalism, is nowhere better shown than in its attempt to draw parallels between the black power movement and the philosophy of Booker T. Washington. Accommodation stood at the center of Washington's thought; accommodation is explicitly and forcefully rejected by the ideology symbolized in the "black power" slogan. As Carmichael and Hamilton wrote, "Black people in the United States must raise hard questions which challenge the very nature of the society itself: its long-standing values, beliefs, and institutions."

What we miss in the Kerner Commission Report is the capacity to ask "hard questions." The Commission members are to be saluted for their instinct that "white racism" is the culprit. They are to be faulted for their inability or unwillingness to pursue this theme.

A new realization is dawning in white America. Under the insistent prodding of articulate blacks plus a few unusual whites, the so-called "Negro Problem" is being redefined. Just possibly the racial sickness in our society is not, as we have so long assumed, rooted in the black and presumably "pathological" subculture but in the white and presumably "healthy" dominant culture. If indeed it turns out that "*the* problem" is finally and deeply a white problem, the solution will have to be found in a restructured white society.

Institutional racism is a term which describes practices in the United States nearly as old as the nation itself. The term, however, appears to be of recent coinage, possibly first used by Stokely Carmichael and Charles V. Hamilton in their widely read book, *Black Power.**

TOWARD A DEFINITION

The murder by KKK members and law enforcement officials of three civil rights workers in Mississippi was an act of individual racism. That the sovereign state of Mississippi refused to indict the killers was institutional racism. The individual act by racist bigots went unpunished in Mississippi because of policies, precedents, and practices that are an integral part of that state's legal institutions. A store clerk who suspects that black children in his store are there to steal candy but white children are there to purchase candy, and who treats the children differently, the blacks as probable delinquents and the whites as probable customers, also illustrates individual racism. Unlike the Mississippi murderers, the store clerk is not a bigot and may not even consider himself prejudiced, but his behavior is shaped by racial stereotypes which have been part of his unconscious since childhood. A university admissions policy which provides for entrance only to students who score high on tests designed primarily for white suburban high schools necessarily excludes black ghetto-educated students. Unlike the legal policies of Mississippi, the university admission criteria are not intended to be racist, but the university is pursuing a course which perpetuates institutional racism. The difference, then, between individual and institutional racism is not a difference in intent or of visibility. Both the individual act of racism and the racist institutional

*Stokely Carmichael and Charles Hamilton, *Black Power: The Politics of Liberation in America* (New York: Vintage Books, 1967).

policy may occur without the presence of conscious bigotry, and both may be masked intentionally or innocently.

In an attempt to understand "institutional racism" it is best to consider first what institutions are and what they do in a society. Institutions are fairly stable social arrangements and practices through which collective actions are taken. Medical institutions, for instance, marshal talents and resources of society so that health care can be provided. Medical institutions include hospitals, research labs, and clinics, as well as organizations of medical people such as doctors and nurses. The health of all of us is affected by general medical policies and by established practices and ethics. Business and labor, for example, determine what is to be produced, how it is to be produced, and by whom and on whose behalf products will be created. Public and private schools determine what is considered knowledge, how it is to be transmitted to new generations, and who will do the teaching. Legal and political institutions determine what laws regulate our lives, how and by whom they are enforced, and who will be prosecuted for which violations.

Institutions have great power to reward and penalize. They reward by providing career opportunities for some people and foreclosing them for others. They reward as well by the way social goods and services are distributed—by deciding who receives training and skills, medical care, formal education, political influence, moral support and self-respect, productive employment, fair treatment by the law, decent housing, self-confidence, and the promise of a secure future for self and children. No society will distribute social benefits in a perfectly equitable way. But no society need use race as a criterion to determine who will be rewarded and who punished. Any nation that permits race to affect the distribution of benefits from social policies is racist.

It is our thesis that institutional racism is deeply embedded in American society. Slavery was only the earliest and most blatant practice. Political, economic, educational, and religious policies cooperated with slaveholders to "keep the nigger in his place." Emancipation changed little. Jim Crow laws as well as residential and employment discrimination guaranteed that black citizens re-mained under the control of white citizens. Second-class citizenship quickly became a social fact as well as a legal status. Overt institutional racism was widely practiced throughout American society at least until World War II.

With desegregation in the armed forces and the passage of various civil rights bills, institutional racism no longer has the status of law. It is perpetuated nonetheless, sometimes by frightened and bigoted individuals, sometimes by good citizens merely carrying on "business as usual," and sometimes by well-intentioned but naive reformers. An attack on institutional racism is clearly the next task for Americans, white and black, who hope to obtain for their children a society less tense and more just than the one of the mid-1960's. It is no easy task. Individual, overt racist acts, such as the shotgun slaying of civil rights workers, are visible. Techniques of crime detection can be used to apprehend guilty parties, and, in theory, due process of law will punish them. To detect institutional racism, especially when it is unintentional or when it is disguised, is a very different task. And even when institutional racism is detected, it is seldom clear who is at fault. How can we say who is responsible for residential segregation, for poor education in ghetto schools, for extraordinarily high unemployment among black men, for racial stereotypes in history textbooks, for the concentration of political power in white society? . . . In understanding how deeply racist practices are embedded in the American experience and values, we can come to a fuller understanding of how contemporary social institutions have adapted to their heritage.

FALSE RESPONSE
AND SOCIAL ILLUSIONS

There are two illusions underlying the forms of false response . . .

The first illusion is that the condition of the black population is steadily improving and that it will continue to improve without drastic changes in our approach to the problem. The second myth is that poverty and racism are best fought *within* the black community. . . .

The second false assumption, that the poverty of the ghettos is best attacked directly through the War on Poverty, welfare, and the countless other ghetto-oriented programs, has caused white people to overlook the more basic issue of racist attitudes and institutions that shut black people off from the instruments of self-determination. A problem cannot be solved unless it is attacked at its roots, but when the roots are found entwined in the lives, communities, and occupations of white people, it is far easier for them to place the blame elsewhere than to face up to their own responsibility. The result has been an overemphasis on poverty. Since the black man's hell is created by both poverty and racism, given the choice, white policy-makers prefer to see black resentment and protest as being due to poverty. Vast welfare bureaucracies and anti-poverty programs are created to buy off and placate the rage of the black community. In the meantime, the white hegemony and wealth remain intact.

Unless this misdirection is understood and corrected, white liberals will continue to waste their energies on blunders in the black community without appreciably altering racial inequities. . . .

THE WAY OUT: LOOKING AT WHITE SOCIETY

It is not easy to suggest unusual remedies. . . .

We believe solutions will be found only as the people band together to demand a reordering of priorities and a new system of popular participation in decision-making. . . .

An individual working alone can do very little about racism in American institutional life; he will be swallowed up by the sheer size of the problem. To work for institutional change it is necessary to develop a force for change in the community, and no one person can constitute that force. Therefore, a first suggestion would be that the individual get together with friends, fellow workers, and neighbors in the area who share similar concerns. Initially, the group must develop a rough analysis of the ways local institutions operate and how they contribute to the subordination and exploitation of black people.

Second, the organization must get down to specific issues as soon as possible. Most American people are tired of sweeping generalities and vague statements. If they are seriously ready to work on racism, then they should be able to dig right into a particular issue that has a bearing on their own lives.

Perhaps the real question is one of commitment, whether or not white people really want to do something. It appears that many people who seem to be asking "What can I do?" actually are asking "What can I do without changing anything?" If there is no commitment to changing the institutions of white society, the concerned white citizen can do little about racism. In order to combat racism effectively in our present society, we must overcome our fears of change and be willing to work actively to reorder our society.

For too long American society has believed in the mythology that social ills are in truth nothing but the aggregate of individual defects. If a black man is unemployed or uneducated or poorly housed, it must be due to some failure to "achieve" on his part. Or, if we do not directly place blame on his character defects, we suggest that there is some prejudiced employer or inadequate teacher or bigoted realtor who is bringing about the condition. As our analysis attempts to make clear, . . . some social ills are not adequately explained by simply alluding to individual defects. There are social ills which are structured into the very operations of the society, which are inevitable given the institutional arrangements. It is this premise which bids us urge the concerned white to think in terms of organization and new institutions if he would do something about racism. We remind the reader of our dedication phrase: "Institutions made by men can be changed by men."

51. VISCERAL RACISM

Irving Thalberg

At a meeting shortly before his death, Malcolm X was asked by a young white listener: "What contribution can youth, especially students who are disgusted with racism, make to the black struggle for freedom?" Malcolm X's reply has become a familiar one: "Whites who are sincere should organize among themselves and figure out some strategy to break down prejudice that exists in white communities. . . . This has never been done."[1]

I will not offer strategies, but I will do what I can with fairly standard philosophical techniques to delineate one target for action. I hope that the social phenomenon I analyze is what polemical writers had in view when they coined the term 'visceral racism.' At any rate the phenomenon is worth bringing into sharper focus; and therefore I will keep the emotively charged term 'racism' out of my discussion as much as possible. Nevertheless when I do for convenience use the expression 'visceral racism', I want it to be clear that I am not belaboring old-fashioned white supremacy doctrines and practices. Adherents of white supremacy are still both numerous and influential; but I doubt that further analysis is needed to understand or to attack their position. What I examine here is more protectively camouflaged and philosophically challenging.

Not a 'latent' form of white supremacy. The main components of the earlier tradition I take to be: (a) factual claims that, in various respects, black people are 'inferior'; (b) normative conclusions, drawn from such factual claims, about how others ought to treat black Americans; (c) regional and national customs of discriminatory treatment that are vindicated by these normative conclusions.[2] All these elements appear in Chief Justice Taney's account of the status of slaves and free Negroes under the U.S. Constitution. Writing immediately before the Civil War in the *Dred Scott* decision, Taney says:

They had for more than a century . . . been regarded as beings of an inferior order, and altogether unfit to associ-

ate with the white race . . .; and so far inferior, that they had no rights which the white man was bound to respect (19 How. [60 U.S.] 392 [1857]).

An equally frank statement is Senator Tillman's apology for the discriminatory post-Reconstruction customs of his state:

In 1876, . . . the people of South Carolina had been living under negro rule for eight years. There was a condition bordering upon anarchy. . . . There was no incentive to labor. . . .

They were taxing us to death and confiscating our property. We felt the very foundations of our civilization crumbling beneath our feet, [*sic*] that we were sure to be engulfed by the black flood of barbarians. . . . In desperation we determined to take the government away from the negroes.

We reorganized the Democratic party with one plank, . . . namely that "this is a white man's country and white men must govern it." (*Congressional Record*, 59th Congress, 1907, pp. 1440–1)

In more recent times, 'respectable' white supremacists have been less forthright about their intention to subjugate blacks. On the other hand, a few biologists and social scientists have plugged *lacunae* in the vague theory of racial inferiority. Their most interesting hypotheses are the Negroid *homo sapiens* evolved much later, and from different sub-*sapiens* ancestors, than Caucasoids; and that the resulting differences in Negroid and Caucasoid brain morphology still determine such things as school achievement and crime rates. Along with data from archeology and brain physiology, comparative psychometric studies of children in the Georgia public schools from 1954 to 1962 have been introduced as evidence for such 'inferiority' hypotheses.[3] This evidence, the leading theories, and especially the normative conclusions that have been drawn from scientific theories of racial inferiority, all have received thorough criticism in scientific and popular journals.[4] So I will turn to contrasts between white supremacist and visceral racist attitudes. . . .

Reprinted from *The Monist*, vol. 56, no. 1 (Jan. 1972), pp. 43–50, 60–63, with the permission of the author and the publisher.

By visceral racism I will mean a set of un-acknowledged attitudes that afflict me and most other 'unprejudiced' whites, especially middle-class liberals. These attitudes are mainly dispositions to perceive and to describe social events in which black people figure. Our most noticeable proclivities are, first, to structure and report such events in a manner that 'screens out' social inequalities which are glaringly evident to black observers; and secondly to represent black people as helplessly dependent upon the white majority. The overall tendency is for 'visceral' whites to regard themselves as doing just about as well as can be expected with 'the race problem'. Of course they never regard themselves as the problem! Examples will emphasize how the visceral racist does not want to think of himself as hostile toward blacks or indifferent to their individual and collective aspirations.

This sketch explains why the visceral inclinations that I shall analyze here are not dissimulated white supremacy attitudes. To recognize your viscerally racist dispositions is *not* to avow that deep down you think black people are all over-sexed savages, or that you really like the caste system we have. It is to notice the protective cocoon of ignorance and distortion that we have spun about ourselves.

Before I review the inequities that we thereby manage to ignore, I want to answer a natural objection from liberal white readers. Many will indignantly complain, "I've never had any hostile feelings toward black people, so how can you call me a visceral or other kind of racist?"

Not 'feelings'. The visceral dispositions I'm analyzing do not consist in sensations or emotions. In this regard, white supremacist and viscerally racist inclinations are similar. . . .

Now the peculiarity of viscerally racist attitudes, according to the hypothesis I will develop, is that a person with these attitudes systematically ignores features of the social situation of black people in this country. . . . The visceral racist will not throw a brick through the window of a new black neighbor. He won't assault black children who are bussed to the neighborhood school. But what does he do to protect them? Doesn't he let the redneck do his dirty-work for him? In general, doesn't he support institutions that oppress black people in nearly every area of social life? Right; and that is why I want

to diagnose his visceral inclinations to misperceive our society as progressing with all deliberate speed toward equality.

For the benefit of nonmilitants, I will explain briefly the claim that there is almost no practical difference for the majority of blacks under liberals and their 'reformed' institutions, in comparison with the old days. No doubt there are more lucky blacks who 'make it' nowadays. Certainly more vote. Fewer lynchings occur. Blacks are no longer obliged to display humility and gratitude. Otherwise the statistics on the *vast majority* of black people in America show little alteration. Except for temporary economic gains during World War II and the Korean War, most blacks have continued to enjoy a very small share of the nation's fabled prosperity. Typically, the 500 largest industrial corporations earn around 40% of the gross national product. About 7,000 companies with 100 or more employees do 90% of manufacturing and 80% of the sales. About 1.6% of the population owns more than 80% of the stock of these top corporations and others. As you would expect, members of this group control corporate and government policy. Blacks have not gotten into this 1.6% group that owns and runs the country. The few whites who belong to it are usually inheritors of wealth. Most stock ends up in the hands of white women, because of their longevity.[5]

Turning to black wage-earners, experts attribute to them between 55% and 70% of the salary that whites receive for equivalent work.[6] Incidentally, the percentage *declines* when we consider blacks with 'higher' positions and more formal education, thus refuting the myth that serious study and 'drive' will be differentially rewarded. Working-class blacks are twice as likely to be unemployed or laid off. In nearly every profession—including our own, academic philosophy—blacks are grossly under-represented. The same is true with skilled trades. Labor unions have driven blacks out of some fields. This happened with locomotive engineers and firemen in the South. Construction workers' unions have kept blacks out. And in automotive industry, unions have confined blacks to low-paying, no-seniority positions.[7]

Black consumers face similar hindrances. They pay more to buy or rent deteriorated housing. Mortgages are nearly unavailable to a black homebuyer. If he obtains one, he will pay higher interest than whites do. Neighborhood segregation is rising, and black children attend increasingly segregated schools, where considerably less is spent per pupil than in white areas. Barely 2% of elective offices at all levels of government are held by blacks—and this marks a relatively big step forward during the last few years. In their relations with government, notably police, most blacks have made no progress at all. Black citizens and property-owners are virtually without police protection, while harrassment from police has grown. Ten to seventeen times as many black people are arrested for major violent crimes.[8] Large numbers, including 'bystanders', fall victims of unprovoked attacks by police. Their property rights, and Fourth Amendment immunity to arbitrary search and seizure, are violated constantly by police. Blacks still constitute the majority of the more than 200,000 inmates of federal and state prisons and reformatories, and are the least likely to have received an impartial trial.

All in all, this lack of progress since the passing of white supremacy appears to confirm Dr. King's foreboding. He wrote in 1963:

I have almost reached the regrettable conclusion that the Negro's great stumbling block in the stride toward freedom is not the White Citizen's Council-er or the Ku Klux Klanner, but the white moderate who is more devoted to "order" than to justice. . . . Shallow understanding from people of goodwill is more frustrating than absolute misunderstanding from people of ill will.[9]

It's hard to believe that the visceral racist manages to ignore all this. But as I shall illustrate, he sometimes even turns the situation upside down, and imagines that with all the current 'favoritism' toward blacks, there is discrimination against whites! In any case, my method is straightforward. Rather than suspect most 'well-meaning' whites of hypocrisy, I will look for patterns of selective and distorted perception of this background when they describe social occurrences involving black people. . . . The test for my analysis is therefore simple. I will ask, of readily available though relatively crude data, whether or not they qualify as evidence for a viscerally racist outlook. Take this pungent interview:

Ray Walczak, 44, works as a gig grinder . . . in Milwaukee. As he walked off his shift not long ago, he saw across the street the Rev. James Groppi and a group of black militants picketing for more jobs.

"Look at that," Ray Walczak said. "Bastards don't want jobs. If you offered them jobs now, 90 per cent of them would run like hell. I tell you, people on relief get better jobs, got better homes, than I've got. You're better off now not working. The colored people are eating steak, and this Polack bastard is eating chicken.

"Damn right I'm bitter. The Polish race years ago didn't go out and riot and ruin people's property. I've been in the shops since I was 16 . . . if I live to be a hundred I'll probably be doing the same job.

"The only raise I ever got was a union raise . . . never a merit raise . . . We're peons, just numbers."[10]

That particular worker does not think himself privileged; but if you compare his situation with that of his potential black competitors, he is. There is an interesting distortion in his claim that blacks do not really want the meager opportunities he has. There is even a slight contradiction between his statement that they "don't want jobs" and his complaint that "people on relief get better jobs"; but perhaps this indicates that he is candidly expressing attitudes that conflict. Naturally he assumes that black protesters are on relief!

More explicit animosity toward blacks appears in another interview:

Ernest (Pee Wee) Hayes is 58, and for 37 years he has worked at the Armco steel plant in Middletown, Ohio. . . .

"We do all the work and the niggers have got it made. They keep closing and closing in, working their way into everything. Last 3 or 4 months you can't even turn on that damn TV without seeing a nigger. They're even playing cowboys. We briarhoppers ain't gonna stand for it. And 90% of Middletown is briarhoppers.

"My man got beat, Wallace. We need someone to wake 'em up. Shake 'em up. Kill 'em."[11]

This second worker is clearly a white supremacist, because in addition to being hostile toward blacks, he recognizes that they do not presently have the same opportunities he has, and he intends to keep things that way.

How about the first worker? I think that my analysis helps us notice distortions as well as white supremacist elements in his diatribe. One particular theme in that interview is worth examining further, because it is so common in discussions I've heard. The theme is that workers like this man have suffered to win the few advantages they have. They started working before they could complete high school, and they accepted miserable wages for long hours, under hazardous conditions. They joined the union movement, got fired and took beatings. How can you expect them to give up the few advantages they won, and step aside to benefit blacks? On this view, schemes for preferential recruitment of blacks, admission to apprenticeship programs, and promotion, all seem like 'favoritism' and 'discrimination in reverse'.

Why are these misdescriptions of economic reality? First, while it is true that white workers suffered, fought and took their knocks, it is a distortion to forget that black workers did also. Moreover, as we noticed in Section 3, labor unions regularly betrayed black workers, forcing companies to put them out of jobs they already had, and refusing to admit and represent them. Thus fatal ambiguities begin to appear in the claim that white workers gained the advantages they have by struggling. If you ask, "Struggling against whom, and advantages over whom?", the answer in each case is: "Employers *and* black workers." Now the struggle does not sound so much like 'the good fight' any more. And the privileges no longer appear to be *privileges for laborers in general.* We notice that they are to a considerable extent 'white-skin privileges', unfair advantages over potential black competitors. The case for white workers looks very twisted.

How about the 'sacrifice' and 'favoritism' themes? These are again gross distortions. In the first place, there is a confusion between actuality and possibility. So far, very few blacks have gotten into industrial and craft unions, apprenticeship programs and supervisory positions. Thus in actual fact, whites have made no sacrifices, and no favoritism has been shown to black workers. At most the complaint might be that *if* blacks eventually get what they demand, this *would be* the result. But the second point to raise here is: 'Would it be favoritism, and would there be sacrifices?' If you agree that white workers' advantages are unfair advantages, then how can you describe it as a 'sacrifice' when they must renounce them? Black workers

have not called for the firing of whites. No renunciation of their legitimate privilege *as workers* is at issue: only their undeserved privileges as *white workers. To end these privileges is no more a sacrifice than it is a sacrifice when you must return someone's property, whether you took it deliberately or by mistake, or whether you got it from your parents.*

In connection with the 'favoritism' theme, what distorts things is the omission of all-important historical background. Consider preferential hiring programs in the setting of 350 years of gross favoritism toward white laborers and craftsmen. Then it hardly sounds unfair when blacks announce: "Until we get our share, you will have to *wait longer* than usual for the new jobs, for promotions and for admission to apprenticeship programs." It is not favoritism toward blacks when whites lose their illegal monopoly.

White workers and their union representatives who describe economic circumstances in the manner I've been analyzing certainly display visceral racism. But the hitch is that when you expose these and similar distortions, many workers will become explicitly antagonistic towards blacks. How many? That is for trained interviewers to find out. At this stage of exploring a person's attitudes, does it make any difference whether you have a visceral racist or a white supremacist on your hands? Besides the ideological and theoretical differences I've noted, there might be a practical difference when someone is intellectually 'up against the wall.' The acknowledged white supremacist will want to preserve current inequalities. Visceral racists like ourselves, once we have stopped misperceiving things, have strong professed reasons to work for immediate and drastic change.

NOTES

1. In G. Breitman, ed., *Malcolm X Speaks* (New York: Grove Press, 1966), p. 221.

2. For general analyses of prejudice and discriminatory behavior, consult the following: G. W. Allport, *The Nature of Prejudice* (New York: Addison-Wesley, 1954); G. E. Simpson and J. M. Yinger, *Racial and Cultural Minorities* (New York: Harper & Row, 1965); B. Lindzey and E. Aronson, eds., *Prejudice and Ethnic Relations* (New York: Addison-Wesley, 1969); H. Tajfel, "Cognitive Aspects of Prejudice," *Journal of Social Issues,* 25, No. 4, (1969), 79–97.

3. Psychometric studies are: Robert T. Osborne, *Racial Differences in School Achievement* (Monograph No. 3 in a series published by *Mankind Quarterly* [Edinburgh, Scotland], 1962);

and Audrey M. Shuey, *The Testing of Negro Intelligence* (Lynchburg, Va., 1958). More general theories are put forth in Wesley C. George, *The Biology of the Race Problem,* a 1962 study commissioned by the Governor of Alabama; and in Carleton Putnam, *Evolution and Race: New Evidence* (New York: National Putnam Letters Committee, 1962). Both George and Putnam draw their conclusions from the theoretical work and archeological research of Carleton S. Coon, as published in such books as *The Origin of Races* (New York: Alfred A. Knopf, 1962).

4. For example, Theodosius Dobzhansky's review of Coon: "A Debatable Account of the Origin of Races," *Scientific American* 208, No. 2 (1963), 169–172. See also the exchange of letters between Coon and Dobzhansky (*Ibid.,* 208, No. 4 [1963], 12–14).

5. For convenient and abundant documentation, largely based on government statistics and other 'respectable' sources, consult Ferdinand Lundberg, *The Rich and the Super Rich* (New York: Bantam Books, 1969), esp. pp. 12–20, 295–298, 354–355, 927–946.

6. The lower figure is given by Thomas F. Mayer, on the basis of U.S. Bureau of Census figures for 1939 and 1947–62, in his useful résumé, "The Position and Progress of Black America," reprinted by Radical Education Project (Ann Arbor, 1967). *The Report of the National Advisory Commission on Civil Disorders* (Washington, D.C.: Government Printing Office, 1968) gives the higher figure for 23 cities it surveyed. Since Mayer draws upon a wide variety of official and scholarly sources, I generally paraphrase his summary of the situation in jobs, housing, and education.

7. For typical railroad cases, see *Steele v. L. and N. R. Co.,* 323 U.S. 192 (1944), and *Railroad Trainmen v. Howard,* 343 U.S. 768 (1951). In Chicago during the Summer of 1969, the Coalition for United Community Action established that of 87,783 union workers in 19 building trades, only 2,251 were black, Latin, or from a similar minority. On the automotive industry, my source is Robert Dudnick, *Black Workers in Revolt* (New York: Guardian Pamphlets, 1969). For broader background, see Ray Marshall, *The Negro and Organized Labor* (New York: John Wiley & Sons, Inc., 1965), and (with V. M. Briggs, Jr.) *The Negro and Apprenticeship* (Baltimore: Johns Hopkins, 1967).

8. This last figure comes from a report by the National Commission on the Causes and Prevention of Violence, summarized in the *Chicago Sun-Times,* November 24, 1969, pp. 5, 18.

9. "Letter from a Birmingham City Jail," reprinted in *Civil Disobedience,* ed. by H. A. Bedau (New York: Pegasus, 1969), p. 81.

10. From Lemon, *The Troubled American,* as serialized in the Chicago *Daily News,* October 29, 1970, p. 6.

11. Lemon, *The Troubled American,* as serialized in the Chicago *Daily News,* October 30, 1970, p. 6.

Sexual Discrimination

52. SEXUAL POLITICS

Kate Millett

. . . In introducing the term "sexual politics," one must first answer the inevitable question "Can the relationship between the sexes be viewed in a political light at all?" The answer depends on how one defines politics.[1] This essay does not define the political as that relatively narrow and exclusive world of meetings, chairmen, and parties. The term "politics" shall refer to power-structured relationships, arrangements whereby one group of persons is controlled by another. By way of parenthesis one might add that although an ideal politics might simply be conceived of as the arrangement of human life on agreeable and rational principles from whence the entire notion of power *over* others should be banished, one must confess that this is not what constitutes the political as we know it, and it is to this that we must address ourselves.

The following sketch, which might be described as "notes toward a theory of patriarchy," will attempt to prove that sex is a status category with political implications. Something of a pioneering effort, it must perforce be both tentative and imperfect. Because the intention is to provide an overall description, statements must be generalized, exceptions neglected, and subheadings overlapping and, to some degree, arbitrary as well.

The word "politics" is enlisted here when speaking of the sexes primarily because such a word is eminently useful in outlining the real nature of their relative status, historically and at the present. It is opportune, perhaps today even mandatory, that we develop a more relevant psychology and philosophy of power relationships beyond the simple conceptual framework provided by our traditional formal politics. Indeed, it may be imperative that we give some attention to defining a theory of politics which treats of power relationships on grounds less conventional than those to which we are accustomed.[2] I have therefore found it pertinent to define them on grounds of personal contact and interaction between members of well-defined and coherent groups: races, castes, classes, and sexes. For it is precisely because certain groups have no representation in a number of recognized political structures that their position tends to be so stable, their oppression so continuous.

In America, recent events have forced us to acknowledge at last that the relationship between the races is indeed a political one which involves the general control of one collectivity, defined by birth, over another collectivity, also defined by birth. Groups who rule by birthright are fast disappearing, yet there remains one ancient and universal scheme for the domination of one birth group by another—the scheme that prevails in the area of sex. The study of racism has convinced us that a truly political state of affairs operates between the races to perpetuate a series of oppressive circumstances. The subordinated group has inadequate redress through existing political institutions, and is deterred thereby from organizing into conventional political struggle and opposition.

Quite in the same manner, a disinterested examination of our system of sexual relationship must point out that the situation between the sexes now, and throughout history, is a case of that phenomenon Max Weber defined as *herrschaft*, a relationship of dominance and subordinance.[3] What goes largely unexamined, often even unacknowl-

edged (yet is institutionalized nonetheless) in our social order, is the birthright priority whereby males rule females. Through this system a most ingenious form of "interior colonization" has been achieved. It is one which tends moreover to be sturdier than any form of segregation, and more rigorous than class stratification, more uniform, certainly more enduring. However muted its present appearance may be, sexual dominion obtains nevertheless as perhaps the most pervasive ideology of our culture and provides its most fundamental concept of power.

This is so because our society, like all other historical civilizations, is a patriarchy.[4] The fact is evident at once if one recalls that the military, industry, technology, universities, science, political office, and finance—in short, every avenue of power within the society, including the coercive force of the police, is entirely in male hands. As the essence of politics is power, such realization cannot fail to carry impact. What lingers of supernatural authority, the Deity, "His" ministry, together with the ethics and values, the philosophy and art of our culture—its very civilization—as T. S. Eliot once observed, is of male manufacture.

If one takes patriarchal government to be the institution whereby that half of the populace which is female is controlled by that half which is male, the principles of patriarchy appear to be twofold: male shall dominate female, elder male shall dominate younger. However, just as with any human institution, there is frequently a distance between the real and the ideal; contradictions and exceptions do exist within the system. While patriarchy as an institution is a social constant so deeply entrenched as to run through all other political, social, or economic forms, whether of caste or class, feudality or bureaucracy, just as it pervades all major religions, it also exhibits great variety in history and locale. In democracies,[5] for example, females have often held no office or do so (as now) in such minuscule numbers as to be below even token representation. Aristocracy, on the other hand, with its emphasis upon the magic and dynastic properties of blood, may at times permit women to hold power. The principle of rule by elder males is violated even more frequently.

I. IDEOLOGICAL

Hannah Arendt[6] has observed that government is upheld by power supported either through consent or imposed through violence. Conditioning to an ideology amounts to the former. Sexual politics obtains consent through the "socialization" of both sexes to basic patriarchal polities with regard to temperament, role, and status. As to status, a pervasive assent to the prejudice of male superiority guarantees superior status in the male, inferior in the female. The first item, temperament, involves the formation of human personality along stereotyped lines of sex category ("masculine" and "feminine"), based on the needs and values of the dominant group and dictated by what its members cherish in themselves and find convenient in subordinates: aggression, intelligence, force, and efficacy in the male; passivity, ignorance, docility, "virtue," and ineffectuality in the female. This is complemented by a second factor, sex role, which decrees a consonant and highly elaborate code of conduct, gesture and attitude for each sex. In terms of activity, sex role assigns domestic service and attendance upon infants to the female, the rest of human achievement, interest, and ambition to the male. The limited role allotted the female tends to arrest her at the level of biological experience. Therefore, nearly all that can be described as distinctly human rather than animal activity (in their own way animals also give birth and care for their young) is largely reserved for the male. Of course, status again follows from such an assignment. Were one to analyze the three categories one might designate status as the political component, role as the sociological, and temperament as the psychological —yet their interdependence is unquestionable and they form a chain. Those awarded higher status tend to adopt roles of mastery, largely because they are first encouraged to develop temperaments of dominance. That this is true of caste and class as well is self-evident.

II. BIOLOGICAL

Patriarchal religion, popular attitude, and to some degree, science as well[7] assumes these psycho-social distinctions to rest upon biological differences between the sexes, so that where culture is acknowledged as shaping behavior, it is said to do no more than cooperate with nature. Yet the temperamental distinctions created in partriarchy ("masculine" and "feminine" personality traits) do not appear to originate in human nature, those of role and status still less.

The heavier musculature of the male, a secondary sexual characteristic and common among mammals, is biological in origin but is also culturally encouraged through breeding, diet and exercise. Yet it is hardly an adequate category on which to base political relations *within civilization*.[8] Male supremacy, like other political creeds, does not finally reside in physical strength but in the acceptance of a value system which is not biological. Superior physical strength is not a factor in political relations—vide those of race and class. Civilization has always been able to substitute other methods (technic, weaponry, knowledge) for those of physical strength, and contemporary civilization has no further need of it. At present, as in the past, physical exertion is very generally a class factor, those at the bottom performing the most strenuous tasks, whether they be strong or not.

It is often assumed that patriarchy is endemic in human social life, explicable or even inevitable on the grounds of human physiology. Such a theory grants patriarchy logical as well as historical origin. . . .

The question of the historical origins of patriarchy—whether patriarchy originated primordially in the male's superior strength, or upon a later mobilization of such strength under certain circumstances—appears at the moment to be unanswerable. It is also probably irrelevant to contemporary patriarchy, where we are left with the realities of sexual politics, still grounded, we are often assured, on nature. Unfortunately, as the psycho-social distinctions made between the two sex groups which are said to justify their present political relationship are not the clear, specific, measurable and neutral ones of the physical sciences, but are instead of an entirely different character—vague, amorphous, often even quasi-religious in phrasing —it must be admitted that many of the generally understood distinctions between the sexes in the more significant areas of role and temperament, not to mention status, have in fact, essentially cultural, rather than biological, bases. Attempts to prove that temperamental dominance is inherent in the male (which for its advocates, would be tantamount to validating, logically as well as historically, the patriarchal situation regarding role and status) have been notably unsuccessful. Sources in the field are in hopeless disagreement about the nature of sexual differences, but the most reasonable among them have despaired of the ambition of any definite equation between temperament and biological nature. It appears that we are not soon to be enlightened as to the existence of any significant inherent differences between male and female beyond the bio-genital ones we already know. Endocrinology and genetics afford no definite evidence of determining mental-emotional differences.[9]

Not only is there insufficient evidence for the thesis that the present social distinctions of patriarchy (status, role, temperament) are physical in origin, but we are hardly in a position to assess the existing differentiations, since distinctions which we know to be culturally induced at present so outweigh them. Whatever the "real" differences between the sexes may be, we are not likely to know them until the sexes are treated differently, that is alike. And this is very far from being the case at present. Important new research not only suggests that the possibilities of innate temperamental differences seem more remote than ever, but even raises questions as to the validity and permanence of psycho-sexual identity. In doing so it gives fairly concrete positive evidence of the overwhelmingly *cultural* character of gender, i.e. personality structure in terms of sexual category.

Although there is no biological reason why the two central functions of the family (socialization and reproduction) need be inseparable from or even take place within it, revolutionary or utopian efforts to remove these functions from the family have been so frustrated, so beset by difficulties, that most experiments so far have involved a gradual return to tradition. This is strong evidence of how basic a form patriarchy is within all societies, and of how pervasive its effects upon family members.

bers. It is perhaps also an admonition that change undertaken without a thorough understanding of the sociopolitical institution to be changed is hardly productive. And yet radical social change cannot take place without having an effect upon patriarchy. And not simply because it is the political form which subordinates such a large percentage of the population (women and youth) but because it serves as a citadel of property and traditional interests. Marriages are financial alliances, and each household operates as an economic entity much like a corporation. As one student of the family states it, "the family is the keystone of the stratification system, the social mechanism by which it is maintained.". . .[10]

III. EDUCATIONAL AND ECONOMIC

Since education and economy are so closely related in the advanced nations, it is significant that the general level and style of higher education for women, particularly in their many remaining segregated institutions, is closer to that of Renaissance humanism than to the skills of mid-twentieth-century scientific and technological society. Traditionally patriarchy permitted occasional minimal literacy to women while higher education was closed to them. While modern patriarchies have, fairly recently, opened all educational levels to women,[11] the kind and quality of education is not the same for each sex. This difference is of course apparent in early socialization, but it persists and enters into higher education as well. Universities, once places of scholarship and the training of a few professionals, now also produce the personnel of a technocracy. This is not the case with regard to women. Their own colleges typically produce neither scholars nor professionals nor technocrats. Nor are they funded by government and corporations as are male colleges and those co-educational colleges and universities whose primary function is the education of males.

As patriarchy enforces a temperamental imbalance of personality traits between the sexes, its educational institutions, segregated or co-educational, accept a cultural programing toward the generally operative division between "masculine" and "feminine" subject matter, assigning the humanities and certain social sciences (at least in their lower or marginal branches) to the female—and science and technology, the professions, business and engineering to the male. Of course the balance of employment, prestige and reward at present lie with the latter. Control of these fields is very eminently a matter of political power. One might also point out how the exclusive dominance of males in the more prestigious fields directly serves the interests of patriarchal power in industry, government, and the military. And since patriarchy encourages an imbalance in human temperament along sex lines, both divisions of learning (science and the humanities) reflect this imbalance. The humanities, because not exclusively male, suffer in prestige: the sciences, technology, and business, because they are nearly exclusively male reflect the deformation of the "masculine" personality, e.g., a certain predatory or aggressive character.

IV. PSYCHOLOGICAL

The aspects of patriarchy already described have each an effect upon the psychology of both sexes. Their principal result is the interiorization of patriarchal ideology. Status, temperament, and role are all value systems with endless psychological ramifications for each sex. Patriarchal marriage and the family with its ranks and division of labor play a large part in enforcing them. The male's superior economic position, the female's inferior one have also grave implications. The large quantity of guilt attached to sexuality in patriarchy is overwhelmingly placed upon the female, who is, culturally speaking, held to be the culpable or the more culpable party in nearly any sexual liaison, whatever the extenuating circumstances. A tendency toward the reification of the female makes her more often a sexual object than a person. This is particularly so when she is denied human rights through chattel status. Even where this has been partly amended the cumulative effect of religion and custom is still very powerful and has enormous psychological consequences. Woman is still denied sexual freedom and the biological control over her body through the cult of virginity, the double standard, the prescription against abortion, and in

many places because contraception is physically or psychically unavailable to her.

The continual surveillance in which she is held tends to perpetuate the infantilization of women even in situations such as those of higher education. The female is continually obliged to seek survival or advancement through the approval of males as those who hold power. She may do this either through appeasement or through the exchange of her sexuality for support and status. As the history of patriarchal culture and the representations of herself within all levels of its cultural media, past and present, have a devastating effect upon her self image, she is customarily deprived of any but the most trivial sources of dignity or self-respect. In many patriarchies, language, as well as cultural tradition, reserve the human condition for the male. With the Indo-European languages this is a nearly inescapable habit of mind, for despite all the customary pretense that "man" and "humanity" are terms which apply equally to both sexes, the fact is hardly obscured that in practice, general application favors the male far more often than the female as referent, or even sole referent, for such designations.[12]

When in any group of persons, the ego is subjected to such invidious versions of itself through social beliefs, ideology, and tradition, the effect is bound to be pernicious. This, coupled with the persistent though frequently subtle denigration women encounter daily through personal contacts, the impressions gathered from the images and media about them, and the discrimination in matters of behavior, employment, and education which they endure, should make it no very special cause for surprise that women develop group characteristics common to those who suffer minority status and a marginal existence. A witty experiment by Philip Goldberg proves what everyone knows, that having internalized the disesteem in which they are held, women despise both themselves and each other.[13] This simple test consisted of asking women undergraduates to respond to the scholarship in an essay signed alternately by one John McKay and one Joan McKay. In making their assessments the students generally agreed that John was a remarkable thinker, Joan an unimpressive mind. Yet the articles were identical: the reaction was dependent on the sex of the supposed author. . . .

Perhaps patriarchy's greatest psychological weapon is simply its universality and longevity. A referent scarcely exists with which it might be contrasted or by which it might be confuted. While the same might be said of class, patriarchy has a still more tenacious or powerful hold through its successful habit of passing itself off as nature. Religion is also universal in human society and slavery was once nearly so; advocates of each were fond of arguing in terms of fatality, or irrevocable human "instinct"—even "biological origins." When a system of power is thoroughly in command, it has scarcely need to speak itself aloud; when its workings are exposed and questioned, it becomes not only subject to discussion, but even to change. Such a period is the one next under discussion.

NOTES

1.   The American Heritage Dictionary's fourth definition is fairly approximate: "methods or tactics involved in managing a state or government." *American Heritage Dictionary* (New York: American Heritage and Houghton Mifflin, 1969). One might expand this to a set of strategems designed to maintain a system. If one understands patriarchy to be an institution perpetuated by such techniques of control, one has a working definition of how politics is conceived in this essay.

2.   I am indebted here to Ronald V. Samson's *The Psychology of Power* (New York: Random House, 1968) for his intelligent investigation of the connection between formal power structures and the family and for his analysis of how power corrupts basic human relationships.

3.   "Domination in the quite general sense of power, i.e. the possibility of imposing one's will upon the behavior of other persons, can emerge in the most diverse forms." In this central passage of *Wirtschaft und Gesellschaft* Weber is particularly interested in two such forms: control through social authority ("patriarchal, magisterial, or princely") and control through economic force. In patriarchy as in other forms of domination "that control over economic goods, i.e. economic power, is a frequent, often purposively willed, consequence of domination as well as one of its most important instruments." Quoted from Max Rheinstein's and Edward Shil's translation of portions of *Wirtschaft und Gesellschaft* entitled *Max Weber on Law in Economy and Society* (New York: Simon and Schuster, 1967), pp. 323–24.

4.   No matriarchal societies are known to exist at present. Matrilineality, which may be, as some anthropologists have held, a residue or a transitional stage of matriarchy, does not constitute an exception to patriarchal rule, it simply channels the power held by males through female descent—, e.g. the Avunculate.

5.   Radical democracy would, of course, preclude patriarchy. One might find evidence of a general satisfaction with a less than perfect democracy in the fact that women have so rarely held power within modern "democracies."

6.   Hannah Arendt, "Speculations on Violence," *The New York Review of Books,* Vol. XII No. 4, February 27, 1969, p. 24.

7.   The social, rather than the physical sciences are referred to here. Traditionally, medical science had often subscribed to such beliefs. This is no longer the case today, when the best medical research points to the conclusion that sexual stereotypes have no bases in biology.

8.   "The historians of Roman laws, having very justly remarked that neither birth nor affection was the foundation of the Roman family, have concluded that this foundation must be found in the power of the father or husband. They make a sort of primordial institution of this power; but they do not explain how this power was established, unless it was by the superiority of strength of the husband over the wife, and of the father over the children. Now, we deceive ourselves sadly when we thus place force as the origin of law. We shall see farther on that the authority of the father or husband, far from having been the first cause, was itself an effect; it was derived from religion, and was established by religion. Superior strength, therefore, was not the principle that established the family." Numa Denis Fustel de Coulanges, *The Ancient City* (1864). English translation by Willard Small (1873), Doubleday Anchor Reprint, pp. 41–42. Unfortunately Fustel de Coulanges neglects to mention how religion came to uphold patriarchal authority, since patriarchal religion is also an effect, rather than an original cause.

9.   No convincing evidence has so far been advanced in this area. Experimentation regarding the connection between hormones and animal behavior not only yields highly ambivalent results but brings with it the hazards of reasoning by analogy to human behavior. For a summary of the arguments see David C. Glass (editor), *Biology and Behavior* (New York: Rockefeller University and the Russell Sage Foundation, 1968).

10.   William J. Goode, *The Family,* (Englewood Cliffs, N.J., Prentice-Hall, 1964) p. 80.

11.   We often forget how recent an event is higher education for women. In the U.S. it is barely one hundred years old; in many Western countries barely fifty. Oxford did not grant degrees to women on the same terms as to men until 1920. In Japan and a number of other countries universities have been open to women only in the period after World War II. There are still areas where higher education for women scarcely exists. Women do not have the same access to education as do men. The Princeton Report stated that "although at the high school level more girls than boys receive grades of 'A,' roughly 50% more boys than girls go to college." *The Princeton Report to the Alumni on Co-Education* (pamphlet), Princeton, N.J. 1968, p. 10. Most other authorities give the national ratio of college students as two males to one female. In a great many countries it is far lower.

12.   Languages outside the Indo-European group are instructive. Japanese, for example, has one word for man (*oto*)*ko*), another for woman (*o*)*nna*) and a third for human being (*ningen*). It would be as unthinkable to use the first to cover the third as it would be to use the second.

13.   Philip Goldberg, "Are Women Prejudiced Against Women?" *Transaction,* April 1968.

53. THE INEVITABILITY OF PATRIARCHY

Steven Goldberg

THE FEMINIST ASSUMPTION

The view of man and woman in society that implicitly underlies all of the arguments of the feminists is this: there is nothing inherent in the nature of human beings or of society that necessitates that any role or task (save those requiring great strength or the ability to give birth) be associated with one sex or the other;[1] there is no natural order of things decreeing that dyadic and social authority must be associated with men, nor is there any reason why it must be men who rule in every society. Patriarchy, matriarchy, and "equiarchy" are all equally possible and—while every society may invoke "the natural order of things" to justify its particular system—all the expectations we have of men and women are culturally determined and have nothing to do with any sort of basic male or female nature.[2]

There is nothing internally contradictory in such a hypothesis, indeed, it is an ideal place from which to begin an empirical investigation into the nature of man, woman, and society. However, the feminist does not use this as a heuristic first step but unquestioningly accepts it as true. . . .

AGGRESSION AND ATTAINMENT

. . . I believe that in the past we have been looking in the wrong direction for the answer to the question of why every society rewards male roles with higher status than it does female roles (even when the male tasks in one society are the female tasks in another). While it is true that men are always in the positions of authority from which status tends to be defined, male roles are not given high status primarily *because* men fill these roles; men fill these roles because their biological aggression "advantage" can be manifested *in any non-child related area rewarded by high status in any society*. (Again: the line of reasoning used . . . demonstrates only that the biological factors we discuss would make the

social institutions we discuss inevitable and does not preclude the existence of other forces also leading in the same direction; there may be a biologically based tendency for women to prefer male leadership, but there need not be for male attainment of leadership and high-status roles to be inevitable.) . . . this aggression "advantage" can be most manifested and can most enable men to reap status rewards *not* in those relatively homogeneous, collectivist primitive societies in which both male and female must play similar economic roles if the society is to survive or in the monarchy (which guarantees an occasional female leader); this biological factor will be given freest play in the complex, relatively individualistic, bureaucratic, democratic society which, of necessity, must emphasize organizational authority and in which social mobility is relatively free of traditional barriers to advancement. There were more female heads of state in the first two-thirds of the sixteenth century than in the first two-thirds of the twentieth.

The mechanisms involved here are easily seen if we examine any roles that males have attained by channeling their aggression toward such attainment. We will assume for now that equivalent women could *perform* the tasks of roles as well as men if they could attain the roles.[3] Here we can speak of the corporation president, the union leader, the governor, the chairman of an association, or any other role or position for which aggression is a precondition for attainment. Now the environmentalist and the feminist will say that the fact that all such roles are nearly always filled by men is attributable not to male aggression but to the fact that women have not been allowed to enter the competitive race to attain these positions, that they have been told that these positions are in male areas, and that girls are socialized away from competing with boys in general. Women *are* socialized in this way, but again we must ask why. If innate male aggression has nothing to do with male attainment of positions of authority and status in the political, academic, scientific, or financial spheres, if aggression has nothing to do with the reasons

367

why *every* society socializes girls away from those areas which are given high status and away from competition in general, then why is it never the *girls* in any society who are socialized toward these areas, why is it never the nonbiological roles played by women that have high status, why is it always boys who are told to compete, and why do women never "force" men into the low-status, non-maternal roles that women play in every society?

These questions pose no problem if we acknowledge a male aggression that enables men to attain any nonbiological role given high status by any society. For one need merely consider the result of a society's *not* socializing women away from competitions with men, from its *not* directing girls toward roles women are more capable of playing than are men or roles with status low enough that men will not strive for them. No doubt some women would be aggressive enough to succeed in competitions with men and there would be considerably more women in high-status positions than there are now. But most women would lose in such competitive struggles with men (because men have the aggression advantage) and so most women would be forced to live adult lives as failures in areas in which the society had *wanted them to succeed*. It is women, far more than men, who would never allow a situation in which girls were socialized in such a way that the vast majority of them were doomed to adult lifetimes of failure to live up to their own expectations. Now I have no doubt that there is a biological factor that gives women the desire to emphasize maternal and nurturance roles, but the point here is that we can accept the feminist assumption that there is no female propensity of this sort and still see that a society must socialize women away from roles that men will attain through their aggression. For if women did not develop an alternative set of criteria for success their sense of their own competence would suffer intolerably. It is undeniable that the resulting different values and expectations that are attached to men and women will tend to work against the aggressive woman while they work for the man who is no more aggressive. But this is the unavoidable result of the fact that most men are more aggressive than most women so that this woman, who is as aggressive as the average man, but more aggressive

than most women, is an exception. Furthermore, even if the sense of competence of each sex did not necessitate society's attaching to each sex values and expectations based on those qualities possessed by each sex, observation of the majority of each sex by the population would "automatically" lead to these values and expectations being attached to men and women.

SOCIALIZATION'S CONFORMATION TO BIOLOGICAL REALITY

Socialization is the process by which society prepares children for adulthood. The way in which its goals conform to the reality of biology is seen quite clearly when we consider the method in which testosterone generates male aggression (testosterone's serially developing nature). Preadolescent boys and girls have roughly equal testosterone levels, yet young boys are far more aggressive than young girls. Eva Figes has used this observation to dismiss incorrectly the possibility of a hormone-aggression association.[4] Now it is quite probable that the boy is more aggressive than the girl for a purely biological reason. We have seen that it is simplistic to speak simply in terms of hormone levels and that there is evidence of male-female differences in the behavior of infants shortly after birth (when differential socialization is not a plausible explanation of such differences). The fetal alteration of the boy's brain by the testosterone that was generated by his testes has probably left him far more sensitive to the aggression-related properties of the testosterone that is present during boyhood than the girl, who did not receive such alteration. But let us for the moment assume that this is not the case. This does not at all reduce the importance of the hormonal factor. For even if the boy is more aggressive than the girl only because the society allows him to be, the boy's socialization still flows from society's acknowledging biological reality. Let us consider what would happen if girls have the same innate aggression as boys and if a society did not socialize girls away from aggressive competitions. Perhaps half of the third-grade baseball team would be female. As many girls as boys would frame their expectations in masculine values and girls would develop not their feminine abilities but their masculine ones. During adolescence, however, the same assertion of the male chromosomal program that causes the boys to grow beards raises their testosterone level, and their potential for aggression, to a level far above that of the adolescent woman. If society did not teach young girls that beating boys at competitions was unfeminine (behavior inappropriate for a woman), if it did not socialize them away from the political and economic areas in which aggression leads to attainment, these girls would grow into adulthood with self-images based not on succeeding in areas for which biology has left them better prepared than men, but on competitions that most women could not win. If women did not develop feminine qualities as girls (assuming that such qualities do not spring automatically from female biology) then they would be forced to deal with the world in the aggressive terms of men. They would lose every source of power their feminine abilities now give them and they would gain nothing. . . .

The . . . most crucial of the feminist fallacies involves the confusion of cause and function. We need not involve ourselves in a detailed discussion of causation here; a simple example should suffice. A jockey is small because biology made him that way. There may be an element of feedback here in that the jockey might well weigh more if society did not reward his weighing as little as possible, but the causation involved in the determination of his physical characteristics is certainly primarily biological. The function that his size plays in society, its manifestation in his role of jockey, is not biological, but society's putting his size to use. Likewise, the economic functions that sexual differentiation requires do not cause the differentiation. The biological element of male aggression will manifest itself in any economic system. It is useless for the Marxist to attempt to disprove the inevitability of male attainment of authority and status positions by demonstrating that males attain such positions in a capitalist society. They do in societies with primitive, feudal, and socialist economies also. Because the social and economic must conform to the biological, we can change any variable and patriarchy will not be diminished. Political rule is male whether the institutions relevant to private property, control of the means of production, and class

stratification are as minimally present as is possible or as advanced as is found in any society. It is male whether a society is patrilineal, matrilineal, or bilateral; patrilocal, matrilocal, or neolocal; white, black, or heterogeneous; racist, separatist, or equalitarian; primitive, preindustrial, or technological; Shintoist, Catholic, or Zoroastrian; monarchical, totalitarian, or democratic; Spartan, Quaker, or Bourbon; ascetic, hedonist, or libertine. It makes no difference whether a society has a value system that specifically forbids women from entering areas of authority or, like Communist China, an ideological and political commitment to equal distribution of authority positions. One cannot "disprove" the inevitability of biological factors manifesting themselves by demonstrating the function that they serve in a political or economic system. No system could operate that did not conform to, and utilize, the reality that constitutes it. In short, the fallacy here is the reasoning that concludes that men rule because of the nature of the political-economic system and ignores the reality that the possible varieties of political-economic systems are limited by, and must conform to, the nature of man.

NOTES

1. "*It is time that we realized that the whole structure of male and female personality is entirely imposed by social conditioning.* All the possible traits of human personality have in this conditioning been *arbitrarily* assigned into two categories; thus aggression is masculine, passivity feminine. . . ." [Emphasis added]. (Kate Millett, *Barnard Alumnae,* Spring, 1970, p. 28.) This statement expresses the assumption which underpins all of Dr. Millett's *Sexual Politics* (New York: Doubleday, 1970).

2. The best presentation of the feminist assumption is unquestionably John Stuart Mill's *The Subjection of Women.* As an impassioned plea for women's rights Mill's essay is both moving and illuminating. As an attempt to explain the etiology of sexually differentiated behavior and institutions it is indefensible. One is tempted, given the fact that the author of the essay was Mill, to ascribe its inadequacies to the fact that little of the relevant anthropological evidence, and none of the relevant hormonal evidence, was available at the time. But the weakness of Mill's analysis is attributable even more to the fallacious reasoning that his preconceived conclusions demanded. For example, Mill argues that we can have no conception of the limits of possibility imposed by innate sexual differences, or even of whether such limits exist, because no society has been composed of one sex; thus he does not even attempt to explain why the conceptions of male and female held by his society are not reversed in any other society. Similarly Mill attempts to dismiss the possibility of the determinativeness of innate sexual

differences by invoking the irrelevant fact that slave owners defended slavery with the invocation of physiological racial differences that do not exist; this fact is correct, of course, but it casts no more doubt on the likelihood that innate sexual differences are determinative to sexual differences in behavior and institutions than it does on the certainty that physiology is determinative to the ability to give birth. Mill's reasoning has been accepted without question by modern feminist writers.

3. I assume this for the present in order to demonstrate that these will be male roles even if women can *perform* these roles as well as men when they can attain them. It should be pointed out, however, that the line between attainment and performance is not always clear in a bureaucratic society or in leadership in any

society; much of the performance of an executive or leader concerns his ability to maintain the authority which his position gives him. Therefore, it is possible that the greater innate male aggression, particularly when opposed to the lesser innate female aggression, leads to *performance* by the male which is superior to that of the female. This does not, of course, mean that the male at any level of the hierarchy has an advantage over the exceptional woman who was aggressive enough to attain a comparable position, but it might indicate that men in general have an innate advantage over women in general which is relevant to the *performance* of bureaucratic and leadership roles.

4. Eva Figes, *Patriarchal Attitudes* (Greenwich, Conn.: Fawcett World, 1971), p. 8.

54. SEX ROLES: THE ARGUMENT FROM NATURE

Joyce Trebilcot

I am concerned here with the normative question of whether, in an ideal society, certain roles should be assigned to females and others to males. In discussions of this issue, a great deal of attention is given to the claim that there are natural psychological differences between the sexes. Those who hold that at least some roles should be sex roles generally base their view primarily on an appeal to such natural differences, while many of those advocating a society without sex roles argue either that the sexes do not differ in innate psychological traits or that there is no evidence that they do.[1] In this paper I argue that whether there are natural psychological differences between females and males has little bearing on the issue of whether society should reserve certain roles for females and others for males.

Let me begin by saying something about the claim that there are natural psychological differences between the sexes. The issue we are dealing with arises, of course, because there are biological

differences among human beings which are bases for designating some as females and others as males. Now it is held by some that, in addition to biological differences between the sexes, there are also natural differences in temperament, interests, abilities, and the like. In this paper I am concerned only with arguments which appeal to these psychological differences as bases of sex roles. Thus I exclude, for example, arguments that the role of jockey should be female because women are smaller than men or that boxers should be male because men are more muscular than women. Nor do I discuss arguments which appeal directly to the reproductive functions peculiar to each sex. If the physiological processes of gestation or of depositing sperm in a vagina are, apart from any psychological correlates they may have, bases for sex roles, these roles are outside the scope of the present discussion.

It should be noted, however, that virtually all those who hold that there are natural psychological differences between the sexes assume that these differences are determined primarily by differences in biology. According to one hypothesis, natural psychological differences between the sexes are due at least in part to differences between female and male nervous systems. As the male fetus develops in the womb, the testes secrete a

From Joyce Trebilcot, "Sex Roles: The Argument From Nature," *Ethics* vol. 85, no. 3 (April 1975), pp. 249–255. Published by the University of Chicago Press and reprinted with their permission and with the permission of the author. Copyright © 1975 by The University of Chicago Press.

An earlier version of this paper was read for the meeting of the American Philosophical Association, Western Division, April 1974.

hormone which is held to influence the growth of the central nervous system. The female fetus does not produce this hormone, nor is there an analogous female hormone which is significant at this stage. Hence it is suggested that female and male brains differ in structure, that this difference is due to the prenatal influence of testicular hormone, and that the difference in brains is the basis of some later differences in behavior.[2]

A second view about the origin of allegedly natural psychological differences between the sexes, a view not incompatible with the first, is psychoanalytical. It conceives of feminine or masculine behavior as, in part, the individual's response to bodily structure. On this view, one's more or less unconscious experience of one's own body (and in some versions, of the bodies of others) is a major factor in producing sex-specific personality traits. The classic theories of this kind are, of course, Freud's; penis envy and the castration complex are supposed to arise largely from perceptions of differences between female and male bodies. Other writers make much of the analogies between genitals and genders: the uterus is passive and receptive, and so are females; penises are active and penetrating, and so are males.[3] But here we are concerned not with the etiology of allegedly natural differences between the sexes but rather with the question of whether such differences, if they exist, are grounds for holding that there should be sex roles.

That a certain psychological disposition is natural only to one sex is generally taken to mean in part that members of that sex are more likely to have the disposition, or to have it to a greater degree, than persons of the other sex. The situation is thought to be similar to that of height. In a given population, females are on the average shorter than males, but some females are taller than some males. . . . The shortest members of the population are all females, and the tallest are all males, but there is an area of overlap. For psychological traits, it is usually assumed that there is some degree of overlap and that the degree of overlap is different for different characteristics. Because of the difficulty of identifying natural psychological characteristics, we have of course little or no data as to the actual distribution of such traits.

I shall not undertake here to define the concept of role, but examples include voter, librarian, wife, president. . . . A sex role is a role performed only or primarily by persons of a particular sex. Now if this is all we mean by "sex role," the problem of whether there should be sex roles must be dealt with as two separate issues: "Are sex roles a good thing?" and "Should society enforce sex roles?" One might argue, for example, that sex roles have value but that, even so, the demands of individual autonomy and freedom are such that societal institutions and practices should not enforce correlations between roles and sex. But the debate over sex roles is of course mainly a discussion about the second question, whether society should enforce these correlations. The judgment that there should be sex roles is generally taken to mean not just that sex-exclusive roles are a good thing, but that society should promote such exclusivity.

In view of this, I use the term "sex role" in such a way that to ask whether there should be sex roles is to ask whether society should direct women into certain roles and away from others, and similarly for men. A role is a sex role then (or perhaps an "institutionalized sex role") only if it is performed exclusively or primarily by persons of a particular sex *and* societal factors tend to encourage this correlation. These factors may be of various kinds. Parents guide children into what are taken to be sex-appropriate roles. Schools direct students into occupations according to sex. Marriage customs prescribe different roles for females and males. Employers and unions may refuse to consider applications from persons of the "wrong" sex. The media carry tales of the happiness of those who conform and the suffering of the others. The law sometimes penalizes deviators. Individuals may ridicule and condemn role crossing and smile on conformity. Societal sanctions such as these are essential to the notion of sex role employed here.

I turn now to a discussion of the three major ways the claim that there are natural psychological differences between the sexes is held to be relevant to the issue of whether there should be sex roles.

1. INEVITABILITY

It is sometimes held that if there are innate psychological differences between females and males, sex roles are inevitable. The point of this argument is not, of course, to urge that there should be sex roles, but rather to show that the normative question is out of place, that there will be sex roles, whatever we decide. The argument assumes first that the alleged natural differences between the sexes are inevitable; but if such differences are inevitable, differences in behavior are inevitable; and if differences in behavior are inevitable, society will inevitably be structured so as to enforce role differences according to sex. Thus, sex roles are inevitable.

For the purpose of this discussion, let us accept the claim that natural psychological differences are inevitable. . . . Does it follow that there must be sex roles, that is, that the institutions and practices of society must enforce correlations between roles and sex?

Surely not. Indeed, such sanctions would be pointless. Why bother to direct women into some roles and men into others if the pattern occurs regardless of the nature of society? Mill makes the point elegantly in *The Subjection of Women:* "The anxiety of mankind to interfere in behalf of nature, for fear lest nature should not succeed in effecting its purpose, is an altogether unnecessary solicitude."[4]

It may be objected that if correlations between sex and roles are inevitable, societal sanctions enforcing these correlations will develop because people will expect the sexes to perform different roles and these expectations will lead to behavior which encourages their fulfillment. This can happen, of course, but it is surely not inevitable. One need not act so as to bring about what one expects.

Indeed, there could be a society in which it is held that there are inevitable correlations between roles and sex but institutionalization of these correlations is deliberately avoided. What is inevitable is presumably not, for example, that every woman will perform a certain role and no man will perform it, but rather that most women will perform the role and most men will not. For any individual, then, a particular role may not be inevitable. Now suppose it is a value in the society in question that people should be free to choose roles according to their individual needs and interests. But then there should not be sanctions enforcing correlations between roles and sex, for such sanctions tend to force some individuals into roles for which they have no natural inclination and which they might otherwise choose against.

I conclude then that, even granting the assumptions that natural psychological differences, and therefore role differences, between the sexes are inevitable, it does not follow that there must be sanctions enforcing correlations between roles and sex. Indeed, if individual freedom is valued, those who vary from the statistical norm should not be required to conform to it.

2. WELL-BEING

The argument from well-being begins with the claim that, because of natural psychological differences between the sexes, members of each sex are happier in certain roles than in others, and the roles which tend to promote happiness are different for each sex. It is also held that if all roles are equally available to everyone regardless of sex, some individuals will choose against their own well-being. Hence, the argument concludes, for the sake of maximizing well-being there should be sex roles: society should encourage individuals to make "correct" role choices.

Suppose that women, on the average, are more compassionate than men. Suppose also that there are two sets of roles, "female" and "male", and that because of the natural compassion of women, women are happier in female than in male roles. Now if females and males overlap with respect to compassion, some men have as much natural compassion as some women, so they too will be happier in female than in male roles. Thus, the first premise of the argument from well-being should read: Suppose that, because of natural psychological differences between the sexes, *most* women are happier in female roles and *most* men in male roles. The argument continues: If all roles are equally available to everyone, some of the women who would be happier in female roles will choose against their own well-being, and similarly for men.

Now if the conclusion that there should be sex roles is to be based on these premises, another assumption must be added—that the loss of potential well-being resulting from societally produced adoption of unsuitable roles by individuals in the overlapping areas of the distribution is *less* than the loss that would result from "mistaken" free choices if there were no sex roles. With sex roles, some individuals who would be happier in roles assigned to the other sex perform roles assigned to their own sex, and so there is a loss of potential happiness. Without sex roles, some individuals, we assume, choose against their own well-being. But surely we are not now in a position to compare the two systems with respect to the number of mismatches produced. Hence, the additional premise required for the argument, that overall well-being is greater with sex roles than without them, is entirely unsupported.

Even if we grant, then, that because of innate psychological differences between the sexes members of each sex achieve greater well-being in some roles than in others, the argument from well-being does not support the conclusion that there should be sex roles. In our present state of knowledge, there is no reason to suppose that a sex role system which makes no discriminations within a sex would produce fewer mismatches between individuals and roles than a system in which all roles are open equally to both sexes.

3. EFFICIENCY

If there are natural differences between the sexes in the capacity to perform socially valuable tasks, then, it is sometimes argued, efficiency is served if these tasks are assigned to the sex with the greatest innate ability for them. Suppose, for example, that females are naturally better than males at learning foreign languages. This means that, if everything else is equal and females and males are given the same training in a foreign language, females, on the average, will achieve a higher level of skill than males. Now suppose that society needs interpreters and translators and that in order to have such a job one must complete a special training program whose only purpose is to provide persons for these roles. Clearly, efficiency is served if only individuals with a good deal of natural ability are selected for training, for the time and effort required to bring them to a given level of proficiency is less than that required for the less talented. But suppose that the innate ability in question is normally distributed within each sex and that the sexes overlap. . . . If we assume that a sufficient number of candidates can be recruited by considering only persons in the shaded area, they are the only ones who should be eligible. There are no men in this group. Hence, although screening is necessary in order to exclude nontalented women, it would be inefficient even to consider men, for it is known that no man is as talented as the talented women. In the interest of efficiency, then, the occupational roles of interpreter and translator should be sex roles; men should be denied access to these roles but women who are interested in them, especially talented women, should be encouraged to pursue them.

This argument is sound. That is, if we grant the factual assumptions and suppose also that efficiency for the society we are concerned with has some value, the argument from efficiency provides one reason for holding that some roles should be sex roles. This conclusion of course is only prima facie. In order to determine whether there should be sex roles, one would have to weigh efficiency, together with other reasons for such roles, against reasons for holding that there should not be sex roles. The reasons against sex roles are very strong. They are couched in terms of individual rights—in terms of liberty, justice, equality of opportunity. Efficiency by itself does not outweigh these moral values. Nevertheless, the appeal to nature, if true, combined with an appeal to the value of efficiency, does provide one reason for the view that there should be sex roles.

The arguments I have discussed here are not the only ones which appeal to natural psychological differences between the sexes in defense of sex roles, but these three arguments—from inevitability, well-being, and efficiency—are, I believe, the most common and the most plausible ones. The argument from efficiency alone, among them, provides a reason—albeit a rather weak reason—for thinking that there should be sex roles. I suggest, therefore, that the issue of natural psychological differences between women and men does not deserve the central place it is given, both traditionally and currently, in the literature on this topic.

It is frequently pointed out that the argument from nature functions as a cover, as a myth to make patriarchy palatable to both women and men. Insofar as this is so, it is surely worthwhile exploring and exposing the myth. But of course most of those who use the argument from nature take it seriously and literally, and this is the spirit in which I have dealt with it. Considering the argument in this way, I conclude that whether there should be sex roles does not depend primarily on whether there are innate psychological differences between the sexes. The question is, after all, not what women and men naturally are, but what kind of society is morally justifiable. In order to answer this question, we must appeal to the notions of justice, equality, and liberty. It is these moral concepts, not the empirical issue of sex differences, which should have pride of place in the philosophical discussion of sex roles.

NOTES

1. For support of sex roles, see, for example, Aristotle, *Politics,* book 1; and Erik Erikson, "Womanhood and the Inner Space," *Identity: Youth and Crisis* (New York: W. W. Norton & Co., 1968). Arguments against sex roles may be found, for example, in J. S. Mill, "The Subjection of Women," in *Essays on Sex Equality: John Stuart Mill and Harriet Taylor Mill,* ed. Alice S. Rossi (Chicago: University of Chicago Press, 1970); and Naomi Weisstein, "Psychology Constructs the Female," in *Women in Sexist Society,* ed. Vivian Gornick and Barbara K. Moran (New York: Basic Books, 1971).

2. See John Money and Anke A. Ehrhardt, *Man and Woman, Boy and Girl* (Baltimore: Johns Hopkins Press, 1972).

3. For Freud, see, for example, "Some Psychological Consequences of the Anatomical Distinctions between the Sexes," in *Sigmund Freud: Collected Papers,* ed. James Strachey (New York: Basic Books, 1959), 5:186–97. See also Karl Stern, *The Flight from Woman* (New York: Farrar, Straus & Giroux, 1965), chap. 2; and Erikson.

4. Mill, p. 154.

Reverse Discrimination

55. REVERSE DISCRIMINATION AS UNJUSTIFIED

Lisa H. Newton

I have heard it argued that "simple justice" requires that we favor women and blacks in employment and educational opportunities, since women and blacks were "unjustly" excluded from such opportunities for so many years in the not so distant past. It is a strange argument, an example of a possible implication of a true proposition advanced to dispute the proposition itself, like an octopus absent-mindedly slicing off his head with a stray tentacle.

Reprinted from Lisa H. Newton, "Reverse Discrimination as Unjustified," *Ethics,* vol. 83, no. 4 (1973), pp. 308–312. Copyright 1973 by The University of Chicago Press. Reprinted with the permission of the author and the publisher.

A fatal confusion underlies this argument, a confusion fundamentally relevant to our understanding of the notion of the rule of law.

Two senses of justice and equality are involved in this confusion. The root notion of justice, progenitor of the other, is the one that Aristotle (*Nicomachean Ethics* 5. 6; *Politics* 1. 2, 3. 1) assumes to be the foundation and proper virtue of the political association. It is the condition which free men establish among themselves when they "share a common life in order that their association bring them self-sufficiency"—the regulation of their relationship by law, and the establishment, by law, of equality before the law. Rule of law is the name and pattern of this justice; its equality stands against the inequalities—of wealth, talent, etc.—otherwise obtaining among its participants, who by virtue of that equality are called "citizens." It is an achievement —complete, or, more frequently, partial—of certain people in certain concrete situations. It is fragile and easily disrupted by powerful individuals who discover that the blind equality of rule of law is inconvenient for their interests. Despite its obvious instability, Aristotle assumed that the establishment of justice in this sense, the creation of citizenship, was a permanent possibility for men and that the resultant association of citizens was the natural home of the species. At levels below the political association, this rule-governed equality is easily found; it is exemplified by any group of children agreeing together to play a game. At the level of the political association, the attainment of this justice is more difficult, simply because the stakes are so much higher for each participant. The equality of citizenship is not something that happens of its own accord, and without the expenditure of a fair amount of effort it will collapse into the rule of a powerful few over an apathetic many. But at least it has been achieved, at some times in some places; it is always worth trying to achieve, and eminently worth trying to maintain, wherever and to whatever degree it has been brought into being.

Aristotle's parochialism is notorious; he really did not imagine that persons other than Greeks could associate freely in justice, and the only form of association he had in mind was the Greek *polis*. With the decline of the *polis* and the shift in the center of political thought, his notion of justice underwent a sea change. To be exact, it ceased to represent a political type and became a moral ideal: the ideal of equality as we know it. This ideal demands that all men be included in citizenship—that one Law govern all equally, that all men regard all other men as fellow citizens with the same guarantees, rights, and protections. Briefly, it demands that the circle of citizenship achieved by any group be extended to include the entire human race. Properly understood, its effect on our associations can be excellent: it congratulates us on our achievement of rule of law as a process of government but refuses to let us remain complacent until we have expanded the associations to include others within the ambit of the rules, as often and as far as possible. While one man is a slave, none of us may feel truly free. We are constantly prodded by this ideal to look for possible unjustifiable discrimination, for inequalities not absolutely required for the functioning of the society and advantageous to all. And after twenty centuries of pressure, not at all constant, from this ideal, it might be said that some progress has been made. To take the cases in point for this problem, we are now prepared to assert, as Aristotle would never have been, the equality of sexes and of persons of different colors. The ambit of American citizenship, once restricted to white males of property, has been extended to include all adult free men, then all adult males including ex-slaves, then all women. The process of acquisition of full citizenship was for these groups a sporadic trail of half-measures, even now not complete; the steps on the road to full equality are marked by legislation and judicial decisions which are only recently concluded and still often not enforced. But the fact that we can now discuss the possibility of favoring such groups in hiring shows that over the area that concerns us, at least, full equality is presupposed as a basis for discussion. To that extent, they are full citizens, fully protected by the law of the land.

It is important for my argument that the moral ideal of equality be recognized as logically distinct from the condition (or virtue) of justice in the political sense. Justice in this sense exists *among* a citizenry, irrespective of the number of the populace included in that citizenry. Further, the moral ideal is parasitic upon the political virtue, for "equality" is unspecified—it means nothing until we are told in what respect that equality is to be realized. In a political context, "equality" is specified as "equal rights"—equal access to the public realm, public goods and offices, equal treatment under the law—in brief, the equality of citizenship. If citizenship is not a possibility, political equality is unintelligible. The ideal emerges as a generalization of the real condition and refers back to that condition for its content.

Now, if justice (Aristotle's justice in the political sense) is equal treatment under law for all citizens, what is injustice? Clearly, injustice is the violation of that equality, discriminating for or against a group of citizens, favoring them with special immunities and privileges or depriving them of those guaranteed to the others. When the southern employer refuses to hire blacks in white-collar jobs, when Wall Street will only hire women as secretaries with new titles, when Mississippi high schools routinely flunk all black boys above ninth grade, we have examples of injustice, and we work to restore the equality of the public realm by ensuring that equal opportunity will be provided in such cases in the future. But of course when the employers and the schools *favor* women and blacks, the same injustice is done. Just as the previous discrimination did, this reverse discrimination violates the public equality which defines citizenship and destroys the rule of law for the areas in which these favors are granted. To the extent that we adopt a program of discrimination, reverse or otherwise, justice in the political sense is destroyed, and none of us, specifically affected or not, is a citizen, a bearer of rights—we are all petitioners for favors. And to the same extent the ideal of equality is undermined, for it has content only where justice obtains, and by destroying justice we render the ideal meaningless. It is, then, an ironic paradox, if not a contradiction in terms, to assert that the ideal of equality justifies the violation of justice; it is as if one should argue, with William Buckley, that an ideal of humanity can justify the destruction of the human race.

Logically, the conclusion is simple enough: all discrimination is wrong prima facie because it violates justice, and that goes for reverse discrimination too. No violation of justice among the citizens may be justified (may overcome the prima facie objection) by appeal to the ideal of equality, for that ideal is logically dependent upon the notion of justice. Reverse discrimination, then, which attempts no other justification than an appeal to equality, is wrong. But let us try to make the conclusion more plausible by suggesting some of the implications of the suggested practice of reverse discrimination in employment and education. My argument will be that the problems raised there are insoluble, not only in practice but in principle.

We may argue, if we like, about what "discrimination" consists of. Do I discriminate against blacks if I admit none to my school when none of the black applicants are qualified by the tests I always give? How far must I go to root out cultural bias from my application forms and tests before I can say that I have not discriminated against those of different cultures? Can I assume that women are not strong enough to be roughnecks on my oil rigs, or must I test them individually? But this controversy, the most popular and well-argued aspect of the issue, is not as fatal as two others which cannot be avoided: if we are regarding the blacks as a "minority" victimized by discrimination, what is a "minority"? And for any group—blacks, women, whatever—that has been discriminated against, what amount of reverse discrimination wipes out the initial discrimination? Let us grant as true that women and blacks were discriminated against, even where laws forbade such discrimination, and grant for the sake of argument that a history of discrimination must be wiped out by reverse discrimination. What follows?

First, are there other groups which have been discriminated against? For they should have the same right of restitution. What about American Indians, Chicanos, Appalachian Mountain whites, Puerto Ricans, Jews, Cajuns, and Orientals? And if these are to be included, the principle according to which we specify a "minority" is simply the criterion of "ethnic (sub) group," and we're stuck with every hyphenated American in the lower-middle class clamoring for special privileges for *his* group —and with equal justification. For be it noted, when we run down the Harvard roster, we find not only a scarcity of blacks (in comparison with the proportion in the population) but an even more striking scarcity of those second-, third-, and fourth-generation ethnics who make up the loudest voice of Middle America. Shouldn't they demand *their* share? And eventually, the WASPs will have to form their own lobby, for they too are a minority. The point is simply this: there is no "majority" in America who will not mind giving up just a bit of their rights to make room for a favored minority. There are only other minorities, each of which is discriminated against by the favoring. The initial injustice is then repeated dozens of times, and if each minority is granted the same right of restitution as the others, an entire area of rule governance is dissolved into a pushing and shoving match between self-interested groups. Each works to catch the public eye and political popularity by whatever means of advertising and power politics lend themselves to the effort, to capitalize as much as possible on temporary popularity until the restless mob picks another group to feel sorry for. Hardly an edifying spectacle, and in the long run no one can benefit: the pie is no larger—it's just that instead of setting up and enforcing rules for getting a piece, we've turned the contest into a free-for-all, requiring much more effort for no larger a reward. It would be in the interests of all the participants to reestablish an objective rule to govern the process, carefully enforced and the same for all.

Second, supposing that we do manage to agree in general that women and blacks (and all the others) have some right of restitution, some right to a privileged place in the structure of opportunities for a while, how will we know when that while is up? How much privilege is enough? When will the guilt be gone, the price paid, the balance restored? What recompense is right for centuries of exclusion? What criterion tells us when we are done? Our experience with the Civil Rights movement shows us that agreement on these terms cannot be presupposed: a process that appears to some to be going at a mad gallop into a black takeover appears to the rest of us to be at a standstill. Should a practice of reverse discrimination be adopted, we may safely predict that just as some of us begin to see "a satisfactory start toward righting the balance," others of us will see that we "have already gone too far in the other direction" and will suggest that the discrimination ought to be reversed again. And such disagreement is inevitable, for the point is that we could not *possibly* have any criteria for evaluating the kind of recompense we have in mind. The context presumed by any discussion of restitution is the context of rule of law: law sets the rights of men and simultaneously sets the method for remedying the violation of those rights. You may exact suffering from others and/or damage payments for yourself if and only if the others have violated your rights; the suffering you have endured is not sufficient reason for them to suffer. And remedial rights exist only where there is law: primary human rights are useful guides to legislation but cannot stand as reasons for awarding remedies for injuries sustained. But then, the context presupposed by any discussion of restitution is the context of preexistent full citizenship. No remedial rights could exist for the excluded; neither in law nor in logic does there exist a right to *sue* for a standing to sue.

From these two considerations, then, the difficulties with reverse discrimination become evident. Restitution for a disadvantaged group whose rights under the law have been violated is possible by legal means, but restitution for a disadvantaged group whose grievance is that there was no law to protect them simply is not. First, outside of the area of justice defined by the law, no sense can be made of "the group's rights," for no law recognizes that group or the individuals in it, qua members, as bearers of rights (hence *any* group can constitute itself as a disadvantaged minority in some sense and demand similar restitution). Second, outside of the area of protection of law, no sense can be made of the violation of rights (hence the amount of the recompense cannot be decided by any objective criterion). For both reasons, the practice of reverse discrimination undermines the foundation of the very ideal in whose name it is advocated; it destroys justice, law, equality, and citizenship itself, and replaces them with power struggles and popularity contests.

56. THE JUSTIFICATION OF REVERSE DISCRIMINATION

Tom L. Beauchamp

In recent years government policies intended to ensure fairer employment and educational opportunities for women and minority groups have engendered alarm. Target goals, timetables, and quotas seem to many citizens to discriminate against more talented applicants who are excluded yet would be accepted on their merits were it not for the preferential advancement of others. Such government policies are said to create a situation of "reverse discrimination." By balancing or compensating for past discrimination against persons on the basis of morally irrelevant characteristics (race, sex, nationality, and religion), these policies now require discrimination in favor of such persons and therefore against the members of other previously favored classes. These policies seem unfairly discriminatory to some because they violate basic principles of justice and equal protection. I believe this conclusion to be reasonable but incorrect, and in this paper I argue that some government policies which would result in reverse discrimination are appropriate and justifiable.

Most all published discussions on this subject known to me are opposed to public policies which would permit reverse discrimination. Among those writers who would permit policies of reverse discrimination, a fairly standard approach is taken: They attempt to justify reverse discrimination by showing that under certain conditions compensation owed for *past* wrongs justifies (for varying reasons) *present* policies productive of reverse discrimination. *This is not my argument;* and it is important to see that it is not. I draw only weak obligations from the claims of compensatory justice; I contend only that because of past wrongs to classes of persons we have *special and strong* obligations to see that these wrongs do not continue. My argument differs from more usual ones since I hold

Reprinted from Tom L. Beauchamp, "The Justification of Reverse Discrimination," in W. T. Blackstone and Robert Heslep, eds., *Social Justice and Preferential Treatment* (Athens, Ga: University of Georgia Press, 1976). Reprinted by permission of the publisher.

that reverse discrimination is permitted and even required in order that we might eliminate *present* discriminatory practices against classes of persons. I adduce factual evidence for this claim of present, continuing discrimination.

As will become apparent, I construe the issue of reverse discrimination as *primarily* a factual one, and as only secondarily an ethical one. My factual argument is based on factual evidence which establishes the following: There exist discriminatory social attitudes and selection procedures so deeply entrenched in contemporary society that they are almost certainly ineradicable by good faith measures in an acceptable period of time. My ethical contention is that because these crippling conditions exist, policies producing reverse discrimination are justified. These policies are morally *permitted* because they are social measures necessary for the protection of those harmed by invidious social attitudes and selection procedures.[1] A stronger thesis is that such policies are morally *required* and not merely morally permitted. I also support this stronger contention on grounds that past discriminatory practices have created a special and strong obligation to erase invidious discrimination and ensure equal protection of the law. Hence these policies are morally required (by compensatory justice) under the kind of incorrigible social conditions I discuss in my factual arguments.

I proceed by first establishing a principled framework for resolving moral issues about the justifiability of reverse discrimination. I then discuss the factual evidence of present discriminatory practices and the difficulties which attend weak attempts to offset or overcome such bias. . . .

ARGUMENTS AGAINST REVERSE DISCRIMINATION

My moral argument is intended to show that policies productive of reverse discrimination are compatible with basic principles of justice and utility. This is not to say that no injustices result from the occurrence of reverse discrimination, but it is to say that these injustices can be justified.

For moral philosophy the main issues of reverse discrimination may be formulated as follows: Under what conditions, if any, are policies resulting in reverse discrimination justified? Can basic ethical principles of justice and utility be successfully employed for the justification of reverse discrimination? Conceivably other ethical principles, such as beneficence, might be invoked. But since justice and utility are universally recognized as the most directly relevant principles, I shall confine my discussion to them, beginning with justice.

An initial difficulty must be faced in any appeal to principles of justice. Since there are different theories of justice, and different kinds of justice recognized within the different theories, it might be thought that a comprehensive theory of justice must be defended before problems of reverse discrimination can be intelligently discussed. Fortunately, for our purposes, this difficulty may be largely ignored, for two reasons. First, we can without prejudicing the arguments successfully operate with two rather minimal principles of justice, both of which derive from Aristotle and both of which receive wide acceptance as at least necessary, even if not sufficient, conditions of justice. The first is the principle of *formal equality*. It says that equals must be treated equally and unequals unequally; or, more fully stated, it says that "No person should be treated unequally, despite all differences with other persons, until such time as it has been shown that there is a difference between them relevant to the treatment at stake." One demand of the principle is the egalitarian ideal of equal consideration of persons: Every person is to be evaluated on his or her merit when there is equal opportunity to compete. The problem with the principle is notoriously more in its abstractness than in any deficiency of content. That equals ought to be treated equally, by law and elsewhere, is not likely to stir disagreement. But who is equal and who unequal? Presumably all citizens should have equal political rights, equal access to public services, and should receive equal treatment under the law. But almost all would allow that distinctions based on experience, merit, and position do sometimes introduce criteria justifying differential treatment. Whether

race, sex, and religion similarly justify differential treatment under some conditions is more controversial. This issue of the appropriate *application* of the principle of formal equality is one that we shall be considering.

The second principle of justice deserving explicit statement is the principle of *compensatory justice*. It says that whenever an injustice has been committed, just compensation or reparation is owed the injured parties. The idea is to restore, so far as possible, the state of affairs prior to the injury or injustice which created the need for compensation, and also to benefit the injured parties in a manner proportional to the injury or loss suffered. The compensation might be to groups or to individuals, but in either case the same justifying principle is used. It is now a widespread view that groups invidiously discriminated against in the proximate and remote past, including women, blacks, North American Indians, and French Canadians, should be recompensed for these injustices by compensatory policies, at least in those cases where injury is traceable to particular persons. I shall be discussing not merely whether some form of compensation is deserved, but the more controversial question whether such compensation might justifiably result in reverse discrimination. I shall not, however, argue that compensatory claims by themselves justify direct monetary reparations or quota allotments to classes of persons. My account is weaker: Compensatory justice both (1) demands that we make an especially vigorous attempt to discover *present* discrimination against classes of persons discriminated against in the past and (2) creates a *special* obligation to eliminate such present discriminatory treatment wherever it is found. I will take for granted that this weakened claim about obligations generated by compensatory justice is reasonable, and that any society which fails to act on this obligation is an unjust society, whether or not this failure is intentional.

Recently a rather large literature has emerged in which the attempt is made to show that policies causing reverse discrimination violate the above (and perhaps other) principles of justice. It is argued in this literature that since reverse discriminatory policies create injustices they cannot be justified. The most widely circulated form of the argument makes a direct appeal to the principle of formal equality. The following is a typical example of this basic argument:

Now, if justice (Aristotle's justice in the political sense) is equal treatment under the law for all citizens, what is injustice? Clearly, injustice is the violation of that equality, discriminating for or against a group of citizens, favoring them with special immunities and privileges or depriving them of those guaranteed to the others. . . . But, of course, when the employers and the schools *favor* women and blacks, the same injustice is done. Just as the previous discrimination did, this reverse discrimination violates the public equality which defines citizenship and destroys the rule of law for the areas in which these favors are granted. To the extent that we adopt a program of discrimination, reverse or otherwise, justice in the political sense is destroyed, . . . [and] the ideal of equality is undermined, for it has content only where justice obtains.. . . . [Reverse discrimination] destroys justice, law, equality, and citizenship itself, and replaces them with power struggles and popularity contests.[2] . . .

ARGUMENT FOR REVERSE DISCRIMINATION

I want to concede from the outset that policies of reverse discrimination can create serious and perhaps even tragic injustices. One must be careful, however, not to draw an overzealous conclusion from this admission. Those who argue that reverse discrimination creates injustices often say that because of the injustice such policies are *unjust.* I think by this use of "unjust" they generally mean "not justified" (rather than "not sanctioned by justice"). But this conclusion does not follow merely from the arguments thus far mentioned. A policy can create and even perpetuate injustices, as violations of the principle of formal equality, and yet be justified by other reasons. It would be an injustice in this sense to fire either one of two assistant professors with exactly similar professional credentials, while retaining the other of the two; yet the financial condition of the university or compensation owed the person retained might provide compelling reasons which justify the action. The first reason supporting the dismissal is utilitarian in character, and the other derives from the principle of compensatory justice. This shows both that there can be conflicts between different justice-

regarding reasons and also that violations of the principle of formal equality are not in themselves sufficient to render an action unjustifiable.

A proper conclusion, then—and one which I accept—is that all discrimination, including reverse discrimination, is prima facie immoral, because a basic principle of justice creates a prima facie duty to abstain from such treatment of persons. But no absolute duty is created come what may, for we might have conflicting duties of sufficient weight to justify such injustices. The latter is the larger thesis I wish to defend: Considerations of compensatory justice and utility are conjointly of sufficient weight in contemporary society to neutralize and overcome the quite proper presumption of immorality in the case of some policies productive of reverse discrimination.

FACTUAL EVIDENCE OF INCORRIGIBLE DISCRIMINATORY PRACTICES

I now turn away from moral considerations to factual ones. It is difficult to avoid accepting two important claims: (a) that the law ought never to sanction any discriminatory practices (whether plain old unadorned discrimination or reverse discrimination), and (b) that such practices can be eradicated by bringing the full weight of the law down on those who engage in discriminatory practices. The first claim is a moral one, the second a factual one. I contend in this section that it is unrealistic to believe, as *b* suggests, that in contemporary society discriminatory practices *can* be eradicated by legal measures which do not permit reverse discrimination. And because they cannot be eradicated, I think we ought to relax our otherwise unimpeachably sound reservations against allowing any discriminatory practices whatever.

My argument is motivated by the belief that racial, sexual, and no doubt other forms of discrimination are not antique relics but are living patterns which continue to warp selection and ranking procedures. In my view the difference between the present and the past is that discriminatory treatment is today less widespread and considerably less blatant. But its reduction has produced apathy; its subtleness has made it less visible and considerably more difficult to detect. Largely because of the reduced visibility of racism and sexism, I suggest, reverse discrimination now strikes us as all too harsh and unfair. After all, quotas and preferential treatment have no appeal if one assumes a just, primarily nondiscriminatory society. Since the presence or absence of seriously discriminatory conditions in our society is a factual matter, empirical evidence must be adduced to show that the set of discriminatory attitudes and selection procedures I have alleged to exist do in fact exist. The data I shall mention derive primarily from historical, linguistic, sociological, and legal sources.

STATISTICAL EVIDENCE

Statistical imbalances in employment and admission are often discounted, because so many variables can be hypothesized to explain why, for nondiscriminatory reasons, an imbalance exists. We can all think of plausible nondiscriminatory reasons why 22% of Harvard's graduate students in 1969 were women but its tenured Arts and Sciences Faculty in the Graduate School consisted of 411 males and 0 females.[3] But sometimes we are able to discover evidence which supports the claim that skewed statistics are the result of discrimination. Quantities of such discriminatory findings, in turn, raise serious questions about the real reasons for suspicious statistics in those cases where we have *not* been able to determine these reasons—perhaps because they are so subtle and unnoticed. I shall discuss each factor in turn: (a) statistics which constitute prima facie but indecisive evidence of discrimination; (b) findings concerning discriminatory reasons for some of these statistics; and (c) cases where the discrimination is probably undetectable because of its subtleness, and yet the statistical evidence is overwhelming.

(a) A massive body of statistics constituting prima facie evidence of discrimination has been assembled in recent years. Here is a tiny but diverse fragment of some of these statistical findings.[4] (1) Women college teachers with identical credentials in terms of publications and experience are promoted at almost exactly one-half the rate of their male counterparts. (2) In the United States women graduates of medical schools in 1965 stood at 7%, as compared with 36% in Germany. The gap in the number of women physicians was

similar. (3) Of 3,000 leading law firms surveyed in 1957 only 32 reported a woman partner, and even these women were paid much less (increasingly so for every year of employment) than their male counterparts. (4) 40% of the white collar positions in the United States are presently held by women, but only 10% of the management positions are held by women, and their pay again is significantly less (70% of clerical workers are women). (5) 8,000 workers were employed in May 1967 in the construction of BART (Bay Area Rapid Transit), but not a single electrician, ironworker, or plumber was black. (6) In the population as a whole in the United States, 3 out of 7 employees hold white collar positions, but only 1 of 7 blacks holds such a position, and these latter jobs are clustered in professions which have the fewest jobs to offer in top-paying positions.

(b) I concede that such statistics are far from decisive indicators of discrimination. But when further evidence concerning the reasons for the statistics is uncovered, they are put in a perspective affording them greater power—clinching power in my view. Consider (3)—the statistics on the lack of women lawyers. A survey of Harvard Law School alumnae in 1970 provided evidence about male lawyers' attitudes.[5] It showed that business and legal firms do not generally expect the women they hire to become lawyers, that they believe women cannot become good litigators, and that they believe only limited numbers of women should be hired since clients generally prefer male lawyers. Surveys of women applicants for legal positions indicate they are frequently either told that a women will not be hired, or are warned that "senior partners" will likely object, or are told that women will be hired to do only probate, trusts, and estate work. (Other statistics confirm that these are the sorts of tasks dominantly given to women.) Consider also (5)—a particular but typical case of hiring in blue-collar positions. Innumerable studies have shown that most of these positions are filled by word-of-mouth recruitment policies conducted by all-white interviewers (usually all-male as well). In a number of decisions of the Equal Employment Opportunity Commission, it has been shown that the interviewers have racially biased attitudes and that the applications of blacks and women are systematically handled in unusual ways, such as never even being filed. So serious and consistent have such violations been that the EEOC has publicly stated its belief that word-of-mouth recruitment policies without demonstrable supplementary and simultaneous recruitment in minority group communities is in itself a "prima facie violation of Title VII".[6] Gertrude Ezorsky has argued, convincingly I believe, that this pattern of 'special ties' is no less present in professional white-collar hiring, which is neither less discriminatory nor more sensitive to hiring strictly on the basis of merit.[7]

(c) Consider, finally, (l)—statistics pertaining to the treatment of women college teachers. The Carnegie Commission and others have assembled statistical evidence to show that in even the most favorable construal of relevant variables, women teachers have been discriminated against in hiring, tenuring, and ranking. But instead of summarizing this mountain of material, I wish here to take a particular case in order to illustrate the difficulty in determining, on the basis of statistics and similar empirical data, whether discrimination is occurring; and yet where even courts have been forced to find satisfactory evidence of discrimination. In December 1974 a decision was reached by the Commission Against Discrimination of the Executive Department of the State of Massachusetts regarding a case at Smith College where the two Complainants were women who were denied tenure and dismissed by the English Department.[8] The women claimed sex discrimination and based their case on the following: (1) Women at the full professor level in the university declined from 54% in 1958 to 21%, and in the English department from 57% in 1960 to 11% in 1972. These statistics compared unfavorably at all levels with Mt. Holyoke's, a comparable institution (since both have an all female student body and are located in Western Massachusetts). (2) Thirteen of the department's fifteen associate and full professorships belonged to men. (3) The two tenured women had obtained tenure under "distinctly peculiar experiences" including a stipulation that one be only part-time and that the other not be promoted when given tenure. (4) The department's faculty members conceded that tenure standards were applied subjectively, were vague, and lacked the kind of precision which would avoid discriminatory application. (5) The women denied tenure were at no time given ad-vance warning that their work was deficient. Rather, they were given favorable evaluations of their teaching and were encouraged to believe they would receive tenure. (6) Some stated reasons for the dismissals were later demonstrated to be rationalizations, and one letter from a senior member to the tenure and promotion committee contradicted his own appraisal of teaching ability filed with the department. (7) The court accepted expert testimony that any deficiencies in the women candidates were also found in male candidates promoted and given tenure during this same period, and that the women's positive credentials were at least as good as the men's.

The Commissioner's opinion found that "the Complainants properly used statistics to demonstrate that the Respondents' practices operate with a discriminatory effect." Citing *Parham v. Southwestern Bell Telephone Co.,*[9] the Commissioner argued that "in such cases extreme statistics may establish discrimination as a matter of law, without additional supportive evidence." But in this case the Commissioner found abundant additional evidence in the form of "the historical absence of women," "word-of-mouth recruitment policies" which operate discriminatorily, and a number of "subtle and not so subtle, societal patterns" existent at Smith.[10] On December 30, 1974, the Commissioner ordered the two women reinstated with tenure and ordered the department to submit an affirmative action program within 60 days.

This case is interesting because there is little in the way of clinching proof that the members of the English department actually held discriminatory attitudes. Yet so consistent a pattern of *apparently* discriminatory treatment must be regarded, according to this decision, as *de facto* discriminatory. The Commissioner's ruling and other laws are quite explicit that "intent or lack thereof is of no consequence." If a procedure constitutes discriminatory treatment, then the parties discriminated against must be recompensed. Here we have a case where irresistible statistics and other sociological evidence of "social exclusion" and "subtle societal patterns" provide convincing evidence that strong, court backed measures must be taken because nothing short of such measures is sufficiently strong to overcome the discriminatory pattern, as the Respondent's testimony in the case verifies.[11]

Some understanding of the attitudes underlying the statistical evidence thus far surveyed can be gained by consideration of some linguistic evidence now to be mentioned. It further supports the charge of widespread discrimination in the case of women and of the difficulty in changing discriminatory attitudes.

LINGUISTIC EVIDENCE

Robert Baker has assembled some impressive linguistic evidence which indicates that our language is male-slanted, perhaps male chauvinistic, and that language about women relates something of fundamental importance concerning the males' most fundamental conceptions of women.[12] Baker argues that as the term "boy" once expressed a paternalistic and dominating attitude toward blacks (and was replaced in our conceptual structure because of this denigrating association), so there are other English terms which serve similar functions in regard to women (but are not replaced because not considered by men as in need of replacement). Baker assembles evidence both from the language itself and from surveys of users of the language to show the following.

(a) Substitutions for "Woman"

The term "woman" is broadly substitutable for and frequently interchanged in English sentences such as 'Who is that ——— over there?' by terms such as those in the following divisions:

A. Neutral Categories	B. Animal Categories	C. Plaything Categories
lady	chick	babe
gal	bird	doll
girl	fox	cuddly thing
broad	vixen	
(sister)	filly	
	bitch	

D. Gender Categories	E. Sexual Categories
skirt	snatch
hem	cunt
	ass
	twat
	piece
	lay
	pussy

Baker notes that (1) while there are differences in the frequency of usage, all of these terms are standard enough to be recognizable at least by most male users of the language; (2) women do not typically identify themselves in sexual categories; and (3) typically only males use the nonneutral categories (B–E). He takes this to be evidence—and I agree—that the male conception of women differs significantly from the female conception and that the categories used by the male in classifying women are "prima facie denigrating." He then argues that it is clearly and not merely prima facie denigrating when categories such as C and E are used, as they are either derived from playboy male images or are outright vulgarities. Baker argues that it is most likely that B and D are similarly used in denigrating ways. His arguments center on the metaphorical associations of these terms, but the evidence cannot be further pursued here.

Although Baker does not remark that women do not have a similar language for men, it seems to be important to notice this fact. Generally, any negative categories used by women to refer to men are as frequently or more frequently used by men to apply to women. This asymmetrical relation does not hold, of course, for the language used by whites and blacks for denigrating reference. This fact perhaps says something about how blacks have caught onto the impact of the language as a tool of denigrating identification in a way women have yet to do, at least in equal numbers. It may also say something about the image of submissiveness which many women still bear about themselves—an image blacks are no longer willing to accept.

(b) The Language of Sexual Intercourse

Baker argues that the conception of sexual intercourse in our culture depicts women more as objects of sexual exploitation than as persons with the same entitlements as males. He analyzes the many terms that are synonymously used with "had sexual intercourse with" ("screwed," "layed," "fucked," "balled," "humped," "diddled with," etc.). He shows—again quite convincingly in my view—that: (1) Male names are the subjects of sentences with active constructions, while names for females require passive constructions. That is, we conceive of the male as doing the action and the female as the recipient, and therefore conceive of the two as having different sexual roles. (2) This linguistic difference cannot be explained merely in terms of the sexual differences in physiology (as "screw," e.g. suggests), since many other words could be chosen ("engulfing," e.g.) but never are. (3) Most of the terms used to portray the male's action are also terms used to indicate that a person is harming another person ("screwed," "had," and "fucked," e.g.) and that the language itself would indicate that we see the woman as "being taken advantage of." (4) Similarly terms such as "prick" used expressly to refer to the male are words in our language for one who hurts or is abusive or brutalizing.

Baker concludes from his linguistic studies that "sexual discrimination permeates our conceptual structure. Such discrimination is clearly inimical to any movement toward sexual egalitariansim and virtually defeats its purpose at the outset." [13] His conclusion may somewhat overreach his premises, but when combined with the corroborating statistical evidence previously adduced, it seems apt. Linguistic dispositions lead us to categorize persons and events in discriminatory ways which are sometimes glaringly obvious to the categorized, but accepted as "objective" by the categorizer. My contention, derived from Baker's . . . is that cautious, good faith movements toward egalitarianism such as affirmative action guidelines *cannot* succeed short of fundamental conceptual and ethical revisions. And since the probability of such revisions approximates zero (because discriminatory attitudes are covertly embedded in language and cultural habit), radical expedients are required to bring about the desired egalitarian results, expedients which may result in reverse discrimination.

CONCLUSIONS

Irving Thalberg has argued, correctly I believe, that the gravest contemporary problems with racism stem from its "protectively camouflaged" status, which he calls "visceral." Thalberg skillfully points to a number of attitudes held by those whites normally classified as unprejudiced which indicate that racism still colors their conception of social facts. [14] John Stuart Mill argued a similar thesis in the nineteenth century about sexism. [15] Virginia Held has recently argued the additional thesis that under present, legally acceptable policies and programs of 'gradual improvement' in the hiring of women and nonwhites, it will take decades to achieve equality

of occupational opportunity. [16] My alliance with such positions ought by now to be obvious. But my overall intentions and conclusions are somehat different. I hold that because of the peculiarly concealed nature of the protective camouflage under which sexism and racism have so long thrived, it is not a reasonable expectation that the lightweight programs now administered under the heading of affirmative action will succeed in overcoming discriminatory treatment.

NOTES

1. I do not claim that policies productive of reverse discrimination are necessary for the elimination of every particular case of invidious discriminatory treatment. Obviously some nonreverse discriminatory measures will on some occasions suffice. My claim is that without such policies the problems of intractable discriminatory treatment in society at large cannot be resolved.

2. Lisa H. Newton, "Reverse Discrimination as Unjustified," *Ethics,* Vol. 83 (1973), pp. 310, 312.

3. From "Statement of Dr. Bernice Sandler," *Discrimination Against Women: Congressional Hearings on Equal Rights in Education and Employment* (New York: R. R. Bowker Company, 1973), ed. Catharine R. Stimpson, pp. 61, 415. Hereafter *Discrimination Against Women.*

4. All of the statistics and quotations cited are taken from the compilations of data in the following sources: (1) Kenneth M. Davidson, Ruth B. Ginsburg, and Herma H. Kay, eds., *Sex-Based Discrimination: Text, Cases, and Materials* (Minneapolis: West Publishing Company, 1974), esp. Ch. III. Hereafter *Sex-Based Discrimination.* (2) *Discrimination Against Women,* esp. pp. 397–441 and 449–502. (3) Alfred W. Blumrosen, *Black Employment and the Law* (New Brunswick, New Jersey: Rutgers University Press, 1971), esp. pp. 107, 122f. (4) *The Federal Civil Rights Enforcement Effort—1971,* A Report of the United States Commission on Civil Rights.

5. *Discrimination Against Women,* pp. 505f.

6. *Sex-Based Discrimination,* p. 516.

7. "The Fight Over University Women," *The New York Review of Books,* Vol. XXI (May 16, 1974), pp. 32–39.

8. *Maurianne Adams and Mary Schroeder v. Smith College,* Massachusetts Commission Against Discrimination, Nos. 72-S-53, 72-S-54 (December 30, 1974). Hereafter *The Smith College Case.*

9. 433 F.2d 421, 426 (8 Cir. 1970).

10. *The Smith College Case,* pp. 23, 26.

11. *Ibid.,* pp. 26f.

12. Robert Baker, " 'Pricks' and 'Chicks': A Plea for Persons," in Richard Wasserstrom, ed., *Today's Moral Problems* (New York: Macmillan Publishing Company, 1975), pp. 152–70.

13. *Ibid.,* p. 170.

14. "Visceral Racism," *The Monist,* Vol. 56 (October 1972), pp. 43–63, and reprinted in Wasserstrom, *op. cit.*

15. *On the Subjection of Women* (London: Longmans, Green, Reades, and Dyer, 1869), and especially as partially reprinted in Tom L. Beauchamp, ed., *Ethics and Public Policy* (Englewood Cliffs, New Jersey: Prentice-Hall, Inc., 1975), pp. 11–19.

16. "Reasonable Progress and Self-Respect," *The Monist,* Vol. 57 (1973), pp. 12–27, and reprinted in Beauchamp, *op. cit.*

57. DEFUNIS V. ODEGAARD
(U.S. SUPREME COURT, 1974)

EDITOR'S NOTE

The DeFunis case, perhaps the best known legal case involving alleged reverse discrimination, brings to the fore a number of the moral and constitutional issues involved in reverse discrimination. Marco DeFunis applied for admission to the University of Washington Law School in 1971. He was denied admission to the first-year law class which was restricted to 150 students and for which there were 1600 applicants. He filed suit in a Washington trial court, claiming that the admissions committee of the law school unfairly discriminated against him on the basis of race in violation of the Fourteenth Amendment of the Constitution. A mandatory injunction against the law school was granted at the trial court and DeFunis was admitted. Subsequently, the trial court judgment was reversed on appeal by the Washington Supreme Court, which held that the admissions policy of the law school did not violate the Constitution. DeFunis then appealed to the U.S. Supreme Court, which stayed the judgment of the Washington Supreme Court, thereby permitting DeFunis to continue in law school. Since DeFunis was in his last quarter of law school when the court finally considered his case, it was subsequently declared moot. The case was not a class action suit and DeFunis no longer needed remedy. The decision and rationale of the Supreme Court of the State of Washington is presented below, followed by Justice Douglas' dissent in which he discusses the merits of the case.

DE FUNIS V. ODEGAARD

The essence of plaintiff's Fourteenth Amendment argument is that the law school violated his right to equal protection of the laws by denying him admission, yet accepting certain minority applicants with lower PFYAs than plaintiff who, but for their minority status, would not have been admitted.

To answer this contention we consider three implicit, subordinate questions: (A) Whether race

82 Wn.2d 11,507 P.2d 1169; from *Washington Reports* 2dS 82 (1973), pp. 24–42.

can ever be considered as one factor in the admissions policy of a state law school or whether racial classifications are *per se* unconstitutional because the equal protection of the laws requires that law school admissions be "color-blind"; (B) if consideration of race is not *per se* unconstitutional, what is the appropriate standard of review to be applied in determining the constitutionality of such a classification; and (C) when the appropriate standard is applied does the specific minority admissions policy employed by the law school pass constitutional muster?

A

Relying solely on *Brown v. Board of Educ.,* 347 U.S. 483, 98 L. Ed. 873, 74 S. Ct. 686, 38 A.L.R.2d 1180 (1954), the trial court held that a state law school can never consider race as one criterion in its selection of first-year students. In holding that all such racial classifications are *per se* unconstitutional, the trial court stated in its oral opinion:

Since no more than 150 applicants were to be admitted the admission of less qualified resulted in a denial of places to those otherwise qualified. The plaintiff and others in this group have not, in my opinion, been accorded equal protection of the laws guaranteed by the Fourteenth Amendment.

In 1954 the United States Supreme Court decided that public education must be equally available to all regardless of race.

After that decision the Fourteenth Amendment could no longer be stretched to accommodate the needs of any race. Policies of discrimination will inevitably lead to reprisals. In my opinion the only safe rule is to treat all races alike, and I feel that is what is required under the equal protection clause.

In *Brown v. Board of Educ., supra,* the Supreme Court addressed a question of primary importance at page 493:

Does segregation of children in public schools solely on the basis of race, even though the physical facilities and other "tangible" factors may be equal, deprive the children of the minority group of equal educational opportunities? We believe that it does.

385

The court in *Brown* held the equal protection clause of the Fourteenth Amendment prohibits state law from requiring the operation of racially segregated, dual school systems of public education and requires that the system be converted into a unitary, nonracially segregated system. In so holding, the court noted that segregation inevitably stigmatizes Black children:

To separate them from others of similar age and qualifications solely because of their race generates a feeling of inferiority as to their status in the community that may affect their hearts and minds in a way unlikely ever to be undone.

Brown v. Board of Educ., supra at 494. Moreover, "The impact is greater when it has the sanction of the law; for the policy of separating the races is usually interpreted as denoting the inferiority of the negro group." *Brown* at 494.

[2] *Brown* did not hold that all racial classifications are *per se* unconstitutional; rather, it held that invidious racial classifications—*i.e.,* those that stigmatize a racial group with the stamp of inferiority—are unconstitutional. Even viewed in a light most favorable to plaintiff, the "preferential" minority admissions policy administered by the law school is clearly not a form of invidious discrimination. The goal of this policy is not to separate the races, but to bring them together. And, as has been observed,

Preferential admissions do not represent a covert attempt to stigmatize the majority race as inferior; nor is it reasonable to expect that a possible effect of the extension of educational preferences to certain disadvantaged racial minorities will be to stigmatize whites.

O'Neil, *Preferential Admissions: Equalizing the Access of Minority Groups to Higher Education,* 80 Yale L.J. 699, 713 (1971).

While *Brown v. Board of Educ., supra,* certainly provides a starting point for our analysis of the instant case, we do not agree with the trial court that *Brown* is dispositive here. Subsequent decisions of the United States Supreme Court have made it clear that in some circumstances a racial criterion *may* be used—and indeed in some circumstances *must* be used—by public educational insti-

tutions in bringing about racial balance. School systems which were formerly segregated de jure[1] now have an affirmative duty to remedy racial imbalance.

In Green v. County School Bd., 391 U.S. 430, 20 L. Ed. 2d 716, 88 S. Ct. 1689 (1963), the Supreme Court considered a school board's adoption of a "freedom-of-choice" plan which allowed a student to choose his own public school. No student was assigned or admitted to school on the basis of race. In holding that, on the facts presented, the plan did not satisfy the board's duty to create a unitary, nonracial system, the court stated at pages 437–40:

In the context of the state-imposed segregated pattern of long standing, the fact that in 1965 the Board opened the doors of the former "white" school to Negro children and of the "Negro" school to white children merely begins, not ends, our inquiry whether the Board has taken steps adequate to abolish its dual, segregated system.

. . . The burden on a school board today is to come forward with a plan that promises realistically to work, and promises realistically to work *now*.

. . .

As Judge Sobeloff has put it,

" 'Freedom of choice' is not a sacred talisman; it is only a means to a constitutionally required end—the abolition of the system of segregation and its effects. If the means prove effective, it is acceptable, but if it fails to undo segregation, other means must be used to achieve this end. The school officials have the continuing duty to take whatever action may be necessary to create a 'unitary, nonracial system.' " *Bowman v. County School Board,* 382 F.2d 326, 333 (C. A. 4th Cir. 1967) (concurring opinion).

Pursuing this principle further, the Supreme Court in *Swann v. Charlotte-Mecklenburg Bd. of Educ.,* 402 U.S. 1, 16, 28 L. Ed. 2d 554, 91 S. Ct. 1267 (1971), unanimously held that school authorities, in seeking to achieve a unitary, nonracial system of public education, need not be "color-blind", but may consider race as a valid criterion when considering admissions and producing a student body. . . .

[4] However, plaintiff contends that cases such as *Green v. County School Bd., supra,* and *Swann v. Charlotte-Mecklenburg Bd. of Educ., supra,* are inapposite here since none of the students there in-

volved were deprived of an education by the plan to achieve a unitary school system. It is questionable whether defendants deprived plaintiff of a legal education by denying him admission.[2] But even accepting this contention, arguendo, the denial of a "benefit" on the basis of race is not necessarily a *per se* violation of the Fourteenth Amendment, if the racial classification is used in a compensatory way to promote integration. . . .

B

[6] Generally, when reviewing a state-created classification alleged to be in violation of the equal protection clause of the Fourteenth Amendment, the question is whether the classification is reasonably related to a legitimate public purpose. And, in applying this "rational basis" test "[A] discrimination will not be set aside if any state of facts reasonably may be conceived to justify it." *McGowan v. Maryland,* 366 U.S. 420, 426, 6 L. Ed. 2d 393, 81 S. Ct 1101 (1961).

However, where the classification is based upon race, a heavier burden of justification is imposed upon the state. In overturning Virginia's antimisegenation law, the Supreme Court explained this stricter standard of review:

The clear and central purpose of the Fourteenth Amendment was to eliminate all official state sources of invidious racial discrimination in the States. [Citations omitted.]

. . . At the very least, the Equal Protection Clause demands that racial classifications, especially suspect in criminal statutes, be subjected to the "most rigid scrutiny," [citation omitted] and, if they are ever to be upheld, they must be shown to be necessary to the accomplishment of some permissible state objective, independent of the racial discrimination which it was the object of the Fourteenth Amendement to eliminate. . . .

There is patently no legitimate overriding purpose independent of invidious racial discrimination which justifies this classification.

Loving v. Virginia, 388 U.S. 1, 10-11, 18 L. Ed. 2d 1010, 87 S. Ct. 1817 (1967). *Accord, McLaughlin v. Florida,* 379 U.S. 184, 13 L. Ed. 2d 222, 85 S. Ct. 283 (1964); *Hunter v. Erickson,* 393 U.S. 385, 21 L. Ed. 2d 616, 89 S. Ct. 557 (1969).

It has been suggested that the less strict "rational basis" test should be applied to the consideration of race here, since the racial distinction is being used to redress the effects of past discrimination; thus, because the persons normally stigmatized by racial classifications are being benefited, the action complained of should be considered "benign" and reviewed under the more permissive standard. However, the minority admissions policy is certainly not benign with respect to nonminority students who are displaced by it. *See* O'Neil, *Preferential Admissions: Equalizing the Access of Minority Groups to Higher Education,* 80 Yale L.J. 699, 710 (1971).

The burden is upon the law school to show that its consideration of race in admitting students is necessary to the accomplishment of a compelling state interest.

C

[7] It can hardly be gainsaid that the minorities have been, and are, grossly underrepresented in the law schools—and consequently in the legal profession—of this state and this nation. We believe the state has an overriding interest in promoting integration in public education. In light of the serious underrepresentation of minority groups in the law schools, and considering that minority groups participate on an equal basis in the tax support of the law school, we find the state interest in eliminating racial imbalance within public legal education to be compelling.

The legal profession plays a critical role in the policy making sector of our society, whether decisions be public or private, state or local. That lawyers, in making and influencing these decisions, should be cognizant of the views, needs and demands of all segments of society is a principle beyond dispute. The educational interest of the state in producing a racially balanced student body at the law school is compelling.

Finally, the shortage of minority attorneys—and, consequently, minority prosecutors, judges and public officials—constitutes an undeniably compelling state interest.[3] If minorities are to live within the rule of law, they must enjoy equal representation within our legal system.

[10] Once a constitutionally valid state interest has been established, it remains for the state to

show the requisite connection between the racial classification employed and that interest. The consideration of race in the law school admissions policy meets the test of necessity here because racial imbalance in the law school and the legal profession is the evil to be corrected, and it can only be corrected by providing legal education to those minority groups which have been previously deprived. . . .

We hold that the minority admissions policy of the law school, and the denial by the law school of admission to plantiff, violate neither the equal protection clause of the fourteenth amendment to the United States Constitution nor article 1, section 12 of the Washington State Constitution. . . .

As a final point, plaintiff argues that the consideration of race here was arbitrary because no inquiry was made into the background of each minority applicant to make certain that the individual was in fact educationally, economically and culturally deprived. However, the mere fact that a minority applicant comes from a relatively more affluent home does not mean that he has not been subjected to psychological harm through discrimination. *See Hobson v. Hansen, supra* at 482. Likewise, every minority lawyer is critically needed, whether he be rich or poor. A showing of actual deprivation is unnecessary for the accomplishment of the compelling state interests here.

Plaintiff has failed to show that the policy and procedures of the law school in denying him admission were so unreasoned and in disregard of the facts and circumstances as to constitute arbitrary and capricious action.

NOTES

1.   "De jure" segregation generally refers to "segregation directly intended or mandated by law or otherwise issuing from an official racial classification," *Hobson v. Hansen,* 269 F. Supp. 401, 492 (D.D.C. 1967), *aff'd sub nom. Smuck v. Hobson,* 408 F.2d 175 (D.C. Cir. 1969), or, in other words, to segregation which has, or had, the sanction of law. In the context of public education the United States Supreme Court has expanded the meaning of the term "de jure segregation." [T]o comprehend any situation in which the activities of school authorities have had a racially discriminatory impact contributing to the establishment or continuation [of racial imbalance] . . . *State ex rel. Citizens Against Mandatory Bussing v. Brooks,* 80 Wn.2d 121, 130, 492 P.2d 536 (1972).

Where the segregation is inadvertent and without the assistance or collusion of school authorities, and is not caused by any "state action," but rather by social, economic and other determinants, it will be referred to as "de facto" herein. *See* Fiss, *Racial Imbalance in the Public Schools: the Constitutional Concepts,* 78 Harv. L. Rev. 564, 565–66, 584, 598 (1965).

2.   Plaintiff alleged in his complaint that he had previously applied to and been accepted by the law school at each of the following universities: University of Oregon, University of Idaho, Gonzaga University and Willamette University.

3.   See O'Neil, *Preferential Admissions: Equalizing Access to Legal Education,* supra note 12 (in the original text).

58. DISSENTING OPINION IN DEFUNIS V. ODEGAARD

Justice William O. Douglas

Mr. Justice DOUGLAS, dissenting.

I agree with Mr. Justice BRENNAN that this case is not moot, and because of the significance of the issues raised I think it is important to reach the merits.

From DeFunis v. Odegaard (decided April 23, 1974; 94 *Supreme Court* Reporter 1704 (1974), pp. 1708–1719). Notes deleted.

The University of Washington Law School received 1601 applications for admission to its first-year class beginning in September 1971. There were spaces available for only about 150 students, but in order to enroll this number the school eventually offered admission to 275 applicants. All applicants were put into two groups, one of which was considered under the minority admissions program. Thirty-seven of those offered admission had indicated on an optional question on their application that their "dominant" ethnic origin was either Black, Chicano, American Indian, or Filipino, the four groups included in the minority admissions program. Answers to this optional question were apparently the sole basis upon which eligibility for the program was determined. Eighteen of these 37 actually enrolled in the law school.

In general, the admissions process proceeded as follows: An index called the Predicted First Year Average (Average) was calculated for each applicant on the basis of a formula combining the applicant's score on the Law School Admission Test (LSAT) and his grades in his last two years in college. On the basis of its experience with the previous years' applications, the admissions committee, consisting of faculty, administration, and students, concluded that the most outstanding applicants were those with averages above 77; the highest average of any applicant was 81. Applicants with averages above 77 were considered as their applications arrived by random distribution of their files to the members of the committee who would read them and report their recommendations back to the committee. As a result of the first three committee meetings in February, March, and April 1971, 78 applicants from this group were admitted, although virtually no other applicants were offered admission this early. By the final conclusion of the admissions process in August 1971, 147 applicants with averages above 77 had been admitted, including all applicants with averages above 78, and 93 of 105 applicants with averages between 77 and 78.

Also beginning early in the admissions process was the culling out of applicants with averages below 74.5. These were reviewed by the Chairman of the Admissions Committee, who had the authority to reject them summarily without further consideration by the rest of the Committee. A small number of these applications were saved by the Chairman for committee consideration on the basis of information in the file indicating greater promise than suggested by the Average. Finally during the early months the Committee accumulated the applications of those with averages between 74.5 and 77 to be considered at a later time when most of the applications had been received and thus could be compared with one another. Since DeFunis' average was 76.23, he was in this middle group.

Beginning in their May meeting the Committee considered this middle group of applicants, whose folders had been randomly distributed to committee members for their recommendations to the Committee. Also considered at this time were remaining applicants with averages below 74.5 who had not been summarily rejected, and some of those with averages above 77 who had not been summarily admitted, but instead held for further consideration. Each committee member would consider the applications competitively, following rough guidelines as to the proportion who could be offered admission. After the Committee had extended offers of admission to somewhat over 200 applicants, a waiting list was constructed in the same fashion, and was divided into four groups ranked by the Committee's assessment of their applications. DeFunis was on this waiting list, but was ranked in the lowest quarter. He was ultimately told in August 1971 that there would be no room for him.

Applicants who had indicated on their application forms that they were either Black, Chicano, American Indian, or Filipino were treated differently in several respects. Whatever their averages, none were given to the Committee Chairman for consideration of summary rejection, nor were they distributed randomly among committee members for consideration along with the other applications. Instead all applications of Black students were assigned separately to two particular committee members: a first year Black law student on the Committee, and a professor on the Committee who had worked the previous summer in a special program for disadvantaged college students considering application to law school. Applications from among the other three minority groups were assigned to an assistant dean who was on the Committee. The minority applications, while considered competively with one another, were never directly compared to the remaining applications, either by the subcommittee or by the full committee. As in the admissions process generally, the Committee sought to find "within the minority category, those persons who we thought had the highest probability of succeeding in law school." In reviewing the minority applications, the Committee attached less weight to the Predicted First Year Average "in making a total judgmental evaluation as to the relative ability of the particular applicant to succeed in law school." 82 Wash.2d 11, 21, 507 P.2d 1169, 1175. In its publicly distributed Guide to Applicants, the Committee explained that "[a]n applicant's racial or ethnic background was considered as one factor in our general attempt to convert formal credentials into realistic predictions."

Thirty-seven minority applicants were admitted under this procedure. Of these, 36 had Predicted First Year Averages below DeFunis' 76.23, and 30 had averages below 74.5, and thus would ordinarily have been summarily rejected by the Chairman. There were also 48 nonminority applicants admitted who had Predicted First Year Averages below DeFunis. Twenty-three of these were returning veterans, see n. 2, *supra,* and 25 others presumably admitted because of other factors in their applications making them attractive candidates despite their relatively low averages.

It is reasonable to conclude from the above facts that while other factors were considered by the Committee, and were on occasion crucial, the Predicted First Year Average was for most applicants a heavily weighted factor, and was at the extremes virtually dispositive. A different balance was apparently struck, however, with regard to the minority applicants. Indeed, at oral argument, the law school advised us that were the minority applicants considered under the same procedure as was generally used, none of those who eventually enrolled at the law school would have been admitted.

The educational policy choices confronting a University Admissions Committee are not ordinarily a subject for judicial oversight; clearly it is not for us but for the law school to decide which tests to employ, how heavily to weigh recommendations from professors or undergraduate grades, and what level of achievement on the chosen criteria are sufficient to demonstrate that the candidate is qualified for admission. What places this case in a special category is the fact that the school did not choose one set of criteria but two, and then determined which to apply to a given applicant on the basis of his race. The Committee adopted this policy in order to achieve "a reasonable representation" of minority groups in the law school. 82 Wash.2d 11, 20, 507 P.2d 1169, 1175. Although it may be speculated that the Committee sought to rectify what it perceived to be cultural or racial biases in the Law School Admission Test or in the candidates' undergraduate records, the record in this case is devoid of any evidence of such bias, and the school has not sought to justify its procedures on this basis.

Although testifying that "[w]e do not have quota . . ." the law school dean explained that "[w]e want a reasonable representation. We will go down to reach if we can," without "taking people who are unqualified in an absolute sense . . ." (Statement of Facts, at 420.) By "unqualified in the absolute sense" the Dean meant candidates who "have no reasonable probable likelihood of having a chance at succeeding in the study of law. . . ." (*Ibid.*) But the Dean conceded that in "reaching," the school does take "some minority students who at least, viewed as a group, have a less such likelihood than the majority student group taken as a whole." (*Id.,* at 423.)

"Q. Of these who have made application to go to the law school, I am saying you are not taking the best qualified?

"A. In total?

"Q. In total.

"A. In using this definition, yes." (*Id.,* at 423–424.)

It thus appears that by the Committee's own assessment, it admitted minority students who, by the tests given, seemed less qualified than some white students who were not accepted, in order to achieve a "reasonable representation." In this regard it may be pointed out that for the year 1969–1970—the year before the class to which DeFunis was seeking admission—the Law School reported an enrollment of eight Black students out of a total of 356. (Defendants' Exh. 7.) That percentage, approximately 2.2%, compares to a percentage of Blacks in the population of Washington of approximately 2.1%.

The Equal Protection Clause did not enact a requirement that Law Schools employ as the sole criterion for admissions a formula based upon the LSAT and undergraduate grades, nor does it proscribe law schools from evaluating an applicant's prior achievements in light of the barriers that he had to overcome. A Black applicant who pulled himself out of the ghetto into a junior college may thereby demonstrate a level of motivation, perseverance and ability that would lead a fairminded admissions committee to conclude that he shows more promise for law study than the son of a rich alumnus who achieved better grades at Harvard. That applicant would not be offered admission because he is Black, but because as an individual he has shown he has the potential, while the Harvard man may have taken less advantage of the vastly superior opportunities offered him. Because of the weight of the prior handicaps, that Black applicant may not realize his full potential in the first year of law school, or even in the full three years, but in the long pull of a legal career his achievements may far outstrip those of his classmates whose earlier records appeared superior by conventional criteria. There is currently no test available to the admissions committee that can predict such possibilities with assurance, but the committee may nevertheless seek to gauge it as best as it can, and weigh this factor in its decisions. Such a policy would not be limited to Blacks, or Chicanos or Filipinos or American Indians, although undoubtedly groups such as these may in practice be the principle beneficiaries of it. But a poor Appalachian white, or a second generation Chinese in San Francisco, or some other American whose lineage is so diverse as to defy ethnic labels, may demonstrate similar potential and thus be accorded favorable consideration by the committee.

The difference between such a policy and the one presented by this case is that the committee would be making decisions on the basis of individual attributes, rather than according a preference solely on the basis of race. To be sure, the racial preference here was not absolute—the committee did not admit all applicants from the four favored groups. But it did accord all such applicants a preference by applying, to an extent not precisely ascertainable from the record, different standards by which to judge their applications, with the result that the committee admitted minority applicants who, in the school's own judgment, were less promising than other applicants who were rejected. Furthermore, it is apparent that because the admissions committee compared minority applicants only with one another, it was necessary to reserve some proportion of the class for them, even

if at the outset a precise number of places were not set aside. That proportion, apparently 15 to 20%, was chosen, because the school determined it to be "reasonable," although no explanation is provided as to how that number rather than some other was found appropriate. Without becoming embroiled in a semantic debate over whether this practice constitutes a "quota," it is clear that given the limitation on the total number of applicants who could be accepted, this policy did reduce the total number of places for which DeFunis could compete—solely on account of his race. Thus, as the Washington Supreme Court concluded, whatever label one wishes to apply to it, "the minority admissions policy is certainly not benign with respect to nonminority students who are displaced by it." 82 Wash.2d 11, 32, 507 P.2d 1169, 1182. A finding that the state school employed a racial classification in selecting its students subjects it to the strictest scrutiny under the Equal Protection Clause.

The consideration of race as a measure of an applicant's qualification normally introduces a capricious and irrelevant factor working an invidious discrimination, Anderson v. Martin, 375 U.S. 399, 402, 84 S. Ct. 454, 455, 11 L.Ed.2d 430; Loving v. Virginia, 388 U.S. 1, 10, 87 S.Ct. 1817, 1822, 18 L.Ed.2d 1010; Harper v. Virginia State Board of Elections, 383 U.S. 663, 668, 86 S.Ct. 1079, 1082, 16 L.Ed.2d 169. Once race is a starting point educators and courts are immediately embroiled in competing claims of different racial and ethnic groups that would make difficult manageable standards consistent with the Equal Protection Clause. "The clear and central purpose of the Fourteenth Amendment was to eliminate all official state sources of invidious racial discrimination in the States." Loving, supra, 388 U.S. at 10, 87 S.Ct., at 1823. The law school's admissions policy cannot be reconciled with that purpose, unless cultural standards of a diverse rather than a homogeneous society are taken into account. The reason is that professional persons, particularly lawyers, are not selected for life in a computerized society. The Indian who walks to the beat of Chief Seattle of the Muckleshoot Tribe in Washington has a different culture than Examiners at Law Schools.

The key to the problem is the consideration of each application *in a racially neutral way*. Since LSAT reflects questions touching on cultural backgrounds, the admissions committee acted properly in my view in setting minority applications apart for separate processing. These minorities have cultural backgrounds that are vastly different from the dominant Caucasian. Many Eskimos, American Indians, Filipinos, Chicanos, Asian Indians, Burmese, and Africans come from such disparate backgrounds that a test sensitively tuned for most applicants would be wide of the mark for many minorities.

The melting pot is not designed to homogenize people, making them uniform in consistency. The melting pot as I understand it is a figure of speech that depicts the wide diversities tolerated by the First Amendment under one flag. See Morrison and Emmager, The Growth of the American Republic (1950) vol. II, c. VIII. Minorities in our midst who are to serve actively in our public affairs should be chosen on talent and character alone, not on cultural orientation or leanings.

I do know, coming as I do from Indian country—in Washington, that many of the young Indians know little about Adam Smith or Karl Marx but are deeply imbued with the spirit and philosophy of Chief Robert B. Jim of the Yakimas, Chief Seattle of the Muckleshoots and Chief Joseph of the Nez Perce which offer competitive attitudes towards life, fellow man, and nature.

I do not know the extent to which Blacks in this country are imbued with ideas of African Socialism. Leopold Senghor and Sekon Torae, most articulate of African leaders, have held that modern African political philosophy is not oriented either to marxism or to capitalism. How far the reintroduction into educational curricula of ancient African art and history has reached the minds of young Afro-Americans I do not know. But at least as respects Indians, Blacks, and Chicanos—as well as those from Asian cultures—I think a separate classification of these applicants is warranted, lest race be a subtle force in eliminating minority members because of cultural differences.

Insofar as LSAT tests reflect the dimensions and orientation of the Organization Man they do a disservice to minorities. I personally know that admissions tests were once used to eliminate Jews. How many other minorities they aim at I do not know. My reaction is that the presence of an LSAT test is

sufficient warrant for a school to put racial minorities into a separate class in order better to probe their capacities and potentials.

This does not mean that a separate LSAT test be designed for minority racial groups, although that might be a possibility. The merits of the present controversy cannot in my view be resolved on this record. A trial would involve the disclosure of hidden prejudices, if any, against certain minorities and the manner in which substitute measurements of one's talents and character were employed in the conventional tests. I could agree with the majority of the Washington Supreme Court only, if on the record, it could be said that the law school's selection was racially neutral. The case, in my view, should be remanded for a new trial to consider, *inter alia,* whether the established LSAT tests should be eliminated so far as racial minorities are concerned.

This does not mean that a separate LSAT test must be designed for minority racial groups, although that might be a possibility. The reason for the separate treatment of minorities as a class is to make more certain that racial factors do not militate *against an applicant or on his behalf.*

There is no constitutional right for any race to be preferred. The years of slavery did more than retard the progress of Blacks. Even a greater wrong was done the whites by creating arrogance instead of humility and by encouraging the growth of the fiction of a superior race. There is no superior person by constitutional standards. A DeFunis who is white is entitled to no advantage by reason of that fact; nor is he subject to any disability, no matter his race or color. Whatever his race, he had a constitutional right to have his application considered on its individual merits in a racially neutral manner. . . .

The argument is that a "compelling" state interest can easily justify the racial discrimination that is practiced here. To many "compelling" would give members of one race even more than *pro rata* representation. The public payrolls might then be deluged say with Chicanos because they are as a group the poorest of the poor and need work more than others, leaving desperately poor individual Blacks and whites without employment. By the same token large quotas of blacks or browns could be added to the Bar, waiving examinations required of other groups, so that it would be better racially balanced. The State, however, may not proceed by racial classification to force strict population equivalencies for every group in every occupation, overriding individual preferences. The Equal Protection Clause commands the elimination of racial barriers, not their creation in order to satisfy our theory as to how society ought to be organized. The purpose of the University of Washington cannot be to produce Black lawyers for Blacks, Polish lawyers for Poles, Jewish lawyers for Jews, Irish lawyers for the Irish. It should be to produce good lawyers for Americans and not to place First Amendment barriers against anyone. That is the point at the heart of all our school desegregation cases, from Brown v. Board of Education, 347 U.S. 483, 74 S.Ct. 686, 98 L.Ed. 873, through Swann v. Charlotte-Mecklenburg Board of Educ., 402 U.S. 1, 91 S.Ct. 1267, 28 L. Ed.2d 554. A segregated admissions process creates suggestions of stigma and caste no less than a segregated classroom, and in the end it may produce that result despite its contrary intentions. One other assumption must be clearly disapproved, that Blacks or Browns cannot make it on their individual merit. That is a stamp of inferiority that a State is not permitted to place on any lawyer.

If discrimination based on race is constitutionally permissible when those who hold the reins can come up with "compelling" reasons to justify it, then constitutional guarantees acquire an accordionlike quality. Speech is closely brigaded with action when it triggers a fight, Chaplinsky v. New Hampshire, 315 U.S. 568, 62 S.Ct. 766, 86 L.Ed. 1031, as shouting "fire" in a crowded theatre triggers a riot. It may well be that racial strains, racial susceptibility to certain diseases, racial sensitiveness to environmental conditions that other races do not experience may in an extreme situation justify differences in racial treatment that no fair-minded person would call "invidious" discrimination. Mental ability is not in the category. All races can compete fairly at all professional levels. So far as race is concerned, any state-sponsored preference to one race over another in that competition is in my view "invidious" and violative of the Equal Protection Clause.

The problem tendered by this case is important and crucial to the operation of our constitutional system; and educators must be given leeway. It may well be that a whole congeries of applicants in the marginal group defy known methods of selection. Conceivably, an admissions committee might conclude that a selection by lot of say the last 20 seats is the only fair solution. Courts are not educators; their expertise is limited; and our task ends with the inquiry whether judged by the main purpose of the Equal Protection Clause—the protection against racial discrimination—there has been an "invidious" discrimination.

We would have a different case if the suit were one to displace the applicant who was chosen in lieu of DeFunis. What the record would show concerning his potentials would have to be considered and weighed. The educational decision, provided proper guidelines were used, would reflect an expertise that courts should honor. The problem is not tendered here because the physical facilitites were apparently adequate to take DeFunis in addition to the others. My view is only that I cannot say by the tests used and applied he was invidiously discriminated against because of his race.

I cannot conclude that the admissions procedure of the Law School of the University of Washington that excluded DeFunis is violative of the Equal Protection Clause of the Fourteenth Amendment. The judgment of the Washington Supreme Court should be vacated and the case remanded for a new trial.

SUGGESTIONS FOR FURTHER READING

RACIAL DISCRIMINATION

Allport, G. W. *Nature of Prejudice.* Cambridge, Mass.: Addison-Wesley, 1954.

Bedau, Hugo, ed. *Justice and Equality.* Englewood Cliffs, N.J.: Prentice-Hall, 1971.

Benedict, Ruth. *Race and Racism.* London: Routledge & Kegan Paul, 1942.

Bettelheim, Bruno, and Janowitz, Morris. *Social Change and Prejudice.* New York: Collier-MacMillan (1964).

Blackstone, William T. "On The Meaning and Justification of the Equality Principle." *Ethics* 77 (1967).

Broderick, Francis L., and Meier, August, eds. *Negro Protest Thought in the Twentieth Century.* New York: Bobbs-Merrill, 1965.

Carmichael, Stokely, and Hamilton, Charles. *Black Power.* New York: Random House, 1967.

Melden, A. I., ed. *Human Rights.* Belmont, Calif., Wadsworth, 1970.

Myrdal, Gunner. *An American Dilemma.* New York: Harper and Brothers, 1944.

Spiegelberg, Herbert. "A Defense of Human Equality." *Philosophical Review* 53 (1944).

Tussman, Joseph, ed. *Supreme Court on Racial Discrimination.* New York: O.U.P. (1963).

SEXUAL DISCRIMINATION

Beauvoir, Simone de. *The Second Sex.* New York, Alfred A. Knopf, 1957.

Davidson, Kenneth N., Ginsburg, Ruth Bader, and Kay, Herma Hill. *Text, Cases, and Materials on Sex-Based Discrimination.* St. Paul, Minn.: West Publishing Co., 1974.

Firestone, Shulamith. *The Dialectic of Sex: The Case for Feminist Revolution.* New York: William Morrow, 1970.

Flexner, Eleanor. *Century of Struggle: The Woman's Rights Movement in the United States.* Cambridge, Mass.: Harvard University Press, 1959.

Friedan, Betty. *The Feminine Mystique.* New York: W. W. Norton, 1963.

Gornick, Vivian, and Moran, Barbara K., eds. *Women in Sexist Society.* New York: Signet Books, 1972.

Jagger, Alison. "On Sexual Equality." *Ethics* 84 (1974).

Lucas, J. R. "Because You Are A woman." *Philosophy* 48 (1973).

Nichols, Jack. *Men's Liberation.* New York: Penguin Books, 1975.

Rossi, Alice S., ed. *Essays on Sex Equality by John Stuart Mill and Harriett Taylor Mill.* Chicago: University of Chicago Press, 1970.

Tanner, Leslie B., ed. *Voices From Women's Liberation.* New York: Signet Books, 1971.

"Women's Liberation: Ethical, Social and Political Issues." *Monist* 57 (1973).

REVERSE DISCRIMINATION

Bayles, Michael D. "Compensatory Reverse Discrimination in Hiring." *Social Theory and Practice* 2 (1973).

Bitter, Boris J. *The Case for Black Reparations.* New York: Random House, 1973.

Blackstone, William T. "Reverse Discrimination and Compensatory Justice." *Social Theory and Practice* 3 (1975).

Bedau, H. A. "Compensatory Justice and the Black Manifesto." *The Monist* 56 (1972).

Dorsen, N., ed. *The Rights of Americans.* New York: Random House, 1971.

Ginger, Ann Fagan, ed. *DeFunis v. Odegaard and the University of Washington: The University Admissions Case.* Oceana Publications, Dobbs-Ferry, 1974. 3 vols.

Goldman, Alan H. "Limits to the Justification to Reverse Discrimination." *Social Theory and Practice* 3 (1975).

Hughes, Graham. "The Right to Special Treatment." In *The Rights of Americans,* edited by Norman Dorsen. New York: Pantheon Books, 1971.

Lichtman, J. "The Ethics of Compensatory Justice." *Law in Transition Quarterly* 1 (1964).

Nagel, Thomas. "Equal Treatment and Compensatory Discrimination." *Philosophy and Public Affairs* 2 (1973).

Nickel, J. W. "Discrimination and Morally Relevant Characteristics." *Analysis* 32 (1972).

Seabury, T. "HEW and the Universities." *Commentary,* February 1972.

Simon, Robert. "Preferential Hiring: A Reply to Judith Jarvis Thomson." *Philosophy and Public Affairs* 3 (1974).

Thomson, Judith. "Preferential Hiring." *Philosophy and Public Affairs* 2 (1973).

Chapter 7   Love and Sexuality

PHILOSOPHICAL QUESTIONS ABOUT SEX AND LOVE

As it has been said of many a visiting speaker, so it might be said of the topics love and sexuality that they "need no introduction." What may need some explanation, however, is the way in which these familiar subjects can become the objects of a distinctively philosophical interest. Philosophers have raised at least three different kinds of questions about love and sexuality. There are, first of all, conceptual questions challenging us to get clear about what we mean by the terms "sex" and "love" and how they are related one to the other. How are we properly to understand the activities denoted by these words? What are their essential characteristics and their most common counterfeits and corruptions? Then there are ethical questions requiring us to evaluate proposed norms for the governance of sexual conduct. Is there a specifically sexual morality? If so, how are its norms related to, or derived from, the moral principles that apply more generally to all human conduct? If there is nothing morally distinctive about sexual activity, how are we to explain the near-obsessive concern of traditional moralists with it? Moral philosophers also seek to describe the place of sex and love among human values and how they contribute to human well-being. Finally there are questions of "institutional design" for the social philosopher. What are the alternatives to the institutions of monogamous marriage and the family? Can a case be made, at least in principle, that alternative arrangements would be socially more useful? If not, what is it about the marriage bond or the "nuclear family" that confer on them their special value or unique significance?

Philosophers, of course, have no monopoly on ethical and evaluative questions, or on questions of institutional design. Moralists, theologians, political leaders, and social scientists also have a great deal to say about such matters, and that diversity of approach is reflected in the authors of the articles in this section, only three of whom are professional philosophers (Baker, Russell, and Nagel). Of the others, Margaret Drabble is a novelist; C. S. Lewis was a professor of English, a writer of fiction, and a lay theologian in the Anglican Church; Millard Schumaker was trained in philosophy but teaches in a department of religion; Tyler is a professor of English; Fasteau is a lawyer; May is a practicing psychoanalyst; Peele is a social psychologist.

HISTORICALLY IMPORTANT CONCEPTS OF LOVE

If our answers to the ethical and evaluative questions about sex and love are to be clear of confusion and argued for with precision, we should have some prior concern with the conceptual questions they presuppose, and if we are to give clear and precise analyses of the concepts of sex and love, we should begin at the *very* beginning, with the meanings of terms. The word "love" in modern English is used to stand for a great variety of responses (attitudes, feelings, dispositions) which share a certain family resemblance, but which differ from one another in such important ways that clarity might require that we refer to them by separate terms. The more interesting of these responses were given separate names by the ancient Greeks, and it will be convenient to use the ancient Greek terms to refer to them whenever necessary to avoid confusion or equivocation.

The Greeks of the Hellenistic period (that is, after Alexander the Great) had three different words for what we might think of as three different types of love: *philia, agape,* and *eros. Philia* refers to the attitudes that characterize ordinary friendship. Friends "like" one another in the sense that they enjoy one another; they like being together. Typically friendships are based on common interests, and the more interests shared the solider the basis of the friendship. Baseball fans may enjoy playing, practicing, witnessing, discussing, or analyzing baseball together, and yet find one another bores in other respects. But if they also share strong interests in politics, camping, philosophy, and gossip, their friendship is likely to be stronger and closer. The friendship will be stronger still if it rests on common interests in a second sense of "interest"—not merely "the propensity to attend to and be stirred by a certain class of objects" (e.g. an interest in baseball, music, or mathematics) but "a stake in a certain outcome, standing to gain or lose depending on some issue of events" (e.g., having an interest in the profits of a corporation, in the main-

tenance of peace and prosperity, in the outcome of a horse race, a stock transaction, or an election). In this second sense of interest, two friends have "common interests" when they stand to gain or lose together from the same causes. Friends with shared interests (in either sense) will have more in common still if they work cooperatively in pursuit of common goals; if they are partners, teammates, or collaborators. In such roles, a kind of loyalty, at first merely instrumental in rendering the cooperation efficient, eventually becomes habitual and turns into a personal bond that survives the enterprises that were its original occasion. Finally, as the association of friends endures through the years, it is strengthened by still another element: common recollections of shared experiences in the past. Shared memories in turn often give rise to, or reinforce, reciprocal feelings of affection. *Philia* is thus itself a blend of diverse elements for which our own language has separate names: "liking," "enjoying," "loyalty," "affection."

Aristotle, in his famous analysis of *philia* (*Nicomachean Ethics,* Books 8 and 9), distinguished three basic kinds of friendships: those grounded on pleasure (enjoyment of one another's company), those based on utility or mutual advantage (as in a business partnership), and those based on reciprocal excellence of character. The third type of friendship is the rarest and highest, Aristotle thought, because it involves a cherishing of the superior qualities of the other's character as ends in themselves quite apart from any amusement or utility they might have on individual occasions. Truly excellent people who are friends of this kind might treasure one another much as they would prize fine works of art or other intrinsically valuable objects. Aristotle's third kind of *philia* thus involves still another element with a separate name, the response we call in English "admiration," or "esteem." As Aristotle understood this element, there is something personal and also something impersonal in it. On the one hand, to admire excellent friends in the appropriate way is to admire them for their own sake, not for what they can do for us. It is to love them for what they are, not for their pleasure-causing or utility. But in another way this response is austerely impersonal, since the admired person is loved only for his or her good qualities; if the person were to lose his or her excellences, there would be nothing left to "love." Aristotle indeed speaks of this "highest form of love" as "love of the good," that is, of qualities of excellence in the abstract, as they may or may not be exemplified in this, that, or the other concrete person. One can contrast that impersonal and judgmental response with the intensely personal love of a parent for his or her child, which may well remain constant even though the character of the child should prove to be bitterly disappointing. Parental love is clearly something other than "philia."

The second kind of love distinguished by the Greeks they called *agape,* and that word was the term used by the writers of the New Testament for what has come to be called "Christian love." (The Latin term is *caritas;* in the King James version of the bible it is translated as "charity.") In contrast to Aristotle's "highest form of *philia,*" there is nothing abstract and impersonal about *agape*—a love that can be directed even at someone known to be severely deficient in virtues of character or otherwise unlikeable. A parent, for example, can give very low "moral grades" to her child without faltering in her love. *Agape* in the pre-Christian sense of the Hellenistic Greeks meant "thoughtful good will, pure and simple, unpossessive and independent of the response of its object."[1] To love another person in this sense is to have a steady desire and ready disposition to promote the other's good or well-being, to advance his or her interests, to protect him or her from harm, whatever the

consequences might be for one's other personal interests. Many Christian moral theologians have made the readiness to *sacrifice* oneself for the loved one part of the meaning of *agape,* and so interpreted, *agape* is the word translated as "love" in the "Great Commandment" of Jesus that people love one another.

The basic idea of *agape* is familiar enough from ordinary life. Sometimes parents, spouses, and others so love one another that it is impossible to separate their own interests from those of the loved one; what harms one necessarily harms the other. Christian doctrines *about agape,* however, raise various philosophical riddles that still divide moral theologians, and which have led to further refinements and complications of sense in the Christian conception of *agape.* One riddle (addressed in the selection from Millard Schumaker) is how love can be *commanded.* If *agape* is a passion, or emotion, or feeling, then it would seem that we cannot simply will it into being as an act of dutiful obedience. No one has such secure control over his or her feelings. On the other hand, if *agape* is simply an obedient disposition to do good to others, then it is a kind of love that can be wholly cold-blooded and unfeeling. Helping others merely out of a sense of duty is the sort of thing that is normally contrasted with acting from love. A second closely related riddle is whether or how *agape* can be felt toward everyone equally. We can *respect* the rights of every human being to decent treatment at the hands of his fellows, but again, *respect* is something normally contrasted with love. One can respect the human rights of a wicked person whom one loathes, and act accordingly, but one cannot loathe and *love* (in any usual sense) at the same time.

The third word the Greeks used for love was *eros.* There is no record of the word *agape* in the writings of philosophers during the early period of Plato and Aristotle. During that period the word *eros* served to mark the contrast with *philia,* much as we might distinguish lovers from mere friends. *Eros* is much more passionate than *philia.* Indeed it can be utterly obsessive, an elemental force, or a "divine madness." In some Greek theories of nature *eros* was the basic creative energy that could "move worlds." In the psyches of individual human beings it has a strength that threatens to overcome reason.

Since the characteristic (but not exclusive) object of *eros* is another human being, the word tended to be used mainly for passionate "craving" love between persons, and finally it evolved in sense (at least in such English derivatives as "erotic") to suggest "sexual love," that is, love expressed physically through caresses and "sex acts." *Eros* was thought to be essentially a kind of desire whose aim is to *possess* its object, and sexual desire itself was conceived as the expression of some life force (compare Spinoza's *conatus* and Freud's *libido*) built centrally into human nature.

TAKING SEX SERIOUSLY

This section opens with a short story by the English novelist Margaret Drabble. The plot of that tale need not be repeated here, but surely a major point of the story is that the desire to be sexually attractive to others remains powerful—to some, unaccountably powerful—even among those sophisticated and intellectually enlightened persons who can find no rationale for it. Why should it matter to a person of solid achievement who knows the true value of things and the proper objects of pride and esteem that an equally talented person should admire her legs? Why should a sexually meaningful glance be "better than words, better than friendship"? Such a comparative judgment seems irrational to the point of perversity, yet in the story the evaluation is a sincere one reflected in the character's feelings and satisfactions, a brute psychological fact, despite all the "reasons" against it. The story should convince most readers that however philosophers and moralists come to terms with sex in the end, they must begin by taking it seriously indeed.

Robert Tyler needs no such admonition. He begins his article with the acknowledgment that sex is "miraculous and a mystery," and then asks us to consider what the consequences of a more matter-of-fact, scientific attitude toward the sexual realm might be. Suppose we liberate ourselves from centuries of guilt, shame, and neurotic obsession and take sex in a "healthy natural way." No more prurience and "dirty-minded" lust; no more repression and guilt. Down with pornographers and puritans both! The resultant picture, surprisingly, is not as

appealing as we might have supposed. The new reformers with their ideology of healthy-mindedness would change sex from "the ultimate dirty secret and the most titillating of sins" to an item in the same category as "calorie counting or bowel movements." Upon consideration, not all of us (even those of us who detest pornos and prudes alike) would find the change altogether satisfactory.

What is needed, if Tyler's analysis is correct, is some model of sexuality other than that shared by the pornos and prudes, on the one hand, and that of the hygienic reformers, on the other. Tyler gives no help here, but his brief essay poses the problem vividly. There *have* been other models proposed than that of the "dirty secret" and that of joint calisthenics, but the baffled reader may find many of the alternatives equally disappointing. One historically important conception of sex is the "spiritual model" so favored by Havelock Ellis, the English pioneer in the scientific study of sex. There was nothing "matter-of-fact" or casual in his account (!):

Apart from any sexual craving, the complete spiritual contact of two persons who love each other can only be attained through some act of rare intimacy. No act can be quite so intimate as the sexual embrace. In its accomplishment, for all who have reached a reasonably human degree of development, the communion of bodies becomes the communion of souls. The outward and visible sign has been the consummation of an inward and spiritual grace. "I would base all my sex teaching to children and young people on the beauty and sacredness of sex;" [wrote a woman correspondent] "sex intercourse is the great sacrament of life. He that eateth and drinketh unworthily eateth and drinketh his own damnation, but it may be the most beautiful sacrament between two souls who have no thought of children." To many the idea of a sacrament seems merely ecclesiastical, but that is a misunderstanding. The word "sacrament" is the ancient Roman name of a soldier's oath of military allegiance, and the idea, in the deeper sense, existed long before Christianity, and has ever been regarded as the physical sign of the closest possible union with some great spiritual reality. From our modern standpoint we may say . . . that the sexual embrace, worthily understood, can only be compared with music and with prayer."[2]

Ellis seeks to escape the dilemma of conceiving sex either as a dirty-minded secret or a healthy-minded science by treating it as a sacrament in a secular religion of love.

SEX STEREOTYPES

Conceptual confusion does not necessarily impede practice and cause unhappiness. Otherwise philosophers (who worry more than others about the meanings of concepts) would be the most paralyzed and unhappy of people. Even a certain amount of confusion about the proper model for interpreting sex is quite consistent with having a tolerable sex life. The way we conceive of the sexes themselves, however, cannot help but affect all of us in the most profound ways. Robert Baker looks to our language, plausibly enough, for evidence of the attitudes toward sex and the sexes that predominate in our culture. The impolite words and phrases he examines are familiar to all of us, but it comes as a rude and depressing shock nevertheless to see that the attitudes embedded in everyday modes of masculine speech are so utterly contemptuous of women. Many of them reveal a male conception of women as pets, domesticated servants, animals to be hunted down for sport, mindless or dependent objects, or depersonalized organs of sex. The very act of sex itself (if customary modes of masculine expression are to be taken seriously) is something done *to* (not for or with) someone. To "screw" someone is to deceive, hurt, or take advantage of her. Baker draws what seems to be the clear inference from the linguistic facts: "We conceive of the male sexual role as that of hurting the person in the female role." Baker's purpose is not so much to explain this puzzling and deplorable fact as to establish it as fact and suggest ways of changing it. He shares the latter purpose with the women's movement, but he differs from some feminists in distrusting the slogan that women are not to be thought of as "sex objects." (Surely that slogan is pointless, he might well suggest, if it conflicts with the gist of the Drabble story.)

Marc Feigen Fasteau has written a whole book[3] describing the prevalent masculine self-conception in our culture and the harmful effect of sex stereotypes on both men and women. The male stereotype described by Fasteau is a shared standard or "yardstick against which we measure ourselves as men."[4] It is not "manly" to experience certain emotions, to accept them, express them, acknowledge them without shame. One's manliness must be proved over and over again in challenge after challenge. A truly manly man is all self-confidence and is never out of control of himself or of external events. As a result it has been characteristically masculine in our culture to be incompetent at personal intimacy, to repress tenderness, to fail to see distress signals, to fear all emotions associated with being vulnerable. And thoroughly to botch sexual relationships.

An habitually contemptuous attitude toward women is part and parcel of the complex of attitudes Fasteau attributes to the masculine mystique. He traces the growth of that attitude from early childhood in the chapter of his book reprinted here. From the beginning boys are expected to separate themselves from girls and treat them as potential sources of the infection of weakness, dependence, and silliness. The worst thing possible is to be like a girl or a "sissy." Despised traits are then attributed to all females, often totally without factual warrant. Above all, men must maintain a certain toughness to females, lest they betray themselves as emotionally dependent or vulnerable. It is the masculine role to be always in control.

Elsewhere in his book Fasteau concedes that there may once have been some utility in the traditional sex roles when they more or less fit the economic and biological circumstances, and before they became so fixed and rigid. But in our day their predominant tendency is pernicious and their psychological effects crippling. In his final chapter Fasteau allows himself to hope:

Perhaps in the future, our lives will be shaped by a view of personality which will not assign fixed ways of behaving to individuals on the basis of sex. Instead, it would acknowledge that each person has the potential to be—depending on the circumstances—both assertive *and* yielding, independent *and* dependent, job *and* people—oriented, strong *and* gentle, in short both "masculine" and "feminine"; that the most effective and happy individuals are likely to be those who have accepted and developed both these "sides" of themselves; and that to deny either is to mutilate and deform; that human beings, in other words, are naturally androgynous.[5]

SEXUAL ETHICS

When it was first published in 1929, Bertrand Russell's *Marriage and Morals* was considered a radical and daring book. The positions defended in it were so shocking to some Americans that when a New York student's parent sought a court injunction barring Russell from being a visiting professor a few years later, the court proceeded to find him "unfit" to teach at the City College of New York despite his great academic distinction. Nearly fifty years later, Russell's views, while not universally triumphant by any means, are very widely held, and much of what he advocated—sex education for children, "companionate marriage" for college students, and relaxation of censorship—have been put into practice. Russell's views are thoroughly modern, and if not altogether respectable, at least not shocking and strange. To this day no one has argued more effectively than he for the new sexual morality.

In one important respect Russell anticipated Robert Tyler's thesis that the prudish and the prurient have one thing in common, the conviction that sex is somehow "dirty." Russell argues that the ideas of sexual decency and sexual indecency are logical correlatives—a person can't have one without the other. It is better, he insists, not to introduce children to either notion but rather to let them satisfy their natural curiosity about sexual matters in the same straightforward and unashamed way they do in other areas of life. In that way they will avoid both the damaging neuroses of the prudes and the offensive "dirty-mindedness" of the pornography addicts. "Nine-tenths of the appeal of pornography," Russell concludes, "is due to the indecent feelings concerning sex which moralists inculcate in the young."

Russell's book has become a classic statement of the case against the traditional sexual morality, and the widespread acceptance in our time of the "natural and wholesome" attitude toward sex he advocated in its place is what led Tyler to express his skeptical misgivings about efforts to demythologize sex. Russell's biographer Alan Wood expressed similar reservations more assertively in 1957:

Russell's . . . fundamental mistake was to imply that there was nothing strange about sex, and that any atmosphere of mystery was solely due to the obscurantism of the Victorian moralists whom he loathed. They believed that children should be kept in artificial ignorance about sex; Russell went to the other extreme and wrote as though it should be possible to tell children all about it. If the mystery could be taken out of something as marvelous as mathematics, why not out of sex?[6]

Whether or not Russell's remedies would solve all social problems concerning sex can be debated. That he accurately documented the evil consequences of the "Victorian" alternative, however, can scarcely be questioned in our day.

C. S. Lewis was by no means a "Victorian moralist" of the sort detested by Russell, but he was a prominent Anglican theologian, seriously concerned to defend the traditional Christian teachings about sex and marriage interpreted in an enlightened and humane way. Christianity, as Lewis interprets it, "thoroughly approves of the body," and its sexual ethic is not at "the center of Christian morality" in any case. Lewis therefore is one traditional moralist who is not obsessed with the sinfulness or "dirtiness" of carnal pleasures. Indeed, he prefers to think of sexual desires on the model of ordinary bodily appetites like those of food and drink. Pressing that comparison, he argues that something has gone awry with the sexual appetite in our time in that it is "in ludicrous and preposterous excess of its function." Writers on both sides of the disagreement over sexual morality commonly invoke in this way the analogy between sexual desire and the appetite for food and drink. It would be a useful exercise for the student reader to think through that analogy as carefully and critically as possible.

Lewis's defense of the Christian ideal of marriage is notable for its discussion of a kind of love he thinks unnecessary for a sound marriage and necessarily short-lived even when it is the original reason for getting married, namely that referred to by the idiom "being in love." That love of this thrilling kind doesn't last (indeed *can't* last) is often taken to be a reason against fidelity or permanent commitment in marriage. Lewis rejoins that it is a simple mistake to identify the love that is "the important thing in marriage" with "being in love," in the first place.

SEX AND PERVERSION

Thomas Nagel discusses another topic in the moral critique of sexual activity, that of a "sexual perversion." The very idea of a perversion presupposes the prior idea of a "natural function" or "characteristic object" from which one can depart in actual (perverted) practice. Note that "depart from" is morally neutral language, unlike such terms as "abused," "corrupted," and "misused," which express condemnation. Nagel thinks that a preference for eating labels off soup cans (rather than drinking soup), or eating only when violently forced to (only painful submission to force creates the appetite), or when the food is flesh from a large living animal—these would be gastronomical perversions. Whether they are to be morally condemned presumably depends on more than their descriptions as perversions. Perhaps some perversions in some circumstances are morally permissible. Nagel's main concern, in any event, is to analyze the concept of "sexual perversion," not to condemn or defend. And to do that job, he must first present an adequate analysis of the natural structure, function, and object of distinctively sexual desire.

The bulk of Nagel's essay then consists of his own analysis of sexual attraction as "multi-level interpersonal awareness." The natural object of sexual desire, he maintains, is always a particular person (not kinds of persons or qualities of persons, but an individual whole person). Qualities of a person no doubt are what originally attract us to him or her, but the person who is the object of the desire transcends the qualities that make him or her attractive. Sexual attraction can exist at various "levels" of awareness; characteristically it exists simultaneously at several levels. *A* is attracted by various of the qualities he perceives in *B*. *B* becomes aware of *A*'s being attracted to her; she notices him and is attracted in turn by his qualities, *but also,* at a "higher level," by her recognition that he is attracted by her. She betrays her desire deliberately or inadvertently to *A,* who is now aware that an attractive person is attracted to him and that makes *her* attractive, at a higher level, to him. She senses that he is now attracted by what he perceives to be her second-level attraction to him and that further excites her, now at the third-level of awareness. And so on. "Some version of this overlapping system of distinct sexual perceptions and interactions is the basic framework of any full-fledged sexual relation," so that "relations involving only

part of the complex are significantly incomplete." It is absolutely essential to distinctively sexual activity that (1) one have a living person as partner; (2) that both oneself and one's partner be aroused, and (3) not *merely* aroused, but aroused by the awareness of the other's desire. Insofar as any of these conditions fails the "encounter" is not a full-fledged, distinctively sexual one.

Nagel's conclusion is not merely an analytical one, that is, a proposed definition of the realm of the sexual. It is also inevitably evaluative: incomplete or "perverted" sex is not "good." But that does not mean that it is *morally* bad (necessarily) or that it is always to be avoided or condemned. It simply means that it is not *good sex.* In a similar way we might say that "junk food" is not *good food* while not meaning to condemn every instance of it, or to condemn its users morally.

ALTRUISTIC LOVE AND ITS CORRUPTIONS

Of the three broad types of love distinguished by the Greeks, only *agape* (in both its general pre-Christian sense and its more specific, distinctively Christian sense) need be genuinely altruistic. When our love for another is *agape* we care for the other's well-being as an end in itself, not *only* as a means to our own amusement, profit, edification, or titillation. It is possible, on the other hand, to like, or enjoy, or even admire a person primarily for "what he can do for us," either in the way of *philia* or of *eros.* When one strongly loves another in the manner of *philia* or *eros,* one will cherish one's relationship to that person, make every effort to preserve it, and feel crushed with loss when the relationship ends. But one's grief will be largely self-regarding; its focus will be on what *I* have lost. And if one perceives that the loved one will be better off when the relationship ceases, that will be little consolation. But if one loves the other person in the sense of *agape* (as well as *philia* and *eros*—the three can coexist), then one will rejoice for that person's sake that the end of the relationship has made him or her better off. In cases of this kind, self-regarding *philia* and *eros* can conflict with altruistic *agape;* the lover can both want to keep the loved one *and* want to let go. "I cannot live without you" conflicts with "How good that you will live better without me." Fortunately this kind of conflict, except perhaps in the hearts of parents as their children achieve maturity and independence, is not common. In many marriages, for example, circumstances permit the three kinds of love to live together in peace, and actually complement and reenforce one another.

The final two essays in this section deal with troublesome aspects of the concept of altruistic love. It is important to Millard Schumaker to distinguish the realm of love (in all proper and ordinary senses of the term including the special Christian sense of *agape*) from another moral realm, that of law, justice, duty, rights, and shares. There cannot be a duty to love, for to love out of a sense of duty is not to love at all. Nor can there be duties *to give gifts, to sacrifice* one's own due or share, *to forgive,* to *waive one's rights,* or to do anything else that is a basic expression of love. To love another person is to be prepared to do these things out of genuine inclination, freely and whole-heartedly. Otherwise the concept is incoherent. The morality of love then is a supererogatory morality, one that goes beyond duty, and rests on something wholly other than requirement.

Indeed, it would be more than "incoherent" to say that one could be morally required to give gifts, sacrifice shares, waive rights, and the like; it would be unjust. We have rights *not* to give gifts (gratuitous offerings), *not* to sacrifice (what we have a right to keep), *not* to give up (what is rightly ours). To require sacrifices is to violate rights, which is another way of saying "to commit injustice." But the whole point of the morality of love, Schumaker insists, is that standing on one's rights is morally insufficient. Christian morality, according to Schumaker, is far from exhausted in its enumeration of rules, rights, and duties; rather it consists also in the teaching that "it is a mistake to insist always upon one's rights and that the best and most authentic life arises out of the willingness to give freely of oneself and one's share without insisting upon equivalent compensation."

The inadequacy of duty-based conceptions of love and of interpretations of morality that restrict its scope to the realm of justice is well illustrated by a passage in D. H. Lawrence's moving novel *Sons*

and Lovers, quoted by the English philosopher Bernard Mayo in his ethics text:

[After the funeral of his mother] Paul went home and busied himself supplying the guests with drinks. His father sat in the kitchen with Mrs. Morel's relatives, "superior" people, and wept, and said what a good lass she'd been, and how he'd tried to do everything he could for her—everything. He had striven all his life to do what he could for her, and he'd nothing to reproach himself with. She was gone, but he'd done his best for her. He wiped his eyes with his white handkerchief. He'd nothing to reproach himself for, he repeated. All his life he'd done his best for her.

And that is how he tried to dismiss her. He never thought of her personally. Everything deep in him he denied.[7]

Even if we assume (contrary to the facts in the novel) that this grieving hypocrite had always done his duty to his wife and never once violated her rights, he had never done *more* than that in his legalistically "just and proper" but totally loveless marriage. Perhaps not once had he violated a specific Christian "rule," but he had violated Jesus's "Great Commandment" (as Schumaker interprets it) by being the sort of small-minded legalistic person he was. Mayo comments tersely: "Such is the ethics of duty. Notice Lawrence's comment on the man who tries to persuade himself that the morality of duty is the whole of morality: the best that such a man can say is that he has *nothing to reproach himself with:* 'everything deep in him he denied.' "[8]

Stanton Peele casts a skeptical glance at a quite different kind of corruption of the ideal of altruistic love, that involved in some of the most intensely "romantic" love affairs and suspiciously "close" marriages. Couples who are, as we say, "totally wrapped up in one another," almost oblivious to the great social world outside them, sworn to stay in that unnatural state "till death do us part," and unable even to conceive of living independent lives are like nothing so much as drug addicts, Peele maintains, in the way they use and rely on one another. Each person, in such couples, can find security only in the other, and unaccustomed separation brings on painful "withdrawal symptoms." Despite rationalizations and self-delusions, people who are fused together in such a way as to constrict rather than enlarge their individuality can have no genuine regard of an altruistic kind for the mate as a separate person. Rather they form an *"égoisme à deux,"* as much a "perversion" of love as a shoe-fetish is of sex. There is really nothing appealing or "romantic" in being "hooked" on someone, the lyrics of a thousand popular songs to the contrary. Germaine Greer makes Peele's point succinctly: "The hallmark of egotistical love, even when it masquerades as altruistic love, is the negative answer to the question 'Do I want my love to be happy more than I want him to be with me?' " Peele's task as a psychologist is to document the destructive effects on human personality of the egotistic masquerade, and this he does convincingly.

Joel Feinberg

NOTES

1. A. Campbell Garnett, *Ethics, A Critical Introduction* (New York: Ronald Press, 1960), p. 83.

2. Havelock Ellis, *On Life and Sex: Essays of Love and Virtue* Vol. 1 (Garden City, N.Y.: Garden City Publishing Co., 1947) pp. 68–69. First published in 1922.

3. Marc Feigen Fasteau, *The Male Machine* (New York: Dell Publishing Co., 1976).

4. Ibid., p. 2.

5. Ibid., p. 196.

6. Alan Wood, *Bertrand Russell The Passionate Skeptic* (New York: Simon and Schuster, 1958), p. 167.

7. As quoted in Bernard Mayo, *Ethics and the Moral Life* (London: Macmillan and New York: St. Martin's Press, 1958), p. 208.

8. Ibid., p. 209.

59. *A SUCCESS STORY*

Margaret Drabble

This is a story about a woman. It couldn't have been told a few years ago: perhaps even five years ago it couldn't have been told. Perhaps it can't really be told now. Perhaps I shouldn't write it, perhaps it's a bad move to write it. But it's worth risking. Just to see.

This woman was a playwright. She was one of the few successful women playwrights, and she had had a hard time on the way up, for she came from a poor background, from a part of the country hostile to the arts, from a family which had never been to the theater in its life. She wasn't really working class: more lower middle class, which made her success all the more remarkable, as her plays didn't have shock value, they were quite complicated and delicate. But they worked: they were something new. She made her way up: first of all she was assistant stagehand at her local repertory, then she worked in the office at a larger provincial theater as she didn't really have much interest in life behind the scenes—and all the while she was writing her plays. The first one was put on by the rep she was working in, and it was very much noticed. Kathie (that was her name—Kathie Jones) used to say modestly that it was noticed because she was a woman, and women playwrights were a rarity, and there was something in what she said. But her modesty couldn't explain why she went on writing, professionally, had her plays transferred to the West End, had them filmed, and did really very nicely. She was good at the job, and that was why she succeeded. She was also good, somewhat to her own surprise, at all the things that went along with the job, and which had kept women out of the job for so long: she was good at explaining herself, at arguing with megalomaniac directors, at coolly sticking to her own ideas, at adapting when things really couldn't be made to work. She had good judgment, she was

calm and professional, she could stand up for herself.

She was not, of course, world famous, let us not give the impression that she was an international name. No, she was a success in her own country, in her own medium. Some of the gossip columns thought her worth mentioning, some of them didn't. Not that there was much to mention: she was a quiet, hardworking girl, with her own friends, her own circle of close friends—some of them writers, one or two friends from the early days at Grammar School in the Midlands, one or two journalists. She was considered rather exclusive by some, and she was. She didn't much care for a gay social life, partly because she hadn't time, partly because she hadn't been brought up to it and didn't quite know how to cope. She lived with a man who was a journalist, and who traveled a great deal: he was always going off to Brazil and Vietnam and up Everest. He was an exceptionally good-natured man, and they got on well together. Sometimes she was sorry when he went away, but she was always so busy that she didn't miss him much, and anyway it was so interesting when he came back. He, for his part, loved her, and had confidence in her.

So really, one could say that her life had worked out very nicely. She had a job she liked, a reputation, a good relationship, some good friends, a respectable though fluctuating income. At the time of this story, she was in her early thirties, and had written five successful plays and several film scripts. She had a play running at a lucrative little theater in the West End, and was amusing herself by working on a television adaptation of a play by Strindberg. Her man was away: he was in Hungary, but he would be back soon, he would be back at the end of the week. At the moment at which we close in upon her, she was just putting the phone down after speaking to him: they had exchanged news, she had told him what was in his post which she always opened for him, he had said that he loved her and was looking forward to coming back and kissing her all over but particularly between her stockings and her suspenders, if she would please wear such antiquated garments on his return to greet him. Then he told her to enjoy her evening; she was just about to go out to a rather grand party. So she was smiling, as she put down the telephone.

She was quite a nice-looking woman. This we have not mentioned till this point, because it ought not to be of any importance. Or ought it? Well, we shall see. Anyway, she wasn't bad-looking, though she was nothing special. She had rather a long, large-featured face, with a large nose: she had big hands and large bones. Some people thought her beautiful, but others thought she was really plain. You know the type. As a child, she had been plain, as her mother had never tired of saying, and consequently she had no confidence in her appearance at all. Nowadays she didn't care much, she was happy anyway, and as long as her lover continued to take an interest in the serious things of life, like her legs, then she wasn't much interested in looking in the mirror. In fact, she hardly ever did, except to brush her hair, and she wore the same clothes most of the time, until they wore out. But tonight was different. She would have to have a look at herself, at least. So when she'd put the phone down she went into the bathroom to have a look.

Tonight was rather a special, grand sort of party, not the usual kind of thing, so she'd put on her best dress, a long green-blue dress that she'd once thought suited her rather old-fashioned looks. She wasn't so sure, now, she wasn't at all sure what she looked like these days, the older she got the more variable she seemed to be. Not that it mattered much, one way or the other. But one might as well wear one's best dress, once in a while. She'd bought it for one of her own first nights, years ago, and hadn't worn it much since. She didn't go to her own first nights any more, or anyone else's for that matter. It had cost a lot of money, for those days. (Not that she spent much money on clothes now—in fact she spent less.) Staring at herself, hitching it a bit at the shoulder, she wondered whether she'd put it on because she was still, whatever she told herself, slightly nervous about the kind of do she was going to. Surely not. Surely not, these days. Why should she care?

The party she was going to was being given by one of the grandest (socially speaking) theatrical entrepreneurs in London. And there she was going to meet the hero of her childhood dreams. It was all quite romantic. His name was Howard Jago (quite the right sort of name, but people like that have that kind of name) and he was one of the biggest American writers of his generation. He had written plays that made her heart bleed when she was sixteen. They still, oddly enough, moved her profoundly.

She admired him more than she admired any other living writer. He hadn't kept up with the play writing—she knew well enough that playwrights, compared with other writers, have a short working life—but he was now doing screenplays, and also a certain amount of political journalism. He had published a couple of novels, which she had liked immensely: he seemed indefatigable.

When she was a child, she had wanted more than anything to meet him. She had even written him a fan letter telling him so. He did not reply. Probably it never reached him.

She had had several opportunities to meet him before, as he was quite often in Europe, and was published by her publishers. But she had always declined.

Why had she declined? Was she afraid of being bored or disappointed? Afraid of not being disappointed? Was she afraid that he might not have heard of her (when, by the rules of the game, he should have done) or might find her boring? Combing her hair, now, looking at herself in the mirror, she wondered. Perhaps she had simply been too busy, on other occasions: or Dan had been at home and had not wanted to go. He didn't care for grand parties, and neither as a rule did she. They preferred to get very drunk quietly at home among friends: that was their favorite form of social life.

She couldn't work out why she hadn't wanted to meet him before: nor why, now, she had decided that she would.

She put him out of her mind, as she went downstairs and found herself a taxi. There would be plenty of other people there that she would know.

And so indeed there were. She knew nearly everybody, by sight or in person. She thought with some relief, as she looked round the massive house in Belgravia, and its glittering inhabitants—film stars in outré garments, diplomats, writers, cabinet ministers, actors, actresses—she thought that at least she didn't have to feel nervous any more. In a way that took some of the thrill away, but it was much pleasanter to be comfortable than thrilled. Being thrilled had always been so exhausting, and such a letdown in the end. Nowadays, she sought and found more lasting pleasures. Nevertheless, she had been very different once. Ambitious, she must have been, or she wouldn't have found herself here at all, would she? And, as she talked to a friend and kept an eye open for Howard Jago, she said to herself, If I'd known twenty years ago that I would ever find myself here, in a room like this, with people looking like this, I *would* have been delighted. A pity, really, that one couldn't have had that particular thrill then—the thrill of knowing. It wasn't worth much now.

The house was enormous. Tapestries hung on the walls and statues stood in corners. The paintings were by Francis Bacon and Bonnard and Matthew Smith and Braque.

After a while, she saw her host approaching her. He was leading Howard Jago in her direction: Howard Jago was doing his rounds. He looked as she had imagined him: wild, heavy, irregular, a bit larger than life-size, the kind of man who looks even bigger than he looks on the television. (She had caught a glimpse or two of him on the television.)

"And this," said her host, "is one of the people you particularly asked to meet. This is Kathie Jones."

Kathie smiled, politely. Jago shook her hand.

"I enjoyed your play the other night," said Jago, politely. He looked as though he was being careful. He looked as though he might be a little drunk.

"That's very kind of you," said Kathie. "I must tell you how very much I have always admired your work."

"I've admired it . . ." and she was going to say, since I was a child, which would have been true, but had to stop herself because it might have been a rude reflection on his age, and went on with ". . . I've admired it ever since I first found it."

They looked at each other, with assessment, and smiled civilly. Kathie couldn't think of anything else to say. She had remembered, suddenly, exactly why she hadn't wanted to meet him: she hadn't wanted to meet him because she knew he was a womanizer, she knew it from a friend of hers, an

actress, who'd had a bad time with him in New York. He can't help it, her friend had said, he's a real sod, he hates women, you know, but he just has to get off with them, he can't let them alone. . . .

The memory paralyzed her. She wondered why she hadn't thought of it earlier. It was obvious, anyway, from his work, that he had a thing about women, that he didn't like them and had to have them. He was a great enough writer for it not to matter to her: it was a measure of his greatness, for she did care about such things considerably.

She thought with a sudden nice physical recollection of Dan, who liked women, and loved her in particular, to her great delight.

She stood there, and smiled, and said nothing. Or rather, she said, "And how long are you in London this time, Mr. Jago?"

And he replied, with equal banality. It's all right, she was saying to herself, it's safe. It doesn't matter. (What did she mean by that?)

And as she listened to him, she saw approaching a film actress, a lady of considerable glamour, approaching with some purpose. "Howard, Howard, *there* you are, I *lost* you," she wailed, throwing her arm around his neck, possessively, her bosom heaving, her necklace sparkling: she started to stroke his graying hair, passionately, as she turned to greet Kathie. "Why hello, *Kathie*," she said, "what a surprise, I haven't seen you in *years*. Howard went to see your play, was he telling you? . . . Oh look, Howard, there's Martin—" and she marched him off: but Kathie Jones had already turned away. Well rid of him, she thought herself. He was drunk: he swayed slightly as Georgina grabbed him. Georgina was well away. She was a young lady with a will of iron. She was quite amusing on some occasions. Kathie wished them joy, and turned to look for a sympathetic friend, thinking as she went that the poor sixteen-year-old child she had been would have been shocked, shocked beyond anything, to have missed the opportunity to ask him, to hear him speak, even, of what he felt about, perhaps, the freedom of the will (one of his themes) and evolution (yet another). She smiled to herself, and went and talked to some publishers. They were much more interesting than Howard Jago had had a chance to be.

It was a couple of hours before he came back to her. She had been enjoying herself. There was plenty to drink, and some very good buffet food, and some people she knew well and some she hadn't seen for ages: she had been drinking quite steadily, and was sitting on a settee with an actress and her husband and another couple she'd never met before, laughing, very loudly, all of them, choking almost, over some anecdote about a play of hers, when he came back. He was looking more morose than before, and more obviously drunk. As he approached, Kathie made space for him on the settee by her, as he clearly intended to sit: they were still laughing over the story, as he sat. "Hello again," she said, turning to him, secure now, expecting nothing, willing to include him in the circle. "Do you know Jenny, and Bob . . ."

"Yes, yes," he said crossly, "I know everyone, I've met everyone in this place. I want to get out."

"Why don't you go, then?" asked Kathie, politely, slightly at a loss: and even as she spoke, she saw Georgina bearing down on them. Jago saw her too, and flinched: he rose to his feet, pulling Kathie to hers.

"Come on," he said, "let's get out of here." She was thrilled. She had never heard anyone talk like that except in a movie. And Howard Jago turned his back on Georgina, with calculated offense, and marched Kathie across the room, gripping her elbow, again in a way that she had only seen in the movies.

He paused, as they reached the bar, having shaken off their pursuer.

"You're not alone, are you?" he then said, turning to her with an amazing predictable heavy old-world gallantry. "It's not possible that the best-looking and most intelligent woman in the room could have come here alone, is it?"

"Yes, I'm alone," said Kathie.

"Where's your man, then?"

"He's in Hungary," said Kathie.

"I've had enough of this party," said Howard Jago. "Let's get out of it, for Christ's sake."

"I don't know . . ." said Kathie. "I should say goodbye . . ."

"There's no need to say good-bye," he said. "Come on. Let's get out."

She hesitated.

He took her arm.

She went.

They went downstairs and looked for a taxi: they found one easily, as it was that kind of district. They got into it. Then he said, again as though in a play or a film written by some playwright infinitely inferior to either of them, "Where shall we go, to my place or yours?"

"Yours," she said. "But only for a little while. I have to get home. I've a script conference in the morning." She was lying.

"Jesus," he said, looking at her legs, actually moving the skirt of her dress so that he could look at her legs, "you've got a beautiful pair of legs."

"They're nothing special," she said, which was true.

They arrived at his hotel, just off Bond Street. They got out, and went into the hotel, and up to his room. He asked the night porter to bring them a drink.

The room was large and expensive. Kathie sat in a chair. So did he. They drank the drink, and talked about the party, and about the people at it—their host, and Georgina, and various other playwrights, and the actress he had made so unhappy in New York the year before. Kathie knew exactly what she was doing: nothing on earth would induce her to get into that bed. She made it clear, as one does make it clear. They laughed a lot, and rang for some more drinks and a sandwich, and talked a lot of nonsense. She felt him move away. He had sense, after all. And she said she ought to go, he looked at her, and said, "Ah, I'm too old for you, you know."

But he can't have said this with much conviction, or she wouldn't have responded with the awful line she then delivered (which she had said, years before, to an Italian actor in Rome)—"You shouldn't try," she said, smiling falsely, "to seduce innocent girls from the country."

He laughed, also falsely. She kissed him: they parted.

She went down and got a taxi and was in bed and asleep in half an hour.

And that is the end of the story. They were to meet again, over the years, at similar parties, and he was to remark again upon her legs and her looks. They never had any serious conversation. But that isn't part of the story.

The point is: What did she think about this episode? She emerges not too badly from it, anyone would agree. She behaved coolly but not censoriously: she said some silly things, but who doesn't in such a silly situation? She had no regrets on her own behalf, though a few on behalf of that sixteen-year-old girl who had somehow just missed the opportunity of a lifetime. She had grown up so differently from what she had imagined. And she had some regrets about her image of the man. It was spoiled, she had to admit it (not quite forever, because oddly enough some years later she went to see one of his early plays and felt such waves of admiration flowing through her, drowning her resentments, as though his old self were still speaking, and she listening, in some other world without ages). But for years and years, she thought she was never going to be able to take his work seriously again, and when she described the evening to Dan, she was so rude about him and his boorish chauvinist masculine behavior that Dan, who usually sided with her and was as indignant as she was about such matters, actually began to feel quite sorry for Howard Jago, and to take his part. *Poor* Mr. Jago, he would say, fondly, whenever his name came up, *poor* Mr. Jago, he would say, lying safely between Kathie's legs, *what* a disappointing evening, I feel quite sorry for him, picking you, my love.

But that isn't all. It ought to be all, but it isn't. For Kathie, when she told the story to Dan, was lying. She tried to lie when she told it to herself, but she didn't quite succeed. She was an honest woman, and she knew perfectly well that she had received more of a thrill through being picked up by Howard Jago at a party, even picked up as she had been, casually, to annoy another woman—she had received more of a thrill from this than she would have got from any discussion, however profound,

of his work and hers. She would trade the whole of his work, willingly, and all the lasting pleasure it had given, for that silly remark he had made about her legs. She would rather he fancied her, however casually, than talked to her. She would rather he liked her face than her plays.

It's an awful thing to say, but she thought of his face, looking at her, heavy, drunk, sexy, battered, knowing, and wanting her, however idly: and it gave her a permanent satisfaction, that she'd been able to do that to him, that she'd been able to make a man like him look at her in that way. It was better than words, better than friendship.

It's an awful thing to say, but that's how some women are. Even nice, sensible, fulfilled, happy women like Kathie Jones. She would try to excuse herself, sometimes: she would say, I'm only like this because I was a plain child, I need reassurance. But she couldn't fool herself. Really, she knew that she was just a woman, and that's how some women are.

Some people are like that. Some men are like that, too. Howard Jago was exactly like that. People like admiration more than anything. Whatever can one do about it? Perhaps one shouldn't say this kind of thing. One ought not to have said such things, even five years ago, about a woman like Kathie Jones. The opposite case, for political reasons, had to be stated. (This is only a story, and Howard Jago didn't really hate women, any more than Kathie hated men.) But Kathie Jones is all right now. The situation is different, the case is made. We can say what we like about her now, because she's all right. I think.

60. PORNOS AND PRUDES UNITE!

Robert L. Tyler

Sex remains a mystery. Casanova had to admit this after investigating and exploring the field for a lifetime; Plato puzzled over sex and came up with some odd theories; Freud saw it as a force as potent as death in shaping human destiny. It still resists

This article first appeared in *The Humanist* (July/August 1971) and is reprinted by permission.

cooling or being translated to punch cards. But we really do not need testimonials, like celebrities in television commercials, to prove the point. By looking to our own lives or observing our friends, we can see the fabulous quality of sex—its strange pushes and pulls; the rich fantasies it generates to get us through subway rides, committee meetings, or marriages; and the weird and kinky shapes it gives personalities; its diffidences and exhibitionisms; all the myths it has spawned in learned books or on the walls of men's rooms. Sex is really incredible. If we take a couple of steps backward for perspective, the spectacle is in danger of collapsing and the drama of dissipating. What a furious tooting and pounding over the mere tumescence and detumescence of certain organs, over neural itches, over the straining for output of a complex physiological system. Like the bright young woman in the 1920's novel who was taken to see a whorehouse circus, we can say from a two-steps-backward perspective, "How *medical*!"

This perspective, in a word, is the normal viewpoint of the scientist—the satisfied, married, or gay gynecologist, let us say, or of Kinsey and his type, when work is progressing smoothly and the data are not being contaminated. Picture such a man of science strolling through his laboratory-clinic, checking the blood-pressure readings from the wires and tubes trailing off a couple copulating on a table; noting the mucous membrane changes around an engorged clitoris; testing his jocular bedside manner on a nervous subject who, with the help of French postcards, is struggling to ready himself for an experiment. Such images can dry up lust as quickly as pictures of the interior of a churning stomach can stop the appetite of a gourmet.

But this scientific, two-steps-backward perspective is wonderfully useful and therapeutic because it enables one to see clearly the tortured, guilt-ridden, repressive, and sickly side of sexuality that runs through human history and that, as human reality, has made, and makes, Freud credible and relevant. It is liberating to tell a guilty masturbator —if any remains—the physiological "facts" and cool things down. The couple screwing for science on the lab table, with wires attached, with motion picture cameras grinding away to capture it all in Kodacolor, serves us all well.

Science as science, however (even sexology, from physiological to psychological ramifications) can only be concerned with what is. To assume that its neutral vision, the sight of the spectacle from two steps backward, can prescribe some correct practice or attitude is, alas, mistaken. Here in this hot area, as in all others, lies the "duality of fact and decision," as the philosophers call it. Science is always neutral, seeking the facts and their theoretical connections. The scientific study of sex will not automatically supply us with some "right" attitudes or behavior. But correct information is always useful for making decisions, even if the information can never *be* the decision, even if the "is" can never stand in for the "should." Whatever is done with the data derived from those brave sexual laboratory experimenters can be good, bad, or indifferent. It can, for example, relieve anxieties based upon myth and misinformation. And that, of course, would be all to the good. It can perhaps loosen up tight people. It could also provide us with some peculiar stag movies, and that might be good also— but probably only indifferent.

Yet there is loose in the land a sexual moralist who bases his preaching, or so he thinks, on what "science" says. He *knows*, like Moses or somebody, that science can supply that liberating two-steps-backward perspective; that it can "cool" and "cure." By a kind of prophetic extrapolation from the glories of the laboratory-clinic this healthy-minded sexual reformer envisions a world of healthy and natural sex, a world free once and for all of guilt, kinkiness, compulsion, neurosis. He has truly a utopian vision—one that is frightening to anyone who gets a peculiar charge out of sex partly because it *is* miraculous and a mystery; because it is dangerous, like cigarette smoking or skiing; and because it can lead to such possible horrors as short engagements, love-making without deodorants, compulsive monogamy, and even love.

What would the new utopia be like, free of all extravagance, neurosis, or even gaiety? Attitudes supporting it would obviously begin at home. Infants of the future would be exposed to the healthy naturalness of sex—as if rural mankind for millennia had not been so exposed. Children would grow up taking general nudity as matter-of-factly as breakfast cereal. And if perchance the child should wander into a bedroom while his parents were making love, he would say simply and truthfully, "I was looking for my baseball mitt." And his somewhat preoccupied, good unflappable parents would reply calmly and rationally, "Try looking in the hall closet, son."

All this wholesomeness in the home would be reinforced at school by more formal sex education. In the lower grades instruction might be nothing more relentless than free information upon demand and a lot of casual nudity, where it comes most naturally, in physical education. As the student entered junior high school and puberty, the instruction would become more practical. No colored charts of genitalia; no animated cartoon of spermatozoa swimming upstream like determined salmon. Sex education would be practice, as healthy-minded and natural as swimming lessons or volley ball. We can perhaps even envision the courses, beginning with the simple and moving along to the more complex. "Copulation I" might well be the first. Then we could advance to "Mutual Adjustment I," involving a kind of musical chairs game on the gym mats. From there we would eventually arrive at the finer points, perhaps reversing the order of learning from those older, unenlightened days of guilty fumbling and contortions at the drive-in movies. Really advanced courses—Yoga and Ancient Oriental Technique, for example—could probably be left for college, where they would be electives. By the time the student was out of high school he or she would be an experienced, healthy-minded, sexually adequate young adult. If students entered the curriculum from old-fashioned and unenlightened homes, they might run into serious blocks; but wise counseling over the 12 years of the program could probably overcome the handicap in most cases.

We need not elaborate. We can certainly agree that such a new order, if achieved, would rid the world of most of the agony that seems to have attached itself to sex, from Abelard and Heloise to the characters in a Tennessee Williams play. But we might also agree that the reform had succeeded at a considerable price, by eliminating what might sometimes be ecstasy with the pain and by reducing the whole matter to hygiene—like calisthenics or jogging.

Reactionaries, of course, would be appalled by this utopia. Appalled, in fact, might be an understatement. As is apparent in the organized opposition to the much more modest sex education plans now afoot, there is a powerful interest in our society that would fight in the streets against such a change. Most of the clergy would object, as would many of the wistful middle-aged who resent the young, together with all those ideologues who think sex is part of the "international Communist conspiracy." From the perspectives of traditional values, opposition would be understandable. If sex

is the ultimate dirty secret and the most titillating of sins, any attempt to defuse it, to "cool" it, to place it in a category with calorie counting or bowel movements, would be the worst kind of acquiescence to evil.

But politics and utopias sometimes make strange bedfellows. Or perhaps bedfellows, in some cases, make strange politics. Like old-guard Republican isolationists and Henry Wallace Progressives, or like right-wing anarchists and elements of the new left, the prude and the porno might discover a reason for political alliance. The two poles can sometimes recognize a common danger they must face from the center. Granting the reflex opposition to our sexual utopia by the prude, does the honest porno really want to see the sexual revolution succeed under the leadership of the "sexologists"? Does he really want his whole marvelous game reduced to such trampoline exercises?

Obviously, both the prude and the porno have an interest in common. They are not really each other's worst enemy. The threat to both is that fateful flip-flop in perception, that two-steps-backward perspective. Oddly enough, the prude and the porno need each other. Their strange battle over censorship, for example, is only a half-battle. It is almost a *pas de deux.* Without the definitions both sides share, there would be no battle. In the new utopia pornography should become as quaint as prudery. What need does a healthy Swedish exerciser have for a literature of fantasy and titillation? In the new dispensation, *Fanny Hill* would become merely a curious social document from a benighted age, riddled with scientific error, as dull as a social Darwinist sociology book is today. A stag movie would become emotionally meaningless, like a Japanese Noh play to the average television audience. Why all that incomprehensible snicker and sneer, that aura of sin and secrecy and of kicking over traces, about something we all did in our sophomore year on the mats at old Baxter High?

So the prude and the porno should consider their common interests. They have a common enemy. But in their marriage of political convenience they must still somehow keep their old, gamey mistrust of each other. If they really discovered their need for each other they would both be in danger of taking that dangerous two steps backward. And then the common enemy would have won all.

61. ''PRICKS'' AND ''CHICKS'': A PLEA FOR ''PERSONS''

Robert Baker

There is a school of philosophers who believe that one starts philosophizing not by examining whatever it is one is philosophizing about but by examining the words we use to designate the subject to be examined. I must confess my allegiance to this school. The import of my confession is that this is an essay on women's liberation.

There seems to be a curious malady that affects those philosophers who in order to analyze anything must examine the way we talk about it; they seem incapable of talking about anything without talking about their talk about it—and, once again, I must confess to being typical. Thus I shall argue, first, that the way in which we identify something reflects our conception ot it; second, that the conception of women embedded in our language is male chauvinistic; third, that the conceptual revisions proposed by the feminist movement are confused; and finally, that at the root of the problem are both our conception of sex and the very structure of sexual identification.

IDENTIFICATION AND CONCEPTION

I am not going to defend the position that the terms we utilize to identify something reflect our conception of it; I shall simply explain and illustrate a simplified version of this thesis. Let us assume that any term that can be (meaningfully) substituted for x in the following statements is a term used to identify something: "Where is the x?" "Who is the x?" Some of the terms that can be substituted for x in the above expressions are metaphors; I shall

refer to such metaphors as metaphorical identifications. For example, southerners frequently say such things as "Where did that girl get to?" and "Who is the new boy that Lou hired to help out at the filling station?" If the persons the terms apply to are adult Afro-Americans, then "girl" and "boy" are metaphorical identifications. The fact that the metaphorical identifications in question are standard in the language reflects the fact that certain characteristics of the objects properly classified as boys and girls (for example, immaturity, inability to take care of themselves, need for guidance) are generally held by those who use identifications to be properly attributable to Afro-Americans. One might say that the whole theory of southern white paternalism is implicit in the metaphorical identification "boy" (just as the rejection of paternalism is implicit in the standardized Afro-American forms of address, "man" and "woman," as in, for example, "Hey, man, how are you?").

Most of what I am going to say in this essay is significant only if the way we metaphorically identify something is not a superficial bit of conceptually irrelevant happenstance but rather a reflection of our conceptual structure. Thus if one is to accept my analysis he must understand the significance of metaphorical identifications. He must see that, even though the southerner who identifies adult Afro-American males as "boys" feels that this identification is "just the way people talk"; but for a group to talk that way it must think that way. In the next few paragraphs I shall adduce what I hope is a persuasive example of how, in one clear case, the change in the way we identified something reflected a change in the way we thought about it.

Until the 1960s, Afro-Americans were identified by such terms as "Negro" and "colored"

From Robert Baker, " 'Pricks' and 'Chicks': A Plea for 'Persons,' " in *Philosophy and Sex*, ed. by Robert Baker and Frederick Ellison, 1975.© 1971, 1973, 1975, 1977. Reprinted by permission of Prometheus Books.

(the respectable terms) and by the more disreputable "nigger," "spook," "kink," and so on. Recently there has been an unsuccessful attempt to replace the respectable identifications with such terms as "African," and "Afro-American," and a more successful attempt to replace them with "black." The most outspoken champions of this linguistic reform were those who argued that nonviolence must be abandoned for Black Power (Stokely Carmichael, H. Rap Brown), that integration must be abandoned in favor of separation (the Black Muslims: Malcolm X, Muhammad Ali), and that Afro-Americans were an internal colony in the alien world of Babylon who must arm themselves against the possibility of extermination (the Black Panthers: Eldridge Cleaver, Huey Newton). All of these movements and their partisans wished to stress that Afro-Americans were different from other Americans and could not be merged with them because the differences between the two was as great as that between black and white. Linguistically, of course, "black" and "white" are antonyms; and it is precisely this sense of oppositeness that those who see the Afro-American as alienated, separated, and nonintegratable wish to capture with the term "black." Moreover, as any good dictionary makes clear, in some contexts "black" is synonymous with "deadly," "sinister," "wicked," "evil," and so forth. The new militants were trying to create just this picture of the black man—civil rights and Uncle Tomism are dead, the ghost of Nat Turner is to be resurrected, Freedom Now or pay the price, the ballot or the bullet, "Violence is as American as cherry pie." The new strategy was that the white man would either give the black man his due or pay the price in violence. Since conceptually a "black man" was an object to be feared ("black" can be synonymous with "deadly," and so on), while a "colored man" or a "Negro" was not, the new strategy required that the "Negro" be supplanted by the "black man." White America resisted the proposed linguistic reform quite vehemently, until hundreds of riots forced the admission that the Afro-American was indeed black.

Now to the point: I have suggested that the word "black" replaced the word "Negro" because there was a change in our conceptual structure. One is likely to reply that while all that I have said above is well and good, one had, after all, no choice about the matter. White people are identified in terms of their skin color as whites; clearly, if we are to recognize what is in reality nothing but the truth, that in this society people are conscious of skin color, to treat blacks as equals is merely to identify them by their skin color, which is black. That is, one might argue that while there was a change in words, we have no reason to think that there was a parallel conceptual change. If the term "black" has all the associations mentioned above, that is unfortunate; but in the context the use of the term "black" to identify the people formerly identified as "Negroes" is natural, inevitable, and, in and of itself, neutral; black is, after all, the skin color of the people in question. (Notice that this defense of the natural-inevitable-and-neutral conception of identification quite nicely circumvents the possible use of such seemingly innocuous terms as "Afro-American" and "African" by suggesting that in this society it is *skin color* that is the relevant variable.)

The great flaw in this analysis is that the actual skin color of virtually all of the people whom we call "black" is not black at all. The color tones range from light yellow to a deep umber that occasionally is literally black. The skin color of most Afro-Americans is best designated by the word "brown." Yet "brown" is not a term that is standard for identifying Afro-Americans. For example, if someone asked, "Who was the brown who was the architect for Washington, D.C.?" we would not know how to construe the question. We might attempt to read "brown" as a proper name ("Do you mean Arthur Brown, the designer?"). We would have no trouble understanding the sentence "Who was the black (Negro, colored guy, and so forth) who designed Washington, D.C.?" ("Oh, you mean Benjamin Banneker"). Clearly, "brown" is not a standard form of identification for Afro-Americans. I hope that it is equally clear that "black" has become the standard way of identifying Afro-Americans not because the term was natural, inevitable, and in the context, neutral, but because of its occasional synonymy with "sinister" and because as an antonym to "white" it best fitted the conceptual needs of those who saw race relations in terms of intensifying and insurmountable antonymies. If one accepts this point, then one must admit that there is a close connection between the way in which we identify things and the way in which we conceive them—and thus it should be also clear why I wish to talk about the way in which women are identified in English.[1] (Thus, for example, one would expect Black Muslims, who continually use the term "black *man*"—as in "the black *man*'s rights"—to be more male chauvinistic than Afro-Americans who use the term "black *people*" or "black *folk*.")

WAYS OF IDENTIFYING WOMEN

It may at first seem trivial to note that women (and men) are identified sexually; but conceptually this is extremely significant. To appreciate the significance of this fact it is helpful to imagine a language in which proper names and personal pronouns do not reflect the sex of the person designated by them (as they do in in our language). I have been told that in some oriental languages pronouns and proper names reflect social status rather than sex, but whether or not there actually exists such a language is irrelevant, for it is easy enough to imagine what one would be like. Let us then imagine a language where the proper names are sexually neutral (for example, "Xanthe"), so that one cannot tell from hearing a name whether the person so named is male or female, and where the personal pronouns in the language are "under" and "over." "Under" is the personal pronoun appropriate for all those who are younger than thirty, while "over" is appropriate to persons older than thirty. In such a language, instead of saying such things as "Where do you think *he* is living now?" one would say such things as "Where do you think *under* is living now?"

What would one say about a cultural community that employed such a language? Clearly, one would say that they thought that for purposes of intelligible communication it was more important to know a person's age grouping than the person's height, sex, race, hair color, or parentage. (There are many actual cultures, of course, in which people are identified by names that reflect their parentage; for example, Abu ben Adam means Abu son of Adam.) I think that one would also claim that this people would not have reflected these differences in the pronominal structure of their language if they did not believe that the differences between unders and overs was such that a statement would

frequently have one meaning if it were about an under and a different meaning if it were about an over. For example, in feudal times if a serf said, "My lord said to do this," that assertion was radically different from "Freeman John said to do this," since (presumably) the former had the status of a command while the latter did not. Hence the conventions of Middle English required that one refer to people in such a way as to indicate their social status. Analogously, one would not distinguish between pronominal references according to the age differences in the persons referred to were there no shift in meaning involved.

If we apply the lesson illustrated by this imaginary language to our own, I think that it should be clear that since in our language proper nouns and pronouns reflect sex rather than age, race, parentage, social status, or religion, we believe one of the most important things one can know about a person is that person's sex. (And, indeed, this is the first thing one seeks to determine about a newborn babe—our first question is almost invariably "Is it a boy or a girl?") Moreover, we would not reflect this important difference pronominally did we not also believe that statements frequently mean one thing when applied to males and something else when applied to females. Perhaps the most striking aspect of the conceptual discrimination reflected in our language is that man is, as it were, essentially human, while woman is only accidentally so.

This charge may seem rather extreme, but consider the following synonyms (which are readily confirmed by any dictionary). "Humanity" is synonymous with "mankind" but not with "womankind." "Man" can be substituted for "humanity" or "mankind" in any sentence in which the terms "mankind" or "humanity" occur without changing the meaning of the sentence, but significantly, "woman" cannot. Thus, the following expressions are all synonymous with each other: "humanity's great achievements," "mankind's great achievements," and "man's great achievements." "Woman's great achievements" is not synonymous with any of these. To highlight the degree to which women are excluded from humanity, let me point out that it is something of a truism to say that "man is a rational animal," while "woman is a rational animal" is quite debatable. Clearly, if "man" in the first assertion embraced both men and women, the second assertion would be just as much a truism as the first.[2] Humanity, it would seem, is a male prerogative. (And hence, one of the goals of women's liberation is to alter our conceptual structure so that someday "mankind" will be regarded as an improper and vestigial ellipsis for "humankind," and "man" will have no special privileges in relation to "human being" that "woman" does not have.[3])

The major question before us is, how are women conceived of in our culture? I have been trying to answer this question by talking about how they are identified. I first considered pronominal identification; now I wish to turn to identification through other types of noun phrases. Methods of nonpronominal identification can be discovered by determining which terms can be substituted for "woman" in such sentences as "Who is that woman over there?" without changing the meaning of the sentence. Virtually no term is interchangeable with "woman" in that sentence for all speakers on all occasions. Even "lady," which most speakers would accept as synonymous with "woman" in that sentence, will not do for a speaker who applies the term "lady" only to those women who display manners, poise, and sensitivity. In most contexts, a large number of students in one or more of my classes will accept the following types of terms as more or less interchangeable with "woman." (An asterisk indicates interchanges acceptable to both males and females; a plus sign indicates terms restricted to black students only. Terms with neither an asterisk nor a plus sign are accepted by all males but are not normally used by females.)

A. NEUTRAL TERMS: *lady, *gal, *girl (especially with regard to a coworker in an office or factory), *+sister, *broad (originally in the animal category, but most people do not think of the term as now meaning pregnant cow).

B. ANIMAL: *chick, bird, fox, vixen, filly, bitch (Many do not know the literal meaning of the term. Some men and most women construe this use as pejorative; they think of "bitch" in the context of "bitchy," that is, snappy, nasty, and so forth. But a large group of men claim that it is a standard nonpejorative term of identification—which may perhaps indicate that women have come to be thought of as shrews by a large subclass of men.)

C. PLAYTHING: babe, doll, cuddly.

D. GENDER (association with articles of clothing typically worn by those in the female gender role): skirt, hem.

E. SEXUAL: snatch, cunt, ass, twat, piece (of ass, and so forth), lay, pussy (could be put in the animal category, but most users associated it with slang expression indicating the female pubic region), +hammer (related to anatomical analogy between a hammer and breasts). There are many other usages, for example, "bunny," "sweat hog," but these were not recognized as standard by as many as 10 percent of any given class.

The students in my classes reported that the most frequently used terms of identification are in the neutral and animal classifications (although men in their forties claim to use the gender classifications quite a bit) and that the least frequently used terms of identification are sexual. Fortunately, however, I am not interested in the frequency of usage but only in whether the use is standard enough to be recognized as an identification among some group or other. (Recall that "brown" was not a standardized term of identification and hence we could not make sense out of "Who was the brown who planned Washington, D.C.?" Similarly, one has trouble with "Who was the breasts who planned Washington, D.C.?" but not with "Who was the babe (doll, chick, skirt, and so forth) who planned Washington, D.C.?")

Except for two of the animal terms, "chick" and "broad"—but note that "broad" is probably neutral today—women do not typically identify themselves in sexual terms, in gender terms, as playthings, or as animals; *only males use nonneutral terms to identify women.* Hence, it would seem that there is a male conception of women and a female conception. Only males identify women as "foxes," "babes," "skirts," or "cunts" (and since all the other nonneutral identifications are male, it is reasonable to assume that the identification of a woman as a "chick" is primarily a male conception that some women have adopted).

What kind of conception do men have of women? Clearly they think that women share certain properties with certain types of animals, toys, and playthings; they conceive of them in terms of the clothes associated with the female gender role; and, last (and, if my classes are any indication, least frequently), they conceive of women in terms of those parts of their anatomy associated with sexual intercourse, that is, as the identification "lay" indicates quite clearly, as sexual partners.

The first two nonneutral male classifications, animal and plaything, are prima facie denigrating (and I mean this in the literal sense of making one like a "nigger"). Consider the animal classification. All of the terms listed, with the possible exception of "bird," refer to animals that are either domesticated for servitude (to *man*) or hunted for sport. First, let us consider the term "bird." When I asked my students what sort of birds might be indicated, they suggested chick, canary (one member, in his forties, had suggested "canary" as a term of identification), chicken, pigeon, dove, parakeet, and hummingbird (one member). With the exception of the hummingbird, which like all the birds suggested is generally thought to be diminutive and pretty, all of the birds are domesticated, usually as pets (which reminds one that "my pet" is an expression of endearment). None of the birds were predators or symbols of intelligence or nobility (as are the owl, eagle, hawk, and falcon); nor did large but beautiful birds seem appropriate (for example, pheasants, peacocks, and swans). If one construes the bird terms (and for that matter, "filly") as applicable to women because they are thought of as beautiful, or at least pretty, *then there is nothing denigrating about them.* If, on the other hand, the common properties that underlie the metaphorical identification are domesticity and servitude, then they are indeed denigrating (as for myself, I think that both domesticity and prettiness underlie the identification). "Broad," of course, is, or at least was, clearly denigrating, since nothing renders more service to a farmer than does a pregnant cow, and cows are not commonly thought of as paradigms of beauty.

With one exception all of the animal terms reflect a male conception of women either as domesticated servants or as pets, or as both. Indeed, some of the terms reflect a conception of women first as pets and then as servants. Thus, when a pretty, cuddly little chick grows older, she becomes a very useful servant—the egg-laying hen.

"Vixen" and "fox," variants of the same term, are the one clear exception. None of the other animals with whom women are metaphorically identified are generally thought to be intelligent, aggressive, or independent—but the fox is. A chick is a soft, cuddly, entertaining, pretty, diminutive, domesticated, and dumb animal. A fox too is soft, cuddly, entertaining, pretty, and diminutive, but it is neither dependent nor dumb. It is aggressive, intelligent, and a minor predator—indeed, it preys on chicks—and frequently outsmarts ("outfoxes") men.

Thus the term "fox" or "vixen" is generally taken to be a compliment by both men and women, and compared to any of the animal or plaything terms it is indeed a compliment. Yet, considered in and of itself, the conception of a woman as a fox is not really complimentary at all, for the major connection between *man* and fox is that of predator and prey. The fox is an animal that men chase, and hunt, and kill for sport. If women are conceived of as foxes, then they are conceived of as prey that is fun to hunt.

In considering plaything identifications, only one sentence is necessary. *All the plaything identifications are clearly denigrating since they assimilate women to the status of mindless or dependent objects.* "Doll" is to male paternalism what "boy" is to white paternalism.

Up to this point in our survey of male conceptions of women, every male identification, without exception, has been clearly antithetical to the conception of women as human beings (recall that "man" was synonymous with "human," while "woman" was not). Since the way we talk of things, and especially the way we identify them, is the way in which we conceive of them, any movement dedicated to breaking the bonds of female servitude must destroy these ways of identifying and hence of conceiving of women. Only when both sexes find the terms "babe," "doll," "chick," "broad," and so forth, as objectionable as "boy" and "nigger" will women come to be conceived of as independent *human beings.*

The two remaining unexamined male identifications are gender and sex. There seems to be nothing objectionable about gender identifications per se. That is, women are metaphorically identified as skirts because in this culture, skirts, like women, are peculiarly female. Indeed, if one accepts the view that the slogan "female and proud" should play the same role for the women's liberation movement that the slogan "Black is beautiful" plays for the black-liberation movement, then female clothes should be worn with the same pride as Afro clothes.(Of course, one can argue that the skirt, like the cropped-down Afro, is a sign of bondage, and hence both the item of clothing and the identification with it are to be rejected—that is, cropped-down Afros are to Uncle Tom what skirts are to Uncle Mom.)

The terms in the last category are obviously sexual, and frequently vulgar. For a variety of reasons I shall consider the import and nature of these identifications in the next section.

MEN OUGHT NOT TO THINK OF WOMEN AS SEX OBJECTS

Feminists have proposed many reforms, and most of them are clearly desirable, for example, equal opportunity for self-development, equal pay for equal work, and free day-care centers. One feminist proposal, however, is peculiarly conceptual and deeply perplexing. I call this proposal peculiarly conceptual because unlike the other reforms it is directed at getting people to think differently. The proposal is that *men should not think of women (and women should not think of themselves) as sex objects*. In the rest of this essay I shall explore this nostrum. I do so for two reasons: first, because the process of exploration should reveal the depth of the problem confronting the feminists; and second, because the feminists themselves seem to be entangled in the very concepts that obstruct their liberation.

To see why I find this proposal puzzling, one has to ask what it is to think of something as a sex object.

If a known object is an object that we know, an unidentified object is an object that we have not identified, and a desired object is an object that we desire, what then is a sex object? Clearly, a sex object is an object we have sex with. Hence, to think of a woman as a sex object is to think of her as someone to have sexual relations with, and when the feminist proposes that men refrain from thinking of women in this way, *she is proposing that men not think of women as persons with whom one has sexual relations*.

What are we to make of this proposal? Is the feminist suggesting that women should not be conceived of in this way because such a conception is "dirty"? To conceive of sex and sex organs as dirty is simply to be a prude. "Shit" is the paradigm case of a dirty word. It is a dirty word because the item it designates is taboo; it is literally unclean and untouchable (as opposed to something designated by what I call a curse word, which is not untouchable but rather something to be feared—"damn" and "hell" are curse words; "piss" is a dirty word). If one claims that "cunt" (or "fuck") is a dirty word, then one holds that what this term designates is unclean and taboo; thus one holds that the terms for sexual intercourse or sexual organs are dirty, one has accepted puritanism. If one is a puritan and a feminist, then indeed one ought to subscribe to the slogan *men should not conceive of women as sexual objects*. What is hard to understand is why anyone but a puritan (or, perhaps, a homosexual) would promulgate this slogan; yet most feminists, who are neither lesbians nor puritans, accept this slogan. Why? . . .

Consider the terms we use to identify coitus, or more technically, terms that function synonymously with "had sexual intercourse with" in a sentence of the form "A had sexual intercourse with B." The following is a list of some commonly used synonyms (numerous others that are not as widely used have been omitted, for example, "diddled," "laid pipe with"):

screwed
laid
fucked
had
did it with (to)
banged
balled
humped
slept with
made love to

Now, for a select group of these verbs, names for males are the subjects of sentences with active constructions (that is, where the subjects are said to be doing the activity); and names for females require passive constructions (that is, they are the recipients of the activity—whatever is done is done to them). Thus, we would not say "Jane did it to Dick," although we would say "Dick did it to Jane." Again, Dick bangs Jane, Jane does not bang Dick; Dick humps Jane, Jane does not hump Dick. In contrast, verbs like "did it with" do not require an active role for the male; thus, "Dick did it with Jane, and Jane with Dick." Again, Jane may make love to Dick, just as Dick makes love to Jane; and Jane sleeps with Dick as easily as Dick sleeps with Jane. (My students were undecided about "laid." Most thought that it would be unusual indeed for Jane to lay Dick, unless she played the masculine role of seducer-aggressor.)

The sentences thus form the following pairs. (Those nonconjoined singular noun phrases where a female subject requires a passive construction are marked with a cross. An asterisk indicates that the sentence in question is not a sentence of English if it is taken as synonymous with the italicized sentence heading the column.[4])

Dick had sexual intercourse with Jane
Dick screwed Jane†
Dick laid Jane†
Dick fucked Jane†
Dick had Jane†
Dick did it to Jane†
Dick banged Jane†
Dick humped Jane†
Dick balled Jane(?)
Dick did it with Jane
Dick slept with Jane
Dick made love to Jane

Jane had sexual intercourse with Dick
Jane was banged by Dick
Jane was humped by Dick
*Jane was done by Dick
Jane was screwed by Dick
Jane was laid by Dick
Jane was fucked by Dick
Jane was had by Dick
Jane balled Dick (?)
Jane did it with Dick
Jane slept with Dick
Jane made love to Dick
*Jane screwed Dick
*Jane laid Dick
*Jane fucked Dick
*Jane had Dick
*Jane did it to Dick

*Jane banged Dick
*Jane humped Dick

These lists make clear that within the standard view of sexual intercourse, males, or at least names for males, seem to play a different role than females, since male subjects play an active role in the language of screwing, fucking, having, doing it, and perhaps, laying, while female subjects play a passive role.

The asymmetrical nature of the relationship indicated by the sentences marked with a cross is confirmed by the fact that the form "—ed with each other" is acceptable for the sentences not marked with a cross, but not for those that require a male subject. Thus:

Dick and Jane had sexual intercourse with each other
Dick and Jane made love to each other
Dick and Jane slept with each other
Dick and Jane did it with each other
Dick and Jane balled with each other (*?)
*Dick and Jane banged with each other
*Dick and Jane did it to each other
*Dick and Jane had each other
*Dick and Jane fucked each other
*Dick and Jane humped each other
*(?) Dick and Jane laid each other
*Dick and Jane screwed each other

It should be clear, therefore, that our language reflects a difference between the male and female sexual roles, and hence that we conceive of the male and female roles in different ways. The question that now arises is, What difference in our conception of the male and female sexual roles requires active constructions for males and passive for females?

One explanation for the use of the active construction for males and the passive construction for females is that this grammatical asymmetry merely reflects the natural physiological asymmetry between men and women: the asymmetry of "to screw" and "to be screwed," "to insert into" and "to be inserted into." That is, it might be argued that the difference between masculine and feminine grammatical roles merely reflects a difference naturally required by the anatomy of males and females. This explanation is inadequate. Anatomical differences do not determine how we are to conceptualize the relation between penis and vagina during intercourse. Thus one can easily imagine a society in which the female normally played the active role during intercourse, where female subjects required active constructions with verbs indicating copulation, and where the standard metaphors were terms like "engulfing"—that is, instead of saying "he screwed her," one would say "she engulfed him." It follows that the use of passive constructions for female subjects of verbs indicating copulation does not reflect differences determined by human anatomy but rather reflects those generated by human customs.

What I am going to argue next is that the passive construction of verbs indicating coitus (that is, indicating the female position) can *also* be used to indicate that a person is being harmed. I am then going to argue that the metaphor involved would only make sense if we conceive of the female role in intercourse as that of a person being harmed (or being taken advantage of).

Passive constructions of "fucked," "screwed," and "had" indicate the female role. They also can be used to indicate being harmed. Thus, in all of the following sentences, Marion plays the female role: "Bobbie fucked Marion"; "Bobbie screwed Marion"; "Bobbie had Marion"; "Marion was fucked"; "Marion was screwed"; and "Marion was had." All of the statements are equivocal. They might literally mean that someone had sexual intercourse with Marion (who played the female role); or they might mean, metaphorically, that Marion was deceived, hurt, or taken advantage of. Thus, we say such things as "I've been screwed" ("fucked," "had," "taken," and so on) when we have been treated unfairly, been sold shoddy merchandise, or conned out of valuables. Throughout this essay I have been arguing that metaphors are applied to things only if what the term *actually* applies to shares one or more properties with what the term *metaphorically* applies to. Thus, the female sexual role must have something in common with being conned or being sold shoddy merchandise. The only common property is that of being harmed, deceived, or taken advantage of. *Hence we conceive of a person who plays the female sexual role as someone who is being harmed* (that is, "screwed," "fucked," and so on).

It might be objected that this is clearly wrong, since the unsignated terms do not indicate some-

one's being harmed, and hence we do not conceive of having intercourse as being harmed. The point about the unsignated terms, however, is that they can take both females and males as subjects (in active constructions) and thus *do not pick out the female role.* This demonstrates that we conceive of sexual roles in such a way that only females are thought to be taken advantage of in intercourse.

The best part of solving a puzzle is when all the pieces fall into place. If the subjects of the passive construction are being harmed, presumably the subjects of the active constructions are doing harm, and, indeed, we do conceive of these subjects in precisely this way. Suppose one is angry at someone and wishes to express malevolence as forcefully as possible without actually committing an act of physical violence. If one is inclined to be vulgar one can make the sign of the erect male cock by clenching one's fist while raising one's middle finger, or by clenching one's fist and raising one's arm and shouting such things as "screw you," "up yours," or "fuck you." In other words, one of the strongest possible ways of telling someone that you wish to harm him is to tell him to assume the female sexual role relative to you. Again, to say to someone "go fuck yourself" is to order him to harm himself, while to call someone a "mother fucker" is not so much a play on his Oedipal fears as to accuse him of being so low that he would inflict the greatest imaginable harm (fucking) upon that person who is most dear to him (his mother).

Clearly, we conceive of the male sexual roles as that of hurting the person in the female role—but lest the reader have any doubts, let me provide two further bits of confirming evidence: one linguistic, one nonlinguistic. One of the English terms for a person who hurts (and takes advantage of) others is the term "prick." This metaphorical identification would not make sense unless the bastard in question (that is, the person outside the bonds of legitimacy) was thought to share some characteristics attributed to things that are literally pricks. As a verb, "prick" literally means "to hurt," as in "I pricked myself with a needle"; but the usage in question is as a noun. As a noun, "prick" is a colloquial term for "penis." Thus, the question before us is what characteristic is shared by a penis and a person who harms others (or, alternatively, by a penis and by being stuck by a needle). Clearly, no physical characteristic is relevant (physical characteristics might underlie the Yiddish metaphorical attribution "schmuck," but one would have to analyze Yiddish usage to determine this); hence the shared characteristic is nonphysical; the only relevant shared nonphysical characteristic is that both a literal prick and a figurative prick are agents that harm people.

Now for the nonlinguistic evidence. Imagine two doors: in front of each door is a line of people; behind each door is a room; in each room is a bed; on each bed is a person. The line in front of one room consists of beautiful women, and on the bed in that room is a man having intercourse with each of these women in turn. One may think any number of things about this scene. One may say that the man is in heaven, or enjoying himself at a bordello; or perhaps one might only wonder at the oddness of it all. One does not think that the man is being hurt or violated or degraded—or at least the possibility does not immediately suggest itself, although one could conceive of situations where this was what was happening (especially, for example, if the man was impotent). Now, consider the other line. Imagine that the figure on the bed is a woman and that the line consists of handsome, smiling men. The woman is having intercourse with each of these men in turn. It immediately strikes one that the woman is being degraded, violated, and so forth—"that poor woman."

When one man fucks many women he is a playboy and gains status; when a woman is fucked by many men she degrades herself and loses stature.

Our conceptual inventory is now complete enough for us to return to the task of analyzing the slogan that men ought not to think of women as sex objects.

I think that it is now plausible to argue that the appeal of the slogan "men ought not to think of women as sex objects," and the thrust of much of the literature produced by contemporary feminists, turns on something much deeper than a rejection of "scoring" (that is, the utilization of sexual "conquests" to gain esteem) and yet is a call neither for homosexuality nor for puritanism.

The slogan is best understood as a call for a new conception of the male and female sexual roles. If the analysis developed above is correct, our present conception of sexuality is such that to be a man

is to be a person capable of brutalizing women (witness the slogans "The marines will make a man out of you!" and "The army builds *men*!" which are widely accepted and which simply state that learning how to kill people will make a person more manly). Such a conception of manhood not only bodes ill for a society led by such men, but also is clearly inimical to the best interests of women. It is only natural for women to reject such a sexual role, and it would seem to be the duty of any moral person to support their efforts—to redefine our conceptions not only of fucking, but of the fucker (man) and the fucked (woman).

This brings me to my final point. We are a society preoccupied with sex. As I noted previously, the nature of proper nouns and pronouns in our language makes it difficult to talk about someone without indicating that person's sex. This convention would not be part of the grammar of our language if we did not believe that knowledge of a person's sex was crucial to understanding what is said about that person. Another way of putting this point is that sexual discrimination permeates our conceptual structure. Such discrimination is clearly inimical to any movement toward sexual egalitarianism and virtually defeats its purpose at the outset. (Imagine, for example, that black people were always referred to as "them" and whites as "us" and that proper names for blacks always had an "x" suffix at the end. Clearly any movement for integration as equals would require the removal of these discriminatory indicators. Thus at the height of the melting-pot era, immigrants Americanized their names: "Bellinsky" became "Bell," "Burnstein" became "Burns," and "Lubitch" became "Baker.")

I should therefore like to close this essay by proposing that contemporary feminists should advocate the utilization of neutral proper names and the elimination of gender from our language (as I have done in this essay); and they should vigorously protest any utilization of the third-person pronouns "he" and "she" as examples of sexist discrimination (perhaps "person" would be a good third-person pronoun)—for, as a parent of linguistic analysis once said, "The limits of our language are the limits of our world."

NOTES

1. The underlying techniques used in this essay were all developed (primarily by Austin and Strawson) to deal with the

problems of metaphysics and epistemology. All I have done is to attempt to apply them to other areas; I should note, however, that I rely rather heavily on metaphorical identifications, and that first philosophy tends not to require the analysis of such superficial aspects of language. Note also that it is an empirical matter whether or not people do use words in a certain way. In this essay I am just going to assume that the reader uses words more or less as my students do; for I gathered the data on which words we use to identify women, and so on, simply by asking students. If the reader does not use terms as my students do, then what I say may be totally inapplicable to him. The linguistic surveys on which this article is based were done on samples of student language at Wayne State University (Detroit) and Wayne County Community College (inner city centers: Detroit) during the 1970–1971 academic year. A number of surveys conducted by students at Union College in 1973 and 1974 indicate different usages. Whereas in the first survey active female constructions for verbs indicating sexual intercourse (e.g. 'Jane laid Dick') were regarded as deviant, later surveys found these constructions to be acceptable. This may be explained by differences in the class structure (since Union College students are predominately white upper middle class, while WSU students are lower middle class and the WCCC students were from the black inner city), or by some more pervasive changes in conception of the woman's role.

2.   It is also interesting to talk about the technical terms that philosophers use. One fairly standard bit of technical terminology is "trouser word." J. L. Austin invented this bit of jargon to indicate which term in a pair of antonyms is important. Austin called the important term a "trouser word" because "it is the use which wears the trousers." Even in the language of philosophy, to be important is to play the male role. Of course, the antifeminism implicit in the language of technical philosophy is hardly comparable to the male chauvinism embedded in commonplaces of ordinary discourse.

3.   Although I thought it inappropriate to dwell on these matters in the text, it is quite clear that *we* do *not* associate many positions with females—as the following story brings out. I related this conundrum both to students in my regular courses and to students I teach in some experimental courses at a nearby community college. Among those students who had not previously heard the story, only native Swedes invariably resolved the problem; less than half of the students from an upper-class background would get it (eventually), while lower-class and black students virtually never figured it out. Radical students, women, even members of women's liberation groups fared no better than anyone else with their same class background. The story goes as follows: A little boy is wheeled into the emergency room of a hospital. The surgeon on emergency call looks at the boy and says, "I'm sorry I cannot operate on this child; he is my son." The surgeon was not the boy's father. In what relation did the surgeon stand to the child? Most students did not give any answer. The most frequent answer given was that the surgeon had fathered the boy illegitimately. (Others suggested that the surgeon had divorced the boy's mother and remarried and hence was not legally the boy's father.) Even though the story was related as a part of a lecture on women's liberation, at best only 20 percent of the written answers gave the correct and obvious answer—the surgeon was the boy's mother.

4.   For further analysis of verbs indicating copulation see "A Note on Conjoined Noun Phrases," *Journal of Philosophical Linguistics*, vol. 1, no. 2, Great Expectations, Evanston, Ill. Reprinted with "English Sentences Without Overt Grammatical Subject," in Zwicky, Salus, Binnick, and Vanek, eds., *Studies Out in Left Field: Defamatory Essays Presented to James D. McCawley* (Edmonton: Linguistic Research, Inc., 1971). The puritanism in our society is such that both of these articles are pseudonymously published under the name of Quang Phuc Dong; Mr. Dong, however, has a fondness for citing and criticizing the articles and theories of Professor James McCawley, Department of Linguistics, University of Chicago. Professor McCawley himself was kind enough to criticize an earlier draft of this essay. I should also like to thank G. E. M. Anscombe for some suggestions concerning this essay.

62. THE ROOTS OF MISOGYNY

Marc Feigen Fasteau

1

Jeffrey, a friend's son, is seven years old and likes a girl of the same age who lives in his apartment building. But when he learned that she was going to transfer to his school, he got an agitated look on his face. "It'll spoil everything," he said. And it nearly has. The other boys in his class tease him and beat him up if they see him playing with her. Things got so bad that one day, when his mother came to

Reprinted by permission of McGraw-Hill Book Company from Marc Feigen Fasteau, *The Male Machine* (1975), pp. 36–50.

school to walk Jeffrey and his friend back to his house so they could play together, the girl, without a word, carefully walked ten yards behind so the other boys wouldn't think Jeffrey was going to play with her. When she and Jeffrey had a fight, her ultimate act of betrayal was to tell the boys that she and Jeffrey had sleep-over dates. She knew he would catch hell from them.

In a second-grade class I visited, I asked the boys whether they played with the girls. Obviously expecting approval, they told me proudly that they didn't. One was embarrassed enough to start a fight when the other boys accused him of liking a particular girl.

A subscriber to *Ms.* magazine, in a letter to the editor, described a scene in which a five-year-old boy was being teased by four other boys of about the same age. Unable to endure any more, pushed to the point of tearful rage, he turned to the leader of the group and, with a look of pure hatred, screamed the most horrible insult he could think of: "You girl!"[1]

This antipathy of little boys toward little girls is so common as to be unremarkable. A "girls—ugh!" line is a standard part of family style television comedies involving pre-pubescent boys, one which calls forth universal sympathetic recognition from grown men. The "funny story" at the end of a CBS network news broadcast one night, for example, was how a twelve-year-old had won a championship horseshoe-pitching match in which his thirteen-year-old brother had also competed. The twelve-year-old had provoked the older boy, who had responded by hitting him, and injuring his own throwing hand, thus hampering his performance the next day. How had the victor precipitated the fight, asked the newscaster? Cut to filmed interview with the kid: "I called him a girl," he said, and he grinned the grin of someone who thinks he has done something expected and amusing. Cut back to matching grin of comfortable male complicity from the newscaster as he says, ". . . and good night from CBS News."[2]

It is a wishful delusion to believe that this kind of hostility toward females is merely a passing phase that somehow disappears with time. It is not. Elaborated and layered over with other feelings, it is the key to the way adult men feel about women. Let us look at its roots.

As early as ages four and five, boys learn what is expected of them as males and restrict themselves to what they believe are suitably masculine activities.[3] What this means in large part is not being like a girl, or, what is the same thing, not being a "sissy." A few years later, they are quite capable of expanding on this point. Eight- and eleven-year-old boys in a study of sex role pressures on male children, by psychologist Ruth Hartley, described girls in these terms:

They have to stay close to the house; they are expected to play quietly and be gentler than boys; they are often afraid; they must not be rough; they have to keep clean; they cry when they are scared or hurt; they are afraid to go to rough places like rooftops and empty lots; their activities consist of "fopperies" like playing with dolls, fussing over babies and sitting and talking about dresses; they need to know how to cook, sew, and take care of children, but spelling and arithmetic are not as important for them as for boys.[4]

This image of girls, reeking of limitation and restraint, is not just the product of parental and peer-group indoctrination. Our schools also do their share in perpetrating it. For example, California's first-grade reading text, published by Harper & Row, paints this picture of girls and their proper relationship to boys:

[Mark and Janet are brother and sister. Janet gets new skates. She tries them and falls.]
    "Mark! Janet!" said Mother. "What is going on here?"
    "She cannot skate," said Mark. "I can help her. I want to help her. Look at her, Mother. Just look at her. She is just like a girl. She gives up."
    [Mother forces Janet to try again.]
    "Now you see," said Mark. "Now you can skate. But just with me to help you."
    [Janet, needless to say, never makes a similar remark to Mark.][5]

This is not atypical. A survey of thirty commonly used children's textbooks[6] showed females were described more often than males as lazy and incapable of direct action as well as more likely to give up easily, collapse in tears, betray secrets, and act on petty or selfish motives. Nearly all the adult female characters (found in only four percent of stories with an adult protagonist) were shown as assistants to men. Madame Curie, for example, appears as little more than a helpmate to her husband and another male scientist. Among the descriptions of present-day professionals, there was only one working female, a scientist. The three other male scientists in the same chapter are shown working alone on projects demanding originality and exacting mental effort, while the text and picture caption for the woman scientist state that she is not working independently and that the idea she is testing was assigned to her by others. Given this picture of females, it is not surprising that the boys in the Hartley study described their own characteristics as the polar opposites:

[Boys] have to be able to fight in case a bully comes along; they have to be athletic; they have to be able to run fast; they must be able to play rough games; they need to know how to play many games—curbball, baseball, basketball, football; they need to be smart; they need to be able to take care of themselves; they should know what girls don't know—how to climb, how to make a fire, how to carry things; they should have more ability than girls; they need to know how to stay out of trouble; they need to know arithmetic and spelling more than girls do.[7]

The "not like a girl" aspects of being a boy come out even more clearly in the answers to Hartley's question, "What is expected of boys?" which gets at behavior tacitly approved by grownups:

They believe grown-ups expect them to be noisy; to get dirty; to mess up the house; to be naughty; to be "outside" more than girls are; not to be cry-babies; not to be "softies," not to be "behind" like girls are; and to get into trouble more than girls do. Moreover, boys are not allowed to do the kind of things that girls usually do, but girls may do the kind of things that boys do.[8]

The situation is practically perfect for inducing anxiety. The ideal toward which a boy's parents and peers pressure him is vague and elusive, defined as much by what he should *not* do and be as by what is approved, and, most important, calling for total repression of his feelings of vulnerability and dependence. Fathers, believing in a slightly more grown-up version of the same ideal, try to conceal from their sons the few departures from the male ideal they permit themselves or cannot avoid, thereby passing on the same dehumanized image of masculinity. The result, Hartley says, is "an overstraining to be masculine, a virtual panic at being caught doing anything traditionally defined as feminine, and hostility toward anything even hinting at 'femininity,' including females themselves."[9]

The mechanism is familiar. When we fear and dislike qualities in ourselves, we "project" this hostility onto others who remind us of or have the unwanted characteristics. Jews who wish they were WASPs dislike other Jews who "act Jewish." Blacks who are insecure in their middle-class style avoid and dislike "funky" ghetto blacks who remind them of their origins. Women whose self-esteem is threatened by their own frustration with their roles as housewives feel hostility toward women who

articulate these feelings. In the same way, boys want so desperately to be different from girls that anything that appears to close the gap, any similarity in behavior that they are aware of, is frightening. My neighborhood tree-house gang, for example, arranged the foot- and hand-holds leading up to our tree house so "no girls can get up there." There were no secret male rituals we wanted to indulge in; it just made us feel different and more manly to keep girls out.

Of course, boys don't see the male and female roles as merely different. To be a boy—prospectively a man—is clearly superior. Although many girls want for a period of time to be boys and do their best to act like boys (so many in fact that we have a word—*tomboy*—to describe them), very few boys want to be girls.[10] Naturally, they project these differences into the future. The boys in Hartley's study thought grown women are, among other things, fearful, indecisive, stay-at-homes, physically weak, squeamish about seeing blood, unadventurous, more easily hurt and killed than men, and afraid of getting wet or getting an electric shock. They thought that women "have a way of doing things the wrong way," that they scream instead of taking charge in emergencies, fuss over children's grades, and very easily become jealous and envy their husbands (although it is conceded that they make their children feel good). Of women's traditional activities they said,

"They are always at those crazy household duties and don't have time for anything else." "Their work is just regular drudging." "Women do things like cooking and washing and sewing because that's all they can do." "Women haven't enough strength in the head or in the body to do most jobs."[11]

By contrast, they thought that grown men had to be strong, protect women and children in emergencies, do rough, dirty and unpleasant work, earn money, care for their children and get along with their wives, and that they get tired a lot. On the positive side, however, men are usually in charge of things, they mess up the house, "mostly do what they want to do," decide how to spend the money, and get first choice of the most comfortable chair. Although they get mad a lot, they laugh and make jokes more than women. They are more fun to be with than mothers, more exciting to have around, and they have the best ideas.[12] With this vision of the future, what boy (or girl, until the pressure of social and physical reality becomes too great) would not choose the male role with its dual load of responsibilities and enticing perquisites?

Consciousness of these perquisites begins very early. My kindergarten informant, a self-assured girl of five, reported how it was when the boys and girls played Red Light—Green Light—One—Two—Three together. For readers who have forgotten or who didn't go to kindergarten, the leader of the game stands at the front of the room, with eyes covered and says "Red Light—Green Light—One—Two—Three" as fast as possible, while the other players try to move up as close to the front of the room as they can. When the leader opens her or his eyes, any player still moving has to go back to the starting line. My informant reported that the boys would readily go back to the starting line when caught by a boy leader but that when she or another girl was the leader they would refuse to go back. In her case, one came up, pushed her aside, and, restoring the natural order of things, pronounced himself the leader.

In adult life, the expression of these attitudes may be muted because of sexual attraction, the demands of family life, and social disapproval of open hostility to women. But, underneath, they remain, reinforced through the years by our institutions and culture, shaping nearly every aspect of men's adult relationships with women, and never to be outgrown.

2

Most grown men no longer state openly their opinions about the nature of women, especially if those opinions mark women out as clearly inferior and destined for subordination. No one today will pronounce, as Nietzsche once did, that a man "must conceive of woman as a possession, as property that can be locked, as something predestined for service and achieving her perfection in that."[13] The growing incredulity and militance of women has imposed a degree of caution and camouflage. Open antagonism and contempt, Mary Ellmann has pointed out, has largely retreated into fiction, "the

conventional sanctuary of unimpeachable utterance."[14] A more acceptable posture is that of wishful reverence for the "real woman" of yore—"women aren't women any more."[15] Nevertheless, as the literature of the women's movement and numerous psychological surveys[16] convincingly demonstrate, the image of the ideal woman as passive, illogical, able to express tender feelings, security-minded, oriented toward home and children, vain, self-effacing, unambitious, and dependent on and subordinate to men still pervades our culture. Individual men may be more enlightened as to particular elements of the feminine stereotype—the idea that women should not work or not work seriously, for example—but when these men are required to accept the ramifications of such enlightenment in their personal lives a swift regression can usually be observed. Some classic lines are: "Someone has to take care of the children and she's better at it." "Her job is important, but when I get home I want a Martini ready and waiting." "Of course I want my wife to be well informed, but I don't like her disagreeing with me when we're out with other people." "I agree that women deserve equal job opportunities, just like blacks, but I can't put Linda in charge of the whole department—I mean, I could never work for a woman." "No, I don't want my wife to throw the game when we play tennis. She should play as hard and as well as she can. Things just got uncomfortable when she started beating me regularly, so we stopped playing. She doesn't have anything else to do all week except to go to those damn tennis lessons, you know."

Changes in men's beliefs about women have so far been superficial, at the level of intellect rather than feeling. Under pressure from our egalitarian ethic and the women's movement, more socially conscious men are beginning to agree in general terms to ideas about women which they are emotionally unable to accept in their personal relationships. The realization that they may not in fact be superior to, or even very different from the women they live or work with is frightening—and fear produces hostility. This reaction, as one would expect, is strongest among men who most need the prop of male superiority. A survey of twenty thousand readers of *Psychology Today,* for example, showed:

Men who are uncomfortable over the prospect of equal women are also more uneasy with women in general (30 percent compared to 14 percent of the whole male sample); they have deceived women more often in order to have sex (31 percent of the threatened men said "frequently" compared to 23 percent of the others); the majority of their good friends are men (61 percent compared to 53 percent); and—most strikingly—they are three times as likely as unthreatened men to have negative reactions to intercourse (18 percent to 5 percent). Indeed, the more threatened a man was, the more likely he was to attribute sexual problems to members of the women's movement.[17]

Antagonism to the aims of the women's movement has also triggered a resurgence of efforts, scholarly and otherwise, to prove that sex roles are "natural," the result of genetic and hormonal differences between men and women rather than social learning. A mainstay of this school in recent years has been the drawing of analogies between human beings and other primates.[18] Among certain species of baboons, for example, patterns of organization have been observed which appear to be roughly analogous to those alleged to be "inherent" in human beings: the males, especially the largest and strongest, protect the troop from predators, direct its movements, and keep order; the females take care of the young, stay near the center of the troop, and extend their sexual favors most readily to the males highest in prestige and authority; positions of authority among males are established through a combination of prowess in ritualized combat and the ability to form and maintain alliances with other powerful males. If the instinctual programing for these behaviors is built into our evolutionary cousins because of its survival value, the argument goes, is it not logical that the formation of analogous patterns in human communities is due to the survival value and persistence of similar programing in us? If so, attempts to do away with sex roles will be futile, as Lionel Tiger suggests in Men in Groups,[19] or, as George Gilder asserts in Sexual Suicide[20] with less logic but more conviction, will create havoc by overriding biological imperatives.

But analogies between humans and primates fail in two ways. First, the behavioral generalizations about the animal world on which they are based often turn out to be instances of inaccurate projections of human stereotypes onto animals. Take "mothering" for example. The extent to which the father assumes the burden of caring for the young varies enormously among primates, ranging from infanticide to carrying and caring for the infant at all times except when it is being nursed.[21] The adult male rhesus monkey usually has little or no relationship with infants, yet recent experiments have shown that when the mother is not available to perform the parenting function a male will perform it quite adequately.[22]

Much has also been made of the critical evolutionary role of aggression in animal life: Since the aggressive tendencies in males had such strong survival value in our precursor species, it is argued that they must persist as an instinctual drive in human males. In the last few years, however, more refined observations of animal aggression have destroyed the foundations of this argument. Fights which lead to serious injury or death are extremely rare among animals of the same species living in normal, non-laboratory conditions. Much intraspecific fighting is ritualized, with no serious injury inflicted (rival stags locking horns, for example). Virtually all intraspecific aggression is subject to inhibitory mechanisms that prevent major injury or death (the weaker of two quarreling wolves, when in danger of serious injury, will expose his belly and throat to the other, who then stops the attack and walks away).[23] Presumably these inhibitions exist in animals because they have survival value for the species. However helpful to our survival they would be, there are no such rigid inhibitions on human aggression.

This points to the second, and fundamental, error in these arguments by analogy: Human beings are radically distinguished from all other animals by their freedom from instinctual determination. We have less instinctual knowledge than baboons when we are born, but our capacity for varying responses is infinitely greater. Self-consciousness, the need for self-esteem, and the ability to create and manipulate complex symbolic systems—found only in humans and made possible by a uniquely large neocortex—allow human beings to ascribe a wide range of different meanings to the same event and to act accordingly. Animals do not measure their actions against a conscious internal ideal; they may defend their young, but they will not die for an idea, a country, or to prove to themselves that they are qualified members of their sex.[24]

With human beings it is extremely difficult to separate out the influences of anatomy and conditioning on the development of sex roles and identity because different treatment of boys and girls begins literally at birth.[25] During the first two years, for example, mothers talk to and smile at girl babies more than boy babies. Boys are touched—kissed, hugged, rocked etc.—more for the first six months (perhaps because of their greater irritability), but after that they are touched less than girls. Beginning when boy babies are six months old, mothers are more likely to discourage them than girls from seeking physical contact by picking them up and facing them away or by distracting their attention with objects of some kind, probably out of a belief that it is more important for boys to develop autonomy.

Drs. John Money and Anke Ehrhardt[26] overcame the usual parallelism between upbringing and biological sex by studying a particular kind of hermaphrodite, genetic females born with female internal sex organs but masculine-looking external genitalia. If diagnosed at birth, the condition can be corrected by surgical feminization and cortisone treatment to suppress the overproduction of androgen that produced the ambiguous genitalia.* If left untreated, the girl develops all the secondary sexual characteristics—facial hair, large muscles, narrow hips, lower voice—of a boy. To isolate out the effect of conditioning, Money and Ehrhardt compared three pairs of such cases.[27]

In the first pair, one was diagnosed at birth and given the prescribed feminizing treatment; the other was misdiagnosed as a boy until age three-and-a-half, when the correct diagnosis was made but it was decided to allow the child to continue living as a boy. Appropriate surgery was done and cortisone therapy used to delay puberty until the normal age. In each case, gender identity and sex role—measured by traditional indices of "feminine" and "masculine" interests and proclivities—followed the sex of assignment.

In the second pair, one was also reared as a boy and the other as a girl. But treatment of a child raised as a girl was delayed until she was twelve, when masculine secondary sex characteristics had already begun to appear. The other child had been misdiagnosed and raised as a genetic male, but, as the result of a mistaken treatment with cortisone through age thirteen, had undergone substantial breast development. Despite their discordant hormonal sex, secondary sex characteristics, and ambiguous external genitals, both children firmly identified themselves as members of the sex of rearing, thought of their secondary sex characteristics as deformities they were eager to be rid of, were attracted sexually to members of the opposite sex, and displayed interests generally considered characteristic of their assigned sex.* For example, the child raised as a boy liked to hunt, fish, and race his motorbike. Treatment for both was in accordance with this gender identity.

In the final pair, each child had requested and, after investigation, received a sex reassignment, one from boy to girl and the other from girl to boy. In both cases, as in other requests for sex change studied by Money, it was found that parents had never really made up their minds about whether the child was a boy or a girl and had transmitted this ambiguity to the child.

Money and Ehrhardt also studied a pair of school-age identical twins. Both were born as normal males, but one lost his penis in a circumcision

*In a comparison of such fetally androgenized girls diagnosed and treated at birth with a control group of normal girls, Money and Ehrhardt reported that more of the girls with adrenogenital syndrome were "tomboys" as measured by their own and their parents' assessment, preference for athletic "boys" games, lesser concern with fashionably feminine clothes and adornment, lesser although substantial interest in marriage and babies, and a greater interest in having a career other than or in addition to being a housewife. (There was no higher degree of lesbianism or aberrant sexual behavior than in the control group.) The authors speculated that the differences may have been the result of a "masculinizing" effect of androgen on the fetal brain,[28] but this conclusion seems unwarranted. As endrocinologist Estelle Ramey has written, parental concern and ambiguity about the sexual identity of the girls with adrenogenital syndrome was conveyed to these children despite corrective procedures, and this difference in postnatal experience would account for the reported variations in behavior.[29]

*An early study of thirty-one such females brought up as women despite prolonged exposure to excess androgens both in utero and postnatally, and despite externally male sex characteristics uncorrected through puberty, showed that all but five tested out as typical American women in virtually all aspects of behavior, life goals, and self-image.[30]

accident and was reassigned as a girl in infancy and given the first stage of surgical reconstruction. "Her behavior as a little girl," Money and Ehrhardt reported, "is in remarkable contrast to the little-boy behavior of her identical twin brother."

After about eighteen months, Money and Ehrhardt have concluded, the influence of conditioning on gender identity is so strong that it is impossible to reassign effectively the sex of a child raised as a member of the other sex, regardless of the child's genetic, gonadal, and hormonal situation. It is easier and more advisable to use hormone therapy and surgery to bring the child's body into conformity with her or his learned sex role than to undo the effects of conditioning.[31]

Historically, the traditional sex roles must have grown out of practical arrangements necessary to childbearing in primitive societies. Women were either nursing infants or pregnant much of their adult lives, conditions which limited their mobility, while hunting game for food put a premium on men's physical strength and speed. A division of labor in which women stayed at home and took care of the children and men went out and hunted made sense. The greater physical strength of men may also have had something to do with their primacy within the primitive family: in the absence of restraining norms, the threat of superior force is an effective means of establishing dominance.

Today, the male/female division of labor, with all its complicated psychological, political, economic and cultural elaborations, is obsolete. It has lost whatever correspondence with objective conditions it may once have had. In America today physical strength and speed of foot are of negligible importance, especially in more highly valued and rewarded work. Women spend only a small part of their lives bearing children and even for most of that period are not incapacitated from tasks that men perform.

3

Because masculine and feminine behavior patterns are not biologically determined, men and women have a disorderly tendency to exhibit traits reserved for the other sex. Keeping the stereotypes straight can be a difficult task for the traditionalist.

"The base of male conceit," according to Norman Mailer, is "that men [can] live with truths too unsentimental for women."[32] But what is less sentimental than the prosaic "feed-the-children-before-you-spend-our-last-few-dollars-printing-your-manifesto" attitude of which women are accused? And what is more romantic and sentimental than the charge of the light brigade or the grand schemes of dynastic, commercial, and national empire which only men are said to have the scope to conceive? What, for example, are we to make of Ian Fleming's observation about his arch-masculine hero, James Bond: "Like all harsh, cold men, he was easily tipped over into sentiment"?[33]—an observation recently confirmed for our junior counterspies by a study conducted by William Kephart of the University of Pennsylvania. Kephart found that over a lifetime the American male becomes infatuated and falls in love more often than the female, while women see their boy friends' faults more clearly and are much less driven by romantic compulsions. . . .

For the most part, men handle the problem of keeping the stereotypes straight with a variation on the scheme of opposites. Where the general categories fail, men fall back on describing women as the opposite of what they, as individuals, think they are like, and even as the opposite of what they are like at any given moment. This device, needless to say, is used unconsciously, allowing the speaker to maintain an image of himself as consistent, an important masculine trait.

But if the twists and turns of definition as to what behavior can be considered masculine and what feminine can sometimes be obscure, the basic assumptions and imperatives which shape men's attitudes toward women come through loud and clear. First, we—men and women both—believe in the either/or theory of human personality even if we do not always conform to it: a person who is tough is always tough; a person who is tender and soft is always tender and soft; we do not expect people to be tough in one situation and tender in another according to the demands of the occasion, to have both responses in their repertoires. Second, men believe that to be masculine they have to be radically different from women. Third, men believe they are better than women and that, in order to retain their masculine self-image when they deal with women, they must dominate and outperform them in every area except child rearing, homemaking, amateur culture, and the management of social life. Fourth, the areas assigned to women are thought of as less important and difficult than those assigned to men, and men, to keep their masculine identification and status, try to stay out of them.. . . .

NOTES

1. *Ms.* (July 1973), p. 8.
2. CBS Evening News, August 17, 1973.
3. Ruth Hartley, "Sex Role Pressure in the Socialization of the Male Child," *Psychological Reports,* Vol. 5 (1959), p. 458.
4. *Ibid.,* pp. 461–62.
5. Virginia Kidd, "Now You See" (unpublished paper, Sacramento State College).
6. Marjorie B. U'Ren, "The Image of Women in Textbooks," in Vivian Gornick and Barbara K. Moran (eds.), *Women in Sexist Society* ([Basic Books: 1971] Signet ed.: 1971), pp. 318–28.
7. Hartley, *op. cit.,* pp. 460–61.
8. *Ibid.,* p. 461.
9. *Ibid.,* p. 458.
10. Inge Broverman, *et al.,* "Sex-Role Stereotypes: A Current Appraisal," *Journal of Social Issues,* Vol. 28 No. 2 (1972), pp. 59, 65. Between five to twelve times as many women as men recall having wished they were of the opposite sex. Moreover, investigators have found that both boys and girls between six and ten years express greater preference for "masculine" things and activities than for "feminine" things and activities.
11. Hartley, *op. cit.,* p. 462.
12. *Ibid.,* p. 461.
13. Friedrich Nietzsche, "Women De-Feminized," reprinted in Betty Roszak and Theodore Roszak (eds.), *Masculine/Feminine* (Harper Colophon: 1969), p. 7.
14. Mary Ellmann, *Thinking About Women* (Harcourt, Brace & World: 1968), p. 60.
15. See, for example, Robert Graves, *Mammon and the Black Goddess* (Doubleday: 1965), pp. 101–14, reprinted in Roszak and Roszak, *op. cit.,* pp. 31–38.
16. Broverman, *et al., op. cit.,* p. 59.
17. Carol Tavris, "Woman and Man," *Psychology Today,* Vol. 5 No. 10 (March 1972), pp. 83–84.
18. E.g., Konrad Lorenz, *On Aggression* (Harcourt, Brace & World: 1966); Anthony Storr, *Human Aggression* (Atheneum: 1968).
19. Lionel Tiger, *Men in Groups* (Random House: 1969); Steven Goldberg, *The Inevitability of Patriarchy* (William Morrow: 1973).
20. George Gilder, *Sexual Suicide* (Quadrangle: 1973).
21. G. D. Mitchell, "Paternalistic Behavior Among Primates," *Psychological Bulletin,* Vol. 71 No. 6 (1969), p. 399.
22. G. D. Mitchell, W. Redican, and J. Gomby, "Lesson from a Primate: Males Can Raise Babies," *Psychology Today* (April 1974), p. 63.
23. L. Harrison Mathews, "Overt Fighting in Mammals," in J. O. McCarthy and E. J. Ebling (eds.), *The Natural History of Aggression* (Academic Press: 1964).
24. For a thorough analysis of the differences which make analysis between animal and human behavior treacherous, see Gregory Rochlin, *Man's Aggression* (Gambit: 1973), Chapter III.
25. Michael Lewis, "Parents and Children: Sex Role Development," *School Review,* Vol. 80 (February 1972), p. 229.
26. John Money and Anke Ehrhardt, *Man & Woman, Boy & Girl* (Johns Hopkins Press: 1972).
27. *Ibid.,* pp. 151–66.
28. *Ibid.,* pp. 95–116.
29. Estelle Ramey, "Sex Hormones and Executive Ability," *Annals of the New York Academy of Sciences,* (Vol. 28 (1973), p. 237:

An examination of the data reveals that of the 15 girls studied, 7 were thought at birth to be . . . males with undescended testicles. Presumably the proud parents were told they had a son. The sex assignment was changed within the first 7 months in this group but it is a matter of some importance that in these, as in all the other cases, the sex ambiguity was a problem for the parents from the time of birth. The effect of parental concern about the true sex identity of these children despite medical corrective procedures must inevitably have conditioned their behavior towards the child and the child's response. For example, the data reveal that in at least half of the matched control groups of normal children, sex education was derived in large part from communication in the home while the adrenogenital children reported as the chief source of information the hospital input. These children were examined frequently as regards their genitalia and could not have escaped the knowledge that they were not entirely the little girls that their parents might have wished for.

How is one to interpret the finding of a greater career interest in these young girls as compared to normal adolescent girls in this society? For Freudians it is tempting to postulate that fetal masculinization of the brain induces the development of a special neuronal pathway for "career orientation." It is more likely, however, that a girl who sees herself as less desirable as a woman then her peer group may seek other avenues of ego development.

Lower interest in motherhood and personal adornment—the latter clearly a cultural variable, since in many human societies it is men who wear the feathers—are also explainable on the basis of uncertainties and fears of inadequacy.

30. J. L. Hampson and G. H. Hampson, "The Ontogenesis of Sexual Behavior in Man," in W. C. Young (ed.), *Sex and Internal Secretions* (Williams & Wilkins: 1961).
31. Money and Ehrhardt, *op. cit.,* p. 13.
32. Norman Mailer, "The Prisoner of Sex," *Harper's Magazine* (March 1971), p. 50.
33. Ian Fleming, *Casino Royale* (Macmillan: 1953), p. 149.

63. MARRIAGE AND MORALS

Bertrand Russell

FROM CHAPTER VIII
THE TABOO ON SEX KNOWLEDGE

In the attempt to build up a new sexual morality, the first question we have to ask ourselves is not, How should the relations of the sexes be regulated? but, Is it good that men, women and children should be kept in artificial ignorance of facts relating to sexual affairs? My reason for putting this question first is that, as I shall try to persuade the reader in this chapter, ignorance on such matters is extraordinarily harmful to the individual, and therefore no system whose perpetuation demands such ignorance can be desirable. Sexual morality, I should say, must be such as to commend itself to well-informed persons and not to depend upon ignorance for its appeal. This is part of a wider doctrine which, though it has never been held by governments or policemen, appears indubitable in the light of reason. That doctrine is that right conduct can never, except by some rare accident, be promoted by ignorance or hindered by knowledge. It is, of course, true that if A desires B to act in a certain manner which is in A's interest but not in B's, it may be useful to A to keep B in ignorance of facts which would show B where his true interest lies. This fact is well understood on the Stock Exchange, but is not generally held to belong to the higher departments of ethics. It covers a large part of governmental activity in concealing facts; for example, the desire which every Government feels to prevent all mention of a defeat in war, for the knowledge of a defeat may lead to the downfall of the Government, which, though usually in the na-

tional interest, is, of course, not in the interest of the Government. Reticence about sexual facts, though it belongs in the main to a different department, has had its origin, at least in part, in a similar motive. It was at first only females who were to be kept ignorant, and their ignorance was desired as a help towards masculine domination. Gradually, however, women acquiesced in the view that ignorance is essential to virtue, and partly through their influence it came to be thought that children and young people, whether male or female, should be as ignorant as possible on sexual subjects. At this stage the motive ceased to be one of domination and passed into the region of irrational taboo. . . .

The traditional course with children was to keep them in as great a degree of ignorance as parents and teachers could achieve. They never saw their parents naked, and after a very early age (provided housing accommodation was sufficient) they did not see their brothers or sisters of the opposite sex naked. They were told never to touch their sexual organs or speak about them; all questions concerning sex were met by the words "Hush, hush" in a shocked tone. They were informed that children were brought by the stork or dug up under a gooseberry bush. Sooner or later they learnt the facts, usually in a more or less garbled form, from other children, who related them secretly, and, as a result of parental teaching, regarded them as "dirty." The children inferred that their father and mother behaved to each other in a way which was nasty and of which they themselves were ashamed, since they took so much trouble to conceal it. They learnt also that they had been systematically deceived by those to whom they had looked for guidance and instruction. Their attitude towards their parents, towards marriage, and towards the opposite sex was thus irrevocably poisoned. Very few men or women who have had a conventional upbringing have learnt to feel decently about sex and marriage. Their education has taught them that deceitfulness and lying are considered virtues by parents and teachers; that sexual relations, even within marriage, are more or less disgusting, and that in propagating the species men are yielding to their animal nature while women are submitting to a painful duty. This attitude has made marriage unsatisfying both to men and to women, and the lack of instinctive satisfaction has turned to cruelty masquerading as morality.

The view of the orthodox moralist* on the question of sex knowledge may, I fancy, be fairly stated as follows:

The sexual impulse is a very powerful one, showing itself in different forms at different stages of development. In infancy it takes the form of a desire to touch and play with certain parts of the body; in later childhood it takes the form of curiosity and love of "dirty" talk, while in adolescence it begins to take more mature forms. There is no doubt that sexual misconduct is promoted by sexual thoughts, and that the best road to virtue is to keep the young occupied in mind and body with matters wholly unconnected with sex. They must, therefore, be told nothing whatever about sex; they must as far as possible be prevented from talking about it with each other, and grown-ups must pretend that there is no such topic. It is possible by these means to keep a girl in ignorance until the night of her marriage, when it is to be expected that the facts will so shock her as to produce exactly that attitude towards sex which every sound moralist considers desirable in women. With boys the matter is more difficult, since we cannot hope to keep them completely ignorant beyond the age of 18 or 19 at latest. The proper course with them is to tell them that masturbation invariably leads to insanity, while intercourse with prostitutes invariably leads to veneral disease. Neither of these assertions is true, but they are white lies, since they are made in the interests of morality. A boy should also be taught that in no circumstances is conversation on sexual subjects permissible, not even in marriage. This increases the likelihood that when he marries

*This includes the police and the magistrates, but hardly any modern educators.

he will give his wife a disgust of sex and thus preserve her from the risk of adultery. Sex outside marriage is sin; sex within marriage is not sin, since it is necessary to the propagation of the human species, but is a disagreeable duty imposed on man as a punishment for the Fall, and to be undertaken in the same spirit in which one submits to a surgical operation. Unfortunately, unless great pains are taken, the sexual act tends to be associated with pleasure, but by sufficient moral care this can be prevented, at any rate in the female. It is illegal in England to state in print that a wife can and should derive sexual pleasure from intercourse. (I have myself heard a pamphlet condemned as obscene in a court of law on this among other grounds.) It is on the above outlook in regard to sex that the attitude of the law, the church, and the old-fashioned educators of the young is based.

Before considering the effect of this attitude in the realm of sex, I should like to say a few words about its consequences in other directions. The first and gravest consequence, in my opinion, is the hampering of scientific curiosity in the young. Intelligent children wish to know about everything in the world; they ask questions about trains and motor-cars and airplanes, about what makes rain and about what makes babies. All these curiosities are to the child on exactly the same level; he is merely following what Pavlov calls the "What-is-it?" reflex, which is the source of all scientific knowledge. When the child in pursuit of the desire for knowledge learns that this impulse in certain directions is considered wicked, his whole impulse of scientific curiosity is checked. He does not at first understand what kinds of curiosity are permissible and what kinds are not: if it is wicked to ask how babies are made it may, for aught the child can tell, be equally wicked to ask how airplanes are made. In any case he is driven to the conclusion that scientific curiosity is a dangerous impulse, which must not be allowed to remain unchecked. Before seeking to know anything, one must anxiously enquire whether this is a virtuous or a vicious kind of knowledge. And since sexual curiosity is generally very strong until it has become atrophied, the child is led to the conclusion that knowledge which he desires is wicked, while the only virtuous knowledge is such as no human being could possibly desire—for example, the multiplication table. The pursuit of knowledge, which is one of the spontaneous impulses of all healthy children, is thus destroyed, and children are rendered artificially stupid. I do not think it can be denied that women who have had a conventional education are on the average stupider than men, and I believe this to be largely due to the fact that in youth they are more effectively choked off from the pursuit of sex knowledge.

In addition to this intellectual damage, there is in most cases a very grave moral damage. As Freud first showed, and as every one intimate with children soon discovers, the fables about the stork and the gooseberry bush are usually disbelieved. The child thus comes to the conclusion that parents are apt to lie to him. If they lie in one matter, they may lie in another, so that their moral and intellectual authority is destroyed. Moreover, since parents lie where sex is concerned, the children conclude that they themselves also may lie on such topics. They talk with each other about them, and very likely they practise masturbation in secret. In this way they learn to acquire habits of deceit and concealment, while owing to their parents' threats, their lives become clouded with fear. The threats of parents and nurses as to the bad consequences of masturbation have been shown by psycho-analysis to be a very frequent cause of nervous disorders, not only in childhood but in adult life also.

The effects of the conventional treatment of sex in dealing with the young are therefore to make people stupid, deceitful and timorous, and to drive a not inconsiderable percentage over the border line into insanity or something like it.

To a certain extent these facts are now recognized by all intelligent people who have to deal with the young; they have, however, not yet become known to the law and those who administer it as is evident from the case quoted at the beginning of this chapter. Thus the situation is at present that every well-informed person who has to deal with children is compelled to choose whether he will break the law or whether he will cause the children under his charge irreparable moral and intellectual damage. It is difficult to change the law, since very many elderly men are so perverted that their pleasure in sex depends upon the belief that sex is wicked and nasty. I am afraid no reform can be hoped for until those who are now old or middle-aged have died.

So far we have been considering the bad effects of conventional methods outside the sphere of sex; it is time to consider the more definitely sexual aspects of the question. One of the aims of the moralist is undoubtedly to prevent obsession with sexual subjects; such obsession is at present extraordinarily frequent. . . . Far the best way to prevent young people from being obsessed with sex is to tell them just as much about it as they care to know.

In saying this I am not arguing *a priori,* but on a basis of experience. What I have observed among the children in my school has shown conclusively, to my mind, the correctness of the view that nastiness in children is the result of prudery in adults. My own two children (a boy aged 7, and a girl aged 5) have never been taught that there is anything peculiar either about sex or about excretion, and have so far been shielded to the utmost possible extent from all knowledge of the idea of decency, with its correlative indecency. They have shown a natural and healthy interest in the subject of where babies come from, but not so much as in engines and railways. Nor have they shown any tendency to dwell upon such topics either in the absence or in the presence of grown-up people. With regard to the other children in the school, we have found that if they came to us at the age of 2 or 3, or even 4, they developed exactly like our own children; those, however, who came to us at the age of 6 or 7 had already been taught to regard anything connected with the sexual organs as improper. They were surprised to find that in the school such matters were spoken of in the same tone of voice as was employed about anything else, and for some time they enjoyed a sense of release in conversations which they felt to be indecent; finding, however, that the grown-ups did nothing to check such conversations, they gradually wearied of them, and became nearly as clean-minded as those who had never been taught decency. They now get merely bored when children new to the school attempt to start conversations which they fondly believe to be improper. Thus by letting fresh air on to the subject, it has become disinfected, and the noxious germs which it breeds when kept in darkness have been dissipated. I do not believe that it is possible by any other method to get a group of children whose attitude towards subjects usually considered improper is so wholesome and decent. . . .

Many people will agree that these consequences of the law against obscene publications are regrettable, but they will nevertheless hold that such a law is necessary. I do not myself believe that it is possible to frame a law against obscenity which will not have these undesirable consequences, and in view of this fact, I should myself be in favour of having no law whatever upon the subject. The argument in favour of this thesis is twofold: on the one hand, that no law can forbid the bad without forbidding the good also, and on the other hand, that publications which are undoubtedly and frankly pornographic would do very little harm if sex education were rational. . . .

There is, however, a further ground for objecting to censorship, and that is that even frank pornography would do less harm if it were open and unashamed than it does when it is rendered interesting by secrecy and stealth. In spite of the law, nearly every fairly well-to-do man has in adolescence seen indecent photographs, and has been proud of obtaining possession of them because they were difficult to procure. Conventional men are of opinion that such things are extraordinarily injurious to others, although hardly one of them will admit that they have been injurious to himself. Undoubtedly they stir a transient feeling of lust, but in any sexually vigorous male such feelings will be stirred in one way if not in another. The frequency with which a man experiences lust depends upon his own physical condition, whereas the occasions which rouse such feelings in him depend upon the social conventions to which he is accustomed. To an early Victorian man a woman's ankles were sufficient stimulus, whereas a modern man remains unmoved by anything up to the thigh. This is merely a question of fashion in clothing. If nakedness were the fashion, it would cease to excite us, and women would be forced, as they are in certain savage tribes, to adopt clothing as a means of making themselves sexually attractive. Exactly similar considerations apply to literature and pictures: what was exciting in the Victorian Age would leave the men of a franker epoch quite unmoved. The more prudes restrict the permissible degree of sexual appeal, the less is required to make such an appeal effective. Nine-tenths of the appeal of pornography is due to the indecent feelings concerning sex which moralists inculcate in the young; the other tenth is physiological, and will occur in one way or another whatever the state of the law may be. On these grounds, although I fear that few will agree with me, I am firmly persuaded that there ought to be no law whatsoever on the subject of obscene publications.

The taboo against nakedness is an obstacle to a decent attitude on the subject of sex. Where young children are concerned, this is now recognized by many people. It is good for children to see each other and their parents naked whenever it so happens naturally. There will be a short period, probably at about three years old, when the child is interested in the differences between his father and his mother, and compares them with the differences between himself and his sister, but this period is soon over, and after this he takes no more interest in nudity than in clothes. So long as parents are unwilling to be seen naked by their children, the children will necessarily have a sense that there is a mystery, and having that sense they will become prurient and indecent. There is only one way to avoid indecency, and that is to avoid mystery. . . .

FROM CHAPTER XII
TRIAL MARRIAGE

Judge Ben B. Lindsey, who was for many years in charge of the juvenile court at Denver, and in that position had unrivalled opportunities for ascertaining the facts, proposed a new institution which he calls "companionate marriage." Unfortunately he has lost his official position, for when it became known that he used it rather to promote the happiness of the young than to give them a consciousness of sin, the Ku Klux Klan and the Catholics combined to oust him. Companionate marriage is the proposal of a wise conservative. It is an attempt to introduce some stability into the sexual relations of the young, in place of the present promiscuity. He points out the obvious fact that what prevents the young from marrying is lack of money, and that money is required in marriage partly on account of children, but partly also because it is not the thing for the wife to earn her own living. His view is that young people should be able to enter upon a new kind of marriage, distinguished from ordinary marriage by three characteristics. First, that there should be for the time being no intention of having children, and that accordingly the best available birth control information should be given to the young couple. Second, that so long as there are no children and the wife is not pregnant, divorce should be possible by mutual consent. And third, that in the event of divorce, the wife should not be entitled to alimony. He holds, and I think rightly, that if such an institution were established by law, a very great many young people, for example, students at universities, would enter upon comparatively permanent partnerships, involving a common life, and free from the Dionysiac characteristics of their present sex relations. He brings evidence to bear that young students who are married do better work than such as are unmarried. It is indeed obvious that work and sex are more easily combined in a quasi-permanent relation than in the scramble and excitement of parties and drunken orgies. There is no reason under the sun why it should be more expensive for two young people to live together than to live separately, and therefore the economic reasons which at present lead to postponement of marriage would no longer operate. I have not the faintest doubt that Judge Lindsey's proposal, if embodied in the law, would have a very beneficent influence, and that this influence would be such as all might agree to be a gain from a moral point of view.

Nevertheless, Judge Lindsey's proposals were received with a howl of horror by all middle-aged persons and most of the newspapers throughout the length and breadth of America. It was said that he was attacking the sanctity of the home; it was said that in tolerating marriages not intended to lead at once to children he was opening the floodgates to legalized lust; it was said that he enormously exaggerated the prevalence of extramarital sexual relations, that he was slandering pure American womanhood, and that most business men remained cheerfully continent up to the age of thirty or thirty-five. All these things were said, and I try to think that among those who said them there were some who believed them. I listened to many invectives against Judge Lindsey, but I came away with the impression that the arguments which were regarded as decisive were two. First, that Judge Lindsey's proposals would not have been approved by Christ; and, second, that they were not approved by eminent divines in the present day. The second of these arguments appeared to be considered the more weighty, and indeed rightly, since the other is purely hypothetical, and incapable of being substantiated. I never heard any person advance any argument even pretending to show that Judge Lindsey's proposals would diminish human happiness. This consideration, indeed, I was forced to conclude, is thought wholly unimportant by those who uphold traditional morality.

For my part, while I am quite convinced that companionate marriage would be a step in the right direction, and would do a great deal of good, I do not think that it goes far enough. I think that all sex relations which do not involve children should be regarded as a purely private affair, and that if a man and a woman choose to live together without having children, that should be no one's business but their own. I should not hold it desirable that either a man or a woman should enter upon the serious business of a marriage intended to lead to children without having had previous sexual experience. There is a great mass of evidence to show that the first experience of sex should be with a person who has previous knowledge. The sexual act in human beings is not instinctive, and apparently never has been since it ceased to be performed *a tergo* [from the back]. And apart from this argument, it seems absurd to ask people to enter upon a relation intended to be lifelong, without any previous knowledge as to their sexual compatibility. It is just as absurd as it would be if a man intending to buy a house were not allowed to view it until had completed the purchase. The proper course, if the biological function of marriage were adequately recognized, would be to say that no marriage should be legally binding until the wife's first pregnancy. At present a marriage is null if sexual intercourse is impossible, but children, rather than sexual intercourse, are the true purpose of marriage, which should therefore be not regarded as consummated until such time as there is a prospect of children. This view depends, at least in part, upon that separation between procreation and mere sex which has been brought about by contraceptives. Contraceptives have altered the whole aspect of sex and marriage, and have made distinctions necessary which could formerly have been ignored. People may come together for sex alone, as occurs in prostitution, or for companionship involving a sexual element, as in Judge Lindsey's companionate marriage, or finally, for the purpose of rearing a family. These are all different, and no morality can be adequate to modern circumstances which confounds them in one indiscriminate total. . . .

FROM CHAPTER XIX
SEX AND INDIVIDUAL WELL-BEING

In the present chapter I propose to recapitulate things said in earlier chapters as regards the effects of sex and sexual morals upon individual happiness and well-being. In this matter we are not concerned only with the actively sexual period of life, nor with actual sex relations. Sexual morality affects childhood, adolescence, and even old age, in all kinds of ways, good or bad according to circumstances.

Conventional morality begins its operations by the imposition of taboos in childhood. A child is taught, at a very early age, not to touch certain parts of the body while grown-up people are looking. It is taught to speak in a whisper when expressing an excretory desire, and to preserve privacy in performing the resultant action. Certain parts of the body and certain acts have some peculiar quality not readily intelligible to the child, which invests them with mystery and a special interest. Certain intellectual problems, such as where babies come from, must be thought over in silence, since the answers given by grown-ups are either evasive or obviously untrue. I know men, by no means old, who, when in infancy they were seen touching a certain portion of their body, were told with the utmost solemnity: "I would rather see you dead than doing that." I regret to say that the effect in producing virtue in later life has not always been all that conventional moralists might desire. Not infrequently threats are used. It is perhaps not so

common as it used to be to threaten a child with castration, but it is still thought quite proper to threaten him with insanity. Indeed, it is illegal in the State of New York to let him know that he does not run the risk unless he thinks he does. The result of this teaching is that most children in their earliest years have a profound sense of guilt and terror which is associated with sexual matters. This association of sex with guilt and fear goes so deep as to become almost or wholly unconscious. I wish it were possible to institute a statistical enquiry, among men who believe themselves emancipated from such nursery tales, as to whether they would be as ready to commit adultery during a thunder storm as at any other time. I believe that ninety per cent of them, in their heart of hearts, would think that if they did so they would be struck by lightning. . . .

Childhood and youth form a period in life when pranks and naughtiness and performance of forbidden acts are natural, spontaneous and not regrettable except when carried too far. But infraction of sex prohibitions is treated by grown-up people quite differently from any other breach of rules, and is therefore felt by the child to belong to a quite different category. If a child steals fruit from the larder you may be annoyed, you may rate the child soundly, but you feel no moral horror, and you do not convey to the child the sense that something appalling has occurred. If, on the other hand, you are an old-fashioned person and you find him masturbating, there will be a tone in your voice which he will never hear in any other connection. This tone produces an abject terror, all the greater since the child probably finds it impossible to abstain from the behaviour that has called forth your denunciation. The child, impressed by your earnestness, profoundly believes that masturbation is as wicked as you say it is. Nevertheless, he persists in it. Thus the foundations are laid for a morbidness which probably continues through life. From his earliest youth onward, he regards himself as a sinner. He soon learns to sin in secret, and to find a half-hearted consolation in the fact that no one knows of his sin. Being profoundly unhappy, he seeks to avenge himself on the world by punishing those who have been less successful than himself in concealing a similar guilt. Being accustomed to deceit as a child, he finds no difficulty in practising it in later life. Thus he becomes a morbidly introverted hypocrite and persecutor as a result of his parents' ill-judged attempt to make him what they consider virtuous.

It is not guilt and shame and fear that should dominate the lives of children. Children should be happy and gay and spontaneous; they should not dread their own impulses; they should not shrink from the exploration of natural facts. They should not hide away in the darkness all their instinctive life. They should not bury in the depths of the unconscious impulses which, even with their utmost endeavours, they cannot kill. If they are to grow into upright men and women, intellectually honest, socially fearless, vigorous in action and tolerant in thought, we must begin from the very beginning to train them so that these results may be possible. Education has been conceived too much on the analogy of the training of dancing bears. Every one knows how dancing bears are trained. They are put on a hot floor, which compels them to dance because their toes are burnt if they remain in contact with it. While this is done, a certain tune is played to them. After a time the tune suffices to make them dance, without the hot floor. So it is with children. While a child is conscious of his sexual organ, grown-ups scold him. In the end, such consciousness brings up a thought of their scolding and makes him dance to their tune, to the complete destruction of all possibility of a healthy or happy sexual life. . . .

Most young men, in their early adult years, go through troubles and difficulties of a quite unnecessary kind in regard to sex. If a young man remains chaste, the difficulty of control probably causes him to become timid and inhibited, so that when he finally marries he cannot break down the self-control of past years, except perhaps in a brutal and sudden manner, which leads him to fail his wife in the capacity of a lover. If he goes with prostitutes, the dissociation between the physical and the idealistic aspects of love which has begun in adolescence is perpetuated, with the result that his relations with women ever after have to be either Platonic or, in his belief, degrading. Moreover, he runs a grave risk of venereal disease. If he has affairs with girls of his own class, much less harm is done,

but even then the need of secrecy is harmful, and interferes with the development of stable relations. Owing partly to snobbery and partly to the belief that marriage ought immediately to lead to children, it is difficult for a man to marry young. Moreover, where divorce is very difficult, early marriage has great dangers, since two people who suit each other at twenty are quite likely not to suit each other at thirty. Stable relations with one partner are difficult for many people until they have had some experience of variety. If our outlook on sex were sane, we should expect university students to be temporarily married though childless. They would in this way be freed from the obsession of sex which at present greatly interferes with work. They would acquire that experience of the other sex which is desirable as a prelude to the serious partnership of a marriage with children. And they would be free to experience love without the concomitants of subterfuge, concealment, and dread of disease, which at present poison youthful adventures.

For the large class of women who, as things are, must remain permanently unmarried, conventional morality is painful and, in most cases, harmful. I have known, as we all have, unmarried women of strict conventional virtue who deserve the highest admiration from every possible point of view. But I think the general rule is otherwise. A woman who has had no experience of sex and has considered it important to preserve her virtue has been engaged in a negative reaction, tinged with fear, and has therefore, as a rule, become timid, while at the same time instinctive, unconscious jealousy has filled her with disapproval of normal people, and with a desire to punish those who have enjoyed what she has forgone. Intellectual timidity is an especially common concomitant of prolonged virginity. Indeed, I am inclined to think that the intellectual inferiority of women, in so far as it exists, is mainly due to the restraint upon curiosity which the fear of sex leads them to impose. There is no good reason for the unhappiness and waste involved in the lifelong virginity of those women who cannot find an exclusive husband. The present situation, in which this necessarily occurs very frequently, was not contemplated in the earlier days of the institution of marriage, since in those days the numbers of the sexes were approximately equal.

Undoubtedly, the existence of a great excess of women in many countries affords a very serious argument in favour of modifications of the conventional moral code.

Marriage, the one conventionally tolerated outlet for sex, itself suffers from the rigidity of the code. The complexes acquired in childhood, the experiences of men with prostitutes, and the attitude of aversion from sex instilled into young ladies in order to preserve their virtue, all militate against happiness in marriage. A well-brought-up girl, if her sexual impulses are strong, will be unable to distinguish, when she is courted, between a serious congeniality with a man and a mere sex attraction. She may easily marry the first man who awakens her sexually, and find out too late that when her sexual hunger is satisfied she has no longer anything in common with him. Everything has been done in the education of the two to make her unduly timid and him unduly sudden in the sexual approach. Neither has the knowledge on sexual matters that each ought to have, and very often initial failures, due to this ignorance, make the marriage ever after sexually unsatisfying to both. Moreover, mental as well as physical companionship is rendered difficult. A woman is not accustomed to free speech on sexual matters. A man is not accustomed to it, except with men and prostitutes. In the most intimate and vital concern of their mutual life, they are shy, awkward, even wholly silent. The wife, perhaps, lies awake unsatisfied and hardly knowing what it is she wants. The man perhaps has the thought, at first fleeting and instantly banished, but gradually becoming more and more insistent, that even prostitutes are more generous in giving than his lawful wife. He is offended by her coldness, at the very moment, perhaps, that she is suffering because he does not know how to rouse her. All this misery results from our policy of silence and decency.

In all these ways, from childhood through adolescence and youth, and on into marriage, the older morality has been allowed to poison love, filling it with gloom, fear, mutual misunderstanding, remorse, and nervous strain, separating into two regions the bodily impulse of sex and the spiritual impulse of ideal love, making the one beastly and the other sterile. It is not so that life should be lived. The animal and the spiritual natures should not be at war. There is nothing in either that is incompatible with the other, and neither can reach its full fruition except in union with the other. The love of man and woman at its best is free and fearless, compounded of body and mind in equal proportions; not dreading to idealize because there is a physical basis, not dreading the physical basis lest it should interfere with the idealization. Love should be a tree whose roots are deep in the earth, but whose branches extend into heaven. But love cannot grow and flourish while it is hedged about with taboos and superstitious terrors, with words of reprobation and silences of horror. The love of man and woman and the love of parents and children are the two central facts in the emotional life of man. While degrading the one, conventional morality has pretended to exalt the other, but in fact the love of parents for children has suffered through the degradation of the love of parents for each other. Children who are the fruit of joy and mutual fulfilment can be loved in a way more healthy and robust, more in accordance with the ways of nature, more simple, direct, and animal, and yet more unselfish and fruitful, than is possible to parents starved, hungry, and eager, reaching out to the helpless young for some fragment of the nutriment that has been denied them in marriage, and in so doing, warping infant minds and laying the foundation of the same troubles for the next generation. To fear love is to fear life, and those who fear life are already three parts dead.

64. SEXUAL MORALITY AND CHRISTIAN MARRIAGE

C. S. Lewis

SEXUAL MORALITY

Today I am going to talk about Christian morality as regards sex, what Christians call the virtue of chastity. This is the most unpopular of the Christian virtues. There is no getting away from it: the old Christian rule is, "Either marriage, with complete faithfulness to your partner, or else total abstinence." Now this is so difficult and so contrary to our instincts, that obviously either Christianity is wrong or our sexual instinct, as it now is, has gone wrong. One or the other. Of course, being a Christian, I think it is the instinct which has gone wrong.

But I have other reasons for thinking so. The biological purpose of sex is children, just as the biological purpose of eating is to repair the body. Now if we eat whenever we feel inclined and just as much as we want, it's quite true that most of us will eat too much: but not terrifically too much. One man may eat enough for two, but he doesn't eat enough for ten. The appetite goes a little beyond its biological purpose, but not enormously. But if a healthy young man indulged his sexual appetite whenever he felt inclined, and if each act produced a baby, then in ten years he might easily populate a small village. This appetite is in ludicrous and preposterous excess of its function.

Or take it another way. You can get a large audience together for a strip-tease act—that is, to watch a girl undress on the stage: now suppose you came to a country where you could fill a theatre by simply bringing a covered plate on to the stage and then slowly lifting the cover so as to let every one see, just before the lights went out, that it contained a mutton chop or a bit of bacon, wouldn't you think that in that country something had gone wrong with the appetite for food? And wouldn't anyone who had grown up in a different world

Reprinted with permission of Macmillan Publishing Co., Inc. from *Christian Behaviour* by C. S Lewis. Copyright 1943 by Macmillan Publishing Co., Inc., renewed 1971 by Arthur Owen Barfield and Alfred Cecil Harwood. Also reprinted by permission of Collins Publishers, London, England.

think there was something equally queer about the state of the sex instinct among us?

Here's a third point. You find very few people who want to eat things that really aren't food or to do other things with food instead of eating it. In other words, perversions of the food appetite are rare. But perversions of the sex instinct are numerous, hard to cure, and frightful. I am sorry to have to go into all these details, but I must. The reason why I must is that you and I, for the last twenty years, have been fed all day long on good solid lies about sex. We've been told, till one's sick of hearing it, that sexual desire is in the same state as any of our other natural desires and that if only we give up the silly old Victorian idea of hushing it up, everything in the garden will be lovely. It's just not true. The moment you look at the facts, and away from the propaganda, you see that it isn't.

They'll tell you sex has become a mess because it was hushed up. But for the last twenty years it has *not* been hushed up. It has been chattered about all day long. Yet it is still in a mess. If hushing up had been the cause of the trouble, ventilation would have set it right. But it hasn't. I think it is the other way round. I think the human race originally hushed it up because it had become such a mess. Modern people are always saying, "Sex is nothing to be ashamed of." They may mean two things. They may mean, "There is nothing to be ashamed of in the fact that the human race reproduces itself in a certain way, nor in the fact that it gives pleasure." If they mean that, they are right. Christianity says the same. It is not the thing, nor the pleasure, that's the trouble. The old Christian teachers said that if man had never fallen, sexual pleasure, instead of being less than it is now, would actually have been greater. I know some muddleheaded Christians have talked as if Christianity thought that sex, or the body, or pleasure were bad in themselves. But they were wrong. Christianity is almost the only one of the great religions which thoroughly approves of the body—which believes that matter is good, that God Himself once took on a human body, that some kind of body is going to be given to us even in Heaven and is going to be an essential part of our happiness, our beauty, and our energy. Christianity has glorified marriage more than any other religion: and nearly all the greatest love poetry in the world has been produced by Christians. If anyone says that sex, in itself, is bad, Christianity contradicts him at once. But, of course, when people say, "Sex is nothing to be ashamed of," they may mean "the state into which the sexual instinct has now got is nothing to be ashamed of."

If they mean that, I think they are wrong. I think it is everything to be ashamed of. There is nothing to be ashamed of in enjoying your food: there would be everything to be ashamed of if half the world made food the main interest of their lives and spent their time looking at pictures of food and dribbling and smacking their lips. I don't say you and I are individually responsible for the present situation. Our ancestors have handed over to us organisms which are warped in this respect: and we grow up surrounded by propaganda in favour of unchastity. There are people who want to keep our sex instinct inflamed in order to make money out of us. Because, of course, a man with an obsession is a man who has very little sales-resistance. The moral question is, given that situation, what we do about it.

If we really want to be cured, I think we shall be. I mean, if a man tries to go back to the Christian rule, if he makes up his mind either to abstain from sex altogether or to marry one woman and stick to her, he may not completely succeed, especially at first. But as long as he picks himself up each time and starts again as well as he can, he'll be on the right track. He won't damage his central self beyond repair. Those who really want help will get it. The difficulty, of course, is the really wanting it. It is quite easy to think you want something when you don't really. A famous Christian long ago said that when he was a young man he prayed constantly for chastity: but only after several years he came to realise that, while his lips were saying, "Oh, God, make me chaste," his real wishes were secretly adding, "But please don't do it for a few years yet." This catch occurs in prayers on other subjects too.

Now for two final remarks. Don't misunderstand what psychology teaches us about repressions. It teaches us that repressed sex is dangerous. But many people who repeat this don't know that "repression" is a technical term. "Repressing" an impulse does not mean having a conscious desire and resisting it. It means being so frightened of some impulse that you don't let it become conscious at all, so that it goes down into the subconscious and causes trouble. Resisting a conscious desire is quite a different matter, and never did anyone any harm yet. The second remark is this. Although I've had to speak at some length about sex, I want to make it as clear as I possibly can that the centre of Christian morality is not here. If anyone thinks that Christians regard unchastity as *the* great vice, he is quite wrong. The sins of the flesh are bad, but they are the least bad of all sins. All the worst pleasures are purely spiritual: the pleasure of putting other people in the wrong, of bossing and patronising and spoiling sport, and back-biting; the pleasures of power, of hatred. You see, there are two things inside me, competing with the human self which I must try to become. They are the Animal self, and the Diabolical self. The Diabolical self is the worse of the two. That is why a cold, self-righteous prig who goes regularly to Church may be far nearer to hell than a prostitute. But, of course, it is better to be neither.

CHRISTIAN MARRIAGE

The last Talk was mainly negative. I discussed what was wrong with the sexual impulse in man, but said very little about how it *ought* to work—in other words, about Christian marriage. There are two reasons why I do not particularly want to deal with marriage. The first is that the Christian doctrines on this subject are extremely unpopular. The second is that I have never been married myself, and, therefore, can speak only at second hand. But in spite of that, I feel I can hardly leave the subject out in a series of Talks on Christian morals.

The Christian idea of marriage is based on Christ's words that a man and wife are to be regarded as a single organism—for that is what the words "one flesh" would be in modern English. And the Christians believe that when He said this He was not expressing a sentiment but stating a fact —just as one is stating a fact when one says that a lock and its key are one mechanism, or that a violin and a bow are one musical instrument. The inventor of the human machine was telling us that its two halves, the male and the female, were made to be combined together in pairs, not simply on the sexual level, but totally combined. The monstrosity of sexual intercourse outside marriage is that those who indulge in it are trying to isolate one kind of union (the sexual) from all the other kinds of union which were intended to go along with it and make up the total union. The Christian attitude doesn't mean that there is anything wrong about sexual pleasure, any more than about the pleasure of eating. It means that you mustn't isolate that pleasure and try to get it by itself, any more than you ought to try to get the pleasures of taste without swallowing and digesting, by chewing things and spitting them out again.

As a consequence, Christianity teaches that marriage is for life. There is, of course, a difference here between different Churches: some don't admit divorce at all; some allow it reluctantly in very special cases. It is a great pity that Christians should disagree about such a question; but for an ordinary layman the thing to notice is that the Churches all agree with one another about marriage a great deal more than any of them agrees with the outside world. I mean, they all regard divorce as something like cutting up a living body, as a kind of surgical operation. Some of them think the operation so violent that it can't be done at all; others admit it as a desperate remedy in extreme cases. They are all agreed that it is more like having both your legs cut off than it is like dissolving a business partnership or even deserting a regiment. What they all disagree with is the modern view that it is a simple readjustment of partners, to be made whenever people feel they are no longer in love with one another, or when either of them falls in love with someone else.

Now this is just where misunderstanding arises. People who are defending easy divorce often say, "Surely love is the important thing in marriage." In a sense, yes. Love is the important thing—perhaps the only important thing—in the whole universe. But it depends what you mean by "Love." What most people mean by Love, when they are talking about marriage, is what is called "being in love." Now "being in love" may be a good reason for getting married, though, as far as I can see, it is not a

perfect one, for you can fall in love with someone most unsuitable, and even with someone you don't really (in the deeper sense) *like,* or trust. But being in love is not the deeper unity which makes man and wife one organism. I am told (indeed I can see by looking round me) that being in love doesn't last. I don't think it was ever intended to. I think it's a sort of explosion that starts up the engine; it's the pie-crust, not the pie. The real thing, I understand, is something far deeper—something you can live on. I think you can be madly in love with someone you would be sick of after ten weeks: and I'm pretty sure you can be bound heart and soul to someone about whom you don't at that moment feel excited, any more than you feel excited about yourself.

If you disagree with me, of course, you'll say, "He knows nothing about it, he's not married." You may quite possibly be right. But before you say that, do make quite sure that you are judging me by what you really know from your own experience and from watching the lives of your friends, and not by ideas you have derived from novels and films. This is not so easy to do as people think. Our experience is coloured through and through by books and plays and the cinema, and it takes patience and skill to disentangle the things we have really learned from life for ourselves.

One thing people get from books is the idea that if you have married the right person you may expect to go on "being in love" for ever. As a result, when they find they are not, they think this proves they have made a mistake and are entitled to a change—not realising that, when they have changed, the glamour will presently go out of the new love just as it went out of the old one. In this department of life, as in every other, thrills come at the beginning and don't last. The sort of thrill a boy has at the first idea of flying won't go on when he has joined the R.A.F. and is really learning to fly. The thrill you feel on first seeing some delightful place dies away when you really go to live there. Does this mean it would be better not to learn to fly and not to live in the beautiful place? By no means. In both cases, if you go through with it, the dying away of the first thrill will be compensated for by a quieter and more lasting kind of interest. What's more (and I can hardly find words to tell you how important I think this) it is just the people who are ready to submit to the loss of the thrill and settle down to the sober interest, who are then most likely to meet *new* thrills in some quite different direction. The man who has learned to fly and become a good pilot will suddenly discover music; the man who has settled down to live in the beauty-spot will discover gardening.

This is, I think, one little part of what Christ meant by saying that a thing won't really live unless it first dies. It's just no good trying to *keep* any thrill: that's the very worst thing you can do. Let the thrill go—let it die away—go on through that period of death into the quieter interest and happiness that follow—and you'll find you are living in a world of *new* thrills all the time. But if you decide to *live* on thrills and try to prolong them artificially, they will all get weaker and weaker, and fewer and fewer, and you will be a bored, disillusioned old man for the rest of your life. It is because so few people understand this that you find many middle-aged men and women maundering about their lost youth, at the very age when new horizons ought to be appearing and new doors opening all round them. It is so much better fun to learn to swim than to go on endlessly (and hopelessly) trying to get back the feeling you had when you first went paddling as a small boy!

Another notion we get from novels and plays is that "falling in love" is something quite irresistible; something that just happens to one, like measles. And because they believe this, some married people just throw up the sponge and give in when they find themselves attracted by a new acquaintance. But I am inclined to think that these irresistible passions are much rarer in real life than in books, at any rate when one is grown up. When we meet someone beautiful and clever and sympathetic, of course we *ought,* in one sense, to admire and love these good qualities. But is it not very largely in our own choice whether this love shall, or shall not, turn into what we call "being in love"? No doubt, if our minds are chockful of novels and plays and sentimental songs, and our bodies full of alcohol, we shall *turn* any love we feel into that kind of love: just as if you have a rut in your path all the rain-water will run into that rut, and if you wear blue spectacles everything you see will turn blue. But that will be our own fault.

Before leaving the question of divorce, I should like to distinguish two things which are very often confused. The Christian conception of marriage is one: the other is the quite different question—how far Christians, if they are voters or members of Parliament, ought to try to force their views of marriage on the rest of the community by embodying them in the divorce laws. A great many people seem to think that if you are a Christian yourself you should try to make divorce difficult for every one. I don't think that at all. At least I know I'd be very angry if the Mohammedans tried to prevent the rest of us from drinking wine. My own view is that the Churches should frankly recognise that the majority of the British people are not Christians and therefore can't be expected to live Christian lives. There ought to be two distinct kinds of marriage: one governed by the State with rules enforced on all citizens, the other governed by the Church with rules enforced by her on her own members. The distinction ought to be quite sharp, so that a man knows which couples are married in a Christian sense and which are not. . . .

65. *SEXUAL PERVERSION*

Thomas G. Nagel

There is something to be learned about sex from the fact that we possess a concept of sexual perversion. I wish to examine the concept, defending it against the charge of unintelligibility and trying to say exactly what about human sexuality qualifies it to admit of perversions. But let me make some preliminary comments about the problem before embarking on its solution.

Some people do not believe that the notion of sexual perversion makes sense, and even those who do, disagree over its application. Nevertheless, I think it will be widely conceded that if the concept is viable at all, it must meet certain general conditions. First, if there are any sexual perversions, they will have to be sexual desires or practices that can be plausibly described as in some sense unnatural, though the explanation of this natural/unnatural distinction is, of course, the main problem. Second, certain practices, such as shoe fetishism, bestiality, and sadism will be perversions if anything is; other practices, such as unadorned sexual intercourse, will not be; and about still others there is controversy. Third, if there are perversions, they will be unnatural sexual *inclinations* rather than merely unnatural practices adopted not from inclination but for other reasons. I realize that this is at variance with the view, maintained by some Roman Catholics, that contraception is a sexual perversion. But although contraception may qualify as a deliberate perversion of the sexual and reproductive functions, it cannot be significantly described as a *sexual* perversion. A sexual perversion must reveal itself in conduct that expresses an unnatural *sexual* preference. And although there might be a form of fetishism focused on the employment of contraceptive devices, that is not the usual explanation for their use.

I wish to declare at the outset my belief that the connection between sex and reproduction has no bearing on sexual perversion. The latter is a concept of psychological, not physiological interest, and it is a concept that we do not apply to the lower animals, let alone to plants, all of which have reproductive functions that can go astray in various ways (think, for example, of seedless oranges). Insofar as we are prepared to regard higher animals as perverted, it is because of their psychological, not their anatomical similarity to humans. Furthermore, we do not regard as a perversion every deviation from the reproductive function of sex in humans: sterility, miscarriage, contraception, abortion.

Another matter that I believe has no bearing on the concept of sexual perversion is social disapproval or custom. Anyone inclined to think that in each society the perversions are those sexual practices of which the community disapproves should consider all of the societies that have frowned upon adultery and fornication. These have not been regarded as unnatural practices, but have been thought objectionable in other ways. What is regarded as unnatural admittedly varies from culture to culture, but the classification is not a pure expression of disapproval or distaste. In fact it is often regarded as a *ground* for disapproval, and that suggests that the classification has an independent content.

1

I am going to attempt a psychological account of sexual perversion, which will depend on a specific psychological theory of sexual desire and human sexual interactions. To approach this solution I wish first to consider a contrary position, one that provides a basis for skepticism about the existence of any sexual perversions at all, and perhaps about

This article is reprinted from the *Journal of Philosophy* 66, no. 1 (January 16, 1969), with the permission of the publisher and author.

the very significance of the term. The skeptical argument runs as follows:

Sexual desire is simply one of the appetites, like hunger and thirst. As such it may have various objects, some more common than others perhaps, but none in any sense "natural." An appetite is identified as sexual by means of the organs and erogenous zones in which its satisfaction can be to some extent localized, and the special sensory pleasures that form the core of that satisfaction. This enables us to recognize widely divergent goals, activities, and desires as sexual, since it is conceivable in principle that anything should produce sexual pleasure and that a nondeliberate, sexually charged desire for it should arise (as a result of conditioning, if nothing else). We may fail to empathize with some of these desires, and some of them, like sadism, may be objectionable on extraneous grounds, but once we have observed that they meet the criteria for being sexual, there is nothing more to be said on *that* score. Either they are sexual or they are not: sexuality does not admit of imperfection, or perversion, or any other such qualification—it is not that sort of affection.

This is probably the received radical position. It suggests that the cost of defending a psychological account may be to deny that sexual desire is an appetite. But insofar as that line of defense is plausible, it should make us suspicious of the simple picture of appetites on which the skepticism depends. Perhaps the standard appetites, like hunger, cannot be classed as pure appetites in that sense either, at least in their human versions.

Let us approach the matter by asking whether we can imagine anything that would qualify as a gastronomical perversion. Hunger and eating are importantly like sex in that they serve a biological function and also play as significant role in our inner lives. It is noteworthy that there is little temptation to describe as perverted an appetite for substances that are not nourishing. We should probably not consider someone's appetites as perverted if he liked to eat paper, sand, wood, or cotton. Those are merely rather odd and very unhealthy tastes: they lack of the psychological complexity that we expect of perversions. (Coprophilia, being already a sexual perversion, may be disregarded.) If, on the other hand, someone liked to eat cookbooks or mag-

azines with pictures of food in them, and preferred these to ordinary food—or if when hungry he sought satisfaction by fondling a napkin or ashtray from his favorite restaurant—then the concept of perversion might seem appropriate (in fact it would be natural to describe this as a case of gastronomical fetishism). It would be natural to describe as gastronomically perverted someone who could eat only by having food forced down his throat through a funnel, or only if the meal were a living animal. What helps in such cases is the peculiarity of the desire itself, rather than the inappropriateness of its object to the biological function that the desire serves. Even an appetite, it would seem, can have perversions if in addition to its biological function it has a significant psychological structure.

In the case of hunger, psychological complexity is provided by the activities that give it expression. Hunger is not merely a disturbing sensation that can be quelled by eating; it is an attitude toward edible portions of the external world, a desire to relate to them in rather special ways. The method of ingestion—chewing, savoring, swallowing, appreciating the texture and smell—is an important component of the relation, as is the passivity and controllability of the food (the only animals we eat live are helpless mollusks). Our relation to food depends also on our size: we do not live upon it or burrow into it like aphids or worms. Some of these features are more central than others, but any adequate phenomenology of eating would have to treat it as a relation to the external world and a way of appropriating bits of that world, with characteristic affection. Displacements or serious restrictions of the desire to eat could then be described as perversions, if they undermined the direct relation between man and food that is the natural expression of hunger. This explains why it is easy to imagine gastronomical fetishism, voyeurism, exhibitionism, or even gastronomical sadism and masochism. Indeed, some of these perversions are fairly common.

If we can imagine perversions of an appetite like hunger, it should be possible to make sense of the concept of sexual perversion. I do not wish to imply that sexual desire is an appetite—only that being an appetite is no bar to admitting of perversions. Like hunger, sexual desire has as its characteristic object a certain relation with something in the external world; only in this case it is usually a person rather than an omelet, and the relation is considerably more complicated. This added complication allows scope for correspondingly complicated perversions.

2

The fact that sexual desire is a feeling about other persons may tempt us to take a pious view of its psychological content. There are those who believe that sexual desire is properly the expression of some other attitude, like love, and that when it occurs by itself it is incomplete and unhealthy—or at any rate subhuman. (The extreme Platonic version of such a view is that sexual practices are all vain attempts to express something they cannot in principle achieve: this makes them all perversions, in a sense.) I do not believe that any such view is correct. Sexual desire is complicated enough without having to be linked to anything else as a condition for phenomenological analysis. It cannot be denied that sex may serve various functions—economic, social, altruistic—but it also has its own content as a relation between persons, and it is only by analyzing that relation that we can understand the conditions of sexual perversion.

It is very important that the object of sexual attraction is a particular individual, who transcends the properties that make him attractive. When different persons are attracted to a single person for different reasons—eyes, hair, figure, laugh, intelligence—we feel that the object of their desire is nevertheless the same, namely, that person. There is even an inclination to feel that this is so if the lovers have different sexual aims, if they include both men and women, for example. Different specific attractive characteristics seem to provide enabling conditions for the operation of a single basic feeling, and the different aims all provide expressions of it. We approach the sexual attitude toward the person through the features that we find attractive, but these features are not the objects of that attitude.

This is very different from the case of an omelet. Various people may desire it for different reasons, one for its fluffiness, another for its mushrooms, another for its unique combination of aroma and visual aspect; yet we do not enshrine the transcendental omelet as the true common object of their affections. Instead we might say that several desires have accidentally converged on the same object: any omelet with the crucial characteristics would do as well. It is not similarly true that any person with the same flesh distribution and way of smoking can be substituted as object for a particular sexual desire that has been elicited by those characteristics. It may be that they will arouse attraction whenever they recur, but it will be a new sexual attraction with a new particular object, not merely a transfer of the old desire to someone else. (I believe this is true even in cases where the new object is unconsciously identified with a former one.)

The importance of this point will emerge when we see how complex a psychological interchange constitutes the natural development of sexual attraction. This would be incomprehensible if its object were not a particular person, but rather a person of a certain *kind*. Attraction is only the beginning, and fulfillment does not consist merely of behavior and contact expressing this attraction, but involves much more.

The best discussion of these matters that I have seen is in part three of Sartre's *Being and Nothingness*.[1] Since it has influenced my own views, I shall say a few things about it now. Sartre's treatment of sexual desire and of love, hate, sadism, masochism, and further attitudes toward others, depends on a general theory of consciousness and the body that we can neither expound nor assume here. He does not discuss perversion, partly because he regards sexual desire as one form of the perpetual attempt of an embodied consciousness to come to terms with the existence of others, an attempt that is as doomed to fail in this form as it is in any of the others, which include sadism and masochism (if not certain of the more impersonal deviations) as well as several nonsexual attitudes. According to Sartre, all attempts to incorporate the other into my world as another subject, that is, to apprehend him as at once an object for me and a subject for whom I am an object, are unstable and doomed to collapse into one or the other of the two aspects. Either I reduce him entirely to an object, in which case his subjectivity escapes the possession or appropriation I can extend to that object; or I become merely an object for him, in which case I am no longer in a position to appropriate his subjectivity. Moreover, neither of these aspects is stable: each is continually in danger of giving way to the other. This has the consequence that there can be no such thing as a *successful* sexual relation, since the deep aim of sexual desire cannot in principle be accomplished. It seems likely, therefore, that this view will not permit a basic distinction between successful, or complete, and unsuccessful, or incomplete, sex and therefore cannot admit the concept of perversion.

I do not adopt this aspect of the theory, nor many of its metaphysical underpinnings. What interests me is Sartre's picture of the attempt. He says that the type of possession that is the object of sexual desire is carried out by "a double reciprocal incarnation" and that this is accomplished, typically in the form of a caress, in the following way: "I make myself flesh in order to impel the Other to realize *for-herself* and *for me* her own flesh, and my caresses cause my flesh to be born for me in so far as it is for the Other flesh *causing her to be born as flesh.*"[2] The incarnation in question is described variously as a clogging or troubling of consciousness, which is inundated by the flesh in which it is embodied.

The view I am going to suggest—I hope in less obscure language—is related to Sartre's, but differs in allowing sexuality to achieve its goal on occasion and thus in providing the concept of perversion with a foothold.

Sexual desire involves a kind of perception, but not merely a single perception of its object, for in the paradigm case of mutual desire there is a complex system of superimposed mutual perceptions —not only perceptions of the sexual object, but perceptions of oneself. Moreover, sexual awareness of another involves considerable self-awareness to begin with—more than is involved in ordinary sensory perception. The experience is felt as an assault on oneself by the view (or touch, or whatever) of the sexual object.

Let us consider a case in which the elements can be separated. For clarity we will restrict ourselves initially to the somewhat artificial case of desire at a distance. Suppose a man and a woman, whom we may call Romeo and Juliet, are at opposite ends of a cocktail lounge with many mirrors on its walls, permitting unobserved observation and even mutual unobserved observation. Each of them is sipping a martini and studying other people in the mirrors. At some point Romeo notices Juliet. He is moved, somehow, by the softness of her hair and the diffidence with which she sips her martini, and this arouses him sexually. Let us say that X *senses* Y whenever X regards Y with sexual desire. (Y need not be a person, and X's apprehension of Y can be visual, tactile, olfactory, and so on, or purely imaginary. In the present example we shall concentrate on vision.) So Romeo senses Juliet, rather than merely noticing her. At this stage he is aroused by an unaroused object; so he is more in the sexual grip of his body than she of hers.

Let us suppose, however, that Juliet now senses Romeo in another mirror on the opposite wall, though neither of them yet knows that he is seen by the other (the mirror angles provide three-quarter views). Romeo then begins to notice in Juliet the subtle signs of sexual arousal: heavylidded stare, dilating pupils, a faint flush. This of course renders her much more bodily, and he not only notices but senses this as well. His arousal is nevertheless still solitary. But now, cleverly calculating the line of her stare without actually looking her in the eyes, he realizes that it is directed at him through the mirror on the opposite wall. That is, he notices, and moreover senses, Juliet sensing him. This is definitely a new development, for it gives him a sense of embodiment, not only through his own reactions, but also through the eyes and reactions of another. Moreover, it is separable from the initial sensing of Juliet, for sexual arousal might begin with a person's sensing that he is sensed and being assailed by the perception of the other person's desire rather than merely by the perception of the person.

But there is a further step. Let us suppose that Juliet, who is a little slower than Romeo, now senses that he senses her. This puts Romeo in a position to notice, and be aroused by, her arousal at being sensed by him. He senses that she senses that he senses her. This is still another level of arousal, for he becomes conscious of his sexuality through his awareness of its effect on her and of her awareness that this effect is due to him. Once she takes the same step and senses that he senses her sensing him, it becomes difficult to state, let alone imagine, further iterations, though they may be logically distinct. If both are alone, they will presumably turn to look at each other directly, and the proceedings will continue on another plane. Physical contact and intercourse are perfectly natural extensions of this complicated visual exchange, and mutual touch can involve all the complexities of awareness present in the visual case, but with a far greater range of subtlety and acuteness.

Ordinarily, of course, things happen in a less orderly fashion—sometimes in a great rush—but I believe that some version of this overlapping system of distinct sexual perceptions and interactions is the basic framework of any full-fledged sexual relation and that relations involving only part of the complex are significantly incomplete. The account is only schematic, as it must be to achieve generality. Every real sexual act will be psychologically far more specific and detailed, in ways that depend not only on the physical techniques employed and on anatomical details but also on countless features of the participants' conceptions of themselves and of each other, which become embodied in the act. (It is a familiar enough fact, for example, that people often take their social roles and the social roles of their partners to bed with them.)

The general schema is important, however, and the proliferation of levels of mutual awareness it involves is an example of a type of complexity that typifies human interactions. Consider aggression, for example. If I am angry with someone, I want to make him feel it, either to produce self-reproach by getting him to see himself through the eyes of my anger and to dislike what he sees, or to produce reciprocal anger or fear by getting him to perceive my anger as a threat or attack. What I want will depend on the details of my anger, but in either case it will involve a desire that the object of that anger be aroused. This accomplishment constitutes the fulfillment of my emotion through domination of the object's feelings.

Another example of such reflexive mutual recognition is to be found in the phenomenon of meaning, which appears to involve an intention to produce a belief or other effect in another by bringing about this recognition of one's intention to produce that effect. (That result is due to H. P. Grice,[3] whose position I shall not attempt to reproduce in detail.) Sex has a related structure: it involves a desire that one's partner be aroused by the recognition of one's desire that he or she be aroused.

It is not easy to define the basic types of awareness and arousal of which these complexes are composed, and that remains a lacuna in this discussion. I believe that the object of awareness is the same in one's own case as it is in one's sexual awareness of another, although the two awarenesses will not be the same, the difference being as great as that between feeling angry and experiencing the anger of another. All stages of sexual perception are varieties of identification of a person with his body. What is perceived is one's own or another's *subjection* to or *immersion* in his body, a phenomenon that has been recognized with loathing by St. Paul and St. Augustine, both of whom regarded "the law of sin which is in my members" as a grave threat to the dominion of the holy will.[4] In sexual desire and its expression the blending of involuntary response with deliberate control is extremely important. For Augustine, the revolution launched against him by his body is symbolized by erection and the other involuntary physical components of arousal. Sartre too stresses the fact that the penis is not a prehensile organ. But mere involuntariness characterizes other bodily processes as well. In sexual desire the involuntary responses are combined with submission to spontaneous impulses: not only one's pulse and secretions but one's actions are taken over by the body; ideally, deliberate control is needed only to guide the expression of those impulses. This is to some extent also true of an appetite like hunger, but the takeover there is more localized, less pervasive, less extreme. One's whole body does not become saturated with hunger as it can with desire. But the most characteristic feature of a specifically sexual immersion in the body is its ability to fit into the complex of mutual perceptions that we have described. Hunger leads to spontaneous interactions with food; sexual desire leads to spontaneous interactions with other persons, whose bodies are asserting their sovereignty in the same way, producing involuntary reactions and spontaneous impulses in *them*. These reactions are perceived, and the perception of them is perceived, and that perception is in turn perceived; at each step the domination of the person by his body is reinforced, and the sexual partner becomes more possessible by physical contact, penetration, and envelopment.

Desire is therefore not merely the perception of a preexisting embodiment that in turn enhances the original subject's sense of himself. This explains why it is important that the partner be aroused, and not merely aroused, but aroused by the awareness of one's desire. It also explains the sense in which desire has unity and possession as its object: physical possession must eventuate in creation of the sexual object in the image of one's desire, and not merely in the object's recognition of that desire or in his or her own private arousal. (This may reveal a male bias. I shall say something about that later.)

3

To return, finally, to the topic of perversion: I believe that various familiar deviations constitute truncated or incomplete versions of the complete configuration and may therefore be regarded as perversions of the central impulse.

In particular, narcissistic practices and intercourse with animals, infants, and inanimate objects seem to be stuck at some primitive version of the first stage. If the object is not alive, the experience is reduced entirely to an awareness of one's own sexual embodiment. Small children and animals permit awareness of the embodiment of the other, but present obstacles to reciprocity, to the recognition by the sexual object of the subject's desire as the source of his (the object's) sexual self-awareness.

Sadism concentrates on the evocation of passive self-awareness in others, but the sadist's engagement is itself active and requires a retention of deliberate control that impedes awareness of himself as a bodily subject of passion in the required sense. The victim must recognize him as the source of his own sexual passivity, but only as the active source. De Sade claimed that the object of sexual desire was to evoke involuntary responses from one's partner, especially audible ones. The infliction of pain is no doubt the most efficient way to accomplish this, but it requires a certain abrogation

of one's own exposed spontaneity. All this, incidentally, helps to explain why it is tempting to regard as sadistic an excessive preoccupation with sexual technique, which does not permit one to abandon the role of agent at any stage of the sexual act. Ideally one should be able to surmount one's technique at some point.

A masochist on the other hand imposes the same disability on his partner as the sadist imposes on himself. The masochist cannot find a satisfactory embodiment as the object of another's sexual desire but only as the object of his control. He is passive not in relation to his partner's passion but in relation to his nonpassive agency. In addition, the subjection to one's body characteristic of pain and physical restraints is of a very different kind from that of sexual excitement: pain causes people to contract rather than dissolve.

Both of these disorders have to do with the second stage, which involves the awareness of oneself as an object of desire. In straightforward sadism and masochism other attentions are substituted for desire as a source of the object's self-awareness. But it is also possible for nothing of that sort to be substituted, as in the case of a masochist who is satisfied with self-inflicted pain or of a sadist who does not insist on playing a role in the suffering that arouses him. Greater difficulties of classification are presented by three other categories of sexual activity: elaborations of the sexual act, intercourse of more than two persons, and homosexuality.

If we apply our model to the various forms that may be taken by two-party heterosexual intercourse, none of them seem clearly to qualify as perversions. Hardly anyone can be found these days to inveigh against oral-genital contact, and the merits of buggery are urged by such respectable figures as D. H. Lawrence and Norman Mailer. There may be something vaguely sadistic about the latter technique (in Mailer's writings it seems to be a method of introducing an element of rape), but it is not obvious that this has to be so. In general, it would appear that any bodily contact between a man and a woman that gives them sexual pleasure is a possible vehicle for the system of multilevel interpersonal awareness that I have claimed is the basic psychological content of sexual interaction. Thus a liberal platitude about sex is upheld.

About multiple combinations the least that can be said is that they are bound to be complicated. If one considers how difficult it is to carry on two conversations simultaneously, one may appreciate the problems of multiple simultaneous interpersonal perception that can arise in even a small-scale orgy. It may be inevitable that some of the component relations should degenerate into mutual epidermal stimulation by participants otherwise isolated from each other. There may also be a tendency toward voyeurism and exhibitionism, both of which are incomplete relations. The exhibitionist wishes to display his desire without needing to be desired in return; he may even fear the sexual attentions of others. A voyeur, on the other hand, need not require any recognition at all by his object, certainly not a recognition of the voyeur's arousal.

It is not clear whether homosexuality is a perversion if that is measured by the standard of the described configuration, but it seems unlikely. For such a classification would have to depend on the possibility of extracting from the system a distinction between male and female sexuality; and much that has been said so far applies equally to men and women. Moreover, it would have to be maintained that there was a natural tie between the type of sexuality and the sex of the body and that two sexualities of the same type could not interact properly.

Certainly there is much support for an aggressive-passive distinction between male and female sexuality. In our culture the male's arousal tends to initiate the perceptual exchange; he usually makes the sexual approach, largely controls the course of the act, and of course penetrates whereas the woman receives. When two men or two women engage in intercourse they cannot both adhere to these sexual roles. The question is how essential the roles are to an adequate sexual relation. One relevant observation is that a good deal of deviation from these roles occurs in heterosexual intercourse. Women can be sexually aggressive and men passive, and temporary reversals of role are not uncommon in heterosexual exchanges of reasonable length. If such conditions are set aside, it may be urged that there is something irreducibly perverted in attraction to a body anatomically like one's own. But alarming as some people in our

culture may find such attraction, it remains psychologically unilluminating to class it as perverted. Certainly if homosexuality is a perversion, it is so in a very different sense from that in which shoe-fetishism is a perversion, for some version of the full range of interpersonal perceptions seems perfectly possible between two persons of the same sex.

In any case, even if the proposed model is correct, it remains implausible to describe as perverted every deviation from it. For example, if the partners in heterosexual intercourse indulge in private heterosexual fantasies, that obscures the recognition of the real partner and so, on the theory, constitutes a defective sexual relation. It is not, however, generally regarded as a perversion. Such examples suggest that a simple dichotomy between perverted and unperverted sex is too crude to organize the phenomena adequately.

I shall close with some remarks about the relation of perversion to good, bad, and morality. The concept of perversion can hardly fail to be evaluative in some sense, for it appears to involve the notion of an ideal or at least adequate sexuality that the perversions in some way fail to achieve. So, if the concept is viable, the judgment that a person or practice or desire is perverted will constitute a sexual evaluation, implying that better sex, or a better specimen of sex, is possible. This in itself is a very weak claim since the evaluation might be in a dimension that is of little interest to us. (Though, if my account is correct, that will not be true.)

Whether it is a moral evaluation, however, is another question entirely, one whose answer would require more understanding of both morality and perversion than can be deployed here. Moral evaluation of acts and of persons is a rather special and very complicated matter and by no means are all of our evaluations of persons and their activities moral evaluations. We make judgments about people's beauty or health or intelligence that are evaluative without being moral. Assessments of their sexuality may be similar in that respect.

Furthermore, moral issues aside, it is not clear that unperverted sex is necessarily *preferable* to the perversions. It may be that sex that receives the highest marks for perfection *as sex* is less enjoyable than certain perversions, and if enjoyment is considered very important, that might outweigh considerations of sexual perfection in determining rational preference.

That raises the question of the relation between the evaluative content of judgments of perversion and the rather common *general* distinction between good and bad sex. The latter distinction is usually confined to sexual acts, and it would seem, within limits, to cut across the other: even someone who believed, for example, that homosexuality was a perversion could admit a distinction between better and worse homosexual sex, and might even allow that good homosexual sex could be better *sex* than not very good unperverted sex. If this is correct, it supports the position—if judgments of perversion are viable at all—that they represent only one aspect of the possible evaluation of sex, even *qua sex.* Moreover it is not the only important aspect: certainly sexual deficiencies that evidently do not constitute perversions can be the object of great concern.

Finally, even if perverted sex is to that extent not so good as it might be, bad sex is generally better than none at all. This should not be controversial: it seems to hold for other important matters, like food, music, literature, and society. In the end, one must choose from among the available alternatives, whether their availability depends on the environment or on one's own constitution. And the alternatives have to be fairly grim before it becomes rational to opt for nothing.

NOTES

1. Trans. Hazel E. Barnes (New York: Philosophical Library, 1956).
2. Ibid., p. 391. Sartre's italics.
3. "Meaning," *Philosophical Review* 66, no. 3 (July 1957): 377–88.
4. See Romans 7:23, and the *Confessions,* Book 8, v.

Altruistic Love and Its Corruptions

66. LOVING AS FREELY GIVING

Millard Schumaker

Jesus said: "This I command you, to love one another" (Jn. 15. 17), and his command in all its majesty has come to be known as the "Great Commandment". What is the status of this Great Commandment in contemporary moral theology? Usually it is treated as a moral requirement (sometimes as the *only* moral requirement), that is, as a duty— an injunction placing the Christian under a moral obligation. Thus, the moral theologian commits himself to the proposition that it is morally right to love one's neighbour and morally wrong not to love one's neighbour, in the sense that failure to love

constitutes a violation of morality. I want to argue that this claim is incoherent and therefore unacceptable and to propose an alternative interpretation of the character of the Great Commandment which is both internally consistent and also helpful in coming to an understanding of the Christian claim with respect to the character of genuinely human life.

Considering the fact that Christians tend to think of love primarily as *agape,* or self-sacrificial love, I shall begin my argument with an analysis of the concept of sacrifice. There is a use of the word "sacrifice" where it means that one has meritoriously given up something to which he was entitled. Paul Weiss has suggested that when we speak of the sacrifices of heroes we have just this

From Millard Schumaker, *Moral Poise* (Edmonton, Alberta: St. Stephens College, 1977), pp. 9–14. Reprinted by permission of the author and publisher.

kind of thing in mind. "In sacrifice", he argues, "we return more than we ever owed and surely, so far as other men are concerned, give them much more than is their due from us". [Paul Weiss, "Sacrifice and Self-Sacrifice", *The Review of Metaphysics, 2* (1947), 82.] Sacrifice, therefore, when the word is used in this way, is never demanded by justice and cannot result from an effort to fulfill moral obligations. A. A. Spir has also insisted that sacrifice goes beyond justice and moral obligation: "To enforce sacrifice is to violate law and at the same time to debase the very nature of morality itself . . . That is why a man will often refuse to fulfill even a trifling demand and yet be ready to do ten times as much of his own free will". [*Right and Wrong* (Edinburgh: University of Saint Andrews, 1954), 27f. Originally published in 1879.]

This is to say that while it is often morally possible to volunteer a sacrifice, it is never morally possible to demand that another sacrifice. To demand that someone else do more than he owes is the very essence of injustice; but injustice is always and necessarily wrong; thus, it is always wrong to demand sacrifice. This use of the word "sacrifice" is almost always the use being made of the word when we speak of sacrificing for the sake of others. Thus, if a man claims to have sacrificed for the sake of his children in feeding and clothing them, we usually (although there are exceptions) dismiss his claim as absurd because as a parent he is dutybound to provide for his children and we therefore feel that he has given up nothing except that which it was not his to keep. But if a man claims to have sacrificed in order to send his son to university, we might well accept his claim because parents are usually not considered to be under strict obligation to provide such an education.

The point is that to give someone his due is to give a person what is his and therefore not to give up anything at all; but sacrifice, in the relevant sense of the word, must be a giving up of one's own. I can, after all, only give up my own if it is rightfully mine; and if it is mine by rights, then I cannot, logically cannot, be rightly required to give it up. It follows, therefore, that there can be no duty to sacrifice.

In general, what is true of self-sacrifice is true also of gifts. On any standard definition of "gift"

they cannot be owed or required. Everyone seems agreed that gifts cannot be owed and can therefore never be claimed as rights, but occasionally people suggest that under certain circumstances we are nevertheless duty-bound to give gifts. A. C. Ewing, for example, argued that a duty to give gifts exists despite the fact that no one ever has a right to them and that this fact indicates that duties are not necessarily correlated with rights. [*The Individual, the State, and World Government* (New York: The Macmillan Company, 1947), 20.] But it seems to me that this paradoxical claim is really an abuse of the word "gift" designed to patch an inadequate moral theory. Aside from question-begging references to certain theories of duty, I know of no reason to think that one might have a duty to give a gift.

It is the case that on occasion one *should* give gifts, and it is presumably this fact which led Ewing to claim that it is sometimes right and even a duty to give gifts. But although Ewing's theory of obligation forced him to conclude that the giving of gifts might sometimes be a duty, the ordinary usage does not really support the claim. Here the decisive evidence consists in the fact that one always has a right not to give a gift. It follows that one need never give a gift, and therefore the giving of gifts cannot be a moral requirement.

It is instructive to think about the word "gift" as it is used in the special context of the law. In the law of contracts a gift is something the property in which is voluntarily transferred to another without the expectation or receipt of an equivalent. To say that gifts are voluntarily transferred is to contrast them with wages or payments; unlike them, the gift is not required. And to say that gifts do not require receipt of an equivalent is to contrast them with that which is traded or sold. What the law has in mind when it speaks of a "gift" is roughly consistent with what the common man means when he speaks of a gift. It is, therefore, self-contradictory to claim that anyone could have a duty to give a gift.

Having made these comments about the concepts of sacrifice, and gift-giving, I want now to discuss the related concepts of friendship and love. There is something very odd about a sentence like "I am John's friend because I am morally required to be" and therefore something very wrong with the claim that men have a duty to do the works which arise out of friendship. It is true that there is a small class of actions which might be called the "duties of friendship"—e.g., being steadfast in times of trial. But it is a necessary condition of the correct use of the word "friend" that the individual so described be willing to do more than such duties require.

The concept of moral requirement takes its form in part by way of contrast with the concept of inclination; hence, an act is a duty only if one ought to do it even if he is inclined not to. And the point is that friendship is not the sort of thing about which this can be said: one simply cannot be a true friend in the full sense of the term unless he wants to be. Furthermore, I am of the opinion that he ought not even to try; it is enough to be civil. Consider this sentence: "John is my best friend, but he wouldn't be if I could find a way to end it". The sentence is odd just because to utter it is to end the friendship, and therefore any future "friendly" actions become mere pretence. Thus, for logical reasons one cannot be a friend solely in response to the call of duty. The point is this: while some friendly actions are also duties, not all are: friends are (by definition) willing when appropriate to sacrifice for one another, to give gifts to one another, and to forgive one another. Furthermore, when we say of someone that he is a friend we mean in part to call attention to just this willingness.

Consider also the closely related concept of love. It has become a commonplace that love cannot be commanded. And it has become just as commonplace, at least among moral theologians, to counter this claim by suggesting that while love taken as an emotion cannot be commanded, love taken as an attitude or willingness to act in a certain way can be commanded. Thus, Joseph Fletcher willingly admits that affections cannot be turned off and on "like water from a faucet"; but he argues that "kindness, generosity, mercy, patience, concern, 'righteous indignation' ", etc. which count as manifestations of Christian love require not affection but a disposition of the will. And such willing, he argues, can be commanded. [*Moral Responsibility* (Philadelphia: The Westminster Press, 1967), 21.] Fletcher thinks that if he can prove that love is a matter of willing an action rather than a matter of feelings and emotions, that then he will have proved that love can be commanded; and many other theologians and moral philosophers have thought the same.

But this is a mistake. For the alleged fact that "love" is the name of a feeling is not the only thing which stands in the way of the legitimacy of commanding love. If something is a proper subject of moral requirement, then it must be something which can be done out of a sense of duty, out of conscientiousness. But love cannot be done out of a sense of duty. D. Z. Phillips, for example, has pointed out that to say that one loves his wife out of a sense of duty is the same as to say that one really does not love her at all. ["The Christian Conception of Love", *Christian Ethics and Contemporary Philosophy,* Ian T. Ramsey, ed. (New York: The Macmillan Company, 1966), 314.] Why is this so? In part, it is so because we allow the fact that a person will not sacrifice, will not give gifts, and will not forgive someone to count decisively against the claim that he loves (on either the affectional or the volitional model), even if he is within his rights—as he always is—in refusing these things. Love, as Bernard Haring has said, is ever ready to surrender its own rights in favour of others. [*The Law of Christ* (Westminster, Maryland: The Newman Press, 1963), I.523.] But, as I have shown, the surrender of genuine rights cannot, for conceptual reasons, be morally required. It follows that love cannot be required.

I am not arguing that love is an emotion and since emotions cannot be assumed upon demand love cannot rightly be required; instead, I am arguing that love implies the willingness to go beyond requirement, such that it would be self-contradictory to say, for example, "John loves Mary, but he would never be moved to sacrifice for her, or to give her a gift, or to forgive her when she offended him". It seems clear enough that if a person consistently stands on his rights with respect to someone else even in situations adverse to that other, that this is sufficient to count against any claim that he loves her.

What would be involved, then, in requiring love? We would be insisting that one must do something in the way of supererogatory action. In one sense, such a command cannot be obeyed since, for example, to give a "gift" on demand is not to give a gift at all but to pay tribute (as to a pirate). In another sense, such a command can be obeyed since one can give what if freely given would have been a gift; but the command itself is then necessarily an unjust one. And so, an ethic which considered love to be morally required is in one sense an incoherent one and in another sense an unjust encroachment upon the individual's legitimate rights.

What I have just said about love and about certain related concepts applies to any sort of morality whatever and therefore applies to Christian ethics. The moral theologian cannot claim exemption from this analysis unless he is prepared to abandon the whole network of concepts which surround the concept of love in the ordinary language. And he really cannot do this because the price is too high: the series of ideas in question is already used prominently and crucially within the biblical witness and the theological tradition. And so, because the theologian is committed to the thesis that one can sacrifice for others, that one can give gifts, that one can forgive offences, etc., he is forced already to accept the thesis that love cannot be a moral requirement; that is, he must accept the fact that loving acts are not necessarily the sorts of things which one ought to do even when not so inclined.

But many theologians will find this claim very difficult, protesting that the Christian has no alternative but to consider love to be a moral requirement since Christian morality is grounded in Jesus's words: "A new commandment I give to you, that you love one another". Surely the theologian is not at liberty to ignore these words and surely this passage unavoidably marks love as a moral and religious requirement? But this is precisely what I want to deny; for I feel constrained to point out that if the moral theologian insists upon interpreting the Great Commandment as imposing a moral requirement, then he is committed to all the conceptual difficulties to which I have called attention. The fact that it is the God-man who is said to require love cannot make the requirement any more intelligible or any less unjust than it would be if uttered by someone with less impressive credentials.

But my critics may persevere: nonetheless, they might protest, Jesus *commands* us to love. How can a commandment be also non-obligatory? To this I reply that a more reasonable translation of the texts would be: "This I 'command' you, to love one another"—with the punctuation indicating that this is a "command" which is not a command, but instead the functional equivalent of the notion of command in other conceptions of morality. In this way, the response of love is to Christians, what the response of obedience is to some others, in much the same way as Christians are "soldiers" of Christ even though they are in fact the very antithesis of the military, as Jesus is "King" even though he is the very antithesis of political power, as the Gospel is the "Law" of Pauline Christians even though it is the very antithesis of the (alleged) Pharisaic morality. Understood in this way, the Great Commandment becomes an invitation to forsake the heteronomous ethic of servile obedience and consequent hierarchical order for a new ethic of friendship and its consequence of graceful giving and grateful receiving.

And so I want to make a new and unorthodox suggestion: I want to suggest that this and similar passages be interpreted as counsels, or advice, rather than as commands. I am suggesting that the Great Commandment must be understood as a supererogatory Counsel of Perfection: it does not delineate what one must do on pain of otherwise being wrong; it delineates what one should do if one wants to live a truly human life, and live it more abundantly.

But something more must be said: this counsel is also the cornerstone of the Christian conception of the moral life; and so the counsel cannot be considered as optional or dispensable; it must be seen as essential to any Christian ethic. But how can a principle which qualifies only as a counsel and not as a moral requirement also be essential? The answer is that this is possible only if the idea of supererogation is itself a central notion in the ethic. And I want to suggest that precisely this is the case in Christian ethics.

Christian ethics presupposes and builds upon Jewish conceptions of justice and fair play and the resultant system of rights and duties which arise out of the social order. Jesus himself spent surprisingly little time discussing those principles of justice; he seems to have been, in general, content that the scribes and Pharisees had done an adequate job of elaborating the requirements and privileges of righteousness in the strict sense. Jesus' own ethical concern seems to have been somewhat differently oriented; he seems to have been more concerned to point out the merits of surrendering one's own rights and volunteering oneself to others. Thus, Jesus proclaimed that "unless your righteousness exceeds that of the scribes and Pharisees, you will never enter the kingdom of heaven". The point of this remark is lost unless one remembers that the scribes and Pharisees were *very* righteous, at least in the strict sense of fulfilling their duties and never going beyond their rights. Since the scribes and Pharisees virtually fulfilled the Law, to exceed their righteousness entails giving up rights and assuming tasks which could be avoided without any violation of morality.

I am suggesting, then, that it is possible to see Christian morality as a radically supererogatory morality; it consists in part in the claim that it is a mistake to insist always upon one's rights and that the best and most authentic life arises out of the willingness to give freely of oneself and one's share without insisting upon equivalent compensation. To accept this evaluation of rights and their place in human life is part of what is involved in accepting the Christian ethic. Unless one is prepared to agree that people should often be willing to do things which they cannot rightly be required to do, one cannot properly be thought to have accepted the Christian ethic. In this sense, Christian morality is fundamentally and essentially a supererogatory morality; it is a morality which itself goes beyond requirement.

And so, although the Reformers erred in rejecting the concept of supererogation, the Medieval theologians erred as well; for they assigned the wrong scope to supererogation when they argued that poverty, chastity, and obedience are supererogatory but that love is not. In tying the concept of supererogation in this way to the Evangelical Counsels, the Medieval theologians trivialized the doctrine and lost a valuable key to the character of Christian morality. The fact that Christian morality is fundamentally and essentially a supererogatory morality explains why the Great Commandment is central to the Faith even though it is not a requirement: to make love central is in part to suggest that people should not always stand on their rights. And the claim of the Church seems to be that only when one ceases to insist upon his own does genuinely human life begin.

But if Christian morality is radically supererogatory in character, what counts as minimally acceptable conduct from the point of view of the Faith? This question has been the great stumbling-block in discussions of supererogation in the theological tradition. Traditionally, obeying God's command counted as the *minimum religionis*. But if Christian morality is radically supererogatory in character, then obedience to command clearly cannot be enough, especially considering that Jesus claimed that only those who go beyond the righteousness of the scribes and Pharisees will see the Kingdom of God.

I would suggest that the correct interpretation of the New Testament claim is this: in part, Jesus is suggesting that salvation comes only to those who cease to be concerned with discovering minimal means of compliance. If I am right in thinking that Jesus in this way advocates the supererogatory way of love as the truly humanizing way, then it would seem correct also to suggest that to seek minimums is to miss the point of human life, that it is to fail to be truly human. And to miss the truly human life— can that not be understood as the contradictory to being saved; is it not to be lost?

Jesus said, "whoever would save his life will lose it, and whoever loses his life for my sake will find it" and many similar things. Surely in part this can be understood as implying that whoever insists always upon his rights is lost, but whoever will waive them for the sake of the truth of love is living a life worthy of a man. And so, when supererogation is seen as central to the Christian life, then there is no longer any *minimum religionis* at all: there is no minimal standard of compliance. But this is not to say that one must be perfect to be saved; it is only to say that salvation entails the willingness to give freely and ungrudgingly of oneself. Only such a willingness allows for exceeding the righteousness of the scribes and Pharisees.

67. LOVE AND ADDICTION

Stanton Peele
(with Archie Brodsky)

'TIL DEATH DO US PART

Several years ago I began to think that what people call love can sometimes be an addiction. It was my way of making sense of some observations about drugs and about people. This was in the late 1960s, at the height of the drug explosion, when reports on acid-tripping and speedfreaking (along with the use of marijuana and heroin) were widely broadcast. At that time, newspapers and magazines began to print tables of drugs to enlighten the public about what effects these drugs had. Two things struck me in reading these tables—first, how many misconceptions I and the people I knew had about drugs, and second, how much inexact information the tables themselves contained. The assumptions I and others were making about the power of psychoactive drugs did not seem justified by any existing evidence. To me this signaled a large undefined area where the motivations and attitudes of people who took drugs could come into play. It also indicated basic fears and irrationalities in our society about drugs and what they could do.

At about the same time, though for unrelated reasons, I was beginning to look more critically at the concept of romantic love with which I had grown up. In today's open society, many varieties of male-female relationships can readily be observed in life, in motion pictures, in novels, in song lyrics. What I saw in these contexts was often disconcerting. Relationships which supposedly entailed some notion of growing together were really based mostly on security and the comfort of spending as much time as possible with someone totally sensitized to one's needs. In those cases, loving another person actually seemed to bring about a contraction in the scope of one's life. What made such relationships stand out for me was the feeling

Stanton Peele with Archie Brodsky, *Love and Addiction* (Taplinger, 1975). Copyright © 1975 by Stanton Peele with Archie Brodsky. Reprinted by permission of Taplinger Publishing Co., Inc., and Sphere Books, Ltd.

that there was something fundamental in their nature that made them this way. I could think of only one word to describe it: addiction. The individuals involved were hooked on someone whom they regarded as an object; their need for the object, their "love," was really a dependency. . . .

What comes through . . . is a sense of waste—of seeing individual identities distorted, and individual possibilities circumscribed, by an intensely felt pressure to seek security in one other person. It is a universal pattern, expressed in a variety of personal styles. My reaction eventually was to consider just how closely this pattern fit the addiction model. As an illustration, I have put together a composite case which conveys the essence of relationships like the three that have been described. Since this is meant to be a straightforwardly schematic example of addiction, I have deliberately kept it free of distracting detail and complicated motivations. . . . Bruce and Vicky's relationship is smooth and harmonious, its terms mutually agreeable.

AN EGOISME A DEUX

Vicky and Bruce are individual human beings in body only; they are constantly struggling to overcome the separation of skin that is the one barrier to their total union. Their backgrounds explain some of the story. Both of them grew up, comfortable and protected, in a suburb of Los Angeles. From an early age they thought in terms of professional careers and a domestic existence. Bruce, who graduated from high school a year ahead of Vicky, turned down a scholarship to an Ivy League university he had always dreamed of attending. Instead, unwilling to leave Vicky, he went to a university in the Los Angeles area. Vicky followed him there a year later. She hadn't wanted to go too far from her parents, and in fact she lived at home rather than on campus, just as Bruce had done the year before so that he could be near her. The couple made the hour-long trip to and from school every day together, and they continued to see each other in the comfortable settings of their old neighborhood and their parents' homes. It was as if they were biding time, waiting simply to reach an age when they could marry without arousing comment. Their lack of experience with other people at college naturally did not give them a chance to gain a very accurate impression of themselves as others saw them. The result was that they didn't develop adult qualities that might have made them attractive to people who didn't already know and love them.

And there you have it. Two people reluctant to leave the security of their high school relationship, probably as much from a fear of disappointing each other, and of never finding anything better for themselves, as from inherent desire, had joined themselves together " 'til death do us part." In the meantime, they had missed the opportunity to live away from home, an experience their upper-middle-class parents would willingly have subsidized. The price they extracted from each other for the sacrifices involved in maintaining the relationship was the constant reassurance of each other's company. Having spent so much of themselves simply to stay together, they both felt the relationship owed them a great deal. And, to justify this commitment, they steadily inflated each other's worth to the point where nothing else seemed of any consequence to them.

They soon gave up whatever independent interests they had. Vicky discarded the idea of joining the college drama club because it would have taken too much of her time from Bruce. They did not see much of their old friends, most of whom had gone away to college. Nor did they make new friends at the university, except a few classroom friends. They talked about courses and teachers with these people, and together went to occasional parties with them, but because so little of their free time was spent on campus, these outside relationships didn't amount to anything. The couple grew more and more clinging, turned to each other for more and more of what they wanted, and gradually severed all connections with the rest of the world except for school and their parents.

Vicky and Bruce got married upon Bruce's graduation. Together, they decided to move to San Francisco for their graduate training. Bruce was to go to law school, while Vicky planned to take her Ph.D. in history after completing her senior year at a college in the area. Not that she had any intention of being a historian. She found her history courses boring and, worse, tremendously stressful. Constrained but not inspired by the curriculum during her undergraduate years, she had made her way through with the help of stimulants and tranquilizers. One may wonder why she didn't rise up against this agony and get off the academic treadmill, but it is not surprising that a person so little disposed to question the security of her family home and her marriage would not seek something more purposeful than continued, meaningless academic activity. In fact, she saw no alternative for herself while her husband was in law school.

Vicky and Bruce were concerned about moving so far away from their families. However, they enjoyed regular weekend visits from their parents. They frequently returned these visits, carefully dividing their time between the two families, as well as bringing them together for joint gatherings. And they had hardly arrived in San Francisco before they began making detailed plans for their eventual return to Los Angeles, where they would buy a house near both families once Bruce was earning a lawyer's income and their San Francisco "bohemian" period had come to an end.

At this point they settled into the kind of married life described in the account at the beginning of this chapter. Marriage gave their relationship, blessed with parental indulgence from the beginning, the added comforts of a home life. Occasionally they roused themselves to attend an evening lecture or other university cultural event. However, their penetration into San Francisco never went much deeper than that. With few friends, their social life was as limited and superficial as it had been in college, and although they espoused topical viewpoints, they were certainly not part of the new West Coast scene.

Thus two underdeveloped egos merged into what D. H. Lawrence called an *égoisme à deux:* two people banded together, not because of love or an increasing understanding of each other, but rather because of their overentanglement and mutual self-deprivation. With each step in their growing interdependence, Bruce and Vicky broke a few more of the ties they had had with other people, things, and activities. And as these disappeared, they hung on to each other that much more frantically to bolster themselves against an increasingly alien environment.

We can partially trace the genesis of these addictive personalities in Vicky's and Bruce's upbringing. Neither of them had broken from a childhood dependence on their parents. They approached all experience outside the family as somehow external to themselves. Although they were both successful students, and both accepted the yoke of school's demands, their schoolwork had little meaning for them, and they spoke of it cynically. Nor were they capable of forming relationships outside the family, but for one—with each other. It was as though this isolated excursion drained them of all the energy they might have applied toward knowing other people.

Their parents had been so generous, so quick to bend the environment to Bruce and Vicky's needs, that they could not realize how they were limiting their children's experience. When Vicky became involved with Bruce, her parents, with his parents' blessing, turned over their beach house to the young lovers, and rented a smaller place at Lake Arrowhead. The couple could go to the beach house and be together without interference. Except, of course, it was total interference, for the young people were never allowed to develop distinct wills of their own. Vicky had no reason to go out into the world when her mother and father were so attentive to her needs, so appreciative of her charm and intelligence, that she could not have hoped to find better treatment anywhere else. Moving straight from her parents' home to her husband's, this woman never had the experience of living alone, on her own emotional resources, and probably never will. In this way, Vicky's and Bruce's parents incorporated every stage of their children's growth except for the last stage, independence—not only a healthy separation from the home, but a true psychological independence; something a person carries with him or her for all time. And it is this kind of self-completion which instills the integrity that every real coming together of two or more individuals presupposes.

THE PARALLEL WITH OPIATE ADDICTION

How does this story resemble the more familiar pattern of addiction we see in habitual drug users? Showing just how deep the resemblance goes is what this book is about. The addict is a person who never learns to come to grips with his world, and who therefore seeks stability and reassurance through some repeated, ritualized activity. This activity is reinforced in two ways—first, by a comforting sensation of well-being induced by the drug or other addictive object; second, by the atrophy of the addict's other interests and abilities and the general deterioration of his life situation while he is preoccupied with the addiction. As alternatives grow smaller, the addiction grows larger, until it is all there is. A true addict progresses into a monomania, whether the object of addiction is a drug or a lover. Vicky and Bruce's sheltered childhoods denied them the self-confidence and the well-formed enthusiasms that a complete life is built on. As a result, they fastened on each other as a daily habit, and this habit became the *raison d'être* of their existence.

It is important to note the vicious cycle at work here. The addict's lack of internal direction or purpose creates the need for ritualized escape in the first place, and is in turn exacerbated by exclusive involvement with the addiction and abandonment of the substance of a normal life. Operating on the personal malaise an addict feels, drugs give him an artificial sense of self-sufficiency that removes what small motivation he has for complicated or difficult pursuits. Similarly, Vicky and Bruce came to each other originally in a state of ennui, without interests that extended deep enough to engage them. Once they found each other, they became even less motivated to cultivate friends or apply themselves to their work in any but the most external way. Their dependency, like the drug addict's, could only increase as other concerns dropped off.

The one major feature of the addiction cycle that the case of Vicky and Bruce does not directly illustrate is withdrawal—the addict's anguished reaction to an interruption of his supply. Vicky and Bruce organized their environment so totally around each other that there never was the slightest threat of a breakup. The couple had at some cost resisted even temporary separations, as when Bruce resigned himself to a school he didn't like in order to stay with his fiancée. Lovers often do suffer withdrawal symptoms when breakups occur. With Vicky and Bruce, the passion for staying together was in large part a fear and avoidance of withdrawal. Vicky and Bruce are like the well-to-do, respectable opiate addict who is able to guarantee that he will never have to feel the pain of withdrawal.

Addiction to a person is just an extension of the social side of all addictions. People who share an addiction form a private world for themselves. For example, a group of people who are addicted to the same drug tend to give their experience a collective interpretation which is incomprehensible to those outside the group. They are not concerned with this discrepancy because only the approval of other group members matters to them. The same is true for Vicky and Bruce, with their family and household rituals, their exclusive concern to please each other, and their inflated estimation of themselves. In fact, an addictive romantic relationship like theirs is the smallest, most isolated group possible. . . .

"LOVE" AS AN ADDICTION

There is an understandable resistance to the idea that a human relationship can be equivalent psychologically to a drug addiction. Yet it is not unreasonable to look for addiction between lovers when psychologists find the roots of drug addiction in childhood dependency needs and stunted family relationships. Chein, Winick, and other observers interpret drugs to be a kind of substitute for human ties. In this sense, addictive love is even more directly linked to what are recognized to be the sources of addiction than is drug dependence.

Almost everyone knows of people who replace romantic relationships with other kinds of escapes, including drug escapes, at least until the next relationship comes along. . . . I know of a man who started drinking heavily after a long-time woman friend left him. He wrote about his reactions at the time of the breakup:

Since Linda left I mainly just lie in bed. I'm just too weak to move, and I have the chills all the time. . . . I've been

crying a lot. . . . I try to calm myself by drinking the scotch my sister left here. . . . I feel so horrible, so dispossessed—like the real me doesn't exist anymore.

He couldn't sleep, and his heartbeat sometimes sped up frighteningly when he wasn't doing anything. These are symptoms of acute withdrawal. We know they can occur—perhaps quite often in certain groups and at certain ages—when one is deprived of a lover. Popular music sings paeans to the experience as a hallmark of true love: "When I lost my baby, I almost lost my mind . . . Since you left me baby, my whole life is through." What is there about love that produces withdrawal in people we have all known, maybe even in ourselves? Can we envision a kind of love that does *not* bring such devastation in its wake? Let us look closely at how "love" can be an addiction, and how addictive love differs from genuine love. . . .

Love is an ideal vehicle for addiction because it can so exclusively claim a person's consciousness. If, to serve as an addiction, something must be both reassuring and consuming, then a sexual or love relationship is perfectly suited for the task. If it must also be patterned, predictable, and isolated, then in these respects, too, a relationship can be ideally tailored to the addictive purpose. Someone who is dissatisfied with himself or his situation can discover in such a relationship the most encompassing substitute for self-contentment and the effort required to attain it.

When a person goes to another with the aim of filling a void in himself, the relationship quickly becomes the center of his or her life. It offers him a solace that contrasts sharply with what he finds everywhere else, so he returns to it more and more, until he needs it to get through each day of his otherwise stressful and unpleasant existence. When a constant exposure to something is necessary in order to make life bearable, an addiction has been brought about, however romantic the trappings. The ever-present danger of withdrawal creates an everpresent craving. . . .

ERICH FROMM: A POSITIVE CONCEPT OF LOVE

Love is the opposite of interpersonal addiction. A love relationship is based on a desire to grow and to expand oneself through living, and a desire for one's partner to do the same. Anything which contributes positively to a loved one's experience is welcomed, partly because it enriches the loved one for his own sake, and partly because it makes him a more stimulating companion in life. If a person is self-completed, he can even accept experiences which cause a lover to grow away from him, if that is the direction in which the lover's fulfillment must take her. If two people hope to realize fully their potential as human beings—both together and apart—then they create an intimacy which includes, along with trust and sharing, hope, independence, openness, adventurousness, and love.

When we speak of a desire for intimacy that resects the loved one's integrity, we naturally think of Erich Fromm's classic work *The Art of Loving*. Fromm's theme is that man or woman can only achieve love when he has realized himself to the point where he can stand as a whole and secure person. "Mature *love*," Fromm states, "is *union under the condition of preserving one's integrity,* one's individuality." It requires "a state of intensity, awakeness, enhanced vitality, which can only be the result of a productive and active orientation in many other spheres of life." This permits us, as lovers, to manifest an *"active concern for the life and the growth of that which we love."*

Unless we have reached this state, and "unless we have faith in the persistence of our self, our feeling of identity is threatened and we become dependent on other people whose approval then becomes the basis for our feeling of identity." In that case, we are in danger of experiencing union *without* integrity. Such a union is a "full commitment in all aspects of life," but one which lacks an essential ingredient, a regard for the rest of the world:

If a person loves only one other person and is indifferent to the rest of his fellow men, his love is not love but a symbiotic attachment, or an enlarged egotism.

These comments, and much else that Fromm writes, reveal a sharp awareness of the potential for addiction inherent in the "powerful striving" man feels for "interpersonal fusion." Fromm notes that two passionately attracted people "take the intensity of the infatuation, this being 'crazy' about each other, for proof of the intensity of their love,

while it may only prove the degree of their preceding loneliness.". . .

CRITERIA FOR LOVE VS. ADDICTION

In Fromm's notion of integrity in love and Greer's emphasis on self-actualization and personal pride, we have the elements of a positive concept of love. By contrasting this model with that of addictive love, we can develop specific criteria for assessing the character of our relationships. These criteria follow from our more general standards for distinguishing between the addictive and the non-addictive approach to life. They are points at which a relationship either expresses health and the promise of growth, or leans toward addiction:

1. Does each lover have a secure belief in his or her own value?
2. Are the lovers improved by the relationship? By some measure outside of the relationship are they better, stronger, more attractive, more accomplished, or more sensitive individuals? Do they value the relationship for this very reason?
3. Do the lovers maintain serious interests outside the relationship, including other meaningful personal relationships?
4. Is the relationship integrated into, rather than being set off from, the totality of the lovers' lives?
5. Are the lovers beyond being possessive or jealous of each other's growth and expansion of interests?
6. Are the lovers also friends? Would they seek each other out if they should cease to be primary partners?

These standards represent an ideal, and as such they cannot be fulfilled completely even by the healthiest relationships. But given that every relationship is bound to contain some elements of addiction, we can still tell what makes one predominantly addictive. This occurs, as in drug addiction, when a single overwhelming involvement with one thing serves to cut a person off from life, to close him or her off to experience, to debilitate him, to make him less open, free, and positive in dealing with the world.

Interpersonal addiction need not be a one-to-one affair. An addict may form successive or simultaneous relationships, either because he or she never allows himself to become seriously involved, or because he can't find a partner who completely accepts him. In all cases, however, addiction has at its center a diminished sense of self. The addict uses relationships to seal off his inner self from a frightening environment. In the process, the already weakened self ceases to develop, and the addict's life contracts further.

D. H. Lawrence used the term *égoisme à deux* to describe the overgrown, quasi-permanent connection between two lovers. Like any form of addiction, an *égoisme à deux* involves people who have not received from life a self-completeness that would enable them to come to an experience whole in themselves. The result is that they are drawn to an object—the lover—which can secure their shallow or fragmented selves. But they become trapped by this object, because even as it stabilizes them, it prevents them from extending themselves outward to meet other people or events that they encounter. As their inadequacy and rigidity worsen, each must lean more heavily on the other. Thus they draw each other into an increasingly closed, isolated, and mutually protective relationship.

Because the partners in an addictive relationship are motivated more by their own needs for security than by an appreciation of each other's personal qualities, what they want most from each other is the reassurance of constancy. Thus they are likely to demand unchallenged acceptance of themselves as they are, including their blemishes and peculiarities. In exchange, they are willing to tolerate passively all similar quirks in each other's makeup. In fact, to justify their total involvement, the lovers may identify each other's idiosyncrasies as their standards for attractiveness. In this way they create a private world which others can't enter and would not want to enter.

Such lovers do, of course, require each other to change in certain ways. But the adaptations expected or demanded are entirely toward each other and do not entail an improved ability to deal with other people or the environment. On the contrary, the changes one partner requests of the other to better satisfy his own needs are almost always harmful to the other's general development as a person. The lovers are not concerned if an "inward" adjustment is a debilitating one overall. In fact, a lessened ability to cope with anything or anyone else is welcomed in the other as a stronger guarantee of allegiance to the relationship. This is why jealousy and possessiveness are so much a part of addictive love. It is why an addict actually hopes that his lover will not meet new people and enjoy the world, since this suggests competing ties and interests that would make her less dependent on him. As Germaine Greer's penetrating analysis puts it:

The hallmark of egotistical love, even when it masquerades as altruistic love, is the negative answer to the question "Do I want my love to be happy more than I want him to be with me?" As soon as we find ourselves working at being indispensable, rigging up a pattern of vulnerability in our loved ones, we ought to know that our love has taken the socially sanctioned form of egotism. Every wife who slaves to keep herself pretty, to cook her husband's favorite meals, to build up his pride and confidence in himself at the expense of his sense of reality, to be his closest and effectively his only friend, to encourage him to reject the consensus of opinion and find reassurance only in her arms is binding her mate to her with hoops of steel that will strangle them both. Every time a woman makes herself laugh at her husband's often-told jokes she betrays him. The man who looks at his woman and says, "What would I do without you?" is already destroyed. His woman's victory is complete, but it is Pyrrhic. Both of them have sacrificed so much of what initially made them lovable to promote the symbiosis of mutual dependence that they scarcely make up one human being between them.

Paradoxically, at the stage where they have rejected the rest of the world—when they need each other most—the lovers have become least critical and aware of each other as unique individuals. The partner is just *there,* a completely necessary point of certainty in a bewildering and dangerous world. Under these conditions, acceptance of another is not a recognition of that person's integrity. Where need is so intense, there is no room in the lovers' minds for such a concept of dignity, either the other person's or one's own. Their lack of feeling for themselves makes them want to be absorbed by each other, and their lack of self-development and ability to express themselves individually makes it possible for them to be so engulfed.

Then, too, the lover's ultimate lack of interest in each other gives the lie to the romantic notion of addicted love as a kind of intense passion. The intensity that we see is that of desperation, not of a desire to know each other better. In healthy relationships the growing attachment to another person goes with a growing appreciation of that person; among these relationships are those inspiring love affairs where two people continually find new facets of each other to admire and delight in. In addiction what is apparent is not the intensity of passion, but its shallowness. There is no emotional risk in this sort of relationship, or, at least, the addict tries to eliminate that risk as much as possible. Because he is so vulnerable, what the addict is ideally striving for is perfect invulnerability. He only gives of himself in exchange for the promise of safety.

From this perspective, love at first sight becomes understandable in the sense that addiction to heroin on the first injection is understandable. A description by an addict in *The Road to H* of his first shot of heroin can apply equally well to the addicted lover's experience: "I felt I always wanted to feel the same way as I felt then." Both addicts have discovered something reassuring that they hope will never change. From the turmoil of their inner worlds, they recognize and latch on to the one sensation they have encountered which they feel can bring them peace.

Addicted lovers see each other more and more in order to maintain this secure state. They settle into each other, requiring ever more frequent interactions, until they find themselves consistently together, unable to endure significant separations. When they are apart, they long for each other. The two people have grown together to such an extent that, as in our example of Vicky and Bruce in Chapter 1, neither feels like a whole person when alone. This is the development of tolerance in a relationship. The excitement that originally brought the lovers together has dissipated, yet the lovers are less able than before to be critical of their arrangement. Even if their contact degenerates into constant conflict, they cannot part.

As with heroin and its irrecoverable euphoria, or cigarettes smoked in routine excess, something initially sought for pleasure is held more tightly *after* it ceases to provide enjoyment. Now it is being maintained for negative rather than positive reasons. The love partner must be there in order to satisfy a deep, aching need, or else the addict begins to feel withdrawal pain. His emotional security is so dependent on this other individual around whom he has organized his life, that to be deprived of the lover would be an utter shock to the system of his existence. If the world he has built with the lover is destroyed, he desperately tries to find some other partner so as to reestablish his artificial equilibrium. For as with heroin and other addictions, it is traumatic for addict lovers to reenter the broader world with which they have lost touch. "It was as though I was lost in a dream world," they say, "I thought everything we did was so cool, and now I see it was all so sick."

The addictive foundations of such a relationship are revealed when it ends in an abrupt, total, and vindictive breakup. Since the relationship has been the person's one essential contact point with life, its removal necessarily leaves him in a disoriented agony. Because the involvement has been so total, its ending must be violent. Thus it is possible for two people who have been the most intimate of friends suddenly to turn around and hate each other, because they have been thinking more of themselves than each other all along. The exploitation that has been going on throughout the relationship simply becomes more overt when the breakup occurs; then the two ex-lovers withdraw emotionally, perhaps to the point of trying to hurt each other. Such betrayals are most striking when a lover breaks off from an established relationship in favor of a new partner who better satisfies his or her needs. Only where "love" is a self-serving device can an external accident destroy the feelings that two people supposedly have for each other. The addict's haphazard, seemingly innocent couplings are more volatile and more destructive than those formed by people who maintain a questioning attitude toward their lives and relationships.

When there is a willingness to examine one's motivations and behavior toward others, the idea of addiction can be treated not as a threatening diagnosis, but as a means for heightening the awareness of some dangers which are very common in relationships. By establishing the antithesis of addiction, we can delineate an ideal with which to oppose the tendencies toward self-suppression and suppression of others that can appear in love. Just as it is important to keep the addictive elements that are somewhere present in all human contact from becoming full-blown addictions, it is at least equally valuable to expand the positive, life-seeking potential that also exists within any relationship.

A loving relationship, as Erich Fromm makes clear, is predicated on the psychological wholeness and security of the individuals who come to it. Out of their own integrity, the lovers seek a constant, nondisruptive growth for each other and for the relationship. Respecting the people they are and have been, and the lives they have formed, they try to maintain the prior interests and affections they have known. Where possible, they want to incorporate these things into the relationship, in order to broaden the world they share. They also reserve the time—and the feeling—to keep up those activities or friendships which it would be impossible or inappropriate to offer each other.

Because they are well-composed individuals before the relationship is conceived, their approach to that relationship is not frantic. They may be passionately attracted and want very much to become better friends, but they also recognize there are points at which pressure and intensity are hurtful to what they desire. They accept the need for privacy and for different viewpoints and tastes, they realize that forcing certain commitments or declarations is unwise and ultimately self-defeating, and they appreciate that it takes time for two people to know each other and to discover the extent and depth of their compatibility. They can now carry over to their relationship together the same good feelings that they have about themselves as whole, secure, and reasonable people.

What makes this relationship fulfilling to them, what convinces them that it is love, is their seeing that what they have together is particularly rewarding among the alternatives that each of them has. Rather than making the relationship dry or emotionless, this perspective enables them to give without reserve as mature people who know why they love and sacrifice, and why they can inspire these feelings in someone else. The fact that they are discriminating makes clear that their choice of each other has been made on both sides out of something other than desperation, and thus cannot be blown away by a chance wind. There is no reason for them to doubt that their feeling for each other is genuine, substantial, and long-lived, and hence there is no reluctance to explore life both within the relationship and outside it.

The impetus for this exploration is the life instinct of the individuals involved: They were growing beings before they met, and they entered upon their union as a positive choice for continued growth, only this time to be carried out in conjunction with—though not exclusively with—another person. The lovers approach the relationship itself as an opportunity for growth. They want to understand more about it, about themselves, and about each other. For this reason, a love relationship necessarily becomes deeper, out of the experience the lovers share, and out of their constant desire to uncover new facets of their connection and to better understand its old facets. Each of the lovers wants to become a better person and wants the other to become a better person, both out of a love for that person and a desire to see the best things happen to him or her, and out of the knowledge that this will make him or her—and oneself—a more stimulating, accomplished, happy person to love and be with.

For these things to come about, a loving relationship must be a helping relationship. The lovers have to support each other in their areas of weakness and their areas of strength, though with a different attitude toward each. The first is understood as something undesirable which it may be hard to change. The second is welcomed, admired, utilized, and expanded. In both cases, there is a loving attention, an appreciation of each other's individuality, and a striving to bring out what is best in each other. To do this may require gentle but persistent reminders, on the one hand, or encouragement and congratulations on the other. But the aim of both is the same: support for one's partner to become the best human being he or she is reasonably capable of being.

While it is impossible to overstate the role of nurturance and reassurance in love, it is also true that love itself is demanding and sometimes exhausting. The issue between addiction and love is whether the demands will be preordained and immediately self-serving, or whether they will be in the service of some larger sense of individual and mutual progress. The exhaustion that sometimes results from intense contact between two people can be due either to the self-disgust and despair of addiction, or to an impatience and dismay at seeing challenges go unmet. Human emotion necessarily involves risk. The risk may stem from the possibility that a rigid coupling will be cataclysmically disrupted by some new, unanticipated experience, or from the chance that two people who do not allow their lives to be totally defined will evolve in different directions. There is always this danger in love; to deny it is to deny love. But where the people involved are genuine and self-sustaining, and where they have been in love, the parting—made with whatever pain and regret—will not be the end of them as individuals or as loving friends.

This feeling of existential confidence in oneself and one's relationships is hard to achieve, and may only very rarely be encountered. A host of social forces work against it, and, as a result, it is unfortunately easier to find examples of addiction than of self-fulfillment in love.

SUGGESTIONS FOR FURTHER READING

GENERAL

Baker, Robert, and Elliston, Frederick, eds. *Philosophy and Sex.* Buffalo, N. Y.: Prometheus Books, 1975.

Taylor, Gordon. *Sex In History.* London: Panther Books, 1965

SEX ROLES AND STEREOTYPES

Gould, Carol C., and Wartofsky, Marx W., eds. *Women and Philosophy: Toward a Theory of Liberation.* New York: G. P. Putnam's Sons, 1976.

Greer, Germaine. *The Female Eunuch.* New York: McGraw-Hill, 1971.

Mead, Margaret. *Male and Female.* New York: William Morrow, 1949.

SEXUAL ETHICS

Atkinson, Ronald. *Sexual Morality.* New York: Harcourt Brace Jovanovich, 1965.

Cohen, Carl. "Sex, Birth Control, and Human Life." *Ethics* 79 (1969): Reprinted in Baker and Elliston, *Philosophy and Sex,* pp. 150–65.

Ellis, Albert. *Sex Without Guilt.* New York: Lyle Stuart, 1958.

Ellis, Havelock. *On Life and Sex: Essays of Love and Virtue.* Garden City, N. Y.: Garden City Publishing Co., 1947.

Guyon, René. *The Ethics of Sexual Acts.* New York: Alfred A. Knopf, 1948.

Lindsey, B. B., and Evans, W. *The Companionate Marriage.* New York: Arno, 1972.

Lippman, Walter. *A Preface to Morals.* New York: Macmillan, 1929, pp. 285–313.

Pope Paul VI. *Humanae Vitae.* Encyclical Letter. 1968.

Purtill, Richard L. *Thinking About Ethics.* Englewood Cliffs, N.J: Prentice-Hall, 1976, chapter 7.

Ruddick, Sara. "Better Sex." In *Philosophy and Sex,* edited by Baker and Elliston, pp. 83–104.

Wasserstrom, Richard A. "Is Adultery Immoral?" In *Today's Moral Problems,* edited by R. A Wasserstrom. New York: Macmillan, 1975.

Whiteley, C. H., and Whiteley, W. M. *Sex and Morals.* New York: Basic Books, 1967.

Wilson, John. *Logic and Sexual Morality.* Baltimore, Md.: Penguin Books, 1956.

SEXUAL PERVERSION

Anscombe, G. E. M. "Conception and Chastity." An Address to the Bristol Newman Circle. *The Human World,* May 1972, pp. 9–30.

Goldman, Alan H. "Plain Sex." *Philosophy and Public Affairs* 6 (1977), pp. 267–87.

Leiser, Burton M. *Liberty, Justice, and Morals: Contemporary Value Conflicts.* New York: Macmillan, 1973, chapters 2–4.

Margolis, Joseph. "The Question of Homosexuality." In *Philosophy and Sex,* edited by Baker and Elliston, pp. 288–304.

Slote, Michael. "Inapplicable Concepts and Sexual Perversion." In *Philosophy and Sex,* edited by Baker and Elliston, pp. 261–67.

Solomon, Robert. "Sex and Perversion." In *Philosophy and Sex,* edited by Baker and Elliston, pp. 268–87.

CONCEPTS AND CORRUPTIONS OF LOVE

Bertocci, Peter A. *Sex, Love, and the Person.* Mission, Kansas: Sheed & Ward, 1967.

Fromm, Erich. *The Art of Loving.* New York: Harper & Row, 1956.

Mayeroff, Milton. *On Caring.* New York: Harper & Row, 1971.

Outka, Gene. *Agape: An Ethical Analysis.* New Haven, Conn.: Yale University Press, 1972.

Singer, Irving. *The Nature of Love: Plato to Luther.* New York: Random House, 1966.

Taylor, Richard. *Good and Evil.* New York: Macmillan, 1970, chapters 15–17.

Williams, Daniel Day. *The Spirit and the Forms of Love.* New York: Harper & Row, 1968.

Chapter 8   Liberty and Its Limitation

Good laws function to safeguard individual and societal rights and liberties. They are intended to insure either that we are *free to* do something we wish or that we are *free from* some undesirable danger. But the law has two sides. By ensuring liberty to one set of persons, the law may restrict the liberty of others. A law by its very function is coercive because it places a limit on what was formerly an open option. It is often said that we trade some liberties either for the insurance of other liberties or for some form of protection by the state. The acceptability of these liberty-limiting laws ultimately depends upon the adequacy of the justification offered for them; and when an adequate justification is not forthcoming, the law can easily become an instrument of oppression. Despite this danger no one, save perhaps an anarchist, would deny that *some* laws should exist which restrict certain types of behavior. As Hobbes pointed out, without laws which bind everyone in society, life would be not only intolerable, but probably rather short. Yet which sorts of activities and which types of behavior are appropriate for legal restriction? In what instances does protection of the rights of individuals require that restrictions be placed on freedoms of others (and perhaps even on certain freedoms of those individuals themselves)? Every article in this chapter attempts to address some aspect of these two questions.

THE VALID LIMITS OF HUMAN LIBERTY

LIBERTY-LIMITING PRINCIPLES

We may begin our understanding of these questions by setting out in systematic fashion the moral grounds that are commonly advanced to justify the limitation of individual human liberties. Four "liberty-limiting principles," which are frequently defended and which form the organizing scheme for this chapter, are especially noteworthy:

1. The Harm Principle: A person's liberty is justifiably restricted to prevent *harm to others*.
2. The Principle of Paternalism: A person's liberty is justifiably restricted to prevent *harm to self*.
3. The Principle of Legal Moralism: A person's liberty is justifiably restricted to prevent that person's *immoral behavior*.
4. The Offense Principle: A person's liberty is justifiably restricted to prevent *offense to others*.

The harm principle is a widely accepted liberty-limiting principle. Indeed it is universally recognized that the law may properly interfere with a person's liberty when that person is causing harm to others. (The category of *harm to others* is here understood to cover not only personal injury but also damage to public institutions and the general social welfare.) But there remains much debate concerning whether any of the other three liberty-limiting principles is a *legitimate* liberty-limiting principle. Each section in this chapter addresses this issue by treating at least one of these principles.[1]

Each of these supplementary principles proclaims that there is a valid limit on one's *right* to do something. The paternalistic principle limits one's right to place oneself in a situation of danger; the offense principle can be used to limit the right to disseminate certain forms of printed material; and legal moralism may limit one's right to be sexually different. The subject of this chapter is whether restrictions—even if highly qualified—may ever *validly* be placed on one's right to freedom of expression in these ways. It might be said that the chapter deals with a conflict between our very firm belief that one ought to be free to do whatever one pleases (commensurate with a like freedom for others) and another firm belief that there are limits to the scope of this freedom.

HISTORY OF THESE PRINCIPLES

Questions about the scope of the harm principle and about whether the other principles are justified have been discussed by many moral philosophers. But John Stuart Mill's monograph *On Liberty* (1859) continues to occupy an especially prominent position. For this reason a selection from it is placed first in the present chapter.

Mill inquired after the nature and limits of social control over the individual. The following passage is his own summary of his central theses:

The object of this Essay is to assert one very simple principle. . . . That principle is, that the sole end for which mankind are warranted, individually or collectively, in interfering with the liberty of action of any of their number, is self-protection. That the only purpose for which power can be rightfully exercised over any member of a civilized community, against his will, is to prevent harm to others. His own good, either physical or moral, is not a sufficient warrant. He cannot rightfully be compelled to do or forbear because it will be better for him to do so, because it will make him happier, because in the opinion of others, to do so would be wise, or even right. These are good reasons for remonstrating with him, or reasoning with him or persuading him, or entreating him, but not for compelling him, or visiting him with any evil in case he do otherwise. To justify that, the conduct from which it is desired to deter him must be calculated to produce evil to someone else. The only part of the conduct of anyone, for which he is amenable to society, is that which concerns others. In the part which merely concerns himself, his independence is, of right, absolute.

Mill supposed he had articulated a general ethical principle which properly restricts social control over individual liberty, regardless whether such control is legal, religious, economic, or of some other type. Mill defended his views with the utilitarian argument that such a principle, however dangerous to prevailing social beliefs, would produce the best possible conditions both for social progress and for the development of individual talents.

It is important to notice that Mill's position explicitly declares all the aforementioned liberty-limiting principles except the harm principle to be morally unjustified. He quite directly rules out "legal moralism," for example. Since Mill, a great deal of ethical and legal literature has been generated concerning whether legal moralism is a valid justifying principle. Even in some prominent public debates, Mill's general position has often been quoted and defended. For example, in the 1950s in England the validity of legal restrictions on prostitution and homosexuality was publicly debated, and one crucial report, by the Wolfenden Committee, read at several points as if it were an application of Mill's general political-social theory As we shall see in some detail when we come to the topic of legal moralism in this Introduction, the committee maintained that while the law must govern matters of public harm and decency, *private* morality is not a matter to be legislated.

Until recently, in both law and ethics the concern with Mill's prohibition of legal moralism almost completely overshadowed discussion of his prohibition of the paternalistic and offense principles. Debates about paternalism during this same time seem to have been confined almost exclusively to special issues, such as the acceptability or unacceptability of involuntary hospitalization for reasons of insanity. Much the same is true of offensiveness, where virtually the sole issue was literary censorship. On the other hand, there has recently been a revival of interest in the literature of ethical theory on paternalism and offense—more so even than on legal moralism.

MILL'S CRITICS

On Liberty remains the most widely quoted, supported, and criticized document on the subject of social liberty. Many recent pieces of literature on paternalism, legal moralism, and censorship devote substantial space either to an attack upon or a defense of Mill's arguments. Some of Mill's critics deal with his general theory of the limits of liberty, rather than with any specific *application* to such problems as sexual freedom. One such critic is found in the opening section of this chapter. Richard Taylor attacks Mill's "principle of liberty" as useless, because it is so broad that it can (contrary to Mill's intentions) be used in support of virtually any criminal legislation. Taylor argues that Mill is so unspecific in his manner of drawing the line between proper and improper governmental intervention that a government is left free to draw that line wherever it wishes. Taylor also contends that if Mill's notion of harm is given a narrow interpretation (e.g., as bodily harm), then even serious nonbodily invasions by one person of another's freedom would not be restricted; but if Mill's notion of harm is given a broad definition, then virtually no freedom would be permitted at all. Taylor concludes that since Mill gives us no acceptable general principle(s) of liberty, we are still in need of an adequate statement of individual rights and of the proper interests of society.

PATERNALISM AND THE FREEDOM TO TAKE RISKS

The word *paternalism* is loosely used to refer to practices of treating individuals in the way a father treats his children. But in ethical theory the word has a more restricted meaning. "Paternalism" is used here to refer to practices which restrict the liberty of individuals, without their consent, where the justification for such actions is either the prevention of some harm they might do to themselves or the production of some benefit for them which they might not otherwise secure. The main ethical issue centers on whether paternalistic justifications are morally acceptable. The paternalistic principle, as it will be referred to here, says that limiting the liberty of individuals is justified if through *their own actions* they would produce serious harm *to themselves* or would fail to secure an important benefit. Those who support this general principle argue that it is justified to use the principle under certain conditions. Those who oppose paternalism argue that the principle itself is not a valid moral principle under any conditions.

Many kinds of actions, rules, and laws are commonly justified by appeal to the paternalistic principle. Examples include laws which protect drivers by requiring seat belts and motorcycle helmets, rules which do not permit a subject of biomedical research voluntarily to assume a risk when it is too great, court orders for blood transfusions when it is known that patients do not wish them, various forms of involuntary commitment to mental hospitals, and intervention to stop "rational" suicides. Laws are the usual public vehicle for the translation of paternalistic justifications into policy. No doubt this is so because laws serve the major function in most societies of placing a limit on what would otherwise be an unregulated state of affairs. But actions and policies can have paternalistic justifications, just as laws can.

Two law cases have been selected for inclusion in this section because they illustrate problems in contemporary law concerning whether paternalistic justifications are or are not valid. In the first case—*American Motorcycle Association v. Davids*—Judge Miller quotes Mill and relies extensively on his views about liberty. Miller argues that requiring motorcyclists and other riders to wear crash helmets for paternalistic reasons is an instance of a kind of logic which "could lead to unlimited [state] paternalism." He acknowledges that highway safety is a relevant reason for legal restrictions in cases where *other* persons are involved, but not where the cyclist alone is involved. He also quotes Justice Brandeis on "the right to be let alone" to the effect that we ought to be especially on guard to protect human liberty when government becomes overprotective by virtue of its beneficence. Much like the Wolfenden Report, Miller's legal opinion reads almost as if it were an immediate application of Mill's social philosophy.

However, this is not true of the second law case included in this chapter, *State v. Eitel*. In his opinion in this case, Judge Mann argues that "we ought to admit frankly that the purpose of the helmet [requirement] is to preserve the life and health of the cyclist"—not some other highway safety purpose. He thus construes the issue as precisely one of paternalism. Such paternalistic laws he finds ac-

ceptable, both on a common-sense basis and on a constitutional basis. He points out that suicide, for example, has been "a common-law crime for centuries." Judge Mann even appeals to Mill as a basis for his opinion, quoting Mill to the effect that "no person is an entirely isolated being," and therefore cannot perform actions free of responsibilities to other persons. It is clear that Judges Miller and Mann have fundamental disagreements on two points. First, they differ over their understandings of Mill, and second, they differ over whether suicide laws are relevant models of paternalistic justifications. In the end their opinions tend to show that the issue of paternalism is as unsettled in contemporary American constitutional law as it is in philosophy.

On a separate matter, there exist some interesting recent law cases where a patient has given informed consent to cessation or has rationally refused therapy. Courts have decided sometimes in favor of the patient and sometimes in favor of those who override patient wishes by administering the therapy. Some kinds of patient refusal, where doctors agree not to administer therapy, are generally accepted to be cases of (passive) euthanasia; yet euthanasia is illegal in many jurisdictions where such practices commonly occur. Justifications for overruling a patient's refusal of therapy or for not allowing a practice such as voluntary euthanasia need not be paternalistic; but they often are paternalistic, and in some cases it is hard to imagine what the justification could be if not paternalistic.

Notoriously, patients have refused treatments such as blood transfusions because their *religious* convictions do not permit such treatment. But ethical problems of patient refusal involve broader issues than those of freedom of religious exercise. A patient might refuse these same treatments for non-religious reasons, and the case might or might not involve emergency measures. Refusal of treatment also encompasses problems of proxy refusal in the case of children and certain classes of incompetent patients, though in most cases the focus is on refusal by competent adult patients. A major moral and legal question in life-threatening cases of refusal is whether a patient should be judicially compelled to accept such treatment. If the moral requirement of obtaining informed consent is a basic moral principle governing medical practice, it might seem that a patient's informed refusal would be decisive, whether the decision was reached on religious or non-religious grounds. Many regard such a right to refuse as fundamental in a free society, both in medical and other contexts. Moreover, there is a long tradition in the law that invasion of a person's body without valid consent is an assault; and doctors are as subject to this legal sanction as anyone else.

On the other hand, many persons do not think that patients' rights at the end of life include a right to "allow themselves to die." According to those who share this view, there are at least some circumstances where competent, non-consenting patients should be *required* to accept lifesaving medical therapies. Different reasons have been cited in defense of this view. Some regard a refusal of lifesaving treatment as patently unreasonable, even if "competently" decided. Others think the state often has a "compelling interest" in preventing such deaths. Another reason for forcing therapy, closely connected to that of unreasonableness, is overtly paternalistic: the competent adult person's liberty of choice is limited for his or her own good in order to prevent harm from befalling the person. This kind of paternalistic intervention occurred in the interesting case of Dr. Symmers, who—with complete information on his own case—asked his colleagues to take no steps to prolong his life if he suffered another cardiovascular collapse, yet was resuscitated against his wishes.[2] Still another reason for coercive treatment challenges the *validity* of the patient's refusal on the grounds that patients in life-and-death situations do not possess the requisite mental or emotional stability to make an informed choice.

Many physicians feel strongly that in these cases they are morally required (perhaps by the Hippocratic Oath) to prevent harm to patients. On the other hand, they also believe that it is a moral obligation to grant a patient's request whenever it is a true exercise of liberty. The issue here is not, of course, whether doctors acutally know what is best for their patients. The issue is whether the patient has a right to make such a decision (when informed and voluntary) even when it *is* harmful to that patient.

THE NATURE AND TYPES OF PATERNALISM

Some disagreement persists concerning proper use of the word "paternalism." If a definition is used which is as loose as H. L. A. Hart's—"the protection of people against themselves"—misunderstandings readily follow. Legislation intended to help citizens protect themselves from inadvertent acts, such as mutilating their hands in garbage disposals, would on this definition seem paternalistic. In his article reprinted in this chapter, Gerald Dworkin has provided a more careful definition: paternalism is "the interference with a person's liberty of action justified by reasons referring exclusively to the welfare, good, happiness, needs, interests or values of the person being coerced." As we shall later see, the selection by Beauchamp in this chapter challenges some aspects of Dworkin's understanding of paternalism.

Joel Feinberg[3] has distinguished two types of paternalism, one based on protection from self-inflicted harm and the other based on the production of benefit. While Feinberg elaborates this distinction exclusively in regard to *state* coercion, his analysis may be adapted to fit all forms of paternalism by distinguishing the following two types of paternalism:

1. Harm paternalism: The justification of liberty limitation to protect individuals from self-inflicted harm.
2. Benefit paternalism: The justification of liberty limitation to benefit the persons whose liberty is limited.

This distinction is important since it is widely held that benefit paternalism is more difficult to justify than harm paternalism. However, Feinberg has also distinguished two other forms of paternalism, and this second distinction is of even greater significance than the first. The distinction is between strong and weak forms of paternalism, where the *weak form* is explained as follows:

[One] has the right to prevent self-regarding conduct only when it is substantially nonvoluntary or when temporary intervention is necessary to establish whether it is voluntary or not.

The class of nonvoluntary cases includes cases where there is consent but not adequately informed consent. The *strong form* holds that it is proper to protect or benefit a person by liberty-limiting measures *even when his contrary choices are informed and voluntary.*

A substantial problem is generated by this second distinction. Virtually everyone acknowledges that some forms of weak paternalism are justified (e.g., preventing a person under the influence of LSD from killing himself). If, then, *some* forms of paternalism are justified, the problem of paternalism for ethical theory is that of deciding under what conditions the paternalistic principle may be used and under what conditions it may not be used. The difficulty with this approach is that weak paternalism may not be paternalism in any interesting sense, because it may not be a liberty-limiting principle which is *independent* of the harm principle. For this reason some writers have restricted the meaning of the word "paternalism" to strong paternalism, as does Beauchamp in this section. The strategy he employs is to show that when the harm principle is properly understood, the paternalistic principle is morally useless. Still other writers, in contrast, have *expanded* the word "paternalism" to cover weak, strong, and *other* (alleged) types of paternalism.

In the literature on paternalism, two main positions have been adopted: (1) "justified paternalism" and (2) "anti-paternalism." Dworkin supports the first of these views in this chapter, while Mill represents the latter and Beauchamp comes to Mill's defense (against Dworkin's attack).

The Justification of Paternalism

Any supporter of a wide-reaching paternalistic principle will specify with care precisely which goods, needs, and interests warrant paternalistic protection. In most recent formulations, it has been said that the state is justified in interfering with a person's liberty if by its interference it protects the person against his own actions where those actions are extremely and unreasonably risky (waterfall-rafting, for example), or are potentially dangerous and irreversible in effect (as some drugs are). Even among supporters of justified paternalism it is widely accepted that it takes a heavy burden of justification to limit free actions by competent persons, especially since there is never direct subject consent (even if there might be proxy consent or direct consent by agreement to be placed under a paternalistic power). According to this position, paternalism could be justified only if the evils prevented from occurring to the person are greater than the evils (if any) caused by interference with their liberty, and if it is universally justified under relevantly similar circumstances to always treat persons in this way. Dworkin defends this sort of position in the present chapter. Dworkin believes that paternalism should be looked at as a form of "social insurance policy" which fully rational persons would take out in order to protect themselves. Such persons would know, for example, that they might be strongly tempted at times to make decisions which are far-reaching, potentially dangerous and irreversible, while at other times they might suffer extreme psychological or social pressures to do something which they truly believe to be too risky to be worth performing (e.g., where one's honor is put in question by being challenged to fight). In still other cases Dworkin believes there might be dangers which persons do not sufficiently understand or appreciate but which are relevant to their conduct (e.g,, one might not know the facts about research on smoking). Dworkin concludes that we all ought to agree to a limited grant of legislative power to enact paternalistic laws.

Anti-Paternalistic Individualism

Some believe that paternalism is never justified, whatever the conditions. This position is basically the one supported by Mill in the opening essay in this chapter, though it can be supported on grounds other than the utilitarian ones offered by Mill. While it is now widely believed that Mill's argument fails in one or more crucial ways, there have been attempts to employ his strategy of permitting only the harm principle as the basis for justified limitations of liberty. Roughly this position is defended in the present chapter by Beauchamp. Against Dworkin he argues that Mill's original standard, the harm principle, is sufficient by itself to insure adequate protection by the state against harms that might befall individuals. He agrees with

Judge Miller that the principle of paternalism ought not to be recognized as a valid principle for restricting liberty, because it allows (in principle) too much restriction. It is the serious adverse consequences of giving such power to the state that motivates Beauchamp to reject Dworkin's view that the fully rational person would accept paternalism. In the end their disagreement seems to turn on whether acceptance of the principle of paternalism as valid would create a situation where, as Dworkin puts it, the "ignorance, ill-will and stupidity" of those in power might be used to override legitimate, though risky, exercises of freedom. Dworkin believes the risk of such unwarranted interference is worth taking in order to gain a kind of personal and social insurance policy, and Beauchamp believes the stakes are too high to make it worth the risk.

LEGAL MORALISM AND SEXUAL LIBERTIES

We are all opposed to having a moral view alien to our own forced on us by an external authority. Hence, when we approach discussions of legal moralism, or the legal enforcement of morality as such, we are immediately inclined to be sceptical that it can be justified. On the other hand, the justification of many laws in our society is based on some form of moral belief, and this fact indicates that there is moral content already in our laws. The harm principle itself is a moral principle which provides the primary basis for massive numbers of laws; and certainly immoral conduct is no trivial matter, as we all know from our own reactions to the indiscretions of politicians. Perhaps, then, it is legitimate to enforce moral views as such *if* they are of overwhelming importance to moral stability in a society. Perhaps what are known as "morals offenses," or offenses against morality and human decency, should be subject to legal sanctions even though they do not actually produce physical or psychological *harm* to the individuals involved.

These are questions concerning what *kinds* of moral content and what *degree* of moral content should be allowed in our laws. The issue is whether, in a pluralistic society, deviant moral conduct of any sort, however serious and controversial, is sufficient justification for limiting freedom by making such behavior illegal. This issue is especially troublesome when sexual acts are widely regarded in a society as sexual perversions, and yet are also purely private affairs involving only consenting adults. Homosexuality is the most frequently mentioned example, but the ethical problems involving sanctions on sexual activity extend far beyond this single issue.

CRIMES WITHOUT VICTIMS

In considering how laws should function with reference to moral questions, especially those focused on sexual conduct, it is useful to distinguish between (1) crimes in which there is no victim because no person is directly harmed and everyone involved voluntarily consents, and (2) crimes in which there is a victim. Prostitution, homosexuality, gambling, smoking marijuana, and sexual stimulation in "massage parlors" are now familiar examples of crimes without victims. Rape—whether heterosexual or homosexual—is clearly a crime which does have a victim. The ethical issue is whether crimes without victims should be considered crimes at all. Perhaps legal restrictions on homosexuality, for example, constitute unwarranted restrictions of liberty. It may be that even if the citizens of a state consider homosexual acts perverse, society should nonetheless allow individuals the personal freedom to engage in homosexual relations (and perhaps even marriage) between consenting adults, in the same way it allows such relations between heterosexual partners.

Each of the following actions—which are not limited to matters of sexual morality—has been considered a candidate for legislation on grounds of its immoral nature:

1. Private use of pornographic films.
2. Private use of drugs which have no socially harmful consequences.
3. Voluntary euthanasia.
4. Prostitution.
5. Gambling.
6. Suicide.
7. Homosexual behavior.

Since Mill's *On Liberty* was published, many attempts either to enforce morals or to eliminate existing enforcements have been made, but the Wolfenden Committee Report mentioned previously has become the classical case. This committee had been established in 1954 in response to complaints that aspects of English law dealing with homosexuality and prostitution were ineffective and unjust. The committee recommended both that English criminal law be amended so that homosexuality not be a crime, if engaged in by consenting adults, and that there be no change in existing laws (which did not hold acts of prostitution intrinsically illegal). Their recommendations at several points noticeably resembled Mill's views. The committee first argued that firm distinctions should be drawn between crime and sin and between public decency and private morality. They then maintained that while the law must govern matters of public decency, private morality is not a matter to be legislated since "the function of the criminal law" is "to preserve public order and decency, to protect the citizen from what is offensive or injurious, and to provide sufficient safeguards against exploitation and corruption of others." They further maintained that it should not be considered the purpose of the law "to intervene in the private lives of citizens, or to seek to enforce any pattern of behavior" unless the above outlined purposes of the law were shown relevant. The clear intent of the committee was to say that unless it could be shown that public indecency or personal exploitation were involved, the law should not prohibit activities such as homosexuality and prostitution. Their justification for this recommendation, which is both legal and ethical in character, was simply that the state does not and should not have the right to restrict any private moral actions which affect only the consenting adults involved. The state should not have this right, they argued, because of the supreme importance both social ethics and the law place on "individual freedom of choice and action in matters of private morality . . . which is, in brief and crude terms, not the law's business."

Lord Patrick Devlin is the most prominent spokesman in opposition to both Mill and the Wolfenden Report. His article, reprinted below, is in many respects another historical landmark. Lord Devlin argues that society has the right to enforce "public morality" because society cannot exist, or

at least remain secure, without preserving a basic community of moral ideas which determine how citizens are to control their lives. The community's common moral convictions concerning behavior constitute, for Devlin, its "moral structure." He allows that society must tolerate "the maximum individual freedom that is consistent with the integrity of society." But he also maintains that society is justified, as a matter of principle, in legislating against privately conducted immoral conduct *if* that conduct is of the sort likely to be injurious to society by endangering the moral order of society necessary for its preservation. Adultery, for example, cannot be tolerated because it would undermine the institution of marriage, which Devlin takes to be indispensable for the stability of society. He also contends that homosexuality and prostitution undermine the moral fabric of society. Each can quite properly be legislated against, he argues, because the integrity and very existence of society are threatened if such laws do not exist.

H. L. A. Hart has been Devlin's leading critic, as well as a selective defender of both Mill and the Wolfenden Report. He argues that a heavy burden of justification, not merely proof of moral wrongness, is required for legislation against acts such as homosexuality, because the coercive power of laws may create frustration and misery of a special degree for those legislated against. Hart regards Devlin's conclusion that the fabric of society is endangered as insufficiently argued. He thinks it is merely a disguised conservative defense of the conventional moral order and that it attempts to sweep all legal restrictions against allegedly immoral practices (e.g., bigamy, killings, and dishonesty) under the same rug, as if there were no morally relevant difference between them and as if morality were a single, indivisible whole without separate justifications for its separate principles. Hart also distinguishes between *positive* morality (that actually accepted in a culture) and *critical* morality (those principles used to criticize both social institutions and rules of positive morality). He argues that Devlin seriously confuses the two, and that this confusion leads to a mistaken general view of *legal* enforcement. While Hart is willing to agree with Devlin that the loss of certain shared moral principles might well threaten the very existence of some society, he argues that there is no empirical evidence to indicate that sexually deviant practices lead to a disintegration of common morality. Unlike treason, Hart reasons, sexual deviancy neither threatens the existence of society nor tends to undermine respect for morality in general. Indeed, Hart thinks changes in sexual laws are more analogous to constitutional amendments which are intended to advance a culture's appreciation and toleration of individual freedoms.

In the selections located in this chapter immediately prior to those by Devlin and Hart, two judges dispute the legal merits of a Virginia statute governing sodomy and homosexuality. The arguments they advance, though resting substantially on a Constitutional basis, mirror many of the same themes found in Devlin and Hart. In the opening and majority opinion, written by Senior Circuit Judge Bryan, it is argued that Virginia's statute making sodomy a crime is not unconstitutional and is warranted by the dangers inherent in not having such a statute. Judge Bryan argues that the Constitution of the United States closely protects marital privacy but *not* those sexual intimacies outside of marriage which the law "has always forbidden and which can have no claim to social protection" (the words of Justice Harlan). Judge Bryan clearly believes a state has the right to regulate not only homosexuality, but adultery, fornication, and incest as well. He seems to have two reasons for this view. The first is that such regulations are not unconstitutional and have a long history in law. The second is that the state does have a compelling interest in such regulation, since children can be harmed by exposure to such practices. Judge Bryan therefore thinks such crimes are not "victimless."

In a dissenting opinion which forms the second article in this section, District Judge Merhige argues that there is no Constitutional basis for the proscription of sexual intimacies between consenting adults. In sharp difference from Judge Bryan's interpretation of previous Supreme Court cases on privacy, Judge Merhige believes such cases stand "for the principle that every individual has a right to be free from unwarranted governmental intrusion into one's decisions on private matters of intimate concern." Since he takes all choices of sexual partners to be such a private matter, he believes the Virginia statute to be un-

constitutional. Judge Merhige regards such freedoms as specifically guaranteed by the Due Process clause. He does acknowledge that no such freedom is beyond state control *if* a compelling state interest such as contact with minors or public displays is involved. However, the judge believes that in the present case, and in the case of homosexual relations in general, no evidence has been provided "which even impliedly demonstrate[s] that homosexuality causes society any significant harm."

ARGUMENTS FOR AND AGAINST LEGAL MORALISM

In the literature on moral enforcement thus far discussed, there are two main positions on the acceptability of the principle of legal moralism: Lord Devlin believes it can be justified and attempts to specify the conditions under which it is justified; Mill is totally opposed to any use of legal moralism, and Hart responds to Devlin in Mill's defense. The major issue between these disputing parties, as by now should be evident, is whether the immorality of any human action can ever, *solely because immoral*, provide a sufficient justification for making that type of action illegal. The following are the major arguments used in support of these positions.

The Arguments for Legal Moralism

Two main arguments are advanced in support of legal moralism. The first is an argument from the principle of democratic rule. The argument is that if some practice is regarded as an outrageously immoral action by the vast majority of citizens in a community, this in itself is sufficient to justify making the behavior illegal. It is maintained that both the principle of democratic rule and the institution of morality must be protected even at the expense of a risk to individual liberties. In democracies it is the weight of community sentiment which makes the law, and laws provide the standards of justice. Any majority-sanctioned law is valid and appropriate, unless unconstitutional. There is no tradition in Western democracies, ethical or legal, which stipulates that morality cannot be legislated against. For these reasons the supporters of this view conclude that a society is perfectly justified in protecting itself by legislating against at least some immoral actions. Lord Devlin pays tribute, if not full allegiance, to this view when he concludes that: (1) a society is partially constituted by a "community of ideas," including moral ideas "about the way its members *should* behave and govern their lives"; and (2) if homosexuality is "a vice so abominable that its mere presence is an offense . . . I do not see how society can be denied the right to eradicate it."

The second argument for legal moralism is based on the social necessity of morality. It is argued that the legal enforcement of morals is justified whenever threats to moral rules challenge the very order of society itself. The thesis is that just as law and order through government are necessary to a stable society, so moral conformity is essential to a society's very continuation. Sometimes the justification seems to be purely pragmatic ("if you want to survive as a society, then you must preserve your moral canons"), while at other times it seems to be an argument from society's inherent right to protect its existence. On either view, individual liberties are said to be protected when but only when they do not erode those standards essential to the life of society. All supporters of this view agree that we ought to be cautious in declaring a practice intolerably immoral. But the point remains, they insist, that we have the *right* to pass criminal laws enforcing morality if they are required. Lord Devlin again pays allegiance to this view when he argues that "society may use the law to preserve morality in the same way as it uses it to safeguard *anything* else that is essential to its existence."

The Argument Against Legal Moralism

This argument springs from Mill's principle that state coercion is never permissible unless an individual's actions produce harm to others. That is, the harm principle alone justifies limitation of individual liberty. Mill's view requires tolerance of all ethical perspectives, it is argued, and is not in the slightest in conflict with principles which require legal protection from harmful acts. Although there are several forms of this argument, the thrust of each is the following: Any attempt to make immoral conduct illegal (criminal), when the conduct is *not harmful* to others, is unacceptable because it directly violates the principle of individual liberty. But suppose the conduct were harmful. If one is to be justifiably punished under law it must be because one's action *harms* someone else, not because a particular *moral practice* is involved. That any particular moral belief or practice is involved should be an irrelevant factor, so far as the law is concerned. According to this argument, the law should never be based on views that a certain moral perspective is intolerable, but rather should be based on the view that harmful treatment is always intolerable. Though he never quite phrases his point this way, Mill seems generally to support this line of thought, as does the Wolfenden Report.

Tom L. Beauchamp

NOTES

1. Joel Feinberg's discussion of these principles provided a model for these formulations. *Social Philosophy* (Englewood Cliffs, N.J.: Prentice-Hall, 1973), Chapters 2–3, esp. p. 33. Principles 2–4 are said to be supplementary liberty-limiting principles, because they supplement the grounds for restricting liberty presented by the harm principle.

2. Jay Katz, Alexander Morgan Capron, and Eleanor Swift Glass, eds., *Experimentation with Human Beings* (New York: Russell Sage Foundation, 1972), p. 709.

3. Feinberg, *Social Philosophy,* pp. 33ff; and "Legal Paternalism," *Canadian Journal of Philosophy* 1 (1971): 105–24, esp. 113–16.

68. ON LIBERTY

John Stuart Mill

INTRODUCTORY

The struggle between Liberty and Authority is the most conspicuous feature in the portions of history with which we are earliest familiar, particularly in that of Greece, Rome, and England. But in old times this contest was between subjects, or some classes of subjects, and the government. By liberty was meant protection against the tyranny of the political rulers. The rulers were conceived (except in some of the popular governments of Greece) as in a necessarily antagonistic position to the people whom they ruled. They consisted of a governing One, or a governing tribe or caste, who derived their authority from inheritance or conquest, who, at all events, did not hold it at the pleasure of the governed, and whose supremacy men did not venture, perhaps did not desire, to contest, whatever precautions might be taken against its oppressive exercise. Their power was regarded as necessary, but also as highly dangerous; as a weapon which they would attempt to use against their subjects, no less than against external enemies. To prevent the weaker members of the community from being preyed upon by innumerable vultures, it was needful that there should be an animal of prey stronger than the rest, commissioned to keep them down. But as the king of the vultures would be no less bent upon preying on the flock, than any of the minor harpies, it was indispensable to be in a perpetual attitude of defence against his beak and claws. The aim, therefore, of patriots, was to set limits to the power which the ruler should be suffered to exercise over the community; and this limitation was what they meant by liberty. It was attempted in two ways. First, by obtaining a recognition of certain immunities, called political liberties or rights, which it was to be regarded as a

From John Stuart Mill, *On Liberty,* originally published in 1859 in England.

breach of duty in the ruler to infringe, and which if he did infringe, specific resistance, or general rebellion, was held to be justifiable. A second, and generally a later expedient, was the establishment of constitutional checks; by which the consent of the community, or of a body of some sort, supposed to represent its interests, was made a necessary condition to some of the more important acts of the governing power. To the first of these modes of limitation, the ruling power, in most European countries, was compelled, more or less, to submit. It was not so with the second; and to attain this, or when already in some degree possessed, to attain it more completely, became everywhere the principal object of the lovers of liberty. And so long as mankind were content to combat one enemy by another, and to be ruled by a master, on condition of being guaranteed more or less efficaciously against his tyranny, they did not carry their aspirations beyond this point.

A time, however, came, in the progress of human affairs, when men ceased to think it a necessity of nature that their governors should be an independent power, opposed in interest to themselves. It appeared to them much better that the various magistrates of the State should be their tenants or delegates, revocable at their pleasure. In that way alone, it seemed, could they have complete security that the powers of government would never be abused to their disadvantage. By degrees, this new demand for elective and temporary rulers became the prominent object of the exertions of the popular party, wherever any such party existed; and superseded, to a considerable extent, the previous efforts to limit the power of rulers. As the struggle proceeded for making the ruling power emanate from the periodical choice of the ruled, some persons began to think that too much importance had been attached to the limitation of the power itself. *That* (it might seem) was a resource against rulers whose interests were habitually opposed to those of the people. What was now wanted was, that the rulers should be identified with the people; that their interest and will should be the interest and will of the nation. The nation did not need to be protected against its own will. There was no fear of its tyrannizing over itself. . . .

. . . The will of the people . . . practically means, the will of the most numerous or the most active *part* of the people; the majority, or those who succeed in making themselves accepted as the majority: the people, consequently, *may* desire to oppress a part of their number; and precautions are as much needed against this, as against any other abuse of power. The limitation, therefore, of the power of government over individuals, loses none of its importance when the holders of power are regularly accountable to the community, that is, to the strongest party therein. This view of things, recommending itself equally to the intelligence of thinkers and to the inclination of those important classes in European society to whose real or supposed interests democracy is adverse, has had no difficulty in establishing itself; and in political speculations 'the tyranny of the majority' is now generally included among the evils against which society requires to be on its guard.

Like other tyrannies, the tyranny of the majority was at first, and is still vulgarly, held in dread, chiefly as operating through the acts of the public authorities. But reflecting persons perceived that when society is itself the tyrant—society collectively over the separate individuals who compose it —its means of tyrannizing are not restricted to the acts which it may do by the hands of its political functionaries. Society can and does execute its own mandates: and if it issues wrong mandates instead of right, or any mandates at all in things with which it ought not to meddle, it practises a social tyranny more formidable than many kinds of political oppression, since, though not usually upheld by such extreme penalties, it leaves fewer means of escape, penetrating much more deeply into the details of life, and enslaving the soul itself. Protection, therefore, against the tyranny of the magistrate is not enough: there needs protection also against the tyranny of the prevailing opinion and feeling; against the tendency of society to impose, by other means than civil penalties, its own ideas and practices as rules of conduct on those who dissent from

them; to fetter the development, and, if possible, prevent the formation, of any individuality not in harmony with its ways, and compel all characters to fashion themselves upon the model of its own. There is a limit to the legitimate interference of collective opinion with individual independence: and to find that limit, and maintain it against encroachment, is as indispensable to a good condition of human affairs, as protection against political despotism.

But though this proposition is not likely to be contested in general terms, the practical question, where to place the limit—how to make the fitting adjustment between individual independence and social control—is a subject on which nearly everything remains to be done. All that makes existence valuable to any one, depends on the enforcement of restraints upon the actions of other people. Some rules of conduct, therefore, must be imposed, by law in the first place, and by opinion on many things which are not fit subjects for the operation of law. What these rules should be, is the principal question in human affairs; but if we except a few of the most obvious cases, it is one of those which least progress has been made in resolving. . . .

. . . There is, in fact, no recognised principle by which the propriety or impropriety of government interference is customarily tested. People decide according to their personal preferences. Some, whenever they see any good to be done, or evil to be remedied, would willingly instigate the government to undertake the business; while others prefer to bear almost any amount of social evil, rather than add one to the departments of human interests amenable to governmental control. And men range themselves on one or the other side in any particular case, according to this general direction of their sentiments; or according to the degree of interest which they feel in the particular thing which it is proposed that the government should do, or according to the belief they entertain that the government would, or would not, do it in the manner they prefer; but very rarely on account of any opinion to which they consistently adhere, as to what things are fit to be done by a government. And it seems to me that in consequence of this absence of rule or principle, one side is at present as often wrong as the other; the interference of government is, with about equal frequency improperly invoked and improperly condemned.

The object of this Essay is to assert one very simple principle, as entitled to govern absolutely the dealings of society with the individual in the way of compulsion and control, whether the means used be physical force in the form of legal penalties, or the moral coercion of public opinion. That principle is, that the sole end for which mankind are warranted, individually or collectively, in interfering with the liberty of action of any of their number, is self-protection. That the only purpose for which power can be rightfully exercised over any member of a civilized community, against his will, is to prevent harm to others. His own good, either physical or moral, is not a sufficient warrant. He cannot rightfully be compelled to do or forbear because it will be better for him to do so, because it will make him happier, because, in the opinions of others, to do so would be wise, or even right. These are good reasons for remonstrating with him, or reasoning with him, or persuading him, or entreating him, but not for compelling him, or visiting him with any evil in case he do otherwise. To justify that, the conduct from which it is desired to deter him, must be calculated to produce evil to some one else. The only part of the conduct of any one, for which he is amenable to society, is that which concerns others. In the part which merely concerns himself, his independence is, of right, absolute. Over himself, over his own body and mind, the individual is sovereign.

It is, perhaps, hardly necessary to say that this doctrine is meant to apply only to human beings in the maturity of their faculties. We are not speaking of children, or of young persons below the age which the law may fix as that of manhood or womanhood. Those who are still in a state to require being taken care of by others, must be protected against their own actions as well as against external injury. For the same reason, we may leave out of consideration those backward states of society in which the race itself may be considered as in its nonage. The early difficulties in the way of spontaneous progress are so great, that there is seldom any choice of means for overcoming them; and a ruler full of the spirit of improvement is warranted in the use of any expedients that will attain an end, perhaps otherwise unattainable. Despotism is a legitimate mode of government in dealing with barbarians, provided the end be their improvement. . . .

No society in which these liberties are not, on the whole, respected, is free, whatever may be its form of government; and none is completely free in which they do not exist absolute and unqualified. The only freedom which deserves the name, is that of pursuing our own good in our own way, so long as we do not attempt to deprive others of theirs, or impede their efforts to obtain it. Each is the proper guardian of his own health, whether bodily, or mental and spiritual. Mankind are greater gainers by suffering each other to live as seems good to themselves, than by compelling each to live as seems good to the rest. . . .

OF THE LIBERTY OF THOUGHT AND DISCUSSION

The time, it is to be hoped, is gone by, when any defence would be necessary of the 'liberty of the press' as one of the securities against corrupt or tyrannical government. No argument, we may suppose, can now be needed, against permitting a legislature or an executive, not identified in interest with the people, to prescribe opinions to them, and determine what doctrines or what arguments they shall be allowed to hear. This aspect of the question, besides, has been so often and so triumphantly enforced by preceding writers, that it needs not be specially insisted on in this place. Though the law of England, on the subject of the press, is as servile to this day as it was in the time of the Tudors, there is little danger of its being actually put in force against political discussion, except during some temporary panic, when fear of insurrection drives ministers and judges from their propriety; and, speaking generally, it is not, in constitutional countries, to be apprehended, that the government, whether completely responsible to the people or not, will often attempt to control the expression of opinion, except when in doing so it makes itself the organ of the general intolerance of the public. Let us suppose, therefore, that the government is entirely at one with the people, and never thinks of exerting any power of coercion unless in agreement with what it conceives to be their voice. But I deny the right of the people to exercise such coercion, either by themselves or by their government. The power itself is illegitimate. The best government has no more title to it than the worst. It is as noxious, or more noxious, when exerted in accordance with public opinion, than when in opposition to it. If all mankind minus one, were of one opinion, and only one person were of the contrary opinion, mankind would be no more justified in silencing that one person, than he, if he had the power, would be justified in silencing mankind. Were an opinion a personal possession of no value except to the owner; if to be obstructed in the enjoyment of it were simply a private injury, it would make some difference whether the injury was inflicted only on a few persons or on many. But the peculiar evil of silencing the expression of an opinion is, that it is robbing the human race; posterity as well as the existing generation; those who dissent from the opinion, still more than those who hold it. If the opinion is right, they are deprived of the opportunity of exchanging error for truth: if wrong, they lose, what is almost as great a benefit, the clearer perception and livelier impression of truth, produced by its collision with error. . . .

OF THE LIMITS TO THE AUTHORITY OF SOCIETY OVER THE INDIVIDUAL

What, then, is the rightful limit to the sovereignty of the individual over himself? Where does the authority of society begin? How much of human life should be assigned to individuality, and how much to society?

Each will receive its proper share, if each has that which more particularly concerns it. To individuality should belong the part of life in which it is chiefly the individual that is interested; to society, the part which chiefly interests society.

Though society is not founded on a contract, and though no good purpose is answered by inventing a contract in order to deduce social obligations from it, every one who receives the protection of society owes a return for the benefit, and the fact of living in society renders it indispensable that each should be found to observe a certain line of conduct towards the rest. This conduct consists, first, in not injuring the interests of one another; or rather certain interests, which, either by express legal provision or by tacit understanding, ought to be con-

sidered as rights; and secondly, in each person's bearing his share (to be fixed on some equitable principle) of the labours and sacrifices incurred for defending the society or its members from injury and molestation. These conditions society is justified in enforcing, at all costs to those who endeavour to withhold fulfilment. Nor is this all that society may do. The acts of an individual may be hurtful to others, or wanting in due consideration for their welfare, without going the length of violating any of their constituted rights. The offender may then be justly punished by opinion, though not by law. As soon as any part of a person's conduct affects prejudicially the interests of others, society has jurisdiction over it, and the question whether the general welfare will or will not be promoted by interfering with it, becomes open to discussion. But there is no room for entertaining any such question when a person's conduct affects the interests of no persons besides himself, or needs not affect them unless they like (all the persons concerned being of full age, and the ordinary amount of understanding). In all such cases there should be perfect freedom, legal and social, to do the action and stand the consequences. . . .

But the strongest of all the arguments against the interference of the public with purely personal conduct, is that when it does interfere, the odds are that it interferes wrongly, and in the wrong place. On questions of social morality, of duty to others, the opinion of the public, that is, of an overruling majority, though often wrong, is likely to be still oftener right; because on such questions they are only required to judge of their own interests; of the manner in which some mode of conduct, if allowed to be practised, would affect themselves. But the opinion of a similar majority, imposed as a law on the minority, on questions of self-regarding conduct, is quite as likely to be wrong as right; for in these cases public opinion means, at the best, some people's opinion of what is good or bad for other people; while very often it does not even mean that; the public, with the most perfect indifference, passing over the pleasure or convenience of those whose conduct they censure, and considering only their own preference. There are many who consider as an injury to themselves any conduct which they have a distaste for, and resent it as an outrage to their feelings; as a religious bigot, when charged with disregarding the religious feelings of others, has been known to retort that they disregard his feelings, by persisting in their abominable worship or creed. But there is no parity between the feeling of a person for his own opinion, and the feeling of another who is offended at his holding it; no more than between the desire of a thief to take a purse, and the desire of the right owner to keep it. And a person's taste is as much his own peculiar concern as his opinion or his purse. It is easy for any one to imagine an ideal public, which leaves the freedom and choice of individuals in all uncertain matters undisturbed, and only requires them to abstain from modes of conduct which universal experience has condemned. But where has there been seen a public which set any such limit to its censorship? or when does the public trouble itself about universal experience? In its interferences with personal conduct it is seldom thinking of anything but the enormity of acting or feeling differently from itself; and this standard of judgment, thinly disguised, is held up to mankind as the dictate of religion and philosophy, by nine-tenths of all moralists and speculative writers. These teach that things are right because they are right; because we feel them to be so. They tell us to search in our own minds and hearts for laws of conduct binding on ourselves and on all others. What can the poor public do but apply these instructions, and make their own personal feelings of good and evil, if they are tolerably unaminous in them, obligatory on all the world? . . .

69. MILL'S CLASSICAL DEFENSE OF LIBERTY

Richard Taylor

The problem of liberty is first of all a problem concerning the creation of criminal law—the prohibitory part of the law that attaches penalties to certain behavior. Civil law is related to liberty in a quite different way, generally providing the means to the ends people seek, rather than restricting them through the definition of crimes.

Thus, legislation involves many things, some of overwhelming importance. It is through legislation that agents of government spread poisons over our land, killing insects and, of course, birds and fish; that they despoil our fields and forests to build big highways; they also build and equip universities, care for the poor, regulate industry, communications, and so on, endlessly. But legislation of this kind, important as it is, does not bear directly on the problem of liberty. We shall instead be concerned with legislation, the explicit (and not the incidental) object of which is to regulate conduct.

From Richard Taylor, *Freedom, Anarchy, and the Law: An Introduction to Political Philosophy,* © 1973, pp. 55–60. Reprinted by permission of Prentice-Hall, Inc., Englewood Cliffs, New Jersey.

This is law that defines felonies, misdemeanors and offenses.

Our first question, then, comes to this: To what extent is such legislation justified? Is it justified at all? Since all such law delimits the natural freedom of the individual, is any such law proper? If so, then by what principle, if any? Is there any conduct which may *not* properly be forbidden by law? If, for example, assault may properly be forbidden under threat by the state, may not also the wearing of strange dress, the desecration of symbols, the eating of shellfish or insects, and so on? At what line, if any, may we draw the reasonable limits of social freedom and those of criminal legislation?

It is widely thought that this question was answered once and for all by John Stuart Mill, and that all that is needed henceforth is an appreciation of his grand principle of liberty and an understanding of the invincible arguments by which he defended it. Even men of such sophisticated legal and philosophical thought as H. L. A. Hart suppose that Mill has defined the principle of liberty, and that his successors need only to expound and defend it.[1] Hardly any students pass through college without having read the famous essay *On Liberty,* and the prevailing view is that it leaves little more to be said.

This is not so. Mill's essay is a declamation and not a cogent philosophical treatise. As an ideological tract it is, perhaps, inspiring. Some can perhaps derive from it a certain attitude, a certain partisan feeling for freedom, an appreciation of philosophy in the service of a noble cause; but one does not in fact find there a coherent principle of liberty. Our first task will be to establish that point and then try to supply the answer for which Mill was groping.

THE FAILURE OF MILL'S PRINCIPLE

It will not be necessary to review the whole of Mill's *On Liberty* because the error in it is central and can be exhibited at once. Essentially it is this: That the principle of liberty, as Mill formulates it, can be used in support of *any* criminal legislation whatsoever. No law, however oppressive or frivolous, really violates it. And clearly, a "principle" of liberty that is not violated by *any* legislation or practice is not a principle at all. It is only a vague and meaningless exhortation.

MILL'S FORMULATION

Mill expressed his central thesis in these words:

. . . the sole end for which mankind are warranted, individually or collectively, in interfering with the liberty of action of any of their number, is self-protection (p. 956).[2]

The principle is expressed by Mill in other ways, which he evidently took to be simply alternative ways of saying the same thing, but which in fact render the thing totally ambiguous. Thus, to the foregoing he immediately adds:

. . . the only purpose for which power can be rightfully exercised over any member of a civilized community, against his will, is to prevent harm to others (Ibid.).

and then further, that to justify applying compulsion to anyone

the conduct from which it is desired to deter him must be calculated to produce evil to someone else (Ibid.).

And on the next page Mill expresses his principle one more way by saying

there is a sphere of action in which society, as distinguished from the individual, has, if any, only an indirect interest; comprehending all that portion of a person's life and conduct which affects only himself, or if it also affects others, only with their free, voluntary, and undeceived consent and participation (p. 957).

Elsewhere in his essay Mill offers still other formulations of this basic idea, but none, I think, which removes the defect contained in these.

That defect is not the falsity of the principle as variously formulated. Certainly the upholder of freedom nods approval of the sentiment expressed in these declarations. The defect is rather that no coherent principle has been formulated. That is to say, if one is seeking a philosophical principle that defines the proper line of governmental and societal interference in the life of the individual, then he does not find it here, for no such line has been drawn at all. A government, however free or despotic, could draw that line in any manner it might choose, and then in complete consistency cite Mill's principle to justify the result.

THE NARROW INTERPRETATION OF "HARM"

To see this, consider the crucial expressions "self-protection," "harm to others," and "evil to someone else." What, for instance, does *harm to another* consist in? Shall we construe this narrowly, limiting it, say, to bodily injury? Of course not, for the principle would then not allow for protection from such things as theft and fraud. A man could walk off with all his neighbor's livestock and, if charged with overstepping the bounds of liberty, point out in complete truth that he had inflicted no bodily injury on anyone and had, therefore, on Mill's principle as thus construed, harmed no one. Construing the notion of *harm* in this narrow way has the immediate consequence of expanding individual liberty far beyond any reasonable limit and leaves us free to commit any offense to others that falls short of bodily injuring them. *Harming* and *injuring* must accordingly encompass much more than just *wounding*.

THE WIDER INTERPRETATION OF "HARM"

If, to overcome the difficulty just cited, we construe the idea of harm more broadly, we find that the principle becomes so restrictive as to permit no real freedom whatever. If we say, for example, that *harming* a man consists not merely of injury to his body, but to any of his deepest interests, then of course we bring such things as theft and fraud within its meaning. Men do have a deep interest in the security of their property as well as of their persons. But unfortunately, men have *other* deep interests as well which no believer in freedom supposes for a minute should never be foiled.

Thus, there are men who have a deep interest in such things as religion, patriotism, public manners, the preservation of wildlife, and so on, without end. Now if we say that no one shall be permitted to do anything that would foil, frustrate, or damage any such interest held by anyone, this will be about equivalent to saying that no one may do anything at all. The whole of the criminal law would be summed up in saying that all actions are prohibited. And a principle having that consequence can hardly be called a principle of liberty.

AN EXAMPLE

Consider a village whose life centers about the practice of religion. Such villages can still be found in the remoter reaches of Quebec. And now let us suppose that someone settles himself down in that village with the avowed and determined mission of doing all he can, through spoken and written persuasion, to unsettle the religion of these villagers, undermine their faith, and break the grip of the Church upon them. Concerning such a state of affairs we can certainly say, *first,* that if this village is in fact a free society, then this iconoclast can by no means be prevented from pursuing his destructive mission with all industry and vigor, assuming, of course, that his instruments are those of persuasion and not physical violence; and *second,* that such activity on his part nevertheless *hurts* the vil-

lagers, in the sense of "hurts" that is now before us. That is, it does most manifestly frustrate and damage a deep interest of its members, or is at least calculated to. Indeed, it is not hard to imagine that their resentment of such activity might be greater than if this outsider undertook to steal all their cattle.

Mill's principle, as thus literally interpreted, does not work, for if it is applied to such a society, with a broad interpretation placed upon the crucial concept of "hurting others," the immediate result is the destruction of the most elementary liberties anyone could claim, such as freedom in the expression of theological opinion. When we consider that there are narrow-minded people (and in fact whole societies of them) who have a deep interest in such things as uniformity of manners and dress, sabbatarian observances, respect for traditional cultural values, and so on, and feel deeply injured by deviations from these, we see how little protection of individual liberty is provided by Mill's principle.

ALTERNATIVE FORMULATIONS OF THE PRINCIPLE

In none of his formulations does Mill ever appear to overcome this difficulty. It seems inherent in the principle itself. Thus, when he insists that the liberty of the individual encompasses "all that portion of a person's life and conduct which affects only himself " (p. 957), and that within that realm an individual should be left alone, the obvious response is that no such portion of one's life and conduct exists. *Everything* one does, though it may be no more than the expression of an opinion sincerely held or the display of eccentric manners or dress, affects others. Nor does it do any good to add, as Mill does, that in case one's conduct affects others, this must be "only with their free, voluntary, and undeceived consent and participation." Reverting to our example of the pious village, it is no principle of liberty that the villagers must freely and voluntarily *consent* to the expression of offensive opinions as a condition of their being enunciated. This is exactly equivalent to saying that every opinion to which anyone objects may be legitimately silenced, without in any way infringing the freedom of the speaker. And this is absurd.

The difficulty is clearly insuperable. Either such

expressions as "hurting others," "protection," "affecting others," or "evil to others" are given a narrow interpretation, or they are not. If interpreted narrowly, then men must, in the name of freedom, be permitted to do whatever they please, short of physically assaulting their fellows. But if not interpreted narrowly, then men may, in accordance with Mill's principle, be restrained in the most elementary expressions of freedom such as the expression of opinion or even the display of manners or the pursuit of life styles offensive to others. So however the principle is understood, the result is absurd.

EFFECTS OF MILL'S FORMULATION UPON HIS OWN PHILOSOPHY

This difficulty sometimes infects Mill's development of his own ideas, occasionally with serious result. For example, he decides, in the light of his principle, that a man who chooses a life of idleness may be judicially punished in case his idleness affects others adversely—his family, for example. Should we not observe that there are very few men whose idleness, were they to choose it, would not adversely affect someone, perhaps seriously? Mill draws the same conclusion with respect to such things as drunkenness and extravagance. One is free to be a drunk provided this does not adversely affect others. What others? And how adversely? Mill specifically mentions one's children and one's creditors—but having mentioned these, at what point shall we stop? Shall we include representatives of the Christian Temperance League? If not, why not? Indeed, the whole principle virtually explodes in its author's face when he finds that it permits the judicial restraint of those whose styles of conduct are "offenses against decency" and "violations of good manners," and draws the appropriate inference (p. 1027) that such behavior should indeed be suppressed! Clearly, this is no principle of liberty at all, but an instrument for grinding men down to conform to someone's conception of "decency" and "good manners."

At one point Mill declares that every man should observe a certain line of conduct toward others, such conduct consisting, he says, of "not injuring the interests of one another" (p. 1008). What interests? The interests these others may have in such things as decency and good manners? As if detecting the difficulty here, Mill adds the qualification, "or rather, certain interests, which, either by express legal provision or by tacit understanding, ought to be considered as rights." At the beginning of his essay, however, Mill had forsworn any appeal to the idea of an abstract right (p. 957). But quite apart from this, the qualification hardly helps, for "express legal provision" can be made for the prohibition of any practice whatever, and "tacit understanding" can similarly extend to anything—to bad manners, for example. Nor is the difficulty overcome by Mill's appeal, elsewhere (p. 1023), to the opinion of society concerning what it considers requisite for its protection. Uniformity of theological opinion, for example, as well as obeisance to the flag and other trappings of the state, have been and in fact still are thought by some societies to be requisite for their protection. Again we have, then, no principle of liberty here at all, but a slogan that can be put to any use one wishes, either for the expansion or the abolishment of individual freedom.

THE NEED FOR A CLEAR PRINCIPLE

Still, the problem Mill dealt with—which is nothing less than the age-old problem of liberty—is one of overwhelming importance. What Mill tried and failed to do is still desperately in need of being done. We do need a philosophical principle of liberty, one that is coherent and meaningful and, above all, one that does not merely presuppose the very distinctions it is intended to make. It is no principle of liberty, for example, to say that every man should have the right to do what he wishes, provided he does not infringe on the rights of others—for that only defines the idea of an individual right by presupposing it and leaves us with absolutely nothing. What is needed is a statement of what men's rights ought to be in a free society, and such a statement is not going to tell us much if it assumes the concept of a right, undefined and unexplained.

NOTES

1.   See H. L. A. Hart, *Law, Liberty and Morality* (New York: Vintage Books, Random House & Alfred A. Knopf, Inc., 1963).
2.   All quotations are from *English Philosophers from Bacon to Mill,* ed. E. A. Burtt (New York: Random House, Inc., 1939).

70. OPINION IN AMERICAN MOTORCYCLE ASSOCIATION v. DAVIDS

Judge A. C. Miller

This is a review of a summary judgment granted in a proceeding requesting a declaration of rights as to the constitutionality of the amendment to the Motor Vehicle Code requiring motorcyclists and riders to wear crash helmets.

Plaintiffs challenge the act on the grounds that it violates the due process and reserved powers clauses of the Michigan Constitution and the due process, equal protection and right of privacy provisions of the Ninth and Fourteenth Amendments of the Constitution of the United States.

The statute in question reads as follows:

A person operating or riding on a motorcycle or motor driven cycle shall wear a crash helmet approved by the department of state police. The department shall promulgate rules for the implementation of this section in accordance with the provisions of Act No. 88 of the Public Acts of 1943, as amended, being sections 24.71 to 24.80 of the Compiled Laws of 1948, and subject to Act No. 197 of the Public Acts of 1952, as amended, being sections 24.101 to 24.110 of the Compiled Laws of 1948.

Failure to wear the helmet by either the driver or rider of a motorcycle subjects such persons to criminal penalties provided for violation of the motor vehicle code.

It is contended by the plaintiffs that the legislative concern is solely related to the safety of the motorcyclist and passenger and can have no possible relationship to the safety and well-being of other persons, much less the public at large. Based on the premise that the individual in our society is still master of his fate and captain of his soul, plaintiffs cite the following maxim:

The maxims are, first, that the individual is not accountable to society for his actions, insofar as these concern the interests of no person but himself. . . .[1]

From 158 N. W. 2d 72.

There is support in the language of Michigan Supreme Court decisions for this maxim. In People v. Armstrong (1889), 73 Mich. 288, 295, 41 N.W. 275, 277, 2 L. R. A. 721, the Court said:

Under our constitution and system of government the object and aim is to leave the subject entire master of his own conduct, except in the points wherein the public good requires some direction or restraint. . . .

The only case found in which the police power has been urged to require one to protect himself from himself is Mugler v. State of Kansas (1887). . . . In that case the prohibition law of Kansas was attacked as a deprivation of property without due process of law. The broad implications of such regulations were argued as follows:

It is, however, contended, that, although the state may prohibit the manufacture of intoxicating liquors for sale or barter within her limits, for general use as a beverage, "no convention or legislature has the right, under our form of government, to prohibit any citizen from manufacturing for his own use, or for export, or storage, any article of food or drink not endangering or affecting the rights of others." The argument made in support of the first branch of this proposition, briefly stated, is, that in the implied compact between the state and the citizen, certain rights are reserved by the latter, which are guaranteed by the constitutional provision protecting persons against being deprived of life, liberty, or property, without due process of law, and with which the State cannot interfere; that among those rights is that of manufacturing for one's use either food or drink; and that while, according to the doctrines of the commune, the state may control the tastes, appetites, habits, dress, food, and drink of the people, our system of government, based upon the individuality and intelligence of the citizen, does not claim to control him, except as to his conduct to others, leaving him the sole judge as to all that only affects himself. (pp. 659–660, 8 S.Ct. p. 296.)

In this case the Court sustained the legislation because to permit individual manufacture "would tend to cripple, if it did not defeat, the effort to guard the community" . . . and ruled:

No one may rightfully do that which the law-making power, upon reasonable grounds, declares to be prejudicial to the general welfare. . . .

No such enforcement problem can be urged to sustain the legislation here in question.

Does a direct relationship to the public, health, safety and welfare exist in the present case?

It is urged that the motorcycle is susceptible to loss of control because it has just two wheels and that other vehicles frequently pick up stones from the road or roadside and throw them at the head of the cyclist causing him to lose control and cross the centerline or otherwise injure others. This was the basis of two New York rulings. . . .

Nevertheless, such reasoning is obviously a strained effort to justify what is admittedly wholesome legislation. If the purpose truly were to deflect flying objects, rather than to reduce cranial injuries, a windshield requirement imposed on the manufacturer would bear a reasonable relationship to the objective and not vary from the norm of safety legislation customarily imposed on the manufacturer for the protection of the public rather than upon the individual.

The Attorney General further contends that the State has an interest in the "viability" of its citizens and can legislate to keep them healthy and self-supporting. This logic could lead to unlimited paternalism. A further contention pertains to the doctrine of *parens patriae,* the special relationship of the State to youth, but this has little merit since the statute is not so limited.

[1] There can be no doubt that the State has a substantial interest in highway safety. In Smith v. Wayne County sheriff. . .the court said:

It is well settled that the Legislature has the power to control and regulate the use of the highways, . . .

but the difficulty with adopting this as a basis for decision is that it would also justify a requirement that automobile drivers wear helmets or buckle their seat belts for their own protection!

These arguments all prove too much. As stated in Shelton v. Tucker (1960) . . .

In a series of decisions this Court has held that, even though the governmental purpose be legitimate and substantial, that purpose cannot be pursued by means that broadly stifle fundamental personal liberties when the end can be more narrowly achieved. . . .

Legislation must meet the test set forth in the recent case of Grovers Dairy company v. McIntyre . . . quoting Roman Catholic Archbishop of Detroit v. Village of Orchard Lake (1952), . . . as follows:

The test of legitimacy of the exercise of the police power is "the existence of a real and substantial relationship between the exercise of those powers in a particular manner in a given case and the public health, safety, morals, or the general welfare."

This statute has a relationship to the protection of the individual motorcyclist from himself, but not to the public health, safety and welfare.

A discussion of the problem leads one to speculate on an analogy to suicide. This was a common law crime, . . . but it is not a statutory crime in Michigan. Our attorney general has opined that we did not adopt that part of the common law because of the abhorrent penalty. . . .

Plaintiffs rely also upon the reserved powers under the Ninth Amendment to the United States Constitution and cites the recent decision[2] wherein Justice Goldberg, concurring, invoked this amendment to invalidate a Connecticut statute making the use of contraceptives a criminal offense. In holding that the use of contraceptives by the individual was a private right of the individual free from State coercion and control, he equated this right with the right "to be let alone". Justice Louis Brandeis stated this principle in his famous dissent in Olmstead v. United States (1928), . . .

The makers of our Constitution . . . sought to protect Americans in their beliefs, their thoughts, their emotions and their sensations. They conferred, as against the government, the right to be let alone—the most comprehensive of rights and the right most valued by civilized men. . . .

Experience should teach us to be most on our guard to protect liberty when the government's purposes are beneficent. Men born to freedom are naturally alert to repel invasion of their liberty by evilminded rulers. The greatest dangers to liberty lurk in insidious encroachment by men of zeal, well-meaning but without understanding.

The precedential consequences of "stretching our imagination" to find a relationship to the public health, safety and welfare, require the invalidation of this statute.

Reversed, but without costs, it being a public question.

NOTES

1.   John Stuart Mill, *Utilitarianism, Liberty and Representative Government,* E. P. Dutton & Co. Inc. (1950 ed., p. 201).
2.   Griswold v. State of Connecticut (1965) 381 U.S. 479, 494, 85 S.Ct. 1678, 1687, 14 L.Ed.2d 510, 521.

71. OPINION IN STATE v. EITEL

Judge Robert T. Mann

Any man's death diminishes me.
John Donne, *Devotions XVII.*

No one pretends that actions
should be as free as opinions.
John Stuart Mill, *On Liberty.*

Does a motorcyclist have a constitutional right to ride the highways without the protective helmet and goggles or face mask the legislature says he must wear? The trial judge thought so. Michigan and Louisiana courts have agreed. But others have upheld similar statutes, declaring that the danger of flying stones is likely to distract the cyclist and send him hurtling into the path of motorists, or that "it is to the interest of the State to have strong, robust, healthy citizens, capable of self-support, of bearing arms, and of adding to the resources of the country." We approve without hesitation the requirement of protection for the eyes. Any collision between the naked eyeball of the cyclist and the dirt increasingly airborne in our time is likely to pose a menace to others. But we ought to admit frankly that the purpose of the helmet is to preserve the life and health of the cyclist, and for some more divinely ordained and humanely explicable purpose than the service of the state.

From 227 Southern Reporter, 2d series (1971), 490F.

The search for precedent is often frustrated, but we believe that society has an interest in the preservation of the life of the individual for his own sake. Suicide, for example, has been a common-law crime for centuries. But we find uneasiness in American legislatures and courts when dealing with self-preservation. They are inclined to require *others* to furnish the individual the means for his own protection. Employers are required to furnish safety equipment; automobile manufacturers are required to furnish seat belts. Or they incline to emphasize protection of *others* rather than *self.* Those religious cultists who handle snakes were forbidden to do so in the name of public safety, for example.

[1,2] We hold that the legislature may impose a minimal inconvenience which affords effective protection against a significant possibility of grave or fatal injury. We have known the pleasure of wind in our faces, but it is relative: death has come with increasing and alarming frequency to motorcyclists in recent years. Seventy-seven per cent of the motorcycle accident deaths studied by a California physician were caused by craniocerebral injury with no potentially fatal trauma to other parts of the body. A New York legislative report, citing the rapid increase in number of motorcycle accidents, stated that 89.2% of these accidents resulted in injury or death and that almost all fatalities in-

volved head injuries, most of which could have been avoided or ameliorated by the use of a proper helmet. An orthopedic surgeon testified in this case that he had cared for six persons injured in motorcycle crashes while wearing protective helmets. None had severe head injury. The inconvenience to the person will vary, but the danger is real and the protection reasonably adapted to its avoidance.

[3] These unwilling cyclists must obey this law. We admire John Stuart Mill's Essay on Liberty, which their counsel cite to persuade us that the State of Florida has unconstitutionally infringed Eitel's and Thompson's right to be let alone. But Mill said there that "no person is an entirely isolated being; it is impossible for a person to do anything seriously or permanently hurtful to himself, without mischief reaching at least to his near connections, and often far beyond them." If he falls we cannot leave him lying in the road. The legislature may constitutionally conclude that the cyclist's right to be let alone is no more precious than the corresponding right of ambulance drivers, nurses and neurosurgeons.

[4] The statute requires that the protective equipment meet the standards of the highway Safety Act of 1966. Standard 4.4.3, promulgated after the enactment but before the effective date of the Florida act, leaves the specifications to the state. The Department of Public Safety adopted Chapter 295G of its Rules months before these charges were brought. We find no unconstitutional delegation of power, nor any vagueness here. Indeed, we think it wise for the Legislature, which stated its purpose with sufficient clarity, to leave to administrative officials the specification of impact strength and the like.

Reversed and remanded.

72. PATERNALISM

Gerald Dworkin

I take as my starting point the "one very simple principle" proclaimed by Mill in *On Liberty*. . . . I assume that no one with the possible exception of extreme pacifists or anarchists questions the correctness of the first half of the principle. This essay is an examination of the negative claim embodied in Mill's principle—the objection to paternalistic interferences with a man's liberty.

I

By paternalism I shall understand roughly the interference with a person's liberty of action justified by reasons referring exclusively to the welfare, good, happiness, needs, interests or values of the person being coerced. One is always well-advised to illustrate one's definitions by examples but it is not easy to find "pure" examples of paternalistic interferences. For almost any piece of legislation is justified by several different kinds of reasons and even if historically a piece of legislation can be shown to have been introduced for purely paternalistic motives, it may be that advocates of the legislation with an anti-paternalistic outlook can find sufficient reasons justifying the legislation without appealing to the reasons which were originally adduced to support it. Thus, for example, it may be that the original legislation requiring motorcyclists to wear safety helmets was introduced for purely paternalistic reasons. But the Rhode Island Supreme Court recently upheld such legislation on the grounds that it was "not persuaded that the legislature is powerless to prohibit individuals from pursuing a course of conduct which could conceivably result in their becoming public

From Gerald Dworkin, "Paternalism," reprinted from *The Monist*, vol. 56, no. 1, with the permission of the author and the publisher.

charges," thus clearly introducing reasons of a quite different kind. Now I regard this decision as being based on reasoning of a very dubious nature but it illustrates the kind of problem one has in finding examples. The following is a list of the kinds of interferences I have in mind as being paternalistic.

II

1. Laws requiring motorcyclists to wear safety helmets when operating their machines.
2. Laws forbidding persons from swimming at a public beach when lifeguards are not on duty.
3. Laws making suicide a criminal offense.
4. Laws making it illegal for women and children to work at certain types of jobs.
5. Laws regulating certain kinds of sexual conduct, e.g. homosexuality among consenting adults in private.
6. Laws regulating the use of certain drugs which may have harmful consequences to the user but do not lead to anti-social conduct.
7. Laws requiring a license to engage in certain professions with those not receiving a license subject to fine or jail sentence if they do engage in the practice.
8. Laws compelling people to spend a specified fraction of their income on the purchase of retirement annuities. (Social Security)
9. Laws forbidding various forms of gambling (often justified on the grounds that the poor are more likely to throw away their money on such activities than the rich who can afford to).
10. Laws regulating the maximum rates of interest for loans.
11. Laws against duelling.

In addition to laws which attach criminal or civil penalties to certain kinds of action there are laws, rules, regulations, decrees, which make it either difficult or impossible for people to carry out their plans and which are also justified on paternalistic grounds. Examples of this are . . . civil commitment procedures when these are specifically justified on the basis of preventing the person being committed

from harming himself. . . . [and] putting fluorides in the community water supply. . . .

III

Bearing these examples in mind let me return to a characterization of paternalism. . . .

. . . We may first divide paternalistic interferences into "pure" and "impure" cases. In "pure" paternalism the class of persons whose freedom is restricted is identical with the class of persons whose benefit is intended to be promoted by such restrictions. Examples: the making of suicide a crime, requiring passengers in automobiles to wear seat-belts, requiring a Christian Scientist to receive a blood transfusion. In the case of "impure" paternalism in trying to protect the welfare of a class of persons we find that the only way to do so will involve restricting the freedom of other persons besides those who are benefitted. . . .

Paternalism then will always involve limitations on the liberty of some individuals in their own interest but it may also extend to interferences with the liberty of parties whose interests are not in question.

IV

Finally, by way of some more preliminary analysis, I want to distinguish paternalistic interferences with liberty from a related type with which it is often confused. Consider, for example, legislation which forbids employees to work more than, say, 40 hours per week. It is sometimes argued that such legislation is paternalistic for if employees desired such a restriction on their hours of work they could agree among themselves to impose it voluntarily. But because they do not the society imposes its own conception of their best interests upon them by the use of coercion. Hence this is paternalism.

Now it may be that some legislation of this nature is, in fact, paternalistically motivated. I am not denying that. All I want to point out is that there is another possible way of justifying such measures which is not paternalistic in nature. It is not paternalistic because as Mill puts it in a similar context such measures are "required not to overrule the judgment of individuals respecting their own interest, but to give effect to that judgment: they being unable to give effect to it except by concert, which concert again cannot be effectual unless it receives validity and sanction from the law."[1]. . . .

. . . In these cases compulsion is not used to achieve some benefit which is not recognized to be a benefit by those concerned, but rather because it is the only feasible means of achieving some benefit which *is* recognized as such by all concerned. This way of viewing matters provides us with another characterization of paternalism in general. Paternalism might be thought of as the use of coercion to achieve a good which is not recognized as such by those persons for whom the good is intended. Again while this formulation captures the heart of the matter—it is surely what Mill is objecting to in *On Liberty*—the matter is not always quite like that. For example when we force motorcyclists to wear helmets we are trying to promote a good—the protection of the person from injury—which is surely recognized by most of the individuals concerned. It is not that a cyclist doesn't value his bodily integrity; rather, as a supporter of such legislation would put it, he either places, perhaps irrationally, another value or good (freedom from wearing a helmet) above that of physical well-being or, perhaps, while recognizing the danger in the abstract, he either does not fully appreciate it or he underestimates the likelihood of its occurring. But now we are approaching the question of possible justifications of paternalistic measures and the rest of this essay will be devoted to that question.

V

I shall begin for dialectical purposes by discussing Mill's objections to paternalism and then go on to discuss more positive proposals.

An initial feature that strikes one is the absolute nature of Mill's prohibitions against paternalism. It is so unlike the carefully qualified admonitions of Mill and his fellow Utilitarians on other moral issues. . . .

Clearly the operative premise here is [that "We either cannot advance the interests of the individual by compulsion, or the attempt to do so involves evil which outweigh the good done;"] and it is

bolstered by claims about the status of the individual as judge and appraiser of his welfare, interests, needs, etc. . . . These claims are used to support the following generalizations concerning the utility of compulsion for paternalistic purposes. . . .

But the strongest of all the arguments against the interference of the public with purely personal conduct is that when it does interfere, the odds are that it interferes wrongly and in the wrong place.[2]

All errors which the individual is likely to commit against advice and warning are far outweighed by the evil of allowing others to constrain him to what they deem his good.[3]

Performing the utilitarian calculation by balancing the advantages and disadvantages we find that:

Mankind are greater gainers by suffering each other to live as seems good to themselves, than by compelling each other to live as seems good to the rest.[4]. . . .

. . . This is clearly the main channel of Mill's thought and it is one which has been subjected to vigorous attack from the moment it appeared—most often by fellow Utilitarians. The link that they have usually seized on is, as Fitzjames Stephen put it, the absence of proof that the "mass of adults are so well acquainted with their own interests and so much disposed to pursue them that no compulsion or restraint put upon them by any others for the purpose of promoting their interest can really promote them."[5] Even so sympathetic a critic as Hart is forced to [this] conclusion. . . . [Now] Mill does not declare that there should never be government interference with the economy but rather that

. . . in every instance, the burden of making out a strong case should be thrown not on those who resist but on those who recommend government interference. Letting alone, in short, should be the general practice: every departure from it, unless required by some great good, is a certain evil.[6]

In short, we get a presumption not an absolute prohibition. The question is why doesn't the argument against paternalism go the same way?

I suggest that the answer lies in seeing that in addition to a purely utilitarian argument Mill uses another as well. As a Utilitarian Mill has to show, in Fitzjames Stephen's words, that:

Self-protection apart, no good object can be attained by any compulsion which is not in itself a greater evil than the absence of the object which the compulsion obtains. [7]

To show this is impossible; one reason being that it isn't true. Preventing a man from selling himself into slavery (a paternalistic measure which Mill himself accepts as legitimate), or from taking heroin, or from driving a car without wearing seatbelts may constitute a lesser evil than allowing him to do any of these things. A consistent Utilitarian can only argue against paternalism on the grounds that it (as a matter of fact) does not maximize the good. It is always a contingent question that may be refuted by the evidence. But there is also a non-contingent argument which runs through *On Liberty*. When Mill states that "there is a part of the life of every person who has come to years of discretion, within which the individuality of that person ought to reign uncontrolled either by any other person or by the public collectively" he is saying something about what it means to be a person, an autonomous agent. It is because coercing a person for his own good denies this status as an independent entity that Mill objects to it so strongly and in such absolute terms. To be able to choose is a good that is independent of the wisdom of what is chosen. . . .

. . . The main consideration for not allowing such a contract is the need to preserve the liberty of the person to make future choices. This gives us a principle—a very narrow one—by which to justify some paternalistic interferences. Paternalism is justified only to preserve a wider range of freedom for the individual in question. How far this principle could be extended, whether it can justify all the cases in which we are inclined upon reflection to think paternalistic measures justified remains to be discussed. What I have tried to show so far is that there are two strains of argument in Mill—one a straight-forward Utilitarian mode of reasoning and one which relies not on the goods which free choice leads to but on the absolute value of the choice itself. The first cannot establish any absolute prohibition but at most a presumption and indeed a fairly weak one given some fairly plausible assumptions about human psychology; the second while a stronger line of argument seems to me to allow on its own grounds a wider range of paternalism than might be suspected. I turn now to a consideration of these matters.

VI

We might begin looking for principles governing the acceptable use of paternalistic power in cases where it is generally agreed that it is legitimate. Even Mill intends his principles to be applicable only to mature individuals, not those in what he calls "non-age". What is it that justifies us in interfering with children? The fact that they lack some of the emotional and cognitive capacities required in order to make fully rational decisions. . . . Extensions of paternalism are argued for by claiming that in various respects, chronologically mature individuals share the same deficiencies in knowledge, capacity to think rationally, and the ability to carry out decisions that children possess. Hence in interfering with such people we are in effect doing what they would do if they were fully rational. Hence we are not really opposing their will, hence we are not really interfering with their freedom. The dangers of this move have been sufficiently exposed by Berlin in his Two Concepts of Liberty. I see no gain in theoretical clarity nor in practical advantage in trying to pass over the real nature of the interferences with liberty that we impose on others. Still the basic notion of consent is important and seems to me the only acceptable way of trying to delimit an area of justified paternalism.

Let me start by considering a case where the consent is not hypothetical in nature. Under certain conditions it is rational for an individual to agree that others should force him to act in ways in which, at the time of action, the individual may not see as desirable. If, for example, a man knows that he is subject to breaking his resolves when temptation is present, he may ask a friend to refuse to entertain his requests at some later stage.

A classical example is given in the Odyssey when Odysseus commands his men to tie him to the mast and refuse all future orders to be set free, because he knows the power of the Sirens to enchant men with their songs. . . .

. . . However in . . . this case . . . the measure to be enforced is specifically requested by the party involved and at some point in time there is genuine consent and agreement on the part of those persons whose liberty is infringed. Such is not the case for the paternalistic measures we have been speaking about. What must be involved here is not consent to specific measures but rather consent to a system of government, run by elected representatives, with an understanding that they may act to safeguard our interests in certain limited ways.

I suggest that since we are all aware of our irrational propensities, deficiencies in cognitive and emotional capacities and avoidable and unavoidable ignorance it is rational and prudent for us to in effect take out "social insurance policies". We may argue for and against proposed paternalistic measures in terms of what fully rational individuals would accept as forms of protection. Now, clearly since the initial agreement is not about specific measures we are dealing with a more-or-less blank check and therefore there have to be carefully defined limits. What I am looking for are certain kinds of conditions which make it plausible to suppose that rational men could reach agreement to limit their liberty even when other men's interests are not affected.

Of course as in any kind of agreement schema there are great difficulties in deciding what rational individuals would or would not accept. Particularly in sensitive area of personal liberty, there is always a danger of the dispute over agreement and rationality being a disguised version of evaluative and normative disagreement.

Let me suggest types of situations in which it seems plausible to suppose that fully rational individuals would agree to having paternalistic restrictions imposed upon them. It is reasonable to suppose that there are "goods" such as health which any person would want to have in order to pursue his own good—no matter how that good is conceived. This is an argument that is used in connection with compulsory education for children but it seems to me that it can be extended to other goods which have this character. Then one could agree

that the attainment of such goods should be promoted even when not recognized to be such, at the moment, by the individuals concerned.

An immediate difficulty that arises stems from the fact that men are always faced with competing goods and that there may be reasons why even a value such as health—or indeed life—may be overridden by competing values. Thus the problem with the Jehovah's Witness and blood transfusions. It may be more important for him to reject "impure substances" than to go on living. The difficult problem that must be faced is whether one can give sense to the notion of a person irrationally attaching weights to competing values.

Consider a person who knows the statistical data on the probability of being injured when not wearing seat belts in an automobile and knows the types and gravity of the various injuries. He also insists that the inconvenience attached to fastening the belt every time he gets in and out of the car outweighs for him the possible risks to himself. I am inclined in this case to think that such a weighing is irrational. Given his life-plans which we are assuming are those of the average person, his interests and commitments already undertaken, I think it is safe to predict that we can find inconsistencies in his calculations at some point. I am assuming that this is not a man who for some conscious or unconscious reasons is trying to injure himself nor is he a man who just likes to "live dangerously". I am assuming that he is like us in all the relevant respects but just puts an enormously high negative value on inconvenience—one which does not seem comprehensible or reasonable. . . .

. . . But why may we not extend our interference to what we might call evaluative delusions? After all in the case of cognitive delusions we are prepared, often, to act against the expressed will of the person involved. If a man believes that when he jumps out the window he will float upwards—Robert Nozick's example—would not we detain him, forcibly if necessary? The reply will be that this man doesn't wish to be injured and if we could convince him that he is mistaken as to the consequences of his action he would not wish to perform the action. But part of what is involved in claiming that a man who doesn't fasten his seatbelts is attaching an irrational weight to the inconvenience of fastening them is that if he were to be involved in an accident and severely injured he would look back and admit that the inconvenience wasn't as bad as all that. So there is a sense in which if I could convince him of the consequences of his action he also would not wish to continue his present course of action. . . .

Some of the decisions we make are of such a character that they produce changes which are in one or another way irreversible. Situations are created in which it is difficult or impossible to return to anything like the initial stage at which the decision was made. In particular some of these changes will make it impossible to continue to make reasoned choices in the future. I am thinking specifically of decisions which involve taking drugs that are physically or psychologically addictive and those which are destructive of one's mental and physical capacities.

I suggest we think of the imposition of paternalistic interferences in situations of this kind as being a kind of insurance policy which we take out against making decisions which are far-reaching, potentially dangerous and irreversible. Each of these factors is important. Clearly there are many decisions we make that are relatively irreversible. In deciding to learn to play chess I could predict in view of my general interests in games that some portion of my free-time was going to be preempted and that it would not be easy to give up the game once I acquired a certain competence. But my whole life-style was not going to be jeopardized in an extreme manner. Further it might be argued that even with addictive drugs such as heroin one's normal life plans would not be seriously interfered with if an inexpensive and adequate supply were readily available. So this type of argument might have a much narrower scope than appears to be the case at first.

A second class of cases concerns decisions which are made under extreme psychological and sociological pressures. I am not thinking here of the making of the decision as being something one is pressured into—e.g. a good reason for making duelling illegal is that unless this is done many people might have to manifest their courage and integrity in ways in which they would rather not do so—but rather of decisions such as that to commit suicide

which are usually made at a point where the individual is not thinking clearly and calmly about the nature of his decision. In addition, of course, this comes under the previous heading of all-too-irrevocable decision. Now there are practical steps which a society could take if it wanted to decrease the possibility of suicide—for example not paying social security benefits to the survivors or as religious institutions do, not allowing such persons to be buried with the same status as natural deaths. I think we may count these as interferences with the liberty of persons to attempt suicide and the question is whether they are justifiable.

Using my argument schema the question is whether rational individuals would consent to absolute prohibition but I do think it is reasonable for them to agree to some kind of enforced waiting period. . . .

A third class of decisions—these are not supposed to be disjoint—involves dangers which are either not sufficiently understood or appreciated correctly by the persons involved. Let me illustrate, using the example of cigarette smoking, a number of possible cases.

1. A man may not know the facts—e.g. smoking between 1 and 2 packs a day shortens life expectancy 6.2 years, the costs and pain of the illness caused by smoking, etc.

2. A man may know the facts, wish to stop smoking, but not have the requisite willpower.

3. A man may know the facts but not have them play the correct role in his calculation because, say, he discounts the danger psychologically because it is remote in time and/or inflates the attractiveness of other consequences of his decision which he regards as beneficial.

In case 1 what is called for is education, the posting of warnings, etc. In case 2 there is no theoretical problem. We are not imposing a good on someone who rejects it. We are simply using coercion to enable people to carry out their own goals. (Note: There obviously is a difficulty in that only a subclass of the individuals affected wish to be prevented from doing what they are doing.) In case 3 there is a sense in which we are imposing a good on someone since given his current appraisal of the facts he doen't wish to be restricted. But in another sense we are not imposing a good since what is being claimed—and what must be shown or at least argued for—is that an accurate accounting on his part would lead him to reject his current course of action. Now we all know that such cases exist, that we are prone to disregard dangers that are only possibilities, that immediate pleasures are often magnified and distorted.

If in addition the dangers are severe and far-reaching we could agree to allowing the state a certain degree of power to intervene in such situations. The difficulty is in specifying in advance, even vaguely, the class of cases in which intervention will be legitimate.

A related difficulty is that of drawing a line so that it is not the case that all ultra-hazardous activities are ruled out, e.g. mountain-climbing, bull-fighting, sports-car racing, etc. There are some risks—even very great ones—which a person is entitled to take with his life.

A good deal depends on the nature of the deprivation—e.g. does it prevent the person from engaging in the activity completely or merely limit his participation—and how important to the nature of the activity is the absence of restriction when this is weighed against the role that the activity plays in the life of the person. In the case of automobile seat belts, for example, the restriction is trivial in nature, interferes not at all with the use or enjoyment of the activity, and does, I am assuming, considerably reduce a high risk of serious injury. Whereas, for example, making mountain climbing illegal prevents completely a person engaging in an activity which may play an important role in his life and his conception of the person he is.

In general the easiest cases to handle are those which can be argued about in the terms which Mill thought to be so important—a concern not just for the happiness or welfare, in some broad sense, of the individual but rather a concern for the autonomy and freedom of the person. I suggest that we would be most likely to consent to paternalism in those instances in which it preserves and enhances for the individual his ability to rationally consider and carry out his own decisions.

I have suggested in this essay a number of types of situations in which it seems plausible that rational men would agree to granting the legislative powers of a society the right to impose restrictions on what Mill calls "self-regarding" conduct. However, rational men knowing something about the resources of ignorance, ill-will and stupidity available to the law-makers of a society—a good case in point is the history of drug legislation in the United States—will be concerned to limit such intervention to a minimum. I suggest in closing two principles designed to achieve this end.

In all cases of paternalistic legislation there must be a heavy and clear burden of proof placed on the authorities to demonstrate the exact nature of the harmful effects (or beneficial consequences) to be avoided (or achieved) and the probability of their occurrence. The burden of proof here is twofold—what lawyers distinguish as the burden of going forward and the burden of persuasion. That the authorities have the burden of going forward means that it is up to them to raise the question and bring forward evidence of the evils to be avoided. Unlike the case of new drugs where the manufacturer must produce some evidence that the drug has been tested and found not harmful, no citizen has to show with respect to self-regarding conduct that is not harmful or promotes his best interests. In addition the nature and cogency of the evidence for the harmfulness of the course of action must be set at a high level. To paraphrase a formulation of the burden of proof for criminal proceedings—better 10 men ruin themselves than one man be unjustly deprived of liberty.

Finally I suggest a principle of the least restrictive alternative. If there is an alternative way of accomplishing the desired end without restricting liberty then although it may involve great expense, inconvenience, etc. the society must adopt it.

NOTES

1.   J. S. Mill, *Principles of Political Economy* (New York: P. F. Collier and Sons, 1900), p. 442.

2.   Mill, *Utilitarianism* and *On Liberty* (Fontana Library Edition, ed. M. Warnock, London, 1962), p. 214.

3.   *Ibid.*, p. 207

4.   *Ibid.*, p. 138.

5.   J. F. Stephens, *Liberty, Equality, Fraternity* (New York: Henry Holt & Co., n.d.), p. 24.

6.   *Ibid.*, II, 451.

7.   Stephen, p. 49.

73. A CRITIQUE OF PATERNALISM

Tom L. Beauchamp

Recently ethical and legal philosophers have shown a revival of interest in whether paternalistic reasons are ever good reasons for the limitation of individual liberties in the form of coercive laws. A special target has been John Stuart Mill, whose searching criticisms of paternalism in *On Liberty* are now widely regarded as too sweeping and insufficiently guarded. Against these recent trends in philosophy I argue in this paper that: (1) Mill's critique of paternalism is in all essentials sustainable; (2) Even his most sympathetic critics (especially Dworkin and Hart) have not demonstrated that paternalism is justified; (3) Paternalistic reasons for behavioral control are both common and dangerous, yet are, like all forms of paternalism, irrelevant to the justification of coercive limitation of liberty.

I shall first briefly survey a few selected examples of paternalistic justifications. . . . I then pass on to general philosophical concerns about the nature and merit of paternalism, including a defense of Mill against Dworkin and other critics.

EXAMPLES OF PATERNALISTIC JUSTIFICATIONS

Dworkin has provided many useful examples of paternalistic justifications, and there is no need to repeat them. However, I do wish to point out that paternalistic justifications are not only common, as Hart rightly points out, but potentially dangerous as well. I will mention two examples to illustrate this point.

(A) INVOLUNTARY COMMITMENT AND THERAPY ON GROUNDS OF INSANITY

Involuntary commitment to therapeutic environments is common. The justification offered for both commitment and forced therapy is often overtly paternalistic. Sometimes language as vague as the "patient's need for treatment" is used, and at other times "dangerous to self" and in "need of

custody" suffice by law as criteria of commitment. Forced bio-behavioral therapeutic techniques are legally permitted after the patient has been committed. The first and most crucial coercive act requiring justification, however, is the commitment itself. A typical problem case is that of Mrs. Catherine Lake, who suffered from arteriosclerosis causing temporary confusion and mild loss of memory, interspersed with times of mental alertness and rationality. All parties agreed that Mrs. Lake never harmed anyone or presented any threat of danger, yet she was committed to a mental institution because she often seemed in a confused and defenseless state. At her trial, while apparently fully rational, she testified that she knew the risk of living outside the hospital and preferred to take that risk rather than be in the hospital environment. The Court of Appeals denied her petition, arguing that she is "mentally ill," "is a danger to herself . . . and is not competent to care for herself." The legal justification cited by the Court was a statute which "provides for involuntary hospitalization of a person who is 'mentally ill and, because of that illness, is likely to injure himself '. . . ."[1] Such reasoning is widespread today, despite forceful arguments by psychiatrists that the harmless "mentally sick" are often competent to make rational judgments.

(B) EUGENIC STERILIZATION

Eugenic sterilization laws are still in effect in over half the states in the U.S. The retarded have been a special target, since they along with criminals, epileptics, alcoholics, and other vulnerable groups have been alleged to have genetically rooted mental and physical disabilities. Since the retarded are often childlike and unaware of their responsibilities, the rearing of children is frequently a heavy burden. For such reasons it has been considered in their own best interest that they be sterilized, even if they do not agree or fail to comprehend the decision.[2] Irvin B. Hill, writing about the sterilization of mentally deficient persons in prison, argues as follows:

From Tom L. Beauchamp, "Paternalism and Bio-Behavioral Control," reprinted from *The Monist*, Vol. 60, No. 1, with the permission of the author and the publisher.

A mentally deficient person is not a suitable parent for either a normal or a subnormal child, and children would be an added burden to an already handicapped individual, who does well to support himself. It would be unfair to the state, *to the individual,* and particularly *to his potential children,* to permit his release without the *protection* of sterilization. . . .

. . . It has been the policy of the State of Oregon to sterilize mentally deficient persons before releasing them from its institution and . . . this program has been of benefit from economic, social, *and eugenic* standpoints. . . . It *assists the individual* in his transition to a non-institutional life; and it relieves the state of the financial burden. . . .[3]

While not a pure paternalistic justification for eugenic control, it is partially paternalistic and is the kind of reasoning which, once canonized into law, can easily become purely paternalistic in coercive environments. Free and informed consent is unlikely in the context of penal institutions, especially when one is dealing with mentally deficient persons. They can be bribed with offers of freedom and intimidated by threats that their confinement will be extended. Although we now know both that most retarded persons are born from parents of normal intelligence and that the retarded often have children of normal intelligence, prison and other custodial environments continue to give rise to the sort of paternalistically motivated interventions suggested by Hill.

I have intentionally chosen two examples of paternalism where the use of paternalistic justifications can have serious and even devastating effects. No doubt there are many innocuous cases of paternalistic justifications, including most of those cited by Dworkin. But, as we shall see, perhaps the major question about paternalism arises because of the harmful consequences produced by its use. My only point thus far is that *some* of those consequences cannot be classified as innocuous.

THE NATURE AND TYPES OF PATERNALISM

Paternalistically motivated laws are thought to be justified because they work to prevent persons from harming themselves. This justification for limiting individual liberty presumably supplements more widely accepted justifications such as the prevention of harm by others and the maintenance of public order. Whether paternalistic reasons are *good* reasons will occupy us momentarily, but first some agreement must be reached concerning proper use of the word "paternalism." If one operates with a definition as loose as H. L. A. Hart's— "the protection of people against themselves"[4]— misunderstandings readily follow. Legislation intended to help citizens protect themselves from inadvertent acts, such as mutilating their hands in garbage disposals, would on this definition seem paternalistic. Dworkin has provided a better definition, which I accept with only two innocuous modifications (in brackets): Paternalism is "the [coercive] interference with a person's liberty of action justified by [protective or beneficent] reasons referring exclusively to the welfare, good, happiness, needs, interests or values of the person being coerced."[5]

Joel Feinberg has quite properly distinguished two types of paternalism,[6] strong and weak. He explains the weak form as follows (113, 116):

The state has the right to prevent self-regarding harmful conduct only when it is substantially nonvoluntary or when temporary intervention is necessary to establish whether it is voluntary or not.

The class of nonvoluntary cases includes cases where there is consent but not adequately informed consent. The strong form holds that the state has the right to coercively protect or benefit a person even when his contrary choices are informed and voluntary. The problem with this distinction, as Feinberg himself argues, is that "weak paternalism" is not paternalism in any interesting sense, because it is not a liberty limiting principle *independent* of the "harm to others" principle (113, 124). For this reason I restrict use of the term "paternalism" to strong paternalism. However, it is important to see that the "temporary intervention" mentioned above is both coercive and justified on what might deceptively appear to be paternalistic grounds. Mill believed that a person ignorant of a potential danger which might befall him could justifiably be restrained, so long as the coercion was temporary and only for the purpose of rendering the person informed, in which case he would be free to choose whatever course he wished. Mill regarded this—correctly, I think—as temporary but justified coercion which is not "real infringement" of liberty:

If either a public officer or anyone else saw a person attempting to cross a bridge which had been ascertained to be unsafe, and there were no time to warn him of his danger, they might seize him and turn him back, without any real infringement of his liberty; for liberty consists in doing what one desires, and he does not desire to fall into the river.[7]

It is not a question of protecting a man *against himself* or of interfering with his *liberty of action*. He is not *acting* at all in regard to his danger. He needs protection from something which is precisely *not himself*, not his intended action, not in any remote sense of his own making. While I am here embellishing Mill, this seems to me clearly the direction of his argument. Mill goes on to say that once the man has been fully informed and understands the dangers of the bridge, then he should be free to traverse it, if he wishes. I shall be arguing in support of Mill's conclusions, and I shall call this justification of *temporary* intervention "Mill's proviso."

MILL'S ANTI-PATERNALISTIC INDIVIDUALISM AND "JUSTIFIED PATERNALISM"

Dworkin, Hart, and any supporter of a limited paternalism attempt to specify with care precisely which goods, needs, interests, etc. are acceptable as reasons for intervention with one's liberty of action. Dworkin and Hart largely agree that the state is justified in coercively interfering with a person's liberty if by its interference it protects the person against his own actions where those actions are extremely and unreasonably risky (waterfall-rafting, e.g.), or are genuinely not in the person's own best interest when his best interest is knowable by the state (as some believe in the case of suicide), or are potentially dangerous and irreversible in effect (as some drugs are). Perhaps Dworkin's fundamental condition justifying interference is that the state justifiably protects a subject against himself if the interference avoids serious evils which the person might cause to himself

through decisions which are far-reaching, potentially dangerous and irreversible, and where no rational alternative is more highly valued by the person.

Dworkin and Hart proceed by citing practices most would agree are justified and sometimes spring from paternalistic motives. It is then assumed that if the conditions justifying these (paternalistically motivated) practices can be listed, they are independent of the harm principle, and paternalism has been justified. Accordingly, no Mill-supportive example can dent or falsify such an analysis, because it has already been assumed (not, I think, *argued*) that instances of *justified paternalism* have been given. Now *if* the methodology and the assumptions just mentioned are admitted, I do not believe this thesis can be gainsaid. The defender of Mill must capitulate.

AN ALTERNATIVE TO PATERNALISM

But it is precisely these assumptions that should be challenged. The coercive measures these philosophers cite do generally seem to me justified. Their tactic goes wrong, I suggest, in assuming that the actual justifying conditions in these cases are *paternalistic* ones rather than Mill's original standard of individual harm. Mill's harm principle may need rigorous embellishment, but, properly qualified, it seems to me to specify the only valid grounds for intervention. The allegedly independent liberty limiting principle called "paternalism" is gratuitous. I now proceed to an argument for this contention.

I propose in defense of Mill and as the proper account, that one of the following two conditions, as applicable, is necessary for, and (prima facie) sufficient for, the justification of coercive interventions (though I shall here be concerned to defend their necessity only against paternalism and not against all possible alternative justifying principles):

(I)   There exist supportable grounds for believing that an individual or group or institution serving the public interest has been or will be *injured* (wrongfully harmed) by the actions or negligence of others. (Deliberately exploitative actions provide the strongest, though not the only grounds for injury claims. Informed consent only negatives injury, not harm; however one might give informed consent and still be injured if treated in a way not specifically consented to.)

(II) There exist supportable grounds for believing that an individual or group of individuals has been or will be physically or mentally harmed by some cause or condition which is to that party not known or not within its control or both (and which has not been intentionally manipulated by other persons, in which case the event would fall under I rather than II).

I have intentionally used the concept of injury in (I) rather than the concept of harm. My intention is to evade certain difficulties with Mill's notion of harm. As Feinberg has pointed out, one may consent to actions and still be *harmed,* whether those actions are his own or others'. However, we might still want to say that such a person was not *injured,* i.e., not done an injustice or wrongfully harmed, because he consented.

Dworkin and Hart present troublesome cases which center on situations where persons are (a) ignorant and (b) less than fully voluntary in acting. All ignorance cases can be handled, I believe, by Mill's proviso. Once someone is adequately informed (assuming this is possible and assuming the person is able to act on the information), the decision should rest with the agent. Cases of involuntary acts or less than fully voluntary acts are more troublesome only because there are degrees of voluntariness. Fully involuntary acts are not especially difficult, however, nor did they seem so to Mill. Feinberg has this point just right:

Neither should we expect anti-paternalistic individualism to deny protection to a person from his own non-voluntary choices, for insofar as the choices are not voluntary they are just as alien to him as the choices of someone else (F, 112 [48]).

Such harmful "actions" involve harms caused by conditions either unknown to the relevant persons or beyond their control, and *for this reason* are

subject to coercive intervention, as condition II specifies.

Still, what are we to say about those actions which are partially voluntary and partially involuntary—e.g., those performed under behavior control devices such as subliminal advertising, and drug therapy, or in circumstances involving alcoholic stimulation, mob-inspired enthusiasm, retardation, and neurotic compulsion? I see no reason why all these cases should not be treated like ignorance cases. We may (assuming objectivity and knowledge on our part) justifiably protect a man from harm which might result directly from his drunkenness or retardation. To the extent one protects him from causes beyond his knowledge and control, to that extent (subject perhaps to further specific qualifications) one justifiably intervenes. If a potentially injurable person genuinely has "cloudy judgment" or is being deceived through ignorance, his choices are substantially nonvoluntary. And if he can be injured *because* of these conditions, we may justifiably restrain his action. But once informed of the dangers of this action, if and when a context can be provided where voluntary choice is meaningfully possible, he cannot justifiably be further restrained. Mrs. Lake provided us earlier with an excellent anti-paternalistic example where coercion is *not* justified. Severely retarded persons provide a useful example where coercion *is* justified. Those with minimal or no language skills are not capable of voluntary choice. It is sometimes contended, however, that they must be protected against themselves by involuntary sterilization, in order that they not enter into sexual relations. This piece of paternalism has matters reversed. Such persons seldom have sexual relations unless exploited by others. Any coercion should be aimed at protecting them from exploitation and should be justified by the harm principle. There are less intrusive means to the end of protection than sterilization. Also, if such persons can be taught language skills and acquire a meaningful measure of free choice, our obligations to them are altered, and coercion would no longer be justified. The case is similar with non-rational behavior control techniques, which typically are used to alter the "choices" a man makes, without his understanding or consenting to the alterations. To the extent such actions truly are controlled, it is meaningless to say they are chosen, though no doubt the degree of control and voluntariness rest on a multi-level continuum.

It might be thought that my objections to Dworkin and Hart are pseudo-objections because these philosophers *mean* by "paternalism" something closely akin to, if not in fact identical with, what I take to be justifications on the grounds of harm and injury. There is some evidence to support this objection. Hart, for example, uses cases of paternalism where interventions are justified because the protection is against exploitation or harm (H, 33 f). However, it does seem to me unlikely that the boundaries drawn by Hart and Dworkin could be construed to coincide with my own. The reason is simple. Each of these philosophers argues that Mill's conclusions led to restrictions which are too strict. Since I have drawn my boundaries in a manner relevantly similar to Mill's, theirs must be different and their objections to Mill's analysis also objections to my analysis.

A more promising objection is that the same coercive paternalistic interferences which I presumably would disallow on harm principle grounds are allowed, through the back door, on grounds of injury by exploitation (in condition I). I think this too cannot be correct. As I am using the word "exploitation" it is simply a special means of producing injury. It is not something different from the process of injuring. Hence it cannot allow all the same coercive interferences as Hart and Dworkin allow. Their whole purpose in sanctioning paternalism is to *supplement* Mill's harm principle with an *independent* liberty-limiting principle. I have been attempting to combat this extension. It is, of course, theoretically possible that *extensionally* all or many cases of "justified paternalism" happen to involve cases of exploitation. I doubt this, but even if it were so, either it would be only accidentally so or it would indicate that we do not need a principle to supplement the harm principle.

THE JUSTIFICATION OF JUSTIFYING PRINCIPLES

Reasonable and informed persons differ concerning those actions which should and should not be coercively restrained; they also differ over the acceptability of those justifying principles invoked as grounds for such interventions. They can disagree vigorously over the proper interpretation of cases such as those I have advanced. Nowhere do they disagree more than in the area of cases which some take to be (1) *hard cases* in test of the sufficiency of a particular principle to justify interference (as, say, suicide and slavery are hard cases for the harm principle) or (2) *hard core cases* favoring the sufficiency of a principle (as, say, the mentally ill needing treatment are considered by some hard core cases for paternalistic principles). One person's clinching paradigm may be the butt of another's attack. In such cases we often say that two disputants cannot bring their moral intuitions into harmony. So in the present dispute over paternalism, it might be argued, I am simply unable to bring my Mill-aligned intuitions into accord with those of Dworkin and Hart; yet there are cases which have an attractive moral sway in the direction of paternalism. Cases of suicide, slavery, treatment of the retarded, and drug controls are examples. So can anything be done to adjudicate our differences?

First, a couple of methodological points are in order. I would agree that the systematic use of examples has its limits and may yield inconclusive results. I share the scepticism of those contemporary philosophers who believe that reliance upon intuition and upon quasi-legal notions such as the "outweighing" of one right or principle by another may ultimately fail to resolve important issues. Also, I am prepared to agree that ethical argument by analysis of examples is not purely descriptive of our common ethical beliefs, and hence is not simply a matter of systematically bringing general intuitions into harmony. Often such argument is *revisionary* of our ethical beliefs. Examples shock intuition and alter belief. In the end disagreements such as, say, mine with Dworkin, may largely reduce to arguments concerning why moral beliefs ought to be readjusted. To argue, then, that paternalism is never justified may well be a way of arguing that we ought to regard it as never justified. I accept the view that moral philosophy should be in the business of providing such arguments.

Why, then, ought paternalism to be judged unacceptable? The dominant reason is that paternalistic principles are too broad and hence justify too much. Robert Harris has correctly pointed out that Hart's description of paternalism would in principle "justify the imposition of a Spartan-like regimen requiring rigorous physical exercise and abstention from smoking, drinking, and hazardous pastimes."[8] The more thoughtful restrictions on paternalism proposed by Dworkin and Feinberg would disallow this sort of extreme, but still leave unacceptable latitude, especially in contexts where bio-behavioral controls are most likely to be abused. Prison environments and therapeutic agencies have thrived on the use of paternalistic justifications. Paternalism potentially gives prison wardens, psychosurgeons, and state officials a good reason for coercively using most any means in order to achieve ends they believe in the subject's best interest. It is demonstrable that allowing this latitude of judgment is dangerous and acutely uncontrollable. This is as true of Feinberg, Hart, and Dworkin's hard core cases in favor of paternalism as it is elsewhere.

Paternalists, then, leave us with unresolved problems concerning the scope of the principle. Suppose, for example, that a man risks his life for the advance of medicine by submitting to an unreasonably risky experiment, an act which most would think not in his own interest. Are we to commend him or coercively restrain him? Paternalism strongly suggests that it would be permissible to coercively restrain such a person. Yet if that is so, then the state is permitted to restrain coercively its morally heroic citizens, not to mention its martyrs, if they act—as such people frequently do—in a manner "harmful" to themselves. I do not see how paternalism can be patched up by adding further conditions about the actions of heroes and martyrs. It would increasingly come to bear the marks of an ad hoc and gratuitous principle which is not genuinely independent of the harm principle.

It is universally acknowledged that the harm principle justifiably permits coercive interventions. No other justifying principle occupies such a noncontroversial status. Perhaps this will and ought to change. But before we agree to supplementary liberty limiting principles, it would seem the better part of caution to be as certain as possible that the harm principle will not suffice and that the evils the supplementary principles enable us to prevent are greater than the evils they inadvertently permit.

NOTES

1. The relevant court documents are found in Jay Katz, Joseph Goldstein, and Alan M. Dershowitz, *Psychoanalysis, Psychiatry, and Law* (New York: The Free Press, 1967), pp. 552–54, 710–13. Informed sources have told me that Mrs. Lake was freed after repeated petitioning.

2. The history of such justifications in American society can be found in Kenneth M. Ludmerer, *Genetics and American Society* (Baltimore: The Johns Hopkins University Press, 1972) and in Mark H. Haller, *Eugenics* (New Brunswick, New Jersey: Rutgers University Press, 1963).

3. Irvin B. Hill, "Sterilizations in Oregon," *American Journal of Mental Deficiency*, Vol. 54 (1950), p. 403. Italics added.

4. H. L. A. Hart, *Law, Liberty, and Morality* (Stanford: Stanford University Press, 1963), p. 31. Hereafter abbreviated *H*.

5. Gerald Dworkin, "Paternalism," *The Monist*, Vol. 56 (January, 1972), p. 65. Hereafter abbreviated *D*.

6. "Legal Paternalism," *The Canadian Journal of Philosophy*, Vol. I (1971), pp. 105–24. This paper is reworked in *Social Philosophy* (Englewood Cliffs: Prentice-Hall, 1973). Hereafter both are abbreviated *F*, with references to the latter in brackets. The distinction mentioned above is best made in *Social Philosophy*, p. 33 and in his " 'Harmless Immoralities' and Offensive Nuisances," *Issues in Law and Morality*, ed. N. S. Care and T. K. Trelogan (Cleveland: Case Western Reserve Press), pp. 83 f.

7. Mill, *On Liberty* (Indianapolis: Liberal Arts Press, 1956), p. 117. Feinberg deals with this example (112 [49]), but I am unsure whether he believes Mill's conclusion correct.

8. "Private Consensual Adult Behavior: The Requirement of Harm to Others in the Enforcement of Morality," 14 *UCLA Law Review* (1967), p. 585n.

74. MAJORITY OPINION IN DOE v. COMMONWEALTH'S ATTORNEY FOR THE CITY OF RICHMOND

Judge Bryan

BRYAN, Senior Circuit Judge:
[1, 2] Virginia's statute making sodomy a crime is unconstitutional, each of the male plaintiffs aver, when it is applied to his active and regular homosexual relations with another *adult male, consensually* and *in private*.[1] They assert that local State officers threaten them with prosecution for violation of this law, that such enforcement would deny them their Fifth and Fourteenth Amendments' assurance of due process, the First Amendment's protection of their rights of freedom of expression, the First and Ninth Amendments' guarantee of privacy, and the Eighth Amendment's forbiddance of cruel and unusual punishments. . . .

So far as relevant, the Code of Virginia, 1950, as amended, provides:

§18.1–212. Crimes against nature.—If any person shall carnally know in any manner any brute animal, or carnally know any male or female person by the anus or by or with the mouth, or voluntarily submit to such carnal knowledge, he or she shall be guilty of a felony and shall be confined in the penitentiary not less than one year nor more than three years.

[3] Our decision is that on its face and in the circumstances here it is not unconstitutional. No judgment is made upon the wisdom or policy of the statute. It is simply that we cannot say that the statute offends the Bill of Rights or any other of the Amendments and the wisdom or policy is a matter for the State's resolve.

I. Precedents cited to us as *contra* rest exclusively on the precept that the Constitution condemns State legislation that trespasses upon the

privacy of the incidents of marriage, upon the sanctity of the home, or upon the nurture of family life. This and only this concern has been the justification for nullification of State regulation in this area. Review of plaintiffs' authorities will reveal these as the principles underlying the referenced decisions.

In *Griswold v. Connecticut* . . . (1965), plaintiffs' chief reliance, the Court has most recently announced its views on the question here. Striking down a State statute forbidding the use of contraceptives, the ruling was put on the right of marital privacy—held to be one of the specific guarantees of the Bill of Rights—and was also put on the sanctity of the home and family. Its thesis is epitomized by the author of the opinion, Mr. Justice Douglas, in his conclusion:

We deal with a right of privacy older than the Bill of Rights—older than our political parties, older than our school system. Marriage is a coming together for better or for worse, hopefully enduring and intimate to the degree of being sacred. It is an association that promotes a way of life, not causes; a harmony in living, not political faiths; a bilateral loyalty, not commercial or social projects. Yet it is an association for as noble a purpose as any involved in our prior decisions. [p. 486, 85 S.Ct. p. 1682.]

That *Griswold* is premised on the right of privacy and that homosexual intimacy is denunciable by the State is unequivocally demonstrated by Mr. Justice Goldberg in his concurrence, p. 499, 85 S.Ct. 1678, in his adoption of Mr. Justice Harlan's dissenting statement in *Poe v. Ullman* . . . (1961):

Adultery, *homosexuality* and the like are sexual intimacies *which the State forbids* . . . but the intimacy of husband

From 403 Federal Supplement 1975, pp. 1200–1203.

and wife is necessarily an essential and accepted feature of the institution of marriage, an institution which the State not only must allow, but which always and in every age it has fostered and protected. *It is one thing when the State exerts its power either to forbid extramarital sexuality . . . or to say who may marry, but it is quite another when,* having acknowledged a marriage and the intimacies inherent in it, it undertakes to regulate by means of the criminal law the details of that intimacy. (Emphasis added.)

Equally forceful is the succeeding paragraph of Justice Harlan:

In sum, even though the State has determined that the use of contraceptives is as iniquitous as any act of extramarital sexual immorality, the intrusion of the whole machinery of the criminal law into the very heart of marital privacy, requiring husband and wife to render account before a criminal tribunal of their uses of that intimacy is surely *a very different thing indeed from punishing those who establish intimacies which the law has always forbidden and which can have no claim to social protection* . . . (Emphasis added.). . .

With his standing, what he had further to say in *Poe v. Ullman,* supra, is worthy of high regard. On the plaintiffs' effort presently to shield the practice of homosexuality from State incrimination by according it immunity when committed in private as against public exercise, the Justice said this:

Indeed to attempt a line between public behavior and that which is purely consensual or solitary would be to withdraw from community concern a range of subjects with which every society in civilized times has found it necessary to deal. The laws regarding marriage which provide both when the sexual powers may be used and the legal and societal context in which children are born and brought up, as well as *laws forbidding adultery, fornication and homosexual practices which express the negative of the proposition,* confining sexuality to lawful marriage, form a pattern so deeply pressed into the substance of our social life that any Constitutional doctrine in this area must build upon that basis. . . . (Accent added.)

Again:

Thus, I would not suggest that *adultery, homosexuality, fornication and incest are immune* from criminal enquiry, *however privately practiced.* So much has been explicitly

recognized in acknowledging the State's rightful concern for its people's moral welfare. . . . But not to discriminate between what is involved in this case and either the traditional offenses against good morals or crimes which, though they may be committed anywhere, *happen to have been committed or concealed in the home,* would entirely misconceive the argument that is being made. . . . (Accent added.)

Many states have long had, and still have, statutes and decisional law criminalizing conduct depicted in the Virginia legislation. . . .

[4] II. With no authoritative judicial bar to the proscription of homosexuality—since it is obviously no portion of marriage, home or family life—the next question is whether there is any ground for barring Virginia from branding it as criminal. If a State determines that punishment therefor, even when committed in the home, is appropriate in the promotion of morality and decency, it is not for the courts to say that the State is not free to do so.

[5] Furthermore, if the State has the burden of proving that it has a legitimate interest in the subject of the statute or that the statute is rationally supportable, Virginia has completely fulfilled this obligation. Fundamentally, the State action is simply directed to the suppression of crime, whether committed in public or in private. Both instances, as *California,* supra, recognizes, are within the reach of the police power.

[6] Moreover, to sustain its action the State is not required to show that moral delinquency actually results from homosexuality. It is enough for upholding the legislation to establish that the conduct is likely to end in a contribution to moral delinquency. Plainly, it would indeed be impracticable to prove the actuality of such a consequence, and the law is not so exacting.

If such a prospect or expectation was in the mind of the General Assembly of Virginia, the prophecy proved only too true in the occurrences narrated in *Lovisi v. Slayton,* . . . now on appeal in the Fourth Circuit. The graphic outline by the District Judge there describes just such a sexual orgy as the Statute was evidently intended to punish. The Lovisis, a married couple, advertised their wish "to meet people" and in response a man came to Virginia to meet the Lovisis on several occasions. In one instance the three of them participated in acts of fellatio. Photographs of the conduct were taken by a set camera and the acts were witnessed by the wife's daughters, aged 11 and 13. The pictures were carried by them to school.

Although a questionable law is not removed from question by the lapse of any prescriptive period, the longevity of the Virginia statute does testify to the State's interest and its legitimacy. It is not an upstart notion; it has ancestry going back to Judaic and Christian law. The immediate parentage may be readily traced to the Code of Virginia of 1792. All the while the law has been kept alive, as evidenced by periodic amendments, the last in the 1968 Acts of the General Assembly of Virginia, c. 427.

In sum, we believe that the sodomy statute, so long in force in Virginia, has a rational basis of State interest demonstrably legitimate and mirrored in the cited decisional law of the Supreme Court. . . .

The prayers for a declaratory judgment and an injunction invalidating the sodomy statute will be denied.

75. MINORITY OPINION IN DOE v. COMMONWEALTH'S ATTORNEY FOR THE CITY OF RICHMOND

Judge Merhige

MERHIGE, District Judge (dissenting).

I am in full accord with the majority as to their conclusion that this action does not fit within the compass of Fed. R.Civ.P. 23. Regretfully, however, my views as to the constitutionality of the statute in question, as it applies to consenting adults acting in the privacy of their homes, does not conform with theirs. In my view, in the absence of any legitimate interest or rational basis to support the statute's application we must, without regard to our own proclivities and reluctance to judicially bar the state proscription of homosexuality, hold the statute as it applies to the plaintiffs to be violative of their rights under the Due Process Clause of the Fourteenth Amendment to the Constitution of the United States. The Supreme Court decision in *Griswold v. Connecticut,* . . . (1965), is, as the majority points out, premised on the right of privacy, but I fear my brothers have misapplied its precedential value through an apparent over-adherence to its factual circumstances.

The Supreme Court has consistently held that the Due Process Clause of the Fourteenth Amendment protects the right of individuals to make personal choices, unfettered by arbitrary and purposeless restraints, in the private matters of marriage and procreation. . . . I view those cases as standing for the principle that every individual has a right to be free from unwarranted governmental intrusion into one's decisions on private matters of intimate concern. A mature individual's choice of an adult sexual partner, in the privacy of his or her own home, would appear to me to be a decision of the utmost private and intimate concern. Private consensual sex acts between adults are matters, absent evidence that they are harmful, in which the state has no legitimate interest.

To say, as the majority does, that the right of privacy, which every citizen has, is limited to matters of marital, home or family life is unwarranted under the law. Such a contention places a distinction in marital-nonmarital matters which is inconsistent with current Supreme Court opinions and is unsupportable.

From 403 Federal Supplement 1975, pp. 1203–1205.

In my view, the reliance of the majority on Mr. Justice Harlan's dissenting statement in *Poe v. Ullman* . . . (1961), is misplaced. An analysis of the cases indicates that in 1965 when *Griswold,* which invalidated a statute prohibiting the use of contraceptives by married couples, was decided, at least three of the Court,* relying primarily on Mr. Justice Harlan's dissent in *Poe v. Ullman,* and Mr. Justice Harlan himself, would not have been willing to attach the right of privacy to homosexual conduct. In my view, *Griswold* applied the right of privacy to its particular factual situation. That the right of privacy is not limited to the facts of *Griswold* is demonstrated by later Supreme Court decisions. After *Griswold,* by virtue of *Eisenstadt v. Baird* . . . (1972), the legal viability of a marital-nonmarital distinction in private sexual acts if not eliminated, was at the very least seriously impaired. In *Eisenstadt, supra,* the Court declined to restrict the right of privacy in sexual matters to married couples:

Yet the marital couple is not an independent entity with a mind and heart of its own, but an association of two individuals each with a separate intellectual and emotional makeup. If the right of privacy means anything, it is the right of the *individual,* married or single, to be free from unwarranted governmental intrusion into matters so fundamentally affecting a person as the decision whether to bear or beget a child. . . .

In significantly diminishing the importance of the marital-nonmarital distinction, the Court to a great extent vitiated any implication that the state can, as suggested by Mr. Justice Harlan in *Poe v. Ullman,* forbid extra-marital sexuality, and such implications are no longer fully accurate.

It is one thing when the State exerts its power either to forbid extra-marital sexuality altogether, or to say who may marry, but it is quite another when, having acknowledged a marriage and the intimacies inherent in it, it undertakes to regulate by means of the criminal law the details of that intimacy. . . . (1961 Harlan dissenting).

Griswold, supra, in its context, applied the right of privacy in sexual matters to the marital relationship. *Eisenstadt* . . . however, clearly demonstrates that the right to privacy in sexual relation-

ships is not limited to the marital relationship. Both *Roe* . . . and *Eisenstadt* . . . cogently demonstrate that intimate personal decisions or private matters of substantial importance to the well-being of the individuals involved are protected by the Due Process Clause. The right to select consenting adult sexual partners must be considered within this category. The exercise of that right, whether heterosexual or homosexual, should not be proscribed by state regulation absent compelling justification.

This approach does not unqualifiedly sanction personal whim. If the activity in question involves more than one participant, as in the instant case, each must be capable of consenting, and each must in fact consent to the conduct for the right of privacy to attach. For example, if one of the participants in homosexual contact is a minor, or force is used to coerce one of the participants to yield, the right will not attach. . . . Similarly, the right of privacy cannot be extended to protect conduct that takes place in publicly frequented areas. . . . However, if the right of privacy does apply to specific courses of conduct, legitimate state restriction on personal autonomy may be justified only under the compelling state interest test. . . .

The defendants, represented by the highest legal officer of the state, made no tender of any evidence which even impliedly demonstrated that homosexuality causes society any significant harm. No effort was made by the defendants to establish either a rational basis or a compelling state interest so as to justify the proscription of § 8.1–212 of the Code of Virginia, presently under attack. To suggest, as defendants do, that the prohibition of homosexual conduct will in some manner encourage new heterosexual marriages and prevent the dissolution of existing ones is unworthy of judicial response. In any event, what we know as men is not forgotten as judges—it is difficult to envision any substantial number of heterosexual marriages being in danger of dissolution because of the private sexual activities of homosexuals.

On the basis of this record one can only conclude that the sole basis of the proscription of homosexuality was what the majority refers to as the promotion of morality and decency. As salutary a legislative goal as this may be, I can find no authority for intrusion by the state into the private dwelling of a citizen. . . . The Supreme Court has made it clear that fundamental rights of such an intimate facet of an individual's life as sex, absent circumstances warranting intrusion by the state, are to be respected. My brothers, I respectfully suggest, have by today's ruling misinterpreted the issue—the issue centers not around morality of decency, but the constitutional right of privacy.

I respectfully note my dissent.

From *The Enforcement of Morals* by Patrick Devlin. © Oxford University Press 1965. Reprinted by permission of Oxford University Press.

[EDITORS' NOTE: The United States Supreme Court on March 29, 1976, affirmed the majority decision without opinion. Justices Brennan, Marshall, and Stevens noted probable jurisdiction and would have voted to hear oral arguments.]

NOTES

Griswold v. Connecticut, supra, 381 U.S. 479, 486, 85 S.Ct. 1678 (1964) (Goldberg, J., with whom Chief Justice Warren and Brennan, J., join, concurring).

76. MORALS AND THE CRIMINAL LAW

Patrick Devlin

I think it is clear that the criminal law as we know it is based upon moral principle. In a number of crimes its function is simply to enforce a moral principle and nothing else. The law, both criminal and civil, claims to be able to speak about morality and immorality generally. Where does it get its authority to do this and how does it settle the moral principles which it enforces? Undoubtedly, as a matter of history, it derived both from Christian teaching. But I think that the strict logician is right when he says that the law can no longer rely on doctrines in which citizens are entitled to disbelieve. It is necessary therefore to look for some other source.

In jurisprudence . . . everything is thrown open to discussion and, in the belief that they cover the whole field, I have framed three interrogatories addressed to myself to answer:

1. Has society the right to pass judgement at all on matters of morals? Ought there, in other words, to be a public morality, or are morals always a matter for private judgement?
2. If society has the right to pass judgement, has it also the right to use the weapon of the law to enforce it?

3. If so, ought it to use that weapon in all cases or only in some; and if only in some, on what principles should it distinguish?

[1] I shall begin with the first interrogatory and consider what is meant by the right of society to pass a moral judgement, that is, a judgement about what is good and what is evil. The fact that a majority of people may disapprove of a practice does not of itself make it a matter for society as a whole. Nine men out of ten may disapprove of what the tenth man is doing and still say that it is not their business. There is a case for a collective judgement (as distinct from a large number of individual opinions which sensible people may even refrain from pronouncing at all if it is upon somebody else's private affairs) only if society is affected. Without a collective judgement there can be no case at all for intervention. Let me take as an illustration the Englishman's attitude to religion as it is now and as it has been in the past. His attitude now is that a man's religion is his private affair; he may think of another man's religion that it is right or wrong, true or untrue, but not that it is good or bad. In earlier times that was not so; a man was denied the right to practise what was thought of as heresy, and heresy was thought of as destructive of society.

The language [in] . . . the Wolfenden Report suggests the view that there ought not to be a collective judgement about immorality *per se*. Is this what is meant by 'private morality' and 'individual freedom of choice and action'? Some people sincerely believe that homosexuality is neither immoral nor unnatural. Is the 'freedom of choice and action' that is offered to the individual, freedom to decide for himself what is moral or immoral, society remaining neutral; or is it freedom to be immoral if he wants to be? The language of the Report may be open to question, but the conclusions at which the Committee arrive answer this question unambiguously. If society is not prepared to say that homosexuality is morally wrong, there would be no basis for a law protecting youth from 'corruption' or punishing a man for living on the 'immoral' earnings of a homosexual prostitute, as the Report recommends.[1] This attitude the Committee make even clearer when they come to deal with prostitution. In truth, the Report takes it for granted that there is in existence a public morality which condemns homosexuality and prostitution. What the Report seems to mean by private morality might perhaps be better described as private behaviour in matters of morals.

This view—that there is such a thing as public morality—can also be justified by *a priori* argument. What makes a society of any sort is community of ideas, not only political ideas but also ideas about the way its members should behave and govern their lives; these latter ideas are its morals. Every society has a moral structure as well as a political one: or rather, since that might suggest two independent systems, I should say that the structure of every society is made up both of politics and morals. Take, for example, the institution of marriage. Whether a man should be allowed to take more than one wife is something about which every society has to make up its mind one way or the other. In England we believe in the Christian idea of marriage and therefore adopt monogamy as a moral principle. Consequently the Christian institution of marriage has become the basis of family life and so part of the structure of our society. It is there not because it is Christian. It has got there because it is Christian, but it remains there because it is built into the house in which we live and could not be removed without bringing it down. The great majority of those who live in this country accept it because it is the Christian idea of marriage and for them the only true one. But a non-Christian is bound by it, not because it is part of Christianity but because, rightly or wrongly, it has been adopted by the society in which he lives. It would be useless for him to stage a debate designed to prove that polygamy was theologically more correct and socially preferable; if he wants to live in the house, he must accept it as built in the way in which it is.

We see this more clearly if we think of ideas or institutions that are purely political. Society cannot tolerate rebellion; it will not allow argument about the rightness of the cause. Historians a century later may say that the rebels were right and the Government was wrong and a percipient and conscientious subject of the State may think so at the time. But it is not a matter which can be left to individual judgement.

The institution of marriage is a good example for my purpose because it bridges the division, if there is one, between politics and morals. Marriage is part of the structure of our society and it is also the basis of a moral code which condemns fornication and adultery. The institution of marriage would be gravely threatened if individual judgements were permitted about the morality of adultery; on these points there must be a public morality. But public morality is not to be confined to those moral principles which support institutions such as marriage. People do not think of monogamy as something which has to be supported because our society has chosen to organize itself upon it; they think of it as something that is good in itself and offering a good way of life and that it is for that reason that our society has adopted it. I return to the statement that I have already made, that society means a community of ideas; without shared ideas on politics, morals, and ethics no society can exist. Each one of us has ideas about what is good and what is evil; they cannot be kept private from the society in which we live. If men and women try to create a society in which there is no fundamental agreement about good and evil they will fail; if, having based it on common agreement, the agreement goes, the society will disintegrate. For society is not something that is kept together physically; it is held by the invisible bonds of common thought. If the bonds were too far relaxed the members would drift apart. A common morality is part of the bondage.

The bondage is part of the price of society; and mankind, which needs society, must pay its price. . . .

[2] You may think that I have taken far too long in contending that there is such a thing as public morality, a proposition which most people would readily accept, and may have left myself too little time to discuss the next question which to many minds may cause greater difficulty: to what extent should society use the law to enforce its moral judgements? But I believe that the answer to the first question determines the way in which the second should be approached and may indeed very nearly dictate the answer to the second question. If society has no right to make judgements on morals, the law must find some special justification for entering the field of morality: if homosexuality and prostitution are not in themselves wrong, then the onus is very clearly on the lawgiver who wants to frame a law against certain aspects of them to justify the exceptional treatment. But if society has the right to make a judgement and has it on the basis that a recognized morality is as necessary to society as, say, a recognized government, then society may use the law to preserve morality in the same way as it uses it to safeguard anything else that is essential to its existence. If therefore the first proposition is securely established with all its implications, society has a prima facie right to legislate against immorality as such.

The Wolfenden Report, notwithstanding that it seems to admit the right of society to condemn homosexuality and prostitution as immoral, requires special circumstances to be shown to justify the intervention of the law. I think that this is wrong in principle and that any attempt to approach my second interrogatory on these lines is bound to break down. I think that the attempt by the Committee does break down and that this is shown by the fact that it has to define or describe its special circumstances so widely that they can be supported only if it is accepted that the law is concerned with immorality as such.

The widest of the special circumstances are described as the provision of 'sufficient safeguards against exploitation and corruption of others, particularly those who are specially vulnerable because they are young, weak in body or mind, inex-perienced, or in a state of special physical, official or economic dependence.'[2] The corruption of youth is a well-recognized ground for intervention by the State and for the purpose of any legislation the young can easily be defined. But if similar protection were to be extended to every other citizen, there would be no limit to the reach of the law. The 'corruption and exploitation of others' is so wide that it could be used to cover any sort of immorality which involves, as most do, the co-operation of another person. Even if the phrase is taken as limited to the categories that are particularized as 'specially vulnerable,' it is so elastic as to be practically no restriction. This is not merely a matter of words. For if the words used are stretched almost beyond breaking-point, they still are not wide enough to cover the recommendations which the Committee make about prostitution.

Prostitution is not in itself illegal and the Committee do not think that it ought to be made so.[3] If prostitution is private immorality and not the law's business, what concern has the law with the ponce or the brothel-keeper or the householder who permits habitual prostitution? The Report recommends that the laws which make these activities criminal offences should be maintained or strengthened and brings them (so far as it goes into principle; with regard to brothels it says simply that the law rightly frowns on them) under the head of exploitation.[4] There may be cases of exploitation in this trade, as there are or used to be in many others, but in general a ponce exploits a prostitute no more than an impresario exploits an actress. The Report finds that 'the great majority of prostitutes are women whose psychological makeup is such that they choose this life because they find in it a style of living which is to them easier, freer and more profitable than would be provided by any other occupation. . . . In the main the association between prostitute and ponce is voluntary and operates to mutual advantage.[5] The Committee would agree that this could not be called exploitation in the ordinary sense. They say: 'It is in our view an oversimplification to think that those who live on the earnings of prostitution are exploiting the prostitute as such. What they are really exploiting is the whole complex of the relationship between prostitute and customer; they are, in effect, exploiting the human weaknesses which cause the customer to seek the prostitute and the prostitute to meet the demand.'[6]

All sexual immorality involves the exploitation of human weaknesses. The prostitute exploits the lust of her customers and the customer the moral weakness of the prostitute. If the exploitation of human weaknesses is considered to create a special circumstance, there is virtually no field of morality which can be defined in such a way as to exclude the law.

I think, therefore, that it is not possible to set theoretical limits to the power of the State to legislate against immorality. It is not possible to settle in advance exceptions to the general rule or to define inflexibly areas of morality into which the law is in no circumstances to be allowed to enter. Society is entitled by means of its laws to protect itself from dangers, whether from within or without. Here again I think that the political parallel is legitimate. The law of treason is directed against aiding the king's enemies and against sedition from within. The justification for this is that established government is necessary for the existence of society and therefore its safety against violent overthrow must be secured. But an established morality is as necessary as good government to the welfare of society. Societies disintegrate from within more frequently than they are broken up by external pressures. There is disintegration when no common morality is observed and history shows that the loosening of moral bonds is often the first stage of disintegration, so that society is justified in taking the same steps to preserve its moral code as it does to preserve its government and other essential institutions.[7] The suppression of vice is as much the law's business as the suppression of subversive activities; it is no more possible to define a sphere of private morality than it is to define one of private subversive activity. It is wrong to talk of private morality or of the law not being concerned with immorality as such or to try to set rigid bounds to the part which the law may play in the suppression of vice. There are no theoretical limits to the power of the State to legislate treason and sedition, and likewise I think there can be no theoretical limits to legislation against immorality. You may argue that if a man's sins affect only himself it cannot be the concern of society. If he chooses to get drunk every night in the privacy of his own home, is any one except himself the worse for it? But suppose a quarter or a half of the population got drunk every night, what sort of society would it be? You cannot set a theoretical limit to the number of people who can get drunk before society is entitled to legislate against drunkenness. The same may be said of gambling. The Royal Commission on Betting, Lotteries, and Gaming took as their test the character of the citizen as a member of society. They said: 'Our concern with the ethical significance of gambling is confined to the effect which it may have on the character of the gambler as a member of society. If we were convinced that whatever the degree of gambling this effect must be harmful we should be inclined to think that it was the duty of the state to restrict gambling to the greatest extent practicable.'[8]

[3] In what circumstances the State should exercise its power is the third of the interrogatories I have framed. But before I get to it I must raise a point which might have been brought up in any one of the three. How are the moral judgements of society to be ascertained? By leaving it until now, I can ask it in the more limited form that is now sufficient for my purpose. How is the law-maker to ascertain the moral judgements of society? It is surely not enough that they should be reached by the opinion of the majority; it would be too much to require the individual assent of every citizen. English law has evolved and regularly uses a standard which does not depend on the counting of heads. It is that of the reasonable man. He is not to be confused with the rational man. He is not expected to reason about anything and his judgment may be largely a matter of feeling. It is the viewpoint of the man in the street—or to use an archaism familiar to all lawyers—the man in the Clapham omnibus. He might also be called the right-minded man. For my purpose I should like to call him the man in the jury box, for the moral judgement of society must be something about which any twelve men or women drawn at random might after discussion be expected to be unanimous. This was the standard the judges applied in the days before Parliament was as active as it is now and when they laid down rules of public policy.

They did not think of themselves as making law but simply as stating principles which every right-minded person would accept as valid. It is what Pollock called 'practical morality', which is based not on theological or philosophical foundations but 'in the mass of continuous experience half-consciously or unconsciously accumulated and embodied in the morality of common sense.' He called it also 'a certain way of thinking on questions of morality which we expect to find in a reasonable civilized man or a reasonable Englishman, taken at random.'[9]

Immorality then, for the purpose of the law, is what every right-minded person is presumed to consider to be immoral. Any immorality is capable of affecting society injuriously and in effect to a greater or lesser extent it usually does; this is what gives the law its *locus standi*. It cannot be shut out. But—and this brings me to the third question—the individual has a *locus standi* too; he cannot be expected to surrender to the judgement of society the whole conduct of his life. It is the old and familiar question of striking a balance between the rights and interests of society and those of the individual. . . .

. . . It is possible to make general statements of principle which it may be thought the legislature should bear in mind when it is considering the enactment of laws enforcing morals.

I believe that most people would agree upon the chief of these elastic principles. There must be toleration of the maximum individual freedom that is consistent with the integrity of society. It cannot be said that this is a principle that runs all through the criminal law. Much of the criminal law that is regulatory in character—the part of it that deals with *malum prohibitum* rather than *malum in se*—is based upon the opposite principle, that is, that the choice of the individual must give way to the convenience of the many. But in all matters of conscience the principle I have stated is generally held to prevail. It is not confined to thought and speech; it extends to action, as is shown by the recognition of the right to conscientious objection in war-time; this example shows also that conscience will be respected even in times of national danger. The principle appears to me to be peculiarly appropriate to all questions of morals. Nothing should be punished by the law that does not lie beyond the limits of tolerance. It is not nearly enough to say that a majority dislike a practice; there must be a real feeling of reprobation. Those who are dissatisfied with the present law on homosexuality often say that the opponents of reform are swayed simply by disgust. If that were so it would be wrong, but I do not think one can ignore disgust if it is deeply felt and not manufactured. Its presence is a good indication that the bounds of toleration are being reached. Not everything is to be tolerated. No society can do without intolerance, indignation, and disgust;[10] they are the forces behind the moral law, and indeed it can be argued that if they or something like them are not present, the feelings of society cannot be weighty enough to deprive the individuals of freedom of choice. I suppose that there is hardly anyone nowadays who would not be disgusted by the thought of deliberate cruelty to animals. No one proposes to relegate that or any other form of sadism to the realm of private morality or to allow it to be practised in public or in private. It would be possible no doubt to point out that until a comparatively short while ago nobody thought very much of cruelty to animals and also that pity and kindliness and the unwillingness to inflict pain are virtues more generally esteemed now than they have ever been in the past. But matters of this sort are not determined by rational argument. Every moral judgement, unless it claims a divine source, is simply a feeling that no right-minded man could behave in any other way without admitting that he was doing wrong. It is the power of a common sense and not the power of reason that is behind the judgements of society. But before a society can put a practice beyond the limits of tolerance there must be a deliberate judgement that the practice is injurious to society. There is, for example, a general abhorrence of homosexuality. We should ask ourselves in the first instance whether, looking at it calmly and dispassionately, we regard it as a vice so abominable that its mere presence is an offence. If that is the genuine feeling of the society in which we live, I do not see how society can be denied the right to eradicate it. Our feeling may not be so intense as that. We may feel about it that, if confined, it is tolerable, but that if it spread it might be gravely injurious; it is in this way that most societies look upon fornication, seeing it as a natural weakness which must be kept within bounds but which cannot be rooted out. It becomes then a question of balance, the danger to society in one scale and the extent of the restriction in the other. On this sort of point the value of an investigation by such a body as the Wolfenden Committee and of its conclusions is manifest.

The limits of tolerance shift. This is supplementary to what I have been saying but of sufficient importance in itself to deserve statement as a separate principle which law-makers have to bear in mind. I suppose that moral standards do not shift; so far as they come from divine revelation they do not, and I am willing to assume that the moral judgements made by a society always remain good for that society. But the extent to which society will tolerate—I mean tolerate, not approve—departures from moral standards varies from generation to generation. It may be that over-all tolerance is always increasing. The pressure of the human mind, always seeking greater freedom of thought, is outwards against the bonds of society forcing their gradual relaxation. It may be that history is a tale of contraction and expansion and that all developed societies are on their way to dissolution. I must not speak of things I do not know; and anyway as a practical matter no society is willing to make provision for its own decay. I return therefore to the simple and observable fact that in matters of morals the limits of tolerance shift. Laws, especially those which are based on morals, are less easily moved. It follows as another good working principle that in any new matter of morals the law should be slow to act. By the next generation the swell of indignation may have abated and the law be left without the strong backing which it needs. But it is then difficult to alter the law without giving the impression that moral judgement is being weakened. This is now one of the factors that is strongly militating against any alteration to the law on homosexuality.

A third elastic principle must be advanced more tentatively. It is that as far as possible privacy should be respected. This is not an idea that has ever been made explicit in the criminal law. Acts or words done or said in public or in private are all brought within its scope without distinction in principle. But there goes with this a strong reluctance on the part of judges and legislators to sanction invasions of privacy in the detection of crime. The police have no more right to trespass than the ordinary citizen has; there is no general right of search; to this extent an Englishman's home is still his castle. The Government is extremely careful in the exercise even of those powers which it claims to be undisputed. Telephone tapping and interference with the mails afford a good illustration of this. . . .

This indicates a general sentiment that the right to privacy is something to be put in the balance against the enforcement of the law. Ought the same sort of consideration to play any part in the formation of the law? Clearly only in a very limited number of cases. When the help of the law is invoked by an injured citizen, privacy must be irrelevant; the individual cannot ask that his right to privacy should be measured against injury criminally done to another. But when all who are involved in the deed are consenting parties and the injury is done to morals, the public interest in the moral order can be balanced against the claims of privacy. The restriction on police powers of investigation goes further than the affording of a parallel; it means that the detection of crime committed in private and when there is no complaint is bound to be rather haphazard and this is an additional reason for moderation. These considerations do not justify the exclusion of all private immorality from the scope of the law. I think that, as I have already suggested, the test of 'private behaviour' should be substituted for 'private morality' and the influence of the factor should be reduced from that of a definite limitation to that of a matter to be taken into account. Since the gravity of the crime is also a proper consideration, a distinction might well be made in the case of homosexuality between the lesser acts of indecency and the full offence, which on the principle of the Wolfenden Report it would be illogical to do.

NOTES

1. Para. 76.
2. Para. 13.
3. Paras. 224, 285, and 318.

4. Paras. 302 and 320.

5. Para. 223.

6. Para. 306.

7. It is somewhere about this point in the argument that Professor Hart in *Law, Liberty and Morality* discerns a proposition which he describes as central to my thought. He states the proposition and his objection to it as follows (p. 51). 'He appears to move from the acceptable proposition that *some* shared morality is essential to the existence of any society [this I take to be the proposition on p. 12] to the unacceptable proposition that a society is identical with its morality as that is at any given moment of its history, so that a change in its morality is tantamount to the destruction of a society. The former proposition might be even accepted as a necessary rather than an empirical truth depending on a quite plausible definition of society as a body of men who hold certain moral views in common. But the latter proposition is absurd. Taken strictly, it would prevent us saying that the morality of a given society had changed, and would compel us instead to say that one society had disappeared and another one taken its place. But it is only on this absurd criterion of what it is for the same society to continue to exist that it could be asserted without evidence that any deviation from a society's shared morality threatens its existence.' In conclusion (p. 82) Professor Hart condemns the whole thesis in the lecture as based on 'a confused definition of what a society is'.

I do not assert that *any* deviation from a society's shared morality threatens its existence any more than I assert that *any* subversive activity threatens its existence. I assert that they are both activities which are capable in their nature of threatening the existence of society so that neither can be put beyond the law.

For the rest, the objection appears to me to be all a matter of words. I would venture to assert, for example, that you cannot have a game without rules and that if there were no rules there would be no game. If I am asked whether that means that the game is 'identical' with the rules, I would be willing for the question to be answered either way in the belief that the answer would lead to nowhere. If I am asked whether a change in the rules means that one game has disappeared and another has taken its place, I would reply probably not, but that it would depend on the extent of the change.

Likewise I should venture to assert that there cannot be a contract without terms. Does this mean that an 'amended' contract is a 'new' contract in the eyes of the law? I once listened to an argument by an ingenious counsel that a contract, because of the substitution of one clause for another, had 'ceased to have effect' within the meaning of a statutory provision. The judge did not accept the argument; but if most of the fundamental terms had been changed, I daresay he would have done.

The proposition that I make in the text is that if (as I understand Professor Hart to agree, at any rate for the purposes of the argument) you cannot have a society without morality, the law can be used to enforce morality as something that is essential to a society. I cannot see why this proposition (whether it is right or wrong) should mean that morality can never be changed without the destruction of society. If morality is changed, the law can be changed. Professor Hart refers (p. 72) to the proposition as 'the use of legal punishment to freeze into immobility the morality dominant at a particular time in a society's existence'. One might as well say that the inclusion of a penal section into a statute prohibiting certain acts freezes the whole statute into immobility and prevents the prohibitions from ever being modified.

8. (1951) Cmd. 8190, para. 159.

9. *Essays in Jurisprudence and Ethics* (1882), Macmillan, pp. 278 and 353.

10. These words which have been much criticized, are considered again in the Preface at p. viii.

77. THE ENFORCEMENT OF MORALS

H. L. A. Hart

Much dissatisfaction has for long been felt in England with the criminal law relating to both prostitution and homosexuality, and in 1954 the committee well known as the Wolfenden Committee was appointed to consider the state of the law. This committee reported[1] in September 1957 and recommended certain changes in the law on both topics. As to homosexuality they recommended by a

Reprinted from *Law, Liberty, and Morality* by H. L. A. Hart, with the permission of the publishers, Stanford University Press. © 1963 by the Board of Trustees of the Leland Stanford Junior University.

majority of 12 to 1 that homosexual practices between consenting adults in private should no longer be a crime; as to prostitution they unanimously recommended that, though it should not itself be made illegal, legislation should be passed "to drive it off the streets" on the ground that public soliciting was an offensive nuisance to ordinary citizens. . . .

What concerns us here is less the fate of the Wolfenden Committee's recommendations than the principles by which these were supported. These are strikingly similar to those expounded by

Mill in his essay *On Liberty*. Thus section 13 of the Committee's Report reads:

[The] function [of the criminal law], as we see it, is to preserve public order and decency, to protect the citizen from what is offensive or injurious and to provide sufficient safeguards against exploitation or corruption of others, particularly those who are specially vulnerable because they are young, weak in the body or mind or inexperienced. . . .

This conception of the positive functions of the criminal law was the Committee's main ground for its recommendation concerning prostitution that legislation should be passed to suppress the offensive public manifestations of prostitution, but not to make prostitution itself illegal. Its recommendation that the law against homosexual practices between consenting adults in private should be relaxed was based on the principle stated simply in section 61 of the Report as follows: "There must remain a realm of private morality and immorality which is, in brief and crude terms, not the law's business."

It is of some interest that these developments in England have had near counterparts in America. In 1955 the American Law Institute published with its draft Model Penal Code a recommendation that all consensual relations between adults in private should be excluded from the scope of the criminal law. Its grounds were (*inter alia*) that "no harm to the secular interests of the community is involved in atypical sex practice in private between consenting adult partners";[2] and "there is the fundamental question of the protection to which every individual is entitled against state interference in his personal affairs when he is not hurting others."[3] . . .

It is perhaps clear from the foregoing that Mill's principles are still very much alive in the criticism of law, whatever their theoretical deficiencies may be. But twice in one hundred years they have been challenged by two masters of the Common Law. The first of these was the great Victorian judge and historian of the Criminal Law, James Fitzjames Stephen. His criticism of Mill is to be found in the sombre and impressive book *Liberty, Equality, Fraternity*,[4] which he wrote as a direct reply to Mill's essay *On Liberty*. It is evident from the tone of this book that Stephen thought he had found crushing arguments against Mill and had demonstrated that the law might justifiably enforce morality as such or, as he said, that the law should be "a persecution of the grosser forms of vice."[5] Nearly a century later, on the publication of the Wolfenden Committee's report, Lord Devlin, now a member of the House of Lords and a most distinguished writer on the criminal law, in his essay on *The Enforcement of Morals*[6] took as his target the Report's contention "that there must be a realm of morality and immorality which is not the law's business" and argued in opposition to it that "the suppression of vice is as much the law's business as the suppression of subversive activities." . . .

Though [the arguments of these legal writers] are at points confused, they certainly still deserve the compliment of rational opposition. They are not only admirably stocked with concrete examples, but they express the considered views of skilled, sophisticated lawyers experienced in the administration of the criminal law. Views such as theirs are still quite widely held especially by lawyers both in England and in this country; it may indeed be that they are more popular, in both countries, than Mill's doctrine of Liberty.

Before we consider the detail of these arguments, it is, I think, necessary to appreciate three different but connected features of the question with which we are concerned. . . .

. . . The question is one *about* morality, but it is important to observe that it is also itself a question *of* morality. It is the question whether the enforcement of morality is morally justified; so morality enters into the question in two ways. The importance of this feature of the question is that it would plainly be no sufficient answer to show that in fact in some society—our own or others—it was widely regarded as morally quite right and proper to enforce, by legal punishment, compliance with the accepted morality. No one who seriously debates this question would regard Mill as refuted by the simple demonstration that there are some societies in which the generally shared morality endorses its own enforcement by law, and does so even in those cases where the immorality was thought harmless to others. The existence of societies which condemn association between white and coloured persons as immoral and punish it by law still leaves our question to be argued. It is true that Mill's critics have often made much of the fact that English law does in several instances, apparently with the support of popular morality, punish immorality as such, especially in sexual matters; but they have usually admitted that this is where the argument begins, not where it ends. I shall indeed later claim that the play made by some legal writers with what they treat as examples of the legal enforcement of morality "as such" is sometimes confused. But they do not, at any rate, put forward their case as simply proved by pointing to these social facts. Instead they attempt to base their own conclusion that it is morally justifiable to use the criminal law in this way on principles which they believe to be universally applicable, and which they think are either quite obviously rational or will be seen to be so after discussion.

Thus Lord Devlin bases his affirmative answer to the question on the quite general principle that it is permissible for any society to take the steps needed to preserve its own existence as an organized society,[7] and he thinks that immorality—even private sexual immorality—may, like treason, be something which jeopardizes a society's existence. Of course many of us may doubt this general principle, and not merely the suggested analogy with treason. We might wish to argue that whether or not a society is justified in taking steps to preserve itself must depend both on what sort of society it is and what the steps to be taken are. If a society were mainly devoted to the cruel persecution of a racial or religious minority, or if the steps to be taken included hideous tortures, it is arguable that what Lord Devlin terms the "disintegration"[8] of such a society would be morally better than its continued existence, and steps ought not to be taken to preserve it. Nonetheless Lord Devlin's principle that a society may take the steps required to preserve its organized existence is not itself tendered as an item of English popular morality, deriving its cogency from its status as part of our institutions. He puts it forward as a principle, rationally acceptable, to be used in the evaluation or criticism of social institutions generally. And it is surely clear that anyone who holds the question whether a society has the "right" to enforce morality, or whether it is morally

permissible for any society to enforce its morality by law, to be discussable at all, must be prepared to deploy some such general principles of critical morality. In asking the question, we are assuming the legitimacy of a standpoint which permits criticism of the institutions of any society, in the light of general principles and knowledge of the facts.

To make this point clear, I would revive the terminology much favoured by the Utilitarians of the last century, which distinguished "positive morality," the morality actually accepted and shared by a given social group, from the general moral principles used in the criticism of actual social institutions including positive morality. We may call such general principles "critical morality" and say that our question is one of critical morality about the legal enforcement of positive morality.

A second feature of our question worth attention is simply that it is a question of *justification*. In asking it we are committed at least to the general critical principle that the use of legal coercion by any society calls for justification as something *prima facie* objectionable to be tolerated only for the sake of some countervailing good. For where there is no *prima facie* objection, wrong, or evil, men do not ask for or give *justifications* of social practices, though they may ask for and give *explanations* of these practices or may attempt to demonstrate their value.

It is salutary to inquire precisely what it is that is *prima facie* objectionable in the legal enforcement of morality; for the idea of legal enforcement is in fact less simple than is often assumed. It has two different but related aspects. One is the actual punishment of the offender. This characteristically involves depriving him of liberty of movement or of property or of association with family or friends, or the infliction upon him of physical pain or even death. All these are things which are assumed to be wrong to inflict on others without special justification, and in fact they are so regarded by the law and morality of all developed societies. To put it as a lawyer would, these are things which, if they are not justified as sanctions, are delicts or wrongs.

The second aspect of legal enforcement bears on those who may never offend against the law, but are coerced into obedience by the threat of legal punishment. This rather than physical restrictions is what is normally meant in the discussion of political arrangements by restrictions on liberty. Such restrictions, it is to be noted, may be thought of as calling for justification for several quite distinct reasons. The unimpeded exercise by individuals of free choice may be held a value in itself with which it is *prima facie* wrong to interfere; or it may be thought valuable because it enables individuals to experiment—even with living—and to discover things valuable both to themselves and to others. But interference with individual liberty may be thought an evil requiring justification for simpler, utilitarian reasons; for it is itself the infliction of a special form of suffering—often very acute—on those whose desires are frustrated by the fear of punishment. This is of particular importance in the case of laws enforcing a sexual morality. They may create misery of a quite special degree. For both the difficulties involved in the repression of sexual impulses and the consequences of repression are quite different from those involved in the abstention from "ordinary" crime. Unlike sexual impulses, the impulse to steal or to wound or even kill is not, except in a minority of mentally abnormal cases, a recurrent and insistent part of daily life. Resistance to the temptation to commit these crimes is not often, as the suppression of sexual impulses generally is, something which affects the development or balance of the individual's emotional life, happiness, and personality.

Thirdly, the distinction already made, between positive morality and principles of critical morality, may serve to dissipate a certain misunderstanding of the question and to clarify its central point. It is sometimes said that the question is not whether it is morally justifiable to enforce morality as such, but only *which* morality may be enforced. Is it only a utilitarian morality condemning activities which are harmful to others? Or is it a morality which also condemns certain activities whether they are harmful or not? This way of regarding the question misrepresents the character of, at any rate, modern controversy. A utilitarian who insists that the law should only punish activities which are harmful adopts this as a critical principle, and, in so doing,

he is quite unconcerned with the question whether a utilitarian morality is or is not already accepted as the positive morality of the society to which he applies his critical principles. If it is so accepted, that is not, in his view, the reason why it should be enforced. It is true that if he is successful in preaching his message to a given society, members of it will then be compelled to behave as utilitarians in certain ways, but these facts do not mean that the vital difference between him and his opponent is only as to the content of the morality to be enforced. For as may be seen from the main criticisms of Mill, the Utilitarian's opponent, who insists that it is morally permissible to enforce morality as such, believes that the mere fact that certain rules or standards of behaviour enjoy the status of a society's positive morality is the reason—or at least part of the reason—which justifies their enforcement by law. No doubt in older controversies the opposed positions were different: the question may have been whether the state could punish only activities causing secular harm or also acts of disobedience to what were believed to be divine commands or prescriptions of Natural Law. But what is crucial to the dispute in its modern form is the significance to be attached to the historical fact that certain conduct, no matter what, is prohibited by a positive morality. The utilitarian denies that this has any significance sufficient to justify its enforcement; his opponent asserts that it has. These are divergent critical principles which do not differ merely over the content of the morality to be enforced, but over a more fundamental and, surely, more interesting issue.

NOTES

1.   Report of the Committee on Homosexual Offences and Prostitution (CMD 247) 1957.
2.   American Law Institute Model Penal Code, Tentative Draft No. 4, p. 277.
3.   *Ibid.,* p. 278.
4.   Second edition, London, 1874.
5.   *Ibid.,* p. 162.
6.   Oxford University Press, 1959.
7.   *The Enforcement of Morals,* pp. 13–14.
8.   *Ibid.,* pp. 14–15.

GENERAL: ON LIBERTY-LIMITING PRINCIPLES

Acton, J. *Essays on Freedom and Power.* Boston: Beacon Press, 1948.

Berlin, I. *Four Essays on Liberty.* New York: Oxford University Press, 1970.

Hart, H. L. A. *Law, Liberty, and Morality.* New York: Vintage Books, 1963.

McCloskey, H. J. "Mill's Liberalism." *Philosophical Quarterly* 13 (1963). (See also the reply by A. Ryan in *Philosophical Quarterly* 14 [1964].)

Popper, K. R. *The Open Society and Its Enemies.* Princeton, N.J.: Princeton University Press, 1966.

Radcliff, Peter, ed. *Limits of Liberty.* Belmont, Calif.: Wadsworth, 1966.

Rees, J. C. *Mill and His Early Critics.* Leicester: University College, 1956.

Russell, Bertrand. *John Stuart Mill, Lecture on a Master Mind.* Published for the British Academy by the Oxford University Press, 1955, from the *Proceedings of the British Academy,* 41.

PATERNALISM

Bayles, Michael D. "Criminal Paternalism." In *The Limits of Law: Nomos XV,* edited by J. Roland Pennock and John W. Chapman, pp. 174–88. New York: Lieber-Atherton, 1974.

Beauchamp, Tom L., and Walters, LeRoy. *Contemporary Issues in Bioethics.* Encino, Calif.: Dickenson Publishing Co., 1977. Especially Chapters 4 and 11.

Engelhardt, H. Tristram, Jr. "Rights and Responsibilities of Patients and Physicians." In *Medical Treatment of the Dying: Moral Issues,* edited by Michael D. Bayles and Dallas M. High. Cambridge, Mass.: Schenkman Publishing Co., 1976.

Feinberg, Joel. "Legal Paternalism." *The Canadian Journal of Philosophy* 1 (1971): 105–24.

————. *Social Philosophy.* Englewood Cliffs, N.J.: Prentice-Hall, 1973. Chapters 2–3.

Gert, Bernard, and Culver, Charles M. "Paternalistic Behavior." *Philosophy and Public Affairs* 6 (1976): 45–57.

Kittrie, Nicholas. *The Right to be Different: Deviance and Enforced Therapy.* Baltimore, Md.: Johns Hopkins University Press, 1971.

Murphy, Jeffrie G. "Incompetence and Paternalism." *Archives for Philosophy of Law and Social Philosophy* 40 (1974): 465–86.

Szasz, Thomas. *Ideology and Insanity.* Garden City, N. Y.: Doubleday, 1970. Espcially Chapters 2 and 9.

MORAL ENFORCEMENT

Devlin, Lord Patrick. *The Enforcement of Morals.* Oxford: Oxford University Press, 1964.

Devlin, Lord Patrick. "Law, Democracy, and Morality." *University of Pennsylvania Law Review* 110 (1962).

Dworkin, Ronald. "Lord Devlin and the Enforcement of Morals." *Yale Law Journal* 75 (May 1966).

Hart, H. L. A. "Immorality and Treason." *The Listener* (July 1959). Reprinted in *The Law as Literature,* edited by L. J. Blom-Cooper, Bodley Head, 1961.

Hughes, Graham. "Morals and the Criminal Law." *Yale Law Journal* 71 (1962).

Mitchell, B. *Law, Morality and Religion in a Secular Society.* London: Oxford University Press, 1967.

"Private Consensual Adult Behavior: The Requirement of Harm to Others in the Enforcement of Morality." *U.C.L.A. Law Review* 14 (1967).

Rostow, Eugene. "The Enforcement of Morals." *Cambridge Law Journal* (1960). Reprinted in *The Sovereign Prerogative,* edited by E. Rostow. New Haven, Conn. Yale University Press, 1962.

Wasserstrom, Richard, ed. *Morality and the Law.* Belmont, Calif.: Wadsworth, 1971.

"Wolfenden Report." Report of the Committee on Homosexual Offences and Prostitution, 1957, Cmd. 247.

Wollheim, Richard. "Crime, Sin and Mr. Justice Devlin." *Encounter* (November 1959).

Wootton, Barbara. *Crime and the Criminal Law.* London: Stevens and Sons, 1963.

OFFENSIVENESS: PORNOGRAPHY AND CENSORSHIP

Bayles, Michael. "Comments on Feinberg: Offensive Conduct and the Law." In *Issues in Law and Morality.* edited by N. S. Care and T. K. Trelogan. Cleveland, Ohio: Case Western Reserve Press, 1973.

Chandos, John, ed. "To Deprave and Corrupt . . ." New York: Association Press, 1962.

Clor, Harry M. *Obscenity and Public Morality.* Chicago: The University of Chicago Press, 1969.

Feinberg, Joel. "Harmless Immoralities and Offensive Nuisances," In *Issues in Law and Morality,* edited by N. S. Care and T. K. Trelogan. Cleveland, Ohio: Case Western Reserve Press, 1973. With a Reply to Bayles.

Feinberg, Joel. *Social Philosophy.* Englewood Cliffs, N.J.: Prentice-Hall, 1973. Chapters Two and Three.

Henkin, Louis. "Morals and the Constitution: The Sin of Obscenity." *Columbia Law Review* 35 (1967).

Holbrook, David, ed. *The Case Against Pornography.* New York: The Library Press, 1973.

Leiser, Burton M. *Liberty, Justice and Morals.* New York: Macmillan, 1973, Chapter VI.

The Report of the Commission on Obscenity and Pornography. Washington, D.C.: U.S. Government Printing Office, 1970.

Simons, G. L. *Pornography Without Prejudice.* London: Abelard-Schuman, 1972.

Chapter 9   Belief in God

Religion is not a problem for all human beings. Some are reared within a given faith and they die within that faith with hardly a side journey. For others religion is a problem, both intellectual and practical. They want to know whether there is evidence for the articles of faith, and they want to know what will happen to them if they are in or out of the fold.

Is there a God? What is He like? Do we have souls? Do they survive bodily death? What is the evidence for these beliefs? These are some of the intellectual questions asked. What will happen if I do not believe? Will I go to hell? Will my life lose direction and significance? Will I become immoral? If I reject the church, will I suffer—socially and economically? Is it wrong to rear children outside of the church? These are some of the practical problems which accompany the intellectual ones.

Perhaps it would be nice simply to avoid these problems. Decide not to decide. But if William James is correct, one cannot decide not to decide. Religion confronts one with a "momentous, forced, live" option. The effort to avoid that option by being an agnostic, by withholding belief either for or against God's existence, is equivalent to choosing non-belief. Unlike some classical philosophers and theologians, James maintained that the existence of God cannot be established by reason. Neither can it be disproven. His solution: we must decide on pragmatic grounds. We must ask ourselves, "Which, of the actual and possible consequences of belief or non-belief, is most to our advantage and carries the least risk?" James answers unequivocally that belief in God is to our advantage now and in a future life, if there is a future life. Eternal salvation depends on belief in God. Why run the risk of that loss by disbelief? Even if it turns out that there is no God, nothing is lost by the belief stance and everything may be gained. This purely pragmatic approach to belief in God offends the sensibilities of some believers and non-believers alike. But we must keep in mind the assumption from which it springs, namely, that rational proof or disproof of God's existence is impossible.

The selections in this chapter deal with a number of traditional and contemporary challenges to belief in God and various responses to those challenges. Due to space limitations, positions which focus basically on the concept of God and religion in the West are represented. Eastern perspectives are represented in other selections in this book.

THE CHALLENGE TO BELIEF IN GOD

THE INTELLECTUAL CHALLENGE

Religious scepticism has a long history, perhaps as old as religion itself. We need not recount that history. It is well-known that for centuries scepticism was *sub rosa* underground activity, for open sceptics paid a price, generally the highest price. Plato ordained death for nonbelievers, and the history of Christianity is replete with acts of torture, mutilation, imprisonment, and killing for disbelief, even for deviation from orthodoxy. Thousands were burned at the stake. Disbelief was seen as depravity itself; and reason, Luther claimed, which leads one to that depravity, is a "whore," who robs one of the Kingdom of Heaven. We must "tear out the eyes of reason," he says, if one is to be a Christian.

The tradition of burning at the stake is now dead. That of "tearing out the eyes of reason" remains, and we will turn to that religious stance in a moment. First, what is the intellectual challenge to religion? It must be observed initially that for centuries there was no effort to rest the Christian faith on reason. The tenets of religion were grounded in revelation, authority, and faith in that authority. In fact, many theologians held that faith must precede understanding. St. Anselm insisted that nothing can be explained ultimately without the framework provided by faith. This stance is by no means dead today. It is the basis of neo-orthodoxy, sometimes called *fideism.*[1] In any case many theologians, classical and contemporary, decided that the tenets of faith could be defended on rational grounds as well. So rational theology, the effort to demonstrate the existence of God by reason, appeared alongside revealed theology. Several different arguments were advanced, particularly by St. Anselm,[2] St. Thomas,[3] William Paley,[4] and subsequent theologians. These classical arguments are known as the ontological, cosmological, and design (teleological) arguments.

Each of these arguments was set forth in somewhat different form but basically they came to this: The *ontological* argument asserted that God's existence could be proven by the very concept of God. Our concept of God is that of a Necessary Being, a Perfect Being who creates everything else. But perfection entails existence—otherwise God would lack something. He would not be perfect. Therefore, God necessarily exists. The argument is deductive and wholly *a priori* (it uses no empirical premises).

The *cosmological* argument utilizes an empirical premise since it refers to our experience of causation in nature, but it attempts to move deductively to the conclusion that God exists. Briefly, it argues in this way: we are aware of cause and effect relationships in nature, and we assume that every effect must have a cause. This fact itself, however, can only be explained by the conclusion that there is an Uncaused Cause (God) who originated or set the whole sequence of causes and effects in motion. Not to make this assumption leads one to logical absurdities.

The *design* or *teleological* argument for God's existence is of a different type. It is inductive rather than deductive. It does not attempt to prove with absolute certainty that God exists or that one is involved in self-contradiction or logical absurdities in denying the existence of God. It argues more modestly that God's existence can be proven to a high degree of probability. The fact of life, the complexity of life, the order and regularity of nature, the apparent design and purposive adaptation of different forms of life—all of this justifies the inductive conclusion that nature and the universe as a whole had a Designer (God). How else account for the apparent design which stares us in the face?

Even in the heyday of rational theology, there were severe doubts about the adequacy of these nts. Those doubts became outright rejection with the emergence of the philosophical theories of Immanuel Kant[5] and David Hume[6] and the further development and acceptance of science and the scientific method. That rejection comes out loud and clear in Bertrand Russell's essay. The ontological argument fails, critics argue, because the factual conclusion that God exists cannot be derived solely from purely *a priori* premises—from the concept of God. Even if it is granted that the concept of a Perfect Being entails existence, that only shows that if one is to have a proper concept of God, one must think of Him as existing. It does not prove that He exists. Further, existence is not a predicate or a property.

The cosmological argument fails, critics held, because the fact of causal relationships in nature does not require an Uncaused Cause. The notion of an infinite causal chain is not logically absurd. Further, to assume that every effect has a cause and then speak of an Uncaused Cause (God) is a logical inconsistency. Also, even if there were an Uncaused Cause, there are no grounds for assuming that that Cause is the Christian God.

The design argument fails for a variety of reasons, critics argued. Some felt that Charles Darwin's theory of natural selection provided a satisfactory naturalistic account of the origin of life, rendering a super-naturalistic account unnecessary. The *Origin of Species* (1859) bothered other believers and theologians much less. They adapted the Darwinian theory to Christianity, seeing the evolutionary process as God's way of creating. The crushing blow to the design argument, some say, came not from Darwin but from the pen of David Hume in his *Dialogues Concerning Natural Religion*. There is order and regularity in nature, Hume agrees. But we cannot properly infer anything about the cause or origin of the entire universe from that fact. ". . . [A]ll inferences . . . concerning fact are founded on experience, and . . . all experimental reasonings are founded on the supposition that similar causes prove similar effects, and similar effects similar causes."[7] But we experience only a very small part of the universe. We cannot "pronounce decisively concerning the origin of the whole" from this small part. The design argument also invokes an improper analogy between a watch and a watchmaker and the universe and a Universe-

maker (God), Hume contends. For both watches and watchmakers are within our experience, whereas the universe and Universe-makers are not. Hence we have no empirical base for inferring anything about the origin or cause of the universe. Furthermore, within our limited experience of a small corner of the world, there are different "principles" or phenomena operating—intelligence, instinct, vegetation, and generation. Why extrapolate to the nature of the origin of the whole from just one of these principles—intelligence? Also, Hume continues, amidst all the order and goodness of the world, there is apparent disorder and evil. He grants that, even in the face of these objections, God may still exist. But the design argument does not and cannot prove that existence.

The above is a brief, oversimplified summary of the traditional rational arguments for God's existence and of the response of the philosophical sceptic. Since the eighteenth century, few have attempted to base a theology on such arguments. Much of religion and theology returned (it had really never left) to the appeal to revelation and faith. God's existence is not provable inductively or deductively, but it is known through faith and revelation (in the Bible and elsewhere).

Thus, Soren Kierkegaard asserts, it is through subjectivity, not objective scientific tests and logic, that we come to understand religious truth. The central tenet of Christianity, Kierkegaard states, is that Jesus is God, the doctrine of the Incarnation.[8] This belief, he agrees, flies in the face of reason; it is utterly absurd. It violates the principle of non-contradiction, for the completely eternal and transcendent cannot also be finite and historical. Yet, it is to be believed. It must be believed, if one is to be a Christian.

Kierkegaard and fideists in this tradition, like Karl Barth,[9] put religion totally beyond the pale of rational critique. Science, with logical reasoning, has its domain; religion, its own domain, and ne'er the 'twain shall meet. This stance has its advantages. Religion is protected by an iron curtain. But it has its disadvantages, for in an age in which science and its canons of reasoning dominate the landscape, a faith which is absurd and irrational, in which even rational discourse about its basic tenets is excluded by the rules of the game, may lose its hold on the minds of men. Furthermore, all additions to the community of faith must be by non-rational (even irrational) conversion. For these reasons, a strict fideism, in particular the Kierkegaardian variety in which the central tenet of faith is an "absurdity," is rejected by many Christians. They cling to what Kierkegaard rejected, namely, that historical records of Biblical events can provide rational underpinning for the faith.

THE PSYCHOLOGICAL CHALLENGE

Aside from the undermining of the traditional rational arguments for God's existence by Kant, Hume, Darwin, Huxley,[10] Russell, and others, the rational grounds of faith were challenged further by Ludwig Feuerbach, Karl Marx, and Sigmund Freud. Feuerbach[11] argued that Christians who adopt a transcendent concept of God, in which God's characteristics are unlike anything human and are unknowable, cut God off from all human experience. This leads to complete scepticism. On the other hand, when the concept and attributes of God are tied to human experience, Feuerbach finds that "the secret of theology is anthropology." That is, human beings simply have projected their own image onto the universe as a whole. Feuerbach states that "[man has] given objectivity to himself but has not recognized the object as his own nature." To understand religion we must understand ourselves, and change ourselves (become mature).

Marx[12] carried Feuerbach a few steps further. Religion is not merely the result of the projection of human traits onto the universe. Human beings are the product of their social relations, their class relationships, and their economic relationships. Religion is the result of the totality of social relationships and it performs a specific function among those relationships. In effect, it is an "opiate of the masses," a kind of drug which diverts social attention from the reality of earth to the unreality of heaven and which helps to perpetuate the exploitive relationship between the bourgeoise and proletarian classes. It prevents one from facing the facts and from assuming the responsibility for changing the world for the better. To understand religion fully we must grasp the role it plays in the relationships of economic classes; and to change those exploitive relationships we must rid ourselves of the opiate that is religion.

For Feuerbach religion is a sign of emotional immaturity. For Marx it is both that and an evil which perpetuates oppression. For Freud religion is an illusion, a psychological crutch which provides security and protection against the contingency and threat of harsh reality. Freud offers a psychoanalytic explanation of the anthropomophism to which Feuerbach points. Humans picture the universe as created by a being resembling themselves, "undisguisedly called 'father,' " much as they picture their own earthly origin. And just as the earthly father loves us, provides for our immediate needs, gives the authority of moral guidelines, and enables us to overcome "the terrifying impression of helplessness," the image of God the Father enables humans to overcome their sense of cosmic helplessness, satisfies the need for moral order, and provides a framework for security. In childhood the feeling of insecurity is exceedingly intense. An earthly father enables us to adjust, and . . . "the recognition that this helplessness lasts throughout life made it necessary to cling to the existence of a father, but this time a more powerful one."

All of this is an illusion from which man must awake in his maturity, Freud insists. Mature persons accept reality for what it is, and they base their beliefs on evidence. There is no evidence for the sort of Father of which Christians speak. The widespread belief that there is such a Being is a neurosis which must be cured. Freud thought that humankind could be cured of the ill of religion, that humans would learn to stand on their own two feet and accept the responsibility for their own moral code, for their own behavior, and their own happiness. This will occur as humankind develops mentally and emotionally—as the canons of reasoning of science and the results of the application of those canons in the various sciences gain acceptance.

Freud sets forth his explanation of religion not as a dogma but as a plausible genetic account of religion and as a hypothesis which is testable. If humankind turns away from religion as it matures, the hypothesis is presumably confirmed. If not, not. But Freud also carefully distinguishes his genetic account of religion from the justifying grounds for the truth or falsity of religious belief. In his genetic account he points to wish-fulfillment as the cause of religion, and he calls religion an illusion because it is based on that wish-fulfillment. But, for Freud, the illusory state of the belief in God does not render the belief in God false. God may exist and hence the belief in God may be true even if the origin of the belief is wish-fulfillment. If confirming evidence turns up that there is a God, Freud is willing to agree that the illusory belief in God may be true. But in the absence of such evidence and given the fact that the phenomenon of religion can be so satisfactorily explained by the wish-fulfillment theory, Freud shifts the burden of proof to the believer; and he makes it clear that for him the scientific evidence renders the belief false.

The impact of the Freudian analysis of belief in God and his challenge to the believer, along with those of Feuerbach and Marx, has been very significant. These analyses have contributed heavily to a general movement in which traditional theism is losing its grip on the minds of modern people. As Nietzsche declares in his essay, "God is dead . . . and we have killed him. . . . At last the horizon appears free again to us."

THE MORAL CHALLENGE

Some theologians and philosophers, as we have noted, have felt that science and religion need not clash head-on, that the respective domains, methods, and objectives of science and religion differ so greatly that conclusions from one do not and cannot conflict with conclusions from the other. This is the solution of fideism and neo-orthodoxy. We have pointed to the advantages and disadvantages of this stance. Yet others hold that although there can be no inductive or deductive proof of the existence of God or the immortality of the soul, such beliefs might be warranted, even required, on *moral* grounds. Thus Kant, after arguing that all rational arguments for God's existence fail, goes on to argue that the beliefs in God, freedom, and immortality are necessary postulates to make sense of morality. These postulates are unprovable. Yet, if we do not operate on them, the entire institution of morality—the belief that persons are responsible for their acts, that reward and punishment will at some time be properly meted out for the kind of life one lives, that there is an objective standard for measuring the rightness and wrongness of acts—all of this will collapse and, with it, moral behavior itself. Kierkegaard joins Kant in calling for this "leap of faith" in order to make morality and our very lives intelligible and significant.

William James takes a somewhat similar position in his pragmatic arguments for accepting both the existence of God and indeterminism ("free will"). There is an important difference, however, between the Jamesean approach (and that of Blaise Pascal) and the Kant-Kierkegaard stance. Though James does stress that religion, when accepted, can add great significance to one's life, he does not take the stronger stand that life or morality is meaningless without God. He and Pascal both emphasize that, given the fact that a rational decision about the existence of God is impossible, we are fully justified in opting for belief on "passional" grounds and that such an option will help give meaning to one's life. But, at least as important, they declare, is that less risk is involved for the believer. As Pascal says, " . . . you ought to stake your all on God; for though you surely risk a finite loss by this procedure, any finite loss is reasonable if there is but the possibility of an infinite gain."[13]

We are here less concerned with the "less risk" stance of James and Pascal than with the Kant-Kierkegaard emphasis that morality and life itself would be meaningless without belief in God. But the following observations about the James-Pascal thesis are in order: The risk to which they point (the loss of eternal salvation for the unbeliever) assumes a certain concept of God, namely, one in which God is the sort of Being who would punish an unbeliever. Why assume that? If God created us in His image and if this means that our rationality constitutes a "spark of divinity," as the Stoics would put it, might He not praise rather than punish a non-believer—a sceptic or agnostic—for trying desperately to adjust his or her beliefs to the available evidence? Is it not just possible that a Being who gave us rationality, who wanted us in His image, expects us to use those capacities and in fact may reward the non-believer for adjusting his beliefs to the facts (given the paucity of evidence) and punish the believer who facilely ignores evidence contrary to his belief and who violates an "ethics of belief," to use W. K. Clifford's phrase?[14] The risk seems to depend on the concept of God invoked. Even if James' premises are correct—that all available and possible evidence will permit no rational decision either way (and we must keep in mind that some theologians like John Hick suggest that more evidence for God's existence may be available in the next life), why assume that God would punish the non-believer?

What about the claim that morality and life itself are maningless without belief in God? This controversy involving the relationship between God and morality goes back at least to Plato's *Euthyphro* where it is asked: "Is that which is right right because God wills it, or does God will that which is right because it is right?" If one opts for the former, then there is no distinction between something being right and God willing it. If one opts for the latter, then there is a standard of rightness to which even God conforms and which is the basis for his willing certain acts. The latter leaves morality independent of the existence of God and of our belief in the existence of God.

Now the religious believer himself, in speaking of God as "good" and of His will as being "right," seems to assume that there is a difference between "goodness" and "rightness" and God's will. For, as Bertrand Russell points out in his essay, the believers assume that they are saying something significant when they that God is good. They are not merely uttering the tautology that God is God or that good is good. "If you are going to say, as theologians do, that God is good, you must then say that right and wrong have some meaning, which is independent of God's fiat."

If these purely logical or conceptual points are correct, they demonstrate not only that we must have some concept of good or right prior to saying that God is good but also that ethics is logically independent of religion. Even if one accepts theism, one's moral beliefs are not completely dependent on one's concept of God. If anything, just the contrary! In order to have the concept of God as a being who is perfectly good and who is worthy of worship, and to significantly ascribe the characteristic "goodness" or "rightness" to Him, one must have some prior concept of goodness or rightness.

The above is a *logical* point which we can perceive by elucidating the meaning of the statement, "God is good." But a telling empirical argument against the Kant-Kierkegaard thesis is that many cultures and millions of persons have no concept of God, particularly the personal God of Christianity; and yet they seem to live significant, meaningful lives. They have functioning moral codes and be-

havior systems in their Godless worlds. Millions of Buddhists, Marxists, Humanists, Confucianists, Utilitarians, and the like fall into this category. These ways of life and codes of behavior fly in the face of the claim that morality and a meaningful life require belief in God. It cannot be doubted that many millions feel that life would lose its significance and that morality would be groundless without God. But, for many others, this is not the case. They believe life has meaning and there are good reasons for acting morally even in a godless world.

The above establishes the independence of ethics and religion. It establishes nothing about the adequacy of any given code. On this score, believers generally argue that their religious code of ethics is far more adequate than a secular code. Christians, for example, cite the ethics of Christ as far superior to any secular ethic. An ethic of love and obedience to God has it all over a purely humanist ethic or an ethic of utility, it is urged. Obviously, some independent standard of adequacy is needed to debate this issue, if one is to avoid begging the question. But in such a debate it may be wise to remind ourselves that, along with the great principles of the Christian ethic, there are rules and attitudes in that ethic which many find morally questionable. Bertrand Russell speaks of "defects in the moral character" of Christ from whence much of that ethic emanates—of his belief in Hell and everlasting punishment. Others may not put the point quite so aggressively as Russell. However, those Biblical passages in which Christ is reputed to have said, "The Son of Man shall send forth his angels, and they shall gather out of His Kingdom all things that offend, and them which do inequity, and shall cast them into a furnace of fire; and there shall be wailing and gnashing of teeth;"[15] and, again, "Depart from me, ye cursed, into everlasting fire"[16]—the moral views in these passages worry even those within the Christian faith. Eternal suffering for a finite amount of sin is hardly a fair shake. The Christian doctrine of Hell has undoubtedly caused an immense amount of suffering. Witness the religious fanatics who populate our mental asylums in large numbers. And recall the terror and cruelty which subscribers to the faith and to the Church as the vehicle of that faith inflicted on millions.

Perhaps both the Christian ethic and secular

ones could do with some improvement. But one thing is certain. The non-believer cannot be simply written off as a destroyer of morality. Nor does the broader thesis that the life of a non-believer lacks significance seem to hold any water. In fact the brunt of the moral challenge, many hold, falls squarely on the shoulders of the traditional theist and the Christian ethicist, not so much on the utilitarian or humanist. There is more than a little doubt that current religious-establishment stances on issues including contraception, abortion, the population problem, the world food crisis, the rights of women, and so on are adequate ones; whereas many feel that the more flexible secular ethics of the humanist and the utilitarian offer far more viable solutions to the pressing moral problems which confront us, hence a more adequate ethic for our time than the traditional Christian one. Perhaps the Christian ethic is more adequate than it appears at first blush. But, at the very least we may conclude that the moral challenge to the faith has added significantly to the negative impact upon religion of the intellectual and psychological challenges.

THE LINGUISTIC CHALLENGE

We turn now to a fourth challenge to religion, one which has had a great deal of contemporary impact and in fact underlies much of the "Honest-to-God" and "Death-of-God" theologies. We will call this challenge the linguistic challenge. It is obviously related to what we earlier called the intellectual challenge, which questioned the adequacy of the the traditional proofs of the existence of God. But this challenge goes even further and questions the very significance or intelligibility of the claims of religion which purport to be true. Thus, it is a challenge to believer and non-believer alike, to those who proclaim that God exists and to those who deny that God exists; for both affirmer and denier assume that the claim(s) they affirm and deny are meaningful, intelligible claims. The linguistic sceptics challenge this root assumption. For them the purported claim that God exists cannot even be false, for it is not a genuine or intelligible claim. The intelligibility or meaningfulness of a purported claim is an issue which is logically prior to the question of whether that claim is true or false, and basic religious claims fail the intelligibility test.

What is the intelligibility or meaningfulness test? Is there a single test? Going back at least to Hume, we have considerable philosophical concern with the significance or meaningfulness of knowledge-claims. Hume distinguishes knowledge-claims into those involving "matters-of-fact" and those involving "relations-of-ideas." The former are claims verifiable by reference to empirical facts; the latter, by reference simply to the meaning of the concepts used in the claim. (For example, the statement "all equiangular triangles are equilateral" is true because the definition of "equiangular" includes "equilateral.") Hume suggested that all knowledge-claims which fit neither of these categories be cast into the flames, for they can contain nothing but "sophistry and illusion." Much of theology, he thought, fit neither category.

Philosophers like R. B. Braithwaite agree that religion is not a cognitive enterprise. Its function is not to give us knowledge of a transcendent Being or reality. Religion is not, however, simply a "retreat into silence"; nor are religious beliefs simply expressions of emotion. Rather those beliefs involve "stories," "tales," "myths," and "allegories" and these stories or propositions are "thought of by the religious man in connection with his resolution to follow the way of life advocated by his religion."[17] The import of the religious stories is psychological and causal, not cognitive. They need not be believed. They need not even be consistent. Their role is simply that of support in adopting and living a certain way of life. Basically, Braithwaite assimilates key religious claims to moral ones. The statement, for example, "God is love," is interpreted as a declaration of an intention to follow a loving way of life.

Acceptance of this analysis of religion retains the meaningfulness of religion in a sense. But not in the cognitive sense. The price to be paid for acceptance of it is obvious. Religion is relegated to a psychological support role for morality.

Another response to the verificationist-linguistic challenge bears mention because, while it denies that key religious claims are *straightforward* empirical claims (and to that extent agrees with the verificationist critique), it refuses to accept a Braithwaitean reduction of religion to morality. This response is that of Richard Hare in his "The Simple Believer." Hare's "simple believer" is an anthropomorphite whose beliefs fly in the face of the findings of science. What, if anything, can be salvaged of his beliefs when one attempts to reconcile them with science? The answer of the verificationist is, nothing. Hare disagrees. He grants that the anthropomorphism of the "simple believer" is false. But belief in God can still be defended by stepping outside of the verificationist framework of thought. Hare's defense seems to draw heavily on the philosophical thought of David Hume but without embracing Hume's scepticism. Recall that Hume classified knowledge-claims into basically "relations-of-ideas" and "matter-of-fact," and he tried to fit most everything into these cupboards. But there were beliefs which would not fit these cupboards, beliefs which "flow in upon one with the force of a sensation." He called them "natural beliefs" and included among them belief in the external world, the identity of the self, and in real causal connections in nature. These beliefs are presuppositions, or the framework within which all inference and explanation take place. They are neither relations-of-ideas or matters-of-fact, yet they are very significant beliefs.

Hare picks up this sort of approach to fundamental religious claims. "There are," he declares, "beliefs which are not beliefs in the truth of assertions, in this narrow sense, and yet which are fundamental to our whole life in the world, and still more to our doing anything like science." The scientist believes in regularity and causal laws in nature. It is an assumption without which the whole notion of scientific prediction would be senseless. And yet, belief in such laws is not an ordinary empirical belief, the sort of belief which is falsifiable in principle for scientists. Quite the contrary, scientists will permit nothing to count against that belief. If they did, they would cease to be scientists. Thus, "we may say that the belief of the scientist is one kind of religious belief." Science and religion, though they differ in important respects, are, in this sense, in the same boat.

In effect, Hare is challenging the adequacy of the logical cupboards of the verificationist-falsificationist. The neat division of all significant beliefs into "relations-of-ideas" (analytic truths) and "matters-of-fact" (synthetic truths) is inadequate. Both human life and human knowledge are more complex than that.

The views of Hare and other philosophers open —it would be more accurate to say reopen—some epistemological doors for religion. Theology may not recapture all of the glitter of those days when it was heralded as queen of the sciences. But it may avoid the completely emasculated status offered it by Braithwaite—that of a story-telling handmaiden for morality.

GOD AND EVIL

The final part of the readings in this chapter, the essays by Dostoevsky, Rubenstein, Hume, and Hick, deal with that challenge to belief in God which is generally called the "problem of evil." One of the greatest obstacles to belief in God, one which has utterly destroyed the faith of many, is the immense amount of evil and suffering in the world. How can a Being who presumably is both perfectly good and omnipotent, having the power to prevent such evil and suffering, permit it to happen? Can the existence of evil be reconciled with the existence of a God who is thought to be both all-powerful and infinitely good? In the face of that evil, must one give up the belief in God's perfect goodness, retaining the belief in his omnipotence? On this option the object of one's worship changes radically. Some would say that such a Being no longer merits one's worship. On the other hand, if one retains belief in God's perfect goodness but gives up belief in his omnipotence, a fundamental theological tenet, at least for the Christian, is breached. God would be seen as a finite force in the universe, along with other forces.

There have been a number of arguments set forth to show that evil and suffering are compatible with the existence of an all-powerful and infinitely good God. Few have been willing simply to deny the reality of evil, solving the problem by conceiving of evil as an illusion, a mere appearance due to man's finite perspective. If we could but see everything from God's perspective, this position holds, those things which appear evil would be seen as, in reality, good and a contribution to a good whole. This "explanation" gets rid of the problem by denying the problem. Generally, evil is seen as quite real but necessary for God's purpose. Thus, it has been argued that God permits natural evils—disease, earthquakes, floods, droughts and so on—

for several reasons: To enable us to appreciate the good in contrast to the bad and to enable us to develop strength of character. He permits moral evil to occur because, otherwise, humans could not be free and responsible beings—they would be automatons. With the freedom given to human beings, there is necessarily the risk that they will do great evil.

These responses, pressed by Professor John Hick in his essay, have satisfied many believers. But not others—they have asked whether God could not accomplish His purposes without permitting quite so much evil to occur. Could not humans learn to appreciate the good in contrast to the bad, function as free, responsible agents, and develop strength of character within a scheme of things in which there is a great deal less moral and natural evil? What of seemingly superfluous evil and suffering—the suffering of innocent children, which Dostoevsky discusses in *The Brothers Karamozov,* and the slaughter of millions of Jews, which Rubenstein discusses in *After Auschwitz?* What are we to believe about God after Auschwitz?, Rubenstein asks. In the face of such atrocities, the traditional concept of a personal and loving God, a God who is omnipotent, omniscient, and perfectly good, must be relinquished. We must reconcile ourselves to "making the very best one can of a limited and tragic existence," Rubenstein argues. Dostoevsky goes a step further. Even if there were a God whose plan for the universe required, for some reason incomprehensible to us, the torturing and suffering of innocent children and acts of genocide, that God must be rejected. Such inhumanity in the name of cosmic harmony is morally unacceptable. Dostoevsky declares: "I don't want harmony. From love of humanity I don't want it. I would rather be left with the unavenged suffering."

Among the philosophers who have dealt with this issue, David Hume is one of the most perceptive. He does not claim that the existence of evil and suffering is incompatible with the existence of an omnipotent and infinitely good God. But he does claim that it is strong prima facie evidence against the hypothesis that such a Being exists. Nor will he permit, methodologically, the appeal to some future life or experience where present evils, injustices and sufferings are rectified. "To establish one hypothesis upon another," Hume declares, "is building entirely in the air."

Professor John Hick, on the other hand, apparently rejects Hume's methodological strictures, for he employs exactly the argument which Hume would not permit. Evil and suffering, both natural and moral, are required for "soul-making," he maintains. That is, they are required if man is to be a free and responsible being. As for apparently superfluous evil—the suffering of innocent children and acts of genocide—Hick states that "the Christian answer must be in terms of a future good which is great enough to justify all that has happened on the way to it." For Hume, however, the appeal to some future life and future good to rectify present evil is simply building one hypothesis upon another. It does enable the believer to maintain that the existence of God and evil are compatible (which Hick calls the "method of negative theodicy"). But is building one hypothesis upon another philosophically acceptable?

William T. Blackstone

NOTES

1. See Karl Barth, *Kirchliche Dogmatik* (1932); also Soren Kierkegaard, *Concluding Unscientific Postscript* (1846).
2. St. Anselm, *Proslogium,* in *A Scholastic Miscellany,* edited and translated by Eugene R. Fairweather, Library of Christian Classics, Vol. X (Philadelphia, Pa.: Westminister Press, 1956).
3. St. Thomas, *Summa Theologia,* in *The Basic Writings of St. Thomas Aquinas,* edited by Anton C. Pegis (New York: Random House, 1945).
4. William Paley, *Natural Theology* (1802).
5. Immanuel Kant, *Critique of Pure Reason* (1781); *Critique of Practical Reason* (1788); *Religion Within the Bounds of Mere Reason* (1793).
6. David Hume, *A Treatise of Human Nature* (1739); *An Enquiry Concerning Human Understanding* (1758); *Dialogues Concerning Natural Religion* (1779).
7. David Hume, *Dialogues Concerning Natural Religion* (1779).
8. *Concluding Unscientific postscript,* translated by David Swenson, completed and edited by Walter Lowrie (Princeton, N.J.: Princeton University Press, 1944).
9. Karl Barth, *Kirchliche Dogmatik* (1932).
10. Thomas Huxley, *Science and Christian Tradition* (1896).
11. Ludwig Feuerbach, *The Essence of Christianity* (1855).
12. Karl Marx, *Theses on Feuerbach* (1845).
13. Blase Pascal, *Pensees* (1658).
14. W. K. Clifford, "The Ethics of Belief," in his *Lectures and Essays* (1879).
15. Matthew 13: 41–42; quoted by Russell, in this chapter's selection.
16. Matthew 25: 41.
17. R. B. Braithwaite, *An Empiricist's View of the Nature of Religious Belief* (New York: Cambridge University Press, 1955), p. 23.

78. *WHY I AM NOT A CHRISTIAN*

Bertrand Russell

As your Chairman has told you, the subject about which I am going to speak to you tonight is "Why I Am Not a Christian." Perhaps it would be as well, first of all, to try to make out what one means by the word *Christian.* It is used these days in a very loose sense by a great many people. Some people mean no more by it than a person who attempts to live a good life. In that sense I suppose there would be Christians in all sects and creeds; but I do not think that that is the proper sense of the word, if only because it would imply that all the people who are not Christians—all the Buddhists, Confucians, Mohammedans, and so on—are not trying to live a good life. I do not mean by a Christian any person who tries to live decently according to his lights. I think that you must have a certain amount of definite belief before you have a right to call yourself a Christian. The word does not have quite such a full-blooded meaning now as it had in the times of St. Augustine and St. Thomas Aquinas. In those days, if a man said that he was a Christian it was known what he meant. You accepted a whole collection of creeds which were set out with great precision, and every single syllable of those creeds you believed with the whole strength of your convictions.

WHAT IS A CHRISTIAN?

Nowadays it is not quite that. We have to be a little more vague in our meaning of Christianity. I think, however, that there are two different items which are quite essential to anybody calling himself a

Christian. The first is one of a dogmatic nature—namely, that you must believe in God and immortality. If you do not believe in those two things, I do not think that you can properly call yourself a Christian. Then, further than that, as the name implies, you must have some kind of belief about Christ. The Mohammedans, for instance, also believe in God and in immortality, and yet they would not call themselves Christians. I think you must have at the very lowest the belief that Christ was, if not divine, at least the best and wisest of men. If you are not going to believe that much about Christ, I do not think you have any right to call yourself a Christian. Of course, there is another sense, which you find in *Whitaker's Almanack* and in geography books, where the population of the world is said to be divided into Christians, Mohammedans, Buddhists, fetish worshipers, and so on; and in that sense we are all Christians. The geography books count us all in, but that is a purely geographical sense, which I suppose we can ignore. Therefore I take it that when I tell you why I am not a Christian I have to tell you two different things: first, why I do not believe in God and in immortality; and, secondly, why I do not think that Christ was the best and wisest of men, although I grant him a very high degree of moral goodness.

But for the successful efforts of unbelievers in the past, I could not take so elastic a definition of Christianity as that. As I said before, in olden days it had a much more full-blooded sense. For instance, it included the belief in hell. Belief in eternal hell-fire was an essential item of Christian belief until pretty recent times. In this country, as you know, it ceased to be an essential item because of a decision of the Privy Council, and from that decision the Archbishop of Canterbury and the Archbishop of York dissented; but in this country our religion is settled by Act of Parliament, and therefore the Privy Council was able to override their Graces and hell was no longer necessary to a Christian. Consequently I shall not insist that a Christian must believe in hell.

THE EXISTENCE OF GOD

To come to this question of the existence of God: it is a large and serious question, and if I were to attempt to deal with it in any adequate manner I should have to keep you here until Kingdom Come, so that you will have to excuse me if I deal with it in a somewhat summary fashion. You know, of course, that the Catholic Church has laid it down as a dogma that the existence of God can be proved by the unaided reason. That is a somewhat curious dogma, but it is one of their dogmas. They had to introduce it because at one time the freethinkers adopted the habit of saying that there were such and such arguments which mere reason might urge against the existence of God, but of course they knew as a matter of faith that God did exist. The arguments and the reasons were set out at great length, and the Catholic Church felt that they must stop it. Therefore they laid it down that the existence of God can be proved by the unaided reason and they had to set up what they considered were arguments to prove it. There are, of course, a number of them, but I shall take only a few.

THE FIRST-CAUSE ARGUMENT

Perhaps the simplest and easiest to understand is the argument of the First Cause. (It is maintained that everything we see in this world has a cause, and as you go back in the chain of causes further and further you must come to a First Cause, and to that First Cause you give the name of God.) That argument, I suppose, does not carry very much weight nowadays, because, in the first place, cause is not quite what it used to be. The philosophers and the men of science have got going on cause, and it has not anything like the vitality it used to have; but, apart from that, you can see that the argument that there must be a First Cause is one that cannot have any validity. I may say that when I was a young man

and was debating these questions very seriously in my mind, I for a long time accepted the argument of the First Cause, until one day, at the age of eighteen, I read John Stuart Mill's Autobiography, and I there found this sentence: "My father taught me that the question 'Who made me?' cannot be answered, since it immediately suggests the further question 'Who made God?' " That very simple sentence showed me, as I still think, the fallacy in the argument of the First Cause. If everything must have a cause, then God must have a cause. If there can be anything without a cause, it may just as well be the world as God, so that there cannot be any validity in that argument. It is exactly of the same nature as the Hindu's view, that the world rested upon an elephant and the elephant rested upon a tortoise; and when they said, "How about the tortoise?" the Indian said, "Suppose we change the subject." The argument is really no better than that. There is no reason why the world could not have come into being without a cause; nor, on the other hand, is there any reason why it should not have always existed. There is no reason to suppose that the world had a beginning at all. The idea that things must have a beginning is really due to the poverty of our imagination. Therefore, perhaps, I need not waste any more time upon the argument about the First Cause.

THE NATURAL-LAW ARGUMENT

Then there is a very common argument from natural law. That was a favorite argument all through the eighteenth century, especially under the influence of Sir Isaac Newton and his cosmogony. People observed the planets going around the sun according to the law of gravitation, and they thought that God had given a behest to these planets to move in that particular fashion, and that was why they did so. That was, of course, a convenient and simple explanation that saved them the trouble of looking any further for explanations of the law of gravitation. Nowadays we explain the law of gravitation in a somewhat complicated fashion that Einstein has introduced. I do not propose to give you a lecture on the law of gravitation, as interpreted by Einstein, because that again would take some time; at any rate, you no longer have the sort of natural law that you had in the Newtonian system, where, for some reason that nobody could understand, nature behaved in a uniform fashion. We now find that a great many things we thought were natural laws are really human conventions. You know that even in the remotest depths of stellar space there are still three feet to a yard. That is, no doubt, a very remarkable fact, but you would hardly call it a law of nature. And a great many things that have been regarded as laws of nature are of that kind. On the other hand, where you can get down to any knowledge of what atoms actually do, you will find they are much less subject to law than people thought, and that the laws at which you arrive are statistical averages of just the sort that would emerge from chance. There is, as we all know, a law that if you throw dice you will get double sixes only about once in thirty-six times, and we do not regard that as evidence that the fall of the dice is regulated by design; on the contrary, if the double sixes came every time we should think that there was design. The laws of nature are of that sort as regards a great many of them. They are statistical averages such as would emerge from the laws of chance; and that makes this whole business of natural law much less impressive than it formerly was. Quite apart from that, which represents the momentary state of science that may change tomorrow, the whole idea that natural laws imply a lawgiver is due to a confusion between natural and human laws. Human laws are behests commanding you to behave a certain way, in which way you may choose to behave, or you may choose not to behave; but natural laws are a description of how things do in fact behave, and being a mere description of what they in fact do, you cannot argue that there must be somebody who told them to do that, because even supposing that there were, you are then faced with the question "Why did God issue just those natural laws and no others?" If you say that he did it simply from his own good pleasure, and without any reason, you then find that there is something which is not subject to law, and so your train of natural law is interrupted. If you say, as more orthodox theologians do, that in all the laws which God issues he had a reason for giving those laws rather than others—the reason, of course, being to create the best universe, although you would

never think it to look at it—if there were a reason for the laws which God gave, then God himself was subject to law, and therefore you do not get any advantage by introducing God as an intermediary. You have really a law outside and anterior to the divine edicts, and God does not serve your purpose, because he is not the ultimate lawgiver. In short, this whole argument about natural law no longer has anything like the strength that it used to have. I am traveling on in time in my review of the arguments. The arguments that are used for the existence of God change their character as time goes on. They were at first hard intellectual arguments embodying certain quite definite fallacies. As we come to modern times they become less respectable intellectually and more and more affected by a kind of moralizing vagueness.

THE ARGUMENT FROM DESIGN

The next step in this process brings us to the argument from design. You all know the argument from design: everything in the world is made just so that we can manage to live in the world, and if the world was ever so little different, we could not manage to live in it. That is the argument from design. It sometimes takes a rather curious form; for instance, it is argued that rabbits have white tails in order to be easy to shoot. I do not know how rabbits would view that application. It is an easy argument to parody. You all know Voltaire's remark, that obviously the nose was designed to be such as to fit spectacles. That sort of parody has turned out to be not nearly so wide of the mark as it might have seemed in the eighteenth century, because since the time of Darwin we understand much better why living creatures are adapted to their environment. It is not that their environment was made to be suitable to them but that they grew to be suitable to it, and that is the basis of adaptation. There is no evidence of design about it.

When you come to look into this argument from design, it is a most astonishing thing that people can believe that this world, with all the things that are in it, with all its defects, should be the best that omnipotence and omniscience have been able to produce in millions of years. I really cannot believe it. Do you think that, if you were granted omnipotence and omniscience and millions of years in which to perfect your world, you could produce nothing better than the Ku Klux Klan or the Fascists? Moreover, if you accept the ordinary laws of science, you have to suppose that human life and life in general on this planet will die out in due course: it is a stage in the decay of the solar system; at a certain stage of decay you get the sort of conditions of temperature and so forth which are suitable to protoplasm, and there is life for a short time in the life of the whole solar system. You see in the moon the sort of thing to which the earth is tending —something dead, cold, and lifeless.

I am told that that sort of view is depressing, and people will sometimes tell you that if they believed that, they would not be able to go on living. Do not believe it; it is all nonsense. Nobody really worries much about what is going to happen millions of years hence. Even if they think they are worrying much about that, they are really deceiving themselves. They are worried about something much more mundane, or it may merely be a bad digestion; but nobody is really seriously rendered unhappy by the thought of something that is going to happen to this world millions and millions of years hence. Therefore, although it is of course a gloomy view to suppose that life will die out—at least I suppose we may say so, although sometimes when I contemplate the things that people do with their lives I think it is almost a consolation—it is not such as to render life miserable. It merely makes you turn your attention to other things.

THE MORAL ARGUMENTS FOR DEITY

Now we reach one stage further in what I shall call the intellectual descent that the Theists have made in their argumentations, and we come to what are called the moral arguments for the existence of God. You all know, of course, that there used to be in the old days three intellectual arguments for the existence of God, all of which were disposed of by Immanuel Kant in the *Critique of Pure Reason;* but no sooner had he disposed of those arguments than he invented a new one, a moral argument, and that quite convinced him. He was like many people: in intellectual matters he was skeptical, but in moral matters he believed implicitly in the maxims that he had imbibed at his mother's knee. That illustrates

what the psychoanalysts so much emphasize—the immensely stronger hold upon us that our very early associations have than those of later times.

Kant, as I say, invented a new moral argument for the existence of God, and that in varying forms was extremely popular during the nineteenth century. It has all sorts of forms. One form is to say that there would be no right or wrong unless God existed. I am not for the moment concerned with whether there is a difference between right and wrong, or whether there is not: that is another question. The point I am concerned with is that, if you are quite sure there is a difference between right and wrong, you are then in this situation: Is that difference due to God's fiat or is it not? If it is due to God's fiat, then for God himself there is no difference between right and wrong, and it is no longer a significant statement to say that God is good. If you are going to say, as theologians do, that God is good, you must then say that right and wrong have some meaning which is independent of God's fiat, because God's fiats are good and not bad independently of the mere fact that he made them. If you are going to say that, you will then have to say that it is not only through God that right and wrong came into being, but that they are in their essence logically anterior to God. You could, of course, if you liked, say that there was a superior deity who gave orders to the God who made this world, or could take up the line that some of the gnostics took up—a line which I often thought was a very plausible one—that as a matter of fact this world that we know was made by the devil at a moment when God was not looking. There is a good deal to be said for that, and I am not concerned to refute it.

THE ARGUMENT FOR THE REMEDYING OF INJUSTICE

Then there is another very curious form of moral argument, which is this: they say that the existence of God is required in order to bring justice into the world. In the part of this universe that we know there is great injustice, and often the good suffer, and often the wicked prosper, and one hardly knows which of those is the more annoying; but if you are going to have justice in the universe as a whole you have to suppose a future life to redress the balance of life here on earth. So they say that there must be a God, and there must be heaven and hell in order that in the long run there may be justice. That is a very curious argument. If you looked at the matter from a scientific point of view, you would say, "After all, I know only this world. I do not know about the rest of the universe, but so far as one can argue at all on probabilities one would say that probably this world is a fair sample, and if there is injustice here the odds are that there is injustice elsewhere also." Supposing you got a crate of oranges that you opened, and you found all the top layer of oranges bad, you would not argue, "The underneath ones must be good, so as to redress the balance." You would say, "Probably the whole lot is a bad consignment"; and that is really what a scientific person would argue about the universe. He would say, "Here we find in this world a great deal of injustice, and so far as that goes that is a reason for supposing that justice does not rule in the world; and therefore so far as it goes it affords a moral argument against deity and not in favor of one." Of course I know that the sort of intellectual arguments that I have been talking to you about are not what really moves people. What really moves people to believe in God is not any intellectual argument at all. Most people believe in God because they have been taught from early infancy to do it, and that is the main reason.

Then I think that the next most powerful reason is the wish for safety, a sort of feeling that there is a big brother who will look after you. That plays a very profound part in influencing people's desire for a belief in God.

THE CHARACTER OF CHRIST

I now want to say a few words upon a topic which I often think is not quite sufficiently dealt with by Rationalists, and that is the question whether Christ was the best and the wisest of men. It is generally taken for granted that we should all agree that that was so. I do not myself. I think that there are a good many points upon which I agree with Christ a great deal more than the professing Christians do. I do not know that I could go with Him all the way, but I could go with Him much further than most professing Christians can. You will remember that He said, "Resist not evil: but whosoever shall smite thee on thy right cheek, turn to him the other

also." That is not a new precept or a new principle. It was used by Lao-tse and Buddha some 500 or 600 years before Christ, but it is not a principle which as a matter of fact Christians accept. I have no doubt that the present Prime Minister,* for instance, is a most sincere Christian, but I should not advise any of you to go and smite him on one cheek. I think you might find that he thought this text was intended in a figurative sense.

Then there is another point which I consider excellent. You will remember that Christ said, "Judge not lest ye be judged." That principle I do not think you would find was popular in the law courts of Christian countries. I have known in my time quite a number of judges who were very earnest Christians, and none of them felt that they were acting contrary to Christian principles in what they did. Then Christ says, "Give to him that asketh of thee, and from him that would borrow of thee turn not thou away." That is a very good principle. Your Chairman has reminded you that we are not here to talk politics, but I cannot help observing that the last general election was fought on the question of how desirable it was to turn away from him that would borrow of thee, so that one must assume that the Liberals and Conservatives of this country are composed of people who do not agree with the teaching of Christ, because they certainly did very emphatically turn away on that occasion.

Then there is one other maxim of Christ which I think has a great deal in it, but I do not find that it is very popular among some of our Christian friends. He says, "If thou wilt be perfect, go and sell that which thou hast, and give to the poor." That is a very excellent maxim, but, as I say, it is not much practiced. All these, I think, are good maxims, although they are a little difficult to live up to. I do not profess to live up to them myself; but then, after all, it is not quite the same thing as for a Christian.

DEFECTS IN CHRIST'S TEACHING

Having granted the excellence of these maxims, I come to certain points in which I do not believe that one can grant either the superlative wisdom or the superlative goodness of Christ as depicted in

* Stanley Baldwin.

the Gospels; and here I may say that one is not concerned with the historical question. Historically it is quite doubtful whether Christ ever existed at all, and if He did we do not know anything about Him, so that I am not concerned with the historical question, which is a very difficult one. I am concerned with Christ as He appears in the Gospels, taking the Gospel narrative as it stands, and there one does find some things that do not seem to be very wise. For one thing, He certainly thought that His second coming would occur in clouds of glory before the death of all the people who were living at that time. There are a great many texts that prove that. He says, for instance, "Ye shall not have gone over the cities of Israel till the Son of Man be come." Then He says, "There are some standing here which shall not taste death till the Son of Man comes into His kingdom"; and there are a lot of places where it is quite clear that He believed that His second coming would happen during the lifetime of many then living. That was the belief of His earlier followers, and it was the basis of a good deal of His moral teaching. When He said, "Take no thought for the morrow," and things of that sort, it was very largely because He thought that the second coming was going to be very soon, and that all ordinary mundane affairs did not count. I have, as a matter of fact, known some Christians who did believe that the second coming was imminent. I knew a parson who frightened his congregation terribly by telling them that the second coming was very imminent indeed, but they were much consoled when they found that he was planting trees in his garden. The early Christians did really believe it, and they did abstain from such things as planting trees in their gardens, because they did accept from Christ the belief that the second coming was imminent. In that respect, clearly He was not so wise as some other people have been, and He was certainly not superlatively wise.

THE MORAL PROBLEM

Then you come to moral questions. There is one very serious defect to my mind in Christ's moral character, and that is that He believed in hell. I do not myself feel that any person who is really profoundly humane can believe in everlasting pun-

ishment. Christ certainly as depicted in the Gospels did believe in everlasting punishment, and one does find repeatedly a vindictive fury against those people who would not listen to His preaching—an attitude which is not uncommon with preachers, but which does somewhat detract from superlative excellence. You do not, for instance find that attitude in Socrates. You find him quite bland and urbane toward the people who would not listen to him; and it is, to my mind, far more worthy of a sage to take that line than to take the line of indignation. You probably all remember the sort of things that Socrates was saying when he was dying, and the sort of things that he generally did say to people who did not agree with him.

You will find that in the Gospels Christ said, "Ye serpents, ye generation of vipers, how can ye escape the damnation of hell." That was said to people who did not like His preaching. It is not really to my mind quite the best tone, and there are a great many of these things about hell. There is, of course, the familiar text about the sin against the Holy Ghost: "Whosoever speaketh against the Holy Ghost it shall not be forgiven him neither in this World nor in the world to come." That text has caused an unspeakable amount of misery in the world, for all sorts of people have imagined that they have committed the sin against the Holy Ghost, and thought that it would not be forgiven them either in this world or in the world to come. I really do not think that a person with a proper degree of kindliness in his nature would have put fears and terrors of that sort into the world.

Then Christ says, "The Son of Man shall send forth His angels, and they shall gather out of His kingdom all things that offend, and them which do iniquity, and shall cast them into a furnace of fire; there shall be wailing and gnashing of teeth"; and He goes on about the wailing and gnashing of teeth. It comes in one verse after another, and it is quite manifest to the reader that there is a certain pleasure in contemplating wailing and gnashing of teeth, or else it would not occur so often. Then you all, of course, remember about the sheep and the goats; how at the second coming He is going to divide the sheep from the goats, and He is going to say to the goats, "Depart from me, ye cursed, into everlasting fire." He continues, "And these shall go away into everlasting fire." Then He says again, "If thy hand offend thee, cut it off; it is better for thee to enter into life maimed, than having two hands to go into hell, into the fire that never shall be quenched; where the worm dieth not and the fire is not quenched." He repeats that again and again also. I must say that I think all this doctrine, that hell-fire is a punishment for sin, is a doctrine of cruelty. It is a doctrine that put cruelty into the world and gave the world generations of cruel torture; and the Christ of the Gospels, if you could take Him as His chroniclers represent Him, would certainly have to be considered partly responsible for that.

There are other things of less importance. There is the instance of the Gadarene swine, where it certainly was not very kind to the pigs to put the devils into them and make them rush down the hill to the sea. You must remember that He was omnipotent, and He could have made the devils simply go away; but He chose to send them into the pigs. Then there is the curious story of the fig tree, which always rather puzzled me. You remember what happened about the fig tree. "He was hungry; and seeing a fig tree afar off having leaves, He came if haply He might find anything thereon; and when He came to it He found nothing but leaves, for the time of figs was not yet. And Jesus answered and said unto it: 'No man eat fruit of thee hereafter for ever' . . . and Peter . . . saith unto Him: 'Master, behold the fig tree which thou cursedst is withered away.' " This is a very curious story, because it was not the right time of year for figs, and you really could not blame the tree. I cannot myself feel that either in the matter of wisdom or in the matter of virtue Christ stands quite as high as some other people known to history. I think I should put Buddha and Socrates above Him in those respects.

THE EMOTIONAL FACTOR

As I said before, I do not think that the real reason why people accept religion has anything to do with argumentation. They accept religion on emotional grounds. One is often told that it is a very wrong thing to attack religion, because religion makes men virtuous. So I am told; I have not noticed it. You know, of course, the parody of that argument

in Samuel Butler's book, *Erewhon Revisited.* You will remember that in *Erewhon* there is a certain Higgs who arrives in a remote country, and after spending some time there he escapes from that country in a balloon. Twenty years later he comes back to that country and finds a new religion in which he is worshiped under the name of the "Sun Child," and it is said that he ascended into heaven. He finds that the Feast of the Ascension is about to be celebrated, and he hears Professors Hanky and Panky say to each other that they never set eyes on the man Higgs, and they hope they never will; but they are the high priests of the religion of the Sun Child. He is very indignant, and he comes up to them, and he says, "I am going to expose all this humbug and tell the people of Erewhon that it was only I, the man Higgs, and I went up in a balloon." He was told, "You must not do that, because all the morals of this country are bound round this myth, and if they once know that you did not ascend into heaven they will all become wicked"; and so he is persuaded of that and he goes quietly away.

That is the idea—that we should all be wicked if we did not hold to the Christian religion. It seems to me that the people who have held to it have been for the most part extremely wicked. You find this curious fact, that the more intense has been the religion of any period and the more profound has been the dogmatic belief, the greater has been the cruelty and the worse has been the state of affairs. In the so-called ages of faith, when men really did believe the Christian religion in all its completeness, there was the Inquisition, with its tortures; there were millions of unfortunate women burned as witches; and there was every kind of cruelty practiced upon all sorts of people in the name of religion.

You find as you look around the world that every single bit of progress in humane feeling, every improvement in the criminal law, every step toward the diminution of war, every step toward better treatment of the colored races, or every mitigation of slavery, every moral progress that there has been in the world, has been consistently opposed by the organized churches of the world. I say quite deliberately that the Christian religion, as organized in its churches, has been and still is the principal enemy of moral progress in the world.

HOW THE CHURCHES HAVE RETARDED PROGRESS

You may think that I am going too far when I say that that is still so. I do not think that I am. Take one fact. You will bear with me if I mention it. It is not a pleasant fact, but the churches compel one to mention facts that are not pleasant. Supposing that in this world that we live in today an inexperienced girl is married to a syphilitic man; in that case the Catholic Church says, "This is an indissoluble sacrament. You must endure celibacy or stay together. And if you stay together, you must not use birth control to prevent the birth of syphilitic children." Nobody whose natural sympathies have not been warped by dogma, or whose moral nature was not absolutely dead to all sense of suffering, could maintain that it is right and proper that that state of things should continue.

That is only an example. There are a great many ways in which, at the present moment, the church, by its insistence upon what it chooses to call morality, inflicts upon all sorts of people undeserved and unnecessary suffering. And of course, as we know, it is in its major part an opponent still of progress and of improvement in all the ways that diminish suffering in the world, because it has chosen to label as morality a certain narrow set of rules of conduct which have nothing to do with human happiness; and when you say that this or that ought to be done because it would make for human happiness, they think that has nothing to do with the matter at all. "What has human happiness to do with morals? The object of morals is not to make people happy."

FEAR, THE FOUNDATION OF RELIGION

Religion is based, I think, primarily and mainly upon fear. It is partly the terror of the unknown and partly, as I have said, the wish to feel that you have a kind of elder brother who will stand by you in all your troubles and disputes. Fear is the basis of the whole thing—fear of the mysterious, fear of defeat, fear of death. Fear is the parent of cruelty, and therefore it is no wonder if cruelty and religion have gone hand in hand. It is because fear is at the basis of those two things. In this world we can now begin a little to understand things, and a little to master them by help of science, which has forced its way step by step against the Christian religion, against the churches, and against the opposition of all the old precepts. Science can help us to get over this craven fear in which mankind has lived for so many generations. Science can teach us, and I think our own hearts can teach us, no longer to look around for imaginary supports, no longer to invent allies in the sky, but rather to look to our own efforts here below to make this world a fit place to live in, instead of the sort of place that the churches in all these centuries have made it.

WHAT WE MUST DO

We want to stand upon our own feet and look fair and square at the world—its good facts, its bad facts, its beauties, and its ugliness; see the world as it is and be not afraid of it. Conquer the world by intelligence and not merely by being slavishly subdued by the terror that comes from it. The whole conception of God is a conception derived from the ancient Oriental despotisms. It is a conception quite unworthy of free men. When you hear people in church debasing themselves and saying that they are miserable sinners, and all the rest of it, it seems contemptible and not worthy of self-respecting human beings. We ought to stand up and look the world frankly in the face. We ought to make the best we can of the world, and if it is not so good as we wish, after all it will still be better than what these others have made of it in all these ages. A good world needs knowledge, kindliness, and courage; it does not need a regretful hankering after the past or a fettering of the free intelligence by the words uttered long ago by ignorant men. It needs a fearless outlook and a free intelligence. It needs hope for the future, not looking back all the time toward a past that is dead, which we trust will be far surpassed by the future that our intelligence can create.

79. THE WILL TO BELIEVE

William James

In the recently published Life by Leslie Stephen of his brother, Fitz-James, there is an account of a school to which the latter went when he was a boy. The teacher, a certain Mr. Guest, used to converse with his pupils in this wise: "Gurney, what is the difference between justification and sanctification? —Stephen, prove the omnipotence of God!" etc. In the midst of our Harvard freethinking and indifference we are prone to imagine that here at your good old orthodox College conversation continues to be somewhat upon this order; and to show you that we at Harvard have not lost all interest in these vital subjects, I have brought with me tonight something like a sermon on justification by faith to read to you.—I mean an essay in justification of faith, a defence of our right to adopt a believing attitude in religious matters, in spite of the fact that our merely logical intellect may not have been coerced. 'The Will to Believe,' accordingly, is the title of my paper.

I have long defended to my own students the lawfulness of voluntarily adopted faith; but as soon as they have got well imbued with the logical spirit, they have as a rule refused to admit my contention to be lawful philosophically, even though in point of fact they were personally all the time chock-full of some faith or other themselves. I am all the while, however, so profoundly convinced that my own position is correct, that your invitation has seemed to me a good occasion to make my statements more clear. Perhaps your minds will be more open than those with which I have hitherto had to deal. I will be as little technical as I can, though I must begin by setting up some technical distinctions that will help us in the end.

Let us give the name of *hypothesis* to anything that may be proposed to our belief; and just as the electricians speak of live and dead wires, let us speak of any hypothesis as either *live* or *dead*. A live hypothesis is one which appeals as a real possibility to him to whom it is proposed. If I ask you to believe in the Mahdi, the notion makes no electric connection with your nature,—it refuses to scintillate with any credibility at all. As an hypothesis it is completely dead. To an Arab, however (even if he be not one of the Mahdi's followers), the hypothesis is among the mind's possibilities: it is alive. This shows that deadness and liveness in an hypothesis are not intrinsic properties, but relations to the individual thinker. They are measured by his willingness to act. The maximum of liveness in an hypothesis means willingness to act irrevocably. Practically, that means belief; but there is some believing tendency wherever there is willingness to act at all.

Next, let us call the decision between two hypotheses an *option*. Options may be of several kinds. They may be—1. *living* or *dead;* 2. *forced* or *avoidable;* 3. *momentous* or *trivial;* and for our purposes we may call an option a *genuine* option when it is of the forced, living, and momentous kind.

1. A living option is one in which both hypotheses are live ones. If I say to you: "Be a theosophist or be a Mohammedan," it is probably a dead option, because for you neither hypothesis is likely to be alive. But if I say: "Be an agnostic or be a Christian," it is otherwise: trained as you are, each hypothesis makes some appeal, however small, to your belief.

2. Next, if I say to you: "Choose between going out with your umbrella or without it," I do not offer you a genuine option, for it is not forced. You can easily avoid it by not going out at all. Similarly, if I say, "Either love me or hate me," "Either call my theory true or call it false," your option is avoidable. You may remain indifferent to me, neither loving nor hating, and you may decline to offer any judgment as to my theory. But if I say, "Either accept this truth or go without it," I put on you a forced option, for there is no standing place outside of the alternative. Every dilemma based on a complete logical disjunction, with no possibility of not choosing, is an option of this forced kind.

3. Finally, if I were Dr. Nansen and proposed to you to join my North Pole expedition, your option would be momentous; for this would probably be your only similar opportunity, and your choice now

An address to the Philosophical Clubs of Yale and Brown Universities. Published in the *New World,* June 1896.

would either exclude you from the North Pole sort of immortality altogether or put at least the chance of it into your hands. He who refuses to embrace a unique opportunity loses the prize as surely as if he tried and failed. *Per contra,* the option is trivial when the opportunity is not unique, when the stake is insignificant, or when the decision is reversible if it later prove unwise. Such trivial options abound in the scientific life. A chemist finds an hypothesis live enough to spend a year in its verification: he believes in it to that extent. But if his experiments prove inconclusive either way, he is quit for his loss of time, no vital harm being done. . . .

The thesis I defend is, briefly stated, this: *Our passional nature not only lawfully may, but must, decide an option between propositions whenever it is a genuine option that cannot by its nature be decided on intellectual grounds; for to say, under such circumstances, "Do not decide but leave the question open," is itself a passional decision,—just like deciding yes or no,—and is attended with the same risk of losing the truth.* The thesis thus abstractly expressed will, I trust, soon become quite clear. . . .

One more point, small but important, and our preliminaries are done. There are two ways of looking at our duty in the matter of opinion,—ways entirely different, and yet ways about whose difference the theory of knowledge seems hitherto to have shown very little concern. *We must know the truth;* and *we must avoid error,*—these are our first and great commandments as would-be knowers; but they are not two ways of stating an identical commandment, they are two separable laws. Although it may indeed happen that when we believe the truth A, we escape as an incidental consequence from believing the falsehood B, it hardly ever happens that by merely disbelieving B we necessarily believe A. We may in escaping B fall into believing other falsehoods, C or D, just as bad as B; or we may escape B by not believing anything at all, not even A.

Believe truth! Shun error!—these, we see, are two materially different laws; and by choosing between them we may end by coloring differently our whole intellectual life. We may regard the chase for truth as paramount, and the avoidance of error as secondary; or we may, on the other hand, treat the avoidance of error as more imperative and let truth take its chance. Clifford, in the instructive passage which I have quoted, exhorts us to the latter course. Believe nothing, he tells us, keep your mind in suspense forever rather than by closing it on insufficient evidence incur the awful risk of believing lies. You, on the other hand, may think that the risk of being in error is a very small matter when compared with the blessings of real knowledge, and be ready to be duped many times in your investigation rather than postpone indefinitely the chance of guessing true. I myself find it impossible to go with Clifford. We must remember that these feelings of our duty about either truth or error are in any case only expressions of our passional life. Biologically considered, our minds are as ready to grind out falsehood as veracity and he who says, "Better go without belief forever than believe a lie!" merely shows his own preponderant private horror of becoming a dupe. He may be critical of many of his desires and fears, but this fear he slavishly obeys. He cannot imagine any one questioning its binding force. For my own part I have also a horror of being duped, but I can believe that worse things than being duped may happen to a man in this world: so Clifford's exhortation has to my ears a thoroughly fantastic sound. It is like a general informing his soldiers that it is better to keep out of battle forever than to risk a single wound. Not so are victories either over enemies or over nature gained. Our errors are surely not such awfully solemn things. In a world where we are so certain to incur them in spite of all our caution, a certain lightness of heart seems healthier than this excessive nervousness on their behalf. At any rate, it seems the fittest thing for the empiricist philosopher. . . .

Well, of course, I agree as far as the facts will allow. Wherever the option between losing truth and gaining it is not momentous, we can throw the chance of *gaining truth* away, and at any rate save ourselves from any chance of *believing falsehood,* by not making up our minds at all till objective evidence has come. In scientific questions, this is almost always the case. . . .

The question next arises: Are there not somewhere forced options in our speculative questions, and can we (as men who may be interested at least as much in positively gaining truth as in merely escaping dupery) always wait with impunity till the coercive evidence shall have arrived? It seems *a priori* improbable that the truth should be so nicely adjusted to our needs and powers as that. In the great boardinghouse of nature, the cakes and the butter and the syrup seldom come out so even and leave the plates so clean. Indeed, we should view them with scientific suspicion if they did.

Moral questions immediately present themselves as questions whose solution cannot wait for sensible proof. A moral question is a question not of what sensibly exists, but of what is good, or would be good if it did exist. Science can tell us what exists; but to compare the *worths,* both of what exists and of what does not exist, we must consult not science, but what Pascal calls our heart. Science herself consults her heart when she lays it down that the infinite ascertainment of fact and correction of false belief are the supreme goods for man. . . .

Turn now from these wide questions of good to a certain class of questions of fact, questions concerning personal relations, states of mind between one man and another. *Do you like me or not?*—for example. Whether you do or not depends, in countless instances, on whether I meet you halfway, am willing to assume that you must like me, and show you trust and expectation. The previous faith on my part in your liking's existence is in such cases what makes your liking come. But if I stand aloof, and refuse to budge an inch until I have objective evidence, until you shall have done something apt, as the absolutists say, *ad extorquendum assensum meum,* ten to one your liking never comes. How many women's hearts are vanquished by the mere sanguine insistence of some man that they *must* love him! he will not consent to the hypothesis that they cannot. The desire for a certain kind of truth here brings about that special truth's existence; and so it is in innumerable cases of other sorts. Who gains promotions, boons, appointments, but the man in whose life they are seen to play the part of live hypotheses, who discounts them, sacrifices other things for their sake before they have come, and takes risks for them in advance? His faith acts on the powers above him as a claim, and creates its own verification. . . . There are, then, cases where a fact cannot come at all

unless a preliminary faith exists in its coming. *And where faith in a fact can help create the fact,* that would be an insane logic which should say that faith running ahead of scientific evidence is the 'lowest kind of immorality' into which a thinking being can fall. Yet such is the logic by which our scientific absolutists pretend to regulate our lives! In truths dependent on our personal action, then, faith based on desire is certainly a lawful and possibly an indispensable thing.

But now, it will be said, these are all childish human cases, and have nothing to do with great cosmical matters, like the question of religious faith. Let us then pass on to that. Religions differ so much in their accidents that in discussing the religious question we must make it very generic and broad. What then do we now mean by the religious hypothesis? Science says things are; morality says some things are better than other things; and religion says essentially two things.

First, she says that the best things are the more eternal things, the overlapping things, the things in the universe that throw the last stone, so to speak, and say the final word. "Perfection is eternal,"— this phrase of Charles Secretan seems a good way of putting this first affirmation of religion, an affirmation which obviously cannot yet be verified scientifically at all.

The second affirmation of religion is that we are better off even now if we believe her first affirmation to be true.

Now, let us consider what the logical elements of this situation are *in case the religious hypothesis in both its branches be really true.* (Of course, we must admit that possibility at the outset. If we are to discuss the question at all, it must involve a living option. If for any of you religion be a hypothesis that cannot, by any living possibility be true, then you need go no farther. I speak to the 'saving remnant' alone.) So proceeding, we see, first, that religion offers itself as a *momentous* option. We are supposed to gain, even now, by our belief, and to lose by our non-belief, a certain vital good. Secondly, religion is a *forced* option, so far as that good goes. We cannot escape the issue by remaining sceptical and waiting for more light, because, although we do avoid error in that way *if religion be untrue* we lose the good, *if it be true,* just as certainly as if we positively chose to disbelieve. It is as if a man should hesitate indefinitely to ask a certain woman to marry him because he was not perfectly sure that she would prove an angel after he brought her home. Would he not cut himself off from that particular angel possibility as decisively as if he went and married some one else? Scepticism, then, is not avoidance of option: it is option of a certain particular kind of risk. *Better risk loss of truth than chance of error,*—that is your faith vetoer's exact position. He is actively playing his stake as much as the believer is: he is backing the field against the religious hypothesis, just as the believer is backing the religious hypothesis against the field. To preach scepticism to us as a duty until 'sufficient evidence' for religion be found, is tantamount therefore to telling us, when in presence of the religious hypothesis, that to yield to our fear of its being error is wiser and better than to yield to our hope that it may be true. It is not intellect against all passions, then; it is only intellect with one passion laying down its law. And by what, forsooth, is the supreme wisdom of this passion warranted? Dupery for dupery, what proof is there that dupery through hope is so much worse than dupery through fear? I, for one, can see no proof; and I simply refuse obedience to the scientist's command to imitate his kind of option, in a case where my own stake is important enough to give me the right to choose my own form of risk. If religion be true and the evidence for it be still insufficient, I do not wish, by putting your extinguisher upon my nature (which feels to me as if it had after all some business in this matter), to forfeit my sole chance in life of getting upon the winning side,—that chance depending, of course, on my willingness to run the risk of acting as if my passional need of taking the world religiously might be prophetic and right. . . .

I, therefore, for one, cannot see my way to accepting the agnostic rules for truth-seeking, or wilfully agree to keep my willing nature out of the game. I cannot do so for this plain reason, that *a rule of thinking which would absolutely prevent me from acknowledging certain kinds of truth if those kinds of truth were really there, would be an irrational rule.* That for me is the long and short of the formal logic of the situation, no matter what the kinds of truth might materially be. . . .

80. THE SIMPLE BELIEVER

R. M. Hare

I am going to introduce you to the situation, as I see it, by telling you a story. There was once a Simple Believer. If you asked him, "Is there a God?" he would reply, "Of course." And if you then asked him, "What is he like?" he would say "He is something like a man (for it says in the Bible that God made man in his own image); and he lives in Heaven, which is a place far up in the sky; and he

From R. M. Hare, "The Simple Believer," the first of three Nathaniel Taylor lectures delivered at the Yale Divinity School in December 1968. Copyright © 1973 by R. M. Hare, published in Gene Outka and John Reeder, Jr., editors, *Religion and Morality,* Anchor Press/Doubleday, Garden City, N. Y. Reprinted with the permission of the author. [Ed. note: The argument presented in this selection is continued in the second half of the Doubleday article.]

made both Heaven and Earth in six days in the year 4004 B.C., as you can find by doing some calculations based on the information given in the Bible. He made it in the manner described in Genesis; and he continues to rule the world by causing things to happen in it according to his will; and especially he causes things to happen which are for the good of those that believe in him; for God is loving, etc."

This sort of belief satisfied the Simple Believer until, at an impressionable age, he met another person, whom I will call the Simple Unbeliever. The Simple Unbeliever said, "Surely you don't believe *that* any more? We know now, for it has been established by science, that a being like a man couldn't possibly live up in the sky." (The conversation took place before the days of space travel.) "If you know any science at all, you know that he couldn't survive for a moment; and in any case, if he did exist on some star, how could he intervene from that distance in our affairs? And as for him making the world in 4004 B.C., we know that the world is much older than that. And he couldn't intervene in the world, since we know—for science tells us—that the world proceeds on its way by immutable scientific laws; so how could he make any difference to what happens in the world?"

The Simple Believer's faith was considerably shaken by all this; for he found on reflection and inquiry that most people believe that what science says, is true, and in his heart of hearts he believed so too. The picture that the Simple Unbeliever gave of the findings of science was, indeed, crude and oversimplified; but that could be remedied without altering its impact upon his former simple beliefs. Fortunately, while he was in this state of incipient doubt, he met a third person, whom I will call the Sophisticated Believer. The Sophisticated Believer set the Simple Believer's doubts at rest by saying, "You have been taking the Bible too literally. Of course, if you have these 'literal and low conceptions of sacred beings,'[1] your beliefs won't stand up against the latest scientific discoveries. If you want to survive the advance of empirical science, you must at all costs *keep out of the way* of the scientists; and this isn't at all difficult. Of course God (God the Father, that is) isn't like a man to look at—the Thirty-nine Articles say that he has neither body, parts, nor passions. And of course Genesis is only legend, although it is of deep symbolical significance. The Creation certainly wasn't like it says in Genesis, and there's no need to believe that it happened in 4004 B.C. You have been taking much too literally the statement that God made the world in six days—'day' here is to be interpreted as meaning an epoch of very great but unspecified length, so that the Genesis story (so far as chronology goes, at any rate) can be reconciled with whatever science discovers about the age of the universe. This is an example of what I mean by 'keeping out of the scientists' way'; you must be careful to say nothing that they can ever disprove. And in the same way to say that God rules the world is not to say anything that science would contradict. Aren't the laws of science the very best evidence that the world is ordered by a mastermind? For everywhere we turn we see things happening, not just by chance and haphazard, but according to the most precise laws. In believing in God, you aren't asked to believe anything about the world except what common sense and science (which is organized common sense) would allow. Religion is not about material things but about the things of the spirit."

This sort of comfort satisfied the Simple Believer, until he met the Simple Unbeliever again. This time the Simple Unbeliever had been reading Freud, and all about Pavlov's dogs. When he heard what the Sophisticated Believer had said about the things of the spirit, he exclaimed, "But that won't do either now, you know. The distinction between the spiritual and the material is nothing but what Ryle calls a 'Cartesian myth.'[2] Scientists don't only find out the laws that govern what you call the material world, but also those that govern what you call the things of the spirit. We can often give very good explanations of people's religious beliefs, for example, in terms of their early upbringing. No doubt if I knew more about *your* early upbringing I could account for your religious beliefs. The phenomena which you call spiritual and those which you call material are all just phenomena; science will explain them all in the end by the methods which have been so successful hitherto. Of course not everything has been explained yet; but that is a stimulus to us to go on looking for the true scientific explanations of things. Your talk about the things of the spirit is just an impediment to our researches, because it makes people think that there is something in the way people behave which is out of the reach of scientific inquiry. The Sophisticated Believer was quite right to tell you to keep out of the way of the scientists—I only wish you would; but to succeed in doing so you will have to move faster and farther than he thinks."

The Simple Believer was of course troubled by this; so he went hurrying back to the Sophisticated Believer, who had been of such assistance to him before, in the hope that he would provide an answer. And he did provide an answer; for if a believer is sophisticated enough, he can provide an answer to anything. He said, "You mustn't be upset by this kind of thing. When I said, the last time we met, that religion did not contradict science, I didn't mean to confine myself to what are called the physical sciences. I included the biological sciences; and, now that psychology has become respectable, I have no hesitation in including that too. Of course the religious believer doesn't want to contradict the psychologist, any more than he wants to contradict the physiologist. Come to that, he doesn't want to contradict *anybody*. Even when the religious person and the psychologist are talking about the same sort of phenomena, they are talking about them in a quite different way. When St. Francis gets swellings on his hands, the psychologist calls it 'hysterical stigmatization'; but the Christian will call it a miracle. And both will be perfectly right. In general, science is concerned with counting, measuring, observing, and predicting; religion is concerned with worship. Therefore it is quite impossible for the statements of the two to contradict one another. Statements about God creating and loving the world are statements of a different logical category from those about nebulae or atoms or bacteria or neurones; and so a person can go on making both kinds of statement without being in any way inconsistent. That is to say, it is perfectly possible to be a scientist and a religious believer at the same time—why, look at all the people who do it!"

While the Sophisticated Believer was offering this comfort, and the Simple Believer was on the way to being comforted, they did not notice that a friend of theirs was standing nearby and listening to what they were saying. He was there quite by accident, and had not meant to join in the conversation at all. But what he heard was too much for him, and he burst in, "But I don't see what the devil is left of your religion after you have said this. Your religious utterances used to consist of plain assertions about the existence of a Being about whose character, though exalted and mysterious, you had at any rate some idea. But now, in your determination to say nothing that anybody could disagree with, you have been surreptitiously whittling down your religion until there's nothing left of it but words, and a warm and womblike feeling that still sometimes comes over you when you utter them. Surely you must have heard of the invisible gardener!"

The two Believers both said that they hadn't heard of the invisible gardener; so the Sophisticated Unbeliever (as I will call him) went to the library and got out *New Essays in Philosophical Theology*,[3] and started to read from Flew's article (from which, by the way, I stole the example about St. Francis which I have just used). He chose Flew's version of the parable, not Wisdom's original one,[4] because it made the point more clearly.

Once upon a time two explorers came upon a clearing in the jungle. In the clearing were growing many flowers and many weeds. One explorer says, "Some gardener must tend this plot." The other disagrees, "There is no gardener." So they pitch their tents and set a watch. No gardener is ever seen. "But perhaps he is an invisible gardener." So they set up a barbed-wire fence. They electrify it. They patrol with bloodhounds. (For they remember how H. G. Wells's *The Invisible Man* could be both smelt and touched though he could not be seen.) But no shrieks ever suggest that some intruder has received a shock. No movements of the wire ever betray an invisible climber. The bloodhounds never give cry. Yet still the Believer is not convinced. "But there is a gardener, invisible, intangible, insensible to electric shocks, a gardener who has no scent and makes no sound, a gardener who comes secretly to look after the garden which he loves." At last the Sceptic despairs, "But what remains of your original assertion? Just how does what you call an invisible, intangible, eternally elusive gardener differ from an imaginary gardener or even from no gardener at all?"

By the time he had finished, the Simple Believer was in a bad way; for its point was only too clear to him. You see, he had started off by thinking that he was making perfectly good assertions about the existence of a being called God, and had in his imagination some sort of idea about what this being was like. Then, when he met the Simple Unbeliever, he came to see that what he had been saying was literally false. At first, when he discovered that a being of the sort he had been imagining couldn't live in the sky, he was comforted by the Sophisticated Believer's telling him that of course he had the wrong ideas about God; God did indeed exist, but he was not quite the sort of being that he had been imagining, and his location was not spatial in the way that he had thought; that in a sense he was everywhere and yet nowhere; that his hand was visible where no hand (no literal hand, that is to say) was visible; that God's love was manifested even in events which, in our normal use of words, we should not regard as manifestations of love, or even of hate, but just as things that happen in the world. But as the process went on, it had begun to be a bit beyond him. He did at least understand the old literal ideas about God, even if they were false; but these new ideas—well, even if they were true, it was so very hard to say what they meant, and they seemed so far removed from the God he used to worship. True, he still got the old warm feeling when he thought about religion; but even that was beginning to fade away a bit.

And then he thought of another thing. His father was a clergyman, and his grandfather had been a bishop; and so he had naturally sometimes had occasion to try to persuade people, whose faith was going or gone, to come back into the fold. He had heard his father doing this in the pulpit, and he had tried in his private conversation to reproduce, and indeed to improve on, his father's arguments. But it did not seem to work, somehow. The trouble was that the people he was trying to reconvert (quite ordinary people) did not seem to understand what it was they were being asked to believe in. They would say things like this: "You tell us to go to church; but why? We understand you when you say that a certain man at the beginning of the A.D.s, whom we can agree was a very good man if all that you say about him is true, was wrongfully and painfully executed; but we don't see what this has got to do with our enduring even much less discomfort and a great deal of boredom by going to church now. When you start talking about God our mind somehow shuts up—and all the bright new liturgical gimmicks that your father is so keen on don't open it up again. We don't know what it is you are saying. You say God answers prayer. But when somebody prays to God and the thing prayed for doesn't happen, you say, 'God has thought it better not to answer this one; and of course he knows best.' But in that case what do you *mean* when you say God answers prayer?"

They just did not seem to understand what it was they were supposed to believe; and he found it hard to explain to them. He could have explained to them the things he believed in before he met the Simple Unbeliever; but he didn't really believe in *them* himself any more. And these new things that the Sophisticated Believer told him he ought to believe were somehow so difficult to explain, or even to understand. And after he had heard about the invisible gardener, the frightening thought occurred to him that the reason why he found it so difficult to explain what he was saying was that he wasn't really saying anything.

The Simple Believer's grandfather, as I have said, was a bishop, and he wrote a book about fossils that was a best seller among the faithful. In it he proved conclusively, in his own opinion, that fossils were of very recent origin, and certainly more recent than 4004 B.C.; that they all dated from round about the biblical date for the Flood. And so he thought he had proved the literal truth of the Genesis account, and saved the faith from the attacks of the scientists who were trying to subvert it. The Simple Believer had read his grandfather's book, and very good hard-hitting stuff it was; but it did not seem to help him in his present difficulty. His grandfather had thought he was having a real battle: it said in the Bible that the world was made in 4004 B.C.; and here were all these geologists and paleontologists saying that it was much older, and it was his job as a bishop to refute them. But what was it the job of his grandson the Simple Believer to refute or prove? For the worrying thing was that he did not believe any longer the things his grandfather was trying to prove—good solid assertions like "The world was made in 4004 B.C." No; *he* believed the scientists that his grandfather was attacking; his grandfather had lost that battle, for all his hard hitting.

But that would not have mattered if there were something substantial left now to fight about; the trouble was that, as a result of the Sophisticated Believer's qualifications, the faith had become so insubstantial that it was hard to see what one was supposed to defend. That perhaps explained why Christians were, taken all in all, so very like other people; in all the things that mattered they seemed to think just like anybody else. In his grandfather's day, if you were a Christian you thought one thing, and if you were not you thought something very different. You disagreed, for example, about the date and manner of the beginning of the world. But now, what are the Christian and the non-Christian disagreeing about? For the Christians have, on the advice of sophisticated believers, conceded all the points to the scientists that the scientists required. And so it came about that, while in his grandfather's day those who attacked Christianity were saying that its affirmations were false, in the Simple Believer's day, which is our own, the most dangerous and up-to-date attack comes from those who say that they are meaningless, that they assert nothing. And a great deal of public opinion has come round to the attackers' point of view.

So you can understand why the Simple Believer was unhappy. What was he to do? He did not feel that he could go back to the simple assertions of his grandfather, which the scientists had overthrown; but yet he did not any longer see much substance in the consolations of the Sophisticated Believer. If he went back to views of his grandfather, he would be saying what he believed to be false; but if he said what the Sophisticated Believer wanted him to say, he would be uttering words without meaning. It was when the Simple Believer was in this dilemma that I first got to know him. I understood his predicament very well, for it was one I had been in myself, and to a great extent was in still. He came to me for philosophical advice; but I was at a loss to know what to say to him. Would it be best, perhaps, to seek out some simple slick way of comforting him? The philosopher always has in his armory plenty of snap refutations that will readily deceive the inexpert. He does not always like to use these devices; but in defending what you think really matters, all's fair. The trouble is that, even if I could outwit the Sophisticated Unbeliever by any logical trick, I should not think that I had thereby helped the Simple Believer much. It would be like proving that the evidence of fossils was no good; it might deceive the layman for a time, but sooner or later the truth would prevail. After all, the God the Simple Believer believed in was a God of Truth; and it would be odd to try to defend faith in him by spurious arguments.

Nevertheless, I did very much want to help the Simple Believer—I will call him from now on the Believer, for he is simple no longer. There seemed to me to be something about his faith that put me to

shame—something whose loss would make the world a worse place. And in so far as I had a little (though perhaps only a little) of this something myself, I wanted to strengthen it rather than destroy it; and for this purpose the Believer, for all his philosophical difficulties and perplexities, was a great example and source of strength to me. He might get into a muddle in his thought when sophisticated people tied him into knots; but to know him was to know that these knots somehow did not matter. If any of you know any people of the type I am describing, you know what I mean.

So in the end I hit upon this method. Instead of trying to teach the Believer what he ought to believe, I sought instead to learn from him what he really did believe. This is a thing that cannot be done entirely by kindness. It entails preventing the victim getting away with any evasions and confusions; and so sometimes I seemed to be trying to undermine his faith. I kept on dinning into him the arguments of the Sophisticated Unbeliever, and had sometimes even to appear a Sophisticated Unbeliever myself. But I felt that the brutality was worth while—for what I was trying to do was no less than to find out what it was about his faith that really made him different—and believe me it did make him different—from other men. It was this that I wanted to find out, and if possible imitate.

I soon came to the conclusion that what the Believer believed in weren't *assertions* in the narrow sense, as the term was used by the Sophisticated Unbeliever. At least, though he may have believed some assertions in this narrow sense, they were not central to his faith. By this I mean that they could be abandoned or modified without his losing that whose basis I was seeking to discover. This much was shown by his readiness to abandon these assertions when Unbelievers cast serious doubt upon them in argument. Of course, in a sense, what the Believer believed in were assertions. But I did not want to perform the usual philosophical trick of saying, "It all depends what you mean by an assertion." This is often a useful thing to say—but only as a prelude to taking each of the things that might be meant in turn, and examining its consequences. So to start with, I saw no harm in accepting the Sophisticated Unbeliever's criterion of what were and were not assertions—the criterion was, you remember, that if the utterance was to express an assertion, there had to be something which, if it occurred, would constitute a disproof of the assertion. But I did not want to admit that all meaningful utterances expressed assertions in this sense; for after all there are plenty of utterances which are quite meaningful and yet do not in this sense express assertions—for example, imperatives, questions, expressions of wishes, and so on. There are, moreover, beliefs which are not beliefs in the truth of assertions, in this narrow sense, and yet which are fundamental to our whole life in this world, and still more to our doing anything like science.

Let me explain this last point. Suppose you believed that everything that happens, happens by pure chance, and that therefore the regularities that we have observed so far in the phenomena around us have all been quite fortuitous; that the world might start behaving tomorrow in a quite different manner, or in no consistent manner at all. Then it is obvious that we should not be able to make any scientific predictions about what was going to happen, and our science would become quite useless. It is only because we believe that there are some causal laws to be discovered, that we think it worth while to set about discovering them. But what sort of belief is this? Is it a belief in the truth of an assertion, in the Sophisticated Unbeliever's sense? Let us apply the test to it. "Just what would have to happen, not merely (morally and wrongly) to *tempt*, but also (logically and rightly) to *entitle*" the scientist to stop believing in or looking for causal laws?[5] The answer to this seems to be, as in the case of the religious believer and his God, "Nothing that could happen could have this effect."

Suppose that a scientist has a hypothesis which he is testing by experiment, and the experiment shows him that his hypothesis was false. He then, after trying the experiment again once or twice to make sure there has been no silly mistake, says, "My hypothesis was wrong; I must try a new one." That is to say, he does not stop believing in, or looking for, regularities in the world which can be stated in the form of scientific "laws"; he abandons this particular candidate for the status of a law, but only in order to look for another candidate. Thus, *whatever* happens, he still goes on looking for laws;

nothing can make him abandon the search, for to abandon the search would be to stop being a scientist. He is just like the religious believer in this; in fact, we may say that the belief of the scientist is one kind of religious belief—a kind, moreover, which is not incompatible with what is called Christian belief, for it is part of it.[6]

I want to emphasize this point, because it is the most important that I have to make. When the scientist refuses to give up his search for causal explanations of things, even when any number of proposed explanations fail, he is acting in an essentially religious manner. Therefore, if you want to know what religion is, this is one of the very best illustrations to take. When the scientist says, "There must *be* an explanation of this, although none of the explanations that we have thought of so far work," he is manifesting just that refusal to doubt, which in religious contexts we call *faith*. And indeed it *is* faith; for the scientist does not *know* that there is an explanation. For all he knows there may be no explanation. Indeed, even when he thinks he has found the explanation, how does he know that it is an explanation? For what is and what is not an explanation of something is not a question that can be settled by any sort of proof or appeal to the facts. To say that something is an explanation of something else is to hold just the kind of belief that the Sophisticated Unbeliever said was not belief in the truth of an assertion.

So then, to be a scientist is to be a kind of believer. And the Sophisticated Believer was quite right—perhaps it was the only thing he was right about—when he said that religion did not contradict science. But this is not, as he thought, because religion and science are different kinds of thing; it is because, though different in many respects, in this one crucial respect they are the same kind of thing. And, as I said, scientific belief is not incompatible with Christian belief. It is rather a *part* of Christian belief. It is a part of Christian belief to believe in the possibility of explaining things by means of scientific laws.

But scientific belief is not the whole of Christian belief. There are whole fields of human conduct outside the laboratory where scientific belief does not give us the answers to the questions we are (or ought to be) asking. It does not give us these answers, not because it is wrong, but because it does not apply in those fields. I will mention only one of those fields, that of morality. We cannot decide by experimental methods or by observation what we ought to do. That I ought to do this or that is another of those beliefs which I have to accept or reject (for what I do depends on this decision) but which are excluded by the Sophisticated Unbeliever's test from the realm of assertions. It is only if he ignores such questions that the scientist is able to make do with so limited a faith.

NOTES

1. The phrase is taken from Hogarth's inscription beneath his print "Enthusiasm Delineated."
2. Gilbert Ryle, *The Concept of Mind* (London: Hutchinson, 1949), chap. I.
3. Anthony Flew, "Theology and Falsification," *New Essays in Philosophical Theology,* eds. Anthony Flew and Alasdair MacIntyre (London: SCM Press, 1955), p. 96; also reprinted in *The Existence of God,* ed. John Hick (New York: Macmillan, 1964), p. 225.
4. John Wisdom, "Gods," *Proceedings of the Aristotelian Society,* XIV (1944/45); reprinted in *Logic and Language,* I, ed. A. Flew (Oxford Blackwell, 1952); and in Wisdom, *Philosophy and Psychoanalysis* (Oxford: Blackwell, 1953).
5. A. Flew, "Theology and Falsification," p. 99.
6. See, e.g., P. E. Hodgson, in *The Tablet,* June 21, 1969.

81. THE END OF BELIEF IN GOD

Friedrich Nietzsche

THE MADMAN

Have you not heard of that madman who lit a lantern in the bright morning hours, ran to the market place, and cried incessantly, "I seek God! I seek God!" As many of those who do not believe in God were standing around just then, he provoked much laughter. Why, did he get lost? said one. Did he lose his way like a child? said another. Or is he hiding? Is he afraid of us? Has he gone on a voyage? or emigrated? Thus they yelled and laughed. The madman jumped into their midst and pierced them with his glances.

"Whither is God" he cried. "I shall tell you. *We have killed him*—you and I. All of us are his murderers. But how have we done this? How were we able to drink up the sea? Who gave us the sponge to wipe away the entire horizon? What did we do when we unchained his earth from its sun? Whither is it moving now? Whither are we moving now? Away from all suns? Are we not plunging continually? Backward, sideward, forward, in all direc-

From Nietzsche's *The Gay Science,* first published in 1882. Trans. and edited by Walter Kaufman, *The Portable Nietzsche* (New York: The Viking Press) pp. 95–6, 447–8. Copyright 1954, 1968, by The Viking Press. Reprinted by permission.

tions? Is there any up or down left? Are we not straying as through an infinite nothing? Do we not feel the breath of empty space? Has it not become colder? Is not night and more night coming on all the while? Must not lanterns be lit in the morning? Do we not hear anything yet of the noise of the gravediggers who are burying God? Do we not smell anything yet of God's decomposition? Gods too decompose. God is dead. God remains dead. And we have killed him. How shall we, the murderers of all murderers, comfort ourselves? What was holiest and most powerful of all that the world has yet owned has bled to death under our knives. Who will wipe this blood off us? What water is there for us to clean ourselves? What festivals of atonement, what sacred games shall we have to invent? Is not the greatness of this deed too great for us? Must not we ourselves become gods simply to seem worthy of it? There has never been a greater deed; and whoever will be born after us—for the sake of this deed he will be part of a higher history than all history hitherto."

Here the madman fell silent and looked again at his listeners; and they too were silent and stared at him in astonishment. At last he threw his lantern on the ground, and it broke and went out. "I come too early," he said then; "my time has not come yet. This tremendous event is still on its way, still wandering—it has not yet reached the ears of man. Lightning and thunder require time, the light of the stars requires time, deeds require time even after they are done, before they can be seen and heard. This deed is still more distant from them than the most distant stars—*and yet they have done it themselves.*"

It has been related further that on that same day the madman entered divers churches and there sang his *requiem aeternam deo.* Led out and called to account, he is said to have replied each time, "What are these churches now if they are not the tombs and sepulchers of God?"

THE BACKGROUND OF OUR CHEERFULNESS

The greatest recent event—that "God is dead," that the belief in the Christian God has ceased to be believable—is even now beginning to cast its first shadows over Europe. For the few, at least, whose eyes, whose *suspicion* in their eyes, is strong and sensitive enough for this spectacle, some sun seems to have set just now. . . . In the main, however, this may be said: the event itself is much too great, too distant, too far from the comprehension of the many even for the tidings of it to be thought of as having *arrived* yet, not to speak of the notion that many people might know what has really happened here, and what must collapse now that this belief has been undermined—all that was built upon it, leaned on it, grew into it; for example, our whole European morality. . . .

Even we born guessers of riddles who are, as it were, waiting on the mountains, put there between today and tomorrow and stretched in the contradiction between today and tomorrow, we firstlings and premature births of the coming century, to whom the shadows that must soon envelop Europe really *should* have appeared by now—why is it that even we look forward to it without any real compassion for this darkening, and above all without any worry and fear for *ourselves?* Is it perhaps that we are still too deeply impressed by the first consequences of this event—and these first consequences, the consequences for *us,* are perhaps the reverse of what one might expect: not at all sad and dark, but rather like a new, scarcely describable kind of light, happiness, relief, exhilaration, encouragement, dawn? Indeed, we philosophers and "free spirits" feel as if a new dawn were shining on us when we receive the tidings that "the old god is dead"; our heart overflows with gratitude, amazement, anticipation, expectation. At last the horizon appears free again to us, even granted that it is not bright; at last our ships may venture out again, venture out to face any danger; all the daring of the lover of knowledge is permitted again; the sea, *our* sea, lies open again; perhaps there has never yet been such an "open sea."

82. HUMAN SUFFERING AND GOD'S GOODNESS

Fyodor Dostoevsky

"Listen! I took the case of children only to make my case clearer. Of the other tears of humanity with which the earth is soaked from its crust to its centre, I will say nothing. I have narrowed my subject on purpose. I am a bug, and I recognize in all humility that I cannot understand why the world is arranged as it is. Men are themselves to blame, I suppose: they were given paradise, they wanted freedom, and stole fire from heaven, though they knew they would become unhappy, so there is no need to pity them. With my pitiful, earthly, Euclidian understanding, all I know is that there is suffering and that there are none guilty; that cause follows effect, simply and directly; that everything flows and finds its level—but that's only Euclidian nonsense, I know that, and I can't consent to live by it! What comfort is it to me that there are none guilty and that cause follows effect simply and directly, and that I know it—I must have justice, or I will destroy myself. And not justice in some remote infinite time and space, but here on earth, and that I could see myself. I have believed in it. I want to see it, and if I am dead by then, let me rise again, for if it all happens without me, it will be too unfair. Surely I haven't suffered, simply that I, my crimes and my sufferings, may manure the soil of the future harmony for somebody else. I want to see with my own eyes the hind lie down with the lion and the victim rise up and embrace his murderer. I want to be there when every one suddenly understands what it has all been for. All the religions of the world are built on this longing, and I am a believer. But then there are the children, and what am I to do about them? That's a question I can't

answer. For the hundredth time I repeat, there are numbers of questions, but I've only taken the children, because in their case what I mean is so unanswerably clear. Listen! If all must suffer to pay for the eternal harmony, what have children to do with it, tell me, please? It's beyond all comprehension why they should suffer, and why they should pay for the harmony. Why should they, too, furnish material to enrich the soil for the harmony of the future? I understand solidarity in sin among men. I understand solidarity in retribution, too; but there can be no such solidarity with children. And if it is really true that they must share responsibility for all their fathers' crimes, such a truth is not of this world and is beyond my comprehension. Some jester will say, perhaps, that the child would have grown up and have sinned, but you see he didn't grow up, he was torn to pieces by the dogs, at eight years old. Oh, Alyosha, I am not blaspheming! I understand, of course, what an upheaval of the universe it will be, when everything in heaven and earth blends in one hymn of praise and everything that lives and has lived cries aloud: 'Thou art just, O Lord, for Thy ways are revealed.' When the mother embraces the fiend who threw her child to the dogs, and all three cry aloud with tears, 'Thou art just, O Lord!' then, of course, the crown of knowledge will be reached and all will be made clear. But what pulls me up here is that I can't accept that harmony. And while I am on earth, I make haste to take my own measures. You see, Alyosha, perhaps it really may happen that if I live to that moment, or rise again to see it, I, too, perhaps, may cry aloud with the rest, looking at the mother embracing the child's torturer, 'Thou art just, O Lord!' but I don't want to cry aloud then. While there is still time, I hasten to protect myself and so I renounce the higher harmony altogether. It's not worth the tears

Fyodor Dostoevsky, *The Brothers Karamazov,* trans. by Constance Garnett (New York: The Macmillan Co., 1912), 256–259. Reprinted by permission of Macmillan Publishing Co. and William Heinemann Ltd.

of that one tortured child who beat itself on the breast with its little fist and prayed in its stinking outhouse, with its unexpiated tears to 'dear, kind God'! It's not worth it, because those tears are unatoned for. They must be atoned for, or there can be no harmony. But how? How are you going to atone for them? Is it possible? By their being avenged? But what do I care for avenging them? What do I care for a hell for oppressors? What good can hell do, since those children have already been tortured? And what becomes of harmony, if there is hell? I want to forgive. I want to embrace. I don't want more suffering. And if the sufferings of children go to swell the sum of sufferings which was necessary to pay for truth, then I protest that the truth is not worth such a price. I don't want the mother to embrace the oppressor who threw her son to the dogs! She dare not forgive him! Let her forgive him for herself, if she will, let her forgive the torturer for the immeasurable suffering of her mother's heart. But the sufferings of her tortured child she has no right to forgive; she dare not forgive the torturer, even if the child were to forgive him! And if that is so, if they dare not forgive, what becomes of harmony? Is there in the whole world a being who would have the right to forgive and could forgive? I don't want harmony. From love for humanity I don't want it. I would rather be left with the unavenged suffering. I would rather remain with my unavenged suffering and unsatisfied indignation, *even if I were wrong.* Besides, too high a price is asked for harmony; it's beyond our means to pay so much to enter on it. And so I hasten to give back my entrance ticket, and if I am an honest man I am bound to give it back as soon as possible. And that I am doing. It's not God that I don't accept, Alyosha, only I most respectfully return Him the ticket."

"That's rebellion," murmured Alyosha, looking down.

"Rebellion? I am sorry you call it that," said Ivan earnestly. "One can hardly live in rebellion, and I want to live. Tell me yourself, I challenge you—answer. Imagine that you are creating a fabric of human destiny with the object of making men happy in the end, giving them peace and rest at last, but that it was essential and inevitable to torture to death only one tiny creature—that baby beating its breast with its fist, for instance—and to found that edifice on its unavenged tears, would you consent to be the architect on those conditions? Tell me, and tell the truth."

"No, I wouldn't consent," said Alyosha softly.

"And can you admit the idea that men for whom you are building it would agree to accept their happiness on the foundation of the unexpiated blood of a little victim? And accepting it would remain happy for ever?"

"No, I can't admit it. Brother," said Alyosha suddenly, with flashing eyes, "you said just now, is there a being in the whole world who would have the right to forgive and could forgive? But there is a Being and He can forgive everything, all and for all, because He gave His innocent blood for all and everything. You have forgotten Him, and on Him is built the edifice, and it is to Him they cry aloud, 'Thou art just, O Lord, for Thy ways are revealed!' "

83. AFTER AUSCHWITZ

Richard L. Rubenstein

There are decided affinities between the theological insights expressed in this work and those of the contemporary Christian radical theologians. We have had some of the same teachers and we react to the same moment in history. Nevertheless, we react differently because our experience of the world has been so very different. I suspect that we part company most radically over what I regard as the Christian radical theologian's inability to take seriously the tragic vision. The tragic vision permeates these writings. How could it have been otherwise after Auschwitz?

. . . [T]o many European and American thinkers the real challenge to religion does not come from the order of nature. The real challenge comes in the social sciences and in literature. It is here that the limitations, the conflicts, the ironies, and the inevitable tragedies of human existence are felt. Nature is far more sympathetic to human self-fulfillment than is man himself. Man is a problem to himself. Human evil has done far more harm throughout the ages than natural catastrophe. The real objections against a personal or theistic God come from the irreconcilability of the claim of god's perfection with the hideous human evil tolerated by such a God.

In *The Brothers Karamazov,* Dostoevsky puts into the mouth of the atheist Ivan the final, irrefutable, and unanswerable objection to a personal or theistic conception of God. In the chapter on Rebellion, Ivan first offers example after example of the cruelty of man to man and of *God's implication in that cruelty if He has the power to control it.* He then demonstrates that the only possible religious answer is that human suffering will be justified in the final Divine harmony at the end of history. He rejects this suggestion, saying: "I renounce the higher harmony altogether. It's not worth the tears of that one tortured child who beat itself on the breast with its little fist and prayed . . . with its unexpiated tears to 'dear God.' "

A God who tolerates the suffering of even one innocent child is either infinitely cruel or hopelessly indifferent. Our ancestors attempted to solve this problem by projecting the existence of another world wherein this world's cruelties would be rectified. We cannot accept such a solution and we would do well to recognize the disguised yet nonetheless strong criticism of God's government of this world implied in their fantasy of another world in which He would ultimately do a better job . . . modern man cannot believe in a personal God. Nevertheless, I believe that the moral and psychological objections are more telling than the objections arising from the physical sciences. . . .

This leads to the question of whether a God-idea can or even should be "that upon which man relies to give meaning to his life." . . . But need the mature man rely upon anything beyond his ability to create his own meanings out of the matrix of responsibilities, destinies, affiliations, roles, and relationships in which he finds himself? From the strictly naturalistic point of view, I find the suggestion that a God-idea does something toward the creation of meanings both extraneous and unnecessary. From the psychological point of view it may very well be possible to show that dependence upon a God-idea for meanings is to some degree unhealthy. To seek to find life's meanings with the support of a God-idea is to lean upon a crutch. Men can and ought to learn to stand upon their own resources. This does not mean that every man can or should come to an inherently private and subjective understanding of what life's meanings are for him. Quite the contrary, the real significance of ethnic religion is that it continually reminds us of the community of experience, wisdom, insight, and common need.

Were [one] to be . . . naturalistic in his doctrine of man . . ., he would see man as essentially a tragic, ironic figure of extremely limited possibilities. He would certainly reject the conception of this-

Richard L. Rubenstein, *After Auschwitz* (New York: Bobbs-Merrill Co., 1966), Preface x–xi, 86–90. Reprinted with the permission of the author.

worldly or other-worldly salvation as an illusion. In a real sense every human advance is also a retreat; salvation is unattainable. Only a modicum of ability on the part of the mature man to make the most of what he is and has and to learn to love his necessities can be expected in a universe which is *not* so constituted as to make for human satisfaction.

Behind the pragmatic arguments of some religious naturalists that we must act as if this world were capable of fulfilling human salvation is their fear that a radical pessimism about human possibilities will stultify all attempts to make the most of man's limited existence. I think this is both factually untrue and psychologically unsound. There is something morally and psychologically satisfying in making the very best one can of a limited and tragic existence. Nor is it the gloomy and humorless philosophy that it is often represented as being. Reality is infinitely more comforting than fiction, even the fictions with which we falsely attempt to deceive ourselves. Man can learn to live in a world without myth or fantasy about himself or his possibilities. Freud is a very good case in point. His pessimism did not prevent him from devoting his life to the task of liberating men from those unnecessary and unreal fears which enslaved them. The knowledge that life is bracketed between two oblivions does not cause life to stop nor does it make those joys which are attainable less joyful.

84. IS THE EXISTENCE OF GOD COMPATIBLE WITH THE EXISTENCE OF EVIL?

David Hume

And is it possible, Cleanthes, said Philo, that after all these reflections, and infinitely more, which might be suggested, you can still persevere in your anthropomorphism, and assert the moral attributes of the Deity, his justice, benevolence, mercy, and rectitude, to be of the same nature with these virtues in human creatures? His power we allow infinite: Whatever he wills is executed: But neither man nor any other animal are happy: Therefore he does not will their happiness. His wisdom is infinite: He is never mistaken in choosing the means to any end: But the course of nature tends not to human or animal felicity: Therefore it is not established for that purpose. Through the whole compass of human knowledge, there are no inferences more certain and infallible than these. In what respect, then, do his benevolence and mercy resemble the benevolence and mercy of men?

Epicurus's old questions are yet unanswered. Is he willing to prevent evil, but not able? then is he impotent. Is he able, but not willing? then is he malevolent. Is he both able and willing? whence then is evil?

You ascribe, Cleanthes (and I believe justly) a purpose and intention to nature. But what, I beseech you, is the object of that curious artifice and machinery, which she has displayed in all animals? The preservation alone of individuals and propagation of the species. It seems enough for her purpose, if such a rank be barely upheld in the universe, without any care or concern for the happiness of the members that compose it. No resource for this purpose: No machinery, in order merely to give pleasure or ease: No fund of pure joy and contentment: No indulgence without some want or necessity accompanying it. At least, the few phenomena of this nature are overbalanced by opposite phenomena of still greater importance.

From David Hume, *Dialogues Concerning Natural Religion*, first published in 1779.

Our sense of music, harmony, and indeed beauty of all kinds, gives satisfaction, without being absolutely necessary to the preservation and propagation of the species. But what racking pains, on the other hand, arise from gouts, gravels, megrims, tooth-aches, rheumatisms; where the injury to the animal-machinery is either small or incurable? Mirth, laughter, play, frolic, seem gratuitous satisfactions, which have no farther tendency: Spleen, melancholy, discontent, superstition, are pains of the same nature. How then does the divine benevolence display itself, in the sense of you anthropomorphites? None but we mystics, as you were pleased to call us, can account for this strange mixture of phenomena, by deriving it from attributes, infinitely perfect, but incomprehensible.

And have you at last, said Cleanthes smiling, betrayed your intentions, Philo? Your long agreement with Demea did indeed a little surprise me; but I find you were all the while erecting a concealed battery against me. And I must confess, that you have now fallen upon a subject worthy of your noble spirit of opposition and controversy. If you can make out the present point, and prove mankind to be unhappy or corrupted, there is an end at once of all religion. For to what purpose establish the natural attributes of the Deity, while the moral are still doubtful and uncertain?

You take umbrage very easily, replied Demea, at opinions the most innocent, and the most generally received even amongst the religious and devout themselves: And nothing can be more surprising than to find a topic like this, concerning the wickedness and misery of man, charged with no less than atheism and profaneness. Have not all pious divines and preachers, who have indulged their rhetoric on so fertile a subject; have they not easily, I say, given a solution of any difficulties which may attend it? This world is but a point in comparison of the universe: This life but a moment in comparison of eternity. The present evil phenomena, therefore, are rectified in other regions, and in some future period of existence. And the eyes of men, being then opened to larger views of things, see the whole connection of general laws, and trace, with adoration, the benevolence and rectitude of the Deity, through all the mazes and intricacies of his providence.

No! replied Cleanthes, No! These arbitrary suppositions can never be admitted, contrary to matter of fact, visible and uncontroverted. Whence can any cause be known but from its known effects? Whence can any hypothesis be proved but from the apparent phenomena? To establish one hypothesis upon another is building entirely in the air; and the utmost we ever attain, by these conjectures and fictions, is to ascertain the bare possibility of our opinion; but never can we, upon such terms, establish its reality.

The only method of supporting divine benevolence (and it is what I willingly embrace) is to deny absolutely the misery and wickedness of man. Your representations are exaggerated: Your melancholy views mostly fictitious: Your inferences contrary to fact and experience. Health is more common than sickness: Pleasure than pain: Happiness than misery. And for one vexation which we meet with, we attain, upon computation, a hundred enjoyments.

Admitting your position, replied Philo, which yet is extremely doubtful, you must, at the same time, allow, that, if pain be less frequent than pleasure, it is infinitely more violent and durable. One hour of it is often able to outweigh a day, a week, a month of our common insipid enjoyments: And how many days, weeks, and months are passed by several in the most acute torments? Pleasure, scarcely in one instance, is ever able to reach ecstasy and rapture: And in no one instance can it continue for any time at its highest pitch and altitude. The spirits evaporate; the nerves relax; the fabric is disordered; and the enjoyment quickly degenerates into fatigue and uneasiness. But pain often, Good God, how often! rises to torture and agony; and the longer it continues, it becomes still more genuine agony and torture. Patience is exhausted; courage languishes; melancholy seizes us; and nothing terminates our misery but the removal of its cause, or another event, which is the sole cure of the evil, but which, from our natural folly, we regard with still greater horror and consternation.

But not to insist upon these topics, continued Philo, though most obvious, certain, and important; I must use the freedom to admonish you, Cleanthes, that you have put this controversy upon a most dangerous issue, and are unawares introducing a total scepticism into the most essential articles of natural and revealed theology. What! no method of fixing a just foundation for religion, unless we allow the happiness of human life, and maintain a continued existence even in this world, with all our present pains, infirmities, vexations, and follies, to be eligible and desirable! But this is contrary to every one's feeling and experience: It is contrary to an authority so established as nothing can subvert: No decisive proofs can ever be produced against this authority; nor is it possible for you to compute, estimate, and compare all the pains and all the pleasures in the lives of all men and of all animals: And thus by your resting the whole system of religion on a point, which, from its very nature, must for ever be uncertain, you tacitly confess, that that system is equally uncertain.

But allowing you, what never will be believed; at least, what you never possibly can prove, that animal, or at least, human happiness, in this life, exceeds its misery; you have yet done nothing: For this is not, by any means, what we expect from infinite power, infinite wisdom, and infinite goodness. Why is there any misery at all in the world? Not by chance surely. From some cause then. Is it from the intention of the Deity? But he is perfectly benevolent. Is it contrary to his intention? But he is almighty. Nothing can shake the solidity of this reasoning, so short, so clear, so decisive; except we assert, that these subjects exceed all human capacity, and that our common measures of truth and falsehood are not applicable to them; a topic, which I have all along insisted on, but which you have, from the beginning, rejected with scorn and indignation.

But I will be contented to retire still from this intrenchment: For I deny that you can ever force me in it: I will allow, that pain or misery in man is *compatible* with infinite power and goodness in the Deity, even in your sense of these attributes: What are you advanced by all these concessions? A mere possible compatibility is not sufficient. You must *prove* these pure, unmixed, and uncontrollable attributes from the present mixed and confused phenomena, and from these alone. A hopeful undertaking! Were the phenomena ever so pure and unmixed, yet being finite, they would be insufficient for that purpose. How much more, were they are also so jarring and discordant?

Here, Cleanthes, I find myself at ease in my argument. Here I triumph. Formerly, when we argued concerning the natural attributes of intelligence and design, I needed all my sceptical and metaphysical subtilty to elude your grasp. In many views of the universe, and of its parts, particularly the latter, the beauty and fitness of final causes strike us with such irresistible force, that all objections appear (what I believe they really are) mere cavils and sophisms; nor can we then imagine how it was ever possible for us to repose any weight on them. But there is no view of human life, or of the condition of mankind, from which, without the greatest violence, we can infer the moral attributes, or learn that infinite benevolence, conjoined with infinite power and infinite wisdom, which we must discover by the eyes of faith alone. It is your turn now to tug the labouring oar, and to support your philosophical subtilties against the dictates of plain reason and experience.

I scruple not to allow, said Cleanthes, that I have been apt to suspect the frequent repetition of the word, *infinite*, which we meet with in all theological writers, to savour more of panegyric than of philosophy, and that any purposes of reasoning, and even of religion, would be better served, were we to rest contented with more accurate and more moderate expressions. The terms, *admirable, excellent, superlatively great, wise,* and *holy;* these sufficiently fill the imaginations of men; and any thing beyond, besides that it leads into absurdities, has no influence on the affections or sentiments. Thus, in the present subject, if we abandon all human analogy, as seems your intention, Demea, I am afraid we abandon all religion, and retain no conception of the great object of our adoration. If we preserve human analogy, we must for ever find it impossible to reconcile any mixture of evil in the universe with infinite attributes; much less, can we ever prove the latter from the former. But supposing the Author

of nature to be finitely perfect, though far exceeding mankind; a satisfactory account may then be given of natural and moral evil, and every untoward phenomenon be explained and adjusted. A less evil may then be chosen, in order to avoid a greater: Inconveniences be submitted to, in order to reach a desirable end: And in a word, benevolence, regulated by wisdom, and limited by necessity, may produce just such a world as the present. You, Philo, who are so prompt at starting views, and reflections, and analogies; I would gladly hear, at length, without interruption, your opinion of this new theory; and if it deserve our attention, we may afterwards, at more leisure, reduce it into form.

My sentiments, replied Philo, are not worth being made a mystery of; and therefore, without any ceremony, I shall deliver what occurs to me with regard to the present subject. It must, I think, be allowed, that, if a very limited intelligence, whom we shall suppose utterly unacquainted with the universe, were assured, that it were the production of a very good, wise, and powerful Being, however finite, he would, from his conjectures, form *beforehand* a different notion of it from what we find it to be by experience; nor would he ever imagine, merely from these attributes of the cause, of which he is informed, that the effect could be so full of vice and misery and disorder, as it appears in this life. Supposing now, that this person were brought into the world, still assured, that it was the workmanship of such a sublime and benevolent Being; he might, perhaps, be surprised at the disappointment: but would never retract his former belief, if founded on any very solid argument; since such a limited intelligence must be sensible of his own blindness and ignorance, and must allow, that there may be many solutions of those phenomena, which will for ever escape his comprehension. But supposing, which is the real case with regard to man, that this creature is not antecedently convinced of a supreme intelligence, benevolent, and powerful, but is left to gather such a belief from the appearances of things: this entirely alters the case, nor will he ever find any reason for such a conclusion. He may be fully convinced of the narrow limits of his understanding; but this will not help him in forming an inference concerning the goodness of superior powers, since he must form that inference from what he knows, not from what he is ignorant of. The more you exaggerate his weakness and ignorance, the more diffident you render him, and give him the greater suspicion, that such subjects are beyond the reach of his faculties. You are obliged, therefore, to reason with him merely from the known phenomena, and to drop every arbitrary supposition or conjecture. . . .

Look round this universe. What an immense profusion of beings, animated and organized, sensible and active! You admire this prodigious variety and fecundity. But inspect a little more narrowly these living existences, the only beings worth regarding. How hostile and destructive to each other! How insufficient all of them for their own happiness! How contemptible or odious to the spectator! The whole presents nothing but the idea of a blind nature, impregnated by a great vivifying principle, and pouring forth from her lap, without discernment or parental care, her maimed and abortive children.

Here the Manichean system occurs as a proper hypothesis to solve the difficulty: And no doubt, in some respects, it is very specious, and has more probability than the common hypothesis, by giving a plausible account of the strange mixture of good and ill which appears in life. But if we consider, on the other hand, the perfect uniformity and agreement of the parts of the universe, we shall not discover in it any marks of the combat of a malevolent with a benevolent Being. There is indeed an opposition of pains and pleasures in the feelings of sensible creatures: But are not all the operations of nature carried on by an opposition of principles, of hot and cold, moist and dry, light and heavy? The

true conclusion is, that the original source of all things is entirely indifferent to all these principles, and has no more regard to good above ill than to heat above cold, or to drought above moisture, or to light above heavy.

There may *four* hypotheses be framed concerning the first causes of the universe: *that* they are endowed with perfect goodness, *that* they have perfect malice, *that* they are opposite and have both goodness and malice, *that* they have neither goodness nor malice. Mixed phenomena can never prove the two former unmixed principles. And the uniformity and steadiness of general laws seem to oppose the third. The fourth, therefore, seems by far the most probable.

What I have said concerning natural evil will apply to moral, with little or no variation; and we have no more reason to infer, that the rectitude of the supreme Being resembles human rectitude than that his benevolence resembles the human. Nay, it will be thought, that we have still greater cause to exclude from him moral sentiments, such as we feel them; since moral evil, in the opinion of many, is much more predominant above moral good than natural evil above natural good.

But even though this should not be allowed, and though the virtue, which is in mankind, should be acknowledged much superior to the vice: yet so long as there is any vice at all in the universe, it will very much puzzle you anthropomorphites, how to account for it. You must assign a cause for it, without having recourse to the first cause. But as every effect must have a cause, and that cause another; you must either carry on the progression *in infinitum,* or rest on that original principle, who is the ultimate cause of all things.

85. THE PROBLEM OF EVIL

John Hick

To many, the most powerful positive objection to belief in God is the fact of evil. Probably for most agnostics it is the appalling depth and extent of human suffering, more than anything else, that makes the idea of a loving Creator seem so implausible and disposes them toward one or another of the various naturalistic theories of religion.

As a challenge to theism, the problem of evil has traditionally been posed in the form of a dilemma: if God is perfectly loving, he must wish to abolish evil; and if he is all-powerful, he must be able to abolish evil. But evil exists; therefore God cannot be both omnipotent and perfectly loving.

Certain solutions, which at once suggest themselves, have to be ruled out so far as the Judaic-Christian faith is concerned.

To say, for example (with contemporary Christian Science), that evil is an illusion of the human mind, is impossible within a religion based upon the stark realism of the Bible. Its pages faithfully reflect the characteristic mixture of good and evil in human experience. They record every kind of sorrow and suffering, every mode of man's inhumanity to man and of his painfully insecure existence in the world. There is no attempt to regard evil as anything but dark, menacingly ugly, heart-rending, and crushing. In the Christian scriptures, the climax of this history of evil is the crucifixion of Jesus, which is presented not only as a case of utterly unjust suffering, but as the violent and murderous rejection of God's Messiah. There can be no doubt, then, that for biblical faith, evil is unambiguously evil, and stands in direct opposition to God's will.

Again, to solve the problem of evil by means of the theory (sponsored, for example, by the Boston "Personalist" School)[1] of a finite deity who does the best he can with a material, intractable and co-eternal with himself, is to have abandoned the basic premise of Hebrew-Christian monotheism; for the theory amounts to rejecting belief in the infinity and sovereignty of God.

John Hick, *Philosophy of Religion*, © 1963, pp. 40–47. Reprinted by permission of Prentice-Hall, Inc., Englewood Cliffs, New Jersey.

Indeed, any theory which would avoid the problem of the origin of evil by depicting it as an ultimate constituent of the universe, coordinate with good, has been repudiated in advance by the classic Christian teaching, first developed by Augustine, that evil represents the going wrong of something which in itself is good.[2] Augustine holds firmly to the Hebrew-Christian conviction that the universe is *good*—that is to say, it is the creation of a good God for a good purpose. He completely rejects the ancient prejudice, widespread in his day, that matter is evil. There are, according to Augustine, higher and lower, greater and lesser goods in immense abundance and variety; but everything which has being is good in its own way and degree, except in so far as it may have become spoiled or corrupted. Evil—whether it be an evil will, an instance of pain, or some disorder or decay in nature—has not been set there by God, but represents the distortion of something that is inherently valuable. Whatever exists is, as such, and in its proper place, good; evil is essentially parasitic upon good, being disorder and perversion in a fundamentally good creation. This understanding of evil as something negative means that it is not willed and created by God; but it does not mean (as some have supposed) that evil is unreal and can be disregarded. On the contrary, the first effect of this doctrine is to accentuate even more the question of the origin of evil.

Theodicy,[3] as many modern Christian thinkers see it, is a modest enterprise, negative rather than positive in its conclusions. It does not claim to explain, nor to explain away, every instance of evil in human experience, but only to point to certain considerations which prevent the fact of evil (largely incomprehensible though it remains) from constituting a final and insuperable bar to rational belief in God.

In indicating these considerations it will be useful to follow the traditional division of the subject. There is the problem of *moral evil* or wickedness: why does an all-good and all-powerful God permit this? And there is the problem of the *non-moral evil* of suffering or pain, both physical and mental: why has an all-good and all-powerful God created a world in which this occurs?

Christian thought has always considered moral evil in its relation to human freedom and responsibility. To be a person is to be a finite center of freedom, a (relatively) free and self-directing agent responsible for one's own decisions. This involves being free to act wrongly as well as to act rightly. The idea of a person who can be infallibly guaranteed always to act rightly is self-contradictory. There can be no guarantee in advance that a genuinely free moral agent will never choose amiss. Consequently, the possibility of wrongdoing or sin is logically inseparable from the creation of finite persons, and to say that God should not have created beings who might sin amounts to saying that he should not have created people.

This thesis has been challenged in some recent philosophical discussions of the problem of evil, in which it is claimed that no contradiction is involved in saying that God might have made people who would be genuinely free and who could yet be guaranteed always to act rightly. A quote from one of these discussions follows:

If there is no logical impossibility in a man's freely choosing the good on one, or on several occasions, there cannot be a logical impossibility in his freely choosing the good on every occasion. God was not, then, faced with a choice between making innocent automata and making beings who, in acting freely, would sometimes go wrong: there was open to him the obviously better possibility of making beings who would act freely but always go right. Clearly, his failure to avail himself of this possibility is inconsistent with his being both omnipotent and wholly good.[4]

A reply to this argument is suggested in another recent contribution to the discussion.[5] If by a free action we mean an action which is not externally compelled but which flows from the nature of the agent as he reacts to the circumstances in which he finds himself, there is, indeed, no contradiction between our being free and our actions being "caused" (by our own nature) and therefore being in principle predictable. There is a contradiction, however, in saying that God is the cause of our acting as we do but that we are free beings in relation to God. There is, in other words, a con-

tradiction in saying that God has made us so that we shall of necessity act in a certain way, and that we are genuinely independent persons in relation to him. If all our thoughts and actions are divinely predestined, however free and morally responsible we may seem to be to ourselves, we cannot be free and morally responsible in the sight of God, but must instead be his helpless puppets. Such "freedom" is like that of a patient acting out a series of post-hypnotic suggestions: he appears, even to himself, to be free, but his volitions have actually been pre-determined by another will, that of the hypnotist, in relation to whom the patient is not a free agent.

A different objector might raise the question of whether or not we deny God's omnipotence if we admit that he is unable to create persons who are free from the risks inherent in personal freedom. The answer that has always been given is that to create such beings is logically impossible. It is no limitation upon God's power that he cannot accomplish the logically impossible, since there is nothing here to accomplish, but only a meaningless conjunction of words[6]—in this case "person who is not a person." God is able to create beings of any and every conceivable kind; but creatures who lack moral freedom, however superior they might be to human beings in other respects, would not be what we mean by persons. They would constitute a different form of life which God might have brought into existence instead of persons. When we ask why God did not create such beings in place of persons, the traditional answer is that only persons could, in any meaningful sense, become "children of God," capable of entering into a personal relationship with their Creator by a free and uncompelled response to his love.

When we turn from the possibility of moral evil as a correlate of man's personal freedom to its actuality, we face something which must remain inexplicable even when it can be seen to be possible. For we can never provide a complete causal explanation of a free act; if we could, it would not be a free act. The origin of moral evil lies forever concealed within the mystery of human freedom.

The necessary connection between moral freedom and the possibility, now actualized, of sin throws light upon a great deal of the suffering which afflicts mankind. For an enormous amount of human pain arises either from the inhumanity or the culpable incompetence of mankind. This includes such major scourges as poverty, oppression and persecution, war, and all the injustice, indignity, and inequity which occur even in the most advanced societies. These evils are manifestations of human sin. Even disease is fostered to an extent, the limits of which have not yet been determined by psychosomatic medicine, by moral and emotional factors seated both in the individual and in his social environment. To the extent that all of these evils stem from human failures and wrong decisions, their possibility is inherent in the creation of free persons inhabiting a world which presents them with real choices which are followed by real consequences.

We may now turn more directly to the problem of suffering. Even though the major bulk of actual human pain is traceable to man's misused freedom as a sole or part cause, there remain other sources of pain which are entirely independent of the human will, for example, earthquake, hurricane, storm, flood, drought, and blight. In practice, it is often impossible to trace a boundary between the suffering which results from human wickedness and folly and that which falls upon mankind from without. Both kinds of suffering are inextricably mingled together in human experience. For our present purpose, however, it is important to note that the latter category does exist and that it seems to be built into the very structure of our world. In response to it, theodicy, if it is wisely conducted, follows a negative path. It is not possible to show positively that each item of human pain serves the divine purpose of good; but, on the other hand, it does seem possible to show that the divine purpose as it is understood in Judaism and Christianity could not be forwarded in a world which was designed as a permanent hedonistic paradise.[7]

An essential premise of this argument concerns the nature of the divine purpose in creating the world. The skeptic's assumption is that man is to be viewed as a completed creation and that God's purpose in making the world was to provide a suitable dwelling-place for this fully-formed creature. Since God is good and loving, the environment which he has created for human life to inhabit

The problem is essentially similar to that of a man who builds a cage for some pet animal. Since our world, in fact, contains sources of hardship, inconvenience, and danger of innumerable kinds, the conclusion follows that this world cannot have been created by a perfectly benevolent and all-powerful deity.[8]

Christianity, however, has never supposed that God's purpose in the creation of the world was to construct a paradise whose inhabitants would experience a maximum of pleasure and a minimum of pain. The world is seen, instead, as a place of "soul-making" in which free beings, grappling with the tasks and challenges of their existence in a common environment, may become "children of God" and "heirs of eternal life." A way of thinking theologically of God's continuing creative purpose for man was suggested by some of the early Hellenistic Fathers of the Christian Church, especially Irenaeus. Following hints from St. Paul, Irenaeus taught that man has been made as a person in the image of God but has not yet been brought as a free and responsible agent into the finite likeness of God, which is revealed in Christ.[9] Our world, with all its rough edges, is the sphere in which this second and harder stage of the creative process is taking place.

This conception of the world (whether or not set in Irenaeus' theological framework) can be supported by the method of negative theodicy. Suppose, contrary to fact, that this world were a paradise from which all possibility of pain and suffering were excluded. The consequences would be very far-reaching. For example, no one could ever injure anyone else: the murderer's knife would turn to paper or his bullets to thin air; the bank safe, robbed of a million dollars, would miraculously become filled with another million dollars (without this device, on however large a scale, proving inflationary); fraud, deceit, conspiracy, and treason would somehow always leave the fabric of society undamaged. Again, no one would ever be injured by accident: the mountain-climber, steeplejack, or playing child falling from a height would float unharmed to the ground; the reckless driver would never meet with disaster. There would be no need to work, since no harm could result from avoiding work; there would be no call to be concerned for others in time of need or danger, for in such a world there could be no real needs or dangers.

To make possible this continual series of individual adjustments, nature would have to work by "special providences" instead of running according to general laws which men must learn to respect on penalty of pain or death. The laws of nature would have to be extremely flexible: sometimes gravity would operate, sometimes not; sometimes an object would be hard and solid, sometimes soft. There could be no sciences, for there would be no enduring world structure to investigate. In eliminating the problems and hardships of an objective environment, with its own laws, life would become like a dream in which, delightfully but aimlessly, we would float and drift at ease.[10]

One can at least begin to imagine such a world. It is evident that our present ethical concepts would have no meaning in it. If, for example, the notion of harming someone is an essential element in the concept of a wrong action, in our hedonistic paradise there would be no wrong actions—nor any right actions in distinction from wrong. Courage and fortitude would have no point in an environment in which there is, by definition, no danger or difficulty. Generosity, kindness, the *agape* aspect of love, prudence, unselfishness, and all other ethical notions which presuppose life in a stable environment, could not even be formed. Consequently, such a world, however well it might promote pleasure, would be very ill adapted for the development of the moral qualities of human personality. In relation to this purpose it would be the worst of all possible worlds.

It would seem, then, that an environment intended to make possible the growth in free beings of the finest characteristics of personal life, must have a good deal in common with our present world. It must operate according to general and dependable laws; and it must involve real dangers, difficulties, problems, obstacles, and possibilities of pain, failure, sorrow, frustration, and defeat. If it did not contain the particular trials and perils which —subtracting man's own very considerable contribution—our world contains, it would have to contain others instead.

To realize this is not, by any means, to be in possession of a detailed theodicy. It is to understand that this world, with all its "heartaches and the thousand natural shocks that flesh is heir to," and environment so manifestly not designed for the maximization of human pleasure and the minimization of human pain, may be rather well adapted to the quite different purpose of "soul-making."[11]

These considerations are related to theism as such. Specifically, Christian theism goes further in the light of the death of Christ, which is seen paradoxically both (as the murder of the divine Son) as the worst thing that has ever happened and (as the occasion of man's salvation) as the best thing that has ever happened. As the supreme evil turned to supreme good, it provides the paradigm for the distinctively Christian reaction to evil. Viewed from the standpoint of Christian faith, evils do not cease to be evils; and certainly, in view of Christ's healing work, they cannot be said to have been sent by God. Yet, it has been the persistent claim of those seriously and wholeheartedly committed to Christian discipleship that tragedy, though truly tragic, may nevertheless be turned, through man's reaction to it, from a cause of despair and alienation from God to a stage in the fulfillment of God's loving purpose for that individual. As the greatest of all evils, the crucifixion of Christ, was made the occasion of man's redemption, so good can be won from other evils. As Jesus saw his execution by the Romans as an experience which God desired him to accept, an experience which was to be brought within the sphere of the divine purpose and made to serve the divine ends, so the Christian response to calamity is to accept the adversities, pains, and afflictions which life brings, in order that they can be turned to a positive spiritual use.[12]

At this point, theodicy points forward in two ways to the subject of life after death, which is to be discussed in the following chapter.

First, although there are many striking instances of good being triumphantly brought out of evil through a man's or a woman's reaction to it, there are many other cases in which the opposite has happened. Sometimes obstacles breed strength of character, dangers evoke courage and unselfishness, and calamities produce patience and moral steadfastness. But sometimes they lead, instead, to resentment, fear, grasping selfishness, and disintegration of character. Therefore, it would seem that any divine purpose of soul-making which is at work in earthly history must continue beyond this life if it is ever to achieve more than a very partial and fragmentary success.

Second, if we ask whether the business of soul-making is worth all the toil and sorrow of human life, the Christian answer must be in terms of a future good which is great enough to justify all that has happened on the way to it.

NOTES

1. Edgar Brightman's *A Philosophy of Religion* (Englewood Cliffs, N.J.: Prentice-Hall, Inc., 1940), chaps 8–10, is a classic exposition of one form of this view.

2. See Augustine's *Confessions,* Book VII, chap. 12; *City of God,* Book XII, chap. 3; *Enchiridion,* chap. 4.

3. The word "theodicy," from the Greek *theos* (God) and *dike* (righteous), means the justification of God's goodness in the face of the fact of evil.

4. J. L. Mackie, "Evil and Omnipotence," *Mind* (April, 1955), 209. A similar point is made by Antony Flew in "Divine Omnipotence and Human Freedom," *New Essays in Philosophical Theology.* An important critical comment on these arguments is offered by Ninian Smart in "Omipotence, Evil and Supermen," *Philosophy* (April, 1961), with replies by Flew (January, 1962) and Mackie (April, 1962).

5. Flew, in *New Essays in Philosophical Theology.*

6. As Aquinas said, ". . . nothing that implies a contradiction falls under the scope of God's omnipotence." *Summa Theologica,* Part I, Question 25, article 4.

7. From the Greek *hedone,* pleasure.

8. This is the nature of David Hume's argument in his discussion of the problem of evil in his *Dialogues,* Part XI.

9. See Irenaeus' *Against Heresies,* Book IV, chaps. 37 and 38.

10. Tennyson's poem, *The Lotus-Eaters,* well expresses the desire (analyzed by Freud as a wish to return to the peace of the womb) for such "dreamful ease."

11. This brief discussion has been confined to the problem of human suffering. The large and intractable problem of animal pain is not taken up here. For a discussion of it see, for example, Nels Ferré, *Evil and the Christian Faith* (New York: Harper and Row, Publishers, Inc., 1947), chap. 7; and Austin Farrer, *Love Almighty and Ills Unlimited* (New York: Doubleday & Company, Inc., 1961), chap. 5.

12. This conception of providence is stated more fully in John Hick, *Faith and Knowledge* (Ithaca: Cornell University Press, 1957), chap. 7, some sentences from which are incorporated in this paragraph.

SUGGESTIONS FOR FURTHER READING

THE CHALLENGE TO BELIEF IN GOD

Alston, William P., ed. *Religious Belief and Philosophical Thought.* New York: Harcourt, Brace & World, 1963.

Christian, William. *Meaning and Truth in Religion.* Princeton, N.J.: Princeton University Press, 1964.

Ducasse, C. J. *A Philosophical Scrutiny of Religion.* New York: Ronald Press, 1953.

Ferre, Frederick. *Language, Logic, and God.* London: Eyre & Spottiswoode Ltd., 1962.

Hick, John, ed. *The Existence of God.* New York: Macmillan, 1964.

Hick, John. *Faith and Knowledge.* 2d ed. Ithaca, N.Y.: Cornell University Press, 1966.

Kaufmann, Walter. *Critique of Religion and Philosophy.* New York: Harper and Row, 1958.

Kaufmann, Walter. *The Faith of a Heretic.* Garden City, N.Y.: Doubleday, 1961.

MacIntyre, Alasdair, and Paul Ricoeur. *The Religious Significance of Atheism.* New York: Columbia University Press, 1961.

Martin, C. B. *Religious Belief.* Ithaca, N.Y.: Cornell University Press, 1959.

Mitchell, Basil, ed. *Faith and Logic.* London: George Allen & Unwin Ltd., 1957.

Paton, H. J. *The Modern Predicament.* N.Y.: Collier Books, 1962.

Smart, Ninian. *Reasons and Faiths.* London: Routledge & Kegan Paul, 1958.

Stace, W. T. *Religion and the Modern Mind.* New York: J. B. Lippincott Company, 1960.

Tillich, Paul. *Dynamics of Faith.* New York: Harper & Row, 1957.

THE LIMITS OF THEOLOGICAL KNOWLEDGE

Altizer, Thomas, J. J. *Toward A New Christianity: Readings in the Death of God Theology.* New York: Harcourt, Brace & World, 1967.

Blackstone, William T. *The Problem of Religious Knowledge.* Englewood Cliffs, N.J.: Prentice-Hall, 1963.

Edwards, D. L., and Robinson, J. A. T. eds. *The Honest to God Debate.* Philadelphia, Pa.: The Westminster Press, 1963.

Flew, Antony. *God and Philosophy.* London: Hutchinson's, 1966.

Flew, Antony, and MacIntyre, Alasdair, eds. *New Essays in Philosophical Theology*. New York: Macmillan, 1955.

Hamilton, William. *The New Essence of Christianity*. New York: Association Press, 1961.

High, Dallas M., ed. *New Essays on Religious Language*. New York: Oxford University Press, 1969.

Hook, Sidney, ed. *Religious Experience and Truth*. New York: New York University Press, 1961.

Ice, J. L., and Carey, J. J. *The Death of God Debate*. Philadelphia, Pa.: The Westminster Press, 1967.

Murchland, Bernard, ed. *The Meaning of the Death of God*. New York: Random House, 1967.

Nielsen, Kai. "Can Faith Validate God-talk?" *Theology Today* 20 (1963).

Nielsen, Kai. "The Intelligibility of God-talk." *Religious Studies,* 6 (1970).

Nielsen, Kai. "Language and the Concept of God." *Question,* January 1969.

Ramsey, Ian. *Religious Language*. London: Student Christian Movement Press, 1957.

Santoni, Ronald E., ed. *Religious Language and the Problem of Religious Knowledge*. Bloomington, Ind.: Indiana University Press, 1968.

GOD AND EVIL

Bible, Book of Job.

Cahn, Steven. "The Book of Job: The Great Dissent." *Reconstructionist* 31 (1965).

Hick, John. *Evil and the God of Love*. New York: Harper & Row, 1966.

Joad, Cyril E. *God and Evil*. New York: Harper & Brothers, 1943.

Jung, C. G. *Answer to Job*. Translated by R. F. C. Hull. New York: Meridian Books, World Publishing Company, 1954.

McCloskey, H. J. "The Problem of Evil." *The Journal of Bible and Religion* 30 (1962).

Niebuhr, Reinhold. *Moral Man and Immoral Society*. New York: Charles Scribners Sons, 1932.

Phillips, D. Z., ed. *Religion and Understanding*. Oxford: Basil Blackwell, 1967.

Pike, Nelson. "Hume on Evil." *The Philosophical Review* 72 (1963).

Tennant, Frederick Robert. *Philosophical Theory*. Vols. I and II. Cambridge: The University Press, 1928, 1930.

Tsanoff, Radoslav. *The Nature of Evil*. New York: MacMillan, 1931.

Chapter 10   The Meaning of Life

SCIENCE AND THE SENSE OF FUTILITY

It would scarcely have occurred to anyone during the medieval period to ask about the meaning of life or to wonder whether human existence has any point or purpose. The Christian world view was unquestioningly accepted and believed without reservation by the vast majority of Europeans, from serfs to philosophers. The elements of that picture of the world are familiar to all of us. Both the origin and the destiny of the human race are parts of a comprehensive overarching Divine plan. God created the universe (of which our earth was thought to be the fixed center around which revolved the sun and other stars) primarily for the purpose of providing a temporary abode for human beings. Men and women were made in God's own image, and the rest of created nature was made for their purposes. The world itself is stage setting for a moral drama in which humans are tested by temptation, condemned for their failings, and finally offered salvation through the sacrifice of Jesus Christ. After the fall from grace, the conditions of human life on earth became a vale of tears, but the sacraments of the church and obedience to the moral commandments of God make possible an after-life of eternal felicity and direct consciousness of Divinity, just as the misuse of free will could bring Divine condemnation and eternal punishment. Our life on earth then is a brief preliminary to an eternal life after death. It is the latter that "really matters" and provides to the former all its meaning, its purpose, and its point.

The modern scientific view of the world has caused many revisions, at least in the details, of the medieval picture. It is no longer possible, for example, for a scientifically minded person to believe that the world was created in 4,004 B.C., that the sun revolves about the earth, that heaven is located "in the sky above our heads" and hell "in the ground beneath our feet."[1] More than this, commitment to the scientific view of things has caused many (but of course by no means all) persons to reject the essentials of the medieval conception altogether. Many of these persons have continued to lead active purposeful lives, free of doubts and anxieties about the worth and significance of their activities, but many others have discovered that the collapse of the medieval belief system has left their lives seeming empty and ultimately pointless. To these sensitive persons, the absence of a Divine plan and an eternal life gives the universe charted by science the aspect of an "alien world." The British statesman Arthur Balfour (1848–1930) has expressed this unhappy conception as well as any (though the reader should also read the selection by Bertrand Russell in this section for an equally eloquent description):

Man, so far as natural science by itself is able to teach us, is no longer the final cause [goal or purpose] of the universe, the Heaven-descended heir of all the ages. His very existence is an accident, his story a brief and transitory episode in the life of one of the meanest of the planets. Of the combination of causes which first converted a dead organic compound into the living progenitors of humanity, science, indeed, as yet knows nothing. It is enough that from such beginnings famine, disease, and mutual slaughter, fit nurses of the future lords of creation, have gradually evolved, after infinite travail, a race with conscience enough to feel that it is vile, and intelligence enough to know that it is insignificant. We survey the past and see that its history is of blood and tears, of helpless blundering, of wild revolt, of stupid acquiescence, of empty aspirations. We sound the future, and learn that after a period, long compared with the individual life, but short indeed compared with the divisions of time open to our investigation, the energies of our system will decay, the glory of the sun will be dimmed, and the earth, tideless and inert, will no longer tolerate the race which has for a moment disturbed its solitude. Man will go down into the pit, and all his thoughts will perish. The uneasy consciousness, which in this obscure corner has for a brief space broken the contented silence of the universe, will be at rest. Matter will know itself no longer. "Imperishable monuments" and "immortal deeds," death itself, and love stronger than death, will be as though they had never been. Nor will anything that *is* be better or be worse for all that the labor, genius, devotion, and suffering of man have striven through countless ages to effect.[2]

The scientific world view alone, unsupplemented by the affirmation of a Divine plan, or of human immortality, or even of the survival of human achievement, thus causes many to feel despair and a sense of futility.

There appear to be three positions (and more) open to us on this question. We can agree that the naturalistic world view that is the product of the unsupplemented scientific outlook is incompatible with what for the moment we can vaguely call "optimism," and then go on to *affirm* that world view. In that case we are committed to the conclusion that a kind of cosmic pessimism of the sort defended in this section by the German philosopher, Arthur Schopenhauer (1788–1860), is the only appropriate attitude toward the world. Alternatively, we can adhere to the view that naturalism and optimism are incompatible, but *deny* that naturalism is true, thus leaving open the possibility that optimism might be reasonable. This second position, of course, is that of most forms of the great western world religions, Judaism, Islam, and Christianity. ("Optimism" in this sense need not be a cheerful attitude. If one holds that most human beings are doomed to eternal damnation, then one has, unlike the "pessimists," an answer to the question of the "meaning," point, or purpose of human existence. But it is an answer that can cause little joy.) Third, one can assert that naturalism and optimism *are* compatible after all, and affirm naturalism, thus also leaving the door open to optimism as a reasonable response to the human situation. The third position is that of most of the philosophical schools represented in this section, though what passes as an "optimistic" response varies from school to school, and in some cases may strike the reader as gloomy and unconsoling indeed.

THE MEANINGS OF "MEANING" AND "PURPOSE"

The analytic philosopher who has no ideological ax to grind will approach this maze of beliefs and emotions with proper caution, making distinctions that might otherwise be blurred, sorting out questions, and focusing on logically crucial subsidiary issues. Unless these preliminary tasks are satisfactorily performed, it will be difficult to acquire the wisdom to deal with the main question. Let us begin then by examining critically the question "What is the meaning of life?" The perplexity that prompts this question, of course, finds expression in a number of different ways: Does life have any point, significance, or importance? Does it all add up to anything in the end? Or is it pointless, senseless, empty, unimportant, insignificant, or absurd? The reader, however, should beware of taking all of these formulations as equivalent; failure to distinguish among distinguishable concepts can trap us into equivocations and subtle logical errors.

The first distinction to make in interpreting our primary questions is suggested by a counter-question: *Whose* life? Questions about "meaningfulness" and the like seem at first to make a lot more sense when asked about various individual human lives than when asked about "life in general." According to common sense, at least, some lives do have meaning, point, importance, etc., and some lives do not. Some have more, some less, some none at all. But the people who pose our original questions are not relying on common sense. They want to know, in the face of arguments for cosmic pessimism, whether *any life at all* can have meaning, even those lives that seem to common sense to be most blessed. Those who conclude that life (in general) can have no meaning might be prepared to concede that by common sense criteria some lives are less meaningless than others; their pessimistic way of putting this, however, might be to say that all lives are meaningless, but some are more so than others! In any case, we can distinguish two broadly different ways of interpreting our original question, and for the moment at least, certify both as well worth our consideration:

1. What is it that in fact confers meaning on the careers of those whose lives *are* (relatively) meaningful, at least by common sense standards?
2. What, if anything, is the meaning of human life in general?

If the second question is answered negatively in the manner of the cosmic pessimist, it leads quickly to a third:

3. If human life has no meaning, why is that the case? Exactly what is missing? What would it take to confer meaning on human existence?

If pessimists cannot even conceive of what meaningful existence *would* be like, then they must be using absurdly high standards that no conceivable state of affairs could satisfy, and it is not even clear what they are saying when they deny that human existence has any meaning.

When we turn next to the crucial term "meaning," we see immediately that various other distinctions must be made. Consider some of the different things we might mean when we use the word "meaning" in other contexts:

1. Conventional signs and symbols such as words, sentences, musical notation, mathematical symbols, and telegraphic codes are said to have meaning in the sense that they refer, or point to, objects beyond themselves. Proper names like "Margaret Mead" refer to particular persons, in this case to Margaret Mead. More general words like "red" stand for qualities that can exist in various times and places and "refer to" all the objects that have those properties. What gives symbols their meanings in this sense is some prior convention of usage.
2. Sounds, signs, gestures, and the like are often said to mean what the speaker or gesturer intends to convey by them either in the absence of a general convention or even in defiance of such a convention. My meaning is what *I* mean or intend, and if *I* mean by "red" what other people mean by "blue," so be it. Thus "the meaning" of a word in a natural language is determined by understood conventions of usage, whereas the speaker's meaning is determined only by his or her own intentions.
3. Objects and occurrences are often said to have a "natural meaning" that derives neither from human conventions nor from indi-

viduals' intentions. Thus we say that a falling barometer *means* (points to, is evidence of) a coming storm, or that the meaning of red on litmus paper is acidity. In general the meaning of a natural sign is something that stands in regular causal relations with it: its inferred cause or consequence.

4. Works of art—novels, stories, plays, paintings, sculpture, dance (but rarely musical compositions)—are sometimes said to have a meaning. Sometimes when we speak of "the meaning" of a particular work of art, we refer to the artist's intentions, what he or she intended to convey. Sometimes, however, we may wish to refer to something that is wholly independent of the artist's actual intentions. We may even disagree with the artist about what his work really or truly means. It is not easy to explain this sense of "meaning," though we seem to understand it well enough in ordinary discourse. Not only do we not refer by it to the artist's intentions; neither do we merely apply understood conventions; nor do we claim, necessarily, to be referring to something outside the work of art that it "points to" or "stands for," in the way a natural sign implicates its cause or effect. Rather we refer to some internal characteristic of the object that gives it its primary "significance," draws our interest and appreciation, and confers on it its peculiar value or merit. Its "meaning" is the key to its understanding, what one has to grasp about it in order fully to apprehend and admire it as a work of art.

5. Finally, we sometimes speak of the actions or activities of human beings as having a meaning. Often when we do so, we do not apply arbitrary symbolic conventions or interpret natural signs, nor infer the actor's intentions ("the meaning" of the person's actions may not be anything he or she intends to convey to observers), nor display the key to a sympathetic appreciation of what is observed. Rather we describe what we take to be the actor's *purpose* in acting, the organizing plan, or aim, or goal behind his or her movements that renders them coherent, as opposed to merely random. It may be a good purpose or a bad one, but insofar as it introduces order, continuity, and pattern to a person's activities it can be called their "meaning."

It is no doubt true that common threads run through these various senses, that there are various overlapping elements that account for the fact that this one word, "meaning," has been given five different jobs to do. But it is important to emphasize nevertheless that the jobs *are* different, especially if our aim is to clarify a question that applies the ambiguous term "meaning" to life as a whole.

We can probably assume with safety that when people inquire about the "meaning" of life, they do not use the word in either sense 1 or 2. They are not applying some sort of linguistic analogy to the world. There are no linguistic conventions that give a sense to the whole world in a manner analogous to that in which conventions of English usage give a sense to the word "dog" or the word "red." A theist might think of all existence as a kind of "statement" made by God, so that when theists inquire about "the meaning of life" they are asking what God intends to convey by that statement. This interpretation should not be dismissed out of hand, although it is perhaps unusual theologically, and it does involve the complication that if in the beginning there was only God, there was no one to whom "the statement" could be addressed. Human beings, on this interpretation, are themselves both part of the statement and the party to whom the statement is addressed. Perhaps human life can be said to have "meaning" in our third sense, that in which natural signs like weather vanes have meaning. The existence of intelligent human life on this planet "means," among other things, that the earth has an atmosphere of a certain kind (inferred causal condition) and (perhaps) that other planets in the solar system are bound to be visited one day (inferred causal consequence). But this is surely not the sense of "meaning" in the phrase "the meaning of life." The most likely candidates then for plausible interpretation of our question are the closely related senses 4, which applies the aesthetic analogy, and 5, which turns our inquiry into a question about *purpose*. We turn to the latter sense now.

The word "purpose" is hardly less complex than the word "meaning." At the start we can distinguish two broadly different uses of the word:

1. A person's purpose in acting is his or her conscious goal, end, or aim—what that person wishes to produce as a consequence of the action, or that element in the expected consequences for the sake of which he or she undertakes the action. Often the answer to the question "Why did you do so and so?" is a statement of the actor's purpose in doing so and so—"in order to bring about such and such." Note that only conscious animals or persons can "have purposes" in this sense.

2. In a quite different but no doubt derivative sense, mere things can be said to "have purposes" too. But the purpose of a created thing is not *its* conscious aim, but rather the goal in the mind of its producer for the sake of which it was created. Thus the purpose of a coffee cup (to hold coffee) is not the conscious aim of that handled porcelain object itself, for such objects can have no aims of their own. Rather it is the purpose in the mind of the artisan who designed and produced it.

The second sense of "having a purpose" might usefully be contrasted also with the closely related notion of having a *function:*

3. The function of a component of a complex organism (e.g., the heart or liver in a human body) or of a component of a complex machine (e.g., a carburetor in an automobile) is the role it actually plays in the functioning of the larger system of which it is a part. In the case of machinery the function of a component part usually (but not necessarily) corresponds with its purpose, that is, with the job it was consciously designed to do. Scientists, however, normally speak of the function of biological organs in a way that implies nothing about their "purpose" (that is, the conscious aim of their designers). A biologist might interpret the question "What is the function of human life?" as a request for an account of the role our species plays in the larger ecological systems of which it is a part. This is an important question, but clearly not the one normally intended when one asks for "the meaning of life."

Applying the two broadly different senses of "purpose" to our question about the meaning of human life, we derive two distinct questions:

1. *Purpose of life.* If we are using the word "purpose" in the second sense distinguished above, we are treating "life" as a kind of artifact of some conscious producer. The purpose of "life" is simply a reflection of the conscious aim of the artisan who produced it. If I am speaking of *my* life (or *my* existence) when I pose this question, I may be asking (although this is not very likely) what my parents had in mind, if anything, when they decided (if they did so decide) to have the child who turned out to be me. Perhaps *their* purpose was to insure against an impoverished old age, or to have somebody else about to love and be loved by, or even to contribute to the world a person with certain talents or virtues. Still, it is hardly consistent with my sense of personal autonomy and dignity to think of "my purpose," or "the purpose of my life" as simply a reflection of theirs. Most persons who have even a mere minimum of pride will find it impossible to think of themselves as mere products of their parents' will with no voice of their own in the shaping of their "purpose." Some philosophers have claimed that it is degrading to think of oneself as "having a purpose" in this sense at all, even if the conscious aim that one embodies is that of God. Kurt Baier writes: "If, at a garden party, I ask a man in livery 'What is your purpose?' I am insulting him. I might as well have asked 'What are you *for?*' Such questions reduce him to the level of a gadget, a domestic animal [bred for a specific purpose], or perhaps a slave."[3] A person is not any kind of artifact, Baier insists, not even a

divine artifact. Others, of course, disagree. At least a self-conscious artifact who knows "what he is for" is unlikely to suffer cosmic anxieties about the "meaning" or "purpose" of his life. The "insulting" or "degrading" character of the question is diminished, moreover, if we ask what is the purpose (in the present sense) of human life in general, or even, more abstractly, of all the universe. The problem with these more abstract questions is that they boggle the mind and resist all reasoning. Only a prior commitment to a theological doctrine can enable one to find sense in them or to grope towards an anxiety-calming answer.

2. *Purpose in life.* If, on the other hand, it is the first sense of "purpose" distinguished above that we are employing when we seek the purpose of our lives, our question has a quite different, and in many cases, a less perplexing, character. Since the question is about *my* conscious goals, I need only consider the direction in which I have aimed my own life in order to answer it. However, when people pose this question to themselves they rarely think of it as a question calling for a mere description of their own aims. Rather it is thought to be a practical problem calling for a personal decision: Insofar as the direction of my life is subject to my own control, what should my ultimate purposes be? What goals and objectives should I select? If the "meaning" of my life is the "purpose" in my life, then it is not something I discover by looking, but something I create as I go along.

Partly because the subject is more amenable to their methods, philosophers have had more to say about the purpose *in* life than about the purpose *of* human existence. And indeed that topic often is directly relevant to the quest for "the meaning of life." Persons whose lives have no clear direction, pattern, and order, and don't know how to go about creating them, persons who are aimless drifters, persons who find "all the uses of this world weary, flat, stale, and unprofitable," these are very often the ones for whom life is "full of sound and fury

signifying nothing." It is a short step from finding oneself to be without serious purposes of one's own to regarding one's life as "meaningless."

The phrase "purpose in life" can be misleading in its simplicity. Almost everyone has many purposes, as opposed to one single purpose, in his or her life. There have been some men and women, however, whose purposes exhibit a striking unity imposed by one superior overriding goal that controls and determines their specific projects and activities. On this matter, analytic philosophy contributes still another useful distinction:

1. A person might have a single *dominant end* (for example, his or her own happiness, wealth, or power; the triumph of a worthy cause; the production of a great work of art; service to God) that is the object of a single prime desire. This is unusual, however. Such a person, if not thought of as a saint or a hero, is often regarded as a monomaniac or a fanatic.

2. On the other hand, a person might have as his or her ultimate goal a single *inclusive end,* namely, the desire that all his or her other goals, whatever they might be, should be achieved. This inclusive end is a higher-level desire, a desire about desires, not just one constituent desire among others. In the words of Anthony Kenny, it is "the desire of the orderly and harmonious gratification of a number of other desires."[4] Many or even most normal persons have such a governing desire; often it goes under the name of the desire for "happiness." But the very existence of an inclusive end presupposes that there be a multiplicity of other—"first level" —purposes from which it is derived. One might also note that "harmony," an elementary aesthetic concept, is involved in the very conception of an inclusive end.

With the exception of those persons whose conative lives are very simple and whose purposes are very few, those who achieve the "inclusive ends" in their lives do so by means of a kind of *life-plan* that orders desires and purposes in a hierarchical structure, relegating to its proper place each passing impulse, specific desire, general means, intermediate end, and ulterior purpose. (A wise life-plan will also leave room for spontaneity, flexibility, and growth.) As Plato was the first to point out, our desires can be put into three basic categories: desires for things valued only as means to other things (instrumental goods), desires for things valued for their own sakes (intrinsic goods), and desires for things valued *both* as means and also in themselves. Sometimes we put up with travel only because it is a necessary means for getting to our destination, other times we find ourselves at a destination only because our travel, undertaken entirely for its own sake (think of a pleasant walk or ride in the country) happened to bring us there; sometimes we value the trip both for its own inherent pleasures and because it is the only way to get to a destination that is also valued for its own sake. The application of these distinctions to life itself is now a commonplace.

An intelligent life-plan will also distinguish among desires in respect to their ulteriority. At the lowest level are those various "passing wants" of the moment—to drink a cup of coffee, to chat with a friend, to see a film, to take a nap—that are the very stuff of life and cannot be altogether ignored, much as they may need disciplining, each to wait its turn. In an ascending order we also have desires of an intermediate and a highest range of ulteriority. First, there are immediate wants whose fulfillments, unlike the desire, say, to have an ice cream cone, are linked up either as means or as necessary conditions to the advancement of more ulterior goals: the desire to get enough exercise for health, enough rest to do one's work efficiently, enough money to pay one's expenses. Health and financial sufficiency generally are themselves objects of still more ultimate desires, and are valued as elements of our welfare without whose maintenance we cannot achieve our higher good, or well-being, as determined by our still more ultimate goals. The latter are well characterized by Charles Stevenson as *focal aims,* which are ends (note the plural) which are also means to many other divergent ends. Unlike a particular holiday trip to a destination (our earlier example), however, focal aims are *ultimate* ends, at least as ultimate as ends are ever likely to be for most people. A focal aim, says Stevenson, is

"an end which is also such an exceptionally important means to so many divergent ends that if anything else is not a means to this [or to another focal aim] it will be without predominating value."[5] Typical examples of focal aims are building a dream house (an end in itself also valued as a means to the entertainment of house guests, to the private pursuit of studies and pleasures, to hours of aesthetic contemplation, and so on); the achievement of political office (which can be an end in itself to those who value power, and also a means to the advancement of favorite causes and policies); the solution of an important scientific problem (a challenge in its own right, but also a means to the further advance of knowledge and technology, to say nothing of personal glory); raising a family to adulthood; achieving security in leisure.

We flourish insofar as we promote the whole economy of our structured goals and make progress toward the harmonious fulfillment of our focal aims. If we add to this picture the steady spawning of new projects and enterprises directed both towards new and continuing goals (this to obviate the possibility of a static "final" fulfillment as a plausible human aspiration), then we have a credible account of human happiness, but one that presupposes the existence of focal aims already present.

As one fully works out this conception of "purpose in life," it approximates more and more closely the meaningfulness expressed in the fourth sense of "meaning" distinguished above, that in which art objects are said to have meaning. And indeed the aesthetic model for the meaningful life has occurred to many.[6] In particular, the meaningful life is not only happy, it is rich and various, balanced and harmonious, exhibiting a fine proportioning of instrumental and intrinsic satisfactions, neither constantly postponing gratification, nor wallowing in it in forfeiture of future gains and achievements. The focal aims of such a life are (to vary the metaphor) its governing themes and motifs; the way they are pursued, its distinctive style. The variety of meaningful lives, on this aesthetic conception, is as great as the variety of human values themselves, and there is no more a single model for all lives than for all works of art. Not even the life of humble domesticity is excluded, as the protagonist in Maugham's novel, *Of Human*

Bondage, discovered in the end: "He thought of his desire [inclusive end] to make a design, intricate and beautiful, out of the myriad, meaningless facts of life: had he not seen also that the simplest pattern, that in which a man was born, worked, married, had children, and died, was likewise the most perfect?"

THE MEANINGS OF "VALUE" AND "WORTHWHILENESS"

The questions discussed above about the meaning and purpose of life need to be further distinguished, as a group, from questions about the *value* and *worthwhileness* of life. Most would agree that if a life has meaning or purpose, then it has value and worthwhileness, but there is great controversy over the truth of the converse of that proposition. Some insist that if a life has no purpose (in the first sense of "purpose," namely that it is part of an eternal plan involving an afterlife, from which it gets its point) then it cannot have value or be worthwhile. Others insist that life can be worth living, that "the good life" is possible, even if life is "meaningless" (fulfilling no external planner's purpose) and, by cosmic standards, brief. The question is surely an open one, not to be settled simply by equating "meaning" and "value" in our definitions. It may be incorrect to say that a meaningless life can nevertheless be a good life, but it is no logical contradiction.

Value and worthwhileness should also be distinguished one from the other. A life with value is a good life, one which must be judged favorably, given high marks, admired, and sought after. We not only approve of another's good life; we must also envy it and seek the same for ourselves. Goodness is something to be treasured, pursued, gloried in, and satisfied by; it is the proper object of such positive attitudes. Of course goodness is a matter of degree. Some good lives are better than others. Some are barely good on balance; others are superlatively good. For most, the good life requires personal excellence and skill, but also a lot of good luck. An unlucky life spent in squalor and disease is not likely to be a very good life for anyone. It surely makes sense to call some people's lives "bad lives," or poor lives, or wretched lives. But it does not follow from the fact that a life was not good that it was not worthwhile. (One must always consider the alternative, as the ancient joke puts it.) In general, to say of a particular thing that it is not a good thing of its kind is not to imply that it is not worth keeping, that one might as well throw it away. One might have a very poor automobile indeed and yet find it better than nothing. Similarly, even a very poor life can be worth living. Only the most wretched life will lead a rational person to ponder suicide.

We can now formulate a whole new set of questions that are broader than our original questions about meaning and purpose. Whatever we may think about the presence or absence of a "cosmic purpose and destiny" for human existence, we can still ask such questions as "What makes any life valuable?" "What is the test of a good life?" "Is my life worthwhile?" "Is any life worthwhile?" Most of the selections that follow in this section either deny that life has a cosmic purpose, or else ignore the question. Nevertheless, they do not take questions about the goodness or worthwhileness of life to be foreclosed by their scepticism about cosmic purposes and destinies. To repeat: whether the absence of cosmic purpose renders life valueless or not worth living must be presented at the start as an open question to be settled one way or the other by argument.

For that reason, the terms "Optimism" and "Pessimism" should be reserved for affirmations and denials of value or worthwhileness, and not applied to views about the presence or absence of a cosmic purpose as such. Some writers are Pessimists *because* they deny immortality and cosmic design; that denial is the ground or reason for their Pessimism. Other writers are Optimists *even though* they deny cosmic purpose; their Optimism is supported by reasons of other kinds.

THE MEANINGS OF "OPTIMISM" AND "PESSIMISM"

What then should we mean by the initially vague terms "Optimism" and "Pessimism"? An extreme Pessimist, either because he denies cosmic purpose and survival of death, or for some other reason, denies that life is worth living at all. That is virtually tantamount to recommending suicide. A less extreme Pessimist will deny that the good life is possible for any human beings, whatever their circumstances, either because death and the dissolution of achievement are inevitable, or for some other reason. Still, the moderate Pessimist will not deny that lives are worth living anyway. A more empirically minded Pessimist may admit that good lives are possible, but insist that because of such evils *in* life as war, disease, poverty, and cruelty, such lives are difficult and rare. That would be to base Pessimism on grounds other than the absence of cosmic design and immortality. Similarly, Optimism may be (but rarely is) extreme, holding that human life as such is necessarily good; or moderate, holding that many or most human lives are good; or weak, holding that human effort, in principle, can succeed in making lives better and better, whatever their present condition.

Optimism and Pessimism, spelled with capital letters, are philosophical doctrines making judgments about reality purportedly based on reasons; they are not mere expressions of cheerful or gloomy moods. In ordinary discourse where we are not referring to philosophical doctrines, we think of the optimist (spelled with a small "o") as a person with a cheerful and hopeful temperament who is disposed to put a favorable construction on things, and a pessimist (with a small "p") as a person of gloomy or despairing temperament who is constantly inclined to anticipate harms and evils. But it is a notorious truth that many philosophical Pessimists have been persons of cheerful temperament, and some philosophical Optimists have been pessimistic indeed in their everyday lives. We must be concerned here only with the truth or falsity of the doctrines and the cogency of their supporting reasons, whatever the temperaments of their proponents.

One way of interpreting philosophical Optimism and Pessimism is to take them to be affirmations of the *appropriateness* of certain attitudes toward life, positive ones for the Optimist, negative ones for the Pessimist. That would be a good start in understanding the doctrines, for we often take the appropriateness or inappropriateness of responses to be matters for objective judgments supportable by reasons. People who yawn at (what we take to be)

hilarious comedy are objectively blind or opaque, we think, deficient in wit, "humorless," and the like. Similarly, people who laugh at tragedies or express pleasure at the sufferings of others, we think of as "morally blind," and their responses, for whatever cause, grossly inappropriate. Optimism and Pessimism similarly affirm the objective appropriateness of either "positive" or "negative" attitudes toward life. The trouble with this characterization is that it artificially simplifies the great range of responses philosophers have recommended, many of which are much too subtle or complex to be called simply "positive" or "negative." Either of these vague "ism" words can be defined as the view that the human condition (or the universe, or reality, or whatever) is such that the appropriate attitude toward one's own life (or human life generally) is . . . what? Take your choice: earnestness, hope, joy, despair, resentment, scorn, defiance, resignation, tears, laughter, irony, a sense of tragedy, or pathos, or comedy, pleasure-seeking, pain-avoiding, emotional intensity, emotional renunciation. Systems of reasons and arguments supporting these and other more subtle responses to life as uniquely appropriate and reasonable have been given names that make up one of the main galleries of philosophical "isms": Epicureanism, Stoicism, Platonism, Romanticism, Existentialism, and Self-Realization. It is much more important to assess the merits of these specific theories than to attempt to settle the essentially vague question whether their recommended attitudes are "positive" or "negative," "optimistic" or "pessimistic."

COSMIC PESSIMISM

The opening selection, "On the Vanity of Existence" by Arthur Schopenhauer, gives eloquent expression to a Pessimism based on the vanity (the word in this context has the sense of "in-vain-ness") of all human effort. To be sure, we spend our lives striving after goals that seem important to us, but there is something essentially negative, according to Schopenhauer, in the very process of goal seeking. When we desire something, we are in a kind of negative state of disequilibrium; something we want is missing, and that absence is uncomfortable, even painful. We strive then to escape the pain or discomfort until we are back in a state of equilibrium again, all pain gone. If we maintain that state, Schopenhauer claims, we experience nothing "positive," no genuine pleasure or satisfaction, merely an absence of pain, which at first pleases us as a kind of relief, but soon is converted either to boredom or to new painful hungers. That is all life offers in consolation as we drift inevitably downhill through sickness and decrepitude to death and the eternity of non-being from which we began. Nothing makes life even worthwhile. Schopenhauer's Pessimism is uncompromising.

The remaining selections all recommend attitudes and ways of living that are thought to give value or at least worthwhileness to life, even though death may be final and life unredeemed by some external purpose.

EPICUREANISM

The school founded by Epicurus (342 B.C.–270 B.C.) had an important influence on the lives of ancient Greeks and Romans who lived in discouragingly turbulent and dangerous times. Like its main rival in the Hellenistic period, Stoicism, it offered a kind of "guarantee" of a happiness or well-being that is immune to the fluctuations of fortune. Epicurus himself taught his students and friends in a famous house and garden in Athens. His subtle teachings about the importance of simple pleasures and plain living were widely misinterpreted, and he was made subject to ridicule in his own time and for centuries after. The Stoic sage Epictetus, addressing Epicurus in his *Discourses,* wrote for example, "This is the life of which you pronounce yourself worthy: eating, drinking, copulation, evacuation, and snoring." Actually Epicurus himself, as Santayana says, was regarded by his disciples as a kind of saint, constantly cheerful, gentle, and abstemious. Surely he was no kind of voluptuary. The epicurean quatrain in the *Rubaiyat* of Omar—"A Book of verses underneath the bough; a jug of wine, a loaf of bread, and thou beside me singing in the wilderness—Oh, wilderness were paradise enow."—can conjure up romantic images in a modern mind, but insofar as its intent is consistently Epicurean, the emphasis is on the simplicity of the good life—simple food and drink in moderate amounts, books of poetry, simple friendship, unspoiled nature. In modern times, alas, the word "epicurean" (with a small "e") has come to suggest gluttony, fancy cooking, and sensuous debauches. Nothing could have been further from the founder's intentions!

The chief good, according to Epicureanism, is pleasure; the chief evil, pain. Some pains (bad-tasting medicine, calesthenics) can be instrumental goods leading to greater pleasures in the long run. Some pleasures (excessive eating and drinking, romantic love) can be instrumental evils leading to greater pains in the long run. The wise person will live his or her life in such a way as to create the greatest balance of pleasure over pain in the long run. All goods other than pleasure (knowledge, friendship, health, money, etc.) are good as means only. We can ask of all of them "What are they good for?" and the answer in every case is that they lead to pleasure. It makes no sense, on the other hand, to ask what pleasure is "good for."

The Epicureans distinguished two kinds of pleasure. Desires, they thought (anticipating Schopenhauer), are all essentially negative, unstable, and painful. The pleasures attending the actual process of attaining a desired end (for example, the pleasures experienced in the process of satisfying hunger) are *dynamic* pleasures. The pleasures of being in the restored state of equilibrium (for example, the quiescence of hunger after one has satisfied it) are *static* pleasures. Dynamic pleasures are the more exciting ones, but nevertheless, the static pleasures are much to be preferred, since they are unalloyed and do not depend on the prior existence of pain (e.g., great hunger) as a stimulus to desire. (Bertrand Russell comments that "Epicurus, it seems, would wish, if it were possible, to be always in the state of having eaten moderately, never in that of voracious desire to eat."[7]) Schopenhauer to the contrary, there is nothing "boring" about the quiet pleasures. Rather there is a calm and mellow satisfaction in the contemplation of one's painless condition; in engaging in simple activities and friendly conversations untroubled by turbulent emotions and compulsive drives; in those pleasures of the senses, like the scent of a rose, that do not presuppose hunger or painful desire; and in recollection and anticipation of the same.

Pleasures, according to Epicureanism, are never as intense as pains. An attack of acute indigestion, for example, clearly outweighs the pleasure of gluttony. The way to the most pleasant life, therefore, is not so much by seeking pleasures as by avoiding pains, and thereby attaining the superior pleasure that consists in, or presupposes, the absence of pain. Epicurus lived on bread and water, adding moderate portions of cheese only at "banquets."

How could the Epicureans "guarantee" happiness in the face of a remorseless impersonal universe and extremely insecure social institutions? Like the Stoics, they taught that wise people cannot help but be happy, for they have at their disposal an infallible technique: Do not invest your hopes and passionate desires in an uncertain future; give no hostages to fortune; uproot desires for material things; cultivate simplicity; remind yourself of your pleasures, present, past, and future. (William DeWitt Hyde tells of the "Epicurean" student at Bowdoin College who had the dormitory janitor wake him at 4:30 each morning so that he might experience the pleasure of knowing that he could go back to sleep again for another hour.[8]) Physical pain, of course, is a great evil and impossible to avoid altogether. But the more intense pains tend to be relatively brief, Epicurus thought, and prolonged pain can be endured through mental discipline and the habit of thinking happy things in spite of it. (An ancient Epicurean claimed that he could be happy on the rack.) And if all else fails, there is always suicide, an entry into a painless realm that must come anyway sooner or later.

The great Epicurean imperative is: Live so as to avoid fear. Anxiety, worry, and the more specific fears are the primary causes of human suffering, and the main sources of fear, Epicurus taught, are religion (with its stories of angry deities and posthumous punishments) and death, thought of as total extinction. Most Epicurean sages thought that the gods exist but do not trouble themselves with human affairs. They are, in fact, themselves perfect Epicureans living untroubled immortal lives free of burdensome cares and emotions—certainly free of *anger* toward mere mortals. The universe itself consists basically of nothing but material atoms and an infinite void. The atoms are in constant random motion and often collide with one another, some-times combining to form large, more complex, material objects. When these random collections of atoms are stuck or hooked together in a stable fashion, the material objects they compose persist for long stretches of time. When they are unstable, they decompose, and their constituent atoms fly off once more into the void and further collisions. Material objects come and go; only the atoms go on forever.

Epicurus's directions for reconciling oneself to death are given concise formulation in the epic philosophical work *On The Nature of Things (De Rerum Natura)* by the Roman poet Lucretius (*circa* 96–55 B.C.). In effect Lucretius attempts to *argue* his reader out of the fear of death. Death is not some dreadful state which we will someday be in, he argues, for if death is simply non-being, as Epicurus teaches, then it is nothing to us, since "where we are death is not yet, and where death is, we are no more." It should therefore trouble neither the living nor the dead, "for it is not found with the living and the dead exist no longer."

The section on Epicureanism begins with excerpts from the "Rubaiyat" ("Quatrains") of Omar Khayyam (Omar, the tent maker), a Persian scientist, poet, and Epicurean philosopher who lived at about the time of the Norman conquest of England. The poem is faithful to the Epicurean world view and evokes with unexcelled clarity the bittersweet feelings such a picture can evoke in a person of more or less Epicurean leanings, but it departs perhaps from the founder's spirit of moderation in its enthusiasm for "the taste of the grape." It does contain quatrains that express the thought—"Eat, drink and be merry, for tomorrow we shall die," which perhaps exceed the cautious directives of Epicurean sages. The intriguing philosophical point in that admonition is the force of the word "for" (because) in "for tomorrow we may die." How, we might wonder, is the certainty of death a *reason* for seeking pleasure? The section printed here from *A Shropshire Lad,* the famous Epicurean work of the English poet A. E. Housman (1859–1936), conveys in remarkably moving lines what might be thought to be the very unpoetic Epicurean strictures against overindulgence, and also describes, through its retelling of the legend of King Mithridates, an important Epicurean technique for immunizing oneself to life's inevitable evils. Finally, the Spanish-American philosopher George Santayana (1863–1952) interprets Lucretius's arguments about death and makes a shrewd criticism of them.

STOICISM

While one could hardly speak of a "Christian Epicureanism" without paradox and contradiction, there *have* been Christian Stoics. Indeed, elements of Stoic teaching, borrowed or developed independently, can be found in the teachings of all the great world religions. Few small tracts have had as great and varied influence as the *Enchiridion* ("Manual") of the Roman Stoic philosopher Epictetus (*circa* 50 A.D.–130 A.D.). The son of a woman slave, Epictetus himself served as a personal slave to a secretary of the Emperor Nero, before he became a free man. Later, like many other philosophers, he was exiled from Rome and wandered through the Greek world before settling in Epirus, where he founded his famous school. The *Enchiridion* consists of notes taken in shorthand by his student, one Flavius Arrian.

Like Epicureanism, Stoicism is an effort to discover "meaning" in a chaotic world, and restore happiness in a frighteningly insecure world, and freedom in a world of servitude. Also like Epicureanism it proposed a discipline and "guaranteed" its success. In reconstructing Epictetus's philosophy from the few written fragments that have come down to us, perhaps it is best to begin with two implicit definitions. Though it is no doubt a simplification of his actual teachings, we can ascribe to Epictetus the view that *happiness* consists basically of satisfaction of desire, and that *freedom* is essentially the absence of constraint to one's desires. (One is perfectly free when one can do whatever one wants.) The second step is to state the basic distinction introduced by Epictetus in his very first paragraph as it should properly be interpreted. The distinction is an exhaustive one, stating two categories into one or another of which all the things and events of the world can be placed. There are things that are *totally* (that word is essential) within our power, and things that are *not totally* within our power. The first group contains our

opinions, aims, desires, aversions, tastes, convictions, attitudes, purposes, and in general, how we react to the world. The second group contains everything else including our health, the condition of our bodies, the state and extent of our property, our talents, our reputations, our status or job, even our continued existence, which can be squelched at any time by unforeseen accidents.

The argument that follows from these definitions and from the basic distinction is designed to establish the Stoic guarantee, and it is simplicity itself. You are absolutely and entirely in control of what you desire. Now if all you desire to do is what you are certain to be able to do, then you will be able to do whatever you want, and your perfect freedom is guaranteed. Moreover, if you desire only things that you are certain to get, you can never be frustrated or disappointed; thus your perfect happiness is assured. "Show me a man who is sick and happy, who is in danger and happy, in disgrace and happy. Show me him—by Zeus, I am asking to be shown a Stoic!"

So far, Stoicism is remarkably similar to Epicureanism in urging a drastic cutback of our desires. The distinctive Stoic doctrine, however, is its answer to the crucial question, "What, and what alone, is it then that one should desire, care for, seek after?" The answer is the Stoic imperative: seek only your own virtue. The English word "virtue" with its Victorian accretions of meaning and its associations of priggishness is entirely incapable of expressing Epictetus's intent. We would be much closer to his meaning if we substituted "excellence of character," "moral worth," or "personal integrity." Such excellence, Stoicism insists, is the sole intrinsic good, but as luck would have it, if it is also the object of one's sole ultimate desire, it yields the derivative good of happiness necessarily as a dividend. If we aim at happiness directly we will not get it, but if we aim at excellence, which is entirely within our power, and give not a damn for *anything* else, then we cannot fail to be happy.

In what then does personal excellence consist? Once more the answer is simple. Personal excellence consists in trying one's best to do one's *duty*. According to the Stoic view, any rational being can discover his or her objective duty, and while external force, internal weakness, or bad luck can prevent one from doing one's duty, nothing can prevent one from trying one's best to do so. If the phrase "subjective duty" is defined in terms of the internal states entirely within our control—our proper attitudes and earnest efforts and attempts—then nothing can ever prevent us from performing our subjective duty, and it is in that faithful performance that personal excellence consists. The objective duty that we must seek always to discharge is discovered by reason according to two formulas: one involves the notion of "my station and its duties," the other the idea of "living according to nature."

Our duties follow, according to the Stoics, from the very conception of the social roles we play, the stations we occupy, the relations we stand in. Ask what any "role-word" means and the answer will be a definition in terms of duties. A father is a man whose duties are (or whose job is). . . . A teacher is a person whose duties are. . . . A student is a person whose duties are. . . . And similarly for "daughter," "son," "philosopher," "soldier," etc. It takes no special revelation to know that a mother's duty is to give loving care and protection to her children, that a soldier's duty is to obey the orders of his superiors, and so on. Similarly (but this is much harder) one can derive "the duties of a person as such" by pondering the nature of the "role" whose name is "human being." The Roman Stoics frequently employed military metaphors (an *enchiridion* is a manual for a combat officer) and theatrical analogies: "Remember that you are an actor in a drama of such sort as the Author chooses—if short, then a short one; if long, then a long one. If it be his pleasure that you should enact a poor man, or a cripple, or a ruler, or a private citizen, see that you act it well. For this is *your* business—to act well the given part, but to choose it belongs to another." A metaphor drawn from card games can make this same point: what cards you are dealt is a matter of luck beyond your control. No matter how you play, if your cards are consistently bad you will lose. But it is within your power to play every hand as well as possible, win or lose. "Fortune is up to fate; excellence is up to me."

The ancient Stoics appealed to "nature" in two ways. First, they refer to "instinctive strivings" and dispositions that "nature appears to have implanted in us," in parents, an affection for their children, in all persons a kind of social bond. "From this impulse is developed the sense of mutual attraction which unites human beings as such"; hence the purely social duties and the duties of patriotism are in accord with nature. So are duties, such as the imparting of knowledge, derived from our "natural" concern for posterity. So are duties derived from our natural impulse to protect the weak. But how, we might ask, can such things be worth pursuing for their own sakes, if, as we were told earlier, only one's own virtue is good in itself, and we are not to give a damn for anything else? The answer is that imparting knowledge, defending one's country, protecting the weak, etc. *are* indifferent things to the wise person, but apparently "among different things some are more indifferent than others"! More precisely, these things are not goods, strictly speaking, but are appropriate or deserving objects of choice and thus possessed of "a certain amount of positive value (*axia*)." Actually it is the knowing and conscientious pursuit of them which is truly good, and "in accord with nature," not the objects themselves. It is in the correct aiming (intention) and not in the actual hitting of the mark (result) that absolute goodness exists. In short, act as if hitting the target (provided by your "nature") is important in order that you might aim well, not the other way around.

The other Stoic formula referring to "nature" directs us always to act "in harmony with nature," that is to identify our will with nature's (or with God's or Zeus's). Learn to love fate; become one with nature; welcome whatever happens; identify your mind with the *reason* of the world, the beautifully ordered inner workings of the material processes whose mind is God. "Demand not that events should happen as you wish, but wish them to happen as they do happen, and you will get on well."

The Stoic moral philosophy is the most extreme example of a "deontological ethic," that is, a system of moral teachings based simply on "duty" rather than on the production of good consequences. Stoics are not virtuous in order to do good; they do good in order to be virtuous. They do their duty for the sake of moral excellence, but excellence itself is sought for its own sake. If a Stoic husband has a fatally sick wife, he will conscientiously and tirelessly do his duty as a husband to the very end, treating her pain, comforting her, consoling her. He does these admirable things not because he cares emotionally what happens to her one way or the other; *all* he cares about is his *own* personal excellence. Bertrand Russell thus parodies the whole Stoic ethic in a nutshell: "Certain things are vulgarly considered goods, but this is a mistake; what *is* good is a will directed toward securing these false goods for other people."[9]

Stoicism thus has a kind of make-believe character that comports well with its theatrical metaphors. To some, it is a morality of pose and gesture that has no place for genuine feelings. Stoics might well concede this charge with the reply that they know the meaning of life in the only way that is possible, namely, in the way actors know the "meaning" of their role and art. And the true Stoic will have no fear of death and eternal non-existence (which are entirely beyond his power) but only of not dying well, with dignity and a kind of moral beauty. While alive, the Stoic's integrity is literally priceless; there is no more ultimate currency in which its value can be registered.

In addition to the selection from Epictetus, two other pieces sound Stoic themes. The *Bhagavad-Gita* or "Song of God" is part of a great Sanskrit epic poem in which the basic philosophy and theology of Hinduism is expounded. The brief selections included here describe the plight of Arjuna, a conscientious but morally confused member of the warrior caste, as he prepares to enter battle in a cruel internecine war. He turns to his chariot driver, the incarnate God Krishna, for teaching and counsel. Why should Arjuna kill his brothers? How can a wise and virtuous man of *any* caste desire the death and suffering of others? How can he even desire that his side win if the outcome is largely beyond his control? Krishna's full answer requires the exposition of the whole Vedantic philosophy, but the parts included here recall the western Stoic emphasis on the "aim" rather than the target. Arjuna will learn his lesson and then fight *fiercely* but in a spirit of total indifference to the success or failure of his efforts. His one and only animating desire will be to do his duty as a member of the warrior caste. That it is even possible psy-

chologically for strenuous and effective efforts to be produced by such motivation is one of the surprising insights common to Hinduism, Roman Stoicism, and some forms of Christianity. Krishna disavows the theory that calls for "renunciation" of all desire, but advocates what he calls "non-attachment" or "abandonment of the fruits of action." The translators of the *Gita* say of this way of "acting without fear and without desire" that:

The Christians call it "holy indifference" and the Hindus "non-attachment." But names are slightly misleading. They suggest coldness and lack of enthusiasm. That is why people often confuse non-attachment with fatalism, when actually they are opposites. The fatalist simply does not care. He will get what is coming to him. Why make any effort? But the doer of non-attached action is the most conscientious of men. Freed from fear and desire, he offers everything he does as a sacrament of devotion to his duty. All work becomes equally and vitally important. It is only toward the results of work—success or failure, praise or blame—that he remains indifferent. When action is done in this spirit, Krishna teaches, it will lead us to the knowledge of what lies behind action, behind all life: the ultimate Reality.[10]

The final selection on Stoicism is a modern poem that voices an attitude many Stoics had toward death. We cannot live forever; that is beyond our power. Nor can we always choose when and how we shall die; that too is not up to us. But while we must die, there is no necessity that we die badly, in terror or despair, and in many cases we can die nobly in the manner demanded by our own integrity, with an appropriateness to the circumstances that evinces the "moral beauty" so prized by Stoics.

PLATONISM

One of the best known efforts to find some redeeming point in the face of what is thought to be an alien and hostile universe is that of the great English philosopher Bertrand Russell (1872–1970) in his famous essay "A Free Man's Worship," first published in 1903. To one who comes to this essay after reading Epictetus, the elements of Stoicism in it are quite striking. People have control only over their inner lives, Russell contends, and in this freedom "to criticize, to know, and in imagination to create is [man's] superiority to the restless forces that control his outward life." Renunciation of material desires and indignant passions is still another Stoic theme. But there are also in this essay overtones of the grand tradition of Western thought that begins with Plato, particularly in Russell's urge to "burn with passion for eternal things." (The Platonism implicit in this essay is made explicit in some of Russell's other writings.)

One of Plato's most important doctrines is that there exists an intelligible world available to our minds but not perceivable by our senses. Indeed, this world of eternal "Forms," or conceptual prototypes, is the true object of all genuine theoretical knowledge. Geometry, for example, is about dimensionless points and one-dimensional lines, but there are no such "objects" in the world revealed to us by our senses, only crude marks made with pencil or chalk, "points" that have dimensions, and "lines" made of dust particles of irregular shapes. Mathematical truths are not *about* the things we see, although obviously they can be given useful application to the empirical world. Rather they are about a mathematical realm of "ideas" or "forms" that is only imperfectly exemplified in experience. This realm of forms is located no place in space or time. The forms are literally "eternal," that is, not in time at all. There is no time at which five plus seven began to equal twelve, and there will never be a time at which the Pythagorean theorem will cease to be correct. These are therefore "eternal truths." Indeed there is a sense in which *all* truths are both eternal and aspatial. A sentence written in symbols or spoken in words comes into existence at a place and time and ceases to be after it is uttered or erased, but the proposition asserted by the words, that which the words *mean,* exists at no particular place in space, and never begins or ceases to exist. It is the sort of entity with which our minds can come into contact in thought, but which our senses alone can never discover. There is a sense then in which it is "more real" than the transitory events and objects of sense experience. And just as a meaning is that which is common to many different and spoken sentences though not to be identified with any one of them, so a concept is something general or abstract shared in common

by many individual or particular things. Redness is what this, that, and the other red thing have in common and treeness is what this, that, and the other trees share, that which makes them intelligible to us as trees. Redness, treeness, dogness, humanness, are among the objects of our thought when we reason about physics, botany, zoology, and psychology. They are no more located in some particular place or vulnerable to the corrosion of time than are points, lines, and (say) the number five.

Eternal objects, therefore, have a fundamental kind of existence, if anything *more real* than that of things that exist in space and time. Eternal existence, in this Platonic sense, is not mere everlastingness. An everlasting thing, if there were such, would exist in time *immortally,* that is, never ceasing to exist. But Platonic eternity has nothing to do with time in the first place, and it doesn't even make sense to say that an eternal object could "cease to exist." When a free human being employs his or her rational faculties to "criticize, know, and in imagination create," he or she then comes into direct contact with eternal reality in the Forms, or ultimate objects, of thought. These include not only propositions, mathematical entities, and scientific concepts, but also the forms of Goodness and Beauty themselves whose direct apprehension in moral theory and aesthetic experience is, for a Platonist, the highest pitch of human achievement and the key to the meaning of the world. To live forever in time would be as nothing compared to being in direct contact for a moment with eternity.

ROMANTICISM

"Sensitive, emotional, preferring color to form, the exotic to the familiar, eager for novelty, for adventure, above all for the vicarious adventure of fantasy, reveling in disorder and uncertainty, insistent on the uniqueness of the individual to the point of making a virtue of eccentricity, the typical Romantic will hold that he cannot be typical, for the very concept of the 'typical' suggests the work of the pigeonholing intellect he scorns."[11] What greater contrast could be imagined to the Epicurean, the Stoic, and the Platonist! Epicurus, Lucretius, and Housman would have us renounce worldly desires, moderate our appetites, extinguish our emotions, all for the sake of avoiding distress and insecurity. The Romantic, on the contrary, lives to the hilt, throws caution to the winds, and cultivates grand passions even though he or she must live dangerously to do so. Epictetus remains "non-attached" to the fruits of his actions and teaches himself not to care about the external events of his world. The Romantic, on the contrary, packs into his or her consciousness as much of the world as possible—variegated images, the "ecstasy and sorrow" of love, enthusiasms of every kind. To live without truly caring about the things that are beyond one's control, and without feeling deeply, indeed as deeply as possible, is to a Romantic to live as an inhuman automaton. Platonists dwell on abstractions. Romantics, on the contrary, glorify their uniqueness, celebrate their particularity, and think of particulars as the true stuff of reality.

Perhaps "Romanticism," unlike the schools discussed earlier, is less a specific set of doctrines than a characteristic temperament uniting a disparate set of artists, critics, poets, and philosophers among whom there is, otherwise, only a family resemblance. In any case the appeal of the romantic mood (if that is all it is) is nowhere more effectively transmitted than in the concluding chapter of *The Renaissance* by the British art critic Walter Pater (1839–1894). But there is also a genuinely philosophical doctrine in that essay that the "reality" and ultimate value of life is to be found in the immediacy of one's experience, itself a continuous flow or (in Pater's other metaphor) a burning flame whose nature can only be falsified and destroyed by the analytic intellect that attempts to capture it in general concepts.

EXISTENTIALISM

Existentialism is the hardest of all the "isms" in this section to define, being merely a label for certain tendencies common to writers of quite diverse views. (See also the introduction to chapter 3, pp. 124–125.) Walter Kaufmann has noticed that these writers (like the nineteenth-century Romanticists) tend to be a highly individualistic lot, many or most of whom object to all ism-labels, including even "Existentialism." Half seriously, he suggests that all

they have in common is "a marked aversion for each other."[12] There have been important Catholic (Gabriel Marcel), Protestant (Karl Jaspers), and Jewish (Martin Buber) writers who are commonly called "Existentialists," but perhaps the best known to the general public are the out and out Atheists, Jean-Paul Sartre (1905–) and Albert Camus (1913–1960). Both of these writers were gifted literary men whose philosophies were often expressed in stories, novels, and plays.

The concept of the absurd is the key Existentialist idea. In other writings Sartre has described what he takes to be a kind of metaphysical absurdity. Being or existence as such, abstracted from the characteristics of the various things that do exist, is "just there," oppressively dense to our insight and purpose, contingent, uncreated, ultimately inexplicable. Only those objects on which we have artificially imposed our concepts or purposes seem at all intelligible. But as soon as we look beyond those features we have projected into the world, to pure being, or being *en soi* (in itself) we find "absurdity," and that discovery can make the head swim with the "existential emotions" Sartre describes so vividly in his novel, *Nausea*.

There is also a kind of *moral* absurdity in the human condition. Persons have another kind of being from that of mere things. We exist *pour soi* (for oneself) in that we are aware of ourselves and can make choices. Indeed we cannot avoid making choices, since in most circumstances not to choose is itself a kind of choice. Our freedom to choose, however, is a kind of absurdity, since in our most important practical dilemmas there is no criterion of rational choice available for us to apply, no preestablished valid moral principles, no external realm of values. In short, it is false that there is always a "sufficient reason" for choosing one way or another; yet we *must* choose, for all that, since the alternative results cannot be a matter of indifference. So the crucial choices of life and death must be "existential leaps" in the dark. In that way we *create* our values, formulate our principles, and determine our characters. The responsibility is chilling; the freedom is dreadful; the situation at once inescapable and absurd. And to make it worse, having to decide in partial ignorance of the likely consequences renders us vulnerable to perverse twists of fate that can defeat our purposes altogether, and that is absurdity compounded.

Yet the Existentialist heroes and heroines do not renounce the world. Like the Stoics they treasure their personal integrity far more than the consequences (in that absurd external world) of their choices, and also like the Stoics, they act without hope, knowing that they must be beaten in the end. Their commitment to the world is something they welcome and devote themselves to, even though it is ultimately as groundless and non-rational as the existence of the world itself. Unlike the Stoics (and more like the Romantics) they do *care* about things; they commit their emotions to the (otherwise) groundless values they have themselves created. But "romantic" is a term of disparagement in the Existentialist's vocabulary. The Extentialist acts entirely without illusions: no *Don Quixote* he (except for his unavoidable absurdity). Life is not an exciting adventure tale full of noble pursuit of noble ideals. On the contrary, it is necessary to look absurdity right in the face without flinching and take one's leap. "Life," writes Camus, "is all the better if it has no meaning." The Existentialist dies unreconciled, proud, and scornful. (Some unsympathetic critics find this picture itself somewhat "romantic" in the very sense disparaged by Existentialists, since it is more than a little self-celebrating and self-glorifying, in the style of the heroes of adventurous romance.)

SELF-REALIZATION

The ancient Greek myth of Sisyphus, condemned by the gods to spend eternity repeatedly pushing a huge boulder up to the top of a hill from which it rolls down again, was thought by Camus to be a very exact symbol of the absurdity of human life and work. It is easy enough for most of us to recall moods in which that symbolism was applicable. People stand in line in supermarkets to purchase food which they need to stay alive and healthy, in order that they might work, in order that they might get money, in order, once more, that they might shop for food, and so on, around the circle again and again. We clean up our dishes and our homes and instantly get them dirty again, to be cleaned up once more, and so on. Richard Taylor, of the University of Rochester, finds it easy to share

Camus' insight that all human life exhibits that same futility, especially when our lives are viewed from some distance or from a hypothetical judgment place in future time. But Taylor adds a twist to the old legend. He has us imagine that the gods "wax perversely merciful" and implant in Sisyphus a compulsive urge to push large boulders or, to vary the supposition, that they designed him in the first place so that it is *in his nature* to push stones. Taylor's hypothetical deity would be merciful, he thinks, because there are inherent rewards in doing what comes naturally. But nevertheless, Taylor shares Camus' view that even in the amended version of the legend, Sisyphus' activity, his life, his inherited "nature," his very existence would still be absurd, without rhyme or reason.

Taylor's view thus combines the Existentialist's perception of absurdity with a very ancient and optimistic conception of the good life, unrepresented in this collection, because of its difficult philosophical technicalities. That tradition derives from Aristotle (B.C. 384–322) and was adapted to Christian teachings in the system of the thirteenth-century philosopher, St. Thomas Aquinas. Every basic species, according to Aristotle, has an essence (properties that make it the sort of thing it is and not another sort of thing), and an end (*telos*) or goal, the achievement of which constitutes its own highest good. Thus, the essential human attributes of rational animality (and all that they imply) are realized most fully in a human life that achieves its natural end, which Aristotle described as a full lifetime of vigorous self-fulfilling activity performed with excellence. The "good for man," then, is a life that actualizes people's distinctively human capacities, discharges their inherited propensities, and converts their highest potential into something actual. It is, in short, the life of *fulfillment,* something essentially different from mere enjoyment (which can be utterly passive, as in drug-induced euphoria), though it can yield enjoyment as a kind of byproduct. Aristotle found nothing absurd in human existence, differing in that respect from Taylor and Camus, but he would agree emphatically with Taylor that the good life (absurd or not) is that in which people succed to the fullest extent in doing that which is in their (highest) nature to do.

Joel Feinberg

NOTES

1. John Hick, "Christianity," in *The Encyclopedia of Philosophy,* edited by Paul Edwards (New York: Macmillan, 1967), p. 107.

2. Arthur Balfour, *Foundations of Belief* (London, 1895), pp. 29–31.

3. Kurt Baier, *The Meaning of Life,* Inaugural Lecture, Canberra University College, 1957, p. 20.

4. Anthony Kenny, "Happiness," *Proceedings of the Aristotelian Society* 66 (1965–66). Reprinted in *Moral Concepts,* edited by Joel Feinberg (London: Oxford University Press, 1969), p. 48.

5. Charles L. Stevenson, *Ethics and Language* (New Haven, Conn.: Yale University Press, 1944), p. 203.

6. See especially R. W. Hepburn, "Questions About the Meaning of Life," *Religious Studies,* Vol. I (1966), pp. 125–40.

7. Bertrand Russell, *A History of Western Philosophy* (New York: Simon & Schuster, 1945), p. 244.

8. William DeWitt Hyde, *The Five Great Philosophies of Life* (New York: Macmillan, 1952), p. 22. The student was Thomas B. Reed, who later became Speaker of the U.S. House of Representatives.

9. Bertrand Russell, *History of Western Philosophy,* pp. 268–69.

10. Swami Prabhavananda and Christopher Isherwood, *The Song of God, Bhagavad-Gita* (New York: New American Library, 1944), Appendix II, "The Gita and War," p. 139.

11. Crane Brinton, "Romanticism," in *The Encyclopedia of Philosophy,* edited by Paul Edwards (New York: Macmillan, 1967), p. 206.

12. Walter Kaufmann, *Existentialism from Dostoievsky to Sartre* (New York: Meridian Books, 1957), p. 11.

86. *THE VANITY OF EXISTENCE*

Arthur Schopenhauer

This vanity finds expression in the whole way in which things exist; in the infinite nature of Time and Space, as opposed to the finite nature of the individual in both; in the ever-passing present moment as the only mode of actual existence; in the interdependence and relativity of all things; in continual Becoming without ever Being; in constant wishing and never being satisfied; in the long battle which forms the history of life, where every effort is checked by difficulties, and stopped until they are overcome. Time is that in which all things pass away; it is merely the form under which the will to live—the thing-in-itself and therefore imperishable—has revealed to it that its efforts are in vain; it is that agent by which at every moment all things in our hands become as nothing, and lose any real value they possess.

That which *has been* exists no more; it exists as little as that which has *never* been. But of everything that exists you must say, in the next moment, that it has been. Hence something of great importance now past is inferior to something of little importance now present, in that the latter is a *reality,* and related to the former as something to nothing.

A man finds himself, to his great astonishment, suddenly existing, after thousands and thousands of years of non-existence: he lives for a little while; and then, again, comes an equally long period when he must exist no more. The heart rebels against this, and feels that it cannot be true. The crudest intellect cannot speculate on such a subject without having a presentiment that Time is something ideal in its nature. This ideality of Time and Space is the key to every true system of metaphysics; because it provides for quite another order of things than is to be met with in the domain of nature. This is why Kant is so great.

Of every event in our life we can say only for one moment that it *is;* for ever after, that it *was.* Every evening we are poorer by a day. It might, perhaps, make us mad to see how rapidly our short span of time ebbs away, if it were not that in the furthest depths of our being we are secretly conscious of our share in the exhaustible spring of eternity, so that we can always hope to find life in it again.

Consideration of the kind, touched on above, might, indeed, lead us to embrace the belief that the greatest *wisdom* is to make the enjoyment of the present the supreme object of life; because that is the only reality, all else being merely the play of thought. On the other hand, such a course might just as well be called the greatest *folly:* for that which in the next moment exists no more, and vanishes utterly, like a dream, can never be worth a serious effort.

The whole foundation on which our existence rests is the present—the ever-fleeting present. It lies, then, in the very nature of our existence to take the form of constant motion, and to offer no possibility of our ever attaining the rest for which we are always striving. We are like a man running downhill, who cannot keep on his legs unless he runs on, and will inevitably fall if he stops; or, again, like a pole balanced on the tip of one's finger; or like a planet, which would fall into its sun the moment it ceased to hurry forward on its way. Unrest is the mark of existence.

In a world where all is unstable, and nought can endure, but is swept onwards at once in the hurrying whirlpool of change; where a man, if he is to keep erect at all, must always be advancing and moving, like an acrobat on a rope—in such a world, happiness is inconceivable. How can it dwell where, as Plato says, *continual Becoming and never Being* is the sole form of existence? In the first place, a man never is happy, but spends his whole life in striving after something which he thinks will make him so; he seldom attains his goal, and when

From "The Vanity of Existence," by Arthur Schopenhauer, in *The Essays of Arthur Schopenhauer,* translated by T. Bailey Saunders, 1951. Reprinted with the permission of George Allen & Unwin Ltd.

he does, it is only to be disappointed; he is mostly shipwrecked in the end, and comes into harbor with masts and rigging gone. And then, it is all one whether he has been happy or miserable; for his life was never anything more than a present moment always vanishing; and now it is over.

At the same time it is a wonderful thing that, in the world of human beings as in that of animals in general, this manifold restless motion is produced and kept up by the agency of two simple impulses —hunger and the sexual instinct; aided a little, perhaps, by the influence of boredom, but by nothing else; and that, in the theatre of life, these suffice to form the *primum mobile* of how complicated a machinery, setting in motion how strange and varied a scene!

On looking a little closer, we find that inorganic matter presents a constant conflict between chemical forces, which eventually works dissolution; and on the other hand, that organic life is impossible without continual change of matter, and cannot exist if it does not receive perpetual help from without. This is the realm of *finality;* and its opposite would be *an infinite existence,* exposed to no attack from without, and needing nothing to support it; the realm of eternal peace; some timeless, changeless state, one and undiversified; the negative knowledge of which forms the dominant note of the Platonic philosophy. It is to some such state as this that the denial of the will to live opens up the way.

The scenes of our life are like pictures done in rough mosaic. Looked at close, they produce no effect. There is nothing beautiful to be found in them, unless you stand some distance off. So, to gain anything we have longed for is only to discover how vain and empty it is; and even though we are always living in expectation of better things, at the same time we often repent and long to have the past back again. We look upon the present as something to be put up with while it lasts, and serving only as the way towards our goal. Hence most people, if they glance back when they come to the end of life, will find that all along they have been living *ad interim:* they will be surprised to find that the very thing they disregarded and let slip by unenjoyed, was just the life in the expectation of which they passed all their time. Of how many a man may it not

be said that hope made a fool of him until he danced into the arms of death!

Then again, how insatiable a creature is man! Every satisfaction he attains lays the seeds of some new desire, so that there is no end to the wishes of each individual will. And why is this? The real reason is simply that, taken in itself, Will is the lord of all worlds: everything belongs to it, and therefore no one single thing can ever give it satisfaction, but only the whole, which is endless. For all that, it must rouse our sympathy to think how very little the Will, this lord of the world, really gets when it takes the form of an individual; usually only just enough to keep the body together. This is why man is so very miserable.

Life presents itself chiefly as a task—the task, I mean, of subsisting at all, *gagner sa vie.* If this is accomplished, life is a burden, and then there comes the second task of doing something with that which has been won—of warding off boredom, which, like a bird of prey, hovers over us, ready to fall wherever it sees a life secure from need. The first task is to win something; the second, to banish the feeling that it has been won; otherwise it is a burden.

Human life must be some kind of mistake. The truth of this will be sufficiently obvious if we only remember that man is a compound of needs and necessities hard to satisfy; and that even when they are satisfied, all he obtains is a state of painlessness, where nothing remains to him but abandonment to boredom. This is direct proof that existence has no real value in itself; for what is boredom but the feeling of the emptiness of life? If life—the craving for which is the very essence of our being—were possessed of any positive intrinsic value, there would be no such thing as boredom at all: mere existence would satisfy us in itself, and we should want for nothing. But as it is, we take no delight in existence except when we are struggling for something; and then distance and difficulties to be overcome make our goal look as though it would satisfy us—an illusion which vanishes when we reach it; or else when we are occupied with some purely intellectual interest—when in reality we have stepped forth from life to look upon it from the outside, much after the manner of spectators at a play. And even sensual pleasure itself means nothing but a struggle and aspiration, ceasing the moment its aim is attained. Whenever we are not occupied in one of these ways, but cast upon existence itself, its vain and worthless nature is brought home to us; and this is what we mean by boredom. The hankering after what is strange and uncommon —an innate and ineradicable tendency of human nature—shows how glad we are at any interruption of that natural course of affairs which is so very tedious.

That this most perfect manifestation of the will to live, the human organism, with the cunning and complex working of its machinery, must fall to dust and yield up itself and all its strivings to extinction —this is the naive way in which Nature, who is always so true and sincere in what she says, proclaims the whole struggle of this will as in its very essence barren and unprofitable. Were it of any value in itself, anything unconditioned and abso-lute, it could not thus end in mere nothing.

If we turn from contemplating the world as a whole, and, in particular, the generations of men as they live their little hour of mock-existence and then are swept away in rapid succession; if we turn from this, and look at life in its small details, as presented, say, in a comedy, how ridiculous it all seems! It is like a drop of water seen through a microscope, a single drop teeming with *infusoria;* or a speck of cheese full of mites invisible to the naked eye. How we laugh as they bustle about so eagerly, and struggle with one another in so tiny a space! And whether here, or in the little span of human life, this terrible activity produces a comic effect.

It is only in the microscope that our life looks so big. It is an indivisible point, drawn out and magnified by the powerful lenses of Time and Space.

Epicureanism

87. THE RUBAIYAT

Omar Khayyam

VII

Come, fill the Cup, and in the fire of Spring
Your Winter-garment of Repentance fling:
  The Bird of Time has but a little way
To flutter—and the Bird is on the Wing. . . .

XII

A Book of Verses underneath the Bough,
A Jug of Wine, a Loaf of Bread—and Thou
  Beside me singing in the Wilderness—
Oh, Wilderness were Paradise enow!

XIII

Some for the Glories of This World; and some
Sigh for the Prophet's Paradise to come;
  Ah, take the Cash, and let the Credit go,
Nor heed the rumble of a distant Drum! . . . .

XVI

The Worldly Hope men set their Hearts upon
Turns Ashes—or it prospers; and anon,
  Like Snow upon the Desert's dusty Face,
Lighting a little hour or two—is gone.

XVII

Think, in this batter'd Caravanserai
Whose Portals are alternate Night and Day,
  How Sultán after Sultán with his Pomp
Abode his destined Hour, and went his way. . . .

From *The Rubaiyat* of Omar Khayyam, translated by Edward Fitzgerald. Fifth edition of the translation, 1879.

XXI

Ah, my Belovéd, fill the Cup that clears
TO-DAY of Past Regrets and Future Fears:
  To-morrow!—Why, To-morrow I may be
Myself with Yesterday's Sev'n Thousand Years.

XXII

For some we loved, the loveliest and the best
That from his Vintage rolling Time hath prest,
  Have drunk their Cup a Round or two before,
And one by one crept silently to rest.

XXIII

And we, that now make merry in the Room
They left, and Summer dresses in new bloom
  Ourselves must we beneath the Couch of Earth
Descend—ourselves to make a Couch—for whom?

XXIV

Ah, make the most of what we yet may spend,
Before we too into the Dust descend;
  Dust into Dust, and under Dust to lie
Sans Wine, sans Song, sans Singer, and—sans End!

XXV

Alike for those who for TO-DAY prepare,
And those that after some TO-MORROW stare,
  A Muezzín from the Tower of Darkness cries
"Fools! your Reward is neither Here nor There."

XXVII

Myself when young did eagerly frequent
Doctor and Saint, and heard great argument
  About it and about: but evermore
Came out by the same door where in I went.

XXVIII

With them the seed of Wisdom did I sow,
And with mine own hand wrought to make it grow;
  And this was all the Harvest that I reap'd—
"I came like Water, and like Wind I go."

XXIX

Into this Universe, and *Why* not knowing
Nor *Whence,* like Water willy-nilly flowing;
  And out of it, as Wind along the Waste,
I know not *Whither,* willy-nilly blowing. . . .

XXXV

Then to the lip of this poor earthen Urn
I lean'd, the Secret of my Life to learn:
  And Lip to Lip it murmur'd—"While you live
Drink!—for, once dead, you never shall return. . ."

LXIII

Oh, threats of Hell and Hopes of Paradise!
One thing at least is certain—*This* Life flies;
  One thing is certain and the rest is Lies;
The Flower that once has blown for ever dies.

LXIV

Strange, is it not? that of the myriads who
Before us pass'd the door of Darkness through,
  Not one returns to tell us of the Road,
Which to discover we must travel too. . . .

LXVII

Heav'n but the Vision of fulfill'd Desire,
And Hell the Shadow from a Soul on fire,
  Cast on the Darkness into which Ourselves,
So late emerged from, shall so soon expire.

LXVIII

We are no other than a moving row
Of Magic Shadow-shapes that come and go
  Round with the Sun-illumined Lantern held
In Midnight by the Master of the Show;

LXIX

But helpless Pieces of the Game He plays
Upon this Chequer-board of Nights and Days;
  Hither and thither moves, and checks, and slays,
And one by one back in the Closet lays.

LXXI

The Moving Finger writes; and, having writ,
Moves on: nor all your Piety nor Wit
  Shall lure it back to cancel half a Line,
Nor all your Tears wash out a Word of it.

LXXII

And that inverted Bowl they call the Sky,
Whereunder crawling coop'd we live and die,
  Lift not your hands to *It* for help—for It
As impotently moves as you or I.

LXXIII

With Earth's first Clay They did the Last Man
knead,
And there of the Last Harvest sow'd the Seed:
  And the first Morning of Creation wrote
What the Last Dawn of Reckoning shall read.

LXXIV

YESTERDAY *This* Day's Madness did prepare;
TO-MORROW'S Silence, Triumph, or Despair:
  Drink! for you know not whence you came, nor
why;
Drink! for you know not why you go, nor where.

88. A SHROPSHIRE LAD

A. E. Housman

LXII

"Terence, this is stupid stuff:
You eat your victuals fast enough;
There can't be much amiss, 'tis clear,
To see the rate you drink your beer.
But oh, good Lord, the verse you make,
It gives a chap the belly-ache.
The cow, the old cow, she is dead;
It sleeps well, the hornéd head:
We poor lads, 'tis our turn now
To hear such tunes as killed the cow.
Pretty friendship 'tis to rhyme
Your friends to death before their time
Moping melancholy mad:
Come, pipe a tune to dance to, lad."

Why, if 'tis dancing you would be,
There's brisker pipes than poetry.

From A. E. Housman, *Collected Poems*. Reprinted by permission of The Society of Authors, Jonathan Cape Ltd., and Holt Rinehart & Winston, Inc.

Say, for what were hop-yards meant,
Or why was Burton* built on Trent?
Oh many a peer of England brews
Livelier liquor than the Muse,
And malt does more than Milton can
To justify God's ways to man.
Ale, man, ale's the stuff to drink
For fellows whom it hurts to think:
Look into the pewter pot
To see the world as the world's not.
And faith, 'tis pleasant till 'tis past:
The mischief is that 'twill not last.
Oh I have been to Ludlow fair
And left my necktie God knows where,
And carried half way home, or near,
Pints and quarts of Ludlow beer:
Then the world seemed none so bad,
And I myself a sterling lad;
And down in lovely muck I've lain,
Happy till I woke again.

*A beer-serving "pub." [ed.]

Then I saw the morning sky:
Heigho, the tale was all a lie;
The world, it was the old world yet,
I was I, my things were wet,
And nothing now remained to do
But begin the game anew.

Therefore, since the world has still
Much good, but much less good than ill,
And while the sun and moon endure
Luck's a chance, but trouble's sure,
I'd face it as a wise man would,
And train for ill and not for good.
'Tis true, the stuff I bring for sale
Is not so brisk a brew as ale:
Out of a stem that scored the hand
I wrung it in a weary land.
But take it: if the smack is sour,
The better for the embittered hour;
It should do good to heart and head
When your soul is in my soul's stead;

And I will friend you, if I may,
In the dark and cloudy day.

There was a king reigned in the East:
There, when kings will sit to feast,
They get their fill before they think
With poisoned meat and poisoned drink.
He gathered all that springs to birth
From the many-venomed earth;
First a little, thence to more,
He sampled all her killing store;
And easy, smiling, seasoned sound,
Sate the king when healths went round.
They put arsenic in his meat
And stared aghast to watch him eat;
They poured strychnine in his cup
And shook to see him drink it up:
They shook, they stared as white's their shirt:
Them it was their poison hurt.
—I tell the tale that I heard told.
Mithridates, he died old.

89. LUCRETIUS

George Santayana

. . . To say that the soul is material has a strange and barbarous sound to modern ears. We live after Descartes, who taught the world that the essence of the soul was consciousness; and to call consciousness material would be to talk of the blackness of white. But ancient usage gave the word soul a rather different meaning. The essence of the soul was not so much to be conscious as to govern the formation of the body, to warm, move, and guide it. And if we think of the soul exclusively in this light, it will not seem a paradox, it may even seem a truism, to say that the soul must be material. For how are we to conceive that preëxisting consciousness should govern the formation of the

body, move, warm, or guide it? A spirit capable of such a miracle would in any case not be human, but altogether divine. The soul that Lucretius calls material should not, then, be identified with consciousness, but with the ground of consciousness, which is at the same time the cause of life in the body. This he conceives to be a swarm of very small and volatile atoms, a sort of ether, resident in all living seeds, breathed in abundantly during life and breathed out at death.

Even if this theory were accepted, however, it would not prove the point which Lucretius has chiefly at heart, namely, that an after-life is impossible. The atoms of the soul are indestructible, like all atoms; and if consciousness were attached to the fortunes of a small group of them, or of one only (as Leibniz afterwards taught), consciousness would continue to exist after these atoms had escaped from the body and were shooting through

Reprinted by permission of the publishers from *Three Philosophical Poets: Lucretius, Dante, and Goethe,* by George Santayana, Cambridge, Mass.: Harvard University Press (Harvard Studies in Comparative Literature), copyright © 1910 by Harvard University; © renewed 1938 by George Santayana.

new fields of space. Indeed, they might be the more aroused by that adventure, as a bee might find the sky or the garden more exciting than the hive. All that Lucretius urges about the divisibility of the soul, its diffused bodily seat, and the perils it would meet outside fails to remove the ominous possibility that troubles him.

To convince us that we perish at death he has to rely on vulgar experience and inherent probability: what changes is not indestructible; what begins, ends; mental growth, health, sanity, accompany the fortunes of the body as a whole (not demonstrably those of the soul-atoms); the passions are relevant to bodily life and to an earthly situation; we should not be ourselves under a different mask or in a new setting; we remember no previous existence if we had one, and so, in a future existence, we should not remember this. These reflections are impressive, and they are enforced by Lucretius with his usual vividness and smack of reality. Nothing is proved scientifically by such a deliverance, yet it is good philosophy and good poetry; it brings much experience together and passes a lofty judgment upon it. The artist has his eye on the model; he is painting death to the life.

If these considerations succeed in banishing the dread of an after-life, there remains the distress which many feel at the idea of extinction; and if we have ceased to fear death, like Hamlet, for the dreams that may come after it, we may still fear death instinctively, like a stuck pig. Against this instinctive horror of dying Lucretius has many brave arguments. Fools, he says to us, why do you fear what never can touch you? While you still live, death is absent; and when you are dead, you are so dead that you cannot know you are dead, nor regret it. You will be as much at ease as before you were born. Or is what troubles you the childish fear of being cold in the earth, or feeling its weight stifling you? But you will not be there; the atoms of your soul—themselves unconscious—will be dancing in some sunbeam far away, and you yourself will be nowhere; you will absolutely not exist. Death is by definition a state that excludes experience. If you fear it, you fear a word.

To all this, perhaps, Memmius, or some other recalcitrant reader, might retort that what he shrank from was not the metaphysical state of being dead, but the very real agony of dying. Dying is

something ghastly, as being born is something ridiculous; and, even if no pain were involved in quitting or entering this world, we might still say what Dante's Francesca says of it: *Il modo ancor m' offende,*—"I shudder at the way of it." Lucretius, for his part, makes no attempt to show that everything is as it should be; and if our way of coming into this life is ignoble, and our way of leaving it pitiful, that is no fault of his nor of his philosophy. If the fear of death were merely the fear of dying, it would be better dealt with by medicine than by argument. There is, or there might be, an art of dying well, of dying painlessly, willingly, and in season,— as in those noble partings which Attic gravestones depict,—especially if we were allowed, as Lucretius would allow us, to choose our own time.

But the radical fear of death, I venture to think, is something quite different. It is the love of life. Epicurus, who feared life, seems to have missed here the primordial and colossal force he was fighting against. Had he perceived that force, he would have been obliged to meet it in a more radical way, by an enveloping movement, as it were, and an attack from the rear. The love of life is not something rational, or founded on experience of life. It is something antecedent and spontaneous. It is that Venus Genetrix which covers the earth with its flora and fauna. It teaches every animal to seek its food and its mate, and to protect its offspring; as also to resist or fly from all injury to the body, and most of all from threatened death. It is the original impulse by which good is discriminated from evil, and hope from fear.

Nothing could be more futile, therefore, than to marshal arguments against that fear of death which is merely another name for the energy of life, or the tendency to self-preservation. Arguments involve premises, and these premises, in the given case, express some particular form of the love of life; whence it is impossible to conclude that death is in no degree evil and not at all to be feared. For what is most dreaded is not the agony of dying, nor yet the strange impossibility that when we do not exist we should suffer for not existing. What is dreaded is the defeat of a present will directed upon life and its various undertakings. Such a present will cannot be argued away, but it may be weakened by contradictions arising within it, by the irony of experience, or by ascetic discipline. To introduce ascetic discipline, to bring out the irony of experience, to expose the self-contradictions of the will, would be the true means of mitigating the love of life; and if the love of life were extinguished, the fear of death, like smoke rising from that fire, would have vanished also.

Indeed, the force of the great passage against the fear of death, at the end of the third book of Lucretius, comes chiefly from the picture it draws of the madness of life. His philosophy deprecates covetousness, ambition, love, and religion; it takes a long step towards the surrender of life, by surrendering all in life that is ardent, on the ground that it is painful in the end and ignominious. To escape from it all is a great deliverance. And since genius must be ardent about something, Lucretius pours out his enthusiasm on Epicurus, who brought this deliverance and was the saviour of mankind. Yet this was only a beginning of salvation, and the same principles carried further would have delivered us from the Epicurean life and what it retained that was Greek and naturalistic: science, friendship, and the healthy pleasures of the body. Had it renounced these things also, Epicureanism would have become altogether ascetic, a thorough system of mortification, or the pursuit of death. To those who sincerely pursue death, death is no evil, but the highest good. No need in that case of elaborate arguments to prove that death should not be feared, because it is nothing; for in spite of being nothing—or rather because it is nothing—death can be loved by a fatigued and disillusioned spirit, just as in spite of being nothing—or rather because it is nothing—it must be hated and feared by every vigorous animal.

One more point, and I have done with this subject. Ancient culture was rhetorical. It abounded in ideas that are verbally plausible, and pass muster in a public speech, but that, if we stop to criticize them, prove at once to be inexcusably false. One of these rhetorical fallacies is the maxim that men cannot live for what they cannot witness. What does it matter to you, we may say in debate, what happened before you were born, or what may go on after you are buried? And the orator who puts such a challenge may carry the audience with him, and raise a laugh at the expense of human sincerity. Yet the very men who applaud are proud of their ancestors, care for the future of their children, and are very much interested in securing legally the execution of their last will and testament. What may go on after their death concerns them deeply, not because they expect to watch the event from hell or heaven, but because they are interested ideally in what that event shall be, although they are never to witness it. Lucretius himself, in his sympathy with nature, in his zeal for human enlightenment, in his tears for Iphigenia, long since dead, is not moved by the hope of observing, or the memory of having observed, what excites his emotion. He forgets himself. He sees the whole universe spread out in its true movement and proportions; he sees mankind freed from the incubus of superstition, and from the havoc of passion. The vision kindles his enthusiasm, exalts his imagination, and swells his verse into unmistakable earnestness.

If we follow Lucretius, therefore, in narrowing the sum of our personal fortunes to one brief and partial glimpse of earth, we must not suppose that we need narrow at all the sphere of our moral interests. On the contrary, just in proportion as we despise superstitious terrors and sentimental hopes, and as our imagination becomes self-forgetful, we shall strengthen the direct and primitive concern which we feel in the world and in what may go on there, before us, after us, or beyond our ken. If, like Lucretius and every philosophical poet, we range over all time and all existence, we shall forget our own persons, as he did, and even wish them to be forgotten, if only the things we care for may subsist or arise. He who truly loves God, says Spinoza, cannot wish that God should love him in return. One who lives the life of the universe cannot be much concerned for his own. After all, the life of the universe is but the locus and extension of ours. The atoms that have once served to produce life remain fit to reproduce it; and although the body they might animate later would be a new one, and would have a somewhat different career, it would not, according to Lucretius, be of a totally new species; perhaps not more unlike ourselves than we are unlike one another, or than each of us is unlike himself at the various stages of his life.

The soul of nature, in the elements of it, is then, according to Lucretius, actually immortal; only the human individuality, the chance composition of those elements, is transitory; so that, if a man could care for what happens to other men, for what befell him when young or what may overtake him when old, he might perfectly well care, on the same imaginative principle, for what may go on in the world for ever. The finitude and injustice of his personal life would be broken down; the illusion of selfishness would be dissipated; and he might say to himself, I have imagination, and nothing that is real is alien to me.

Stoicism

90. THE ENCHIRIDION

Epictetus

1. There are things which are within our power, and there are things which are beyond our power. Within our power are opinion, aim, desire, aversion, and, in one word, whatever affairs are our own. Beyond our power are body, property, reputation, office, and, in one word, whatever are not properly our own affairs.

Now the things within our power are by nature free, unrestricted, unhindered; but those beyond our power are weak, dependent, restricted, alien. Remember, then, that if you attribute freedom to things by nature dependent and take what belongs to others for your own, you will be hindered, you will lament, you will be disturbed, you will find fault both with gods and men. But if you take for your own only that which is your own and view what belongs to others just as it really is, then no one will ever compel you, no one will restrict you; you will find fault with no one, you will accuse no one, you will do nothing against your will; no one will hurt you, you will not have an enemy, nor will you suffer any harm.

Aiming, therefore, at such great things, remember that you must not allow yourself any inclination, however slight, toward the attainment of the others; but that you must entirely quit some of them, and for the present postpone the rest. But if you would have these, and possess power and wealth likewise, you may miss the latter in seeking

Reprinted from *The Enchiridion* by Epictetus, translated by Thomas W. Higginson (Indianapolis: Bobbs-Merrill, 1948).

the former; and you will certainly fail of that by which alone happiness and freedom are procured.

Seek at once, therefore, to be able to say to every unpleasing semblance, "You are but a semblance and by no means the real thing." And then examine it by those rules which you have; and first and chiefly by this: whether it concerns the things which are within our own power or those which are not; and if it concerns anything beyond our power, be prepared to say that it is nothing to you.

2. Remember that desire demands the attainment of that of which you are desirous; and aversion demands the avoidance of that to which you are averse; that he who fails of the object of his desires is disappointed; and he who incurs the object of his aversion is wretched. If, then, you shun only those undesirable things which you can control, you will never incur anything which you shun; but if you shun sickness, or death, or poverty, you will run the risk of wretchedness. Remove [the habit of] aversion, then, from all things that are not within our power, and apply it to things undesirable which are within our power. But for the present, altogether restrain desire; for if you desire any of the things not within our own power, you must necessarily be disappointed; and you are not yet secure of those which are within our power, and so are legitimate objects of desire. Where it is practically necessary for you to pursue or avoid anything, do even this with discretion and gentleness and moderation.

3. With regard to whatever objects either delight the mind or contribute to use or are tenderly beloved, remind yourself of what nature they are, beginning with the merest trifles: If you have a favorite cup, that it is but a cup of which you are fond of—for thus, if it is broken, you can bear it; if you embrace your child or your wife, that you embrace a mortal—and thus, if either of them dies, you can bear it.

4. When you set about any action, remind yourself of what nature the action is. If you are going to bathe, represent to yourself the incidents usual in the bath—some persons pouring out, others pushing in, others scolding, others pilfering. And thus you will more safely go about this action if you say to yourself, "I will now go to bathe and keep my own will in harmony with nature." And so with regard to every other action. For thus, if any impediment arises in bathing, you will be able to say, "It was not only to bathe that I desired, but to keep my will in harmony with nature; and I shall not keep it thus if I am out of humor at things that happen."

5. Men are disturbed not by things, but by the views which they take of things. Thus death is nothing terrible, else it would have appeared so to Socrates. But the terror consists in our notion of death, that it is terrible. When, therefore, we are hindered or disturbed, or grieved, let us never impute it to others, but to ourselves—that is, to our own views. It is the action of an uninstructed person to reproach others for his own misfortunes; of one entering upon instruction, to reproach himself; and one perfectly instructed, to reproach neither others nor himself.

6. Be not elated at any excellence not your own. If a horse should be elated, and say, "I am handsome," it might be endurable. But when you are elated and say, "I have a handsome horse," know that you are elated only on the merit of the horse. What then is your own? The use of the phenomena of existence. So that when you are in harmony with nature in this respect, you will be elated with some reason; for you will be elated at some good of your own.

7. As in a voyage, when the ship is at anchor, if you go on shore to get water, you may amuse yourself with picking up a shellfish or a truffle in your way, but your thought ought to be bent toward the ship, and perpetually attentive, lest the captain should call, and then you must leave all these things, that you may not have to be carried on board the vessel, bound like a sheep; thus likewise in life, if, instead of a truffle or shellfish, such a thing as a wife or a child be granted you, there is no objection; but if the captain calls, run to the ship, leave all these things, and never look behind. But if you are old, never go far from the ship, lest you should be missing when called for.

8. Demand not that events should happen as you wish; but wish them to happen as they do happen, and you will go on well.

9. Sickness is an impediment to the body, but not to the will unless itself pleases. Lameness is an impediment to the leg, but not to the will; and say this to yourself with regard to everything that happens. For you will find it to be an impediment to something else, but not truly to yourself.

10. Upon every accident, remember to turn toward yourself and inquire what faculty you have for its use. If you encounter a handsome person, you will find continence the faculty needed; if pain, then fortitude; if reviling, then patience. And when thus habituated, the phenomena of existence will not overwhelm you.

11. Never say of anything, "I have lost it," but, "I have restored it." Has your child died? It is restored. Has your wife died? She is restored. Has your estate been taken away? That likewise is restored. "But it was a bad man who took it." What is it to you by whose hands he who gave it has demanded it again? While he permits you to possess it, hold it as something not your own, as do travelers at an inn. . . .

14. If you wish your children and your wife and your friends to live forever, you are foolish, for you wish things to be in your power which are not so, and what belongs to others to be your own. So likewise, if you wish your servant to be without fault, you are foolish, for you wish vice not to be vice but something else. But if you wish not to be disappointed in your desires, that is in your own power. Exercise, therefore, what is in your power. A man's master is he who is able to confer or remove whatever that man seeks or shuns. Whoever then would be free, let him wish nothing, let

him decline nothing, which depends on others; else he must necessarily be a slave.

15. Remember that you must behave as at a banquet. Is anything brought round to you? Put our your hand and take a moderate share. Does it pass by you? Do not stop it. Is it not yet come? Do not yearn in desire toward it, but wait till it reaches you. So with regard to children, wife, office, riches; and you will some time or other be worthy to feast with the gods. . . .

16. When you see anyone weeping for grief, either that his son has gone abroad or that he has suffered in his affairs, take care not to be overcome by the apparent evil, but discriminate and be ready to say, "What hurts this man is not this occurrence itself—for another man might not be hurt by it—but the view he chooses to take of it." As far as conversation goes, however, do not disdain to accommodate yourself to him and, if need be, to groan with him. Take heed, however, not to groan inwardly, too.

17. Remember that you are an actor in a drama of such sort as the Author chooses—if short, then in a short one; if long, then in a long one. If it be his pleasure that you should enact a poor man, or a cripple, or a ruler, or a private citizen see that you act it well. For this is your business—to act well the given part, but to choose it belongs to another. . . .

19. You can be unconquerable if you enter into no combat in which it is not in your own power to conquer. When therefore, you see anyone eminent in honors or power, or in high esteem on any other account, take heed not to be bewildered by appearances and to pronounce him happy; for if the essence of good consists in things within our own power there will be no room for envy or emulation. But, for your part, do not desire to be a general, or a senator, or a consul, but to be free; and the only way to this is a disregard of things which lie not within our own power.

20. Remember that it is not he who gives abuse or blows, who affronts, but the view we take of these things as insulting. When, therefore, anyone provokes you, be assured that it is your own opinion which provokes you. Try, therefore, in the first place, not to be bewildered by appearances. For if you once gain time and respite, you will more easily command yourself.

21. Let death and exile, and all other things which appear terrible, be daily before your eyes, but death chiefly; and you will never entertain an abject thought, nor too eagerly covet anything. . . .

26. The will of nature may be learned from things upon which we are all agreed. As when our neighbor's boy has broken a cup, or the like, we are ready at once to say, "These are casualties that will happen"; be assured, then, that when your own cup is likewise broken, you ought to be affected just as when another's cup was broken. Now apply this to greater things. Is the child or wife of another dead? There is no one who would not say, "This is an accident of mortality." But if anyone's own child happens to die, it is immediately, "Alas! how wretched am I!" It should be always remembered how we are affected on hearing the same thing concerning others. . . .

29. In every affair consider what precedes and what follows, and then undertake it. Otherwise you will begin with spirit, indeed, careless of the consequences, and when these are developed, you will shamefully desist. "I would conquer at the Olympic Games." But consider what precedes and what follows, and then, if it be for your advantage, engage in the affair. You must conform to rules, submit to a diet, refrain from dainties; exercise your body, whether you choose it or not, at a stated hour, in heat and cold; you must drink no cold water, and sometimes no wine—in a word, you must give yourself up to your trainer as to a physician. Then, in the combat, you may be thrown into a ditch, dislocate your arm, turn your ankle, swallow an abundance of dust, receive stripes [for negligence], and, after all, lose the victory. When you have reckoned up all this, if your inclination still holds, set about the combat. Otherwise, take notice, you will behave like children who sometimes play wrestlers, sometimes gladiators, sometimes blow a trumpet, and sometimes act a tragedy, when they happen to have seen and admired these shows. Thus you too will be at one time a wrestler, and another a gladiator; now a philosopher, now an orator; but nothing in earnest. Like an ape you mimic all you see, and one thing after another is sure to please you, but is out of favor as soon as it becomes familiar. For you have never entered upon anything considerately; nor after having sur-

veyed and tested the whole matter, but carelessly, and with a halfway zeal. Thus some, when they have seen a philosopher and heard a man speaking like Euphrates[1]—though, indeed, who can speak like him?—have a mind to be philosophers, too. Consider first, man, what the matter is, and what your own nature is able to bear. If you would be a wrestler, consider your shoulders, your back, your thighs; for different persons are made for different things. Do you think that you can act as you do and be a philosopher, that you can eat, drink, be angry, be discontented, as you are now? You must watch, you must labor, you must get the better of certain appetites, must quit your acquaintances, be despised by your servant, be laughed at by those you meet; come off worse than others in everything—in offices, in honors, before tribunals. When you have fully considered all these things, approach, if you please—that is, if, by parting with them, you have a mind to purchase serenity, freedom, and tranquillity. If not, do not come hither; do not, like children, be now a philosopher, then a publican, then an orator, and then one of Caesar's officers. These things are not consistent. You must be one man, either good or bad. You must cultivate either your own reason or else externals; apply yourself either to things within or without you—that is, be either a philosopher or one of the mob.

30. Duties are universally measured by relations. Is a certain man your father? In this are implied taking care of him, submitting to him in all things, patiently receiving his reproaches, his correction. But he is a bad father. Is your natural tie, then, to a *good* father? No, but to a father. Is a brother unjust? Well, preserve your own just relation toward him. Consider not what *he* does, but what *you* are to do to keep your own will in a state conformable to nature, for another cannot hurt you unless you please. You will then be hurt when you consent to be hurt. In this manner, therefore, if you accustom yourself to contemplate the relations of neighbor, citizen, commander, you can deduce from each the corresponding duties. . . .

32. When you have recourse to divination, remember that you know not what the event will be, and you come to learn it of the diviner; but of what nature it is you knew before coming; at least, if you are of philosophic mind. For if it is among the things not within our own power, it can by no means be either good or evil. Do not, therefore, bring with you to the diviner either desire or aversion—else you will approach him trembling—but first clearly understand that every event is indifferent and nothing to *you,* of whatever sort it may be; for it will be in your power to make a right use of it, and this no one can hinder. . . .

33. . . . It is not necessary for you to appear often at public spectacles; but if ever there is a proper occasion for you to be there, do not appear more solicitous for any other than for yourself—that is, wish things to be only just as they are, and only the best man to win; for thus nothing will go against you. But abstain entirely from acclamations and derision and violent emotions. And when you come away, do not discourse a great deal on what has passed and what contributes nothing to your own amendment. For it would appear by such discourse that you were dazzled by the show. . . .

34. If you are dazzled by the semblance of any promised pleasure, guard yourself against being bewildered by it; but let the affair wait your leisure, and procure yourself some delay. Then bring to your mind both points of time—that in which you shall enjoy the pleasure, and that in which you will repent and reproach yourself, after you have enjoyed it—and set before you, in opposition to these, how you will rejoice and applaud yourself if you abstain. And even though it should appear to you a seasonable gratification, take heed that its enticements and allurements and seductions may not subdue you, but set in opposition to this how much better it is to be conscious of having gained so great a victory.

35. When you do anything from a clear judgment that it ought to be done, never shrink from being seen to do it, even though the world should misunderstand it; for if you are not acting rightly, shun the action itself; if you are, why fear those who wrongly censure you? . . .

44. These reasonings have no logical connection: "I am richer than you, therefore I am your superior." "I am more eloquent than you, therefore I am your superior." The true logical connection is rather this: "I am richer than you, therefore my possessions must exceed yours." "I am more eloquent than you, therefore my style must surpass

yours." But you, after all, consist neither in property nor in style.

45. Does anyone bathe hastily? Do not say that he does it ill, but hastily. Does anyone drink much wine? Do not say that he does ill, but that he drinks a great deal. For unless you perfectly understand his motives, how should you know if he acts ill? Thus you will not risk yielding to any appearances but such as you fully comprehend. . . .

48. The condition and characteristic of a vulgar person is that he never looks for either help or harm from himself, but only from externals. The condition and characteristic of a philosopher is that he looks to himself for all help or harm. The marks of a proficient are that he censures no one, praises no one, blames no one, accuses no one; says nothing concerning himself as being anybody or knowing anything. When he is in any instance hindered or restrained, he accuses himself; and if he is praised, he smiles to himself at the person who praises him; and if he is censured, he makes no defense. But he goes about with the caution of a convalescent, careful of interference with anything that is doing well but not yet quite secure. He restrains desire; he transfers his aversion to those things only which thwart the proper use of our own will; he employs his energies moderately in all directions; if he appears stupid or ignorant, he does not care; and, in a word, he keep watch over himself as over an enemy and one in ambush.

49. When anyone shows himself vain on being able to understand and interpret the works of Chrysippus,[2] say to yourself: "Unless Chrysippus had written obscurely, this person would have had nothing to be vain of. But what do I desire? To understand nature, and follow her. I ask, then, who interprets her; and hearing that Chrysippus does, I have recourse to him. I do not understand his writ-

ings. I seek, therefore, one to interpret *them*." So far there is nothing to value myself upon. And when I find an interpreter, what remains is to make use of his instructions. This alone is the valuable thing. But if I admire merely the interpretation, what do I become more than a grammarian, instead of a philosopher, except, indeed, that instead of Homer I interpret Chrysippus? When anyone, therefore, desires me to read Chrysippus to him, I rather blush when I cannot exhibit actions that are harmonious and consonant with his discourse. . . .

51. . . . Upon all occasions we ought to have these maxims ready at hand:

Conduct me, Zeus, and thou, O Destiny,
Wherever your decrees have fixed my lot.
I follow cheerfully; and, did I not,
Wicked and wretched, I must follow still.[3]

Who'er yields properly to Fate is deemed
Wise among men, and knows the laws of Heaven.[4]

And this third:

"O Crito, if it thus pleases the gods, thus let it be."[5] "Anytus and Melitus may kill me indeed; but hurt me they cannot."[6]

NOTES

1. Euphrates was a philosopher of Syria, whose character is described, with the highest encomiums, by Pliny the Younger, *Letters* I. 10.
2. Chrysippus(*c.* 280–207 B.C.) was a philosopher whose works were generally accepted as the authoritative interpretation of orthodox Stoic philosophy.
3. Cleanthes, in Diogenes Laertius, quoted also by Seneca, *Epistle* 107.
4. Euripides, Fragments.
5. Plato, *Crito,* Chap. XVII.
6. Plato, *Apology,* Chap. XVIII.

91. THE BHAGAVAD-GITA

I. THE SORROW OF ARJUNA[1]

DHRITARASHTRA:

Tell me, Sanjaya, what my sons and the sons of Pandu did, when they gathered on the sacred field of Kurukshetra eager for battle?

(In the following verses, Sanjaya describes how Duryodhana, seeing the opposing army of Pandavas in array, went to Drona, his teacher, and expressed his fear that their own army was the weaker of the two, although numerically larger. He named the leading warriors on either side. This is one of the catalogue-passages to be found in nearly all epics. It need not be translated in full.

In order to raise Duryodhana's failing courage, Bhisma, the commander-in-chief, sounded his conch-shell horn. But this was ill-advised—for the enemy chieftains immediately blew their horns in reply, and made much more noise. The trumpeting 'resounded through heaven and earth,' we are told. Arjuna now addresses Krishna, his friend and charioteer.)

ARJUNA:

Krishna the changeless,
Halt my chariot
There where the warriors,
Bold for the battle,
Face their foemen.
Between the armies
There let me see them,
The men I must fight with,
Gathered together
Now at the bidding
Of him their leader,
Blind Dhritarashtra's
Evil offspring:
Such are my foes
In the war that is coming.

SANJAYA (TO DHRITARASHTRA):

Then Krishna, subduer of the senses, thus requested by Arjuna, the conqueror of sloth,[2] drove that most splendid of chariots into a place between the two armies, confronting Bhisma, Drona and all those other rulers of the earth. And he said: 'O Prince, behold the assembled Kurus!'

Then the prince looked on the array, and in both armies he recognized fathers and grandfathers, teachers, uncles, sons, brothers, grandsons, fathers-in-law, dear friends, and many other familiar faces.

When Kunti's son saw all those ranks of kinsmen he was filled with deep compassion, and he spoke despairingly, as follows:

ARJUNA:

Krishna, Krishna,
Now as I look on
These my kinsmen
Arrayed for battle,
My limbs are weakened,
My mouth is parching,
My body trembles,
My hair stands upright,
My skin seems burning,
The bow Gandiva
Slips from my hand,
My brain is whirling
Round and round,
I can stand no longer:
Krishna, I see such
Omens of evil!
What can we hope from
This killing of kinsmen?
What do I want with
Victory, empire,
Or their enjoyment?
O Govinda,[3]
How can I care for
Power or pleasure,
My own life, even,
When all these others,
Teachers, fathers,
Grandfathers, uncles,
Sons and brothers,
Husbands of sisters,
Grandsons and cousins,
For whose sake only
I could enjoy them

Reprinted from *The Song of God Bhagavad-Gita*. Translated by Swami Prabhavananda and Christopher Isherwood. Reprinted with the permission of the Vedanta Society of Southern California.

Stand here ready
To risk blood and wealth
In war against us?

Knower of all things,
Though they should slay me
How could I harm them?
I cannot wish it:
Never, never,
Not though it won me
The throne of the three worlds;
How much the less for
Earthly lordship!

Krishna, hearing
The prayers of all men,
Tell me how can
We hope to be happy
Slaying the sons
Of Dhritarashtra?
Evil they may be,
Worst of the wicked,
Yet if we kill them
Our sin is greater.
How could we dare spill
The blood that unites us?
Where is joy in
The killing of kinsmen?

Foul their hearts are
With greed, and blinded:
They see no evil
In breaking of blood-bonds,
See no sin
In treason to comrades.
But we, clear-sighted,
Scanning the ruin
Of families scattered,
Should we not shun
This crime, O Krishna?

We know what fate falls
On families broken:
The rites are forgotten,
Vice rots the remnant
Defiling the women,
And from their corruption
Comes mixing of castes:
The curse of confusion
Degrades the victims
And damns the destroyers.

The rice and the water
No longer are offered;
The ancestors also
Must fall dishonoured
From home in heaven.
Such is the crime
Of the killers of kinsmen:
The ancient, the sacred,
Is broken, forgotten.
Such is the doom
Of the lost, without caste-rites:
Darkness and doubting
And hell for ever.

What is the crime
I am planning, O Krishna?
Murder most hateful,
Murder of brothers!
Am I indeed
So greedy for greatness?

Rather than this
Let the evil children
Of Dhritarashtra
Come with their weapons
Against me in battle:
I shall not struggle,
I shall not strike them.
Now let them kill me,
That will be better.

SANJAYA:

Having spoken thus, Arjuna threw aside his arrows
and his bow in the midst of the battlefield. He sat
down on the seat of the chariot, and his heart was
overcome with sorrow.

II. THE YOGA OF KNOWLEDGE

SANJAYA:

Then his eyes filled with tears, and his heart grieved
and was bewildered with pity. And Sri Krishna
spoke to him, saying:

SRI KRISHNA:

Arjuna, is this hour of battle the time for scruples
and fancies? Are they worthy of you, who seek
enlightenment? Any brave man who merely hopes
for fame or heaven would despise them.

What is this weakness? It is beneath you. Is it for nothing men call you the foe-consumer? Shake off this cowardice, Arjuna. Stand up.

ARJUNA:

Bhisma and Drona are noble and ancient, worthy of the deepest reverence. How can I greet them with arrows, in battle? If I kill them, how can I ever enjoy my wealth, or any other pleasure? It will be cursed with blood-guilt. I would much rather spare them, and eat the bread of a beggar.

Which will be worse, to win this war, or to lose it? I scarcely know. Even the sons of Dhritarashtra stand in the enemy ranks. If we kill them, none of us will wish to live.

Is this real compassion that I feel, or only a delusion? My mind gropes about in darkness. I cannot see where my duty lies. Krishna, I beg you, tell me frankly and clearly what I ought to do. I am your disciple. I put myself into your hands. Show me the way.

Not this world's kingdom,
Supreme, unchallenged,
No, nor the throne
Of the gods in heaven,
Could ease this sorrow
That numbs my senses!

SANJAYA:

When Arjuna, the foe-consuming, the never-slothful, had spoken thus to Govinda, ruler of the senses, he added: 'I will not fight,' and was silent. . . .

III. KARMA YOGA

ARJUNA:

But, Krishna, if you consider knowledge of Brahman superior to any sort of action, why are you telling me to do these terrible deeds?

Your statements seem to contradict each other. They confuse my mind. Tell me one definite way of reaching the highest good.

SRI KRISHNA:

I have already told you that, in this world, aspirants may find enlightenment by two different paths. For the contemplative is the path of knowledge: for the active is the path of selfless action.

Freedom from activity is never achieved by abstaining from action. Nobody can become perfect by merely ceasing to act. In fact, nobody can ever rest from his activity[4] even for a moment. All are helplessly forced to act, by the gunas.

A man who renounces certain physical actions but still lets his mind dwell on the objects of his sensual desire, is deceiving himself. He can only be called a hypocrite. The truly admirable man controls his senses by the power of his will. All his actions are disinterested. All are directed along the path to union with Brahman.

Activity is better than inertia. Act, but with self-control. If you are lazy, you cannot even sustain your own body.

The world is imprisoned in its own activity, except when actions are performed as worship of God. Therefore you must perform every action sacramentally, and be free from all attachments to results. . . .

I established the four castes, which correspond to the different types of guna and karma. I am their author; nevertheless, you must realize that I am beyond action and changeless. Action does not contaminate me. I have no desire at all for the fruits of action. A man who understands my nature in this respect will never become the slave of his own activity. Because they understood this, the ancient seekers for liberation could safely engage in action. You, too, must do your work in the spirit of those early seers.

What is action? What is inaction? Even the wise are puzzled by this question. Therefore, I will tell you what action is. When you know that, you will be free from all impurity. You must learn what kind of work to do, what kind of work to avoid, and how to reach a state of calm detachment from your work. The real nature of action is hard to understand.

He who sees the inaction that is in action, and the action that is in inaction, is wise indeed. Even when he is engaged in action he remains poised in the tranquillity of the Atman.

The seers say truly
That he is wise
Who acts without lust or scheming
For the fruit of the act:

His act falls from him,
Its chain is broken,
Melted in the flame of my knowledge.
Turning his face from the fruit,
He needs nothing:
The Atman is enough.
He acts, and is beyond action.

Not hoping, not lusting,
Bridling body and mind,
He calls nothing his own:
He acts, and earns no evil.

What God's Will gives
He takes, and is contented.
Pain follows pleasure,
He is not troubled:
Gain follows loss,
He is indifferent:
Of whom should he be jealous?
He acts, and is not bound by his action.

When the bonds are broken
His illumined heart
Beats in Brahman:
His every action
Is worship of Brahman:
Can such acts bring evil?
Brahman is the ritual,
Brahman is the offering,
Brahman is he who offers
To the fire that is Brahman.
If a man sees Brahman
In every action,
He will find Brahman.[5] . . .

V. THE YOGA OF RENUNCIATION

ARJUNA:

You speak so highly of the renunciation of action;
yet you ask me to follow the yoga of action. Now
tell me definitely: which of these is better?

SRI KRISHNA:

Action rightly renounced brings freedom:
Action rightly performed brings freedom:
Both are better
Than mere shunning of action.

When a man lacks lust and hatred,
His renunciation does not waver.
He neither longs for one thing
Nor loathes its opposite:
The chains of his delusion
Are soon cast off.

The yoga of action, say the ignorant,
Is different from the yoga of the knowledge of
Brahman.

The wise see knowledge and action as one:
They see truly.
Take either path
And tread it to the end:
The end is the same.
There the followers of action
Meet the seekers after knowledge
In equal freedom.

It is hard to renounce action
Without following the yoga of action.
This yoga purifies
The man of meditation,
Bringing him soon to Brahman.

When the heart is made pure by that yoga,
When the body is obedient,
When the senses are mastered,
When man knows that his Atman
Is the Atman in all creatures,
Then let him act,
Untainted by action.

The illumined soul
Whose heart is Brahman's heart
Thinks always: 'I am doing nothing.'
No matter what he sees,
Hears, touches, smells, eats;
No matter whether he is moving,
Sleeping, breathing, speaking,
Excreting, or grasping something with his
hand,
Or opening his eyes,
Or closing his eyes:
This he knows always:
'I am not seeing, I am not hearing:
It is the senses that see and hear
And touch the things of the senses.'

He puts aside desire,
Offering the act to Brahman.

The lotus leaf rests unwetted on water:
He rests on action, untouched by action.

To the follower of the yoga of action,
The body and the mind,
The sense-organs and the intellect
Are instruments only:
He knows himself other than the instrument
And thus his heart grows pure.

United with Brahman,
Cut free from the fruit of the act,
A man finds peace
In the work of the spirit.
Without Brahman,
Man is a prisoner,
Enslaved by action,
Dragged onward by desire.

Happy is that dweller
In the city of nine gates[6]
Whose discrimination
Has cut him free from his act:
He is not involved in action,
He does not involve others.

Do not say:
'God gave us this delusion.'
You dream you are the doer,
You dream that action is done,
You dream that action bears fruit.
It is your ignorance,
It is the world's delusion
That gives you these dreams.

The Lord is everywhere
And always perfect:
What does He care for man's sin
Or the righteousness of man? . . .

XVIII. THE YOGA OF RENUNCIATION

ARJUNA:

I want to learn the truth about renunciation and non-attachment. What is the difference between these two principles?

SRI KRISHNA:

The sages tell us that renunciation means the complete giving-up of all actions which are motivated by desire. And they say that non-attachment means abandonment of the fruits of action.

Some philosophers declare that all kinds of action should be given up, because action always contains a certain measure of evil. Others say that acts of sacrifice, almsgiving and austerity should not be given up. Now you shall hear the truth of this matter.

Acts of sacrifice, almsgiving and austerity should not be given up: Their performance is necessary. For sacrifice, almsgiving and austerity are a means of purification to those who rightly understand them. But even these acts must be performed without attachment or regard for their fruits. Such is my final and considered judgment.

Renunciation is said to be of three kinds. If a man, in his ignorance, renounces those actions which the scriptures ordain, his renunciation is inspired by tamas. If he abstains from any action merely because it is disagreeable, or because he fears it will cause him bodily pain, his renunciation is inspired by rajas. He will not obtain any spiritual benefit from such renunciation. But when a man performs an action which is sanctioned by the scriptures, and does it for duty's sake only, renouncing all attachment and desire for its fruits, then his renunciation is inspired by sattwa.

When a man is endowed with spiritual discrimination and illumined by knowledge of the Atman, all his doubts are dispelled. He does not shrink from doing what is disagreeable to him, nor does he long to do what is agreeable. No human being can give up action altogether, but he who gives up the fruits of action is said to be non-attached.

To those who have not yet renounced the ego and its desires, action bears three kinds of fruit—pleasant, unpleasant, and a mixture of both. They will be reaped in due season. But those who have renounced ego and desire will reap no fruit at all, either in this world or in the next. . . .

NOTES

1. The accent is on the first syllable.
2. Arjuna is traditionally supposed to have lived entirely without sleep. We may take this to mean that he had overcome all forms of laziness.

3. One of the names of Sri Krishna, meaning Giver of Enlightenment.

4. Here 'activity' includes mental action, conscious and subconscious.

5. This verse is chanted by all Hindu monks as a grace before meals. In this case 'the fire' is regarded as the fire of hunger.

6. The human body.

92. THE CHOICE

Hilary Corke

I have known one bound to a bed by wrist and ankle,
Scarred by the whips of a wasting ache,
Who, at the point of entering of the needle,
Looked once around to take
The final view, then spoke;
The echo of that terribly witty joke
Pursued the surgeon to his home in Kew,
Deafened a nurse all night, and leaden lay
On the heart of a thick-skinned anesthetist
Long after they'd dispatched his ended clay.

That one lies in Oxford and is its earth.
Also, a bright-eyed woman in Germany,
In a sightless trap, far below ground,
Of which another held the key,
Surveyed without visible alarm
Or twitching of a pinioned arm
The instruments set out upon a table;
Then from her mouth there flowed a resolute
Stream of satire deliciously edged until
The tormentor tormented stopped it with a boot.

She fell as ash, not bones, in Herzen fields.
All brave men breathe her when the wind
Blows east from Danube. And Tom Caine,
When the Imperial was mined
And water had flooded all but the wireless room,
Spoke without audible gloom
From fifty fathoms down for fifteen hours
To his messmates on land, told several stories,
Then to a doctor carefully described
Asphyxiation's onset and his doom.

He is grown water and surrounds the pole
If ever you dip a cup in any sea
Tom Caine is in it somewhere. On the whole
Men die asleep or else disgracefully;
But not all men. Perhaps we are never,
By any average mountain, wood, or river,
More than a heart's breadth from the dust
Of one who laughed with nothing left to lose.
Who saw the joke beneath the mammoth's foot?
And what shall I choose, if I am free to choose?

Reprinted by permission; © 1961 The New Yorker Magazine, Inc.

93. *A FREE MAN'S WORSHIP*

Bertrand Russell

1. To Dr. Faustus in his study Mephistopheles told the history of the Creation, saying:

"The endless praises of the choirs of angels had begun to grow wearisome; for, after all, did he not deserve their praise? Had he not given them endless joy? Would it not be more amusing to obtain undeserved praise, to be worshipped by beings whom he tortured? He smiled inwardly, and resolved that the great drama should be performed.

"For countless ages the hot nebula whirled aimlessly through space. At length it began to take shape, the central mass threw off planets, the planets cooled, boiling seas and burning mountains heaved and tossed, from black masses of cloud hot sheets of rain deluged the barely solid crust. And now the first germ of life grew in the depths of the ocean, and developed rapidly in the fructifying warmth into vast forest trees, huge ferns springing from the damp mould, sea monsters breeding, fighting, devouring, and passing away. And from the monsters, as the play unfolded itself, Man was born, with the power of thought, the knowledge of good and evil, and the cruel thirst for worship. And Man saw that all is passing in this mad, monstrous world, that all is struggling to snatch, at any cost, a few brief moments of life before Death's inexorable decree. And Man said: 'There is a hidden purpose, could we but fathom it, and the purpose is good; for we must reverence something, and in the visible world there is nothing worthy of reverence.' And Man stood aside from the struggle, resolving that God intended harmony to come out of chaos by human efforts. And when he followed the instincts which God had transmitted to him from his ancestry of beasts of prey, he called it Sin, and asked God to forgive him. But he doubted whether he could be justly forgiven, until he invented a divine Plan by which God's wrath was to have been appeased. And seeing the present was bad, he made it yet worse, that thereby the future might be better. And he gave God thanks for the strength that enabled him to forgo even the joys that were possible. And God smiled, and when he saw that Man had become perfect in renunciation and worship, he sent another sun through the sky, which crashed into Man's sun; and all returned again to nebula.

" 'Yes,' he murmured, 'it was a good play; I will have it performed again.' "

Such, in outline, but even more purposeless, more void of meaning, is the world which Science presents for our belief. Amid such a world, if anywhere, our ideals henceforward must find a home. That Man is the product of causes which had no prevision of the end they were achieving; that his origin, his growth, his hopes and fears, his loves and his beliefs, are but the outcome of accidental collocations of atoms; that no fire, no heroism, no intensity of thought and feeling, can preserve an individual life beyond the grave; that all the labours of the ages, all the devotion, all the inspiration, all the noonday brightness of human genius, are destined to extinction in the vast death of the solar system, and that the whole temple of Man's achievement must inevitably be buried beneath the débris of a universe in ruins—all these things, if not quite beyond dispute, are yet so nearly certain, that no philosophy which rejects them can hope to stand. Only within the scaffolding of these truths, only on the firm foundation of unyielding despair, can the soul's habitation henceforth be safely built.

2. How, in such an alien and inhuman world, can so powerless a creature as Man preserve his aspirations untarnished? A strange mystery it is that Nature, omnipotent but blind, in the revolutions of her secular hurryings through the abysses of space, has brought forth at last a child, subject still to her power, but gifted with sight, with knowledge of

Reprinted from Bertrand Russell, *Mysticism and Logic,* pp. 46–57,© George Allen & Unwin, Ltd., 1963. Reprinted with the permission of George Allen & Unwin, Ltd., and Harper & Row Publishers, Inc., Barnes & Noble Books.

good and evil, with the capacity of judging all the works of his unthinking Mother. In spite of Death, the mark and seal of the parental control, Man is yet free, during his brief years, to examine, to criticise, to know, and in imagination to create. To him alone, in the world with which he is acquainted, this freedom belongs; and in this lies his superiority to the resistless forces that control his outward life. . . .

When first the opposition of fact and ideal grows fully visible, a spirit of fiery revolt, of fierce hatred of the gods, seems necessary to the assertion of freedom. To defy with Promethean constancy a hostile universe, to keep its evil always in view, always actively hated, to refuse no pain that the malice of Power can invent, appears to be the duty of all who will not bow before the inevitable. But indignation is still a bondage, for it compels our thoughts to be occupied with an evil world; and in the fierceness of desire from which rebellion springs there is a kind of self-assertion which it is necessary for the wise to overcome. Indignation is a submission of our thoughts, but not of our desires; the Stoic freedom in which wisdom consists is found in the submission of our desires, but not of our thoughts. From the submission of our desires springs the virtue of resignation; from the freedom of our thoughts springs the whole world of art and philosophy, and the vision of beauty by which, at last, we half reconquer the reluctant world. But the vision of beauty is possible only to unfettered contemplation, to thoughts not weighted by the load of eager wishes; and thus Freedom comes only to those who no longer ask of life that it shall yield them any of those personal goods that are subject to the mutations of Time.

Although the necessity of renunciation is evidence of the existence of evil, yet Christianity, in preaching it, has shown a wisdom exceeding that of the Promethean philosophy of rebellion. It must be admitted that, of the things we desire, some, though they prove impossible, are yet real goods; others, however, as ardently longed for, do not form part of a fully purified ideal. The belief that what must be renounced is bad, though sometimes false, is far less often false than untamed passion supposes; and the creed of religion, by providing a reason for proving that it is never false, has been the means of purifying our hopes by the discovery of many austere truths.

But there is in resignation a further good element: even real goods, when they are unattainable, ought not to be fretfully desired. To every man comes, sooner or later, the great renunciation. For the young, there is nothing unattainable; a good thing desired with the whole force of a passionate will, and yet impossible, is to them not credible. Yet, by death, by illness, by poverty, or by the voice of duty, we must learn, each one of us, that the world was not made for us, and that, however beautiful may be the things we crave, Fate may nevertheless forbid them. It is the part of courage, when misfortune comes, to bear without repining the ruin of our hopes, to turn away our thoughts from vain regrets. This degree of submission to Power is not only just and right: it is the very gate of wisdom.

3. But passive renunciation is not the whole of wisdom; for not by renunciation alone can we build a temple for the worship of our own ideals. Haunting foreshadowings of the temple appear in the realm of imagination, in music, in architecture, in the untroubled kingdom of reason, and in the golden sunset magic of lyrics, where beauty shines and glows, remote from the touch of sorrow, remote from the fear of change, remote from the failures and disenchantments of the world of fact. In the contemplation of these things the vision of heaven will shape itself in our hearts, giving at once a touchstone to judge the world about us, and an inspiration by which to fashion to our needs whatever is not incapable of serving as a stone in the sacred temple.

Except for those rare spirits that are born without sin, there is a cavern of darkness to be traversed before that temple can be entered. The gate of the cavern is despair, and its floor is paved with the gravestones of abandoned hopes. There Self must die; there the eagerness, the greed of untamed desire must be slain, for only so can the soul be freed from the empire of Fate. But out of the cavern the Gate of Renunciation leads again to the daylight of wisdom, by whose radiance a new insight, a new joy, a new tenderness, shine forth to gladden the pilgrim's heart.

When, without the bitterness of impotent rebellion, we have learnt both to resign ourselves to the outward rule of Fate and to recognise that the non-human world is unworthy of our worship, it becomes possible at last so to transform and refashion the unconscious universe, so to transmute it in the crucible of imagination, that a new image of shining gold replaces the old idol of clay. In all the multiform facts of the world—in the visual shapes of trees and mountains and clouds, in the events of the life of man, even in the very omnipotence of Death —the insight of creative idealism can find the reflection of a beauty which its own thoughts first made. In this way mind asserts its subtle mastery over the thoughtless forces of Nature. The more evil the material with which it deals, the more thwarting to untrained desire, the greater is its achievement in inducing the reluctant rock to yield up its hidden treasures, the prouder its victory in compelling the opposing forces to swell the pageant of its triumph. Of all the arts, Tragedy is the proudest, the most triumphant; for it builds its shining citadel in the very centre of the enemy's country, on the very summit of his highest mountain; from its impregnable watchtowers, his camps and arsenals, his columns and forts, are all revealed; within its walls the free life continues, while the legions of Death and Pain and Despair, and all the servile captains of tyrant Fate, afford the burghers of that dauntless city new spectacles of beauty. Happy those sacred ramparts, thrice happy the dwellers on that all-seeing eminence. . . .

But the beauty of Tragedy does but make visible a quality which, in more or less obvious shapes, is present always and everywhere in life. In the spectacle of Death, in the endurance of intolerable pain, and in the irrevocableness of a vanished past, there is a sacredness, an overpowering awe, a feeling of the vastness, the depth, the inexhaustible mystery of existence, in which, as by some strange marriage of pain, the sufferer is bound to the world by bonds of sorrow. In these moments of insight, we lose all eagerness of temporary desire, all struggling and striving for petty ends, all care for the little trivial things that, to a superficial view, make up the common life of day by day; we see, surrounding the narrow raft illumined by the flickering light of human comradeship, the dark ocean on whose rolling waves we toss for a brief hour; from the great night without, a chill blast breaks in upon our refuge; all the loneliness of humanity amid hostile forces is concentrated upon the individual soul, which must struggle alone, with what of courage it can command, against the whole weight of a universe that cares nothing for its hopes and fears. Victory, in this struggle with the powers of darkness, is the true baptism into the glorious company of heroes, the true initiation into the overmastering beauty of human existence. From that awful encounter of the soul with the outer world, renunciation, wisdom, and charity are born; and with their birth a new life begins. To take into the inmost shrine of the soul the irresistible forces whose puppets we seem to be —Death and change, the irrevocableness of the past, and the powerlessness of man before the blind hurry of the universe from vanity to vanity—to feel these things and know them is to conquer them.

This is the reason why the Past has such magical power. The beauty of its motionless and silent pictures is like the enchanted purity of late autumn, when the leaves, though one breath would make them fall, still glow against the sky in golden glory. The Past does not change or strive; like Duncan, after life's fitful fever it sleeps well; what was eager and grasping, what was petty and transitory, has faded away, the things that were beautiful and eternal shine out of it like stars in the night. Its beauty, to a soul not worthy of it, is unendurable; but to a soul which has conquered Fate it is the key of religion.

4. The life of Man, viewed outwardly, is but a small thing in comparison with the forces of Nature. The slave is doomed to worship Time and Fate and Death, because they are greater than anything he finds in himself, and because all his thoughts are of things which they devour. But, great as they are, to think of them greatly, to feel their passionless splendour, is greater still. And such thought makes us free men; we no longer bow before the inevitable in Oriental subjection, but we absorb it, and make it a part of ourselves. To abandon the struggle for private happiness, to expel all eagerness of temporary desire, to burn with passion for eternal things—this is emancipation, and this is the free man's worship. . . .

Brief and powerless is Man's life; on him and all his race the slow, sure doom falls pitiless and dark.

Blind to good and evil, reckless of destruction, omnipotent matter rolls on its relentless way; for Man, condemned to-day to lose his dearest, to-morrow himself to pass through the gate of darkness, it remains only to cherish, ere yet the blow falls, the lofty thoughts that ennoble his little day; disdaining the coward terrors of the slave of Fate, to worship at the shrine that his own hands have built; undismayed by the empire of chance, to preserve a mind free from the wanton tyranny that rules his outward life; proudly defiant of the irresistible forces that tolerate, for a moment, his knowledge and his condemnation, to sustain alone, a weary but unyielding Atlas, the world that his own ideals have fashioned despite the trampling march of unconscious power.

Romanticism

94. CONCLUSION from THE RENAISSANCE

Walter Pater

To regard all things and principles of things as inconstant modes or fashions has more and more become the tendency of modern thought. Let us begin with that which is without—our physical life. Fix upon it in one of its more exquisite intervals, the moment, for instance, of delicious recoil from the flood of water in summer heat. What is the whole physical life in that moment but a combination of natural elements to which science gives their names? But those elements, phosphorus and lime and delicate fibres, are present not in the human body alone: we detect them in places most remote from it. Our physical life is a perpetual motion of them—the passage of the blood, the waste and repairing of the lenses of the eye, the modification of the tissues of the brain under every ray of light and sound—processes which science reduces to simpler and more elementary forces. Like the elements of which we are composed, the action of these forces extends beyond us: it rusts iron and ripens corn. Far out on every side of us those elements are broadcast, driven in many currents; and birth and gesture and death and the springing of violets from the grave are but a few out of ten thousand resultant combinations. That clear, perpetual outline of face and limb is but an image of ours, under which we group them—a design in a web, the actual threads of which pass out beyond it. This at least of flame-like our life has, that it is but the concurrence, renewed from moment to moment, of forces parting sooner or later on their ways.

Or, if we begin with the inward world of thought and feeling, the whirlpool is still more rapid, the flame more eager and devouring. There it is no longer the gradual darkening of the eye, the gradual fading of colour from the wall—movements of the shore-side, where the water flows down indeed, though in apparent rest—but the race of the midstream, a drift of momentary acts of sight and passion and thought. At first sight experience seems to bury us under a flood of external objects, pressing upon us with a sharp and importunate reality, calling us out of ourselves in a thousand forms of action. But when reflexion begins to play upon those objects they are dissipated under its influence; the cohesive force seems suspended like

From Walter Pater, The "Conclusion" from *The Renaissance*. First published in 1873.

some trick of magic; each object is loosed into a group of impressions—colour, odour, texture—in the mind of the observer. And if we continue to dwell in thought on this world, not of objects in the solidity with which language invests them, but of impressions, unstable, flickering, inconsistent, which burn and are extinguished with our consciousness of them, it contracts still further: the whole scope of observation is dwarfed into the narrow chamber of the individual mind. Experience, already reduced to a group of impressions, is ringed round for each one of us by that thick wall of personality through which no real voice has ever pierced on its way to us, or from us to that which we can only conjecture to be without. Every one of those impressions is the impression of the individual in his isolation, each mind keeping as a solitary prisoner its own dream of a world. Analysis goes a step farther still, and assures us that those impressions of the individual mind to which, for each one of us, experience dwindles down, are in perpetual flight; that each of them is limited by time, and that as time is infinitely divisible, each of them is infinitely divisible also; all that is actual in it being a single moment, gone while we try to apprehend it, of which it may ever be more truly said that it has ceased to be than that it is. To such a tremulous wisp constantly re-forming itself on the stream, to a single sharp impression, with a sense in it, a relic more or less fleeting, of such moments gone by, what is real in our life fines itself down. It is with this movement, with the passage and dissolution of impressions, images, sensations, that analysis leaves off—that continual vanishing away, that strange, perpetual weaving and unweaving of ourselves. . . .

. . . The service of philosophy, of speculative culture, towards the human spirit, is to rouse, to startle it to a life of constant and eager observation. Every moment some form grows perfect in hand or face; some tone on the hills or the sea is choicer than the rest; some mood of passion or insight or intellectual excitement is irresistibly real and attractive to us,—for that moment only. Not the fruit of experience, but experience itself, is the end. A counted number of pulses only is given to us of a variegated, dramatic life. How may we see in them all that is to be seen in them by the finest senses? How shall we pass most swiftly from point to point, and be present always at the focus where the greatest number of vital forces unite in their purest energy?

To burn always with this hard, gemlike flame, to maintain this ecstasy, is success in life. In a sense it might even be said that our failure is to form habits: for, after all, habit is relative to a stereotyped world, and meantime it is only the roughness of the eye that makes any two persons, things, situations, seem alike. While all melts under our feet, we may well grasp at any exquisite passion, or any contribution to knowledge that seems by a lifted horizon to set the spirit free for a moment, or any stirring of the senses, strange dyes, strange colours, and curious odours, or work of the artist's hands, or the face of one's friend. Not to discriminate every moment some passionate attitude in those about us, and in the very brilliancy of their gifts some tragic dividing of forces on their ways, is, on this short day of frost and sun, to sleep before evening. With this sense of the splendour of our experience and of its awful brevity, gathering all we are into one desperate effort to see and touch, we shall hardly have time to make theories about the things we see and touch. What we have to do is to be for ever curiously testing new opinions and courting new impressions, never acquiescing in a facile orthodoxy of Comte, or of Hegel, or of our own. Philosophical theories or ideas, as points of view, instruments of criticism, may help us to gather up what might otherwise pass unregarded by us. "Philosophy is the microscope of thought." The theory or idea or system which requires of us the sacrifice of any part of this experience, in consideration of some interest into which we cannot enter, or some abstract theory we have not identified with ourselves, or of what is only conventional, has no real claim upon us.

One of the most beautiful passages of Rousseau is that in the sixth book of the *Confessions,* where he describes the awakening in him of the literary sense. An undefinable taint of death had clung always about him, and now in early manhood he believed himself smitten by mortal disease. He asked himself how he might make as much as possible of the interval that remained; and he was not biased by anything in his previous life when he decided that it must be by intellectual excitement, which he found just then in the clear, fresh writings of Voltaire. Well! we are all *condamnés* as Victor Hugo says: we are all under sentence of death but with a sort of indefinite reprive—*les hommes sont tous condamnés à mort avec des sursis idéfinis:* we have an interval, and then our place knows us no more. Some spend this interval in listlessness, some in high passions, the wisest, at least among "the children of this world," in art and song. For our one chance lies in expanding that interval, in getting as many pulsations as possible into the given time.

Great passions may give us this quickened sense of life, ectasy and sorrow of love, the various forms of enthusiastic activity, disinterested or otherwise, which come naturally to many of us. Only be sure it is passion—that it does yield you this fruit of a quickened, multiplied consciousness. Of such wisdom, the poetic passion, the desire of beauty, the love of art for its own sake, has most. For art comes to you proposing frankly to give nothing but the highest quality to your moments as they pass, and simply for those moments' sake.

Existentialism

95. *ABSURD FREEDOM and THE MYTH OF SISYPHUS*

Albert Camus

ABSURD FREEDOM

. . . I hold certain facts from which I cannot separate. What I know, what is certain, what I cannot deny, what I cannot reject—this is what counts. I can negate everything of that part of me that lives on vague nostalgias, except this desire for unity, this longing to solve, this need for clarity and cohesion. I can refute everything in this world surrounding me that offends or enraptures me, except this chaos, this sovereign chance and this divine equivalence which springs from anarchy. I don't know whether this world has a meaning that transcends it. But I know that I do not know that meaning and that it is impossible for me just now to know it. What can a meaning outside my condition mean to me? I can understand only in human terms. What I touch, what resists me—that is what I understand. And these two certainties—my appetite for the absolute and for unity and the impossibility of reducing this world to a rational and reasonable principle—I also know that I cannot reconcile them. What other truth can I admit without lying, without bringing in a hope I lack and which means nothing within the limits of my condition?

If I were a tree among trees, a cat among animals, this life would have a meaning, or rather this problem would not arise, for I should belong to this world. I should *be* this world to which I am now opposed by my whole consciousness and my whole insistence upon familiarity. This ridiculous reason is what sets me in opposition to all creation. I cannot cross it out with a stroke of the pen. What I believe to be true I must therefore preserve. What seem to me so obvious, even against me, I must support. And what constitutes the basis of that conflict, of that break between the world and my mind, but the awareness of it? If therefore I want to preserve it, I can through a constant awareness, ever revived, ever alert. This is what, for the moment, I must remember. At this moment the absurd, so obvious and yet so hard to win, returns to a man's life and finds its home there. At this moment, too, the mind can leave the arid, dried-up path of lucid effort. That path now emerges in daily life. It encounters the world of the anonymous impersonal pronoun "one," but henceforth man enters in with his revolt and his lucidity. He has forgotten how to hope. This hell of the present is his Kingdom at last. All problems recover their sharp edge. Abstract evidence retreats before the poetry of forms and colors. Spiritual conflicts become embodied and return to the abject and magnificent shelter of man's heart. None of them is settled. But all are transfigured. Is one going to die, escape by the leap, rebuild a mansion of ideas and forms to one's own scale? Is one, on the contrary, going to take up the heart-rending and marvelous wager of the absurd? Let's make a final effort in this regard and draw all our conclusions. The body, affection, creation, action, human nobility will then resume their places in this mad world. At last man will again find there the wine of the absurd and the bread of indifference on which he feeds his greatness.

Let us insist again on the method: it is a matter of persisting. At a certain point on his path the absurd man is tempted. History is not lacking in either religions or prophets, even without gods. He is asked to leap. All he can reply is that he doesn't fully understand, that it is not obvious. Indeed, he does not want to do anything but what he fully understands. He is assured that this is the sin of pride, but he does not understand the notion of sin; that perhaps hell is in store, but he has not enough imagination to visualize that strange future; that he is losing immortal life, but that seems to him an idle consideration. An attempt is made to get him to admit his guilt. He feels innocent. To tell the truth, that is all he feels—his irreparable innocence. This is what allows him everything. Hence, what he demands of himself is to live *solely* with what he knows, to accommodate himself to what is, and to bring in nothing that is not certain. He is told that nothing is. But this at least is a certainty. And it is with this that he is concerned: he wants to find out if it is possible to live *without appeal.*

Now I can broach the notion of suicide. It has already been felt what solution might be given. At this point the problem is reversed. It was previously a question of finding out whether or not life

clear, on the contrary, that it will be lived all the better if it has no meaning. Living an experience, a particular fate, is accepting it fully. Now, no one will live this fate, knowing it to be absurd, unless he does everything to keep before him that absurd brought to light by consciousness. Negating one of the terms of the opposition on which he lives amounts to escaping it. To abolish conscious revolt is to elude the problem. The theme of permanent revolution is thus carried into individual experience. Living is keeping the absurd alive. Keeping it alive is, above all, contemplating it. Unlike Eurydice, the absurd dies only when we turn away from it. One of the only coherent philosophical positions is thus revolt. It is a constant confrontation between man and his own obscurity. It is an insistence upon an impossible transparency. It challenges the world anew every second. Just as danger provided man the unique opportunity of seizing awareness, so metaphysical revolt extends awareness to the whole of experience. It is that constant presence of man in his own eyes. It is not aspiration, for it is devoid of hope. That revolt is the certainty of a crushing fate, without the resignation that ought to accompany it.

This is where it is seen to what a degree absurd experience is remote from suicide. It may be thought that suicide follows revolt—but wrongly. For it does not represent the logical outcome of revolt. It is just the contrary by the consent it presupposes. Suicide, like the leap, is acceptance at its extreme. Everything is over and man returns to his essential history. His future, his unique and dreadful future—he sees and rushes toward it. In its way, suicide settles the absurd. It engulfs the absurd in the same death. But I know that in order to keep alive, the absurd cannot be settled. It escapes suicide to the extent that it is simultaneously awareness and rejection of death. It is, at the extreme limit of the condemned man's last thought, that shoelace that despite everything he sees a few yard away, on the very brink of his dizzying fall. The contrary of suicide, in fact, is the man condemned to death.

That revolt gives life its value. Spread out over the whole length of a life, it restores its majesty to that life. To a man devoid of blinders, there is no finer sight than that of the intelligence at grips with a reality that transcends it. The sight of human

That discipline that the mind imposes on itself, that will conjured up out of nothing, that face-to-face struggle have something exceptional about them. To impoverish that reality whose inhumanity constitutes man's majesty is tantamount to impoverishing him himself. I understand then why the doctrines that explain everything to me also debilitate me at the same time. They relieve me of the weight of my own life, and yet I must carry it alone. At this juncture, I cannot conceive that a skeptical metaphysics can be joined to an ethics of renunciation.

Consciousness and revolt, these rejections are the contrary of renunciation. Everything that is indomitable and passionate in a human heart quickens them, on the contrary, with its own life. It is essential to die unreconciled and not of one's own free will. Suicide is a repudiation. The absurd man can only drain everything to the bitter end, and deplete himself. The absurd is his extreme tension, which he maintains constantly by solitary effort, for he knows that in that consciousness and in that day-to-day revolt he gives proof of his only truth, which is defiance. This is a first consequence. . . .

THE MYTH OF SISYPHUS

The gods had condemned Sisyphus to ceaselessly rolling a rock to the top of a mountain, whence the stone would fall back of its own weight. They had thought with some reason that there is no more dreadful punishment than futile and hopeless labor.

If one believes Homer, Sisyphus was the wisest and most prudent of mortals. According to another tradition, however, he was disposed to practice the profession of highwayman. I see no contradiction in this. Opinions differ as to the reasons why he became the futile laborer of the underworld. To begin with, he is accused of a certain levity in regard to the gods. He stole their secrets. Aegina, the daughter of Aesopus, was carried off by Jupiter. The father was shocked by that disappearance and complained to Sisyphus. He, who knew of the abduction, offered to tell about it on condition that Aesopus would give water to the citadel of Corinth. To the celestial thunderbolts he preferred the benediction of water. He was punished for this in

the underworld. Homer tells us also that Sisyphus had put Death in chains. Pluto could not endure the sight of his deserted, silent empire. He dispatched the god of war, who liberated Death from the hands of her conqueror.

It is said also that Sisyphus, being near to death, rashly wanted to test his wife's love. He ordered her to cast his unburied body into the middle of the public square. Sisyphus woke up in the underworld. And there, annoyed by an obedience so contrary to human love, he obtained from Pluto permission to return to earth in order to chastise his wife. But when he had seen again the face of this world, enjoyed water and sun, warm stones and the sea, he no longer wanted to go back to the infernal darkness. Recalls, signs of anger, warnings were of no avail. Many years more he lived facing the curve of the gulf, the sparkling sea, and the smiles of earth. A decree of the gods was necessary. Mercury came and seized the impudent man by the collar and, snatching him from his joys, led him forcibly back to the underworld, where his rock was ready for him.

You have already grasped that Sisyphus is the absurd hero. He *is,* as much through his passions as through his torture. His scorn of the gods, his hatred of death, and his passion for life won him that unspeakable penalty in which the whole being is exerted toward accomplishing nothing. This is the price that must be paid for the passions of this earth. Nothing is told us about Sisyphus in the underworld. Myths are made for the imagination to breathe life into them. As for this myth, one sees merely the whole effort of a body straining to raise the huge stone, to roll it and push it up a slope a hundred times over; one sees the face screwed up, the cheek tight against the stone, the shoulder bracing the clay-covered mass, the foot wedging it, the fresh start with arms outstretched, the wholly human security of two earth-clotted hands. At the very end of his long effort measured by skyless space and time without depth, the purpose is achieved. Then Sisyphus watches the stone rush down in a few moments toward that lower world whence he will have to push it up again toward the summit. He goes back down to the plain.

It is during that return, that pause, that Sisyphus interests me. A face that toils so close to stones is already stone itself! I see that man going back down with a heavy yet measured step toward the torment of which he will never know the end. That hour like a breathing-space which returns as surely as his suffering, that is the hour of consciousness. At each of those moments when he leaves the heights and gradually sinks toward the lairs of the gods, he is superior to his fate. He is stronger than his rock.

If this myth is tragic, that is because its hero is conscious. Where would his torture be, indeed, if at every step the hope of succeeding upheld him? The workman of today works every day in his life at the same tasks, and this fate is no less absurd. But it is tragic only at the rare moments when it becomes conscious. Sisyphus, proletarian of the gods, powerless and rebellious, knows the whole extent of his wretched condition: it is what he thinks of during his descent. The lucidity that was to constitute his torture at the same time crowns his victory. There is no fate that cannot be surmounted by scorn. . . .

If the descent is thus sometimes performed in sorrow, it can also take place in joy. This word is not too much. Again I fancy Sisyphus returning toward his rock, and the sorrow was in the beginning. When the images of earth cling too tightly to memory, when the call of happiness becomes too insistent, it happens that melancholy rises in man's heart: this is the rock's victory, this is the rock itself. The boundless grief is too heavy to bear. These are our nights of Gethsemane. But crushing truths perish from being acknowledged. Thus, Oedipus at the outset obeys fate without knowing it. But from the moment he knows, his tragedy begins. Yet at the same moment, blind and desperate, he realizes that the only bond linking him to the world is the cool hand of a girl. Then a tremendous remark rings out: "Despite so many ordeals, my advanced age and the nobility of my soul make me conclude that all is well." Sophocles' Oedipus, like Dostoevsky's Kirilov, thus gives the recipe for the absurd victory. Ancient wisdom confirms modern heroism.

One does not discover the absurd without being tempted to write a manual of happiness. "What! by such narrow ways—?" There is but one world, however. Happiness and the absurd are two sons of the same earth. They are inseparable. It would be a mistake to say that happiness necessarily springs from the absurd discovery. It happens as well that the feeling of the absurd springs from happiness. "I conclude that all is well," says Oedipus, and that remark is sacred. It echoes in the wild and limited universe of man. It teaches that all is not, has not been, exhausted. It drives out of this world a god who had come into it with dissatisfaction and a preference for futile sufferings. It makes of fate a human matter, which must be settled among men.

All Sisyphus' silent joy is contained therein. His fate belongs to him. His rock is his thing. Likewise, the absurd man, when he contemplates his torment, silences all the idols. In the universe suddenly restored to its silence, the myriad wondering little voices of the earth rise up. Unconscious, secret calls, invitations from all the faces, they are the necessary reverse and price of victory. There is no sun without shadow, and it is essential to know the night. The absurd man says yes and his effort will henceforth be unceasing. If there is a personal fate, there is no higher destiny, or at least there is but one which he concludes is inevitable and despicable. For the rest, he knows himself to be the master of his days. At that subtle moment when man glances backward over his life, Sisyphus returning toward his rock, in that slight pivoting he contemplates that series of unrelated actions which becomes his fate, created by him, combined under his memory's eye and soon sealed by his death. Thus, convinced of the wholly human origin of all that is human, a blind man eager to see who knows that the night has no end, he is still on the go. The rock is still rolling.

I leave Sisyphus at the foot of the mountain! One always finds one's burden again. But Sisyphus teaches the higher fidelity that negates the gods and raises rocks. He too concludes that all is well. This universe henceforth without a master seems to him neither sterile nor futile. Each atom of that stone, each mineral flake of that night-filled mountain, in itself forms a world. The struggle itself toward the heights is enough to fill a man's heart. One must imagine Sisyphus happy.

96. THE MEANING OF LIFE

Richard Taylor

The question whether life has any meaning is difficult to interpret, and the more one concentrates his critical faculty on it the more it seems to elude him, or to evaporate as any intelligible question. One wants to turn it aside, as a source of embarrassment, as something that, if it cannot be abolished, should at least be decently covered. And yet I think any reflective person recognizes that the question it raises is important, and that it ought to have a significant answer.

If the idea of meaningfulness is difficult to grasp in this context, so that we are unsure what sort of thing would amount to answering the question, the idea of meaninglessness is perhaps less so. If, then, we can bring before our minds a clear image of meaningless existence, then perhaps we can take a step toward coping with our original question by seeing to what extent our lives, as we actually find them, resemble that image, and draw such lessons as we are able to from the comparison.

MEANINGLESS EXISTENCE

A perfect image of meaninglessness, of the kind we are seeking, is found in the ancient myth of Sisyphus. Sisyphus, it will be remembered, betrayed divine secrets to mortals, and for this he was condemned by the gods to roll a stone to the top of a hill, the stone then immediately to roll back down, again to be pushed to the top by Sisyphus, to roll down once more, and so on again and again, *forever.* Now in this we have the picture of meaningless, pointless toil, of a meaningless existence that is absolutely *never* redeemed. It is not even redeemed by a death that, if it were to accomplish nothing more, would at least bring this idiotic cycle to a close. If we were invited to imagine Sisyphus struggling for awhile and accomplishing nothing, perhaps eventually falling from exhaustion, so that we might suppose him then eventually turning to something having some sort of promise, then the meaninglessness of that chapter of his life would not be so stark. It would be a dark and dreadful dream, from which he eventually awakens to sunlight and reality. But he does not awaken, for there is nothing for him to awaken to. His repetitive toil is his life and reality, and it goes on forever, and it is without any meaning whatever. Nothing ever comes of what he is doing, except simply, more of the same. Not by one step, nor by a thousand, nor by ten thousand does he even expiate by the smallest token the sin against the gods that led him into this fate. Nothing comes of it, nothing at all.

This ancient myth has always enchanted men, for countless meanings can be read into it. Some of the ancients apparently thought it symbolized the perpetual rising and setting of the sun, and others the repetitious crashing of the waves upon the shore. Probably the commonest interpretation is that it symbolizes man's eternal struggle and unquenchable spirit, his determination always to try once more in the face of overwhelming discouragement. This interpretation is further supported by that version of the myth according to which Sisyphus was commanded to roll the stone *over* the hill, so that it would finally roll down the other side, but was never quite able to make it.

I am not concerned with rendering or defending any interpretation of this myth, however. I have cited it only for the one element it does unmistakably contain, namely, that of a repetitious, cyclic activity that never comes to anything. We could contrive other images of this that would serve just as well, and no myth-makers are needed to supply the materials of it. Thus, we can imagine two persons transporting a stone—or even a precious gem, it does not matter—back and forth, relay style. One carries it to a near or distant point where it is received by the other; it is returned to its starting point, there to be recovered by the first, and the process is repeated over and over. Except in this relay nothing counts as winning, and nothing brings the contest to any close, each step only leads to a repetition of itself. Or we can imagine two groups of prisoners, one of them engaged in digging a prodigious hole in the ground that is no sooner finished than it is filled in again by the other group, the latter then digging a new hole that is at once filled in by the first group, and so on and on endlessly.

Now what stands out in all such pictures as oppressive and dejecting is not that the beings who enact these roles suffer any torture or pain, for it need not be assumed that they do. Nor is it that their labors are great, for they are no greater than the labors commonly undertaken by most men most of the time. According to the original myth, the stone is so large that Sisyphus never quite gets it to the top and must groan under every step, so that his enormous labor is all for naught. But this is not what appalls. It is not that his great struggle comes to nothing, but that his existence itself is without meaning. Even if we suppose, for example, that the stone is but a pebble that can be carried effortlessly, or that the holes dug by the prisoners are but small ones, not the slightest meaning is introduced into their lives. The stone that Sisyphus moves to the top of the hill, whether we think of it as large or small, still rolls back every time, and the process is repeated forever. Nothing comes of it, and the work is simply pointless. That is the element of the myth that I wish to capture.

Again, it is not the fact that the labors of Sisyphus continue forever that deprives them of meaning. It is, rather, the implication of this: that they come to nothing. The image would not be changed by our supposing him to push a different stone up every time, each to roll down again. But if we supposed that these stones, instead of rolling back to their places as if they had never been moved, were assembled at the top of the hill and there incorporated, say, in a beautiful and enduring temple, then the aspect of meaninglessness would disappear. His labors would then have a point, something would come of them all, and although one could perhaps still say it was not worth it, one could not say that the life of Sisyphus was devoid of meaning altogether. Meaningfulness would at least have made an appearance, and we could see what it was.

That point will need remembering. But in the meantime, let us note another way in which the image of meaninglessness can be altered by making only a very slight change. Let us suppose that the gods, while condemning Sisyphus to the fate just described, at the same time, as an afterthought, waxed perversely merciful by implanting in him a strange and irrational impulse; namely, a compulsive impulse to roll stones. We may if we like, to make this more graphic, suppose they accomplish this by implanting in him some substance that has this effect on his character and drives. I call this perverse, because from our point of view there is clearly no reason why anyone should have a persistent and insatiable desire to do something so pointless as that. Nevertheless, suppose that is Sisyphus' condition. He has but one obsession, which is to roll stones, and it is an obsession that is only for the moment appeased by his rolling them—he no sooner gets a stone rolled to the top of the hill than he is restless to roll up another.

Now it can be seen why this little afterthought of the gods, which I called perverse, was also in fact merciful. For they have by this device managed to give Sisyphus precisely what he wants—by making him want precisely what they inflict on him. However it may appear to us, Sisyphus' fate now does not appear to him as a condemnation, but the very reverse. His one desire in life is to roll stones, and he is absolutely guaranteed its endless fulfillment. Where otherwise he might profoundly have wished surcease, and even welcomed the quiet of death to release him from endless boredom and meaninglessness, his life is now filled with mission and meaning, and he seems to himself to have been given an entry to heaven. Nor need he even fear death, for the gods have promised him an endless opportunity to indulge his single purpose, without concern or frustration. He will be able to roll stones *forever*.

What we need to mark most carefully at this point is that the picture with which we began has not really been changed in the least by adding this supposition. Exactly the same things happen as before. The only change is in Sisyphus' view of them. The picture before was the image of meaningless activity and existence. It was created precisely to be an image of that. It has not lost that meaninglessness, it has now gained not the least shred of meaningfulness. The stones still roll back as before, each phase of Sisyphus' life still exactly resembles all the others, the task is never completed, nothing comes of it, no temple ever begins to rise, and all this cycle of the same pointless thing over and over goes on forever in this picture as in the other. The *only* thing that has happened is this: Sisyphus has been reconciled to it, and indeed more, he has been led to embrace it. Not, however, by reason or persuasion, but by nothing more rational than the potency of a new substance in his veins.

THE MEANINGLESSNESS OF LIFE

I believe the foregoing provides a fairly clear content to the idea of meaninglessness and, through it, some hint of what meaningfulness, in this sense, might be. Meaninglessness is essentially endless pointlessness, and meaningfulness is therefore the opposite. Activity, and even long, drawn-out and repetitive activity, has a meaning if it has some significant culmination, some more or less lasting end that can be considered to have been the direction and purpose of the activity. But the descriptions so far also provide something else; namely, the suggestion of how an existence that is objectively meaningless, in this sense, can nevertheless acquire a meaning for him whose existence it is.

Now let us ask: Which of these pictures does life in fact resemble? And let us not begin with our own lives, for here both our prejudices and wishes are great, but with the life in general that we share with the rest of creation. We shall find, I think, that it all has a certain pattern, and that this pattern is by now easily recognized.

We can begin anywhere, only saving human existence for our last consideration. We can, for example, begin with any animal. It does not matter where we begin, because the result is going to be exactly the same.

Thus, for example, there are caves in New Zealand, deep and dark, whose floors are quiet pools and whose walls and ceilings are covered with soft light. As one gazes in wonder in the stillness of these caves it seems that the Creator has reproduced there in microcosm the heavens themselves, until one scarcely remembers the enclosing presence of the walls. As one looks more closely, however, the scene is explained. Each dot of light identifies an ugly worm, whose luminous tail is meant to attract insects from the surrounding darkness. As from time to time one of these insects draws near it becomes entangled in a sticky thread lowered by the worm, and is eaten. This goes on month after month, the blind worm lying there in the barren stillness waiting to entrap an occasional bit of nourishment that will only sustain it to another bit of nourishment until. . . . Until what? What great thing awaits all this long and repetitious effort and makes it worthwhile? Really nothing. The larva just transforms itself finally to a tiny winged adult that lacks even mouth parts to feed and lives only a day or two. These adults, as soon as they have mated and laid eggs, are themselves caught in the threads and are devoured by the cannibalist worms, often without having ventured into the day, the only point to their existence having now been fulfilled. This has been going on for millions of years, and to no end other than that the same meaningless cycle may continue for another millions of years.

All living things present essentially the same spectacle. The larva of a certain cicada burrows in the darkness of the earth for seventeen years, through season after season, to emerge finally into the daylight for a brief flight, lay its eggs, and die— this all to repeat itself during the next seventeen years, and so on to eternity. We have already noted, in another connection, the struggles of fish, made only that others may do the same after them and that this cycle, having no other point than itself, may never cease. Some birds span an entire side of the globe each year and then return, only to insure that others may follow the same incredibly long path again and again. One is led to wonder what the point of it all is, with what great triumph this ceaseless effort, repeating itself through millions of years, might finally culminate, and why it should go on and on for so long, accomplishing nothing, getting nowhere. But then one realizes that there is no point to it at all, that it really culminates in nothing, that each of these cycles, so filled with toil, is to be followed only by more of the same. The point of any living thing's life is, evidently, nothing but life itself.

This life of the world thus presents itself to our eyes as a vast machine, feeding on itself, running on and on forever to nothing. And we are part of that life. To be sure, we are not just the same, but the differences are not so great as we like to think; many are merely invented, and none really cancels the kind of meaninglessness that we found in Sisyphus and that we find all around, wherever anything lives. We are conscious of our activity. Our goals, whether in any significant sense we choose them or not, are things of which we are at least partly aware and can therefore in some sense appraise. More significantly, perhaps, men have a history, as other animals do not, such that each generation does not precisely resemble all those before. Still, if we can in imagination disengage our wills from our lives and disregard the deep interest each man has in his own existence, we shall find that they do not so little resemble the existence of Sisyphus. We toil after goals, most of them—indeed every single one of them—of transitory significance and, having gained one of them, we immediately set forth for the next, as if that one had never been, with this next one being essentially more of the same. Look at a busy street any day, and observe the throng going hither and thither. To what? Some office or shop, where the same things will be done today as were done yesterday, and are done now so they may be repeated tomorrow. And if we think that, unlike Sisyphus, these labors do have a point, that they culminate in something lasting and, independently of our own deep interests in them, very worthwhile, then we simply have not considered the thing closely enough. Most such effort is directed only to the establishment and perpetuation of home and family; that is, to the begetting of others who will follow in our steps to do more of the same. Each man's life thus resembles one of Sisyphus' climbs to the summit of his hill, and each day of it one of his steps; the difference is that whereas Sisyphus himself returns to push the stone up again, we leave this to our children. We at one point imagined that the labors of Sisyphus finally culminated in the creation of a temple, but for this to make any difference it had to be a temple that would at least endure, adding beauty to the world for the remainder of time. Our achievements, even though they are often beautiful, are mostly bubbles; and those that do last, like the sand-swept pyramids, soon become mere curiosities while around them the rest of mankind continues its perpetual toting of rocks, only to see them roll down. Nations are built upon the bones of their founders and pioneers, but only to decay and crumble before long, their rubble then becoming the foundation for others directed to exactly the same fate. The picture of Sisyphus is the picture of existence of the individual man, great or unknown, of nations, of the race of men, and of the very life of the world.

On a country road one sometimes comes upon the ruined hulks of a house and once extensive buildings, all in collapse and spread over with weeds. A curious eye can in imagination reconstruct from what is left a once warm and thriving life, filled with purpose. There was the hearth, where a family once talked, sang, and made plans; there were the rooms, where people loved, and babes were born to a rejoicing mother; there are the musty remains of a sofa, infested with bugs, once bought at a dear price to enhance an ever-growing comfort, beauty, and warmth. Every small piece of junk fills the mind with what once, not long ago, was utterly real, with children's voices, plans made, and enterprises embarked upon. That is how these stones of Sisyphus were rolled up, and that is how they became incorporated into a beautiful temple, and that temple is what now lies before you. Meanwhile other buildings, institutions, nations, and civilizations spring up all around, only to share the same fate before long. And if the question "What for?" is now asked, the answer is clear: so that just this may go on forever.

The two pictures—of Sisyphus and of our own lives, if we look at them from a distance—are in outline the same and convey to the mind the same image. It is not surprising, then, that men invent ways of denying it, their religions proclaiming a heaven that does not crumble, their hymnals and prayer books declaring a significance to life of which our eyes provide no hint whatever.* Even our philosophies portray some permanent and last-

---

* A popular Christian hymn, sung often at funerals and typical of many hymns, expresses this thought:
Swift to its close ebbs out life's little day;
Earth's joys grow dim, its glories pass away;
Change and decay in all around I see:
O thou who changest not, abide with me.

ing good at which all may aim, from the changeless forms invented by Plato to the beatific vision of St. Thomas and the ideals of permanence contrived by the moderns. When these fail to convince, then earthly ideals such as universal justice and brotherhood are conjured up to take their places and give meaning to man's seemingly endless pilgrimage, some final state that will be ushered in when the last obstacle is removed and the last stone pushed to the hilltop. No one believes, of course, that any such state will be final, or even wants it to be in case it means that human existence would then cease to be a struggle; but in the meantime such ideas serve a very real need.

THE MEANING OF LIFE

We noted that Sisyphus' existence would have meaning if there were some point to his labors, if his efforts ever culminated in something that was not just an occasion for fresh labors of the same kind. But that is precisely the meaning it lacks. And human existence resembles his in that respect. Men do achieve things—they scale their towers and raise their stones to their hilltops—but every such accomplishment fades, providing only an occasion for renewed labors of the same kind.

But here we need to note something else that has been mentioned, but its significance not explored, and that is the state of mind and feeling with which such labors are undertaken. We noted that if Sisyphus had a keen and unappeasable desire to be doing just what he found himself doing, then, although his life would in no way be changed, it would nevertheless have a meaning for him. It would be an irrational one, no doubt, because the desire itself would be only the product of the substance in his veins, and not any that reason could discover, but a meaning nevertheless.

And would it not, in fact, be a meaning incomparably better than the other? For let us examine again the first kind of meaning it could have. Let us suppose that, without having any interest in rolling stones, as such, and finding this, in fact, a galling toil, Sisyphus did nevertheless have a deep interest in raising a temple, one that would be beautiful and lasting. And let us suppose he succeeded in this, that after ages of dreadful toil, all directed at this

final result, he did at last complete his temple, such that now he could say his work was done, and he could rest and forever enjoy the result. Now what? What picture now presents itself to our minds? It is precisely the picture of infinite boredom! Of Sisyphus doing nothing ever again, but contemplating what he has already wrought and can no longer add anything to, and contemplating it for an eternity! Now in this picture we have a meaning for Sisyphus' existence, a point for his prodigious labor, because we have put it there; yet, at the same time, that which is really worthwhile seems to have slipped away entirely. Where before we were presented with the nightmare of eternal and pointless activity, we are now confronted with the hell of its eternal absence.

Our second picture, then, wherein we imagined Sisyphus to have had inflicted on him the irrational desire to be doing just what he found himself doing, should not have been dismissed so abruptly. The meaning that picture lacked was no meaning that he or any one could crave, and the strange meaning it had was perhaps just what we were seeking.

At this point, then, we can reintroduce what has been until now, it is hoped, resolutely pushed aside in an effort to view our lives and human existence with objectivity; namely, our own wills, our deep interest in what we find ourselves doing. If we do this we find that our lives do indeed still resemble that of Sisyphus, but that the meaningfulness they thus lack is precisely the meaningfulness of infinite boredom. At the same time, the strange meaningfulness they possess is that of the inner compulsion to be doing just what we were put here to do, and to go on doing it forever. This is the nearest we may hope to get to heaven, but the redeeming side of that fact is that we do thereby avoid a genuine hell.

If the builders of a great and flourishing ancient civilization could somehow return now to see archaeologists unearthing the trivial remnants of what they had once accomplished with such effort —see the fragments of pots and vases, a few broken statues, and such tokens of another age and greatness—they could indeed ask themselves what the point of it all was, if this is all it finally came to. Yet, it did not seem so to them then, for it was just the building, and not what was finally built, that gave their life meaning. Similarly, if the builders of the ruined home and farm that I described a short while ago could be brought back to see what is left, they would have the same feelings. What we construct in our imaginations as we look over these decayed and rusting pieces would reconstruct itself in their very memories, and certainly with unspeakable sadness. The piece of a sled at our feet would revive in them a warm Christmas. And what rich memories would there be in the broken crib? And the weed-covered remains of a fence would reproduce the scene of a great herd of livestock, so laboriously built up over so many years. What was it all worth, if this is the final result? Yet, again, it did not seem so to them through those many years of struggle and toil, and they did not imagine they were building a Gibraltar. The things to which they bent their backs day after day, realizing one by one their ephemeral plans, were precisely the things in which their wills were deeply involved, precisely the things in which their interests lay, and there was no need then to ask questions. There is no more need of them now—the day was sufficient to itself, and so was the life.

This is surely the way to look at all of life—at one's own life, and each day and moment it contains; of the life of a nation; of the species; of the life of the world; and of everything that breathes. Even the glow worms I described, whose cycles of existence over the millions of years seem so pointless when looked at by us, will seem entirely different to us if we can somehow try to view their existence from within. Their endless activity, which gets nowhere, is just what it is their will to pursue. This is its whole justification and meaning. Nor would it be any salvation to the birds who span the globe every year, back and forth, to have a home made for them in a cage with plenty of food and protection, so that they would not have to migrate any more. It would be their condenmation, for it is the doing that counts for them, and not what they hope to win by it. Flying these prodigious distances, never ending, is what it is in their veins to do, exactly as it was in Sisyphus' veins to roll stones, without end, after the gods had waxed merciful and implanted this in him.

A human being no sooner draws his first breath than he responds to the will that is in him to live. He no more asks whether it will be worthwhile, or whether anything of significance will come of it, than the worms and the birds. The point of his living is simply to be living, in the manner that it is his nature to be living. He goes through his life building his castles, each of these beginning to fade into time as the next is begun; yet, it would be no salvation to rest from all this. It would be a condemnation, and one that would in no way be redeemed were he able to gaze upon the things he has done, even if these were beautiful and absolutely permanent, as they never are. What counts is that one should be able to begin a new task, a new castle, a new bubble. It counts only because it is there to be done and he has the will to do it. The same will be the life of his children, and of theirs; and if the philosopher is apt to see in this a pattern similar to the unending cycles of the existence of Sisyphus, and to despair, then it is indeed because the meaning and point he is seeking is not there—but mercifully so. The meaning of life is from within us, it is not bestowed from without, and it far exceeds in both its beauty and permanence any heaven of which men have ever dreamed or yearned for.

SUGGESTIONS FOR FURTHER READING

Barnes, Hazel E. *The Literature of Possibility: A Study in Humanistic Existentialism.* Lincoln, Neb.: University of Nebraska Press, 1959.

Brinton, Crane. "Romanticism." In *The Encyclopedia of Philosophy,* edited by Paul Edwards. New York: Macmillan, 1967.

Britton, Karl. *Philosophy and the Meaning of Life.* New York: Cambridge University Press, 1969.

Edwards, Paul. "Life, Meaning and Value of." In *Encyclopedia of Philosophy,* edited by Paul Edwards. New York: Macmillan, 1967.

Farrington, Benjamin. *The Faith of Epicurus.* New York: Basic Books, 1967.

Hadas, Moses, ed. *The Essential Works of Stoicism.* New York: Bantam Books, 1961.

Hepburn, Ronald. *Christianity and Paradox.* New York: Pegasus, 1958.

Hochberg, Herbert. "Albert Camus and the Ethic of Absurdity." *Ethics* 75 (1964–65): 87–102.

Hyde, William DeWitt. *The Five Great Philosophies of Life.* New York: Macmillan, 1952. An extremely readable exposition of Epicureanism, Stoicism, Platonism, Aristotelianism, and the philosophy of Christian love, presented in that order as increasing in degree of plausibility.

Joske, W. D. "Philosophy and the Meaning of Life." *Australasian Journal of Philosophy* 52, (August 1974): 93–104.

Kaplan, Abraham. *The New World of Philosophy.* New York: Random House, 1961, Lecture 3, "Existentialism," and Lecture 9, "Zen."

Kaufmann, Walter, ed. *Existentialism from Dostoievsky to Sartre.* New York: Meridian Books, 1957.

Langer, Susanne K. *Feeling and Form: A Theory of Art.* New York: Charles Scribner's Sons, 1953. See chapter 18, "The Comic Rhythm," and chapter 19, "The Tragic Rhythm"; penetrating accounts of the comic and tragic responses both to art and to life.

Lewis, C. S. "De Futilitate." In *Christian Reflections.* Grand Rapids,: Mich: William Eerdmans, 1967, pp. 57–75.

Nagel, Thomas. "The Absurd." *Journal of Philosophy* 68 (1971): 716–22, 725–27. A very important article.

Norton, David L. *Personal Destinies: A Philosophy of Ethical Individualiam.* Princeton, N.J.: Princeton University Press, 1977. An important new book in the tradition of self-realization.

Pater, Walter. *Marius the Epicurean.* New York: Random House Modern Library. A fuller statement and development of Pater's views.

Sanders, Steven, and Cheney, David R., Eds. *The Meaning of Life: Questions, Answers and Analysis.* Englewood Cliffs, N.J.: Prentice-Hall, 1980. A definitive collection.

Santayana, George. *Dialogues in Limbo.* Ann Arbor, Mich.: The University of Michigan Press, 1957. See especially Dialogues I–V. Dramatic presentations of Santayana's neo-Epicurean philosophy.

Schopenhauer, Arthur. *The Will to Live, Selected Writings.* Edited by Richard Taylor. Garden City, N.Y.: Doubleday Anchor Books, 1962. Taylor contributes a helpful introduction.

White, R. C. "The Meaning of Life." *Australasian Journal of Philosophy* 53 (August 1975): 148–50. Makes some very helpful distinctions.

Wienpahl, Paul. *The Matter of Zen: A Brief Account of Zazen.* New York: New York University Press, 1964.

Wood, Alan. *Bertrand Russell: The Passionate Skeptic.* New York: Simon and Schuster, 1958.